READINGS IN

Sociology

Readings in Sociology

FIFTH EDITION

edited by **Edgar A. Schuler**
MICHIGAN STATE UNIVERSITY

Thomas Ford Hoult
ARIZONA STATE UNIVERSITY

Duane L. Gibson
MICHIGAN STATE UNIVERSITY

Wilbur B. Brookover
MICHIGAN STATE UNIVERSITY

THOMAS Y. CROWELL COMPANY
NEW YORK ESTABLISHED 1834

 Published simultaneously in Canada by Fitzhenry & Whiteside, Ltd., Toronto

Manufactured in the United States of America

1 2 3 4 5 6 7 8 9 10

Library of Congress Cataloging in Publication Data

SCHULER, EDGAR ALBERT, 1905- 5th ed.
Readings in sociology.

Originally published in 1952 under title: Outside readings in sociology.
1. Sociology—Addresses, essays, lectures.
I. Hoult, Thomas Ford, Gibson, Duane L., Brookover, Wilbur B., joint comp. II. Title

HM51.S353 1974 301'.08 74-4452
ISBN 0-690-00461-3

Preface to the Fifth Edition

With this fifth edition of *Readings in Sociology,* as with each of the preceding editions, we have sought selections which would exemplify the concepts and principles of sociology rather than explore in depth their theoretical dimensions. We leave the latter critical function to instructor and text. Because it is our intent to be illustrative rather than analytical, we have again drawn our selections not only from the work of sociologists and scholars in related disciplines but also from the writings of essayists, journalists, and novelists. We have sought for illustrative material on topics and issues about which we believe students are, or ought to be, concerned, thus providing them an opportunity to examine these problems from a sociological perspective. Moreover, we have tried to deal with issues that are significant rather than trivial, persistent rather than transient.

Because of the effort continuously to update our material, if those who used the first edition—who may well be the parents of our students today—were to open this book, they would find the *content* almost completely different although the *approach* would be found to be much the same. Only fifteen of the original ninety-six selections are to be found in this edition and they remain because they represent enduring statements and classic expositions. Furthermore, this fifth edition has been so thoroughly revised that forty-eight of the ninety-seven selections found here differ from those in the fourth edition.

We can conceive of no more appropriate way to express the purpose which guided our decisions in making the selections for this edition than the statement which introduced the first edition: "Believing in the possibility of genuine *liberal education,* [we] have sought to provide an orientation that will expand the reader's horizon and human concern beyond his own immediate place and time; to inculcate a truly scientific humility in the face of diverse peoples, customs and beliefs; and to affirm [our] own belief in the values of a maturing social science for our own democratic society, and for an increasingly rich and humane life for all peoples everywhere."

That statement of purpose seems to us, in the light of recent public events, to be even more pertinent than when it was first written. Certainly, today more than ever, we need youth who, on the one hand, are willing and able to move from a solid ethical and moral base to use their knowledge for the betterment of life for all; we need youth who exhibit intellectual leadership and are capable of defending their own liberty and that of others; we need youth who can detect the misuse of power under whatever complexion it may assume and, detecting it, can defeat its exercise; we need youth who cannot be seduced by demagogues or overawed by the erudite obfuscations of pretentious pedants; we need youth who recognize the right—rather, the obligation—to exhibit moral indignation at evidence of wrongdoing and who have the competence to set matters aright. It is clear, then, that we have come down resoundingly on the side of the need to take moral stands and with this book we unashamedly demonstrate it. And if it encourages our readers to examine issues critically and take their own moral stands we shall feel suitably recompensed.

We wish here to thank the many authors and publishers who have made their work available for inclusion in this book. Individual acknowledgments appear in footnotes accompanying each selection, as well as brief biographical notes about each author.

Librarians and library staffs of the following libraries were of great assistance to us in our work: Michigan State University, Lakeland (Florida) Public Library, the Polk Community College Library (Winter Haven, Florida), the Roux Library of Florida Southern College, and the Hayden Library of Arizona State University. Thanks should also be directed to Nancy Gendell, editor in the Institute for Community Development at Michigan State University, who assumed responsibility for revising and updating the biographical data on the authors of the selections. James Ballin and Julie Robinson helped to prepare the tables which correlate the selections in this work with leading texts.

Prospective selections were recommended, and other kinds of professional assistance were kindly given, by the following sociologists and others: Jo Ann Ebert, Larry Roush, and Paul Thompson, Polk Community College; Burton Wright III, Florida Technological University; Charles E. Fuller and Peter P. Jonitis, Florida Southern College; Linda Brookover Bourque, UCLA; John H. Useem, Michigan State University; Joan Greene and Herman Makler, Thomas Y. Crowell, Co.; Lewis A. Kirshner, M.D., Research Associate, Harvard Health Services; Betty Schuler, Lake County (Ohio) Comprehensive Mental Retardation Program; Joel Schulman, writer; and Virginia Schulman, formerly a senior attorney with the Mid-Hudson Valley Legal Services Project in Upstate New York. The generosity and helpfulness of these individuals is gratefully acknowledged by the editors.

To them, and to our capable and dedicated secretarial colleagues at Michigan State University—Almeda Ritter, office manager of the Institute for Community Development, and Betty White and Judy Walters, Department of Urban and Metropolitan Studies—we wish to express our deep appreciation.

We wish also to acknowledge a debt to those students and professional colleagues who through their comments regarding the content of earlier editions have helped to shape our decisions regarding selections to be used, and by their continued use of the earlier editions encouraged us to undertake the preparation of this fifth edition.

Finally, we feel it appropriate to dedicate this book to our wives, who have contributed to this and earlier editions in unnumbered ways—Kay Schuler, Chris Hoult, Wynne Gibson, and Edna Brookover.

E. A. S. D. L. G.
T. F. H. W. B. B.

Contents

Part IV

SOCIAL ORGANIZATION: TYPES OF GROUP RELATIONSHIPS

Part V

SOCIAL ORGANIZATION: COLLECTIVE BEHAVIOR

Part VI

SOCIAL ORGANIZATION: STRATIFICATION AND MOBILITY

Part VII

SOCIAL ORGANIZATION: INSTITUTIONS AND ASSOCIATIONS

Part VIII

SOCIAL ORGANIZATION: COMMUNITY AND ECOLOGY

Part IX

SOCIAL PROCESSES

Prologue

Social Science in Liberal Education

PERSPECTIVES OF STUART CHASE, PETER BERGER, ROBERT REDFIELD, AND ROBERT BIERSTEDT

Those who study sociology have a right to ask, "What can sociology do for me?" To help answer this question are brief statements by four writers and scholars. They have been chosen because, with varying emphasis, they see sociology as valuable, not only because of its utility in our jobs and in our communities, but also because it can help us improve the quality of our lives and realize our capabilities as human beings—the mark of the liberally educated. It is the editors' hope that many of the later selections, chosen with great care, will exemplify Bierstedt's position that "Sociology has an honorable place in the realm of humane letters and it belongs with the liberal arts as well as with the sciences."

Stuart Chase

. . . . .

To cope with the tough problems ahead of us we should be able to see all the way around them. Experts and specialists are invaluable, but, as specialists, they see only the trees, sometimes only the twigs under the trees. We need power to see the woods. We need generalists who do not get lost in the trees. This does not mean two kinds of people, for everyone is a specialist in some degree, perhaps as a typist, perhaps as a nuclear physicist. It means more room in our minds for the overall view, especially for relationships and balancing of alternatives.

. . . The competence of the specialist today has overawed the intelligent layman until he says: "It's way over my head; I'll leave it to the experts." How often do we all say or think something like that? Yet it is a dangerous attitude in this day and age. It tends to create an oligarchy of knowledge, which can become a monopoly of power, a series of tight little principalities with no minds left to survey the whole country.

I know a generalist who is also a learned specialist. He has written me that he would like to tell his specialist confreres: "Wake up! Live at the level of your time! Crawl out of that talent-trap which you refer to as your 'field' and look around. You may learn something about the only era you will ever live in, and about the only species you will ever be a member of. You will certainly learn something about yourself!"

To leave learning exclusively to specialists is not only dangerous but weak. It deprives civilized people of an essential part of their life on earth, something that many primitive peoples have naturally exercised —the full expression of curiosity, honestly

Source: Stuart Chase, *Some Things Worth Knowing* (New York: Harper & Row, 1958).

Stuart Chase is the author of many interpretive works in social science, especially in economics and communications. He has been an investigator for the Federal Trade Commission and has been a consultant for many organizations, among which are the United States Treasury, SEC, and UNESCO. Among his many books are *The Proper Study of Mankind, The Economy of Abundance,* and, more recently, *The Most Probable World* and *Danger Man Talking.*

confronting the mystery of existence, trying to understand their world and themselves. It is pitiful to retreat from this facing of life, especially at a time when so much new knowledge is coming in. Even if the astrophysicists have shown the universe to be far grander and more complex than we used to think, shall we say: "It's all beyond me," and turn our backs and go indoors? Or shall we look up with new wonder and delight, trying to imagine the vast recesses of the whirling sky? Similarly for the marvels unfolding before the electronic microscope, and for new aspects of human behavior now being revealed.

. . . . .

A mature mind combines reliable information with good judgment, and one definition of good judgment is appreciation of relationships between fields of information. . . .

The intelligent layman . . . also wants to know what knowledge is available to promote negotiation and accommodation between the great powers. This is a question in the area of the behavioral sciences.

He wants to understand too what can be done to lessen tension between the races, and between worker and employer, and how to improve community relations. He would especially like to understand himself better, and why he often has so much trouble doing what he thinks he ought to do, and how he can get on more happily with his family, and in his personal relations generally.

Aside from these rather practical motives a good generalist possesses a healthy curiosity. . . . How and where [Homo sapiens] originally developed, how he survived as a hunter for many thousands of years, as a farmer and city dweller for a few more thousands; the purpose of his excess brain capacity even beyond what he needs for the intricate skills of language – these are some of the mysteries. The study of various cultures (where indeed the behavioral sciences begin) answers some questions but raises others: for example, which traits are common to man of every age and place, which are unique in a given society or even individual; why can the same complex customs arise independently in widely separate cultures?

. . . . .

. . . Specialists have distorted the environment of the world today and pulled human behavior out of scale. Generalists are needed in great numbers to offset what the specialists are doing to us. To put it in another way, we need more specialists equipped with wide perspective, to exert critical judgment on what they are doing as specialists. This, I take it, was Robert Oppenheimer's motive when he demurred about working on the hydrogen bomb: his general philosophy came in conflict with his expert knowledge. Almost everyone, as I said earlier, is both specialist and generalist; but the latter function has grown more and more neglected as specialties become more complex and demanding.

In *Fables for Our Time,* James Thurber imagines a conference of ostriches concerned with the loss of their ability to fly. One of them named Oliver complains that men can fly sitting down, while ostriches cannot fly at all. "The old ostrich glared at Oliver severely, first with one eye and then with the other. 'Man is flying too fast for a world that is round,' he said. 'Soon he will catch up with himself, in a great rear-end collision, and man will never know that what hit Man from behind was Man.' "

Peter Berger

Any intellectual activity derives excitement from the moment it becomes a trail of discovery. In some fields of learning this is the discovery of worlds previously unthought and unthinkable. This is the excitement of the astronomer or of the nuclear physicist on the antipodal boundaries of the realities that man is capable of conceiving. But it can also be the excitement of bacteriology or geology. In a different way it can be the excitement of the linguist discovering new realms of human expression or of the anthropologist exploring human customs in faraway countries. In such discovery, when undertaken with passion, a widening of awareness, sometimes a veritable transformation of consciousness, occurs. The universe turns out to be much more wonder-full than one had ever dreamed. The excitement of sociology is usually of a different sort. Sometimes, it is true, the sociologist penetrates into worlds that had previously been quite unknown to him—for instance, the world of crime, or the world of some bizarre religious sect, or the world fashioned by the exclusive concerns of some group such as medical specialists or military leaders or advertising executives. However,

Source: Peter L. Berger, *Invitation to Sociology* (New York: Doubleday, 1963), pp. 20–24, 175. Copyright © 1963 by Peter L. Berger. Reprinted by permission of Doubleday & Company, Inc.
Peter L. Berger is professor of sociology and chairman of the Council on International and Regional Studies at the New School for Social Research. Sociological theory, the sociology of religion, and the sociology of politics are among his special interests. In addition to *Invitation to Sociology*, he has written *Noise of Solemn Assemblies and Precarious Vision* and *The Sacred Canopy*.

much of the time the sociologist moves in sectors of experience that are familiar to him and to most people in his society. He investigates communities, institutions and activities that one can read about every day in the newspapers. Yet there is another excitement of discovery beckoning in his investigations. It is not the excitement of coming upon the totally unfamiliar, but rather the excitement of finding the familiar becoming transformed in its meaning. The fascination of sociology lies in the fact that its perspective makes us see in a new light the very world in which we have lived all our lives. This also constitutes a transformation of consciousness. Moreover, this transformation is more relevant existentially than that of many other intellectual disciplines, because it is more difficult to segregate in some special compartment of the mind. The astronomer does not live in the remote galaxies, and the nuclear physicist can, outside his laboratory, eat and laugh and marry and vote without thinking about the insides of the atom. The geologist looks at rocks only at appropriate times, and the linguist speaks English with his wife. The sociologist lives in society, on the job and off it. His own life, inevitably, is part of his subject matter. Men being what they are, sociologists too manage to segregate their professional insights from their everyday affairs. But it is a rather difficult feat to perform in good faith.

The sociologist moves in the common world of men, close to what most of them would call real. The categories he employs in his analyses are only refinements of the categories by which other men live—power, class, status, race, ethnicity. As a result, there is a deceptive simplicity and obviousness about some sociological investigations. One reads them, nods at the familiar scene, remarks that one has heard all this before and don't people have better things to do than to waste their time on truisms – until one is suddenly brought up against an insight that radically questions everything one had previously assumed about this familiar scene. This is the point at which one begins to sense the excitement of sociology.

Let us take a specific example. Imagine a sociology class in a Southern college where almost all the students are white Southerners. Imagine a lecture on the subject of the racial system of the South. The lecturer is talking here of matters that have been familiar to his students from the time of their infancy. Indeed, it may be that they are much more familiar with the minutiae of this system than he is. They are quite bored as a result. It seems to them that he is only using more pretentious words to describe what they already know. Thus he may use the term "caste," one commonly used now by American sociologists to describe the Southern racial system. But in explaining the term he shifts to traditional Hindu society, to make it clearer. He then goes on to analyze the magical beliefs inherent in caste tabus, the social dynamics of commensalism and connubium, the economic interests concealed within the system, the way in which religious beliefs relate to the tabus, the effects of the caste system upon the industrial development of the society and vice versa – all in India. But suddenly India is not very far away at all. The lecture then goes back to its Southern theme. The familiar now seems not quite so familiar any more. Questions are raised that are new, perhaps raised angrily, but raised all the same. And at least some of the students have begun to understand that there are functions involved in this business of race that they have not read about in the newspapers (at least not those in their hometowns) and that their parents have not told them – partly, at least, because neither the newspapers nor the parents knew about them.

It can be said that the first wisdom of sociology is this – things are not what they seem. This too is a deceptively simple statement. It ceases to be simple after a while. Social reality turns out to have many layers of meaning. The discovery of each new layer changes the perception of the whole.

Anthropologists use the term "culture shock" to describe the impact of a totally new culture upon a newcomer. . . .

. . . The first encounters with polygamy or with puberty rites or even with the way some nations drive their automobiles can be quite a shock to an American visitor. With the shock may go not only disapproval or disgust but a sense of excitement that things can *really* be that different from what they are at home. To some extent, at least, this is the excitement of any first travel abroad. The experience of sociological discovery could be described as "culture shock" minus geographical displacement. In other words, the sociologist travels at home – with shocking results.

. . . The discovery, for instance, that his own church has considerable money invested in the missile industry or that a few blocks from his home there are people who engage in cultic orgies may not be drastically different in emotional impact. Yet we would not want to imply that sociological discoveries are always or even usually outrageous to moral sentiment. Not at all. What they have in common with exploration in distant lands, however, is the sudden illumination of new and unsuspected facets of human existence in society. This is the excitement and the humanistic justification of sociology.

People who like to avoid shocking discoveries, who prefer to believe that society is just what they were taught in Sunday

School, who like the safety of the rules and the maxims of what Alfred Schuetz has called the "world-taken-for-granted," should stay away from sociology. People who feel no temptation before closed doors, who have no curiosity about human beings, who are content to admire scenery without wondering about the people who live in those houses on the other side of that river, should probably also stay away from sociology. They will find it unpleasant or, at any rate, unrewarding. People who are interested in human beings only if they can change, convert or reform them should also be warned, for they will find sociology much less useful than they hoped. And people whose interest is mainly in their own conceptual constructions will do just as well to turn to the study of little white mice. Sociology will be satisfying, in the long run, only to those who can think of nothing more entrancing than to watch men and to understand things human.

. . . . .

We maintain that the teaching of sociology is justified insofar as a liberal education is assumed to have a more than etymological connection with intellectual liberation. Where this assumption does not exist, where education is understood in purely technical or professional terms, let sociology be eliminated from the curriculum. It will only interfere with the smooth operation of the latter, provided, of course, that sociology has not also been emasculated in accordance with the educational ethos prevailing in such situations. Where, however, the assumption still holds, sociology is justified by the belief that it is better to be conscious than unconscious and that consciousness is a condition of freedom. To attain a greater measure of awareness, and with it of freedom, entails a certain amount of suffering and even risk. An educational process that would avoid this becomes simple technical training and ceases to have any relationship to the civilizing of the mind. We contend that it is part of a civilized mind in our age to have come in touch with the peculiarly modern, peculiarly timely form of critical thought that we call sociology.

Robert Redfield

. . . . .

It is part of a general education to understand, in the first place, that there is a social science, as distinct from commonsense knowledge about society and as distinct from social reform. Every educated person should know that to a great extent society can be studied objectively and systematically, as can starfish or the action of glaciers. One can get impersonal, organized, verifiable knowledge about housing, crime, and race relations, as one can get such knowledge about any other phenomena of nature. An educated person will know how to distinguish the scientific way of attacking a social problem from those ways of attacking it which are more generally practiced around him. He will understand that in a great many instances people do something about a social problem be-

Source: Robert Redfield, "Research in the Social Sciences: Its Significance for General Education," *Social Education* (December 1941), pp. 568–75. Reprinted by permission of the publisher

Robert Redfield (1897–1958) was chairman of the Department of Anthropology and Distinguished Service Professor at the University of Chicago. His chief interests lay in ethnological studies. From 1930 to 1947 he directed ethnological field work in Yucatan and Guatemala. Among his books are *The Folk Culture of Yucatan, The Primitive World and Its Transformations, The Little Community,* and *The Social Uses of Science.*

cause they feel badly about it rather than because they understand it and that what they do corresponds with their feelings rather than with the facts underlying the problem. He will understand that this is true, whether the action taken be to write a letter to the newspapers, to pass a law, or to demand changes in the school curriculum. It is a part of general education to understand that scientific knowledge is different from feeling strongly about something and from common-sense knowledge and that it is a more secure basis for social action than either.

The successful teacher of the social studies will make clear that there is a difference between the analysis of processes, which are matters of efficiency, and other objective judgments. The citizen must know what are his values, and he should understand how to act so as to protect or realize them. The uneducated person confuses values and processes, ends and means; a good education in social science will help to keep them distinct.

As a part of this understanding, the educated man or woman will have been taught that a social problem is not a simple thing. Social problems are closely intermeshed with one another. If one makes a beginning with the problem of housing, one finds that it is only one aspect of the larger problem of national insecurity. It is also related to the problem of the national income and to that of the national health. The solutions given in the form of new housing projects or in zoning laws encounter the problems of racial intolerance. It follows from this that a social problem does not mean the same thing to everybody.

. . . The problem of housing looks very different to laymen, landowners, builders, tax officials, and city planners, and . . . full understanding of the problem depends upon special scientific knowledge of economists, sociologists, and students of government. The contribution of social-science research to a general education is not made use of when a social problem is presented to young people as if it existed with simple reference to some social ideal. It is not made use of if the problem is presented as if all one had to do was to take note of the social injustice attending the present state of things. That is not functional education; it does not prepare the young person for life.

A further contribution which social-science research can make to general education is the understanding that although social science is like physical or biological science in that it is objective, systematic description of the world around us, it differs from physical and biological science in that all the facts and all the problems are controversial. The social scientist is studying, chiefly, to put it strongly, himself, and one cannot help feeling and caring about one's self. We, as human beings, care about the institutions and social problems which the social scientist studies. Therefore it is harder for the social scientist to maintain objectivity than it is for the physicist, and it is harder for Society, with a capital "S," to keep from interfering with the social scientist than with the physicist. This is one of the elements of understanding of social-science research which belongs in a general education. If social problems are presented . . . so as to communicate this general knowledge of the nature of social science it will be made clear to the learner that the mere facts of social science lie within a realm of controversy and prejudice. As Professor Wirth has pointed out even the number of people living in a given city of the United States is a controversial matter in the sense that if the city has been losing population the Chamber of Commerce will not want the fact to get abroad. The number of people unemployed in this country is a controversial fact, first, in the sense that various interest groups care as to what criterion is selected for determining who is unemployed, and, second, because even if it is decided who are unemployed, various groups will interpret the fact according to their interests. For some employers there will be just enough unemployed to assure a labor reserve, while for other of our citizens these same unemployed constitute a problem of providing relief.

At the same time the educated man or woman will understand that this special difficulty under which the social scientist labors has its compensation in a special advantage enjoyed by the social scientist and understanding of the nature of social-science research is not complete until another general characteristic of it is recognized. It is a peculiarity of the scientific method as applied to man in society that the investigator can get a more intimate knowledge of his subject matter than can the physicist of his, just because he is part of it. The physical scientist learns of his subject matter only as caliper and scales can tell him about it. The social scientist can ask questions of his subject matter and get answers, and he can project his own humanity imaginatively into the subject matter and so increase his understanding of it. The contribution of social-science research to a general education is provided in part by an understanding of the advantages and the dangers of this essential characteristic of social-science research. The social scientist does not abolish his own prejudices any more than he abolishes his own human nature. But he controls prejudice by making it explicit. So, too, he develops controlled use of his human insights. It is more important to a general education that the individual knows that there is a problem of using and controlling the human faculty of insight as a scientific instrument than that he know the latest facts with regard to any problem studied by that method.

The humanistic aspect of social science is the aspect of it that is today not well appreciated. Social science is essentially scientific in that its propositions describe, in general terms, natural phenomena; in that it returns again and again to special experience to verify and to modify these propositions. It tells what is, not what ought to be. It investigates nature. It strives for objectivity, accuracy, competency. It employs hypotheses and formal evidence; it values negative cases; and, when it finds a hypothesis to be unsupported by the facts, it drops it for some other which is. But these are all aspects of social science so well known that it is tedious to list them again. What is less familiar, but equally true, is that to create the hypothesis, to reach the conclusion, to get, often, the very first real datum as to what are A's motives or what is the meaning of this odd custom or that too-familiar institution, requires on the part of one who studies persons and societies, and not rocks or proteins, a truly humanistic and freely imaginative insight into people, their conventions and interests and motives, and that this requirement in the social scientist calls for gifts and for a kind of education different from that required of any physicist and very similar to what is called for in a creative artist.

If this be seen, it may also be seen that the function of social science in our society is a double function. Social science is customarily explained and justified by reason of what social science contributes to the solution of particular problems that arise in the management of our society, as a help in getting particular things done. As social scientists we take satisfaction in the fact that today, as compared with thirty years ago, social scientists are employed because their employers think that their social science is applicable to some practical necessity. Some knowledge of techniques developed in social science may be used: to select taxicab drivers that are not likely to have accidents; to give vocational guidance; to discover why one business enterprise has labor troubles while a similar enterprise does not; to make more effective some governmental program carried into farming communities. . . .

All these contributions to efficiency and adjustment may be claimed with justice by social scientists. What is also to be claimed, and is less commonly stressed, is that social science contributes to that general understanding of the world around us which, as we say, "liberalizes," or "enriches." The relation of social science to humanistic learning is reciprocal. Social scientists need humanistic learning the better to be social scientists. And the understanding of society, personality, and human nature which is achieved by scientific methods returns to enrich that humanistic understanding without which none can become human and with which some few may become wise. Because its subject matter is humanity, the contribution of social science to general, liberal education is greater than is the contribution of those sciences with subject matter that is physical. In this respect also, creative artist and social scientist find themselves side by side. The artist may reveal something of universal human or social nature. So too may the social scientist. No one has ever applied, as a key to a lock, Sumner's *Folkways* or Tawney's *Religion and the Rise of Capitalism* or James's *The Varieties of Religious Experience.* These are not the works of social science that can be directly consulted and applied when a government office or a business concern has an immediate problem. But they are the books of lasting influence. Besides what influence they have upon those social scientists who come to work in the government office, or the business concern, in so far as they are read and understood and thought about by men and women who are not social scientists, or even as they are communicated indirectly by those who have read them to others, they are part of humanistic education, in the broad sense. Releasing us from our imprisonment in the particular, we are freed by seeing how we are exemplifications of the general. For how many young people has not Sumner's book, or Veblen's book, or some work by Freud, come as a swift widening of the doors of vision, truly a liberation, a seeing of one's self, perhaps for the first time, as sharing the experiences, the nature, of many other men and women? So I say that social science, as practiced, is something of an art and that, as its best works are communicated, it has something of the personal and social values of all the arts.

Robert Bierstedt

Sociology has an honorable place in the realm of humane letters and it belongs with the liberal arts as well as with the sciences. We have seldom been able to escape the

Source: Robert Bierstedt, "Sociology and Humane Learning," *American Sociological Review* 25, no. 1 (February 1960): 8–9. Reprinted by permission of the American Sociological Association.

Robert Bierstedt is professor of sociology and anthropology at New York University. He has served in an editorial capacity on the *American Sociological Review* and the *American Journal of Sociology.* In 1960–61 he was executive officer of the American Sociological Association. His chief interests include sociological theory and control, and he is the author of *The Social Order, The Making of Society,* and *Emile Durkheim.*

public belief that it is the principal business of sociology to solve social problems; and the identification of our discipline with such problems is too well known to require comment. That sociology might also have something to do with culture in the narrower and nonsociological sense of intellectual cultivation seems seldom to have occurred to anyone, including sociologists.

I invite your attention, therefore, to the fact that sociology, like the other arts, is one of the ornaments of the human mind, that its literature extending from Plato to our contemporaries is in a great and humane tradition, that sociology—like all of the liberal arts—liberates us from the provincialisms of time and place and circumstance, that the social order is a study worthy of a free man, and that society itself, like every other thing that has ever agitated the restless and inquisitive mind of man, is a fit and dignified subject of inquiry.

Part I

Sociology and Society

1.

THE TRANSITION TO SCIENCE IN HUMAN RELATIONS

George A. Lundberg

Sociology consists of the scientific study of human groups and human interaction. To consider sociology a science means that we stand ready to observe human behavior as scientists would observe any natural phenomenon and to look for systematic regularities in this human behavior. In this selection Lundberg, long an exponent of the rigorous application of the natural science approach to the study of human behavior, describes some of the practical results of this approach and presents the steps that he felt must be taken if the social sciences are to help achieve a more rational "management of social relations." Public opinion polling, characterized here as one of the best known of social science methods, seems to have achieved high credibility faster than Lundberg could have thought possible if the media's reporting of the numerous national polls on various subjects of current interest is a valid criterion.

I. CONSENSUS ON METHODS

I have expressed the view that the best hope for man in his present social predicament lies in a type of social science strictly comparable to the other natural sciences. We have reviewed some of the objections that have been urged both by physical and social scientists to this proposal. I am not under the illusion that my argument can be established conclusively in so brief a compass. Actually, of course, only time and future scientific development can finally demonstrate the validity of the position which I have outlined.

In the meantime, we are confronted with the necessity of proceeding on *some* hypothesis as to the way out of our difficulties. It is generally agreed, even by those who differ most radically as to the proper approach, that our first need is a unified, coherent theory on which to proceed. A society cannot achieve its adjustments by mutually incompatible or contradictory behavior, any more than can an individual organism. However we may differ on details and on ends, we must agree on certain broad means, certain principles of action toward whatever ends we do agree upon.

In short, we all apparently agree with Comte's appraisal of the situation as he saw

Source: George A. Lundberg, *Can Science Save Us?*, 2d ed. (London: Longmans, Green, 1947), pp. 42–51.

The author (1895–1966) was professor emeritus of sociology, University of Washington. He was the editor of *Sociometry,* 1941–1945, and served as consultant to the National Resources Planning Board for many years. Among his publications are *Foundations of Sociology, Social Research,* and *Sociology,* of which he was the co-author. He was a past president of the American Sociological Association.

it a hundred years ago. Speaking of the theological, the metaphysical, and the positive scientific approaches, he said: "Any one of these might alone secure some sort of social order: but, while the three coexist, it is impossible for us to understand one another upon any essential point whatever."

Of course there are some who find in our present predicament merely further evidence of the futility of the scientific approach in human affairs. They overlook the fact that, actually, science has as yet not been tried on social problems. Consequently, they advocate a return to theology, or "the" classics, either in their historic forms or in new versions in which the advocates of these approaches personally can play the role of major prophets. If I could see any chance of bringing about a return to theology or "the" classics, I might give it serious consideration, because any one unified approach might be better than two or more contradictory ones. But I see no such possibility in the long run. The commitments we have already made to science, chiefly in our technological culture, are of such character that we can neither go back nor stand still.

Our technological developments and our methods of communication have resulted in a fundamental interdependence which dominates our lives. This state of affairs requires, as we shall see, that we bring our social arrangements into line with this basic technological pattern, rather than vice versa. This basic technological pattern unquestionably rests upon natural science. On this ground, rather than on any assumption of absolute or intrinsic superiority of science as a philosophy of life, I think the following conclusion is inescapable: *In our time and for some centuries to come, for better or for worse, the sciences, physical and social, will be to an increasing degree the accepted point of reference with respect to which the validity (Truth) of all knowledge is gauged.*

II. WHAT CAN BE DONE—SOME EXAMPLES

What are some examples of types of work by social scientists that are of vast importance in managing human relations?

When we speak of *types* of work by social scientists, we are obviously announcing an undertaking so large as to prevent even a summary within the confines of this book. There are at least five well-recognized social sciences, and if we use the larger category of "behavioral science," the number rises to twelve or more. The social sciences are well-recognized in the sense that they are firmly established as departments in nearly all leading universities and colleges as well as in professional, industrial, and governmental circles. Over a hundred journals publish every year hundreds of research reports of studies large and small, designed to yield new knowledge or to test and refine previous conclusions and to predict behavior under stipulated conditions. We shall confine ourselves to a few illustrations selected chiefly because they are individually of interest to more than one of the social sciences. Readers interested in more comprehensive accounts, including methodological details, will find a large literature readily available.

For our present purpose we shall not here become involved in the question of the degree of scientific refinement attained in the different sciences. My argument has been based in large part on what appears to me to be warranted anticipations regarding *future developments* of the social sciences. Here I shall rather take the view that, *even with their present shortcomings,* the social sciences must be taken seriously. The recent (1960) elevation of the Office of Social Sciences to full divisional status in the National Science Foundation is an indication of this growing recognition.

The work of such agencies as the Census Bureau is known to all and is more or less taken for granted. Without the data and the analyses which it provides, the administration of public affairs would certainly dissolve in chaos and perhaps in civil war. It is equally certain that no international organization can function without an elaborate organization of this kind to provide the essential facts regarding people and their characteristics and activities. Perhaps the most permanently valuable contribution of the ill-fated League of Nations was its establishment of an international statistical bureau which managed to survive until taken over by the larger information agencies of the United Nations. The Office of Population Research at Princeton University has engaged in detailed studies of local and international population trends in various parts of the world and has predicted the future areas of population pressure. This knowledge is of the utmost practical importance in the administration of national and international organizations of any kind. The Scripps Foundation, the Milbank Memorial Fund, and many others are engaged in similar or related work of a character that measures up very well to the standards of the physical sciences.

Social scientists have also been prominent in pointing out one of the most serious of the world's *problems,* namely, the problem of overpopulation. As a result of the drastic decline in the death rate resulting from the application of medical science, world population is increasing at an unprecedented rate. For example, although it took thousands of years for the human species to reach the number of one billion of living people (about 1830) it required only one century to add the second billion. It is now taking less than thirty-five years for the world population to add a third billion—probably before 1965. The United Nations' population experts estimate that it will take only fifteen years to add a fourth billion, and another ten years to add the fifth billion if present rates should continue. The idea that any expansion of the food supply could do more than temporarily alleviate the starvation of people under such rates of population increase is merely a confusion of wishful thinking with stern realities.

However, just as the application of science to health and sanitation has produced this situation, science has provided the means for its control. Further improvements in the latter are highly likely and imminent. The distinctively social problem of securing the widespread adoption of known methods of control involves a number of problems of a type not yet fully solved, but under extensive inquiry by social scientists. In the meantime we have an example of successful population control in the case of postwar Japan. We are not here concerned with these problems in themselves, but with the role of scientifically gathered and analyzed human social data in the prediction of future population, and the solution of a problem which some regard as more dangerous than nuclear war. Also in other ways, statistics of individual countries, and the data collected by the United Nations organization, are of fundamental importance to the work of many scientists engaged in a wide variety of particular projects. Human ecology, which cuts across the conventional boundaries of demography, geography, sociology, economics, political science (and perhaps others), has produced very impressive work both of applied and theoretical significance.

Reliable and objective knowledge of other peoples and cultures constitutes another field in which social scientists have made distinguished contributions. This knowledge has thrown a flood of light on our own civilization and permits the formulation and test of hypotheses regarding human behavior patterns in general. The Human Relations Area Files contain, systematically filed and indexed, virtually all present reliable knowledge regarding some two hundred cultures. To make a long story short, if a researcher happens to be interested in some subject as, for example, divorce, crime, education, law (and about a thousand other topics), in other cultures, he can go to one of the twenty or more libraries which subscribe to the File, and find all the known information on any or all of these subjects for each of about two hundred cultures. The information is neatly filed away in a separate drawer for each subject. Information which it might take years to locate as scattered in hundreds of books in a library can be secured in a few hours from the File. The importance of this kind of knowledge and its ready availability in facilitating our contacts with people of other lands and cultures became very evident during and after World War II.

We [have recognized] the importance of instruments and methods of observation and measurement in the social as well as in the physical sciences. Social scientists have produced revolutionary developments in this field in the last thirty years. Thousands of such instruments have been invented by means of which vocational aptitudes, success in college and other undertakings, and social behavior of great variety can be accurately measured and predicted. Instruments and scales for the measurement of attitudes have opened vast new fields for investigation.

Perhaps the best known, but by no means the only one, of these devices is the public opinion poll. We have in this technique an illustration of how a development in the social sciences may be as significant for the future of social organization as many physical inventions have been in our industrial development. The mechanisms by which the "public will" can make itself reliably felt in government and community action has always been in the foreground of political discussion. With the expansion of the areas in which public opinion must operate, many students of the problem have despaired of the capacity of the town meeting technique adequately to make operative the "public will." In the face of this situation, the scientific public opinion poll constitutes an instrument which cheaply and accurately permits us to learn the beliefs, the attitudes, and the wishes of the rank and file of the population. Public opinion polls are at present frequently thought of as interesting devices mainly for predicting the outcome of elections. They do permit such prediction, but this is a very minor aspect of their full possible importance. Polls were extensively used in the armed forces in World War II as a guide to the administration of the invaded areas, the return of the armed forces after the war, and in many other ways.

Public opinion polling may be a device through which can be resolved one of the principal impasses of our time, namely, the apparent irreconcilability of authoritarian control on the one hand and the "public will" on the other. It may be that through properly administered public opinion polls professionalized public officials can give us all the efficiency now claimed for authoritarian centralized administration and yet have that administration at all times subject to the dictates of a more delicate barometer of the peoples' wills than is provided by all the technologically obsolete paraphernalia of traditional democratic processes. In short, it is not impossible that as the advancing technology in the physical adjustments of our lives leads to a threatened breakdown of democracy, so an improved social research instrument may restore and even increase the dominance of the people's voice in the control of human society.

The time may come when the reliable polling of public opinion will be a science comparable to meteorology. Charts of all kinds of social weather, its movements and trends, whether it be anti-Semitism, anti-Negro sentiment, or mob-mindedness will be at the disposal of the administrators of the people's will in every land. A barometer of international tension has been designed to detect reliably and early the tensions that lead to war. It is true that mere knowledge of these tensions does not necessarily operate to alleviate them. But it is also true that a reliable diagnosis of the tension and an understanding of the feelings and sentiments that underlie tensions is essential for an effective approach to the problem.

"Statesmen" will doubtless continue for some time to value their intuitions more highly than scientific prediction. Pious platitudes doubtless will continue to be heard about the "unpredictability" of human behavior. It remains a fact that social scientists predicted within a fraction of 1 percent the actual voting behavior of sixty-eight million voters in the U.S.A. in the presidential election of 1960. The pollsters have been doing so regularly since 1936 with a maximum error of 6 percent. Nor are such results limited to voting behaviors. The late Professor Stouffer of Harvard predicted, also within a fraction of 1 percent, the number of discharged soldiers after World War II who would take advantage of the educational privileges of the G.I. Bill of Rights. Hundreds of other cases could be reported from a great variety of fields of human social behavior, including the vast areas of market research.

To those who constantly have their minds on quick and dramatic solutions to the world's troubles this type of research is likely to seem offensively trivial—a kind of fiddling while Rome burns. "Writers" are fond of referring contemptuously to basic scientific work as an "ivory tower" and as "lecturing on navigation while the ship sinks." Navigation today is what it is because some people were willing to study the *principles* of their subject while their individual ships went down, instead of rushing about with half-baked advice as to how to save ships that could not be saved, or were not worth saving anyway. As A. J. Carlson has recently said: "The failure of bacteria to survive in close proximity to certain moulds looked trivial at first, but few informed people would label the discovery of that initial fact *trivial* today."

So much, then, for a few illustrations, rather than a summary, of the type of work that is being done and that needs to be done in the social sciences. Is there enough of it being done? Clearly not, or we would not need to flounder as we are in national and international affairs, pursuing diametrically opposite courses within the same decade. Can the social sciences ever hope to catch up with the other sciences, the increasingly rapid advance of which constantly creates new social problems? Certainly we can, if we devote ourselves to the business with something like the seriousness, the money, and the equipment that we have devoted to physical research. Consider how the physical scientists are today given vast resources to concentrate on the invention of a new submarine detector or a new bomb, not to mention the peacetime occupations of these scientists with penicillin and sulpha drugs. Obviously, I am not criticizing this action. On the contrary, it is the way to proceed if you want results. Is there anything like that going on regarding the world organization and its numerous subsidiary problems, all of them important to peace and prosperity?

Comparatively speaking, there is almost nothing that could be called fundamental research into the basic nature of human relations. To be sure, there are endless petty projects, surveys, conferences, oratory, and arguments by representatives of pressure groups, as if argument ever settled any scientific questions. Of basic social research there is very little. Why isn't there more? It is not yet realized that scientific knowledge is relevant to successful world organization. We still think that common sense, good will, eloquent leaders, and pious hopes are sufficient when it comes to management of social relations.

2.

POPULATION STUDIES: FERTILITY IN TAIWAN

James E. Haney

This selection, which examines a successful attempt to teach family planning in Taiwan, demonstrates the practical value of sociology. On the basis of the experiment described here, one may infer that sociological knowledge can be used to influence social change in a desired direction. The reader is also invited to study this selection as an illustration of the rigor that characterizes high quality experimental research in the social sciences.

The Population Studies Center has been engaged in fertility studies in Taiwan since 1962 in programs sponsored by the provincial health department of Taiwan and sup-

Source: James E. Haney, *Research News* 29, no. 10 (Ann Arbor: University of Michigan, Office of Research Administration, April 1969): 3–11. A book-length treatment of this study is found in Ronald Freedman and John Y. Takeshita, *Family Planning in Taiwan* (Princeton: Princeton University Press, 1969). Reprinted by permission of the publisher.

James E. Haney is a senior editor of *Research News,* publication of the Office of Research Administration, the University of Michigan, and has written numerous articles for it.

ported by the Population Council, a private U.S. foundation. The Taiwan Population Studies Center, established with the assistance of the U–M Center, has set basic policies and conducted the field work. The U–M group has provided training assistance and consultation, and has participated in joint work on research analyses. The principal object of the research has been to understand the population changes underway and to test the efficacy of various means of accelerating a slow decline in fertility that began in 1958. Taiwan has become increasingly urbanized and industrialized recently, with fairly widespread education and literacy, transportation, communications, and medical facilities. Its population also has few religious or cultural objections to contraception; less than 5 percent of the women in any age group believe that the number of children they bear is up to "fate" or "providence." The island has thus been suitable for an experimental program designed to study various means of accelerating what is known as the "demographic transition"—a trend in which birth rates decline following a decline in death rates. In various Western countries this transition required, on the average, about 50 years.

In 1962, Taichung, a city of about 325,000, was selected for a sample-survey and two small pilot-projects designed to measure contraceptive knowledge, attitudes, and practices. The pilot-projects explored the acceptability of modern contraceptives, the pill and the intrauterine device (IUD), in relation to older means of contraception, abortion, and sterilization. (Although abortion is illegal in Taiwan, the law is not strictly enforced.) An experimental program covering all of Taichung was then set up to test a number of important questions concerning the diffusion of contraceptive knowledge and practices. Although other large-scale family planning programs have possessed some of the features of this program, they have had few provisions for analyzing their own effectiveness. The Taiwan program is one of the largest social science studies ever conducted under some approximation of experimental conditions.

The preprogram survey indicated that Taichung's married couples were having more children than they wanted. A significant minority of them were attempting family planning, but they were not well informed, and their efforts were too ineffective to achieve their goals. Based on this situation the Taiwanese designed an action-study program to answer the following questions:

1. How much can the practice of family planning be increased by a massive information and service campaign of short duration? This was perhaps the single most important question to be answered by the study. In 1962 there was no example anywhere in the world of a program for a large population that was successful in substantially changing the proportion of people practicing contraception.

2. Must both husbands and wives be approached in an education program, or is it enough to approach the wife alone? Most programs had concentrated on reaching wives. The failure of many of them to achieve significant results was often attributed to the hostility or indifference of husbands, but this view had rarely been tested. It was important to know whether the additional effort is worthwhile, because reaching husbands as well as wives is difficult and expensive.

3. Can family planning ideas be spread cheaply and simply by mail? Most programs involve expensive person-to-person contacts by field workers. Given sufficient literacy among a population, mail campaigns could have great potential. Within a given

budget, the number of acceptors might be much greater, even though the proportion of people influenced to accept might be much smaller than through personal contacts.

4. Can direct communication to systematically spaced subgroups of a population indirectly affect a much larger population by a diffusion of information from the points of direct contact? What are the dynamics of "circulation" effects? Will the population itself spread the desired innovation, and, if so, how large an initial effort is required to prime this process? To communicate directly with each couple of childbearing age is expensive. Word-of-mouth diffusion probably was mainly responsible for spreading ideas about family planning in Western countries and in Japan over long periods of time and without organized programs. To what extent can centers of direct communication speed up this process?

5. Does a new innovation in contraception, the IUD, influence diffusion and acceptances? Significant numbers of women were beginning to use the IUD at the outset of the Taichung study. It was necessary to test its relative acceptability, whether it would diffuse rapidly, and whether some potential disadvantages would create special problems.

6. Would a significant adoption of family planning actually accelerate the decline in fertility already evident in Taichung and Taiwan? The recognition that child mortality had greatly declined was already influencing couples to want less children and to think of adopting contraception. Could the program effects be separated from a fertility decline that might be expected to accelerate even in the absence of any program?

7. What demographic and social characteristics of the couples are most important in determining whether they accept family planning in an organized program? Which is more important: the pressures of growing family size, or education and other signs of modernization? How do the characteristics of acceptors in the program compare with those of couples who had adopted family limitation prior to the program? Are the younger women readier than others to adopt family planning?

8. What are the characteristics of couples who express an intention to accept family planning but do not do so? Who express an intention not to, but do? It was important to learn how the demographic and social characteristics of the couples affect their intentions, whether the intentions predict behavior, and whether the reasons given to explain intentions help to discriminate between acceptors and nonacceptors.

9. Is the recent fertility of those accepting family planning high enough so that their use of contraception will produce a distinct reduction in birth rates? If the couples who accept family planning via the program are above average in their fecundability, the program is potentially more effective.

10. Which characteristics of the couples are related to persistence in effective use of contraception once it is adopted? High acceptance rates in a program mean little unless the acceptors continue to use contraception.

11. How does the discussion and perception of what others are doing affect acceptances? This question relates to the diffusion of information through informal contacts. Studies elsewhere have since shown diffusion to be an important factor (in Chicago, Kentucky, Korea, Puerto Rico, Thailand, and Japan).

Providing a data base to attempt to answer these questions required a rather sophisticated action program designed to reach 36,000 married couples of Taichung with wives 20–39 years old. For statistical purposes, however, Taichung was already organized into about 2,400 *lin*'s—neighborhood units containing an average of about 20 households, each including about 12 married women aged 20–39. For purposes of the experiment, the city was divided into three wedge-shaped sectors, placing about one-third of the lins in each sector. The sectors were roughly equated initially on fertility, rural-urban distribution, occupational composition, and educational levels.

Four different "treatments" were devised for application to individual lins:

1. *Everything—husband and wife.* These lins received all of the stimuli of the program: personal visits to both husbands and wives by trained health workers, mailings of information to newlyweds and couples with at least two children, and neighborhood meetings that mixed entertainment with information about family planning, including slides, film strips, flip charts, etc.

2. *Everything—wife only.* This treatment included all of the major stimuli except the personal visit to the husband.

3. *Mailings.* This treatment involved no personal visits or neighborhood meetings, but a series of mailings of letters and pamphlets to newlyweds and couples with at least two children. The mailings provided general information on methods, rationale, location of clinics, etc., and included a return-post device for requesting more information or a personal visit from a field worker.

4. *Nothing.* In this treatment, no effort was made to reach the couples directly. There were, however, posters in these areas, because posters had been distributed throughout the city. Also, some meetings were held at the *li* level (a neighborhood unit of about 350 households).

The three sectors of about 800 lins each were differentiated in terms of the proportion of lins within each sector that received a given "treatment." The sectors were designated as heavy-, medium-, or light-density, according to the percentage of their lins to receive the "Everything" treatment. In the heavy-density sector, half of the lins received an Everything treatment; in the medium-density sector, one-third of them; and in the light-density sector, one-fifth of them. The remaining lins in each sector were divided equally between "Mail" and "Nothing" treatments. Once these percentages of lin treatments were assigned, the lin treatments within each sector were randomly distributed throughout the sector.

All of the couples in the lins receiving a particular treatment supposedly received the same set of prescribed stimuli (or none) regardless of the density sector in which they were located. The difference lay only in the percentage of surrounding lins receiving the same or another treatment. That is, Nothing lins in the heavy-density sector bordered many more lins that were receiving an Everything treatment than did Nothing lins in the light-density sector.

In addition to the specific treatments, posters were placed throughout the city; some city-wide mass media messages were broadcast; and meetings were held with such occupational groups as the farmers' association and the pedicab drivers' association. In the course of the program, some 12,000 initial home visits were made and 500 neighborhood meetings were held. More than 20,000 follow-up home visits of various kinds were made. Family planning services and supplies were offered at ten clinics located throughout the city. Information, services, and supplies were offered with respect to the diaphragm, jelly, foam tablets, condom, withdrawal, rhythm, oral pills, and the IUD, although no effort was made to set up procedures that would test the attractiveness of different methods. Except for the oral pills and the IUD, which were available only at the clinics, supplies were available on request from field workers during home visits or group meetings. There was a nominal charge, except for indigents, for any kind of contraceptive device or chemicals accepted. A charge of $.75 was made for an IUD insertion or for a set of 20 oral pills.

How were all of the data obtained? The data base was compiled from three sources: (1) an Intensive Survey of 2,443 women interviewed prior to and following the experimental program. This was a probability, cross-section sample of all wives of child-bearing age in the city; (2) a Household Survey interview of the more than 11,000 women in the Everything lins; and (3) the clinic records of all women who were acceptors, regardless of where they came from. These clinic records also included answers to the Household Survey questions. Clinic records were linked to the Household Survey records for those acceptors who were interviewed in either the Household Survey sample or the Intensive Survey sample. It was therefore possible to relate the characteristics of the respondent on a survey to whether she later became an acceptor.

The survey instruments and clinical records established an extensive data base of demographic and social characteristics, including detailed information on marriage, births, pregnancies, household composition, fecundity, family size, attitudes and practices relating to family planning, reading skills and habits, wife's background, husband's background, occupation, and income, and household facilities. Questions on household facilities included some relating to the social and economic status of the household in terms of conveniences associated with economic and technological "modernity" – whether or not the couple had a bicycle, motorcycle, clock or watch, newspaper subscription, radio, record player, electric fan, electric rice cooker, or sewing machine. Ownership of these objects is an indication of economic modernization, of a transition to a market economy. The number of these objects owned was found to be much more closely related to the educational level of the couple than to their household income. Modernization is broadly defined as a shift from dependence on relatively self-contained local institutions to participation in larger social, economic, and political units. Such a shift implies a change in the division of labor: Family and village units give up many functions to larger units not based on kinship ties. Education and literacy are relevant to this process. It was not surprising to find that several indicators of modernization were linked to the preprogram practice of birth control. A more significant finding was that, once the program began, these indicators of modernization were no longer indicative of who accepted family planning in the program. This is important, because most of the population in developing countries is in less modern categories.

. . . . .

What were the major results of the study? As of the end of 1962, when the program began, 36 percent of all married couples in Taichung had practiced some form of birth control. By July of 1965 this figure had risen to 51.2 percent, and it is now estimated to be about 60 percent. Much of this rise is believed to be directly attributable to the program, but it is difficult to separate these program effects from social and economic influences outside the program. The experiment did establish, however, that demographic variables are much more important than social and economic variables in determining who becomes an acceptor. Demographic variables indicate in various ways the stages of the family life-cycle, and their relation to the desired number and sex of children. The acceptance rate increased markedly with increasing numbers of children, with increasing numbers of sons, and with increasing age or years of marriage. It was also high among couples who had already tried to limit their family's size. On the other hand, nine social and economic variables, including wife's education and husband's occupation, were only weakly correlated with acceptances.

By July of 1965 the vast majority of acceptors (86 percent) had chosen the new IUD. The Taichung program was the first to have introduced the IUD on a large scale in a developing country; its educational material stressed the IUD and traditional methods, rather than the pill. Yet a similar mass campaign based on the pills might have had equal or greater success in such a population. The Taichung experiment did not definitively answer the question of which method of contraception is the most suitable in such a population. A substantial minority of acceptors removed the IUD after a time, for various reasons. A three-year follow-up did indicate, however, that the great majority of couples who accepted an IUD had reduced their birth rates sharply. Even if they gave up the IUD, they found other ways to limit further family growth.

What conclusions can be drawn from results of the variation in densities and treatments in Taichung? Four stand out:

1. Contacting the husband as well as the wife in home visits was not discernibly more effective than contacting only the wife. The principal method chosen (the IUD) is pertinent here. Moreover, the probability of a high incidence of agreement between the spouses about the need for family planning would often make contacts with the husband redundant.

2. The direct personal contacts in the Everything lins produced more acceptances, but this is less remarkable than the substantial acceptance rates obtained in neighborhoods in which the influence was almost entirely by diffusion.

3. The use of letters was not effective in Taichung. The acceptance rate in the Mail lins was no higher than in the Nothing lins. The letters mentioned only that family planning information could be obtained from a field worker upon request, or from the nearest health station. Possibly they might have been more effective if they had been keyed specifically to the IUD. In Seoul, Korea, however, in a similar experiment, mailings keyed to the IUD failed to produce any significant effects. Since the Taichung experiment, mass mailings keyed to the IUD and addressed to couples with a very recent birth have been highly effective in Taiwan.

4. The heavy-density sector yielded acceptance rates distinctly higher than the medium- and light-density sectors. Contrary to expectation, results in these other two sectors did not differ in any consistent, meaningful way. These results led to the conclusion that for most purposes the 12-fold experimental design could be collapsed into four cells by reducing the four treatments to a dichotomy—Everything and Nothing—and reducing the three density sectors to another dichotomy—heavy and light.

In the heavy-density sector there was relatively little difference in IUD acceptances between the Everything and the Nothing lins, after sufficient time had passed. In relation to the three major subperiods of the study, a small advantage in the Everything lins during the first period was neutralized in the second period and reversed in the third, indicating an extremely effective diffusion process. During the second period, when free insertion of the IUD was offered, the rate of acceptances in Nothing lins in the heavy-density sector was actually higher than in the Everything lins. These heavy-density Nothing lins also had a higher IUD acceptance rate than the Nothing lins in the light-density sector. The intensive treatment made a significant difference initially, but as time progressed the IUD diffused so widely throughout the city as to minimize the initial differences in treatment. It is significant also that diffusion did not stop at the city's border. As much as 26 percent of all of the acceptances in the experimental period came from outside Taichung, where no formal effort had been made to recruit them. By July, 1965, 30 percent of all acceptances were from outside the city, and 97 percent of these acceptors had chosen the IUD.

About one-half of the acceptors within the city reported having heard of the program through a neighbor, friend, or relative, and 67 percent of the acceptors from outside the city gave this as their source of information. Other important sources of information were the regular health station personnel, who had good rapport with the public in their routine health service activities. Some of the health station nurses in outlying areas brought in groups of women for IUD insertions. Finally, the program's home visitors, who apparently talked to people outside of the Everything lins in addition to making their scheduled home visits, helped to circulate information.

One of the consequences of the diffusion process was the increased perception of support from relatives, friends, and neighbors. Wives interviewed before and after the intensive program were asked whether some or many of their relatives, friends, and neighbors were using family limitation methods. When the "before" and "after" responses were compared, results indicated a significant drop in the "don't know" answers, and definite shifts toward perception of more use of contraception among relatives, friends, and neighbors. The greatest changes in awareness occurred in Everything lins, but there were also significant changes in the Mail and Nothing lins. The increase in the perceptions that significant "others" were practicing contraception related positively to acceptance in the program. "Before" and "after" responses indicated that acceptance rates were related less to increased *discussion* about family limitation than to increased *perception* of its use by others; whether more discussion with significant "others" took place was evidently less important than whether people believed that more of their primary contacts were actually adopting family limitation.

Although 854 neighborhood group meetings were originally planned, only about 500 were held, owing to a shortage of personnel and unexpected difficulties in assembling a group in some areas. But this situation inadvertently provided an opportunity for an independent test of the influence of group meetings. The meetings were rated as "effective," "somewhat effective," or "ineffective" by the field workers who conducted them, immediately after they were held and before the workers could know what the response in acceptances would be. Results indicated that a higher proportion of meetings were rated as effective in the high-density sector than in the other two sectors. Yet, despite the relatively high acceptance rates in the Everything lins taken as a whole, almost one-third of the Everything lins had no acceptances by the end of the first period. But this phenomenon was much less common in lins that had had effective or somewhat effective meetings.

An examination of the reliability of expressed intentions indicated that they were a useful but not very reliable predictor of later actions. Women had been asked whether they intended to adopt birth control "soon" or "later" or not at all. Of all women interviewed, 15 percent said they would act "soon" and 38 percent said "later." Yet by July of 1965, thirty months after the program began, only 19 percent of all home-visited cases had accepted. Stated intentions to adopt family planning were, however, more predictive than demographic and social characteristics considered alone.

Many of the program acceptors in Taichung and elsewhere were women over 30 and of relatively high parity (number of live births). Because women over 30 have a much lower average fertility than younger women, some observers are pessimistic about the capacity of such programs for reducing fertility. The Taichung acceptors were, however, whatever their age, a selected high-fertility group. Acceptors in their 30's had recent fertility rates not much below the average fertility levels of women in their 20's. It is therefore unsafe to assume that such acceptances can have little impact on the birth rate.

When the Taichung experiment was begun, almost all family planning programs were concentrating on influencing large numbers of couples to begin using contraception. Little attention was given to problems of continuation and termination. An assumption concerning the IUD, only sometimes made explicit, was that continuation rates would be high. Theoretically, the IUD could remain in place for years and would require no recurrent decisions concerning its use. It soon became apparent that, in Taiwan and elsewhere, despite the many advantages of the IUD, many couples were terminating its use. Most terminations resulted from voluntary removal of the device for medical or other reasons. In some cases the IUD produced side effects such as bleeding, headaches, backaches, etc. Although these side effects were diagnosed as not serious from a medical point of view, and were believed to be psychological in origin in a substantial proportion of the cases, nevertheless the symptoms were very real to the women involved.

In Taichung, 34 percent of IUD acceptors had terminated the use of the first device within one year after the initial insertion, and 51 percent had done so within two years. The results were disappointing to those who expected the IUD to be the perfect contraceptive. Yet, so far as is known, no other contraceptive has even as good a record for continuation over a period of a year or two in a mass program in a developing country. Preliminary reports of experiments underway with the pill in Taiwan and Korea indicate lower continuation rates than for the IUD. Moreover, the rate of termination of first insertions is less significant when reinsertions are considered; 29 percent of those who terminated had at least one subsequent reinsertion. A comparison of continuation rates for IUD acceptors and for women who accepted traditional methods of contraception indicates that IUD acceptors had much higher rates of continuation and much lower pregnancy rates.

Without careful study, termination rates for the IUD cannot be extrapolated from one population to another. Even within a single society, it is risky to extrapolate from a particular stratum to the whole society. The frequent practice of basing IUD studies on special clinic samples or on the population of experimental health areas is especially suspect as a basis for generalizing to a whole population. These special populations frequently receive a quality of medical care and attention not generally available elsewhere, and this can affect termination rates considerably. It is even more risky to attempt to develop some universal coefficient that will translate the number of IUD insertions into the "number of births averted," as is so often done. The number of births averted will depend, first, upon the termination rate, which is not a constant. Secondly, it will depend upon a number of other nonconstant factors: the fertility of the couples prior to the insertion, on what they would do if there were no insertion, and on what they do about alternative methods after the use of an IUD is terminated. Administrators who demand a fixed universal number that translates acceptances into births averted, without research on the local situation, can be given an answer based on an arbitrary set of assumptions. But actual results may prove to be far different.

What are the implications of the Taichung experience for population planning programs in other countries? There is a natural tendency to reject out of hand the experience of Taiwan or Korea for programs in such places as India, Pakistan, Indonesia, or Egypt. The argument is that Taiwan and Korea are so much more developed and so much farther along the road of demographic transition that they are not comparable with countries in which literacy, per-capita income, availability of medical personnel, evidence of preexisting birth control practice, etc., is much less. The basic premise of this argument is that birth control practice and declining birth rates occur only when a society has passed a minimal threshold of economic and social change. A counterargument is that no one knows what specific changes in mortality or in social structure are necessary preconditions for specific changes in birth control practice and fertility. Recent studies of the history of demographic transition in Europe have challenged some premises of theories relating to the European fertility decline—premises central to much theorizing and prediction concerning the future fertility of developing countries. Many of the generalizations about developing countries seem to be based on the dubious assumption that these countries stand socially where Europe was before its fertility began to decline—that developing countries are no different today than they were 25 or 50 or 100 years ago, when their mortality levels and kinship-centered social structures were probably strongly supportive of high-fertility norms and behavior. They have, in fact, changed in several ways. Lower mortality is profoundly affecting internal demographic pressures. The elite, as well as increasing numbers of the nonelite, have been linked to other countries through the mass media and the market place. There are rapidly changing levels of aspirations for consumer goods, education, better health, etc. These changes have proceeded further in urban and educated strata than in the mass of these populations, but even remote villages of India show evidence of linkage to a wider national and world community, of an incongruous juxtaposition of new and traditional ideas and objects. Even though it may be true that population programs cannot be completely successful without profound social changes with respect to the role of women, industrialization, social security outside the family, etc., it can still be argued that family planning programs are justified in conjunction with the pursuit of more general social and economic transformations.

One argument for the idea that India, for

example, is "not ready" for a Taiwan-type program is that the Indian program of many years has not been very successful. For years, however, the Indian program was poorly staffed and inadequately organized. Recently there has been considerable increase in efforts, expenditures, and acceptance rates. The test of what would happen with an "all-out" program in India has not yet been made; no systematic program has been conducted in any large unit of the country over a reasonable period of years. The point is not that such a program would be greatly successful, but that it needs to be tested.

It is possible to assume that the past failure of a country like India to carry out a systematic program is an endemic symptom of the lack of development. This may be true, but, again, this argument has not really been tested. India and Pakistan are unevenly developed. The most advanced parts of the population would presumably respond most readily to a program effort. This is an argument for concentrating effort in some areas and strata more than others. For various reasons, quite a different policy is being followed in many important programs. Resources and efforts are spread rather thinly and uniformly throughout the country. This would appear to ignore some motivational aspects, including the provision of social support for actions that millions view with considerable ambivalence.

An argument commonly advanced against current programs is that even if they are successful in helping to reduce the average number of children per family from seven to four, the "population problem" will not be solved. There are several answers to this: If the ideal goal for some countries may be an average of two children per family, it is still necessary to move through the average size of four to attain the ultimate goal of two. Programs that legitimate the idea that birth control can limit family growth at three or four children also spread the idea that birth control can be used to achieve any desired family size. The emphasis in current programs on reaching those who want no more children (rather than trying to change values about desired family size) is ethically justifiable, politically practical, and pedagogically sound.

The power of diffusion demonstrated in Taichung (and, later, throughout Taiwan) may very well indicate that programs should concentrate their efforts at a number of focal points, rather than spreading them thinly over an entire population. Everything possible, consistent with truth, should be done to increase awareness in the population that birth control is accepted by trusted members of their primary group. This reduces "pluralistic ignorance" —the situation in which many people accept an idea but believe that everyone else is against it. In line with this idea, ten acceptors in each of ten villages may be much more effective than one acceptor in each of 100 villages. While respondents in a survey may say "yes" or "no" to the question of "do you want more children" or "do you want birth control," the Taiwan experience indicates that what most people mean is "maybe."

Primary attention should be given to couples who feel themselves to be under demographic pressure. This includes couples who say they want no more children, and also those who have had the moderate number of children and sons that they want. The goal of reaching younger or lower-parity women is much more difficult to attain.

Programs should also be organized so that primary attention is given to the continuing practice of birth control by acceptors, rather than to the continued use of any particular method in the program. Evidence from Taichung, from Taiwan, and from Korea is that high termination rates for the IUD, for example, do not mean the end of birth control practice.

Every major family planning program should include means of evaluating itself. Although the evaluation activities in Taichung and Taiwan had many inadequacies, they provided several advantages: The initial surveys helped to alleviate doubts about the feasibility of such a program, and led to a program larger than was originally planned. The quick reporting of results from the Taichung experience helped to provide a basis for rapid expansion to an island-wide program. When anecdotal reports of IUD terminations worried administrators, follow-up surveys helped to define the magnitude of the problem. Information indicating that IUD-terminated cases were finding other means of limiting their birth rates was relevant to questions about whether it was important to invest in programs designed to reduce termination rates. Information about the fact that older and higher-parity acceptors still had high fecundability provided reassurance that the program was reaching women whose actions could make a difference, for both their families and for the general population.

The Taichung study was the first step toward an island-wide program that by the end of 1968 had provided services to 500,000 couples. Social changes throughout Taiwan are now under joint study by the Taiwan and Michigan research groups. Although this larger program is reaching the less modern strata of the population, it is still evident that the practice of birth control is strongly associated with modernization and development. It is still an open question whether organized family planning programs will be successful in reaching the rural, illiterate, tradition-directed masses in countries that lack an elite strata or centers of influence of the kind found in Taiwan. This question has been decided neither by historical evidence nor recent experience. Certain developmental changes are very likely important to reducing fertility: more education, particularly for women; involvement in markets that transcend the local economy; links with other societies through such mass media as the newspaper, radio, television, etc. Such changes have profound effects on population growth rates, but family planning programs can also make an important contribution. The types of programs suitable for particular populations must, however, be selected with care. In assessing proposed programs, several factors must be considered: their ethical acceptability, presumed effectiveness, and technical, political, economic, and administrative feasibility. A weakness in any of these six aspects can limit a beautiful paper plan to little more than that – paper. And if such a plan is put into operation, it can become very expensive paper.

3.

WHAT DO ATTITUDE SURVEYS TELL US?

Paul F. Lazarsfeld

Sociologists are commonly accused by laymen of "elaborating the obvious"—of investing time, energy, and dollars in studies which, in the end, only reveal "what everybody already knows." But there are dangers inherent in too-heavy dependence on commonsensical generalizations about attitudes and behavior, as Paul Lazarsfeld dramatically demonstrates here. He makes his point as a part of a review of two publications which set forth the findings of extensive attitude surveys conducted by the army during World War II—the results of which were used in a new and wholly unprecedented fashion to improve the selection, training, assignment, and morale of American soldiers.

It will be helpful to consider the special role played by attitude surveys in contemporary social science. Although surveys are only one of the many techniques available, at the moment they undoubtedly constitute the most important and promising step forward that has been made in recent years.

The limitations of survey methods are obvious. They do not use experimental techniques; they rely primarily on what people say, and rarely include objective observations; they deal with aggregates of individuals rather than with integrated communities; they are restricted to contemporary problems—history can be studied only by the use of documents remaining from earlier periods.

In spite of these limitations survey methods provide one of the foundations upon which social science is being built. The finding of regularities is the beginning of any science, and surveys can make an important contribution in this respect. For it is necessary that we know what people usually do under many and different circumstances if we are to develop theories explaining their behavior. Furthermore, before we can devise an experiment we must know what problems are worthwhile; which should be investigated in greater detail. Here again surveys can be of service.

Finding regularities and determining criteria of significance are concerns the social sciences have in common with the natural sciences. But there are crucial differences between the two fields of inquiry. The world of social events is much less "visible" than the realm of nature. That bodies fall to the ground, that things are hot or cold, that iron becomes rusty, are all immediately obvious. It is much more

---

Source: Paul F. Lazarsfeld, "The American Soldier—An Expository Review," *The Public Opinion Quarterly* 13, no. 3 (Fall 1969): 378–80. Reprinted by permission.

Sociologist and educator, the author is professor emeritus at Columbia University where he taught social sciences. He was formerly director of the Bureau of Applied Social Research and is a former president of the American Sociological Association. He coauthored *The People's Choice, Continuities in Social Research,* and *Language of Social Research.*

difficult to realize that ideas of right and wrong vary in different cultures; that customs may serve a different function from the one which the people practising them believe they are serving; that the same person may show marked contrasts in his behavior as a member of a family and as a member of an occupational group. The mere description of human behavior, of its variation from group to group and of its changes in different situations, is a vast and difficult undertaking. It is this task of describing, sifting and ferreting out interrelationships which surveys perform for us. And yet this very function often leads to serious misunderstandings. For it is hard to find a form of human behavior that has not already been observed somewhere. Consequently, if a study reports a prevailing regularity, many readers respond to it by thinking "of course that is the way things are." Thus, from time to time, the argument is advanced that surveys only put into complicated form observations which are already obvious to everyone.

Understanding the origin of this point of view is of importance far beyond the limits of the present discussion. The reader may be helped in recognizing this attitude if he looks over a few statements which are typical of many survey findings and carefully observes his own reaction. A short list of these, with brief interpretive comments, will be given here in order to bring into sharper focus probable reactions of many readers.

1. Better educated men showed more psycho-neurotic symptoms than those with less education. (The mental instability of the intellectual as compared to the more impassive psychology of the man-in-the-street has often been commented on.)
2. Men from rural backgrounds were usually in better spirits during their Army life than soldiers from city backgrounds. (After all, they are more accustomed to hardships.)
3. Southern soldiers were better able to stand the climate in the hot South Sea Islands than Northern soldiers. (Of course, Southerners are more accustomed to hot weather.)
4. White privates were more eager to become noncoms than Negroes. (The lack of ambition among Negroes is almost proverbial.)
5. Southern Negroes preferred Southern to Northern white officers. (Isn't it well known that Southern whites have a more fatherly attitude toward their "darkies"?)
6. As long as the fighting continued, men were more eager to be returned to the States than they were after the German surrender. (You cannot blame people for not wanting to be killed.)

We have in these examples a sample list of the simplest type of interrelationships which provide the "bricks" from which our empirical social science is being built. But why, since they are so obvious, is so much money and energy given to establish such findings? Would it not be wiser to take them for granted and proceed directly to a more sophisticated type of analysis? This might be so except for one interesting point about the list. *Every one of these statements is the direct opposite of what actually was found.* Poorly educated soldiers were more neurotic than those with high education; Southerners showed no greater ability than Northerners to adjust to a tropical climate; Negroes were more eager for promotion than whites; and so on.

If we had mentioned the actual results of the investigation first, the reader would have labelled these "obvious" also. Obviously something is wrong with the entire argument of "obviousness." It should really be turned on its head. Since every kind of human reaction is conceivable, it is of great importance to know which reactions actually occur most frequently and under what conditions; only then will a more advanced social science develop.

4.

MANIFEST AND LATENT FUNCTIONS

Robert K. Merton

One of the tasks of sociology is to explore the "functions" performed by the institutions, organizations, and groups in society and the relations among them. Some functions are *manifest,* that is, intended and recognized by participants in the system; other functions are *latent,* that is, neither intended nor recognized. In this selection, Robert K. Merton examines the functions of political machines in both their manifest and latent dimensions. Some of the latent functions described are ones of which we do not approve. As Merton points out, however, we cannot hope to eliminate them unless we are prepared to restructure our social and political arrangements so that the needs met by the latent functions are satisfied by other, and acceptable, means or unless a change is rendered which eliminates these needs altogether.

SOME FUNCTIONS OF THE POLITICAL MACHINE

Without presuming to enter into the variations of detail marking different political machines—a Tweed, Vare, Crump, Flynn, Hague are by no means identical types of bosses—we can briefly examine the functions more or less common to the political machine, as a generic type of social organization. We neither attempt to itemize all the diverse functions of the political machine nor imply that all these functions are similarly fulfilled by each and every machine.

The key structural function of the Boss is to organize, centralize and maintain in good working condition "the scattered fragments of power" which are at present dispersed through our political organization. By this centralized organization of political power, the Boss and his apparatus can satisfy the needs of diverse subgroups in the larger community which are not adequately satisfied by legally devised and culturally approved social structures.

To understand the role of bossism and the machine, therefore, we must look at two types of sociological variables: (1) the *structural context* which makes it difficult, if not impossible, for morally approved structures to fulfill essential social functions, thus leaving the door open for political machines (or their structural equivalents) to fulfill these functions and (2) the subgroups whose distinctive needs are left unsatisfied, except

Source: Robert K. Merton, *Social Theory and Social Structure* (N.Y.: The Free Press, 1949), pp. 71–81. Copyright 1949 by The Free Press. Reprinted by permission of Macmillan Publishing Co., Inc.

The author is Giddings Professor of Sociology, Columbia University, and associate director of the Bureau of Applied Social Research. He is a past president of the American Sociological Association. His main interests include the sociology of professions, the sociology of science, sociological theory, and mass communications. He is the author of *On Theoretical Sociology* and *On The Shoulders of Giants,* and the coeditor of *Sociology Today* and *Reader in Bureaucracy.*

for the latent functions which the machine in fact fulfills.

Structural Context

The constitutional framework of American political organization specifically precludes the legal possibility of highly centralized power and, it has been noted, thus "discourages the growth of effective and responsible leadership. The framers of the Constitution, as Woodrow Wilson observed, set up the check and balance system 'to keep government at a sort of mechanical equipoise by means of a standing amicable contest among its several organic parts.' They distrusted power as dangerous to liberty: and therefore they spread it thin and erected barriers against its concentration." This dispersion of power is found not only at the national level but in local areas as well. "As a consequence," Sait goes on to observe, "when *the people or particular groups* among them demanded positive action, no one had adequate authority to act. The machine provided an antidote."

The constitutional dispersion of power not only makes for difficulty of effective decision and action but when action does occur it is defined and hemmed in by legalistic considerations. In consequence, there develops "a much *more human system* of partisan government, whose chief object soon became the circumvention of government by law. . . . The lawlessness of the extraofficial democracy was merely the counterpoise of the legalism of the official democracy. The lawyer having been permitted to subordinate democracy to the Law, the Boss had to be called in to extricate the victim, which he did after a fashion and for a consideration."

Officially, political power is dispersed. Various well-known expedients were devised for this manifest objective. Not only was there the familiar separation of powers among the several branches of the government but, in some measure, tenure in each office was limited, rotation in office approved. And the scope of power inherent in each office was severely circumscribed. Yet, observes Sait in rigorously functional terms, "Leadership is necessary; and *since* it does not develop readily within the constitutional framework, the Boss provides it in a crude and irresponsible form from the outside."

Put in more generalized terms, *the functional deficiencies of the official structure generate an alternative (unofficial) structure to fulfill existing needs somewhat more effectively.* Whatever its specific historical origins, the political machine persists as an apparatus for satisfying otherwise unfulfilled needs of diverse groups in the population. By turning to a few of these subgroups and their characteristic needs, we shall be led at once to a range of latent functions of the political machine.

FUNCTIONS OF THE POLITICAL MACHINE FOR DIVERSE SUBGROUPS

It is well known that one source of strength of the political machine derives from its roots in the local community and the neighborhood. The political machine does not regard the electorate as a vague, undifferentiated mass of voters. With a keen sociological intuition, the machine recognizes that the voter is primarily a man living in the specific neighborhood, with specific personal problems and personal wants. Public issues are abstract and remote; private problems are extremely concrete and immediate. It is not through the generalized appeal to large public concerns that the machine operates, but through the direct, quasi-feudal relationships between local representatives of the machine and voters in their neighborhood. Elections are won in the precinct.

The machine welds its link with ordinary men and women by elaborate networks of personal relations. Politics is transformed into personal ties. The precinct captain "must be a friend to every man, assuming, if he does not feel, sympathy with the unfortunate, and utilizing in his good works the resources which the boss puts at his disposal." The precinct captain is forever a friend in need. In our prevailingly impersonal society, the machine, through its local agents, fulfills the important social *function of humanizing and personalizing all manner of assistance* to those in need. Food-baskets and jobs, legal and extralegal advice, setting to rights minor scrapes with the law, helping the bright poor boy to a political scholarship in a local college, looking after the bereaved – the whole range of crises when a feller needs a friend, and, above all, a friend who knows the score and who can do something about it – all these find the everhelpful precinct captain available in the pinch.

To assess this function of the political machine adequately, it is important to note not only the fact that aid *is* provided but *the manner in which it is provided.* After all, other agencies do exist for dispensing such assistance. Welfare agencies, settlement houses, legal aid clinics, medical aid in free hospitals, public relief departments, immigration authorities – these and a multitude of other organizations are available to provide the most varied types of assistance. But in contrast to the professional techniques of the welfare worker which may typically represent in the mind of the recipient the cold, bureaucratic dispensation of limited aid following upon detailed investigation of *legal* claims to aid of the "client," are the unprofessional techniques of the precinct captain who asks no questions, exacts no compliance with legal rules of eligibility and does not "snoop" into private affairs.

For many, the loss of "self-respect" is too high a price for legalized assistance. In contrast to the gulf between the settlement house workers who so often come from a different social class, educational background and ethnic group, the precinct worker is "just one of us," who understands what it's all about. The condescending lady bountiful can hardly compete with the understanding friend in need. In *this struggle between alternative structures for fulfilling the nominally same function* of providing aid and support to those who need it, it is clearly the machine politician who is better integrated with the groups which he serves than the impersonal, professionalized, socially distant and legally constrained welfare worker. And since the politician can at times influence and manipulate the official organizations for the dispensation of assistance, whereas the welfare worker has practically no influence on the political machine, this only adds to his greater effectiveness. More colloquially and also, perhaps, more incisively, it was the Boston wardleader, Martin Lomasny, who described this essential function to the curious Lincoln Steffens: "I think," said Lomasny, "that there's got to be in every ward somebody that any bloke can come to – no matter what he's done – and get help. *Help, you understand; none of your law and justice, but help.*"

The "deprived classes," then, constitute one subgroup for whom the political machine clearly satisfies wants not adequately satisfied in the same fashion by the legitimate social structure.

For a second subgroup, that of business (primarily "big" business but also "small"), the political boss serves the function of providing those political privileges which entail immediate economic gains. Business corporations, among which the public utilities (railroads, local transportation companies, communications corporations, electric light) are simply the most conspicuous in this regard, seek special political dispensations which will enable them to stabilize their situation and to near their objective of maximizing profits. Interestingly enough, corporations often want to avoid a chaos of uncontrolled competition. They want the greater security of an economic czar who controls, regulates and organizes competition, providing this czar is not a public official with his decisions subject to public scrutiny and public control. (The latter would be "government control," and hence taboo.) The political boss fulfills these requirements admirably.

Examined for a moment apart from any "moral" considerations, the political apparatus of the Boss is effectively designed to perform these functions with a minimum of inefficiency. Holding the strings of diverse governmental divisions, bureaus and agencies in his competent hands, the Boss rationalizes the relations between public and private business. He serves as the business community's ambassador in the otherwise alien (and sometimes unfriendly) realm of government. And, in strict businesslike terms, he is well-paid for his economic services to his respectable business clients. In an article entitled, "An Apology to Graft," Steffens suggested that "Our economic system, which held up riches, power and acclaim as prizes to men bold enough and able enough to buy corruptly timber, mines, oil fields and franchises and 'get away with it,' was at fault." And, in a conference with a hundred or so of Los Angeles business leaders, he described a fact well known to all of them: the Boss and his machine were an *integral part* of the organization of the economy. "You cannot build or operate a railroad, or a street railway, gas, water, or power company, develop and operate a mine, or get forests and cut timber on a large scale, or run any privileged business, without corrupting or joining in the corruption of the government. You tell me privately that you must, and here I am telling you semi-publicly that you must. And that is so all over the country. And that means that we have an organization of society in which, *for some reason,* you and your kind, the ablest, most intelligent, most imaginative, daring, and resourceful leaders of society, are and must be against society and its laws and its all-around growth."

Since the demand for the services of special privileges are built into the structure of the society, the Boss fulfills diverse functions for this second subgroup of business-seeking-privilege. These "needs" of business, as presently constituted, are not adequately provided for by "conventional" and "culturally approved" social structures; consequently, the extralegal but more-or-less efficient organization of the political machine comes to provide these services. To adopt an *exclusively* moral attitude toward the "corrupt political machine" is to lose sight of the very structural conditions which generate the "evil" that is so bitterly attacked. To adopt a functional outlook on the political machine is not to provide an apologia, but a more solid base for modifying or eliminating the machine, *providing* specific structural arrangements are introduced either for eliminating these effective demands of the business community or, if that is the objective, of satisfying these demands through alternative means.

A third set of distinctive functions fulfilled by the political machine for a special subgroup is that of providing alternative channels of social mobility for those otherwise excluded from the more conventional avenues for personal "advancement." Both the sources of this special "need" (for social mobility) and the respect in which the political machine comes to help satisfy this need can be understood by examining the structure of the larger culture and society. As is well known, the American culture lays enormous emphasis on money and power as a "success" goal legitimate for all members of the society. By no means alone in our inventory of cultural goals, it still remains among the most heavily endowed with positive affect and value. However, certain subgroups and certain ecological areas are notable for the relative absence of opportunity for achieving these (monetary and power) types of success. They constitute, in short, subpopulations where "the cultural emphasis upon pecuniary success has been absorbed, but where there is *little access to conventional and legitimate* means for attaining such success. The conventional occupational opportunities of persons in (such areas) are almost completely limited to manual labor. Given our cultural stigmatization of manual labor, and its correlate, the prestige of white-collar work," it is clear that the result is a tendency to achieve these culturally approved objectives *through whatever means are possible.* These people are on the one hand, "asked to orient their conduct toward the prospect of accumulating wealth [and power] and, on the other, they are largely denied effective opportunities to do so institutionally."

It is within this context of social structure that the political machine fulfills the basic function of providing avenues of social mobility for the otherwise disadvantaged. Within this context, even the corrupt political machine and the racket "represent the triumph of amoral intelligence over morally prescribed 'failure' when the channels of vertical mobility are closed or narrowed *in a society which places a high premium on economic affluence [power], and social ascent for all its members."* As one sociologist has noted on the basis of several years of close observation in a "slum area":

> The sociologist who dismisses racket and political organizations as deviations from desirable standards thereby neglects some of the major elements of slum life. . . . *He does not discover the functions they perform for the members* [of the groupings in the slum]. The Irish and later immigrant peoples have had the greatest difficulty in finding places for themselves in our urban social and economic structure. Does anyone believe that the immigrants and their children could have achieved their present degree of social mobility without gaining control of the political organization of some of our largest cities? The same is true of the racket organization. *Politics and the rackets have furnished an important means of social mobility for individuals, who, because of ethnic background and low class position,* are blocked from advancement in the "respectable" channels.

This, then, represents a third type of function performed for a distinctive subgroup. This function, it may be noted in passing, is fulfilled by the *sheer* existence and operation of the political machine, for it is in the machine itself that these individuals and subgroups find their culturally induced needs more or less satisfied. It refers to the services which the political apparatus provides for its own personnel. But seen in the wider social context we have set forth, it no longer appears as *merely* a means of self-aggrandizement for profit-hungry and power-hungry *individuals,* but as an organized provision for *subgroups* otherwise excluded or restricted from the race for "getting ahead."

Just as the political machine performs services for "legitimate" business, so it operates to perform not dissimilar services for "illegitimate" business: vice, crime and rackets. Once again, the basic sociological role of the machine in this respect can be more fully appreciated only if one temporarily abandons attitudes of moral indignation, to examine with all moral innocence the actual workings of the organization. In this light, it at once appears that the subgroup of the professional criminal, racketeer, gambler, has basic similarities of organization, demands and operation to the subgroup of the industrialist, man of business, speculator. If there is a Lumber King or an Oil King, there is also a Vice King or a Racket King. If expansive legitimate business organizes administrative and financial syndicates to "rationalize" and to "integrate" diverse areas of production and business enterprise, so expansive rackets and crime organize syndicates to bring order to the otherwise chaotic areas of production of illicit goods and services. If legitimate business regards the proliferation of small business enterprises as wasteful and inefficient, substituting, for example the giant chain stores for the hundreds of corner groceries, so illegitimate business adopts the same businesslike attitude, and syndicates crime and vice.

Finally, and in many respects, most important, is the basic similarity, if not near-identity, of the economic role of "legitimate" business and "illegitimate" business. *Both are in some degree concerned with the provision of goods and services for which there is an economic demand.* Morals aside, they are both business, industrial and professional enterprises, dispensing goods and services which some people want, for which there is a market in which goods and services are transformed into commodities. And, in a prevalently market society, we should expect appropriate enterprises to arise whenever there is a market demand for given goods or services.

As is well known, vice, crime and the rackets *are* "big business." Consider only that there have been estimated to be about 500,000 professional prostitutes in the United States, and compare this with the approximately 200,000 physicians and 200,000 nurses. It is difficult to estimate which have the larger clientele: the professional men and women of medicine or the professional men and women of vice. It is, of course, difficult to estimate the economic assets, income, profits and dividends of illicit gambling in this country and to compare it with the economic assets, income, profits and dividends of, say, the shoe industry, but it is altogether possible that the two industries are about on a par. No precise figures exist on the annual expenditures on illicit narcotics, and it is probable that these are less than the expenditures on candy, but it is also probable that they are larger than the expenditure on books.

It takes but a moment's thought to recognize that, *in strictly economic terms,* there is no relevant difference between the provision of licit and illicit goods and services. The liquor traffic illustrates this perfectly. It would be peculiar to argue that prior to 1920 (when the 18th amendment became effective), the provision of liquor constituted an economic service, that from 1920 to 1933, its production and sale no longer constituted an economic service dispensed in a market, and that from 1934 to the present, it again took on a serviceable aspect. Or, it would be *economically* (not morally) absurd to suggest that the sale of bootlegged liquor in the dry state of Kansas is less a response to a market demand than the sale of publicly manufactured liquor in the neighboring wet state of Missouri. Examples of this sort can of course be multiplied many times over. Can it be held that in European countries, with registered and legalized prostitution, the prostitute contributes an economic service, whereas in this country, lacking legal sanction, the prostitute provides no such service? Or that the professional abortionist is in the economic market where he has approved legal status and that he is out of the economic market where he is legally taboo? Or that gambling satisfies a specific demand for entertainment in Nevada, where it is one of the largest business enterprises of the largest city in the state, but that it differs essentially in this respect from movie houses in the neighboring state of California?

The failure to recognize that these businesses are only *morally* and not *economically* distinguishable from "legitimate" businesses has led to badly scrambled analysis. Once the economic identity of the two is recognized, we may anticipate that if the political machine performs functions for "legitimate big business" it will be all the more likely to perform not dissimilar functions for "illegitimate big business." And, of course, such is often the case.

The distinctive function of the political machine for their criminal, vice and racket clientele is to enable them to operate in satisfying the economic demands of a large market without due interference from the government. Just as big business may contribute funds to the political party warchest to ensure a minimum of governmental interference, so with big rackets and big crime. In both instances, the political machine can, in varying degrees, provide "protection." In both instances, many features of the structural context are identical: (1) market demands for goods and services; (2) the operators' concern with maximizing gains from their enterprises; (3) the need for partial control of government which might otherwise interfere with these activities of businessmen; (4) the need for an efficient, powerful and centralized agency to provide an effective liaison of "business" with government.

Without assuming that the foregoing pages exhaust either the range of functions or the range of subgroups served by the political machine, we can at least see that *it presently fulfills some functions for these diverse subgroups which are not adequately fulfilled by culturally approved or more conventional structures.*

Several additional implications of the functional analysis of the political machine can be mentioned here only in passing, although they obviously require to be developed at length. First, the foregoing analysis has direct implications for *social engineering.* It helps explain why the periodic efforts at "political reform," "turning the rascals out" and "cleaning political house" are typically short-lived and ineffectual. It exemplifies a basic theorem: *any attempt to eliminate an existing social structure without providing adequate alternative structures for fulfilling the functions previously fulfilled by the abolished organization is doomed to failure.* (Needless to say, this theorem has much wider bearing than the one instance of the political machine.) When "political reform" confines itself to the manifest task of "turning the rascals out," it is engaging in little more than sociological magic. The reform may for a time bring new figures into the political limelight; it may serve the casual social function of reassuring the electorate that the moral virtues remain intact and will ultimately triumph; it may actually effect a turnover in the personnel of the political machine; it may even, for a time, so curb the activities of the machine as to leave unsatisfied the many needs it has previously fulfilled. But, inevitably, unless the reform also involves a "re-forming" of the social and political structure such that the existing needs are satisfied by alternative structures or unless it involves a change which eliminates these needs altogether, the political machine will return to its integral place in the social scheme of things. *To seek social change, without due recognition of the manifest and latent functions performed by the social organization undergoing change, is to indulge in social ritual rather than social engineering.* The concepts of manifest and latent functions (or their equivalents) are indispensable elements in the theoretic repertoire of the social engineer. In this crucial sense, these concepts are not "merely" theoretical (in the abusive sense of the term), but are eminently practical. In the deliberate enactment of social change, they can be ignored only at the price of considerably heightening the risk of failure.

A second implication of our analysis of the political machine also has a bearing upon areas wider than the one we have considered. The "paradox" has often been noted that the supporters of the political machine include both the "respectable" business class elements who are, of course, opposed to the criminal or racketeer and the distinctly "unrespectable" elements of the underworld. And, at first appearance, this is cited as an instance of very strange bedfellows. The learned judge is not infrequently called upon to sentence the very racketeer beside whom he sat the night before at an informal dinner of the political bigwigs. The district attorney jostles the exonerated convict on his way to the back room where the Boss has called a meeting. The big business man may complain almost as bitterly as the big racketeer about the "extortionate" contributions to the party fund demanded by the Boss. Social opposites meet—in the smoke-filled room of the successful politician.

In the light of a functional analysis all this of course no longer seems paradoxical. Since the machine serves both the business man and the criminal man, the two seemingly antipodal groups intersect. This points to a more general theorem: *the social functions of an organization help determine the structure (including the recruitment of personnel involved in the structure), just as the structure helps determine the effectiveness with which the functions are fulfilled.* In terms of social status, the business group and the criminal group are indeed poles apart. But status does not fully determine behavior and the interrelations between groups. Functions modify these relations. Given their distinctive needs, the several subgroups in the large society are "integrated," whatever their personal desires or intentions, by the centralizing structure which serves these several needs. In a phrase with many implications which require further study, *structure affects function and function affects structure.*

5.

THE JUKE MYTH

Samuel Hopkins Adams

In this amusing account, Samuel Hopkins Adams illustrates the importance, to science in general and to social science in particular, of carefully gathered data. It has been fortunate for the healthy development of sociology that today's standards of data collection and interpretation are radically different from those that prevailed when the Juke study was considered sound research. Another important change has occurred in our basic theory of human behavior. Early in this century, as the popularity of the Juke study illustrates, most people were convinced that the behavior of humans is largely inborn. This emphasis on genetic determination of human behavior, particularly intelligence, has been revived in recent years, but the great majority of the scientists knowledgeable in this area agree that most human behavior is learned. Selection 7, written by psychologists Boyer and Walsh, and 8, written by biologist Lewontin, present the more common view among social scientists. This and the following selection by Cole illustrate the tendency to accept data which fit our preconceived beliefs regardless of their validity. A close reading of these reports of invalid conclusions from an earlier period of American history should help sharpen the reader's skill in objective examination of the evidence in other studies of human social behavior.

No other family in American annals is so well and unfavorably known as the Jukes. The name is a synonym for depravity. What the Rothschilds embody in finance the Jukes represent in misdemeanor. If there were an International Hall of Ill Fame they would get top billing.

And they never existed otherwhere than in the brain of an amateur criminologist. Richard L. Dugdale did not precisely invent them; rather, he compiled them from an assortment of human derelicts whom he collected after a method peculiarly his own, for the purpose of bolstering his theory of criminal heredity. He passed on his findings to posterity in his *magnum opus, The Jukes: A Study in Crime, Pauperism, Disease, and Insanity.*

This classic has permeated the sociology of nations. Geneticists like Giddings, East, and Walter have swallowed it whole. The New York State Prison Association sponsored it. Putnam's brought out three large editions, which were accepted as sociological gospel. Dugdale became the recognized authority on crime. His qualifications as an expert are peculiar. When the Dugdale family came to this country from England in 1851 Richard was ten years old. It was intended that he should go to college. After three years of schooling in New York

Source: Samuel Hopkins Adams, *Saturday Review* 38, no. 14 (April 2, 1955): 48–49.

The author (1871–1958) was a distinguished essayist and a former staff member of *McClure's Magazine*. Among his works are *The Santa Fe Trail, Erie Canal,* and *Grandfather Stories.*

something went awry in his education. He left school and became assistant to a sculptor. In the evenings he attended classes at Cooper Union, where he won something of a reputation as a debater on social topics.

His career, if such it were, was interrupted by the departure of the family to try farming in the Middle-west. The venture was unsuccessful. The Dugdales returned to New York and Richard turned his hands to manufacturing. He was then twenty-three. The business failed. Richard had a nervous breakdown and withdrew from active endeavor. "For four years I could neither earn nor learn," he records. Such was his technical equipment as a sociologist.

The Jukes came into his life quite by chance. He happened to be in a Kingston, N.Y., police court in 1873, where a youth was on trial for receiving stolen goods. Five relatives were present as witnesses. They came of a breed, to quote the incipient investigator, "so despised that their family name had come to be used generically as a term of reproach." They were alleged to live like haggards of the rock, in the caves of a nearby lake region. "Crime-cradles," our author calls the locality. He was a neat hand at a phrase.

He invented the name Juke for the clan.

The fact that the Juke at the bar of justice was acquitted in no wise discouraged young Dugdale. He made inquiries about the others present. An uncle of the accused is set down as a burglar. No proof is adduced. Two male cousins had been charged with pushing a boy over a cliff, one of whom was convicted. The remaining witnesses, two girls, he lists as harlots. By the Dugdale method "under the heading of harlots are included all women who have made lapses, however seldom." This is fairly indicative of his standards of investigation and attribution.

With this auspicious start he canvassed the neighborhood for further specimens.

> With comparatively little inquiry [he writes], it was found that out of twenty-nine male adults, the immediate blood relations of the six, seventeen were criminals and fifteen others convicted of some degree of offense.

Impressed by this suggestive ratio—as who would not be by thirty-two out of a possible twenty-nine?—Dugdale went sleuthing back through the generations until he came upon an old Dutch reprobate who kept a turnpike hostelry in Orange County about the middle of the eighteenth century. Old Max appears to have been a sporting character. Several illegitimate children were imputed to him. He enjoyed a local reputation for drinking, gaming, and wenching, divertissements fairly general in those lusty pioneer days. He became Exhibit A in the Dugdale rogues' gallery, though nothing criminal appears in his record.

Max had two legitimate sons who married into a family of six sisters. With the discovery of the sisterhood Dugdale really hits his stride. The family line of the six is obscure; it "has not been absolutely ascertained," he admits. "One, if not all, of them were illegitimate," he surmises, on what grounds he does not explain. Delia is recorded as a "harlot before marriage," and Bell as a "harlot after marriage." Clara, he notes (presumptively with reluctance), was "reputed chaste." She did, however, marry a man who shot a neighbor. Effie's reputation was unknown to author Dugdale.

Another sister *circa* 1760 is Dugdale's prize specimen. "Margaret, Mother of Criminals," he calls her, although her name was Ada. Apt alliteration's artful aid again! To her goes the credit for "the distinctly criminal line of the family." But, what family? For all that he reveals

Margaret-Ada, of unascertained parentage, may have been a Van Rensselaer, a Livingston, a Saltonstall, a Biddle, or the granddaughter of the original Joe Doakes. To be sure, he later characterizes the whole lot as "belonging to the Juke blood." Pure assumption. As their derivation was unknown and they were suspectedly illegitimate anyway, how could Dugdale or anybody else know anything of their ancestry?

As a "Mother of Criminals" Margaret (or Ada) hardly lives up to her name. Her daughter is designated as a harlot, but, by way of palliation perhaps, our author adds, "not industrious." One son was a laborer, "somewhat industrious." The other, a farmer, is stigmatized as having been "indolent" and "licentious in youth." The same might be said of some eminent non-Jukes, including Robert Burns and the Apostle Paul.

Margaret-Ada was married to one of Old Max's sons. She had a son of her own, whom Dugdale holds to be coresponsible for the evil Juke inheritance. But this son was a Juke only in name. He was illegitimate. Dugdale says so.

Thus, the notorious criminal-Juke strain derives on one side from a progenitor who was not criminal (Old Max) and on the other from a line which was not Juke except by Dugdale fiat. (Margaret-Ada through her illegitimate son.)

It sufficed Dugdale. He had his theory; now he set out after supporting facts. He made a year's tour of prisons, almshouses, and asylums, collecting Jukes. The result he published in 1875. It is still regarded by those who have not read it, and even some who have, as an authoritative document. It established the Jukes as the type-family of degeneration.

Dugdale invented a terminology to go with his Jukes. His thesis is based, so he states, upon "Positive Statistics and Conjectural Statistics . . . Conjectural Statistics consists in Political Arithmetic and the Theory of Probabilities.". This recondite process "reduces the method of study to one of historico-biographical synthesis united to statistical analysis," which sounds as if it might have come out of Lewis Carroll.

Applying this yardstick, Dugdale lists 709 alleged Jukes of whom 507 were social detrimentals. Such conventional crimes as murder, arson, rape, and robbery, quite lacking in proof for the most part, are cited. But there were not enough of them to support satisfactorily the Dugdale political arithmetic and theory of probabilities. So he fattens up the record with entries like the following:

Reputed sheep-stealer, but never caught.
Thief, but never caught.
Petty thief, though never convicted.
Guilty of murder, but escapes punishment.
Unpunished and cautious thief.
Bastardy prosecution.
Supposed to have attempted rape.
Cruelty to animals.
Habitual criminal.
Impossible to get any reliable information, but it is evident that at nineteen he was a leader in crime.

And such scattered attributions as "pauper," "harlot," "brothelkeeper," "vagrant," "lazy," "intemperate," "drunkard," "immoral," "lecherous," etc., etc., etc. There was also a "contriver of crime," and a hardened character who, in addition to frequenting a saloon, was accused of breaking a deaf man's ear-trumpet. Like the Juke who started it all, he was acquitted. It did not matter to our investigator; the non-breaker of the ear trumpet comes down the ages, embalmed in criminal history.

All this might seem rather attenuated evidence on which to indict an entire family. It sufficed Dugdale. He followed the long and proliferating branches of the clan through the generations and worked out a diagram as framework for the composite portrait. This he calls "Leading Facts."

		Consanguinity		
		F		
C	Prostitution	O	Illegitimacy	P
		R		A
R		N		U
		I		P
I	Exhaustion	C	Intemperance	E
		A		R
M		T		I
		I		S
E	Disease	O	Extinction	M
		N		
		Not Consanguineous		

In other words, *fornication* [the italics are his], either consanguineous or not, is the backbone of their habits, flanked on the one side by *pauperism,* on the other by *crime.* The secondary features are *prostitution,* with its complement of *bastardy,* and its resultant of miseducated childhood; *exhaustion,* with its complement, *intemperance,* and its resultant, unbalanced minds; and *disease,* with its complement, *extinction.*

Dugdale's investigations into hygiene and morality are on a par with his criminological efforts. Insanity, epilepsy, deformity, impotency, and tuberculosis appear to have been as typical Juke phenomena as thievery, bastardy, and general lawlessness. Some of the evidence cited is calculated to astonish students of heredity. For example, it is recorded that the original Max went blind and transmitted the affliction to his posterity. As he lost his sight late in life, after his children were born, it is difficult to see how he can be held responsible for their blindness unless he poked them in the eye with a burnt stick.

Our author's figures on tuberculosis are confident, but where he found them is left a mystery. Nobody bothered to keep statistics in those days. Still more difficult would it have been to gather reliable data on venereal disease. Yet our conjectural statistician specifies, in one branch of the Jukes, forty harlots who contaminated 440 men, presumably eleven-per-harlot. In another genealogical line he states that $23\frac{1}{2}$ percent of the females were immoral. That $\frac{1}{2}$ percent is fairly awe-inspiring.

Not until long after the author's death did anyone rise to challenge his thesis. The late Thomas Mott Osborne, of prison-reform fame and at one time president of that same prison association which certified the Dugdale revelations, studied the Juke records with growing skepticism. Himself a practised investigator, he raised questions about the Dugdale methods which that author might have found awkward to answer.

Whence, Mr. Osborne wished to know, did Dugdale derive those cocksure figures on disease, insanity, and death? Vital statistics at the time of his inquiry were practically nonexistent. How did he acquire his data on criminality when court records for the period were notoriously unreliable, if, indeed, they were available at all? What genealogical method did he use in tracing back the Juke line through the mazes of its prevalent bastardy, for a century and a quarter? Legitimate family lines, Mr. Osborne pointed out, were difficult enough to trace; illegitimate were flatly impossible, beyond a generation or two. Further, the objector indicated, a specially trained sociological investigator would have required at least three years to do the work which Dugdale completed in one.

Analyzing the indicated method of investigation, Mr. Osborne suggested that Dugdale based it on a formula of retroactive hypothesis as follows:

That every criminal was a putative Juke.

That every Juke was a presumptive criminal.

By the system which Dugdale employed in tracing down his Jukes, Mr. Osborne concluded, it would be possible to asperse the morality, sanity, and legitimacy of any family in America. As for the Jukes, they were "pure folklore."

Another dissident raised objections in *The Clinical Review* for April 1902. Was it credible, Edmund Andrews asked, that Old Max possessed "such a miraculous energy of vicious propagation that, by his sole vital force, he begat and transmitted the degeneracy of all the Jukes for five generations?" Each descendant in the fifth generation, the critic pointed out, had fifteen other progenitors. Why assign his or her lawless, shiftless, or bawdy habits to Max any more than to any other of the uncharted Jukes or Jakes or Jeeks or Jenkins? A sturdy breeder like Max might well be the ancestor of a couple of thousand great-great-grandchildren, 1,500 of whom, for all that Dugdale knew to the contrary, might have been missionaries.

"It is sheer nonsense," Mr. Andrews contends "to suppose that he (a fifth-generation Juke degenerate) got them all (his vicious proclivities) from that one lazy, but jovial old Rip Van Winkle, the original Juke."

These were but voices crying in a wilderness. To scotch a good, sturdy historical fake, once it has got its growth, is impossible. Nine-tenths of America devoutly believes that Robert Fulton invented the steamboat and that Abner Doubleday was the founder of baseball. So the Jukes will doubtless continue to furnish texts to trusting sociologists, and no great harm done.

But they are in the wrong category. The proper place of a Juke is not in criminology. It is in mythology.

6.

A WITNESS AT THE SCOPES TRIAL

Fay-Cooper Cole

Facts never speak for themselves. For the scientist they speak in terms of theoretical assumptions. For the layman they are interpreted to fit his basic beliefs. If, for example, one assumed the earth was flat, then data that suggested that the world has a spherical shape could be discounted as optical illusions. Action would likewise be affected; sailors who believed the world was flat would hesitate to sail far from land. Similarly, if one believed that our species was created just as it exists today—a conception that was widely accepted for centuries—then one would hardly be motivated to search for data tracing human development through the ages. This is the significance of the Scopes trial as discussed by Fay-Cooper Cole. It represented the most famous and dramatic public test of the traditional belief about the nature of humankind. By 1925, almost all respected scientists had accepted the theory that human behavior was a product of evolutionary forces. This theory has profoundly affected teaching

Source: Fay-Cooper Cole, *Scientific American* 200, no. 1 (January 1959): 121–30.

The author (1881–1961) was professor of anthropology at the University of Chicago. He has done archaeological work in the United States and abroad. His books include *Peoples of Malaysia, Kincaid—A Prehistoric Illinois Metropolis,* and *The Bukidnon of Mindanao.*

and research in social science and religion, but opposition has again recently arisen to the teaching of evolution in California and Tennessee. Equal time must now be devoted to alternate theories in the latter. It should be noted, in any event, that the theory does not and cannot say anything about man's ultimate beginnings.

"This is Clarence Darrow," said the voice at the other end of the wire, "I suppose you have been reading the papers, so you know Bryan and his outfit are prosecuting that young fellow Scopes. Well, Malone, Colby and I have put ourselves in a mess by offering to defend. We don't know much about evolution. We don't know whom to call as witnesses. But we do know we are fighting your battle for academic freedom. We need the help of you fellows at the University, so I am asking three of you to come to my office to help lay plans."

That afternoon in Darrow's office three of us from the University of Chicago—Horatio Hackett Newman, professor of biology; Shailer Mathews, dean of the Divinity School; and I—met to outline the strategy for what turned out to be one of the most publicized trials of the century. The Scopes trial proved also to be a historic occasion in the cause of popular understanding of science. A century ago the educated world was shaken by the discoveries of Charles Darwin and Alfred Russel Wallace, and the evidence they presented for the evolution of life on this planet. In 1959, as we celebrate the centenary of the *Origin of Species,* few informed persons, if any, question the theory of evolution. However, the century has witnessed several attempts to stifle investigation and outlaw the teaching of the theory. The best known of these was the Scopes trial, held in Dayton, Tenn., in 1925. The trial resulted in an immense revival of public interest in Darwin and in evolution; there has been no comparable effort since then to suppress this advance in man's understanding of himself and the world he lives in.

To understand the trial and what lay back of it, one must recall the climate of the 1920s. It was a time of uncertainty, unrest and repression. We had just emerged from a world war. Old standards were badly shaken; the young were labeled "the lost generation"; intolerance was rampant. The Ku Klux Klan was on the march, not only in the South but in the North as well. In many towns in Illinois, Indiana and other parts of the Midwest, staid business men—even members of the clergy—put on "white nighties" and burned fiery crosses to put the Negro, the Jew, the Catholic and the immigrant "in their places." The Fundamentalists, under the leadership of William Jennings Bryan, had organized in some 20 states and were putting pressure on all institutions of learning to curb the teaching of science, particularly evolution, which they considered in contradiction to the Bible. Prohibitive bills had been passed in Tennessee and Mississippi and were pending in six other states.

Then came the great opportunity. In the little town of Dayton the high-school science teacher and football coach, 24-year-old John Thomas Scopes, found himself engaged in a discussion of the new law with George W. Rappelyea, a young mining engineer and superintendent of the local coal mines. Scopes expressed bewilderment that the state should supply him with a textbook that presented the theory of evolution, yet make him a lawbreaker if he taught the theory. Rappelyea agreed that it was a crazy law and clearly unconstitutional. Then suddenly he asked: "Why don't I have you arrested for teaching evolution from that text and bring the whole thing to an end?" Scopes replied: "Fair enough."

Scopes was duly arrested. But neither of the principals had any idea of what they were starting. Within a few hours the Chattanooga papers carried the story. Soon it was spread across the nation. The Fundamentalists were quick to realize the opportunity to dramatize their battle against evolution. Bryan and his associates offered their services to the Prosecution. They were accepted. Here was big news.

At this point, it happened, three lawyers met in New York City for a conference on some business matters. They were Clarence Darrow, controversialist and defender of unpopular causes; Bainbridge Colby, an eminent corporation lawyer and, like Bryan, a former Secretary of State; and Dudley Field Malone, a leading Catholic layman and a fashionable barrister. Their conversation turned to the Tennessee situation. One said: "It is a shame. That poor teacher, who probably doesn't know what it is all about, is to be sacrificed by the Fundamentalists." Another said: "Someone ought to do something about it." The third replied: "Why don't we?" Through the American Civil Liberties Union they offered to defend young Scopes. Their offer was accepted.

This was real news! Bryan, three times candidate for the presidency of the U.S., the great Fundamentalist leader and orator, on one side. On the other, three of the nation's most famous lawyers, including Darrow, master jury-pleader. The papers were full of the story.

This was the background of Darrow's call to me and of our meeting at his office in Chicago early in the summer of 1925. By telephone, wire and letter we proceeded to assemble a panel of expert witnesses: scientists to testify on the theory of evolution and theologians to give evidence on the history and interpretation of the Bible. In addition to Newman, Mathews and myself, our panel finally included Kirtley Mather, professor of geology at Harvard; Jacob G. Lipman, director of the New Jersey Agricultural Experiment Station at Rutgers University; W. C. Curtis, professor of zoology at the University of Missouri; Wilbur Nelson, state geologist of Tennessee; Maynard Metcalf, professor of zoology at Johns Hopkins University; Charles Judd, head of the University of Chicago School of Education; and Rabbi Herman Rosenwasser of San Francisco, a noted Hebrew scholar. All of us, along with our counsel, undertook to go to Dayton at our own expense and to serve without fee.

The trial was scheduled for Friday, July 10. But long before that date the town was crowded with newspapermen, Fundamentalist supporters and others who were just curious. No one was willing to house "the heretics," that is, the scientific witnesses and defense attorneys. So an old "haunted house" on a hill overlooking the town was fitted out as a dormitory.

When I reached town, I took care not to associate myself at once with the Defense group, and was able to wander about for a time listening to the talk of the local people. For the most part they were extremely partisan to the Fundamentalist cause. But they were apprehensive of the famous Darrow, and they were not yet aware of his plan to present expert testimony on evolution and the scriptures.

That evening I joined the group at the "haunted house" and there met young Scopes for the first time. He was a fine, clean-cut young man, a little shy and apparently overwhelmed by the controversy he had stirred up. He expressed amazement that famous lawyers like Darrow, Colby, Malone and Arthur Garfield Hays (counsel to the American Civil Liberties Union) should come to his defense, and that a group of well-known scientists should join them.

Little happened on the first day of the trial beyond the selection of the jury. A panel was offered, and Darrow accepted it without change after a casual examination. But he did bring out the fact that 11 jurors were Fundamentalist church members. All admitted that they knew little about science or evolution. One said that the only Darwin he had ever heard about ran a local notion store. One could not read or write.

The events of Sunday provided us with an interesting insight into the local climate of opinion. Charles Francis Potter, a liberal Unitarian minister and writer who had been invited to conduct services at the Methodist-Episcopal church, was barred from the pulpit by the parishioners. Meanwhile Bryan addressed an overflow house at the Southern Methodist church. That afternoon, in an open courtyard in the center of town, Bryan talked to an immense audience. He said he welcomed the opportunity to bring "this slimy thing, evolution, out of the darkness. . . . Now the facts of religion and evolution would meet at last in a duel to the death." It was a fine example of Bryan's oratory, and it swept the crowd.

The court opened on Monday with a prayer in which a local clergyman urged God to preserve his sacred word against attack. It was a scarcely veiled plea to the jury.

The Defense filed a motion to quash the indictment on the ground that the act violated the Constitution of the State of Tennessee and Section 1 of the Fourteenth Amendment of the Constitution of the United States, which extends the Bill of Rights to limit action by the governments of the states. The Defense argued further that the indictment was contrary to a U.S. Supreme Court decision which says: "The law knows no heresy, and is committed to the support of no dogma, nor to the establishment of any sect." In support of this attack on the indictment, the Defense declared that it wished to offer the testimony of scientists and biblical scholars. These expert witnesses, the Defense contended, would show that there was no necessary conflict between evolution and Christianity.

Though the Defense asked that judgment on its motion to dismiss should be reserved until its witnesses had been heard, Judge John T. Raulston ordered the argument to proceed. On motion of the Prosecution, he sent the jury from the courtroom. Apparently the introduction of scientific witnesses had taken Bryan and his associates by surprise. Their ultimate response to our efforts to argue the underlying issues of the case was to lose them the trial in the minds of the American people.

That afternoon Darrow pressed for dismissal with an eloquent attack on ignorance and bigotry. Coatless in the sweltering courtroom, tugging at his suspenders, he paced up and down, firing shot after shot at the Prosecution. He stressed the danger to freedom of press, church and school if men like Bryan could impose their opinions and interpretations on the law of the land. "The fires of bigotry and hate are being lighted," he said. "This is as bold an attempt to destroy learning as was ever made in the Middle Ages. . . . The statute says you cannot teach anything in conflict with the Bible." He argued that in the U.S. there are over 500 churches and sects which differ over certain passages in the Bible. If the law were to prevail, Scopes would have to be familiar with the whole Bible and all its interpretations; among all the warring sects, he would have to know which one was right in order not to commit a crime.

Darrow said: "Your Honor, my client is here because ignorance and bigotry are rampant, and that is a mighty strong combination. . . . If today you can make teaching of evolution in the public schools a crime, tomorrow you can make it a crime to teach it in the private schools. At the next session of the Legislature you can ban books and newspapers. You can set Catholic against Protestant, and Protestant against Protestant, when you try to foist your own religion upon the minds of men. If you can do the one, you can do the other. After a while, Your Honor, we will find ourselves marching backward to the glorious days of the 16th century when bigots lighted the fagots to burn men who dared to bring any intelligence and enlightenment to the human mind."

The speech made a profound impression. Townspeople agreed that anything might happen with that man Darrow around. Judge Raulston adjourned court until Wednesday in order that he might consider the motion to quash.

That night, as we gathered in our haunted house for a conference, a terrific storm swept the town. When a brilliant flash of lightning struck nearby, Darrow said: "Boys, if lightning strikes this house tonight . . . !"

Tuesday was a quiet day. At Rappelyea's office, where he had been invited to take advantage of the secretarial facilities, Potter found that the stenographer would not take dictation from any Unitarian minister. Rappelyea himself was arrested three times for speeding in the course of his service to us as guide and chauffeur. We were besieged by Holy Rollers, who came in from the hills to convert us. We also had to protect ourselves from a supporter. H. L. Mencken had come to town. His vitriolic articles so antagonized the people we wanted most to reach that we had to persuade him to leave the scene.

After the jury was sworn in on Wednesday, the Court ruled against the Defense motion to quash the indictment. The law, said Judge Raulston, did not deprive anyone of speech, thought or opinion, for no one need accept employment in Tennessee. He ruled the law constitutional, saying that the public has the right to say, by legislative act or referendum, whether Latin, chemistry or astronomy might be taught in its schools.

The Prosecution then called the county superintendent of schools, the heads of the school board and seven students. All testified to what Scopes had taught. Darrow limited his cross-examination to establishing simply that the State had furnished the textbook. After offering the King James version of the Bible as an exhibit, the Prosecution rested.

The first witness for the Defense was Maynard Metcalf. A recognized scientist, he was also an eminent Congregational layman and teacher of one of the largest Bible classes in the country. Darrow established his competence as a witness, then asked a question on evolution. The Prosecution at once challenged the testimony as irrelevant; according to them the only question was: Did Scopes violate the law?

The judge agreed to hear arguments on this point the next day. Meanwhile he excused the jury, with instructions not to enter the courtroom or to remain within hearing of the loudspeakers. A lot of angry jurors filed out. They had not only lost their reserved seats, but also were barred from the proceedings entirely.

The trial reached its high point on Thursday. After an impassioned plea by the

State's Attorney against the admission of expert testimony, Bryan took over for the Prosecution. Instead of making good on his challenge of "a duel to the death," he argued against the presentation of scientific evidence. He said that the jury did not need the help of scientists or Bible experts to decide the facts and to interpret the law: "The law is what the people decided." He then presented an enlargement of the picture of the evolutionary tree from the textbook Scopes had used; it showed man in a circle with other mammals. Bryan shouted: "Talk about putting Daniel in the lions' den. How dare these scientists put man in a little ring with lions and tigers and everything that smells of the jungle. . . . One does not need to be an expert to know what the Bible says. . . . Expert testimony is not needed!"

With that speech Bryan lost the argument with the press and with the radio audience. When Malone had finished his reply, Bryan had also lost the argument, for a time, with most of his Dayton followers.

Malone was a Patrick Henry that day. He asked whether our children are to know nothing of science beyond that permitted by certain sects. "I have never seen greater need for learning," he declared, "than is exhibited by the Prosecution, which refuses information offered by expert witnesses. . . . Why this fear of meeting the issue? Mr. Bryan has said this is to be a duel to the death. I know little about dueling, Your Honor, but does it mean that our only weapon, the witnesses, is to be taken away while the Prosecution alone carries the sword? This is not my idea of a duel. . . . We do not fear all the truth they can present as facts. We are ready. We stand with progress. We stand with science. We stand with intelligence. We feel that we stand with the fundamental freedoms in America. We are not afraid. Where is the fear? We defy it." Then, turning toward Bryan and pointing his finger, he cried: "There is the fear!"

The crowd went out of control—cheering, stamping, pounding on desks—until it was necessary to adjourn court for 15 minutes to restore order.

I was sitting next to the aisle. Beside me was a Chattanooga policeman, one of the squad brought in to protect us from the Ku Klux Klan. As Malone finished, my guard beat the desk in front of me so hard with his club that a corner of the desk broke off. His chief came up and asked: "Why didn't you cheer when Malone made that speech?" My guard replied: "Hell. What did you think I was doing? Rapping for order?"

We had won for the day. Even the hostile crowd was with us.

That night Darrow said: "Today we have won, but by tomorrow the judge will have recovered and will rule against us. I want each one of you to go to the stenographer's room the first thing in the morning and prepare a statement for the press, saying what you would have said if allowed to testify in court."

As we were preparing our statements next morning, Judge Raulston looked in. I was nearest to the door. He asked what we were doing. When I told him, he asked the others in turn. Then he went to Darrow and told him he must not release the testimony: "It might reach the jury." Darrow replied: "Your Honor, you can do what you please with that jury. You can lock it up, but you cannot lock up the American people. The testimony will be released."

When court resumed, the judge ruled against us on all points. Rising and pushing his long hair from his forehead, Darrow spoke slowly and clearly. "The outcome is plain. We expect to protect our rights in some other court. Is that plain?" The judge replied: "I hope, Colonel Darrow, you don't attempt to reflect upon the Court." To which Darrow drawled: "Your Honor has the right to hope." The insult was deliberate. For an instant there was complete silence; then the judge mumbled that he had the right to do something else. A moment later he adjourned court until Monday.

Public reaction to the ruling was emphatic, and Bryan's prestige was shaken. Townspeople admitted to me, one of the "heretics," that they could not understand why Bryan had backed down. They asked: "What can you do now, if you can't talk?"

On Monday Darrow apologized to the Court, momentarily relieving the tension. Then, in order to secure the foundation for appeal, Hays read into the record the prepared statements of the scientific and other scholarly witnesses, and concluded by placing in evidence three versions of the Bible that differed from one another and from the King James version submitted by the Prosecution. Suddenly Hays electrified the crowd with the announcement that the Defense wished to call Bryan to the stand "as a biblical witness."

Darrow submitted Bryan to grueling examination. In reply to Darrow's questions Bryan stated that he accepted the Bible literally as God's revealed word. What he didn't understand he accepted on simple faith. He believed that Eve was the first woman, created from Adam's rib; that God had sent childbirth pains to all women because of her transgression; that the snake must crawl on its belly because it tempted Eve; that everything outside the Ark, except fish, perished in the flood; that all existing animals had descended from the pairs saved by Noah; that all men spoke one language until the Tower of Babel; and that present languages had developed since then. Only once did he falter, when he admitted that the seven days of creation might mean seven epochs. He conceded that he was not familiar with the work of archaeologists, who had uncovered civilizations more than 5,000 years old, but he declared that he had never had much interest in those scientists who disputed the Bible. Repeatedly the State's Attorney tried to stop the questioning, but always Bryan replied: "No. Let it go on. I am not afraid to defend my religion."

Finally Malone intervened, saying he would have asked the same questions, but only to challenge Bryan's literal interpretation of the King James version. As a churchman and a Christian, however, he objected to any effort by counsel for the State to pin Darrow's views of religion on the defense. "I don't want this case to be changed by Mr. Darrow's agnosticism or Mr. Bryan's brand of religion." Malone further observed that this was supposed to be a trial by jury, yet the jury had not been permitted in the court for more than 15 minutes since being sworn in.

On Tuesday Judge Raulston struck the examination of Bryan from the record. The only question remaining, he said, was: What did Scopes teach? To this ruling Darrow replied: "Your Honor, we are wasting time. You should call the jury and instruct it to bring in a verdict of guilty." The court did so, and Scopes was fined $100.

Scopes had come on to graduate study in geology at the University of Chicago when the Tennessee Supreme Court heard Darrow's appeal and at last handed down its decision in January, 1927. The court narrowly affirmed the antievolution statute, but threw out the $100 fine on a technicality. It brought an end to the formal proceedings by advising the State to desist from further prosecution: "We see nothing to be gained by prolonging the life of this bizarre case."

The Defense was also content to accept the Court's advice. No attempt at repression has ever backfired so impressively. Where one person had been interested in evolution before the trial, scores were reading and inquiring at its close. Within a year the prohibitive bills which had been pending in other states were dropped or killed. Tennessee had been made to appear so ridiculous in the eyes of the nation that other states did not care to follow its lead.

At the University of Chicago I had been teaching modest-sized classes. When the University resumed in the autumn my lecture hall was filled. Students were standing along the walls and sitting in the windows. I thought I was in the wrong room. When I asked a boy at the door what class was meeting, he replied: "Anthropology. The prof who teaches it defended that fellow Scopes." From that time on Introductory Anthropology had to be limited to lecture-hall capacity. My mail, mostly hostile, increased until the University gave up trying to put it in my box, but tied it in bundles and sent it to my office.

Some time after the trial I was summoned to the office of Frederick Woodward, acting president of the University. He handed me a long document, a series of resolutions from a Southern Baptist conference. They took the University to task for the part members of its faculty had taken in the trial, taking note of the University's strong Baptist origins. They voiced objections to Professors Judd, Newman and Mathews, but reserved the real condemnation for me—the witness on human evolution. I was "a snake in the grass corrupting the youth of a nation," and so on, concluding with "and we have been investigating Professor Cole still further, and we find that he is not even a Baptist."

I began to laugh, but the president said: "This is no laughing matter. You are a rather new man here, but already we have more demands for your removal than any other man who has been on our faculty. These resolutions are typical and were considered of such importance that they were read yesterday at the meeting of the Board of Trustees." "Yes," I replied. "And what did they do?" He reached across his desk and handed me a piece of paper. They had raised my salary.

Part II

Environmental Factors

7.

INNATE INTELLIGENCE: AN INSIDIOUS MYTH?

William H. Boyer and Paul Walsh

A long-standing controversy in American social science concerns the relative importance of heredity and environment in the development of human behavior, especially school achievement. This controversy has recently been rekindled by the claim that lower-class and black children are unable to learn in school as other children do. The basis for this claim is the presumed genetic differences among children. In both this selection and the next, the authors examine evidences of such genetic individual differences and the possibility that such differences are the result of environmental force. They also demonstrate that our educational system is based upon the model of unequal innate abilities. The resulting public policy and educational practice tend to reinforce the differences that are observed.

In societies where power and privilege are not equally distributed, it has always been consoling to those with favored positions to assume that nature has caused the disparity. When man himself creates unequal opportunity, he can be obliged or even forced to change his social system. But if nature creates inequality, man need only bow to supreme forces beyond his control, and the less fortunate must resign themselves to their inevitable disadvantage.

The metaphysics of natural inequality has served aristocracies well. The Greeks had wealth and leisure as a result of the labor of slaves. Plato expressed the wisdom of the established order with the claim that nature produces a hierarchy of superiority in which philosophers, such as himself, emerge at the top. Aristotle's belief that all men possess a rational faculty had more heretical potential, but it was not difficult to believe that some men are more rational than others.

In later periods, nations that possessed economic superiority explained their advantages on the basis of innate superiority. Sir Francis Galton was convinced that the English were superior and that the propertied classes were even more superior than the general population. They were the repository of what was the most biologically precious in mankind.

The democracies of the new world shattered many elements of the old order, and brought a new, radical, equalitarian outlook. In principle, if not always in practice,

Source: William Boyer and Paul Walsh, "Are Children Born Unequal?" *Saturday Review* 41, no. 42 (October 19, 1968): 61–3, 77–9.

William H. Boyer, professor emeritus of psychology at the University of Idaho, is presently professor of psychology at Colorado State University, Fort Collins. His major interests include learning and psychometrics.

Paul Walsh coauthored this article with Professor Boyer when they were both at the University of Hawaii, where Professor Walsh was a member of the Department of Education.

man became equal before the law, and the idea of "the worth of the individual" established a principle of moral equality. Yet legal and moral equalitarianism did not necessarily mean that men were intellectually equal. So the assumption upon which American schools and the American market place developed was that democracy should mean *equal opportunity for competition among people who are genetically unequal.* This creed has satisfied the requirements of modern wisdom even for the more liberal founding fathers such as Thomas Jefferson, and it equally fit into the social Darwinism of an emerging industrial society.

In contemporary American education many of these assumptions remain. People are usually assumed to be not only different in appearance, but also innately unequal in intellectual capacity and therefore unequal in capacity to learn. The contemporary creed urges that schools do all they can to develop *individual* capacities, but it is usually assumed that such capacities vary among individuals. Ability grouping is standard practice and begins in the earliest grades. Intelligence tests and the burgeoning armory of psychometric techniques increasingly facilitate ability tracking, and therefore the potentially prosperous American can usually be identified at an early age. If it is true that people have inherently unequal capacities to learn, the American educational system is built on theoretical bedrock, and it helps construct a social order based on natural superiority. But if people actually have inherently equal capacities, the system is grounded in quicksand and reinforces a system of arbitrary privilege.

Four types of evidence are typically offered to prove that people are innately different in their capacity to learn. The first is self-evidential, the second is observational, the third is logical-theoretical, and the fourth is statistical.

The self-evidential position is based on high levels of certainty which include a strong belief in the obviousness of a conclusion. Many people are very certain that there is an innate difference between people in intellectual capacity. However, such tenacity of feeling is not itself a sufficient basis for evidence, for it offers no method of cross-verification. The mere certainty of a point of view regarding the nature of intelligence must be discounted as an adequate basis for verification.

The observation of individual differences in learning capacity cannot be dismissed as a basis for evidence; useful information for hypotheses requiring further verification can be obtained in this way. For instance, parents may notice different rates of learning among their children. People from different social classes learn and perform at different levels. The city child may learn particular skills more rapidly than the rural child. Observations require some care if they are to produce reliable evidence, but it is possible to observe carefully, and such observation can be cross-verified by other careful observers.

But if people learn particular tasks at different rates, does it follow that people must therefore be *innately* different in their learning capacity? It does *not* necessarily follow. Increasingly, as we know more about the role of environment, we see that there are not only differences between cultures, but also differences within cultures. Even within families, no child has the same environment as the others. Being born first, for instance, makes that child different; he is always the oldest sibling. A whole host of variables operates so that the environment as perceived by an individual child has elements of uniqueness (and similarity) with other children raised in proximity.

Observational evidence can be a useful part of the process of understanding when it raises questions that can be subjected to more conclusive evidence, but it is often used as a way of selectively verifying preconceived notions which are endemic in the culture. Western culture is strongly rooted in the belief in a natural intellectual hierarchy. Few observers have been taught to make observations based on assumptions of natural intellectual equality. Observational evidence must be carefully questioned, for it is often based on a metaphysic of differential capacity which encourages selective perception and a priori categories of explanation. Yet these preconceptions are rarely admitted as an interpretive bias of the observer.

Theories based on carefully obtained data provide a more adequate basis for reaching a defensible position on the nature-nurture controversy than either of the previous procedures. A general theory in the field of genetics or psychology which fits available information would be a relevant instrument for making a deduction about the nature of intelligence. If a logical deduction could be made from a more general theory about heredity and environment to the more specific question of innate intellectual capacity, the conclusion would be as strong as the theory. Such deduction is a commonly used procedure.

Both genetic and psychological theories have often been used to support the belief in inherited intelligence. Genetic connections between physical characteristics such as eye color, hair color, and bodily stature are now clearly established. Certain disease propensity has a genetic basis, yet the best established research is now between single genes and specific physical traits. It is commonplace to assume that if a hereditary basis for differential physical traits has been established, there is a similar connection between genes and intelligence. The conclusion, however, does *not* necessarily follow. Intelligence defined as the capacity to profit by experience or as the ability to solve problems is not a function of a single gene. Whatever the particular polygenetic basis for learning, it does not follow that intellectual capacity is variable because physical traits are variable. Current genetic theory does not provide an adequate basis for deducing a theory of abilities.

Similarly, the Darwinian theory of natural selection is often used to ascribe superiority to those in the upper strata of a hierarchical society. Yet a system of individual economic competition for survival is actually a very recent phenomenon in human history, characteristic of only a few societies, primarily in the eighteenth, nineteenth, and early twentieth centuries. It is very likely that it is irrelevant to genetic natural selection because of its recent origin. American immigration came largely from the lower classes, a fact which could condemn America to national inferiority if the Darwinian theory were used. In the long span of human history, most societies have relied mainly on cooperative systems or autocratic systems for their survival, and individual competition is an untypical example drawn largely from the unique conditions of Western, particularly American experience.

Psychological theories which emphasize individual difference have often assumed that the descriptive differences in physical characteristics, personality, and demonstrated ability are all due largely to heredity. Psychology has had strong historical roots in physiology, but as social psychologists and students of culture have provided new understanding of the role of experience, hereditarian explanation has shifted toward environmentalism. Even the chemical and anatomical characteristics of the brain are now known to be modifiable by experience. Psychologists such as Ann Anastasi point out that, "In view of available genetic knowledge, it appears improbable that social differentiation in physical traits was accompanied by differentiation with regard to genes affecting intellectual or personality development."

Anthropologists, with their awareness of the effects of culture, are the least likely to place credence in the genetic hypothesis. Claude Levi-Strauss, a social anthropologist, claims that all men have equal intellectual potentiality, and have been equal for about a million years. Whether or not this is true, it is clear that the best-supported general genetic or psychological theory does not validate the conclusion that individual intellectual capacity is innately unequal.

Statistical studies under controlled conditions, on the other hand, can provide some of the most reliable information. For instance, when animals are genetically the same, there is the possibility of inferring genetic characteristics through experimental studies. Identical twins develop from the separation of a single egg and have identical genetic inheritance. If human twins could be raised under controlled experimental conditions, much could be learned about the respective role of heredity and environment. Many studies have been made of twins, but none under sufficiently controlled experimental conditions. The results, therefore, permit only speculative conclusions. Most twins are so similar that unless they are separated they are likely to be treated alike. When they are separated, in most cases, one twin is moved to a family of the same social class as the other twin. And people of similar appearance tend to be treated similarly – a large, handsome child is not usually treated the same as a short, unattractive child. The resultant similarity of IQ scores of separate twins has not been surprising.

Even if particular identical twins were to show marked differences in ability when they live in substantially different environments, as they occasionally do, the evidence does not prove the *environmentalist* thesis unless a significantly large number of random cases is compared with a similarly random selection of nonidentical twins. In a small sample, difference could be due to the experience deprivation of one twin. It is possible to stultify any type of development, and so the variation between identical twins, identified in some studies up to forty points, by no means disproves the hereditarian position. Consequently, current studies do not provide conclusive statistical evidence to support either position over the other.

The second most commonly used statistical evidence to show the hereditary basis of intelligence is the constancy of IQ scores at different age periods. Usually, IQ scores do not change appreciably, but occasionally the changes are dramatic. It is now understood that a standard IQ test is culturally loaded toward middle-class values, and so the general constancy of most IQ scores can be explained as the expected result of limited mobility between social class and the resultant constancy of subcultural experiences. So even the statistical "evidence," so often used to support a belief in innate intelligence, is really not conclusive.

Studies of innate intelligence, then, have not produced conclusive evidence to justify the claim for an innate difference in individual intellectual capacity. Equally, there has not been conclusive evidence that the innate potential between people is equal. The research is heavily marked by the self-serving beliefs of the researchers. Psychologists have usually created "intelligence" tests which reflect their own values, predetermining that their own scores will be high. When they have discovered they are high, they have often proclaimed such tests to be indicators of innate superiority.

Many studies are built on simpleminded assumptions about the nature of environment. Psychological environment is related to the subject. A researcher who says that two children live in the "same" environment is quite wrong, for the environment that each child perceives may be quite different from that perceived by the researcher.

Also, it is often assumed that environment is only postnatal, but evidence is now available on the role of prenatal environment, both psychologically and nutritionally. Malnutrition of a pregnant mother can, and often does, have permanent debilitating psychological and physiological effects on her child. Certain diseases contracted by the mother (measles, for example) and certain drugs (thalidomide, for instance) can produce destructive "environmental" effects which limit intellectual capacities. Clearly, people do demonstrate varying capacities to learn, but they have had varying prenatal and postnatal opportunities. If they are female, they are generally treated differently than if they are male. Negroes are treated different from whites—one social class is treated different from another. The *kind* of employment people engage in has a profound effect on what they become. They probably become different through different treatment and different experience, yet our institutions, reflecting our culture, usually operate on the assumption that such differences in ability are innate.

There are at least three ability models which can be supported by current evidence. Each is based on different assumptions about human nature and therefore provides a basis for different social philosophies and different conceptions of government and education.

The first model assumes a great variety of innate ability and a high level of intellectual demand on the average person. In this model, there are hereditary geniuses and idiots, while most people have an intellectual capacity about equal to the demands of their society.

The second model assumes that the innate ability potential of everyone (who has not been injured pre- or postnatally) is equal and far exceeds the normal demand level. (The actual opportunities a person has may produce differential *performance* similar to model No. 1.)

The third model assumes the possibility of some variation, but since all of the ability potential is well beyond the normal demand level, the variation makes virtually no operational difference.

In an economic or educational system, model No. 1 would justify the usual culling, sorting, and excluding through screening devices to create a "natural" hierarchy of ability. It would also justify the common belief in "equal opportunity for competition between unequals," where sorting is achieved through competition.

Both models two and three would justify maximum social effort to develop the abilities of all people, and the failure to achieve high levels of ability in all people would constitute social failure rather than individual failure. American society, with its considerable disparity of wealth and power,

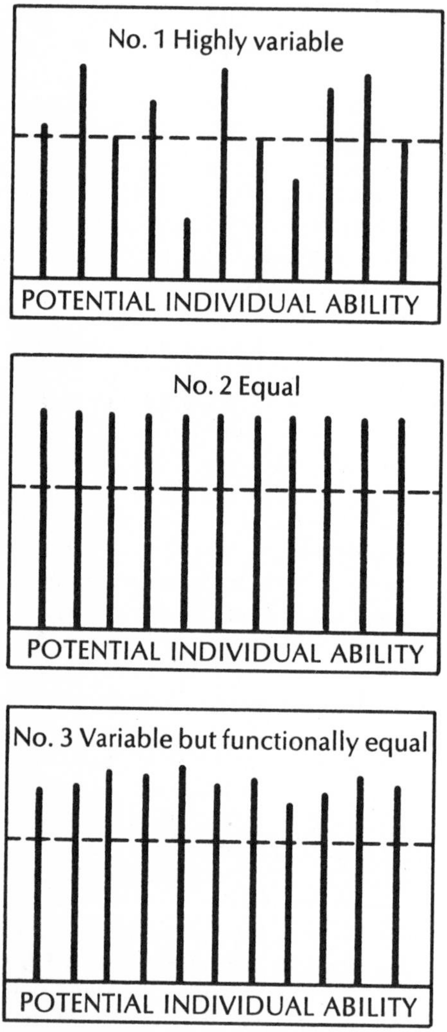

Ability Models *Each model is based on different assumptions about the nature of potential human ability. The dashed line indicates the intellectual level at which individuals must function to meet the requirements of society.*

is largely a success based on the inequality assumed in the first of the three models. It is largely a failure based on the equality assumed in the second and third models.

Schools make little effort to develop the kind of equal ability assumed in models two and three. IQ tests are widely used to identify presumed differences in innate ability so that culling and grouping can make the management of the school easier and more efficient. The disastrous effects of the schools on lower class children are now finally becoming known. The "compensatory" concept has gained some headway, but most educators are so overloaded with work and so traditional in outlook that the schools have become partners with the economic system in reinforcing a system of privilege that usually panders to the children of those in power and finds metaphysical excuses to make only minor gestures toward the less fortunate. The "special programs for the gifted" would be more accurately labeled "special programs for the privileged," for the gifted are primarily the children from socioeconomic classes which provide the most opportunities. The less fortunate (usually lower class children) are ordinarily neglected or convinced that they are innately inferior. Once they become convinced, the prophesy is soon realized.

Part of the problem is the way "intelligence" is defined. It can be defined in many different ways, each leading to a somewhat different educational direction. We can view it as environmental adaptation, as ability to solve problems, as ability to use logical convergent thinking, or it can emphasize divergent thinking and the creation of ideas and problems. When intelligence is defined as abstract verbal-conceptual ability drawing on the modal experiences of middle class environment, as it is in most IQ tests, a selection has been made which excludes many other plausible and often more useful definitions.

The capacity to become intelligent does, of course, have a genetic basis. A cat is not capable of becoming a psychologist. But this does not mean that demonstrated differences in intelligence among psychologists are innate. What is particularly important is whether intelligence is defined primarily as the input or the output. The input is not subject to control, but the output depends on experience; so it is intelligence as output that should be the central concern of the educator.

Until the particular beliefs, which are endemic in many cultures, including American culture, are seen to be part of the heritage of an ancient, anachronistic, elitist tradition, there is little likelihood that the official liberal and equalitarian goals of many modern nations are likely to be realized, even though the wealth of modern technology gives every promise that they are capable of being achieved. Government, industry, education, and virtually all other institutions are now part of the problem, hobbled by a metaphysics of innate inequality. Elitist assumptions about the meaning of ability permeate all fields of education. When teachers of music, mathematics, art, or physical education find that a student doesn't demonstrate the requisite ability, they often reject him (low grades can be a form of rejection). Then counselors shuttle the student to courses where he shows "ability." All this assumes that the school should not develop abilities, but only grant them opportunity to be expressed. The Rousseauian belief in the preexisting self is widespread.

The environmental hypothesis may be wrong, but if it is, it should be shown to be wrong only after a society has done everything possible to develop the abilities of people. We should begin with prenatal care, and should eliminate the experience of economic deprivation, ghettoized living, and elitist schools and businesses. *Lacking definitive scientific evidence about human potentialities, social policy should be based on moral considerations.* We should base our policy on the most generous and promising assumptions about human nature rather than the most niggardly and pessimistic. Men will do their best only when they assume they are capable. Liberal assumptions and conservative assumptions about human nature create their own self-fulfilling prophesies. We now create millions of people who think of themselves as failures—as social rejects. Their sense of frustration and despair is a travesty on the potentialities of an affluent nation.

Poor teaching is protected in the American educational system through the assumption that the child doesn't have the ability. An American environmentalist commitment (toward liberal rather than totalitarian goals) would aim at *creating* ability, at *increasing* intelligence, at *developing* interests. The meaning of "education" would need to be broader than merely institutional schooling. It should also include community responsibility, especially for business and the mass media, which must supplement the work of the school if Americans are to receive more equal educational opportunity. This requires more social planning and more public responsibility than Americans have previously been willing to undertake.

Most American institutions, including the schools, still base their policy largely on the old conservative ideology. This outlook resists change and condemns many to inferiority. Ideological rigidity is not exclusive to the United States; in fact, many other nations are even more rigid. Yet the expanding wealth produced by modern technology is beginning to encourage the have-nots within the United States and throughout the world to demand their share by force and violence if necessary. Violence is likely to be an increasingly common road to social change unless a new public morality based on new assumptions about human potentiality is translated into both foreign and domestic policy. It is not merely racism which bogs down American progress, but also the more pervasive belief in intellectual inequality. The failure to develop the abilities of people was useful to the early American aristocracy and to the power elite of an industrial-scarcity economy. But modern economies of abundance flourish through the maximum development of the abilities of people. There is potentially plenty for all. More widespread development of the capabilities of people would not only add greatly to the wealth of nations, but it can also permit people to participate in a social and cultural renaissance.

Aside from the compelling moral obligation to create equal opportunities within nations and even between nations, the excluded millions in the world are starting to force the changes which should have occurred long ago. Some of them don't believe they are inferior, and they are understandably impatient about changing the old processes of exclusion. All institutions, including the schools, will either need to reexamine their self-consoling elitist beliefs and create real and equal opportunity, or else risk that violence and revolution will increasingly become the dominant instruments of social change.

8.

RACE AND INTELLIGENCE

Richard C. Lewontin

The doctrine that differences in behavior among individuals and groups result from genetic differences developed long before either biological or social scientific evidence was available. Early in this century it was the dominant belief, as indicated in selection 6, "The Juke Myth." Since that time much of the heredity-environment research and argument has focused on the particular areas of behavior measured by intelligence tests. Arthur Jensen, William Shockley, Richard Herrnstein, and others have revived the doctrine as the explanation of the lower I.Q. scores found more commonly among black and lower-class whites as compared with middle-class whites in the U.S. This genetic explanation of I.Q. differences, now popularly identified as Jensenism, has been widely challenged by social scientists and

Source: Richard C. Lewontin, *Bulletin of the Atomic Scientists* 26 (March 1970): 2–8.

Richard C. Lewontin is professor of zoology and mathematical biology at the University of Chicago. He is a Fellow of the American Academy of Arts and Sciences.

frequently attributed to the racist beliefs in American culture. The data on which Jensen and others base their conclusion that intelligence is largely inherited are subject to other interpretations. In this article Richard C. Lewontin, a biologist, dissects the Jensen paper which precipitated the recent controversy and concludes Jensen is wrong.

In the Spring of 1653 Pope Innocent X condemned a pernicious heresy which espoused the doctrines of "total depravity, irresistable grace, lack of free will, predestination and limited atonement." That heresy was Jansenism and its author was Cornelius Jansen, Bishop of Ypres.

In the winter of 1968 the same doctrine appeared in the "Harvard Educational Review." That doctrine is now called "jensenism" by the "New York Times Magazine" and its author is Arthur R. Jensen, professor of educational psychology at the University of California at Berkeley. It is a doctrine as erroneous in the twentieth century as it was in the seventeenth. I shall try to play the Innocent.

Jensen's article, "How Much Can We Boost I.Q. and Scholastic Achievement?" created such a furor that the "Review" reprinted it along with critiques by psychologists, theorists of education and a population geneticist under the title "Environment, Heredity and Intelligence." The article first came to my attention when, at no little expense, it was sent to every member of the National Academy of Sciences by the eminent white Anglo-Saxon inventor, William Shockley, as part of his continuing campaign to have the Academy study the effects of interracial mating. It is little wonder that the "New York Times" found the matter newsworthy, and that Professor Jensen has surely become the most discussed and least read essayist since Karl Marx. I shall try, in this article, to display Professor Jensen's argument, to show how the structure of his argument is designed to make his point and to reveal what appear to be deeply embedded assumptions derived from a particular world view, leading him to erroneous conclusions.

. . . . . .

I shall say little or nothing about the critiques of Jensen's article, which would require even more space to criticize than the original article itself.

THE POSITION

Jensen's argument consists essentially of an elaboration on two incontrovertible facts, a causative explanation and a programmatic conclusion. The two facts are that black people perform, on the average, more poorly than whites on standard I.Q. tests, and that special programs of compensatory education so far tried have not had much success in removing this difference. His causative explanation for these facts is that I.Q. is highly heritable, with most of the variation among individuals arising from genetic rather than environmental sources. His programmatic conclusion is that there is no use in trying to remove the difference in I.Q. by education since it arises chiefly from genetic causes and the best thing that can be done for black children is to capitalize on those skills for which they are biologically adapted. Such a conclusion is so clearly at variance with the present egalitarian consensus and so clearly smacks of a racist elitism, whatever its merit or motivation, that a very careful analysis of the argument is in order.

The article begins with the pronouncement: "Compensatory education has been tried and it apparently has failed." A documentation of that failure and a definition of compensatory education are left to the end of the article for good logical and pedagogical reasons. Having caught our attention by whacking us over the head with a two-by-four, like that famous trainer of mules, Jensen then asks:

"What has gone wrong? In other fields, when bridges do not stand, when aircraft do not fly, when machines do not work, when treatments do not cure, despite all the conscientious efforts on the part of many persons to make them do so, one begins to question the basic assumptions, principles, theories, and hypotheses that guide one's efforts. Is it time to follow suit in education?"

Who can help but answer that last rhetorical question with a resounding "Yes"? What thoughtful and intelligent person can avoid being struck by the intellectual and empirical bankruptcy of educational psychology as it is practiced in our mass educational systems? The innocent reader will immediately fall into close sympathy with Professor Jensen, who, it seems, is about to dissect educational psychology and show it up as a prescientific jumble without theoretic coherence or prescriptive competence. But the innocent reader will be wrong. For the rest of Jensen's article puts the blame for the failure of his science not on the scientists but on the children. According to him, it is not that his science and its practitioners have failed utterly to understand human motivation, behavior and development but simply that the damn kids are ineducable.

The unconscious irony of his metaphor of bridges, airplanes and machines has apparently been lost on him. The fact is that in the twentieth century bridges do stand, machines do work and airplanes do fly, because they are built on clearly understood mechanical and hydrodynamic principles which even moderately careful and intelligent engineers can put into practice. In the seventeenth century that was not the case, and the general opinion was that men would never succeed in their attempts to fly because flying was impossible. Jensen proposes that we take the same view of education and that, in the terms of his metaphor, fallen bridges be taken as evidence of the unbridgeability of rivers. The alternative explanation, that educational psychology is still in the seventeenth century, is apparently not part of his philosophy.

This view of technological failure as arising from ontological rather than epistemological sources is a common form of apology at many levels of practice. Anyone who has dealt with plumbers will appreciate how many things "can't be fixed" or "weren't meant to be used like that." Physicists tell me that their failure to formulate an elegant general theory of fundamental particles is a result of there not being any underlying regularity to be discerned. How often men, in their overweening pride, blame nature for their own failures. This professionalist bias, that if a problem were soluble it would have been solved, lies at the basis of Jensen's thesis which can only be appreciated when seen in this light.

Having begun with the assumption that I.Q. cannot be equalized, Jensen now goes on to why not. He begins his investigation with a discussion of the "nature of intelligence," by which he means the way in which intelligence is defined by testing and the correlation of intelligence test scores with scholastic and occupational performance. A very strong point is made that I.Q. testing was developed in a western industrialized society specifically as a prognostication of success in that society by the generally accepted criteria. He makes a special point of noting that psychologists' notions of status and success have a high correlation with those of the society at large, so that it is entirely reasonable that tests created by psychologists will correlate highly with conventional measures of success. One might think that this argument, that I.Q. testing is "culture bound," would militate against Jensen's general thesis of the biological and specifically genetical basis of I.Q. differences. Indeed, it is an argument often used against I.Q. testing for so-called "deprived" children, since it is supposed that they have developed in a subculture that does not prepare them for such tests. What role does this "environmentalist" argument play in Jensen's thesis? Is it simply evidence of his total fairness and objectivity? No. Jensen has seen, more clearly than most, that the argument of the specific cultural origins of I.Q. testing and especially the high correlation of these tests with occupational status cuts both ways. For if the poorer performance of blacks on I.Q. tests has largely genetic rather than environmental causes, then it follows that blacks are also genetically handicapped for other high status components of Western culture. That is, what Jensen is arguing is that differences between cultures are in large part genetically determined and that I.Q. testing is simply one manifestation of those differences.

In this light we can also understand his argument concerning the existence of "general intelligence" as measured by I.Q. tests. Jensen is at some pains to convince his readers that there is a single factor, *g*, which, in factor analysis of various intelligence tests, accounts for a large fraction of the variance of scores. The existence of such a factor, while not critical to the argument, obviously simplifies it, for then I.Q. tests would really be testing for "something" rather than just being correlated with scholastic and occupational performance. While Jensen denies that intelligence should be reified, he comes perilously close to doing so in his discussion of *g*.

Without going into factor analysis at any length, I will point out only that factor analysis does not give a unique result for any given set of data. Rather, it gives an infinity of possible results among which the investigator chooses according to his tastes and preconceptions of the models he is fitting. One strategy in factor analysis is to pack as much weight as possible into one factor, while another is to distribute the weights over as many factors as possible as equally as possible. Whether one chooses one of these or some other depends upon one's model, the numerical analysis only providing the weights appropriate for each model. Thus, the impression left by Jensen that factor analysis somehow naturally or ineluctably isolates one factor with high weight is wrong.

"TRUE MERIT"?

In the welter of psychological metaphysics involving concepts of "crystallized" as against "fluid" intelligence, "generalized" intelligence, "intelligence" as opposed to "mental ability," there is some danger of losing sight of Jensen's main point: I.Q. tests are culture bound and there is good reason that they should be, because they are predictors of culture bound activities and values. What is further implied, of course, is that those who do not perform well on these tests are less well suited for high status and must paint barns rather than pictures. We read that "We have to face it: the assortment of persons into occupational roles simply is not 'fair' in any absolute sense. The best we can hope for is that true merit, given equality of opportunity, act as a basis for the natural assorting process." What a world view is there revealed! The most rewarding places in society shall go to those with "true merit" and that is the best we can hope for. Of course, Professor Jensen is safe since, despite the abject failure of educational psychology to solve the problems it has set itself, that failure does not arise from lack of "true merit" on the part of psychologists but from the natural intransigence of their human subjects.

Having established that there are differences among men in the degree to which they are adapted to higher status and high satisfaction roles in Western society, and having stated that education has not succeeded in removing these differences, Jensen now moves on to their cause. He raises the question of "fixed" intelligence and quite rightly dismisses it as misleading. He introduces us here to what he regards as the two real issues. "The first issue concerns the genetic basis of individual differences in intelligence; the second concerns the stability or constancy of the I.Q. through the individual's lifetime." Jensen devotes some three-quarters of his essay to an attempt to demonstrate that I.Q. is developmentally rather stable, being to all intents and purposes fixed after the age of eight, and that most of the variation in I.Q. among individuals in the population has a genetic rather than environmental basis. Before looking in detail at some of these arguments, we must again ask where he is headed. While Jensen argues strongly that I.Q. is "culture bound," he wishes to argue that it is not environmentally determined. This is a vital distinction. I.Q. is "culture bound" in the sense that it is related to performance in a Western industrial society. But the determination of the ability to perform culturally defined tasks might itself be entirely genetic. For example, a person suffering from a genetically caused deaf-mutism is handicapped to different extents in cultures requiring different degrees of verbal performance, yet his disorder did not have an environmental origin.

Jensen first dispenses with the question of developmental stability of I.Q. Citing Benjamin Bloom's survey of the literature, he concludes that the correlation between test scores of an individual at different ages is close to unity after the age of eight. The inference to be drawn from this fact is, I suppose, that it is not worth trying to change I.Q. by training after that age. But such an inference cannot be made. All that can be said is that, given the usual progression of educational experience to which most children are exposed, there is sufficient consistency not to cause any remarkable changes in I.Q. That is, a child whose educational experience (in the broad sense) may have ruined his capacity to perform by the age of eight is not likely to experience an environment in his later years that will do much to alter those capacities. Indeed, given the present state of educational theory and practice, there is likely to be a considerable reinforcement of early performance. To say that children do not change their I.Q. is not the same as saying they cannot. Moreover, Jensen is curiously silent on the lower correlation and apparent plasticity of I.Q. at younger ages, which is after all the chief point of Bloom's work.

THE GENETIC ARGUMENT

The heart of Jensen's paper is contained in his long discussion of the distribution and inheritance of intelligence. Clearly he feels that here his main point is to be established. The failure of compensatory education, the developmental stability of I.Q., the obvious difference between the performance of blacks and whites can be best understood, he believes, when the full impact of the findings of genetics is felt. In his view, insufficient attention has been given by social scientists to the findings of geneticists, and I must agree with him. Although there are exceptions, there has been a strong professional bias toward the assumption that human behavior is infinitely plastic, a bias natural enough in men whose professional commitment is to changing behavior. It is as a reaction to this tradition, and as a natural outcome of his confrontation with the failure of educational psychology, that Jensen's own opposite bias flows, as I have already claimed.

The first step in his genetical argument is the demonstration that I.Q. scores are normally distributed or nearly so. I am unable to find in his paper any explicit statement of why he regards this point as so important. From repeated references to Sir Francis Galton, filial regression, mutant genes, a few major genes for exceptional ability and assortative mating, it gradually emerges that an underlying normality of the distribution appears to Jensen as an important consequence of genetic control of I.Q. He asks: ". . . is intelligence itself—not just our measurements of it—really normally distributed?" Apparently he believes that if intelligence, quite aside from measurement, were really normally distributed, this would demonstrate its biological and genetical status. Aside from a serious epistemological error involved in the question, the basis for his concern is itself erroneous. There is nothing in genetic theory that requires or even suggests that a phenotypic character should be normally distributed, even when it is completely determined genetically. Depending upon the degree of dominance of genes, interaction between them, frequencies of alternative alleles at the various gene loci in the population and allometric growth relations between various parts of the organism transforming primary gene effects, a character may have almost any unimodal distribution and under some circumstances even a multimodal one.

After establishing the near-normality of the curve of I.Q. scores, Jensen goes directly to a discussion of the genetics of continuously varying characters. He begins by quoting with approbation E. L. Thorndike's maxim: "In the actual race of life, which is not to get ahead, but to get ahead of somebody, the chief determining factor is heredity." This quotation along with many others used by Jensen shows a style of argument that is not congenial to natural scientists, however it may be a part of other disciplines. There is a great deal of appeal to authority and the acceptance of the empirically unsubstantiated opinions of eminent authorities as a kind of relevant evidence. We hear of "three eminent geneticists," or "the most distinguished exponent [of genetical methods], Sir Cyril Burt." The irrelevance of this kind of argument is illustrated precisely by the appeal to E. L. Thorndike, who, despite his eminence in the history of psychology, made the statement quoted by Jensen in 1905, when nothing was known about genetics outside of attempts to confirm Mendel's paper. Whatever the eventual truth of his statement turns out to be, Thorndike made it out of his utter ignorance of the genetics of human behavior, and it can only be ascribed to the sheer prejudice of a Methodist Yankee.

HERITABILITY

To understand the main genetical argument of Jensen, we must dwell, as he does, on the concept of heritability. We cannot speak of a trait being molded by heredity, as opposed to environment. Every character of an organism is the result of a unique interaction between the inherited genetic information and the sequence of environments through which the organism has passed during its development. For some traits the variations in environment have little effect, so that once the genotype is known, the eventual form of the organism is pretty well specified. For other traits, specification of the genetic makeup may be a very poor predictor of the eventual phenotype because even the smallest environmental effects may affect the trait greatly. But for all traits there is a many-many relationship between gene and character and between environment and character. Only by a specification of both the genotype and the environmental sequence can the character be predicted. Nevertheless, traits do vary in the degree of their genetic determination and this degree can be expressed, among other ways, by their heritabilities.

The distribution of character values, say I.Q. scores, in a population arises from a mixture of a large number of genotypes. Each genotype in the population does not have a unique phenotype corresponding to it because the different individuals of that genotype have undergone somewhat different environmental sequences in their development. Thus, each genotype has a distribution of I.Q. scores associated with it. Some genotypes are more common in the population so their distributions contribute heavily to determining the overall distribution, while others are rare and make little contribution. The total variation in the population, as measured by the variance, results from the variation between the mean I.Q. scores of the different genotypes and the variation around each genotypic mean. The heritability of a measurement is defined as the ratio of the variance due to the differences between the genotypes to the total variance in the population. If this heritability were 1.0, it would mean that all the variation in the population resulted from differences between genotypes but that there was no environmentally caused variation around each genotype mean. On the other hand, a heritability of 0.0 would mean that there was no genetic variation because all individuals were effectively identical in their genes, and that all the variation in the population arose from environmental differences in the development of the different individuals.

Defined in this way, heritability is not a concept that can be applied to a trait in general, but only to a trait in a particular population, in a particular set of environments. Thus, different populations may have more or less genetic variation for the same character. Moreover, a character may be relatively insensitive to environment in a particular environmental range, but be extremely sensitive outside this range. Many such characters are known, and it is the commonest kind of relation between character and environment. Finally, some genotypes are more sensitive to environmental fluctuation than others so that two populations with the same genetic variance but different genotypes, and living in the same environments, may still have different heritabilities for a trait.

The estimation of heritability of a trait in a population depends on measuring individuals of known degrees of relationship to each other and comparing the observed correlation in the trait between relatives with the theoretical correlation from genetic theory. There are two difficulties that arise in such a procedure. First, the exact theoretical correlation between relatives, except for identical twins, cannot be specified unless there is detailed knowledge of the mode of inheritance of the character. A first order approximation is possible, however, based upon some simplifying assumptions, and it is unusual for this approximation to be badly off.

A much more serious difficulty arises because relatives are correlated not only in their heredities but also in their environments. Two sibs are much more alike in the sequence of environments in which they developed than are two cousins or two unrelated persons. As a result, there will be an overestimate of the heritability of a character, arising from the added correlation between relatives from environmental similarities. There is no easy way to get around this bias in general so that great weight must be put on peculiar situations in which the ordinary environmental correlations are disturbed. That is why so much emphasis is placed, in human genetics, on the handful of cases of identical twins raised apart from birth, and the much more numerous cases of totally unrelated children raised in the same family. Neither of these cases is completely reliable, however, since twins separated from birth are nevertheless likely to be raised in families belonging to the same socioeconomic, racial, religious and ethnic categories, while unrelated children raised in the same family may easily be treated rather more differently than biological sibs. Despite these difficulties, the weight of evidence from a variety of correlations between relatives puts the heritability of I.Q. in various human populations between .6 and .8. For reasons of his argument, Jensen prefers the higher value but it is not worth quibbling over. Volumes could be written on the evaluation of heritability estimates for I.Q. and one can find a number of faults with Jensen's treatment of the published data. However, it is irrelevant to questions of race and intelligence, and to questions of the failure of compensatory education, whether the heritability of I.Q. is .4 or .8, so I shall accept Jensen's rather high estimate without serious argument.

The description I have given of heritability, its application to a specific population in a specific set of environments and the difficulties in its accurate estimation are all discussed by Jensen. While the emphasis he gives to various points differs from mine, and his estimate of heritability is on the high side, he appears to have said in one way or another just about everything that a judicious man can say. The very judiciousness of his argument has been disarming to geneticists especially, and they have failed to note the extraordinary conclusions that are drawn from these reasonable premises. Indeed, the logical and empirical hiatus between the conclusions and the premises is especially striking and thought-provoking in view of Jensen's apparent understanding of the technical issues.

The first conclusion concerns the cause of the difference between the I.Q. distributions of blacks and whites. On the average, over a number of studies, blacks have a distribution of I.Q. scores whose mean is about 15 points—about 1 standard deviation—below whites. Taking into account the lower variance of scores among blacks than among whites, this difference means that about 11 percent of blacks have I.Q. scores above the mean white score (as compared with 50 percent of whites) while 18 percent of whites score below the mean black score (again, as compared to 50 percent of blacks). If, according to Jensen, "gross socioeconomic factors" are equalized between the tested groups, the difference in means is reduced to 11 points. It is hard to know what to say about overlap between the groups after this correction, since the standard deviations of such equalized populations will be lower. From these and related observations, and the estimate of .8 for the heritability of I.Q. (in white populations, no reliable estimate existing for blacks), Jensen concludes that:

> . . . all we are left with are various lines of evidence, no one of which is definitive alone, but which, viewed altogether, make it a not unreasonable hypothesis that genetic factors are strongly implicated in the average Negro-white intelligence difference. The preponderance of evidence is, in my opinion, less consistent with a strictly environmental hypothesis than with a genetic hypothesis, which, of course, does not exclude the influence of environment on its interaction with genetic factors.

Anyone not familiar with the standard litany of academic disclaimers ("not unreasonable hypothesis," "does not exclude," "in my opinion") will, taking this statement at face value, find nothing to disagree with since it says nothing. To contrast a "strictly environmental hypothesis" with "a genetic hypothesis which . . . does not exclude the influence of the environment" is to be guilty of the utmost triviality. If that is the only conclusion he means to come to, Jensen has just wasted a great deal of space in the "Harvard Educational Review." But of course, like all cant, the special language of the social scientist needs to be translated into common English. What Jensen is saying is: "It is pretty clear, although not absolutely proved, that most of the difference in I.Q. between blacks and whites is genetical." This, at least, is not a trivial conclusion. Indeed, it may even be true. However, the evidence offered by Jensen is irrelevant.

IS IT LIKELY?

How can that be? We have admitted the high heritability of I.Q. and the reality of the difference between the black and the white distributions. Moreover, we have seen that adjustment for gross socio-economic level still leaves a large difference. Is it not then likely that the difference is genetic? No. It is neither likely nor unlikely. There is no evidence. The fundamental error of Jensen's argument is to confuse heritability of a character within a population with heritability of the difference between two populations. Indeed, between two populations, the concept of heritability of their difference is meaningless. This is because a variance based upon two measurements has only one degree of freedom and so cannot be partitioned into genetic and environmental components. The genetic basis of the difference between two populations bears no logical or empirical relation to the heritability within populations and cannot be inferred from it, as I will show in a simple but realistic example. In addition, the notion that eliminating what appear a priori to be major environmental variables will serve to eliminate a large part of the environmentally caused difference between the populations is biologically naive. In the context of I.Q. testing, it assumes that educational psychologists know what the major sources of environmental difference between black and white performance are. Thus, Jensen compares blacks with American Indians whom he regards as far more environmentally disadvantaged. But a priori judgments of the importance of different aspects of the environment are valueless, as every ecologist and plant physiologist knows. My example will speak to that point as well.

Let us take two completely inbred lines of corn. Because they are completely inbred by self-fertilization, there is no genetic variation in either line, but the two lines will be genetically different from each other. Let us now plant seeds of these two inbred lines in flower pots with ordinary potting soil, one seed of each line to a pot. After they have germinated and grown for a few weeks we will measure the height of each plant. We will discover variation in height from plant to plant. Because each line is completely inbred, the variation in height within lines must be entirely environmental, a result of variation in potting conditions from pot to pot. Then the heritability of plant height in both lines is 0.0. But there will be an average difference in plant height between lines that arises entirely from the fact that the two lines are genetically different. Thus the difference between lines is entirely genetical even though the heritability of height is 0!

Now let us do the opposite experiment. We will take two handsful from a sack containing seed of an open-pollinated variety of corn. Such a variety has lots of genetic variation in it. Instead of using potting soil, however, we will grow the seed in vermiculite watered with a carefully made up nutrient, Knop's solution, used by plant physiologists for controlled growth experiments. One batch of seed will be grown on complete Knop's solution, but the other will have the concentration of nitrates cut in half and, in addition, we will leave out the minute trace of zinc salt that is part of the necessary trace elements (30 parts per billion). After several weeks we will measure the plants. Now we will find variation within seed lots which is entirely genetical since no environmental variation within lots was allowed. Thus heritability will be 1.0. However, there will be a radical difference between seed lots which is ascribable entirely to the difference in nutrient levels. Thus, we have a case where heritability within populations is complete, yet the difference between populations is entirely environmental!

But let us carry our experiment to the end. Suppose we do not know about the difference in the nutrient solutions because it was really the carelessness of our assistant that was involved. We call in a friend who is a very careful chemist and ask him to look into the matter for us. He analyzes the nutrient solutions and discovers the obvious—only half as much nitrates in the case of the stunted plants. So we add the missing nitrates and do the experiment again. This time our second batch of plants will grow a little larger but not much, and we will conclude that the difference between the lots is genetic since equalizing the large difference in nitrate level had so little effect. But, of course, we would be wrong for it is the missing trace of zinc that is the real culprit. Finally, it should be pointed out that it took many years before the importance of minute trace elements in plant physiology was worked out because ordinary laboratory glassware will leach out enough of many trace elements to let plants grow normally. Should educational psychologists study plant physiology?

Having disposed, I hope, of Jensen's conclusion that the high heritability of I.Q. and the lack of effect of correction for gross socioeconomic class are presumptive evidence for the genetic basis of the difference between blacks and whites, I will turn to his second erroneous conclusion. The article under discussion began with the observation, which he documents, that compensatory education for the disadvantaged (blacks, chiefly) has failed. The explanation offered for the failure is that I.Q. has a high heritability and that therefore the difference between the races is also mostly genetical. Given that the racial difference is genetical, then environmental change and educational effort cannot make much and cannot close the gap very much between blacks and whites. I have already argued that there is no evidence one way or the other about the genetics of interracial I.Q. differences. To understand Jensen's second error, however, we will suppose that the difference is indeed genetical. Let it be entirely genetical. Does this mean that compensatory education, having failed, must fail? The supposition that it must arises from a misapprehension about the fixity of genetically determined traits. It was thought at one time that genetic disorders, because they were genetic, were incurable. Yet we now know that inborn errors of metabolism are indeed curable if their biochemistry is sufficiently well understood and if deficient metabolic products can be supplied exogenously. Yet in the normal range of environments, these inborn errors manifest themselves irrespective of the usual environmental variables. That is, even though no environment in the normal range has an effect on the character, there may be special environments, created in response to our knowledge of the underlying biology of a character, which are effective in altering it.

But we do not need recourse to abnormalities of development to see this point. Jensen says that "there is no reason to believe that the I.Q.'s of deprived children, given an environment of abundance, would rise to a higher level than the already privileged children's I.Q.'s." It is empirically wrong to argue that if the richest environment experience we can conceive does not raise I.Q. substantially, that we have exhausted the environmental possibilities. In the seventeenth century the infant mortality rates were many times their present level at all socioeconomic levels. Using what was then the normal range of environments, the infant mortality rate of the highest socioeconomic class would have been regarded as the limit below which one could not reasonably expect to reduce the death rate. But changes in sanitation, public health and disease control—changes which are commonplace to us now but would have seemed incredible to a man of the seventeenth century—have reduced the infant mortality rates of "disadvantaged" urban Americans well below those of even the richest members of seventeenth century society. The argument that compensatory education is hopeless is equivalent to saying that changing the form of the seventeenth century gutter would not have a pronounced effect on public sanitation. What compensatory education will be able to accomplish when the study of human behavior finally emerges from its prescientific era is anyone's guess. It will be most extraordinary if it stands as the sole exception to the rule that technological progress exceeds by manyfold what even the most optimistic might have imagined.

The real issue in compensatory education does not lie in the heritability of I.Q. or in the possible limits of educational technology. On the reasonable assumption that ways of significantly altering mental capacities can be developed if it is important enough to do so, the real issue is what the goals of our society will be. Do we want to foster a society in which the "race of life" is "to get ahead of somebody" and in which "true merit," be it genetically or environmentally determined, will be the criterion of men's earthly reward? Or do we want a society in which every man can aspire to the fullest measure of psychic and material fulfillment that social activity can produce? Professor Jensen has made it fairly clear to me what sort of society he wants.

I oppose him.

9.

A STUDY OF VALUES

Evon Z. Vogt and
John M. Roberts

If it can be shown that the inborn characteristics of people in communities do not differ significantly, and at the same time one observes that such groups solve similar problems quite differently, then the differences must be ascribed to the learned factors which not only sociologists and anthropologists but, increasingly, educated people in general call "culture." This point is illustrated by Evon Z. Vogt and John M. Roberts as they demonstrate that persons basically similar biologically, but having different cultures, may settle in the same general geographical area and yet develop markedly different modes of life.

"No tenet of intellectual folklore has been so damaging to our life and times as the cliché that 'science has nothing to do with values.' If the consideration of values is to be the exclusive property of religion and the humanities, a scientific understanding of human experience is impossible."

In these words the anthropologist Clyde Kluckhohn recently defined a major challenge and frontier of social research. The forming and choosing of values is a central concern of all men and societies. Conceptions of the desirable, the fitting and the good vary widely among the world's 3,000 or so cultures. They strongly influence the selection of the modes, the means and the ends of human behavior. The social scientist cannot view "man in culture" as conditioned only by economic forces and biological impulses. People see the world through cultural lenses compounded of particular combinations of values; they respond in different ways in accordance with their differing values. We must recognize that people are not just "driven" by situational pressures: they are also "pulled" by the ideals and goals of their cultures.

As we advance the frontiers of the social sciences it becomes increasingly clear that values must be studied as a part of our actual subject matter and not left entirely to the humanists and philosophers. Values are, in fact, the subject of an increasing number of investigations today. But how can values be brought under the same kind of objective study as linguistic systems and the techniques of salmon fishing?

Source: Evon Z. Vogt and John M. Roberts, "A Study of Values," *Scientific American* 195, no. 1 (July 1956): 25–30.

Evon Z. Vogt is professor of anthropology at Harvard University. American ethnology is one of his major concerns in the broader field of social anthropology. Among his books are *Modern Homesteaders, Navaho Veterans,* and, most recently, *The Zincantecos of Mexico: A Modern Maya Way of Life.*

John M. Roberts is professor of anthropology at Cornell University. His areas of study in the general field of cultural anthropology include southwestern ethnology, small group cultures, and primitive law and government. He is author of *Three Navaho Households, Zuni Law,* and *Zuni Daily Life.*

The apparent difficulty is reduced if we recall that the object of such study is not to make an ethical judgment of goodness or badness. We want to know, rather, how values function in organizing behavior. Since it is virtually impossible to experiment with human cultures, the social scientist must find his laboratory situation ready-made. Preferably he should be able to observe and compare the role of values in one or two cultures other than his own. Ideally he will find a situation where he can observe variations in values against a background in which other variables are relatively constant.

This article is concerned with . . . the region south of Gallup, N.M., where communities of five different cultural traditions—Zuñi and Navaho Indians, Mormons, Catholic Spanish-Americans and Protestant-American homesteaders from Texas—all contend with the same high-altitude semiarid environment. Since our research has not yet reached the phase of synthesis and final theory construction, it is still too early to summarize the project's overall results. At this stage, however, we are able to report that the Gallup region has given us a practically ideal laboratory for investigation of the manifold questions presented by the role of values in human life.

The value study . . . has engaged the collaboration of 30 investigators from the disciplines of anthropology, sociology, psychology, philosophy, history, government and law. They have approached their common concern with values through a wide variety of topical interests, such as religion, cultural change, politics, land use, child rearing, adult personality, mythology, music and graphic arts. The full battery of research techniques—direct observation, participant observation, personal interviews, group discussions, interaction analysis, psychological tests and questionnaires—is represented in the immense documentation now assembled. Since the populations of the five communities are small (3,000 Zuñis, 650 Navahos, 700 Spanish-Americans, 250 Mormons, 250 Texans) it has been possible to emphasize intensive methods and reduce the problems of sampling and statistical analysis which attend so much social research. The extensive existing literatures on some of the cultures have helped to give the study historical depth.

In all its undertakings the values study has been faced with the delicate problem of rapport and public relations in the five communities. No research could be conducted that might endanger future investigations. Among the Zuñi, for example, it has so far not been politic to study prayers, ceremonials and other religious matters at close range. Because we have had to be careful to protect individuals and groups in every way, this is the first overall account of the project to be published outside a few specialized professional journals and monographs.

The geography of the Gallup region establishes some much-needed constants for a study that is otherwise bedeviled by a multiplicity of uncontrolled variables. Each of the peoples of the five cultures see the same plateau and mesa country, sparsely covered with gramagrass, sagebrush, pinyon and juniper and with stands of ponderosa pines at the higher elevations. All of the people must contend with the same fluctuation in rainfall, averaging only 12 to 15 inches per year, and with the short, changeable growing season typical of the American Southwest at this 7,000-foot altitude. There are permanent springs in the region, but the small Zuñi River, a tributary of the Little Colorado, is the only year-round stream. Soils, however, are fertile and productive when watered.

To meet the problems of making a living

in this landscape, each of the five communities has essentially the same technology available to it. In face-to-face contact with one another for a generation or more, all have been subjected to markedly similar historical pressures. These pressures have mounted during the last 10 years, as hard-surfaced roads, telephone lines and public power have spread through their country. The five communities remain distinct, however, and present significant contrasts.

Each of the cultures, for example, has worked out its own solution for the problem of physical survival. The Zuñis, oldest of the peoples in the region, conduct a long-established irrigation agriculture supplemented by stock-raising and by crafts, notably the making of silver jewelry. The Navahos were originally roving hunters and gatherers and came into the region only a century ago; they have become dry farmers and sheepherders with wage work providing an increasing percentage of their income as contact with our American culture becomes more extensive. Livestock ranching and wage work provide the principal income for the three Spanish-American villages, which were settled about 75 years ago. The Mormons, also established in this region since the 1880's, have been conspicuously successful at irrigation farming; they also engage in livestock ranching and wage work. The Texans staked out the last Homestead Act lands in the region during the 1930's, as refugees from the dust bowl to the east; they raise cattle and carry on a commercial and largely mechanized dry-land farming, with pinto beans as their principal crop.

The five cultures present corresponding contrasts in their community organization and family life. The sedentary Zuñis spend their winters in the stone houses of their large central pueblo, moving in the agricultural season to three farming villages. Their social structure is based on the matrilocal household (with the husband living with his wife's kinfolk), matrilineal clans, and various priesthoods and other religious groupings. The Navahos also have matrilocal extended families and matrilineal clans. They are less tightly organized, however, and families dwell in widely scattered hogans: hexagonal log houses with dirt roofs. As compared to the other two non-Indian cultures, the Mormons resemble the Zuñis in having a strong sense of identity with their community. Their life centers around the single village of Ramah, where the values study maintains its field headquarters. For the Spanish-Americans the family and the Catholic church are paramount institutions. The Texan homesteads are scattered over several townships; their identity is loosely maintained by competing Protestant churches and cliques.

The values study seeks answers to a number of questions that are suggested by the differences among these five cultures. It has set out to define, first of all, the value system of each of them and to establish the role that values play in making these cultures different from one another. The changes in values that are occurring in each culture represent another important line of inquiry. Of equal challenge is the question of why their different value systems persist, despite their contact with each other and their exposure to the same environmental pressures.

One of the most promising areas of investigation is the connection between the values and the social structures of the various communities. For example, the Spanish-Americans lay strong emphasis upon "lineality" – the view that social relations are desirable when they are consistent with the hierarchy of their society. In their communities younger relatives are subordinate to older kinsmen, females to males, and the *peón* to his *patrón.* The secular structure gears into the hierarchically arranged Catholic church with its offices extending from the parish priest through the bishops, archbishops, cardinals and on up to the Pope. Much the same type of hierarchy is found in the sacred world of the Spanish-Americans, from the local images of the saints up to the Deity.

The Texan homesteaders, in marked contrast, place a strong American-frontier stress upon individualistic social relations in which each man is expected to be self-reliant and to be "his own boss." The social order of the community is composed of relatively isolated families, each living on its own farm and competing with other families for position and prestige. Instead of the single, hierarchically arranged church, the homesteaders subscribe to no less than 10 competing Christian denominations, each distinguished by a slightly different doctrine and type of service.

The Texan homesteaders fail to understand why "anybody wants to live all bunched up in a little village and take orders from the big landholders and the priests." The Spanish-Americans say of the Texans that "everybody tries to be his own *patrón.*"

The Mormons present still another picture. The formal structure of the Mormon church has hierarchical aspects with lines of authority running upward from the local ward bishops through the state presidents to the 12 apostles and church president in Salt Lake City, Utah. But within this framework the local community enjoys much autonomy to work out its own affairs, and great value is placed upon collateral, cooperative economic and social relationships. Around the village and the large cohesive family system there is a proliferation of cooperatives in economic affairs. The little village of Ramah boasts a mutual irrigation company, a cooperative land and cattle company and a cooperative dairy. The spirit of individualistic competition which pervades the Texan community is consciously suppressed in favor of the values of cooperation in the Mormon village.

These values have deep roots in Mormon history. Joseph Smith, the founder of the church, proposed the "law of consecration" which required that all who had surplus wealth must impart it through the church to the poor. Although this "law" was abandoned as early as 1838, the values it expressed lent a strong cooperative bias to much of later Mormon activity. The compact village settlement was a social invention of the Mormons, motivated by a sense of urgent need to prepare a dwelling place for the "Savior" at "His second coming." Through the years cooperation became a strong defense against "persecution" by the "gentiles," first in the Middle West and later in the Far West, when the political and legal movements to stamp out Mormon polygamy came to a head. The cooperative spirit was also strongly reinforced in the arid West by the requirements of irrigation agriculture—the construction of storage reservoirs, the building and maintaining of networks of ditches, and the necessity of organized arrangements for the distribution of scarce water supplies among the various farms within a village.

The Spanish-Americans, Texans and Mormons, different as they are, belong to a single major historical tradition which contrasts with that of the Zuñis and Navahos. In former times Zuñi was ruled by a theocracy. Today personal relationships among the Zuñis are organized in a complicated series of interlocking religious, kinship and secular units, in which the individual strikes a delicate balance with external authority. No true Zuñi wishes to live away from Zuñi, particularly in the wintertime. The Zuñis have been characterized as having a kind of "middle of the road," "avoidance of excess" approach to life, in the manner of the ancient Greeks. Although this characterization must be qualified, it still symbolizes the Zuñi ideal.

While both Mormons and Zuñis can be characterized as "cooperative" and both societies manifest important linkages between their cooperative value systems and the requirements of irrigation agriculture, there are some interesting differences between them. In the Mormon community the values of cooperation are propounded by a single organized church which embraces the entire community. The Zuñi spirit of cooperation is expressed and institutionalized in the activities of a whole series of priesthoods, dancing groups and curing societies, in which the individual Zuñi may hold two or more memberships. Cooperation is stressed also as a matter of Zuñi kinship obligation. Kinship is important to the Mormons, but sustained kinship-based activity seldom goes beyond the closest relatives. In Zuñi there are large groups of near and distant relatives to whom one owes duties and from whom one derives benefits and position.

The Navahos, with their scattered hogans are more like the Texans in their settlement pattern. Except near agencies and railroad towns, they have no villages. From the core of the extended matrilineal family the Navaho views his relationships as reaching outward to include an ever-widening circle of kinsmen, some of whom he may rarely, if ever, see during the course of a year or more. Until recent times the Navahos have had no organized political leadership, the "tribe" consisting merely of a series of local bands which shared the same language and customs.

Although the Texans and Navahos can be characterized as being less communally inclined and more "individualistic" than the Mormons and Zuñis, there are, again, interesting differences in pattern and emphasis. The Texan focus is upon the individual farmer and his immediate family engaged in a competitive struggle with others for economic wealth and social prestige within the community. The Navaho sense of kinship involves no idea of striving and competing. Navahos cooperate easily with kinsmen and neighbors when the occasion arises, such as the work of putting on the larger ceremonials. But there are no organized and regular cooperative activities on a community-wide basis, unless these are actively promoted by Indian Service officials or other whites.

Differences in culture can thus be related to differences in values. The relationship comes into sharper focus when we consider the varying cultures in the context of their adjustment to their relatively unvarying natural environment, the constant in our laboratory situation. First we shall describe the general orientations of the five groups toward nature and time. Then we shall see how the values thus expressed relate to the way each of the groups reacts to the environmental problem of drought.

The Spanish-Americans have what might be called a "normal curve" view of the workings of nature. Out of so many children born, so many die before maturity; from every row of seeds, only so many plants come up; and out of every 10 or so summers, two or three are bound to be without rain. One can do little but accept what comes. Corresponding to this view of nature is an orientation in time that lays stress upon the present, as opposed to the past, which slowly recedes into obscurity, or to the even more elusive future. Life flows secure in the traditional familial mold; the important thing is the present, with its immediate drama, color and spontaneity. It is foolish to work too hard, and to worry about the future is even more ridiculous. About the mysteries of the world neither curiosity nor knowledge extend much beyond a shrug of the shoulders and a "*Quién sabe?*" These Spanish-American values find concrete expression in the traditional fiesta, a combined religious and recreational affair which is conducted each year in honor of the patron saint of the village. Catholic Masses and processions, combined with drinking, dancing, singing and visiting, express at once the solemn traditionalism and the love of present excitement and drama in the life of the small Spanish-American village.

By contrast the Texan frontier homesteaders manifest a drive for mastery over the workings of nature. Nature is defined as something to be controlled and exploited by man for his own ends and material comfort. The homesteader therefore equips himself with the most modern type of tractor, practices modern farming methods and attempts to extend even further his control over nature in the face of great odds in this semiarid environment. The past can be forgotten, even rejected, and the present is merely a step along the road to the future. If the crops fail, there is always the hope that "next year we'll make it." There is strong perennial optimism that "progress" will continue and that their crossroads will eventually grow into a modern city. While the homesteaders feel that their Spanish-American neighbors are lazy and "not getting any place," the latter feel just as strongly that the homesteaders are senselessly working themselves to death in a life in which one should live fully in the present.

The Mormon villagers share with the Texan homesteaders the view that mastery over nature is desirable. Indeed, in some respects they carry this idea much farther, for they hold the theological view that the Mormon people have "put on the uniform of the flesh" and live out this earthly life in order to learn about and attain mastery over gross matter. "The Latter-Day Saints," as the Mormons call themselves, have developed a work-health-education-recreation value complex to guide their activities: work to gain mastery over the world; health to keep man effective in the struggle for continuing progress; education to accelerate his progress; and recreation to strengthen both man's body and the community he lives in. Like the Texans, they emphasize the future, but not so much for the purpose of economic development as for participation in the eternal progress of the universe in which man himself progresses toward godhood.

To the Zuñi the universe looks very different. He neither feels that he is a master of nature nor that he is its victim. In his colorful and beautiful religion he has developed techniques of cooperating with nature. This attitude is of course sustained by a body of realistic information on ways to make a living in a difficult environment. The Zuñi equivalent of the Spanish-American fiesta has an important place in his life, but he is less taken with its recreational aspects. He lives in the present, but in many things, much more than any of his neighbors, he looks back to the past. It is a glorious past, an ancient mythological time when Zuñis came up from the "wombs" of the earth, wandered around, and finally settled at "the middle place," where their descendants to this day still maintain a shrine to mark the center of the universe.

The Navahos resemble the Spanish-Americans and the Zuñis in their orientation to nature and time. Like the Zuñis, the Navahos view man as having an integral part to play in a general cosmic scheme. But they see the universe as more powerful than man and profoundly threatening. In dealing with nature circumspection is the best guide to action, and fear is the dominant emotional theme. Yet the Navaho is not completely fatalistic. There are small things one can do to maintain and restore harmony in the scheme. Thus individual curing ceremonials, performed with care, can keep matters from becoming worse. The present is the important time-dimension, but the Navahos also recall a "holy people" who came up from the underworld, created four sacred mountains and the "earth surface people" and then departed for their permanent homes in the six directions: east, south, west, north, zenith and nadir.

For all five cultures the annual drought is a serious common concern. Each group responds differently to this problem in terms of its distinctive value-orientation. The Zuñis increase the intensity and tempo of their ceremonial activity; they give more attention to the planting of prayer feathers and to the fasting and prayers of the rain priests. This is in line with their view of the ultimate harmony of nature; man need only do his part and the gods will do the rest. With centuries of summer rains to testify to the soundness of this view, Zuñi is deeply opposed to rainmaking with airplanes and silver iodide.

The Navahos also tend to respond to drought by increasing ceremonial activity. But they are not so certain of the efficacy of their rainmaking ceremonies. They direct less ritual to that purpose and are more humble in the face of a more threatening universe.

The Spanish-Americans, on the other hand, seem to do little or nothing about drought beyond collecting in small groups on the plaza to talk about it. In their view, to attempt to alter the course of natural events by ceremonial is as useless as trying to alter it by rainmaking.

Against the ceremonial response of the Zuñis and Navahos and the fatalistic response of the Spanish-Americans, the behavior of the Mormons and Texans draws a dramatic contrast. They actively support the artificial rainmaking projects, they reduce their livestock herds and crop acreages, and they organize to enlist government aid in meeting the drought conditions. The Navahos and Zuñis, in contrast, have to be forced by the government to practice acreage restriction in bad years.

Ceremonial and ritual responses are not entirely lacking, however, in the Mormon and Texan communities. Mormons occasionally say prayers in church for rain. The Texans have held special prayer meetings during droughts; indeed, the governor of Texas set aside a special day for such meetings during a severe southwestern drought. A minority within each community also feels that seeding the clouds is "interfering with the work of the Lord." But the majority responds in the vein expressed by one of the more articulate farmers in the Texan community, who declared: "The Lord will look down and say, 'Look at those poor ignorant people. I gave them the clouds, the airplanes and the silver iodide, and they didn't have the sense to put them together.' "

Thus systems of values may promote and justify radically different modes of behavior among people confronted with the same objective problem. Why do such different values persist in the same tiny region among peoples living so close to one another? There appear to be at least two basic aspects to this question. First, we know that the values are intricately related to the total structure of each culture. Accordingly, unless the structure breaks down completely, values will tend to persist as functional parts of the whole. Second, we have also discovered that face-to-face contacts between the five cultural groups have not always encouraged the easy communication and interaction which might eventually level the differences between them. In fact, some of the intercultural contacts appear to have reinforced, rather than changed, the original value systems. There is, for example, good evidence that Navahos and Zuñis cling tenaciously to certain of their aboriginal values precisely because missionaries and other agents of white culture bring strong pressure upon them to change.

10.

THE AMISH: A CULTURAL ISLAND

John Hostetler

One can learn about the concept of culture either by examining a cultural island within one's own society or by comparing the codes of behavior in different societies. This selection represents the former approach. Hostetler's examination of strongly traditional Amish codes of behavior and the symbols associated with these codes helps us to understand not only the meaning of culture, but also the ways in which groups such as the Amish resist assimilation into the larger society.

THE AMISH CHARTER

We turn now to the moral principles of the contemporary Amish community. By moral we mean that which is considered right and

Source: John A. Hostetler, *Amish Society* (Baltimore, Md.: The Johns Hopkins Press, 1963).

John A. Hostetler is professor of sociology and anthropology at Temple University. He was born in Mifflin County, Pennsylvania, and was reared as an Amishman, but he left his Plain Folk community to pursue an education. His special interests include social change, problems of the marginal man, and cultural anthropology. His research and numerous publications have focused on the Amish, Mennonites, and Hutterites. He is the author of *Annotated Bibliography on the Amish,* which was awarded the International Folklore Prize, University of Chicago; *The Sociology of Mennonite Evangelism; Education and Marginality in the Communal Society of the Hutterites;* and *The Hutterites in North America.*

wrong, and the principles for which life is worth living. The fundamentals of right and wrong are made relevant in the life of the society. Behavior in the Amish community is oriented to absolute values, involving a conscious belief in religious and ethical ends, entirely for their own sake, and quite independent of any external rewards. This orientation to *Wert-rational,* or absolute values, requires of the individual certain unconditional demands. Regardless of any possible cost to themselves, the members are required to put into practice what is required by duty, honor, personal loyalty, and religious calling. The fundamental values and common ends of the group, recognized by the people and accepted by them, have been designated as the charter. A charter need not be reduced to writing to be effective in the little community; it may be thought of as the common purpose of the community, corresponding to a desire or a set of motives embodied in tradition. Although Amish life is oriented to absolute values, there is an almost automatic reaction to habitual stimuli that guides behavior in a course which has been repeatedly followed. Behavior is traditionally oriented by belief and the habit of long experience.

The Amish view of reality is conditioned by a dualistic world view. They believe, as have many other ascetic brotherhoods, that light and truth coexist with the powers of darkness and falsehood. Purity and goodness are in conflict with impurity and evil. The rejection of the world is based upon this dualistic conception of reality and is manifest in specific life situations. While the Amish share this fundamental doctrine of the two worlds with other believers, it becomes a reality to the Amish, while to many Christian people it is greatly modified.

Separation from the World

To the Amish there is a divine spiritual reality, the Kingdom of God, and a Satanic Kingdom that dominates the present world. It is the duty of a Christian to keep himself "unspotted from the world" and separate from the desires, intent, and goals of the worldly person. Amish preaching and teaching draws upon passages from the Bible which emphasize the necessity of separation from the world. Two passages, perhaps the most often quoted, epitomize for the Amishman the message of the Bible. The first is: "Be not conformed to this world, but be ye transformed by the renewing of your mind that ye may prove what is that good and acceptable and perfect will of God." This to the Amishman means among other things that one should not dress and behave like the world. The second is: "Be ye not unequally yoked together with unbelievers; for what fellowship hath righteousness with unrighteousness? and what communion hath light with darkness?" This doctrine forbids the Amishman from marrying a non-Amish person or from being in business partnership with an outsider. It is applied generally to all social contacts that would involve intimate connections with persons outside the ceremonial community. This emphasis upon literalness and separateness is compatible with the Amish view of themselves as a "chosen people" or "peculiar people."

The principle of separation conditions and controls the Amishman's contact with the outside world; it colors his entire view of reality and being. Bible teaching is conditioned by the totality of the traditional way of life. Compatible with the doctrine of separation is the doctrine of nonresistance. By the precepts of Christ, the Amish are forbidden to take part in violence and war. In time of war they are conscientious objectors, basing their stand on biblical texts, such as "My kingdom is not of this world: if my kingdom were of this world, then would my servant fight." The Amish have no rationale for self-defense or for defending their possessions. Like many early Anabaptists they are "defenseless Christians." Problems of hostility are met without retaliation. The Amish farmer, in difficulty with the hostile world around him, is admonished by his bishop to follow the example of Isaac: after the warring Philistines had stopped up all the wells of his father Abraham, Isaac moved to new lands and dug new wells. This advice is taken literally, so that in the face of hostility, the Amish move to new locations without defending their rights.

The Amish share with the Mennonites the principles of Anabaptism as evidenced by their common endorsement of the Dortrecht Confession. Both practice adult rather than infant baptism, nonresistance and refusal to bear arms, and refusal to swear an oath, and both refrain from holding public office. Religion tends to be pervasive and associated with a total way of life, not a specialized activity. The Amish today differ from the Mennonites mainly in the extent to which external changes have affected the groups. The Amish are more literal in the observance of certain practices such as fasting and shunning, in practical informal mutual aid, and in keeping the young on the farm. The Mennonites have been readier to accept changes and to incorporate them into their religious values. Mennonites are technologically modern, and they generally accept higher education. Furthermore, during the nineteenth century they founded institutions of higher education to train missionaries. Mennonites developed along the lines of modern Protestantism, while the Amish have retained literalism, limited education, and agrarianism.

The Amish are "otherworldly" minded, in contrast to the many Christian churches that are concerned with making the world a better place in which to live. The Amish show little interest in improving the world or their environment. They profess to be "strangers and pilgrims" in the present world.

. . . . .

Amish preaching and moral instruction emphasize self-denial and obedience to the teaching of the Word of God, which is equated with the rules of the church. All ministers constantly warn their members to beware of worldliness. Long passages from the Old Testament are retold, giving prominence to crucial events in the lives of Abraham, Isaac, Jacob, Joseph, and Moses. The escape of the Israelites from Egyptian bondage and Moses's giving of the law are sermon themes; punishments meted out to the lawbreakers are emphasized. The themes: "Offenders were executed for breaking the law," and "we are not better than they," are emphatically stressed. The choice put before the congregation is to obey or die. To disobey the church is to die. To obey the church and strive for "full fellowship," that is, complete harmony with the order of the church, is to have *lebendige Hoffnung,* a living hope of salvation. An Amish person simply puts faith in God, obeys the order of the church, and patiently hopes for the best.

Separation from the world is a basic tenet of the Amish charter; yet the Amish are not highly ethnocentric in their relationships with the outside world. They accept as a matter of course other people as they are, without attempting to convert them to the Amish way of life. But for those who are born into the Amish society, the sanctions for belonging are deeply rooted in the belief in separatism.

The people of the little community have an "inside view" as well as a contrasting "outside view" of things. The doctrine of separation shapes the "outside view," and in discussing further aspects of the Amish charter we turn now to the "inside view."

The Vow of Obedience

The ceremony of baptism may be viewed as a rite of passage from youth to adulthood, but it also reveals the "inside view" of things. The meaning of baptism to the individual and the community reflects ethos. Taking the baptismal vow admits one to full fellowship in the church. When young people reach late adolescence, they are urged to become members of the church. In their sermons, ministers challenge young people to join the church. The parents are concerned that young people take this step. In most cases no overt urging by the parents is necessary, since it is normal for young people to follow the role expectation and be baptized. No young person could be married in the Amish church without first being baptized in the faith.

After the spring communion, a class of instructions is held for all those who wish to join the church. This is known as *die Gemee nooch geh,* or literally, "to follow the church." The applicants meet with the ministers on Sunday morning at worship service in the *Kämmerli,* the consultation room where the ordained customarily meet. The ministers very simply acquaint the applicants for baptism with the incidents in the Bible that suggest the right relationship with God. At the same time the *Regel und Ordnung* (rules and order) of the Amish church are explained. After six or eight periods of instruction, roughly from May to August, a day is set for the baptismal service. The consent of the members is obtained to receive the applicants into fellowship. Baptism occurs prior to the fall *Ordnungsgemee* (preparatory service), which is followed by *Grossgemee* (communion). Great emphasis is placed upon the difficulty of walking the "straight and narrow way." The applicants are told that it is better not to make a vow than to vow and later break it; on a Saturday prior to baptism they are asked to meet with the ministers where they are given opportunity to "turn back" if they so desire. The young men are asked to promise that they will accept the duties of a minister should the lot ever fall on them.

. . . . .

The Rules for Living

Once the individual has been baptized, he is committed to keep the *Ordnung* or the rules of the church. For a single person this means keeping one's behavior more in line with the rules than before. With marriage the individual assumes responsibility for keeping the rules as well as for "building the church," which means taking an active part in promoting the rules. The little Amish community is distinctive from other church groups in that the rules governing life are traditional ways not specified in writing. These rules can be known only by being a participant. The rules for living tend to form a body of sentiments that are essentially a list of taboos within the environment of the small Amish community.

All Amish members know the *Ordnung* of their church district and these generally remain oral and unwritten. Perhaps most rules are taken for granted and it is usually those questionable or borderline issues which are specified in the *Ordnung*. These rules are repeated at the *Ordnungsgemee* just preceding communion Sunday. They must have been unanimously endorsed by the ordained body. At the members' meeting following the regular service they are presented orally, after which members are asked to give assent. If there is any change from previous practice, allowing a new innovation or adaptation, this change is not announced. The former taboo is simply not mentioned. A unanimous expression of unity and "peace" with the *Ordnung* makes possible the communion. But without unity there can be no communion.

The following *Ordnung* of a contemporary group, published in English, appears to be representative of the Old Order Amish, except for those portions indicated by brackets. That it appears in print at all is evidence of change from the traditional practice of keeping it oral. This *Ordnung* allows a few practices not typically sanctioned by the Old Order: the giving of tithes, distribution of tracts, belief in assurance of salvation, and limited missionary activity.

ORDNUNG OF A CHRISTIAN CHURCH

Since it is the duty of the church, especially in this day and age, to decide what is fitting and proper and also what is not fitting and proper for a Christian to do (in points that are not clearly stated in the Bible), we have considered it needful to publish this booklet listing some rules and ordinances of a Christian Church.

We hereby confess to be of one faith with the 18 articles of Faith adopted at Dortrecht, 1632, also with nearly all if not all articles in booklet entitled "Article und Ordnung der Christlichen Gemeinde."

No ornamental bright, showy formfitting, immodest or silklike clothing of any kind. Colors such as bright red, orange, yellow and pink not allowed. Amish form of clothing to be followed as a general rule. Costly Sunday clothing to be discouraged. Dresses not shorter than halfway between knees and floor, nor over eight inches from floor. Longer advisable. Clothing in every way modest, serviceable and as simple as scripturally possible. Only outside pockets allowed are on work eberhem or vomas and pockets on large overcoats. Dress shoes, if any, to be plain and black only. No high heels and pump slippers, dress socks, if any, to be black except white for foot hygiene for both sexes. A plain, unshowy suspender without buckles.

Hat to be black with no less than 3-inch rim and not extremely high in crown. No stylish impression in any hat. No pressed trousers. No sweaters.

Prayer covering to be simple, and made to fit head. Should cover all the hair as nearly as possible and is to be worn wherever possible. [Pleating of caps to be discouraged.] No silk ribbons. Young children to dress according to the Word as well as parents. No pink or fancy baby blankets or caps.

Women to wear shawls, bonnets, and capes in public. Aprons to be worn at all times. No adorning of hair among either sex such as parting of hair among men and curling or waving among women.

A full beard should be worn among men and boys after baptism if possible. No shingled hair. Length at least half-way below tops of ears.

No decorations of any kind in buildings inside or out. No fancy yard fences. Linoleum, oilcloth, shelf and wall paper to be plain and unshowy. Overstuffed furniture or any luxury items forbidden. No doilies or napkins. No large mirrors (fancy glassware), statues or wall pictures for decorations.

[No embroidery work of any kind.] Curtains either dark green rollers or black cloth. No boughten dolls.

No bottle gas or high line electrical appliances. Stoves should be black if bought new.

Weddings should be simple and without decorations. [Names not attached to gifts.]

No ornaments on buggies or harness.

Tractors to be used only for such things that can hardly be done with horses. Only either stationary engines or tractors with steel tires allowed. No airfilled rubber tires.

Farming and related occupations to be encouraged. Working in cities or factories not permissible. Boys and girls working out away from home for worldly people forbidden except in emergencies.

Worldly amusements as radios, card playing [party games], movies, fairs, etc., forbidden.

[Reading, singing, tract distribution, Bible games, relief work, giving of tithes, etc., are encouraged.]

Musical instruments or different voice singing not permissible. No dirty, silly talking or sex teasing of children.

Usury forbidden in most instances. No government benefit payments or partnership in harmful associations. No insurance. No photographs.

No buying or selling of anything on Sunday. It should be kept according to the principles of the Sabbath. [Worship of some kind every Sunday.]

[Women should spend time doing good or reading God's Word instead of taking care of canaries, goldfish or house flowers.]

Church confession is to be made if practical where transgression was made. If not, a written request of forgiveness should be made to said church. All manifest sins to be openly confessed before church before being allowed to commune. I Tim. 5, 20. A period of time required before taking new members into full fellowship.

Because of great falling away from sound doctrine, we do not care to fellowship, that is hold communion, with any churches that allow or uphold any unfruitful works of darkness such as worldliness, fashionable attire [bed-courtship, habitual smoking or drinking, old wives fables, nonassurance of salvation, anti-missionary zeal] or anything contrary to sound doctrine.

The rules of the Amish church cover the whole range of human experience. In a society where the goal is directed toward keeping the world out, there are many taboos, and customs become symbolic. There are variations in what is allowed from one community to another in the United States and Canada. Custom is regional and therefore not strictly uniform. The most universal of all Amish norms across the United States and Canada are the following: no electricity, telephones, central-heating systems, automobiles, or tractors with pneumatic tires; required are beards but not moustaches for all married men, long hair (which must be parted in the center, if allowed at all), hooks-and-eyes on dresscoats, and the use of horses for farming and travel. No formal education beyond the elementary grades is a rule of life.

The *Ordnung* is an essential part of the Amish charter. It is the way in which the moral postulates of society are expressed and carried out in life. The charter is constantly subjected to forces of change, a source of conflict to be discussed later.

The Punishment of the Disobedient

A moral principle in the little Amish community is the practice of *Bann und Meidung.* These words rendered in English mean excommunication and shunning. *Meidung* was the crucial question in the controversy that gave rise to the Amish as a sect movement in their secession from the Swiss Brethren. This doctrine was intrinsic in the Anabaptist movement from its very beginning and appeared in the earliest confession of faith. The Anabaptist concept of the church was that it should be a pure church of believers only; persons who fall into sin must be first excommunicated, then shunned. Menno Simons taught that the ban applies to "all—great and small, rich and poor, without any respect of persons, who once passed under the Word but have now fallen back, those living or teaching offensively in the house of the Lord—until they repent." The method of dealing with a backslider is that given by Christ in Matthew 18:15–17, and "If he neglect to hear the church, let him be unto thee as a heathen man and a publican." In other words, a person who has broken his vow and will not mend his ways must be expelled just as the human body casts off an ulcer or infectious growth. Through the years the *Meidung* has been applied in different ways. The doctrine among the Mennonites of Holland and Switzerland was of a mild character, in which the offender was excluded from communion. But a stricter conception of the ban was advanced by Jakob Ammann. The strict interpretation requires shunning of all (1) members who leave the Amish church to join another and (2) members who marry outside the brotherhood. *Meidung* requires that members receive no favors from the excommunicated person, that they do not buy from or sell to an excommunicated person, that no member shall eat at the same table with an excommunicated person, and if the case involves husband or wife, they are to suspend their usual marital relations.

The Amish make no effort to evangelize or proselyte the outsider, nor are they concerned with the redemption of the outside society to the extent that they wish to draw members from the outer society into the brotherhood. It is their primary concern to keep their own baptized members from slipping into the outer world, or into other religious groups. With greater mobility and ease of travel and communication, isolation is breaking down, and Amish solidarity is threatened by more and more of their members wanting to become like outsiders. The Amish leaders meet this threat with the ban. Members who wish to have automobiles, radios, or the usual comforts of modern living, face the threat of being excommunicated and shunned. Thus the ban is used as an instrument of discipline, not only for the drunkard or the adulterer, but for the person who transgresses the order of the church. It is a powerful instrument for keeping the church intact and for preventing members from involvement in the wider society.

The meaning of *Bann und Meidung* is made clearer if we understand how it works in life situations. Let us take the case of a young man whom we shall fictitiously name Joseph. Joseph grew up in a very strict Amish home, under the guidance of parents who were known for their orthodoxy. He was baptized at the age of twenty. Three years after his baptism Joseph was excommunicated and shunned. Charges laid against him included the following: he had attended a revival meeting, began to chum with excommunicated persons, bought an automobile, and began to attend a Mennonite church.

Joseph was excommunicated with the counsel of the assembly and was informed in their presence. After being asked to leave the service he thought to himself: "It is strange to think that I am now to be 'mited.' I don't feel very comfortable." At home, the young man was shunned: he could no longer eat at the family table. He ate at a separate table, with the younger children, or after the baptized persons finished eating. Joseph was urged to mend his ways, to make good his broken promise. His normal work relations and conversational pattern were strained. Several times he attended preaching services with his family. Since members may not accept services, goods, or favors from excommunicated members, he could not take his sisters to church, even if he used a buggy instead of his offensive automobile, but they could drive a buggy and take him along. It was not long until Joseph accepted employment with a non-Amish person and began using his automobile for transportation to and from home. When shunned friends came to his home for conversation, Joseph's parents met them at the gate and turned them away. It was not long until father and mother asked him to leave home. He explained: "I had to move away from home or my parents could not take communion. My parents were afraid that younger persons in the family would be led astray. They didn't exactly chase me off the place, but I was no longer welcome at home."

One of the purposes of excommunication is to restore the erring member by showing him his lost condition so that he will turn to repentance. The excommunication service itself is a painful and sober procedure. John Umble's description is fitting: "The excommunication of members was an awful and solemn procedure. The members to be expelled had been notified in advance and were present. An air of tenseness filled the house. Sadfaced women wept quietly; stern men sat with faces drawn. The bishop arose; with trembling voice and with tears on his cheek he announced that the guilty parties had confessed their sin, that they were cast off from the fellowship of the church and committed to the devil and all his angels (*dem Teufel und allen seinen Engeln übergeben*). He cautioned all the members to exercise 'shunning rigorously.' "

Once an individual is in a state of *Bann* (or *Bond* as the Amish call it), members are to receive no favors from him. In a very real sense he is "an outcast, rejected of God and man. His only hope is not to die before he should be reinstated, lest he should be an outcast also in the world to come."

Among the Amish communities today there are numerous divisions as a result of differing opinions on shunning. The moderate interpretation of the ban, taken by most of the midwestern groups, holds that moral transgressors should be excommunicated and shunned, but if the offender is restored to another Christian church of the nonresistant faith then shunning should no longer be applied. But this, according to the adherents of the strict ban, is a departure from Jakob Ammann. In speaking of a former Amish member who joined the Mennonites a bishop told the writer: "The only way for us to lift the ban is for him to make peace with the Old Order church, going back to one of them and living his promise he made in his baptismal vow on his knees before God and the church. It does not need to be here but in any of the churches that are in peace with us." According to this view, an excommunicated person must be shunned for life unless he restores his previous relationship with the group. The ban becomes an effective means of dispensing with the offender. By shunning him in all social relations, he is given a status that minimizes the threat to other members of the community. This perpetuation of the controversy undoubtedly aids the Old Order group to remain distinct and socially isolated.

Closeness to Nature

The little Amish community has a strong affinity for the soil and for nature. Unlike science, which is occupied with the theoretical reconstruction of the order of the world, the Amish view comes from direct contact with nature by the reality of work. The physical world is good, and in itself not corrupting or evil. The beautiful is apprehended in the universe, by the orderliness of the seasons, the heavens, the world of growing plants as well as the many species of animals, and by the forces of living and dying. While it is wrong to attend a show in a theater, it is not uncommon for an Amish family to visit the zoo or the circus to see the animals God has made.

The Amishman feels contact with the world through the working of his muscles and the aching of his limbs. In the little Amish community toil is proper and good, religion provides meaning, and the bonds of family and church provide human satisfaction and love.

The charter of Amish life requires members to limit their occupation to farming or closely associated activity such as operating a saw mill, carpentry, or mason work.

In Europe the Amish lived in rural areas, always having close association with the soil, so that the community was entirely agrarian in character. It is only in America that the Amish have found it necessary to make occupational regulations for protection from the influence of urbanism.

The preference for rural living is reflected in attitudes and in the informal relations of group life, rather than in an explicit dogma. For the Amish, God is manifest more in closeness to nature, in the soil and in the weather, and among plants and animals, than he is in the man-made city. Hard work, thrift, and mutual aid find sanction in the Bible. The city by contrast is held to be the center of leisure, of non-productive spending, and often of wickedness. The Christian life, they contend, is best maintained away from the cities. God created Adam and Eve to "replenish the earth, and subdue it; and have dominion over the fish of the sea, and over the fowl of the air, and over every living thing that moveth upon the earth." In the same way, man's highest place in the universe today is to care for the things of creation. One Amishman said, "The Lord told Adam to replenish the earth and to rule over the animals and the land—you can't do that in cities." Another said, "While the Lord's blessings were given to the people who remained in the country, sickness and ruination befell Sodom. Shows, dances, parties, and other temptations ruin even the good people who now live in cities. Families are small in cities; in the city you never know where your wife is, and city women can't cook. People go hungry in the cities but you will never starve if you work hard in the country."

The Amish have generally prospered on the land more often than their neighbors. Lancaster County, Pennsylvania, which is the center of Amish life, has long been distinguished as the garden spot of the nation, representing an intensive kind of farming on relatively small holdings. Their success is based upon long experience with agricultural practices in the Old World and upon a philosophy of work and thrift.

. . . . .

. . . The Amish attribute their material success in farming to divine blessing.

The main objective of their farming, as Walter Kollmorgen has pointed out, "is to accumulate sufficient means to buy enough land to keep all the children on farms. To this end the Amish work hard, produce abundantly, and save extensively."

. . . . .

There are other moral directives in the little community but these form the essential core of what is viewed as right and wrong. The view of life and of man's place in the total scheme of things are determined by the sacred guides to life. These guides are: a biblical view of separation from the world, the vow of obedience, observance of the *Ordnung,* upholding the true doctrine of shunning, and living close to the God-created environment. In all of these tradition plays an important part. The people of the little Amish community tend to regard the ways of their ancestors as sacred and to believe that these time-hallowed practices should be carefully guarded.

THE SYMBOLIC COMMUNITY

The Amish community is a multibonded community. The members are held together not by a single interest but by many symbolic ties which they have in common. The ecologic and ceremonial functions are bounded by the limits of horse-and-buggy travel. But there exists also a symbolic community made up of many social rules for living and a culture that has set definite boundaries. A member of the Amish faith is bound to the norms and practices of his social group. He is a member of the in-group or *unser Satt Leit* (our sort of people) and is marked by certain symbols. The outgroup is *anner Satt Leit* (other sorts of people), who are distinguished by their symbols. This sharp line of distinction gives rise to a general principle by which in-groups tend to stereotype out-groups, and any threat from an out-group tends to intensify the cohesion of the in-group.

Before observing in detail the intimately shared activities which make the Amish community a multibonded one, it is well to note the overall complexity of these ties. Language provides a guide to a social reality that is different from that of other people. All new members with rare exceptions are offspring and they are assimilated gradually by a majority of the old members. Physical property, including farms that were the abodes of the forefathers, and preference for certain soils and topography come to have sentimental attachment. Common traditions and ideals which have been revered by the whole community from generation to generation embody the expectations of all. All relatives are Amish or of Amish descent. There are formal church rules that guide the members in their conduct with each other and with outsiders. The specialists, the lifetime ordained persons, carry on the functions of the church and enable it to act as a unit in maintaining separation from the world. The size of each church district is kept to a minimum, enabling it to function as a small, intimate, and informally controlled group, whereas largeness would make consensus more difficult. There are special means to resist shock such as mutual aid in times of fire, death, and sickness. The life of the community is prolonged because the basic needs of the individual are met from the cradle to the grave. The Amish baby grows up strongly attached to those of his kind and remains indifferent to contacts outside his culture. The tendency to symbolize all of life provides a basis for action in meeting the future. It assures internal unity and community longevity.

Symbols, Convention, and Tradition

Symbols form an important maintenance function in everyday life. The symbols are different from the non-Amish or "English" symbols. In the world around them, the Amish see the symbols of worldly civilization. They are such objects as the cathedral, the skyscraper, the modernistically designed automobile and house, the television set, the missile, and modern ways of clothing the body. To the Amishman these symbols represent the world. They are a reminder of danger to him and are to be avoided.

The Amish have their own symbolism which provides a basis for common consciousness and a common course of action. We may hypothesize that in a simple society like the Amish the people themselves become symbolic, and not their achievements as in world civilization. The horse and buggy, the beard of the married man, and the styles of dress—all take on symbolic meaning. All Amish know that this is the accepted way of doing things, and symbolism becomes an effective means of social control as the nonconformist can quickly be detected from the conformist. Symbols which are universal in all Amish communities include the following: hooks-and-eyes on the Sunday coat and vest of all men, trouser styles that have no fly-closing but a flap that buttons along the waist, wide-brimmed black-felt hats for men, white organdy caps for women, plain rather than patterned or striped dresses for women, uncut hair for women, and long hair cut in bangs for men. All these symbols together constitute a world of social reality, a way of life that teaches how people should live and what they should imitate.

An illustration of convention which is symbolic is the way courtesy is expressed among the Amish. Acts rather than words perform this function. In a small society where convention is understood few words are needed between actor and alter to make meanings precise. Words of courtesy, as expressed by the English-speaking world, are conspicuously absent among members of the Amish family and community. The dialect contains few if any words of endearment between husband and wife, but young people of courting age frequently employ English words of endearment. Amish parents who hear "English" couples exchange words like "honey" and "sweetheart" have remarked that such a relationship is probably anything but "sweet." There are no words in the Amish spoken language that correspond to "pardon me" or "excuse me." Children might use such English terms in their play but persistence in using them in family relationships would not be approved. They would be accused of trying to be "society" persons. "Oops" is sometimes used to indicate that a certain act was not intentional. "Please" and "thank you" are not a part of table manners nor a part of everyday conversation, but children are taught to say *Denki* (thank you) and *Wilkomm* (you are welcome) when giving or receiving gifts on special occasions.

Acts of politeness are much more characteristic than words. The wife may brush the husband's hat on Sunday morning before he gets around to it. The act requires no "thank you." If the husband is thoughtful he will carry the toddler, help his wife into the carriage, and tuck the blankets around her. Belching is a normal occurrence around the dinner table and conceived as a sign of good appetite with no thought of discourtesy. A boy who was chewing his food vigorously at the breakfast table was greeted by his older brother with the words: "Fer was machst so wiescht?" (Why do you make so ugly?) The boy did not reply but modified his behavior. However, in the presence of English people the Amish will adopt the polite language of the outsider. An Amish woman walking along a village sidewalk who approached a woman washing her sidewalk said "pardon me" as she stepped over the washed part of the sidewalk.

Symbolism in Amish life performs the functions of communication. When much of life is governed by symbols, fewer words are needed for communication. The conspicuous absence of words of courtesy in the Amish dialect would appear to be a function of the importance of symbols, making such words unnecessary. Like dress patterns, the speech habits have also been preserved in the New World. Polite language in Medieval Europe was characteristic of the nobility and not of the peasant groups. Actions among the Amish speak louder than words of courtesy. Acts and intentions are understood, while words of courtesy which might be adopted from the English language would not be understood. The large number of symbols which function within the Amish society aid the growing Amish child to find his place within the family, the community, and within the world of the Amish people.

The Language of Dress

Anything that can be perceived through the senses can be symbolized, and in Amish society styles of dressing become very important as symbols of group identity. The garb not only admits the individual to full fellowship but also clarifies his role and status within his society.

The hat, for example, distinguishes the Amishman from the outsider and also symbolizes his role within his social structure. When the two-year-old boy discards a dress and begins wearing trousers for the first time, he also receives a stiff jet-black hat with three or more inches of brim. Hat manufacturers produce at least twenty-eight different sizes and a dozen different styles of Amish hats. The bridegroom in Pennsylvania gets a telescopic hat that is worn during the early married years. The hat is distinguished by a permanent crease around the top of the crown. Grandfather's hat has a four-inch crown and a four-inch brim. The bishop's hat has a four- and one-half-inch crown, slightly rounded, and a wide seam around the brim. A hat which has a flatter crown is worn by the rank and file of Amish fathers. The outsider may never notice these differences, or if he does he may regard them as accidental. But to the Amish these symbols indicate whether people are fulfilling the expectations of the group. A young man who wears a hat with a brim that is too narrow is liable for sanction. The very strict Amish congregations can be distinguished from the more progressive ones by the width of the brim and the band around the crown. Thus when the writer's family moved from Pennsylvania to Iowa, one of the first adaptations to make was to take out the scissors and cut off some of the brim. This made my brothers and myself more acceptable to the new community of Amish. At the same time the act symbolized other adaptations that had to be made to adjust to a more "westernized" group of Old Order Amish.

. . . . .

One of the most highly symbolic of all garments among the women is the *Kapp* or head cap worn by every woman and even by infants. Girls from about age twelve to marriage wear a black cap for Sunday dress and a white cap at home. After marriage a white cap is always worn. The size, style and color of caps varies slightly with regions and with degrees of orthodoxy in a single community. The fine pleats ironed into some of these caps requires hours of tedious work. The specific way in which they are made, including the width of the *fedderdeel* (front part) and the *hinnerdeel* (back part), and the width of the pleats and seams are sacred symbols of the community. Though this headpiece has undergone some changes in detail, the present Amish cap is essentially the same as that worn by the Palatine women of earlier centuries. Among most American Mennonites of Swiss-German origin the cap has become a "prayer cap" or "veiling" required of women "when praying or prophesying." (I Corinthians 11:5)

These few illustrations of Amish dress could be supported with still many others. But this is sufficient to indicate how dress styles serve as symbols for a group. The symbols function very effectively in maintaining separatism and continuity. The language of dress forms a common understanding and mutual appreciation among those who share the same traditions and expectations. Dress keeps the insider separate from the world and also keeps the outsider out. These shared conventions are given sacred sanction and biblical justification: *unser Satt Leit* (our sort of people) are distinguishable from *englische Leit* (English people) or *anner Satt Leit* (other people). The attempts by theatricals to reproduce the dress of the Amish never quite measure up to the authentic. They appear ludicrous if not hilarious to the Amish.

The Language of Speech

The Amish community is also a speech community. Language provides familiarity in which individuals find common grounds for understanding. Although the Amish came from Switzerland, from Alsace and Lorraine in France, and from the Rhineland of Germany, yet their conversational speech is remarkably uniform. The reason for this is that they came from the same (Allemanic) dialect-speaking area. Some of the Alsatian Amish could speak French when they arrived in America and a few French words have been incorporated into their dialect which is Pennsylvania Dutch (or German). Dutch in this instance is a usage from "Deutsch" meaning German, and not the language of the Netherlands. The four districts of Amish in Adams County, Indiana, around Berne, speak a Swiss dialect, but it poses no real barrier for interaction with other Amish. An Amish person traveling from Pennsylvania through the midwestern states on a kinship visit can speak his own familiar dialect and be understood.

Linguists have observed that the Amish are trilingual, that is, they can speak three somewhat distinctive yet intermixed tongues. These are: Pennsylvania Dutch, High German, and English. The usage of three distinctive tongues, rather than one or two languages, lends itself to social isolation in that there are speech groupings within the community. Roles and functions tend to organize around each language; thus when speaking English the Amishman tends to think and behave like the English-speaking person.

Pennsylvania Dutch is the familiar tongue of children at home and in informal conversation. It is the mother tongue of children born to Amish parents. Professor Albert Buffington has made it clear that this speech is not a "garbled English" or "corrupted German in the mouths of ignorant people who speak with a heavy accent," but a distinct dialect of the German language. The dialect resembles the Palatine German folk speech. It is, of course, spoken by many Pennsylvania Dutch people who are not Amish.

The second language of the growing Amish child is English. A child is introduced to English when he attends school; as he learns it he also learns that his non-Amish playmates are "English" or *Englisher* in the dialect. They are *anner Satt Leit* (the other sort of people). Amish children learn to speak the two languages without difficulty and without noticeable accent. Upon entering school the child frequently has no English vocabulary, but he readily learns his second language.

English is used when speaking with non-Amish persons in town, at school, or when talking to an "English" visitor or salesman. Thus Amishmen employ the English language on "forced" occasions. An Amish person may shift his conversation from the dialect to English, or from English to the dialect, whichever he finds most convenient for the situation. An outsider as a guest at an Amish table may find that dialect chatter prevails at one end of the table, while one or two members of the family keep the general conversation in English for the benefit of the guest. Frey has described the Amish use of English as "American English built on a framework of Pennsylvania Dutch language patterns and interjected continually with whole or part loan-translations from the dialect." The Amish generally experience little difficulty in speaking correct English.

High German, or more precisely "Amish High German," is used exclusively for the preaching service and at formal ceremonial occasions. . . . . .

The Amish nomenclature denoting an outsider as an *Englischer* has symbolic meaning. Such a general term means that he may be Methodist, Baptist, Lutheran, or anything but Amish. The Mennonites are not classed as English. Since the Mennonites are only a step removed from the Amish they are *Mennischte* and not really as "English" as other people. On the other hand a person of Catholic affiliation is called a *Gedolischer* (from the German word *Katholischer*). Outsiders who are neighbors of the Amish people often refer to the Amish as "The Dutch."

Conversation in the dialect becomes an especially important function of community life as the Amish are very sociable and hospitable people. The Amish devote more space to the subject of visiting in their weekly newspaper than to any other topic. Visits to the homes, preaching services, particularly before and after the service, funerals, weddings, sales, quiltings, barn-raisings, frolics of various kinds, sewings, singings, and Sunday visiting are all occasions for conversing at length.

Controlled and Limited Education

Limiting education to the elementary grades prevents exposure to many areas of scientific knowledge and vocational training. It functions also as a form of boundary maintenance. New inventions and knowledge find their way into the little Amish community by many diffuse and delayed means. As soon as the law will allow, Amish children are taken out of school for work at home. The Amish viewpoint is that "Our people are engaged in some form of agriculture and we feel positive that as farmers we are better off with only a common school education. Education does not build muscle like tilling the soil in the open field and sunshine with lots of hard work. If a boy does little hard work before he is twenty-one, he probably never gets to like it afterward. In other words, he will not amount to much as a farmer."

Conflict over the school question arose in Pennsylvania, a few years later in Ohio, and continues in some areas. Pennsylvania law requires that children attend school until their seventeenth birthday but that children engaged in farm work may be excused through permits when they reach the age of fifteen. The conflict arose when it became clear that some Amish children completed grade eight more than once because their parents were opposed to sending them to high schools. When the parents were summoned to court and refused to pay their fines on grounds that this would admit to being guilty, they were sent to jail. Friends and businessmen paid the fines to release the parents. Some were arrested as many as ten times. The Amish took the position that compulsory attendance beyond the elementary grades interferes with the exercise of their religious liberty. Meanwhile a compromise plan has been worked out in Pennsylvania where pupils who have completed grade eight report to special "Saturday" schools conducted by the Amish themselves. Some of the more progressive Amish groups have allowed their children to enter the high school believing that it is not wrong to comply with the law. The Old Order Amish state that their children are needed for agricultural labor at home and that farming does not require higher education. The Amish leaders believe that exposure to the consolidated high school would constitute a real danger to their future community life. An Amishman who was called to court for challenging the school attendance law said: "We teach our children not to smoke or use profane language and do such things as that. I know most of the high school pupils smoke cigarettes and many girls I guess too. . . . It is better to have them at home. . . ."

The Amish strategy is merely one of withdrawal from the world. In some areas school boards have been able to keep the one-room school open in deference to the Amish, and in other areas where consolidation has occurred the Amish have built their own schools. The establishment of their own schools in recent times is an attempt to avoid participation in the centralized school and to bypass its whole socializing influence, rather than for the purpose of religious indoctrination. However, there seems to be a tendency after several years of experience for some schools to take over from the home the function of teaching religion.

The Old Order Amish are firm in their stand against formal education in the American high school. It is an effective means of maintenance, especially when linked to the doctrine of shunning. With set limits to the amount of knowledge a young person can acquire on one hand, and with the dread of censure (and of excommunication) on the other, one can scarcely find a more effective way of bounding the little community. A person who receives knowledge outside of the Amish bounds equips himself for capable living outside of the Amish community but makes himself liable to the severe sanctions of the ban and shunning. Limited knowledge preserves the existing order of things; it reinforces traditional values by keeping alternate courses of action to a minimum. Traditional values and stereotypes are thus maintained by unfamiliarity with alternate courses of action. Furthermore, questions about in-group practices are kept to a minimum.

11.

BODY RITUAL AMONG THE NACIREMA

Horace Miner

The preceding selection examined a cultural island within our own society. This selection, the author tells us, also examines a culture within the North American continent. Anthropologist Horace Miner metaphorically describes, in what has become in its way a classic statement, some of the unique features of the culture of the "Nacirema." The reader should certainly be able to see his own culture in a new perspective after reading this brief selection.

The anthropologist has become so familiar with the diversity of ways in which different peoples behave in similar situations that he is not apt to be surprised by even the most exotic customs. In fact, if all of the logically possible combinations of behavior have not been found somewhere in the world, he is apt to suspect that they

Source: Horace Miner, *American Anthropologist* 58, no. 3 (1958): 503–7. Reprinted by permission of the American Anthropological Association and the author.

The author is professor of sociology and anthropology at the University of Michigan. He has studied and lectured extensively in Africa.

must be present in some yet undescribed tribe. This point has, in fact, been expressed with respect to clan organization by Murdock (1949:71). In this light, the magical beliefs and practices of the Nacirema present such unusual aspects that it seems desirable to describe them as an example of the extremes to which human behavior can go.

Professor Linton first brought the ritual of the Nacirema to the attention of anthropologists twenty years ago (1936:326), but the culture of this people is still very poorly understood. They are a North American group living in the territory between the Canadian Cree, the Yaqui and Tarahumare of Mexico, and the Carib and Arawak of the Antilles. Little is known of their origin, although tradition states that they came from the east. According to Nacirema mythology, their nation was originated by a culture hero, Notgnihsaw, who is otherwise known for two great feats of strength—the throwing of a piece of wampum across the river Pa-To-Mac and the chopping down of a cherry tree in which the Spirit of Truth resided.

Nacirema culture is characterized by a highly developed market economy which has evolved in a rich natural habitat. While much of the people's time is devoted to economic pursuits, a large part of the fruits of these labors and a considerable portion of the day are spent in ritual activity. The focus of this activity is the human body, the appearance and health of which loom as a dominant concern in the ethos of the people. While such a concern is certainly not unusual, its ceremonial aspects and associated philosophy are unique.

The fundamental belief underlying the whole system appears to be that the human body is ugly and that its natural tendency is to debility and disease. Incarcerated in such a body, man's only hope is to avert these characteristics through the use of the powerful influences of ritual and ceremony. Every household has one or more shrines devoted to this purpose. The more powerful individuals in the society have several shrines in their houses and, in fact, the opulence of a house is often referred to in terms of the number of such ritual centers it possesses. Most houses are of wattle and daub construction, but the shrine rooms of the more wealthy are walled with stone. Poorer families imitate the rich by applying pottery plaques to their shrine walls.

While each family has at least one such shrine, the rituals associated with it are not family ceremonies but are private and secret. The rites are normally only discussed with children, and then only during the period when they are being initiated into these mysteries. I was able, however, to establish sufficient rapport with the natives to examine these shrines and to have the rituals described to me.

The focal point of the shrine is a box or chest which is built into the wall. In this chest are kept the many charms and magical potions without which no native believes he could live. These preparations are secured from a variety of specialized practitioners. The most powerful of these are the medicine men, whose assistance must be rewarded with substantial gifts. However, the medicine men do not provide the curative potions for their clients, but decide what the ingredients should be and then write them down in an ancient and secret language. This writing is understood only by the medicine men and by the herbalists who, for another gift, provide the required charm.

The charm is not disposed of after it has served its purpose, but is placed in the charmbox of the household shrine. As these magical materials are specific for certain ills, and the real or imagined maladies of the people are many, the charmbox is usually full to overflowing. The magical packets are so numerous that people forget what their purposes were and fear to use them again. While the natives are very vague on this point, we can only assume that the idea in retaining all the old magical materials is that their presence in the charmbox, before which the body rituals are conducted, will in some way protect the worshipper.

Beneath the charmbox is a small font. Each day every member of the family, in succession, enters the shrine room, bows his head before the charmbox, mingles different sorts of holy water in the font, and proceeds with a brief rite of ablution. The holy waters are secured from the Water Temple of the community, where the priests conduct elaborate ceremonies to make the liquid ritually pure.

In the hierarchy of magical practitioners, and below the medicine men in prestige, are specialists whose designation is best translated "holy-mouth-men." The Nacirema have an almost pathological horror of and fascination with the mouth, the condition of which is believed to have a supernatural influence on all social relationships. Were it not for the rituals of the mouth, they believe that their teeth would fall out, their gums bleed, their jaws shrink, their friends desert them, and their lovers reject them. They also believe that a strong relationship exists between oral and moral characteristics. For example, there is a ritual ablution of the mouth for children which is supposed to improve their moral fiber.

The daily body ritual performed by everyone includes a mouthrite. Despite the fact that these people are so punctilious about care of the mouth, this rite involves a practice which strikes the uninitiated stranger as revolting. It was reported to me that the ritual consists of inserting a small bundle of hog hairs into the mouth, along with certain magical powders, and then moving the bundle in a highly formalized series of gestures.

In addition to the private mouthrite, the people seek out a holy-mouth-man once or twice a year. These practitioners have an impressive set of paraphernalia, consisting of a variety of augers, awls, probes, and prods. The use of these objects in the exorcism of the evils of the mouth involves almost unbelievable ritual torture of the client. The holy-mouth-man opens the client's mouth and, using the above mentioned tools, enlarges any holes which decay may have created in the teeth. Magical materials are put into these holes. If there are no naturally occurring holes in the teeth, large sections of one or more teeth are gouged out so that the supernatural substance can be applied. In the client's view, the purpose of these ministrations is to arrest decay and to draw friends. The extremely sacred and traditional character of the rite is evident in the fact that the natives return to the holy-mouth-men year after year, despite the fact that their teeth continue to decay.

It is to be hoped that, when a thorough study of the Nacirema is made, there will be careful inquiry into the personality structure of these people. One has but to watch the gleam in the eye of a holy-mouth-man, as he jabs an awl into an exposed nerve, to suspect that a certain amount of sadism is involved. If this can be established, a very interesting pattern emerges, for most of the population shows definite masochistic tendencies. It was to these that Professor Linton referred in discussing a distinctive part of the daily body ritual which is performed only by men. This part of the rite involves scraping and lacerating the surface of the face with a sharp instrument. Special women's rites are performed only four times during each lunar month, but what they lack in frequency is made up in barbarity. As part of this ceremony, women bake their heads in small ovens for about an hour. The theoretically interesting point is that what seems to be a preponderantly masochistic people have developed sadistic specialists.

The medicine men have an imposing temple, or *latipso,* in every community of any size. The more elaborate ceremonies required to treat very sick patients can only be performed at this temple. These ceremonies involve not only the thaumaturge but a permanent group of vestal maidens who move sedately about the temple chambers in distinctive costume and headdress.

The *latipso* ceremonies are so harsh that it is phenomenal that a fair proportion of the really sick natives who enter the temple ever recover. Small children whose indoctrination is still incomplete have been known to resist attempts to take them to the temple because "that is where you go to die." Despite this fact, sick adults are not only willing but eager to undergo the protracted ritual purification, if they can afford to do so. No matter how ill the supplicant or how grave the emergency, the guardians of many temples will not admit a client if he cannot give a rich gift to the custodian. Even after one has gained admission and survived the ceremonies, the guardians will not permit the neophyte to leave until he makes still another gift.

The supplicant entering the temple is first stripped of all his or her clothes. In everyday life the Nacirema avoids exposure of his body and its natural functions. Bathing and excretory acts are performed only in the secrecy of the household shrine, where they are ritualized as part of the bodyrites. Psychological shock results from the fact that body secrecy is suddenly lost upon entry into the *latipso.* A man, whose own wife has never seen him in an excretory act, suddenly finds himself naked and assisted by a vestal maiden while he performs his natural functions into a sacred vessel. This sort of ceremonial treatment is necessitated by the fact that the excreta are used by a diviner to ascertain the course and nature of the client's sickness. Female clients, on the other hand, find their naked bodies are subjected to the scrutiny, manipulation and prodding of the medicine men.

Few supplicants in the temple are well enough to do anything but lie on their hard beds. The daily ceremonies, like the rites of the holy-mouth-men, involve discomfort and torture. With ritual precision, the vestals awaken their miserable charges each dawn and roll them about on their beds of pain while performing ablutions, in the formal movements of which the maidens are highly trained. At other times they insert magic wands in the supplicant's mouth or force him to eat substances which are supposed to be healing. From time to time the medicine men come to their clients and jab magically treated needles into their flesh. The fact that these temple ceremonies may not cure, and may even kill the neophyte, in no way decreases the people's faith in the medicine men.

There remains one other kind of practitioner, known as a "listener." This witchdoctor has the power to exorcise the devils that lodge in the heads of people who have been bewitched. The Nacirema believe that parents bewitch their own children. Mothers are particularly suspected of putting a curse on children while teaching them the secret body rituals. The countermagic of the witchdoctor is unusual in its lack of ritual. The patient simply tells the "listener" all his troubles and fears, beginning with the earliest difficulties he can remember. The memory displayed by the Nacirema in these exorcism sessions is truly remarkable. It is not uncommon for the patient to bemoan the rejection he felt upon being weaned as a babe, and a few individuals even see their troubles going back to the traumatic effects of their own birth.

In conclusion, mention must be made of certain practices which have their base in native esthetics but which depend upon the pervasive aversion to the natural body and its functions. There are ritual fasts to make fat people thin and ceremonial feasts to make thin people fat. Still other rites are used to make women's breasts larger if they are small, and smaller if they are large. General dissatisfaction with breast shape is symbolized in the fact that the ideal form is virtually outside the range of human variation. A few women afflicted with almost inhuman hypermammary development are so idolized that they make a handsome living by simply going from village to village and permitting the natives to stare at them for a fee.

Reference has already been made to the fact that excretory functions are ritualized, routinized, and relegated to secrecy. Natural reproductive functions are similarly distorted. Intercourse is taboo as a topic and scheduled as an act. Efforts are made to avoid pregnancy by the use of magical materials or by limiting intercourse to certain phases of the moon. Conception is actually very infrequent. When pregnant, women dress so as to hide their condition. Parturition takes place in secret, without friends or relatives to assist, and the majority of women do not nurse their infants.

Our review of the ritual life of the Nacirema has certainly shown them to be a magic-ridden people. It is hard to understand how they have managed to exist so long under the burdens which they have imposed upon themselves. But even such exotic customs as these take on real meaning when they are viewed with the insight provided by Malinowski when he wrote (1948:70):

> Looking from far and above, from our high places of safety in the developed civilization, it is easy to see all the crudity and irrelevance of magic. But without its power and guidance early man could not have mastered his practical difficulties as he has done, nor could man have advanced to the higher stages of civilization.

REFERENCES CITED

LINTON, RALPH
1936 The Study of Man. New York, D. Appleton-Century Co.

MALINOWSKI, BRONISLAW
1948 Magic, Science, and Religion. Glencoe, The Free Press.

MURDOCK, GEORGE P.
1949 Social Structure. New York, The Macmillan Co.

12.

FUNDAMENTAL NOTIONS OF THE FOLKWAYS AND OF THE MORES

William Graham Sumner

The manners, usages, folkways, mores, and institutions of every society tend to be regarded by the members of that society as the only right and proper ones. Sumner's famous book, *Folkways,* published in 1906, probably did more than any other to demonstrate the great variety of human behavior patterns thus regarded. As a result, his thesis has induced many people to pause before they say—or even to refrain from thinking—"My ways—our ways—are the only civilized ways of behavior." The terms "folkways" and "mores," first given currency as sociological terms by Sumner, are now a part of our everyday language. The reader should be able to recognize, however, that if Sumner were writing *Folkways* today certain terms such as "savages," would be inappropriate. It is also very probable that he would be less dogmatic, in view of the speedy pace of many kinds of change today, about the universality of changelessness in the folkways and the mores. Such change is illustrated in the selection by Eileen Herbert Jordan which follows.

DEFINITION AND MODE OF ORIGIN OF THE FOLKWAYS

If we put together all that we have learned from anthropology and ethnography about primitive men and primitive society, we perceive that the first task of life is to live. Men begin with acts, not with thoughts. Every moment brings necessities which must be satisfied at once. Need was the first experience, and it was followed at once by a blundering effort to satisfy it. It is generally taken for granted that men inherited some guiding instincts from their beast ancestry, and it may be true, although it has never been proved. If there were such inheritances, they controlled and aided the first efforts to satisfy needs. Analogy makes it easy to assume that the ways of beasts had produced channels of habit and predisposition along which dexterities and other psychophysical activities would run easily. Experiments with newborn animals show that in the absence of

Source: William Graham Sumner, *Folkways,* Centennial Edition (Lexington, Mass.: Ginn and Company, 1940), pp. 1–3, 28–9, 34–5, 66–8.

The author (1840–1910) was one of the pioneer American sociologists with Ward, Giddings, Small, Cooley, and Ross. He was also an economist and a rector. In 1872 he became professor of political and social science at Yale University. He was the second president of the American Sociological Association. He wrote *A History of American Currency* and *What Social Classes Owe to Each Other* and was the coauthor of *The Science of Society.*

any experience of the relation of means to ends, efforts to satisfy needs are clumsy and blundering. The method is that of trial and failure, which produces repeated pain, loss, and disappointments. Nevertheless, it is a method of rude experiment and selection. The earliest efforts of men were of this kind. Need was the impelling force. Pleasure and pain, on the one side and the other, were the rude constraints which defined the line on which efforts must proceed. The ability to distinguish between pleasure and pain is the only psychical power which is to be assumed. Thus ways of doing things were selected, which were expedient. They answered the purpose better than other ways, or with less toil and pain. Along the course on which efforts were compelled to go, habit, routine, and skill were developed. The struggle to maintain existence was carried on, not individually, but in groups. Each profited by the other's experience; hence there was concurrence towards that which proved to be most expedient. All at last adopted the same way for the same purpose; hence the ways turned into customs and became mass phenomena. Instincts were developed in connection with them. In this way folkways arise. The young learn them by tradition, imitation, and authority. The folkways, at a time, provide for all the needs of life then and there. They are uniform, universal in the group, imperative, and invariable. As time goes on, the folkways become more and more arbitrary, positive, and imperative. If asked why they act in a certain way in certain cases, primitive people always answer that it is because they and their ancestors always have done so. A sanction also arises from ghost fear. The ghosts of ancestors would be angry if the living should change the ancient folkways.

THE FOLKWAYS ARE A SOCIETAL FORCE

The operation by which folkways are produced consists in the frequent repetition of petty acts, often by great numbers acting in concert or, at least, acting in the same way when face to face with the same need. The immediate motive is interest. It produces habit in the individual and custom in the group. It is, therefore, in the highest degree original and primitive. By habit and custom it exerts a strain on every individual within its range; therefore it rises to a societal force to which great classes of societal phenomena are due. Its earliest stages, its course, and laws may be studied; also its influence on individuals and their reaction on it. It is our present purpose so to study it. We have to recognize it as one of the chief forces by which a society is made to be what it is. Out of the unconscious experiment which every repetition of the ways includes, there issues pleasure or pain, and then, so far as the men are capable of reflection, convictions that the ways are conducive to societal welfare. These two experiences are not the same. The most uncivilized men, both in the food quest and in war, do things which are painful, but which have been found to be expedient. Perhaps these cases teach the sense of social welfare better than those which are pleasurable and favorable to welfare. The former cases call for some intelligent reflection on experience. When this conviction as to the relation to welfare is added to the folkways they are converted into mores, and, by virtue of the philosophical and ethical element added to them, they win utility and importance and become the source of the science and the art of living.

FOLKWAYS ARE MADE UNCONSCIOUSLY

It is of the first importance to notice that, from the first acts by which men try to satisfy needs, each act stands by itself, and looks no further than the immediate satisfaction. From recurrent needs arise habits for the individual and customs for the group, but these results are consequences which were never conscious, and never foreseen or intended. They are not noticed until they have long existed, and it is still longer before they are appreciated. Another long time must pass, and a higher stage of mental development must be reached, before they can be used as a basis from which to deduce rules for meeting, in the future, problems whose pressure can be foreseen. The folkways, therefore, are not creations of human purpose and wit. They are like products of natural forces which men unconsciously set in operation, or they are like the instinctive ways of animals, which are developed out of experience, which reach a final form of maximum adaptation to an interest, which are handed down by tradition and admit of no exception or variation, yet change to meet new conditions, still within the same limited methods, and without rational reflection or purpose. From this it results that all the life of human beings, in all ages and stages of culture, is primarily controlled by a vast mass of folkways handed down from the earliest existence of the race, having the nature of the ways of other animals, only the topmost layers of which are subject to change and control, and have been somewhat modified by human philosophy, ethics, and religion, or by other acts of intelligent reflection. We are told of savages that "It is difficult to exhaust the customs and small ceremonial usages of a savage people. Custom regulates the whole of a man's actions,—his bathing, washing, cutting his hair, eating, drinking, and fasting. From his cradle to his grave he is the slave of ancient usage. In his life there is nothing free, nothing original, nothing spontaneous, no progress towards a higher and better life, and no attempt to improve his condition, mentally, morally, or spiritually." All men act in this way with only a little wider margin of voluntary variation.

. . . . . .

FOLKWAYS DUE TO FALSE INFERENCE

Folkways have been formed by accident, that is, by irrational and incongruous action, based on pseudoknowledge. In Molembo a pestilence broke out soon after a Portuguese had died there. After that the natives took all possible measures not to allow any white man to die in their country. On the Nicobar islands some natives who had just begun to make pottery died. The art was given up and never again attempted. White men gave to one Bushman in a kraal a stick ornamented with buttons as a symbol of authority. The recipient died leaving the stick to his son. The son soon died. Then the Bushmen brought back the stick lest all should die. Until recently no building of incombustible materials could be built in any big town of the central province of Madagascar, on account of some ancient prejudice. A party of Eskimos met with no game. One of them returned to their sledges and got the ham of a dog to eat. As he returned with the ham bone in his hand he met and killed a seal. Ever afterwards he carried a ham bone in his hand when hunting. The Belenda women (peninsula of Malacca) stay as near to the house as possible during the period. Many keep the door closed. They know no reason for this custom. "It must be due to some now forgotten superstition." Soon after the Yakuts saw a camel for the first time smallpox broke out amongst them. They thought the camel to be the agent of the disease. A woman amongst the same people contracted an endogamous marriage. She soon afterwards became blind. This was thought to be on account of the violation of ancient customs. A very great number of such cases could be collected. In fact they represent the current mode of reasoning of nature people. It is their custom to reason that, if one thing follows another, it is due to it. A great number of customs are traceable to the notion of the evil eye, many more to ritual notions of uncleanness. No scientific investigation could discover the origin of the folkways mentioned, if the origin had not chanced to become known to civilized men. We must believe that the known cases illustrate the irrational and incongruous origin of many folkways. In civilized history also we know that customs have owed their origin to "historical accident,"—the vanity of a princess, the deformity of a king, the whim of a democracy, the love intrigue of a statesman or prelate. By the institutions of another age it may be provided that no one of these things can affect decisions, acts, or interests, but then the power to decide the ways may have passed to clubs, trades unions, trusts, commercial rivals, wire-pullers, politicians, and political fanatics. In these cases also the causes and origins may escape investigation.

HARMFUL FOLKWAYS

There are folkways which are positively harmful. Very often these are just the ones for which a definite reason can be given. The destruction of a man's goods at his death is a direct deduction from other-worldliness; the dead man is supposed to want in the other world just what he wanted here. The destruction of a man's goods at his death was a great waste of capital, and it must have had a disastrous effect on the interests of the living, and must have very seriously hindered the development of civilization. With this custom we must class all the expenditure of labor and capital on graves, temples, pyramids, rites, sacrifices, and support of priests, so far as these were supposed to benefit the dead. The faith in goblinism produced other-worldly interests which overruled ordinary worldly interests. Foods have often been forbidden which were plentiful, the prohibition of which injuriously lessened the food supply. There is a tribe of Bushmen who will eat no goat's flesh, although goats are the most numerous domestic animals in the district. Where totemism exists it is regularly accompanied by a taboo on eating the totem animal. Whatever may be the real principle in totemism, it overrules the interest in an abundant food supply. "The origin of the sacred regard paid to the cow must be sought in the primitive nomadic life of the Indo-European race," because it is common to Iranians and Indians of Hindostan. The Libyans ate oxen but not cows. The same was true of the Phoenicians and Egyptians. In some cases the sense of a food taboo is not to be learned. It may have been entirely capricious. Mohammed would not eat lizards, because he thought them the offspring of a metamorphosed clan of Israelites. On the other hand, the protective taboo which forbade killing crocodiles, pythons, cobras, and other animal enemies of man was harmful to his interests, whatever the motive. "It seems to be a fixed article of belief throughout southern India, that all who have willfully or accidentally killed a snake, especially a cobra, will certainly be punished, either in this life or the next, in one of three ways: either by childlessness, or by leprosy, or by ophthalmia." Where this faith exists man has a greater interest to spare a cobra than to kill it. India furnishes a great number of cases of harmful mores. "In India every tendency of humanity seems intensified and exaggerated. No country in the world is so conservative in its traditions, yet no country has undergone so many religious changes and vicissitudes." "Every year thousands perish of disease that might recover if they would take proper nourishment, and drink the medicine that science prescribes, but which they imagine that their religion forbids them to touch." "Men who can scarcely count beyond twenty, and know not the letters of the alphabet, would rather die than eat food which had been prepared by men of lower caste, unless it had been sanctified by being offered to an idol; and would kill their daughters rather than endure the disgrace of having unmarried girls at home beyond twelve or thirteen years of age." In the last case the rule of obligation and duty is set by the mores. The interest comes under vanity. The sanction of the caste rules is in a boycott by all members of the caste. The rules are often very harmful. "The authority of caste rests partly on written laws, partly on legendary fables or narratives, partly on the injunctions of instructors and priests, partly on custom and usage, and partly on the caprice and convenience of its votaries." The harm of caste rules is so great that of late they have been broken in some cases, especially in regard to travel over sea, which is a great advantage to Hindoos. The Hindoo folkways in regard to widows and child marriages must also be recognized as socially harmful.

. . . . .

THE FOLKWAYS ARE "RIGHT"

The folkways are the "right" ways to satisfy all interests, because they are traditional, and exist in fact. They extend over the whole of life. There is a right way to catch game, to win a wife, to make one's self appear, to cure disease, to honor ghosts, to treat comrades or strangers, to behave when a child is born, on the warpath, in council, and soon in all cases which can arise. The ways are defined on the negative side, that is, by taboos. The "right" way is the way which the ancestors used and which has been handed down. The tradition is its own warrant. It is not held subject to verification by experience. The notion of right is in the folkways. It is not outside of them, of independent origin, and brought to them to test them. In the folkways, whatever is, is right. This is because they are traditional, and therefore contain in themselves the authority of the ancestral ghosts. When we come to the folkways we are at the end of our analysis. The notion of right and ought is the same in regard to all the folkways, but the degree of it varies with the importance of the interest at stake. The obligation of conformable and cooperative action is far greater under ghost fear and war than in other matters, and the social sanctions are severer, because group interests are supposed to be at stake. Some usages contain only a slight element of right and ought. It may well be believed that notions of right and duty, and of social welfare, were first developed in connection with ghost fear and other-worldliness, and therefore that, in that field also, folkways were first raised to mores. "Rights" are the rules of mutual give and take in the competition of life which are imposed on comrades in the in-group, in order that the peace may prevail there which is essential to the group strength.

Therefore rights can never be "natural" or "God-given," or absolute in any sense. The morality of a group at a time is the sum of the taboos and prescriptions in the folkways by which right conduct is defined. Therefore morals can never be intuitive. They are historical, institutional, and empirical.

World philosophy, life policy, right, rights, and morality are all products of the folkways. They are reflections on, and generalizations from, the experience of pleasure and pain which is won in efforts to carry on the struggle for existence under actual life conditions. The generalizations are very crude and vague in their germinal forms. They are all embodied in folklore, and all our philosophy and science have been developed out of them.

THE FOLKWAYS ARE "TRUE"

The folkways are necessarily "true" with respect to some world philosophy. Pain forced men to think. The ills of life imposed reflection and taught forethought. Mental processes were irksome and were not undertaken until painful experience made them unavoidable. With great unanimity all over the globe primitive men followed the same line of thought. The dead were believed to live on as ghosts in another world just like this one. The ghosts had just the same needs, tastes, passions, etc., as the living men had had. These transcendental notions were the beginning of the mental outfit of mankind. They are articles of faith, not rational convictions. The living had duties to the ghosts, and the ghosts had rights; they also had power to enforce their rights. It behooved the living therefore to learn how to deal with ghosts. Here we have a complete world philosophy and a life policy deduced from it. When pain, loss, and ill were experienced and the question was provoked, Who did this to us? the world philosophy furnished the answer. When the painful experience forced the question, Why are the ghosts angry and what must we do to appease them? the "right" answer was the one which fitted into the philosophy of ghost fear. All acts were therefore constrained and trained into the forms of the world philosophy by ghost fear, ancestral authority, taboos, and habit. The habits and customs created a practical philosophy of welfare, and they confirmed and developed the religious theories of goblinism.

. . . . .

DEFINITION OF THE MORES

When the elements of truth and right are developed into doctrines of welfare, the folkways are raised to another plane. They then become capable of producing inferences, developing into new forms, and extending their constructive influence over men and society. Then we call them the mores. The mores are the folkways, including the philosophical and ethical generalizations as to societal welfare which are suggested by them, and inherent in them, as they grow.

TABOOS

The mores necessarily consist, in a large part, of taboos, which indicate the things which must not be done. In part these are dictated by mystic dread of ghosts who might be offended by certain acts, but they also include such acts as have been found by experience to produce unwelcome results, especially in the food quest, in war, in health, or in increase or decrease of population. These taboos always contain a greater element of philosophy than the positive rules, because the taboos contain reference to a reason, as, for instance, that the act would displease the ghosts. The primitive taboos correspond to the fact that the life of man is environed by perils. His food quest must be limited by shunning poisonous plants. His appetite must be restrained from excess. His physical strength and health must be guarded from dangers. The taboos carry on the accumulated wisdom of generations, which has almost always been purchased by pain, loss, disease, and death. Other taboos contain inhibitions of what will be injurious to the group. The laws about sexes, about property, about war, and about ghosts, have this character. They always include some social philosophy. They are both mystic and utilitarian, or compounded of the two.

Taboos may be divided into two classes, (1) protective and (2) destructive. Some of them aim to protect and secure, while others aim to repress or exterminate. Women are subject to some taboos which are directed against them as sources of possible harm or danger to men, and they are subject to other taboos which put them outside of the duties or risks of men. On account of this difference in taboos, taboos act selectively, and thus affect the course of civilization. They contain judgments as to societal welfare.

. . . . .

MORE EXACT DEFINITION OF THE MORES

We may now formulate a more complete definition of the mores. They are the ways of doing things which are current in a society to satisfy human needs and desires, together with the faiths, notions, codes, and standards of well living which inhere in those ways, having a genetic connection with them. By virtue of the latter element the mores are traits in the specific character (ethos) of a society or a period. They pervade and control the ways of thinking in all the exigencies of life, returning from the world of abstractions to the world of action, to give guidance and to win revivification. "The mores [*Sitten*] are, before any beginning of reflection, the regulators of the political, social, and religious behavior of the individual. Conscious reflection is the worst enemy of the mores, because mores begin unconsciously and pursue unconscious purposes, which are recognized by reflection often only after long and circuitous processes, and because their expediency often depends on the assumption that they will have general acceptance and currency, uninterfered with by reflection." "The mores are usage in any group, insofar as it, on the one hand, is not the expression or fulfillment of an absolute natural necessity [e.g. eating or sleeping], and, on the other hand, is independent of the arbitrary will of the individual, and is generally accepted as worthy."

RITUAL

The process by which mores are developed and established is ritual. Ritual is so foreign to our mores that we do not recognize its power. In primitive society it is the prevailing method of activity, and primitive religion is entirely a matter of ritual. Ritual is the perfect form of drill and of the regulated habit which comes from drill. Acts which are ordained by authority and are repeated mechanically without intelligence run into ritual. If infants and children are subjected to ritual they never escape from its effects through life. Galton says that he was, in early youth, in contact with the Mohammedan ritual idea that the left hand is less worthy than the right, and that he never overcame it. We see the effect of ritual in breeding, courtesy, politeness, and all forms of prescribed behavior. Etiquette is social ritual. Ritual is not easy compliance with usage; it is strict compliance with detailed and punctilious rule. It admits of no exception or deviation. The stricter the discipline, the greater the power of ritual over action and character. In the training of animals and the education of children it is the perfection, inevitableness, invariableness, and relentlessness of routine which tells. They should never experience any exception or irregularity. Ritual is connected with words, gestures, symbols, and signs. Associations result, and, upon a repetition of the signal, the act is repeated, whether the will assents or not. Association and habit account for the phenomena. Ritual gains further strength when it is rhythmical, and is connected with music, verse, or other rhythmical acts. Acts are ritually repeated at the recurrence of the rhythmical points. The alternation of night and day produces rhythms of waking and sleeping, of labor and rest, for great numbers at the same time, in their struggle for existence. The seasons also produce rhythms in work. Ritual may embody an idea of utility, expediency, or welfare, but it always tends to become perfunctory, and the idea is only subconscious. There is ritual in primitive therapeutics, and it was not eliminated until very recent times. The patient was directed, not only to apply remedies, but also to perform rites. The rites introduced mystic elements. This illustrates the connection of ritual with notions of magical effects produced by rites. All ritual is ceremonious and solemn. It tends to become sacred, or to make sacred the subject-matter with which it is connected. Therefore, in primitive society, it is by ritual that sentiments of awe, deference to authority, submission to tradition, and disciplinary cooperation are inculcated. Ritual operates a constant suggestion, and the suggestion is at once put in operation in acts. Ritual is strongest when it is most perfunctory and excites no thought. By familiarity with ritual any doctrinal reference which it once had is lost by familiarity, but the habits persist. Primitive religion is ritualistic, not because religion makes ritual, but because ritual makes religion. Ritual is something to be done, not something to be thought or felt. Men can always perform the prescribed act, although they cannot always think or feel prescribed thoughts or emotions. The acts may bring up again, by association, states of the mind and sentiments which have been connected with them, especially in childhood, when the fantasy was easily affected by rites, music, singing, dramas, etc. No creed, no moral code, and no scientific demonstration can ever win the same hold upon men and women as habits of action, with associated sentiments and states of mind, drilled in from childhood. Mohammedanism shows the power of ritual. Any occupation is interrupted for the prayers and prescribed genuflections. The Brahmins also observe an elaborate daily ritual. They devote to it two hours in the morning, two in the evening, and one at midday. Monks and nuns have won the extreme satisfaction of religious sentiment from the unbroken habit of repeated ritual, with undisturbed opportunity to develop emotional effects of it.

THE RITUAL OF THE MORES

The mores are social ritual in which we all participate unconsciously. The current habits as to hours of labor, meal hours, family life, the social intercourse of the sexes, propriety, amusements, travel, holidays, education, the use of periodicals and libraries, and innumerable other details of life fall under this ritual. Each does as everybody does. For the great mass of mankind as to all things, and for all of us for a great many things, the rule to do as all do suffices. We are led by suggestion and association to believe that there must be wisdom and utility in what all do. The great mass of the folkways give us discipline and the support of routine and habit. If we had to form judgments as to all these cases before we could act in them, and were forced always to act rationally, the burden would be unendurable. Beneficent use and wont save us this trouble.

13.

ROBERT C. SORENSEN'S "ADOLESCENT SEXUALITY IN CONTEMPORARY AMERICA"

Eileen Herbert Jordan

As Sumner made clear in the preceding selection, folkways, mores, and taboos, as part of the cultural environment, can define just about any kind of behavior as right or wrong in a particular society. But sometimes, as seems to be true of American society today, there is no consensus regarding what kinds of behavior and social relationships are required or prohibited by the mores. Perhaps no area of human behavior better illustrates our contemporary moral ambiguity and uncertainty than sexuality. The following selection, based on a sociological survey by Robert C. Sorenson, indicates how sexual morality is currently viewed by a sample of American youth.

Long ago when my generation was young —my generation being the parents of today's adolescents—we thought we knew the answers. We accepted the moral ethic

Source: Eileen Herbert Jordan, "Robert C. Sorenson's Adolescent Sexuality in Contemporary America," *Woman's Day Feature Review* (March 1973). Reprinted by permission of World Publishing Company.

A successful free-lance writer, Eileen Herbert Jordan is Books and Fiction editor for *Woman's Day* magazine.

Adolescent Sexual Experience

	All Teen-agers	By Sex		By Age	
		Boys	Girls	13–15	16–19
VIRGINS (All adolescents who have not had sexual intercourse)					
Sexually inexperienced (Virgins with no beginning sexual activities)	22%	20%	25%	39%	9%
Sexual beginners (Virgins who have actively or passively experienced sexual petting)	17%	14%	19%	12%	21%
Unclassified virgins (Virgins who for whatever reason could not be classified in the above groups)	9%	7%	11%	12%	6%
Total	48%	41%	55%	63%	36%
NONVIRGINS (All adolescents who have had sexual intercourse one or more times)					
Serial monogamists (Nonvirgins having a sexual relationship with one person)	21%	15%	28%	9%	31%
Sexual adventurers (Nonvirgins freely moving from one sexual-intercourse partner to another)	15%	24%	6%	10%	18%
Inactive nonvirgins (Nonvirgins who have not had sexual intercourse for more than one year)	12%	13%	10%	15%	10%
Unclassified nonvirgins (Nonvirgins who for whatever reasons could not be classified in the above groups)	4%	7%	1%	3%	5%
Total	52%	59%	45%	37%	64%

handed us; we accepted, for the most part, the dictates of whatever church we belonged to, because, like Mount Everest, they were there. We sang songs like "That Old Black Magic" and "Love and Marriage," which had a line that read, I believe, "go together like a horse and carriage." That was love—old black magic—and that is what followed it, as night followed day—marriage. Sex, when mentioned, which it rarely was, was something a woman withheld—and a man craved. The chapter dealing with sex was clipped from my college textbook on health before I received it. I recall a friend of mine who created a furor by choosing a pale pink wedding gown instead of a white one—the implications of not wearing white at one's wedding being what they were.

Perhaps all of this has made us uniquely incapable of dealing with, or even understanding, the mores and the freedom of the children whom, after our white weddings, we subsequently produced—the children who have now reached their adolescent years. Like the small boy who spotted the

Emperor's lack of clothes, this generation has stood up, pointed a finger at our institutions, our rights and our wrongs, our entire life-style and asked *why?*

In the book, *Adolescent Sexuality in Contemporary America,* we have for the first time a report that comes solely from *them.* Not from the experts, not from the educators, not from the clergy or the parents—"we have so many opinions about things we know so little about," Dr. Sorensen says. "And perhaps our opinions are strongest about one thing we know the least about—our growing children." Dr. Sorensen is the father of three children himself, so there was, from the beginning, a personal element in his concern.

From the statistics and the observations in his survey it is quite clear that, with some youthful instinct, whether right or wrong, young people mainly trust each other. They relate overwhelmingly to their peers—and not to their elders. They condone any course of moral behavior or any moral beliefs held by *anyone*—provided that no one is hurt by them. Formal religion has failed them—half of those questioned (no matter their religious denomination) rarely, if ever, went to religious services. At the same time they feel that they are rather religious. *To me, whenever I want to speak to God it's just me and God. I don't have to go through a priest or a church or anything like that, you know . . .* the comment of one seventeen-year-old girl. Religion, along with everything else, is a personal thing. The church, no matter what church, does not reach them; the church believes that sex is sinful, they say, and this they will not buy.

Although they condemn no one who likes sex for its own sake, most of them believe that it should be accompanied by love and also friendship—and that love and friendship should naturally be accompanied by sex. *It isn't that you just know a girl better after you've had sex with her. It's that you open up with each other and you trust each other, and you find yourself saying things that maybe you never even thought out for yourself before. I get to know a girl a lot better after—better than I used to think I had a right to know anybody*—the opinions of a fifteen-year-old boy.

The automatic tandem of love and marriage exists no more for the majority, despite the sixteen-year-old girl who said *I would not go to bed with a guy unless I were willing to marry him. That's a way of showing a guy you love him. Otherwise it's immoral.* The fact is, at the time of the interview she had had, thus far, intercourse with six boys!

A love affair may lead ideally to marriage, but it need not in order to be a good thing in itself; it may last a week, a month, a year and no longer, and still enrich their lives—that is what love is all about. When it does lead to a permanent union, it is very special. As a sixteen-year-old boy explains it: *When I first saw her, I had a feeling. There was something in her eyes. I could tell she was very definitely a warm person, and then I got to know her. She was warm and passionate and good-looking . . . it grew on me. It's like wine—it aged for the better. If it's really true love, it will last for a long time. After I get married I'll come home from work and walk in my house and see her and there will be love.*

However, when asked, "Are there any reasons you might want to get married other than to give your children a name?" the majority answer was *No.*

There is one thing to remember throughout all of this, however; the general age group of thirteen to nineteen is divided again into those who are between thirteen and fifteen and those between sixteen and nineteen. There are light years between a thirteen-year-old girl and a nineteen-year-old one; there are, for that matter, often years between a thirteen-year-old boy and a thirteen-year-old girl—as anyone who has known both intimately can tell you—so it is important to study the sample as a whole before forming conclusions.

There is also the fact that written parental consent was required before any of the adolescents were permitted to participate in the survey. Whether the children of parents who refused to give consent—out of a sense of conservatism, a reluctance toward such permissiveness—are themselves more conservative, unaccustomed to permissiveness in their life-styles, and would therefore tip the scales in the findings, is a purely speculative matter. The survey covers a number of classifications of sexual experience, which we will break down for purposes of simplification.

THE SEXUALLY INEXPERIENCED

When I want to start I'll know it, a fifteen-year-old girl remarks. *Every kid has to decide for himself . . . When you're so young you don't know anything about life. I'm glad I waited so far . . .* a fifteen-year-old girl and a seventeen-year-old boy.

The sexually inexperienced are not only virgins but also young people with no beginning sexual activities (what I believe my generation called necking or petting). They are a minority in the overall picture, although, not surprisingly, the greatest number fall into the thirteen-to-fifteen age bracket. The break-off year seems to be sixteen, since 90 percent of those who said they had experience in sex had it by their sixteenth birthday.

More than the rest, the inexperienced consider themselves more children than adults, more bound to their parents, more religious—if only because they have not yet broken with tradition. Even in this group, however, one can see signs of the changing ethic. Over half of those questioned denied that any moral issue was involved, but said the reason they had not yet experienced sex was simply because they had not yet met anyone to experience it with! The majority believe that the sex education courses in school are valuable. And despite their deference to parents, 57 percent believe *my generation is going to do a better job of running things than the last generation has done.*

THE SEXUAL BEGINNERS

I don't want my girlfriend to want anything else. We concentrate on each other's needs—and you can't do that when you're having intercourse—or so I've heard, a seventeen-year-old boy. *I guess I started petting when I first started going out . . . heavy petting is I guess touching everything above the waist . . .* a seventeen-year-old girl.

Sexual beginners are virgins who have actively or passively experienced sexual petting. In my day we called it "not going *all the way*"—to many of us, it was the only sex we knew. Today, most adolescents spend a relatively short period of time in the beginning stage, but go on rapidly from there to a complete relationship—though not always with the same partner. What makes them pause often seems to be a certainty that there must be love for there to be sex—and an uncertainty as to what love is.

THE FIRST SEXUAL INTERCOURSE

Time and place change, but everything does not change completely—most of the girls questioned said that the first time they experienced sex they were afraid; most of the boys said they were excited. And, despite the relaxation of the age, the first act of sexual intercourse remains one of the moving moments of life.

I really desperately wanted to say the first time, "Make it good . . ."

What were my feelings? I don't know how to explain them except that they were warm feelings. There's just something about him that was just shining out bright . . . I never wanted to be quitting . . . just go on forever. We don't talk to each other . . . we don't have to talk . . . comments made by two seventeen-year-old girls.

And most of those who did it say they are glad they did.

SERIAL MONOGAMY

The largest group in the survey are the nonvirgins and among these in turn the largest group is what Dr. Sorensen calls the Serial Monogamists. The novel *Love Story* is an example (if only one), he says, of serial monogamy. That is perhaps as good a definition of it as any. Serial monogamists are adolescents who have a sexual relationship with only one person—or, at the least, with only one person at a time.

When I have love and sex, I'm definitely a happier person . . . I really believe that sex and love cut down a lot of your hassles because you know there is someone who cares for you very much . . . a sixteen-year-old serial monagamist.

More than any others polled, the monogamists represent most dramatically the growing trend in the sex habits of teenagers, and their growing belief that what they are doing is an ethical and convenient means of enjoying sex (and sex is always to be enjoyed) without the commitment of marriage. They see the relationship they have as durable and lasting while it exists, but they refuse to say how long that will be.

I wouldn't want somebody to go drastically out of their way and change their lifestyle . . . I don't want anyone to make concessions in the way they think or live, just because we happen to be loving. I want the same freedom myself . . . You can't make a person sign a contract that says, "I will love you forever" . . . That's when things start to fall apart and you get headaches . . . a nineteen-year-old girl.

It is real while it does last just the same—love with all its turmoil.

Sometimes it gets into my head that it's something I don't want to do . . . and I try to explain to him that something just tells me don't. He tries to understand . . . but then he'll just get up and start playing his guitar and it makes me feel very bad because I know he's trying to get his mind off it . . . I want to make him happy—an age-old tale told by a fourteen-year-old monogamist.

I think love is giving yourself to somebody—really giving—and caring for that person more than yourself. It's a kind of loss of all self-concern . . . you just give whatever you can . . . you think of them before anyone else . . . before yourself . . . a sixteen-year-old one.

The closest my age group came to all of this must have been "going steady"—and it's obviously not worthwhile even bothering to compare the two. In a way, however, we wanted the same things. We wanted to be told that we were loved—and we wanted to know that it was true. And love is not without honor still; the great majority of boys believe that it is wrong (though easy) to tell a girl that you love her if you don't. And the great majority of serial monogamists say they love their partners—and wistfully hope that they are loved in return.

THE ADVENTURERS

I think a lot of relationships get started because people dig each other sexually and they get to know each other because of the sex . . . a lot of people can't communicate their feeling of love in any other way . . .

Well, perhaps the way a person looks at you has something to do with it. A wide-eyed look—that's what I look for—a wide-eyed look by the girl. It looks at you as though she wanted something . . . These are the remarks made by a sixteen-year-old girl and an eighteen-year-old boy respectively. They are both what Dr. Sorensen calls the *sexual adventurers.* Adventurers are adolescents who move freely from one sex experience and one partner to another—usually with little or no affection involved. Sex is an end in itself, unconnected with the emotions.

The adventurers are, in many ways, the lost souls of the adolescent world—more at odds with their parents than others, more often products of a broken home, even less religious than their peers, getting poorer grades in school, smoking more marijuana—and three quarters of them admitting they find it hard to accept the idea of obeying the law.

They substitute fantasies for reality, as in the case of the sixteen-year-old girl who explained: *I imagine a scene in a big, beautiful bed, king size, with beautiful satin sheets—just doing everything that was whatever he wanted, I would do. I would talk about our staying in bed all day and all night, just doing whatever we pleased . . .* Or the eighteen-year-old adventuress (who has had intercourse with fifty men) who said: *I'd fantasize about my prince . . . sitting down and thinking and closing my eyes and saying there was someone there . . . it was out of loneliness . . .*

The sad fact that emerges here is that many of these young people, driven by physical passions, find it harder and harder ever to fall in love—and often end up even actively disliking the opposite sex.

Despite a kind of poignancy in their situations, however, the adventurers probably are responsible for much of the bad publicity adolescents on the whole have been receiving—and for much of the concern about them shown by educators, parents and the clergy. If we can take any comfort from these figures, it may be in the fact that if this sample is accurate, there are so few of them. Only 15 percent of all the young people questioned fall into the category, 80 percent of these being boys, and nearly half of the 15 percent concentrated in the South—the only sharp geographic distinction in the whole study. There is the possibility that they will stand out in the survey more than their number justifies—adventurers being more inclined to talk about their exploits than others.

PREGNANCY

Like when I'm having sex, I don't really connect it with getting pregnant . . . I've never been pregnant, you know, and a lot of my friends have, but I just can't picture it happening to me . . . This is a comment made by an eighteen-year-old girl who does not believe in abortion and would have no alternative to having the baby, should she become pregnant; her attitude is typical. On the whole, there is no overwhelming support for abortion recorded here, though many simply regard it as *simpler than birth control.* One of the surprising things that emerges from this study (surprising at least to someone like me, who has coped with the enormous emotional, physical and financial pressures involved with raising children) is the nonchalance of adolescents regarding pregnancy—and the little they do to avoid it.

Theories have abounded that the ease with which the Pill can be obtained today has had an enormous effect on the increase of sexual activity; not so, say the teenagers. While it is the largest single form of birth control they use, 65 percent of them have never used the Pill at all—and the majority often depend blithely on luck or blind chance.

Yet half of all those questioned agreed. "It's immoral to bring an unwanted child into this overpopulated world,"—making us assume that they feel very lucky indeed. Since half of them say they do not believe they will become pregnant if they don't want to, they have a kind of bravado as well.

There is another element, too—part of the fabric of youth, a kind of make-believe . . . *That's like coming right out and admitting I am doing it, you know. I don't want to admit that to myself* . . . This eighteen-year-old girl feels she has preserved her innocence by doing nothing mechanical about the act of sex—she is only one of many.

Should pregnancy happen, the majority of girls want to marry the father of the child and raise the baby. Boys' feelings on the subject are too fragmented to let us form any conclusions, but there are strong hints that the marriage ties that bind cause less hesitancy than the pressures of money. These are, after all, children of an affluent society (54 percent of the total sample in the survey are sons and daughters of families in the ten-thousand-dollar-a-year-and-up wage bracket) and they want all the things they have now, and preferably more, before they take on any responsibility.

. . . . .

Dr. Sorensen feels from his findings, and it would be difficult to disagree with him, that sex among the young is here to stay—and the old illusions, the old black magic, are gone forever. He feels that it is probably a good thing, that when today's love affairs, with their strong ties of friendship and their strong empathy, lead to marriages, they will lead to very good marriages indeed. He points out that three quarters of the boys and girls questioned said that, when they marry, they expect to be married to one person for the rest of their lives.

The trouble is our tendency, when we turn our backs, to push them too fast, too soon. Tenderness, after all, must be learned and affection has to grow. Sex can be swift and transient; love is long. We would be smarter to let the affection out in public and not pressure adolescents into the bedroom. The maiden aunts will not be back, nor will the grandmothers, and it is unlikely that fewer mothers will work than are working now, but a little frank communication between parent and child might go a long way. Love and understanding in the home, the kind of time and protection the home can give, will go a long way toward developing the kind of understanding of love that adolescents will need for the rest of their lives.

14.

WHAT TO DO AS POPULATION EXPLODES, IMPLODES, DISPLODES

Philip M. Hauser

Sociologists have long been interested in demography, the statistical study of population. Their studies have dealt with such aspects of population as density, growth, distribution, migration, vital statistics, and the relationship of all of these elements to social and economic conditions. Increasingly, in recent years, sociologists have also become involved in the question of sheer numbers. What is an optimum population for the U.S.? For the world? Are we in danger of overpopulation? Here a renowned specialist in population research examines the issue of population explosion and other significant demographic concerns.

The problems of population and environment in the United States have received a great deal of attention in recent months. But much that has been said and written has been so distorted that our short-run public zeal may turn into long-run public apathy. Loud assertions that it is already too late to prevent ecological disaster may make a lot of people ask themselves, "Why bother to do anything about it?"

Above all we must get our priorities right. Despite the views of overall environmentalists, it is more important to eliminate Chicago slums than to clean up Lake Michigan.

So important are these problems that we must vaccinate ourselves against a reaction of indifference on the part of the public. So let us explore some of the distortions:

"The population explosion is responsible for environmental pollution."

This statement fails to recognize that even if there is no further growth in population, high levels of production and consumption could increase pollution. Similarly, a continued growth of population need not necessarily increase pollution.

. . . . .

"Technology is to blame for the environmental pollution."

Technology is not an evil but a neutral agent which can be used for good or evil. It has been permitted to produce pollution in the United States, but it can also be used to eliminate it.

"Environmental pollution is caused by the free-enterprise system."

Socialist systems are as concerned about pollution problems as capitalist systems. Russia is worried about caviar production because of pollution in the Caspian Sea.

"Tens of millions of people will starve to death during the 1970s."

Nonsense. For the first time, some Asian

Source: Philip M. Hauser, *Smithsonian* (December 1970): 21–24.

Philip M. Hauser is a professor of sociology at the University of Chicago. He is director of the Population Research Center and has done work in the area of demography and urban sociology.

countries have food surpluses to export—the miracle rice that they do not like to eat themselves. Yet it would be absurd, also, to deny that mankind will face future food shortages. All the "green revolution" of the past few years has done is give man two, three, possibly four decades in which he has an opportunity to decrease population growth.

So population and environmental data must be viewed in perspective. Man not only adapts to his environment but adapts it to his requirements. He has done much to modify nature while increasing his lifespan from 18 or 20 years at the time of the Roman Empire to 70 years in the United States today.

Man or some close kissing cousin has been on this planet for about four million years. During the relatively recent years of his occupation, Man has generated three developments which have profoundly affected his values and actions. These are: the population explosion—the remarkable growth of the species during the three centuries of the modern era; the population implosion—increasing concentration of people on relatively small portions of the earth, in other words, urbanization; the population displosion—increasing heterogeneity, or ethnic and cultural diversity, of people sharing the same locale and activities.

Man is still trying to learn how to live in the world he has created for himself.

The world's population did not reach one billion until about 1850. A second billion people were produced in the next 80 years, and a third billion in only 30 years. If the present birth and mortality trends continue, there are likely to be 7.5 billion people on the earth by the year 2000. The global population, in other words, may increase by as many persons in the next three decades as there are now in the world.

There was insufficient technological development and social organization for cities of 100,000 or more to appear until the time of the Greco-Roman civilization. The proliferation of cities of a million or more began only about 170 years ago. By the United Nations definition of urban (a population of 20,000 or more), the fraction of the world population that was urban in 1800 was only slightly more than two percent, and by the end of this century it may be between 40 and 50 percent.

DIFFERENT PEOPLES CROWDED TOGETHER

The worldwide displosion of the population is more difficult to measure than the explosion and the implosion. For as many years as we have any data, diverse peoples have lived on our planet, but only in our time have so many of them shared common geographic areas, living space and activities. The frictions that this displosion has brought about are evident between the Protestants and the Catholics in Northern Ireland, between the Arabs and the Israelis in the Middle East, between Chinese and Malays in Malaysia, between Muslims and Hindus in India and Pakistan, among the various Hindu groups within India, and between the white and black people of the United States. Such problems can best be understood as part of a transition that is still under way from a preurban to a metropolitan world.

Within the United States, developments have been similar to those in other countries. When our first census was taken in 1790, we were a nation of fewer than four million people. The results of the 1970 census indicate a population of more than 204 million. Short of catastrophe, we seem almost certain to have 300 million people by the end of this century.

A second postwar baby boom has already begun. The products of the first one have reached the reproductive age, and this boom is an echo of that one. In October 1968, for the first time since 1957, the number of births in one month exceeded the number in the same month of the preceding year. A recession tends to decrease marriage and birthrates. The high proportion of people of reproductive age among us now, nevertheless, makes it almost certain that even if the birthrate dips, it will rise again. The women between 20 and 29 are increasing by 35 percent in our country between 1968 and 1975.

Does this mean, as the alarm criers say, that we should have compulsory family limitation now? In my judgment, no.

Look at it this way: The average number of children per completed family in the United States was six in 1800 but has fallen to three. Voluntarily, we have diminished the number of children born during the reproductive life of couples by 50 percent. With present mortality, a zero rate of population growth requires 2.11 children per family. Our country is already close enough to this average to achieve a stable population without any of the sanctions or penalties that frightened persons advocate.

The population implosion gave rise to many of the collective needs to which our governmental system has responded too slowly. Ninety-five percent of the American people lived on farms or in towns of fewer than 2,500 when our first census was taken. Fifty-one percent of us were urban by 1920, and 70 percent by 1960. We have been a predominantly urban country for only half a century, which is less than one lifetime. The transition has brought on the urban crisis.

It is virtually certain that the 100 million persons whom we may add to our total population in the next 30 years will be mostly urban. So metropolises may grow even faster in the future than our nation's total population.

In our country the dramatic story of the black people has highlighted the population displosion. Let me place that story in perspective:

Only 51 percent of the American people were native white of native parentage in 1900. The other 49 percent were foreign-born, second-generation immigrants, blacks or members of other races. As recently as 1960, the latter groups still constituted 30 percent, nearly a third, of our population.

About 89 percent of all nonwhites lived in the South as recently as 1910, and that figure had changed by only two or three percent since 1860. By 1960, however, only 60 percent were in the South.

AMERICAN HERITAGE AND BLACK REVOLT

Even more significantly, the black people have been urbanized more rapidly than the whites. In 1910, before the great internal migratory movement began, 73 percent of all this country's blacks were rural people. Fifty years later, 73 percent were urban. Among the black people, moreover, 23 percent of those 25 or more years old were functionally illiterate. They had not gone beyond the fifth grade in school and had not reached a stage at which they could read a metropolitan newspaper with ease. This was their share of the American heritage. These facts are requisite to understanding the revolt of the blacks.

What are the problems our population history has generated? We have seen effects of the explosion, implosion and displosion throughout both our schools and our economy. The first postwar baby boom swept youngsters through the schools like a tidal wave, completely inundating elementary, secondary and higher education institutions. Now this generation is joining the labor force, and we have high rates of unemployment among youth—especially, of course, among disadvantaged young blacks.

The police report that delinquency and crime are increasing much more rapidly than the population. Standing alone, this statement seems pretty naive to a demographer. During the 1960s the number of youngsters between 15 and 19 years old—from whom, by definition, delinquency comes—was increasing by 46 percent. Delinquency would have increased by reason of the size of this age group even if the delinquency *rate* had remained the same. We did not have a 46 percent increase in police, however, or in reformatories, or in any other agencies that might have prevented or dealt with delinquency.

The automotive insurance companies discovered what reserves were for in the 1960s when the number of persons 20 to 25 years old increased by 54 percent. Few things in our way of life are as dangerous as a male under 25 years of age behind the wheel of an automobile. We are now slaughtering 56,000 people a year with the automobiles on our highways, and a significant part of this toll is a result of the change in the age structure of our population.

How will we deal with these problems?

Although the disadvantaged groups, the poor and uneducated, have large families, their contribution to total population growth in the United States is relatively small. Distributing contraceptives to these people will not suffice to halt the growth.

WHAT CAN FAMILY PLANNING DO?

In the United States the population problem resides mainly in the dominant white middle-class people having third and fourth children. These are the people who must reduce the average number of children per couple from three to 2.11.

But what about minorities and underprivileged peoples of Asia, Latin America and Africa? No one knows yet what family planning will do for them.

We have yet to discover whether peoples who are mired in illiteracy and poverty, isolated as subcultural groups, and living in a traditional type of society, can decrease their birthrate. But we do know there has never been a people on the face of this earth that, having acquired literacy, education and a fair level of living, did not reduce its birthrate.

Personal and social problems as well as physical challenges have been generated by the population implosion. These include crime and delinquency, alcoholism, drug addiction and the revolt of youth. They are characterized at one extreme by the hippies, young folk seeking some way of retreating from our society because they cannot cope with it.

. . . . .

The revolt of women is a further consequence of the population implosion. Urbanization has dramatically changed the role of a woman from that of simply being female to being a human being. Unemployment and underemployment are also ascribable in part at least to the distribution of our people—and demand our attention.

A cultural lag in the relationships between our federal, state and local governments has made it exceedingly difficult to meet the challenges of metropolitanism as a way of life. Although a majority of the people in 39 of our states was urban by 1960, the urban citizenry did not yet control the legislature of a single state.

By deliberately delaying reapportionments, the state legislatures have given us a fine example of civil disobedience. They forced the large percentage of our city people to turn to the federal government for help. The national government has not usurped state rights. State legislatures have made themselves a fifth wheel by ignoring urban problems.

The displosion in population has obviously added to the difficulty of obtaining gratification of new collective needs, and has also brought on a new problem. This is the white backlash to the still rising power of the blacks; it could tear us apart.

I would like to vaccinate against the distortions that may change public zeal into public apathy. Population and environment hucksterism must be given credit for creating awareness, but in overstating anticipated consequences they may boomerang and cause public disillusionment. For example:

Zero population growth, we are told, must be achieved as rapidly as possible, even through a drastic decrease in the birthrate.

To believe in the slogan "Zero Population Growth" is similar to believing in the law of gravitation—it is inevitable. Given the finite dimensions of this planet any rate of population growth will, in the long run, produce saturation. The question is not should there be zero population growth, but at what rate and by what means is it to be achieved.

ZERO GROWTH WILL SOLVE THE YOUTH PROBLEM

There is nothing in prospect in our country that necessitates a negative growth rate. Nor is there any need to put pressure on a couple to have only one child. We can achieve a stable population without any such drastic measures.

Young people's adoption of the zero-population-growth slogan intrigues me. Given our present and anticipated mortality rate, the achievement of zero population growth by the end of this century would increase the average age of the American people from about 27, at present, to 40. The number over 60 would rise from about 12 percent to more than 20 percent. From the standpoint of us elders, that clearly would solve the youth problem.

We must and can grapple with problems of the environment. We must also control fertility and find ways to meet the many other problems posed by the population explosion, implosion and displosion. Both factual and profound philosophical questions are involved in our choice of priorities. Let's not allow pollution to become a smokescreen to distract us from more immediate challenges to mankind.

15.

THE WIND THAT MEANS LIFE TO INDIA

Santha Rama Rau

At least as far back as the ancient Greeks, attempts have been made to explain social behavior as resulting from variations in the physical environment—in climate, topography, soil conditions, natural resources. Although evidence against climatic and geographical determinism is today convincing to most scholars, geographic and climatic elements cannot be ignored in an analysis of social and cultural life. How a society responds to variations in temperature, climate, terrain, and natural resources depends on its culture—knowledge, skills, values—and on its social organization. The selection below describes the struggles of a society with the persistent question of how to deal with a dominant feature of its physical environment—the wind. Note that the behavior of the people in this Indian society is not simply being *determined* by the geographical phenomenon but, rather, the society has sought systematically ways of coping with it, to modify it to serve human ends. As W. D. Wallis has said, "Geographical environment is the cradle in which man's genius awaits the promptings of motives which give him mastery over his fate."

Sometime at the end of every April winds spring up off the west coast of South America and these, so the meteorologists tentatively suggest, travel westward across more than half the world to produce one of the world's most spectacular climatic phenomena. In the early part of their annual journey they are not particularly dramatic winds. They move easily at about fifteen or twenty miles an hour as part of the trade winds of the southern hemisphere, blow across the Marquesas Islands, include Tahiti in their scope and carry with them, for the most part, clear days and warm nights.

By the middle of May the winds have reached the Samoan Islands and continue along the course determined for them by the turning earth. They move across the Ellice Islands, the Solomons and New Guinea, and the long island chain of Indonesia.

In June the winds reach the Indian Ocean, and it is only then that their whole character changes. They sweep entirely out of their course, slacken their speed, acquire a special name and such enormous importance that without them the 500 million people who live in India, Pakistan, Ceylon, Burma, Indo-China and Siam would not be able to survive in their home-

Source: Santha Rama Rau, *New York Times Magazine* (June 8, 1952), pp. 12, 24, 26–27. Copyright 1952 by the New York Times Company. Reprinted by permission of the William Morris Agency, Inc.

Santha Rama Rau is the author of many published works. Among them are the play, *A Passage to India,* and books including *Home to India* and *Gifts of Passage.* She has also had many magazine articles published.

lands. By the time the first rain clouds burst over the Malabar coast those winds have become the great southwest monsoon, India's most valued – and most capricious – blessing.

From the time of the spring equinox onward, as the sun's rays strike the earth more and more directly, the huge land mass of continental Asia begins to heat up. With growing intensity through the weeks that follow, the heat continues unrelieved. In late May and early June temperatures recorded in North India have reached as high as 126 degrees F. The capital city, Delhi, has an average daytime temperature for May of 104 degrees. Then the Government offices and the foreign embassies switch to summer hours – the working day begins at 7:30 A.M. and finishes at 1:30 P.M. A large part of every day becomes devoted simply to avoiding the heat. Chiks (the slatted, bamboo screens) are lowered all day over windows and verandas to keep the interiors of homes and offices cool and shaded from the sun and glare. Only after sunset are windows and houses opened up to the slightly cooler air of evening. Only in the late short twilight do people sit in their gardens or walk in the parks.

The sea's moderating influence does not spread very far inland and only the cities immediately on the coast benefit by reasonably temperate weather. But in the plains of the north and east of the great plateaus of the center of India the heat is a strong and a curiously personal enemy. The earth bakes into a hard cracked surface, rivers dry up entirely or shrink to thin opaque trickles, and all farming comes to a standstill. This is also the season of the Loo, a dreaded, searingly hot wind that blows in from the Rajasthan desert, raises the temperature by 15 or 20 degrees and sweeps the surface soil into dust storms. All kinds of illnesses and nervous ailments are attributed to it, heatstroke, hysteria and uncertain tempers, and, at the first hint of the rising Loo, doors and windows are shut and bolted against its dust, heat and evil influence.

At the end of May the prolonged and acute heat has formed an enormous low pressure area in the atmosphere over India, and something like a huge whirlwind begins to circulate around its edges. As the heat increases, the speed of the air circulation grows until at last it has acquired suction strong enough to reach below the equator and pull the southeastern trade winds into India. Here, as the monsoon, for three months they move east and north across the country pouring out the water accumulated over 10,000 miles of ocean. Eventually they are checked by the great mountain barriers of the Himalayas which serve to contain the monsoon and conserve the major force of the rains for India. This mountain wall makes it possible for parts of Assam to have a rainfall of 450 inches in one summer while beyond the Himalayas Tibet gets between five and ten inches a year.

As the sun enters its autumnal phase, the earth, already cooled by the rains, is further cooled by the sun's declining intensity, and gradually the monsoon retreats from India to rejoin its old route south of the equator. If anything were to interfere with the process – if, for instance, a string of large volcanic islands were to spring up between the African Coast and Cape Gormorin, the southern tip of India, to deflect the monsoon, or if the heat in Central Asia should, by the cooling of the earth, be reduced and the force to pull in the monsoon should vanish – then India would become a desert. Only a thin coastal strip and the banks of the Ganges might remain green and habitable.

It is not surprising, then, that the chief of the Vedic gods, the oldest of all India's deities and the father of the whole pantheon of gods is Indra, the god of rain. A child born under his auspices is certain to be fortunate and prosperous, and the monsoon, his season, is traditionally connected with fertility, production and richness.

For weeks before the rains begin priests in the temples of the west coast compute from ancient scriptures and old astronomical charts the exact date the monsoon will arrive. With equal seriousness (and, according to the priests, hardly more reliable results) scientists and Government meteorologists collect data from their many coastal stations, study advance reports of weather conditions from island outposts in the Indian Ocean and attempt to predict when the rains will come. For days beforehand, prayers and chanting in the temples urge Indra not to withhold his gift. In some parts of India raindances and drumbeats are performed to call the rain. In Delhi, Government officials more prosaically get on with the job of seeing that plans for water storage, more and deeper wells and bigger irrigation schemes are completed in case this year, again, the monsoon should fail.

Some years ago, one of India's former Ministers of Finance, in presenting his budget to the Indian Parliament, opened his speech with the remark, "The Indian budget is a gamble in rain." Just as Indian agriculture depends entirely on the monsoon to provide its water to fill the country's rivers and reservoirs, and to make irrigation possible, so Indian industry relies to a great extent on the same sources for its power. The electric light and power supply in all the major cities depends on the water reserves which, in turn, are replenished only by the monsoon. Without question, the greatest single factor in maintaining the functioning economy of India is the rain of high summer.

Although the monsoon has never entirely failed to appear, there has never been a recorded year in which the rains have been satisfactory in every part of the country. The day the rains break there is an extraordinary relaxing of tension everywhere. Strangers in city streets smile at each other in relief that the heat has broken. Children rush out yelling in excitement to stand in the first downpour and adults touch the damp ground in gratitude. Every newspaper carries the news on the front page, and compares the arrival of this year's rain with previous monsoons. But after a night of singing and exhilaration and thanksgiving, the anxiety begins again.

So many things can go wrong. There can be too much rain all at once and this will cause floods. Lives will be lost, property damaged, and yet more of India's thin, infinitely precious top soil will get washed away. There may be too little rain and that will result in droughts and famine. There may be long breaks in the monsoon which can mean that the seeds which are sown immediately the rains begin don't germinate, or that later, seedlings wither.

The rains may begin too early or too late, and continue too long or end too abruptly. Then crops will rot in the fields before they are ripe for harvesting, or they may dry up before they are fully grown. In fact, one of the most important of the monsoon festivals, Bombay's Coconut Day, comes at the end of the heavy rains. At that time the gods of the ocean are appeased and offerings of food and flowers and fruit are taken down to all the beaches so that the monsoon seas will abate and allow the fishing craft to leave the harbors again. In all the aspects of the arrival, distribution, timing and departure of the monsoon the Indian farmer most of all, the industrialist and the Indian Government must gamble on the rains.

The monsoon, which has been known to give some places thirty inches of rain in one day, can equally give other parts of

India only five inches for the whole year. Normally, over two or three seasons things even themselves out, but the monsoon shortcomings have been so widespread and so consistent as to produce in some areas what is described by the meteorologists as "a chronic condition of the failure of the rains."

. . . . .

16.

MURDER IN EDEN OR THE NEW DOGMA OF MAN'S ORIGIN

Robert Ascher

Among the topics of interest to social scientists is the origin and development of "human" behavior. One of the elements of continuing debate in this regard is the extent to which our behavior is so basically linked to genetically determined forces in the earliest evolutionary stages of our ancestors that we simply cannot change. Two of the most widely known exponents of the position that our behavior—especially our belligerent and aggressive behavior—is inherited and unchangeable are Robert Ardrey and Konrad Lorenz. In the selection below, Robert Ascher questions the validity of the conclusions of Ardrey and Lorenz and presents alternative explanations to the currently popular generalization that man is

Source: Robert Ascher, *The Cornell Plantations* 26, no. 1 (Spring 1970): 7–11. Reprinted by permission of the publisher.

Robert Ascher is professor of archaeology at Cornell University. He has excavated in the United States, Mexico, and Turkey. His articles have appeared in *Science, The American Anthropologist,* and *The American Scientist.* He is the author of *Origins of Man.*

so much like other animals that his behavior results from what Ardrey refers to as "the legacy bequeathed us by those killer apes, our immediate forebears."

In the opening episode of the film 2001 – A Space Odyssey, the emergence of man is depicted in cineomatic splendor. We first see a band of very hairy, glassy-eyed primates scrounging in a bone bed. Next, a member of the band turns his head as if to announce an idea. After some intermediary grunting, the entire band, now all armed with bones, is seen attacking a neighboring band. The neighbors have no implements and are quickly routed. It is made clear to the moviegoer that through these acts proto-man becomes man.

Can this be passed off as just a Hollywood version of how man got started? I think not. Prior to the showing of 2001, increasing numbers of people conceived of man's origin in a way realized in the movie. Moreover, many believed that there was strong evidence to support the Hollywood version, or something like it. Although details vary, the crucial act is ever present: man is born in violence as one primate (or group of primates) armed with implements attacks another primate (or group of primates).

After hearing this gory tale told several times, I probed for its sources. I was most often directed to Ardrey's *African Genesis,* and to *On Aggression* by Konrad Lorenz. I examined these sources: here are examples of what I found. First, from Ardrey: "Far from the truth lay the antique assumption that man had fathered the weapon. The weapon, instead, had fathered man." Turning to Lorenz, we read: "There is evidence that the first inventors of pebble tools, the African Australopithecines promptly used their new weapon to kill not only game, but fellow members of their own species as well." In short, I found that the theme for the human origins episode in 2001 could have been taken from notions in these books.

Nowadays many people write freely about human origins. Everyone knows this was not always the case. Before Darwin, the bible set the outer boundaries for the discussion. Man is more than a hundred years older now, and those upsetting issues about science and religion are supposedly resolved. Why then should one be concerned with a certain twist in the story of human origins? Mainly because the newer version seeks to account for mankind's present behavior in an unacceptable manner. In this essay, I concentrate on crucial evidence for the thesis, namely the nature and use of man's first artifacts.

To begin, suppose we uncritically go along with those who are convinced that man was born in violence. Taking this path, where does it end up? We recall the statement from Ardrey cited above and follow it to the end of the paragraph. "Far from the truth lay the antique assumption that man had fathered the weapon. The weapon, instead, had fathered man." And Ardrey immediately adds: "The mightiest predators had come about as the logical conclusion to an evolutionary transition. With his big brain and his stone handaxes, man annihilated a predecessor who fought only with bones. And if all human history from that date has turned on the development of superior weapons, then it is for very sound reason. It is for genetic necessity." Violent episodes, together with such diverse happenings as the present armaments race and the rise of Hitler youth can be accounted for by what Ardrey variably calls "genetic necessity," or "animal instincts," or "drive." Ardrey clearly means to say that today we act violently toward one another in the sense that we cannot elect to do otherwise. All is determined by our animal ancestry in general, and in particular by "the legacy bequeathed us by those killer apes, our immediate forebears."

One might unfairly dismiss *African Genesis* as the work of a man without proper scientific credentials. Few would dispute the credentials of Konrad Lorenz. Lorenz hopes to explain events such as the dropping of bombs ". . . on sleeping cities, thereby committing hundreds and thousands of children to a horrible death in the flame" by "perfectly good-natured men who would not even smack a naughty child." Incidents like these are "amazing paradoxes," says Lorenz. But, he explains, they fall into place ". . . like the pieces of a jigsaw puzzle, if one assumes that human behavior, and particularly social behavior, far from being determined by reason and cultural tradition alone, is still subject to all the laws prevailing in all phylogenetically adapted instinctive behavior." Our problem started, according to Lorenz, when our vegetable-loving ancestors first used tools. Immediately, as evolutionary time goes, they began to hunt and eat meat. Having none of the natural inhibitions of meat eaters, they became unnaturally aggressive, and killed and even ate one another. There are differences between Ardrey and Lorenz, but on these two essentials they agree (a) man originated in violence, and (b) since we are tied to our origins, we are necessarily violent.

I am not of course the first to discuss *On Aggression* and *African Genesis*. Some reviews imply that the books are appealing because the ideas expressed in them are useful. Let us consider just how the ideas may be used according to those who write in this vein.

There is much aggression in the world, the argument goes, and we do not understand why this should be so. Ardrey and Lorenz have an answer that is direct and requires nothing from us. "It is easy," writes one reviewer, "to accept the idea of an instinctive cause for man's aggression for that explains everything." The answer of Ardrey and Lorenz is not only useful for explaining everything; it works equally well on particular things. Specifically, it has been applied to the Vietnam war, as follows:

"A line of argument like that of Ardrey's, therefore, seems to legitimate our present morality, in regarding the threat system as dominant at all costs, by reference to our biological ancestors. If the names of both antiquity and science can be drawn upon to legitimate our behavior, the moral uneasiness about napalm and the massacre of the innocent in Vietnam may be assuaged." Neither you, nor I, nor the commentators cited above really know how anyone uses the ideas found in these books. The alleged wide readership may reside more in literary merit than in ideology. It may be, as another commentator says, that the works of Ardrey and Lorenz are popular because many people enjoy reading about animals. In any case, if the scientific foundation is difficult to accept, so will be any application dangled from it. It is from two disciplines—ethology and anthropology—that the scientific argument of Ardrey and Lorenz is drawn.

The contribution from ethology is based upon an operation I call *beastomorphizing*. This word is not in the dictionary, so I will describe it by reference to a word that is in the dictionary, namely anthropomorphizing. When one attributes human characteristics to a non-human animal, he is anthropomorphizing. Doing the same thing in the opposite direction, that is, attributing animal characteristics to humans, is beastomorphizing.

The scientific vocabulary of Ardrey and Lorenz includes the term anthropomorphize. I counted five appearances of it in *On Aggression,* and it occurs at least four times in *African Genesis.* It is usually accompanied with the statement that the author knows better than to do this wrong-headed kind of thing. Beastomorphizing is an entirely different matter: it is advanced as a pathway to truth. So much is this the case that one need only describe some particular behavior pattern such as of wild geese. The similarities to human patterns are then clear, and further argument would be, to use Lorenz's term, "superfluous." In this same mode, Ardrey tells us that the ". . . animal foundation for that form of human misconduct known as war, is so obvious as to demand small attention."

This marks an unusual departure in scientific method. The connection between a caged rat, an aquarium fish, and me is not self-evident. It is no easy matter to show that the three of us need oxygen to live, or that we are more closely related to each other than any one of us is related to an ant. To establish the connection between behaviors, one must specifically demonstrate the connection, not simply place them side by side. Those who see a man in the face of a dog are no worse off than those who see a dog in the face of a man. That is to say, beastomorphizing is as suspect as anthropomorphizing.

In the literature, the ethology of Ardrey and Lorenz is picked apart rather fully; by contrast, their anthropology is neglected. The best guess as to why this is so is that few commentators know the available hard evidence concerning man's origin. Instead of confronting the Ardrey-Lorenz origin story point-for-point, I offer a background to help the reader formulate an independent judgment.

A familiar, if minimal, portrait of early man contains four elements: a cave, an artifact, a man, and a source of food. Usually the man is shown peering off into the distance in search of game. This portrait is, first of all, historically significant. The evidence that led to the fall of the literal interpretation of the bible consisted of finding in the same geological deposit, in close association, three kinds of things: the bones of extinct animals, the bones of men, and materials shaped by men. All of the elements could be found, in association as far back as forty thousand years ago, thus extending man's presence on earth ten times that allowed under the biblical model. However, the association is not as common as is often supposed. It is therefore fortunate that enough examples of it were discovered to convince nineteenth-century man of the antiquity of his descent.

The portrait also serves to illustrate how evidence changes with time. The first substantial evidence for the use of caves by man occurs half a million years ago. If we want a portrait prior to that time, we remove the cave. As we move backwards to about one-half million years ago, we pass three species of the genus *Homo.* The man at the cave entrance continuously changes in detail. For example, moving backwards at first he has a chin and then he has none. Toward the two million years mark, we need to choose some form of our ancestor to represent our closest relative. Interpretation of much of the fossil evidence in the last decade is confused; whatever the choice, there will be a clatter of dissent. How much of the man to draw is independent of the kind of man drawn. The bone is the same, whether it be a femur of *Homo erectus* or *Homo sapiens*. The rule is simple: the further back in time, the less there is likely to be. The food source in the portrait is subject to the same rule of decay, and if the source were not attached to a bony skeleton, the chance of its survival as evidence would be close to zero. We can now redraw a portrait that more closely approximates earliest man: this second version consists of a few scraps of animal and human bone and an artifact. Let us focus down on the artifact.

An early man made many things in his lifetime and he dropped them over a wide area. By contrast, one man has one skeleton and this he deposits in one place. The things men made were often fashioned from durable material and they outlasted their maker's bones. The abundance, distribution, and material of man's workmanship should make artifacts the best source for reconstructing behavior. Yet, as we approach our expected origin, it becomes increasingly difficult to tell whether something is or is not an artifact. This is particularly the case if questionable specimens are found in places where auxiliary clues are hard or impossible to find. For example, on an open plain the bones of men and animals are often absent, and the materials shaped by men are mixed with materials altered by natural agencies alone. If artifacts occur in such a setting, they will be outnumbered by hundreds of thousands of similar-looking objects. The expectation is that the earlier the artifact, the simpler it will be. The simpler it is, the more like naturally broken materials it will be. There should be verifiable ways to distinguish a bone or a rock fractured by a man from one that has been changed by other means such as rolling in a rapid stream. Right now, authoritative pronouncement decides the issue, although the first steps away from this have been taken. What if we decide that something was made by man? The next question is: what was it used for? The means for deciding this issue are slightly better than those employed to determine whether something was made by man, but any as-to-use inference is only one of many possibilities. We redraw the portrait of earliest man once again, this time adding something. In the third and final version, there are a few scraps of bone and a broken rock with a question mark on it. It is from evidence such as this that stories about man's origin are woven.

The foregoing provides minimal critical equipment for examining notions about man's origin, violent or otherwise. Let us finally consider a few alternate ways of thinking about the evidence, in particular the cultural evidence. Coda: another piece of critical equipment.

For generations, people thought that simply shaped stones were made in heaven. Michel Mercatus, physician to Pope Clement VIII wrote: "Some people carry them as a protection against lightning, and believe that this power derives from the fact that they are hurled down by the lightning. But it is the place *where* they fall that receives such immunity, and this is a matter of pure chance." This view was recorded sometime before 1590. Modern men call these same rocks artifacts and say that they were made on earth. However, it is still possible to look at the same thing and see different things. J. B. S. Haldane looked at the first one hundred thousand years of stone tools and thought that they might have been made by instinct in the same way, to use his analogy, as spiders weave webs. V. G. Childe looked at somewhat later specimens and thought they showed an implicit knowledge of cause and effect. Childe discovered the origins of scientific thought in stone tools. Robert Ardrey looked at the same things Mercatus, Haldane, and Childe looked at before him, and Ardrey says that ". . . they reveal the continuity of developments in man's cultural efforts is not truly that of the tool; it is that of the weapon."

In her lectures on Stonehenge, Jacquette Hawkes shows sketches of that famous and complex artifact done at different times. In the romantic era, the stones are jagged; in classical times, stones were drawn with smooth lines. "Every age," concludes Miss Hawkes, "has the Stonehenge it deserves—or desires."

A case could be made for the idea that man's early artifacts are more related to aesthetics than to aggression. Early workmanship shows a scarcity in design that compares favorably with many modern concepts of the beautiful. Later artifacts show elaboration that reached beyond any practical functions. These specimens fit yet another concept of the beautiful. Were these shaped stones really weapons that led to the irresistible built-in need to kill members of our own species? Answered directly, thoughts about earliest man and his way of life are mostly reflections of our particular vision of man.

Part III

Person and Group

17.

FINAL NOTE ON A CASE OF EXTREME ISOLATION

Kingsley Davis

For centuries there have been reports of children who were raised by animals or in some other way managed to live in complete isolation from human beings. If such feral men could be found, they would have great significance for social science, since they would provide a crucial means of determining the nature and extent of sociocultural influence on human behavior. Investigation of all reported cases has, however, shown them to have little validity and to be heavily laden with myth and rumor. It is highly doubtful if any child ever lived without at least some human association. In recent years, however, a few verified instances have been found in which extremely limited association with humans has occurred. In this selection Kingsley Davis gives his final report on such a case and makes some comparisons between the child, Anna, and another child, Isabelle, who lived under similar circumstances. One cannot be sure to what extent Anna's failure to achieve the level of socialization of a normal ten-year-old was due to organic deficiency. Clearly, however, a tremendous change took place in her behavior after the isolation was ended. It seems certain that many typically human behavior patterns were not achieved until Anna was able to associate with other humans from whom she could learn such behavior.

Early in 1940 there appeared . . . an account of a girl called Anna.[1] She had been deprived of normal contact and had received a minimum of human care for almost the whole of her first six years of life. At that time observations were not complete and the report had a tentative character. Now, however, the girl is dead, and, with more information available, it is possible to give a fuller and more definitive description of the case from a sociological point of view.

Anna's death, caused by hemorrhagic jaundice, occurred on August 6, 1942. Having been born on March 1 or 6, 1932, she was approximately ten and a half years of

[1] Kingsley Davis, "Extreme Social Isolation of a Child," *American Journal of Sociology,* XLV (January 1940), 554–65.

Source: Kingsley Davis, *American Journal of Sociology* 45 (January 1940): 554–65. Reprinted by permission of The University of Chicago Press and the author.

The author is professor of sociology and Director of International Population and Urban Research at the University of California, Berkeley, and chairman of the National Research Council's Behavioral Science Division. He is past president of the American Sociological Association and has served as United States representative to the Population Commission of the United Nations. His main interests are population, urbanization, and family. Among his books are *Youth in Depression, Human Society,* and *The Pattern of World Urbanization.*

age when she died. The previous report covered her development up to the age of almost eight years; the present one recapitulates the earlier period on the basis of new evidence and then covers the last two and a half years of her life.

EARLY HISTORY

The first few days and weeks of Anna's life were complicated by frequent changes of domicile. It will be recalled that she was an illegitimate child, the second such child born to her mother, and that her grandfather, a widowed farmer in whose house her mother lived, strongly disapproved of this new evidence of the mother's indiscretion. This fact led to the baby's being shifted about.

Two weeks after being born in a nurse's private home, Anna was brought to the family farm, but the grandfather's antagonism was so great that she was shortly taken to the house of one of her mother's friends. At this time a local minister became interested in her and took her to his house with an idea of possible adoption. He decided against adoption, however, when he discovered that she had vaginitis. The infant was then taken to a children's home in the nearest large city. This agency found that at the age of only three weeks she was already in a miserable condition, being "terribly galled and otherwise in very bad shape." It did not regard her as a likely subject for adoption but took her in for a while anyway, hoping to benefit her. After Anna had spent nearly eight weeks in this place, the agency notified her mother to come to get her. The mother responded by sending a man and his wife to the children's home with a view to their adopting Anna, but they made such a poor impression on the agency that permission was refused. Later the mother came herself and took the child out of the home and then gave her to this couple. It was in the home of this pair that a social worker found the girl a short time thereafter. The social worker went to the mother's home and pleaded with Anna's grandfather to allow the mother to bring the child home. In spite of threats, he refused. The child, by then more than four months old, was next taken to another children's home in a nearby town. A medical examination at this time revealed that she had impetigo, vaginitis, umbilical hernia, and a skin rash.

Anna remained in this second children's home for nearly three weeks, at the end of which time she was transferred to a private foster home. Since, however, the grandfather would not, and the mother could not, pay for the child's care, she was finally taken back as a last resort to the grandfather's house (at the age of five and a half months). There she remained, kept on the second floor in an atticlike room because her mother hesitated to incur the grandfather's wrath by bringing her downstairs.

The mother, a sturdy woman weighing about 180 pounds, did a man's work on the farm. She engaged in heavy work such as milking cows and tending hogs and had little time for her children. Sometimes she went out at night, in which case Anna was left entirely without attention. Ordinarily, it seems, Anna received only enough care to keep her barely alive. She appears to have been seldom moved from one position to another. Her clothing and bedding were filthy. She apparently had no instruction, no friendly attention.

It is little wonder that, when finally found and removed from the room in the grandfather's house at the age of nearly six years, the child could not talk, walk, or do anything that showed intelligence. She was in an extremely emaciated and undernourished condition, with skeletonlike legs and a bloated abdomen. She had been fed on virtually nothing except cow's milk during the years under her mother's care.

Anna's condition when found, and her subsequent improvement, have been described in the previous report. It now remains to say what happened to her after that.

LATER HISTORY

In 1939, nearly two years after being discovered, Anna had progressed, as previously reported, to the point where she could walk, understand simple commands, feed herself, achieve some neatness, remember people, etc. But she still did not speak, and, though she was much more like a normal infant of something over one year of age in mentality, she was far from normal for her age.

On August 30, 1939, she was taken to a private home for retarded children, leaving the county home where she had been for more than a year and a half. In her new setting she made some further progress, but not a great deal. In a report of an examination made November 6 of the same year, the head of the institution pictured the child as follows:

> Anna walks about aimlessly, makes periodic rhythmic motions of her hands, and, at intervals, makes guttural and sucking noises. She regards her hands as if she had seen them for the first time. It was impossible to hold her attention for more than a few seconds at a time—not because of distraction due to external stimuli but because of her inability to concentrate. She ignored the task in hand to gaze vacantly about the room. Speech is entirely lacking. Numerous unsuccessful attempts have been made with her in the hope of developing initial sounds. I do not believe that this failure is due to negativism or deafness but that she is not sufficiently developed to accept speech at this time. . . . The prognosis is not favorable. . . .

More than five months later, on April 25, 1940, a clinical psychologist, the late Professor Francis N. Maxfield, examined Anna and reported the following: large for her age; hearing "entirely normal"; vision apparently normal; able to climb stairs; speech in the "babbling stage" and "promise for developing intelligible speech later seems to be good." He said further that "on the Merrill-Palmer scale she made a mental score of 19 months. On the Vineland social maturity scale she made a score of 23 months."

Professor Maxfield very sensibly pointed out that prognosis is difficult in such case of isolation. "It is very difficult to take scores on tests standardized under average conditions of environment and experience," he wrote, "and interpret them in a case where environment and experience have been so unusual." With this warning he gave it as his opinion at that time that Anna would eventually "attain an adult mental level of six or seven years."

The school for retarded children, on July 1, 1941, reported that Anna had reached 46 inches in height and weighed 60 pounds. She could bounce and catch a ball and was said to conform to group socialization, though as a follower rather than a leader. Toilet habits were firmly established. Food habits were normal, except that she still used a spoon as her sole implement. She could dress herself except for fastening her clothes. Most remarkable of all, she had finally begun to develop speech. She was characterized as being at about the two-year level in this regard. She could call attendants by name and bring in one when she was asked to. She had a few complete sentences to express her wants. The report concluded that there was nothing peculiar about her, except that she was feebleminded—"probably congenital in type."

A final report from the school, made on June 22, 1942, and evidently the last report before the girl's death, pictured only a slight advance over that given above. It said that Anna could follow directions, string beads, identify a few colors, build with blocks, and differentiate between attractive and unattractive pictures. She had a good sense of rhythm and loved a doll. She talked mainly in phrases but would repeat words and try to carry on a conversation. She was clean about clothing. She habitually washed her hands and brushed her teeth. She would try to help other children. She walked well and could run fairly well, though clumsily. Although easily excited, she had a pleasant disposition.

INTERPRETATION

Such was Anna's condition just before her death. It may seem as if she had not made much progress, but one must remember the condition in which she had been found. One must recall that she had no glimmering of speech, absolutely no ability to walk, no sense of gesture, not the least capacity to feed herself even when the food was put in front of her, and no comprehension of cleanliness. She was so apathetic that it was hard to tell whether or not she could hear. And all this at the age of nearly six years. Compared with this condition, her capacities at the time of her death seem striking indeed, though they do not amount to much more than a two-and-a-half-year mental level. One conclusion therefore seems safe, namely, that her isolation prevented a considerable amount of mental development that was undoubtedly part of her capacity. Just what her original capacity was, of course, is hard to say; but her development after her period of confinement (including the ability to walk and run, to play, dress, fit into a social situation, and, above all, to speak) shows that she had at least this much capacity—capacity that never could have been realized in her original condition of isolation.

A further question is this: What would she have been like if she had received a normal upbringing from the moment of birth? A definitive answer would have been impossible in any case, but even an approximate answer is made difficult by her early death. If one assumes, as was tentatively surmised in the previous report, that it is "almost impossible for any child to learn to speak, think, and act like a normal person after a long period of early isolation," it seems likely that Anna might have had a normal or near-normal capacity, genetically speaking. On the other hand, it was pointed out that Anna represented "a marginal case, [because] she was discovered before she had reached six years of age," an age "young enough to allow for some plasticity." While admitting, then, that Anna's isolation *may* have been the major cause (and was certainly a minor cause) of her lack of rapid mental progress during the four and a half years following her rescue from neglect, it is necessary to entertain the hypothesis that she was congenitally deficient.

In connection with this hypothesis, one suggestive though by no means conclusive circumstance needs consideration, namely, the mentality of Anna's forebears. Information on this subject is easier to obtain, as one might guess, on the mother's than on the father's side. Anna's maternal grandmother, for example, is said to have been college educated and wished to have her children receive a good education, but her husband, Anna's stern grandfather, apparently a shrewd, hard-driving, calculating farmowner, was so penurious that her ambitions in this direction were thwarted. Under the circumstances her daughter (Anna's mother) managed, despite having to do hard work on the farm, to complete the eighth grade in a country school. Even so, however, the daughter was evidently not very smart. "A schoolmate of [Anna's mother] stated that she was retarded in school work; was very gullible at this age; and that her morals even at this time were discussed by other students." Two tests administered to her on March 4, 1938, when she was thirty-two years of age, showed that she was mentally deficient. On the Stanford Revision of the Binet-Simon Scale her performance was equivalent to that of a child of eight years, giving her an I.Q. of 50 and indicating mental deficiency of "middle-grade moron type."

As to the identity of Anna's father, the most persistent theory holds that he was an old man about seventy-four years of age at the time of the girl's birth. If he was the one, there is no indication of mental or other biological deficiency, whatever one may think of his morals. However, someone else may actually have been the father.

To sum up: Anna's heredity is the kind that *might* have given rise to innate mental deficiency, though not necessarily.

COMPARISON WITH ANOTHER CASE

Perhaps more to the point than speculations about Anna's ancestry would be a case for comparison. If a child could be discovered who had been isolated about the same length of time as Anna but had achieved a much quicker recovery and a greater mental development, it would be a stronger indication that Anna was deficient to start with.

Such a case does exist. It is the case of a girl found at about the same time as Anna and under strikingly similar circumstances. A full description of the details of this case has not been published, but, in addition to newspaper reports, an excellent preliminary account by a speech specialist, Dr. Marie K. Mason, who played an important role in the handling of the child, has appeared. Also the late Dr. Francis N. Maxfield, clinical psychologist at Ohio State University, as was Dr. Mason, has written [a] penetrating analysis of the case. Some of his observations have been included in Professor Zingg's book on feral man. The following discussion is drawn mainly from these enlightening materials. The writer, through the kindness of Professors Mason and Maxfield, did have a chance to observe the girl in April, 1940, and to discuss the features of her case with them.

Born apparently one month later than Anna, the girl in question, who has been given the pseudonym Isabelle, was discovered in November, 1938, nine months after the discovery of Anna. At the time she was found she was approximately six and a half years of age. Like Anna, she was an illegitimate child and had been kept in seclusion for that reason. Her mother was a deaf-mute, having become so at the age of two, and it appears that she and Isabelle had spent most of their time together in a dark room shut off from the rest of the mother's family. As a result Isabelle had no chance to develop speech; when she communicated with her mother, it was by means of gestures. Lack of sunshine and inadequacy of diet had caused Isabelle to become rachitic. Her legs in particular were affected; they "were so bowed that as she stood erect the soles of her shoes came nearly flat together, and she got about with a skittering gait." Her behavior toward strangers, especially men, was almost that of a wild animal, manifesting much fear and hostility. In lieu of speech she made only a strange croaking sound. In many ways she acted like an infant. "She was apparently utterly unaware of relationships of any kind. When presented with a ball for the first time, she held it in the palm of her hand, then reached out and stroked my face with it. Such behavior is comparable to that of a child of six months." At first it was even hard to tell whether or not she could hear, so unused were her senses. Many of her actions resembled those of deaf children.

It is small wonder that, once it was established that she could hear, specialists working with her believed her to be feebleminded. Even on nonverbal tests her performance was so low as to promise little for the future. Her first score on the Stanford-Binet was 19 months, practically at the zero point of the scale. On the Vineland social maturity scale her first score was 39, representing an age level of two and a half years. "The general impression was that she was wholly uneducable and that any attempt to teach her to speak, after so long a period of silence, would meet with failure."

In spite of this interpretation, the individuals in charge of Isabelle launched a systematic and skillful program of training. It seemed hopeless at first. The approach had to be through pantomime and dramatization, suitable to an infant. It required one week of intensive effort before she even made her first attempt at vocalization. Gradually she began to respond, however, and, after the first hurdles had at last been overcome, a curious thing happened. She went through the usual stages of learning characteristic of the years from one to six not only in proper succession but far more rapidly than normal. In a little over two months after her first vocalization she was putting sentences together. Nine months after that she could identify words and sentences on the printed page, could write well, could add to ten, and could retell a story after hearing it. Seven months beyond this point she had a vocabulary of 1,500–2,000 words and was asking complicated questions. Starting from an educational level of between one and three years (depending on what aspect one considers), she had reached a normal level by the time she was eight and a half years old. In short, she covered in two years the stages of learning that ordinarily require six. Or, to put it another way, her I.Q. trebled in a year and a half. The speed with which she reached the normal level of mental development seems analogous to the recovery of body weight in a growing child after an illness, the recovery being achieved by an extra fast rate of growth for a period after the illness until normal weight for the given age is again attained.

When the writer saw Isabelle a year and a half after her discovery, she gave him the impression of being a very bright, cheerful, energetic little girl. She spoke well, walked and ran without trouble, and sang with gusto and accuracy. Today she is over fourteen years old and has passed the sixth grade in a public school. Her teachers say that she participates in all school activities as normally as other children. Though older than her classmates, she has fortunately not physically matured too far beyond their level.

Clearly the history of Isabelle's development is different from that of Anna's. In both cases there was an exceedingly low, or rather blank, intellectual level to begin with. In both cases it seemed that the girl might be congenitally feebleminded. In both a considerably higher level was reached later on. But the Ohio girl achieved a normal mentality within two years, whereas Anna was still markedly inadequate at the end of four and a half years. This difference in achievement may suggest that Anna had less initial capacity. But an alternative hypothesis is possible.

One should remember that Anna never received the prolonged and expert attention that Isabelle received. The result of such attention, in the case of the Ohio girl, was to give her speech at an early stage, and her subsequent rapid development seems to have been a consequence of that. "Until Isabelle's speech and language development, she had all the characteristics of a feebleminded child." Had Anna, who, from the standpoint of psychometric tests and early history, closely resembled this girl at the start, been given a mastery of speech at an earlier point by intensive training, her subsequent development might have been much more rapid.

The hypothesis that Anna began with a sharply inferior mental capacity is therefore not established. Even if she were deficient to start with, we have no way of knowing how much so. Under ordinary conditions she might have been a dull normal or, like her mother, a moron. Even after the blight of her isolation, if she had lived to maturity, she might have finally reached virtually the full level of her capacity, whatever it may have been. That her isolation did have a profound effect upon her mentality, there can be no doubt. This is proved by the substantial degree of change during the four and a half years following her rescue.

Consideration of Isabelle's case serves to show, as Anna's case does not clearly show, that isolation up to the age of six, with failure to acquire any form of speech and hence failure to grasp nearly the whole world of cultural meaning, does not preclude the subsequent acquisition of these. Indeed, there seems to be a process of accelerated recovery in which the child goes through the mental stages at a more rapid rate than would be the case in normal development. Just what would be the maximum age at which a person could remain isolated and still retain the capacity for full cultural acquisition is hard to say. Almost certainly it would not be as high as age fifteen; it might possibly be as low as age ten. Undoubtedly various individuals would differ considerably as to the exact age.

Anna's is not an ideal case for showing the effects of extreme isolation, partly because she was possibly deficient to begin with, partly because she did not receive the best training available, and partly because she did not live long enough. Nevertheless, her case is instructive when placed in the record with numerous other cases of extreme isolation. This and the previous article about her are meant to place her in the record. It is to be hoped that other cases will be described in the scientific literature as they are discovered (as unfortunately they will be), for only in these rare cases of extreme isolation is it possible "to observe *concretely separated* two factors in the development of human personality which are always otherwise only analytically separated, the biogenic and the sociogenic factors."

18.

KILLERS OF THE DREAM: WHEN I WAS A CHILD

Lillian Smith

The previous selection illustrates the importance of association with other human beings in the development of human personality. Since the transmission to children of human habits, attitudes, and beliefs begins very early, and goes on constantly in every family, school, and other groups, we are often not keenly aware of this pervasive social process. In this selection Lillian Smith reveals, with sensitivity and candor, how she was taught a particular pattern of behavior and attitudes considered appropriate for white southern Christian girls of her generation. What is considered right and proper for comparable girls of today cannot be stated with any certainty, for the changes Lillian Smith sought to promote by her writings seem to be definitely on the way to achievement. The soaring eloquence of Martin Luther King, Jr.'s famous "I Have a Dream" speech, for example, may well have been an outgrowth of her poetic formulation of that prophetic vision.

Even its children knew that the South was in trouble. No one had to tell them; no words said aloud. To them, it was a vague thing weaving in and out of their play, like a ghost haunting an old graveyard or whispers after the household sleeps—fleeting mystery, vague menace to which each responded in his own way. Some learned to screen out all except the soft and the soothing; others denied even as they saw plainly, and heard. But all knew that under quiet words and warmth and laughter, under the slow ease and tender concern about small matters, there was a heavy burden on all of us and as heavy a refusal to confess it. The children knew this "trouble" was bigger than they, bigger than their family, bigger than their church, so big that people turned away from its size. They had seen it flash out and shatter a town's peace, had felt it tear up all they believed in. They had measured its giant strength and felt weak when they remembered.

This haunted childhood belongs to every southerner of my age. We ran away from it but we came back like a hurt animal to

Source: Lillian Smith, *Killers of the Dream* (New York: W. W. Norton, 1949), pp. 15–28.

The author (1897–1966), a novelist, held honorary doctorate degrees from Oberlin College and Howard University. During her early career, she was principal of a two-teacher mountain school and later spent three years in China teaching music at a private school. For ten years she was editor and publisher of *South Today.* In 1950 she was granted the Southern Author's Award and also a Special Citation for Distinguished Contribution to American Letters by the National Book Award Committee. Her books include *Strange Fruit, One Hour, The Journey,* and *Now Is the Time.*

its wound, or a murderer to the scene of his sin. The human heart dares not stay away too long from that which hurt it most. There is a return journey to anguish that few of us are released from making.

. . . . .

The mother who taught me what I know of tenderness and love and compassion taught me also the bleak rituals of keeping Negroes in their "place." The father who rebuked me for an air of superiority toward schoolmates from the mill and rounded out his rebuke by gravely reminding me that "all men are brothers," trained me in the steel-rigid decorums I must demand of every colored male. They who so gravely taught me to split my body from my mind and both from my "soul," taught me also to split my conscience from my acts and Christianity from southern tradition.

Neither the Negro nor sex was often discussed at length in our home. We were given no formal instruction in these difficult matters but we learned our lessons well. We learned the intricate system of taboos, of renunciations and compensations, of manners, voice modulations, words, feelings, along with our prayers, our toilet habits, and our games. I do not remember how or when, but by the time I had learned that God is love, that Jesus is His Son and came to give us more abundant life, that all men are brothers with a common Father, I also knew that I was better than a Negro, that all black folks have their place and must be kept in it, that sex has its place and must be kept in it, that a terrifying disaster would befall the South if ever I treated a Negro as my social equal and as terrifying a disaster would befall my family if ever I were to have a baby outside of marriage. I had learned that God so loved the world that He gave His only begotten Son so that we might have segregated churches in which it was my duty to worship each Sunday and on Wednesday at evening prayers. I had learned that while southerners are a hospitable, courteous, tactful people who treat those of their own group with consideration and who as carefully segregate from all the richness of life "for their own good and welfare" thirteen million people whose skin is colored a little differently from my own.

I knew by the time I was twelve that a member of my family would always shake hands with old Negro friends, would speak graciously to members of the Negro race unless they forgot their place, in which event icy peremptory tones would draw lines beyond which only the desperate would dare take one step. I knew that to use the word "nigger" was unpardonable and no well-bred southerner was quite so crude as to do so; nor would a well-bred southerner call a Negro "mister" or invite him into the living room or eat with him or sit by him in public places.

I knew that my old nurse who had cared for me through long months of illness, who had given me refuge when a little sister took my place as the baby of the family, who soothed, fed me, delighted me with her stories and games, let me fall asleep on her deep warm breast, was not worthy of the passionate love I felt for her but must be given instead of half-smiled-at affection similar to that which one feels for one's dog. I knew but I never believed it, that the deep respect I felt for her, the tenderness, the love, was a childish thing which every normal child outgrows, that such love begins with one's toys and is discarded with them, and that somehow—though it seemed impossible to my agonized heart—I too, must outgrow these feelings. I learned to use a soft voice to oil my words of superiority. I learned to cheapen with tears and sentimental talk of "my old mammy" one of the profound relationships of my life. I learned the bitterest thing a child can learn: that the human relations I valued most were held cheap by the world I lived in.

From the day I was born, I began to learn my lessons. I was put in a rigid frame too intricate, too twisting to describe here so briefly, but I learned to conform to its slide-rule measurements. I learned it is possible to be a Christian and a white southerner simultaneously; to be a gentlewoman and an arrogant callous creature in the same moment; to pray at night and ride a Jim Crow car the next morning and to feel comfortable in doing both. I learned to believe in freedom, to glow when the word *democracy* was used, and to practice slavery from morning to night. I learned it the way all my southern people learn it: by closing door after door until one's mind and heart and conscience are blocked off from each other and from reality.

I closed the doors. Or perhaps they were closed for me. One day they began to open again. Why I had the desire or the strength to open them, or what strange accident or circumstance opened them for me would require in the answering an account too long, too particular, too stark to make here. And perhaps I should not have the wisdom that such an analysis would demand of me, nor the will to make it. I know only that the doors opened, a little; that somewhere along that iron corridor we travel from babyhood to maturity, doors swinging inward began to swing outward, showing glimpses of the world beyond, of that bright thing we call "reality."

I believe there is one experience which pushed these doors open, a little. And I am going to tell it here, although I know well that to excerpt from a life and family background one incident and name it as a "cause" of a change in one's life direction is a distortion and often an irrelevance. The hungers of a child and how they are filled have too much to do with the way in which experiences are assimilated to tear an incident out of life and look at it in isolation. Yet, with these reservations, I shall tell it, not because it was in itself a severe trauma, but because it became a symbol of buried experiences that I did not have access to. It is an incident that has rarely happened to other southern children. In a sense, unique. But it was an acting-out, a private production of a little script that is written on the lives of most southern children before they know the words. Though they may not have seen it staged this way, each southerner has had his own private showing.

I should like to preface the account by giving a brief glimpse of my family, hoping the reader, entering my home with me, will be able to blend the edges of this isolated experience into a more full life picture and in doing so will see that it is, in a sense, everybody's story.

I was born and reared in a small Deep South town whose population was about equally Negro and white. There were nine of us who grew up freely in a rambling house of many rooms, surrounded by big lawn, back yard, gardens, fields, and barn. It was the kind of home that gathers memories like dust, a place filled with laughter and play and pain and hurt and ghosts and games. We were given such advantages of schooling, music, and art as were available in the South, and our world was not limited to the South, for travel to far places seemed a natural thing to us, and usually one of the family was in a remote part of the earth.

We knew we were a respected and important family of this small town but beyond this we gave little thought to status. Our father made money in lumber and naval stores for the excitement of making and losing it—not for what money can buy nor the security which it sometimes gives. I do not remember at any time wanting "to be rich" nor do I remember that thrift and saving were ideals which our parents considered important enough to urge upon us. In the family there was acceptance of risk, a mild delight in burning bridges, an expectant "What next?" We were not irresponsible; living according to the pleasure principle was by no means our way of life. On the contrary we were trained to think that each of us should do something of genuine usefulness, and the family thought it right to make sacrifices if necessary, to give each child preparation for such work. We were also trained to think learning important, and books; but "bad" books our mother burned. We valued music and art and craftsmanship but it was people and their welfare and religion that were the foci around which our lives seemed naturally to move. Above all else, the important thing was what we "planned to do." That each of us must do something was as inevitable as breathing for we owed a "debt to society which must be paid." This was a family commandment.

While many neighbors spent their energies in counting limbs on the family tree and grafting some on now and then to give symmetry to it, or in licking scars to cure their vague malaise, or in fighting each battle and turn of battle of the Civil War which has haunted the southern conscience so long, my father was pushing his nine children straight into the future. "You have your heritage," he used to say, "some of it good, some not so good; and as far as I know you had the usual number of grandmothers and grandfathers. Yes, there were slaves, too many of them in the family, but that was your grandfather's mistake, not yours. The past has been lived. It is gone. The future is yours. What are you going to do with it? He asked this question often and sometimes one knew it was but an echo of a question he had spent his life trying to answer for himself. For the future held my father's dreams; always there, not in the past, did he expect to find what he had spent his life searching for.

We lived the same segregated life as did other southerners but our parents talked in excessively Christian and democratic terms. We were told ten thousand times that status and money are unimportant (though we were well supplied with both); we were told that "all men are brothers," that we are a part of a democracy and must act like democrats. We were told that the teachings of Jesus are important and could be practiced if we tried. We were told that to be "radical" is bad, silly too; and that one must always conform to the "best behavior" of one's community and make it better if one can. We were taught that we were superior to hate and resentment, and that no member of the Smith family could stoop so low as to have an enemy. No matter what injury was done us, we must not injure ourselves further by retaliating. That was a family commandment.

We had family prayers once each day. All of us as children read the Bible in its entirety each year. We memorized hundreds of Bible verses and repeated them at breakfast, and said "sentence prayers" around the family table. God was not someone we met on Sunday but a permanent member of our household. It never occurred to me until I was fourteen or fifteen years old that He did not chalk up the daily score on eternity's tablets.

Despite the strain of living so intimately with God, the nine of us were strong, healthy, energetic youngsters who filled days with play and sports and music and books and managed to live most of the time on the careless level at which young lives should be lived. We had our times of anxiety of course, for there were hard lessons to be learned about the soul and "bad things" to be learned about sex. Sometimes I have wondered how we learned them with a mother so shy with words.

She was a wistful creature who loved beautiful things like lace and sunsets and flowers in a vague inarticulate way, and took good care of her children. We always knew this was not her world but one she accepted under duress. Her private world we rarely entered, though the shadow of it lay heavily on our hearts.

Our father owned large business interests, employed hundreds of colored and white laborers, paid them the prevailing low wages, worked them the prevailing long hours, built for them mill towns (Negro and white), built for each group a church, saw to it that religion was supplied free, saw to it that a commissary supplied commodities at a high price, and in general managed his affairs much as ten thousand other southern businessmen managed theirs.

. . . . .

Against this backdrop the drama of the South was played out one day in my life:

A little white girl was found in the colored section of our town, living with a Negro family in a broken-down shack. This family had moved in a few weeks before and little was known of them. One of the ladies in my mother's club, while driving over to her washerwoman's, saw the child swinging on a gate. The shack, as she said, was hardly more than a pigsty and this white child was living with dirty and sick-looking colored folks. "They must have kidnapped her," she told her friends. Genuinely shocked, the clubwomen busied themselves in an attempt to do something, for the child was very white indeed. The strange Negroes were subjected to a grueling questioning and finally grew evasive and refused to talk at all. This only increased the suspicion of the white group. The next day the clubwomen, escorted by the town marshal, took the child from her adopted family despite their tears.

She was brought to our home. I do not know why my mother consented to this plan. Perhaps because she loved children and always showed concern for them. It was easy for one more to fit into our ample household and Janie was soon at home there. She roomed with me, sat next to me at the table; I found Bible verses for her to say at breakfast; she wore my clothes, played with my dolls, and followed me around from morning to night. She was dazed by her new comforts and by the interesting activities of this big lively family; and I was as happily dazed, for her adoration was a new thing to me; and as time passed a quick, childish, and deeply felt bond grew up between us.

But a day came when a telephone message was received from a colored orphanage. There was a meeting at our home. Many whispers. All afternoon the ladies went in and out of our house talking to Mother in tones too low for children to hear. As they passed us at play, they looked at Janie and quickly looked away again, though a few stopped and stared at her as if they could not tear their eyes from her face. When my father came home Mother closed her door against our young ears and talked a long time with him. I heard him laugh, heard Mother say, "But Papa, this is no laughing matter!" And then they were back in the living room with us and my mother was pale and my father was saying, "Well, work it out, Mame, as best you can. After all, now that you know, it is pretty simple."

In a little while my mother called my sister and me into her bedroom and told us that in the morning Janie would return to Colored Town. She said Janie was to have the dresses the ladies had given her and a few of my own, and the toys we had shared with her. She asked me if I would like to give Janie one of my dolls. She seemed hurried, though Janie was not to leave until next day. She said "Why not select it now?" And in dreamlike stiffness I brought in my dolls and chose one for Janie. And then I found it possible to say, "Why is she leaving? She likes us, she hardly knows them. She told me she had been with them only a month."

"Because," Mother said gently, "Janie is a little colored girl."

"But she's white!"

"We were mistaken. She is colored."

"But she looks—"

"She is colored. Please don't argue!"

"What does it mean?" I whispered.

"It means," Mother said slowly, "that she has to live in Colored Town with colored people."

"But why? She lived here three weeks and she doesn't belong to them, she told me so."

"She is a little colored girl."

"But you said yourself she has nice manners. You said that," I persisted.

"Yes, she is a nice child. But a colored child cannot live in our home."

"Why?"

"You know, dear! You have always known that white and colored people do not live together."

"Can she come to play?"

"No."

"I don't understand."

"I don't either," my young sister quavered.

"You're too young to understand. And don't ask me again, ever again, about this!" Mother's voice was sharp but her face was sad and there was no certainty left there. She hurried out and busied herself in the kitchen and I wandered through that room where I had been born, touching the old familiar things in it, looking at them, trying to find the answer to a question that moaned like a hurt thing. . . .

And then I went out to Janie, who was waiting, knowing things were happening that concerned her but waiting until they were spoken aloud.

I do not know quite how the words were said but I told her she was to return in the morning to the little place where she had lived because she was colored and colored children could not live with white children.

"Are you white?" she said.

"I'm white," I replied, "and my sister is white. And you're colored. And white and colored can't live together because my mother says so."

"Why?" Janie whispered.

"Because they can't," I said. But I knew, though I said it firmly, that something was wrong. I knew my mother and father whom I passionately admired had betrayed something which they held dear. And they could not help doing it. And I was shamed by their failure and frightened, for I felt they were no longer as powerful as I had thought. There was something Out There that was stronger than they and I could not bear to believe it. I could not confess that my father, who always solved the family dilemmas easily and with laughter, could not solve this. I knew that my mother who was so good to children did not believe in her heart that she was being good to this child. There was not a word in my mind that said it but my body knew and my glands, and I was filled with anxiety.

But I felt compelled to believe they were right. It was the only way my world could be held together. And, slowly, it began to seep through me: *I was white. She was colored. We must not be together. It was bad to be together. Though you ate with your nurse when you were little, it was bad to eat with any colored person after that. It was bad just as other things were bad that your mother had told you. It was bad that she was to sleep in the room with me that night. It was bad. . . .*

I was overcome with guilt. For three weeks I had done things that white children were not supposed to do. And now I knew these things had been wrong.

I went to the piano and began to play, as I had always done when I was in trouble. I tried to play my next lesson and as I stumbled through it, the little girl came over and sat on the bench with me. Feeling lost in the deep currents sweeping through our house that night, she crept closer and put her arms around me and I shrank away as if my body had been uncovered. I had not said a word, I did not say one, but she knew, and tears slowly rolled down her little white face. . . .

And then I forgot it. For more than thirty years the experience was wiped out of my memory. But that night, and the weeks it was tied to, worked its way like a splinter, bit by bit, down to the hurt places in my memory and festered there. And as I grew older, as more experiences collected around that faithless time, as memories of earlier, more profound hurts crept closer, drawn to that night as if to a magnet, I began to know that people who talked of love and children did not mean it. That is a hard thing for a child to learn. I still admired my parents, there was so much that was strong and vital and sane and good about them and I never forgot this; I stubbornly believed in their sincerity, as I do to this day, and I loved them. Yet in my heart they were under suspicion. Something was wrong.

Something was wrong with a world that tells you that love is good and people are important and then forces you to deny love and to humiliate people. I knew, though I would not for years confess it aloud, that in trying to shut the Negro race away from us, we have shut ourselves away from so many good, creative, honest, deeply human things in life. I began to understand slowly at first but more clearly as the years passed, that the warped, distorted frame we have put around every Negro child from birth is around every white child also. Each is on a different side of the frame but each is pinioned there. And I knew that what cruelly shapes and cripples the personality of one is as cruelly shaping and crippling the personality of the other. I began to see that though we may, as we acquire new knowledge, live through new experiences, examine old memories, gain the strength to tear the frame from us, yet we are stunted and warped and in our lifetime cannot grow straight again any more than can a tree, put in a steel-like twisting frame when young, grow tall and straight when the frame is torn away at maturity.

As I sit here writing, I can almost touch that little town, so close is the memory of it. There it lies, its main street lined with great oaks, heavy with matted moss that swings softly even now as I remember. A little white town rimmed with Negroes, making a deep shadow on the whiteness. There it lies, broken in two by one strange idea. Minds broken. Hearts broken. Conscience torn from acts. A culture split in a thousand pieces. That is segregation. I am remembering: a woman in a mental hospital walking four steps out, four steps in, unable to go further because she has drawn an invisible line around her small world and is terrified to take one step beyond it. . . . A man in a Disturbed Ward assigning "places" to the other patients and violently insisting that each stay in his place. . . . A Negro woman saying to me so quietly, "We cannot ride together on the bus, you know. It is not legal to be human down here."

Memory, walking the streets of one's childhood . . . of the town where one was born.

19.

STATUS AND ROLE

Ralph Linton

Through their behavior in various groups people come to perform certain roles and acquire statuses. Ralph Linton's discussion of these two concepts has become a classic. He examines the theory of status and role with illustrations from both nonliterate and complex societies.

The term *status,* like the term *culture,* has come to be used with a double significance. A *status,* in the abstract, is a position in a particular pattern. It is thus quite correct to speak of each individual as

Source: Ralph Linton, *The Study of Man* (New York: Appleton-Century-Crofts, 1936), pp. 113–21.

The author (1893–1953) was Sterling Professor of Anthropology at Yale University. He was Assistant Curator of North American Ethnology, Field Museum of Natural History. He has been described as one of the greatest anthropologists of the present era. Among his works are *Acculturation in Seven American Indian Tribes; The Cultural Background of Personality; Most of the World: The Peoples of Africa, Latin America, and the East Today;* and *The Tree of Culture.*

having many statuses, since each individual participates in the expression of a number of patterns. However, unless the term is qualified in some way, *the status of* any individual means the sum total of all the statuses which he occupies. It represents his position with relation to the total society. Thus the status of Mr. Jones as a member of his community derives from a combination of all the statuses which he holds as a citizen, as an attorney, as a Mason, as a Methodist, as Mrs. Jones's husband, and so on.

A status, as distinct from the individual who may occupy it, is simply a collection of rights and duties. Since these rights and duties can find expression only through the medium of individuals, it is extremely hard for us to maintain a distinction in our thinking between statuses and the people who hold them and exercise the rights and duties which constitute them. The relation between any individual and any status he holds is somewhat like that between the driver of an automobile and the driver's place in the machine. The driver's seat with its steering wheel, accelerator, and other controls is a constant with ever-present potentialities for action and control, while the driver may be any member of the family and may exercise these potentialities very well or very badly.

A *rôle* represents the dynamic aspect of a status. The individual is socially assigned to a status and occupies it with relation to other statuses. When he puts the rights and duties which constitute the status into effect, he is performing a rôle. Rôle and status are quite inseparable, and the distinction between them is of only academic interest. There are no rôles without statuses or statuses without rôles. Just as in the case of *status,* the term *rôle* is used with a double significance. Every individual has a series of rôles deriving from the various patterns in which he participates and at the same time a *rôle,* general, which represents the sum total of these rôles and determines what he does for his society and what he can expect from it.

Although all statuses and rôles derive from social patterns and are integral parts of patterns, they have an independent function with relation to the individuals who occupy particular statuses and exercise their rôles. To such individuals the combined status and rôle represent the minimum of attitudes and behavior which he must assume if he is to participate in the overt expression of the pattern. Status and rôle serve to reduce the ideal patterns for social life to individual terms. They become models for organizing the attitudes and behavior of the individual so that these will be congruous with those of the other individuals participating in the expression of the pattern. Thus if we are studying football teams in the abstract, the position of quarterback is meaningless except in relation to the other positions. From the point of view of the quarterback himself it is a distinct and important entity. It determines where he shall take his place in the line-up and what he shall do in various plays. His assignment to this position at once limits and defines his activities and establishes a minimum of things which he must learn. Similarly, in a social pattern such as that for the employer-employee relationship the statuses of employer and employee define what each has to know and do to put the pattern into operation. The employer does not need to know the techniques involved in the employee's labor, and the employee does not need to know the techniques for marketing or accounting.

It is obvious that, as long as there is no interference from external sources, the more perfectly the members of any society are adjusted to their statuses and rôles the more smoothly the society will function. In its attempts to bring about such adjustments every society finds itself caught on the horns of a dilemma. The individual's formation of habits and attitudes begins at birth, and, other things being equal, the earlier his training for a status can begin the more successful it is likely to be. At the same time, no two individuals are alike, and a status which will be congenial to one may be quite uncongenial to another. Also, there are in all social systems certain rôles which require more than training for their successful performance. Perfect technique does not make a great violinist, nor a thorough book knowledge of tactics an efficient general. The utilization of the special gifts of individuals may be highly important to society, as in the case of the general, yet these gifts usually show themselves rather late, and to wait upon their manifestation for the assignment of statuses would be to forfeit the advantages to be derived from commencing training early.

Fortunately, human beings are so mutable that almost any normal individual can be trained to the adequate performance of almost any rôle. Most of the business of living can be conducted on a basis of habit, with little need for intelligence and none for special gifts. Societies have met the dilemma by developing two types of statuses, the *ascribed* and the *achieved.* Ascribed statuses are those which are assigned to individuals without reference to their innate differences or abilities. They can be predicted and trained for from the moment of birth. The *achieved* statuses are, as a minimum, those requiring special qualities, although they are not necessarily limited to these. They are not assigned to individuals from birth but are left open to be filled through competition and individual effort. The majority of the statuses in all social systems are of the ascribed type and those which take care of the ordinary day-to-day business of living are practically always of this type.

In all societies certain things are selected as reference points for the ascription of status. The things chosen for this purpose are always of such a nature that they are ascertainable at birth, making it possible to begin the training of the individual for his potential statuses and rôles at once. The simplest and most universally used of these reference points is sex. Age is used with nearly equal frequency, since all individuals pass through the same cycle of growth, maturity, and decline, and the statuses whose occupation will be determined by age can be forecast and trained for with accuracy. Family relationships, the simplest and most obvious being that of the child to its mother, are also used in all societies as reference points for the establishment of a whole series of statuses. Lastly, there is the matter of birth into a particular socially established group, such as a class or caste. The use of this type of reference is common but not universal. In all societies the actual ascription of statuses to the individual is controlled by a series of these reference points which together serve to delimit the field of his future participation in the life of the group.

The division and ascription of statuses with relation to sex seems to be basic in all social systems. All societies prescribe different attitudes and activities to men and to women. Most of them try to rationalize these prescriptions in terms of the physiological differences between the sexes or their different roles in reproduction. However, a comparative study of the statuses ascribed to women and men in different cultures seems to show that while such factors may have served as a starting point for the development of a division the actual ascriptions are almost entirely determined by culture. Even the psychological characteristics ascribed to men and women in different societies vary so much that they can have little physiological basis. Our own idea of women as ministering angels contrasts sharply with the ingenuity of women as torturers among the Iroquois and the sadistic delight they took in the process. Even the last two generations have seen a sharp change in the psychological patterns for women in our own society. The delicate, fainting lady of the middle eighteen-hundreds is as extinct as the dodo.

When it comes to the ascription of occupations, which is after all an integral part of status, we find the differences in various societies even more marked. Arapesh women regularly carry heavier loads than men "because their heads are so much harder and stronger." In some societies women do most of the manual labor; in others, as in the Marquesas, even cooking, housekeeping, and babytending are proper male occupations, and women spend most of their time primping. Even the general rule that women's handicap through pregnancy and nursing indicates the more active occupations as male and the less active ones as female has many exceptions. Thus among the Tasmanians seal-hunting was women's work. They swam out to the seal rocks, stalked the animals, and clubbed them. Tasmanian women also hunted opossums, which required the climbing of large trees.

Although the actual ascription of occupations along sex lines is highly variable, the pattern of sex division is constant. There are very few societies in which every important activity has not been definitely assigned to men or to women. Even when the two sexes cooperate in a particular occupation, the field of each is usually clearly delimited. Thus in Madagascar rice culture the men make the seed beds and terraces and prepare the fields for transplanting. The women do the work of transplanting, which is hard and backbreaking. The women weed the crop, but the men harvest it. The women then carry it to the threshing floors, where the men thresh it while the women winnow it. Lastly, the women pound the grain in mortars and cook it.

When a society takes over a new industry, there is often a period of uncertainty during which the work may be done by either sex, but it soon falls into the province of one or the other. In Madagascar, pottery is made by men in some tribes and by women in others. The only tribe in which it is made by both men and women is one into which the art has been introduced within the last sixty years. I was told that during the fifteen years preceding my visit there had been a marked decrease in the number of male potters, many men who had once practised the art having given it up. The factor of lowered wages, usually advanced as the reason for men leaving one of our own occupations when women enter it in force, certainly was not operative here. The field was not overcrowded, and the prices for men's and women's products were the same. Most of the men who had given up the trade were vague as to their reasons, but a few said frankly that they did not like to compete with women. Apparently the entry of women into the occupation had robbed it of a certain amount of prestige. It was no longer quite the thing for a man to be a potter, even though he was a very good one.

The use of age as a reference point for establishing status is as universal as the use of sex. All societies recognize three age groupings as a minimum: child, adult, and old. Certain societies have emphasized age as a basis for assigning status and have greatly amplified the divisions. Thus in certain African tribes the whole male population is divided into units composed of those born in the same years or within two- or three-year intervals. However, such extreme attention to age is unusual, and we need not discuss it here.

The physical differences between child and adult are easily recognizable, and the passage from childhood to maturity is marked by physiological events which make it possible to date it exactly for girls and within a few weeks or months for boys. However, the physical passage from childhood to maturity does not necessarily coincide with the social transfer of the individual from one category to the other. Thus in our own society both men and women remain legally children until long after they are physically adult. In most societies this difference between the physical and social transfer is more clearly marked than in our own. The child becomes a man not when he is physically mature but when he is formally recognized as a man by his society. This recognition is almost always given ceremonial expression in what are technically known as puberty rites. The most important element in these rites is not the determination of physical maturity but that of social maturity. Whether a boy is able to breed is less vital to his society than whether he is able to do a man's work and has a man's knowledge. Actually, most puberty ceremonies include tests of the boy's learning and fortitude, and if the aspirants are unable to pass these they are left in the child status until they can. For those who pass the tests, the ceremonies usually culminate in the transfer to them of certain secrets which the men guard from women and children.

The passage of individuals from adult to aged is harder to perceive. There is no clear physiological line for men, while even women may retain their full physical vigor and their ability to carry on all the activities of the adult status for several years after the menopause. The social transfer of men from adult to the aged group is given ceremonial recognition in a few cultures, as when a father normally surrenders his official position and titles to his son, but such recognition is rare. As for women, there appears to be no society in which the menopause is given ceremonial recognition, although there are a few societies in which it does alter the individual's status. Thus Comanche women, after the menopause, were released from their disabilities with regard to the supernatural. They could handle sacred objects, obtain power through dreams and practise as shamans, all things forbidden to women of bearing age.

The general tendency for societies to emphasize the individual's first change in age status and largely ignore the second is no doubt due in part to the difficulty of determining the onset of old age. However, there are also psychological factors involved. The boy or girl is usually anxious to grow up, and this eagerness is heightened by the exclusion of children from certain activities and knowledge. Also, society welcomes new additions to the most active division of the group, that which contributes most to its perpetuation and well-being. Conversely, the individual who enjoys the thought of growing old is atypical in all societies. Even when age brings respect and a new measure of influence, it means the relinquishment of much that is pleasant. We can see among ourselves that the aging usually refuse to recognize the change until long after it has happened.

In the case of age, as in that of sex, the biological factors involved appear to be secondary to the cultural ones in determining the content of status. There are certain activities which cannot be ascribed to children because children either lack the necessary strength or have not had time to acquire the necessary technical skills. However, the attitudes between parent and child and the importance given to the child in the family structure vary enormously from one culture to another. The status of the child among our Puritan ancestors, where he was seen and not heard and ate at the second table, represents one extreme. At the other might be placed the status of the eldest son of a Polynesian chief. All the *mana* (supernatural power) of the royal line converged upon such a child. He was socially superior to his own father and mother, and any attempt to discipline him would have been little short of sacrilege. I once visited the hereditary chief of a Marquesan tribe and found the whole family camping uncomfortably in their own front yard, although they had a good house built on European lines. Their eldest son, aged nine, had had a dispute with his father a few days before and had tabooed the house by naming it after his head. The family had thus been compelled to move out and could not use it again until he relented and lifted the taboo. As he could use the house himself and eat anywhere in the village, he was getting along quite well and seemed to enjoy the situation thoroughly.

The statuses ascribed to the old in various societies vary even more than those ascribed to children. In some cases they are relieved of all heavy labor and can settle back comfortably to live off their children. In others they perform most of the hard and monotonous tasks which do not require great physical strength, such as the gathering of firewood. In many societies the old women, in particular, take over most of the care of the younger children, leaving the younger women free to enjoy themselves. In some places the old are treated with consideration and respect; in others they are considered a useless incumbrance and removed as soon as they are incapable of heavy labor. In most societies their advice is sought even when little attention is paid to their wishes. This custom has a sound practical basis, for the individual who contrives to live to old age in an uncivilized group has usually been a person of ability and his memory constitutes a sort of reference library to which one can turn for help under all sorts of circumstances.

In certain societies the change from the adult to the old status is made more difficult for the individual by the fact that the patterns for these statuses ascribe different types of personality to each. This was the case among the Comanche, as it seems to have been among most of the Plains tribes. The adult male was a warrior, vigorous, self-reliant, and pushing. Most of his social relationships were phrased in terms of competition. He took what he could get and held what he had without regard to any abstract rights of those weaker than himself. Any willingness to arbitrate differences or to ignore slights was a sign of weakness resulting in loss of prestige. The old man, on the other hand, was expected to be wise and gentle, willing to overlook slights and, if need be, to endure abuse. It was his task to work for the welfare of the tribe, giving sound advice, settling feuds between the warriors, and even preventing his tribe from making new enemies. Young men strove for war and honor, old men strove for peace and tranquility. There is abundant evidence that among the Comanche the transition was often a difficult one for the individual. Warriors did not prepare for old age, thinking it a better fate to be killed in action. When waning physical powers forced them to assume the new rôle, many of them did so grudgingly, and those who had strong magic would go on trying to enforce the rights which belonged to the younger status. Such bad old men were a peril to young ones beginning their careers, for they were jealous of them simply because they were young and strong and admired by the women. The medicine power of these young men was still weak, and the old men could and did kill them by malevolent magic. It is significant that although benevolent medicine men might be of any age in Comanche folklore, malevolent ones were always old.

20.

IF WE'RE SO SMART, WHY AREN'T WE RICH?

Gloria Steinem

Throughout the long sweep of recorded human history the public dominance of females by males seems undeniable. But this and the selection that follows should make absolutely clear that perhaps the most significant development in the relation between persons and groups in the reader's lifetime is reflected in the full-bodied emergence of the Women's Liberation Movement. In this selection, Gloria Steinem, who is currently a major spokesperson for the movement, convincingly analyzes the economic discrimination that has traditionally characterized the status of women.

There are all those familiar questions. Why are there no great women composers? inventors? painters? Or, a more sophisticated version: isn't it really mothers who

Source: Gloria Steinem, *Ms.* 1, no. 12 (June 1973): 37–39, 125–27. Reprinted by permission of the *Ms.* magazine.

Gloria Steinem, writer and feminist leader, has written many articles and spoken extensively on the women's movement. She is editor of *Ms.* magazine.

train children into sex role stereotypes? Or, sillier but more humiliating since it implies we can't achieve greatness even on our own turf: why are most of the great couturiers men? and the great chefs?

Women may never grow used to those challenges, but we have finally begun to recognize them for what they are: subtler versions of the old vaudeville taunt, "If you're so smart, why aren't you rich?"

In recent years, we've learned some of the answers. Thanks to women's history courses, we now know more about the brave exceptions who *did* compose, invent, or paint; and we can document the power of cultural conditioning, of the sexual caste system that continues to limit most women. Even more important, the Black Movement and other struggles for social justice have helped all of us to realize that the existing distribution of power is not "natural"; that poverty is no proof of unwillingness to work, and wealth is no measure of human value.

There is finally some understanding, therefore, of the real reasons why women of all races are still only 7 percent of the physicians in this country, but 99 percent of registered nurses; of why we are 4 percent of lawyers, but 97 percent of household workers. There is even a weakening of the notion that American women are better off relative to their men than are the women of other industrialized countries. (It's a truism, for instance, that Scandinavian countries are considerably more democratic toward their female citizens than we are, and that women are a far greater percentage of the physicians and other professionals in the Soviet Union than is true here—though all these European societies are still quite patriarchal.)

· · · · ·

Now we are learning that women have been used as a source of unpaid or underpaid labor—whether in offices or factories or in our own kitchens. We are learning that women of all races have suffered not only as cheap labor, but in their role as a means of production; as the producers of workers and soldiers that this expanding country demanded in abnormally large supply. (Early American life was so hard and contraceptive information so suppressed that, until the early part of this century, it was common for a man to survive one or several wives. As a heritage of slavery, black women were even more likely to be thought of as breeders and lowly workers.) Sexist myths were elaborated to justify and enshrine this economic use of women: child-centered lives and unrewarded work became our "natural" domain.

We are just beginning to see racism and sexism as the twin problems of caste. One is more physically cruel and less intimate than the other, but both perpetuate themselves through myths—often the very same myths—of innate inferiority. Both are more ruthless than class, for they can never be changed or escaped. And both have an economic motive: the creation of a cheap labor force that is visibly marked for the job.

But women, black and brown as well as white, suffer from a dimension of economic prejudice that minority men do not; one that prolongs the problem by the very effective device of denying that any problem exists. We are perceived as *already powerful*—at least in relation to men of our own group, and often to society at large.

So, while most people now understand the discrimination that prevented women and minority men from becoming great painters or inventors, there is still the conviction that women exercise some great behind-the-scenes power.

We are said to be domineering or castrating (even if it is only retribution for our limited lives); to be matriarchs; to have more economic power than our counterpart men. We are even supposed to control the economy.

All the stereotypes come to mind: there is the pampered housewife, sitting at home in wall-to-wall comfort while her unfortunate husband works long hours to keep her that way. There are the lazy women getting a free ride on alimony because they were once married, or on welfare because they have children. There are those great figures of American mythology, the rich widows who are supposed to control most of the stock, and travel Europe on the life insurance of some overworked spouse.

. . . . .

And, according to stereotype, it's getting worse. Women are being hired not because they're qualified, but because the employer has a quota to fill. Therefore, women's incomes are shooting up; especially unfortunate since women work for pin money, not because they need to, and are taking jobs away from men. As for black or other minority women, they are widening the gap between themselves and their men: employers hire more minority females than minority males in order to fill two quotas for the price of one.

So goes the Popular Wisdom. It's very convincing. We ourselves often find ourselves believing it about women as a group, even though we personally have had no such experience. As a result, we take sex discrimination less seriously than we would if the very same discrimination were based on race; and we comfort ourselves for the conspicuous absence of women artists, executives, political leaders; and even chefs with the knowledge that, in some basic if rather underhanded way, we really *are* in control of the economy. Back-seat drivers, yes, but drivers nonetheless. It must be true. Isn't that what everybody says?

Looking beyond the stereotype to women's real economic situation isn't easy. As with public opinion polls and other national measures, women as a category are not always broken out of economic statistics. Neither are minority groups; and minority women are the least likely of all to be paid separate attention. But here are some pertinent facts, all collected from the sources listed at the end of this article. There are many surprises, but also confirmations of what our personal experience has told us—even if the economic mythology about women has not.

To take the areas of greatest resentment first, what about unearned wealth and non-salaried income? These are, after all, areas in which women are supposed to be living off the fat of the land.

The Great Alimony Myth. Perhaps it's the news stories about big Hollywood divorce settlements, or perhaps it's just public complaint by the few middle-class men who really do pay unfair alimony. Whatever the reason, the stereotype is very far from the fact. According to judges quoted in a 1965 study by the American Bar Association (the only nationwide report available), temporary alimony is awarded in fewer than 10 percent of all divorces, and serves largely to give the wife enough time to find a job. According to one judge quoted in the study, permanent alimony is awarded in less than 2 percent of divorces; usually when the wife is too old or ill to be employable. As for child support, the average payment is less than half the amount necessary to support a child.

Then there is the problem of collecting. Though nearly all states hold men criminally liable if they do not support their wives and children, most require that families be in "destitute or necessitous circumstances" before action is taken. Many women find they cannot afford the court costs and lawyers' fees, or that the exhusbands simply move away and cannot be found. Though there are no reliable studies on the collection of alimony, the Citizens' Advisory Council on the Status of Women quotes a 1955 study as the only available one on the collection of child support. According to those findings, only 38 percent of fathers were in full compliance with the support order a year after the divorce; 20 percent were in partial compliance (which meant they had made at least one payment); and 42 percent had made no payment at all. Ten years after the divorce, only 13 percent of the fathers were making all payments and 79 percent were making no payments at all.

The Advisory Council notes rather drily that "mistaken ideas about a husband's responsibility for support of wife and children, which have been reinforced by opponents of the Equal Rights Amendment, are a great disservice. . . . Many young women, relying on the belief that marriage means financial security, do not prepare themselves vocationally."

Stocks. Perhaps this is the source of the notion that we control the economy: women *did* once constitute slightly more than half of all stockholders, and are still a big 49.9 percent. But here is the catch. They are far more likely to have small holdings. For instance, women own only 42 percent of the dollar value and 38 percent of the total shares. Furthermore, the stock may belong to the woman in name only. Her husband may want to limit his liability in business investments, for example, or to leave the stock without inheritance tax to her and the children should he die, or be able to say for business or political reasons that the stock belongs not to him but to his wife. (Stock that is in women's names during or after the life of the husband is very often a necessary saving for the support of children.) And, no matter why the stock is attributed to her, it's rare that the woman actually controls it. A New York Stock Exchange study shows, for instance, that 75 percent of all securities transactions are carried out by men.

For whatever reason, very few women have the assets, expertise, or control to get rich in the stock market. In fact, female stockholders are poorer and far more likely to have clerical or sales jobs than are male stockholders.

Pensions, life insurance, and real estate. Pensions are based on salaries. Since women make only 59 percent of what men do, they're bound to feel the pinch at retirement time, too; supposing, that is, that they have not left dreary, futureless jobs too soon to be eligible. (Because money is set aside for pension funds in companies where there is little incentive for women to stay the requisite years, their contributions often end up subsidizing the pensions of men.) Furthermore, pension or retirement plans rarely give the same benefits to families of women as they do to families of men. Accrued benefits may be lost entirely if the woman takes time out when her children are young; and plans often force women to retire earlier—in spite of their longer life expectancy. Finally, the companies with the greatest number of women workers are the least likely to have decent pension plans at all.

Now we come to life insurance. Yes, two-thirds of all beneficiaries *are* women (supposing that the policy hasn't either lapsed or been borrowed against before the holder's death). But the benefits are often low; far less, for instance, than a housewife might have saved had she been paid the estimated worth of her work in the home: currently, about $9,000 a year. And the benefits are frequently spent less for the wife's welfare than for the children's.

Insurance policies taken out on the lives of women constitute only 14 percent of all life insurance. The average size of ordinary policies purchased for men in 1971 was $17,810; for women, it was $6,580.

Real estate has to be included, too, in assessing women's wealth. The Internal Revenue Service hasn't released new figures since 1962, and the IRS only reported this kind of property wealth for individuals with estates worth more than $60,000. In that group, however, there were 2,194,000 men who held $118.3 billion in real estate among them; plus 1,250,000 women who held $69.7 billion. Of course, questions of control and who benefits have to be asked here, just as they do when assessing women's real degree of economic power in the stock market.

So how true is the stereotype of pampered and powerful women of large incomes? One good overall measure is this: if you look at all the people in this country who have incomes of $10,000 a year or more from whatever sources (jobs, alimony, stock dividends, real estate rental, insurance, pensions, gifts; everything), you find that less than 9 percent of them are women. And that includes all the divorcées and rich widows.

. . . . .

Salaried work is an area in which more facts are known, and the Popular Wisdom may be less distant from the truth. It's probably not surprising, for instance, that women workers earn less than $3 for every $5 earned by men. Or that the sex-based differential survives, even where women are not confined to the lower-paying professions. (The 1970 median yearly salaries of women in scientific fields, for instance, were from $1,700 to $5,100 less than those earned by men with similar training and positions.)

But there is still a lot of mythology surrounding relative earning power.

Salaries: male and female, black and white. In 1970, the median incomes for full-time, year-round work went like this:

white men	$9,373
minority men	$6,598
white women	$5,490
minority women	$4,674

These figures, showing that women of all races earn less than men of all races, go against our ingrained beliefs about relative earning power. Race does, however, become the dominant factor going *down* the economic scale, though sex continues as a major influence: 35.5 percent of all black females lived beneath the poverty line in 1971 as opposed to 28.9 percent of black males; but 11.2 percent of white females were below that line, and only 8.5 percent of white males. Sex becomes more of a factor going *up* the income brackets, though race continues as a major influence: in 1971, 46.8 percent of fully employed white males and 17.4 percent of minority males earned over $10,000; while just 8.7 percent of white females and 6.5 percent of black females reached those heights.

Furthermore, education doesn't have as crucial an effect on those trends as we might think. Women with one to three years of college had lower incomes in 1971 than men who had gone to school for only eight years.

It's clear by any measure that black women, with the double stigma of sex and race, come out on the bottom. The fact that they could get jobs (though poorly paid ones, often domestic work) when black men could get none has obscured the economic truth that now, they have the highest unemployment rate of all adults, and the least access to upper income jobs.

Perhaps the economic element of the matriarchal myth is not so much the real power held by black women, as black men's lack of power relative to white men; a fact that has brought black men and black women into economically closer relationship than their white counterparts. In 1970, for instance, the median income of black women was 70 percent that of black men, as opposed to white women whose median income was 59 percent that received by their male counterparts.

. . . . .

The lesson of all male-female comparisons is only that sexism runs from top to bottom of society, and penalizes the minority community by keeping half its number doubly oppressed.

But if we have any doubts about who is really benefiting from this double system of caste, we have only to look at the upper levels. Of all the jobs that pay $15,000 a year or more, for instance, 94 percent are held by white males—leaving a big 6 percent to all women and minority men combined.

Real progress will come only when we stop comparing second-class groups with each other, and direct all our energies toward fundamental change; toward the people who are really in power.

. . . . .

Is women's economic plight getting better? Not in a mass way at all. In fact, the differential between male and female pay has been getting steadily bigger, not smaller; the unemployment rate for women is up about 40 percent in four years; easier divorce laws, though a basic step forward, still have left many women with no job training and few alternatives; child care becomes more expensive and less adequate each year; older women on fixed incomes are suffering from spiraling prices; and the number of women and dependent children on welfare has gone up by nearly five million since 1968. All the recent trends of inflation combined with increased unemployment have hit women very hard.

But there are signs of hope. Job actions and back-pay suits have been successful enough to frighten big companies into at least taking a serious look at their employment policies. So have actions on promotion and hiring, though, at higher levels, we are only approaching tokenism. According to the 1970 census, women have begun to break out of traditionally female occupations, and into formerly male preserves; even into some of the blue-collar jobs. Altogether, women accounted for two-thirds of the employment increase in the 1960s.

But only constant effort, and unified action can begin to lighten women's economic burden. The changes to come must be basic: even equal pay for the women already in the work force would necessitate a major redistribution of wealth.

It will be a long road. The first step is believing in ourselves; understanding that we are indeed smart, even if we aren't rich. And the second is giving up the myths of power, so that we can see our economic plight as it really is.

21.

HUMAN . . . NOT CLASS!

Betty Friedan

Within the Women's Liberation Movement itself some of its leaders are questioning the lengths to which certain of its exponents have gone. Here Betty Friedan, who gave increased impetus to the movement with the publication in 1963 of *The Feminine Mystique,* examines the gains which women have made toward achieving equal status with men but also, in part through introspection, assesses the risks to which extreme positions might lead. She decries the efforts of those who would treat the women's movement as class warfare against men and pleads for *human* liberation and for recognition of the need to learn how to "relate" to those of the opposite sex. The success or failure of the movement cannot help but have repercussions for the interpersonal relations of husband and wife, brother and sister, and all the other male to female relationships. It is appropriate, therefore, to include this selection in the section of this book dealing with person and group.

I have been on too many airplanes lately, traveled too far and fast, feel unrooted, disembodied. Sitting on a 747, too huge, antihuman, this technological monster paralyzed in the Detroit airport because a single computer part has blown a fuse—I only wish I were *home* this Sunday night. But where and what is home for me? There is my apartment in New York and having dinner with Emily, if by chance Emily is also home. My sixteen year old, already two feet out the door, mysteriously involved in her own "interpersonal relations, mommy," as she spells it out for me with the exasperated tolerance our young feel for us as they find their own wings—up and out.

Stalled on the 747, I see in my mind's eye a figure of a man on a Christmas card tumbling through an infinity of space with the message, "The only way to cope with change is to help make it happen."

I am stalled on this plane, on my way home from a conference with my allies in the fight for women's right to choose childbirth or abortion. We have grown so used to our differences, this motley, unlikely crew of feminists, priests, churchwomen, doctors, Zero Population Growth freaks, old socialites and young socialists, and family planning zealots, that we, who used to fight

Source: Betty Friedan, *Social Policy* (March/April 1973), pp. 32–38. This article is extracted from two articles that originally appeared in *McCall's:* "Beyond Women's Liberation" (August 1972) and "We Don't Have to Be That Independent" (January 1973).

Author and feminist leader Betty Friedan was a founder and the first president of the National Organization for Women (NOW). She has been a member of the National Women's Political Caucus. She has written many articles and is the author of *The Feminine Mystique.*

each other suspiciously, now simply fight comfortably together. . . .

The stewardess on the plane tells me that she was one of those forced to resign when she got married and now has been rehired although she is a mother.

But I am tired of the 747's and strangers who are all my comrades in this battle in which I seem to have traveled so far. Concepts that began as fanciful thoughts, a yearning sense of possibility in my own mind and others', are about to be confirmed by the Supreme Court . . . and I suddenly feel disoriented, at loose ends, tired.

At home, in my empty apartment, I sit down and finally read the letters women have been writing to me in such numbers these past months. . . . I don't feel like going to the NOW Board meeting or the Policy Council of the Political Caucus; I am sick of fighting Gloria, Bella, Jill, the power brokers, and the manipulators of the women's movement; I am even sick of trying to explain to the endless reporters the real differences in ideology, direction.

Have I, unthinkably, lost my own nerve for this battle? A song nags at me, just out of memory, and I dust off the record player. Simon and Garfunkel sing, "I'm sitting in a railway station/Got a ticket for my destination/On a tour of one-night stands/My suitcase and guitar in hand/And every step is neatly planned/For every night an endless stream/Of cigarettes and magazines/And each town looks the same to me/ The movies and the factories/And every stranger's face I see/Reminds me that I long to be . . . Homeward Bound . . ."

With all my comings and goings, the organizing, the speaking, the politicking, I haven't had time to read or answer these letters from women. Reading these letters, I feel that once again we have all come to the same place at the same time. How can I find answers to my own search for new directions in your letters looking to me for answers? I feel the same relief you tell me that you feel when I put into words the new questions that are plaguing all of us midway in flight from the feminine mystique. It's as if . . . all of us are somehow trying to catch our breath. After so much change in the 1960s, we are breathless, tired, after nearly ten years of nay-saying. Not that we want to reverse it, wipe it all out, go home again, not that at all—we had to do what we did, we couldn't stay the way we were any longer. But now that change is suddenly more than *words,* not that it is happening—and our lives *are* changing, opening out—we suddenly want something familiar to hold onto. We realize we don't want to say "no" to everything. Do we dare to say out loud that we still need certain familiar roots to warm us (embarrassed in our new sophistication to use words like "home" or "love" or "support" or "dependence" or "trust")? Does that mean we don't really want the equality, the freedom, the independence, the voice of our own we've been fighting for after all?

The relief in your letters reminds me of the sudden sense of almost overwhelming relief in the letters from thousands of women after *The Feminine Mystique* was published in 1963. You said then, "it changed my whole life" just to have it put into words that no matter how much you wanted to be your children's mother, your husband's wife, you needed to put yourself in the equation as a person in your own right and were tired of confessing guilt on the analyst's couch because you no longer felt so happy in your role of mother and wife. That need to realize ourselves as human beings by our own actions in society had been so suppressed, I called it the "problem that has no name." Just giving it a name made women realize they were not guilty and alone, and enabled them to take themselves more seriously, get a job, go back to school, confront the discrimination against them on the job or in school, and then organize to change all the things in society that must be changed if women are to enjoy real equality.

For nearly ten years, then, our consciousness has focused on all the barriers that have kept us from being full people. We acted out our rage at the putdowns we used to take with false smiles in the office or at home, in church or on TV, the rage that we took out on ourselves, our children, and our husbands in bed. The public acting out of that anger made headlines, magazine cover stories, and chic, sophisticated cocktail party banter and jokes. It also changed laws and has begun to change institutions: colleges, offices, unions, political parties, even TV. It took courage for women to act this way in public, and sometimes even more courage for a woman to deal herself into the equation in a new way with her own husband or children or boss. And sometimes it seemed to require her turning altogether on her old way of life and the people in it, leaving a marriage or a home or a job. The reverberations of the movement and the results have been real and complex and not always comfortable at first for everyone involved.

We are almost afraid to face the uncomfortable part of it . . . because we don't want to risk losing it and going back to what we were before. As if we had to be more independent than any human being can really be—completely independent of men, of children—be hard against all softness. I think it is a relief now to realize that we don't have to be that independent, that we can admit our need for love and home, be soft as well as hard with our children and our husbands, admit our dependence on them without giving up our own identity. We have become independent enough to admit our need to be dependent. Maybe we are relieved finally to discuss out loud certain fears, certain discomforts, certain negative feelings, which, if suppressed, if not faced, might boomerang into backlash and force us back.

When we are afraid to face our own negative feelings, we can't tolerate any shading of the blacks and whites; we get stuck and lose our will to go on. You are strong enough to face your own questions that can't be dismissed as either/or, black and white.

Realizing what course we don't want to take, we can move again on our real course; realizing what we don't want to change, we can regain our spirit for the change we can't escape and really need. In changing ourselves, that which we thought we wanted to get rid of may also have changed enough so we can see how much we really want to keep it.

. . . . .

A woman from Sacramento, California (Kris Matzka), writes that the new dialogue "has helped clear up the many contradictions that I've felt within myself. My lack of conviction that we, by virtue of being women, are morally pure, whereas men are in full consciousness heartless exploiters, left me with the fear that I could not see reality. When I was told by a man that I couldn't possibly be a women's libber because I was affectionate and wanted to please him, I wondered why it was necessary to choose between loving a man and being accepted as an equal by him."

Some of you are worried that by admitting these new questions, we will give up our will to go on with the real battle still not finished.

"You are mistaken if you believe women as a whole have won very real gains in the past few years," writes Gloria Parsons of

Costa Mesa, California. "Little has changed for the majority of us."

And Karen Henningsgard of Havre, Montana, argues: "The message is that we should slow down or stop much of what we are doing for fear of male backlash. Not so. Also, to sweep away "class warfare" is rather hasty. After all, haven't women been oppressed as a class? I don't think this can be reversed. It seems better to live through the temporary backlash to come out on the other side and start putting things together in a new way. We must become conscious of ourselves first."

The majority of your letters, however, confirm my own feeling that many women and men who now support the goals of equality for women will be (or have been) alienated by the rhetoric of sex class warfare, especially the young who are already breaking through the old mystiques of masculinity and femininity.

. . . . .

Tim McGlasson of Pomona, California, writes: "This may seem rather odd, a letter from a twelve-year-old male. But I wanted to air a few of my ideas. I am sick to death of the phrase 'male chauvinist pig.' As a long-haired male I have to put up with the prejudices that seem to revolve around long hair. O.K. I'll try to tolerate that. But I cannot stomach the phrase 'male chauvinist pig' any longer. I am almost ready to quit fighting for equal rights for women. What's the use? I'll only be spit in the eye. Besides, there are 'female chauvinist pigs' also. I know plenty. All I'm trying to say is prejudice is a monster. So please, for God's sake, don't feed it."

From Bowie, Maryland, Ms. Bible writes: "So glad to realize that Women's Lib is not just another way of saying 'Make War—Not Love With Men.' Many of my friends and I have found ourselves turning away from anything labeled Women's Liberation for the very reasons you mention. Most of us have a profession, we are fairly well educated, and all of us want the *real* goals Women's Lib set out to attain. But to sacrifice love, home, and men to do that is a little bit too much."

. . . . .

A letter from Marion Piccioni from Sparks, Nevada, gave me new courage: "I am a divorcée who spent six and a half years in Brooklyn with two babies and a husband who was never home. I remember the frustration as if it were yesterday. I have been alone ever since and will probably never marry again. But, like you, I am not a manhater and believe that whatever hurts men hurts all of us."

By the end of 1972 the backlash, both masculine and feminine, that I predicted six months ago surfaced. Two respected, serious writers—Joan Didion and Midge Decter—have published devastating attacks on the women's movement, which they equate with the rhetoric of sex class warfare. Joan Didion's attack on the women's movement . . . was based on the writings of Kate Millett, Germaine Greer, Shulamith Firestone, and lesser known radical feminists as well as Gloria Steinem's magazine, *Ms.* "At the exact dispirited moment when there seemed no one willing to play the proletariat, along came the women's movement and the invention of women as a 'class.' . . . If the family was the last resort of capitalism, then let us abolish the family. . . . Small children could only be odious mechanisms for the spilling and digesting of food, for robbing women of their freedom. . . . Increasingly it seemed that the aversion was to adult sexual life itself: how much cleaner to stay forever children. . . ."

Midge Decter, in a book called *The New Chastity and Other Arguments against Women's Liberation,* tries to dismiss the whole movement for women's equality on the grounds that it is antisexual, antichildbearing, antihousework, anti-individual, and antifreedom. She seemed surprised when I rebutted her in two radio broadcasts with the realities of the women's movement experienced by millions of women throughout America: the fight for good jobs and equal pay, maternity leaves, income tax deductions, the right to abortion and child-care centers, the ability to get a credit card and a mortgage, economic protection in divorce, running for office, and being yourself with men. But as a successful editor and wife of one of the leading editors in the literary establishment, Midge Decter, like the antisexual female chauvinists whose rhetoric she attacks, does not identify with the majority of American women whose real problems at job or school or home, with bosses, children, and husbands, can't be solved either by killing them off in fantasy or pretending they don't exist.

In an even more ominous fantasy of male backlash, Ira Levin, author of *Rosemary's Baby,* has written a ghoulish thriller, *The Stepford Wives,* in which suburban housewives, spurred to rebellion by *me,* incite their husbands to a horrifying revenge; they are murdered one by one and replaced with lifelike robots with breasts of superior measurement and never flagging sweetness in their technically perfect, menial serviceability to children, husband, and home.

More seriously, in real life, on August 26, 1972, the anniversary of women's suffrage, in New York, where in previous years more than 20,000 women and men and children had marched for women's equality, less than 5,000 marched. Radical lesbians and other adherents of sex class warfare took over the march, alienating suburban housewives, working women, welfare mothers, churchwomen, Junior Leaguers, and high school girls who had previously joined forces in unprecedented numbers. If those who preach the rhetoric of sex class warfare succeed in taking over the women's movement, Midge Decter's literary attacks will be mild compared to the fury of the disillusioned and alienated women who were ready to take on the real problems. You who wrote me letters, all who read and understand these words, share responsibility with me not to let this happen.

We must continue to spell out clearly that it's not necessary to turn your back on husband, children, home, or even the beauty parlor to be a liberated woman. In fact, in this era of stalled 747's, bombs in the mail, incessant, bewildering change, permanent future shocks, a very equal, liberated woman can and should be able to admit a need for someone to love and "comfort me."

. . . . .

Female chauvinism may only be a temporary self-indulgence, an excess reaction of rage too long suppressed. In the consciousness-raising groups female chauvinist rhetoric can be indulged in for a while without even touching the test of reality. But if the strident fringe rhetoric is confused with the reality of the movement—if it affects decisions about personal lives and about movement tactics—it could abort the entire movement. We ourselves can only be seduced by our own rhetoric for so long. If our actual situation is unchanged—or if the changes do not create the new life or self we have dreamed of, or even make life worse—we will sink into even further depths of self-pity, self-disgust, and impotent rage. And we will vent that rage on men, who can and must be with us if we are to change society.

The great majority of men and women in America now support the real goals and gains of our movement, according to the

Virginia Slims poll, even those who don't like "women's lib" (I no longer use the term myself: it has been too corrupted by the media and the female chauvinists they exploit). Those real goals—equal pay, equal opportunity for good jobs and the necessary training for them, our own voice in decisions of church and state, an end to practices that discriminate against us, the restructuring of work, home, marriage, child-rearing, and our very morality that this involves—are too important and precarious to jeopardize now. Our movement has grown so fast because of these real needs of women, needs that most men now support.

I have always objected to rhetoric that treats the women's movement as class warfare against men—women oppressed as a class by men, the oppressors. I do not believe that the conditions we are trying to change are caused by a conspiracy for "the economic and social profit of men as a group," as Gloria Steinem sees it. The causes are more complex and burden men as well as benefit them. My definition of feminism is simply that women are people, in the fullest sense of the word, who must be free to move in society with all the privileges and opportunities and responsibilities that are their human and American right. This does not mean class warfare against men, which denies our sexual and human bonds with them, nor does it mean the elimination of children, which denies our human future.

It seems to me that all the women's movement ever was, or needs to be, is a stage in the whole human rights movement, bringing another group—a majority this time—into the mainstream of human society, with all the perils and promises and personal risks this involves. No more, no less. Women needed and still need to organize separately only in order to break through the barriers that prevent our participation as people. But there is no need to shackle ourselves to a new mystique of specialness, glorifying the traits resulting from our isolation from society—some good, some bad—into virtues. No need to create an abstract religion rationalizing or dictating our continued isolation, or justifying special privilege, which exempts us from the risks and tests of merely being human. Female chauvinism could keep us from using the gains we have won, from moving through the door we have opened. It could make men slam the door in our faces.

A male friend of mine, on the verge of switching from supporter to enemy of the women's movement, is paying $17,500 a year in alimony to his first wife. He is hungrily sharing personal responsibility for his children, as well as responsibility with his second wife for the housework and her children. In this, of course, he is not like many other divorced men—only some of them. Men are *not* a class; more and more middle-aged men who played the old masculine role in their marriages and jobs are joining the young who reject the brutal and obsolete masculine mystique of domination.

My particular friend is still being chivalrous. He shows much greater support and respect for his new wife's professional work than she for his. He had always assumed that because of her sex she was more vulnerable than he. Now he is not so sure. "I like everything about her except the way she always puts me down. It's like she is supposed to be free to really be herself now, but if I'm not always the big, strong, perfect man, I'm no good. I'm sick and tired of being treated like an enemy, a brute, no matter what I do. I want a woman who really likes me. My first wife *had* to like me. That didn't count."

He asks if I have read the book about the dropout husband (*Letter to My Wife,* by John Koffend, who describes becoming impotent sexually and then leaving his wife, children, and job to escape to Pago Pago; "the story of a man who had to stop being a husband so he could get back to being a man," the book was advertised). "Maybe Pago Pago is carrying it too far," my friend said to me, "but impotence is the masculine backlash."

If we *make* men the enemy they will surely lash back at us. If we insist on our freedom but keep them in jail, as our breadwinners or scapegoats. If we demand equal treatment from them and still insist on special privilege. Or if we replace a double standard that said a woman had to be twice as good as a man to get the job with a double standard that says a woman deserves the job of *any* man, no matter how good. Do we really want to hit men below the belt?

The women's movement will become bankrupt if it goes that route, because our basic capital is the human rightness of our cause and men's need for our love—and our votes. They also depend on our underpaid or unpaid menial work; the machines or the men they have replaced could take over that. But if in the name of our own moral superiority we do not abide even by the basic customs of honor and decency, then we deserve the backlash. Men are hungry for the soft qualities they've suppressed in themselves in the name of masculinity.

So my own sense, deepened considerably by the kind of letters I have quoted from, is that the women's movement has reached a plateau from which it must find a new direction or retreat in disarray and panic by going home again the old way. That's what started this whole movement after all—the spoiling of love, home, childrearing for women, and thus also for men and children, when we tried to make them our whole lives, submerging ourselves in the feminine mystique and retreating from the fears and challenges of society as we did in the 1950s. But now, I think, deep within us we also fear, and rightly, that society has become too large, cold, frightening, unfamiliar, too rapidly changing to endure without warmth and love to come home to. It is the conditions that trap both men and women in mutual torment instead of love, the old sex roles, that need to be changed. It doesn't have to be either/or.

. . . . . .

In the bleakest month of my own stalled spirit, I was asked to give a lecture in Peoria, Illinois, my hometown, at Bradley College, my mother's alma mater. I have not been back in nearly ten years.

Coming in from the airport. I recognize the old street names, but there is a McDonald's now on Western, around the corner from our old house. The trees in the park look smaller, the streetcar tracks are gone on Main Street, the hotel is now the Peoria Hilton.

I speak in the gym, and although I am used to large crowds I can hardly believe so many people, surely over a thousand, have come out in Peoria to hear me talk about where the women's movement is going. I recognize faces in the crowd—old people's faces, maybe my parents' friends, neighbors. I see my kid brother on an aisle; he looks very elegant with silver streaks in his hair.

The very thought of coming back to Peoria in this capacity had scared me; not for how they would receive me, but for what I might revert to. I always thought I hated Peoria, couldn't wait to get out of there. Now a powerful emotion that I cannot name suddenly makes my chin tremble, and I say: "This is not an ordinary lecture for me. I grew up in this place. My father came here as a boy from Russia, and my mother's father came as a young doctor. My mother went to this college. My roots are in this place. My sense of possibility, whatever in me that started women moving, came from here, from Peoria. They say you can't go home again. And yet you must go home again, affirm your own roots, to know where you are going. It is profoundly moving to me that this revolution that I helped start brings me home, finally, to Peoria."

I speak of women and men and human liberation, not quite what they expected to hear. They listen quietly, do not laugh, and are not hostile.

"Homeward Bound"—the song keeps running in my head as, back home in New York, I move out of my bleak mood, teach my new class at Temple, plan strategy to defend the abortion law, discuss colleges with Emily, and stop playing unnecessary power games with a man I love. I also stop feeling so helpless, hopeless about the women's movement—and about America. When my father and my mother's father and all the men like them from Poland or Ireland or Italy found their way to towns like Peoria, what blueprint of the future did they have to create a way of life for themselves and their children?

Against the shocks of the future, women or men, we must keep rooted in our own present, in whatever of our past has nourished us, in whatever warmth and strength and love we get and give, from our old and our young, our friends and comrades who share our experiences, and those whose differences we finally respect in our new battles as women. Finally we as women must be able to join with the men we can now know and love as friends as well as lovers, and the strangers who become our friends as we move. We take our roots with us as we move into the unknown ahead, for women, for America. I think we may be strong enough to make it if we admit that we are unsure and afraid and depend on each other.

22.

THE TERRITORIES OF THE SELF

Erving Goffman

Among contemporary sociologists, none has done more to call attention to the importance of certain aspects of interpersonal or person-group behavior and relationships than Erving Goffman. He has demonstrated through a number of publications the ability innovatively to observe and imaginatively analyze many previously neglected features of these interactional phenomena. In the following selection he explores the spatial features, and then the nonspatial extensions, of human *territoriality.* The reader, once sensitized to these familiar bits of everyday experience, may recognize them subsequently in all aspects of social life. Although the concept of territoriality has been popularized by others, Goffman has brought it into focus as a legitimate area

Source: Erving Goffman, *Relations in Public: Microstudies of the Public Order* (New York: Basic Books, 1971), pp. 28–41.

The author is Benjamin Franklin professor of anthropology and sociology at the University of Pennsylvania. He is on the board of directors of the American Association for the Abolition of Involuntary Mental Hospitalization.

of sociological interest, and has enriched our understanding of these common patterns of social relationships in American life.

PRESERVES

At the center of social organization is the concept of claims, and around this center, properly, the student must consider the vicissitudes of maintaining them.

To speak closely of these matters, a set of related terms is needed. There is the "good," the desired object or state that is in question; the "claim," namely, entitlement to possess, control, use, or dispose of the good; the "claimant," that is, the party on whose behalf the claim is made; the "impediment," meaning here the act, substance, means, or agency through which the claim is threatened; the "author" (or "counterclaimant"), namely, the party—when there is one—on whose behalf the threat to claims is intended; and finally, the "agents," these being the individuals who act for and represent the claimant and counterclaimant in these matters involving claims.

When we restrict our attention to activity that can only occur during face-to-face interaction, the claimant tends to be an individual (or a small set of individuals) and to function as his own agent. The same can be said of the counterclaimant, but in addition the impediment that occurs in his name is likely to involve his own activity or body. Therefore, conventional terms such as "victim" and "offender" will often be adequate. And one type of claim becomes crucial: it is a claim exerted in regard to "territory." This concept from ethology seems apt, because the claim is not so much to a discrete and particular matter but rather to a field of things—to a preserve—and because the boundaries of the field are ordinarily patrolled and defended by the claimant.

Territories vary in terms of their organization. Some are "fixed"; they are staked out geographically and attached to one claimant, his claim being supported often by the law and its courts. Fields, yards, and houses are examples. Some are "situational"; they are part of the fixed equipment in the setting (whether publicly or privately owned), but are made available to the populace in the form of claimed goods while-in-use. Temporary tenancy is perceived to be involved, measured in seconds, minutes, or hours, informally exerted, raising constant questions as to when the claim begins and when it terminates. Park benches and restaurant tables are examples. Finally, there are "egocentric" preserves which move around with the claimant, he being in the center. They are typically (but not necessarily) claimed long term. Purses are an example. This threefold division is, of course, only valid in degree. A hotel room is a situational claim, yet it can function much like a house, a fixed territory. And, of course, houses in the form of trailers can move around.

The prototypical preserve is no doubt spatial and perhaps even fixed. However, to facilitate the study of comingling—at least in American society—it is useful to extend the notion of territoriality into claims that function like territories but are not spatial, and it is useful to focus on situational and egocentric territoriality. Starting, then, with the spatial, we shall move by steps to matters that are not.

1. *Personal Space:* The space surrounding an individual, anywhere within which an entering other causes the individual to feel encroached upon, leading him to show displeasure and sometimes to withdraw.

A contour, not a sphere, is involved, the spatial demands directly in front of the face being larger than at back. The fixed layout of seats and other interior equipment may restrictively structure available space around the individual in one dimension, as occurs in line or column organization. When two individuals are alone in a setting, then concern about personal space takes the form of concern over straight-line distance.

Given that individuals can be relied upon to keep away from situations in which they might be contaminated by another or contaminate him, it follows that they can be controlled by him if he is willing to use himself calculatedly to constitute that object that the others will attempt to avoid, and in avoiding, move in a direction desired by him. For example, we read of the engaging action of a pickpocket "stall" who uses his body to "pratt in" a mark, that is to cause the mark to hold himself away from a body that is pressing on him, and incidentally hold himself in a position from which his wallet can be reached; similarly we read of the "pratting out" of one bystander whose position prevents theft from another.

It is a central feature of personal space that legitimate claim to it varies greatly according to the accountings available in the setting and that the bases for these will change continuously. Such factors as local population density, purpose of the approacher, fixed seating equipment, character of the social occasion, and so forth, can all influence radically from moment to moment what it is that is seen as an offense. Indeed, in human studies it is often best to consider personal space not as a permanently possessed, egocentric claim but as a temporary, situational preserve into whose center the individual moves.

Take, for example, the social organization of cowaiting. Obviously, to stand or sit next to a stranger when the setting is all but empty is more of an intrusion than the same act would be when the place is packed and all can see that only this niche remains. In theory we might expect also a continuous process of adjustment whereby each arrival and each departure causes alterations throughout. What seems to occur in middle-class society is that arrival creates sequential reallocation but departure leads to somewhat more complex behavior, since an individual who leaves his current niche to take up a freed one produces an open sign that he is disinclined to be as close to his neighbor as he was. (When the two are of opposite sex, there exists the added complication that failure to move away when possible can be taken as a sign of undue interest.) In consequence, a departure may leave an empty place and no change in the remaining allocation, or at least an appropriator may wait for some tactful moment before making use of the newly available resource. In brief, moving in on someone or having oneself moved in on is a less delicate task than removing oneself from proximity to him. In consequence, as say a streetcar empties, there will be a period when two individuals signal by proximity a relationship that does not in fact exist.

All of this may be seen in miniature in elevator behavior. Passengers have two problems: to allocate the space equably, and to maintain a defensible position, which in this context means orientation to the door and center with the back up against the wall if possible. The first few individuals can enter without anyone present having to rearrange himself, but very shortly each new entrant—up to a certain number—causes all those present to shift position and reorient themselves in sequence. Leave-taking introduces a tendency to reverse the cycle, but this is tempered by the countervailing resistance to appearing uncomfortable in an established distance from another. Thus, as the car empties, passengers acquire a measure of uneasiness, caught between two opposing inclinations—to obtain maximum distance from others and to inhibit avoidance behavior that might give offense.

2. *The Stall:* The well-bounded space to which individuals can lay temporary claim, possession being on an all-or-none basis. A scarce good will often be involved, such as a comfortable chair, a table with a view, an empty cot, a telephone booth. In the main, stalls are fixed in the setting, although, for example, at beaches devices such as large towels and mats can be carried along with the claimant and unrolled when convenient, thus providing a portable stall. When seats are built in rows and divided by common armrests (as in theaters), then personal space and stall have the same boundaries. When there is space between seats, then personal space is likely to extend beyond the stall. And, of course, there are stalls such as boxes at the opera which allocate several seats to the exclusive use (on any one social occasion) of a single "party." The availability of stalls in a setting articulates and stabilizes claims to space, sometimes providing more than would have been claimed as personal space, sometimes less—as can be seen, for example, in regard to seats when a class of six-year-olds attends an adult theater or when parents have a meeting in an elementary school room.

It should be noted that a stall can be left temporarily while the leave-taker is sustained in a continuing claim upon it; personal space cannot. Furthermore, often the claimant to a stall will not be an individual but two or more of them who properly share it, as illustrated nicely in public tennis courts and commercial bowling alleys, these being designed to provide a large, well-equipped stall to parties of players for stipulated periods of time. (In our society the most common multiperson stall is the table, there being relatively few too small for more than one person or too large to be claimed by a party of only two.) Personal space, on the other hand, is largely a one-person possession, although in crowded places, such as packed elevators, a small child grasped to a parent may be treated as part of the latter's personal space, and couples engaged in affectional entwinings may also be treated as claiming a single personal space.

The point about stalls, as suggested, is that they provide external, easily visible, defendable boundaries for a spatial claim. Stalls provide a contrast in this regard to personal space, the latter having ever-shifting dimensions. This points up a problem in the organization of American public places. Here, for practical considerations, equipment such as picnic tables or park benches is often built to a size to suggest that each can be claimed as a stall by a participation unit, a "single" or a "with." However, when crowding is such that this allocation would leave some individuals standing, then a rule is understood to apply that gives unaccommodated participation units the right to enforce a fictional division of a stall into two (and occasionally more than two) stalls. Obviously, then, as crowding increases, those already ensconced will begin to have to give up exclusive claim to a stall. An ambiguity results, because there is no well-established principle to order the sequence in which various claimants, already ensconced, will be obliged to give up their exclusiveness. A field is thus opened for personal enterprise. Hence, on buses, streetcars, and trains, seats designed to hold two persons, and fully recognized to be designed to accommodate two strangers when necessary, nonetheless establish for the first arrival a territory he may attempt to retain for himself by standard ruses: he may leave his own possessions on the empty place, thereby marking it for his own and obliging competitors to move (or ask to have moved) something that symbolizes another; he may deny his eyes to those seeking a seat, thereby preventing them from obtaining the fleeting permission that they tend to seek, failure to receive which can cause them to move on to the next available place; he may expose some contaminating part of himself, such as his feet, or allow part of his body to fall on the disputed place, so that those who would use the place invite contamination; and so forth.

3. *Use Space:* The territory immediately around or in front of an individual, his claim to which is respected because of apparent instrumental needs. For example, a gallery goer can expect that when he is close to a picture, other patrons will make some effort to walk around his line of vision or excuse or minimize their momentarily blocking it. Persons holding a conversation over a distance can expect a similar accommodation from nonparticipants whose bodies might block the giving and receiving of conversation management cues. Sportsmen of all kind expect some consideration will be given to the amount of elbow room they require in order to manipulate their equipment, as do convicts using pickaxes to break stone. Gymnasts using a vaulting horse expect that others will "stay out of their way." A crewman obliged to scrub and polish a designated portion of the surface of his warship expects, especially on the day before weekly inspection, to be able to keep everyone away during and right after the cleaning. Note that circumstances can allow the individual to offer instrumental grounds for demanding limits on the level of noise and sound, especially when the source is physically close by.

4. *The Turn:* The order in which a claimant receives a good of some kind relative to other claimants in the situation. A decision-rule is involved, ordering participants categorically ("women and children first," or "whites before blacks"), or individually ("smallest first, then next smallest"), or some mixture of both. Typically claimants are required to have been present in order to establish their claim on a turn, but once this has been done and marked in some way, they may be allowed to absent themselves until their turn comes up. In our Western society, perhaps the most important principle in turn organization is "first come, first served," establishing the claim of an individual to come right after the person "ahead" and right before the person "behind." This decision rule creates a dominance ranking but a paradoxical one, since all other forms of preference are thereby excluded.

Turn-taking requires not only an ordering rule but a claiming mechanism as well. This may be formal, for example, number-tickets, names on a receptionist's list, or informal, as when the individual remains close to the place of service and assumes that a tacit consensus will operate. Sometimes a line or row formation (a queue) will be employed as a collective, mnemonic device, and sometimes this formal device allows the participant to sustain a formally unmarked turn during brief absences. Many queues qualify a with as a claimant, especially where one member can transact all of its business (as in movie queues), and this often leads to permission to join an acquaintance ahead of where one otherwise would have been, since in these cases a single already established in line will be able to act as though he is merely the agent for a with that is just now fully arrived. I want only to add that when turns are held by bodies standing in single file, then each participant will be involved both in maintaining his turn and his personal space. However, since the taking of turns provides a clear reading of events, great reductions of personal space can be tolerated along with attendant bodily contact.

5. *The Sheath:* The skin that covers the body and, at a little remove, the clothes that cover the skin. Certainly the body's sheath can function as the least of all possible personal spaces, the minimal configuration in that regard; but it can also function as a preserve in its own right, the purest kind of egocentric territoriality. Of course, different parts of the body are accorded different concern—indeed this differential concern tells us in part how the body will be divided up into segments conceptually. Among the American middle classes, for example, little effort is made to keep the elbow inviolate, whereas orifice areas are of concern. And, of course, across different cultures, the body will be differently segmented ritually.

6. *Possessional Territory:* Any set of objects that can be identified with the self and arrayed around the body wherever it is. The central examples are spoken of as "personal effects"—easily detachable possessions such as jackets, hats, gloves, cigarette packs, matches, handbags and what they contain, and parcels. We must also include a claimant's copresent dependents because, territorially, they function somewhat like his personal possessions. Finally, there are objects that remain tethered to a particular setting but can be temporarily claimed by persons present, much as can stalls: ashtrays, magazines, cushions, and eating utensils are examples. One might also include here regulative command over mechanical creature-comfort devices: control over radio, television sets, temperature, windows, light, and so forth.

7. *Information Preserve:* The set of facts about himself to which an individual expects to control access while in the presence of others. There are several varieties of information preserve, and there is some question about classing them all together. There is the content of the claimant's mind, control over which is threatened when queries are made that he sees as intrusive, nosy, untactful. There are the contents of pockets, purses, containers, letters, and the like, which the claimant can feel others have no right to ascertain. There are biographical facts about the individual over the divulgence of which he expects to maintain control. And most important for our purposes, there is what can be directly perceived about an individual, his body's sheath and his current behavior, the issue here being his right not to be stared at or examined. Of course, since the individual is also a vehicular unit and since pilots of other such units have a need and a right to track him, he will come to be able to make an exquisite perceptual distinction between being looked at and being stared at, and, God help us, learn to suspect, if not detect, that the latter is being masked by the former; and he will learn to conduct himself so that others come to respond to him in the same way. Incidentally, wherever we find such fine behavioral discriminations, we should suspect that what is at work is the need to keep two different behavioral systems functioning without interference in the same physical area.

8. *Conversational Preserve:* The right of an individual to exert some control over who can summon him into talk and when he can be summoned; and the right of a set of individuals once engaged in talk to have their circle protected from entrance and overhearing by others.

I have touched on eight territories of

the self, all of a situational or an egocentric kind: personal space, stalls, use space, turns, sheath, possessional territory, information preserve, and conversational preserve. One general feature of these several forms of territoriality should be noted: their socially determined variability. Given a particular setting and what is available in it, the extensivity of preserves obviously can vary greatly according to power and rank. Patients in a charity hospital may have to wait until dying before being given a privacy screen around their bed; in middle-class private hospitals, the patient may enjoy this privilege at other times, too, for example, when breast feeding a child. Similarly, clinic patients in a hospital may be discussed by physicians by name, while private patients in the same hospital are given the privacy rights of being referred to by room number. In general, the higher the rank, the greater the size of all territories of the self and the greater the control across the boundaries. (Within a given household, for example, adults tend to have vastly larger territorial claims than do children.) Cutting across these differences, however, there is another—the variation that occurs in the understandings sustained by any one set of individuals as they move from situation to situation. For example, middle-class Americans at Western ski lodges allow their bodies to be stared at and touched-in-passing to a degree that would be considered quite intrusive were this to occur in the public places of their home town. Finally, there are group-cultural differences that crosscut these cross cuttings. For example, there is some evidence that lower-class blacks are more concerned to obtain eyeing avoidance than are lower-class Italians.

23.

G. H. MEAD'S THEORY OF INDIVIDUAL AND SOCIETY

Charles W. Morris

G. H. Mead's great contribution to sociology was his theoretical analysis of the basic relationship between the person and the group. His "social behaviorism" emphasized the crucial function of language and social interaction in the development of human behavior and stressed that the human mind is a social phenomenon. This selection, taken from Charles Morris's introduction to a compilation of Mead's lectures entitled *Mind, Self, and Society,* presents some of the concepts central to his theory. Mead's formulation has come to be known as the "symbolic interaction" theory of behavior.

The transformation of the biologic individual to the minded organism or self takes place, on Mead's account, through the agency of language, while language in turn presupposes the existence of a certain

Source: Charles W. Morris, *Mind, Self and Society* (Chicago: The Chicago University Press, 1934), pp. xx–xxvi.

kind of society and certain physiological capacities in the individual organisms.

The minimal society must be composed of biologic individuals participating in a social act and using the early stages of each other's actions as gestures, that is, as guides to the completion of the act. In the "conversation of gestures" of the dog fight each dog determines his behavior in terms of what the other dog is beginning to do; and the same holds for the boxer, the fencer, and the chick which runs to the hen at the hen's cluck. Such action is a type of communication; in one sense the gestures are symbols, since they indicate, stand for, and cause action appropriate to the later stages of the act of which they are early fragments, and secondarily to the objects implicated in such acts. In the same sense, the gestures may be said to have meaning, namely, they mean the later stages of the oncoming act, and secondarily, the objects implicated: the clenched fist means the blow, the outstretched hand means the object being reached for. Such meanings are not subjective, not private, not mental, but are objectively there in the social situation.

Nevertheless, this type of communication is not language proper; the meanings are not yet "in mind"; the biologic individuals are not yet consciously communicating selves. For these results to transpire the symbols or gestures must become significant symbols or gestures. The individual must know what he is about; he himself, and not merely those who respond to him, must be able to interpret the meaning of his own gesture. Behavioristically, this is to say that the biologic individual must be able to call out in himself the response his gesture calls out in the other, and then utilize this response of the other for the control of his own further conduct. Such gestures are significant symbols. Through their use the individual is "taking the rôle of the other" in the regulation of his own conduct. Man is essentially the rôle-taking animal. The calling out of the same response in both the self and the other gives the common content necessary for community of meaning.

As an example of the significant symbol Mead uses the tendency to call out "Fire!" when smoke is seen in a crowded theater. The immediate utterance of the sound would simply be part of the initiated act, and would be at the best a nonsignificant symbol. But when the tendency to call out "Fire!" affects the individual as it affects others, and is itself controlled in terms of these effects, the vocal gesture has become a significant symbol; the individual is conscious of what he is about; he has reached the stage of genuine language instead of unconscious communications; he may now be said to use symbols and not merely respond to signs; he has now acquired a mind.

In looking for gestures capable of becoming significant symbols, and so of transforming the biologic individual into a minded organism, Mead comes upon the vocal gesture. No other gesture affects the individual himself so similarly as it affects others. We hear ourselves talk as others do, but we do not see our facial expressions, nor normally watch our own actions. For Mead, the vocal gesture is the actual fountainhead of language proper and all derivative forms of symbolism; and so of mind.

Mind is the presence in behavior of significant symbols. It is the internalization

---

Charles W. Morris is professor emeritus at the University of Florida where he taught philosophy. He is the editor of *Works of George H. Mead* and the author of *Six Theories of Mind, Logical Positivism, Pragmatism and Scientific Empiricism,* and *Signs, Language and Behavior.*

within the individual of the social process of communication in which meaning emerges. It is the ability to indicate to one's self the response (and implicated objects) that one's gesture indicates to others, and to control the response itself in these terms. The significant gesture, itself a part of a social process, internalizes and makes available to the component biologic individuals the meanings which have themselves emerged in the earlier, nonsignificant stages of gestural communication. Instead of beginning with individual minds and working out to society, Mead starts with an objective social process and works inward through the importation of the social process of communication into the individual by the medium of the vocal gesture. The individual has then taken the social act into himself. Mind remains social; even in the inner forum so developed thought goes on by one's assuming the rôles of others and controlling one's behavior in terms of such rôle-taking. Since the isolation of the physical thing is for Mead dependent upon the ability to take the rôle of the other, and since thought about such objects involves taking their rôles, even the scientist's reflection about physical nature is a social process, though the objects thought about are no longer social.

. . . . .

It is the same agency of language which on this theory makes possible the appearance of the self. Indeed, the self, mind, "consciousness of," and the significant symbol are in a sense precipitated together. Mead finds the distinguishing trait of selfhood to reside in the capacity of the minded organism to be an object to itself. The mechanism by which this is possible on a behavioristic approach is found in the rôle-taking which is involved in the language symbol. Insofar as one can take the rôle of the other, he can, as it were, look back at himself from (respond to himself from) that perspective, and so become an object to himself. Thus again, it is only in a social process that selves, as distinct from biological organisms, can arise—selves as beings that have become conscious of themselves.

Nor is it merely the process of being aware of one's self that is social: the self that one becomes conscious of in this manner is itself social in form, though not always in content. Mead stresses two stages in the development of the self: the stages of play and the game. In play the child simply assumes one rôle after another of persons and animals that have in some way or other entered into its life. One here sees, writ large as it were, the assumption of the attitudes of others through the self-stimulation of the vocal gesture, whereas later in life such attitudes are more abbreviated and harder to detect. In the game, however, one has become, as it were, all of the others implicated in the common activity—must have within one's self the whole organized activity in order to successfully play one's own part. The person here has not merely assumed the rôle of a specific other, but of any other participating in the common activity; he has generalized the attitude of rôle-taking. In one of Mead's happiest terms and most fertile concepts he has taken the attitude or rôle of the "generalized other."

. . . . .

Through a social process, then, the biologic individual of proper organic stuff gets a mind and a self. Through society the impulsive animal becomes a rational animal, a man. In virtue of the internalization or importation of the social process of communication, the individual gains the mechanism of reflective thought (the ability to direct his action in terms of the foreseen consequences of alternative courses of action); acquires the ability to make himself an object to himself and to live in a common moral and scientific world; becomes a moral individual with impulsive ends transformed into the conscious pursuit of ends-in-view.

Because of the emergence of such an individual, society is in turn transformed. It receives through the reflective social self the organization distinctive of human society; instead of playing his social part through physiological differentiation (as in the case of the insect) or through the bare influence of gestures upon others, the human individual regulates his part in the social act through having within himself the rôles of the others implicated in the common activity. In attaining a new principle of social organization, society has gained a new technique of control, since it has now implanted itself within its component parts, and so regulates, to the degree that this is successfully done, the behavior of the individual in terms of the effect on others of his contemplated action.

24.

RIESMAN ON SOCIETY AND CHARACTER

David Riesman, with
Nathan Glazer and
Reuel Denney

The Lonely Crowd by David Riesman, et al., which was published in the early 1950s created a sensation outside as well as inside the "sociological fraternity." The reason for this is the authors' contention regarding the basic nature of modern Western society. Our society, they assert, has gradually become one in which people are decreasingly "inner-directed" and increasingly "other-directed." To Riesman, et al., the inner-directed person is one whose choices of goals and values are implanted early in life and who pursues them without deviation even though he is con-

Source: David Riesman, Nathan Glazer, and Reuel Denney, *The Lonely Crowd* (New Haven, Conn.: Yale University Press, 1953), pp. 25–40.

David Riesman is the Henry Ford II Professor of Social Sciences at Harvard University. He was trained as a lawyer and served as law clerk to Justice Brandeis. In addition to *The Lonely Crowd,* he wrote *Thorstein Veblen, Individualism Reconsidered and Other Essays, Constraint and Variety in American Education,* and is the coauthor of *The Academic Revolution.*

Nathan Glazer, sociologist, is professor of education and social structure at Harvard University. He wrote *Remembering the Answers* and coauthored *Beyond the Melting Pot.*

Educator and author Reuel Denney is professor of American Studies at the University of Hawaii. He is a member of PEN International and on the advisory board of the *Journal of Social History.* He is the author of *Connecticut River* and *Astonished Muse.*

scious of changing circumstances and alternative behavior in others. The other-directed individual is guided in determining his goals and values through assessing the sentiments of those around him and thus will shift his position as he perceives others changing. These definitions are developed more fully in the following extracts from *The Lonely Crowd.*

In western history the society that emerged with the Renaissance and Reformation and that is only now vanishing serves to illustrate the type of society in which inner-direction is the principal mode of securing conformity. Such a society is characterized by increased personal mobility, by a rapid accumulation of capital (teamed with devastating technological shifts), and by an almost constant *expansion:* intensive expansion in the production of goods and people, and extensive expansion in exploration, colonization, and imperialism. The greater choices this society gives—and the greater initiatives it demands in order to cope with its novel problems—are handled by character types who can manage to live socially without strict and self-evident tradition-direction. These are the inner-directed types.

The concept of inner-direction is intended to cover a very wide range of types. Thus, while it is essential for the study of certain problems to differentiate between Protestant and Catholic countries and their character types, between the effects of the Reformation and the effects of the Renaissance, between the puritan ethic of the European north and west, and the somewhat more hedonistic ethic of the European east and south, while all these are valid and, for certain purposes, important distinctions, the concentration of this study on the development of modes of conformity permits their neglect. It allows the grouping together of these otherwise distinct developments because they have one thing in common: *the source of direction for the individual is "inner" in the sense that it is implanted early in life by the elders and directed toward generalized but nonetheless inescapably destined goals.*

We can see what this means when we realize that, in societies in which tradition-direction is the dominant mode of insuring conformity, attention is focused on securing external *behavioral* conformity. While behavior is minutely prescribed, individuality of character need not be highly developed to meet prescriptions that are objectified in ritual and etiquette—though to be sure, a social character *capable* of such behavioral attention and obedience is requisite. By contrast, societies in which inner-direction becomes important, though they also are concerned with behavioral conformity, cannot be satisfied with behavioral conformity alone. Too many novel situations are presented, situations which a code cannot encompass in advance. Consequently the problem of personal choice, solved in . . . [a tradition-directed period] by channeling choice through rigid social organization, in the period of . . . [inner-direction] is solved by channeling choice through a rigid though highly individualized character.

This rigidity is a complex matter. While any society dependent on inner-direction seems to present people with a wide choice of aims—such as money, possessions, power, knowledge, fame, goodness—these aims are ideologically interrelated, and the selection made by any one individual remains relatively unalterable throughout his life. Moreover, the means to those ends, though not fitted into as tight a social frame of reference as in the society dependent on tradition-direction, are nevertheless limited by the new voluntary associations—for instance, the Quakers, the Masons, the Mechanics' Associations—to which people tie themselves. Indeed, the term "tradition-direction" could be misleading if the reader were to conclude that the force of tradition has no weight for the inner-directed character. On the contrary, he is very considerably bound by traditions: they limit his ends and inhibit his choice of means. The point is rather that a splintering of tradition takes place, connected in part with the increasing division of labor and stratification of society. Even if the individual's choice of tradition is largely determined for him by his family, as it is in most cases, he cannot help becoming aware of the existence of competing traditions—hence of tradition as such. As a result he possesses a somewhat greater degree of flexibility in adapting himself to ever changing requirements and in return requires more from his environment.

. . . . .

A DEFINITION OF OTHER-DIRECTION

The type of character I shall describe as other-directed seems to be emerging in very recent years in the upper middle class of our larger cities: more prominently in New York than in Boston, in Los Angeles than in Spokane, in Cincinnati than in Chillicothe. Yet in some respects this type is strikingly similar to *the* American, whom Tocqueville and other curious and astonished visitors from Europe, even before the Revolution, thought to be a new kind of man. Indeed, travelers' reports on America impress us with their unanimity. The American is said to be shallower, freer with his money, friendlier, more uncertain of himself and his values, more demanding of approval than the European. It all adds up to a pattern which, without stretching matters too far, resembles the kind of character that a number of social scientists have seen as developing in contemporary, highly industrialized, and bureaucratic America: Fromm's "marketer," Mills's "fixer," Arnold Green's "middle class male child."

It is my impression that the middle-class American of today is decisively different from those Americans of de Tocqueville's writings who nevertheless strike us as so contemporary. It is also my impression that the conditions I believe to be responsible for other-direction are affecting increasing numbers of people in the metropolitan centers of the advanced industrial countries. My analysis of the other-directed character is thus at once an analysis of the American and of contemporary man. Much of the time I find it hard or impossible to say where one ends and the other begins. Tentatively, I am inclined to think that the other-directed type does find itself most at home in America, due to certain unique elements in American society, such as its recruitment from Europe and its lack of any feudal past. As against this, I am also inclined to put more weight on capitalism, industrialism, and urbanization—these being international tendencies—than on any character-forming peculiarities of the American scene.

Bearing these qualifications in mind, it seems appropriate to treat contemporary metropolitan America as our illustration of a society—so far, perhaps, the only illustration—in which other-direction is the dominant mode of insuring conformity. It would be premature, however, to say that it is already the dominant mode in America as a whole. But since the other-directed types are to be found among the young, in the larger cities, and among the upper income groups, we may assume that, unless present trends are reversed, the hegemony of other-direction lies not far off.

If we wanted to cast our social character types into social class molds, we could say that inner-direction is the typical character of the "old" middle class—the banker, the tradesman, the small entrepreneur, the technically oriented engineer, etc.—while other-direction is becoming the typical character of the "new" middle class—the bureaucrat, the salaried employee in business, etc. Many of the economic factors associated with the recent growth of the "new" middle class are well known. They have been discussed by James Burnham, Colin Clark, Peter Drucker, and others. There is a decline in the numbers and in the proportion of the working population engaged in production and extraction—agriculture, heavy industry, heavy transport—and an increase in the numbers and the proportion engaged in white-collar work and the service trades. People who are literate, educated, and provided with the necessities of life by an ever more efficient machine industry and agriculture, turn increasingly to the "tertiary" economic realm. The service industries prosper among the people as a whole and no longer only in court circles.

. . . . .

These developments lead, for large numbers of people, to changes in paths to success and to requirement of more "socialized" behavior both for success and for marital and personal adaptation. Connected with such changes are changes in the family and in child-rearing practices. In the smaller families of urban life, and with the spread of "permissive" child care to ever wider strata of the population, there is a relaxation of older patterns of discipline. Under these newer patterns the peer-group (the group of one's associates of the same age and class) becomes much more important to the child, while the parents make him feel guilty not so much about violation of inner standards as about failure to be popular or otherwise to manage his relations with these other children. Moreover, the pressures of the school and the peer-group are reinforced and continued—in a manner whose inner paradoxes I shall discuss later—by the mass media: movies, radio, comics, and popular culture media generally. Under these conditions types of character emerge that we shall here term other-directed. . . . *What is common to all the other-directed people is that their contemporaries are the source of direction for the individual—either those known to him or those with whom he is indirectly acquainted, through friends and through the mass media. This source is of course "internalized" in the sense that dependence on it for guidance in life is implanted early. The goals toward which the other-directed person strives shift with that guidance: it is only the process of striving itself and the process of paying close attention to the signals from others that remain unaltered throughout life.* This mode of keeping in touch with others permits a close behavioral conformity, not through drill in behavior itself, as in the tradition-directed character, but rather through an exceptional sensitivity to the actions and wishes of others.

Of course, it matters very much who these "others" are: whether they are the individual's immediate circle or a "higher" circle or the anonymous voices of the mass media; whether the individual fears the hostility of chance acquaintances or only of those who "count." But his need for approval and direction from others—and contemporary others rather than ancestors—goes beyond the reasons that lead most people in any era to care very much what others think of them. While all people want and need to be liked by some of the people some of the time, it is only the modern other-directed types who make this their chief source of direction and chief area of sensitivity.

. . . . .

. . . We must differentiate the nineteenth-century American—gregarious and subservient to public opinion though he was found to be by Tocqueville, Bryce, and others—from the other-directed American as he emerges today, an American who in his character is more capable of and more interested in maintaining responsive contact with others both at work and at play. This point needs to be emphasized, since the distinction is easily misunderstood. The inner-directed person, though he often sought and sometimes achieved a relative independence of public opinion and of what the neighbors thought of him, was in most cases very much concerned with his good repute and, at least in America, with "keeping up with the Joneses." These conformities, however, were primarily external, typified in such details as clothes, curtains, and bank credit. For, indeed, the conformities were to a standard, evidence of which was provided by the "best people" in one's milieu. In contrast with this pattern, the other-directed person, though he has his eye very much on the Joneses, aims to keep up with them not so much in external details as in the quality of his inner experience. That is, his great sensitivity keeps him in touch with others on many more levels than the externals of appearance and propriety. Nor does any ideal of independence or of reliance on God alone modify his desire to look to the others—and the "good guys" as well as the best people—for guidance in what experiences to seek and in how to interpret them.

25.

BUSINESS AS A CAREER

Victor Lebow

Less than twenty years ago the concept of "The Organization Man" was introduced to represent what appeared to be a pervasive orientation of those employed in the innumerable bureaucratic organizations of society. This orientation was considered to be characterized by people who behaved as though they not only *worked* for an organization but *belonged* to it. Today we find trends toward the opposite extreme—the dissident American youth who has dropped out of the "established social system." Both represent types of relationships between the individual and groups. In the selection that follows Lebow gives his views on why many

Source: Victor Lebow, *Free Enterprise: The Opium of the American People* (New York: Oriole Editions, 1973), pp. 111–18.

Victor Lebow has been an executive, officer, and director of large corporations. He has written articles on economics, advertising, and marketing and his published work has appeared in *Harper's* magazine, *The Nation*, and others. At Columbia University, the author is cochairman of the University Seminar on the Economics of Distribution.

college and university students of this period repudiated business as a possible career and indicated why ". . . it is important that some of these brilliant and idealistic rebels seek out careers in private enterprise." Lebow is an exceptional witness on how the American economic system works because of his personal experience in the business world. He claims that the profit system needs to be radically changed to make it responsible to American society. In accordance with his strategy of enlightened change, his little book, from which this chapter was taken, is dedicated ". . . to the college generation of the 1960s and 1970s upon whom will fall the responsibility for transforming this country by the year 2000 A.D."

Because it shapes our values, business is able to influence our national priorities in the directions most profitable to its operations, and to exercise its veto on ideas and proposals it deems undesirable. Thus, while the nation needs more and better housing, schools, hospitals, it gets mile after mile of new highways. The country lacks efficient mass transportation systems, but it gets more highways, more jet ports, while mile after mile of railroad right-of-way is demolished. This indictment has become familiar and it grows ever more lengthy and detailed with each passing year. But, of course, it is a criticism of State administrations, or of the Congress, or the incumbent national government. Business as an institution, as a system, has been a sacred cow, exempt from criticism, and even from objective study.

It is among the dissident young people, particularly those in the colleges and universities, that rejection of "The System" takes the form of the repudiation of business as a career. There is a spectre haunting American corporations. It is the parade of college and university graduates who are seeking careers in fields other than business.

This is, or should be, a concern for all Americans. For a deep and bitter breach is developing between the young people who repudiate business and the "grey flannel types" who accept it without question. Indeed, for the healthy development of the economy and of the society as a whole, it is important that some of these brilliant and idealistic rebels seek out careers in private enterprise. They may, of course, succumb to its blandishments and rewards, but they may also play a role in the transformation that is bound to come, and, perhaps, they may help make it smoother and less violent than it will otherwise be.

As a nation we have always been suckers for the simplistic solution, and the young generation is equally susceptible. It sounds most attractive to stand Karl Marx on his head and preach that a new consciousness will alter the world. No people has ever been able to dismantle its way of life without destroying its civilization. We live in a time when the scientific and technological developments may need new direction and different emphasis. But this is a most complex civilization, and to retreat to some Nirvana of love, and beads, and Levi's, actually means inviting catastrophe and barbarism.

That the college and university students of the last twenty years have sound reason for their repudiation of much in this society, no sensible person can dispute. "This generation of college students is the best informed, the most intelligent, and the most idealistic this country has ever known," was the opinion of the Cox Commission report on the uprising in Columbia University. Calling the dissenters "kooks" and "social misfits" as Spiro Agnew did, is to embitter the divisions in our society.

It is an oversimplification to ascribe the disaffection of the young to the war in Vietnam alone. The former director of the Peace Corps, Jack H. Vaughn, asserted that young people are angry at the sham they see and hear: "The sham that fighting a war is the way to achieve peace; the sham that life is getting better in a country where cities are sliding rapidly into dilapidation; the sham that a country which permits twenty million black men and women to be second-class citizens is a country animated by the spirit of liberty and dedicated to the principle of equality."

One advertising agency tried to meet the dissent of the young head on with a full page advertisement in *The New York Times,* under the headline, "Has Business Become a Dirty Word?" It argued that college students simply do not know how much business contributes toward the public good for medical research, for victims of fire and flood, for war orphans and refugees. "Look what business is doing for culture, for human values. Opera, ballet and symphony orchestras simply couldn't exist on today's scale without subsidies from business. Neither could museums or libraries. Or repertory theatre . . . Business is helping to enrich minds, to broaden understanding. To improve relations among races, nations, ideologies . . . to improve people's chances of living in peace and dignity . . ."

The refutation is so obvious, it is not worth making. This is the only industrialized country in the world which does not subsidize those cultural institutions the advertisement is listing. However, a more direct answer could be found in *Advertising Age,* which reported some remarks made at a meeting of the Association of National Advertisers by the vice-chancellor of the University of California at Berkeley. He spoke about our "exploitative society . . . with profit rather than human fulfillment as the goal."

This was Dr. William B. Boyd, and he was speaking out of his intimate knowledge of the college population: "Many students assert that a society in which one's behavior is influenced by manipulation undertaken for commercial reasons (for example, one in which we are made anxious about how we smell) is as much the victim of economic determinism as Marx ever thought society to be—with results less hopeful than for Marx." He continued, "When you add the bitter lessons of the civil rights crisis and now the war in Vietnam, when you acknowledge our use of sex to sell merchandise, you will begin to sense the power of their (the students') indictment . . . A generation of youth that rates involvement higher than status will not choose either the same job or the same clothes as its fathers. Neither the carrot nor the whip will drive this new generation. When we reach the moment when the quality of life, rather than its preservation, becomes our true concern, then the attitude of modern youth will have come into its own."

The view many college students take of the corporation seems quite similar to that expressed by the British historian, E. J. Hobsbawm. As he sees it, big business is in fact better business than small business—more dynamic, more efficient, better able to undertake the increasingly complex and expensive tasks of development. However, he says, "The real case against it is not that it is big, but that it is antisocial."

This is a new era dawning. For such opinions, whether these college graduates reject the corporate life altogether or not, threaten the established *milieu.* In earlier years, the radical in his youth became the staid conservative in his mature years. But the very technology which business has so assiduously fostered, the colonial peoples whom business for so long exploited, the vast armaments which private enterprise has produced, all conspire to make the times uncertain, the future clouded, and the cry for change ever more insistent.

A whole young generation is questioning the values, goals, attitudes, and institutions which have brought the world to its present condition. They inherit a burden bequeathed to them in that succession of catastrophes and upheavals that have marked world history since World War I. To them, the rise of Italian fascism and German nazism, the Spanish civil war, and even World War II and the Korean conflicts, are just chapters in their modern history text books, and now they have met the horror of Vietnam. But theirs is the world these events have fathered, the world of nuclear armaments, of planes airborne on the hour carrying atom bombs, of Polaris submarines, of unwanted and illegal wars, of American interventions on behalf of militarists and dictators. They see a land of unimaginable riches in which some forty million people live in poverty. They are witness to the revolution of its Black citizens, they have awakened to the discrimination and injustices perpetrated against the truly native Americans, the Indians, and against our Spanish speaking citizens.

Along with all this, they see business flourishing, indeed profiting from much of the turmoil and destruction, and reaching into every corner of the planet not preempted by Communist control. Today, in fact, one of the largest economic constellations in the world is the American investment in foreign lands. As they understand their own social obligation, the college and university men and women sense a great gap between their sense of commitment and that of private enterprise. All these realizations have helped produce this alienation of so many of the most intelligent of our younger people.

As one business executive put it, after attending a conference of students and executives at Princeton University, "Business will be in a lot of trouble in the years to come if we can't change the minds of some of these kids. We'll be stuck with nothing but the mediocrities."

There are those who shrug off the interest of young people in the environment and in its pollution as just another fad of youth. But involved here, too, is bitter criticism of business practices. In a *Business Week* survey of the views of student leaders on this problem, the degree of concern was high. A Harvard PhD candidate: "The cause of this crisis is unabated capitalism—the easiest way to produce a product is to use the environment as industry's private dumping ground." A Boston University student: "They equate GNP with quality of life, but we can't keep up with the built-in obsolescence. Industry is a giant funnel taking nature and turning out garbage for its own profit. The government doesn't police them—they say growth is not just good, growth is God." A Columbia University graduate student: "Out walking in the Adirondacks, I came over a hill and saw this incredibly barren zone. Not even weeds, just a sign, 'Property of National Lead Co.' Well, this country isn't for private exploitation, it belongs to all of us . . ."

Fortune reported that in the top-ranking colleges from 60 percent to 80 percent of the seniors in *recent* graduating classes had decided not to go to graduate school, proclaiming as they went that "Business is for the birds." Particularly galling has been the fact, in recent years, that graduates with higher academic standing have been avoiding the recruiters, while the men with the lower marks have been accepting the jobs corporations have offered. One public opinion poll revealed the fact that while 23 percent of the general public thought that business leaders were public spirited, only 9 percent of the nation's college students agreed. On a percentage basis, twice as many students as members of the general population felt that business leaders were motivated by "selfish interest" and an even larger proportion considered them "manipulators."

Some business leaders have been frank to admit that "some of what students believe about business was true. And, in all honesty, to some extent it is still true today, though to a rapidly decreasing degree . . ." And some college professors try to be reassuring to the corporations that are concerned about this trend. Professor Andrew Hacker, of Cornell, has written that "Too much has been made of the alleged 'repudiation' of business and the corporate life by the current generation of college students. This may be the case at Swarthmore, Oberlin, and in certain Ivied circles. But, in actual fact, the great majority of undergraduates, who are after all at places like Penn State and Purdue, would like nothing better than a good berth at Ford or Texaco. Indeed, they are even now priming themselves to become the sort of persons these companies would want them to be."

In the atmosphere of the 'Fifties, poisoned by Senator Joe McCarthy, there was practically no expression of dissent nor any reservations about business as a career. But the civil rights movement and the war in Vietnam served to jolt the students of the 'Sixties out of the placidity of the "silent generation" that had preceded them. From what they have been saying, it seems clear that today's college students see a world so distorted, so violent, so wracked by poverty, deprivation, suppression, and discrimination, so corrupt, and so hypocritical, that most of them harbor a cold distrust of all the powers that be.

Yet, the fact remains that it is business that orders the wheels to go 'round in this country, and it is business which commands and oversees the execution of its plans. And while it corrupts, it also rewards its devotees with wealth, with status, with power, with byzantine expense accounts, and with the envy of their less successful fellows. More important is the fact that American private enterprise has developed managerial and administrative skills, a capacity for long-term planning, and the ability to use and exploit technological and scientific developments to a degree unsurpassed. What it lacks is humanity.

As one listens to a few of the more enlightened business leaders there appears some reason for a more hopeful solution to the problem of whether society can survive corporate power. True, one must listen with this dire injunction ever before one's eyes: "Put not your faith in princes." Thus, in a remarkable speech on the need for planning and for explicit national goals, the Chairman of the Board of IBM, Thomas J. Watson, pointed to many of our shortcomings, and ended his statement: "It's a sad thing, a very sad thing, when a nation like this one has to creep into a new decade with its tail between its legs. I don't want to do that again. I want to sail into the 1980's—and I want to see flags flying and hear bands playing. We can do that, I'm convinced, if we're willing to take a hard, cold and constant look at how we're running the biggest enterprise in the world."

Probably no businessman in recent years has so clearly expressed the dilemma of the young as did the Chairman of the Chase Manhattan Bank, David Rockefeller:

"I suppose young people have always had a tendency to feel that their elders have made a botch of the world. But this is the first generation I know of which has publicly proclaimed distrust of anyone over thirty. The cold fact is that many of today's young people regard me and my fellow businessmen as hopelessly corrupt. We are, in their eyes, so crippled by the compromises we have made in order to find a place in what they call 'The Establishment' that we are no longer capable of recognizing the truth or acting upon it . . . The answers that young people themselves supply to this question are not reassuring. On the extreme left, there are some who believe that American society is so evil it must be torn down—that destruction must precede reconstruction. Even among the more moderate majority of youngsters, there is a general conviction that American society stands convicted of not practicing the principles it professes."

Perhaps the career for the college graduate who is dedicated to the changes that must come, is to come into business as a sort of fifth-columnist, to work from within its framework to make it more amenable to the needs of humanity. But it would be naive to believe that, no matter what high-minded protestations may come from business leaders, the essential character of the private enterprise system can be radically altered from within.

The only way changes in the working and the direction of business can be accomplished is through compulsion. And since the college and university students of this decade will be the masters of industry by the end of this century, it would seem incumbent upon the university to prepare the future businessmen for the special character of their careers.

26.

THE END OF SCARCITY?

Daniel Bell

As the year 2000 of the Christian Era inexorably draws near, a new intellectual specialty is emerging, that of the futurologist. Activity of this kind has a long history, but has usually been characterized by a utopian rather than a scientific orientation. However, a half century ago an earlier generation of social scientists set a precedent by examining the past and offering projections for the future in a landmark study commissioned by President Hoover and entitled *Recent Social Trends, 1933.* In this more recent effort of a similar nature, Daniel Bell examines present social trends giving particular attention to the possible future interrelations of people in economic organizations. Though the reader may not readily accept

Source: Daniel R. Bell, "The End of Scarcity," *Saturday Review of the Society* 1, no. 4 (May 1973): 49–53.

The author is professor of sociology at Harvard University. His chief interests are industrial relations and industrial sociology. He is author of *American Marxist Parties, Work in the Life of an American, The Reforming of General Education,* and *Capitalism Today.*

the idea that a rising standard of life means simply more and more of the same goods and services, Bell rightly emphasizes that in the future qualitative changes in social relations may well be more significant than the strictly quantitative changes measured in goods and services.

Not long ago social scientists were predicting dramatic changes in our work habits, the coming of a "leisure society," and—even more remarkably—the end of scarcity as we moved from an industrial to a postindustrial society. More recently we have been warned that, unless we curtail our appetites and learn to control our exploitation of the natural environment, there will be too many people, not enough resources, and more than enough waste and pollution to engulf future generations. Both of these conceptions—a utopian end of scarcity and a catastrophic end of resources—seem to me to be wrong. What is more likely to come is a new and different set of scarcities, a new set of "costs" that previous generations did not have to pay but that must be borne by those inhabiting the postindustrial society.

Central to this discussion is the notion of scarcity, a word given many interpretations, but usually viewed as something absolute rather than relative, in physical rather than economic terms. For a number of writers the idea of a postindustrial society is equated with a postscarcity society. David Riesman, when he first used the term "postindustrial" in 1958, was thinking of a "leisure society" and the sociological problems that might arise when, for the first time in human history, large numbers of persons had to confront the use of leisure time rather than the drudgery of work. Anarchist writers such as Paul Goodman and Murray Bookchin envisage a postscarcity society as one in which technology has freed men from dependence on material things and thus provides the basis for a "free" relation to, rather than dependence on, nature. The elimination of scarcity, as the condition for abolishing all competitiveness and strife, has been the axial principle of all utopian thinking, including Marxist.

Although Marx himself rarely speculated on what the future society would be like, it is clear from every aspect of his work that the condition for socialism, for genuine equality, was economic abundance, the possibility of which lay in the extraordinary accomplishments of the bourgeoisie. In 1848, in a startling panegyric in the Communist Manifesto, Marx wrote that the bourgeoisie "has been the first to show what man's activity can bring about," and has created "during its rule of scarcely 100 years . . . more massive and more colossal productive forces than have all the preceding generations together."

Writing in 1930, John Maynard Keynes pointed out that the worldwide depression then under way was not the "rheumatics of old age" but the "growing pains of overrapid changes . . . between one economic period and another." The "disastrous mistakes" we have made "blind us to what is going on under the surface—to the true interpretation of the trend of things." The underlying trend of things could be seen in two innovations: the discovery of technical efficiency or productivity, and the sustained means for the accumulation of capital.

From the earliest times down to the eighteenth century, Keynes wrote, "there was no very great change in the standard of life of the average man living in the civilized centres of earth." But with the combination of technical efficiency and capital accumulation, mankind had discovered the "magic" of "compound interest," of growth building on growth. "If capital increases, say, 2 percent per annum, the capital equipment of the world will have increased by a half in 20 years, and seven and a half times in 100 years. Think of this in terms of material things—houses, transport, and the like." And to Keynes this meant "in the long run *that mankind is solving its economic problem.* I would predict that the standard of life in progressive countries 100 years hence will be between four and eight times as high as it is today. . . . It would not be foolish to contemplate the possibility of a far greater progress still."

In the decades since Keynes wrote, greater and greater progress, spurred by technological advances, has been envisaged by social scientists. This technological euphoria reached its vertex in 1964 with the statement of a group calling itself The Ad Hoc Committee on the Triple Revolution. "A new era of production has begun," the committee declared; indeed, a new "cybernation revolution" was under way whose "principles of organization are as different from the industrial era as those of the industrial era were different from the agricultural." Cybernation—a term invented by Donald Michael—is "the combination of the computer and the automated self-regulating machine." The increased efficiency of machine systems "is shown in the more rapid increase in productivity per man-hour since 1960, a year that marks the first visible upsurge of the cybernation revolution." Cybernation results "in a system of almost unlimited productive capacity which requires progressively less labor."

. . . . .

Has the economic problem been solved? Will scarcity disappear? Put in the terms that socialist and utopian thinkers have used—nineteenth-century terms—the answer is no, or not for a long time. For one thing the cybernetic revolution quickly proved to be illusory. There were no spectacular jumps in productivity. A detailed study by the President's Commission on Technology, Automation, and Economic Progress, completed in 1966, showed that for the past two decades there had been no sharp changes in the rate of productivity, and, if one looked ahead ten years—the period for which one could identify oncoming technological developments—there were no increases in the offing. In fact, the prospects for the economy were quite the reverse. The expansion of the service sector—a significant feature of the postindustrial society—had become a drag on productivity. The image of a completely automated production economy—with an endless capacity to turn out goods—was simply a social science fiction of the early 1960s.

Paradoxically, the vision of utopia was suddenly replaced by the specter of doomsday. In place of the early Sixties theme of endless plenty, the picture by the end of the decade was one of a fragile planet of limited resources whose finite stocks were being rapidly depleted and whose wastes from soaring industrial production were polluting the air and waters. Now the only way of saving the world was zero growth.

The difficulty with such thinking is that it assumes that no qualitative change takes place, or is even possible. But this is clearly not so. Materials can be recycled. New sources of energy (e.g., solar energy) can be tapped. We do not yet have a full inventory of the mineral and metal resources of the earth (in the oceans, Siberia, the Amazon basin, and elsewhere). And technology makes possible the transmutation of resources. For example, taconite, once thought to be worthless, is now a vast source of iron ore; aluminum oxide, once a curiosity, has now become a source of hundreds of millions of tons of metal reserve because industrial chemistry reduced the cost of extraction. The ecological models take the physical finiteness of the earth as the ultimate bound, but this is fundamentally misleading. Resources are properly measured in economic, not physical, terms, and on the basis of relative costs new investments are made that can irrigate arid land, drain swampy land, clear forests, explore for new resources, or stimulate the process of extraction and transmutation. These methods of adding to the supplies of "fixed resources" have been going on throughout human history.

If in the foreseeable future—say for the next 100 years—there will be neither utopia nor doomsday but the same state that has existed for the last 100 years—namely, the fairly steady advance of "compound interest"—the banality of this fact (how jaded we soon become to the routinization of the spectacular!) should not obscure the extraordinary achievement Keynes called attention to. For the first time in human history, he reminded us, the problem of survival in the bare sense of the word—freedom from hunger and disease—need no longer exist. The question before the human race is not subsistence but standard of living, not biology but sociology. Basic needs are satiable, and the possibility of abundance is real. To that extent, the Marx-Keynes vision of the economic meaning of industrial society is certainly true.

But this is to define the future in nineteenth-century terms, to conceive of scarcity as something to be overcome by the production of goods, and to see society as a game between man and nature, a game man wins when he can wrest enough goods and thereby "conquer" scarcity. When the interaction between man and nature, if not at an end, is less pressing, the primary mode of interaction becomes that among persons—and this is the design of postindustrial society. This new design brings with it a new set of scarcities, not viewed in physical terms as something to be overcome by production, but seen in economic terms measurable in rising costs. For preindustrial society, scarcity is an absolute measure of have or have not. Yet few goods are completely "free," and if we think of scarcity, we have to think of relative costs.

The question used to be: Are there enough material goods, and how do we produce more? The question now becomes: What are the costs of new kinds of services, and how much are we willing to pay?

Thus, if we think of scarcity in terms of cost, the postindustrial society brings with it a whole new set of scarcities. What have become costly in this society are information, coordination, and time. The nineteenth century never thought of these in terms of costs, but now because we have to pay more for them, each is a scarcity. Let us examine them one by one:

THE COSTS OF INFORMATION

The postindustrial society is an information society, and the centrality of information creates some new and different problems for the society to manage. These are:

1. The sheer amount of information that one has to absorb because of the expansion of the different arenas—economic, political, and social—of men's attention and involvement. More information is not complete information; if anything, it makes information more and more incomplete. For example, in the political world one must

keep up with the changing fortunes of several dozen countries and pay consistent attention to political situations in a half-dozen areas of the world simultaneously. And the cost of gathering relevant information necessarily goes up.

2. The increasingly technical nature of the information. Today the discussion of international affairs involves a knowledge of balance of payments, of first- and second-strike nuclear capabilities, and so forth; to judge economic policy on unemployment and inflation, one has to understand the intersects of the Phillips curve, the relation of monetary to fiscal policy, and the like. Information thus becomes more arcane, and one must study a subject more intensively than ever before.

3. The greater need for mediation, or journalistic translation: news is no longer reported but interpreted. There is the question of selection from the vast flow of information; explanation is required because of the technical nature of the information. Not only do journalists have to become more specialized, but the journals themselves become more differentiated in order to explain the new theories to intermediate and mass audiences. The differentiation of journalism inevitably becomes a rising "cost" to the society.

4. The sheer limits of the amount of information one can absorb. There is an outer limit to the span of control of the "bits" of information an individual can "process" at one time. There is equally an outer limit to the amount of information about events one can absorb (or the fields or interests one can pursue). And with the "exponential" growth of knowledge and the multiplication of fields and interests, the knowledge that any individual can retain about the variety of events or the span of knowledge inevitably diminishes. More and more we know less and less.

THE COSTS OF COORDINATION

The postindustrial society is a "game between persons" that requires increasing amounts of coordination, especially when that game is carried on in a visible political arena rather than through the "invisible hand" of the economic marketplace. The costs of coordination can be deducted from this change in the locus of decision making.

1. *Participation.* The expansion of the political arena and the involvement of a greater number of persons means that it takes more time and greater cost to reach a decision and to get anything done. More claimants are involved, interests multiply, caucuses have to meet, demands have to be bargained over, differences have to be mediated—and time and costs mount up as each person or interest wants to have a say. Often one hears the statement that individuals or groups feel "powerless" to affect affairs. But there is probably more participation today than ever before in political life, at all levels of government, and that very increase in participation leads to the multiplication of groups that "check" each other, and thus to the sense of impasse. Thus increased participation paradoxically leads, more often than not, to increased frustration.

2. *Interaction.* With the expansion of the world sensorium, we exchange more telephone calls, travel more often, go to more conferences, meet more people. But at what cost? Either one accepts the fleeting nature of such encounters, or one encounters an "upper bound" that limits the degree of personal interaction. What happens is that the number of contacts and interactions often increases at the expense of one's relatively good friendships. Increasingly, one goes through "cycles" of friendship while at a particular job or place, and then these end or become attenuated as one

moves on to a different job or place. Thus the increase of mobility, spatial and social, has its costs in the multiplication of interactions and networks that one has experienced.

3. *Transaction.* In our definition of freedom we attach a high value to easy mobility and freedom from schedules. We seek to have rapid and easy access from our homes to any other point. Living farther apart, we need to ship more goods—and to ship ourselves—across larger distances. As a result we incur an increasing amount of what one might call *transaction costs,* especially in the form of goods and space devoted to communication and transportation. Two cars per family no longer represent an increase in the standard of living. These are part of the rising transaction costs of the newer affluent lifestyles—and they give rise to larger social costs in the congestion on the roads, the lack of ample parking space, air pollution, and the like. The costs of freedom and mobility in the end become quite high and must be regulated, or the lifestyle becomes self-defeating.

4. *Planning.* Inevitably a complex society, like the large, complex organizations within it, becomes a planning society. The large corporations engage in five-year and even longer-range planning in order to identify new products, estimate capital needs, replace obsolescent plants, train labor, and so on. Necessarily, government begins to plan—in dealing with such questions as renewal of cities, building of housing, planning of medical care, etc. The costs of planning, involving as they do research and consultation, inevitably become more expensive as more and more factors—and claimants—enter into the planning process.

5. *Regulation.* The more income and the greater the abundance in a society, the greater becomes the need for regulation and for an increase in the costs of regulation. It may well be, as Herman Kahn has predicted, that private income in the year 2000 will be $10,000 a person, as against $3,550 in 1965, but that person will not be three times better off, just as a person today, whose income is twice as high as it was 20 years ago, is not twice as well off as he was then. As incomes rise, there is a greater demand for goods or amenities that are by their nature limited: access to parks, to beaches, to vacation homes, to travel. The greater use of these amenities involves more planning, scheduling, and regulation.

The moral is clear: Without appropriate organization the results are apt to be unsatisfactory. But organization, too, has its costs, not only in time, personnel, and money, but in the degree of coercion required. As Mancur Olsen pointed out several years ago in his pathbreaking book *The Logic of Collective Action,* the nature of collective goods or benefits is such that they apply to all in the group, and it is impossible to exclude any member of the group from the benefits. But for this very reason there is often an incentive for each individual not to make a payment of his own accord, since he will receive the benefit once it is extended. This is why, for example, trade unions seek to impose a closed shop or obligatory union membership on all workers in a plant in order to bar a "free ride" for those who do not pay the union dues. For a collective action to be fair, everyone must be required to join the agreement.

Again, greater abundance and more time for leisure create wider choice and more individual options, but also, and paradoxically, the greater need for collective regulation. If all people are to coexist, there is a greater need for a social contract, but for that contract to work it must also be enforceable—which is also a greater cost.

THE COSTS OF TIME

Benjamin Franklin, that practical Yankee, used to say that "time is money," a remark that Max Weber regarded as the heart of the Protestant ethic of calculation. We usually think of time as a cost when applied to production. When a machine is idle—or "downtime"—costs mount up; an efficient manager seeks to get full use of the time of the machine. But consumption also requires time. In the modern economy, which is one of growing abundance, time paradoxically becomes the scarcest element of all. Unlike other economic resources, time cannot be accumulated. In economic terms there is a limited "supply" of time. And like any limited supply, it has a cost. When productivity is low, time is relatively cheap; when productivity is high, time becomes relatively expensive. In short, economic growth entails a general increase in the scarcity of time.

Working time is subject to measurement and allocation. Time, outside of work, is "free time" for play or leisure. But in the postindustrial society that "free time" also becomes subject to measurement and allocation, and the "yield on time" in those activities is brought into parity with the yield on working time.

There are three areas in which this calculus begins to take hold:

1. *Services.* Most of the durable goods we buy—TV sets, autos, houses—have costs in the form of time required for maintenance. An individual can either take these costs out of his own time (e.g., paint the house himself), or engage a service man to do the work. When only a small proportion of people own many goods, it is easy to farm out the maintenance cost. But as productivity rises and the high yield on time spreads throughout the whole society, the price of maintenance services rises, too. Thus the consumer finds he needs more income to buy the maintenance time required for his consumer goods.

2. *Consumption.* The pleasures of consumption take time: the time to read a book, to talk to a friend, to drink a cup of coffee, to travel abroad. In "backward countries" with fewer goods to enjoy, there is more time. But when a man has a sailing boat, a sports car, or a series of concert tickets, he finds that his "free time" is his scarcest resource. If he wants to go to a concert, he may have to rush through his dinner, and since good cooking takes time, he may buy frozen dinners that can be cooked quickly. If he goes to a concert and takes his dinner afterwards, he may have to stay up too late and thus lose sleep in order to get to work "on time." If he could cut down the "on time" requirements, he would have more time, but then he would have to be quite wealthy or retired. So he must ration and allocate his time.

3. *Time-savers.* Since "free time" becomes more and more precious, the consumer will tend to buy those items that require relatively little of his nonwork time and relatively more of his income from work. He will buy items that he can use and then throw away. He will "contract out" various services or maintenances (as he now sends clothes to the dry cleaner's). And to do this, he may have to work longer in order to acquire the kinds of goods and services that give him a high yield on his nonwork time. But the cost may be too high, and he has to begin to reckon his trade-offs. He must calculate relative prices and yields from different allocations of time and money. He may find that because of high maintenance cost he will do

his own laundry or dry cleaning in a self-service store, thus spending part of his time to save money. Or he may want to spend money to save time. In balancing these considerations he begins to plot (without knowing that he is doing technical economics) an indifference curve of differential scales of substitution (of time and money) and the marginal utility of each unit of satisfaction in the different sectors of his expenditures. Low yields have to be transferred to high yields until, at the end, his resources have been so efficiently distributed as to give him an equal yield in all sectors of use. Economic abundance thus reintroduces utility by the back door of time. Man, in his leisure time, has become *homo economicus*.

In cruel fashion, utopia thus stands confounded. The end of scarcity, as it was envisaged by nineteenth-century writers, would bring such a plethora of goods that man would no longer need to delay his gratifications or live like a calculating machine.

And yet it has all been turned around. Industrial society is spectacularly devoted to the production of things. But in the post-industrial society the multiplication of things and their rising custodial costs bring time into the calculus of allocating one's personal activities; men become enslaved to its measurement through marginal utility.

In utopia (as in the market economy) each man is to be free to pursue his own interest, but in the postindustrial society—where the relation among men (rather than between man and nature, or man and things) becomes the primary mode of interaction—the clash of individual interests, each following its own whim, leads necessarily to a greater need for collective regulation and a greater degree of coercion in order to have effective communal action. And when individuals demand full participation in the decisions that affect their lives, the consequence is an increase in information costs and in the time required for bargaining in order to reach agreement.

The end of scarcity, it was believed—the leap from the kingdom of necessity—would be the freeing of time from the inexorable rhythm of economic life. In the end, all time has become an economic calculus. As Auden put it, "Time will say only, I told you so."

Part IV

Social Organization: Types of Group Relationships

27.

PRIMARY GROUPS

Charles Horton Cooley

Professor Cooley, the author of this selection, is recognized as a pioneer in the field of social psychology. One of his very fruitful contributions to sociology is the concept of primary groups as the "nursery of human nature." Here he explains the universality of primary groups and contrasts their characteristics with what we now designate as secondary groups. He carefully defines "human nature," which he declares to be fundamentally the same the world over. Although more recent discoveries have revealed certain limitations in his data, such as his statement in this selection about differences in racial capacities, in most essentials his thinking remains sound and illuminating. Since 1909, when the book containing this selection was published, much progress has been made in developing the scientific research methods of both psychology and sociology; but many of Cooley's ideas, of which the primary-group concept is one, have a timeless quality.

By primary groups I mean those characterized by intimate face-to-face association and cooperation. They are primary in several senses, but chiefly in that they are fundamental in forming the social nature and ideals of the individual. The result of intimate association, psychologically, is a certain fusion of individualities in a common whole, so that one's very self, for many purposes at least, is the common life and purpose of the group. Perhaps the simplest way of describing this wholeness is by saying that it is a "we"; it involves the sort of sympathy and mutual identification for which "we" is the natural expression. One lives in the feeling of the whole and finds the chief aims of his will in that feeling.

It is not to be supposed that the unity of the primary group is one of mere harmony and love. It is always a differentiated and usually a competitive unity, admitting of self-assertion and various appropriative passions; but these passions are socialized by sympathy, and come, or tend to come, under the discipline of a common spirit. The individual will be ambitious, but the chief object of his ambition will be some desired place in the thought of the others, and he will feel allegiance to common standards of service and fair play. So the boy will dispute with his fellows a place on the

Source: Charles Horton Cooley, *Social Organization* (New York: Charles Scribner's Sons, 1909), pp. 23–31.

The author (1864–1929), an American social philosopher, was professor of sociology at the University of Michigan and a president of the American Sociological Association. He made contributions of great range and depth to the field of sociology. Among his important works are *Personal Competition, Human Nature and the Social Order, Social Organization,* and *Social Process.*

team, but above such disputes will place the common glory of his class and school.

The most important spheres of this intimate association and cooperation—though by no means the only ones—are the family, the playgroup of children, and the neighborhood or community group of elders. These are practically universal, belonging to all times and all stages of development; and are accordingly a chief basis of what is universal in human nature and human ideals. The best comparative studies of the family, such as those of Westermarck or Howard, show it to us as not only a universal institution, but as more alike the world over than the exaggeration of exceptional customs by an earlier school had led us to suppose. Nor can any one doubt the general prevalence of playgroups among children or of informal assemblies of various kinds among their elders. Such association is clearly the nursery of human nature in the world about us, and there is no apparent reason to suppose that the case has anywhere or at any time been essentially different.

As regards play, I might, were it not a matter of common observation, multiply illustrations of the universality and spontaneity of the group discussion and cooperation to which it gives rise. The general fact is that children, especially boys after about their twelfth year, live in fellowships in which their sympathy, ambition and honor are engaged even more often than they are in the family. Most of us can recall examples of the endurance by boys of injustice and even cruelty, rather than appeal from their fellows to parents or teachers—as, for instance, in the hazing so prevalent at schools, and so difficult, for this very reason, to repress. And how elaborate the discussion, how cogent the public opinion, how hot the ambitions in these fellowships.

Nor is this facility of juvenile association, as is sometimes supposed, a trait peculiar to English and American boys; since experience among our immigrant population seems to show that the offspring of the more restrictive civilizations of the continent of Europe form self-governing playgroups with almost equal readiness. Thus Miss Jane Addams, after pointing out that the "gang" is almost universal, speaks of the interminable discussion which every detail of the gang's activity receives, remarking that "in these social folkmotes, so to speak, the young citizen learns to act upon his own determination."

Of the neighborhood group it may be said, in general, that from the time men formed permanent settlements upon the land, down, at least, to the rise of modern industrial cities, it has played a main part in the primary, heart-to-heart life of the people. Among our Teutonic forefathers the village community was apparently the chief sphere of sympathy and mutual aid for the commons all through the "dark" and middle ages, and for many purposes it remains so in rural districts at the present day. In some countries we still find it with all its ancient vitality, notably in Russia, where the mir, or self-governing village group, is the main theatre of life, along with the family, for perhaps fifty millions of peasants.

In our own life the intimacy of the neighborhood has been broken up by the growth of an intricate mesh of wider contacts which leaves us strangers to people who live in the same house. And even in the country the same principle is at work, though less obviously, diminishing our economic and spiritual community with our neighbors. How far this change is a healthy development, and how far a disease, is perhaps still uncertain.

Besides these almost universal kinds of

primary association, there are many others whose form depends upon the particular state of civilization; the only essential thing, as I have said, being a certain intimacy and fusion of personalities. In our own society, being little bound by place, people easily form clubs, fraternal societies and the like, based on congeniality, which may give rise to real intimacy. Many such relations are formed at school and college, and among men and women brought together in the first instance by their occupations—as workmen in the same trade, or the like. Where there is a little common interest and activity, kindness grows like weeds by the roadside.

But the fact that the family and neighborhood groups are ascendant in the open and plastic time of childhood makes them even now incomparably more influential than all the rest.

Primary groups are primary in the sense that they give the individual his earliest and completest experience of social unity, and also in the sense that they do not change in the same degree as more elaborate relations, but form a comparatively permanent source out of which the latter are ever springing. Of course they are not independent of the larger society, but to some extent reflect its spirit; as the German family and the German school bear somewhat distinctly the print of German militarism. But this, after all, is like the tide setting back into creeks, and does not commonly go very far. Among the German, and still more among the Russian, peasantry are found habits of free cooperation and discussion almost uninfluenced by the character of the state; and it is a familiar and well-supported view that the village commune, self-governing as regards local affairs and habituated to discussion, is a very widespread institution in settled communities, and the continuator of a similar autonomy previously existing in the clan. "It is man who makes monarchies and establishes republics, but the commune seems to come directly from the hand of God."

In our own cities the crowded tenements and the general economic and social confusion have sorely wounded the family and the neighborhood, but it is remarkable, in view of these conditions, what vitality they show; and there is nothing upon which the conscience of the time is more determined than upon restoring them to health.

These groups, then, are springs of life, not only for the individual but for social institutions. They are only in part moulded by special traditions, and, in larger degree, express a universal nature. The religion or government of other civilizations may seem alien to us, but the children or the family group wear the common life, and with them we can always make ourselves at home.

By human nature, I suppose, we may understand those sentiments and impulses that are human in being superior to those of lower animals, and also in the sense that they belong to mankind at large, and not to any particular race or time. It means, particularly, sympathy and the innumerable sentiments into which sympathy enters, such as love, resentment, ambition, vanity, hero-worship, and the feeling of social right and wrong.

Human nature in this sense is justly regarded as a comparatively permanent element in society. Always and everywhere men seek honor and dread ridicule, defer to public opinion, cherish their goods and their children, and admire courage, generosity, and success. It is always safe to assume that people are and have been human.

It is true, no doubt, that there are differences of race capacity, so great that a large part of mankind are possibly incapable of any high kind of social organization. But these differences, like those among individuals of the same race, are subtle, depending upon some obscure intellectual deficiency, some want of vigor, or slackness of moral fibre, and do not involve unlikeness in the generic impulses of human nature. In these all races are very much alike. The more insight one gets into the life of savages, even those that are reckoned the lowest, the more human, the more like ourselves, they appear. Take for instance the natives of Central Australia, as described by Spencer and Gillen, tribes having no definite government or worship and scarcely able to count to five. They are generous to one another, emulous of virtue as they understand it, kind to their children and to the aged, and by no means harsh to women. Their faces . . . are wholly human and many of them attractive.

And when we come to a comparison between different stages in the development of the same race, between ourselves, for instance, and the Teutonic tribes of the time of Caesar, the difference is neither in human nature nor in capacity, but in organization, in the range and complexity of relations, in the diverse expression of powers and passions essentially much the same.

There is no better proof of this generic likeness of human nature than in the ease and joy with which the modern man makes himself at home in literature depicting the most remote and varied phases of life—in Homer, in the Nibelung tales, in the Hebrew Scriptures, in the legends of the American Indians, in stories of frontier life, of soldiers and sailors, of criminals and tramps, and so on. The more penetratingly any phase of human life is studied the more an essential likeness to ourselves is revealed.

To return to primary groups: the view here maintained is that human nature is not something existing separately in the individual, but a *group-nature or primary phase of society,* a relatively simple and general condition of the social mind. It is something more, on the one hand, than the mere instinct that is born in us—though that enters into it—and something less, on the other, than the more elaborate development of ideas and sentiments that makes up institutions. It is the nature which is developed and expressed in those simple, face-to-face groups that are somewhat alike in all societies; groups of the family, the playground, and the neighborhood. In the essential similarity of these is to be found the basis, in experience, for similar ideas and sentiments in the human mind. In these, everywhere, human nature comes into existence. Man does not have it at birth; he cannot acquire it except through fellowship, and it decays in isolation.

If this view does not recommend itself to common-sense I do not know that elaboration will be of much avail. It simply means the application at this point of the idea that society and individuals are inseparable phases of a common whole, so that wherever we find an individual fact we may look for a social fact to go with it. If there is a universal nature in persons there must be something universal in association to correspond to it.

What else can human nature be than a trait of primary groups? Surely not an attribute of the separate individual—supposing there were any such thing—since its typical characteristics, such as affection, ambition, vanity, and resentment, are inconceivable apart from society. If it belongs, then, to man in association, what kind or degree of association is required to develop it? Evidently nothing elaborate, because elaborate phases of society are transient and diverse, while human nature is comparatively stable and universal. In short the family and neighborhood life is essential to its genesis and nothing more is.

Here as everywhere in the study of society we must learn to see mankind in psychical wholes, rather than in artificial separation. We must see and feel the communal life of family and local groups as immediate facts, not as combinations of something else. And perhaps we shall do this best by recalling our own experience and extending it through sympathetic observation. What, in our life, is the family and the fellowship; what do we know of the we-feeling? Thought of this kind may help us to get a concrete perception of that primary group-nature of which everything social is the outgrowth.

28.

CONTRASTING TYPES OF GROUP RELATIONSHIPS

John B. Holland

Sociologists have introduced a number of terms to characterize types of social relationships. The primary-group concept described in the previous selection, the contrasting secondary-group concept, and the Gemeinschaft and Gesellschaft concepts developed by Ferdinand Tönnies are among those most widely used to identify differing patterns of social interaction. In this selection John Holland defines Gemeinschaft and Gesellschaft and illustrates their usefulness in social analysis.

The individual lives in a world made up of many groups of people. While we think of ourselves as individuals, separate and

Source: John B. Holland, *Source Book for Effective Living,* Leo Haak, ed. (East Lansing: Michigan State University Press, 1950), pp. 196–99.

Professor Holland (1910–1953) was a member of the Department of Sociology and Anthropology and of the Social Science Department at Michigan State University. He was the coauthor of *Community Involvement.*

distinct from all other individuals, we do not, nor can we live without others. We are not only individuals, we are at the same time group members. We participate in many kinds of social groups. More than that we find ourselves at times, both as individuals and as group members, in conflict with other groups. And in a complex modern world we find ourselves affected by still other groups about whom we may be unaware.

The nature of these many associations that we as individuals have with other people is complex, varied, and often difficult to determine. Some progress may be made toward clarifying these relations, however, if we will distinguish between two quite different kinds of human relations. We shall use the classification of Tönnies, a German sociologist, and explore the meaning of the terms Gemeinschaft and Gesellschaft.

Before doing so it is necessary to be critical of any attempt to classify all human relations into only two general categories. Further, rather than thinking of Gemeinschaft and Gesellschaft as two separate and distinct kinds of human relations, it would seem more nearly correct to think of them as occupying the extreme ends of a straight line.

The extreme ends of such a scale represent pure types or polar extremes. Our own concrete and real experiences with other people usually fall somewhere along this scale rather than at one end or the other. Our relations with others are generally in terms of more or less rather than all or none, for usually these relations involve both Gemeinschaft and Gesellschaft. Nevertheless, by clearly defining the polar extremes we may classify many of our relations as an individual in the group, for generally one or the other kind of relationship is predominant. The scale furnishes us with a convenient device to measure many of the kinds of associations we have as group members, though we need not assume that all human relations can be made to fit into one or the other of these categories.

This way of classifying our relations with others is not new. The ideas we are to explore here have been most explicitly developed by Tönnies, but they are really a refinement of the thinking of many others who have gone before. Confucius and Plato, Aristotle and Cicero, St. Augustine and Thomas Aquinas, to mention only a few, have attempted to understand and account for the different kinds of human relationships which they observed. Their classifications are similar to that of Tönnies. This way of looking at people, therefore, is not new, it has been useful to many of the great thinkers of the ages, and it is useful to us because it gives us a new pair of glasses with which we may look at facts which are familiar to all of us.

GESELLSCHAFT RELATIONS

First, let us define Gesellschaft, not because it comes first, but because it is the easiest to explain. A brief definition may be given as "Rational relations based on calculation of individual self-interest." Like all brief statements there are many points covered in that definition. What are some of them?

. . . . .

First of all, our Gesellschaft relations with others are based upon reason and not feeling. Second, we are concerned with our individual self-interest. Third, our obligations are limited to whatever specific contract is stated or implied. Fourth, our relationship with others covers only a specific and clearly-defined area of interest. Fifth, it is not necessary, in fact it is entirely irrelevant whether or not we have any interests in common other than these specific, individual interests which we hope to further by our relationship.

In terms of concrete, flesh and blood people what does this mean? What kind of relations do we have with other people which serve our immediate interests and are largely Gesellschaft in character?

Take an inventory of your daily activities. Whom do you see and what do you do when you are with other people? When you buy a loaf of bread is it primarily an intimate and friendly exchange, or is it a contract between buyer and seller? If you get a check from Veterans Administration do you have a warm personal feeling for the man who signed the check, or do you look to see if it is made out correctly and delivered on time? If you have a part-time job, do you usually prop your feet upon the boss's desk for an hour of friendly conversation, or do you have specific, well-defined duties which you are expected to perform? When you registered at this college, although the cashier may have been very friendly, was this principally Gesellschaft or otherwise? The illustrations could be multiplied indefinitely in terms of your own experiences, but these serve to point out the fact that you and I, living as we do in a complex society, spend a great deal of time busily engaged with the pursuit of our own self-interests. And we have many contacts with other human beings who are likewise concerned with their own interests. In this pursuit of self-interest, people have little reality for us as human beings, as personalities who think, feel, and act, and have personal problems even as we. Because so many of our relations with others are largely Gesellschaft in character it is not surprising that we sometimes fail to recognize the reality of groups and the effect on us and our personalities of our many associations with others.

GEMEINSCHAFT RELATIONS

Just as Gesellschaft is a polar type which characterizes one kind of human relations, so Gemeinschaft is the other. Broadly stated Gemeinschaft is everything that Gesellschaft is not. Gemeinschaft comes logically first in human relations.

Gemeinschaft is easier to define but harder to explain. A brief definition is: "Intimate relations based on sentiment." That is, Gemeinschaft relations are based on the way we feel about people. They are intimate relations. In such contacts with others people are real. Our concern is not with rational calculations and limited obligations but with flesh and blood people and our felt obligations to them.

We may make further contrasts. Whereas in Gesellschaft we enter into a relationship because of rational consideration of individual self-interest, in Gemeinschaft our motives are general and indefinite in character. This is so because they are not carefully calculated but are a part of our feelings. Gemeinschaft relations cover a multitude of interests not well defined at all. For example, if you are married why did you marry? There are many answers, not one or two single, specific reasons. You married for love, to have a home, to raise children, to obtain what we may call psychic security—that is, emotional security and approval. If I ask you why you entered the college bookstore you can tell me exactly. But if I ask you why you married this particular person, why you like certain friends, why you have a friendly feeling for the old home town, it is difficult to explain. This is natural since sentiments and feelings, being nonrational, are hard to explain by rational means. Frequently, however, we feel called upon to justify our feelings and in so doing we depend upon rationalizations which we offer as "good reasons" to explain our behavior.

A second contrast with Gesellschaft relations is that in Gemeinschaft obligations are unspecified and unlimited. There is no specific contract. The burden of proof is on him who would evade an obligation arising out of a Gemeinschaft relation. Let us examine the obligations in marriage. In a general sense a marriage between two people involves a ceremony in which certain obligations are stated. But these are blanket obligations which in the final analysis mean an obligation on each of the marriage partners to help in whatever contingencies arise in their common life together. A married veteran is going to school. There is nothing in the marriage contract which says that his wife will take a full or part-time job to help him in that process. And yet many veterans' wives are doing just that. If a friend of yours is down and out and needs ten dollars there is no written obligation on your part to meet his need. But if you've got the money and if he is a real friend of yours, one for whom you have an intimate and deep-seated liking, you loan him the money, even though you do not expect to get it back.

A third point that may be made about Gemeinschaft relations is that not only are obligations unlimited but they can be ignored only because of the prior obligations of another Gemeinschaft relationship. To illustrate, if you are a doctor you would not, as a husband, ordinarily leave your wife's bridge party. But if it were necessary for you to make an emergency call you would do so. Or again if you were about to meet with a friend who was in a tough spot and needed you to help him regain his bearings, you would cancel the engagement if your child were to be injured or suddenly taken ill. But it should be noted that you are relieved of one Gemeinschaft obligation only because another and higher Gemeinschaft obligation supersedes. You do not customarily ignore Gemeinschaft obligations for Gesellschaft obligations, or if you do we may safely say that there was no deep Gemeinschaft feeling on your part in the first place.

Finally, Gemeinschaft obligations are both moral and ethical in character. I mean by that that individuals in a Gemeinschaft relationship have individual interests but these interests are integrated and a part of the ultimate values of the group. It is safe to say that as a member of a family, insofar as you have intimate feelings for that family, you share in common certain beliefs and ideals. There are certain moral responsibilities that you feel and these moral responsibilities are a part of your individual codes of ethics, your standards, your values. Gemeinschaft relations are shared relations. They extend beyond individual self-interest. In Gemeinschaft relations your individual purposes and ends are integrated and a part of the purposes and ends of the group.

These are the principal characteristics of Gemeinschaft. Relations are intimate and based on feelings or sentiment, not upon reason or calculation. In Gemeinschaft there is what we might call a bond or feeling of belonging. Thus we speak of the bond that unites man and wife or friends or a group of neighbors who are intimately acquainted with each other.

We can illustrate Gemeinschaft concretely for ourselves again in terms of the groups of people with whom we associate in a day. Whom did you see today? How intimately are you concerned with their welfare? Not abstract persons, but real people about whose welfare you are genuinely and personally concerned? What bonds do you have with others and what would it take to break them?

In summary, then, Gemeinschaft relations are intimate relations based on sentiment; Gesellschaft relations are rational relations based on calculation of individual interest. These two types of relations are polar extremes and our actual relations with others vary from extreme, intimate, personal relations with others to extreme, rational calculation of people as means to serve our own immediate ends. It is useful to make this classification because it enables us to analyze more clearly our relations with others and to see in proper perspective our actions as they affect and are affected by others. But even beyond that we need to appraise what is involved in gaining and losing Gemeinschaft relations because we live in a world which is based increasingly upon Gesellschaft. How well each of us personally can survive by rational concern with limited and specific interests alone is a problem which confronts us both as individuals and as group members.

29.

A WALDEN TWO EXPERIMENT

Kathleen Kinkade

Twenty years after Harvard behavioral psychologist B. F. Skinner wrote *Walden Two,* Twin Oaks, an experimental rural commune based on his utopian novel, was established in central Virginia by the author of the following selection and seven of her cofounders. In this publication she describes the types of group relationships developed in Twin Oaks to cope with problems in a very small and intimate community trying to evolve a new life style. Such problems of interaction as gossip, bitching, jealousy, envy, and sex relationships made the development of some minimal group organization necessary. The patterns of marriage, the family, and child care in this commune are also discussed. For the reader who wishes to gain a better understanding of contemporary communal group relations Kathleen Kinkade's candid report is a fascinating introduction: one specimen of a diversified species of organized human groups.

Source: Kathleen Kinkade, *A Walden Two Experiment* (New York: William Morrow, 1973), pp. 147–55, 157–58, 160–61, 164–71.

Kathleen Kinkade is the founder of Twin Oaks Community, a commune based on the philosophy of B. F. Skinner's *Walden Two.*

A SENSE OF COMMUNITY—INTERPERSONAL RELATIONS

The social planning of the founders of Twin Oaks was largely limited to considerations of equality, and especially economic equality. I am not ashamed of that. Achieving a cultural norm that assumes real economic equality is no simple task. The effort we put into this task, which we considered basic and indispensable to our aims, has been repaid, I think, by the smoothness and pleasantness of our daily lives now that the struggle has been won. Our labor and property systems really are fair. We really do all get a fair share of the Community's wealth, such as it is, and the managers and planners really do make the best decisions they can for the benefit of the whole group—they have no reason to do anything else. We have been called "dogmatic" and "doctrinaire" and "rigid" and "nitpicking," but our net result is a peaceful and pleasant life style.

At first I thought that this thorough and determined economic equality, plus a little common sense, would be all that was necessary to insure good human relations. What are most quarrels about, anyway? Do they not arise out of envy? And if we removed the causes of envy, would we not be removing the causes of the quarrels?

I now think that this idea was naïve. It is true that we removed a lot of the causes for discord, and it is true also that we have reaped the rewards of that planning. But there is more to human antagonism than envy, and we do not have the capability of even doing away with all causes for envy. Our systems did not touch the problems of loneliness, rejection, and unrequited love. We had no way of dealing with envy caused by superior social talents or disgruntlements over appointments to public office. We were continually plagued by dissatisfactions over the failure of members to agree on standards of workmanship, cleanliness, or courtesy. In short, there were problems in human behavior that our institutions just didn't reach. They were problems, we would say to each other with wry humor, for "behavioral engineering."

Well, what does that mean? In theory, we were for it, but what is it?

We have never been hindered by the usual conception of behavioral engineering as the manipulation of people's desires and preferences by a group of scientists in white coats, while the poor dupes under their control find themselves helplessly doing things that they really do not want to do, just because they "want to." We had read *Brave New World* and *1984* and were not impressed. The writing is great, the logic downright silly. If there were to be manipulators, we were it. But we would also be the manipulated. We would have to be both puppet and puppet-master. The logic of equalitarianism is inescapable on this point. The board of planners might think of a program for changing behavior, but they would themselves be subject to that program.

We were not hindered, as I said, by silly prejudices, from using behavioral engineering. But we were hindered, nevertheless. It is precisely the equality ethic that makes the problem complicated.

Great strides have been made by the behaviorists in mental hospitals and schools by the use of token economies. The staff are given tokens of some kind. The students or patients are told how they can earn these tokens by certain desirable behavior—doing homework, taking a bath, cleaning up a room, or what have you. The tokens can be traded for sweets or privileges. Behavior quickly conforms to the desired norms without the use of punishment. Fine. But Twin Oaks is different from these institutions in a fundamental way. There is no staff. There are no students. We divide the labor—some people have the labor of making governmental decisions—but we do not seriously have hierarchies. We are all on the same level. Token economies necessitate someone handing out the tokens. Who would do it here? The planners? Resentment over such blatant presumption and authority would topple the government. We would refuse to earn the tokens. We would tear them up and demand our rights to those sweets or privileges as citizens of a people's state. No, token economies operating from a premise of controller-controllee will not do.

. . . . .

The simplest and maybe oldest of all deliberate techniques of social control is the making of rules. Walden Two had them. We have them. They are not backed up by force, but they are there as a kind of guideline and goal. Item Four of Twin Oaks's Behavioral Code says that we will not speak negatively about other members behind their backs. This was our interpretation of the hint in *Walden Two* that "gossip" was prohibited by the Walden Code. Actually, we interpreted "gossip" to mean something quite different from its ordinary connotations. Commenting on someone's love affairs is not considered gossip at Twin Oaks. To call it so is to imply that there is something somehow wrong or shameful about sexual relations, an implication we did not want to make, even indirectly. "Gossip" in our definition is talk that does damage. Exasperated comments on the quality of someone's work is gossip, as are disparaging remarks about personal characteristics. If you have something negative to say, says our rule, say it to the person's face—and when there is nobody else listening. (For this reason the words, "May I speak to you alone?" have an ominous sound.)

Can we do away with negative speech just by writing a rule against it? Experimental evidence backs up common-sense assumptions on this point: No, we cannot. But the rule, viewed as a desirable norm, does have the effect of curbing negative talk—we don't do as much of it as we might. After all, we wrote the rule; we signed a contract saying we would try to go by it; we generally approve of it. So we sometimes lose control and violate our agreement? So what? Tomorrow we can try again.

The antigossip rule has been under attack on various occasions. Pete disliked it, saying that honesty was desirable, even if negative. Several members throughout our history have shared his feeling. They were frustrated that work was not done as well as they wanted, or that somebody left the gate open and the cows got out, and they wanted to complain about it loudly and publicly. Rule Four says they shouldn't. People will even get up and leave the room if they do it. The rule can be changed, of course, any time we find, as a group, that it does not have desirable consequences. But out of the three meetings I can recall on the subject, the conclusion has always been that as a group we really do not want to listen to public statements about other people's sins (or our own). The rule stands.

That leaves us with the question: What *can* one do about frustration with other people's unacceptable behavior? What are we supposed to do when we are just sick and tired of having the cows get out, or seeing the kitchen improperly cleaned—or for that matter, of hearing other people violate the gossip rule? We have tried several structures, all with some success, to handle legitimate criticism.

The first was the appointment of a "Generalized Bastard." Brian thought of the idea, and we unanimously appointed him to the task. It was his job to relay unpleasant information. If I wanted to tell Quincy that he wasn't doing his share of the work, I was supposed to tell Brian, and he would tell Quincy without mentioning my name. Brian quickly found that he lacked the stomach for face-to-face encounters and reduced the system to note-writing. We lived with variations on this system for over three years. Now we have a box with a slot in the top called the "Bitch Box," where we can air our grievances if we lack the courage to go directly to the offender.

It works like this: Suppose I am unhappy about the waste of money involved in making too many automobile trips to Richmond. I notice that one person in particular seems to make extra trips. I write a note for the Bitch Box and can sign it or not. There is no need for me to restrain my temper for the Bitch Box, and my note might go something like this: "I am goddamned sick and tired of seeing Community cars being run back and forth to Richmond for nothing. Three trips have been made this week, in addition to the regularly scheduled one, two of them by John. John doesn't seem to care whether he wastes Community money, Community time, and Community automobiles. He just likes to go for rides. His excuses for this week's trips are pretty weak ones, considering that it costs us $10 a trip in wear and tear and gasoline. I tried to talk to him about it, and he just said he needed to get some things. I say he doesn't need to get those things. He could wait for a regular Richmond trip."

The Bitch Manager would get my note, but he would not deliver it directly to John. He would probably speak to John about automobile trips in general and say something like this: "Some people have been noticing that we have been putting a lot of automobile mileage into trips to Richmond, and someone particularly mentioned your name in this connection, questioning whether the value of the trips was really worth the ten dollars per trip it costs us." John will probably explain why he thought the trips necessary, and the Bitch Manager will probably respond sympathetically. He may or may not relay this information back to me, depending on whether it will be likely to mollify me or just make me madder. In any case several things have been accomplished: I have expressed myself vehemently to someone who cares, without having gossiped in public and made other people uncomfortable; John now knows that trips to Richmond really cost ten dollars each, something he may not have thought of; and John now realizes that his driving does not go unnoticed, a form of gentle pressure that probably helps the situation if he is indeed driving more than he ought.

The Bitch Box helps a little. But it isn't enough. Some interpersonal friction is caused not by illegal or inconsiderate behavior that one can reasonably bitch about, but by overriding personality traits that need to be discussed. It was to this problem that we addressed ourselves when we started the Group Criticism sessions.

In 1969 we had an educational project called Utopia Class. It amounted to a weekly group meeting to read about communities of the past and to discuss the possible applications of their systems, ideas, successes, and failures to Twin Oaks situations. A great many ideas came out of these sessions. One of them was Group Criticism, which we borrowed from Oneida Community. Like the Oneidans, we found each other's behavior less than perfect, and we wondered if smooth group functioning might be helped by more direct information—that is, some regular and accepted means of getting across negative feedback to members. A lot of us professed ourselves willing and interested in hearing what the rest of the group would say about us. It amounted to an invitation to criticize. One of us at a time would volunteer, and the group would gather to talk about the volunteer.

I was writing a journal during this period. I quote from my notes:

Penn. Criticism of Penn tonight. Jenny, Penn and I had all volunteered to be the first subject for Group Criticism, so we tossed a coin, and Penn "won." There was some feeling that this was a bad place to begin, because it was obvious to practically everybody that there wasn't much to criticize in Penn's behavior. He is good, kind, considerate, and fun to be with. What can you say about somebody like that?

Everybody in the Community attended, including the little kids. We read the ground rules aloud. Then we started around the group clockwise. Everybody said something to the effect that they couldn't think of anything to say. Brian's criticism was that Penn sometimes left him and Jenny alone together when his (Penn's) company would have been perfectly welcome. Also that his thinking is irrational, that he believes things that don't have any evidence for them. Dwight criticized Penn's fuzzy thinking ("Maybe you don't think the moon is made of green cheese, but it isn't at all clear why you wouldn't. There's as much evidence for that as for some other things you do believe.") and for his lack of political commitment ("Why don't you join the Community?"). Jenny just said "The same as Brian," and Simon and the children all said Penn let himself be taken advantage of too easily, and that other people had no way of knowing when they were exploiting him, because he accepted exploitation so cheerfully. I said that he had leadership qualities (people tend to do what he does) and that he ought to pay more attention to where he was leading people. My example was the apple diet he and some others have been on. Apple diets don't do much harm, probably, but there must be better things to do.

Penn was pleased and embarrassed by so much oblique praise, and he said he had learned that he hid his faults well. Dwight commented that nobody else would get by so easily. The meeting had the effect of making other people want to be "it," and of setting a tone of helpfulness and courtesy for the meetings that followed. But no meeting since has been so well attended.

Me. About ten people present. Brian said I ought to get the newsletter out oftener than I do. Also that I am too easily bored, which I interpret to mean that I show my boredom too openly. Simon said that I ought to drink a little beer and hang around and party a little—loosen up and be part of the social life instead of worrying about the Community all the time. I understand what he is trying to say, but it amounted to telling me to be somebody else instead of me.

Dwight, from whom I feared the sharpest criticism, confessed to coming unprepared to the session. He said, "I feel that I should have a great deal to say, but I haven't thought it out." I was disappointed. But later he did some thinking and wrote me a criticism in a letter. It was devastating, and I only wish it could have been said in public, where I could hear other people's comments on it. The core of it is what he called "imperial attitudes." He says I exhibit a "condescension toward the group—a certain regal airiness," that I sometimes act "as if Twin Oaks were my duchy." I sense that Dwight is saying (at last) something a lot of people have felt but won't say, and I feel a mixture of defensiveness and gratitude. He cited incidents and quoted comments of mine which I recall with embarrassment. He completely misinterpreted the things I said. But then, probably everybody else misinterpreted them, too. That's the point. I have got to change my verbal behavior!

. . . . .

Criticism sessions went on for a year and a half and have fallen into disuse only in the last few months. I never missed a session, and I feel that I ought to have a better idea than I do of whether or not they have been effective, whether they did more good or more harm. The truth is that I still feel ambivalent about them. They seemed to serve very well the function of reassuring timid and modest people that they are appreciated and liked by the group. They also allowed some of us to let off steam about behavior that particularly annoyed us. Occasionally we could even notice changes after a Criticism.

But the major benefit of the method in my opinion was simply the attitude it induced in us of being admittedly imperfect and willing to listen to the opinions of our peers about our conduct. We said, in effect, "I am not defending my bad behavior; I want to know how I come across; I care what you all think about me." I found myself more tolerant of somebody's foibles if I had already told that person about them.

Also, I am personally glad to have gone through the experience. I certainly know more about my social self than I did before I came here, and I am much more sensitive to group opinion.

Nevertheless I am not unreservedly enthusiastic about Criticism. It did not succeed in its major aim—which was to impart to every member of the group the consciousness of being responsible to the rest. It worked only for volunteers. Dissenters to the system simply did not attend the sessions and did not volunteer to be the subject. They claimed that public criticism was nothing more than authorized gossip, and that it had the same bad effects as the unauthorized kind.

The right not to attend is fundamental to Twin Oaks's sense of liberty. As the number of nonparticipants grew larger in 1971, the subjection of the individual's ego to the criticism process ceased to be the norm. For a long time, too, the people who would volunteer for criticism just weren't the people we were mad at. There wasn't much to say. Interest flagged.

. . . . .

In the last year or so we have been getting members at Twin Oaks who have not been content with our social aims. It is not enough, they say, just to reduce interpersonal friction. The Bitch Box, gossip rule, and Group Criticism could all be dispensed with, they claim, if we all just loved and trusted one another. When I first heard this kind of talk I responded with exasperation and contempt. Sure it would be lovely if we all loved one another, but we don't all love one another, so let's use what techniques we can find to minimize the friction. But the young people joining the Community these last two years have not been willing to settle for that. They do not believe that mutual love and trust are out of our reach. They think that hatred and suspicion and jealousy are just results of misunderstanding, and that increased understanding would bring increased affection. I find this difficult to swallow. I can see a great many antagonisms born of perfectly good understandings, clear perceptions of conflict of interest. My skepticism notwithstanding, I have had a keen interest in every trial we have given to Group Encounter techniques. After all, at least *some* bad feeling is traceable to mistaken perception. What do we have to lose by trying?

. . . . .

WHICH WAY TO THE ORGIES?—SEX, LOVE, MARRIAGE, AND WOMEN'S LIBERATION

"Sex is an interesting question," said B. F. Skinner in an interview for *Mademoiselle,* "because nobody can say anything against it." This is pretty close to the stand Twin Oaks took on sexual morality from the beginning, but we didn't derive it from *Walden Two.* Written in 1947, *Walden Two* portrays a society in which couples marry at an early age in order to get around the problem of adolescent sexual frustration. The fictional community put a high value on abiding affection—loosely equivalent to monogamy, and presumably backed up its value system with behavioral engineering. Not so Twin Oaks. Though most of *Walden Two* was nearly sacred to us, we ignored this solution to the sex problem. We figured Skinner would have written it differently if he had been writing in the sixties instead of the forties. In any case, our standard was freedom, and it continues to be.

It was a freedom that was largely academic in our first year. Monogamy was so common among us in the beginning that single people found life with us intolerable and were immediately forced into more or less monogamous relationships. This pattern broke down in the summer of 1968 when a large number of young people joined the Community at about the same time. From then until now sexual freedom has been the Community's norm, both in theory and in practice.

This, of course, includes monogamy. We don't have anything against monogamy, as long as it is desired by both parties. What we object to is one of a pair's being happily monogamous while the other is not. In such a case, the weight of Twin Oaks's social pressure is against the jealous, possessive person and in favor of the one who wants to get free.

Under these circumstances it is reasonable to wonder how marriages fare at Twin Oaks. There are institutional reasons why marriage should naturally be weaker in community—any community—than on the Outside. No economic bonds link pairs here. Everybody supports himself with his own work. Likewise, children need not provide a vital connection, for the Community will certainly care for its children, regardless of whether their parents like each other or not. In short, the only reason for a married couple to stay married in community is that they like each other.

Out of the nine married couples who have at one time or another been members of Twin Oaks, six stayed married and three broke up. Occasionally a couple will leave the Community because they fear the influence of other available partners on their unstable relationships. Toby was one of these. "I agree with the idea of dissolving the nuclear family," he told us when he left, "but I always thought of it in terms of parent-child, not husband-wife." Toby's wife had begun to prefer other company to his. Their marriage didn't last more than six months after they left the Community, so it is doubtful that, even had they stayed, the Community could have been called responsible for the break.

It isn't always another partner that splits up a marriage. At least once the break came because one partner wanted to leave the Community, and the other refused to go.

Twin Oaks has made marriages as well as broken them. Hal and Gwen met here, Leif and Jenny, Dwight and Sally. We have also provided the courtship scene for visitors who are now married or engaged, including the reporter from *Time* who fell in love with a reporter from *National Geographic.*

Even the pristine arrangements of *Walden Two* left room for nonsexual friendship between men and women, but we had one member who defended his married virtue to precisely the same degree that he would on the Outside—avoiding even the appearance of a compromising situation. This was Pete. Though a sexual liberal—he believed in freedom for others—Pete was very circumspect in his own behavior. Once when he was giving flirtatious Jenny a class in chemistry, she reached out to him to straighten his shirt, which he had buttoned improperly. Pete jerked away from her gesture, saying, "I can button my own shirt." On another occasion, I asked him if he would show me the new calf in the lower pasture, and with some embarrassment he said that I should have Fred show it to me, since viewing new calves was something that he and Rosa had always done together.

Nevertheless, nonsexual friendship across sex lines is commonplace at Twin Oaks. It is particularly common where there is some strong reason to leave sex out of the relationship. If a pair is monogamous, for instance, and everybody in the Community knows it, neither of the pair is thereby cut off from friendship. Partly because of a fairly large age difference, I have not participated much in the mating games here, but I have always had good male friends, people I sit and talk with for hours, take walks with, go for drives with, even travel to other cities with.

Sometimes friendship with the opposite sex is easier than friendship with a person of the same sex. We went through some soul-searching on this subject in 1971. The women discovered that they were competing with each other and saw each other as rivals rather than as potential friends. Just getting together and talking about this helped a lot. Several of the women deliberately sought the company of other women, just to force themselves out of old habits. Men began to do the same. New friendships came about that have been continuously rewarding, lacking the terrible ups and downs of love affairs, making up in stability for what they lack in excitement.

There isn't much I can say about the love affairs themselves. For one thing, I don't know much. Lovemaking continues to be a private thing at Twin Oaks. Even though demonstrative public affection is common, you can't tell just from looking at two Twin Oakers holding hands that they are lovers. They may be and they may not be. Nobody asks, and nobody much cares.

Jealousy, of course, is a problem. Jealousy caused us to lose Carrie and Bonnie in 1969, and it will probably account for some turnover this year and next. We have not solved this problem. We have, however, taken steps to ease it. Sometimes we succeed and sometimes we don't, but for what it's worth, here is what Twin Oaks couples have come up with to help the tensions caused by either multiple relations or changing ones.

One technique is simple scheduling. If a woman cares a lot about two different men, and the men don't like each other, it may be possible for her to agree to spend one day with one, the next with the other. This has been tried various times at Twin Oaks, and it always breaks down after a short time, but it helps to ease the interim. The reason it breaks down is usually that the person in the middle really does prefer one partner to the other and shows it. This leads to withdrawal by the less-preferred partner out of hurt pride.

What has been more successful is for the three to spend a lot of time together as a trio. Thus the people who would otherwise be rivals are able to learn to appreciate each other and to gauge the depth of the affair all around. Even if one of them discovers that things aren't ideal for him or her, at least he or she isn't sitting around alone being tortured by imaginary scenes. It is easier to be right there dealing with a real situation than to be imagining one that may or may not exist.

Multiple relations have succeeded best when both ends of the triangle like each other. Otherwise they are practically impossible in community. In any case, they have not lasted very long. I have sometimes thought that triangles are really just a process of getting gently from one pairing to a different one.

The biggest bulwark against jealousy is our heavy communal disapproval of it. This is why sexual freedom is easier in community than it is on the Outside. Here we stand behind it as a group. Nobody gets group reinforcement for feeling or expressing jealousy. A surprising amount of it is wiped out by that fact alone.

What can't be accounted for by public

pressure can be attributed to personal idealism. Strange as it seems to our parents and the rest of the straight world, the stand against personal possessiveness is a moral stand, and most of us here do not approve of our bad feelings when we have them. Just as a person with a puritan conscience can often control his erotic impulses by reference to what he believes, so a person with a communitarian conscience can control his possessive impulses by reminding himself of what his principles are.

Twin Oaks has taken a firm stand in favor of sexual freedom and nonpossessiveness, and that brings its problems with it. But problems notwithstanding, we did not have any real choice about taking this stand. Any group that settles on monogamy as a norm has to figure out how to defend it. Without a heavy puritan religious bias this is very difficult. Philosophy isn't the only problem with monogamy, either. Sexual rules are hard to enforce in any society, and more so among free-thinking communitarians. The closer people live together, the higher will be the incidence of opportunity for attraction. A commune has to take the choice between dealing with jealousy in an open way or dealing with complicated questions of sin, dalliance, adultery. I conjecture that a group norm of free choice in sexual matters is not only philosophically consistent but literally easier to manage than any compromises would be.

In any case, we are rather pleased with our progress in this area. We are managing fairly well to live what we believe. Members do whatever seems right for them, and wrong choices do not shake the Community itself at all. A good many unconventional sexual arrangements have worked out perfectly smoothly and successfully here, probably because the individuals involved were prepared for them.

There have been three stages in Twin Oaks's sexual revolution. The first was just the step away from the standards that we learned from Mom and Dad, away from a sense of sex being connected with sin. That was the easiest. A lot of our members came here with that battle years behind them. The next was the fight against personal possessiveness and jealousy. That one is harder, but we are winning.

The third step, one that has become necessary partly because of the liberation achieved through the first two, is the ongoing struggle against sexism.

Sexism is the assumption that one's overall worth is measured in terms of one's desirability to the opposite sex. Outside society is heavily sexist, and women, in particular, suffer from it. We weren't conscious of this problem when we started the Community, but when Women's Liberation consciousness hit the rest of the nation, Twin Oaks naturally started thinking about it too. We examined our attitudes, and they were not entirely free of sexism. We still thought of each other in terms of physical attractiveness, and "cute" men and women were rated above plain ones, just as they would be on the Outside. Well, what could we do about it? We have all been raised to respond to certain types of beauty, as well as to status-linked styles of dress, certain hair styles, and so forth. Being products of the youth culture did not change this. True, our women liked only long-haired men and spurned the advances of anyone with a crewcut, but the reasons for this were just the same as the ones that make a sorority girl choose a date on the basis of his acceptable appearance. For a woman the criteria were even more stringent. Twin Oaks men, like men elsewhere, found that they preferred women who didn't chase them but just smiled and waited to be approached, that they were turned on by girls who let them do most of the talking, and most of all that it mattered a great deal to them that women have long hair and bodies that somewhat resembled that of a *Playboy* foldout. Here, as elsewhere, the closer a girl came to the standard stereotypes of beauty, the more she received the attentions of men.

On a sexual level this is very hard to eradicate. Adult sexual responses have already been conditioned to certain kinds of partners. We mean for our children to grow up without these kinds of prejudices, but for ourselves, we are stuck with our conditioning. The only thing that helps this situation is the fact that the longer a member is here, the less physical appearance matters. All of us are beautiful, and the status-giving power of certain kinds of beauty fades after a few months of living together.

On other than strictly sexual levels, there is a great deal we can do about the roles men and women are expected to play. We had meetings on the subject and discussed the problem. Was it true that men did most of the talking at meetings? It was. Was this because the group did not respect women? We thought not. The dismal fact was that many of the women did not know as much as the men, had not thought as much, and therefore did not have as much to say. The remedy, then, was with the women themselves. They began to read more, talk more about Community policy, and then speak up at meetings. In a matter of a few months we had a heavy liberation norm going that drew newcomers into it as soon as they got here. For a while the women tended to discriminate against new male applicants for membership if the applicants were caught making male chauvinist remarks, or even if they openly preferred pretty girls to plain ones. But after a few weeks the women began to relax as they realized their own power as a group. "All males are chauvinists when they first come here," one woman member commented to me, "but in a week or two they learn better."

We are all learning better, but not all at once. So much of our thinking is colored by assumptions about masculinity and femininity that it is hard to get free of them. What we are aiming for is to relate to each other simply as people, appreciating each other as human beings without regard to gender. Even now we are closer to this ideal than most places. We have no sex roles in our work. Both men and women cook and clean and wash dishes; both women and men drive trucks and tractors, repair fences, load hay, slaughter cattle. Managerial responsibility is divided almost exactly equally—this in spite of the fact that our women are on the average two or three years younger than our men.

Sensation seekers looking for communal orgies would be surprised to hear that one of the acceptable behavior patterns at Twin Oaks is celibacy. Once free of the necessity of proving oneself worthy by finding a mate, a person can really decide whether or not he or she is interested in sex. Every once in a while, somebody isn't. And that's all right. Your love life is your own business here, and if you don't want any love life, that's your business, too.

As for orgies, I don't think there are any. I have no way of being sure, of course. We don't have any antiorgy rules or anything. For all I know there may be one every night, and I just haven't been invited. But I doubt it. Sex is very important to us, but at the same time we don't make a big deal of it. It is part of our daily lives, but we rarely discuss it. Like eating and working and going for a walk and playing the guitar, it is a part of the good life.

30.

SOCIAL RELATIONS IN A BUREAUCRACY

George C. Homans

To a person unacquainted with a bureaucracy, with its highly organized and formalized structure and its many specific rules of operation, it would seem that there would be little opportunity for any informal interaction, either in relation to the job or in a purely social sense. Actually, however, the work of large and complex organizations is mediated through a network of many small, interrelated groups as the analysis below demonstrates. This selection by George Homans is based on case materials from Peter Blau's *The Dynamics of Bureaucracy* and the data are examined from the standpoint of Homans's "exchange theory" for the explanation of interpersonal behavior. After reading this selection, the student will find it instructive to analyze, using Homans's approach, a small group which he or she is in a position to observe.

A FEDERAL AGENCY: CONSULTATION AMONG COLLEAGUES

The group consisted of a supervisor, sixteen agents, and one clerk, who formed in 1949 a department in a local branch of a Federal agency that had its headquarters in Washington, D.C. In order to protect the anonymity of the group, the investigator does not tell us what the precise job of the agency was. Broadly it was concerned with the enforcement of a certain set of Federal laws. Since we are not interested in formal organization, and since he was hardly a member of the group, we shall not have much to say about the supervisor; nor was the clerk a member. Our business is with the sixteen agents.

The members of the department were fairly experienced in their work: only one had been with the agency for less than five years. Two held the civil-service grade 9, which was the highest represented among the agents; two were in grade 7; and the rest, the great majority, were in the middle with grade 8. But regardless of their different grades, all did much the same kind of work. Only three were women, and only one was a Negro. On the average an agent spent about 40 percent of his time in the home office, where he had a desk of his own along with the other agents. But because their duties took them often into the field, not all the agents were together in the office at any one time.

Source: George C. Homans, *Social Behavior: Its Elementary Forms* (New York: Harcourt Brace Jovanovich, 1961), pp. 360–77. Abridged. Reprinted by permission of the publisher.

The author is a professor of sociology in the department of Social Relations at Harvard University. His major interests include sociological theory and small groups. In addition to *Social Behavior: Its Elementary Forms,* he has written *The Human Group, English Villagers of the Thirteenth Century,* and *The Nature of Social Science.* He is a past president of the American Sociological Association.

An agents' main duty was investigation. On assignment by the supervisor, he went to the office of a business firm, obtained from it a wide variety of information, then came back to the agency where, from the information he had collected, he wrote a report stating whether or not and in what way the firm had violated Federal law. In order to determine whether a violation had occurred, an agent had to know how a large and complex body of legal rulings applied to the circumstances of a particular case. And since his report might become the basis of legal action against the firm, an agent had to be sure of his facts, his argument, and the clarity of his presentation.

The quality of the reports an agent turned in to the supervisor determined more than anything else the kind of efficiency rating the latter gave him, and this in turn affected his chances for promotion to a higher grade in the civil service. Thus an agent had to do a job difficult in itself, and his success in doing it made a difference to his future. Moreover, unlike the members of many industrial groups, the agents believed strongly in the value of the work the agency was doing, and so were doubly motivated to do it right.

Yet in spite of his long experience, an agent was often in doubt which legal rules might be applicable to the case under consideration and what decision he ought to reach about it. An agent was left free to make his own decision, the only formal rule being that if he had any doubt or question, he was to bring it to the supervisor without consulting any of his colleagues. But like many formal rules, this one was disregarded. Not unnaturally the agents believed that to take a question to the supervisor was to confess one's incompetence and so to prejudice one's efficiency rating; accordingly they did go to their colleagues for help and advice, and the supervisor seems to have winked at the practice.

Although the agents all had much experience, they still recognized that some of their number were better than others at solving the problems that came up over writing reports. Blau's first job was to ask every agent to put all the others in order of their competence as he saw it. The individual rankings were highly in agreement with one another, and they agreed also with the supervisor's ranking of the competence of the different agents.

The investigator next tried to relate the perceived competence of the different agents to the number of times other agents went to them for help and advice. In the course of his observations of behavior in the department, the investigator kept a record of every contact between agents, however brief it might have been, such as a word spoken in passing. He discovered that an agent, while he was in the office, had an average of five contacts per hour with colleagues. Some of these were casual and social conversations, but many were discussions of technical problems. The investigator decided that the latter were probably the longer, and so in studying the distribution of technical consultations he included only contacts that lasted more than three minutes. The investigator also asked every agent to name the other agents whom he consulted when he ran into difficulties with his work.

The results showed a rather marked pattern. As we should expect, the more competent an agent, the more contacts he was apt to receive, and the higher was the esteem in which he was held. But the correlation was not perfect. Two of the agents who their colleagues believed were competent seem to have discouraged people that came to them for help and so to have choked off further advances. As Blau says, "The two experts who were considered uncooperative by their colleagues were generally disliked and received only few contacts. To become accepted, an expert had to share the advantages of his superior skill with his coworkers."

But most agents were ready to help. A few of them, and these among the most competent of all, were consulted by a large number of others, but did not themselves go regularly for advice to any one agent. Thus four agents had no regular partners, but all four were highly competent. Three of them were also very popular as consultants. "These three were by no means isolated from the exchange of advice. On the contrary, they participated so widely in it that they did not spend much time with any single coworker." The fourth agent had only recently been assigned to the department and had not yet been brought into much use as a consultant. The rest of the agents, on the other hand, were apt to take regular partners. Each one of them, though occasionally consulting the few highly competent men, was apt to be especially closely linked with one or two others whose competence was more nearly equal to his own. On any occasion when he needed help, he felt free to consult his partner, as long as he was ready to allow the latter the same kind of privilege in return.

REWARDS AND COSTS OF CONSULTATION

Now let us see what the investigator has to say about the social economics of consultation:

A consultation can be considered an exchange of values; both participants gain something, and both have to pay a price. The questioning agent is enabled to perform better than he could otherwise have done, without exposing his difficulties to the supervisor. By asking for advice, he implicitly pays his respect to the superior proficiency of his colleague. This acknowledgment of inferiority is the cost of receiving assistance. The consultant gains prestige, in return for which he is willing to devote some time to the consultation and permit it to disrupt his own work. The following remark of an agent illustrates this: "I like giving advice. It's flattering, I suppose, if you feel that the others come to you for advice."

The expert who was willing to give advice got various advantages incidental to his rise in esteem. From the consultation he drew renewed confidence in his own capacity to solve technical problems. He might, indeed, pick up ideas useful to him in doing his own work without paying the price of an admission of inferiority. Each of the three most popular consultants, whom many others asked for help, could, moreover, when he needed help in return, scatter his requests among these many and did not need to concentrate them on any single agent, which would have made more conspicuous the fact that it was help he was asking for. As the investigator puts it: "Besides, to refrain from asking any particular individual too many questions helped to maintain his reputation as an expert. Consequently, three of the most popular consultants had no regular partners."

The cost that an expert incurred in getting his prestige is obvious: he had to take time from his own work. "All agents liked being consulted, but the value of any one of very many consultations became deflated for experts, and the price they paid in frequent interruptions became inflated. . . . Being approached for help was too valuable an experience to be refused, but popular consultants were not inclined to encourage further questions."

The investigator is quite explicit that asking a colleague for help incurred an agent costs: "Asking a colleague for guidance was less threatening than asking the supervisor, but the repeated admission of his inability to solve his own problems also undermined the self-confidence of an agent and his standing in the group. The cost of advice became prohibitive, if the consultant, after the questioner had subordinated himself by asking for help, was in the least discouraging—by postponing a discussion or by revealing his impatience during one."

The cost in inferiority of asking a colleague for help was rendered greater in this group than it would have been in some others by the fact that, formally, the agents were not greatly unequal: all held the same job-title, all did the same kind of work, and most of them held the same civil-service grade. A man who is already another's inferior has much less to lose in asking a service of him than one who began as his equal.

That asking for help did indeed incur a man costs is shown by the practice some agents adopted of asking for help while elaborately pretending that they were doing nothing of the sort. Such an agent would bring his problem to a colleague as if it were a case presenting special points of interest well worthy of dispassionate analysis between two discriminating judges. As one of the agents said, "Casey asks me sometimes, too, but he does it with a lot of finesse. He will just seem to ask what my opinion is, not as if he were worried about the question." And the investigator makes the comment: "Such manipulative attempts to obtain advice without reciprocating by acknowledging the need for the other's help were resented. . . . If his advice was needed, the agent demanded that the respect due him be paid by *asking* for his assistance. An official whose deliberate disguise of a consultation was discovered created resentment without averting loss of esteem." In short, this maneuver broke the rules of fair exchange: it attempted to get help without conceding superiority in return. . . .

As we have seen, three of the most competent agents did not enter into partnerships, did not regularly exchange help and advice with particular other agents. Two highly competent agents did take regular partners, but upon the whole partnerships were confined to people of middle and low competence. The investigator implies that it was precisely the costs a man incurred in asking the most competent agents for advice that led the rest to seek out partners among people more nearly of their own rank, with whom they could exchange help without losing status; for the essence of partnership was that if one man asked his partner for help on one occasion, the partner might ask the same favor back on the next. Speaking of the fact that an agent who tried to consult one of his more competent colleagues might meet with a refusal, Blau says:

> To avoid such rejections, agents usually consulted a colleague with whom they were friendly, even if he was not an expert. . . . The establishment of partnerships of mutual consultation virtually eliminated the danger of rejections as well as the status threat implicit in asking for help, since the roles of questioner and consultant were intermittently reversed. These partnerships also enabled agents to reserve their consultations with an expert whom they did not know too well for their most complicated problems.

That is, the advice a man got from his partner might not be of the highest value, but it was purchased at low cost since a partner was apt to be his social equal. And thus he was enabled to save his really difficult problems for the most competent agents, whose advice, since it did come high in confessed inferiority, he did not want to ask often. . . .

. . . Social behavior is an exchange of more or less valuable rewards. The expert agents provided for the others a service that these others found valuable and rare. In return, the experts received much interaction and were able to command from the rest a high degree of esteem, thus establishing a social ranking in the group. But in getting these rewards both parties to the exchange incurred costs—the experts in time taken away from their own work, the others in implicit admissions of inferiority. The costs, moreover, increased and the rewards declined with the number of exchanges, thus tending to cut off further exchange. The experts began to rebuff new requests, and the rest began to hesitate before approaching the experts. Indeed the rest began to look for sources of help they could exploit at lower cost. In the nature of the case, these sources could only be agents more nearly of their own rank than the experts. With such people they could both give and take advice without net loss in esteem.

Finally, most agents met the conditions of distributive justice. For instance, the experts who were ready to give help got much esteem but incurred heavy costs in time taken away from their own work: their costs were proportional to their rewards. Therefore the other agents not only respected but liked them. To win esteem it was not enough to *be* expert: a man had to devote his expert knowledge to the service of others. Thus a couple of agents, known to be competent, who repelled others approaching them with requests for help, were much disliked and left much alone. In failing to enter into exchange at all they had deprived the others of services that the others had come to expect of people with so much to give.

"SOCIAL" INTERACTION

The investigator next turned to the relations between the agents' competence and their more purely "social" behavior. Of the latter he made two different kinds of observations. In his period of watching the group he had kept a record of all the contacts (interactions) an agent received from others, but in mapping out the pattern of consultations he had included only the relatively long contacts—three minutes or more—on the ground that long contacts were more likely than short ones to have to do with the official business of the agency. Now, in mapping out "social" behavior—passing the time of day, gossiping, telling jokes—he included all the contacts an agent received, long or short, and called this a measure of *contacts received*. The investigator also asked each agent to keep a record every day of the colleagues he lunched with. "If a luncheon engagement is defined as eating with one colleague once, the total number of engagements reported (which often included several colleagues on the same day, and the same colleague on repeated days), divided by the number of days on which the respondent went out to lunch from the office, defines the value of this index,"—which the investigator called a measure of an agent's *informal relations*.

He then proceeded to study the interrelations of these three variables: competence, contacts received, and informal relations. For this purpose, he divided the rank-order of the agents on each variable into two parts, but the division did not necessarily come at the midpoint of the distribution. Thus seven agents were rated as high in competence and eight low, but six were rated as high in contacts received and nine low. (One agent transferred out of the department in the course of the study, reducing the total number of the agents considered for the present purpose to fifteen.)

Agents high in competence were statistically likely to be high also in contacts received. Not all were: the two highly competent agents who were unwilling to give the others the benefit of their competence and who were accordingly disliked received few social contacts; but the tendency was in this direction. By the same token, the less competent agents tended statistically to get few contacts.

Perhaps this finding tells us little more than we know already. An expert who was willing to share his knowledge with others was much sought after by the others for consultation, and we know that many of the contacts an expert received were of this sort. But not all were: some were more purely "social." Once a man has won esteem by providing others with rare and valuable services, another reason for their seeking him out comes into play: he is now able to offer a new kind of service. . . .

. . . Some members of a group, those not unduly troubled about their self-respect, seek out social interaction with a member of high status for reasons other than getting the service that first won him the status. But how will a member of high status receive their advances? If he is in any doubt about his status, social contacts with his inferiors will tend to bring him down to their level, and he is apt to rebuff them; but if his status is so firmly established that he need not worry about it, his willingness to allow them social access to him provides them with a new and valuable service and enhances the esteem in which they hold him.

"Contacts received" was measured by the number of interactions a man received in the office, and this might include "Business" contacts as well as "social" ones. The best index of purely "social" contacts was "informal relations," which was measured by luncheons. The investigator found that, statistically speaking, agents of high competence were apt to have few informal relations and agents of low competence to have many. Some of the competent agents did not use their competence to help others; therefore they did not enjoy high status, and the others were not much interested in getting their company for lunch. Some enjoyed a status both high and secure, and could afford to wait until others approached them. And some may not have been quite sure of their high status, which may have led them to rebuff the advances of their inferiors. All of these effects tended to reduce the informal relations of the more competent people. But the less competent people, who on the average were less secure in their status than the more competent ones, tended actively to seek others out for luncheon dates. They sought out the agents of high status if they could get them, but if they could not, they found lunching with somebody better than lunching alone. No doubt man is a gregarious animal and enjoys lunching with his fellows regardless of what it does to his status. Our only point is that differences in status provide additional reasons for (or against) social contacts. By lunching with any one of his fellows an agent of low status could at least make good the fact that he was the other's equal, that he was at least an accepted member of the group. At any rate, the less competent agents "lunched in larger groups than experts and made greater efforts to arrange their work so that they would have to eat alone as rarely as possible." By eating in large groups they necessarily rolled up a high score in informal relations, since each person present at the table added to the score.

Though the competent agents tended to have fewer informal relations than the less competent, lunching more often alone or with fewer companions, the relationship was statistical and did not hold good of all of them. One agent of whom it did not hold good was the one who, in the office, was most encouraging to people who came and asked him for help. He was better liked than any other agent, and became, as we shall soon see, the informal leader of the group. In short, his status was both high and secure. "His great willingness to assist others," the investigator comments, "was his price for maintaining this position." But this was not the only service he did for them: he was also willing to provide them with the secondary reward of lunching with him. "He was particularly hospitable to colleagues who consulted him, and he deliberately fostered informal relations with them. 'If anyone asks me for lunch,' he told the observer, 'I never say, "I have a date with another fellow; I can't." I always say, "Of course, come along."' In contrast to most experts, this agent had very extensive informal relations."

The investigator finally turned to the third of the possible relations between the three variables, the relation between informal relations and contacts received, and he found that agents who had many informal relations (luncheons) were statistically likely to receive many contacts.

. . . . .

It is interesting to reconstruct from the investigator's data what the actual pattern of social engagements among the agents must have been. We shall not give here the tedious reasoning that leads to the reconstruction but only its conclusions. The less competent agents must have lunched with one another a great deal, and in large groups, without the more competent agents being present—indeed the investigator implies as much. The competent agents must also have lunched with one another a good deal without the less competent agents being present—but in small groups. This suggests that they may have rebuffed some of the social advances made to them by the less competent agents. And, finally, some of the less competent managed to get some of the more competent to lunch with them fairly often, in large groups. In fact the investigator tells us that the informal leader was one of the competent men who thus allowed himself to be lunched with by his social inferiors. Equals, then, tended in general to lunch with equals, but some inferiors made successful advances to their superiors in status.

We have here further evidence of the complex interplay of two tendencies we have encountered again and again: a tendency for a man to interact with his superiors in status, and a tendency for him to interact with his equals. A man establishes superior status by providing superior services for others. By the same token, accepting the superior services becomes a cost to a man, since he thereby recognizes his inferiority. Sooner or later he will turn to others who can provide him with services that no doubt reward him less but that also cost him less in inferiority. In the nature of the case, these others can only be his equals. As the partnerships in the Federal agency show, he will turn to his equals for services at work that he can return in kind; but he is particularly apt to turn to them in the "social" field of activity, just because it is *not* the field in which his superiors win their high esteem—and he his low. A secondary development then builds on this primary one. The rest of mankind can "see" the equations of elementary social behavior just as clearly in their way as we social scientists can, and once the relation between social interaction and equality of status is established, it provides new rewards for interaction. By interacting with his fellows a man can then provide evidence for himself and for them that he is at least their equal. Still better, if he can get his superior to interact with him he may do something to raise his apparent status.

ESTEEM AND AUTHORITY

As we have just seen, people of high status tend to receive much interaction. Indeed to maneuver a man into coming to you is to establish the presumption that you are his superior. But people of high status also give much interaction, especially in the sense of originating activity. They tell a relatively large number of others what they ought to do, and the others often do it. The higher the esteem, the higher the authority, is a proposition for which the Federal agency provided much evidence.

Let us consider particularly the agent who the investigator believes was the top informal leader in the department. (The supervisor was of course the formal leader.) He was highly competent at his job, and recognized as being so both by the supervisor and by the other agents. Of the more competent agents, he was also the one most receptive and least discouraging to requests for help from others. That is, he was the most willing to incur the cost of taking time off from his own work. And he was highly popular. . . .

. . . He received high rewards in esteem from the group, but in so doing he incurred, as they saw it, high costs too.

He rewarded the others not only in the business side of their life but in the social one too. He was always ready to accept an invitation to lunch with his social inferiors, and in this he was unlike most of the other competent agents. But the very liberality with which he distributed his favors prevented his becoming identified with any one of the cliques whose members met regularly for lunch. He was in touch with everybody and not exclusively in touch with any single person or subgroup. . . .

. . . The more competent agents tended to take the lead in any undertaking in which several members of the group were engaged. They made most suggestions, and their suggestions were most often followed, whether the question was where to go for lunch or what to do about a project on which a number of agents were working together. And of all the competent agents, the one held in highest esteem was the one who also held highest authority. When a committee was appointed to draft a change in one of the regulations, he dominated the discussion, and his opinion was the one finally adopted. Above all he stood up for the other agents against the supervisor. In this connection the investigator says of him:

> This agent became the informal leader of the group, whose suggestions the others often followed and who acted as their spokesman. For example, in a departmental meeting the supervisor criticized certain deficiencies in the performance of most agents, clearly exempting experts from his criticism. Nevertheless, this official spoke up on behalf of the group and explained that agents could not be blamed for these deficiencies, since a legal regulation that restricted their operations was responsible for them. Generally, the high regard in which this agent was held made his advice and opinion influential among colleagues, and even among superiors.

A man to whom many others come singly for valuable services, in this case advice on how to do their work, and who in rendering the services incurs costs visibly proportional to the esteem they have given him, earns the right to tell them jointly what to do in new conditions that may affect the welfare of many of them, himself among the rest. By serving he becomes a leader. We must always remember that the services he provides need not be ones that you or I should find rewarding or even approve of. Leaders get to be where they are by doing some of the strangest things, and the rest of us are always asking ourselves, "What's he got that I haven't got?"

The answer is that what he has got does actually reward some other men, whether or not it ought to do so, and what he has got is rare in the actual circumstances, whether or not it would be rare in others.

Nor should we lay too much stress on the difference between the followers' coming to him singly and his telling them jointly what to do. In both cases, whether he gives them advice they take or orders they obey, the important point is that he controls their behavior; and the fact that a new occasion may call for his advising them jointly is a nonessential detail. His past behavior has won him the capability of doing so, should the occasion present itself, but it may not. The advice he has given them singly they have in the past rewarded with approval, and so he is more likely to give advice again on a new occasion. He has, as we say, acquired confidence in his ability to give them advice. Nor is it just that he has more confidence but that the others have less: persons whose status is less than his own are persons whose advice has less often won approval in the past, and who are therefore less apt to have the gall to speak up now: what wise ideas they have do them no good if they lack the confidence to come out with them.

The relation between past behavior and present that holds good for the leader holds good also for the followers. Having taken his advice singly and found it rewarding, they are more ready to take it jointly—to obey him when he tells them what to do for their welfare and his own. In doing so, he puts his social capital at hazard, since if they obey and fail to find the outcome rewarding, he has done injury to his esteem and their future willingness to obey. But he has much capital to risk, and if they do find the outcome to their satisfaction, he has replaced his capital and more. Finally, though the leader may lay himself open to the social advances of his followers, he cannot allow himself to get too close to any one of them or any single clique; for frequent social interaction implies equality, and equality between people tends to be incongruent with the fact that one of their number gives orders to the rest. But the best guarantee that he shall not be too close to anyone lies in the very profusion with which he scatters his favors abroad.

NONCONFORMITY AND ISOLATION

A member of a group acquires high esteem by providing rare and valuable services for the other members. But these are obviously not the only services a member can perform: he can also perform services that, without being rare, nevertheless have their value. Prominent among them is conformity to the norms of the group—a norm being a statement of what behavior ought to be, to which at least some members of the group find it valuable that their own actual behavior and that of other members should conform. Since a norm envisages that a relatively large number of members will behave similarly in some respect, conformity to a norm cannot be a rare service: any fool can conform if he will only take the trouble; and therefore if all a man did was conform, he would never get much esteem, though he would always get some. But it does not follow that if conformity will not win a man much esteem, nonconformity will not lose him much—if he has any to lose. For his failure to conform, when the other members see no just reason why he should not, deprives them unfairly of a valuable service, and so earns him their positive hostility.

Among themselves the agents had, over time, worked out several unofficial norms. They felt that no agent, as a maximum, should complete more than the eight cases a month that the supervisor expected of every agent as a minimum. And they felt that no agent should take a report home from the office in order to work on it in the evening. Agents who showed any sign of doing these things were kidded until they stopped. Violation of these norms was an injury to the members of the group, and conformity a value to them, because an agent who finished more than eight cases a month or worked on cases at home might have gotten an advantage over the others in the race for promotion; and if everyone had started to violate the norms, they would all have found themselves, through competition, working harder than they ever had before—not that the supervisor was at all discouraged with the quantity and quality of their present work: the agents were devoted civil servants. In practice, these output norms conspired to perpetuate existing differences in competence, since they prevented slower agents from catching up with their superiors by working harder.

The agents laid an even more severe taboo against reporting to the supervisor that firms had offered them bribes, though by the official rules of the agency they were bound to report such offers. It was not that the agents accepted bribes and wanted to prevent a colleague who was puritanical about such matters from spoiling their game. Far from it: when they suspected that an officer of a firm was working up to offering a bribe, they did their best to cut him off before he could commit himself openly. In the agents' view, it was inevitable that businessmen, given the pressures they worked under, should think of bribery; therefore it ought not to be held against them, and an agent reporting them and so making them subject to legal action was a "squealer." The agents also had a more practical interest in the norm against reporting bribes. If possible an agent was expected to induce the firm he was investigating to obey the law voluntarily and not under the compulsion of legal action expensive to both parties. An offer of a bribe, however tactfully it was made, put into an agent's hand a lever by which he might without legal action get the firm to comply with the law. But it was a lever that became worse than useless once the proffered bribe was officially reported. Indeed the report might make the company all the more ready to fight it out with the government in the courts. Accordingly, agents discouraged all tendencies in their colleagues to "get tough with" and "crack down on" companies, except as a last resort. Should the agency get the reputation of behaving this way, their work would become much more difficult: all companies would meet every agent with automatic hostility, and the chances of persuading them instead of compelling them to compliance would be gone forever. For these reasons most agents felt they had a direct personal interest in seeing that all their colleagues conformed to this norm.

With these norms in mind, let us look at one of the isolates in the department. When we call him an isolate, we mean that he received few social contacts and often lunched alone. Although he appears to have been considered fairly competent, he not only was not ready to use his competence for the benefit of others but spent his time instead turning out more work than the others considered right. Already held in low esteem for behavior of this sort, he proceeded to take a "get tough" attitude toward the firms he investigated; indeed this was generally more apt to be true of the less popular agents than of the more popular ones. And he was the only agent who violated the strongest taboo of all and reported to the supervisor that a bribe had been offered him. The investigator tells us little or nothing about the social background of any of the agents, including this one, and so we cannot tell what features of his past history may have predisposed him to behave as he did. He himself admitted he had made a mistake: though he had violated the norm, he was ready to say it was a good one.

For his action the group had for a time deliberately ostracized him. Cutting off interaction with a member and thus depriving him of any social reward whatever is the most severe punishment a group can inflict on him; in fact he ceases to be a member. But once a man has stood that, he can, so to speak, stand anything; and the group has lost control of him, for it has left him with nothing more to lose. Certainly the department had pretty well lost control of this agent. Though he reported no more bribes, he did much as he pleased in other ways. For instance, the agents felt that he wasted their time by talking a great deal too much in department meetings, where the agents of higher esteem usually took the largest part in the discussion. But in spite of the laughter his remarks provoked, he kept at it and could not be cowed. In a better cause he might have been a hero. The investigator believes that this agent provided only the most conspicuous example of a general tendency: that agents of established low status conformed least closely to the norms of the group, while those of middle status—particularly those, like newcomers, whose esteem was least well established—were the greatest conformers of all.

Social behavior, in a group as elsewhere, is a continuous process of members influencing other members, and the success of influence in the past changes the probability of its success in the future. One result of the process of influence is that the members of a group become differentiated in a more or less stable way—stable so long as external circumstances do not change much. As some members, for instance, succeed in providing, under the influence of requests from others, more valuable services for these others than they can provide for themselves, the members become differentiated in esteem. This fairly stable differentiation in some pattern other than a random one is what we mean by the structure or organization of the group. But the structure is never so stable that it does not itself sow the seeds of further change, and we have been studying a particular example of this. The process of influence that has landed a man at the bottom of the ladder of esteem may render any future influence, so far as it comes from other members, still less likely to succeed with him. Suppose he would ordinarily lose esteem by doing something other than what they want, but he happens as a result of his past behavior to be left without any esteem to lose. If there is any other way in which he finds the action rewarding—and it may be rewarding just because it vexes *them*—the fact that its costs have been reduced to zero raises the odds in favor of his taking it.

A group controls its members by creating rewards for them which it can then threaten to withdraw. If the group has to make good the threat too often, it may wind up with nothing left to withdraw. Its control is always precarious as long as the members have any alternative to accepting the control, such as the alternative offered by another group they can make their escape to. We have been speaking of the low-status member who is going lower. But very high status may have something of the same effect as very low. A man who has so much status to lose that he will not mind if he loses a little of it can afford to try something new and take the risk that it may not turn out to be acceptable to the membership. He too, in his way, is exempt from the control of the group. There are deviates and deviates, some from the point of view of the group are bad deviates, some are good ones. But both are innovators; and if one looked only at the innovations they propose, it would often be hard to tell which is which.

We try to describe what happens in human behavior without taking any moral stand about it—unless laughter is a moral stand. Or rather we take only one stand out of the many open to us. We have nothing to say in favor of conformity or against it. All we have done is point out that a man who does not conform takes certain risks. But a man is born to take risks. Morally we cannot object to him unless he wants his nonconformity made easy, unless he wants to kick the group in the teeth and have it like him too. For then he is being unfair to the rest of us by asking that an exception to the human condition be made in his favor.

31.

THEIR MOTHER, THEIR FATHER, THEIR EVERYTHING

Robert Coles

The preceding selection illustrates the development of informal leadership among the members of a work group made up of relative equals. This selection, on the other hand, explores the dynamics of formal leadership—a person chosen to supervise others, in this case the crew leader of a group of migrant farm workers. The author, Robert Coles, a psychiatrist, depends almost completely on an autobiographical statement by the crew leader to portray the way the leader views his role and the way he believes he is viewed by his followers. The selection graphically portrays a leader role which is both dictatorial and benevolently paternalistic and

Source: Robert Coles, *Migrants Sharecroppers, Mountaineers: Children of Crisis* (Boston: Little, Brown, 1971), pp. 422–31, 433–39.

Robert Coles is research psychiatrist at Harvard University. He is contributing editor of the *New Republic* and on the editorial boards of several magazines devoted to psychology and psychiatry. He is the author of *Children of Crisis: A Study of Courage and Fear*, and, most recently, *Drugs and Youth*.

reflects the complex mix of regard, respect, awe, and hatred with which he is held by the members of his crew. The editors have chosen this particular selection not because it is a typical illustration of leader-follower relationship but because, in its very exaggerated character, it makes more vivid those elements which careful observation will reveal in many superordinate-subordinate relationships. Moreover, the editors have elected to include this material because it deals with a significant issue in our society—the living and working conditions of the half million or more (even the number is uncertain) migrant farm workers who, together with their families, flow in great streams across the United States, providing hand labor for raising, and especially harvesting, the crops whose ripening season varies across the latitudes. (A further examination of this subject may be found in Selection 45.)

For many migrants, the Word has become flesh in the person of "the crew man," which I say not to be smart and sacrilegious but because over and over again I hear those crew leaders described as virtual gods—by people afraid that without crew leaders, without their guidance and constant help and almost infinite direction, all would be lost and no doubt about it, "the earth we work on would turn on us and would take us back," which is how one migrant mother dramatically stated the matter.

The migrant mother quoted above looks upon a crew leader with almost religious devotion. She sees the earth she helps cultivate as something fickle, avaricious and consuming, almost as a person in collusion with the powerful crew leader. The migrant mother has no time to appreciate such psychological and quasi-theological issues. Her words are as good a way as any to give concrete evidence of what a crew leader "means" to his people: "Without him there would be nothing for us to do." She starts out with that foreboding, nihilistic observation and then gets even more ominous: "I truly believe we'd get stuck someplace and never get away, and we'd have nothing, no food or place to stay. Maybe the earth we work on would turn on us and would take us back, just like you hear the minister says might happen one of these days to the whole world, and everyone in it. The crew leader, he's the one who knows how all the people go about their business, and he talks with the growers, and he'll go and see them, you know, before we ever get to their farm. He's the one who recruited us way back. We tried a couple of times to leave him, but it was bad; we tried to get year-round work and we couldn't and it was either sign up with another crew man or go back to our own. We do know him, we said, and he could be worse—although he could be better, I'll say that. He's all we have, though; and there's something I know—and I tell my children all the time: you can't have any choice about a lot of things if you're down and out and your stomach is beating on you to please, please go and get food, any kind of food, just so it'll stop hurting and you don't fall on your face and soon be dead. Now, the crew leader, he *has* to feed you. He has to make sure you get some food. He needs us alive 'on the season,' not dead. He needs us alive to pick, not dead. You see how it is?"

I am not sure I can ever "see how it is." I believe I was able to appreciate her desperate situation, her awful worries, her restlessness, her dread of no less than imminent and utter extinction. I was not able, however, to dismiss what I suppose can be called my middle-class rationality. Why doesn't she free herself of that crew leader, strike out on her own, as some migrants have? Why doesn't she go back home, return to Mississippi, or veer off into one of those cities she comes so near to—New York or Philadelphia, say, or Rochester? I know those alternatives are not without their drawbacks; but she here implied what at other times she has stated outright, and what I have even heard confirmed by crew leaders themselves: migrants are again and again used and abused by their crew leaders, who often are plunderers the equal of any America has managed to produce and tolerate. Why then, I have felt like asking her, or even shouting at her, does she submit to the crew leader, even welcome his presence as next in importance to salvation itself ?

In contrast with me and my stifled questions, the crew leader whose spell dominates her and regulates almost her every move has a very clear idea of what such a woman means, what she is thinking about when she asks me whether I "see how it is." I have used one of his remarks as the title of this section, and perhaps he can help us "see how it is" for migrants as well as himself: "I'm different from the migrant, I know it. I move all over, like them, but they're the sheep and I'm their leader. That's the truth. I try to be good to them. I try to help them out. But I have to shout at them. I have to punish them. They're like children. They're like sheep. It's too bad, how they are. I could have been the same way. The only difference was that one of the growers saw me picking beans, it was about fifteen years ago. I was shouting at my friend, because he was in my way, and I wanted to fill as many bags as I could. The grower called me over and said he liked that, my 'attitude,' he said. He asked me about myself, where I came from and all that kind of thing. So, I told him. It was a story, and I told him all I could remember.

"I told him I was born in Georgia, and my daddy worked on shares, and the bossman one day told us all to get off the land, and fast, because he was turning to cattle, and so we left, as fast as we knew we had to leave. My daddy heard we could get work in Florida, because there are big farms there, so we went there instead of heading for Atlanta, or up to Washington, where his sister and her husband are. My daddy became sick. It broke him, you know, trying to follow the crops. The first year he almost died, and the second year he did die. He loved the work, picking. He never could have lasted a day in a city, sitting there like they do and getting welfare. But he got confused, moving from place to place, and I think he got poisoned by the food in one of the camps, and there was no doctor to come see us. So, I had to take his place, and there was my mother and my two brothers and my two sisters, and we stayed with the crewman that we met when we first came to Florida, and he gave us twenty-five dollars because my daddy died, and he paid to get him buried—it was someplace in Virginia, I think. My mother said she didn't ever want to see the place he's buried, because his soul is gone from the earth, and at least one of us is free of the earth. That was the way she looked at it, you know. She died the next year. I was eighteen then, when we lost her, around that age I think, and I had my younger brothers and sisters with me, and we tried to stay together. Our mother had been sick for a long time before she died, but we never knew from what. No, she never saw a doctor. There was no doctor for us to see in Georgia and once we got on the road the crew leader told us a lot of people have what she had, trouble breathing and the pains in the chest and the stomach.

"The day that grower picked me out to talk to, my mother had been dead a couple of months, I believe. I told him what I've just told you, and he seemed real sorry for me. He asked where my brothers and sisters were. I told him my sister was sick, bad sick, so she was in the camp lying down and the other sister was near her side, trying to give her the help she needed. My two brothers were on the other side of the field, like me, picking beans. He told me I had 'promise.' He told me I was a smart colored man, he could tell. He told me I could be a 'leader,' and I was like him because his mother and daddy died when he was a young man, and they had just come over here from Italy. He said I should stop what I was doing and come and work in the packinghouse. That way I could get a salary, guaranteed every week. Then I could know more about the business; and when it was time to go North, later on, I could take some of the people with me and learn to be a leader. He said he would make sure I went with the best crew leader he knew, better than the one I was working for. He said I could learn from him by helping him. 'You become a leader by learning how, like everything else.' That's what he said. I thought I was imagining things, for a while I did. But he went over and talked to my crew leader and in a second the crew leader was saying, 'Sure, sure,' and I was riding over in the grower's truck to the packinghouse.

"That was the start of it. That was the way I began being a crew man, a crew leader. The grower said you learn to be a leader, but let me tell you, you have to be lucky to be able to learn. If God smiles on you, then you get the chance I did. If He doesn't, you can be the smartest person in the whole world and it won't make any difference at all. I didn't always pick beans that fast, the way I did that day when the grower saw me. My sister Mary was sick that day, like I said, and I wanted to make the most money I could, so we could get her some milk and extra-good food. Then he came along, that big guy, and he was friendly, and he said that he could understand me and he wanted to help—and he did. That summer when we went up through Georgia—we came into Echols County and then over to Valdosta right near where we used to live—my brothers and sisters said it was Momma and Daddy looking down on us that made me a helper to the crew man and on my way to being one. I said it was because of the Italian man, the grower; but Mary said no, it was God's work. Then I told her that if she wanted to think that way, she could, but not me.

"I'm not very much of a believer. I'll admit to that. I don't mind those ministers coming around; they quiet my poeple down. But can anyone really believe what they say? My sister Mary, she's dead. My other sister, I keep her home in Florida, and she's sick. She has tuberculosis. If I didn't have money, if I was a poor bean picker like my people are, my sister would be dead—and my brother too. He also has tuberculosis, just like her! Don't feel sorry for them! They all get one thing or another, pickers do, the migrant people do. They die because their heads drown in cheap wine. They die from a venereal disease. They die because they're drunk, and they fall into a canal or get run over. They die from the other diseases that migrant people get. Everyone gets a disease and dies, but migrant people, they get diseases twenty-five years before other people do. I'm glad I make some money, and I know where to go get a doctor and I can pay him, pay him cash. Doctors are like growers; they pay attention to money. If you have money, they'll take care of you. If you don't, they'll tell you to get the hell out of their office. My sister says the doctors are like the ministers, 'God's people,' she calls them. I get a laugh out of that. I say to her, 'God's people,' yes, they're 'God's people' if you have 'God's dollar bill' for them; and if you don't, then they're the Devil—worse than the Devil, because at least the Devil doesn't pretend to be something other than what he is.

"I try to be as good as the ministers say I should, and I try to help people out, like I'd do if I was a doctor. In a way I *am* a minister and a doctor; I'm the only one my people can turn to if they need advice and help. I'm their mother, their father, their everything. And they're my children, my workers, *my* everything! I have two children, but I never let them or my wife come North with me. It would be terrible for them moving from place to place. It's bad for a family, for children especially. We have a nice house in Belle Glade, Florida and, come May or June, I leave and don't come back until September or October. My wife has all she needs: a refrigerator, a freezer and a big car that's air-conditioned. Our house is air-conditioned. You need air-conditioning in the summer. When we start on the road I lead, and if there's one of my workers who isn't feeling too good, I have him drive with me in my car, because it's air-conditioned. They all keep in line behind my Oldsmobile; we have four big trucks, and the people can sleep in them or beside the road, whichever they want, and depending on the weather, naturally. A few families—four of them—drive their own cars; and I myself can't figure why those people don't go on their own. If I was them, walking in their shoes, I'd go and get my own deal. They know enough by now where they could go, to what farms, and the money they would make would be all theirs. But they're scared, very scared to be alone. One of them told me last year that every time he thought of leaving us, he got dizzy and things would spin around in his head; so he decided to stay with me.

"Well, I'm glad to be taking care of my people. I do anything you can imagine for them. I wake them up in the morning, or else a lot of them would sleep on and on. I tell them what the weather is going to be like. I take them to the field and get them started. Before that I make sure they've had some breakfast in them. I bring them food to prepare. I tell them where to sleep, and I make sure they don't go and fight with each other. That's the worst problem I have; they fight and fight, all the time they do. When they're not drinking they're cutting up real bad, or they're kicking in a door or breaking something. They are little children—that's what I think; they've just never grown up, the way other people do.

"I agree that if they'd be doing different work and not having to move all over, then they'd be different, they'd act different. But there's no other work for them, and they know that. You go and talk with them; they'll all tell you that they're used to going on the road, and they're satisfied. Maybe they're not satisfied, I'll admit that; but they don't know how to leave, and it doesn't enter their mind to leave, no sir, not even as a thought. I believe that. Once a man told me it was like being hooked, you know. He said he was twice hooked; he was hooked on his needle and hooked on picking beans and tomatoes.

"During the day I have to watch them real close. I take them to the field and leave them off. I always tell them I'll *see them in a few minutes.* With my voice I say it so that they know what I mean: I'm going to get some coffee and then, by God, when I return I want to find them *on their knees,* moving along and picking and piling up those baskets and those bags, as many as they can. Later I'll bring along their food to them, of course. I have a man that works for me; he's very good—he can drive the canteen and cook the food and serve it to them. My people are not good at counting and keeping track of things, and I don't want to give them more trouble than they already have. I've learned to be good with arithmetic. I never had much schooling, no more than my people, but if you have to learn, then you do. You don't need any schooling to know how to keep track of your dollars; no, you just find out how by yourself and consider yourself lucky for having the chance. Like I said, I make it easy for my people. I don't give them cards to hand in and have punched each time they eat. They lose the cards, and since they pay for them, it means they've lost money. They have to eat, even if they can't afford to buy the food. Either they eat or they can't work—and that's no good. So, I tell them they're going to get three meals every day while we're on the road. I tell them that I don't care what other crew leaders do; there will be no meal tickets, no punching of cards before they eat, no paying for meals. I tell them they're here with me to work, and that means they've got to eat and sleep, and I'm not going to bother their minds and mine taking money from them for a place to sleep and food to eat. That way they can relax and know they'll be OK as long as we're moving along. That way it's simple and easy for all of us. I pay all the bills—for gas to move us, and the food and everything. I get the money from the growers, and I pay all my bills and expenses, and then I take out my own money, and then I give the families something, so they won't be going all the way from Florida up to New York and back without having some cash left for themselves.

"I'll say this to you, if you want to hear it: I hate to give them money, any at all, *any*. You know why? They throw it away. That's what they do. It's the worst thing in the world to see. I'll hand out the wages to them, and I'll tell them to be careful and save something. I'll tell them to think about how they're going to feel, come a few days, when they can't put their hands on a single cent. They'll one by one say yes sir, yes sir, and there will be so many yeses you'd think the world was changing. I don't think they are lying when they say yes; no, I don't. They mean what they say when they say it, and then they change their minds later on. Actually, they don't change their minds. They have the money and they feel thirsty and they're tired, and they think to themselves that a bottle of wine would be good, so they go and get the wine and they drink it. Soon their money is gone, and if I get mad and tell them they're fools, they say yes sir, like always, and I do believe they mean it, they feel sorry for doing the wrong thing.

"Our people, the migrants, they're not like others. They have to be *told* what to do. If I didn't act strong with them and keep them moving along and let them know what comes next and what they have to do now, then I'd have them all lying around staring up at the sky, drunk as can be; or if they couldn't get their hands on a bottle, then they'd be sitting around and doing nothing and hoping they'd get their next meal somehow. I don't mean to be so down on them. I like them; they're my people. But you see they've all left their homes, and they don't have anyplace to be but with me; and so it's hard on them, and on me, too. They'll bring me all their troubles, you know. If they're fighting or worried over something or they get fits of crying, crying all the time, then I have to fix them up. Don't ask me how I do it. I don't know. I talk with them. I listen to them until my ears are tired and when I can't hear them any longer, because my head is all filled up, I tell them to get back to the truck and sleep, and the next day when we stop someplace, I'll listen some more. They're very up and down, my people are. One minute they're whistling and singing and they'll do dances, even on the trucks while we're moving up North. The next minute they'll be sitting by themselves, staring off into nowhere. You can't get their attention, it seems, no matter what you do. There are times when I expect them never to say another word to me or anyone else; I expect them to kill themselves, they seem so low. I can't predict how they'll be from one day to the other and even one minute to the other; but I've learned my own kind of psychology, I guess you could call it. I saw on television once a man who said every one of us, no matter who he is and no matter if he has gone to school or not, can learn how to read people and figure out what is on their mind, like a psychologist does. I tell a man that I know there's something bothering him, but there'll be a lot *more* bothering him if he doesn't get his work done. I talk like this to my people: 'You've got your pain now, and I appreciate it; but brothers and sisters, you'll be dead and six feet under if you don't go out there and do your picking. So go and work, and you won't have time for all your pain, and then later we'll solve what's ailing you. We will.'

"They always work. They know I'm telling them what's true. They know that if you stop working—that goes for all of us, right?—you die. I'd die if I didn't keep working. I go nuts sitting at home in Florida. I'm supposed to be resting all the time, because the doctor says my blood pressure is high, way up there on his machine. He told my wife I should stop, and stay home and get rest. I told her that we'd soon be without food, and *then* what would the doctor say. I'm like my people; I've got to keep moving with them. What goes for them goes for me. There's no other way for them to live, nor for me, either. We're all lucky we're even alive. A lot of kids I grew up with there near Valdosta, Georgia, they died before they became men or women, before they knew what life is all about, I'll tell you. Maybe they were lucky. I get to wondering myself, like my people do. They'll come and ask me if there's any reason I can tell them why they should stay alive. I tell them I'd rather be alive than dead, and that's all the 'reason' anyone should need. They start telling me we're all dead, the way we keep going—with no rest, and the work and more work and not much money. Of course they stare into me, right into me, as though I'm getting money even if they're not, as though to say that. I tell them sure, I'm getting more, but a lot of difference it really makes. It means my wife lives better, and I have my big car; but that's all. I'm *with* them, and I'm trying *for* them, to do the best that can be done, so that they can work and eat and not starve to death and not be beggars.

. . . . .

"I'm quick to see if one of my people is sick. I try to quiet them down if they're excited and talking about being afraid. I'm the only one they can call upon, like I said, and I'm there, I'm always there to be of help. There's a limit to what I can do, of course. It's expensive to call a doctor. A lot of the places where we are, there's no doctor for miles and miles around. Even when there is one, they want you to bring the person over, and they can keep you and the sick one waiting all day. I've got the growers pushing on me all the time. In this business, it's rush, rush, everything rush. They want me here and then the next place; they want everything harvested, everything that's been planted, in five days or six or seven—or they'll be ruined, ruined for life, to hear them talk. If I start driving my people to doctors all the time, it won't be long before I'm seeing one myself. I already am. He's the one who told me my daddy died of high blood pressure. He's the one who told me I've got the same thing. Maybe every single migrant has it, for all I know. Sometimes we'll be out there in the field. The grower will be on my back, telling me the tomatoes have to be in by the end of the week or he's through, completely destroyed. I'll be pushing on my people to pull those tomatoes in. The sun will be beating down on us. And I'll be looking at my people and thinking to myself that half of them are in real bad trouble, the men and the women and the children. Maybe *all* of them are in trouble, and I should be taking all of them that day to the doctor. But if we don't get the tomatoes in pretty soon, none of us will be eating three meals a day and then we'll *really* need to see a doctor—and he'll tell us to go and eat! And how, I ask you, how will we go and do that, except by getting those tomatoes in, right on time?

"You see, we're all in trouble, that's the truth. Some of those ministers come over and tell me I'm bad because I steal from my workers. They're from some 'migrant ministry,' some organization like that. They're not like the preachers who want to talk about God with my people; instead, 'migrant ministry' people want to test the water we drink in the fields, and they give me long sermons on how bad it is, what they call 'the migrant life.' I asked one minister a little while ago what other kind of life he thought my people could live. Let those ministers go and get jobs for all my men and see how good the jobs will be. They have a look on them, those ministers, as if they've never had to worry about a meal in their life. They speak good; they talk a good line. They look at you as if you're a crook and you belong in jail. They look at you as if they're the angels and you're the biggest sinner in the whole world. I asked them—they don't scare me—what their fathers did to make a living. They didn't answer me, so I knew I had them. I told them to get out and stop bothering me and my people, or I'd take care of them. I said if they can't even answer an honest question I ask, and instead they keep on asking me things, then they can leave and never come back, *never*. They told me, then they did. One had a father who was a teacher, and the other, his father was a lawyer. Now that's wonderful. I told them, 'That's wonderful.' I wasn't being wise. I mean I was; but hell, I wish my daddy could have been a teacher or a lawyer or something like that instead of a slave—that's what he really was, on a plantation in south Georgia.

"I've argued with those ministers plenty, and with others like them. They're all over the country! I've told them that when they can figure out a way to keep me and my men at work all year around in one place, I'll be the first to sign up, and I'll do anything they want me to do. They say I should be 'nicer' to my men. I'm everything to my men. Like I keep on saying, I have to lead them around and tell them when to do every single thing they do. Like I said I'm their mother, their father, their everything. I'd like to give them, each one, a million dollars and a big home and all the wine they want and people to wait on them. I'd like to. I told the ministers that there are plenty of rich churches, and why don't they go to them and get some money and stop preaching at me because of how bad I treat my people, and instead give them a lot of money, a good fat bundle of cash. One of the ministers told me I was 'evading.' He said I was trying to get out of something, and I should be doing more for my people. Should I? Maybe I should. Where would I get the money, though? I'm not a grower. I'm not a rich man. I make some money, and I do it by working all the time and living here one day and up the road the next day. I leave my family and don't see them for half the year, almost. I have a good car, correct. I have air-conditioning in it, correct. I have a good home in Florida, correct. My wife has some nice dresses, correct. I buy my children good clothes, correct. Does that make me into a millionaire? Does that make me a grower, a man who has a hundred jobs to offer?

"What the ministers say is right: we don't live good, we live bad. Why don't they go and talk with the growers, though? Why don't they go and weep on *their* shoulders? You know why? It's because the growers will throw them out without hearing a word from them. It's only suckers like me who listen and listen—until I feel so lousy I'm ready to let those ministers take over. I wish they would. I wish they would come and live with these people here, and not just come around once in a while, checking up on the water and the food and the 'sanitation.' I'm sick and tired of that word they use, 'sanitation.' When they're not complaining on that score, they're telling me I should make my men not drink water from the tap, or I should pay them more. There's always a complaint they have to register. I told them never to come bothering me again; just last week I did. I picked up my gun and told them to leave and not come back. They said I was using my gun on the men; that I was treating them like slaves. What do they know about being a slave? After they left I asked my men if they followed those ministers, if they believed what they said. Not one of my people agreed with them. They all said they never hear them for very long, because they talk too much, and they're trying to stir up trouble. That's what they *are* trying to do, make everyone feel bad and turn us each one against the other. Then the growers would have it even better than they do now. Then they'd have us all on our knees, begging. It's bad enough we're on our knees all day long, picking. I am on my knees, too. I'm on my knees telling my men to work faster, and then I have to stoop over and feel the beans and decide if they are too wet to pick or the time is too soon, all that.

"I beg for my people. I don't only beg for myself but for them. I ask the growers to fix up good cabins and pay the best wages they can. My daddy said never to beg, so I don't, not the begging he spoke of. But I beg. I beg for money, so that the work we do isn't for nothing. I sweat for my people; and they *are* my people. The ministers tell me I have no right to call them that, to call them 'my people.' Whose people are they? You have to belong to someone in this world. I'm *their* crew man, *their* crew leader. They wouldn't leave me for anything, and I wouldn't leave them. I have some money saved up, and I could easily leave. My wife tells me I should. But I won't. Never; I'll never leave my people, and they know it's true, what I'm saying.

"One of my men died a couple of months ago, and I told the others we'd miss him, but we'd keep going; and his brother and his wife, they both came to me and said they wanted to stay with me, and so long as I would keep them, they would stay with me. Then I decided to ask them something. I asked them what they would do if I said no, if I said I was through, and they could go and do what they want and so would I. They didn't answer me. They didn't say a word to me. That's how worried they got. I tried to get them to talk, but they didn't. I asked them if their tongues were all tied down, and they didn't answer me then, either. I asked them if they were ever going to talk again in their whole lives, and they didn't answer me. Then I told them not to worry, and I was only fooling, and there wasn't a chance in the world that I'd give up on them. Right away they started smiling and laughing, and all of a sudden they could talk. They told me I was a great guy, but not to speak like I did, because it made them get scared, and they didn't know what would happen to them if I retired, except that they'd probably end up by the side of the road, dead. Yes sir, that's what they told me; they told me they'd die if I gave up on them. I guess when I do die, they will die. But we all die sooner or later. And in this work, when you go on the road to do harvesting, the chances are it'll be sooner and not later that you die. Even for me, the crew man, that's what the chances are."

I believe I have spent more time talking with him than any other particular person I have met and interviewed in the course of my work with migrant farmers. He is a bundle, a tangle of contradictions. I add tangle to bundle because over time I finally did realize how caught up he is by those contradictions—which can be said to make up his very life. He means just about everything to "his" people, and their extravagant praise of him more than matches any of his own more grandiose self-evaluations. Yet those same people also doubt him, suspect him, hate him—all of which in his own indirect way he can acknowledge. He takes care of dozens of human beings, makes certain that they eat and work, provides shelter for them, listens to their complaints and worries, offers them advice, interprets things to them, reminds them of obligations and responsibilities—he keeps in mind countless birthdays and wedding days and memorial days—and in general mediates between impoverished, uneducated (and it can be said), abandoned or wayward people on the one hand, and the tough, demanding world of agricultural commerce on the other. Yet he also takes *from* the people he takes care of, and for all his explanations, whose length and intensity are remarkable, there is no way he can get around the truth: he rakes in considerable cash, keeps most of it, gives precious little to the migrants who work so hard, sends home thousands and thousands of dollars, while at the same time the families whose toil has produced such an income for him are lucky if they see even one thousand of those dollars in an entire year. The words can be summoned forth and pinned upon him, one after the other: he is protective, shrewd, exploitative, kindhearted, concerned, evasive, cruel, quite definitely authoritative, even (for these sad and lost souls) charismatic; he is a confidence man, a manipulator, a thief, a monster even; he is a middleman in the worst sense of the word, a living reminder of how awful a society can let things get, hence force people to become.

What am I to say? I happen to believe he is more tormented and anguished, more rocked by the awfulness of his life as well as the fate of his people than he can ever possibly realize. Somehow, somewhere in himself, he knows how monstrous it is for everyone—that people should live as migrants do in a country such as this. He says that, many times he does; he almost accuses himself, and he of course turns on the migrants, then rushes to defend them. And I myself rush at this moment to say something: I am not writing about this tragedy in order to turn this man into a hero *or* into a sort of terrible gangster. I suppose if I had to settle on a "position" for myself it would be one that echoes this man's own plaintive (yes, self-pitying) description of his dilemma: he is bound, confined, and controlled by an evil he turns to profit, but at a price, a price his own conscience cannot quite overlook, a price the United States of America continues to find not unbearable. Perhaps the last word on him and his kind—some of whom are worse, some of whom are better, some of whom are crueler, some more compassionate—ought to be left to the grower, a man who has known and fought with and relied upon this particular crew leader for many years: "Hell, it's a hard, hard world we live in. None of us really are secure, certainly not him. He's trying to keep alive and he knows he has to use his fists to do it, the way things are. But I'll tell you one thing about him: he's the kind of guy who turns around every once in a while to see how the next person is doing and to worry about him, all the guys he's pushing and fighting with. He uses people; but they get to him and they bother him. They do. He'll be talking about them and I can see it in his face, in his look: he worries over them. I can't, I admit it. I don't know the migrants. I just know *him*. I hire him, and he brings them to work here on my land. A man like me can't get to worrying, not over the migrants. I have a million other worries to juggle; and if I don't solve them each year, the migrants would even be worse off than they now are—and so would the crew leaders, and me and my brothers, the growers."

32.

BEYOND WORDS: THE STORY OF SENSITIVITY TRAINING AND THE ENCOUNTER MOVEMENT

Kurt W. Back

An examination of types of group relationships—the subject of this section of the book—would be incomplete without considering a phenomenon in our society known variously as sensitivity training, encounter groups, or the human potential movement. Its focus on trust, candor, openness, on the "immediate feedback" of feelings, on the importance of the "here and now" produces, for those who accept it, a unique pattern of interpersonal relationship. Its results have been both praised and criticized; it has been seen both as the path to the New Utopia and as antiintellectual and the use of science to "overcome the scientific view of man." This selection by Back should provide the reader with a sense of the nature of the interaction

Source: Kurt W. Back, *Beyond Words* (New York: Basic Books, 1972), pp. 78–83, 201–11, 229–37.

Kurt W. Back is professor of sociology and psychiatry at Duke University. He is the author of *Slums, Projects and People: Social Psychological Problems of Relocation in Puerto Rico,* and the coauthor of *The June Bug, A Study in Hysterical Contagion.*

which sensitivity training and encounter groups produce. It should also offer the reader an illustration of some of the characteristics of a "social movement," which is the subject of the *next* section of this book. (See especially Selection 35.)

Sensitivity training is novel in accepting the group experience as having value in itself, without recourse to any ultimate aims. Correspondingly, the group experience has become the center of the movement. In earlier times, intense emotional experiences could always be explained as a working of the agency which gave the movement its own flavor, be it religious or political. In these instances the development of the science of pragmatism deemphasized the experience itself while emphasizing the ultimate goals.

The catchword for the sensitivity training movement is "here and now." The term was invented by Moreno in his work on psychodrama, one of the techniques which is basic to much of the work in sensitivity training. In his book *Microcosm,* Philip Slater has contrasted the here-and-now orientation within a group with three other ways in which a group could promote group process: extragroup data, general principles, and personal histories. Classroom teaching concentrates on the relation between extragroup data and general principles. Therapy stresses principally the relation between events in the group and personal history. Academic work may also use the general group process, usually as a way to explain general principles. The uniqueness of sensitivity training is that it uses the present experience only, not as a wedge to get into people's past the way therapy does, and not as a wedge to interpretation as teaching methods do. Concentrating on outside events, interpretation, and verbal discussion is seen as an escape from the present experience and from the essential work of the group.

This new kind of group activity found in sensitivity training needs a justification to become acceptable for its prospective members. Thus we find a mythology of the here and now which is separate from any social psychological theory developed for the professional audience. This myth of the here and now ties in with the tensions within society: the growth of a large prosperous mobile middle-class left without any central belief or controlled ways to get excitement. It rejects history, even personal history, and any enduring structure. It also rejects symbolization. In effect, one of the main techniques of sensitivity training is to make symbols concrete and active. Thus the statement "I hate you" will be quickly acted out in a fight, the statement "I love you" in an embrace, unhappiness in crying, and so on. The implication of this attitude is a complete denial of some recent developments in human history of the importance of abstraction and symbolism.

The cult of the experience is justified by deprecating symbolic statements, especially higher abstractions, and extolling strong sensual experiences, especially the more direct ones. This value shift is carried out in three ways: from symbols to concrete expression, from intellect to emotions, and from the mind to the body. One part of the here-and-now myth, therefore, is the rejection of a language of symbols in favor of direct experience and action; thus, group exercises, which sometimes look like children's games, are really given a deep meaning. One of the more famous of the exercises, called "trust fall," consists of a person falling backward, confident that his partner is going to catch him. Under the conditions of the group, it is highly unlikely that the partner is not going to catch him. While it is true that to an outsider this may look like a ritual, apparently it assumes deep meaning within the group, so that people really feel that this is the only way to express trust. Similar ways of making abstract concepts concrete are embodied in the myth and ritual of many societies. In all cases, participants realize that the concrete form is known to be a substitute or an explanation of the abstract concept. In the mythology of sensitivity training we learn that concreteness is the high road to understanding. Thus one of the early practitioners of sensitivity training in industry, Douglas McGregor, coined the expression "gut learning" as the only kind of learning that has any meaning and will hold. If we do not have to look beyond the present, any record keeping or symbolization of language would be unnecessary. Language is useful only for recurring situations, and to refer to things absent in the present situation.

Allied with this rejection of symbolism is the rejection of the function that makes symbolism possible, the intellect. Attention is directed toward the exalting of emotion or the direct sensual experience. Group experiences become stronger if their meaning is not mediated by thought but accepted directly. This technique of concentrating on feeling and senses has been for a long time the technique of mysticism and of allied techniques. Here again we must stress the fact that in sensitivity training no ulterior aims can be acknowledged, no ideology gives meaning to the experience, and, therefore, the experience has to be celebrated for itself. Thus we find an emphasis on concentration on sensual experience. Exercises comprise simple concentration on one sense organ, such as one's sight, feeling, or hearing. This emphasis extends to whole programs of education based on sensual experience or emotional education or, as it has been called, education for ecstasy.

Using dualistic terminology, we find an emphasis on the body as contrasted to the mind. Bodily exercises have been used, especially by religious groups, for a long time. In fact, some California encounter groups make extensive use of Far Eastern and Indian dance, gymnastics, and physical exercises as an aid in their programs. Other physical exercises have been tried which are based on more modern concepts, from gymnastics to psychoanalysis.

Charlotte Selver, Ida Rolfe, and Alexander Lowen are the more prominent advocates of this somatic aspect. Selver and Rolfe are physiotherapists who have developed complete methods of practice, movement, and exercise intended to lead to a regeneration of the whole person. Lowen is more in the Reichian tradition of psychoanalysis. Like this student and friend of Freud, he poses the liberation of the body, especially the sexual organs, as an equal and even fundamental problem to that of social change. Lowen has developed an integrated psychosomatic "bioenergetic" approach which is intended to release the hidden energy of the body, especially of the lower part. Procedures of sensory awareness or awakening have become the most popular parts of encounter groups and form the subjects of the best-selling publications, notably among them Bernard Gunther's *Sensory Awareness below Your Mind* and *What to Do until the Messiah Comes.* He describes the rationale for this aspect of Esalen as follows:

> I guess largely I feel that most people in our culture tend to carry around a lot of chronic tension, and that they tend to respond largely on the basis of *habit* behavior and often goal-motivated behavior. And what I call sensory awakening is a method to get people to quiet their verbal activ-

ity, to let go their tension and focus their awareness on various parts of the body or various activities or feelings in the body. And of experiencing the *moment,* experiencing what it is they are actually doing as opposed to any kind of concept or conditioned kind of habit behavior.

Sensitivity training represents a reaction to the development of intellectual history. Claude Levi-Strauss has recently distinguished between the savage mind and the modern mind. The savage mind proposes a completely coherent picture of the world in a concrete manner. What the modern mind would consider a symbol is for the savage mind a real fact. He claims that what is metaphor for the modern mind is metonymy for the savage. The modern mind has developed science by deliberately refusing to assume that different realms of experience, such as animals, stars, trees, human actions, and feelings, can be classified in the same way. For the modern mind, these different realms are investigated separately, using purely pragmatic methodology. Mythological thinking, which in a way is what Levi-Strauss means by the savage mind, tries to put everything into a coherent system. The modern mind, represented by the experimentalists, perceives a fact and uses a symbolization of it for easier manipulation, quite conscious that it is only a symbol.

The last four hundred years have gradually seen the increase of the importance of the modern over the savage outlook. While day-by-day activities were always regulated by principles of practicality, they were interpolated into a completely coherent world view. The scientific outlook and its philosophical underpinnings have stressed mainly instrumental value, problem solving, emphasis on the intellect, and a free, almost playful use of symbols. Since the rise of science, there has always been a reaction against the values implicit in science. There are several forms which this reaction can take. One is the belief in ultimate nonrational values, the emphasis on ends over means, and the rejection of certain scientific facts in order to fit into a preconceived world view. This is a conservative, anti-intellectual way which traditional religion has used in its step-by-step fight against new developments in science from Galileo to Darwin to Freud. As these three examples show, scientific thought has usually prevailed, and much of the approach of science has become ingrained in many people. Science may frustrate some aspects of human life. But this frustration does not lead readily to a return to ideas which have preceded scientific development.

Another way to reject the "modern mind" (in Levi-Strauss's sense) is to use some of the procedures and language of science in a mythological sense. The central belief of sensitivity training, the use of behavioral science concepts to go from symbol to event, from cognition to emotion, and from mind to body, may be the first comprehensive attempt of this kind.

The progression of behavioral science to a social movement in sensitivity training illuminates one of the paradoxes of the pragmatic outlook. Pragmatism is the philosophy most attuned to the scientific method. It judges a procedure by its outcomes, by whether or not it works. It rejects explicitly the need to integrate each act and idea into an overarching framework. It is satisfied if an idea is useful for a reasonable time. Thus, pragmatics concentrate on choosing means that can be judged in this way, and are suspicious of ultimate ends that may only arrive in the distant future and be used as a justification for all kinds of mischief in the meantime. The philosophy of sensitivity training follows this logic in its origins from philosophy based on James and Dewey, as well as in continuous resistance to questions about the ultimate aims of the procedures.

The pragmatic orientation of rejecting ultimate aims can easily slip into a perspective of shorter and shorter time spans. A T-group workshop can be accepted for its short-range objective of leaving the participants with good feelings without worry about ultimate aims. But the same can be said about each session, each interaction, each experience. Thus, denial of ultimate ends may lead beyond a rational short-term time perspective to a cult of the instantaneous and sensual experience. Sigmund Koch described the resulting model of human nature in this way:

> The Group Movement is the most extreme excursion thus far of man's talent for reducing, distorting, evading, and vulgarizing his own reality. It is also the most poignant exercise of that talent, for it seeks and promises to do the very reverse. It is adept at the second remove image-making maneuver of evading human reality within the very process of seeking to reembrace it. It seeks to court spontaneity and authenticity by artifice; to combat instrumentalism instrumentally; to provide access to experience by reducing it to a neuter-pap commodity; to engineer autonomy by group pressure; to liberate individuality by group shaping.

Sensitivity training can be seen as a reaction against the scientific outlook by an emphasis on direct, immediate experience. It can be seen as the logical end-point of the transition from the extremely long-range outlook of religion to the middle-range time perspective of science, to the immediacy of the here and now.

. . . . .

[It] has ranged farther and farther away from traditional scientific work. It is treated at best as the outer fringe of group dynamics in discussions of social psychology, and research efforts and theoretical input by people in the movement have decreased almost continually since its inception. By contrast, some adherents of the movement still claim allegiance to social science. Many of them are professionals in the field. Requirements for some sensitivity practitioners include academic training, for example, becoming fellows of NTL, and trainers continue their efforts to legitimize the enterprise through the traditional channels. The relevant professions are becoming more involved in establishing social control. The basic irony lies in the discrepancy between ends and means. Sensitivity training basically aims at the regeneration of man through a deep, almost spiritual, experience, the kind of effort that has traditionally been part of the field of religion. It uses, however, the methods, the language, and some of the ritual of scientific work. One could almost say that, here, science is used to overcome the scientific view of man.

Sensitivity training can be related to the problems of social science and may be seen as a reaction to some of its developments. The central feature of sensitivity training, the strong experience in group interaction, is a very real event, and the conditions that lead to it are central to the concerns of social psychology. During a great part of their history, however, social psychologists have been looking at emotional events, describing them, and talking about their importance, and then gradually giving up the topic in favor of exact language describing other topics. Thus, group processes have been studied for a long time and discussed by many scholars with interesting ideas. Nevertheless, further work following their pioneering efforts has led them to exact but impersonal laboratory experiments or extremely abstract mathematical models. The Lewinian school, from which at least the Bethel experience started, has gone this course. Although Lewin was extremely concerned with human interaction and social problems and the study of real groups, the basic principles he developed have succumbed more and more to detailed analysis. Lewin's successors in group dynamics have gone from natural groups, then from groups of any kind, to work with individuals. The large laboratories supposed to contain whole groups for observation were gradually subdivided into cubicles where one person could be measured in interaction with a tape recorder or a message that presumably came from another person.

It may be argued, and most practitioners in the field of group dynamics would grant it willingly, that this gradual shift in emphasis has led to increased methodological and theoretical precision, the development of several logical, intricate, but consistent miniature theories, and an amount of cumulative research rare in social science. By the same token, however, many topics that could not be treated in this way, that might depend on the actual functioning of groups or somewhat subtle emotional interchanges, have been lost and neglected. Many practitioners in the field, eager young students, and laymen concerned with problems of everyday living have felt a great loss when they compared what they thought was being done in group dynamics with what was actually being done. Recurrently, in the history of the field, less exact but more encompassing new approaches have arisen, even within academic social psychology, to treat such topics as ethnomethodology and associated techniques. However, sensitivity training has also been ready to receive scientists disappointed in rapid progress by traditional methods. Sensitivity training has been sanctioned by its ancestry in group dynamics as a legitimate field for treating group interaction. It has kept up its reputation by advertising itself as able to treat both practically and experimentally the concerns of many in dealing with their personal problems, with the functioning of groups, and especially with the emotional aspects of man and society. It has been ready to receive them in its centers and workshops and to give them the support and experience they needed.

For many people who have come to the sensitivity training centers in search of a rational understanding of group processes, the experience has been a revelation. Many stay for the experience itself, for the enjoyment of working in the field, and forget the original concern with hard science that brought them there. It has become more and more true with sensitivity training that one is either in it or out of it, and that attraction to it has been in the nature of a conversion experience. Within the field of social science, a person who has followed this school and has become a member of the in-group will neglect any doubts or investigations that may undermine the experience. The social support given to sensitivity training, the proliferation of the centers, the attention given to them in the press and other mass media, the attempts of all kinds of organizations to hire consultants and to institute something like sensitivity training in their fields, has made it easy for people to become full members of the movement and to reject any inside analysis. The field given up by experimental group dynamics has been preempted with a vengeance.

This development may explain the paradox of much of sensitivity training, namely, that it is an anti-intellectual movement in the name of science. Its strengths, as well as its weaknesses, derive from this fact. At its best it is an attempt to integrate two aspects of man's existence that are usually kept separate—the analytical, intellectual function and global feelings, emotional attempts to understand man's place in the world. A neat balance between the two may lead to fruitful cross-fertilization. At its worst, however, it may tamper with the procedure of science, introduce questionable emotional practices, and disguise easy excitement as experimental research or proved professional practice. Between these extremes, the system frequently becomes exasperating. Believing the language of the movement, one might look for research, proof, and the acceptability of disproof. In fact, the followers of the movement are quite immune to rational argument or persuasion. The experience they are seeking exists, and the believers are happy in their closed system which shows them that they alone have true insights and emotional beliefs. Given the cultural context in which they are working, however, the high prestige of science, and the necessity of professional control, sensitivity training in general does not want to sell itself as purely a new awakening. Thus it wants not only to become a cult, a new religion of the age of Aquarius, but also to stay on good terms with the scientific establishment. From this dual effort arise certain tensions and new attempts which may show best the place of sensitivity training within social science.

. . . . .

The relation between mind and body, which has been fundamental for the development of modern science, may also be the best example of what can be called the postscientific attitude within the encounter movement. The contrast between mind and body, and the separation of the two, is probably one of the characteristics of Western culture. In part the distinction is implied in Christianity; Descartes used this fact and made the distinction absolute in order to gain freedom for physical science from theological restrictions. One of the effects of this separation has been the development of physical and biological sciences, separate from psychology, psychoanalysis, and the social sciences, keeping the mental and physical aspects as separate and closed systems. It was only after both kinds of science developed that attempts were made to show a relationship between the two and to integrate the two systems. In the late nineteenth and early twentieth centuries, the theories of emotion by James, Lange, and Cannon, Pavlov's conditioning theories, and Freud's theory of symptom formation showed the relationship between the two. The same period saw a frank acknowledgement of the importance of the body and of bodily needs. The original split between mind and body was made with the assumption that the mind was superior and the body was something weak, bad, which one should be ashamed of. Further development in psychosomatic medicine has stressed the profound interaction between mind and body, the importance of bodily well-being for mental adjustment, and the influence of psychic disturbances on physical expression.

The sensitivity training movement has been influenced by several strands of this development. It accepts the importance of the body, and expends much effort in physical exercises. These exercises are there to develop bodily skills, to get a greater variety of new sensations, and also to use physical conditions to attain certain mental states. On the other hand, partly through the influence of Oriental philosophy and religion, encounter centers also use mental control and techniques such as meditation and, perhaps, trancelike states. The movement seems to have had two influences in its consideration of mind-body relationships: the medical, psychosomatic influence which gives an almost physiological definition for mental changes and uses all kinds of techniques to produce those, and the Oriental one with all its attempts to direct training to achieve new and supposedly superior mental states.

. . . . .

Thus the current problem of the relation of sensitivity training to society and to science has developed. One the one hand, sensitivity training is advertised as the movement that rids man of his over-reliance on his overdeveloped brain, especially the cortex, which reverses history, especially the Western history of dominance over nature, and which returns man to his lost garden of innocence. On the other side, sensitivity training is sold to diverse clients as a problem-solving technique, and as a new way of working on the traditional problems of behavioral science. The more the movement expands and becomes part of the popular culture, the more both aspects arouse public attention and concern.

The different factions within sensitivity training have looked for ways to maintain, or regain, scientific respectability. In the activities at NTL and Bethel and their associated laboratories, a continuous attempt has been made to keep in contact with academic science. Faculty delegates are recruited from university or similar professional settings. The failure of concrete evaluation attempts has been especially crucial here. A reaction has been to proclaim that people trained in these laboratories will become special people, members of an invisible, or perhaps visible, fraternity who have experienced something that may or may not be appropriate in their own work or profession. Connected with this are the attempts to introduce sensitivity training as part of the curriculum in some schools or in professional training. This may be an example of the familiar phenomenon of converts proselytizing to maintain the social reality of their own experience. We have seen the different forms this may take, such as a general reform in instruction which fits a lack that the present malaise of academic life has created.

Attempts to teach some of the concepts of human interaction, especially in courses similar to sensitivity training, combine the sometimes dry textbook psychology with immediate experience. This balance is difficult to maintain, and frequently such teaching leads to excitement for excitement's sake and attracts people who are looking either for therapy or a strong emotional experience. The age of most of the students and the general setting would guarantee in any case the occurrence of some rapid change, and the students who experience this change are greatly impressed by the procedure. It is noticeable, however, that many of the main protagonists of this classroom approach have left sensitivity training and say they are no longer part of the movement, that what they are doing is *not* sensitivity training.

A good example of this trend is Richard Mann, who has taught experientially directed courses in group interaction at Harvard and Michigan.

> I don't have interest in training people how to give feedback or get feedback, or make a good group or be democratic, or be open and honest, or any other damn thing. I mean, that is not my goal. My goal is to go in there and let a group develop. You know, groups aren't all that different, and when I think I understand something, I will say, "Hey, I think I see something happening." Or when I feel something, I will say, "Hey, that is really getting me mad," but it is not, it seems to me, with some underlying purpose of training everybody in the new etiquette of how you say, in this kind of somber tone, "Yes, I have a little feedback to give you, and blah, blah, blah." I don't like it. I think it is

Boy Scout moralism, and I think that's the sensitivity training tradition.

Attitudes of this kind exemplify one aspect of the conflict between the emotional experience that is sensitivity training and the demands of hard science. Unwilling to give up the regular procedures in social science, protagonists reject their membership in the clique of sensitivity training and admit only that they use group methods, some more or less orthodox and some of their own devising. In the same way, some of the personnel management people at NTL have left the fold and use group methods in a different context. Among these people, the conflict and ambiguity of the whole field of human relations has led them through different schools of thought, and they may have learned something by having had the experience of having considered sensitivity training.

Perhaps it is the more extreme groups that are looking harder for new ways to adopt scientific respectability. The balance between faith and reason has been precarious wherever one has looked. It is instructive to see how this balance has been worked out in various instances. Recent developments at Esalen are an interesting case in point.

The adoption of the encounter movement by the mass media has in part overwhelmed the encounter centers as well as influenced their development. After all, at a time when restaurants advertise themselves as group encounters with food, going to an encounter session is hardly a novelty and even somewhat conventional. Pure encounter groups have diminished, and the participants at Esalen meetings, as well as at the meetings Esalen holds in San Francisco, are demanding new kinds of programs. The response has been in several directions. One has occurred at Esalen itself, by creating a residential community and acceding in this way to the demand for a complete cultural isolation and riding with the so-called counter-culture. This regime includes work time for the paying customer, organic food, and similar cultural patterns. The second is the more pronounced drive toward occultism, mysticism, and the adoption of cult exercises from the extreme branches of religion around the world. The basic premise of Esalen has always been, at least in the eyes of the founders, an adaptation of Eastern modes of thought into Western science. Encounter groups used this implicitly within the framework of group dynamics and social science. The newer developments have been more explicit about this heritage but lean also on the work of experimental psychology, psychophysiology, and biological sciences. These developments include the new interest in all kinds of physical exercise, massage, osteopathy, and chiropractic, which have all found a home at Esalen.

Thus, interest in group experience per se has decreased at Esalen, and encounter groups are played down in favor of working with individuals. In this work there is a search for exact, scientific instrumentation, the kind of data that can be measured by electronic machines. Science here means neglect of the emotional experience once thought essential for the understanding of groups. However, these experiences still persist with their aura of mystical anti-intellectualism. Thus the attempt is made to obtain the regular data of experimental psychology with the procedures of growth centers and to measure changes within an individual after various forms of treatment. But at the same time, interpretation of these data is made almost intuitively, and the procedure is only used to validate the beliefs of the faithful.

A demonstration of the scientific value of

sensitivity training was put on at Esalen for a group of visiting behavioral and biological scientists. A popular Esalen technique was demonstrated, a kind of chiropractic developed by Ida Rolfe but evaluated only by photographs, without any measuring devices or any standardized conditions. The idea that tape measures or other simple devices could be used was rejected emphatically and almost emotionally. One reason given was lack of funds (apparently the cost of tape measures in comparison with that of Polaroid cameras); another was that measurement was impossible because change depended not on simple linear measures but on the ratio of several such measures. Even under these antiscientific conditions, however, coordinated attempts are being made to attract reputable scientists whose cautious statements can then be easily generalized into wholesale endorsements. Here again, the development has been similar to the one in teaching human relations discussed above. Some interesting research areas, such as the physiological and psychological effects of meditation, have been taken out of the setting of the growth centers and into the laboratory by people who are not necessarily part of the movement. Psychologists and physiologists not necessarily connected or identified with the movement may find some of the ideas enriching. Here also, an individual must choose at some point whether he wants to be a scientist or stay within the encounter movement. Some people are able to do both part-time, at least for a while.

. . . . .

Sensitivity training was born out of a search for a new technique, a new way of conducting human relations training in and through groups. The fundamental principle was process, what happened in the group; it was felt that a democratic, involving, meaningful experience could not lead to objectionable ends. This principle represented the then dominant philosophy of pragmatism and instrumentalism, the retreat from ultimate aims, be they religious or ideological.

This process orientation considers only the time period covered by the sensitivity training program. It implies that if sensitivity training is conducted according to valid rules, then one does not have to worry about any ultimate ends of the program itself. Attention to the means of providing change is better than invoking a utopian ideal and using any means to achieve it. This principle causes its followers to adhere to a middle-range time perspective rather than a long or short time perspective. If the time perspective is lengthened, then the resulting goals and world-encompassing belief systems can be included in the justification of the process. If it is shortened, then single acts, feelings, and pure sensation tend to be valued for themselves alone. The intermediate position, while the most conducive to rational planning, is hard to maintain. [We] have discussed the increasing emphasis on the short-range goals, on the cult of pure experience and sensualism. Nevertheless, a countertrend can also be discerned, toward the development of an all-encompassing ideology of the movement, toward placing sensitivity training into the framework of a new philosophy that will regenerate man, bring about a new kind of society, and find a new center of being which will transcend the traditional faith.

With its explosion in the 1960's, sensitivity training has attracted prophets, philosophers, and Utopians who see in sensitivity training at least some chance for the fulfillment of their future goals. It is also true that the experiences provided by sensitivity training fit well with some of the trends of the decade: the turning away from the technological society, from goal orientation, and from exploitation of nature toward emphasis on individual expression, life based on small groups, cooperation, and lack of social structure. It can be seen that these new aims represent an almost conscious departure from traditional middle-class values or the values of a technological society. That is, productivity in the material sense, long-range time perspective, trust in institutionalized structures, and privacy of the individual are precisely those features within society that are rejected by the sensitivity training movement. In contrast, the ideal group is more expressive than instrumental, has faith in the here and now, is dependent on the needs of the individual, and does not believe any safeguards are necessary either to protect the group procedure from disruption and terror by its members or to protect the individual from being crushed by the group. In this way, sensitivity training has become part of a new radical outlook, and in some respects has been used to symbolize it.

This conjunction brings up the question of the aims of sensitivity training within traditional politics. It is hard to place sensitivity training in this framework, as it has been attacked from both the left and the right.

. . . . .

Perhaps the attacks by both sides of the political spectrum on sensitivity training spring from the same cultural sources. Sensitivity training is neither a method to solve the dire social problems and disadvantages of the poor, as the orthodox left would want it to be, nor is it a method for teaching conformity to traditional values, as the right would want. It is a symptom of the new middle class, of the affluent society, and of the explosion of, and the search for, joy and new kinds of excitement. Thus its escape from the traditional problems of economic need and the dictates of necessity can be the source for the attacks by both sides.

The ideology of sensitivity training, therefore, stands outside the conventional arrangement of political ideologies. This is a carryover of its origin, which was a combination of techniques for producing change, encouraging participatory leadership, promoting sensual awareness, and expanding the ranges of human (especially nonintellectual) potentiality. It is apparent that the first two aims are at loggerheads with the last two. The first set is derived from a rational concern with the pragmatic problems of society. The second set promotes a regeneration of man and, in the extreme, a change of the whole direction of the development of human society. These two aspects we have noted as the two aims of the sensitivity training movement have frequently been irreconcilable. The fact that the movement continues to maintain both wings makes it difficult to fit its basic philosophy to traditional political categories.

How can we describe the ideology of a movement born out of a reaction against ultimate aims, the long-range aim of a movement whose slogan is "here and now"? We can begin with the concept which has been the sacred term of the movement from the beginning: "change." Change was the stated purpose of the early NTL labs, change has been the commodity sold to clients by diverse organizations, and it is what the psych-resorts sell today. The feeling of change can be an immediate experience, but it implies a future effect, however unspecified. The inclusive term for all professionals working in sensitivity training is "change agent," referring again to the process but presumably implying some purpose as well.

An ideology based on change for change's

sake can encompass the different schools of sensitivity training, but it is set off from other ideologies. Those, too, accept change; after all, nobody assumes a present state of perfection. But other ideologies, religious as well as secular, assume a direction, an ideal state first, and then chart the changes that must occur for this state to be achieved. By contrast, sensitivity training seeks change as a good in itself, in this way producing an ideology for the sensation of the moment.

This ideology of change implies a constant search for novelty for its own sake. The fascination with new techniques by encounter group centers leads to neglect of the client's problem and his immediate needs. However, the readiness of sensitivity training to be on the side of change against tradition in any context and its willingness to enlist the powerful group methods for this purpose is seen as a threat by proponents of the established order as well as by those who have some specific change in mind. In its lack of ideology, sensitivity training is not too different from the radical mood of the 1960's.

Many attacks on sensitivity training from laymen stress its similarity to brainwashing techniques, the process of leading innocent people away from old traditions to new values. Ironically, criticism from the scientific community comes from the fact that no real change has been shown, and that probably what is looked at as the destruction of values is mainly the result of the self-selection of participants. The more extreme behavior and expression of surprising new values is less the result of sensitivity training than the use of encounter centers as places to express long-felt ideas and desires by people who elect to attend. Thus, many of the strongest attacks on sensitivity training look very strange to people who have examined the evidence for the effectiveness of sensitivity training.

The philosophy of the movement has developed from an abnormal situation, a situation in which, on the one hand, economic needs were not as salient as they had been, and on the other hand, the traditional religious and cultural values no longer affected a great part of the population. Sensitivity training has become a symbol of the search for new types of positive values, for a new "center" within man, and for similar social expressions. The movement starts from the regeneration of the individual, the way most religions start. In this context, its main claim is the fact that a reconstructed individual, an individual who can express his own feelings, has a chance through sensitivity training to create his own society. According to this view, there is no distinction between social needs and needs of the individual.

This attitude expresses the view of the affluent society, especially the affluent middle class within it, which needs no materialistic help from society but feels only the restrictions that come from it. A final irony is that this ideology represents a return to problem solving. It expresses the same optimism that has carried the rise of technology so far and leads to hope that the intense group experience will solve society's remaining problems. As the rise of technology has satisfied physical needs, while restricting the social needs and helping to mechanize man, so the new social technologists are trying to change man by giving proper attention to change in the expression of man's needs, intense experiences, or other claimed effects of sensitivity training. They say that we can solve all our social problems by abolishing them altogether. This optimistic view amounts to a denial that there is a tragedy within man which arises from the fact that, at some point, social needs and human needs are contradictory, the good of the individual and of the group cannot always be identical, and then one of them has to give.

DILEMMAS OF THE FUTURE

At the end of the 1960's, organizationally as well as ideologically, sensitivity training reached the end of an era. The ideas of sensitivity training are no longer new. A movement committed to change and novelty cannot subsist even on its own innovations. The glamour has faded. Clients have seen intensive group techniques introduced and abandoned; social scientists are waiting for hard research results; even the popular media are abandoning the wide-eyed picture of the breakthrough in human relations and the equally exaggerated picture of the sinister group leader manipulating the group for his nefarious ends. Nevertheless, the groups still attract many participants who need, if only for a short time, a feeling of purpose and meaning in the universe which they have not found in their secular middle-class life.

Projecting the present trends in sensitivity training into the future, the movement is likely to be less a separate movement within or at the borderline of the scientific enterprise. Some of its features are likely to be absorbed by traditional enterprises. The more extreme aspects, on the other hand, are going to become more purely religious or recreational exercises, separated from the present areas of application. Conflicting demands might lead to a split, to separate movements for separate purposes.

Let us see how this would be accomplished in different fields. As far as scientific research is concerned, social psychologists are showing more interest in the nature of affection, love, and trust, as well as hate and aggression. Some aspects of encounter groups as well as some of their terminology may well be taken over for this purpose. In the same way, psychophysiologists are beginning to study meditation and its effects in the laboratory and are returning to experimental psychology's heritage of introspection, to describe meditation and similar exercises in their own terms. At the same time, however, sensitivity groups are coming more and more to approximate religious retreats, Sufi and Yoga centers, halfway houses, and singles' weekends at mountain and beach resorts.

Similarly, group therapists have begun to incorporate exercises first used in sensitivity training into orthodox therapy groups. Management has adopted some intensive techniques without purchasing the whole sensitivity training approach. This selective acceptance of a few new techniques has been the fate of many panaceas and may constitute their essential function. Originators of new systems prepare a whole new package, supposedly theoretically and technically integrated. After some experience, it is found that the main values lie in some of the system's new techniques which are then incorporated under other current systems. Instead of a breakthrough in effecting massive change we have acquired a few useful tools. We might remember that even differential calculus was introduced as an important aspect of a philosophy of the perfection of God.

On the other hand, we might expect some offshoots of therapeutically oriented sensitivity training procedures to exist for a long time. These techniques will become more esoteric and be surrounded by a tighter and tighter clique of true believers.

And we may be sure that they will always find some willing customers.

Finally, what of the future of the movement in the history of ideas? Prediction here is most hazardous; proponents of the movement frequently rely on analogy with previous times. A favorite analogy is the breakdown of classical civilization, the loss of values which had served the Mediterranean people for more than a millennium. They can see sensitivity training as the cutting edge of a movement which brings forth new beliefs, new values, new ways of life that would be as radically different as Christianity was from Classicism. The religious flavor of the movement points in this direction.

Perhaps. But it is always a little presumptuous to see oneself at the moment of supreme crisis at the start of a new era. Other historical analogies may be less grandiose. One which comes to mind is the "Splendid Century" in France. The aristocracy had amassed great affluence but lost its function and purpose and thereby gained a great amount of leisure. Aristocrats spent their time in sensual play and in close examination and discussion of the minutiae of interpersonal relations, which they endowed with enormous meaning. They also were looking for less harmless diversions, such as occultism and intense emotional release. In the meantime the real work of the state was carried on by the establishment of the time.

In the same vein, Peter Berger has predicted that the meaning of the "counterculture" is the surrendering of power positions by the youths of the upper classes to the lower-middle and lower classes. He also maintains that for the ones who do not want to drop out completely, there will always be jobs available as T-group leaders.

Neither of the two analogies fits exactly. We have neither the social nor economic conditions of the Roman Empire or of the French monarchy. Our wealth as well as our leisure are based on the rapid rise of technology and science, and much of our spiritual motive may spring from the need to come to grips with the implications of science. Sensitivity training represents a movement in this context. We can be sure that it will not be the last of its kind. But whether it represents a transition to a new era or merely the sensibility of the newly affluent and leisured, only the future historian can tell.

33.

WHAT MAKES FOR TRUST?

James M. Henslin

The preceding selection examines efforts systematically to develop openness and trust under controlled conditions of experimentally oriented small groups. This article by James Henslin, on the other hand, takes a look at "trust" from another perspective—that of the day-to-day situation faced by those who must engage in an "exchange relationship" with strangers. For these people—in this case cab drivers—must depend upon a variety of social, behavioral, and situational cues to determine whether even to enter into or initiate a relationship, temporary though it usually is for cab drivers and passengers. The reader is encouraged to consider, after reading this selection, the particular cues he or she uses to determine whether to trust a stranger with whom a temporary exchange might be entered into. The reader is also invited to examine this article as an interesting illustration of the research method known as "covert participant observation."

Trust is a fundamental aspect of "any-day/everyday-life-in-society." We all deal with trust all the time. It is with us each day as we go about our regular routines, but it is one of those "taken-for-granted" aspects of "life-in-society" that we seldom analyze. At times we may be sharply aware of our distrust of others and be quite verbal in specifying why. At other times we may be only vaguely aware that we are uneasy and distrustful in the presence of a certain person, being unable even to specify the factors that have led to our distrust. There are also occasions when we are very trusting and comfortable in the presence of others, but when we would be "hard put" to explain just why this was so.

We usually miss the subtlety of our own perceptions when it comes to trust. The probable reason is that most of the behavioral cues by which we are judging the "trustability" of others are finely-honed characteristics about which we have been socialized since we were children. Although these variables are continually affecting our lives, and we routinely make both important and trivial decisions on the basis of them, they are ordinarily below the threshold of our awareness.

As such, if we are asked why we didn't trust a particular person, rather than being able to specify the relevant variables, we might more likely say something like, "I just didn't like the looks of him." And it is true that we "*didn't* like the looks of him." But what are the variables that go into determining whether we like or do not like "the looks" of someone? What determines whether we will trust or distrust someone? To move in the direction of an answer to

Source: James M. Henslin, *Down to Earth Sociology: Introductory Readings* (New York: The Free Press, 1972), pp. 20–32.

James M. Henslin is a professor of sociology at Southern Illinois University. His areas of study include social psychology and deviant behavior.

this question, we shall examine what trust means for the cab driver, looking specifically at what determines whether a cab driver will accept someone as his passenger.

DEFINITION

Erving Goffman has developed useful concepts concerning the *front* of performers (the expressive equipment that serves to define the situation for the observer) that can be utilized as a conceptual framework in analyzing how a cab driver determines whether an individual can be trusted to become his passenger or not. Goffman states that there are three standard parts to front: a general aspect, (1) the *setting* (the background items which supply scenery and props for the performance, e.g., furniture, decor, and physical layout), and two personal aspects, (2) the *appearance* of the performer (the stimuli that tell the observer the social statuses of the performer, e.g., clothing), and (3) the *manner* of the performer (the stimuli that tell the observer the role that the performer will play on a particular occasion or the way in which he will play his role, e.g., being meek or haughty). Goffman adds that the audience ordinarily expects a "fit" or coherence among these standard parts of the front.

Actors are continually offering definitions of themselves to audiences. The audience, by "checking the fit" of the parts that compose the front of the actor, determines whether it will accept or reject the offered definition. *Trust consists of an actor offering a definition of himself and an audience being willing to interact with the actor on the basis of that definition.* If the audience does not accept the definition of the actor and is not willing to interact with the actor on the basis of his proffered definition, the situation is characterized by *distrust.*

Thus trust, more fully, is conceptualized for our purposes as consisting of:

a. The proffering of a definition of self by an actor;
b. Such that when the audience perceives fit between the parts of the front of the actor;
c. And accepts this definition as valid;
d. The audience is willing, without coercion, to engage in interaction with the actor;
e. The interaction being based on the accepted definition of the actor, and;
f. The continuance of this interaction being dependent on the continued acceptance of this definition, or the substitution of a different definition that is also satisfactory to the audience.

TRUST AND ACCEPTING SOMEONE AS A PASSENGER

The major definition people offer of themselves that cab drivers are concerned with is that of "passenger." In trying to hire a cab, an individual is in effect saying to the cab driver, "I am (or more accurately, I want to be) a passenger," i.e., I will fulfill the role-obligations of a passenger. In the driver's view the role obligations of "passenger" include having a destination, being willing to go to a destination for an agreed upon rate, being able and willing to pay the fare, and not robbing or harming the cab driver. If a cab driver accepts someone as a passenger—is interacting with him on the basis of this definition—it means, according to our conceptualization, that trust is present.

How does the cab driver know whether he can accept someone's definition of himself as a passenger and interact with him on the basis of that definition, i.e., how does he know whether he can trust him? This is our major concern here. We shall now try to explicate what enters into such a decision by the cab driver. Table I-1 diagrams the variables which we shall examine.

Table I-1 The Variables Which, in the Cab Driver's View, Lead to Greater or Lesser Trust of One Who Wants To Be (or Has Become) a Passenger

TRUST	*TYPE OF ORDER*		*TIME*
HI	Dispatched order	Regular rider or charge customer	Day
LO	Flag Load	Stranger	Night

TRUST	*CHARACTERISTICS OF LOCATION*				
	Match with Physical Reality	*Social Class*	*Racial Make-up*	*Driver's Knowl-edge of*	*Illumination and Habitation*
HI	Matches (a location)	(a) Upper class (b) Middle class	White	Known to driver	Light, inhabited area
LO	Doesn't match (a non-location)	Lower class (poverty area)	Black (ghetto area)	Strange to driver	Dark, deserted area

TRUST	*CHARACTERISTICS OF PASSENGER*				
	Social Class	*Sex*	*Race*	*Age*	*Sobriety*
HI	(a) Upper class (b) Middle class	Female	White	(a) Very old (b) Very young	(a) Sober (b) "High" (c) Drunk (d) Very Drunk
LO	Lower class (poverty)	Male	Black	Ages between above	(a) Sober (b) "High" (c) Drunk

TRUST	*BEHAVIOR OF PASSENGER*			
	Emergent Behavior	*Sitting Behavior Where*	*How*	*Rationality of Behavior*
HI	Seen to emerge from primary location	(a) In rear, diagonal from driver (b) in front	"Open sitting"	Acts rationally
LO	Not seen to emerge from primary location	In rear, behind driver	Sitting that seems to conceal passenger	Acts irrationally

TRUST	*DISPATCHER*	*PREVIOUS EXPERIENCE WITH A GIVEN VARIABLE*	*SUMMARY OF THE VARIABLES OF THIS TABLE*
HI	(a) Dispatches order without comment (b) Offers assurance	Positive experience: "Known that can be trusted"	Matches any stereotype the driver has of a trusted category
LO	Dispatches order with a warning	(a) Negative experience: "Known that cannot be trusted" (b) No experience: "Not known whether can be trusted"	Matches any stereotype the driver has of a distrusted category

The cab driver typically accepts as passengers those to whom he has been dispatched, especially when he is sent to a middle or upper-class residential area during daylight hours. He is progressively less likely to do so as the time becomes later in hour or as the neighborhood becomes more lower-class or more Negro. When these three conditions of time, social class, and race are combined, he is least likely to accept the passenger.

From his past experiences a driver assumes that he is safer as the *neighborhood* becomes "better." This is even more the case when the passenger emerges from the residence to which the driver has been dispatched. Hence the driver assumes that there is a connection between such a caller and his point of departure. Responsible people whom one can trust to be "good passengers" live in neighborhoods like these. If a caller lives in such an area, he *is* a good passenger; if the caller doesn't actually live there, then he must be "known" by those who do live in the location from which he is now emerging, so it is unlikely that this individual would be anything other than a good passenger. This latter case illustrates "trackability," i.e., the rider can be "traced back" to his point of origin and his association with the residence or with the people who live in that residence. Those who possess the greatest amount of trackability, and in whom the drivers place the greatest trust, are *regular riders* who routinely use cabs in their activities and who consequently become "known" to the drivers. (In many of these cases the interaction between cab drivers and regular riders moves into the personal sphere.)

However, this is not the case when a driver is dispatched to a potential passenger in a neighborhood where, in the driver's view, less responsible types of people live, people who are not as financially established, who do not own their own homes, and whose trackability is low. The drivers view poor or black neighborhoods as an indication of correspondingly less responsibility and trackability on the part of potential passengers. Accordingly, they trust persons from these origins less, and the likelihood increases that they will be rejected as passengers.

The same is true with *time of day*. A driver feels that daylight provides greater trackability, because it is possible to "get a better look at" and to observe much more about his passenger than he is able to at night. This means that he can notice any discrepancies or lack of fit among the parts of the front of the passenger, especially in terms of his appearance and manner. Thus, in a lower-class or black neighborhood the cab driver can "look over good" any potential passenger, whether the passenger either has phoned for a cab or is trying to flag down the driver. He can observe quickly and well any discrepancies about the potential passenger's manner, and in the case of a flag load, determine whether to stop or not. When it is night, the driver simply cannot see as well, so that with the lateness of the hour he is progressively less likely to stop for passengers in such areas.

Night and trust works out in practice the following way. A driver will always enter certain neighborhoods at any time of the night or day, for a dispatched order to a residence. These are the upper and middle class neighborhoods of the city. He is, however, less likely to accept a passenger who is calling from a phone booth in this area because the trackability is lower, and because the connection between the caller and the residents of that neighborhood becomes more tenuous, i.e., it could be anyone calling from a public phone booth, including, and more likely, someone who doesn't "belong there."

Drivers will enter some neighborhoods during the day for a dispatched order and also stop for a flag load, yet at night they will enter only for dispatched orders. That is, the drivers assume that one can trust people at night in this neighborhood if there is a call from an apartment for a cab, but not if a person is flagging from the street. In this type of neighborhood, veteran drivers frequently exhort novice drivers to be very careful to observe that their passenger is actually coming from the house to which they were dispatched, and not from an area nearby the house. If the house has a light on inside, then so much the better. (If there is no light on inside it becomes difficult to tell whether or not the person is actually coming from within the house.)

Finally, there are neighborhoods which drivers will enter for a dispatched order during the day, and perhaps reluctantly stop for flag loads during the day, but which they will not enter at night to pick up any passengers, dispatched or otherwise. This is true of the hard core ghetto of the city studied, St. Louis. The demand for cabs from this area is serviced primarily by a Negro cab firm.

Sex is another variable used by drivers to size up a passenger. Under almost all circumstances a driver will exhibit greater trust for a female passenger than for a male passenger. The following comment by a driver illustrates this trust of the female:

> I was driving down Union and Delmar about two o'clock this morning, and this woman hollered "Taxi." I wouldn't have stopped at that time in the morning, but I saw it was a woman, so I stopped for her. At least I thought it was a woman. And she gets into the cab, and she turns out to be a guy all dressed up like a woman.

Aside from the humor present in this case, the driver furnishes us with an excellent illustration of the differential trust cab drivers have of the female. Union and Delmar is on the fringe of the ghetto, and drivers would ordinarily stop for flag loads during the day there, but not at this time of night. This driver, however, typically stops for a woman in this area at a time when, according to his own statement, he would not think of stopping for a male who was trying to flag him down.

Another determinant of trust is that of *age*. If a passenger is quite aged, the driver will trust him. I was unaware of the influence of this variable until the following took place:

> About midnight I was dispatched to an apartment building where I picked up two men who appeared to be in their seventies or eighties. As we drove along I started to count the money that was in my pocket. Ordinarily every time I accumulated five dollars over enough to make change for a ten I would put the excess away to make certain that it would be safe in case of robbery. I thought to myself, "I should put this away," but then I thought, "No, these guys aren't going to rob me." It was at this point that I realized that I felt safe from robbery because of their ages. One does not ordinarily think of a robber as being an old man. These men were not too spry; they walked with the aid of canes; and they didn't look as though they were physically able to rob me.

The same applies at the other end of the age continuum: children would be more trusted than adults. Very young children, at least, are physically incapable of carrying out a robbery or of harming the driver, and as they become older, until they reach a certain age or size, can do so only with difficulty.

Another relevant personal characteristic is the *degree of sobriety* of the passenger. This variable does not operate by itself, however; it operates rather as a "potentiator." The passenger's degree of sobriety takes on meaning for the driver only in conjunction with other variables. Thus sobriety allows the other variables to retain their meaning, but different levels of intoxication intensify the meaning of the other variables. When a passenger reaches a level of intoxication that is described by drivers as "He is high," then he is more trusted. Such passengers are more likely to increase their tips or be amenable to the driver's suggestions. At the same time, this level of intoxication makes those who do not normally meet the criteria of a passenger even less trusted. The driver views such individuals, when they are "high," as being even more likely than when sober to "try something funny."

When intoxication is greater than "high," and the passenger could be called "drunk," drivers have less trust, regardless of whether he meets the criteria of a good passenger or not. This is because of the basic unpredictability of a drunk, or as the drivers say, "Ya don't know what a drunk is gonna do." Yet when intoxication is to the point where the passenger has little control over his actions (close to being "dead drunk" or "passed out"), trust again increases. Such persons become defined by drivers as being unable to carry out evil intentions even if they wanted to. The person inebriated to this degree, of course, easily becomes prey for the cab driver.

The secondary location, the destination to which the passenger is going, is another variable that determines trust for the cab driver. In the driver's view, the passenger's destination is frequently considered to be a part of the passenger himself. Thus, if a passenger is going to an area that the driver distrusts, his distrust of the area can be transferred to the passenger whom he otherwise trusted. That is, if this same passenger were going to a location that the driver trusted, the driver would not give a second thought about this passenger. If everything else is the same—except that the passenger wants to go to an area that the driver doesn't trust—the driver will begin to wonder about the trustworthiness of his passenger, and he will begin to question the correctness of his original decision to trust this individual as a passenger. He will wonder why his passenger is going into that area, an area which the driver himself doesn't like to enter. Usually the reason becomes apparent: sometimes the driver elicits the information, either directly or indirectly, and sometimes the passenger, aware of the driver's concerns, volunteers the information. Usual reasons for this discrepancy involve such things as the passenger's place of residence versus his place of work (e.g., a black domestic returning by cab to the ghetto), or continuing relationships with friends and relatives who have not moved out of the ghetto, or "slumming" by persons who are out for "kicks" that they can't receive in their usual "haunts."

Another way that the passenger's destination can communicate distrust to the driver is the driver's perception of the destination as a *nonlocation,* i.e., there is no "match" between the location given and a corresponding location in physical reality. For example, a street address is given, but the street does not run as far as the number indicates. In this case, too, he will seek an explanation for the discrepancy, and many times a plausible explanation exists, e.g., the person has read the number incorrectly. If a plausible explanation is not readily available, or if the individual is one for whom low trust exists, this "fiction" will lead to distrust.

If no specific destination is given, this too can lead to distrust. A passenger telling a driver to "just drive around" is suspect unless there is a satisfactory explanation for this lack of a specific destination, e.g., a tourist who wants to see various parts of the city or a woman who wants to be driven around the park because it is a beautiful day. Where the explanation is not available, the driver is likely to suspect that the passenger might be setting him up for robbery.

The secondary location also communicates trust. A passenger who gives as his destination a "good" part of town, or an area that the driver already trusts, is less likely to be under the driver's suspicion than in the above case. In some instances, the secondary location can even mitigate distrust that has developed for other reasons. For example:

> It was about one A.M. I had taken a practical nurse home after her work shift and ended up in part of the ghetto. Since I was next to a stand, I decided to park there. As I was pulling into the space, I saw a man standing at the bus stop which was next to the stand, with his arm held out horizontally and wagging his finger a bit. He was a large black male wearing a dark blue overcoat. He opened the back door of the cab, and my first thought was, "Well, here goes! I'm going to be robbed. I'd better turn on the tape recorder and get this on tape!" After he got in the cab, he said, "I want to go to Richmond Heights. You know where Richmond Heights is?"

Although there was originally a high level of distrust of this passenger, when he gave his destination I was much reassured. My perception at that time of the black community in Richmond Heights was that of a small community of blacks in the midst of middle class whites, a black community that was "solid," composed of black professional and working people. His destination was "paired" with him, and I figured if he was going to where this class of blacks live, that I did not have to worry about being robbed.

Many variables affect trust that are not as easily analyzable as the above variables. Many of these are subtle interactional cues that communicate much to the driver but which are difficult to explicate. Such a variable is the *sitting behavior* of the passenger. It is possible for the passenger to sit in such a way that he communicates "evil intention" to the driver in that his manner doesn't fit the rest of his front or his definition of himself as a trustworthy passenger. In the above case, for example:

> After I was reassured about this passenger because of his destination, I noticed by means of the mirror that he was sitting in a slumped-over position in the extreme right-hand side of the back seat. It seemed that he could be sitting this way to hide his face from me. I decided to turn around and get a good look at him. I turned around and made some innocuous comment about directions, and as I did so I noticed that he was sleeping. When he heard my question his eyes popped open, and he began to respond. It was then obvious that his manner of sitting was due to his sleepiness, and I was again reassured.

Another type of sitting behavior that lessens a driver's trust of his passenger concerns single passengers. A single passenger will almost invariably sit on the right-hand side of the back seat (the side diagonal from the driver), or, at times, in the front seat next to the driver. The driver views either of these positions as being appropriate for his passenger. Occasionally, however, a passenger will sit directly behind the driver in the back seat. This ordinarily makes the driver uncomfortable and wary of the passenger; he begins to wonder why the passenger is sitting there. Interaction between the driver and passenger is more difficult in this position, and the cab driver cannot easily "keep tabs" on what his passenger is doing.

There are additional subtle interaction cues which affect a driver's trust of his passenger. They range from the "looks" of somebody, e.g., "sneaky, slitty eyes," to body posture and beyond. Cab drivers interpret and react to others in stereotypical ways on the basis of the symbols to which they have been socialized. It is obvious that there are any number of such cues, gestures, or symbols that lead to trust or distrust. Most of these are beyond the scope of this analysis except to state the obvious: When the driver deals with symbols to which he has "feelings of distrust" attached, he will distrust the bearer of the symbol, the passenger.

An example of something to which the meaning of distrust has become attached is the sound of one's voice. This was the manifest variable leading to distrust in the following case:

> DISPATCHER: Twenty-third and Choteau . . .
> DRIVER: (( ))
> DISPATCHER: It's fine if you can't. Don't take any chances . . .
> DRIVER: (( ))
> DISPATCHER: I don't like the order myself. *I don't like the sound of the man's voice . . .*

This order was given at 1:10 a.m., and the dispatcher himself was answering incoming calls. According to his statement, there was something about the caller's voice that made him reluctant to dispatch a cab. But what was it about the caller's voice that led to this reaction? It is this type of variable, though both interesting and important in determining trust, to which our data unfortunately does not lend itself for analysis.

Because the dispatcher has a vital role in the communication process of dispatching drivers to passengers, he figures in determining whether a driver will trust a potential passenger to become an actual passenger or not. The above taped conversation concluded with:

> DISPATCHER: No. It is not a Missouri Boiler order! It is not a Missouri Boiler order! It's a terminal railroad man on Twenty-third and Choteau, on Twenty-third street north of Choteau . . .
> DRIVER: (( ))
> DISPATCHER: Let me know if you get the man or if you do not get him . . .

The driver, who wants and needs the order at this slack period of his shift, tries to tie the order in with the "known and trusted." That is, workers getting off the swing shift at Missouri Boiler sometimes take cabs, and they can be trusted. Perhaps this is such an order. But the dispatcher, showing his impatience with the driver's lack of knowledge that the address he gave is not that of Missouri Boiler, tells him that it is not that kind of order and that the caller should be carefully approached if the driver is going to take the order. The dispatcher then does an unusual thing, he makes the dispatched order optional at the discretion of the driver. Ordinarily a dispatched order becomes a "sacred thing" to the driver, not an option. It is a responsibility for which the driver assumes completion and for which he can be fired if he fails to complete. Yet here in the view of both the cab driver and of the dispatcher, the driver need not accept the responsibility for completing an order when the passenger cannot be trusted.

The dispatcher, when he is able, offers assurance to drivers who do not have enough cues to know whether they can trust a passenger or not. The following example illustrates this:

> DISPATCHER: You have to go in the rear of the court to get in there, Driver. We had that last night, so it's all right . . .

The dispatcher is assuring the driver that the people waiting are acceptable as passengers, i.e., that although the driver must drive where he is reluctant to go, in the back where it is perhaps dark, it is all right to do so: this is not a setup for a robbery. How can the dispatcher give such an assurance? As he states, there had been an order from that location the night before and it turned out to be an acceptable passenger. In this case, the setting, "in the rear of the court at night," did not fit the driver's estimation of acceptability for trusting someone to become a passenger, but, because the dispatcher has had a previous rewarding experience with this lack of fit, he knows that it is all right, and he is able to assure the driver.

The passenger of mine who best incorporated most of the above variables of distrust within a single case and who illustrates other variables which have not been explicated was the following:

> About 2:00 A.M. I was dispatched to just within the ghetto, to a hotel which also serves as a house of prostitution. My passenger turned out to be a drunk, elderly, black male, who chose to sit next to me in the front seat. He ordered me to take him to East St. Louis and said, "We're going to a rough neighborhood. Lock your doors. Roll up your windows."
>
> The passenger then began talking to himself. As he did so, I thought he was talking to me, and I said, "What did you say?" He looked up and said, "None of your business!" He then continued talking to himself. As we passed the Atlas Hotel in the 4200 block of Delmar, he made the comment that he should have stopped there and seen someone, but that since we had already passed it I should go on. I said, "No, that's all right. I'll take you there," and I drove around the block to the hotel. He got out and was about to leave when I said, "I'll wait for you, but you'll have to pay what's on the meter." He became rather angry, gave me some money, and then urinated against the side of the cab. I drove on without him.

This man was distrusted because he was a stranger, a male, a black, at night, had been drinking, was coming from the edge of the ghetto, going to a ghetto area, which area was "unknown" to the driver, and acted irrationally by speaking aloud to himself.

The driver has less trust for someone who acts irrationally, just as most members of society would have less trust for someone who exhibited this type of behavior. Because the individual is irrational, predictability of his behavior decreases, while to trust someone means that one can predict his behavior on the basis of acceptance of his identity. This is what cannot be done with someone who does not act as we have learned that "ordinary" persons act.

The driver has less trust for an area that he does not know, i.e., an area whose "layout" he is unfamiliar with, because he cannot easily maneuver his cab or plan and carry out routes in such areas. Control in such situations passes from the driver to the passenger who possesses such knowledge. To enter an interaction with someone who possesses the greater control requires trust that the other individual will not use this control to his advantage and to one's own disadvantage, in this case such things as robbery or not paying the fare.

CONCLUSION

Cabbies will usually accept an actor's definition of himself as belonging to the category "passenger," and they almost without exception will do so when they are dispatched to an order. However, under some circumstances, especially "flag loads," the cab driver will refuse to allow a potential passenger to become his passenger and will not let him ride in his cab. In examining how the cab driver differentiates between those he allows to become his passengers and those he does not, we have attempted to delineate the variables that go into this foundational aspect of our "life-in-society," trust.

Although the specific interaction situation in which trust has been analyzed is that of the cab driver as he goes about his daily routines, the import of this analysis extends beyond the cab driver–passenger interaction situation to all of "life-in-society." The specific variables that lead to trust and distrust change with each situation, but the fundamental principles of evaluating others are the same. Your world is also composed of situations in which people are continually offering you a definition of themselves, and you must, and do, evaluate that definition on the basis of your perception of the fit or misfit among the parts presented which you have learned to associate with that particular front. Your evaluation, as it does with the cabbie, although perhaps based on differing expectations of parts to be associated with particular fronts, leads to a reaction of trust or distrust. Hopefully, through an analysis of the way trust operates in the cabbie's life, you have gained both a clearer perception of the principles underlying trust in your own social world and a more complete understanding of your reactions to others within that world.

Part V

Social Organization: Collective Behavior

34.

THE MEN FROM MARS

John Houseman

Collective behavior depends upon some form of communication functioning within the framework of a shared culture. Under these conditions any enlargement in the available means of communication, such as radio, television, and the communication satellites, increases the potential size of the audience whose attention may be attracted and whose behavior may be influenced for either desirable or undesirable ends through control of the content transmitted. In the selection which follows, John Houseman gives a graphic account of a startling and rather disquieting episode precipitated by a radio program designed only for entertainment. Realism was necessary to ensure the full dramatic effect in its presentation. So skillful was the technique used, however, that thousands believed an actual invasion from Mars was taking place. The panic, the irrational behavior of many people who chanced to tune in, is an interesting example of the propaganda power of radio and television. Houseman rejects the idea that the incident can be dismissed as an example of the "incredible stupidity and gullibility of the American public." Instead, he indicates many other important factors that must be considered in any explanation of the effects stimulated by the broadcast. And those who would argue that this incident, which occurred more than thirty-five years ago, could never happen today, should know that a recent rerun of the same program created much the same reaction, but on a smaller scale, since it was carried on only a single station.

RADIO WAR TERRORIZES U.S.—*N.Y. Daily News, October 31, 1938*

Everybody was excited I felt as if I was going crazy and kept on saying what can we do what difference does it make whether we die sooner or later? We were holding each other. Everything seemed unimportant in the face of death. I was afraid to die, just kept on listening.—*A listener*

Nothing about the broadcast was in the least credible.—*Dorothy Thompson*

The show came off. There is no doubt about that. It set out to dramatize, in terms of popular apprehension, an attempted invasion of our world by hostile forces from the planet Mars. It succeeded. Of the several million American citizens who, on the evening of October 30, 1938, milled about the streets, clung sobbing to one another or drove wildly in all directions to avoid asphyxiation and flaming death, approximately one-half were in terror of Mar-

Source: John Houseman, *Harper's Magazine* 197 (December 1948): 74–82. Copyright 1948 by John Houseman. Reprinted by permission of the author.

Producer, director, John Houseman is director of the drama division of the Juilliard School as well as director in the Phoenix Theater in New York. His recent productions include *Antigone* and *The Losers.* He occupied the Cockefair chair at the University of Missouri in Kansas City in 1971–72.

tians—not of Germans, Japanese, or unknown enemies—but, specifically, of Martians. Later, when the excitement was over and the shadow of the gallows had lifted, some of us were inclined to take credit for more deliberate and premeditated villainy than we deserved. The truth is that at the time, nobody was more surprised than we were. In fact, one of the most remarkable things about the broadcast was the quite haphazard nature of its birth.

In October 1938, the Mercury Theater, of which Orson Welles and I were the founding partners, had been in existence for less than a year. Our first Broadway season had been shatteringly successful—"Julius Caesar," "The Cradle Will Rock," "Shoemaker's Holiday," and "Heartbreak House" in the order of their appearance. In April, Orson, in a straggly white beard, made the cover of *Time* Magazine. In June, the Columbia Broadcasting System offered him a radio show—"The Mercury Theater on the Air," a series of classic dramatizations in the first person singular with Orson as master of ceremonies, star, narrator, writer, director, and producer. He accepted. So, now, in addition to an empty theater, a movie in progress, two plays in rehearsal, and all seven of the chronicle plays of William Shakespeare in preparation, we had a radio show.

We opened on July 11. Among our first thirteen shows were "Treasure Island," "39 Steps," "Abraham Lincoln," "Three Short Stories" (by Saki, Sherwood Anderson, and Carl Ewald), "Jane Eyre," "Julius Caesar" (with running commentary by Kaltenborn out of Plutarch), and "The Man Who Was Thursday." Our second series, in the fall, began with Booth Tarkington's "Seventeen," "Around the World in Eighty Days," and "Oliver Twist." Our fifth show was to be "Life with Father." Our fourth was "The War of the Worlds."

No one, as I remember, was very enthusiastic about it. But it seemed good programming, between the terrors of Dickens' London slums, and the charm of Clarence Day's New York in the nineties, to throw in something of a contrasting and pseudoscientific nature. We thought of Shiel's *Purple Cloud,* Conan Doyle's *Lost World,* and several others before we settled on H. G. Wells' twenty-year-old novel, which neither of us, as it turned out later, remembered at all clearly. It is just possible that neither of us had ever read it.

II

Those were our golden days of unsponsored radio. We had no advertising agency to harass us, no client to cut our withers. Partly because we were perpetually overworked and partly because that was the way we did things at the Mercury, we never seemed to get more than a single jump ahead of ourselves. Shows were created week after week under conditions of soul- and health-destroying pressure. On the whole they were good shows. And we *did* develop a system—of sorts.

It worked as follows: I was editor of the series. With Welles, I chose the shows and then laid them out. The writing, most of it, was done by Howard Koch—earnest, spindly, six-foot-two—a Westchester lawyer turned playwright. To write the first draft of an hour's radio script took him about five days, working about fifteen hours a day. Our associate producer was Paul Stewart, a Broadway actor turned director. His function was to put the broadcast through its first paces and preliminary rehearsals. Every Thursday, musicless and with rudimentary sound effects, a wax record of the show was cut. From this record, played back later that night, Orson would give us his reactions and revisions.

In the next thirty-six hours the script would be reshaped and rewritten, sometimes drastically. Saturday afternoon there was another rehearsal, with sound—with or without Welles. It was not until the last day that Orson really took over.

Sundays, at eight, we went on the air. Beginning in the early afternoon—when Bernard Herrmann arrived with his orchestra of twenty-seven high-grade symphony players—two simultaneous dramas were regularly unfolded in the stale, tense air of Studio Number One: the minor drama of the current show and the major drama of Orson's gargantuan struggle to get it on. Sweating, howling, disheveled, and single-handed he wrestled with Chaos and Time—always conveying an effect of being alone, traduced by his collaborators, surrounded by treachery, ignorance, sloth, indifference, incompetence and—more often than not—down-right sabotage! Every Sunday it was touch and go. As the hands of the clock moved relentlessly toward air time the crisis grew more extreme, the peril more desperate. Often violence broke out. Scripts flew through the air, doors were slammed, batons smashed. Scheduled for six—but usually nearer seven—there was a dress rehearsal, a thing of wild improvisations and irrevocable disaster. (One show was found to be twenty-one minutes overlength, another fourteen and one-half minutes short.)

After that, with only a few minutes to go, there was a final frenzy of correction and reparation, of utter confusion and absolute horror, aggravated by the gobbling of sandwiches and the bolting of oversized milkshakes. By now it was less than a minute to air time. . . .

At that instant, quite regularly week after week—with not one second to spare . . . the titanic buffoonery stopped. Suddenly out of chaos, the show emerged—delicately poised, meticulously executed, precise as clockwork, and smooth as satin. And above us all, like a rainbow over storm clouds, stood Orson on his podium, sonorous and heroic, a leader of men surrounded by his band of loyal followers; a giant in action, serene and radiant with the joy of a hard battle bravely fought—a great victory snatched from the jaws of disaster.

In later years, when the Men from Mars had passed into history, there was some bickering among members of the Mercury as to who, exactly, had contributed precisely what, to that particular evening's entertainment. The truth is that a number of us made a number of essential and incalculable contributions to the broadcast. (Who can accurately assess, for instance, the part played by Johnny Dietz's perfect engineering, in keeping unbroken the shifting illusion of imperfect reality? How much did the original old H. G. Wells, who noisily repudiated us, have to do with it? Or the second assistant sound man? Or individual actors? Or Dr. Goebbels? Or Charlie McCarthy?) Orson Welles had virtually nothing to do with the writing of the script and less than usual to do with its preliminary rehearsals. Yet first and last it was his creation. If there had been a lynching that night, it is Welles the outraged populace would have strung up—and rightly so. Orson was the Mercury. "The War of the Worlds," like everything we did, was his show.

Actually, it was a narrow squeak. Those Men from Mars barely escaped being stillborn. Tuesday afternoon—five days before the show—Howard Koch telephoned. He was in deep distress. After three days of slaving on H. G. Wells' scientific fantasy he was ready to give up. Under no circumstances, he declared, could it be made interesting or in any way credible to modern American ears. Koch was not given to habitual alarmism. To confirm his fears, Annie, our secretary, came to the phone.

She was an acid and emphatic girl from Smith College with fine blond hair, who smelled of fading spring flowers. "You can't do it!" she whined. "Those old Martians are just a lot of nonsense. It's all too silly! We're going to make fools of ourselves! Absolute fools!"

For some reason which I do not clearly remember our only possible alternative for that week was a dreary one—"Lorna Doone." I tried to reach Welles. He was at the theater and wouldn't come to the phone.

The reason he wouldn't come to the phone was that he was in his thirty-sixth successive hour of dress-rehearsing "Danton's Death," a beautiful, fragmentary play by Georg Buechner out of which Max Reinhardt, in an augmented form, had made a successful mass-spectacle in the twenties. Not to be outdone, Orson had glued seventeen hundred masks on to the back wall of the Mercury Theater, and ripped out the entire stage. Day after day actors fell headlong into the ratridden basement, leaped on and off erratically moving elevators, and chanted the "Carmagnole" in chorus under the supervision of Marc Blitzstein.

Unable to reach Welles, I called Koch back. I was severe. I taxed him with defeatism. I gave him false comfort. I promised to come up and help. When I finally got there—around two the next morning—things were better. He was beginning to have fun laying waste the State of New Jersey. Annie had stopped grinding her teeth. We worked all night and through the next day. Wednesday at sunset the script was finished.

Thursday, as usual, Paul Stewart rehearsed the show, then made a record. We listened to it rather gloomily, long after midnight in Orson's room at the St. Regis, sitting on the floor because all the chairs were covered with coils of unrolled and unedited film. We agreed it was a dull show. We all felt its only chance of coming off lay in emphasizing its newscast style—its simultaneous, eyewitness quality.

All night we sat up, spicing the script with circumstantial allusions and authentic detail. Friday afternoon it went over to CBS to be passed by the network censor. Certain name alterations were requested. Under protest and with a deep sense of grievance we changed the Hotel Biltmore to a non-existent Park Plaza, Trans-America to Intercontinent, the Columbia Broadcasting Building to Broadcasting Building. Then the script went over to mimeograph and we went to bed. We had done our best and, after all, a show is just a show. . . .

Saturday afternoon Paul Stewart rehearsed with sound effects but without Welles. He worked for a long time on the crowd scenes, the roar of cannon echoing in the Watchung Hills and the sound of New York Harbor as the ships with the last remaining survivors put out to sea.

Around six we left the studio. Orson, phoning from the theater a few minutes later to find out how things were going, was told by one of the CBS sound men, who had stayed behind to pack up his equipment, that it was not one of our better shows. Confidentially, the man opined, it just didn't come off. Twenty-seven hours later, quite a few of his employers would have found themselves a good deal happier if he had turned out to be right.

III

On Sunday, October 30, at 8:00 P.M., E.S.T., in a studio littered with coffee cartons and sandwich paper, Orson swallowed a second container of pineapple juice, put on his earphones, raised his long white fingers and threw the cue for the Mercury theme—the Tchaikovsky Piano Concerto in B Flat

Minor #1. After the music dipped, there were routine introductions—then the announcement that a dramatization of H. G. Wells' famous novel, *The War of the Worlds,* was about to be performed. Around 8:01 Orson began to speak, as follows:

WELLES

We know now that in the early years of the twentieth century this world was being watched closely by intelligences greater than man's and yet as mortal as his own. We know now that as human beings busied themselves about their various concerns they were scrutinized and studied, perhaps almost as narrowly as a man with a microscope might scrutinize the transient creatures that swarm and multiply in a drop of water. With infinite complacence people went to and fro over the earth about their little affairs, serene in the assurance of their dominion over this small spinning fragment of solar driftwood which by chance or design man has inherited out of the dark mystery of Time and Space. Yet across an immense ethereal gulf minds that are to our minds as ours are to the beasts in the jungle, intellects vast, cool, and unsympathetic regarded this earth with envious eyes and slowly and surely drew their plans against us. In the thirty-ninth year of the twentieth century came the great disillusionment.

It was near the end of October. Business was better. The war scare was over. More men were back at work. Sales were picking up. On this particular evening, October 30, the Crossley service estimated that thirty-two million people were listening in on their radios. . . .

Neatly, without perceptible transition, he was followed on the air by an anonymous announcer caught in a routine bulletin:

ANNOUNCER

. . . for the next twenty-four hours not much change in temperature. A slight atmospheric disturbance of undetermined origin is reported over Nova Scotia, causing a low pressure area to move down rather rapidly over the northeastern states, bringing a forecast of rain, accompanied by winds of light gale force. Maximum temperature 66; minimum 48. This weather report comes to you from the Government Weather Bureau. . . . We now take you to Meridian Room in the Hotel Park Plaza in downtown New York, where you will be entertained by the music of Ramon Raquello and his orchestra.

At which cue, Bernard Herrmann led the massed men of the CBS house orchestra in a thunderous rendition of "La Cumparsita." The entire hoax might well have exploded there and then—but for the fact that hardly anyone was listening. They were being entertained by Charlie McCarthy—then at the height of his success.

The Crossley census, taken about a week before the broadcast, had given us 3.6 percent of the listening audience to Edgar Bergen's 34.7 percent. What the Crossley Institute (that hireling of the advertising agencies) deliberately ignored was the healthy American habit of dial-twisting. On that particular evening, Edgar Bergen in the person of Charlie McCarthy temporarily left the air about 8:12 P.M., E.S.T., yielding place to a new and not very popular singer. At that point, and during the following minutes, a large number of listeners started twisting their dials in search of other entertainment. Many of them turned to us—and when they did, they stayed put! For by this time the mysterious meteorite had fallen at Grovers Mill in New Jersey, the Martians had begun to show their foul leathery heads above the ground, and the New Jersey State Police were racing to the spot. Within a few minutes people all over the United States were praying, crying, fleeing frantically to escape death from the Martians. Some remembered to rescue loved ones, others telephoned farewells or warnings, hurried to inform neighbors, sought information from newspapers or radio stations, summoned ambulances and police cars.

The reaction was strongest at points nearest the tragedy—in Newark, New Jersey, in a single block, more than twenty families rushed out of their houses with wet handkerchiefs and towels over their faces. Some began moving household furniture. Police switchboards were flooded with calls inquiring, "Shall I close my windows?" "Have the police any extra gas masks?" Police found one family waiting in the yard with wet cloths on faces contorted with hysteria. As one woman reported later:

> I was terribly frightened. I wanted to pack and take my child in my arms, gather up my friend and get in the car and just go north as far as we could. But what I did was just sit by one window, praying, listening, and scared stiff, and my husband by the other sniffling and looking to see if people were running. . . .

In New York hundreds of people on Riverside Drive left their homes ready for flight. Bus terminals were crowded. A woman calling up the Dixie Bus Terminal for information said impatiently, "Hurry please, the world is coming to an end and I have a lot to do."

In the parlor churches of Harlem evening service became "end of the world" prayer meetings. Many turned to God in that moment:

> I held a crucifix in my hand and prayed while looking out of my open window for falling meteors. . . . When the monsters were wading across the Hudson River and coming into New York, I wanted to run up on my roof to see what they looked like, but I couldn't leave my radio while it was telling me of their whereabouts.
>
> Aunt Grace began to pray with Uncle Henry. Lily got sick to her stomach. I don't know what I did exactly but I know I prayed harder and more earnestly than ever before. Just as soon as we were convinced that this thing was real, how petty all things on this earth seemed; how soon we put our trust in God!

The panic moved upstate. One man called up the Mt. Vernon Police Headquarters to find out "where the forty policemen were killed." Another took time out to philosophize:

> I thought the whole human race was going to be wiped out—that seemed more important than the fact that we were going to die. It seemed awful that everything that had been worked on for years was going to be lost forever.

In Rhode Island weeping and hysterical women swamped the switchboard of the Providence *Journal* for details of the massacre, and officials of the electric light company received a score of calls urging them to turn off all lights so that the city would be safe from the enemy. The Boston *Globe* received a call from one woman "who could see the fire." A man in Pittsburgh hurried home in the midst of the broadcast and found his wife in the bathroom, a bottle of poison in her hand, screaming, "I'd rather die this way than that." In Minneapolis a woman ran into church screaming, "New York destroyed this is the end of the world. You might as well go home to die I just heard it on the radio."

The Kansas City Bureau of the AP received inquiries about the "meteors" from Los Angeles; Salt Lake City; Beaumont, Texas; and St. Joseph, Missouri. In San Francisco the general impression of listeners seemed to be that an overwhelming force had invaded the United States from the air—was in process of destroying New York and threatening to more westward. "My God," roared an inquirer into a telephone, "where can I volunteer my services, we've got to stop this awful thing!"

As far south as Birmingham, Alabama, people gathered in churches and prayed. On the campus of a Southeastern college——

> The girls in the sorority houses and dormitories huddled around their radios trembling and weeping in each other's arms. They separated themselves from their friends only to take their

turn at the telephones to make long distance calls to their parents, saying goodbye for what they thought might be the last time. . . .

There are hundreds of such bits of testimony, gathered from coast to coast.

IV

At least one book [1] and quite a pile of sociological literature has appeared on the subject of "The Invasion from Mars." Many theories have been put forward to explain the "tidal wave" of panic that swept the nation. I know of two factors that largely contributed to the broadcast's extraordinarily violent effect. First, its historical timing. It came within thirty-five days of the Munich crisis. For weeks, the American people had been hanging on their radios, getting most of their news no longer from the press, but over the air. A new technique of "on-the-spot" reporting had been developed and eagerly accepted by an anxious and news-hungry world. The Mercury Theater on the Air by faithfully copying every detail of the new technique—including its imperfections—found an already enervated audience ready to accept its wildest fantasies. The second factor was the show's sheer technical brilliance. To this day it is impossible to sit in a room and hear the scratched, worn, off-the-air recording of the broadcast, without feeling in the back of your neck some slight draft left over from that great wind of terror that swept the nation. Even with the element of credibility totally removed it remains a surprisingly frightening show.

Radio drama was taken seriously in the thirties—before the Quiz and the Giveaway became the lords of the air. In the work of such directors as Reis, Corwin, Fickett, Welles, Robson, Spier, and Oboler there was an eager, excited drive to get the most out of this new, all too rapidly freezing medium. But what happened that Sunday, up on the twentieth floor of the CBS building was something quite special. Beginning around two, when the show started to take shape under Orson's hands, a strange fever seemed to invade the studio—part childish mischief, part professional zeal.

First to feel it were the actors. I remember Frank Readick (who played the part of Carl Phillips, the network's special reporter) going down to the record library and digging up the Morrison recording of the explosion of the Hindenburg at Lakehurst. This is a classic reportage—one of those wonderful, unpredictable accidents of eyewitness description. The broadcaster is casually describing a routine landing of the giant gasbag. Suddenly he sees something. A flash of flame! An instant later the whole thing explodes. It takes him time—a full second—to react at all. Then seconds more of sputtering ejaculations before he can make the adjustment between brain and tongue. He starts to describe the terrible things he sees—the writhing human figures twisting and squirming as they fall from the white burning wreckage. He stops, fumbles, vomits, then quickly continues. Readick played the record to himself, over and over. Then, recreating the emotion in his own terms, he described the Martian meteorite as he saw it lying inert and harmless in a field at Grovers Mill, lit up by the headlights of a hundred cars—the coppery cylinder suddenly opening, revealing the leathery tentacles and the terrible pale-eyed faces of the Martians within. As they begin to emerge he freezes, unable to translate his vision into words; he fumbles, retches—and then after a second continues.

[1] *The Invasion from Mars* by Hadley Cantril, Princeton University Press, from which many of the above quotations were taken.

A few moments later Carl Phillips lay dead, tumbling over the microphone in his fall—one of the first victims of the Martian Ray. There followed a moment of absolute silence—an eternity of waiting. Then, without warning, the network's emergency fill-in was heard—somewhere in a quiet studio, a piano, close on mike, playing "Clair de Lune," soft and sweet as honey, for many seconds, while the fate of the universe hung in the balance. Finally it was interrupted by the manly reassuring voice of Brigadier General Montgomery Smith, Commander of the New Jersey State Militia, speaking from Trenton, and placing "the counties of Mercer and Middlesex as far west as Princeton and east to Jamesburg" under Martial Law! Tension—release—then renewed tension. For soon after that came an eyewitness account of the fatal battle of the Watchung Hills; and then, once again, that lone piano was heard—now a symbol of terror, shattering the dead air with its ominous tinkle. As it played, on and on, its effect became increasingly sinister—a thin band of suspense stretched almost beyond endurance.

That piano was the neatest trick of the show—a fine specimen of the theatrical "retard," boldly conceived and exploited to the full. It was one of the many devices with which Welles succeeded in compelling, not merely the attention, but also the belief of his invisible audience. "The War of the Worlds" was a magic act, one of the world's greatest, and Orson was just the man to bring it off.

For Welles is at heart a magician whose particular talent lies not so much in his creative imagination (which is considerable) as in his proven ability to stretch the familiar elements of theatrical effect far beyond their normal point of tension. For this reason his productions require more elaborate preparation and more perfect execution than most. At that—like all complicated magic tricks—they remain, till the last moment, in a state of precarious balance. When they come off, they give—by virtue of their unusually high intensity—an impression of great brilliance and power; when they fail—when something in their balance goes wrong or the original structure proves to have been unsound—they provoke, among their audience, a particularly violent reaction of unease and revulsion. Welles' flops are louder than other men's. The Mars broadcast was one of his unqualified successes.

Among the columnists and public figures who discussed the affair during the next few days (some praising us for the public service we had rendered, some condemning us as sinister scoundrels) the most general reaction was one of amazement at the "incredible stupidity" and "gullibility" of the American public, who had accepted as real, in this single broadcast, incidents which in actual fact would have taken days or even weeks to occur. "Nothing about the broadcast," wrote Dorothy Thompson with her usual aplomb, "was in the least credible." She was wrong. The first few minutes of our broadcast were, in point of fact, strictly realistic in time and perfectly credible, though somewhat boring, in content. Herein lay the great tensile strength of the show; it was the structural device that made the whole illusion possible. And it could have been carried off in no other medium than radio.

Our actual broadcasting time, from the first mention of the meteorites to the fall of New York City, was less than forty minutes. During that time men traveled long distances, large bodies of troops were mobilized, cabinet meetings were held, savage battles fought on land and in the air. And millions of people accepted it—emotionally if not logically.

There is nothing so very strange about that. Most of us do the same thing, to some degree, most days of our lives—every time we look at a movie or listen to a broadcast. Not even the realistic theater observes the literal unities; motion pictures and, particularly, radio (where neither place nor time exists save in the imagination of the listener) have no difficulty in getting their audiences to accept the telescoped reality of dramatic time. Our special hazard lay in the fact that we purported to be, not a play, but reality. In order to take advantage of the accepted convention, we had to slide swiftly and imperceptibly out of the "real" time of a news report into the dramatic time of a fictional broadcast. Once that was achieved—without losing the audience's attention or arousing their skepticism, if they could be sufficiently absorbed and bewitched not to notice the transition—then, we felt, there was no extreme of fantasy through which they would not follow us. We were keenly aware of our problem; we found what we believed was the key to its solution. And if, that night, the American public proved "gullible," it was because enormous pains and a great deal of thought had been spent to make it so.

In the script, "The War of the Worlds" started extremely slowly—dull meteorological and astronomical bulletins alternating with musical interludes. These were followed by a colorless scientific interview and still another stretch of dance music. These first few minutes of routine broadcasting "within the existing standards of judgment of the listener" were intended to lull (or maybe bore) the audience into a false security and to furnish a solid base of realistic time from which to accelerate later. Orson, in making over the show, extended this slow movement far beyond our original conception. "La Cumparsita," rendered by "Ramon Raquello, from the Meridian Room of the Hotel Park Plaza in downtown New York," had been thought of as running only a few seconds; "Bobby Millette playing 'Stardust' from the Hotel Martinet in Brooklyn," even less. At rehearsal Orson stretched both these numbers to what seemed to us, in the control room, an almost unbearable length. We objected. The interview in the Princeton Observatory—the clockwork ticking monotonously overhead, the woolly-minded professor mumbling vague replies to the reporters' uninformed questions—this, too, he dragged out to a point of tedium. Over our protests, lines were restored that had been cut at earlier rehearsals. We cried there would not be a listener left. Welles stretched them out even longer.

He was right. His sense of tempo, that night, was infallible. When the flashed news of the cylinder's landing finally came—almost fifteen minutes after the beginning of a fairly dull show—he was able suddenly to spiral his action to a speed as wild and reckless as its base was solid. The appearance of the Martians; their first treacherous act; the death of Carl Phillips; the arrival of the militia; the battle of the Watchung Hills; the destruction of New Jersey—all these were telescoped into a space of twelve minutes without overstretching the listeners' emotional credulity. The broadcast, by then, had its own reality, the reality of emotionally felt time and space.

V

At the height of the crisis, around 8:31, the Secretary of the Interior came on the air with an exhortation to the American people. His words, as you read them now, ten years later, have a Voltairean ring.

(They were admirably spoken—in a voice just faintly reminiscent of the President's—by a young man named Kenneth Delmar, who has since grown rich and famous as Senator Claghorn.)

THE SECRETARY

Citizens of the nation: I shall not try to conceal the gravity of the situation that confronts the country, nor the concern of your Government in protecting the lives and property of its people. However, I wish to impress upon you—private citizens and public officials, all of you—the urgent need of calm and resourceful action. Fortunately, this formidable enemy is still confined to a comparatively small area, and we may place our faith in the military forces to keep them there. In the meantime placing our trust in God, we must continue the performance of our duties, each and every one of us, so that we may confront this destructive adversary with a nation united, courageous, and consecrated to the preservation of human supremacy on this earth. I thank you.

Toward the end of this speech (*circa* 8:22 E.S.T.), Davidson Taylor, supervisor of the broadcast for the Columbia Broadcasting System, received a phone call in the control room, creased his lips, and hurriedly left the studio. By the time he returned, a few moments later—pale as death—clouds of heavy smoke were rising from Newark, New Jersey, and the Martians, tall as skyscrapers, were astride the Pulaski Highway preparatory to wading the Hudson River. To us in the studio the show seemed to be progressing splendidly—how splendidly Davidson Taylor had just learned outside. For several minutes now, a kind of madness had seemed to be sweeping the continent—somehow connected with our show. The CBS switchboards had been swamped into uselessness, but from outside sources vague rumors were coming in of deaths and suicides and panic injuries.

Taylor had requests to interrupt the show immediately with an explanatory station-announcement. By now the Martians were across the Hudson and gas was blanketing the city. The end was near. We were less than a minute from the Station Break. The organ was allowed to swirl out under the slackening fingers of its failing organist and Ray Collins, superb as the "last announcer," choked heroically to death on the roof of Broadcasting Building. The boats were all whistling for a while as the last of the refugees perished in New York Harbor. Finally, as they died away, an amateur shortwave operator was heard from heaven knows where, weakly reaching out for human companionship across the empty world:

2X2L Calling CQ
2X2L Calling CQ
2X2L Calling CQ
Isn't there anyone on the air?
Isn't there anyone?

Five seconds of absolute silence. Then, shattering the reality of World's End—the Announcer's voice was heard, suave and bright:

ANNOUNCER

You are listening to the CBS presentation of Orson Welles and the Mercury Theater on the Air in an original dramatization of *The War of the Worlds,* by H. G. Wells. The performance will continue after a brief intermission.

The second part of the show was extremely well written and most sensitively played—but nobody heard it. It recounted the adventures of a lone survivor, with interesting observations on the nature of human society; it described the eventual death of the Martian invaders, slain—"after all man's defenses had failed by the humblest thing that God in his wisdom had put upon this earth"—by bacteriological action; it told of the rebuilding of a brave new world. After a stirring musical finale, Welles, in his own person, delivered a charming informal little speech about Halloween, which it happened to be.

I remember, during the playing of the final theme, the phone starting to ring in the control room and a shrill voice through the receiver announcing itself as belonging to the mayor of some Midwestern city, one of the big ones. He is screaming for Welles. Choking with fury, he reports mobs in the streets of his city, women and children huddled in the churches, violence and looting. If, as he now learns, the whole thing is nothing but a crummy joke—then he, personally, is coming up to New York to punch the author of it on the nose! Orson hangs up quickly. For we are off the air now and the studio door bursts open. The following hours are a nightmare. The building is suddenly full of people and dark blue uniforms. We are hurried out of the studio, downstairs, into a back office. Here we sit incommunicado while network employees are busily collecting, destroying, or locking up all scripts and records of the broadcast. Then the press is let loose upon us, ravening for horror. How many deaths have we heard of? (Implying they know of thousands.) What do we know of the fatal stampede in a Jersey hall? (Implying it is one of many.) What traffic deaths? (The ditches must be choked with corpses.) The suicides? (Haven't you heard about the one on Riverside Drive?) It is all quite vague in my memory and quite terrible.

Hours later, instead of arresting us, they let us out a back way. We scurry down to the theater like hunted animals to their hole. It is surprising to see life going on as usual in the midnight streets, cars stopping for traffic, people walking. At the Mercury the company is still stoically rehearsing—falling downstairs and singing the "Carmagnole." Welles goes up on stage, where photographers, lying in wait, catch him with his eyes raised up to heaven, his arms outstretched in an attitude of crucifixion. Thus he appeared in a tabloid that morning over the caption, "I Didn't Know What I Was Doing!" The *New York Times* quoted him as saying, "I don't think we will choose anything like this again."

We were on the front page for two days. Having had to bow to radio as a news source during the Munich crisis, the press was now only too eager to expose the perilous irresponsibilities of the new medium. Orson was their whipping boy. They quizzed and badgered him. Condemnatory editorials were delivered by our press-clipping bureau in bushel baskets. There was talk, for a while, of criminal action.

Then gradually, after about two weeks, the excitement subsided. By then it had been discovered that the casualties were not as numerous or as serious as had at first been supposed. One young woman had fallen and broken her arm running downstairs. Later the Federal Communications Commission held some hearings and passed some regulations. The Columbia Broadcasting System made a public apology. With that the official aspects of the incident were closed.

As to the Mercury—our new play, "Danton's Death," finally opened after five postponements. Not even our fantastic publicity was able to offset its generally unfavorable notices. On the other hand, that same week the Mercury Theater on the Air was signed up by Campbell Soups at a most lavish figure.

Of the suits that were brought against us—amounting to over three quarters of a million dollars for damages, injuries, miscarriages, and distresses of various kinds—none was substantiated or legally proved. We did settle one claim however, against the advice of our lawyers. It was the particularly affecting case of a man in Massachusetts, who wrote:

"I thought the best thing to do was to go away. So I took three dollars twenty-five cents out of my savings and bought a ticket. After I had gone sixty miles I knew it was a play. Now I don't have money left for the shoes that I was saving up for. Will you please have someone send me a pair of black shoes size 9B!"

We did.

35.

MASS MOVEMENTS AND INSTITUTIONS: METHODISM

William E. H. Lecky

"The term 'social movement' . . . ," says Rudolf Heberle in the *Encyclopedia of the Social Sciences*, "is being used to denote a wide variety of collective attempts to bring about a change in certain social institutions or to create an entirely new order." Within the broad spectrum of collective behavior types covered by his definition the first and narrower kind is illustrated by the following selection, based on an historian's account of an eighteenth-century English religious mass movement; the second, all-inclusive type is represented by three brief selections on Mao's China (88, 89, 90). Lecky's statement also serves to illustrate Max Weber's concepts of charismatic leadership, in the person of the dynamic Methodist preacher, George Whitefield, and of the movement's "rationalization" through the organizational genius of John Wesley after the

Source: William E. H. Lecky, *Introduction to the Science of Sociology*, Robert G. Park and Ernest W. Burgess, eds. (Chicago: The University of Chicago Press, 1924), pp. 915–24. Copyright 1924 by The University of Chicago Press. Reprinted by permission of the publisher.

William E. H. Lecky (1838–1903) was an Irish historian and essayist. His most important work is *The History of England in the Eighteenth Century* in eight volumes. He was a Liberal Unionist M.P. who opposed Home Rule.

masses of the poor had become its ardent supporters. It is perhaps noteworthy that the fanaticism engendered in the youthful supporters of both these widely divergent movements led to repudiation of their elders' traditional authority held, especially, by parents, teachers, and the religious establishment.

The term Methodist was a college nickname bestowed upon a small society of students at Oxford, who met together between 1729 and 1735 for the purpose of mutual improvement. They were accustomed to communicate every week, to fast regularly on Wednesdays and Fridays, and on most days during Lent; to read and discuss the Bible in common, to abstain from most forms of amusement and luxury, and to visit sick persons and prisoners in the gaol. John Wesley, the future leader of the religious revival of the eighteenth century, was the master-spirit of this society. The society hardly numbered more than fifteen members, and was the object of much ridicule at the university; but it included some men who afterward played considerable parts in the world. Among them was Charles, the younger brother of John Wesley, whose hymns became the favorite poetry of the sect, and whose gentler, more submissive, and more amiable character, though less fitted than that of his brother for the great conflicts of public life, was very useful in moderating the movement, and in drawing converts to it by personal influence. Charles Wesley appears to have originated the society at Oxford; he brought Whitefield into its pale, and besides being the most popular poet he was one of the most persuasive preachers of the movement.

In the course of 1738 the chief elements of the movement were already formed. Whitefield had returned from Georgia, Charles Wesley had begun to preach the doctrine with extraordinary effect to the criminals in Newgate and from every pulpit into which he was admitted. Methodist societies had already sprung up under Moravian influence. They were in part a continuation of the society at Oxford, in part a revival of those religious societies that have been already noticed as so common after the Revolution. The design of each was to be a church within a church, a seedplot of a more fervent piety, the center of a stricter discipline and a more energetic propagandism than existed in religious communities at large. In these societies the old Christian custom of love-feasts was revived. The members sometimes passed almost the whole night in the most passionate devotions, and voluntarily submitted to a spiritual tyranny that could hardly be surpassed in a Catholic monastery. They were to meet every week, to make an open and particular confession of every frailty, to submit to be cross-examined on all their thoughts, words, and deeds. The following among others were the questions asked at every meeting: "What known sin have you committed since our last meeting? What temptations have you met with? How were you delivered? What have you thought, said, or done of which you doubt whether it be sin or not? Have you nothing you desire to keep secret?"

Such rules could only have been accepted under the influence of an overpowering religious enthusiasm, and there was much truth in the judgment which the elder brother of John Wesley passed upon them in 1739. "Their societies," he wrote to their mother, "are sufficient to dissolve all other societies but their own. Will any man of common sense or spirit suffer any domestic to be in a band engaged to relate to five or ten people everything without reserve that concerns the person's conscience how much soever it may concern the family? Ought any married persons to be there unless husband and wife be there together?"

From this time the leaders of the movement became the most active of missionaries. Without any fixed parishes they wandered from place to place, proclaiming their new doctrine in every pulpit to which they were admitted, and they speedily awoke a passionate enthusiasm and a bitter hostility in the Church.

We may blame, but we can hardly, I think, wonder at the hostility all this aroused among the clergy. It is, indeed, certain that Wesley and Whitefield were at this time doing more than any other contemporary clergymen to kindle a living piety among the people. Yet before the end of 1738 the Methodist leaders were excluded from most of the pulpits of the Church, and were thus compelled, unless they consented to relinquish what they considered a Divine mission, to take steps in the direction of separation.

Two important measures of this nature were taken in 1739. One of them was the creation of Methodist chapels, which were intended not to oppose or replace, but to be supplemental and ancillary to, the churches, and to secure that the doctrine of the new birth should be faithfully taught to the people. The other and still more important event was the institution by Whitefield of field-preaching. The idea had occurred to him in London, where he found congregations too numerous for the church in which he preached, but the first actual step was taken in the neighborhood of Bristol. At a time when he was himself excluded from the pulpits at Bristol, and was thus deprived of the chief normal means of exercising his talents, his attention was called to the condition of the colliers at Kingswood. He was filled with horror and compassion at finding in the heart of a Christian country, and in the immediate neighborhood of a great city, a population of many thousands, sunk in the most brutal ignorance and vice, and entirely excluded from the ordinances of religion. Moved by such feelings, he resolved to address the colliers in their own haunts. The resolution was a bold one, for field-preaching was then utterly unknown in England, and it needed no common courage to brave all the obloquy and derision it must provoke, and to commence the experiment in the center of a half-savage population. Whitefield, however, had a just confidence in his cause and in his powers. Standing himself upon a hillside, he took for his text the first words of the sermon which was spoken from the Mount, and he addressed with his accustomed fire an astonished audience of some two hundred men. The fame of his eloquence spread far and wide. On successive occasions, five, ten, fifteen, even twenty thousand were present. It was February, but the winter sun shone clear and bright. The lanes were filled with carriages of the more wealthy citizens, whom curiosity had drawn from Bristol. The trees and hedges were crowded with humbler listeners, and the fields were darkened by a compact mass. The voice of the great preacher pealed with a thrilling power to the outskirts of that mighty throng. The picturesque novelty of the occasion and of the scene, the contagious emotion of so great a multitude, a deep sense of the condition of his hearers and of the momentous importance of the step he was taking, gave an additional solemnity to his eloquence. His rude auditors were electrified. They stood for a time in rapt and motionless attention. Soon tears might be seen forming white gutters down cheeks blackened from the coal mine. Then sobs and groans told how hard hearts were melting at his words. A fire was kindled among the outcasts of Kingswood which burnt long and fiercely, and was destined in a few years to overspread the land.

But for the simultaneous appearance of a great orator and a great statesman, Methodism would probably have smouldered and at last perished like the very similar religious societies of the preceding century. Whitefield was utterly destitute of the organizing skill which could alone give a permanence to the movement, and no talent is naturally more ephemeral than popular oratory; while Wesley, though a great and impressive preacher, could scarcely have kindled a general enthusiasm had he not been assisted by an orator who had an unrivaled power of moving the passions of the ignorant. The institution of field-preaching by Whitefield in the February of 1739 carried the impulse through the great masses of the poor, while the foundation by Wesley, in the May of the same year, of the first Methodist chapel was the beginning of an organized body capable of securing and perpetuating the results that had been achieved.

From the time of the institution of lay preachers Methodism became in a great degree independent of the Established Church. Its chapels multiplied in the great towns, and its itinerant missionaries penetrated to the most secluded districts. They were accustomed to preach in fields and gardens, in streets and lecture-rooms, in market places and churchyards.

. . . . .

It was frequently observed by Wesley that his preaching rarely affected the rich and the educated. It was over the ignorant and the credulous that it exercised its most appalling power, and it is difficult to overrate the mental anguish it must sometimes have produced. Timid and desponding natures unable to convince themselves that they had undergone a supernatural change, gentle and affectionate natures who believed that those who were dearest to them were descending into everlasting fire, must have often experienced pangs compared with which the torments of the martyr were insignificant. The confident assertions of the Methodist preacher and the ghastly images he continually evoked poisoned their imaginations, haunted them in every hour of weakness or depression, discolored all their judgments of the world, and added a tenfold horror to the darkness of the grave.

. . . . .

In the intense religious enthusiasm that was generated, many of the ties of life were snapped in twain. Children treated with contempt the commands of their parents, students the rules of their colleges, clergymen the discipline of their Church. The whole structure of society, and almost all the amusements of life, appeared criminal. The fairs, the mountebanks, the public rejoicings of the people, were all Satanic. It was sinful for a woman to wear any gold ornament or any brilliant dress. It was even sinful for a man to exercise the common prudence of laying by a certain portion of his income. When Whitefield proposed to a lady to marry him, he thought it necessary to say, "I bless God, if I know anything of my own heart, I am free from that foolish passion which the world calls love." "I trust I love you only for God, and desire to be joined to you only by His commands, and for His sake." It is perhaps not very surprising that Whitefield's marriage, like that of Wesley, proved very unhappy. Theaters and the reading of plays were absolutely condemned, and Methodists employed all their influence with the authorities to prevent the erection of the former. It seems to have been regarded as a divine judgment that once, when *Macbeth* was being acted at Drury Lane, a real thunderstorm mingled with the mimic thunder in the witch scene. Dancing was, if possible, even worse than the theater. "Dancers," said Whitefield, "please the devil at every step"; and it was said that his visit to a town usually put "a stop to the dancing-school, the assemblies, and every pleasant thing." He made it his mission to "bear testimony against the detestable diversions of this generation"; and he declared that no "recreations, considered as such, can be innocent."

Accompanying this asceticism we find an extraordinary revival of the grossest superstition. It was a natural consequence of the essentially emotional character of Methodism that its disciples should imagine that every strong feeling or impulse within them was a direct inspiration of God or Satan. The language of Whitefield—the language in a great degree of all the members of the sect—was that of men who were at once continually inspired and the continual objects of miraculous interposition. In every perplexity they imagined that, by casting lots or opening their Bibles at random, they could obtain a supernatural answer to their inquiries.

In all matters relating to Satanic interference, Wesley was especially credulous. "I cannot give up to all the Deists in Great Britain the existence of witchcraft till I give up the credit of all history, sacred and profane." He had no doubt that the physical contortions into which so many of his hearers fell were due to the direct agency of Satan, who tore the converts as they were coming to Christ. He had himself seen men and women who were literally possessed by devils; he had witnessed forms of madness which were not natural, but diabolical, and he had experienced in his own person the hysterical affections which resulted from supernatural agency.

If Satanic agencies continually convulsed those who were coming to the faith, divine judgments as frequently struck down those who opposed it. Every illness, every misfortune that befell an opponent, was believed to be supernatural. Molther, the Moravian minister, shortly after the Methodists had separated from the Moravians, was seized with a passing illness. "I believe," wrote Wesley, "it was the hand of God that was upon him." Numerous cases were cited of sudden and fearful judgments which fell upon the adversaries of the cause. A clergyman at Bristol, standing up to preach against the Methodists, "was suddenly seized with a rattling in his throat, attended with a hideous groaning," and on the next Sunday he died. At Todmorden a minister was struck with a violent fit of palsy immediately after preaching against the Methodists.

. . . . . .

By such anecdotes and by such beliefs a fever of enthusiasm was sustained.

But with all its divisions and defects the movement was unquestionably effecting a great moral revolution in England. It was essentially a popular movement, exercising its deepest influence over the lower and middle classes. Some of its leaders were men of real genius, but in general the Methodist teacher had little sympathy with the more educated of his fellow-countrymen. To an ordinarily cultivated mind there was something extremely repulsive in his tears and groans and amorous ejaculations, in the coarse and anthropomorphic familiarity and the unwavering dogmatism with which he dealt with the most sacred subjects, in the narrowness of his theory of life and his utter insensibility to many of the influences that expand and embellish it, in the mingled credulity and self-confidence with which he imagined that the whole course of nature was altered for his convenience. But the very qualities that impaired his influence in one sphere enhanced it in another. His impassioned prayers and exhortations stirred the hearts of multitudes whom a more decorous teaching had left absolutely callous. The supernatural atmosphere of miracles, judgments, and inspirations in which he moved, invested the most prosaic life with a halo of romance. The doctrines he taught, the theory of life he enforced, proved themselves capable of arousing in great masses of men an enthusiasm of piety which was hardly surpassed in the first days of Christianity, of eradicating inveterate vice, of fixing and directing impulsive and tempestuous natures that were rapidly hastening toward the abyss. Out of the profligate slave-dealer, John Newton, Methodism formed one of the purest and most unselfish of saints. It taught criminals in Newgate to mount the gallows in an ecstasy of rapturous devotion. It planted a fervid and enduring religious sentiment in the midst of the most brutal and most neglected portions of the population, and whatever may have been its vices or its defects, it undoubtedly emancipated great numbers from the fear of death, and imparted a warmer tone to the devotion and a greater energy to the philanthropy of every denomination both in England and the colonies.

36.

VIOLENCE IN AMERICAN HISTORY

The National Commission on the Causes and Prevention of Violence

The mass demonstrations which developed into riots and violence in the past decade illustrate a virulent form of collective behavior. Americans generally condemn both the "mobs" that become violent and the police that overreact to demonstrators. Contemporary criticism of violence seems to assume that such collective behavior is a new phenomenon in civilized America. The National Commission on the Causes and Prevention of Violence, in the following selection, indicates that violence has occurred frequently in our history and examines some of the forces that may produce such behavior.

Because we believe that the past has much to tell us about the present and the future, this Commission has studied the history of violence in America. We wanted

Source: National Commission on the Causes and Prevention of Violence, *Report* (Washington, D.C.: Government Printing Office, 1969).

Created by President Lyndon B. Johnson in June 1968, this commission submitted its final report eighteen months later. The commission was chaired by Dr. Milton S. Eisenhower. Other members were: Congressmen Hale Boggs and William C. McCulloch; senators Philip A. Hart and Roman Hruska; judges A. Leon Higginbotham and Ernest W. McFarland; Ambassador Patricial Harris; Archbishop Terence J. Cooke; Eric Hoffer; Leon Jaworski; Albert E. Jenner, Jr.; and Dr. W. Walter Menninger.

to know whether Americans are more violent today than they have been in the past. We studied historical events which parallel current events in hopes of finding basic principles that might guide us toward solutions. Most of all, however, we sought the broad perspective which would help us and our fellow citizens to understand better the nature, the character, and the dilemma of contemporary America.

This study of history has illuminated for us the causes of violence in this nation and some of the ways to reduce it:

1. America has always been a relatively violent nation. Considering the tumultuous historical forces that have shaped the United States, it would be astonishing were it otherwise.
2. Since rapid social change in America has produced different forms of violence with widely varying patterns of motivation, aggression, and victimization, violence in America has waxed and waned with the social tides. The decade just ending, for example, has been one of our most violent eras—although probably not the most violent.
3. Exclusive emphasis in a society on law enforcement rather than on a sensible balance of remedial action and enforcement tends to lead to a decaying cycle in which resistance grows and becomes ever more violent.
4. For remedial social change to be an effective moderator of violence, the changes must command a wide measure of support throughout the community. Official efforts to impose change that is resisted by a dominant majority frequently prompt counterviolence.
5. Finally, Americans have been, paradoxically, both a turbulent people but have enjoyed a relatively stable republic. Our liberal and pluralistic system has historically both generated and accommodated itself to a high level of unrest, and our turmoil has reflected far more demonstration and protest than conspiracy and revolution.

These are a few of the conclusions we have drawn from our study of American history. It is a source of partial consolation and reassurance that our present pattern of violence falls largely within that tradition and that traditionally violence has subsided as political and social institutions gradually responded to the underlying social dislocations and injustices that caused it. But it is a source of great concern that the very velocity of historical change itself has been vastly accelerated by modern technology. Technological progress causes enormous dislocation and demands for social change; our techniques of instant communications intensify these demands manyfold. Whether our political and social institutions can respond as rapidly as new demands arise will largely determine how much violence we are about to experience.

If we are wise—if we listen carefully and watch closely—we will realize that violence is a social bellwether: dramatic rises in its level and modifications in its form (as is the case today) tell us that something important is happening in our political and social systems.

. . . . .

THE ROOTS OF AMERICAN DISCONTENT

With the 1960s came shock and frustration. It was a decade against itself: the students of affluence were marching in the streets; the nation that had never lost a war to any power was mired in a seemingly endless, unpopular, and possibly unwinnable land war in Asia; the national consciousness was shocked by savage assassinations; and Negro Americans were responding to ostensible victories in civil rights and to their collectively unprecedented prosperity with a paradoxical venting of outrage. It seemed as if America, so long especially blessed by the fates, had suddenly been cheated. Emerging victorious from the world war against fascism, she faced not a century of Pax Americana (as had her British counterparts faced a century of Pax Britannica) but, instead, frustrating cold and hot war abroad and turmoil at home. How could the violent 1960s be explained in the light of our past?

Historical analysis of our national experience and character would suggest that the seeds of our contemporary discontent were to a large extent deeply embedded in those same ostensibly benevolent forces which had contributed to our uniqueness. First, we are indeed a nation of immigrants, but one in which the original dominant immigrant group, the so-called Anglo-Saxons, effectively preempted the crucial levers of economic and political power in government, commerce, and the professions. This elite group has consistently resisted—though by no means with uniform success—the upward strivings of successive "ethnic" immigrant waves. The resultant competitive hierarchy of immigrants has always been highly conducive to violence, but this violence has taken different forms. The Anglo-Americans used their access to the levers of power to maintain their dominance, using legal force surrounded by an aura of legitimacy for such ends as economic exploitation; the restriction of immigration by a national-origin quota system which clearly branded later immigrants from southern and eastern Europe and from Asia as culturally undesirable; the confinement of the original Indian immigrants largely to barren reservations; and the restriction of blacks first to slavery, then to a degraded caste. Periodically in times of national crisis, dominant Anglo-Americans rallied to "nativist" movements that directed violence toward "ethnic" scapegoats: in the 1790s with the Alien and Sedition Acts; in the 1850s with the sectional split; in the decade 1886–96 with unrestricted immigration and labor and racial unrest; in World War I with the Red Scare; in World War II with the Nisei.

But the system was also conducive to violence among competing racial and ethnic groups themselves. The massive New York draft riots of 1863 prompted thousands of poor Irish, who felt the brunt of an inequitable conscription that allowed wealthy men to purchase substitutes, to vent their wrath upon New York's Negroes. Much of the interethnic hostility has flowed from genuine economic competition among lower class Americans, and this source of ethnic antagonism has historically been exacerbated by the tendency of American industrialists to combat union organizers by employing black "scabs" and strikebreakers. This practice most clearly linked two mutually supportive sources of social anxiety: economic threat and status frustration. Given America's unprecedented ethnic pluralism simply being born American conferred no automatic and equal citizenship in the eyes of the larger society. In the face of such reservations, ethnic minorities had constantly to affirm their Americanism through a kind of patriotic ritual which intensified the ethnic competition for status and invited severe and abiding conflict.

The second major formative historical experience was America's prolonged encounter with the frontier. While the frontier experience indubitably strengthened the mettle of the American character, it also witnessed the brutal and brutalizing ousting of the Indians and the forceful incorporation of Mexican and other original inhabitants, and fastened into the American character a tenacious habit of wastefully exploiting our natural resources. Further, it concomitantly created an environment in which, owing to the paucity of law enforcement agencies, a tradition of vigilante "justice" was legitimized. Originally prompted by frontier lawlessness and inspired—or at least rationalized—by the doctrines of self-preservation, the right of revolution, popular sovereignty and the Higher Law, American vigilantism has historically enjoyed powerful ideological support. Vigilantism has persisted as a socially malleable instrument long after the disappearance of the frontier environment that gave it birth, and it has proved quite congenial to an urban setting. The longevity of the Ku Klux Klan and the vitality both of contemporary urban rioting and of the stiffening resistance to it owe much to this tradition.

Third, the revolutionary doctrine that our Declaration of Independence proudly proclaims is mistakenly cited as a model for legitimate violence by contemporary groups such as militant Negroes and radical students who confront a system of both public and private government that they regard as contemptuous of their consent. Entranced by the resurgence of revolution in the underdeveloped world and of international university unrest, radical students and blacks seize upon our early doctrine of the inherent right of revolution and self-determination to justify their rebellion. That their analogies are fatefully problematical in no way dilutes the majesty of our own proud Declaration.

The fourth historic legacy, our consensual political philosophy of Lockean-Jeffersonian liberalism, was premised upon a pervasive fear of governmental power and has reinforced the tendency to define freedom negatively as freedom *from*. As a consequence, conservatives have been able paradoxically to invoke the doctrines of Jefferson in resistance to legislative reforms, and the Sumnerian imperative that "stateways cannot change folkways" has historically enjoyed a wide and not altogether unjustified allegiance in the public eye. Its implicit corollary has been that forceful, and, if necessary, violent local and state resistance to unpopular federal stateways is a legitimate response; both Calhoun and Wallace could confidently repair to a strict construction of the same document invoked by Lincoln and the Warren court.

This ability of the American liberal consensus to encompass widely divergent social views within a common framework of constitutionalism was clearly demonstrated by the failure of Reconstruction following the Civil War. While the taut prohibition of the 13th Amendment permitted no ambiguity concerning slavery, the conservative Supreme Court of the postwar years consistently demonstrated the extraordinary flexibility of judicial construction in largely eviscerating the substance and perverting the purpose of the 14th and 15th Amendments and the social reform of Reconstruction law. The resultant hypocrisy for generations made a mockery of liberal rhetoric and fueled the fires of alienation. Black education became separate and manifestly unequal, yet for a century the local bias of Jeffersonian liberalism effectively blocked federal assistance or intervention. The massive expansion of public education in recent years, together with the social reform of the Second Reconstruction, has to some extent bolstered public faith in the contemporary efficacy and relevance of the American liberal tradition and particularly its commitment to free public education. But this proud commitment has too often been advanced as a panacea wherein America's schools are expected somehow to solve her most deeply-rooted social problems.

The next historic source both of our modern society and our current plight, following Civil War and Reconstruction, has been our industrial revolution and the great internal migration from the countryside to the city. Yet the process occurred with such astonishing rapidity that it produced widespread socioeconomic dislocation in an environment in which the internal controls of the American social structure were loose and the external controls were weak. Urban historian Richard Wade has observed that—

> The cities inherited no system of police control adequate to the numbers or to the rapid increase of the urban centers. The modern police force is the creation of the 20th century; the establishment of genuinely professional systems is historically a very recent thing. Throughout the 18th and 19th century, the force was small, untrained, poorly paid, and part of the political system. In case of any sizeable disorder, it was hopelessly inadequate; and rioters sometimes routed the constabulary in the first confrontation.

Organized labor's protracted and bloody battles for recognition and power occurred during these years of minimal control and maximal social upheaval. The violence of workers' confrontation with their employers was partly the result of a lack of consensus on the legitimacy of workers' protests, partly the result of the lack of means of social control. Workers used force to press their grievances, employers organized violent resistance, and repeatedly state or federal troops had to be summoned to restore order.

The final distinctive characteristic—in many ways perhaps our most distinctive—has been our unmatched prosperity. Ranked celestially with life and liberty in the sacrosanct Lockean trilogy, property has generated a quest and prompted a devotion in the American character that has matched our devotion to equality and, in a fundamental sense, has transformed the idea of equality from the radical leveling of the European democratic tradition into a typically American insistence upon equality of *opportunity*. In an acquisitive society of individuals with unequal talents and groups with unequal advantages, this had resulted in an unequal distribution of the rapid accumulation of abundance that, especially since World War II, has promised widespread participation in the affluent society to a degree unprecedented in history. Central to the notion of "revolutions of rising expectations" is the assumption that improved economic rewards can coincide with and often obscure a degree of *relative* deprivation that generates frustration and can prompt men toward violent protest despite measurable gains. Revolutions have not historically occurred in stagnant and utterly destitute nations; rather, they have occurred in nations in which rising but uneven prosperity at once inspired hope and intensified frustrations and impatience with the old order.

VIOLENCE IN THE AMERICAN TRADITION

Our historical evolution, then, has given our national character a dual nature: we strive for both liberty and equality, which can be—and often in practice are—quite contradictory goals. This is not to suggest that American society is grounded in a fatal contradiction. For all the conflict inherent in a simultaneous quest for liberty and equality, American history is replete with dramatic instances of the successful adjustment of "the system" to the demands of disparate protesting groups. An historical appraisal of these genuine achievements should give pause to contemporary Cassandras who bemoan in self-flagellation how hopelessly wretched we all are. To be sure, these radically disillusioned social critics can find abundant evil in our historical legacy: centuries of Negro slavery, the cultural deracination and near extinction of the Indians, our initiation of atomic destruction—*ad infinitum.* But these radical new social critics in their overcompensations tend to distort the American experience in much the same fashion, although in an opposite direction, as have the more familiar superpatriotic celebrants of American virtuosity. Even so, a careful and honest historical appraisal should remind us that violence has been far more intrinsic to our past than we should like to think.

Although violence has been a disagreeably persistent characteristic of American social life, this recurrent theme of violence has taken different forms in response to America's rapidly changing social context. Historical analysis suggests that while much of the American violence was prompted by environmental conditions that no longer exist, many of the social tensions that produced violence are recurrent and remain of contemporary relevance.

Perhaps the historically violent American episode that is least relevant to our contemporary concerns is the family feud. The famous and colorful clan feuding of Hatfields versus McCoys and Suttons versus Taylors seems to have been triggered by the Civil War in border areas where loyalties were sharply divided and where the large extended family of the 19th century provided both a focus for intense loyalties and a ready instrument of aggression. But this tradition has waned with the fading of the peculiar circumstances that conditioned its birth. It is arguable, however, that the brutalizing traditions associated with the Indian wars have left their callous imprint on our national character long after the estimated 850,000 to one million American Indians had been ruthlessly reduced by 1950 to 400,000. Similarly, the violence associated with the American Revolution, the Civil War, and the two Reconstructions has surely reinforced the ancient notion that the end justifies the means.

Whether the long association with violence of agrarian uprising and the labor movement has permanently faded with changing modern circumstances is fervently to be hoped, but by no means certain. Employer acceptance of unions during and after the New Deal suggests that that long and bloody conflict is largely behind us. But the growing guild-like defensiveness and exclusiveness of especially those unions threatened by automation, together with the persistent reality that the majority of American laborers—especially black workers—remain outside the unions, invite a resurgence of intramural labor unrest. Also, the stubborn persistence of rural poverty constitutes a latent invitation to a resurgence of latter-day populism.

Two other sordid American traditions that have largely waned but that recently have shown some signs of revival are vigilantism and lynching. If vigilantism is defined broadly to include regional and even national movements as well as local organizations, then America's preeminent vigilante movement has been the Ku Klux Klan—or rather, the Ku Klux Klans, for there have essentially been three of them. The original Klan arose in the South in response to radical Reconstruction and, through terror and intimidation, was instrumental in the "redemption" of the southern state governments by white conservatives. The second Klan, by far the largest, was resurrected in Atlanta in 1915 and boomed nationally in the 1920s. Strong in the Midwest and Far West as well as in the South, and making inroads even in the cities, the Klan of the 1920s—despite its traditional racist and xenophobic rhetoric—focused its chastisement less upon

Negroes, Catholics, and Jews than upon white Protestants who were adjudged guilty of violating small-town America's Victorian moral code. The third Klan represented a proliferation of competing Klans in the South in response to the civil rights movement of the 1950s. Generally lacking the prestige and organizational strength of the earlier Klans, the groups of lower-class whites engaged in a period of unrestrained terrorism in the rural and small-town Black Belt South in the 1950s and early 1960s, but have belatedly been brought under greater control.

Lynching, vigilantism's supreme instrument of terror and summary "justice," has been widely practiced in America since the Revolution era, when miscreant Tories were tarred and feathered, and worse. Although lynching is popularly associated with racial mob murder, this pattern is historically a relatively recent one, for prior to the late 19th century, white Americans perforce lynched one another—Negro slaves being far too valuable to squander at the stake. But lynching became predominantly racial from 1882 to 1903, when 1,985 Negroes were murdered in the tragic but successful effort of those years to forge a rigid system of biracial caste, most brutal and explicit in the South but generally reflective of national attitudes. Once the point that this was a white man's country was made, lynching gradually declined. Its recent resurgence in response to the civil rights movement is notorious, but it nowhere approximates its scale at the turn of the century.

The contemporary relevance of political assassination and freelance multiple murder needs no documentation to a nation that has so recently witnessed the murders of John and Robert Kennedy, Dr. Martin Luther King, and, on television, Lee Harvey Oswald—in addition to the chilling mass slaughtering sprees of Charles Whitman in Austin and Richard Speck in Chicago. Historically, political assassination has become a recurrent feature of the American political system only in the South during (the first) Reconstruction and in the New Mexico Territory. Although four American Presidents have been assassinated since 1865, prominent politicians and civil servants occupying the myriad lesser levels of government have been largely immune. Whether the current spate of public murder is an endemic symptom of a new social malaise is a crucial question that history cannot yet answer, other than to observe that precedents in our past are minimal.

Similarly, historical precedents are few regarding massive student and antiwar protests. American students have historically engaged in food riots and succumbed to the annual spring throes of the panty-raid syndrome, but the current wave of campus confrontations is essentially an unprecedented phenomenon—as is the massive and prolonged opposition to the war in Vietnam. But the size of and sophistication of the contemporary college student body are also unprecedented. Now outnumbering America's farmers by almost three million, America's seven million college students confront, largely without votes, a society that nags the conscience of the best of them by sending younger noncollege students off to an unpopular war in Asia, and threatens their security and careers by greeting them with the same grim summons upon graduation. We have lived with these harsh realities before—unpopular wars, inequitable conscription, threatened young men—but never in such potent combination. Unfortunately, in this regard, the past does not have much to tell us; we will have to make our history along uncharted and frightening ways.

But the past has much to tell us about the rioting and crime that have gripped our cities. Urban mobs are as old as the city itself. Colonial seaports frequently were rocked for days by roving mobs—groups of unruly and often drunken men whose energies were shrewdly put to political purpose as Liberty Boys in the American Revolution. Indeed, our two principal instruments of physical control evolved directly in response to 19th-century urban turmoil. The professional city police system replaced the inadequate constabulary and watch-and-ward in response to the urban rioting of the 1840s and 1850s, largely in the Northeast. Similarly, the national guard was organized in order to control the labor violence—or more appropriately, the anti-labor violence—of the 1880s and 1890s.

CONCLUSION

Probably all nations are given to a kind of historical amnesia or selective recollection that masks unpleasant traumas of the past. Certainly, Americans since the Puritans have historically regarded themselves as a latter-day "Chosen People" sent on a holy errand to the wilderness, there to create a New Jerusalem. One beneficent side effect of our current turmoil may be to force a harder and more candid look at our past.

Violence has usually been the lava flowing from the top of a volcano fed by deeper fires of social dislocation and injustice; it has not been stopped solely by capping the top, but has usually subsided when our political and social institutions have managed to make the adjustments necessary to cool the fires below. If our future is to be more just, less violent, less crime-ridden, and free of fear, we obviously must do much better than we are now doing to speed social reform and simultaneously improve the effectiveness of the entire law enforcement system of the nation. Only in an orderly society can we achieve the advances which militants and moderates alike know are required.

37.

THE RELEVANCE OF NONVIOLENT ACTION

Herbert C. Kelman

Every social scientist must somehow reconcile his role as scientist with his role as citizen. In the selection that follows, a distinguished social psychologist illustrates his solution to this problem. Following many years of personal involvement in direct action campaigns, playing the role of an "observing participant," he recommends nonviolent action as "an effective instrument of social change in Negro Americans' current struggle for justice." Writing shortly after the martyrdom of America's greatest exemplar of nonviolent action, Martin Luther King, Jr., Kelman advocates nonviolence because it is "consistent with . . . [his] basic values about human relationships and social change" and because he is "convinced that nonviolent action represents a potentially effective way of producing social change based on principles that are social-psychologically sound."

The early 1960s were a period of excitement and exhilaration in the history of social protest in the United States. The country was emerging from the long winter of the Joseph McCarthy years. A new generation of young people, who had not learned the habit of caution, rediscovered the meaning of personal commitment and social action. The civil rights movement captured the imagination of Negro and white students who, in turn, gave courage to their elders and brought them back into the struggle.

Perhaps the most exciting feature of the civil rights movement during these years was the pattern of social action that it pursued. Though activist and militant, it was firmly committed to nonviolence; though dedicated to creating a new pride and a new image for Negro Americans, it was built on collaboration between the races. Organized nonviolent and interracial struggle against segregation and discrimination was not, of course, invented in 1960. It goes back to the formation of the Congress of Racial Equality in Chicago in 1942. By 1960, CORE chapters had almost two decades of experience in breaking down segregation through the use of the techniques of nonviolent direct action, with many local successes to their credit, mostly in Northern and border states. Nonviolent action became a major force in the South in 1956 with the Montgomery bus boycott, under the leadership of Martin Luther King, Jr., and the formation of the Southern Christian Leadership Conference. It

Source: Herbert C. Kelman, *A Time to Speak: On Human Values and Social Research* (San Francisco: Jossey-Bass, 1968), pp. 231–44, 255–60.

Herbert Kelman is the Richard Clark Cabot professor of Social Ethics at Harvard University. His main interests include social psychology, intergroup conflict, social movements, and political ideology. He is the author of many articles and wrote the book *A Time to Speak: On Human Values and Social Research.*

was in the early 1960s, however, that nonviolent civil rights action began to take on the character of a national mass movement, mobilizing support throughout the country and exerting major influence on official policy.

PRINCIPLES OF NONVIOLENT ACTION

What is nonviolent action? One thing that surely ought to be clear is that nonviolence does not refer to the mere absence of violence—though it seems that both militants, who castigate nonviolence as a counterrevolutionary strategy, and establishmentarians, who embrace it as part of the process of orderly change, are not always aware of that fact. Nonviolence is not to be equated with passive yielding to superior force or with working only through established channels. It is a positive, active, and in fact militant strategy, designed to produce thoroughgoing changes in social patterns.

Though it respects the adversary as a human being and attempts to mobilize his conscience, nonviolent action is not just a moral appeal and a petition to the other that he do the right thing. It is very definitely and deliberately an exercise of power. Barbara Deming puts it very well:

> To resort to power one need not be violent, and to speak to conscience one need not be meek. The most effective action *both* resorts to power *and* engages conscience. Nonviolent action does not have to beg others to "be nice." It can in effect force them to consult their consciences—or to pretend to have them. . . . One brings what economic weight one has to bear, what political, social, psychological, what physical weight. There is a good deal more involved here than a moral appeal. It should be acknowledged both by those who argue against nonviolence and those who argue for it that we, too, rely upon force.

Indeed, a nonviolent confrontation presents real threats to the adversary. By dramatically exposing his unjust practices, by refusing continued cooperation with them, and by replacing them with new patterns, it may threaten him with embarrassment and adverse publicity, with reduction in his economic or political power, and with disruption of the orderly processes he cherishes. It does not, however, threaten to destroy him, and thus leaves open the way for reappraisal, for negotiation, and for rebuilding.

Nonviolent campaigns are most readily identified by the use of techniques of direct action. Various other techniques, however, have always been important parts of the repertoire of nonviolent action, even though they may not be unique to that strategy. Thus, nonviolent action programs overlap with and utilize protest demonstrations, educational campaigns, legislative lobbying, judicial suits, community organization, and negotiations with employers or unions. Typically, they rely on a combination of methods, which vary in dominance, depending on the nature of the problem under attack, the stage in which the campaign finds itself, and the opportunities for action that are available. What defines nonviolent action is not the specific array of techniques that have evolved, but the effort to utilize and develop appropriate techniques that are consistent with a set of basic action principles.

If we view nonviolence as a pragmatic strategy for intergroup conflict, rooted in a Gandhian philosophy of action we can describe these principles as follows:

(1) Nonviolent strategy is built on an active effort to empathize with one's opponent and to understand the perspectives, goals, fears, expectations, and preconceptions that he brings to the situation. To understand the adversary's point of view

does not mean to accept it or to compromise with injustice. Rather, it avoids the type of escalation of conflict that is caused by misperception, and permits actions that are informed by the facts, that are not unnecessarily threatening, and that are conducive to a resolution of conflict in which both sides benefit.

(2) Nonviolent strategy includes continuing efforts to maintain and broaden channels of communication, to step up the level and depth of communication, and to discuss and negotiate all disagreements directly. Even when the conflict has reached a stage of sharp confrontation, there is a readiness to enter into negotiation and to explore mutual interests and possibilities for cooperation.

(3) Nonviolent strategy calls for the deliberate initiation of steps that help to decrease tension, hostility, and reliance on violent means. Janis and Katz stress, in this connection, the importance of "adopting a consistent attitude of *trust* toward the rival group and taking overt actions which demonstrate that one is, in fact, willing to act upon this attitude." By exhibiting trust toward the adversary, by refusing to treat him as an enemy, and by dealing with him in a straightforward and aboveboard manner, one can often induce a reciprocal response on his part.

(4) Nonviolent strategy is committed to eschewing violence in response to hostile moves initiated by the opponent. This commitment is clearly formulated and publicly pronounced. It means refraining from acts of physical or verbal violence against members of the other group and from acts that have the effect of humiliating them, even in the face of clear provocation. It does not, however, mean a passive yielding to coercion on their part. Typically, the strategy involves disciplined nonviolent resistance, marked by a readiness to make personal sacrifices in defense of one's cause.

(5) When it becomes necessary to initiate conflict moves and to engage the opponent in a direct confrontation, nonviolent strategy continues to rely on nonviolent techniques. These techniques are aimed not at defeating the adversary, but at trying to "convert" him, while working for the achievement of concrete, positive objectives.

(6) Wherever possible, nonviolent action confronts a specific practice or law or institutional pattern that is unjust, and consists in a direct or symbolic enactment of an alternative pattern that corresponds to the desired state of affairs. This effort to give concrete expression to the desired state of affairs—to bring into reality, even if only in symbolic and rudimentary fashion, a pattern consistent with social justice—represents the most characteristic and most dramatic feature of the "classical" nonviolent action campaign. Thus, participants in lunch-counter sit-ins or in Freedom Rides refused to accept the established pattern of segregation and—by sitting where they were not supposed to sit—acted out the new pattern with which they hoped to replace it.[1]

[1] Such direct action techniques, however, are usually preceded and always accompanied by a variety of other activities. For example, in Baltimore CORE's campaign against segregated lunch counters in the early 1950s, we went through a series of other steps—including tests to determine existing practices, leaflet distribution, efforts to mobilize the support of various community agencies, and repeated discussions and negotiations with store managers—before mounting a sit-in campaign. Even after sit-ins began, we continued to utilize various other techniques, such as attempts to initiate negotiations between store management and some established community agencies, and attempts to put pressure on the national headquarters of a local store by picketing branches in other cities and by raising the issue at stockholders' meetings. The existence of a direct action campaign, of course, served as an important lever for the other approaches, but it was the convergence of different approaches that finally produced the desired change.

A fundamental feature of these six principles is that they combine firmness and militancy with a conciliatory and open attitude. Participants in nonviolent action try to capitalize on the opponent's strengths rather than his weaknesses, to mobilize his sense of justice and self-interest in support of change rather than resistance to it, to win him over rather than to win over him. At the same time, they are utterly clear about their goals, they are firm in their commitment to a new social pattern, they insist on the opponent's responsibility to accept and promote change, and they leave no doubt that they themselves are prepared to follow through even at great personal cost. They express their militancy not by the suffering that they are prepared to inflict on the opponent, but by the suffering to which they are willing to subject themselves in order to achieve justice. In short, theirs is a militancy that is not confounded with violence and hatred. Their strategy for social change relies on power directed to two tactical purposes: (1) to confront the adversary with the fact that he can no longer rely on their willing cooperation with existing practices and that, at least in symbolic and rudimentary fashion, a new state of affairs has been instituted; and (2) to force the adversary to take active steps in reciprocating the respect, trust, openness, and objectivity that they have shown toward him.

These principles have been applied most readily and effectively in the area of public accommodations, the context in which nonviolent action was originally tailored to the struggle for racial equality in the United States. In campaigns designed to integrate public facilities it is relatively easy to define the specific practice that needs to be changed, to identify a specific adversary, and to find a dramatic and yet self-evident way of symbolically enacting the alternative desired pattern. Other areas, such as discrimination in employment or segregated housing, are not as ideally suited for a classical nonviolent action campaign. In particular, it is difficult to find a focus for direct action and confrontation that has a clear and intrinsic relevance to the old pattern under attack and to the new pattern designed to replace it. An open housing march, for example, is a mechanism of nonviolent confrontation that is only indirectly linked to the housing pattern itself; by marching through a hostile neighborhood the participants are symbolically insisting on their right to be there. If they actually erected houses on vacant lots, or moved into abandoned buildings, the link between action and issue would be as obvious as it was in the case of sit-ins and Freedom Rides. Opportunities for such actions, however, are not readily available.

The challenge to those of us who believe in the efficacy of nonviolent strategy is to develop creative new techniques, embodying the principles of nonviolent action, that are suited to the central problems and the new realities of today—that address themselves to the issues of poverty, of economic and political participation, of the improvement of ghetto life, of the upgrading of educational facilities. Efforts in that direction are under way. The Poor People's Campaign, planned by Martin Luther King before his assassination and now led by Ralph Abernathy, is the major example of such efforts. Proponents of nonviolent action have also suggested "constructive programs"—that is, ways of instituting new states of affairs—that can accompany the Washington campaign. Various self-reliance projects, such as cooperative businesses and services, and community organization efforts in the black ghettoes, though not conceived as components of a nonviolent action campaign, are in fact governed by or at least compatible with the principles of nonviolent action. The question is, Are such efforts relevant to the current situation? Is there still a place for creative innovation in nonviolent action or is nonviolence dead?

THE RELEVANCE OF NONVIOLENCE TODAY

By now almost everyone who is willing and able to listen realizes that, despite the dedication and sacrifices of the civil rights movement, justice and equality for Negro Americans are nowhere in sight. This does not mean that the civil rights movement has failed. Rather, it means that the task is far more difficult and the changes required are far more fundamental than most of us realized. The exclusion of Negroes from American society is so systematic and racism is so thoroughly built into public attitudes and institutional arrangements that a meaningful solution requires a restructuring of the system.

This newly recognized wisdom and the new rhetoric that accompanies it, however, often blind us to the tremendous changes, both in law and social pattern, that have in fact taken place during the past ten years. In his last book, Martin Luther King summed up the important contributions that nonviolent action had made to these changes in the following words:

> It is not overlooking the limitations of nonviolence and the distance we have yet to go to point out the remarkable record of achievements that have already come through nonviolent action. The 1960 sit-ins desegregated lunch counters in more than 150 cities within a year. The 1961 Freedom Rides put an end to segregation in interstate travel. The 1956 bus boycott in Montgomery, Alabama, ended segregation on the buses not only of that city but in practically every city of the South. The 1963 Birmingham movement and the climactic March on Washington won passage of the most powerful civil rights law in a century. The 1965 Selma movement brought enactment of the Voting Rights Law. . . .

The civil rights movement not only has a series of concrete accomplishments to its credit, but it also revolutionized social action in this country by militantly working toward social changes without resort to violence and hatred. King and other Negro Americans have thus taken the lead in reshaping and revitalizing the whole of American society. White America could hardly expect nonviolence in return for the systematic violence to which Negroes had been subjected over the centuries; it surely could not expect the leadership of Negroes in giving new vitality to a society that had excluded them from its benefits. This was indeed an unanticipated blessing, perhaps grounded in part in the very suffering to which the Negro community has been subjected and which prepared it for this unique role in experimenting with radically new and more human forms of social action.

It is not surprising, at least in retrospect, that, as the struggle progresses, its emphasis has moved away from the principles of nonviolence and interracial collaboration as the central pillars of the movement. This development can be traced to the dynamics of the struggle itself, as well as to the new realities that it has created or revealed. Despite many successes, and in large part because of the hopes that these very successes engendered, there came a growing realization of the painful and costly process by which every small change had to be hammered out, of the dependence of the Negro community on white support and good will, of the profound hatred and violence that the movement elicited among some elements of the white community, of the limits beyond which even the "white liberal" was unprepared to go, of the divergencies in interest—and yet communalities in fate—between the Negro middle and lower class and between the Negro populations in the rural South and the urban North, of the irrelevance of civil rights advances to the Negro ghetto dwellers in Watts and in the large cities throughout the country, and of the desperation and isolation of the vast Negro underclass. These conditions ushered in a nationalistic phase of the struggle, in which black unity, black pride, black self-determination, and black leadership have become the central instruments. This nationalistic phase was perhaps inevitable, but its advent was hastened and intensified by the impact of the Vietnam war on our domestic programs.

The current phase is marked by the emergence of a new group of militants, committed to a transformation of the movement and bidding for its leadership by an appeal to nationalist sentiments. As is so often true in nationalist movements, some of these appeals take on an aggressively ethnocentric character. They express contempt and hatred for the white man and are often phrased in the idiom of violence and surrounded with the mystique of guerrilla warfare. The strength and influence of militants of this school are easily exaggerated, in part because they are so vocal and colorful. They represent only one branch of the nationalist revival in the Negro community, and their interpretation of Black Power is certainly not typical of all those who use the term. Charles Hamilton and Nathan Wright, for example, have something quite different in mind when they speak of Black Power. Yet the militant separatists have shifted the center of gravity in the movement and have laid down a powerful challenge to the doctrine of nonviolence. They have contributed to a widespread feeling, particularly in the younger generation, that nonviolent action is irrelevant to the current realities, a relic of the past that only "Uncle Toms," "counterrevolutionaries," and "white liberals" would think of unearthing.[2]

The assassination of Martin Luther King, the most eloquent spokesman for nonviolence and the most beautiful human being in American public life, has added a new poignancy to questions about the relevance of the philosophy for which he lived and died. Again and again we are told that this act of total violence demonstrates the futility of nonviolence and marks the end of the nonviolent phase of the struggle. This is a natural reaction to the anger, to the bitter hurt, to the sense of meaninglessness and despair evoked by the assassination. But once we turn from grief to analysis, can this reaction really be maintained?

Certainly the assassination of Martin Luther King does not provide proof of the ineffectiveness of nonviolence as a strategy, any more than did the assassination of Mohandas Gandhi twenty years ago. It is true that a nonviolent strategy is designed to call forth reciprocal behavior in the adversary, and that proponents of nonviolent action expect the number of casualties to be far lower than those suffered in a violent confrontation. Nonviolence, however, as Gandhi knew, and as King knew and repeatedly said, offers no guarantee against injury and violent death. Nonviolent action is a form of struggle, often carried out in areas in which tensions are high and emotions deep. Proponents of such action are cognizant of the fact that it

[2] Barbara Deming quotes a man who said to her: "You can't turn the clock back now to nonviolence!" She comments, wistfully: "Turn the clock back? The clock has been turned to violence all down through history. Resort to violence hardly marks a move forward. It is nonviolence which is in the process of invention, if only people would not stop short in that experiment."

may activate efforts of ruthless suppression and bring into the open blind hatreds and fears. It is quite possible, therefore, that the level of violence on the part of the adversary may at first increase after a nonviolent action campaign has been initiated, although certainly not to the same extent that it increases after rioting or other forms of violent action.

Although violent responses by the adversary are by no means necessary to the success of a nonviolent action campaign, they may in fact further it. They may mobilize widespread support for the campaign among those who were previously neutral or inactive, as they did in Birmingham and Selma. They may also bring about a gradual change in the adversary himself, as he finds that his own violence continues to be met with nonviolence and with increasing disapproval on the part of bystanders. But whether or not it furthers the campaign, a violent response is an eventuality for which nonviolent actionists must be and have been prepared.

To cite the assassination as evidence for the failure of nonviolence reveals a lack of understanding of what nonviolence means and what Martin Luther King stood for. It is similar to the lack of understanding betrayed by a number of publicists, who, in discussing King's assassination, referred to the "irony" that this nonviolent man met with such a violent death. Nonviolence for King meant active participation in controversy and struggle; he was not dedicated to keeping things calm, smooth, and orderly, but to a militant pursuit of change. As activists, practitioners of nonviolence like Martin Luther King are unique in that they refuse to inflict violence on others but are prepared for the possibility that they may bring it upon themselves. Thus, there was neither irony, nor proof of the inefficacy of nonviolence, in the fact that King met with violent death; it was consistent with his profound commitment and indicative of his extraordinary courage.

Granting, however, that the assassination did not prove the failure of nonviolence, did it not at least demonstrate that the conditions for nonviolent action do not exist today? The assassination, it can be argued, brought out dramatically the profound violence of white America and its determination to crush every effort of the Negro population to achieve a measure of justice. An atmosphere in which the internationally acknowledged spokesman for nonviolence, the man who more than any other refused to abandon faith in America, becomes a prime target for assassination may not be suited to the practice of nonviolence. In this view, then, the assassination as such does not constitute a reason or justification for abandoning nonviolence, but it serves as a symbolic reminder that such a strategy is irrelevant.

I find this a compelling position because I too reacted to the assassination of Martin Luther King with a sense of despair at the relentless violence of American society, both in its internal and external affairs. Yet, on closer reflection, I cannot accept as valid the conclusion that nonviolence is irrelevant to the present situation of our society. In fact, I shall try to show why militant nonviolent action is specifically relevant to our present dilemma, given the changes that need to be achieved and the available means that are capable of achieving them. I am convinced that nonviolent means are far more likely to be effective in producing real changes than the violence now being elevated into a positive value in the romantic mystique and the revolutionary rhetoric of some black militants and their white supporters and provokers. What is wrong with the cult of violence is not that it is too radical, but that it is not radical enough. It relies on the slogans, the methods, and the ways of thinking that have characterized all of the old nationalisms, and, in advocating violence, it is—to use King's words—"imitating the worst, the most brutal and the most uncivilized values of American life." The advocacy of violence may be radical in the sense of using an aggressive style and calling for "extreme" actions. The advocacy of nonviolence, however, is truly radical in its insistence on an analysis that goes to the roots, on a redefinition of ends and means, and on a search for innovative approaches.

Black militants are, understandably, suspicious and resentful of calls for nonviolence that come from—or are seen as coming from—representatives of the establishment. It is indeed hypocritical to demand of Negroes, in a moralizing tone of voice, that they renounce violence when the rest of the society is so saturated with it, particularly at a time when the very men who make these demands are responsible for the brutal and systematic uses of violence in Vietnam. Clearly, these demands derive from a vested interest in maintaining the status quo, which the black militant certainly does not share. It is from the same perspective that some political figures have declared in recent months that "no one has a right to riot." They reveal their complete lack of comprehension of the meaning of the riots by appealing to the legitimacy of the system, when the essential message of the riots is precisely that the system—being unjust—is illegitimate.

My own questioning of the mystique and rhetoric of violence derives, of course, from a very different perspective, formed by a concern with fundamental social change. Nevertheless, as a white man, I hesitate to urge Negroes to commit themselves to nonviolence because of its moral superiority, or even because of its pragmatic advantages. I feel that only Negroes can decide whether they prefer the risks of armed self-defense to the risks of going unarmed, whether they prefer erring in the direction of undue trust of the white society to erring in the direction of undue suspicion, or even whether they prefer expressing their anger to being effective. White men, no matter how deeply involved they may be in the struggles of the Negro community, are not exposed to the same provocations, nor subject to the same consequences, and they have a freedom to withdraw from the struggle that is not available to their Negro comrades. They must be wary, therefore, of any attempt to impose their own moral or strategic preferences on Negroes, for whom these questions represent basic existential choices.[3] But, just as it would be presumptuous for white men to pass moral judgment on the actions of black nationalists, so would it be patronizing to withhold criticism of the premises on which these actions are based, if that criticism derives from an honest and thoughtful analysis of the issues and options.

My analysis has convinced me that violence is self-defeating in Negro Americans' struggle to achieve justice and that nonviolence is ultimately more conducive to genuine change. This analysis is based on the following considerations: (1) The current phase of the struggle calls for tactics of confrontation directed to a realignment of power relationships within the society; (2) Such confrontations, however, can create meaningful and lasting

[3] By the same token, white "revolutionaries" ought to think twice before urging the Negro to adopt a strategy of violence and to form the vanguard of their revolution. In their often self-righteous conviction that they are the only true spokesmen for the oppressed, they may fail to notice that they are imposing their *own* revolution on the Negro rather than supporting *his* struggle.

changes only if they induce white Americans to reexamine their attitudes and to open up the system to full Negro participation; (3) We face, therefore, a real dilemma in that confrontations and demands for changes in power relationships—particularly if they use the postures and rhetoric of violence—tend to alienate white Americans from the Negro population and its cause and to strengthen the barriers to Negro participation through repression and separation; and (4) Nonviolent action offers the most promising resolution to this dilemma, and is thus singularly relevant to the current situation, because it provides confrontations without unduly alienating the white population and challenges to existing power relationships without unduly threatening the integrity of the system.

. . . . .

38.

HOW TO AVOID RIOTS

Dick Gregory

As stated by Kelman in the preceding selection, nonviolent action typically requires "a readiness to make personal sacrifices in defense of one's cause." Few feel compelled, like Martin Luther King, Jr., and his model Gandhi, to make the ultimate sacrifice of giving up one's life for his beliefs. Also important are men like Dick Gregory who are able effectively to combine social activism with humor. In the selection which follows he first gives a moving account of his own family's involvement in his heroic efforts to avoid violence through peaceful demonstrations seeking to achieve change, then with wry humor he reports on the effectiveness of violence when nonviolent methods have failed. Riots can be prevented, Dick Gregory is saying, if those in positions of authority will actually eliminate resented injustices before the patience of those who are unfairly treated is exhausted.

Source: Dick Gregory, *The Shadow That Scares Me* (New York: Doubleday, 1968), pp. 116–19.

Comedian, entertainer, and peace activist, Dick Gregory has made numerous television and college appearances. He is the author of *From the Back of the Bus, Nigger, What's Happening,* and, most recently, *No More Lies.*

During the summer of 1965, I was Peck's Bad Boy in Chicago, according to the press. For a solid month I led nonviolent marches in the city of Chicago. For thirty-one days straight, I boarded a plane each morning in San Francisco, where I was playing a night-club engagement at the hungry i, and flew to Chicago to lead afternoon marches. Then I flew back to San Francisco each evening to go to work. Why did I commute four thousand miles each day for thirty-one days? Because I knew that if the city was being hit by nonviolent demonstrations, there was less chance of rioting in the streets. The nonviolent demonstration gives the ghetto dweller a ray of hope that perhaps the power structure will hear his just demands and do something to alleviate the problems.

It was a real struggle to keep the demonstration alive. If I had not known that this was the only way to avoid violence, I might have been discouraged. I saw my four- and six-year-old daughters get arrested that summer. Think about that. When demonstrators are arrested, the men are taken one place, the women another, and the children still another. My children had never been away from their home and their mother overnight.

But if I ever had any question about being able to justify involving my kids in demonstrations they were answered by my little four-year-old daughter Lynne. When we were being placed in the wagon to go to jail, Lynne said to me, "We're in trouble, aren't we, Daddy?" That night, I cried because of what she said. Tears of anger, really. I was angry that my momma and daddy had not taught me I was in trouble at the age of four. I didn't find out until I was twenty-nine. And here my little four-year-old daughter had a twenty-five-year head start on her father.

We all know of times when kids have been used for wrong. In election frauds in the city of Chicago, kids have voted. And if I read my Bible right, little David was only a boy when he went out to fight Goliath with a slingshot. I was not asking my kids to kill anybody, only to stand up for what was right. And there is no age limit on that.

My wife had a baby that summer on June 16. Since we were running out of demonstrators, I called her on June 18 and said, "Come on out of the hospital, baby, because we are running out of demonstrators and we can't stop this thing now." As long as we held nonviolent demonstrations, there were no riots in the city of Chicago. Even when we were arrested en masse, in acts of civil disobedience halting downtown traffic, there was no violence. Only when the demonstrations stopped did violence erupt on the West Side of Chicago.

Violence results when the power structure fails to respond to the peaceful, nonviolent demonstration. Not only does the power structure fail to consider the just demands of nonviolent demonstrators, it will try to defame and ridicule nonviolent leaders. I was arrested that summer and accused of biting a cop. I stood trial and lost my case. The story of how I lost my case is a study in governmental mockery.

The woman who actually bit the cop came to me and offered to testify on my behalf. I knew she bit the cop; the cop knew she bit him. The trouble came when city hall found out she bit him. The woman was given a job with the poverty program, paying $175 per week, with the stipulation that she not testify in court. The biter is now making more money than the bitten!

There is a pattern of governmental refusal to listen to just demands. The summer riot season in Chicago in 1966 began in the Puerto Rican neighborhood. Many people in Chicago have always wondered why there were no Puerto Rican cops. The official answer from city hall has been, "We don't have anything against Puerto Ricans, but the official height standard for Chicago policemen is five feet, ten inches. Puerto Ricans are just too short."

If Puerto Rican leaders go to city hall and ask that the height requirements be lowered three inches to allow more Puerto Ricans to become policemen, they will be politely but firmly refused. After the Puerto Ricans threw bricks in their neighborhood for three days, the height requirement *was* lowered three inches—an inch per day of rioting. If the riots had lasted a month, there would be job openings on the Chicago police force for Spanish-speaking midgets!

It is a shame that it should take rioting to get Puerto Rican policemen in Chicago. The need for Spanish-speaking policemen in Puerto Rican neighborhoods is crucial. Imagine the problem of communication which is created when the cop on the beat does not understand your language. A man whose wife has just been scalded and seriously burned comes running out of his apartment, grabs the cop, and yells excitedly at him in Spanish. The cop reacts by grabbing his nightstick because he doesn't understand what the excitement is all about.

After the rioting in the Puerto Rican neighborhoods settled down during the summer of 1966, the West Side of Chicago blew up. It is ironic that the rioting in the colored neighborhood started over some water. Negro leaders had been politely asking city hall for some swimming pools. And city hall turned a deaf ear to them. So the residents of the ghetto decided to create their own swimming pools by turning on the fire hydrants. When the cops came to shut the hydrants off, the trouble started. It seems strange to me that white folks should want to cut off the water in a colored neighborhood. They have been trying to run away from hot nigger stink for a hundred years. Instead of turning off the water, they should have brought in some soap.

Since the bricks were thrown all over the West Side of Chicago, it is hard now to walk in that section without stepping into a swimming pool. The government conveniently found forty million dollars after the rioting which did not seem to be available before. It was the same pattern in Los Angeles. Before the rioting, few people had ever heard of the Watts section of Los Angeles. After the bricks were thrown, some two hundred million dollars were poured into that community in emergency funds. As nonviolent demonstrations help to avoid violence in the streets, the refusal of government to respond to the just demands of such demonstrations creates an atmosphere of anger, frustration, and desperation which assures a violent reaction.

39.

THE "MISSING WOMEN" OF ORLEANS

Lynne Ianniello

The phenomenon commonly known as rumor may precipitate such violent types of collective behavior as riots and mob action. Lynne Ianniello, in the following brief but dramatic account, taken from a publication devoted to fighting discrimination, reports the fantastic speed, geographic spread, distortion, and unhappy consequences of an anti-Semitic story circulated in Orleans, France. Initially the incredible rumor was disregarded by the Jews, since it was known by them to be false, but eventually they found organized counteractive efforts were necessary to bring the slander-mongering to an end.

Orleans, France, is a pretty and prosperous city on the right bank of the Loire, 77 miles southwest of Paris. It has handsome public squares, a bronze statue of Joan of Arc—the Maid of Orleans—a Gothic cathedral, a nine-arched bridge, well built houses, quaint crooked streets—and a galloping anti-Semitic rumor reminiscent of the Middle Ages.

Women are disappearing in Orleans, the story goes. Jewish merchants are drugging and kidnapping female customers and selling them into white slavery. Twenty-six women have been victims so far.

The story, a seemingly sick joke or a plot for a bad movie, was at first ignored by Orleans' 600 Jews in a total population of 150,000. But it spread like wildfire.

The police were deluged with anonymous letters and calls. Women reported as victims were found safe in their homes—annoyed at being questioned and completely mystified as to why anyone had reported them missing.

The story persisted and grew in detail. Eight shops, owned by Jewish merchants, were the alleged scenes of "the crimes." In one, Chez Dorphé, a modern apparel store near Orleans' central market, three women were supposed to have been found bound and drugged in the basement. They had gone to shop, people whispered, and "poof, disappeared." The husband of one of the women went to the police and all three were found and rescued "just in time."

Why were there no newspaper reports? "Ah," came the answer, "Jewish gold—$20,000 hushed up the affair."

More details were added. There was supposed to be a tunnel from the apparel store to the shoe store. It was a long tunnel—it connected all the stores.

The main victim of the false story, Henri Licht, manager of Dorphé's, said he laughed when he first heard that people thought he

Source: Lynne Ianniello, *ADL Bulletin,* national publication of the Anti-Defamation League of B'nai B'rith 26, no. 6 (June 1969): 3–4. Reprinted by permission of the publisher and the author.

Author of *Milestones along the March* and editor of *The Ax-Grinders: Critics of our Public Schools,* Lynne Ianniello is the director of press relations for the Anti-Defamation League of B'nai B'rith in New York City.

was dealing in drugs and women. But then it became no laughing matter. His daughter heard the story in school. Students were warned to "be careful." The eight stores were suddenly empty, or serving mere scatterings of male customers or women accompanied by their husbands.

Mr. Licht said crowds gathered outside his shop staring in the windows and pointing. He started receiving vituperous phone calls. Shaking with anger, frustration and disbelief at the incredulous situation, he said: "They accused us in the Middle Ages of stealing children to make matzoh. . . ."

Attempts to track down the rumor proved futile. No one knew who first told the story in Orleans. "I'm certain it was not spontaneous," a high police official said. He added that he was convinced the spreading of the rumor was organized and deliberate.

One explanation, some said, might lie in an article which had appeared in a May issue of a sex-and-crime weekly, *Noir et Blanc,* under the title "The Odious Traps of Women Trafficers." The article spun a tale of a man waiting outside a dress shop in Grenoble for his wife. He grew impatient, went inside, and was told that she had not been there. He never saw her again, according to the article. She had been spirited off, it said, to the "brothels of the Middle East."

Grenoble, near the Italian border, is 250 miles from Orleans. The Orleans' rumor began about two weeks after the issue of *Noir et Blanc* appeared.

But why was the fantastic story believed in Orleans? Mrs. Jacqueline Llados, the non-Jewish manager of a Jewish-owned store, told a reporter she was born in Orleans and had "never seen anything like it."

People came by nudging and pointing, she said. "Business was catastrophic. They were afraid. One of our main customers is a girls' home. They come in and charge things." At the height of the rumor, a sister from the home settled the account and told Mrs. Llados the store was never to serve any of the girls unless they were accompanied by adults.

"None of them have come in since," Mrs. Llados said. "Hardly any women come in alone any more."

People in the street were questioned.

"There's no smoke without fire," said a middle-aged woman.

A young girl, walking home with groceries, declared: "A policeman warned me—I won't go into those stores alone."

A group of teenagers giggled when they were asked if they had heard the story. "Yes," said one of them, "there was a man waiting for his wife. . . ."

. . . . .

"We are always the victims," one shopkeeper said sadly. "When they need a scapegoat, they attack the Jews. That's how it started in 1932. . . ."

He also said that neither he, the other merchants, the authorities or civic leaders knew what to do when they first heard the Orleans' rumor. Some were afraid that to issue denials would spread the story. For nearly two weeks, they did nothing.

By that time, however, the rumor was completely out of hand and it was obvious that something had to be done. Six of the merchants filed a complaint of slander against "parties unknown," thereby setting off a formal police investigation. Maurice Rebaudet, head of the high school parents association, and two merchant organizations denounced the rumors as vicious and false. The two daily Orleans newspapers published the denunciations and added their own.

A committee to fight against the defamation of the Jewish merchants was organized by the writer Louis Guilloux. More than 300 people attended the first meeting and signed a statement expressing friendship and sympathy for "the victims of these odious accusations."

The Representative Council of Jews in France likened the slandering of the merchants to Nazi propaganda tactics and urged the Minister of the Interior to see that those responsible be brought to justice. The League Against Racism and Anti-Semitism also issued a protest and appealed to the police to "unmask the malevolent slanderers" since "public safety is threatened."

Part VI

Social Organization: Stratification and Mobility

40.

NOTES ON THE SERVICE SOCIETY

Alan Gartner and
Frank Riessman

The social class into which one fits is determined, in considerable part, by one's occupation. Studies of social stratification and mobility, therefore, ordinarily deal with occupation as one of the significant elements contributing to one's status. But in times when the very nature of occupations and their assumed contribution to society are undergoing drastic change, it is important to examine these shifts and their potential effect on the social order in general and on the nature of social stratification in particular. In this selection, Alan Gartner and Frank Riessman explore the trend toward what they refer to as the "Service Society" and, although they do not discuss specifically social class and social mobility, the implications of the Service Society for a possible reordering of the criteria for determining social class should be clear to the reader acquainted with the general principles governing the phenomenon of social class.

SERVICE WORK VERSUS SERVICE SOCIETY

To begin with we need to distinguish between the phenomena of service work evidenced by the growing number of workers employed in the service sector (see Tables 1 and 2) and the corollary service society ethos that we consider important. The latter includes values and institutions, a special role for the consumer, and changing work ethic, new leading groups or vanguards, and a political economy that embodies a unique relationship to the state.

Nearly 65 percent of the civilian work force are employed in service production while only 35 percent work in goods production. Sixty-three million people volunteer their services, and millions more provide child care. Over 200 growth centers have arisen in the United States in the last five years, and there are 262 different types of self-help organizations, including Alcoholics Anonymous, Synanon, Recovery, Inc., Gamblers Anonymous, and Weight Watchers. Forty-seven percent of young people between the ages of eighteen and

Source: Alan Gartner and Frank Riessman, *Social Policy* 3, no. 6 (March/April 1973): 62–69. Reprinted by permission of *Social Policy,* published by Social Policy Corporation, New York.

Alan Gartner is the associate director of the New Careers Development Center at New York University. He has also served as the executive director of the Economic Opportunity Council of Suffolk (N.Y.), and before that was Community Relations Director for the Council on Racial Equality (CORE). He is the author of *Paraprofessionals and Their Performance.*

Frank Riessman is professor of educational sociology at New York University and the editor of *Social Policy.* He is the author of *The Culturally Deprived Child* and coauthored, with Alan Gartner, *Children Teach Children.*

Table 1 *Civilian Labor Force (in Millions)* [a]

	Total	Goods-Producing Workers	Services-Producing Workers
1940	49.3	25.6	24.5
1947	51.7	26.3	25.4
1968	80.7	28.9	51.8

[a] This trend is continuing with a projected ratio in 1980 of 32 goods-producing to 68 services-producing workers.

twenty-one are going to college, most of them to community colleges. In addition a service society vocabulary has developed, including words like alternative institutions, counterculture, encounter, human potential, personal liberation, and consciousness raising. But we need to go beyond phenotypic dimensions in order to understand the emerging service society and its potential directions.

At the simplest level the easiest way to characterize the emerging service society is in terms of the number of people employed providing services in proportion to those employed producing goods. The problem is that a diverse range of industries are classified as service production, for example: finance, insurance, real estate, personal services, retail and wholesale trade, transportation and communications as well as health, education, and welfare services. These industries have common elements, but there are crucial differences too.

Although there is value in thinking of the services as a whole, if only to note the broad shifts in the economy, a more refined grouping is necessary to our interest in the human services. Typically the number of people providing human services are underestimated in overall service sector statistics, as are the number of people consuming them. Stanley Moses observes that over 124 million people receive educational and training services, a figure that goes far beyond the usual notion of how many people are in school. His estimate includes people in correspondence courses, TV courses, adult education, etc. Moses notes that this figure has gone up considerably, from 47.1 million in 1940 to 101.0 million in 1965; the projected figure for 1976 is 149.4 million. Bertram Gross estimates that there are six million people involved in providing educational services, in contrast to the usual low estimate of approximately two million teachers.

The human service sector differs from the industrial service sector in ways that are vitally important to the character and quality of the service society. Human services are ostensibly initiated to produce benefit for the recipient; the character of these services is explicitly relational and interpersonal, creating a multiplier effect —producing an impact far beyond the numbers employed.

Thus teachers have the potential to affect huge numbers of people; so do counselors, social workers, psychiatrists, media people, ministers, professors, lawyers, doctors, health workers, day-care workers, family planning specialists.

Another important aspect of these services is that they afford access to other benefits; for example, education provides access to employment and thence to income. Furthermore, the public and the media give special attention to the service institutions, their employees, their consumers, and the issues that surround them, for example, community control. There has been an enormous expansion of what might be called "service consciousness."

Education, mental health, and day care are increasingly seen as basic necessities

Table 2 *Distribution of Employment within the Services-Producing Sector, 1870–1971* [a]

	1870	1900	1920	1940	1947	1971
Transportation and utilities	20%	23%	27%	17%	16%	9%
Trade, finance, real estate, insurance	28%	30%	31%	36%	42%	39%
Personal services	48%	42%	36%	40%	20%	25%
Government	4%	5%	6%	7%	22%	26%

[a] Daniel Bell, "Labor in the Post Industrial Society," *Dissent,* Winter 1972, p. 166.

of life, even as human rights. They are as important as consumer goods. Not only do increasing numbers of people produce the services—which incidentally are largely underestimated in the Gross National Product—but also great numbers are consuming these services as housewives, students, TV viewers.

CONSUMER-INTENSIVE SERVICES

Moreover, as Victor Fuchs points out, service activity tends frequently to involve the "consumer" in the "production" of the service. For example, the bank customer fills out a deposit slip as part of the production of the banking service; the supermarket customer carries his or her goods from the shelves to the checkout counter as a part of the production of the retail trade service.

This special consumer role is of even greater importance in those services of primary interest to us. Indeed just this greater consumer role makes services such as education and health so interesting. Not only is the student, for example, a consumer of the service, that is, learning, but also he or she is a factor in the production of it. Similarly the patient is a factor in the production of his or her own good health, which depends upon the history given to the doctor and willingness to follow the prescribed regimen. The consumer is thus a force of production and the human services are not only labor-intensive but also consumer-intensive.

In addition Margaret Mead calls attention to an increased consumer orientation of the services in a different way. She says there is a "revolt of all the people who are being done good to." She talks of pupils, patients, clients, prisoners all wanting a share of what's going on, and an end to the era "of the great number of professional people who knew best and did good." It may be premature to declare that an era of professional control is over (Daniel Bell says that the conflict between professional and consumer is the postindustrial service sector's equivalent of the industrial era's capitalist versus labor struggle, but there are varied signs of at least a greater, if not preeminent, consumer role.)

Some things are already happening to make the services more consumer-oriented, especially around the alternative institutions. In education the more child-centered free schools have had an impact serving numbers of affluent people, and to some extent they are beginning to influence the traditional educational structure through the emphasis on open classrooms.

In the mental health field encounter groups, sensitivity training, and growth centers have contributed to a new psychotherapy going beyond traditional mental health approaches. (Again not only are the numbers of people working and consuming in these areas significant, but also the effect on consciousness, particularly on the affluent middle class, is striking.)

In the field of health the people's health centers are very important, as are the self-run community day-care centers that are spreading all over the country, frequently outside of or on the fringe of the formal establishment.

Young people have been involved in service giving and service receiving in the area of tutoring and in a great variety of youth-serving endeavors—runaway houses, free clinics, hotlines, educational reform projects, vocational and educational clearing houses, peer counseling groups. All these efforts are concerned with providing services in new ways—less professional, less hierarchical, less expensive, involving a sense of community, including advocacy and the concern for social change, emphasizing consumer responsiveness and accessibility.

The women's movement, with its strong critique of many of the traditional services in the health and mental health fields, also has given rise to new women's health centers, counseling groups, feminist counselors, new abortion and sex education services.

Finally the greatly expanded employment of paraprofessionals has increased service giving and service receiving in the ghettos and among the poor via community mental health programs, neighborhood service centers, family planning centers, as well as in existing institutions such as schools and health agencies. Concomitant with this development there has been a greatly increased interest on the part of the poor in the quality of services, their relevance, accountability, vitality, and their control by the community.

It is interesting to note that the groups who have been most active during the 1960s in putting forward new service-related values and making new demands—the Third World minorities, the youth, the women—are all disproportionately employed (when they are employed) in service work, having been more excluded from manufacturing employment. Women are more often employed in the "demi-professions": social work, nursing, teaching; youth, because of their student credentials, have had more access to the human service occupations; and Blacks and other minorities have been employed at the lower levels of the service spectrum as hospital workers and technicians.

The role of the consumer is significant in this context too. Very often the major values that are espoused by the groups discussed above arise from their consumer as well as their producer roles—from students rather than youth in general, from welfare recipients rather than union members, from service receivers rather than professional service givers, from women's consciousness-raising groups rather than female factory workers. True, the values are spreading contagiously to groups in their worker roles, but the initial spark and the motion seem to come from these groups as consumers less well integrated and socialized in the work force.

The Marxist Ernest Mandel makes an interesting point regarding the role of consumption and its relation to alienation:

> . . . alienation is no longer purely economic but has become social and psychological in nature. For what is the motivation of a system for constantly extending needs beyond the limits of

what is rational? It is to create, purposely and deliberately, permanent and meretricious dissatisfactions in human beings. Capitalism would cease to exist if people were fully and healthily satisfied. The system must provoke continued artificial dissatisfaction in human beings because without that dissatisfaction the sales of new gadgets which are more and more divorced from genuine human needs cannot be increased.

Perhaps these dissatisfactions are a source of both consumerism and alienation, two extremely important features of the emerging service society. We begin to see, then, the very special role of the consumer in this society.

THE UNDERLYING DYNAMIC

Up until now we have talked about the phenomena of this emerging service society, not about how it came to be. Our emerging service society is predicated on the tremendously expanded productivity of industrial production; just as the industrial society was based upon the expansion of agricultural productivity. A major change in the forces of production has taken place over the last thirty years, bringing a vastly expanded productivity without the need for a proportionately expanded labor force.

The state became the instrument for dealing with the special problems produced by the new productivity. At least two basic problems had to be dealt with: the maintaining of purchasing power and the masking of increased unemployment and underemployment. Both problems were met by maintaining large numbers of people off the official labor market in colleges, on welfare, in the Army, on unemployment insurance, pensions, and social security, in the home, in hospitals, in prisons, in part-time jobs, in job training programs. This was all made possible by the huge surplus garnered from the industrial productivity. The society could afford the demands for more education, health services, social services, enabling it to absorb part of the unemployment and provide the consumer buying power that was needed. As a result the consumption of services has become as economically important as the consumption of products in this society.

The capitalist state powerfully conditions what occurs in the human service sectors. With the exception of services organized by the alternative institutions, practically all other human services are provided directly or indirectly by the state. Further the state contributes in very important ways to the education of the human power that provides the services.

As we have said, the service dimensions of our society overlap with and are dependent upon the industrial base. The service society is superimposed upon industrial capitalism. This is not an economic abstraction, but relates very powerfully to different groups of people employed in the various sectors and the respective values emanating from them. The old industrial sector still exists and is very strong, employing large numbers of industrial workers, managers, and technicians. These groups, the upper and middle portions of the working class, form the "old majority." They identify themselves with the old values of the puritan ethic: hard work, material gain, advancement, deferred gratification, and sublimation of sexual desires. They are preoccupied by a high degree of loyalty to the country and are opposed to permissiveness, pampering, and all sorts of liberation efforts. Religion, tradition, and authority are the virtues they expound. This old majority and its industrial and capitalist base have enormous power. The working-class segments of this old majority are most often employed in primary industry, relatively well-paid, highly organized, with generally stable employment.

SPECIAL CONTRADICTIONS OF THE SERVICE SOCIETY

There are a number of special contradictions produced by the service society. . . :

1. The development of large-scale bureaucracy, which in many ways is antithetical to the basic values and character of the human services.
2. The tremendous demand for credentials and the resulting oversupply of overcredentialed people.
3. The emergence of new values of autonomy and creativity with little concern for how the simple routine work of the society is to be accomplished.
4. The continued tremendous importance of the worker role and worker power, but the relative decline of the workplace as the point of motion.
5. Concomitantly the tremendous increase in consumer motion and leadership along with the limitations of consumer power.
6. The fact that the positive motion in the human services seems to derive largely from the alternative institutions and various unpaid activities rather than from the more professionalized formal structures.
7. The basic contradiction wherein the humane service-giving dimensions are constricted by their various uses by the society, state, and professions.

An illustration of this contradiction is the role of free schools and of the new more open education within the public schools. Traditionally organized schools, with their emphasis upon discipline, rigid curricula, hierarchy, and deferral of gratification, were appropriate socialization instruments for both the work of early industrial capitalism and the appropriate consumer roles therein. However, as we move into a new stage of capitalism, with a greater role for service work and related consumption, a different form of school organization is required to socialize future workers and consumers. Here the emphasis upon self-development, the affective, a more cooperative and nonhierarchical structure—themselves positive values—may well be the appropriate modalities for socializing workers who are going to be more engaged in human service work than in factory production, who are going to play increasingly important consumer roles. Used in this way, the radical potential of these values may well be denuded. Of course, the advocates of free schools and more open education are not the handmaidens of the society's managers; but their goals may well suit the new needs of the society.

In addition to these special contradictions, there is the ongoing conflict between the emerging service society and the existing industrial society, with its old majority, traditional values, and basic economic and political power. Meanwhile the service ethos and the progressive forces focused around it remain inchoate to date: weak, undeveloped, fragmented, lacking in self-consciousness.

WHITHER THE SERVICE SOCIETY?

Institutional tension, subcultural conflict—where will the emerging service society go? Will the polarization between the service groups and the old majority increase? How will the battle for the state be resolved? What will happen to the tendencies toward bureaucratization and bigness? What will happen to the alternative institutions? Will they grow, influencing the major structures, or will they remain as small experimental outlets of discontent for trying new forms and for maintaining the basic forms as they are? What will happen to the service crisis in our society? Will the services get better, leading to a real improvement in the quality of life? Will some of the fire and verve found in the alternative institutions find their way into the old services and old professions? Will we go beyond alienation to more positive perspectives? What will happen to all the people acquiring new credentials as a result of educational inflation? Will there be jobs for the enormous numbers acquiring a college degree? Will the rights that were recognized in the 1960s be internalized as part of basic life and practice?

What will happen to privatism, the retreatism of the young and the affluents? Where will the new politics go and the consumer politics of Nader, the ecology activists, the welfare recipients, the tenants, the consumer boycotters, the Alinsky people, and the ripper-offers? Will the new service society vanguards move toward a humanistic socialism or some new forms of egalitarianism or will they become a new elite? Will there be planning, direction, the reduction of waste, rational authority, decentralization, redistribution, controlled growth, or will anarchy, irrationality, competition—careless and unbounded growth—continue to flourish? Will the differences between male and female sex roles diminish? Will new reforms arise that begin to transform the system or will incrementalism prevail?

WHAT IS TO BE DONE?

For the service society to overcome its own contradictions and to move forward to a more advanced form of society, the following seem minimally necessary:

1. There is a need to go beyond one-issue demands and movements to develop an ideology, a theory, a vision, a perspective; there is a need to transcend the "now," the localism, the self.
2. There is a need to go beyond consumer issues and into the workplace and to win segments of the working class.

To some extent the consumer, particularly the underemployed consumer—the women, the youth, the minorities—may be the weak link in the neocapitalist structure. Robbed and alienated, on the one hand, and less well-integrated by the traditional industrial structures, on the other, they are therefore more open to different value influences.

3. The contradictions implied in transition and emergence have to be utilized.
4. The development of new priorities in national life will have to be undertaken, together with a continued fight for the state, for a public sector that actually serves the public.
5. It is clear, and Marcuse has said it very well, that personal and social liberation must be combined with political and economic liberation, that the "long march through the institutions," which is so necessary, must include the political and economic. Although consumer politics has an especially important contribution to make to future politics, it will have to be integrated with electoral politics and worker tactics.

The direction of the emerging service society is not predetermined, but it can go in an egalitarian, liberated direction.

However, if the new service ethos and consumer-sensitized values are extensively to influence American society in the 1970s, they will have to be consciously directed to the task. The women's movement will have to move much more toward working-class women and women on welfare. The youth will have to raise issues in relation to work alienation, not simply issues related to the consumer oriented quality of life. The Blacks and minorities will have to go beyond a go-it-alone orientation and, as James Boggs suggests, will have to take on the basic contradictions of our society.

CONCLUSION

We have noted four features of the service society:

1. The first basic characteristic of the service society is its political economy: the role of the welfare state; the various economic stabilizing functions of the services; the relationship of the new services to the "old" industrial base; and finally the contradiction wherein the human services struggle to be humane and beneficial, while being used to divert dissent and to socialize to new social, cultural, and economic forms.

2. A second basic characteristic of the service society is the tremendous new significance of the consumer and the fact that the services are consumer-intensive; that is, their productivity is uniquely dependent on consumer involvement.

In addition the role of the consumer takes on special force because under neocapitalism the consumer is typically exploited at the point of consumption rather than production, encouraged to be constantly dissatisfied with the products he is overstimulated to purchase—a dissatisfaction bordering on alienation that may spread into many areas, including what we call "consumer politics." It is extremely important to realize that the service society is based upon a highly advanced productivity in the industrial sector and allows large numbers of people, for great portions of their life, to remain outside the work force. These people are essentially hidden, not counted in the labor force, frequently disparaged. They are "dispensable" people as far as production is concerned, *but they are not dispensable as consumers.*

3. The service society, especially via the activity and consciousness of its leading groups—women, youth, and Third World minorities—directly relates to the issues of the quality of life, personal autonomy, and antihierarchical interaction, the importance of human rights, and the question of equality.

4. Finally the service society is characterized by enormous expansion in the production and consumption of the human services, both paid and unpaid. The most significant expansion is occurring in health, education, and welfare services and in government employment. The human services are but a part of the larger services sector, but a number of features magnify their importance. First, as their work is relational in character, they affect a broad consumer population—pupils, clients, patients. Second, vast media and public attention given to the human services has led to considerable "service consciousness." Third, in addition to those services offered in a formal setting by members of the work force, there are similar services provided outside of such settings.

We have, therefore, a series of overlapping phenomena, which together suggest a configuration of potential significance. The data are not altogether clear; emerging phenomena are commonly characterized by unclarity. However, movement along the lines outlined here is manifest and needs to be examined and harnessed in line with an increasingly clear vision of what kind of society we want the emerging service society to reflect.

POSTSCRIPT

Finally the service society and its fragmented vanguards have little awareness of overall directions; thus the new majority is slow to emerge. In fact the service society grows in the womb of a strong (not yet dying) industrial neocapitalist base that can and might accommodate most of the new demands without revolutionary changes.

41.

PORTRAIT OF A STRIVER

John P. Marquand

In an open-class society social mobility is possible but never assured. Even those who are well-educated and relatively well-advantaged find that making one's way up the bureaucratic ladder is not easy. Here J. P. Marquand has portrayed in colorful fiction the picture of a young man "trying to get ahead." The interpersonal relations and the private feelings of an upwardly mobile middle-class man are vividly depicted—the tensions, the insecurities, the delicate finesses, the need to watch every step, and the satisfactions. Graphically illustrated is the importance, if one is to achieve social-financial success in this type of situation, of having many skills other than those required for the mere accurate and rapid performance of one's assigned duties.

Shortly before the outbreak of the European war, Charles had begun taking the eight-thirty. This was a privilege that had raised him above the ruck of younger

Source: John P. Marquand, *Point of No Return* (Boston: Little, Brown, 1949), pp. 16, 17, 18, 19-21, 80-2, 101-2, 107-10.

John P. Marquand (1893–1960) was a well-known American novelist. He also wrote detective stories, short stories, and a play. Among his many works are *The Late George Apley* (awarded a Pulitzer Prize, 1938), *So Little Time, Stopover Tokyo,* and *Thank You Mr. Moto.*

men and of shopworn older ones who had to take the eight-two. It indicated to everyone that his business life had finally permitted him a certain margin of leisure. It meant that he was no longer one of the salaried class who had to be at his desk at nine.

The eight-thirty train was designed for the executive aristocracy, and once Mr. Guthrie Mayhew, not one of the Mayhews who lived on South Street, not George Mayhew, but Guthrie Mayhew, who was president of the Hawthorn Hill Club and also president of Mayhew Brothers at 86 Broadway, had even spoken of getting an eight-thirty crowd together who would agree to occupy one of those club cars with wicker chairs and card tables and a porter, to be attached to the eight-thirty in the morning and again to the five-thirty in the afternoon.

. . . . .

Charles remembered Mr. Mayhew's idea vividly, if only because it had come up at the same time that Mr. Burton had suggested that Charles call him Tony.

Charles could still recall the glow he had felt on this occasion and the sudden moment of elation. Mr. Burton had been shy about it in a very nice way, as an older man is sometimes shy. Charles remembered that Mr. Burton had fidgeted with his onyx pen stand and that first Mr. Burton had called him "feller." It had all happened one evening when they had stayed late talking over the Catlin estate, which was one of the largest accounts in the trust department.

. . . . .

"Now you may remember," Mr. Burton had said, "that Mrs. Burton and I took a little trip in 1933. You hadn't been with us long then, but I don't believe that you or anyone else will forget how tense things were in 1933, and now and then I found I was getting a little taut, so when things eased up I decided to go away somewhere to get a sense of perspective. That was when Mrs. Burton and I went to Bagdad. You ought to go there sometime."

. . . . .

The first morning he and Mrs. Burton had gone to the museum to see the treasure from Ur, parts of which looked like something in a case at Cartier's. You got a lot out of travel if you kept your eyes open. There had been a man in the museum, a queer sort of British archaeologist, who showed him some mud bricks that were actually parts of an account book. When you got used to them, you could see how they balanced their figures; and on one brick, believe it or not, there was even an error in addition, preserved there through the centuries. This had meant a great deal to Mr. Burton.

That clerical error in mud had given him an idea for one of the best speeches he had ever written, his speech before the American Bankers' Association in 1936 at the Waldorf-Astoria. Mr. Burton had opened a drawer and had pulled out a deckle-edged pamphlet.

"Take it home and read it if you have the time," he said, "I dashed it off rather hurriedly but it has a few ideas. It starts with that mistake in addition."

The pamphlet was entitled *The Ancient Art of Banking, by Anthony Burton, President, the Stuyvesant Bank, Delivered before the American Bankers' Association, May 1936.*

"Why, thanks very much, sir," Charles had said, "I certainly will read it." It was not the time to say that he had read the speech already or that for years he had made a point of reading all Mr. Burton's speeches.

"Look here, feller," Mr. Burton said, and he had blushed when he said "feller," "why not cut out this sir business? Why not just call me Tony?"

That was in 1941 but Charles still remembered his great joy and relief, with the relief uppermost, and that he could hardly wait to hear what Nancy would say.

"You know, Charles," Mr. Burton had continued, "Guthrie Mayhew and I have quite an idea. We're going to get hold of Tommy Mapes on the New Haven and see if he can't get us a special car on the eight-thirty. How about getting aboard? My idea is to call it the Crackerbarrel."

"Why, thanks," Charles had said. "I'd like to very much, Tony."

He had worked late that night and he could not remember what train he had taken home, but Nancy had been asleep when he got there.

"Nance," he said, "wake up. I've got something to tell you. Burton's asked me to call him Tony." And Nancy had sat bolt upright in her twin bed.

"Start at the beginning," Nancy had said. "Exactly how did it happen, and don't leave out anything."

They must have talked for a long while, there in the middle of the night. Nancy had known what it meant because she had worked downtown herself.

"Now wait," she had said. "Let's not get too excited. Who else calls him Tony?"

"I don't think anyone else does," Charles had told her, "except the officers, and old Jake when he speaks of him."

"Who's old Jake?" Nancy asked.

It surprised him that Nancy did not know, for she usually kept everything straight, but when he told her that old Jake was a day watchman in the vault who had been there when Mr. Burton had first started at the bank, Nancy had remembered.

"Darling, we ought to have a drink of something, shouldn't we?" she said, but it was pretty late for a drink. "Darling, I knew it would happen sometime. I'm pretty proud of you, Charley."

It was only a week later that they found out that Mr. Burton had also asked Roger Blakesley to call him Tony and they never could find out whom Mr. Burton had asked first.

. . . . .

Though you seldom talked of salaries at the Stuyvesant, your social status was obvious from the position of your desk. Charles occupied one of the two flat mahogany desks that stood in a sort of no man's land between the rolltop desks of the officers and the smaller flattops of lesser executives and secretaries crowding the floor of the bank outside the cages. A green rug extended from the officers' desks, forming a neat and restricted zone that just included Charles's desk and the one beside it which was occupied by Roger Blakesley. Charles could see both their names, Mr. Blakesley and Mr. Gray, in silver letters, and he was pleased to see that he had got there first from the eight-thirty, a minute or two ahead of Roger and Mr. Burton and ahead of everyone else near the windows.

Mr. Burton's desk, which had the best light, was opened already and so was that of Mr. Stephen Merry, the oldest vice-president, and so were all the others except one. This was the desk of Arthur Slade, the youngest vice-president of the Stuyvesant, who had died in a plane accident when returning from the West Coast six months before. The closed desk still gave Charles a curious feeling of incompleteness and a mixed sense of personal gain and loss because he had been more friendly with Arthur Slade than with anyone else in the Stuyvesant—but then you had to die sometime. Once Arthur Slade had sat at Charles's own place but that was before Mr. Walter Harry, who had been president when Charles had first come to the bank, had died of an embolism and everyone had moved like players on bases—Burton to

Harry, Merry to Burton, Slade to the vacant rolltop—and so on down to Charles himself. The Stuyvesant was decorously accustomed to accident and death and now it was moving time again and it was so plain where one of two persons might be moving next that it was embarrassing. Any observing depositor and certainly everyone employed in the bank, right up to the third floor, must have known that either Mr. Blakesley or Mr. Gray would move to Arthur Slade's desk by the window. Undoubtedly they were making side bets out in back as Charles used to himself when he had first come there from Boston. Undoubtedly the clerks and the secretaries and the watchmen had started some sort of pool.

. . . . .

Tony Burton looked very fit, in spite of his white hair and his rolltop desk which both conspired to place him in another generation. For years Charles had accepted him as a model willingly, even though he realized that everyone else above a certain salary rating also used Tony Burton as a perfect sartorial example, and he was pretty sure that Tony himself was conscious of it. Charles never rebelled against this convention because Tony had everything one should expect to find in a president of a first-rate bank. It was amusing but not ridiculous to observe that all the minor executives in the Stuyvesant, as well as the more ambitious clerks, wore conservative double-breasted suits like Tony Burton's at the same time allowing undue rigidity to break out into pin stripes and herringbones, just like Tony Burton's. They all visited the barber once a week. They all had taken up golf, whether they liked it or not, and most of them wore the same square type of wrist watch and the same stainless steel strap. They had adopted Tony Burton's posture and his brisk, quick step and even the gently vibrant inflection of his voice. In fact once at one of those annual dinners for officers and junior executives when everyone said a few words and got off a few local jokes about the bank, Charles had brought the matter up when he had been called upon to speak. Speaking was always an unpleasant ordeal with which he had finally learned to cope successfully largely from imitating Tony. He remembered standing up and waiting for silence, just as Tony waited, with the same faint smile and the same deliberate gaze.

"I should like to drink a toast," he had said, "not to our president but to everyone who tries to look like him. When I walk, I always walk like Tony, because Tony knows just how to walk; and when I talk, I always talk like Tony, because Tony knows just how to talk; and when I dress, I always dress like Tony, in a double-breasted suit. But no matter how I try, I cannot be like Tony. I can never make myself sufficiently astute."

It was the one time in the year, at that annual dinner, when you could let yourself go, within certain limits, and Tony Burton had loved it. He had stood up and waited for the laughter to die down and then he had spoken easily, with just the right pause and cadence. He had said that there were always little surprises at these dinners. He had never realized, for instance, that there could be a poet in the trust department, but poetry had its place. Poetry could teach lessons that transcended pedestrian prose.

"And I'm not too old to learn," Tony Burton had said, "and I'm humbly glad to learn. Sometimes on a starlit night I've wondered what my function was in the Stuyvesant. I'm very glad to know it is that of a clothing dummy. It's a patriotic duty. It's what they want us to be, in Washington."

That was back in 1941, but Tony Burton

still had the same spring to his step, the same unlined, almost youthful face, and the same florid complexion; and he had the same three pictures on his desk, the first of Mrs. Burton in their garden, the second of their three girls standing in profile, like a flight of stairs, and the third of his sixty-foot schooner, the *Wanderlust* (the boat you were invited on once every summer), with Tony Burton in his yachting cap standing at the wheel. Time had marched on. All of the girls had come out and all were married, and the *Wanderlust* had been returned by the navy in deplorable condition, but Tony Burton had no superficial scars.

No matter how well Charles might know him, in that half-intimate, half-formal business relationship, he still had a slight feeling of diffidence and constraint. It was the same feeling that one had toward generals in wartime or perhaps toward anyone with power over one. There was always a vestige of a subservient desire to please and to be careful. You had to know how far to go, how long to laugh, and how to measure every speech.

. . . . .

Sycamore Park had been developed in 1938 on the forty-acre grounds of an old estate and the subdivision had been excellently managed by the local real estate firm of Merton and Pease. As Mr. Merton had said, it was a natural, and he had never understood why someone had not dreamed it up long ago—not too far from the shopping center and the trains, and yet in the neighborhood of other larger places. Every place had its own acre, and no house was to be constructed for a cost of less than thirty thousand dollars. It would have been wiser, perhaps, never to have gone there but to have bought a smaller place.

It would have been wiser, easier, and much safer. He had not at that time been moved up in the trust department and in 1939 all he had was twenty thousand dollars in savings, part of which was in paid-up life insurance. He could never analyze all the urges that made him lay everything on the line in order to live on a scale he could not immediately afford, discounting the possibilities of illness or accident and relying on possibilities of promotion. He only remembered having had an irrational idea that time was of the essence, that he would always stay on a certain business level if he did not take some sort of action, and Nancy too, had shared that feeling.

. . . . .

Not since he had left Clyde had Charles ever felt as identified with any community as he had since he had been asked to join the Oak Knoll Country Club. They were in a brave new world involving all sorts of things, of which he had scarcely dreamed after they had moved to Sycamore Park. This cleavage between past and present, Charles realized, was a part of a chain reaction that started, of course, with one of those shake-ups in the bank. Charles had known that he had been doing well. He had known for a year or so, from the way Mr. Merry and Mr. Burton and particularly Mr. Slade had been giving him little jobs to do, that something was moving him out of the crowd of nonentities around him. He was aware also that Walter Gibbs in the trust department was growing restless. There had been a premonition of impending change, just like the present tension. One day Walter Gibbs had asked him out to lunch and had told him, confidentially, that he was going to move to the Bankers' Trust and that he was recommending Charles for his place. Charles was not surprised, because he had been a good assistant to Walter Gibbs, and he was glad to remember that he had been loyal to his chief, ever since the old days in the statistical department.

"Charley," Walter Gibbs had said, "a lot of people around here have been out to knife me. You could have and you never did, and I appreciate it, Charley."

He had known, of course, for some time that Walter Gibbs was not infallible, that he was fumbling more and more over his decisions and depending more and more on Charles's support, but Walter had taught him a lot.

"Slade keeps butting in," Walter had said, and then he went on to tell the old story which Charles had often heard of conflicting personalities and suspicions. Walter had felt that frankly he was more eligible for a vice-presidency than Slade, and the truth was he had never been the same after Arthur Slade had been selected. "If they don't like you enough to move you up," Walter had said, "it's time to get out, Charley."

God only knew where Walter Gibbs was now. He was gone like others with whom you worked closely once and from whom you were separated. Walter Gibbs was gone with his little jokes and his bifocal glasses and the stooping shoulders that had given him a deceptively sloppy appearance. He was gone with his personality that would never have permitted him to be a vice-president of anything.

Charles was ready, not surprised, when Tony Burton, though of course he did not call him Tony then, had called him downstairs and had asked him if he knew what was coming, that he had been with them for quite a while and that they had all had an eye on him ever since he had done that analysis on chain stores. Even if you were prepared for such a change there was still an unforgettable afterglow, and an illuminating sense of unrealized potentiality. It was a time to be more careful than ever, to measure the new balance of power, and not to antagonize the crowd that you were leaving. One day, it seemed to Charles, though of course it was not one day, he was living in a two-family house in Larchmont that smelled of cauliflower in the evenings, stumbling over the children's rollerskates and tricycles, taking the eight-three in the morning, keeping the budget on a salary of six thousand a year. Then in a day, though of course it was not a day, they were building at Sycamore Park. The children were going to the Country Day School. They were seeing their old friends, but not so often. Instead they were spending Sundays with Arthur Slade. There was a maid to do the work. He was earning eleven thousand instead of six, and he was an executive with a future. New people were coming to call; all sorts of men he had hardly known were calling him Charley. It was a great crowd in Sycamore Park and he was asked to join the Oak Knoll Country Club. They were a great crowd in Sycamore Park.

It would have made quite a story—if it could have been written down—how all those families had come to Sycamore Park. They had all risen from a ferment of unidentifiable individuals whom you might see in any office. They had all once been clerks or salesmen or assistants, digits of what was known as the white-collar class. They had come from different parts of the country and yet they all had the same intellectual reactions because they had all been through much the same sorts of adventures on their way to Sycamore Park. They all bore the same calluses from the competitive struggle, and it was still too early for most of them to look back on that struggle with complacency. They were all in the position of being insecurely poised in Sycamore Park—high enough above the average to have gained the envy of those below them, and yet not high enough so that those above them might not easily push them down. It was still necessary to balance and sometimes even to push a little in Sycamore Park, and there was always the possibility that something might go wrong—for example, in the recession that everyone was saying was due to crop up in the next six or eight months. It was consoling to think that they were no longer in the group that would catch it first, or they would not have been at Sycamore Park—but then they were not so far above it. They were not quite indispensable. Their own turn might come if the recession were too deep. Then no more Sycamore Park, and no more dreams of leaving it for something bigger—only memories of having been there once. It was something to think about as you went over your checkbook on clear, cold winter nights, but it was nothing ever to discuss. It was never wise or lucky to envisage failure. It was better to turn on the phonograph—and someday you would get one that would change the records automatically. It was better to get out the ice cubes and have some friends in and to talk broad-mindedly about the misfortunes of others. It was better to go to the club on Tuesday evenings and to talk about something else—and that was where Charles Gray was going.

42.

THE LOWER CLASS AND THE FUTURE OF INEQUALITY

Sally Bould Van Til and Jon Van Til

Though an equalitarian and demcratic ideology is part of most Americans' cultural heritage, common usage reflects a pragmatic and informal social class system: "middle class" is how most Americans seem to prefer to characterize themselves. Though "upper class" and "lower class" designations are rarely if ever used voluntarily to identify one's own class position, the existence of positions above and below the middle are implicit even though undefined. But the social scientist, unlike the lay person, must define terms objectively and use them rigorously if scientific knowledge is to be gained. The reader is taken behind the scenes in the following selection and given an example of how sociologists are today dealing with a significant and inevitably continuing theoretical

Source: Sally Bould Van Til and Jon Van Til, *Growth and Change: A Journal of Regional Development* 4, no. 1 (January 1973): 10–16.

Sally Bould Van Til teaches sociology at the University of Delaware. She has done work in the areas of industrial economics as well as in stratification and mobility.

Jon Van Til teaches in the department of sociology and anthropology at Swarthmore College. He has done work in the areas of urban and political sociology.

and methodological problem of great difficulty and complexity: how are "the poor . . . different from the rich," and if there are differences between lower and upper class members and groups, why do they exist? We as editors emphatically agree with the authors' position that "coming to grips with the broad policy implications of the empirical evidence" is entirely proper for social scientists.

It is a recurrent problem in social science to measure and evaluate the degree to which the poor are different from the rich and to explain why this may be so. Despite Jenny's assertion in *The Threepenny Opera* that "first comes the belly, then come the morals," many social scientists in the 1960s tended to approach the study of the poor with the hypothesis of a *culture of poverty* as the dominant point of reference. In this article, we review this literature and argue that social scientists have sufficiently advanced their research to support two major contentions. These contentions are: (1) that neither of the two most common perspectives adopted regarding the lower class and its culture has proved to be empirically accurate or theoretically useful; and (2) that recent evidence points to a third perspective, *adaptive drift,* as most adequate in dealing with the problem.

Neither of these points is original, but both ought to be stated forcefully, for they reflect genuine advances in social science over the past decade. Despite recent criticism of the appropriateness of social scientists studying the behavior of the poor, the answer does not lie in denying the legitimacy of such research, but rather in coming to grips with the broad social policy implications of the empirical evidence.

TWO COMMON PERSPECTIVES

The two positions most commonly adopted regarding the orientation of the lower class are those of the culture of poverty and the *blocked opportunity* or *situational* hypotheses. A brief identification of each position, as well as substantiation of the contention that many social scientists have yet to go beyond these positions, may be provided by quoting from a newly edited textbook put together from the work of about fifty eminent sociologists.

> Although virtually all sociologists agree that the behaviors of different classes have both cultural and situational sources, there is considerable disagreement on the relative importance of the two. Many emphasize the cultural sources and speak of "social class subcultures" or of a "culture of poverty." The latter is believed to be a way of life guided by values transmitted from one generation to another, a collective adaptation of the poor to their adverse conditions. . . . Other observers believe that the behaviors attributed to the culture of poverty are actually individual responses to the conditions of economic deprivation and social dishonor. According to this point of view, the values of the poor are basically the same as those of higher strata; however, because of situational restrictions, they do not result in the same overt behaviors.

The authors then outline how each perspective interprets lower-class family life, noting the importance of the differences in policy implied by each view.

> If the situational view is correct, once the social environment of the poor is changed, their behavior will quickly come to resemble that of the solid middle classes. . . . If, however, there is a culture of poverty, many of the poor will not respond readily or at all to increased opportunities and other situational changes. Rather, the values of the poor that are maladaptive in the long run will have to be extinguished, or the society's guardians will have to accept the fact that American middle-class values are perhaps, after

all, not the highest point of moral evolution, that other values may be equally suitable to those who hold them.

Our first contention is that the issue, thus framed, presents a false dilemma, for neither of these two commonly held perspectives on the problem is satisfactory. Despite the attractiveness of the culture of poverty hypothesis to some social scientists and the widespread attention it received from its statement by Oscar Lewis, very little empirical evidence has lent it support. Rejection of the culture of poverty view, however, does not imply acceptance of the situational, blocked opportunity view, which has also proved to be less than adequate.

The Culture of Poverty

The evidence refuting the culture of poverty hypothesis is most clear and comes from careful ethnographic and statistical studies of the behavior and attitudes of the poor. Foremost among the latter is Kriesberg's study of fatherless families among public housing residents, in which he searches exhaustively for cultural differences between his sample of mothers in poverty and a largely near-poor sample of parents in whole families. Neither a homogeneous way of life nor the perpetuation of poverty-specific values is found by Kriesberg. Rather, the poor and the near-poor evince similar high levels of housing aspirations, desire to work, encouragement of achievement and autonomy, and achievement aspiration for their children. The samples differ mainly in the opportunities available to them for jobs, housing, and association with potential neighbors in the various communities in which the projects are located.

Ethnographic Studies. Similar conclusions emerge from the major ethnographic studies of black lower-class communities, most notably those of Liebow, Hannerz, and Valentine. Liebow rejects the cultural view in favor of the situational hypothesis.

> We do not have to see the problem in terms of breaking into a puncture proof circle, of trying to change values, of disrupting the lines of communication between parent and child so that parents cannot make children in their own image, thereby transmitting their culture inexorably, ad infinitum. . . . Of much greater importance for the possibilities of change . . . is the fact . . . that the son goes out and independently experiences the same failures, in the same areas, and for much the same reasons as his father.

Hannerz expands his analysis beyond the street corner and discovers four major forms of adaptation to ghetto life, among which the "mainstreamers" behave in a fashion which directly refutes almost every contention of the culture of poverty position. Charles A. Valentine, in his ongoing research in Blackston (a large-city neighborhood), reports discovering a greater pattern of institutional participation than the culture of poverty theorist would expect.

Research among Mexican Americans has similarly found the culture of poverty view inadequate. Burma notes that while "present-orientation" is common in this cultural context, it is "closely related to what the parent Anglo culture calls fatalism, the feeling that one's destiny is not in one's own hands." Studies of the Puerto Rican poor in New York also provide little support for a hard culture of poverty hypothesis. Sexton finds the Puerto Rican school child proud of his ethnic heritage and achieving well through the first few years of school. Padilla finds that recent migrants on welfare do not hide that fact, but speak openly of the reasons for dependence on aid. By doing so, they make it clear that they were forced to receive welfare aid, that they had no choice but to take it. And Oscar Lewis, the misreading of whom did much to popularize the concept, noted that "the culture of poverty is both an adaptation and a reaction of the poor to their marginal position in a class-stratified, highly individuated, capitalistic society."

SURVEY RESEARCH. Survey research among the poor has also lent little evidence to support the culture of poverty position. With an area probability sample of 1,400 persons, Rokeach and Parker examined differences in the values held by the poor and middle class. Differences in values did exist, but not in areas generally cited as evidence for a self-perpetuating poverty subculture. An exhaustive search of the literature led Rossi and Blum to conclude, similarly, that if one means by the culture of poverty something more than the fact that the poor are different with respect to some behavioral indicators and show higher rates of a wide variety of disabilities, "then the empirical evidence would not support such a view."

Blocked Opportunity

If the culture of poverty hypothesis must be rejected, what of the situational hypothesis? We contend that it too is inadequate, although it is evident that behavior is greatly influenced by what Schorr called the "nonculture of poverty." The extent of existing inequality and the limitations it places upon the poor in achieving the economic security required to support mainstream life-styles are overwhelming. Indeed, pervasive economic insecurity, coupled with severely limited opportunities to achieve economic security, appears to provide sufficient explanation for many of the behavior patterns which have been seen as characteristic of a culture of poverty.

CONCEPTUALIZED REALITY. Dissatisfaction with the blocked opportunity model is not due to any question about the reality of such limitations, but rather derives from the failure of the model, as it is often conceptualized, to recognize fully the complex nature of human beings in social life. It is a basic part of the human condition to develop cultural patterns that facilitate adaptation to external situations. Even in one of the most brutal cases of external limitation, the American experience with slavery, cultural forms are now acknowledged to have emerged which provided the basis for interaction. Such patterns have been termed survival techniques, but their essence is neither technical nor rational, but rather affective. The will to survive is not simply an existential decision, but one which rests as well upon the individual's attachment to an ongoing human community, and the basis of that community interaction is cultural. Culture, as Hannerz argues, is itself delimited by environment, an important part of which is social.

POLICY IMPLICATIONS. On a similar basis we criticize the policy implications of the situational hypothesis. The poor do not live in a cultural vacuum and hence will not react mechanically to new opportunity structures. Past lifeways developed within the stark options of poverty cannot be shed quickly. Early socialization, no matter how limited the environment, is the process of becoming human, and it is not only unrealistic but also arrogant to assume that such socialization is a superficial process which can be swept away by new structural forms.

The poor will alter their behavior when their options increase; the mass media and the public schools provide for their socialization to patterns not found in ghetto streets. But it is doubtful that their past experience will cease to play a role in their behavior. Claude Brown's insight, when he returned to Harlem and became involved in a fracas, is pertinent. "Damn, I thought I had grown out of all that sort of thing. I thought I had grown out of hitting anybody in the street. I thought I had grown out of putting the blame on somebody else. I guess I hadn't." Though evidence is slim in sociological studies, it does point to the persistence of some past behavior patterns among those upwardly mobile from the ranks of the lower class.

ADAPTIVE DRIFT

That the poor, living in poverty, do not respond mechanically to opportunity, as Liebow suggested, is the basic revision of the blocked opportunity model suggested by Hannerz at the end of his ghetto study. The argument was first persuasively stated in Rodman's seminal essay on "The Lower-Class Value Stretch." There Rodman noted that "the lower-class person, without abandoning the general values of the society, develops an alternative set of values. . . . The resultant is a stretched value system with a low degree of commitment to all the values within the range, including the dominant, middle-class values."

The Heterogeneous Poor

Rodman's perspective was substantiated by his own empirical work and by that of S. M. Miller, Frank Riessman, Martin Rein, Pamela Roby, and their associates. Working in Trinidad, Rodman concluded that the lower-class family seeks solutions to its problems by both value-stretching and pragmatic responses. Lower-class individuals are seen as "circumstance-oriented," though their values are "not altogether determined by the circumstances of lower-class life." Miller, Riessman, and Seagull reviewed this literature and found little evidence to support the hypothesized inability of the poor to defer gratification; Miller and Rein summarized their findings as follows.

(1) Great variation occurs among the poor.
(2) There are important differences from many middle-class patterns. . . .
(3) Although many of these patterns and orientations are carried from generation to generation, contemporary influences are important in maintaining them.
(4) Some positive elements of strength, of coping, exist as well as negative ones that make it difficult to handle life.
(5) Many of the poor are open to change, to taking advantage of new possibilities. But in offering new possibilities, their experiences and orientations must be considered.

Hannerz' work documents how, in the lower-class milieu, basic modes of behavior and outlook develop and become shared. They are learned from experience and maintained both by experience and by interaction. These modes of behavior vary from individual to individual, mixing mainstream and ghetto-specific adaptations. The model is probabilistic, not rigidly deterministic.

> Exposure thus gives practically every ghetto dweller opportunities to familiarize himself with a range of modes of behavior and combinations of modes of behavior, from mainstream-oriented to ghetto-specific ways. It is obvious, however, that man is not a mindless cultural automaton. . . . [A cultural] repertoire to some measure constitutes adaptive potential. . . . As far as the individual's evaluation of a mode of behavior is concerned, it is likely that the more often it occurs in his milieu, the greater will be his readiness to find it not only convenient but also morally appropriate.

Current research by Charles Valentine appears to be confirming much of Hannerz' research, as well as Valentine's earlier contention that neither the cultural nor the situational view was adequate and that a third model involving a "heterogeneous subsociety with variable, adaptive subcultures" was required. Valentine's field research in Blackston has led to the preliminary finding that "the most significant cultural similarities and differences of Blackston are associated with ethnic identity or racial status and not with class lines that would indicate a 'culture of poverty.' "

Biculturalism

Elsewhere, Valentine has argued that a bicultural model is more applicable to the study of Afro-American behavior than either deficit or difference models. He notes that many black Americans "are simultaneously enculturated and socialized in two different ways of life," learning and practicing "both mainstream cultures and ethnic cultures at the same time." This biculturalism has also been noted by Burma in his study of Mexican Americans, as well as Padilla and Lewis in their research on Puerto Ricans in New York. Those studied demonstrated a mixing of traits common to the Spanish-speaking subculture and the subculture of poverty. Much of the overall adaptation, Burma further notes, falls in "areas of indifference to or mesh[es] well with the middle-class Anglo culture and hence [is] subject to no normative stress." Thus, the biculturalism of the black and Mexican American poor appears to be demonstrated along both class and ethnic lines, mixing on the one hand middle-class with lower-class behavior, and on the other ethnic and core cultural adaptations. Separating the class and ethnic factors will require a series of studies in varying lower-class milieux, especially among the infrequently studied native white poor.

Adaptive drift, however, differs from biculturalism in a manner similar to Weber's distinction between caste and ethnic segregation: "ethnic coexistences . . . allow each ethnic community to consider its own honor as the highest one." A bicultural individual obtains in his ethnic identity a sense of dignity and legitimacy which is independent of the mainstream system of stratification. For the poor, however, "the belief in their own specific 'honor' " becomes problematic precisely because of their position at the bottom of the system of stratification. Their ambiguous culture represents an attempt to sustain some aspect of self-respect and legitimacy in spite of their position at the tail end of an unequal distribution of class, status, and power. Poverty-specific patterns, distinct from ethnic or racial differences, arise as a result of this situation. As Lewis has indicated, such conditions are especially favorable in industrialized and industrializing countries with predominantly capitalistic economic systems.

The unequal distribution of rewards is legitimized in capitalistic systems by the achievement ethic which implies that one gets what one deserves. Even without full equality of opportunity, however, this ethic is used to justify the present treatment of the poor as marginal misfits. It is the ideology of the *open class* system which on the one hand provides for the socialization of the poor into mainstream culture, while being used on the other hand to justify their unequal treatment by mainstream institutions. These are the conditions which promote behavior patterns described in our concept of adaptive drift. Unless they see themselves as upwardly mobile, the poor cannot risk total commitment to a system of values which defines them as deserving of less than their fellow human beings. There must be an alternative design for living which provides a safety valve for their feelings of self-worth and self-respect, one which they can drift into and out of as circumstances shift.

The Adaptive Drift Model

We suggest that the phrase *adaptive drift* catches the flavor of this lower-class style. The concept of adaptive drift combines the notions of biculturalism, openness, and adaptation to social-environmental circumstances. By "drift," David Matza referred to the ability of the delinquent to move from the criminal to the conventional milieu, physically, socially, and morally, with a minimum of personal disorganization. The process of drift is not a mechanistic or calculated response. Furthermore, it is one which is circumscribed by the larger social environment. The lower-class drifter is not fully bicultural because he cannot risk commitment to either mode—not to the mainstream one because he is not likely to be accepted as a full participant, and not to the poverty one because it lacks much of the reward provided by the larger system. Thus, the lower-class person remains open.

Lower-class Values. Adaptive drift encompasses Rodman's view that lower-class individuals have a wider range of values than middle-class individuals but also possess a lower degree of commitment to any of those values. "As a consequence, they are more open to the possibility of acts that are defined as delinquent by the official representatives of society." Rainwater, similarly, sees a distinctive pattern of lower-class behavior, both existential and evaluative.

> Lower class subculture, then, can be regarded as the historical creation of persons who are disinherited by their society, persons who have adapted to the twin realities of disinheritance and limited functional autonomy for their group by developing existential perspectives on social reality (including the norms and practices of the larger society) that allow them to stay alive and not lose their minds, that allow them some modicum of hope about a reasonably gratifying life, and that preserve for many the slim hope that somehow they may be able to find admittance for themselves and their children to the larger society.

Like Hannerz, Rainwater does not want wholly to abandon the concept of lower-class culture. A lower-class culture exists as a reality for most of the poor, together with a core culture.

Lower-class Behavior. The concept of adaptive drift provides a perspective on lower-class behavior that indicates its situational variability and the retention of learned cultural modes during situational change, and leads to the prediction of a variety of personal and group adaptations in times of increasing affluence. It suggests that in static poverty the poor possess many bicultural traits which they retain in times of change, developing new subcultural forms from experience, much like Stonequist's "marginal man." Thus a tension is established between the self-definition of the lower class and the definition of their behavior applied by the "moral entrepreneurs" of a predominantly middle-class society. The poor are "signified," but they also participate in their own definition.

This marginal status of the poor is clearly demonstrated by examining their dealings with the primary institutions of society outside the family which affect its critical functioning, particularly political, economic, welfare, and educational institutions. These structures both provide the poor with mainstream values and limit them to opportunity structures that do not permit the realization of those values. Further, this gap is recognized by the creation of mainstream definitions that characterize the poor as lazy, undeserving, or subhuman. The poor react to this situation by seeking to adjust to the double bind in which they find themselves—proved inadequate by the denial of opportunity to achieve mainstream status, and confirmed inadequate by their signification as shiftless and undeserving. Thus, it is the interaction of their marginal opportunity with their uneven treatment that leads them to create self-images that are necessarily variable with situational opportunity and the definition of that situation by their peers. They learn the mainstream values, but at the same time learn to be distrustful and cynical, developing alternative values to deal with their marginal status. They remain ever ready to shift their definition of a situation, ever adapting to a world that proves itself mercurial, inconsistent, and usually intractable to purposes they set for themselves.

THE FUTURE OF INEQUALITY

Thus, as the situational model contends, the behavior of the poor is fettered by the limited nature of their opportunities. And, as the culture of poverty hypothesis contends, the poor do develop and adopt values and norms peculiar to their situation. But, as the culture of poverty model does not permit, the evidence is more than clear that the poor possess in their behavioral repertories many mainstream values and normative orientations. And, as the situational model does not recognize, they also develop modes of evaluating reality that cannot be expected to disappear when opportunities change.

Thus, we suggest that there is little reason to believe that should inequalities be reduced, the expoor will behave just as the present middle masses do, or will. The behavior of the poor in the adaptive drift model does not simply reflect an inadequacy of income, nor the lack of opportunity, but rather is the consequence of their marginal position at the bottom of the stratification hierarchy. In the marketplace, they are unable to contribute sufficient net marginal productivity to make their labor worth buying at a decent wage. Furthermore, lacking any substantial claim to status or access to power, they are better able to perceive the importance of these factors in the everyday operation of the social order around them. Unlike Glazer, we are not surprised that the increasing level of welfare payments in New York City has failed to alter substantially the behavior of the poor. Even if we grant the unlikely assumption that these increased payments are adequate as subsistence income, they do not affect the basic conditions of life at the bottom. The poor still pay more for what they get; the housing market and the job market remain the same. The schools to which they send their children have not changed, and their access to good health care is as poor as always. They still face the capriciousness of the welfare department, manipulated by reactionary state legislators. Furthermore they have little power, as always, to effect any changes in these circumstances.

Income equalization as proposed by Rainwater is not sufficient, for equality must be achieved on the other dimensions of stratification as well. The behavior of the poor which reflects their poverty, not their ethnicity, is unlikely to change unless a radically more equal society is created along all dimensions. Lower-class persons have learned, through bitter experience, to perceive privilege; the elimination of privilege in one dimension is not likely to blind them to its persistence in other dimensions. They will reserve their commitment to mainstream values and preserve their own designs for living until the larger society provides not just equality of opportunity but also equality of results.

43.

THE WHITE MAN'S THEORY OF COLOR CASTE

Gunnar Myrdal

Americans pride themselves on the conviction that this country permits social and economic advancement by able and energetic persons. A society which provides for such mobility is said to have an "open-class" system: one in which persons may move freely up, or down, within the socioeconomic hierarchy. At the other extreme is a "closed-class," or "caste," system. The essence of the caste system is that a person's status is completely determined by biological inheritance, or family identification, and that one is prevented from crossing caste lines

Source: Gunnar Myrdal, *An American Dilemma* (New York: Harper & Row, 1944), pp. 57–67.

Gunnar Myrdal is professor of economics at the University of Stockholm in Sweden. He worked with the United Nations on the Economic Commission from 1947 to 1957. His study of the American Negro for the Carnegie Corporation resulted in the classic *An American Dilemma*. Among his other books are *Population: A Problem for Democracy, Economic Theory and Under-Developed Regions,* and *Asian Drama.*

through marriage or by any other means. In his famous study of the black in America, Myrdal shows that some aspects of caste are characteristic of our society, despite popular beliefs to the contrary. In this excerpt, based on data collected about 1940, Myrdal presents the white man's attitudes concerning antiamalgamation—attitudes which have helped to maintain separate black and white social systems in America. These separate systems and the attitudes on which they are based not only persist to this day, but have become more visible throughout our society as blacks have become more militant in their demands for equality and justice now.

Every widening of the writer's experience of white Americans has only driven home to him more strongly that the opinion that the Negro is unassimilable, or, rather, that his amalgamation into the American nation is undesirable, is held more commonly, absolutely, and intensely than would be assumed from a general knowledge of American thoughtways. Except for a handful of rational intellectual liberals—who also, in many cases, add to their acceptance in principle of amalgamation an admission that they personally feel an irrational emotional inhibition against it—it is a rare case to meet a white American who will confess that, if it were not for public opinion and social sanctions not removable by private choice, he would have no strong objection to intermarriage.

The intensity of the attitude seems to be markedly stronger in the South than in the North. Its strength seems generally to be inversely related to the economic and social status of the informant and his educational level. It is usually strong even in most of the noncolored minority groups, if they are above the lowest plane of indifference. To the poor and socially insecure, but struggling, white individual, a fixed opinion on this point seems an important matter of prestige and distinction.

But even a liberal-minded Northerner of cosmopolitan culture and with a minimum of conventional blinds will, in nine cases out of ten, express a definite feeling against amalgamation. He will not be willing usually to hinder intermarriage by law. Individual liberty is to him a higher principle and, what is more important, he actually invokes it. But he will regret the exceptional cases that occur. He may sometimes hold a philosophical view that in centuries to come amalgamation is bound to happen and might become the solution. But he will be inclined to look on it as an inevitable deterioration.[1]

This attitude of refusing to consider amalgamation—felt and expressed in the entire country—constitutes the center in the complex of attitudes which can be described as the "common denominator" in the problem. It defines the Negro group in contradistinction to all the noncolored minority groups in America and all other lower class groups. The boundary between Negro and

[1] The response is likely to be anything but pleasant if one jestingly argues that possibly a small fraction of Negro blood in the American people, if it were blended well with all the other good stuff brought over to the new continent, might create a race of unsurpassed excellence: a people with just a little sunburn without extra trouble and even through the winter; with some curl in the hair without the cost of a permanent wave; with, perhaps, a little more emotional warmth in their souls; and a little more religion, music, laughter, and carefreeness in their lives. Amalgamation is, to the ordinary American, not a proper subject for jokes at all, unless it can be pulled down to the level of dirty stories, where, however, it enjoys a favored place. Referred to society as a whole and viewed as a principle, the anti-amalgamation maxim is held holy; it is a consecrated taboo. The maxim might, indeed, be a remnant of something really in the "mores." It is kept unproblematic, which is certainly not the case with all the rest of etiquette and segregation and discrimination patterns, for which this quality is sometimes erroneously claimed.

white is not simply a class line which can be successfully crossed by education, integration into the national culture, and individual economic advancement. The boundary is fixed. It is not a temporary expedience during an apprenticeship in the national culture. It is a bar erected with the intention of permanency. It is directed against the whole group. Actually, however, "passing" as a white person is possible when a Negro is white enough to conceal his Negro heritage. But the difference between "passing" and ordinary social climbing reveals the distinction between a class line, in the ordinary sense, and a caste line.

This brings us to the point where we shall attempt to sketch, only in an abstract and preliminary form, the social mechanism by which the antiamalgamation maxim determines race relations. This mechanism is perceived by nearly everybody in America, but most clearly in the South. Almost unanimously white Americans have communicated to the author the following logic of the caste situation which we shall call the "*white man's theory of color caste.*"

1. The concern for "race purity" is basic in the whole issue; the primary and essential command is to prevent amalgamation; the whites are determined to utilize every means to this end.
2. Rejection of "social equality" is to be understood as a precaution to hinder miscegenation and particularly intermarriage.
3. The danger of miscegenation is so tremendous that the segregation and discrimination inherent in the refusal of "social equality" must be extended to nearly all spheres of life. There must be segregation and discrimination in recreation, in religious service, in education, before the law, in politics, in housing, in stores and in breadwinning.

This popular theory of the American caste mechanism is, of course, open to criticism. It can be criticized from a valuational point of view by maintaining that hindering miscegenation is not a worthwhile end, or that as an end it is not sufficiently worthwhile to counterbalance the sufferings inflicted upon the suppressed caste and the general depression of productive efficiency, standards of living and human culture in the American society at large—costs appreciated by all parties concerned. This criticism does not, however, endanger the theory which assumes that white people actually are following another valuation of means and ends and are prepared to pay the costs for attaining the ends. A second criticism would point out that, assuming the desirability of the end, this end could be reached without the complicated and, in all respects, socially expensive caste apparatus now employed. This criticism, however adequate though it be on the practical or political plane of discussion, does not disprove that people believe otherwise, and that the popular theory is a true representation of their beliefs and actions.

To undermine the popular theory of the caste mechanism, as based on the antiamalgamation maxim, it would, of course, be necessary to prove that people really are influenced by other motives than the ones pronounced. Much material has, as we shall find, been brought together indicating that, among other things, competitive economic interests, which do not figure at all in the popular rationalization referred to, play a decisive role. The announced concern about racial purity is, when this economic motive is taken into account, no longer awarded the exclusive role as the *basic* cause in the psychology of the race problem.

Though the popular theory of color caste turns out to be a rationalization, this does not destroy it. For among the forces in the minds of the white people are certainly not only economic interests (if these were the only ones, the popular theory would be utterly demolished), but also sexual urges, inhibitions, and jealousies, and social fears and cravings for prestige and security. When they come under the scrutiny of scientific research, both the sexual and the social complexes take on unexpected designs. We shall then also get a clue to understanding the remarkable tendency of this presumably biological doctrine, that it refers only to legal marriage and to relations between Negro men and white women, but not to extramarital sex relations between white men and Negro women.

However these sexual and social complexes might turn out when analyzed, they will reveal the psychological nature of the antiamalgamation doctrine and show its "meaning." They will also explain the compressed emotion attached to the Negro problem. It is inherent in our type of modern Western civilization that sex and social status are for most individuals the danger points, the directions whence he fears the sinister onslaughts on his personal security. These two factors are more likely than anything else to push a life problem deep down into the subconscious and load it with emotions. There is some probability that in America both complexes are particularly laden with emotions. The American puritan tradition gives everything connected with sex a higher emotional charge. The roads for social climbing have been kept more open in America than perhaps anywhere else in the world, but in this upward struggle the competition for social status has also become more absorbing. In a manner and to a degree most uncomfortable for the Negro people in America, both the sexual and the social complexes have become related to the Negro problem.

These complexes are most of the time kept concealed. In occasional groups of persons and situations they break into the open. Even when not consciously perceived or expressed, they ordinarily determine interracial behavior on the white side.

. . . . . .

It has . . . always been a primary requirement upon every Negro leader—who aspires to get any hearing at all from the white majority group, and who does not want to appear dangerously radical to the Negro group and at the same time hurt the "race pride" it has built up as a defense—that he shall explicitly condone the antiamalgamation maxim, which is the keystone in the white man's structure of race prejudice, and forbear to express any desire on the part of the Negro people to aspire to intermarriage with the whites. The request for intermarriage is easy for the Negro leader to give up. Intermarriage cannot possibly be a practical object of Negro public policy. Independent of the Negroes' wishes, the opportunity for intermarriage is not favorable as long as the great majority of the white population dislikes the very idea. As a defense reaction a strong attitude against intermarriage has developed in the Negro people itself. And the Negro people have no interest in defending the exploitative illicit relations between white men and Negro women. This race mingling is, on the contrary, commonly felt among Negroes to be disgraceful. And it often arouses the jealousy of Negro men.

The required soothing gesture toward the antiamalgamation doctrine is, therefore, readily delivered. It is iterated at every convenient opportunity and belongs to the established routine of Negro leadership. For example, Robert R. Moton writes:

> As for amalgamation, very few expect it; still fewer want it; no one advocates it; and only a constantly diminishing minority practise it, and that surreptitiously. It is generally accepted

on both sides of the colour line that it is best for the two races to remain ethnologically distinct.

There seems thus to be unanimity among Negro leaders on the point deemed crucial by white Americans. If we attend carefully, we shall, however, detect some important differences in formulation. The Negro spokesman will never, to begin with, accept the common white premise of racial inferiority of the Negro stock. To quote Moton again.

> . . . even in the matter of the mingling of racial strains, however undesirable it might seem to be from a social point of view, he [the Negro] would never admit that his blood carries any taint of physiological, mental, or spiritual inferiority.

A doctrine of equal natural endowments—a doctrine contrary to the white man's assumption of Negro inferiority, which is at the basis of the antiamalgamation theory—has been consistently upheld. If a Negro leader publicly even hinted at the possibility of inherent racial inferiority, he would immediately lose his following. The entire Negro press watches the Negro leaders on this point.

Even Booker T. Washington, the supreme diplomat of the Negro people through a generation filled with severe trials, who was able by studied unobtrusiveness to wring so many favors from the white majority, never dared to allude to such a possibility, though he sometimes criticized most severely his own people for lack of thrift, skill, perseverance and general culture. In fact, there is no reason to think that he did not firmly believe in the fundamental equality of inherent capacities. Privately, local Negro leaders might find it advisable to admit Negro inferiority and, particularly earlier, many individual Negroes might have shared the white man's view. But it will not be expressed by national leaders and, in fact, never when they are under public scrutiny. An emphatic assertion of equal endowments is article number one in the growing Negro "race pride."

Another deviation of the Negro faith in the antiamalgamation doctrine is the stress that they, for natural reasons, lay on condemning exploitative illicit amalgamation. They turn the tables and accuse white men of debasing Negro womanhood, and the entire white culture for not rising up against this practice as their expressed antagonism against miscegenation should demand. Here they have a strong point, and they know how to press it.

A third qualification in the Negro's acceptance of the antiamalgamation doctrine, expressed not only by the more "radical" and outspoken Negro leaders, is the assertion that intermarriage should not be barred by law. The respect for individual liberty is invoked as an argument. But, in addition, it is pointed out that this barrier, by releasing the white man from the consequences of intimacy with a Negro woman, actually has the effect of inducing such intimacy and thus tends to increase miscegenation. Moton makes this point:

> The Negro woman suffers not only from the handicap of economic and social discriminations imposed upon the race as a whole, but is in addition the victim of unfavourable legislation incorporated in the marriage laws of twenty-nine states, which forbid the intermarriage of black and white. The disadvantage of these statutes lies, not as is generally represented, in the legal obstacle they present to social equality, but rather in the fact that such laws specifically deny to the Negro woman and her offspring that safeguard from abuse and exploitation with which the women of the white race are abundantly surrounded. On the other side, the effect of such legislation leaves the white man, who is so inclined, free of any responsibility attending his amatory excursions across the colour line and leaves the coloured woman without redress for any of the consequences of her defencelessness; whereas white women have every protection,

from fine and imprisonment under the law to enforced marriage and lynching outside the law.

But even with all these qualifications, the antiamalgamation doctrine, the necessity of assenting to which is understood by nearly everybody, obviously encounters some difficulties in the minds of intellectual Negroes. They can hardly be expected to accept it as a just rule of conduct. They tend to accept it merely as a temporary expedient necessitated by human weakness. Kelly Miller thus wrote:

> . . . you would hardly expect the Negro, in derogation of his common human qualities, to proclaim that he is so diverse from God's other human creatures as to make the blending of the races contrary to the law of nature. The Negro refuses to become excited or share in your frenzy on this subject. The amalgamation of the races is an ultimate possibility, though not an immediate probability. But what have you and I to do with ultimate questions, anyway?

And a few years later, he said:

> It must be taken for granted in the final outcome of things that the colour line will be wholly obliterated. While blood may be thicker than water, it does not possess the spissitude or inherency of everlasting principle. The brotherhood of man is more fundamental than the fellowship of race. A physical and spiritual identity of all peoples occupying common territory is a logical necessity of thought. The clear seeing mind refuses to yield or give its assent to any other ultimate conclusion. This consummation, however, is far too removed from the sphere of present probability to have decisive influence upon practical procedure.

The problem is, of course, tied up with the freedom of the individual. "Theoretically Negroes would all subscribe to the right of freedom of choice in marriage even between the two races," wrote Moton. And Du Bois formulates it in stronger terms:

> . . . a woman may say, I do not want to marry this black man, or this red man, or this white man. . . . But the impudent and vicious demand that all colored folk shall write themselves down as brutes by a general assertation of their unfitness to marry other decent folk is a nightmare.

Negroes have always pointed out that the white man must not be very certain of his woman's lack of interest when he rises to such frenzy on behalf of the danger to her and feels compelled to build up such formidable fences to prevent her from marrying a Negro.

With these reservations both Negro leadership and the Negro masses acquiesce in the white antiamalgamation doctrine. This attitude is noted with satisfaction in the white camp. The writer has observed, however, that the average white man, particularly in the South, does not feel quite convinced of the Negro's acquiescence. In several conversations, the same white person, in the same breath, has assured me, on the one hand, that the Negroes are perfectly satisfied in their position and would not like to be treated as equals, and on the other hand, that the only thing these Negroes long for is to be like white people and to marry their daughters.

Whereas the Negro spokesman finds it possible to assent to the first rank of discrimination, namely, that involving miscegenation, it is more difficult for him to give his approval to the second rank of discrimination, namely, that involving "etiquette" and consisting in the white man's refusal to extend the ordinary courtesies to Negroes in daily life and his expectation of receiving certain symbolic signs of submissiveness from the Negro. The Negro leader could not do so without serious risk of censorship by his own people and rebuke by the Negro press. In all articulate groups of Negroes there is a demand to have white men call them by their titles of Mr., Mrs., and Miss; to have white men take off their hats on entering a Negro's house; to be able to enter a white man's house through the front door rather than the back door, and so on. But on the whole, and in spite of the rule that they stand up for "social equality" in this sense, most Negroes in the South obey the white man's rules.

Booker T. Washington went a long way, it is true, in his Atlanta speech in 1895 where he explained that: "In all things that are purely social we [the two races] can be as separate as the fingers, yet one as the hand in all things essential to mutual progress." He there seemed to condone not only these rules of "etiquette" but also the denial of "social equality" in a broader sense, including some of the further categories in the white man's rank order of discrimination. He himself was always most eager to observe the rules. But Washington was bitterly rebuked for this capitulation, particularly by Negroes in the North. And a long time has passed since then; the whole spirit in the Negro world has changed considerably in three decades.

The modern Negro leader will try to solve this dilemma by iterating that no Negroes want to intrude upon white people's private lives. But this is not what Southern white opinion asks for. It is not satisfied with the natural rules of polite conduct that no individual, of whatever race, shall push his presence on a society where he is not wanted. It asks for a general order according to which *all* Negroes are placed under *all* white people and excluded from not only the white man's society but also from the ordinary symbols of respect. No Negro shall ever aspire to them, and no white shall be allowed to offer them.

Thus, on this second rank of discrimination there is a wide gap between the ideologies of the two groups. As we then continue downward in our rank order and arrive at the ordinary Jim Crow practices, the segregation in schools, the disfranchisement, and the discrimination in employment, we find, on the one hand, that increasingly larger groups of white people are prepared to take a stand against these discriminations. Many a liberal white professor in the South who, for his own welfare, would not dare to entertain a Negro in his home and perhaps not even speak to him in a friendly manner on the street, will be found prepared publicly to condemn disfranchisement, lynching, and the forcing of the Negro out of employment. Also, on the other hand, Negro spokesmen are becoming increasingly firm in their opposition to discrimination on these lower levels. It is principally on these lower levels of the white man's rank order of discrimination that the race struggle goes on. The struggle will widen to embrace all the thousand problems of education, politics, economic standards, and so forth, and the frontier will shift from day to day according to varying events.

Even a superficial view of discrimination in America will reveal to the observer: first, that there are great differences, not only between larger regions, but between neighboring communities; and, second, that even in the same community, changes occur from one time to another. There is also, contrary to the rule that all Negroes are to be treated alike, a certain amount of discretion depending upon the class and social status of the Negro in question. A white person, especially if he has high status in the community, is, furthermore, supposed to be free, within limits, to overstep the rules. The rules are primarily to govern the Negro's behavior.

Some of these differences and changes can be explained. But the need for their interpretation is perhaps less than has sometimes been assumed. The variations in discrimination between local communities or from one time to another are often not of primary consequence. All of these thousand and one precepts, etiquettes, taboos, and disabilities inflicted upon the Negro have a common purpose: to express the subordinate status of the Negro people and the exalted position of the whites. They have their meaning and chief function as symbols. As symbols they are, however, interchangeable to an extent: one can serve in place of another without causing material difference in the essential social relations in the community.

The differences in patterns of discrimination between the larger regions of the country and the temporal changes of patterns within one region, which reveal a definite trend, have, on the contrary, more material import. These differences and changes imply, in fact, a considerable margin of variation within the very notion of American caste, which is not true of all the other minor differences between the changes in localities within a single region—hence the reason for a clear distinction. For exemplification it may suffice here to refer only to the differentials in space. As one moves from the Deep South through the Upper South and the Border states to the North, the manifestations of discrimination decrease in extent and intensity; at the same time the rules become more uncertain and capricious. The "color line" becomes a broad ribbon of arbitrariness. The old New England states stand, on the whole, as the antipode to the Deep South. This generalization requires important qualifications, and the relations are in process of change.

The decreasing discrimination as we go from South to North in the United States is apparently related to a weaker basic prejudice. In the North the Negroes have fair justice and are not disfranchised; they are not Jim-Crowed in public means of conveyance; educational institutions are less segregated. The interesting thing is that the decrease of discrimination does *not* regularly follow the white man's rank order. Thus intermarriage, placed on the top of the rank order, is legally permitted in all but one of the Northern states east of the Mississippi. The racial etiquette, being the most conspicuous element in the second rank, is, practically speaking, absent from the North. On the other hand, employment discriminations, placed at the bottom of the rank order, at times are equally severe, or more so, in some Northern communities than in the South, even if it is true that Negroes have been able to press themselves into many more new avenues of employment during the last generation in the North than in the South.

There is plenty of discrimination in the North. But it is—or rather its rationalization is—kept hidden. We can, in the North, witness the legislators' obedience to the American Creed when they solemnly pass laws and regulations to condemn and punish such acts of discrimination which, as a matter of routine, are committed daily by the great majority of the white citizens and by the legislators themselves. In the North, as indeed often in the South, public speakers frequently pronounce principles of human and civic equality. We see here revealed in relief the Negro problem as an American Dilemma.

44.

THE RISE OF THE UNMELTABLE ETHNICS: POLITICS AND CULTURE IN THE SEVENTIES

Michael Novak

White-Anglo-Saxon Protestants—WASPs—generally have been the dominant ethnic group—economically, socially, and politically in American society for many years. In the following selection Michael Novak illustrates unawareness by WASPs of their own ethnicity, the importance of social stratification within that ethnic category, and differentiation among both lower class and elite WASPs. By making several assumptions Novak also comes up with some innovative speculations concerning the political and electoral potential of a coalition of non-WASP groups. Novak's imaginative expression, "the unmeltable ethnics," suggests that, contrary to American precedent, some ethnic groups will not be assimilated in our society. Though his hypothesis is only speculative, he forcefully articulates the ethnics' disenchantment with the dominant WASPish political Establishment and the belief of ethnics in cultural pluralism rather than homogenization masquerading as Americanization. The reader may find it interesting to identify and evaluate Novak's assumptions and decide on the merits of his intriguing political speculation.

Let us suppose that in the 1960s the blacks and the young had their day in the sun. They had maximum publicity. And now it is the ethnics' turn. Perhaps the ethnics can carry our society further, more constructively, more inventively.

Three sets of figures set the political dimensions of the possibilities. There are seventy million Americans in families whose income falls between $5,000 and $10,000 per year. These are 40 percent of all Americans. Secondly, there are seventy million descendants of immigrants from Ireland, Italy, Spain, Greece, Armenia, and the Slavic nations. Thirdly, there are nearly fifty million Catholics.

These three abstract segments overlap considerably. Most Catholics are descendants of such immigrants. Most (it appears) are also in lower-middle-class families by income.

Such persons have special characteristics, needs, and dreams. Their symbolic life, rhetoric, and ways of perceiving are unique. They form a formidable electoral bloc.

In 1960 the percentage of first- and sec-

Source: Michael Novak, *The Rise of the Unmeltable Ethnics: Politics and Culture in the Seventies* (New York: Macmillan, 1971), pp. 19–21, 110–15.

Michael Novak, a contributing editor to *Christianity and Crisis,* has written extensively on religious and social subjects, particularly ethnicity in America. He is the author of *The Rise of the Unmeltable Ethnics.*

ond-generation immigrants in the major cities (larger than 500,000) of the United States was as follows. If one counts the third generation, figures would presumably be larger:

Rank	City	%
1	*New York*	48.6
2	*Boston*	45.5
3	*San Francisco*	43.5
4	*Chicago*	35.9
5	*Buffalo*	35.4
6	*Los Angeles*	32.6
7	*Detroit*	32.2
8	*Seattle*	31.4
9	*Cleveland*	30.9
10	*Pittsburgh*	30.3
11	*Milwaukee*	30.0
12	*Philadelphia*	29.1
13	*San Antonio*	24.0
14	*San Diego*	21.5
15	*Baltimore*	14.8
16	*St. Louis*	14.1
17	*Washington*	12.6
18	*Cincinnati*	12.0
19	*Houston*	9.7
20	*New Orleans*	8.6
21	*Dallas*	6.9

Other reflections on statistics are in order. In 1969 the median age of the American population was 27 years and 8 months. In 1910 it was 24. In 1985 the median American will be six months older than he was in 1969.

According to Scammon and Wattenberg, six out of seven voters are over 30. The median age of voters is 47. Younger voters, whose maximal numbers will lower the median age only slightly, may very well vote Democratic in larger proportions than their elders. But their fundamental values may be opposed to those of the liberal intellectuals. Conceivably, a politics which turned in a new ethnic direction would be closer to their own search for meaning than the classical politics of the Left. It might be possible to invent a political language and a political program that appealed simultaneously to young students and young workers, to those attracted (whether they go to them or not) to communes, and to those attracted (whether they remain in them or not) to ethnic neighborhoods. It is possible that Anglo-Saxon political creativity is exhausted, and that at last America is ready for a substantive contribution from other cultures.

. . . . .

MANY KINDS OF WASP

Growing up in America is a series of new social-cultural explorations. The undifferentiated "them" beyond one's own family, neighborhood, ethnic, religious, and economic group turns out to be exceedingly various. One evening in Boston I attended a party with black families in Roxbury; went for cocktails and dinner at the home of an assistant to the governor in a sheltered, quiet, sylvan hideaway in Cambridge; and finished up with dessert at the small suburban home of a genial Irish lawyer (a federal attorney) who had moved out from an Irish neighborhood to Wellesley. The manners, vocabulary, interests, courtesies, jokes, speech patterns, facial expressions varied from place to place.

When I first came to New York, general schemes like "Jews" shattered in my hands. I wasn't prepared for Jewish cab drivers or Jewish poverty; not for militantly conservative Jews in a teachers' union; not for countless factions, classes, political views, and neatly elaborate hierarchies of status. High in one status did not mean high in another; Jewish disdain—escaping from compressed lips—is crisp. A relatively small number of Jews in New York and Los Angeles set a style for Jewishness that may be foreign to Jews in Cleveland or Utica.

Just as clearly it has become plain to me that there are many different kinds of WASP. In the West Virginia hills there may be bitter hostility to Catholics or indeed to all outsiders, and four or five generations of residence are required before one is accepted as other than an interloper. But West Virginia WASPS would have an attitude toward Boston Brahmins or Wall Street bankers very much like that of Catholics in Dorchester, or Okies in the Southwest. WASP history is often internally tragic and bitter. Poor, forgotten, excluded persons abound.

In a brilliant short study of a single Massachusetts town, Stephen Thernstrom opened my eyes to the poverty and degradation exercised by upper-class WASPS for lower-class WASPS. He helped me to see more vividly how threatening to poor WASPS cheap immigrant labor must have been. One can sympathize with their terror. Thernstrom also shows how the image of a small-town community, where everyone knew everyone, slipped from uneasy reality into sheer fantasy two centuries ago. Far from being free and egalitarian, early American culture was severely based on class power, authority from on high, and little or no participation by the poor:

> In the 18th-century community the political structure encouraged habits of obedience and deference, habits promising stability and unity. Parties were abhorred, "fashions" despised. Repeated unanimous votes in their town meetings revealed the powerful centripetal influence of local political institutions.
>
> At mid-century the town meeting disappeared, the size and complexity which made Newburyport a city demanded a more rationalized, impersonal form of government. Voting became an anonymous act, and social constraints supporting political deference were thereby weakened. Party competition was now fierce and chaotic.
>
> The competing political parties were not sharply polarized along class lines in 1850, and both were controlled by respectable middle-class citizens. . . . Not a single laborer was included on an 1852 list of the 72 members of the Democratic vigilance committees in the wards. The lower class was politically passive; laborers and operatives exercised their franchise less frequently than citizens of higher status.

The extent to which upper-class WASP convictions rest upon high authority, distance, and direct application of force runs so contrary to the stated ideology of the Constitution, the Declaration of Independence, and the Gettysburg Address that the swift dependence of silver-haired establishmentarians on brute force always jangles one's mental images forcibly. Upper-class WASPS picture themselves as defending uniquely Anglo-Saxon liberties and a distinctive egalitarianism. Still, in the eyes of many of them, they are clearly defending order, *their* order, and they believe in beating down challenges swiftly and efficiently. The White House, GOP leaders assembled, and the Republican governors meeting in San Juan speedily came to Governor Rockefeller's defense after he had bloodily crushed the prisoners' rebellion at Attica. He did "what he had to do." They commended his "forcefulness."

The old WASP family, like other ethnic families, had a tradition of subjection. Thernstrom notes: "The seventeenth-century Puritan family had been not only 'a little church and a little commonwealth,' but also 'a school wherein the first principles and grounds of government and subjection are learned.' Every member of the community had to belong to some family, the agency through which social stability was maintained." This tradition of stability, subjection, the severe internalization of order, seems to lie behind a certain

WASP suspicion of other looser ethnic groups, and gives historical depth to our perception of the symbolic meaning of "law and order." The point of force is "to teach a lesson" that was, unfortunately, not learned in the family. People of good families, meanwhile, seldom feel the weight of the law even when they err, for there are many testimonies to their "good character" and "upbringing." (The support of David Rockefeller for William Bundy as a suitable editor for *Foreign Affairs* is a classic of upper-class WASP solidarity. How could anyone impugn the character of "one of us"? Similarly, the Yankee grandmother of a young lawyer wanted for allegedly passing a gun to George Jackson at San Quentin tells a television audience that whatever the young man did, "he did from conscience.")

Upper-class WASP traditions of democratic liberty depended very highly on strict family discipline and internalized order. They flourished best in small towns and rural environments, where families could be in stricter control of their offspring. As *social* conceptions, these traditions have been under enormous strains, even among WASPS, for over a century.

> Things *never had* been as rosy as the myths about small-town America in the 19th century would suggest: already in the 1850's: "We don't know each other"; "we have been gradually losing that social knowledge of each other's residences and occupations"; we must "renew the spirit of former times"—these became commonplace utterances as the forces of change reached into quiet villages and towns across the land. The warmth and security of a vanished organic community was an attractive image to set against the realities of the present—the factory, the immigrant, the reign of the market.

But there were other English conceptions, dear to a whole line of liberal thinkers, waiting to take up the slack:

> The rise of the city and the spread of the factory across America was accompanied by a new social creed. According to this complex of ideas, American society was a collection of mobile, freely competing atoms; divisions between rich and poor could not produce destructive social conflict because the status rich or poor was not permanent. If society was in a state of constant circulation, if every man had an opportunity to rise to the top, all would be well.

English conceptions of order, decorum, social planning, the free marketplace (of goods and of ideas), friction-free consensus, etc., dominate American life so thoroughly that most WASPS seem unaware of them as ethnic preferences. For them, such matters are so much a part of their sense of reality, so integral to their own life story, so symbolically familiar, so inherently self-validating, that charges of partiality and bias must seem to them faintly insane. *Their* conception of sanity is, in fact, in question. They are being obliged to see themselves as ethnically one-sided for perhaps the first time. What used to be regarded as dignified reserve is now mocked as uptightness; what used to be regarded as good character is analyzed now for its "hangups"; the individualism of the Marlboro man, once a cherished aspiration, is regarded as alienation; the smooth-talking managerial style of liberal WASP authoritarianism is hissed as manipulative and venal; competitiveness is laughed at by those to whom it is closed. American cultural pluralism, fed by Jews, Blacks, Indians, and other ethnic groups, has thrown WASP ideals into a new and unflattering light.

The recent rise in ethnic assertion is due in large measure to the discrediting of traditional WASP styles in the face of Vietnam, a revisionist history of Teutonic-Nordic prejudice against other races and ethnic groups, and the failure in the cities of WASP conceptions of social planning and social reform. For years, WASPS could comfortably comment on the distant progress of others in "Americanizing" themselves, that is to say, in making themselves into WASPS. Nowadays, the glamor is gone. Who wants to be a WASP? Not even WASPS are certain.

Still, one ought not to be too hard on others. All ethnic groups have their own confusions. All acceded for far too long to the pressures of Americanization—which was really WASPification. Many individuals eagerly accepted it. All have found some good and beautiful things in it.

Besides the many regional varieties of lower-class WASPS, moreover, we should also distinguish between two WASP elites who mutually, it appears, disdain each other: the WASPS of "the northeastern establishment" and the newly rich WASPS of what Kevin Phillips calls "the Sun Belt." The industrialists around Ronald Reagan, the oilmen and new technology of Texas, the booming real estate of Florida—over against the oak-panelled rooms, quiet voices, collections of art, and attachment to civil rights of the Rockefellers, Harrimans, Lodges, and others—may draw the contrasts in power and style clearly enough. And in between these two groups is a third: those small-town lawyers of little class, wealth, or power, whose armpits sweat and whose keys to Playboy clubs compensate for the strict morals of the midwestern Bible Belt, whose legwork is the backbone of Republican power across the land, and whose epigone is Richard Nixon—Nixon the outsider, the nonestablishmentarian, shifty, hardworking, fiercely controlled internally, making himself suffer to convince himself he's on a right path, tough, moralistic, "the last liberal," and president of the United States.

In the country clubs, as city executives, established families, industrialists, owners, lawyers, masters of etiquette, college presidents, dominators of the military, fundraisers, members of blue ribbon communities, realtors, brokers, deans, sheriffs—it is the cumulative power and distinctive styles of WASPS that the rest of us have had to learn in order to survive. WASPS have never had to celebrate Columbus Day or march down Fifth Avenue wearing green. Every day has been their day in America. No more.

45.

FORGOTTEN AMERICANS: THE MIGRANT AND INDIAN POOR

John F. Bauman

The "war against poverty" in the decade of the sixties was predominantly concerned with the urban poor. The parallel civil rights movement was for the most part concerned with discrimination against black Americans. Neither of these movements to achieve a greater measure of equality in the American social structure had an impact on the status of two large segments of the disadvantaged stratum of our society—the migrant workers and Indians. John F. Bauman describes the current conditions of these "forgotten Americans" and identifies some of the historical forces that have contributed to their present disadvantaged status in our society.

When the Kennedy-Johnson administration declared war on American poverty, no one doubted that the main battleground would be the streets and back alleys of American cities. Michael Harrington, Dwight McDonald, Oscar Ornati, John Kenneth Galbraith and other grand strategists of the New Frontier and the Great Society had discovered that "hidden poverty" was the twentieth century canker vitiating the body politic. No one was surprised that this troglodytic misery of the aging and the unorganized was lodged in the city, because the nineteenth century had placed poverty in the gallery of anti-urban imagery. Thus despite the outpourings of agrarian protest in the late nineteenth century, in 1960 poverty remained linked in the American mind with tenements, robbers' roosts and low beer dives.

The slick mid-twentieth century expressways, which whisked affluent suburbanites over, under and through city slums, extinguished moldering neighborhoods and memories of the grinding poverty of the past. Just as effectively, these expressways and turnpikes snuffed out even the blurred recollections of rural poverty. While the "grapes of wrath" still ripened on the vine, midcentury Americans watched John Steinbeck's Joads in their rattletrap jalopy bounce eerily into a surrealistic oblivion.

Not until 1947 did Dale Wright (in *They Harvest Despair*) tell Americans that, while the Great Depression was over, the children of the Joads still roamed the same dusty vineyard roads. Thirteen years later, Edward R. Murrow, in a television documentary entitled "Harvest of Shame," reminded the nation that misery-wracked caravans of itinerant pickers wend their way up, down, and across the country pick-

Source: John F. Bauman, *Current History* 64, no. 382 (June 1973): 364–78. Reprinted by permission of Current History, Inc.

John F. Bauman teaches courses in urban America and black history at California State College, California, Pa., where he is professor of history. He has been studying the welfare structure of Philadelphia, especially during the years 1932 to 1937.

ing beans here, tomatoes there, and reaping for themselves only empty lives of illness and poor education. But although journalists have periodically brought his problem to the attention of the public, the migrant worker himself remains unseen and unaided; he travels at night and is sequestered in a shanty miles from the interstate highways.

The system isolating the American Indian is as effective as a superhighway. In 1960, William A. Brophy and Sophie D. Aberle, *et al.*, in *The Indian: America's Unfinished Business,* wrote that "the economic position of the Indian is less favorable than that of any other American minority group. In most Indian communities the pattern is one of bare subsistence with the result that the worst slums are found on Indian reservations." Yet few discussions of the poverty problem have included the problem of the Indian.

Indians and migrants are among America's least populous minorities; they are also the nation's least powerful minorities. The analogy can easily be extended. A University of Minnesota study team found the Mille Lacs reservation similar to any migrant camp: both are places of "backwardness and mainstream isolation . . . [standing] no chance of individual or group development unless the terrible inequalities of education, occupation, income and other related variables are erased." Where poor education spells bleak prospects for future mobility, the Indian, like the migrant, grabs the fleeting pleasure of alcohol. Both these cultures are also characterized by the tenacity of the family bond. In fact, family dependency and close kinship ties have been a sustaining force for each culture.

Despite similarities, some differences distinguish the migrant's problem from the Indian dilemma. While the subculture of the Joads is the twentieth century creation of large-scale cash-crop farming, American Indian culture is thousands of years old. Migrant families live a vagabond existence, settling only long enough to harvest some of the richest crops in the world. American Indians, on the other hand, have title to almost 50,000,000 acres, but all of it is unfertile land hardly worth the effort to till. Finally, while the migrant suffers from government neglect, ignored by almost every federal social program, the Indian squirms under more than a century of government paternalism.

In 1973, however, both cultures face the prospect of extinction. New developments in crop-picking machinery displace thousands of migrants yearly. At the same time, the lure of the city, the thrust of technology, and the vagaries of federal Indian policy threaten to loosen the ancient grip of Indian tradition. While the migrant accepts his fate, militant Indians battle anew to preserve tribal integrity. Whether challenged by farm technology or federal policy, the number one dragon to be killed is poverty.

Migrant families in America are victims of an exploitative system that spins off generations of dulled offspring. More than a million people are ensnared in the migrant trap; regretfully, a more precise enumeration of America's wandering crop-pickers is unavailable. Mobile populations are difficult to trace. However, one 1966 study tallied some 466,000 different migratory farm workers, not including the 300,000 children and other collateral kin available for work in the fields.

THE PROBLEM OF THE MIGRANT

Three great streams of itinerant farm workers flow through the United States. One begins in California. There, some

39,200 pickers and sorters harvest the lettuce, the oranges and the grapes, and then limp on to Colorado, Utah or Idaho. A similar caravan forms each spring in Texas. Mexicans and Mexican-Americans from the Rio Grande Valley comprise half this gypsy band, which moves from the Texas fields through the midwest as far north as Michigan. A third stream follows the ripening crops from Florida in winter to New Jersey, New York, and Maine in summer. And so it goes. Three or four times a year, the migrant family is uprooted in search of another field, another crop, and another chance to earn a meager subsistence.

Migrants are vocationally a minority, and migrant ranks are comprised largely of ethnic minorities. Negroes, Puerto Ricans, Bahamians, West Indians, Mexican-Americans, and American Indians are all trapped in the migrant web. Blacks and Puerto Ricans made up some 90 percent of New York's migrant work force in 1971. "Stoop laborers," who pick Colorado's sugar beets and peaches, are customarily Spanish-speaking or American Indian, while further north and east Mexican-Americans comprise 80 percent of Michigan's migrant cherry pickers.

While the roots of migrancy are buried in agricultural technology and large-scale "bonanza" farming, much of the misery suffered by the migrants can be attributed to federal farm policy. Some scholars accuse the government of perpetuating an "exceptionalist" labor system which offers no deterrents to exploitation. In brief, the federal Agriculture Adjustment Administration of the 1930's in effect disinherited the human chaff from the marginal lands of Oklahoma, Arkansas, Texas, Missouri and Kansas, and enmeshed generations in a cycle of farm migrancy. Subsequently, migrants were excluded from the minimum wage provisions of the Fair Labor Standards Act, denied bargaining rights under the Wagner Labor Relations Act, and barred from the social welfare benefits of the 1935 Social Security legislation. More recently, child care services, food stamps, surplus food, school lunch programs all available to the resident poor were placed outside the pale of the migrant family.

By excluding itinerant farmworkers from crucial federal legislation and deferring to farm bloc politicians interested in preserving a cheap labor supply, the United States has helped to perpetuate what Ernesto Galarza, a student of farm migrancy, has called a "modified patron system." In Latin America's feudal patron system, the peon was linked to the hacienda overlordship by the patron. In the American model, the crew leader replaced the patron. Few migrants labor without a crew leader or contractor. The crew leader is the recruiter, the camp manager, the work supervisor, the policeman, the banker, and the provider of alcohol and transportation. The grower, wanting a tractable work force, encourages the migrant's physical and social dependence on the crew leader. In migrant camps, crew leaders wield awesome power, appointing lieutenants, dispensing favors, meeting any dissent with the threat of banishment. The power of the crew leader only emphasizes the helplessness of the migrant, who meekly settles for one of the most deprived existences in America.

INADEQUATE WAGES

Crew leaders are, in fact, a vital cog in the migrant subculture which, like other cultures rooted in poverty, endures paltry wages, wretched housing, poor health and poorer education. A glance at recent statistics on farm worker earnings suggests that all farm labor grovels for low wages. In March, 1971, 189,000, or 38.3 percent of America's 494,000 farm laborers earned less than the poverty-line income of $3,034 a year for a rural family of four. Note that 69 percent of the 23,000 black farm laborers—most likely to be migrants—lived below the poverty line. Studies in the last ten years show that many migrants earn between $900 and $1,200 a year. Even with a wife and child in the field, most migrants average only $2,300 a year. State laws establishing minimum wages for migrants (the $1.40 an hour in New York is still below the minimum for industrial labor) mitigate some of the hardships. But they cannot compensate for the 50 to 75 days a year of unemployment due to illness, weather or immature crops.

Out of the approximately $25 a week that a migrant earns picking strawberries on Long Island, New York, he returns $5 to $7 for shelter in a one-room tar-papered shanty in a migrant camp. Often the accommodation is nothing more than a duck shed or a partitioned old barn. Foul outdoor privies are commonplace and the workers frequently cook in an illequipped common kitchen.

In such bleak settings, social relationships are strained. Heavy drinking, gambling, gnawing distrust, and camp violence act as leveling devices which thwart latent leadership and frustrate the unionization efforts of a Cesar Chavez. Inadequate diets contribute to camp lethargy. Malnutrition is endemic. Dr. Peter Chase of the University of Colorado compared the undernourished children he found in Colorado camps to children in Biafra; he reported finding dramatically severe cases of scurvy, rickets, kwaskiorkor and marasmus, all diseases related to protein-calorie deficiencies. A recent outbreak of a typhoid epidemic in a Homestead, Florida, migrant camp in early 1973 underlines abysmally inadequate sanitary facilities. Families bucket water from streams or shallow wells.

Sickly migrants are rarely treated by physicians. A 1957 survey of a group of 225 New York migrants discovered that only half saw a doctor from year to year. One migrant in six visited a dentist, and instances of prenatal, obstetrical or postnatal care were very few. Robert Coles told of children born by the sides of roads or in dingy rooms without running water.

Coles observed that migrant children quickly internalize the defeatism caught in a parent's habitual lament. "What did I do to deserve this?" Migrant children crayon a life of sunless skies, faceless people, and endless roads with "a big fence on each side of a road that we can't get off even if we wanted."

Migrant parents discount the benefits of education for their children; a much more immediate concern is a boost in the family earnings. An American Friends Service Committee study compared child use and abuse on United States farms in 1970 to the sweatshops of the 1930's. For ten hours at a time, children stooped and crawled in the fields baked hard by the sun. According to the committee, over 100,000 children helped harvest California crops in 1970. In that same year, in Aroostook County, Maine, children dug 37 percent of the potato yield. Cassandra Stockburger of the National Committee on the Education of Migrant Children sees little hope for improvement, because migrant children miss eight or more days of school a month. Instead, she favors the quick abolition of agricultural migrancy.

In actual fact, technology is having an erosive effect on migrancy. A 1967 manpower report on the state of the 125,000 migrant population of South Texas warned that mechanization was shrinking the opportunity for unskilled farm labor. Meanwhile, in Michigan, mechanization has teamed with a recent state law establishing rigid standards for migrant camp housing to cut deeply into the migrant work force. In the words of one Michigan farmer, "Putting money into good migrant housing is investing in a dead horse." Instead, Michigan growers have invested in cherry "shakers" and mechanical cucumber-pickers, eliminating hundreds of migrant jobs. Furthermore, the trend toward larger farms and more automation, hallmarks of American agribusiness, demands a more stable and a more skilled labor force. This leaves only the "flash peak" harvest for the migrant. Clearly, the United States must support programs such as the Department of Labor's Rural Manpower Service, which encourages migrants to seek permanent residence. Neither technology nor humanity can forever endure the existence of a twentieth century serfdom that leaves human beings at the mercy of exploiters, the most degraded labor in America.

THE AMERICAN INDIAN

Close to half the American Indians dwell on the 267 federally recognized reservations, pueblos, rancherias, communities, allotments, and other off-reservation lands. Reservations range in size from a few hundred acres to the 25,000-square-mile Navaho reservation, which straddles northern Arizona and northwestern New Mexico and extends into Utah. Regardless of their size, Indian landholdings are economically marginal. A Bureau of Indian Affairs (BIA) soil conservation study listed 14 million reservation acres as "critically eroded," 17 million as "severely eroded" and the 25 million remaining acres as only "slightly eroded."

More important, life on the reservation is marginal also. Reservations are ghettos and have been described as "the purest example of underdeveloped enclaves within the American society." Peter McDonald, chairman of the Navaho, deprecates reservation conditions as "too primitive for most Americans to conceive, . . . a seemingly hopeless poverty." Navaho land is a place of anthill-like hogans with dirt floors and kerosene lamps. In the shadow of Navaho Mountain, Indians sleep on sheepskin mats and cook on makeshift stoves fashioned out of old oil drums. On the Gila River reservation, in an area where 80 acres is considered a bare minimum for profitable cultivation, tribesmen scratch out a feeble existence on 10-acre allotments. In a day when cattle ranching is often a branch of New York- and Chicago-based conglomerates, the Montana Crow ride herd on an average of 48 cattle. The average Navaho sheep flock numbers 50.

It is not strange, then, that poverty stalks Indian hogans as it haunts migrant shacks. The 1967 median income for the Navaho came to $1,900 for a family of 5.4; the national average was $7,720 for a family of 2.8. Incomes on Dakota, Montana and Idaho reservations range between $870 and $1,150. About half of all Indian families have annual incomes of $2,000 or less, and three-fourths earn less than $3,000.

Many Indians, however, earn nothing. Dependency upon AFDC (Aid to Families with Dependent Children) and surplus commodities is a way of life for many Indian families. Unemployment rates climb from as high as 65 percent for the Arizona Apache to 80 percent among the Navaho. Moreover, where jobs exist, Indians usually fail to meet the educational requirements. Of the 163,337 Indians 14 years or over in 1960, almost 16,000 had no schooling, only

19,000 had high school diplomas, and less than 3,000 had college degrees.

Little education and dependency on the Bureau of Indian Affairs breed an oppressive powerlessness reflected in the squalor of Indian life. One study found 76,000 reservation houses below minimum standards. Houses on a typical Cherokee reservation in Oklahoma were constructed of unpainted slabs, partially covered with tarpaper. Cherokee shacks had kitchen sinks but the water had to be hand pumped or bucketed from nearby streams. (In arid Navaho country, water must often be carried five or more miles to the faucetless hogans.) Arizona Apaches still live in wickiups built of poles thatched with beargrass, and sleep on pallets thrown on dirt floors. Navaho hogans are similarly dismal windowless affairs made of logs sealed with mud, and usually shared with a swarm of flies.

Unsanitary, lice-infested houses and unvaried diets (such as the Navaho's fried bread, mutton stew and black coffee) contribute to poor health. Despite significant gains in Indian life expectancy between 1950 and 1970, the Indian infant death rate is still twice that of the nation. Indians, furthermore, still suffer disproportionately from influenza, pneumonia, dysentery, tuberculosis (six times more prevalent among Indians than non-Indians), and trachoma, a virus infection of the eye which has virtually disappeared in the general population. Another disease, alcoholism, ravages the reservation.

Understandably, many Indians escape the reservation and relocate in the city, taking advantage of a 21-year-old federal employment assistance program which provides job training, financial assistance to move, and social services in the city to facilitate adjustment. The 1970 census reported that 55 percent of the Indian population lived in cities. Cities near the reservations like Tulsa, Oklahoma, and Tucson, Arizona, have Indian populations of 9,000 and 15,000 respectively. However, in 1970, more than 9,000 Indians lived in Chicago and over 12,000 Indians made their home in New York.

URBAN INDIANS

Statistics indicate clearly that the urban Indian participates more fully in the work force. Yet Indians, like black Americans, find the city paved with hardship rather than gold. A University of Minnesota study of Indians in the Twin City area found 55 percent working in blue collar occupations and only 8 percent wearing white collars. Another study discovered that half the 225 Indians visiting a Minneapolis hospital lived on welfare; 27 percent of the 225 had incomes under $3,000 a year, and only 25 percent earned more than $6,000 annually.

Indians appear to disagree about the advantages of urban life. Some Indians are afraid that the federal relocation program is a ploy to undermine Indian culture. Militant Indians insist that if there were more opportunities on the reservations more than 75 percent of the urban Indians would return to their kin, to their tribal religion, their fishing and hunting rights and, most important, to their identity.

Students of the Indian maintain that underlying Indian poverty lies the Indian's struggle to preserve his identity in an urban-industrial milieu. Still hovering paternalistically over the struggle looms the United States government and its right arm, the Bureau of Indian Affairs. In fact, federal officialdom has been grinding out Indian policy at least since the exterminatory Cherokee removal of the 1830's. Following the Civil War—inspired in part by

United States "Negro policy"—Americans began a concerted effort to "Americanize" the Indian; but for the Indians Americanization was too often a "join or die" proposition.

Not all the Americanizers were George Custers. Harriet Beecher Stowe labored diligently to bring civilization to the Indian. Then, in 1887, the government inaugurated a Carthaginian plan of assimilation. The Dawes Severalty Act aimed to dissolve the reservations and compel the Indians to melt into the mainstream of American life. Between 1887 and 1934 assimilation failed as a tactic, but not before white greed had decimated Indian life and land. In fact, during this period two-thirds of Indian lands passed into white ownership. The Wheeler-Howard Act of 1934 repealed the Dawes Act and proposed the reconstitution of Indian culture. Whimsically, 20 years later President Dwight D. Eisenhower reversed New Deal Indian policy and resolved to terminate "as fast as possible the special relationship between the American Indian and the federal government." "Termination" eviscerated Indian civilization till the administrations of John F. Kennedy and Lyndon B. Johnson halted the policy.

After 1962, the late Office of Economic Opportunity, and especially the Community Action Program, rekindled reservation life, not so much by lifting the pall of poverty (it did not), but by giving tribes a chance to participate in tribal planning. According to one Indian spokesman, the OEO buttressed the self-confidence of the young so that they could fight for Indian rights. As one Indian put it, "What happens when you free the snake? When he realizes he's free, he begins to move."

Even while the young Indian movement was deciding how to channel this fledgling energy, President Richard Nixon in 1971 hailed the Indian as his favorite minority and invested the Indian tribe with the right of self-determination over reservation affairs. Under President Nixon, the appropriations of the Bureau of Indian Affairs especially for economic development spiraled from $243 million in 1968 to $530 million in 1973.

Not surprisingly, the Nixon administration was shocked at the outbreak of Indian militance at Alcatraz, then in Washington, D.C., and, most recently, at Wounded Knee. But according to the American Indian Movement (AIM), the activists look behind the Nixon concessions and focus on continuing betrayal of the Indian by the BIA. These young Indians regard the bureau as a 150-year-old, highly inefficient, white-dominated bureaucracy which "has stultified our ambitions, corrupted our society, and caused creeping paralysis to set in—economically and socially as well." The AIM accuses the bureau of plotting with "Uncle Tomahawk" tribal "spokesmen" to turn over valuable land and mineral rights to white corporations and, more importantly, the AIM maintains that the bureau demonstrates an absence of sympathy for Indian culture.

The dilemma, then, is how to preserve Indian culture while relieving the deadening poverty of the reservation. Young Indians protest that the city is not the answer. The solution as they see it is the revitalization of the reservation. "Meaningful" Indian education can be provided. For example, at Navaho High School in Gallup, New Mexico, and especially at the experimental Rough Rock Demonstration School, Indians teach Indians in the tribal language, and courses are provided in the ancient tribal arts and crafts.

But while education can build a substratum for "Red Power," a viable economic base is necessary. Although certain tribes, like the Cheyenne River Sioux, have been engaged since 1940 in consolidating their fragmented land holdings, the effort to effect a renascence of the traditional tribal wilderness economy seems doomed to failure. More realistically, experts feel that the reservation must develop some manufacturing "as a necessary concession to economic reality." Sadly, the past history of reservation industrialization is not encouraging. Between 1950 and 1965, the BIA coaxed only 76 firms to relocate on Indian reservations; and by 1968, 20 had ceased operations. Plant managers complained of excessive absenteeism and high turnover rates. By 1971, only three percent of the Indian labor force was working in the less than 200 reservation-based companies.

There have been some breakthroughs. The Red Lake Chippewa and the Rosebud Sioux are negotiating independently with outside corporations, and are showing considerable expertise in developing their fishing and lumber resources. On the Navaho reservation, the Fairchild semiconductor plant employs 880 Navahos, mostly in work that utilizes the women's precision rug-weaving skills for the manufacture of complex circuits. But the ambition of some Indians to find an industrial solution to Indian woes disturbs the traditionalists, old as well as young. Industrialization, with its stress on competition, conflicts with the ancient Indian stress on beauty and social harmony. Industrialization also too often entails the rape of the natural environment; witness the strip mining and power plant development on the Hopi's Black Mesa in Arizona. Thus, the Indian, like the migrant, views technology with a profound ambivalence.

Unfortunately, for both peoples the pace of technology is inexorable, and the manner in which Indian and migrant peoples adjust to technology is crucial if they are to escape the clutch of poverty. It should not be forgotten that the federal government contributed to the plight of both these forgotten peoples. If the bootstraps are to be lifted, if the wellsprings of self-reliance are to be plumbed—and I am alluding deliberately to President Nixon's 1973 Inaugural Address—then Uncle Sam should roll up his sleeves, wade into the mire of migrant and Indian poverty, and join with these "other Americans" in the Herculean task of plumbing and lifting.

46.

SOCIAL MOBILITY IN AMERICA

Department of
Health, Education
and Welfare

Societies vary in the amount of stratification and degree of social mobility which characterize them, but every society has some stratification and some social mobility. Americans believe that our society permits a great deal of social mobility and take pride in the relative freedom of opportunity our society claims it offers for individuals to rise in the strata of prestige, wealth, and power regardless of how low the status of one's family of origin. As the preceding selections have pointed out, formidable barriers of race and ethnicity constitute a sharp contrast between ideological myth and sociological reality. The extent of social mobility in the United States is a subject of great interest among its social scientists. Among the first to study mobility was Pitirim A. Sorokin whose *Social Mobility* was published in 1927. This pioneering research by a migrant from persecution by both Czarist and Bolshevik Russia initiated the development of extensive subsequent analyses of mobility. Only recently, however, has the analytic power of social science methodology been applied on a sufficiently broad population base so dependable knowledge could be gained about social mobility throughout American society, both currently and over time. The analysis of social mobility in this selection from a report of the Department of Health, Education and Welfare draws on research from various sources. The following selections 47, 48, and 49 examine the role of education in social mobility.

HOW MUCH OPPORTUNITY IS THERE?

"America means opportunity." So said Ralph Waldo Emerson over a hundred years ago. Ever since our Nation began, Americans, probably more than others, have believed that the individual should have the opportunity to achieve whatever his talents can bring. They have not enjoyed complete equality of opportunity, but a belief in greater equality of opportunity has always been a part of the American creed.

Source: U.S. Department of Health, Education and Welfare, *Toward a Social Report* (Washington, D.C., Government Printing Office, 1970).

Toward a Social Report was prepared by the staff of the department of Health, Education and Welfare, in the office of Alice M. Rivlin, Assistant Secretary for Planning and Evaluation. Included in the source material for the report were reports submitted by the Panel of Social Indicators, a group of social scientists, and government representatives organized by John Gardner, Secretary of H.E.W. in 1966, to advise the department on the measurement of social change. Daniel Bell chaired the panel.

Although the panel neither wrote nor reviewed the report, the materials submitted by panel members Otis Dudley Duncan, Myrick Freeman, and Harvey Perloff, were important in its formulation.

Thus any inventory of the state of American society must ask how much equality of opportunity we have, and whether there is more or less than there used to be. Complete equality of opportunity exists when the social and economic status a person has is determined by his own abilities and efforts rather than by the circumstances of his birth. If a person's family background or race, for example, affect his ability to "get ahead," then the ideal of equality of opportunity has not been realized.

An improvement throughout the society in the prospects for a high income, an advanced education, or a white collar job, however, does *not* necessarily mean greater *equality* of opportunity. Such improvements in "life chances" for the population as a whole are, of course, important, but they are largely the result of economic progress. We focus on the extent to which a person's status, *relative* to that of others in his society, is determined by his ability and effort, rather than by his social origins. True equality of opportunity means that some families must fall in *relative* social or economic position if others rise. Indeed, many Americans might not want complete equality of opportunity with its extreme emphasis on individual talent, and some might question whether an aristocracy of ability is really preferable to an aristocracy of birth. A society in which the most capable people were always able to rise to positions of leadership, however fair this might seem, could prove intolerable to those who were condemned to failure because they lacked the particular talents valued in that culture. We must, then, temper our desire for more equality of opportunity with the realization that it may also be necessary for the successful and talented to share their good fortune with those less well endowed. But, these issues need not concern us unduly, for no matter how much equality of opportunity there may be in our Nation, most people want more than we now have.

To assess the degree of opportunity and measure its changes over time, we have to be able to determine a man's relative "position" in society, so that we can say whether he has risen or fallen in status. Though there is no one ideal measure of social and economic position, a man's occupation is probably the best single indicator of his socioeconomic level. Other characteristics, like high income, education, social standing, community influence, and membership in prestigious organizations, can also bring high socioeconomic status. The man of independent means and wide influence may have a high standing in his community even if he does not work at a job, and the man in a religious or ethnic minority may be denied access to prestigious organizations in spite of his career success. Thus occupational mobility is not a perfect indicator of social mobility, and we cannot be sure that there is more or less equality of opportunity just because a man's occupational position is more or less dependent on his family background than at some earlier point in our history. Yet changes in occupational mobility probably tell us as much about changes in social mobility as any other single measure we could use. All of the ingredients of a high status usually vary with occupation and are roughly measured by it. In a modern society like the United States, moreover, men are admired primarily for the work they do. Accordingly, we will measure the extent of opportunity by looking at changes in occupational status from one generation to the next, asking in particular how an individual's family background bears on his chances of success. We will also consider how the color of a man's skin affects his position in our society (or at least his economic opportunities). In this first attempt toward a social report, it was not possible to consider other circumstances, such as sex, religion, or national origin, that may limit success in our society. The special problems facing some of these groups are also of great concern to the Nation and it is hoped that any future report can give greater attention to them.

HOW MUCH EQUALITY OF OPPORTUNITY IS THERE?

Earlier in American history, the possibility of moving to the frontier, with its lack of established social structure, was supposed to provide at least some degree of equality of opportunity. The opportunities of the unsettled frontier have vanished, and modern American society has ongoing institutions, established families, and an emphasis on educational credentials that could limit equality of opportunity. A number of observers have been understandably concerned that the extent of equality of opportunity may be decreasing as the Nation's institutions become older and the demands of modern technology place those with an inadequate educational background under an ever greater disadvantage. Among sociologists there has been a debate on the question of whether class lines, as reflected by occupational mobility, have or have not been hardening in the last several decades.

In 1962, the Bureau of the Census conducted a survey of "Occupational Changes in a Generation" which has made it possible to estimate the present extent of opportunity in this country and whether or not there is more or less than there used to be. This survey asked a representative sample of American men not only about their own first occupation, income, education, and the like, but also about their father's usual occupation. A separate survey asked a cross section of the American public what degree of status they thought attached to each occupation, and these responses were used to derive a numerical status "score" (ranging from 0 to 96) for each of 446 detailed Census occupations.[1]

As a result of these two surveys, it is possible to compare the occupational score of each man surveyed in 1962 with the score his father had, and thereby see how much influence the father's relative socioeconomic position had on the ranking of his son. Since the men surveyed were of different ages, it is also possible to get some impression about whether equality of opportunity has been increasing or decreasing by comparing the father-son status relationship of the older men with that of the younger.

The Present State of Opportunity

An analysis of the survey results undertaken by Professors Dudley Duncan and Peter Blau shows that the occupational achievements of the sons were *not* in any large degree explained by the socioeconomic levels of their fathers. To be exact, only 16 percent of the variation in the occupational scores of the men surveyed in 1962 was explained by the father's occupational status.[2] If the data and analyses are

[1] The survey provided prestige ratings for 45 occupations. Census information on the income and education within each occupation was used to assign scores to all other occupations. The procedure was to assume that the relationship between the socioeconomic status of an occupation and the general level of income and education in that occupation was similar to the relationship found to exist between these variables in the 45 occupations for which direct scores were available. It was also known that the relative prestige of various occupations changes very little over time, which made it possible to use the same scores to measure the occupational status of both fathers and sons.

[2] In the language of the statistician, the correlation coefficient relating the occupational scores of fathers and sons was .40.

correct, it follows that the remaining 84 percent of the variation in socioeconomic status among the sons was not related to the socioeconomic status of their fathers. Since there is a probability that the men whose fathers were of high socioeconomic status had on the average somewhat more ability than those whose fathers had lower socioeconomic status, some relationship between status of father and son might be expected even in a society with perfect equality of opportunity. Accordingly, the findings, though extremely tentative, tend to suggest that there is a considerable degree of social mobility in America.[3]

Table 1

*Degree of Relationship * Between Father's Occupation and Respondent's First Job for Four Age Groups, Men 25 to 64 Years Old*

Age (years) in March 1962	
25–34	.380
35–44	.377
45–54	.388
55–64	.384

* Correlation Coefficient.

SOURCE: Peter M. Blau and Otis D. Duncan, *The American Occupational Structure* (New York, John Wiley & Sons, 1967), p. 110.

Trends in Opportunity

There is also some reason to suppose that the degree of equality of opportunity has *not* been declining in recent decades. The oldest group of men surveyed were between 55 and 64 years of age in 1962, and the youngest between 25 and 34, so the oldest group of men held their first jobs about 30 years before the youngest. As table 1 shows, the degree of relationship between the status of father and son is roughly the same for older and younger groups. The relationship appears to be slightly less for the two younger groups than for the two older groups, but it would be a mistake to attach significance to these small changes, and infer that social mobility is increasing. The conclusion should rather be that opportunity and social mobility have shown no tendency to decline.

It might seem that historical changes in the occupational structure, such as the increasing importance of white collar and other high status jobs, have invalidated the conclusions. But, in fact, the statistical analysis that was used tended to abstract from these changes, since it related the *relative*, not the absolute, occupational positions of the men in the two generations. As a result, such changes in occupational structure presumably could not account for the findings.

There is, to be sure, the possibility of other shortcomings in the data or analysis that qualify or invalidate the conclusions. If the material wealth of the fathers of the men surveyed were known, and comparisons made with the wealth or income of the sons, the results might well have been less impressive, since material wealth is presumably easier to pass on from generation to generation than a given occupational status.

These and other qualifications notwithstanding, it is most encouraging that the relative socioeconomic status of the father has only a small influence on the relative socioeconomic status of the son, and that this influence is not increasing.

[3] Some Americans may also wonder whether there is more or less opportunity in the United States than in other parts of the world. At least one study has shown that occupational opportunity, as here measured, is about the same in all industrialized countries. Interestingly enough, however, there is evidence that long distance social mobility—that is, the ability to go from rags to riches in a single generation—is greater in the United States than elsewhere, so there does seem to be a grain of truth in the Horatio Alger myth.

EDUCATION AND OPPORTUNITY

What accounts for the degree of social mobility that we enjoy? And the obstacles to opportunity that remain? Here education plays an important but uncertain role. Education is the principal route to a high status occupation, but it is not obvious whether, on balance, it promotes social mobility. Socioeconomic status influences not only access to higher levels of education, but also the motivation and capacity to learn. In part, then, education is a "transmission belt," whereby initial advantages stemming from the family are maintained for the fortunate, whereas initial disadvantages are perpetuated for the unfortunate. On the other hand, education allows some able people from low status families to rise to a higher relative position in the society. We must assess the extent to which education limits social mobility and also the extent to which it increases it, so that we can evaluate the effect of additional education on equality of opportunity and find educational policies that will further this objective. We look first at the evidence which tends to suggest that education is the means by which parents bequeath superior status to their children.

Education as a Barrier to Mobility

The average person born in this century received more years of schooling than his parents did. As table 2 shows, the average white male born between 1900 and 1934 (aged 35 to 69 in 1969) spent 11 years in school whereas his father who was educated at a much earlier point in time spent only about 8 years in school. But, whenever these men were born, the education they obtained depended to some extent on the education their father received. Thus, fathers who had above-average education for their day have tended to produce sons who were well-educated relative to their own contemporaries. Specifically, for every extra year of education the family head receives, the son tends to get an additional three-tenths or four-tenths of a year of education. It is also clear from table 2 that this relationship between the relative educational attainment of fathers and sons has not changed much since the turn of the century.

Evidently, one way in which high status parents can assure the future success of their children is by providing them with a better than average education. The influence of socioeconomic status on years of schooling is particularly notable where college and graduate education are concerned. This is true even after differences in academic ability have been taken into account, as can be shown by using previously unpublished data from *Project Talent,* and considering only those high school graduates who rank in the top one-fifth of the sample in academic aptitude. If the parents of these relatively able youth are from the top socioeconomic quartile, 82 percent of them will go on to college in the first year after high school graduation. But, if their parents come from the bottom socioeconomic quartile, *only 37 percent* will go on to college in the first year after high school graduation. As table 3 shows, even 5 years after high school graduation, by which time almost everyone who will ever enter college has done so, only 50 percent of these high ability but low status youth will have entered college, and by this time 95 percent of the comparable students from high status families will have entered college. High school graduates from the top socioeconomic quartile who are in the third ability group are more likely to enter college than even the top ability group from the bottom socioeconomic quartile.

Differences in attendance at graduate or

Table 2

Mean Number of School Years Completed by Native White Males and by the Heads of Their Families of Orientation, and Average Relationship of Respondent's to Head's Schooling, by Age, for Men in the Civilian Non-institutional Population of the United States: March 1962

Respondent's year of birth	Family head	Respondent	Average increase in respondent's schooling for each year completed by head
All, 1900–1934	7.9	11.0	.376
1900–1904	7.4	9.4	.401
1905–1909	7.4	10.1	.398
1910–1914	7.5	10.6	.333
1915–1919	7.8	11.1	.336
1920–1924	8.0	11.4	.368
1925–1929	8.3	11.8	.337
1930–1934	8.7	12.0	.366

SOURCE: Beverly Duncan, *Family Factors and School Dropout: 1920–1960,* Cooperative Research Project No. 2258, U.S. Office of Education (Ann Arbor: University of Michigan, 1965), tables 3-1 and 3-2. (Based on data collected by the Bureau of the Census in the Current Population Survey and supplementary questionnaire, "Occupational Changes in a Generation," March 1962.)

professional schools are even more striking. Five years after high school graduation, those high school graduates in the top fifth by ability are *five times more likely to be in a graduate or professional school* if their parents were in the top socioeconomic quartile than if their parents were in the bottom socioeconomic quartile.

There is also a tendency for children from families of low socioeconomic status to perform less well on tests than other children even when they have spent the same number of years in school. This learning differential further accentuates the differences in the initial advantages of children from low and high status families.

How Education Promotes Equality of Opportunity

On the other side of the ledger, we know that there are many factors independent of family socioeconomic status which influence educational attainment, and in turn occupational achievement. These include native mental ability, personality traits, the influence of stimulating teachers, and the like. If educational attainment depends mostly on these and similar factors, it will promote social mobility, by allowing those with ability and ambition to rise to a higher socioeconomic level than their parents. If, on the other hand, education depends on family status it may simply be the means by which successful parents bequeath social and economic advantages to their children.

A statistical analysis, using again the data from the survey of "Occupational Changes in a Generation," tells us something about the role which education plays in promoting social mobility. In this analysis, which is summarized graphically in figure II–1, family background is defined to include father's occupation and education, number of siblings, nativity of birth, color, region of birth, and region of residence. It is evident from figure 2 that some part of the variation in occupational achievement is accounted for by the family

Table 3

Entrance to College, by Ability and Socioeconomic Status (within 5 years after high school graduation)

	Socioeconomic status quartile	Number of high school graduates in group	Number who enter college	Talent loss
Top ability group (100–80%)	1. High	203,000	192,000 (95%)	11,000 (5%)
	2.	153,000	120,000 (79%)	33,000 (21%)
	3.	122,000	82,000 (67%)	40,000 (33%)
	4. Low	60,000	30,000 (50%)	30,000 (50%)
Totals		538,000	424,000 (79%)	114,000 (21%)
Ability group two (80–60%)	1. High	130,000	109,000 (84%)	21,000 (16%)
	2.	143,000	90,000 (63%)	53,000 (37%)
	3.	148,000	78,000 (52%)	70,000 (48%)
	4. Low	94,000	34,000 (36%)	60,000 (64%)
Totals		515,000	311,000 (60%)	204,000 (40%)
Total (top 40%)		1,053,000	735,000 (70%)	318,000 (30%)
Ability group three (60–40%)	1. High	94,000	65,000 (69%)	29,000 (31%)
	2.	135,000	63,000 (46%)	72,000 (54%)
	3.	159,000	55,000 (34%)	104,000 (66%)
	4. Low	148,000	35,000 (24%)	113,000 (76%)
Totals		536,000	218,000 (41%)	318,000 (59%)
Subtotal (1–3 quintiles)		1,600,000	952,000 (60%)	648,000 (40%)

NOTE. Entrance to College means degree-credit only.

SOURCE: The probabilities for these tables are derived from unpublished data from Project Talent, 5-year follow-up surveys of the 1960 twelfth and eleventh grade high school students. The 1965–1966 High School Graduates (*Digest of Educational Statistics,* 1967 edition, Office of Education, U.S. GPO, table 65, "Number of public and nonpublic high school graduates, by sex and State: 1955–66") were then distributed according to the Project Talent probabilities.

background factors we have just mentioned. This is largely because individuals born in favorable circumstances (for example, in well-educated, white families in the North) come to be better educated than those born in less favorable circumstances. But, to a great extent, the educational attainment of a child is due to factors that are independent of his family background, and this education, in turn, helps him achieve a higher occupational status even if he had a disadvantaged family background. Indeed, individual differences in educational attainment that are independent of family background explain more than half of the variation in occupational scores attributable to education.

We can then conclude that social background factors, though important determinants of educational and occupational achievements, are *not* as important as the other factors that influence educational

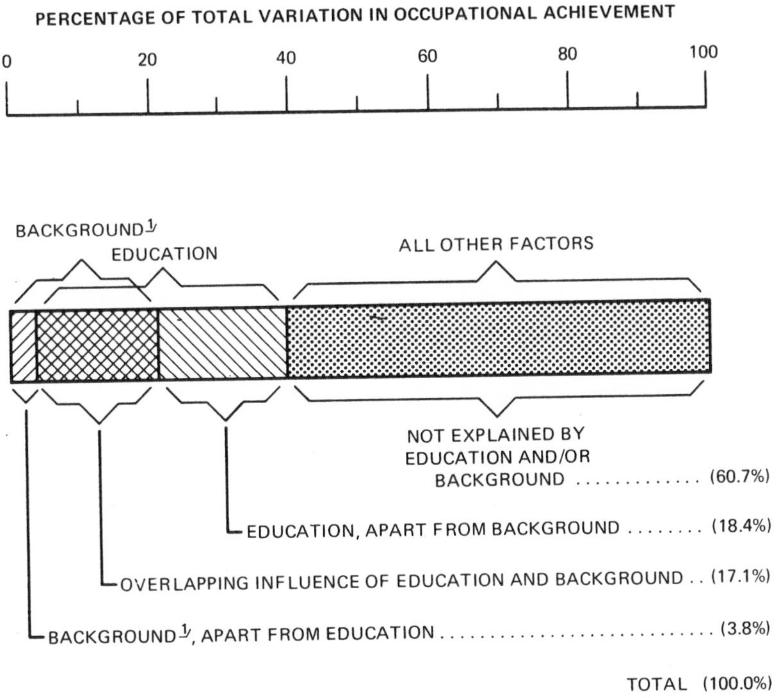

Figure II–1 *Sources of Variation in Occupational Achievement, for Men 20–64 Years Old in Experienced Civilian Labor Force: March 1962. Source: P. M. Blau and O. D. Duncan,* The American Occupational Structure *(New York: Wiley, 1967), Appendix H.*

[1] *Background factors included: family head's occupation, family head's education, number of siblings and sibling position, nativity, color, region of birth and region of residence.*

attainment and thereby allow those of humble birth to rise to the more prestigious occupations. What might be called the democratic discovery of talent through universal education is quantitatively more important than the educational advantages children from high status families enjoy.

Education could, to be sure, do still more to equalize opportunity. If education depended less on family background than it now does then it would give children from families with a low socioeconomic position a still greater opportunity to rise to a higher level. If, for example, the chance to go on to college did not depend so much on the financial resources of one's family, education would enable many more to climb up the ladder of occupational success. Though education could contribute much more to equality of opportunity, the fact that it has already contributed a good deal may explain why we expect so much of it.

OPPORTUNITY AND RACE

There is one glaring exception to the encouraging conclusions we have drawn. The same data that show abundant opportunity for most Americans also show that Negroes have much less occupational mobility than whites. This can be seen by looking at table 4. This table shows the occupational distributions of men whose fathers were in the same occupation, and also distinguishes the occupational distributions of Negroes from all of the others surveyed in the study of "Occupational Changes in a Generation."

The table reveals a striking result: Most Negro men, *regardless of their fathers' occupations,* were working at unskilled or semiskilled jobs. Even if their fathers were in professional, managerial, or proprietary positions, they were usually operatives, service workers, or laborers. Growing up in a family of high socioeconomic status was only a slight advantage for the Negro man. By contrast, the majority of white men with higher white collar backgrounds remained at their father's level and almost half of the white men whose fathers were in clerical or sales work and almost two-fifths of those with a farm or blue collar background moved up into the more prestigious professional and managerial group. But the Negroes from similar origins did not. The Negro man originating at the lower levels is likely to stay there, the white man to move up. The Negro originating at the higher levels is likely to move down; the white man seldom does. The contrast is stark.

Education is an important source of occupational opportunity. Because most Americans can realize their highest ambitions through education, it is often assumed that Negroes can similarly overcome the handicaps of poverty and race. But this has not been so in the past. To be sure, even in minority groups, better educated individuals tend to occupy more desirable occupational positions than do the less educated. Yet the returns on an investment in education are much lower for Negroes than for the general population. Indeed, for a Negro, educational attainment may simply mean exposure to more severe and visible discrimination than is experienced by the dropout or the unschooled.

Thus, in addition to the handicap of being born in a family with few economic or other resources, the average Negro also appears to have less opportunity because of his race alone. Let us examine the relative importance of each of the different types of barriers to success for Negroes.

Figure 2 shows that the average Negro male completed 2.3 fewer years of school than the average white male, that his occupational score is 23.8 points lower, and that his income is $3,790 lower. Much of the shortfall in the relative achievement of Negroes can be attributed to specific causes. One year of the educational gap arises from the fact that Negroes come from disadvantaged families while an additional 0.1 year is the result of the fact that Negroes tend to be born into larger families where resources must be spread among more children. But even with the allowance of 1.1 years of schooling traceable to these disadvantages, there remains an unexplained gap of 1.2 years. Evidently, this must be caused by something other than the initial socioeconomic differences between blacks and whites. Perhaps it is the Negro's knowledge that he will be discriminated against whatever his education.

If we look at the *occupational gap* of 23.8 points, we see that 6.6 points can be ascribed to initial Negro-white differences in family socioeconomic levels and an addi-

Table 4

Mobility from Father's Occupation to 1962 Occupation (percentage distributions), by Race, for Civilian Men 25 to 64 Years Old, March 1962

	1962 Occupation [1]						Total	
Race and father's occupation	High white collar	Lower white collar	Higher manual	Lower manual	Farm	Not in experienced civilian labor force	Percent	Number (000)
Negro								
Higher white collar	10.4	9.7	19.4	53.0	0.0	7.5	100.0	134
Lower white collar	14.5	9.1	6.0	69.1	0.0	7.3	100.0	55
Higher manual	8.8	6.8	11.2	64.1	2.8	6.4	100.0	251
Lower manual	8.0	7.0	11.5	63.2	1.8	8.4	100.4	973
Farm	3.1	3.0	6.4	59.8	16.2	11.6	100.0	1,389
Not reported	2.4	6.5	11.1	65.9	3.1	11.1	100.0	712
Total, percent	5.2	5.4	9.5	62.2	7.7	10.0	100.0	
Total, number	182	190	334	2,184	272	352		3,514
Non-Negro								
Higher white collar	54.3	15.3	11.5	11.9	1.3	5.6	100.0	5,836
Lower white collar	45.1	18.3	13.5	14.6	1.5	7.1	100.0	2,652
Higher manual	28.1	11.8	27.9	24.0	1.0	7.3	100.0	6,512
Lower manual	21.3	11.5	22.5	36.0	1.7	6.9	100.0	8,798
Farm	16.5	7.0	19.8	28.8	20.4	7.5	100.0	9,991
Not reported	26.0	10.3	21.0	32.5	3.9	6.4	100.0	2,666
Total, percent	28.6	11.3	20.2	26.2	6.8	6.9	100.0	
Total, number	10,414	4,130	7,359	9,560	2,475	2,517		36,455

[1] Combinations of census major occupation groups. *Higher white collar:* professional and kindred workers, and managers, officials, and proprietors, except farm. *Lower white collar:* sales, clerical, and kindred workers. *Higher manual:* craftsmen, foremen, and kindred workers. *Lower manual:* operatives and kindred workers, service workers, and laborers, except farm. *Farm:* farmers and farm managers, farm laborers and foremen. Classification by "father's occupation" includes some men reporting on the occupation of a family head other than the father.

SOURCE: Unpublished tables, survey of "Occupational Changes in a Generation."

tional 0.6 to differences in family size. The residual educational gap, already identified, carries over into occupational achievement, lowering the Negro score relative to the white by 4.8 points on the average. There remains a gap, not otherwise accounted for, of 11.8 points. This discrepancy derives from the fact that Negro men with the same schooling and the same family background as a comparable group of white men will have jobs of appreciably lower status. It is surely attributable in part to racial discrimination in hiring, promotion, and other job-related opportunities.

All of the factors mentioned are converted into an *income gap* totaling $3,790. Substantial components of this are due to socioeconomic status and family size

Figure 2 *Differences in means between white (W) and Negro (N) with respect to educatioal attainment, occupational status, and income, with components of differences generated by cumulative effects in a model of the socioeconomic life cycle, for native men, 25 to 64 years old, with nonfarm background and in the experienced civilian labor force: March 1962.*

Years of school completed		1962 occupation score		1961 income (dollars)		Component[1]
(W) 11.7		(W) 43.5		(W) 7,070		
	1.0		6.6		940	(A) [Family]
10.7		36.9		6,130		
	0.1		0.6		70	(B) [Siblings]
10.6		36.3		6,060		
	1.2		4.8		520	(C) [Education]
(N) 9.4		31.5		5,540		
			11.8		830	(D) [Occupation]
		(N) 19.7		4,710		
					1,430	(E) [Income]
				(N) 3,280		
	2.3		23.8		3,790	(T) [Total]

[1] Difference due to:
(A) Socioeconomic level of family of origin (head's education and occupation).
(B) Number of siblings, net of family origin level.
(C) Education, net of siblings and family origin level.
(D) Occupation, net of education, siblings, and family origin level.
(E) Income, net of occupation, education, siblings, and family origin level.
(T) Total difference, (W) minus (N) = sum of components (A) through (E).

SOURCE: O. D. Duncan, "Inheritance of Poverty or Inheritance of Race?" forthcoming.

($1,010), lower educational attainment ($520), and job discrimination ($830), so that disadvantages detectable at earlier stages clearly have an important impact in lowering Negro income compared to white income. But there remains a gap of $1,430 not otherwise accounted for, suggesting that Negro men, relative to a group of white men of comparable family background, educational attainment, and occupational level, still receive much lower wages and salaries. The specific magnitudes obtained in calculations of this kind are not to be taken as firm estimates. Nevertheless, the substantial discrepancies existing between Negro and white attainment suggest that the Negro has severely limited opportunity, not only because his social and economic background place him at a disadvantage, but also because he faces racial discrimination in the school system and in the job market.

What can we conclude about social mobility in America? We have seen that there is opportunity for the great majority of our citizens to improve their relative occupational status through their own efforts. Yet we are far from achieving true equality of opportunity. Economic and social status in our society still depend in a striking way on the color of a man's skin. Until we can eliminate this barrier to full participation, we will not have been faithful to our historic ideals.

47. 48. 49.

THE SCHOOLS AND EQUAL OPPORTUNITY

Mary Jo Bane and Christopher Jencks

EQUAL OPPORTUNITY AND EQUAL RESULTS

James S. Coleman

SOCIAL POLICY, POWER, AND SOCIAL SCIENCE RESEARCH

Kenneth B. Clark

People in most nations around the world look to education as the means of upward social mobility and equalizing opportunity to achieve higher social and economic status. The United States is no exception. The level of education attained is significantly correlated with occupational status and income in the United States as in other countries. However, Christopher Jencks and his associates have concluded, after the analysis of several sets of data relevant to the subject, that educational achievement, when separated from other variables, accounts for little of the difference in adult income or occupation. The first of the next three selections is an article summarizing their findings and conclusions drawn from their subsequently published book, Jencks, et al., *Inequality: A Reassessment of the Effect of Family and Schooling in America.*

Many social scientists have responded to the Jencks publication with critical reviews and counter positions. We have chosen two of these by distinguished social scientists. In selection 48, James Coleman, the codirector of the national study reported in *Equality of Educational Opportunity* notes the differences between equality of opportunity and equality of status or income. He also shows how the same data support the hypothesis that "increasing equality of education does have a strong effect on increasing equality of income." These divergent conclusions are the result of different types of analysis of the same data. This fact demonstrates the important role methods of analysis may play in social research, for inappropriate methods may produce invalid conclusions.

In selection 49, the distinguished black social psychologist, Kenneth Clark, contends that Jencks's conclusions are unjustified and are simply lending support to a segregation and discrimination policy in education. Clark maintains that the conclusions of the Jencks study "in terms of the immediate policy implication is that racial, economic, and academic discrimination in the schools has trivial educational effects. These assertions are of such importance that it is potentially irresponsible to make them without the most rigorous objective verification or refutation." The role of social science research and the responsibility of the social scientist in analysis of major social policy issues is thus brought into sharp focus.

These three selections, and the one that follows, focus on the pervasive social and political issue of the past score of years—segregation and educational inequality. Public concern with the issue arises in part at least because it involves strongly held values in American culture. The right to equality of opportunity is highly valued, but we also believe there are great differences among individuals which should be rewarded with differences in status and income. Education is seen as the means of both maintaining differences and achieving equality of opportunity in the society. These selections *reflect* the importance of the issue in American society.

47. Bane and Jencks

Americans have a recurrent fantasy that schools can solve their problems. Thus it was perhaps inevitable that, after we rediscovered poverty and inequality in the early 1960s, we turned to the schools for

Source: Mary Jo Bane and Christopher Jencks, *Saturday Review of Education* 55 (September 16, 1972): 37–42. Copyright © 1972 by Saturday Review Co. Reprinted by permission of the publisher.

Mary Jo Bane is a research associate at the Center for Educational Policy Research, Harvard University. She has been a contributing editor to the Education portion of *The Saturday Review.*

Christopher Jencks is a professor of education at Harvard University, and on the staff of the Center for the Study of Public Policy at Harvard. He is the author of a controversial report, *Education Vouchers,* for the Office of Equal Opportunity, and of *Inequality: A Reassessment of the Effect of Family and Schooling in America.* He is coauthor of *The Academic Revolution.*

solutions. Yet the schools did not provide solutions, the high hopes of the early-and-middle 1960s faded, and the war on poverty ended in ignominious surrender to the *status quo.* In part, of course, this was because the war in Southeast Asia turned out to be incompatible with the war on poverty. In part, however, it was because we all had rather muddleheaded ideas about the various causes and cures of poverty and inequality.

Today there are signs that some people are beginning to look for new solutions to these perennial problems. There is a vast amount of sociological and economic data that can, we think, help in this effort, both by explaining the failures of the 1960s and by suggesting more realistic alternatives. For the past four years we have been working with this data. Our research has led us to three general conclusions.

First, poverty is a condition of relative rather than absolute deprivation. People feel poor and are poor if they have a lot less money than their neighbors. This is true regardless of their absolute income. It follows that we cannot eliminate poverty unless we prevent people from falling too far below the national average. The problem is economic inequality rather than low incomes.

Second, the reforms of the 1960s were misdirected because they focused only on equalizing opportunity to "succeed" (or "fail") rather than on reducing the economic and social distance between those who succeeded and those who failed. The evidence we have reviewed suggests that equalizing opportunity will not do very much to equalize results, and hence that it will not do much to reduce poverty.

Third, even if we are interested solely in equalizing opportunities for economic success, making schools more equal will not help very much. Differences between schools have very little effect on what happens to students after they graduate.

The main policy implication of these findings is that although school reform is important for improving the lives of children, schools cannot contribute significantly to adult equality. If we want economic equality in our society, we will have to get it by changing our economic institutions, not by changing the schools.

POVERTY AND INEQUALITY

The rhetoric of the war on poverty described the persistence of poverty in the midst of affluence as a "paradox," largely attributable to "neglect." Official publications all assumed that poverty was an absolute rather than a relative condition. Having assumed this, they all showed progress toward the elimination of poverty, since fewer and fewer people had incomes below the official "poverty line."

Yet, despite all the official announcements of progress, many Americans still seemed poor, by both their own standards and their neighbors'. The reason was that most Americans define poverty in relative rather than absolute terms. Public-opinion surveys show, for example, that when people are asked how much money an American family needs to "get by," they typically name a figure about half what the average American family actually receives. This has been true for the last three decades, despite the fact that real incomes (incomes adjusted for inflation) have doubled in the interval.

During the Depression the average American family was living on about $30 a week. A third of all families were living on less than half this amount, which made it natural for Franklin Roosevelt to speak of "one-third of a nation" as illhoused, illclothed, and illfed. By 1964 mean family income was about $160 a week, and the Gallup poll found that the average American thought a family of four needed at least $80 a week to "get by." Even allowing for inflation, this was twice what people had thought necessary during the Depression. Playing it safe, the Johnson administration defined the poverty line at $60 a week for a family of four, but most people felt this was inadequate. By 1970 inflation had raised mean family income to about $200 a week, and the National Welfare Rights Organization was trying to rally liberal support for a guaranteed income of $100 a week.

These changes in the definition of poverty were not just a matter of "rising expectations" or of people's needing to "keep up with the Joneses." The goods and services that made it possible to live on $15 a week during the Depression were no longer available to a family with the same real income ($40 a week) in 1964. Eating habits had changed, and many cheap foods had disappeared from the stores. Housing arrangements had changed, too. During the Depression many people could not afford indoor plumbing and "got by" with a privy. By the 1960s privies were illegal in most places. Those who still could not afford an indoor toilet ended up in buildings that had broken toilets. For these they paid more than their parents had paid for privies.

Examples of this kind suggest that the "cost of living" is not the cost of buying some fixed set of goods and services. It is the cost of participating in a social system. It therefore depends in large part on how much other people habitually spend to participate in the system. Those who fall far below the norm, whatever it may be, are excluded. Accordingly, raising the incomes of the poor will not eliminate poverty if the cost of participating in "mainstream" American life rises even faster. People with incomes less than half the national average will not be able to afford what "everyone" regards as "necessities." The only way to eliminate poverty is, therefore, to make sure everyone has an income at least half the average.

Arguments of this kind suggest not only that it makes more sense to think of "poverty" as a relative rather than an absolute condition but that eliminating poverty, at least as it is usually defined in America, depends on eliminating, or at least greatly reducing, inequality.

SCHOOLING AND OPPORTUNITY

Almost none of the reform legislation of the 1960s involved direct efforts to equalize adult status, power, or income. Most Americans accepted the idea that these rewards should go to those who were most competent and diligent. Their objection to America's traditional economic system was not that it produced inequality but that the rules determining who succeeded and who failed were often unfair. The reformers wanted to create a world in which success would no longer be associated with skin color, economic background, or other "irrelevant" factors, but only with actual merit. What they wanted, in short, was what they called "equal opportunity."

Their strategy for achieving equal opportunity placed great emphasis on education. Many people imagined that if schools could equalize people's cognitive skills this would equalize their bargaining power as adults. Presumably, if every one had equal bargaining power, few people would end up very poor.

This strategy for reducing poverty rested on a series of assumptions that went roughly as follows:

1) Eliminating poverty is largely a matter of helping children born into poverty to rise out of it. Once families escape from poverty, they do not fall back into it. Middle-class children rarely end up poor.

2) The primary reason poor children cannot escape from poverty is that they do not acquire basic cognitive skills. They cannot read, write, calculate, or articulate. Lacking these skills, they cannot get or keep a well-paid job.

3) The best mechanism for breaking this "vicious circle" is educational reform. Since children born into poor homes do not acquire the skills they need from their parents, they must be taught these skills in school. This can be done by making sure that they attend the same schools as middle-class children, by giving them extra compensatory programs in school, by giving their parents a voice in running their schools, or by some combination of all three approaches.

Our research over the last four years suggests that each of these assumptions is erroneous:

1) Poverty is not primarily hereditary. While children born into poverty have a higher than average chance of ending up poor, there is still an enormous amount of economic mobility from one generation to the next. A father whose occupational status is high passes on less than half his advantage to his sons, and a father whose status is low passes along less than half his disadvantage. A family whose income is above the norm has an even harder time passing along its privileges; its sons are typically only about a third as advantaged as the parents. Conversely, a family whose income is below average will typically have sons about a third as disadvantaged as the parents. The effects of parents' status on their daughters' economic positions appear to be even weaker. This means that many "advantaged" parents have some

"disadvantaged" children and vice versa.

2) The primary reason some people end up richer than others is not that they have more adequate cognitive skills. While children who read well, get the right answers to arithmetic problems, and articulate their thoughts clearly are somewhat more likely than others to get ahead, there are many other equally important factors involved. The effects of I.Q. on economic success are about the same as the effects of family background. This means, for example, that if two men's I.Q. scores differ by 17 points—the typical difference between I.Q. scores of individuals chosen at random—their incomes will typically differ by less than $2,000. That amount is not completely trivial, of course. But the income difference between random individuals is three times as large and the difference between the best-paid fifth and the worst-paid fifth of all male workers averages $14,000. There is almost as much economic inequality among those who score high on standardized tests as in the general population.

3) There is no evidence that school reform can substantially reduce the extent of cognitive inequality, as measured by tests of verbal fluency, reading comprehension, or mathematical skill. Eliminating qualitative differences between elementary schools would reduce the range of scores on standardized tests in sixth grade by less than 3 percent. Eliminating qualitative differences between high schools would hardly reduce the range of twelfth-grade scores at all and would reduce by only 1 percent the disparities in the amount of education people eventually get.

Our best guess, after reviewing all the evidence we could find, is that racial desegregation raises black elementary school students' test scores by a couple of points. But most of the test-score gap between blacks and whites persists, even when they are in the same schools. So also: Tracking has very little effect on test scores. And neither the overall level of resources available to a school nor any specific, easily identifiable school policy has a significant effect on students' cognitive skills or educational attainments. Thus, even if we went beyond "equal opportunity" and allocated resources disproportionately to schools whose students now do worst on tests and are least likely to acquire credentials, this would not improve these students' prospects very much.

The evidence does not tell us why school quality has so little effect on test scores. Three possible explanations come to mind. First, children seem to be more influenced by what happens at home than by what happens in school. They may also be more influenced by what happens on the streets and by what they see on television. Second, administrators have very little control over those aspects of school life that do affect children. Reallocating resources, reassigning pupils, and rewriting the curriculum seldom change the way teachers and students actually treat each other minute by minute. Third, even when the schools exert an unusual influence on children, the resulting changes are not likely to persist into adulthood. It takes a huge change in elementary school test scores, for example, to alter adult income by a significant amount.

EQUAL OPPORTUNITY AND UNEQUAL RESULTS

The evidence we have reviewed, taken all together, suggests that equalizing opportunity cannot take us very far toward eliminating inequality. The simplest way of demonstrating this is to compare the economic prospects of brothers raised in the same home. Even the most egalitarian society could not hope to make opportunities for all children appreciably more equal than the opportunities now available to brothers from the same family. Looking at society at large, if we compare random pairs of individuals, the difference between their occupational statuses averages about 28 points on the Duncan "status scale" (the scale runs from 0 to 96 points). The difference between brothers' occupational statuses averages fully 23 points on this same scale. If we compare men's incomes, the difference between random pairs averaged about $6,200 in 1968. The difference between brothers' incomes, according to our best estimate, probably averaged about $5,700. These estimates mean that people who start off equal end up almost as unequal as everyone else. Inequality is not mostly inherited: It is recreated anew in each generation.

We can take this line of argument a step further by comparing people who not only start off in similar families but who also have the same I.Q. scores and get the same amount of schooling. Such people's occupational statuses differ by an average of 21 points, compared to 28 points for random individuals. If we compare their incomes, making the additional assumption that the men have the same occupational status, we find that they differ by an average of about $5,300, compared to $6,200 for men chosen at random.

These comparisons suggest that adult success must depend on a lot of things besides family background, schooling, and the cognitive skills measured by standardized tests. We have no idea what these factors are. To some extent, no doubt, specialized varieties of competence, such as the ability to hit a ball thrown at high speed or the ability to persuade a customer that he wants a larger car than he thought he wanted, play a major role. Income also depends on luck: the range of jobs available when you are job hunting, the amount of overtime work in your plant, good or bad weather for your strawberry crop, and a hundred other unpredictable accidents.

Equalizing opportunity will not, then, do much to reduce economic inequality in America. If poverty is relative rather than absolute, equalizing opportunity will not do much to reduce poverty, either.

IMPLICATIONS FOR EDUCATIONAL POLICY

These findings imply that school reform is never likely to have any significant effect on the degree of inequality among adults. This suggests that the prevalent "factory" model, in which schools are seen as places that "produce" alumni, probably ought to be abandoned. It is true that schools have "inputs" and "outputs," and that one of their nominal purposes is to take human "raw material" (*i.e.,* children) and convert it into something more "useful" (*i.e.,* employable adults). Our research suggests, however, that the character of a school's output depends largely on a single input, the characteristics of the entering children. Everything else—the school budget, its policies, the characteristics of the teachers—is either secondary or completely irrelevant, at least so long as the range of variation among schools is as narrow as it seems to be in America.

These findings have convinced us that the long-term effects of schooling are relatively uniform. The day-to-day internal life of the schools, in contrast, is highly variable. It follows that *the primary basis for evaluating a school should be whether the students and teachers find it a satisfying place to be.* This does not mean we think schools should be like mediocre summer camps, in which children are kept out of trouble but not taught anything. We doubt that a school can be enjoyable for either adults or children unless the children keep learning new things. We value ideas and the life of the mind, and we think that a school that does not value these things is a poor place for children. But a school that values ideas because they enrich the lives of children is quite different from a school that values high reading scores because reading scores are important for adult success.

Our concern with making schools satisfying places for teachers and children has led us to a concern for diversity and choice. People have widely different notions of what a "satisfying" place is, and we believe they ought to be able to put these values into practice. As we have noted, our research suggests that none of the programs or structural arrangements in common use today has consistently different long-term effects from any other. Since the character of a child's schooling has few long-term effects, and since these effects are quite unpredictable, society has little reason to constrain the choices available to parents and children. If a "good school" is one the students and staff find satisfying, no one school will be best for everyone. Since there is no evidence that professional educators know appreciably more than parents about what is good for children, it seems reasonable to let parents decide what kind of education their children should have while they are young and to let the children decide as they get older.

Short-term considerations also seem decisive in determining whether to spend more money on schooling or to spend it on busing children to schools outside their neighborhoods. If extra resources make school life pleasanter and more interesting, they are worthwhile. But we should not try to justify school expenditures on the grounds that they boost adult earnings. Likewise, busing ought to be justified in political and moral terms rather than in terms of presumed long-term effects on the children who are bused. If we want an integrated society, we ought to have integrated schools, which make people feel they have a stake in the well-being of other races. If we want a society in which people are free to segregate themselves, then we should apply that principle to our schools. There is, however, no compelling reason to treat schools differently from other social arrangements, including neighborhoods. Personally, we believe in both open housing and open schools. If parents or students want to take buses to schools in other neighborhoods, school boards ought to provide the buses, expand the relevant schools, and ensure that the students are welcome in the schools they want to attend. This is the least we can do to offset the effects of residential segregation. But we do not believe that forced busing can be justified on the grounds of its long-term benefits for students.

This leads to our last conclusion about educational reform. Reformers are always getting trapped into claiming too much for what they propose. They may want a particular reform—like open classrooms, or desegregation, or vouchers—because they think these reforms will make schools more satisfying places to work. Yet they feel obliged to claim that these reforms will also reduce the number of nonreaders, increase racial understanding, or strengthen family life. A wise reformer ought to be more modest, claiming only that a particular reform will not harm adult society and that it will make life pleasanter for parents, teachers, and students in the short run.

This plea for modesty in school reform will, we fear, fall on deaf ears. Ivan Illich is right in seeing schools as secular churches, through which we seek to improve not ourselves but our descendants. That this process should be disagreeable seems inevitable; one cannot abolish original sin through self-indulgence. That it should be immodest seems equally inevitable; a religion that promises anything less than salvation wins few converts. In school, as in church, we present the world as we wish it were. We try to inspire children with the ideals we ourselves have failed to live up to. We assume, for example, that we cannot make adults live in desegregated neighborhoods, so we devise schemes for busing children from one neighborhood to another in order to desegregate the schools. We all prefer conducting our moral experiments on other people. Nonetheless, so long as we confine our experiments to children, we will not have much effect on adult life.

IMPLICATIONS FOR SOCIAL REFORM

Then how *are* we to affect adult life? Our findings tell us that different kinds of inequality are only loosely related to one another. This can be either encouraging or discouraging, depending on how you look at it. On the discouraging side, it means that eliminating inequality in one area will not eliminate it in other areas. On the encouraging side, it means that inequality in one area does not dictate inequality in other areas.

To begin with, genetic inequality is not a major obstacle to economic equality. It is true that genetic diversity almost inevitably means considerable variation in people's scores on standardized tests. But this kind of cognitive inequality need not imply anything like the present degree of economic inequality. We estimate, for example, that if the only sources of income inequality in America were differences in people's genes, the top fifth of the population would earn only about 1.4 times as much as the bottom fifth. In actuality, the top fifth earns seven times as much as the bottom fifth.

Second, our findings suggest that psychological and cultural differences between families are not an irrevocable barrier to adult equality. Family background has more influence than genes on an individual's educational attainment, occupational status, and income. Nonetheless, if family background were the only source of economic inequality in America, the top fifth would earn only about twice as much as the bottom fifth.

Our findings show, then, that inequality is not determined at birth. But they also suggest that economic equality cannot be achieved by indirect efforts to manipulate the environments in which people grow up. We have already discussed the minuscule effects of equalizing school quality. Equalizing the amount of schooling people get would not work much better. Income inequality among men with similar amounts of schooling is only 5–10 percent less than among men in general. The effect is even less if we include women.

If we want to eliminate economic inequality, we must make this an explicit objective of public policy rather than deluding ourselves into thinking that we can do it by giving everyone equal opportunity to succeed or fail. If we want an occupational structure which is less hierarchical and in which the social distance between the top and the bottom is reduced, we will have to make deliberate efforts to reorganize work and redistribute power within organizations. We will probably also have to rotate jobs, so that no individual held power very long.

If we want an income distribution that is more equal, we can constrain employers, either by tax incentives or direct legislation, to reduce wage disparities between their best- and worst-paid workers. We can make taxes more progressive, and we can provide income supplements to those who do not make an adequate living from wages alone. We can also provide free public services for those who cannot afford to buy adequate services in the private sector. Pursued with vigor, such a strategy can make "poverty" (*i.e.,* having a living standard less than half the national average) virtually impossible. Such a strategy would also make economic "success," in the sense of having, say, a living standard more than twice the national average, far less common than it now is. The net effect would be to make those with the most competence and luck subsidize those with the least competence and luck to a far greater extent than they do today. Unless we are prepared to do this, poverty and inequality will remain with us indefinitely.

This strategy was rejected during the 1960s for the simple reason that it commanded relatively little popular support. The required legislation could not have passed Congress, nor could it pass today. That does not mean that it is the wrong strategy. It simply means that, until we change the political and moral premises on which most Americans now operate, poverty and inequality will persist at pretty much their present level. Intervention in market processes, for example, means restricting the "right" of individuals to use their natural advantages for private gain. Economic equality requires social and legal sanctions—analogous to those that now exist against capricious firing of employees—against inequality within work settings. It also requires that wage rates, which Americans have traditionally viewed as a "private" question to be adjudicated by negotiation between (unequal) individuals or groups, must become a "public" question subject to political control and solution.

In America, as elsewhere, the long-term drift over the past 200 years has been toward equality. In America, however, the contribution of public policy to this drift has been slight. As long as egalitarians assume that public policy cannot contribute to equality directly but must proceed by ingenious manipulations of marginal institutions like the schools, this pattern will continue. If we want to move beyond this tradition, we must establish political control over the economic institutions that shape our society. What we will need, in short, is what other countries call socialism. Anything less will end in the same disappointment as the reforms of the 1960s.

48. Coleman

This could have been an important book. Jencks and his colleagues have had the audacity to assemble and reanalyze a wide range of research on inequality, and have demonstrated a high level of technical skill in doing so. But the book misses the opportunity. To show how it comes to miss the opportunity, I must clarify at the outset certain points about inequalities in society.

Source: James S. Coleman, *Harvard Educational Review* 43, no. 1 (February 1973): 129–34.

James S. Coleman is a professor of sociology at the University of Chicago. He has written *The Adolescent Society* and *Adolescents and the Schools,* and has coauthored *Equality of Educational Opportunity.*

For it is the confusion between different meanings of inequality that leads Jencks and his colleagues to the fundamental difficulties of the book.

INEQUALITY OF RESULT

In every society there are occupational positions that earn different amounts of income. This income is ordinarily in money, though where income taxes are high (as in England and Sweden) or where there are ideological constraints on income inequalities (as in socialist states), a significant portion is paid in direct (untaxed) perquisites. Since these occupations are filled by persons, the differential earnings from different positions give rise to a distribution of income among persons or among families. The skewness of this distribution has historically declined in the United States, with incomes becoming more nearly alike, though a great deal of inequality of income remains.

Thus one meaning of inequality in society is merely the differential distribution of income and other social rewards to different persons. This can be described as "inequality of result." The extent of inequality of result can be measured, though imperfectly, by the degree of skewness in the income distribution. The authors use the coefficient of variation of income to measure this inequality, and show that it has declined from 1.23 in 1929 to 0.75 in 1970. They also present the share of total income held by each fifth of the population, ranging from the lowest-income fifth to the highest. The authors argue that this distribution has become very little more equal in the past twenty-five years (a claim that I will return to), and that this is the matter that concerns them. . . . For example, they say, "The reader should by now have gathered that our primary concern is with equalizing the distribution of income."

INEQUALITY OF OPPORTUNITY

But there is a second sense of inequality as well, one at least as familiar to most Americans as inequality in the sense above. This is inequality of access to those positions which give high income and other social rewards. Inequality in this sense is not measured by the amount of income different persons have; it is measured by the relation of a person's background to the social rewards he comes to gain. If all sons from high-income families come to have high income, and all sons from low-income families come to have low income, then there would be high inequality in this second sense. This is what is meant by "inequality of opportunity," and it is reactions to this inequality that have been the source of recent equalizing movements—for blacks, Chicanos, women, and Indians.

It should be clear that these two meanings of inequality are conceptually distinct. If there are two societies with a given degree of inequality of result, one of them might have total inequality of opportunity, via direct transmission of occupational position and wealth from father to son, while the other might have total equality of opportunity, with a son's income unrelated to that of his father. Of course, at the extreme of perfect income equality, there can be no inequality of opportunity, since there is no opportunity to do better or worse.

Now the curious aspect of this book is that the authors say that they are concerned with inequality of income, and their policy proposals are directed to that inequality. But nearly all their analysis is directed to questions of inequality of opportunity. This is likely the consequence of making a book with many hands. But whatever the source of the difficulty, the result is a book that fails to study appropriately either inequalities of income or inequalities of opportunity.

A DIFFERENT BOOK

If Jencks and his colleagues had pursued the question of why inequalities of income are as great as they are, the book would have differed in two ways from its present form. It would have started with inequality of income, and not waited until the last chapter to consider it. Much of the current book might then have been unnecessary. The questions of inequality of opportunity that they study, such as the relation of family background to income, would have been unnecessary and irrelevant. . . . And if they found, as they argue, that income is not much related to educational attainment or cognitive skills, then there would have been no need to investigate the sources of inequality in educational attainment and in cognitive skills. . . .

A second way in which the book would have differed if it had truly studied inequality of income is that it would have investigated many things it has not investigated. It would have focused not primarily on the inequalities of opportunity among persons, but on the inequalities of reward among occupational positions. These differential rewards depend on a variety of things not touched in *Inequality:* the demand for activities for which skills are scarce, and the control of entrance into highly paid positions, e.g., by professional associations or unions or credentialling systems. It would have looked for the cause of the skewness of the income distribution in societal variables, such as the rate of economic growth or level of unemployment. It cannot be found in the individual variables that they study, such as father's occupation, for those variables are relevant to equality of opportunity, not equality of income. They would have found, among other things, a fact to negate their argument for socialism in the last paragraph of the book: that income inequality in the U.S. dropped more rapidly during the period of rampant capitalism in the early part of this century than it has dropped recently, as more and more controls have been placed on the free functioning of labor markets.

The kind of analysis the book would have engaged in, with variables defined at the societal level rather than the individual level, is exemplified by the relation between education and income. If equalizing educational attainment is to lead to equalization of income, then what should be studied is the relation, over time, between the equality of income and the equality of educational attainment. . . . The inequalities in these two distributions are shown by the coefficient of variation, which is high when inequality is high, and low when inequality is low. The coefficients of variation for corresponding years are shown in Table 1 below (the correspondence chosen is the closest possible for labor force participation of persons educated at particular dates, using the data Jencks presents). That for education is much lower than that for income, but both decline over time. If the coefficient of variation for each at each time is divided by that for 1929, we get the inequality at that date relative to that in 1929. The declines in inequality, as shown below in Table 2, are remarkably similar. Though other explanations could be offered, they suggest that increasing equality of education does have a strong effect on increasing equality of income. The

Table 1

Year	1929	1935–36	1946	1960	1968	1970
Coefficient of variation for income	1.23	1.09	0.87	0.83	0.72	0.75
Coefficient of variation for education	0.42	0.37	0.30	0.28	0.25	0.23
Of people aged: in given year	25–34	22–31	22–31	26–35	29–33	26–30

data are in direct contradiction to the authors' statements, e.g., "Furthermore, the experience of the past twenty-five years suggests that even fairly substantial reductions in the range of educational attainments do not materially reduce economic inequality among adults." But the authors never carry out this kind of analysis at the societal level. Yet it, rather than the individual-level analysis they carry out, is what is relevant to the question of increasing equality of income.

THE CURIOUS NOTION OF "LUCK"

Now none of this is to say that the book was not influenced by the professed interest in equality of income. It was, but in ways that impeded the study of what the book is mostly about, inequality of opportunity. For in their attempt to show that most income inequality is due to luck, they tried to show that it is not much related to anything else, such as family background. By minimizing the importance of family background for educational attainment, for occupational status, and for income, the authors obscure the inequality of opportunity that does exist in American society.

But since most of the analyses in the book are in fact about inequality of opportunity, let me turn to those analyses. Jencks and his colleagues bring together two kinds of studies, partly using existing analyses and partly carrying out reanalyses: studies of the effects during childhood and youth of different resources, including family background, genetic endowment, and school resources on acquisition of cognitive skills and on school attainment (number of years completed); and studies of the effects, during adulthood, of family background, cognitive skills, and educational attainment on occupational status and income.

Briefly, the first kind of these studies shows that cognitive skills and educational attainment derive very little from school resources, but a great deal from family background and IQ. The second kind of studies shows that occupational status and income are dependent both on cognitive skills and educational attainment, but not much on family background, apart from the influence of background on cognitive skills and educational attainment.

It is the results of the latter set of studies that are obscured by the need to show that income is mostly dependent on luck. This is done by a use of statistics that is unusual and, I believe, unwarranted. The use is

Table 2

Year	1929	1935–36	1946	1960	1968	1970
Income	1.0	0.89	0.71	0.67	0.59	0.61
Education	1.0	0.88	0.71	0.67	0.60	0.55

this: studies show a given relationship between background factors and income. This leaves a certain amount of variation in income unexplained by background. The unusual twist that Jencks employs is to attribute this unexplained variation to particular other factors, luck and personality. It is this attribution, particularly the attribution to luck, which provides a major justification for policy proposals to equalize income. But if he had attributed the unexplained variation to variation in effort or other skills unmeasured by IQ tests, which is equally reasonable in the absence of positive evidence, the justification for equalizing income is gone. Or if the unexplained variation were attributed to variation in income by age or to different wage levels in different regions, again the justification for equalizing income is gone or greatly reduced.

There is an extremely wide variation in professional baseball players' incomes, probably unrelated to their level of education or father's occupation; but it is more related to baseball ability than to luck; there is wide variability in college teachers' incomes, again little related to level of education or father's occupation, but more related to age than to luck. But the central point is that the unexplained variation in income is merely unexplained by the variables measured (father's education and occupation, own education, and a measure of cognitive skills), and cannot be attributed to something arbitrarily pulled out of a hat.

EQUAL OPPORTUNITY AN APPROPRIATE GOAL?

The potential importance of a book on "inequality" that treats the range of data in this one lies in the possibility of examining some fundamental questions of moral philosophy in the presence of sociological data on inequality. The recent research on the relation of school outputs to resource inputs that they review, reanalyze, and synthesize, directly raises questions about the ability of the State, even in principle, to equalize opportunity. The fact that each person begins life with a set of private resources, genetic and environmental (the first from his parents and the second largely so), means that in the absence of public resources, children have quite unequal opportunities.

. . . . .

Data of the sort that Jencks brings together should be directed to the question of what investment of resources is most efficient in increasing the capabilities that bring people satisfaction, both intrinsically-derived and extrinsically-derived. To answer that question, the satisfaction derived from public investments in parks, health resources, crime prevention, and a variety of other services must be included as well. But the data that Jencks examines can give a start toward an answer, within a narrower frame. When reexamined from this point of view, the data indicate that those resources which increase cognitive skills and those which increase the number of years of school completed are both effective, and about equally so, in giving the capabilities that lead to prestigeful occupations and high income. It is important to note here that the criterion is not prestigeful occupations and high income, but the capabilities that lead to them, because satisfaction derives from the exercise of those capabilities, and not only from the prestige or money awarded.

This does not mean that investment of public resources in directions other than increasing cognitive skills and level of education do not increase opportunity as well. This is one of the major defects of the existing research: cognitive skills and education level are nearly the only attributes of persons that have been studied in this way. Social skills, entrepreneurial skills, managerial capability, ability to mobilize one's resources toward an end—none of these have been measured in these studies. Thus we do not know how public investment in schools affects them, nor do we know how they affect the individual's level of opportunity to realize satisfactions.

It is also not clear from the existing data just what investment of public resources is most effective in increasing cognitive skills and level of education. What is clear is that improving "school quality" by the standard measures of quality (class size, quality of textbooks, school physical plant, teachers' experience, library size, and others) has little effect on cognitive skills. This kind of negative knowledge exists; apparently innovations in education, together with careful examination of their effects, are necessary to learn positive directions for such investment.

It should also be pointed out that preoccupation with inequality of opportunity and inequality of result in society is probably only a current preoccupation that derives from structured inequalities of opportunity for certain groups like blacks and women. When those are reduced, social attention will likely pass to other questions of social reconstruction, such as how to increase the degree of personal responsibility of persons toward particular other persons.

Nevertheless, there is now, with the existence of a large amount of sociological research on inequality of opportunity and inequality of result, and with the resurgence of interest among moral philosophers in inequality, as manifested in John Rawls's work, the possibility of serious examination of social ideals and social reality in this area. Jencks's book could have begun that examination. Its failure to do so is not lack of technical expertise, for Jencks has shown a good command of that in this book. It is instead the lack of attention to the deeper questions of moral philosophy surrounding the existence of inequality in society.

49. Clark

In its historic decision of May 17, 1954 (*Brown v. Board of Education of Topeka*), the United States Supreme Court ruled that state laws which required or permitted racial segregation in public education violated the equal protection clause of the 14th Amendment of the United States Constitution. In concluding that "Separate educational facilities are inherently unequal," the Court cited the work of social scientists in its pioneering and controversial footnote eleven. This citation demonstrated dramatically that the theories and research findings of social scientists could influence public policy decisions on educational and other social problems. The use of social science research in the making of such important policy decisions raised the question among social scientists of the propriety of their involvement or the validity of their contribution to the decisions.

Source: Kenneth B. Clark, *Harvard Educational Review* 43 (February 1973): 113–21.

Educator and psychologist Kenneth B. Clark is a professor at the City College of New York. His major interest has been the education of children and particularly the integration of schools. He is the author of *Desegregation: An Appraisal of the Evidence, Dark Ghetto,* and *A Relevant War against Poverty.*

Although there were differences of opinion, social scientists in general tended to view the Supreme Court's citation as an indication that their research could have direct social relevance. Social scientists became increasingly involved in research on social and educational problems from which policy implications for social change could be made. Psychologists and sociologists disseminated their theories, findings, and opinions on such important problems as the effects of early childhood deprivation and family instability on the learning ability of children. There was a resurgence of well-publicized social science research and discussion on such problems as the effects of "racial" differences on academic achievement and "intelligence." Theories that posed the concepts of "cultural deprivation" and "genetic inferiority" and explored the effects of racial and economic mixture of school populations on the academic achievement of Negro children were published in professional journals and widely discussed in the mass media.

Without going into the details of the scientific validity or the policy issues raised by these theories, some of the characteristics which they have in common should be noted.

All of the more publicized social science research and theories – and the acceleration of concern of social scientists with problems which have direct educational policy implications – came in the wake of the *Brown* decision, and became part of the political controversy surrounding the desirability, the methods, and the rate of public school desegregation.

Not all of the social science research and theories which proliferated after the *Brown* decision attempted to reverse or to question the social science findings which were cited by the Court. Rather they sought to explore or emphasize other reasons for the academic and psychological inferiority of Negro students. For example, the cultural deprivation theories sought to explain the academic inferiority of Negro students in terms of the inferiority of the student's general and home environment. These theories questioned, implicitly or explicitly, whether segregated schools alone were responsible for the academic inequality of segregated education, and placed emphasis on the larger historical and contemporary patterns of racial discrimination in the society as a whole. This was the specific policy question answered affirmatively by the Supreme Court in the *Brown* decision of 1954.

An even more direct challenge to the social science rationale of the *Brown* decision is found in the racial inferiority theory as expounded and elaborated by Jensen and others. Genetic inferiority theories assert that the academic inferiority of Negro children cannot be understood in terms of segregated or desegregated schools, or in terms of any other remediable environmental factors. Academic retardation in Negro children, for the exponents of these theories, is inevitable and merely one of the manifestations of inherent, genetically determined racial inferiority.

The policy implications of both the post-*Brown* environmental and biological explanations are the same. Changing the racial patterns of the schools through desegregation will not result, to any significant degree, in equality of educational opportunity or, even more importantly, in equality of educational performance for minority-group children. The environmental theories contend that the academic retardation of these children will persist as long as the total pattern of racial discrimination exists and is reinforced by an immutable cultural deprivation which resulted from the unchangeable history of racial rejection. Thus, the seemingly more liberal and contemporary environmentalist explanations are as fatalistic in terms of positive educational change for minority-group children as are the more obvious theories of racial inferiority. If any of these theories are correct, it would seem that regardless of the *Brown* decision—the achievement gap between white and Negro children will remain. Thus, the bulk of the better-publicized social science theories and research published subsequent to the *Brown* decision have persistently suggested to policy makers—intentionally or not—that minority-group children are constricted academically because of either genetic inferiority, cultural inferiority, or a conspiracy of circumstances and fate over which human intelligence and technology could have no control. This implies that there exist no remedies to raise the academic achievement of minority-group children and that the laws of individual differences do not apply to these children in ways in which they apply to more privileged white children. It is now the sophisticated intellectual fashion for many of these studies to suggest that all avenues of social and economic mobility—particularly the avenue of effective education—are closed to these children, thus dooming them to intellectual and personal inferiority. And it would follow, therefore, that the rationale, intent and possibility of eventual successful implementation of the *Brown* decision would be blocked by fundamental error and doomed to failure.*

Probably the most sophisticated recent contribution to this counsel of despair is the Christopher Jencks and associates report on *Inequality: A Reassessment of the Effect of Family and Schooling in America.* My analysis of the book will not address the problems of methodology, accuracy of the findings, or the relationship between alleged findings on the one hand, and interpretations and conclusions on the other. Neither is this analysis primarily concerned with the irritating problem of Jencks's style of presentation. However, it is the judgment of this writer that there is a serious question of propriety when a well-publicized document, which deals with the important issue of racial equality in public education, is presented in an essentially glib, journalistic, smart-alecky manner. The consequences of social scientists dealing with matters of equity and justice through the exploitation of Madison Avenue advertising techniques is a problem which must be faced by serious social scientists and their professional organizations. Jencks's findings and interpretations had been skillfully advertised to the general public through the mass media before other social scientists had had the opportunity to review them critically. By the time this study could be carefully reviewed, the general public, including policy makers, was quoting Jencks's questionable findings as if they were sacred writ. This process highlights a new, fashionable, and most disturbing approach: a group of social scientists, having mastered the art of public relations, are able to confuse scientific validation with effective mass publicity. Given that the mass media have an insatiable need for sensational findings and that journalists are not usually trained to make critical appraisals of the claims of scientists, it is not difficult for the skillful social scientist-public relations expert to phrase his "findings" in such a way as to become an overnight celebrity. When this is supported by the name of a prestigious university and by the backup of the infallible computer, the public's uncritical acceptance of the Olympian utterances of

* See editors' statement in discussion of school climate following Rosenthal and Jacobson selection no. 72—Ed.

the celebrity social scientist is practically guaranteed. This approach makes for seemingly interesting discussions on TV talk shows, but is clearly questionable science.

This problem of social science validation through public relations is closely related to the basic problem addressed in this paper—the policy implications of social science speculations, biases, and "findings." A subtle aspect of the larger problem is that important educational decisions are generally made by non-social scientists. These men are influenced by the publicity which has been generated by social scientists hawking their findings before the findings have been objectively appraised by others in the field. State and local boards of education, legislative bodies, and even the courts make important educational decisions on the basis of well-publicized rather than well-analyzed and validated social science findings because of their need for either factual guidance or support for their biases or rationalizations. There is also the possibility, which is even more disturbing, that science findings have a greater chance of being well-publicized and discussed through the mass media when these findings are consistent with prevailing biases and desires to maintain the status quo—or to reverse positive changes which have already been made. One highly publicized finding of the Jencks report is that education will not reduce socioeconomic inequality; that, in fact, the belief that schools are significant vehicles for social and economic mobility is a delusion, supported neither by the "facts" nor the "findings" of the Jencks study. Related to this overall finding is the assertion that economic status is not determined by skills which are taught in school; and even if it were, that there is no evidence that school reform could in any way effect academic equality among groups. Specifically regarding the relationship between academic performance of minority-group children and school desegregation, the "evidence" suggests that such a relationship is insignificant. Children are more influenced by what happens at home, what happens on the streets, and what they see on television, than by what happens to them in classrooms. Probably the most significant conclusion of this study in terms of immediate policy implications is that racial, economic, and academic discrimination in the schools has trivial educational effects. These assertions are of such importance that it is patently irresponsible to make them without the most rigorous objective verification or refutation.

Jencks's contribution to the increasing social science litany of immobility and despair for minority-group youngsters is a significantly new and novel one. These children are not only blocked by their culture and their genes, but they are now also being blocked by the inherent meaninglessness of the schools. If education itself is of no value then there can be no significance in the struggle to use the schools as instruments for justice and mobility. Jencks has closed the circle. The last possibility of hope for undereducated and oppressed minorities has been dashed. The social scientists have now provided policy makers with the invaluable rationale that, given the insignificance of schools as an instrument for translating the promises of democracy into reality, there is in fact no realistic need either to desegregate schools, decentralize schools, equalize expenditures for schools, or, for that matter, even adequately maintain schools.

From the perspective of this observer, it is a matter of significance, not coincidence, that the closing of the circle of doom comes at a time in American history when Negroes and other darkskinned minorities are increasing their demands for the reality of equal education. It comes at a time when the federal courts have ordered state and local educational policy makers to reorganize the public schools so that previously rejected minorities will share the realities of educational opportunity. It is possible to interpret the tight, interrelated pattern of social science cant as a sophisticated intellectual form of white backlash, a response to the important educational demands and advances achieved in concert with the civil rights movement of the late 1950's and 1960's. The unseemly haste with which policy makers have clutched at these straws of social science for the maintenance of the educational status quo would seem to support an interpretation of congruence between regressive educational policy, and sophisticated, prestigious, and well-publicized social science reports which detail the limitations of public education.

A literal interpretation of the Jencks findings would suggest that one way of dealing with equalization of expenditures as demanded in the *Serrano* and *Rodriguez* cases would be for the courts and policymaking groups to reduce the expenditures in the various school districts to that of the minimum district. If schools are as irrelevant as suggested by Jencks and his associates, and if expenditures in schools bear no relationship to the acquisition of cognitive skills, then it would follow not only that the minimum expended on schools would be acceptable to those school districts which have already reached the tax limits, but that this approach would fulfill the democratic requirement of equality. On its face, this is a preposterous position. In spite of the elaborate pretenses of computer analysis, the Jencks thesis is countered by general observation, folk knowledge, insight, and by our national history—a history in which previously deprived groups of European immigrants, themselves handicapped by the burdens of language and cultural differences, came to America and used public schools as the chief instrument for their own economic and social mobility.

The Jencks report cannot successfully obscure its arrogant demeaning of contemporary social science. To this observer the report betrays its own underlying racial biases and those of similar reports and theories which have in common the unquestioned premise that public schools are impotent—in themselves—in facilitating the educational, social, and political mobility of darkskinned children. White policy makers generally do not find this type of historical and empirical distortion difficult to accept when the victims of educational neglect are nonwhite. These social science rationalizations for the benign neglect or malignant rejection of non-white human beings in America both reflect and reinforce the pervasive racism of America.

It seems incredible that well-trained minds could ignore the facts which demonstrate that there is a consistent relationship between total lifetime income and years of schooling. In addition, it is an embarrassment to restate these facts since it is difficult to comprehend whv or how a group of social scientists who are experienced in educational research could publicly define the primary function of education almost exclusively in terms of economic reward. Unfortunately, nowhere does the Jencks report seriously discuss the educational goals of social sensitivity, respect for justice, and acceptance of differences among human beings. And Jencks and his associates missed, or deliberately ignored, the chance to define as important the need of our educational system to reinforce in children their potential for empathy and dignity.

More specifically, nowhere does this report discuss such critical educational variables as the relationship of the attitudes of teachers and their abilities to respect and conserve the humanity of their students without regard to superficial differences, and to foster cognitive and personal development. Probably the most grievous limitation of this report is that it attempts to understand the role of schools and the problems of inequality in education as if these were isolated from the total complexity of attitudes, values, and institutionalized inequities which characterize this society as a whole. This deficiency is *not* dealt with by the Jencks assertion that inequality in the schools will not be rectified except in the context of a total pattern of economic and political reorganization of the American system. This last minute bow to the radical stance is neither radical nor inconsistent with the report's permeating bias. In effect, it states that present educational inequities cannot now be remedied until some future Utopian political reorganization is obtained—probably by magic. Only then would there be any remedy for educationally neglected children. This is a cruel condemnation of these children to a lifetime of the negative consequences of educational deprivation. These children have but one lifetime within which they can either be destroyed, relegated to the dungheap of human debris, or provided with the necessary skills and strengths to become constructive citizens. They are not expendable—either by the indifferences of politicians, the insensitivity of educators, or the fashionable pseudoscience of academicians.

Social scientists, who by their glib, fatuous willingness to compromise the fundamental humanity of darkskinned children and who by doing so provide public officials with rationalizations for regressive policies of malignant neglect, are not only accessories to the perpetuation of injustices; they become indistinguishable from the active agents of injustice. This role raises the serious question of whether social scientists and the type of research for which they are responsible should be permitted to have any direct role in decisions on important matters of equity, justice, and equality among groups of human beings. Jencks himself asserts that, "Academic opinion has vacillated from one side to the other, according to the political mood of the times." This observation is disturbingly true—although there were no indications that Jencks and his associates were disturbed by this fact and its implications. They did not seem to understand that, in this role of follower of the "political mood," social scientists are indistinguishable from politicians. And certainly they then tend to become dependent upon the politicians for small consultant favors or public exposure, and seemingly for political influence. Under these conditions social scientists, in spite of their scientific pretensions, are no more dependable in the quest for social justice than are other citizens. What should be their primary allegiance in the tortuous quest for truth is subtly subordinated to the temptation to seek power, fame, and political influence. They then, in effect, become politicians, using scientific jargon, methodology, and computers in an attempt to disguise their essentially political role—a disguise facilitated by identification with a prestigious academic institution.

Of course, as citizens of a democracy, social scientists like all other citizens cannot be denied their Constitutional right to seek to influence policy and decisions. Nor can the issue of the subordination of the pursuit of truth to the practical problems of political reality be raised only in regard to certain social scientists. Educators, clergymen, and those social scientists whose political values one identifies with, must also be required to meet the test of objectivity.

Freedom of speech and inquiry must be preserved and protected for all citizens in a democracy—and certainly these rights must be protected for social scientists without regard to their particular social biases. But when social scientists are operating in the important areas of social justice and equity they can claim no special immunity to intense critical scrutiny of their findings, particularly when those findings have clear policy implications. In fact, it is precisely in regard to their policy impact that the findings and interpretations of social scientists must be subjected to the most rigorous critical analysis. In these areas of social justice and equity the contributions of social scientists can only be accepted as merely one of the many considerations to be taken into account in arriving at policy decisions. Even with a methodology which seeks to assure a higher degree of objectivity in arriving at an understanding of social dynamics, social scientists cannot justifiably claim to be immune from class and racial biases which distort their interpretations.

To avoid the dangers of social science collusion with those who control political and economic power in our society, the public must be alerted to the vulnerabilities—the human frailties—of social scientists. There must be continued reliance upon the political, the legislative, and the judicial apparatuses—in spite of their imperfections—for determinations on matters of equity and justice. These democratic processes cannot be permitted to be eroded, no matter how subtly, by a social science posture of omniscience. Nor can the independent search for truth in science be sacrificed on the altars of subservience to political power or of fashionable beliefs and attitudes of the times.

Social scientists must set up an apparatus to monitor scrupulously their own work and involvement in matters affecting social policy. They must assume the responsibility for protecting a gullible public from the seductive pretensions of scientific infallibility which are now increasingly being offered. Social scientists must assume the difficult role of monitoring with vigilance the partnership of regressive politicians and social scientists.

The extent to which the Jencks report starkly highlights these problems, and in so doing alerts responsible social scientists to the need to seek answers and techniques for dealing with them, is the extent to which Christopher Jencks and his associates have inadvertently made a significant and timely contribution to the role of social scientists in seeking to help our society move one step further toward humanity.

50.

THE CASE FOR THE RACIAL INTEGRATION OF THE SCHOOLS

Thomas F. Pettigrew

The relation of education to social stratification and mobility is a basic factor in the American struggle over school desegregation and integration. Now, twenty years after the U.S. Supreme Court decision outlawing segregated schools, the resistance to reorganization of our stratified educational system is pervasive. Social scientists such as the authors of the three preceding selections and Thomas Pettigrew, who prepared the analysis of the current situation presented in this selection, have contributed much to our understanding of this traumatic period in American society. Like the prior selections, this one reveals how the heated controversy in the society may affect the social scientist's interpretation of data. Although the editors might be accused of bias by some, we believe that Pettigrew's analysis of the current case for integration of schools is sound.

I. INTRODUCTION

William McCulloch, the former Republican from Ohio's Fourth Congressional District, served for many years as the ranking minority member of the Judiciary Committee of the U.S. House of Representatives. Last year, the elderly Mr. McCulloch had to endure listening to the testimony of literally dozens of angry "antibusing" witnesses who came before the Committee. Gently, the soft-spoken Ohioan would ask each of these witnesses the same question.

"Do you *really* want to change the basic rules of American society?" And without waiting for an answer, Mr. McCulloch would point out that black Americans had been told for 350 years by white Americans to play by the democratic rules, to eschew violence in favor of the ballot box and court action and the promise of this great nation would apply to them, too. So they did play by the rules right on through to the 1954 Supreme Court ruling outlawing *de jure* racial segregation of the public schools.

"Isn't that your problem?" prodded Mr. McCulloch of each antibusing witness. "Isn't it true that black Americans have played by the rules so well that they've won in the courts. And because they've won you now wish to change the rules on them, to tell them that it was all a lie what we white people have been telling black people all these years. Isn't that what you come before us today to advocate?"

Well, how do we answer the pointed query of the Honorable Mr. McCulloch? *Are* we going to change the basic constitutional rules of our democracy to avoid interracial schools? This question provides

Source: Thomas F. Pettigrew, paper delivered at the Cubberley Conference at Stanford University. Reprinted by permission of the author.

Thomas F. Pettigrew is professor of social psychology at Harvard University. He was the social science consultant for the U.S. Commission on Civil Rights from 1966 to 1971. Among other books, he has written *Racially Separate or Together?*

us with the historical backdrop upon which to consider the case for the racial integration of the schools.

II. THE SCHOOL DESEGREGATION SITUATION TODAY

The fundamental "case for integrated schools," of course, is not grounded in social science findings or even court rulings. It is founded on concepts of justice and the American dream. Yet we meet here at the Cubberley Conference at a bleak time in our national history, a time of scandal and a time when neither justice nor the American dream is in vogue with our national leadership. For almost half a decade now, the President of the United States himself has led and legitimized the effort essentially to reverse the Brown *v.* Board of Education ruling of 1954 through the use of such shibboleths as "busing" and "neighborhood schools."

Still the racial problems of our nation continue to fester and grow worse. The racial integration of the public schools does not constitute a complete solution to these problems, but it is a necessary component of the institutional restructuring that will be required. Indeed, as the political climate in recent years has grown more hostile to it, the practical need for school desegregation has become more obvious. Consequently, this paper points to a future when the United States regains its accustomed confidence and returns to its highest ideals; in short, our discussion will not be constrained by the present national mood.

The present situation in school desegregation is complex. While President Nixon has repeatedly attacked "busing" for integration, the Federal courts have grown impatient with "deliberate speed" and begun ordering sweeping school desegregation. These court orders have particularly affected such southern cities as Richmond, Charlotte, and Memphis, though Denver, Minneapolis and a few other northern cities have recently received similar directives. Public school statistics reflect this trend. Black children in all-black schools declined from 40 percent in 1968 to 12 percent in 1971; and those in predominantly white schools rose from 18 percent in 1968 to 44 percent by 1971. Indeed, the special pressure on the South means that by the fall of 1970 a greater percentage of black children in the South attended majority-white schools than in the North (38 to 28 percent).

But there is another, less positive side to current trends. Many areas without court orders continue to practice massive racial segregation in their public schools as if the racial changes over the past generation had never happened. Cincinnati, for example, still in 1973 has about three-fifths of its pupils attending schools that are over 90 percent of their own race. Moreover, a number of urban districts, such as Louisville and Washington, D.C., achieved considerable school desegregation within their boundaries in past years only to find themselves resegregating as white families continue to move out to the suburbs and black families remain constrained to central city residence through a vast and effective system of racial discrimination in housing. Finally, the growth of interracial schools under court pressure has raised a third and critical issue: How do you go beyond mere desegregation to attain true integration? We shall discuss the distinction between desegregation and integration shortly.

In summary, three problems persist. First, some areas have yet to initiate the school desegregation process even in this last third of the twentieth century. Second, many central cities are becoming overwhelmingly black school districts due to demographic patterns and housing discrimination. Third, those districts with stable desegregation must now achieve genuine racial integration. Add to these problems the negative political climate, and the present state of the school desegregation process can be properly evaluated.

There are four major causes of public school segregation in urban areas, the relative importance of which is not widely understood. The most immediately critical are (1) *long-term trends in racial demography* and (2) *the antimetropolitan nature of school district organization.* Contributing further to the problem are (3) *the effects of private schools* and (4) *intentional segregation within districts.*

The magnitude of the first two of these factors becomes apparent as soon as we check the relevant data. There are approximately 17,000 school districts in the United States with most of the recent consolidation of districts limited to rural areas. Thus, there are still over seventy-five school districts in the Boston metropolitan area and ninety-six in the Detroit metropolitan area. There is pitifully little cooperation between central-city and suburban school systems, and often vast fiscal and social disparities between them. In addition, the 1970 census reveals that 78 percent of all black Americans in metropolitan areas reside within central cities, while 59 percent of all white Americans in metropolitan areas reside in suburbs. This extensive racial separation at the suburban line was evident back in 1950 and 1960, too, but has increased in each of these decades: in 1950 and 1960, black central city percentages were 75 percent and 77 percent while the white suburban percentages spurted from 45 percent and 53 percent to its present 59 percent. The educational implications of these demographic data are made more severe by the fact that younger white families with school-aged children are more likely to be living in the suburbs than metropolitan whites in general. Racial housing trends are not encouraging and offer no hope for extensive relief of school segregation by race in the next generation. Consequently, America would face an enormous problem of *interdistrict* segregation of public schools if there were no patterns of *intradistrict* separation.

But, of course, the nation also faces the task of overcoming sharp racial segregation within such school districts as Cincinnati, Philadelphia, Chicago, New York, and Los Angeles. In cities with large Roman Catholic populations, this intradistrict segregation is unwittingly increased by the absorption of many white children in the parochial school system. Since only about 6 percent of black Americans are Roman Catholics, a large church school system necessarily limits the available pool of school-aged white children for a central city public school system. In Philadelphia, for example, well over half of all school-aged white children in the central city attend Roman Catholic schools. The same general point can be made for other church schools in urban areas—Quaker, Episcopal, Missouri Synod Lutheran, etc. Indeed, urban private schools of all descriptions act in this manner. The South has not had a tradition of private education; but the region has recently shown a sudden interest in it. Thus, white private school enrollment in the South rose from about 300,000 in 1968 to 500,000 in 1971, though this still represents only about 4 percent of the region's public school enrollment.

Finally, though only fourth in significance, the factor of blatant racist leadership cannot be ignored. At the local level, the Hickses and Wallaces of American political life have exacerbated the problem of intradistrict segregation by their open advocacy of separation, careful misplacement and zone-drawing of new facilities, and steadfast refusal to take even the preliminary measures that would ease the problem. But while the public resistance of these antiblack political figures captures the headlines, such structural factors as demographic trends, the antimetropolitan nature of school organization and private-school effects remain more critical.

From this analysis, we can readily appreciate the positive significance of present efforts to achieve *metropolitan*-based educational desegregation and truly democratic, *integrated* classrooms—subjects upon which we shall shortly focus. We can also appreciate the negative significance of present political attempts to perpetuate three basic myths of resistance—the myths of "*de facto* segregation," "the neighborhood school," and "the dangers of busing." Let us consider each of these myths briefly.

III. THE THREE MYTHS OF SEGREGATIONIST RESISTANCE

(1) THE MYTH OF "DE FACTO SEGREGATION." There has long been a sharp discrepancy between the legal and social science views of American race relations. In particular, the legal distinction between *de jure* and *de facto* racial segregation received no empirical support whatsoever in research. This disconfirmation exists even when we recall the derivation of the legal distinction from "the state action" prohibition of the Constitution's Fourteenth Amendment. "State action" need not be an explicit law of a southern state that requires racially separate schools; it may more often be school board decisions of attendance boundaries, new school placement, and the like, as well as city council zoning actions that act to increase residential segregation by race. For public school segregation to be accurately termed *de facto,* then, its origins must be completely untainted with such broadly defined "state action." It can be said with confidence that social science research on American race relations has yet to uncover such *de facto* segregation in any public realm anywhere in the nation. *De jure* racial segregation is the harsh fact of American society; so-called *de facto* segregation is simply a myth.

Increasingly, the federal district courts in northern cities are coming to accept this fact. Judges are ruling in Denver, Minneapolis, and other cities that *de jure* segregation exists in their public schools and must be ended under the *Brown* v. *Board of Education* doctrine just as in southern cities. This trend is what gives the Supreme Court review of the Denver case such broad national significance. Ironically, just as the federal courts slowly throw out the conception of *de facto* segregation, President Nixon has given new life to the myth by ostensibly making it the legal cornerstone of his approach to racial segregation and discrimination.

(2) THE MYTH OF "THE NEIGHBORHOOD SCHOOL." The President has also legitimized the notion that racial and social class desegregation is appropriate only if it can occur in "neighborhood schools." Given the enormity of the housing segregation patterns by race and class, this argument is obviously a not-subtle attempt to maintain homogeneous schools as long as the country possesses homogeneous residential areas.

Additional considerations contribute further evidence as to the speciousness of this contention. To begin with, there are actually relatively few "neighborhood schools" in urban areas today—"neighborhood," that is, in the true Gemeinschaft sense that the school draws its students from a small area where virtually all of the resident families know each other and constitute a genuine community. What "neighborhood school" apparently means to its advocates is "local and conveniently nearby." But then one wonders if it is being upheld as a sacred ideal less for its presumed educational value than as a parental convenience.

Nor can "neighborhood schools" validly be described as "traditionally American." True, the fabled log-cabin school of the frontier had by necessity to be within walking distance of its pupils. But the frontier school was the classic example of a "common school," bringing together American children from all walks of life. To compare the homogeneous local urban school as the historical outgrowth of the heterogeneous rural school is to ignore the powerful social class "desegregating" function of the common school. The concept of "the neighborhood school" has been in educational circles since the Chicago city planners' use of it in the 1890s; yet it did not win popular acclaim and presidential support until the desegregation process gained momentum in recent years. Such timing is enough to make even a prudent person suspicious, especially when the neighborhood school advocates push their case to the point of claiming the nonexistent right of all parents to choose the public school which their children will attend.

Furthermore, there is no evidence of the educational merit of the "neighborhood school." Indeed, if it has to be small it is probably an anachronism and highly inefficient like the corner grocery of bygone decades. But what about parental involvement? There can be doubts raised as to how much parental involvement urban "neighborhood schools" can boast of now. In any event, there is no evidence that there exists a close and negative association between the size of the attendance area and parental involvement, or that only a local school can generate such concern.

(3) THE MYTH OF THE DANGERS OF SCHOOL BUSING. This third myth is the most virulent, and has been given increased currency by numerous politicians including the President. Proposed bills to end all school busing for racial desegregation proliferate; antibusing riders of dubious constitutionality are attached to major national legislation; and Constitutional amendments to end the practice forever receive serious attention.

A curious historian looking back upon this racial era from the perspective of the next century will have to dig hard to explain this national mania. Complicating the task is an array of facts that make school busing a strange target. In 1972, nineteen million pupils (43.5 percent of the total enrollment of public schools) were being regularly transported to school at public expense, a massive effort that requires 256,000 buses traveling 2.2 billion miles at a cost of 1.7 billion dollars annually. Legally authorized in forty-eight states since 1919, fifteen states today permit the transportation of students to private schools at public expense. Clearly, travel-conscious America has no objection whatsoever to the busing of school children *per se*.

The political issue arises only when the transportation is designed to further the racial desegregation of schools. Only *three* percent of all bused students are transported for desegregation; and more public funds are still expended for transportation to racially *segregated* schools than to desegregated schools. Likewise the dangers of bus accidents have been stressed for this three percent while ignored for the remaining 97 percent who are transported for "acceptable" reasons. Moreover, the relevant data reveal that the school bus is by far the safest mode of transportation. In 1968, according to the National Safety Council, the occupant death rate per 100 million passenger miles was 0.06 for school buses as compared to 0.24 for regular buses and 2.40 for automobiles. And the Pennsylvania Commission on Human Relations recently announced that over a five-year period, the State's school children were over three times safer per mile being bused to school rather than walking to school.

So why the national excitement? The movement ostensibly against busing has been forming over the past five years, and gained momentum when federal judges in a number of key cities ordered busing solutions to correct urban patterns of widespread school segregation by race in situations where other alternatives were not available.

Survey data show that once Nixon explicitly legitimized the movement, it rose in strength even among so-called "moderate" white Americans. While 41 percent of a national sample of adult Americans told Harris Survey interviewers in early 1971 that they were unwilling to see school children bused for integration in their communities, 69 percent were unwilling by March of 1972. Opposition was, not surprisingly, most intense in the Deep South and among whites, for blacks *favored* busing for integration in 1972 by 54 to 34 percent. In sharp contrast, by an overwhelming margin of 83 to 15 percent, parents whose children are bused to school for largely nonracial reasons are satisfied with the arrangement. Despite insistent denials, then, a future historian is likely to conclude that "busing" became in our time the polite, culturally sanctioned way to oppose the racial desegregation of the public schools. It's not the distance, stated a white mother in my home town of Richmond, Virginia, candidly, "It's the niggers."

IV. BUT DOES RACIAL INTEGRATION OF THE SCHOOLS "WORK"?

Recently a fourth myth has developed as a part of the movement to turn back the racial clock during the Nixon era. Bluntly, this fourth myth asserts that "science shows busing doesn't work." It originates from a much-publicized article in the summer 1972 issue of the conservative organ, *The Public Interest.* Authored by David Armor, now a sociological consultant to the Rand Corporation, this article claimed to be an objective, "scientific" appraisal of "the evidence on busing." The mass media, as yet unequipped to evaluate material that purports to be social science, soon spread its antiintegration contentions across the nation. Nixon campaigners immediately began to exploit the article as "scientific proof" of the antibusing position; and Armor himself began appearing before congressional committees and in courts throughout the country as an "expert witness" on behalf of maintaining the racial segregation of the public schools.

Soon, however, a critique of Armor's article appeared. It was written by four of his former colleagues at Harvard (including the present author), and it asserted that the Armor article was neither objective, "scientific," nor the complete evidence. The critique maintained that there were four fatal flaws in Armor's antiintegration arguments.

. . . . .

From this assortment of "evidence," Armor concludes authoritatively that "busing" fails on four out of five counts. It does not lead, he argues, to improved achievement, grades, aspirations, and racial attitudes for black children; yet, despite these failures, he admits that desegregated schools do seem somehow to lead more often to college enrollment for black students.

The picture is considerably more positive, as well as more complex, than that painted by Dr. Armor. For example, when specified school conditions are attained, research has repeatedly indicated that desegregated, compared to segregated, schools improve the academic performance of black pupils. Other research has demonstrated that rigidly high and unrealistic aspirations actually deter learning. Thus a slight lowering of such aspirations by school desegregation can lead to better achievement and cannot be regarded as a failure of "busing." And "militancy" and "black consciousness and solidarity" are not negative characteristics, as the article asserts, and their alleged development in desegregated schools could well be regarded as a further success, not a failure, of "busing." Moreover, the evidence that desegregated education sharply expands the life opportunities of black children is more extensive than indicated in the article.

Consequently, Armor's sweeping policy decision against "mandatory busing" is neither substantiated nor warranted.

. . . . .

His antiintegration argument was based on special case data selected carefully to fit the thesis. Obscured in his response was the fact that actually he was begrudgingly in *agreement* with his critics on a number of important points concerning the effects of interracial schools. Marshall Smith, one of the original Harvard critics, has summarized three important points . . . .

1. *Insofar as we can tell from existing research, racial desegregation (induced or voluntary—via busing or other transportation) does not negatively influence and may often benefit the achievement of white students.* In the controversy over the effects of desegregation on the achievement of black students, this important fact appears to have gone relatively unnoticed.

. . . . .

2. *Insofar as we can tell from the existing research, desegregation (induced or voluntary—via busing or other transportation) does not harm and may often benefit the achievement of black students.* Although this may appear to be a controversial statement, in no place . . . is there an indication that . . . black students in desegregated situations do less well on standardized tests than they did prior to desegregating, or than similar black students do in segregated situations.

. . . . .

3. *There are indications that desegregated education increases the chances of black students attending postsecondary educational institutions. . . .* Although authors indicate that more data is needed on this issue, the potential implications are great. As a variety of researchers have recently pointed out, the consequences of increasing years of schooling for later income and occupational status are far greater than the consequences of increasing scores on achievement tests.

There are, to be sure, major points of *disagreement* between Armor and his critics, points that must be emphasized to understand the mythical nature of the "desegregation doesn't work" assertion. Smith provides a cogent summary:

1. *The authors disagree in their interpretation of the achievement data.* Dr. Armor

argues that, while there may be black gains attributable to desegregation, . . . the gain is of no importance since the "gap" between whites and blacks in achievement is not closed. Pettigrew *et al.*, on the other hand, argue that the gains are potentially important and that part of the "gap" is in fact being closed. *The central bone of contention revolves around the definition of "gap."*

. . . . .

There are three different ways of computing the "gap." We can illustrate for New York youngsters:

a) If we compare the difference in their grade levels between the national norms and the scores of black students before and after the desegregation experience, black students have closed the "gap" by 0.1 grade levels.

b) If we compare the difference in grade levels between the national norms and the achievement of blacks before desegregation with the difference in grade level between national norms and the expected achievement of black students (given no desegregation), the black students have closed the "gap" by 0.5 grade levels.

c) If we compare the white students in the same school with the black students in the school, the "gap" has opened by 0.6 grade levels.

The question then is: Which of the three ways of assessing the gap makes more sense? I believe the second definition is educationally, legally, and logically correct. *The "gap" as we normally think of it is the difference between the achievement of black students and the achievement of the national sample of all students, for if black students on the average scored at the fiftieth percentile, we would not be concerned with the "gap."* The only measure which assesses the difference between the national norms in percentiles and the black average is the second definition of "gap." In the New York case, it shows that desegregation is closing this "gap." Simply because the New York desegregation program under investigation is apparently so successful that the white students increase in grade level at faster than an average rate is no reason to discard the conclusion that desegregation is helpful to black students in the study.

2. *A second major point of disagreement surrounds the interpretation of Black Militancy.* Dr. Armor finds that black students . . . in desegregated . . . schools . . . appear to become more "separatist" than do black students in segregated schools. Although all of the means for students appear to be at the nonseparatist end of a continuum, he claims to discern statistically significant differences.

The interpretation of this finding rests in part upon the expectations and predilections of the reader. My own experience in a university setting where majority faculty and students dominate has been to accept and encourage minority students to have pride in their background and heritage—not to reject it. As a vehicle for coping with a new and sometimes hostile environment, group cohesion and a partial rejection of majority norms may be a powerful source of strength for an individual student.

. . . . .

There is an irony in Dr. Armor's argument which stems back to the original findings of the Supreme Court in *Brown.* The High Court found that blacks' identity and pride suffered from segregated education. Should we now be distressed to find that black identity and pride improve from desegregated education ?

. . . . .

In the case of racial desegregation, the findings of social science are that it will not harm and can often enhance the achievement of both black and white students. And the findings of the courts are that the nation has systematically excluded the possibility of blacks going to school with whites in the South and in all of the instances where the courts have ordered desegregation in the North. The rest is politics. Dramatic evidence for this view was provided by the ready acceptance of Dr. Armor's conclusions by those who oppose interracial schools, an acceptance that had little to do with the social science data that presumably related to his conclusions. Indeed, the conclusions received national publicity before the paper was even published.

. . . . .

No responsible observer ever claimed that *all* interracial schools would be "good" schools. It takes little imagination to design desegregated schools that are living hells for both black and white pupils. The question, then, is not: Do *all* interracial schools work well? The key questions, neatly skirted by Armor and other political foes of biracial education, are: How do we make interracial schools effective? And what are the discernible differences now between effective interracial schools and ineffective ones?

The racial desegregation of schools is not a static but a complex, dynamic process. One must search for the critical conditions under which the process seems to be most beneficial for all students. For this purpose, it is important to distinguish between *desegregation* and *integration.* Desegregation is achieved by simply ending segregation and bringing blacks and whites together; it implies nothing about the quality of the interracial interaction. Integration involves positive intergroup contact with cross-racial acceptance and equal dignity and access to resources for both racial groups. Now that desegregation is reasonably widespread, an important question for education—and this Conference—becomes: How do we achieve integration out of desegregation?

Unfortunately, competent research directed specifically upon this question is scarce. But eight conditions that appear to maximize the probability that integration can occur in a school can be tentatively advanced on the basis of laboratory and classroom research, social psychological theory, and observation.

(1) *There must be equal racial access to the school's resources.* This critical condition means far more than just equal group access to books in the libraries and other physical facilities. More importantly, it refers to equal access to the school's sources of social status as well. It is a compelling fact that the two most frequently voiced complaints in desegregated schools revolve around membership in the cheerleading squad and the student government—both sources of student status. Blacks in the minority often note that they are welcome to participate in those activities with universalistic standards such as athletics; but not as welcome in more particularistic activities such as cheerleading and student government leadership. These restrictions upon social status particularly affect black girls, and a number of studies have shown that they tend to have a more difficult time than black boys in newly desegregated schools.

. . . . .

(2) *Classroom—not just school—desegregation is essential if integration is to develop.* This second condition may seem so obvious as not to warrant listing. Yet many of our so-called "desegregated" schools today are essentially internally segregated. This internal segregation is achieved in many not-so-subtle ways, ability grouping

and curriculum separation being prime examples. But sometimes the methods can be quite elaborate. For example, transported minority children in some Riverside, California, schools arrive and leave an hour earlier than untransported white children so that they can have entirely separate reading classes—hardly a practice that facilitates integration. However it is managed, segregation by classroom does not and cannot provide the benefits that generally attend integration.

(3) *Strict ability grouping should be avoided.* The principal means of separating majority and minority pupils within schools is by rigid ability grouping across various subjects. Such grouping is typically based on achievement and I.Q. tests standardized only on majority samples. And ability grouping is increasing in American schools, even penetrating down into the elementary grades. Some grouping by subject matter is, of course, necessary; Algebra 2 must follow Algebra 1, chemistry requires certain basic skills in arithmetic. Rather, it is the across-the-board classification of students into "dull," "average," and "bright" that not only segregates by race and social class, but through labeling sets the aspirations of both teachers and students in concrete and produces self-fulfilling prophecies of achievement. Told they are dumb and treated as if dumb, all but the most rebellious and self-confident pupils become in fact dumb.

. . . . .

A chief obstacle in eliminating across-the-board labeling and tracking of children is presented by teachers who have only been trained to instruct homogeneous ability classes. They, understandably, come to regard ability grouping as a necessary practice as well as a beneficial work condition that makes their task easier. Moreover, it often is perceived as a status differentiating device with teachers holding seniority given the "high" track classes. In a profession that lacks sufficient status differentials, this feature becomes an important function of ability grouping apart from the needs of children. Nevertheless, it leads to the bizarre situation where the most inexperienced teachers are given the greatest professional challenge. It is as if the chief of a hospital's surgical service handled only band-aid cases and the newest interns were given all of the most complex surgical procedures. . . .

(4) *School services and remedial training must be maintained or increased with the onset of desegregation.* Again this condition may appear so obvious as to be unnecessary to mention. Yet it must be listed, for many desegregation programs witness an actual reduction in per student expenditures. Examples include Ann Arbor, Michigan and Riverside and Berkeley, California. Typically there is no reduction in *local* funds, but an overall decrease due to narrowly conceived federal guidelines for the use of Title I monies under the 1965 Elementary and Secondary Education Aid Act. Actually, the Act does not expressly forbid Title I funds for children from low-income families from following the children on the bus to the desegregated school. . . . Yet the fact remains that desegregation and so-called "compensatory education" are most effective when they are combined rather than treated as opposite alternatives.

(5) *Desegregation should be initiated in the early grades.* During the 1950s, the White Citizens' Councils of the deep South provided a noteworthy example of being wrong for the right reasons. They sternly opposed the racial desegregation of the public schools and particularly objected to beginning the process in the primary grades. "It's not fair," they argued; "the

very young children simply wouldn't know any better than to become friends."

Relevant research supports the Citizens' Councils' observation, if not their conclusion. The Coleman Report data show higher achievement among black children who began their interracial schooling in the first five grades. . . .

More relevant for determining the beginning of genuine integration are other results. The Coleman data also indicate that the most positive attitudes toward having interracial classes and blacks as close friends are evinced by white children who begin their interracial schooling in the earliest grades. . . .

Racial isolation is a cumulative process. Its effects over time on children of both races make subsequent integration increasingly more difficult. Separation leads them to grow apart in interests and values. . . . In short, from many perspectives, early interracial intervention seems most desirable.

Recently, the nation witnessed dramatic evidence of this critical condition for obtaining integration. Following the assassination of Dr. Martin Luther King in April of 1968, a series of interracial confrontations and conflicts erupted in many biracial schools. Some observers immediately interpreted this strife as evidence that desegregation "cannot work," that it "only leads to trouble." Yet a diametrically opposite explanation is more plausible. This interracial conflict was centered at the high school level and typically involved black and white students who in the earlier grades had attended largely uniracial schools. The hostile students, then, were unfortunately living what they had been taught; that is, their first eight years of schooling taught them that segregation was the legitimate American norm and did not prepare them for harmonious interracial contact in high school. It was not desegregation that "failed" as such. Rather it was racial segregation in the formative years that had "succeeded" as it has throughout our nation's history to develop distrust and conflict between Americans of different skin colors.

(6) *The need for interracial staffs is critical.* Another correlate of the high school strife following Dr. King's murder underlines the importance of black teachers and administrators in the public schools. One study has shown that high school "disruptions" and racial tensions are far less likely to occur when the black staff percentage is equal to or greater than the black student percentage. To be sure, there are more positive reasons for the development of thoroughly interracial staffs than the prevention of conflict. Genuine integration among students may be impossible to achieve unless the staff furnishes an affirmative model of the process. Black students report a greater sense of inclusion and involvement when blacks, as well as whites, are in authority. And black and white teachers learn the subtleties of the process from each other under optimal intergroup contact conditions—interdependently working toward common goals as equals under authority sanction.

There is growing evidence, too, that the role of the principal is decisive in generating an integrated climate within a school. This fact suggests that it is important not just to have an interracial mix of teachers but a mix of administrators as well. . . .

(7) *Substantial, rather than token, minority percentages are necessary.* Coleman's original analysis of his national data revealed that black children who were the only members of their race in a classroom tended to score either quite high or quite low on both mathematical and reading achievement tests. Such tokenism is psy-

chologically difficult for black children in America where race is so salient. Without the numbers to form a critical mass, black students can come to think of themselves as an unwanted appendage; and white students can overlook the black presence and even perceive it as a temporary situation. But once the minority percentage reaches about 20 percent to 25 percent, a critical mass is formed. Blacks are then a significant part of the school to stay; they are now numerous enough to be filtered throughout the entire school structure, on the newspaper staff and in the honor society as well as in the glee club and on athletic teams. Substantial minority representation, of course, does not guarantee intergroup harmony, but it is clearly a prerequisite for integration. Little wonder that Jencks and Brown find in a reanalysis of Coleman data that schools with 25 percent to 50 percent black enrollment seem to teach their black pupils more than those with 1 percent to 25 percent black enrollment. Tokenism, then, appears not only to exact a heavy psychological cost from black children, but may hold fewer academic benefits for them in addition.

(8) *Finally, race and social class must not be confounded in the interracial school.* When the white children of a biracial school are overwhelmingly from affluent, middle-class families and the black children are overwhelmingly from poor, working-class families, the opportunities to develop integration are severely limited. Such confounding of race and class heightens the probability for conflict. Much of this conflict may be generated by value differences between classes; but in race-conscious America such class conflict is typically seen as race conflict. To meet this eighth condition for the development of integration, the inclusion of working-class white children and middle-class black children is essential. The crucial group in shortest supply are the middle-class blacks, though their absolute numbers have expanded about fourteen times since 1940. The middle-class black child, then, should be seen as an invaluable resource for lowering the correlation within biracial schools between race and class.

VI. SUMMING UP

The basic case for the racial integration of the public schools is founded on our nation's traditional view of justice as well as the American dream. It is a cumulative process with potential academic and attitudinal benefits for both black and white children; but it is not a paternalistic program conducted "for" blacks or "for" whites for that matter. Rather it should be viewed as one component of the massive racial changes required to make viable the United States as an interracial society.

Within this framework, this paper has traced the present situation of school desegregation, listed the principal myths currently in vogue to legitimate racist resistance to the process, and summarized the recent debate on its effects. Finally, the paper maintained that a major task now facing American education is how to develop integration out of desegregation. The conception of intergroup integration put forward is emphatically not an "Anglo-white-middle-class assimilation model." It requires a blending and a mutual dignity and respect of diverse groups and their cultures. Such a development, it is argued here, would be more likely if eight conditions held: equal racial access to the school's resources; thorough classroom desegregation; the avoidance of strict, across-the-board ability grouping; the maintenance of or increase in school services and remedial training; desegregation begun in the early grades; interracial staffs; substantial, rather than token, minority representation; and race and social class both involved in the desegregation.

But will the thorough desegregation—and hopefully, integration—of the public schools of the United States actually ever become a reality? This paper does not claim to be prophetic. It cannot state authoritatively that the separatists, white and black, are wrong when they claim that the nation is too racist, too antiblack, too committed to the 350-year tradition of white domination to ever countenance extensive school integration as described here. However, it can be said that those who hold such pessimistic views and act upon them personally contribute to achieving the grim future they foresee. To avoid participating in such a self-fulfilling prophecy, one must assume the best for the future of American race relations and act accordingly—much as the legal father of the integration movement, Charles Hamilton Houston, did during the even more discouraging decades of the twenties and thirties.

It can also be asserted that integration as described here *is* possible were America somehow to will it.

. . . . .

In the meantime, there is much for educators to be doing professionally. We should not allow lawyers and the courts to determine completely the direction of a process that is basically within our field of competence. Even if the racial integration of the public schools is currently out of political vogue, it is up to us to achieve it within our desegregated schools, to make it "work" effectively. To end where we began, we can contribute to the effort of negatively answering Representative McCulloch's rhetorical question about changing our basic national premises to maintain racial segregation.

Part VII

Social Organization: Institutions and Associations

51.

BUREAUCRACY

Max Weber

All "modern" societies are characterized by highly bureaucratic organizations. This type of structure is common in business and other private social institutions as well as governmental agencies. In this selection Max Weber has systematically analyzed the nature of bureaucracies and demonstrated their necessity. Although this analysis was written over a half-century ago and is based largely on observations of German and other European organizations, no more thorough or sociologically significant statement on the subject has ever appeared.

CHARACTERISTICS OF BUREAUCRACY

Modern officialdom functions in the following specific manner:

I. There is the principle of fixed and official jurisdictional areas, which are generally ordered by rules, that is, by laws or administrative regulations.

1. The regular activities required for the purposes of the bureaucratically governed structure are distributed in a fixed way as official duties.

2. The authority to give the commands required for the discharge of these duties is distributed in a stable way and is strictly delimited by rules concerning the coercive means, physical, sacerdotal, or otherwise, which may be placed at the disposal of officials.

3. Methodical provision is made for the regular and continuous fulfilment of these duties and for the execution of the corresponding rights; only persons who have the generally regulated qualifications to serve are employed.

In public and lawful government these three elements constitute "bureaucratic authority." In private economic domination, they constitute bureaucratic "management." Bureaucracy, thus understood, is fully developed in political and ecclesiastical communities only in the modern state, and, in the private economy, only in the most advanced institutions of capitalism. Permanent and public office authority, with fixed jurisdiction, is not the historical rule but rather the exception. This is so even in large political structures such as those of the ancient Orient, the Germanic and Mongolian empires of con-

Source: Max Weber, *From Max Weber: Essays in Sociology,* H. H. Gerth and C. Wright Mills eds. and trans. (New York: Oxford University Press, 1946), pp. 196–244.

The author (1846–1920) was a German sociologist and political economist. He held the Chair of Political Economy at Freiburg. Weber's sociology is based on his extensive knowledge of economic, political, social, legal, military, and religious fields. He is especially well known for his typological studies of charismatic authority, feudalism, and bureaucracy. He was also a pioneer in the sociology of religion. Among his translated works are *General Economic History, The Protestant Ethic and the Spirit of Capitalism,* and *The Theory of Economic and Social Organization.*

quest, or of many feudal structures of state. In all these cases, the ruler executes the most important measures through personal trustees, table-companions, or court-servants. Their commissions and authority are not precisely delimited and are temporarily called into being for each case.

II. The principles of office hierarchy and of levels of graded authority mean a firmly ordered system of super- and subordination in which there is a supervision of the lower offices by the higher ones. Such a system offers the governed the possibility of appealing the decision of a lower office to its higher authority, in a definitely regulated manner. With the full development of the bureaucratic type, the office hierarchy is monocratically organized. The principle of hierarchical office authority is found in all bureaucratic structures: in state and ecclesiastical structures as well as in large party organizations and private enterprises. It does not matter for the character of bureaucracy whether its authority is called "private" or "public."

When the principle of jurisdictional "competency" is fully carried through, hierarchical subordination—at least in public office—does not mean that the "higher" authority is simply authorized to take over the business of the "lower." Indeed, the opposite is the rule. Once established and having fulfilled its task, an office tends to continue in existence and be held by another incumbent.

III. The management of the modern office is based upon written documents ("the files"), which are preserved in their original or draught form. There is, therefore, a staff of subaltern officials and scribes of all sorts. The body of officials actively engaged in a "public" office, along with the respective apparatus of material implements and the files, make up a "bureau." In private enterprise, "the bureau" is often called "the office."

In principle, the modern organization of the civil service separates the bureau from the private domicile of the official, and, in general, bureaucracy segregates official activity as something distinct from the sphere of private life. Public monies and equipment are divorced from the private property of the official. This condition is everywhere the product of a long development. Nowadays, it is found in public as well as in private enterprises; in the latter, the principle extends even to the leading entrepreneur. In principle, the executive office is separated from the household, business from private correspondence, and business assets from private fortunes. The more consistently the modern type of business management has been carried through the more are these separations the case. The beginnings of this process are to be found as early as the Middle Ages.

It is the peculiarity of the modern entrepreneur that he conducts himself as the "first official" of his enterprise, in the very same way in which the ruler of a specifically modern bureaucratic state spoke of himself as "the first servant" of the state. The idea that the bureau activities of the state are intrinsically different in character from the management of private economic offices is a continental European notion and, by way of contrast, is totally foreign to the American way.

IV. Office management, at least all specialized office management—and such management is distinctly modern—usually presupposes thorough and expert training. This increasingly holds for the modern executive and employee of private enterprises, in the same manner as it holds for the state official.

V. When the office is fully developed,

official activity demands the full working capacity of the official, irrespective of the fact that his obligatory time in the bureau may be firmly delimited. In the normal case, this is only the product of a long development, in the public as well as in the private office. Formerly, in all cases, the normal state of affairs was reversed: official business was discharged as a secondary activity.

VI. The management of the office follows general rules, which are more or less stable, more or less exhaustive, and which can be learned. Knowledge of these rules represents a special technical learning which the officials possess. It involves jurisprudence, or administrative or business management.

The reduction of modern office management to rules is deeply embedded in its very nature. The theory of modern public administration, for instance, assumes that the authority to order certain matters by decree—which has been legally granted to public authorities—does not entitle the bureau to regulate the matter by commands given for each case, but only to regulate the matter abstractly. This stands in extreme contrast to the regulation of all relationships through individual privileges and bestowals of favor, which is absolutely dominant in patrimonialism, at least in so far as such relationships are not fixed by sacred tradition.

THE POSITION OF THE OFFICIAL

All this results in the following for the internal and external position of the official:

I. Office holding is a "vocation." This is shown, first, in the requirement of a firmly prescribed course of training, which demands the entire capacity for work for a long period of time, and in the generally prescribed and special examinations which are prerequisites of employment. Furthermore, the position of the official is in the nature of a duty. This determines the internal structure of his relations, in the following manner: Legally and actually, office holding is not considered a source to be exploited for rents or emoluments, as was normally the case during the Middle Ages and frequently up to the threshold of recent times. Nor is office holding considered a usual exchange of services for equivalents, as is the case with free labor contracts. Entrance into an office, including one in the private economy, is considered an acceptance of a specific obligation of faithful management in return for a secure existence. It is decisive for the specific nature of modern loyalty to an office that, in the pure type, it does not establish a relationship to a *person,* like the vassal's or disciple's faith in feudal or in patrimonial relations of authority. Modern loyalty is devoted to impersonal and functional purposes. Behind the functional purposes, of course, "ideas of culture-values" usually stand. These are *ersatz* for the earthly or supramundane personal master: ideas such as "state," "church," "community," "party," or "enterprise" are thought of as being realized in a community; they provide an ideological halo for the master.

The political official—at least in the fully developed modern state—is not considered the personal servant of a ruler. Today, the bishop, the priest, and the preacher are in fact no longer, as in early Christian times, holders of purely personal charisma. The supramundane and sacred values which they offer are given to everybody who seems to be worthy of them and who asks for them. In former times, such leaders acted upon the personal command of their master; in principle, they were responsible only to him. Nowadays, in spite of the partial survival of the old theory, such religious leaders are officials in the service of a functional purpose, which in the present-day "church" has become routinized and, in turn, ideologically hallowed.

II. The personal position of the official is patterned in the following way:

1. Whether he is in a private office or a public bureau, the modern official always strives and usually enjoys a distinct *social esteem* as compared with the governed. His social position is guaranteed by the prescriptive rules of rank order and, for the political official, by special definitions of the criminal code against "insults of officials" and "contempt" of state and church authorities.

The actual social position of the official is normally highest where, as in old civilized countries, the following conditions prevail: a strong demand for administration by trained experts; a strong and stable social differentiation, where the official predominantly derives from socially and economically privileged strata because of the social distribution of power; or where the costliness of the required training and status conventions are binding upon him. The possession of educational certificates—to be discussed elsewhere—are usually linked with qualification for office. Naturally, such certificates or patents enhance the "status element" in the social position of the official. For the rest this status factor in individual cases is explicitly and impassively acknowledged, for example, in the prescription that the acceptance or rejection of an aspirant to an official career depends upon the consent ("election") of the members of the official body. This is the case in the German army with the officer corps. Similar phenomena, which promote this guildlike closure of officialdom, are typically found in patrimonial and, particularly, in prebendal officialdoms of the past. The desire to resurrect such phenomena in changed forms is by no means infrequent among modern bureaucrats. For instance, they have played a role among the demands of the quite proletarian and expert officials (the *tretyj* element) during the Russian revolution.

Usually the social esteem of the officials as such is especially low where the demand for expert administration and the dominance of status conventions are weak. This is especially the case in the United States; it is often the case in new settlements by virtue of their wide fields for profit-making and the great instability of their social stratification.

2. The pure type of bureaucratic official is *appointed* by a superior authority. An official elected by the governed is not a purely bureaucratic figure. Of course, the formal existence of an election does not by itself mean that no appointment hides behind the election—in the state, especially, appointment by party chiefs. Whether or not this is the case does not depend upon legal statutes but upon the way in which the party mechanism functions. Once firmly organized, the parties can turn a formally free election into the mere acclamation of a candidate designated by the party chief. As a rule, however, a formally free election is turned into a fight, conducted according to definite rules, for votes in favor of one of two designated candidates.

In all circumstances, the designation of officials by means of an election among the governed modifies the strictness of hierarchical subordination. In principle, an official who is so elected has an autonomous position opposite the superordinate official. The elected official does not derive his position "from above" but "from below," or at least not from a superior authority of the official hierarchy but from powerful party men ("bosses"), who also determine his further career. The career of the elected official is not, or at least not primarily, dependent upon his chief in the administration. The official who is not elected but appointed by a chief normally functions more exactly, from a technical point of view, because, all other circumstances being equal, it is more likely that purely functional points of consideration and qualities will determine his selection and career. As laymen, the governed can become acquainted with the extent to which a candidate is expertly qualified for office only in terms of experience, and hence only after his service. Moreover, in every sort of selection of officials by election, parties quite naturally give decisive weight not to expert considerations but to the services a follower renders to the party boss. This holds for all kinds of procurement of officials by elections, for the designation of formally free, elected officials by party bosses when they determine the slate of candidates, or the free appointment by a chief who has himself been elected. The contrast, however, is relative: substantially similar conditions hold where legitimate monarchs and their subordinates appoint officials, except that the influence of the followings are then less controllable.

When the demand for administration by trained experts is considerable, and the party followings have to recognize an intellectually developed, educated, and freely moving "public opinion," the use of unqualified officials falls back upon the party in power at the next election. Naturally, this is more likely to happen when the officials are appointed by the chief. The demand for a trained administration now exists in the United States, but in the large cities, where immigrant votes are "corraled," there is, of course, no educated public opinion. Therefore, popular elections of the administrative chief and also of his subordinate officials usually endanger the expert qualification of the official as well as the precise functioning of the bureaucratic mechanism. It also weakens the dependence of the officials upon the hierarchy. This holds at least for the large administrative bodies that are difficult to supervise. The superior qualification and integrity of federal judges, appointed by the President, as over against elected judges in the United States is well known, although both types of officials have been selected primarily in terms of party considerations. The great changes in American metropolitan administrations demanded by reformers have proceeded essentially from elected mayors working with an apparatus of officials who were appointed by them. These reforms have thus come about in a "Caesarist" fashion. Viewed technically, as an organized form of authority, the efficiency of "Caesarism," which often grows out of democracy, rests in general upon the position of the "Caesar" as a free trustee of the masses (of the army or of the citizenry), who is unfettered by tradition. The "Caesar" is thus the unrestrained master of a body of highly qualified military officers and officials whom he selects freely and personally without regard to tradition or to any other considerations. This, "rule of the personal genius," however, stands in contradiction to the formally "democratic" principle of a universally elected officialdom.

3. Normally, the position of the official is held for life, at least in public bureaucracies; and this is increasingly the case for all similar structures. As a factual rule, *tenure for life* is presupposed, even where the giving of notice or periodic reappointment occurs. In contrast to the worker in a private enterprise, the official normally holds tenure. Legal or actual life-tenure, however, is not recognized as the official's

right to the possession of office, as was the case with many structures of authority in the past. Where legal guarantees against arbitrary dismissal or transfer are developed, they merely serve to guarantee a strictly objective discharge of specific office duties free from all personal considerations. In Germany, this is the case for all juridical and, increasingly, for all administrative officials.

Within the bureaucracy, therefore, the measure of "independence," legally guaranteed by tenure, is not always a source of increased status for the official whose position is thus secured. Indeed, often the reverse holds, especially in old cultures and communities that are highly differentiated. In such communities, the stricter the subordination under the arbitrary rule of the master, the more it guarantees the maintenance of the conventional seigneurial style of living for the official. Because of the very absence of these legal guarantees of tenure, the conventional esteem for the official may rise in the same way as, during the Middle Ages, the esteem of the nobility of office rose at the expense of esteem for the freemen, and as the king's judge surpassed that of the people's judge. In Germany, the military officer or the administrative official can be removed from office at any time, or at least far more readily than the "independent judge," who never pays with loss of his office for even the grossest offense against the "code of honor" or against social conventions of the salon. For this very reason, if other things are equal, in the eyes of the master stratum the judge is considered less qualified for social intercourse than are officers and administrative officials, whose greater dependence on the master is a greater guarantee of their conformity with status conventions. Of course, the average official strives for a civil-service law, which would materially secure his old age and provide increased guarantees against his arbitrary removal from office. This striving, however, has its limits. A very strong development of the "right to the office" naturally makes it more difficult to staff them with regard to technical efficiency, for such a development decreases the career-opportunities of ambitious candidates for office. This makes for the fact that officials, on the whole, do not feel their dependency upon those at the top. This lack of feeling of dependency, however, rests primarily upon the inclination to depend upon one's equals rather than upon the socially inferior and governed strata. The present conservative movement among the Badenia clergy, occasioned by the anxiety of a presumably threatening separation of church and state, has been expressly determined by the desire not to be turned "from a master into a servant of the parish."

4. The official receives the regular *pecuniary* compensation of a normally fixed *salary* and the old age security provided by a pension. The salary is not measured like a wage in terms of work done, but according to "status," that is, according to the kind of function (the "rank") and, in addition, possibly, according to the length of service. The relatively great security of the official's income, as well as the rewards of social esteem, make the office a sought-after position, especially in countries which no longer provide opportunities for colonial profits. In such countries, this situation permits relatively low salaries for officials.

5. The official is set for a "*career*" within the hierarchical order of the public service. He moves from the lower, less important, and lower paid to the higher positions. The average official naturally desires a mechanical fixing of the conditions of promotion: if not of the offices, at least of the salary levels. He wants these conditions

fixed in terms of "seniority," or possibly according to grades achieved in a developed system of expert examinations. Here and there, such examinations actually form a character *indelebilis* of the official and have lifelong effects on his career. To this is joined the desire to qualify the right to office and the increasing tendency toward status group closure and economic security. All of this makes for a tendency to consider the offices as "prebends" of those who are qualified by educational certificates. The necessity of taking general personal and intellectual qualifications into consideration, irrespective of the often subaltern character of the educational certificate, has led to a condition in which the highest political offices, especially the positions of "ministers," are principally filled without reference to such certificates.

. . . . .

TECHNICAL ADVANTAGES OF BUREAUCRATIC ORGANIZATION

The decisive reason for the advance of bureaucratic organization has always been its purely technical superiority over any other form of organization. The fully developed bureaucratic mechanism compares with other organizations exactly as does the machine with the non-mechanical modes of production.

Precision, speed, unambiguity, knowledge of the files, continuity, discretion, unity, strict subordination, reduction of friction and of material and personal costs —these are raised to the optimum point in the strictly bureaucratic administration, and especially in its monocratic form. As compared with all collegiate, honorific, and avocational forms of administration, trained bureaucracy is superior on all these points. And as far as complicated tasks are concerned, paid bureaucratic work is not only more precise but, in the last analysis, it is often cheaper than even formally unremunerated honorific service.

Honorific arrangements make administrative work an avocation and, for this reason alone, honorific service normally functions more slowly; being less bound to schemata and being more formless. Hence it is less precise and less unified than bureaucratic work because it is less dependent upon superiors and because the establishment and exploitation of the apparatus of subordinate officials and filing services are almost unavoidably less economical. Honorific service is less continuous than bureaucratic and frequently quite expensive. This is especially the case if one thinks not only of the money costs to the public treasury—costs which bureaucratic administration, in comparison with administration by notables, usually substantially increases—but also of the frequent economic losses of the governed caused by delays and lack of precision. The possibility of administration by notables normally and permanently exists only where official management can be satisfactorily discharged as an avocation. With the qualitative increase of tasks the administration has to face, administration by notables reaches its limits—today, even in England. Work organized by collegiate bodies causes friction and delay and requires compromises between colliding interests and views. The administration, therefore, runs less precisely and is more independent of superiors; hence, it is less unified and slower. All advances of the Prussian administrative organization have been and will in the future be advances of the bureaucratic, and especially of the monocratic, principle.

Today, it is primarily the capitalist market economy which demands that the official business of the administration be discharged precisely, unambiguously, continuously, and with as much speed as possible. Normally, the very large, modern capitalist enterprises are themselves unequalled models of strict bureaucratic organization. Business management throughout rests on increasing precision, steadiness, and, above all, the speed of operations. This, in turn, is determined by the peculiar nature of the modern means of communication, including, among other things, the news service of the press. The extraordinary increase in the speed by which public announcements, as well as economic and political facts, are transmitted exerts a steady and sharp pressure in the direction of speeding up the tempo of administrative reaction towards various situations. The optimum of such reaction time is normally attained only by a strictly bureaucratic organization.[1]

Bureaucratization offers above all the optimum possibility for carrying through the principle of specializing administrative functions according to purely objective considerations. Individual performances are allocated to functionaries who have specialized training and who by constant practice learn more and more. The "objective" discharge of business primarily means a discharge of business according to *calculable rules* and "without regard for persons."

"Without regard for persons" is also the watchword of the "market" and, in general, of all pursuits of naked economic interests. A consistent execution of bureaucratic domination means the leveling of status "honor." Hence, if the principle of the free-market is not at the same time restricted, it means the universal domination of the "class situation." That this consequence of bureaucratic domination has not set in everywhere, parallel to the extent of bureaucratization, is due to the differences among possible principles by which polities may meet their demands.

The second element mentioned, "calculable rules," also is of paramount importance for modern bureaucracy. The peculiarity of modern culture, and specifically of its technical and economic basis, demands this very "calculability" of results. When fully developed, bureaucracy also stands, in a specific sense, under the principle of *sine ira ac studio.* Its specific nature, which is welcomed by capitalism, develops the more perfectly the more the bureaucracy is "dehumanized," the more completely it succeeds in eliminating from official business love, hatred, and all purely personal, irrational, and emotional elements which escape calculation. This is the specific nature of bureaucracy and it is appraised as its special virtue.

The more complicated and specialized modern culture becomes, the more its external supporting apparatus demands the personally detached and strictly "objective" *expert,* in lieu of the master of older social structures, who was moved by personal sympathy and favor, by grace and gratitude. Bureaucracy offers the attitudes demanded by the external apparatus of modern culture in the most favorable combination.

[1] Here we cannot discuss in detail how the bureaucratic apparatus may, and actually does, produce definite obstacles to the discharge of business in a manner suitable for the single case.

52.

PARKINSON'S LAW

C. Northcote Parkinson

Although this selection was written with tongue in cheek, Parkinson's Law describes one of the most fundamental facts about human society. Human groups, Parkinson says, tend to devise increasingly complicated organized ways of doing things, and then frequently keep on doing these things in the established way even when it would appear, from the standpoint of efficiency, not to make sense to do so. This article, then, serves to illuminate some of the worst features of bureaucracies just as the preceding one, by Weber, emphasizes the more positive elements.

I. PARKINSON'S LAW OR THE RISING PYRAMID

Work expands so as to fill the time available for its completion. General recognition of this fact is shown in the proverbial phrase "It is the busiest man who has time to spare." Thus, an elderly lady of leisure can spend the entire day in writing and dispatching a postcard to her niece at Bognor Regis. An hour will be spent in finding the postcard, another in hunting for spectacles, half an hour in a search for the address, an hour and a quarter in composition, and twenty minutes in deciding whether or not to take an umbrella when going to the mailbox in the next street. The total effort that would occupy a busy man for three minutes all told may in this fashion leave another person prostrate after a day of doubt, anxiety, and toil.

Granted that work (and especially paperwork) is thus elastic in its demands on time, it is manifest that there need be little or no relationship between the work to be done and the size of the staff to which it may be assigned. A lack of real activity does not, of necessity, result in leisure. A lack of occupation is not necessarily revealed by a manifest idleness. The thing to be done swells in importance and complexity in a direct ratio with the time spent. This fact is widely recognized, but less attention has been paid to its wider implications, more especially in the field of public administration. Politicians and taxpayers have assumed (with occasional phases of doubt) that a rising total in the number of civil servants must reflect a growing volume of work to be done. Cynics, in questioning this belief, have imagined that the multiplication of officials must have left some of them idle or all of them able to work shorter hours. But this is a matter in which faith and doubt seem

---

Source: C. Northcote Parkinson, *Parkinson's Law and Other Studies in Administration* (Boston: Houghton Mifflin, 1957), pp. 2–13, 59–69.

Historian, author, C. Northcote Parkinson has written many books. Among his published works are the now-classic *Parkinson's Law: The Pursuit of Progress,* and more recently *Mrs. Parkinson's Law, the Law of Delay,* and *The Life and Times of Horatio Hornblower.*

equally misplaced. The fact is that the number of the officials and the quantity of the work are not related to each other at all. The rise in the total of those employed is governed by Parkinson's Law and would be much the same whether the volume of the work were to increase, diminish, or even disappear. The importance of Parkinson's Law lies in the fact that it is a law of growth based upon an analysis of the factors by which that growth is controlled.

The validity of this recently discovered law must rest mainly on statistical proofs, which will follow. Of more interest to the general reader is the explanation of the factors underlying the general tendency to which this law gives definition. Omitting technicalities (which are numerous) we may distinguish at the outset two motive forces. They can be represented for the present purpose by two almost axiomatic statements, thus: (1) "An official wants to multiply subordinates, not rivals" and (2) "Officials make work for each other."

To comprehend Factor 1, we must picture a civil servant, called A, who finds himself overworked. Whether this overwork is real or imaginary is immaterial, but we should observe, in passing, that A's sensation (or illusion) might easily result from his own decreasing energy: a normal symptom of middle age. For this real or imagined overwork there are, broadly speaking, three possible remedies. He may resign; he may ask to halve the work with a colleague called B; he may demand the assistance of two subordinates, to be called C and D. There is probably no instance in history, however, of A choosing any but the third alternative. By resignation he would lose his pension rights. By having B appointed, on his own level in the hierarchy, he would merely bring in a rival for promotion to W's vacancy when W (at long last) retires. So A would rather have C and D, junior men, below him. They will add to his consequence and, by dividing the work into two categories, as between C and D, he will have the merit of being the only man who comprehends them both. It is essential to realize at this point that C and D are, as it were, inseparable. To appoint C alone would have been impossible. Why? Because C, if by himself, would divide the work with A and so assume almost the equal status that has been refused in the first instance to B; a status the more emphasized if C is A's only possible successor. Subordinates must thus number two or more, each being thus kept in order by fear of the other's promotion. When C complains in turn of being overworked (as he certainly will) A will, with the concurrence of C, advise the appointment of two assistants to help C. But he can then avert internal friction only by advising the appointment of two more assistants to help D, whose position is much the same. With this recruitment of E, F, G, and H the promotion of A is now practically certain.

Seven officials are now doing what one did before. This is where Factor 2 comes into operation. For these seven make so much work for each other that all are fully occupied and A is actually working harder than ever. An incoming document may well come before each of them in turn. Official E decides that it falls within the province of F, who places a draft reply before C, who amends it drastically before consulting D, who asks G to deal with it. But G goes on leave at this point, handing the file over to H, who drafts a minute that is signed by D and returned to C, who revises his draft accordingly and lays the new version before A.

What does A do? He would have every excuse for signing the thing unread, for he has many other matters on his mind. Knowing now that he is to succeed W next year, he has to decide whether C or D should succeed to his own office. He had to agree to G's going on leave even if not yet strictly entitled to it. He is worried whether H should not have gone instead, for reasons of health. He has looked pale recently—partly but not solely because of his domestic troubles. Then there is the business of F's special increment of salary for the period of the conference and E's application for transfer to the Ministry of Pensions. A has heard that D is in love with a married typist and that G and F are no longer on speaking terms—no one seems to know why. So A might be tempted to sign C's draft and have done with it. But A is a conscientious man. Beset as he is with problems created by his colleagues for themselves and for him—created by the mere fact of these officials' existence—he is not the man to shirk his duty. He reads through the draft with care, deletes the fussy paragraphs added by C and H, and restores the thing back to the form preferred in the first instance by the able (if quarrelsome) F. He corrects the English—none of these young men can write grammatically—and finally produces the same reply he would have written if officials C to H had never been born. Far more people have taken far longer to produce the same result. No one has been idle. All have done their best. And it is late in the evening before A finally quits his office and begins the return journey to Ealing. The last of the office lights are being turned off in the gathering dusk that marks the end of another day's administrative toil. Among the last to leave, A reflects with bowed shoulders and a wry smile that late hours, like gray hairs, are among the penalties of success.

. . . . .

II. PLANS AND PLANTS OR THE ADMINISTRATIVE BLOCK

Every student of human institutions is familiar with the standard test by which the importance of the individual may be assessed. The number of doors to be passed, the number of his personal assistants, the number of his telephone receivers—these three figures, taken with the depth of his carpet in centimeters, have given us a simple formula that is reliable for most parts of the world. It is less widely known that the same sort of measurement is applicable, *but in reverse,* to the institution itself.

Take, for example, a publishing organization. Publishers have a strong tendency, as we know, to live in a state of chaotic squalor. The visitor who applies at the obvious entrance is led outside and around the block, down an alley and up three flights of stairs. A research establishment is similarly housed, as a rule, on the ground floor of what was once a private house, a crazy wooden corridor leading thence to a corrugated iron hut in what was once the garden. Are we not all familiar, moreover, with the layout of an international airport? As we emerge from the aircraft, we see (over to our right or left) a lofty structure wrapped in scaffolding. Then the air hostess leads us into a hut with an asbestos roof. Nor do we suppose for a moment that it will ever be otherwise. By the time the permanent building is complete the airfield will have been moved to another site.

The institutions already mentioned—lively and productive as they may be—flourish in such shabby and makeshift surroundings that we might turn with relief to an institution clothed from the outset with convenience and dignity. The outer door, in bronze and glass, is placed centrally in a symmetrical facade. Polished shoes glide quietly over shining rubber to the glittering and silent elevator. The overpoweringly cultured receptionist will murmur with carmine lips into an ice-blue receiver. She will wave you into a chromium armchair, consoling you with a dazzling smile for any slight but inevitable delay. Looking up from a glossy magazine, you will observe how the wide corridors radiate toward departments A, B, and C. From behind closed doors will come the subdued noise of an ordered activity. A minute later and you are ankle deep in the director's carpet, plodding sturdily toward his distant, tidy desk. Hypnotized by the chief's unwavering stare, cowed by the Matisse hung upon his wall, you will feel that you have found real efficiency at last.

In point of fact you will have discovered nothing of the kind. It is now known that a perfection of planned layout is achieved only by institutions on the point of collapse. This apparently paradoxical conclusion is based upon a wealth of archaeological and historical research, with the more esoteric details of which we need not concern ourselves. In general principle, however, the method pursued has been to select and date the buildings which appear to have been perfectly designed for their purpose. A study and comparison of these has tended to prove that perfection of planning is a symptom of decay. During a period of exciting discovery or progress there is no time to plan the perfect headquarters. The time for that comes later, when all the important work has been done. Perfection, we know, is finality; and finality is death.

. . . . .

It is natural . . . to ask at this point whether the Palace of Westminster, where the House of Commons meets, is itself a true expression of parliamentary rule. It represents beyond question a magnificent piece of planning aptly designed for debate and yet provided with ample space for everything else—for committee meetings, for quiet study, for refreshment, and (on its terrace) for tea. It has everything a legislator could possibly desire, all incorporated in a building of immense dignity and comfort. It should date—but this we now hardly dare assume—from a period when parliamentary rule was at its height. But once again the dates refuse to fit into this pattern. The original House, where Pitt and Fox were matched in oratory, was accidentally destroyed by fire in 1843. It would appear to have been as famed for its inconveniences as for its lofty standard of debate. The present structure was begun in 1840, partly occupied in 1852, but incomplete when its architect died in 1860. It finally assumed its present appearance in about 1868. Now, by what we can no longer regard as coincidence, the decline of Parliament can be traced, without much dispute, to the Reform Act of 1867. It was in the following year that all initiative in legislation passed from Parliament to be vested in the Cabinet. The prestige attached to the letters "M.P." began sharply to decline and thenceforward the most that could be said is that "a role, though, a humble one, was left for private members." The great days were over.

. . . . .

But no other British example can now match in significance the story of New Delhi. Nowhere else have British architects been given the task of planning so great a capital city as the seat of government for so vast a population. The intention to found New Delhi was announced at the Imperial Durbar of 1911, King George V being at that time the Mogul's successor on what had been the Peacock Throne. Sir Edwin Lutyens then proceeded to draw up plans for a British Versailles, splendid in conception, comprehensive in detail, masterly in design, and overpowering in scale. But the stages of its progress toward completion correspond with so many steps in political collapse. The Government of India Act of 1909 had been the prelude to all that followed—the attempt on the Viceroy's life in 1912, the Declaration of 1917, the Montagu-Chelmsford Report of 1918 and its implementation in 1920. Lord Irwin actually moved into his new palace in 1929, the year in which the Indian Congress demanded independence, the year in which the Round Table Conference opened, the year before the Civil Disobedience campaign began. It would be possible, though tedious, to trace the whole story down to the day when the British finally withdrew, showing how each phase of the retreat was exactly paralleled with the completion of another triumph in civic design. What was finally achieved was no more and no less than a mausoleum. . . .

The elaborate layout of the Pentagon at Arlington, Virginia, provides another significant lesson for planners. It was not completed until the later stages of World War II and, of course, the architecture of the great victory was not constructed here, but in the crowded and untidy Munitions Building on Constitution Avenue.

Even today, as the least observant visitor to Washington can see, the most monumental edifices are found to house such derelict organizations as the Departments of Commerce and Labor, while the more active agencies occupy half-completed quarters. Indeed, much of the more urgent business of government goes forward in "temporary" structures erected during World War I, and shrewdly preserved for their stimulating effect on administration. Hard by the Capitol, the visitor will also observe the imposing marble-and-glass headquarters of the Teamsters' Union, completed not a moment too soon before the heavy hand of Congressional investigation descended on its occupants.

It is by no means certain that an influential reader of this chapter could prolong the life of a dying institution merely by depriving it of its streamlined headquarters. What he can do, however, with more confidence, is to prevent any organization strangling itself at birth. Examples abound of new institutions coming into existence with a full establishment of deputy directors, consultants, and executives; all these coming together in a building especially designed for their purpose. And experience proves that such an institution will die. It is choked by its own perfection. It cannot take root for lack of soil. It cannot grow naturally for it is already grown. Fruitless by its very nature, it cannot even flower. When we see an example of such planning—when we are confronted for example by the building designed for the United Nations—the experts among us shake their heads sadly, draw a sheet over the corpse, and tiptoe quietly into the open air.

53.

MARRIAGE 1973 STYLE

Charles E. Overholser, Jr.

One of the basic institutional systems found in every society is that of the family, although there are, of course, wide variations in marriage and family organization among societies. And even within a single society, such as the United States today, there are significant differences in the ways in which marriage, family, child rearing, and sex relations are perceived. The range of some of these variations, as seen by a representative sample of American wives, is reflected in this article. Selection 13 also examines an aspect of this institution—but focuses on the adolescent perception, especially with regard to sexuality—and Selection 54 (which follows) reflects some of the patterns common in Sweden.

How do American wives really feel about themselves, their marriages, their husbands, their children? In the light of the tumultuous social changes of the past decade, do they consider marriage outmoded? Has the women's lib movement caused great upheaval in family relationships? How crucial is sexual fulfillment, how much togetherness is enough, how important is a career?

In an effort to find the answer to these—and many other—questions, *Family Circle* commissioned me to conduct an in-depth study—including a projectable national poll of American wives. The results are in—and according to this unique survey, marriage is very much here to stay. Most wives enjoy being married—in fact, more than half, or 58 percent, declared that they're "very happy" in their marriage. But even though happily wed, 31 percent now seek self-realization beyond the traditional roles of wife and mother. Another key finding: Despite the all-pervasive emphasis on sexuality in our culture, most American wives do not consider sexual fulfillment the most important aspect of marriage. More than half agreed that "if a husband is a good provider and is kind and considerate, a wife can be reasonably happy even though she does not feel sexually fulfilled." And, despite the so-called breakdown in sexual morality, nine out of ten married women declared that "no matter what the circumstance, it is wrong for a married woman to have sexual relations with another man." (Of course, these are attitudes, not necessarily reflections of actual behavior. People may say something is "right" and behave a totally inconsistent way.) Another unexpected finding: When it comes to basic attitudes toward marriage, the much-touted generation gap is not nearly as wide as the

Source: Charles E. Overholser, Jr., *Family Circle* (February 1973): 32–4, 136–7. Reprinted by permission of Cowles Communications and the author.

Charles Overholser, Jr., was director of Young & Rubicam International, Inc., and a member of the American Association for Public Opinion Research and the Market Research Council.

gap between people of different educational and cultural backgrounds.

Scientific statistical techniques identical to those used in the best political polls were employed in the *Family Circle* poll. The study consisted of two phases: First, a series of tape-recorded group interviews were conducted, involving wives of various ages and backgrounds. Out of these free-wheeling sessions emerged the key issues, which were used in an extensive, probing questionnaire. In phase two, 952 wives from eighty-two different metropolitan areas and rural counties, and comprising a reliable sampling of the entire country, were asked by trained interviewers to fill out a questionnaire. Unmarried women heading households of their own were also queried to provide background information. All the answers were fed into a computer and tabulated.

What follows is the first in a series of reports on the results. One thing is very evident. Change is in the air. It shows up in the way women regard themselves and the goals they are now seeking. One suburban mother told us:

> I think more and more society is not looking down on a woman who decides that she is an important person. She has to do things that make her feel better mentally. And if she wants to get out of the house and leave her children for a couple of hours, or all day, or whatever, and get a job, more power to her.

And from another wife:

> I think there's more of a 50/50 division in marriage now than there ever was, and this is something difficult for a man to accept. The woman has become more independent mentally and spiritually, so much so that she no longer feels she has to be the little goody housewife, constantly at her husband's beck and call. I think all that's changed.

The women's lib movement at times has been considered out of step with the thinking of the mass of American women. But this was not the case with the suburban women we talked to. They led us to wonder just how much the American woman's view of marriage had been altered.

A VIRTUAL REVOLUTION

If Betty Friedan was right in 1963, when she wrote *The Feminine Mystique,* that only a tiny handful of married women looked for ultimate fulfillment in a life beyond marriage and motherhood, then a virtual revolution has taken place. Today 15 million American wives, or 31 percent of our representative national sample of American wives, agree with this statement: "A woman's ultimate fulfillment in life is the realization of her own personal goals."

These women look for something more in life than marriage and motherhood. One young Philadelphia mother summed it up:

> The first thing is being fulfilled in yourself as a woman and as a person. You must have your own identity, you must know yourself and be complete within yourself. Then you can find fulfillment in a marriage and then motherhood. The most important thing is to be satisfied with the fact that you're a woman.

Still, this new consciousness is by no means universal. Sixty-seven percent of the women in our poll agreed with an opposing, more conventional statement: "A woman's ultimate fulfillment in life is marriage and motherhood."

Our questionnaire also included what turned out to be a very difficult question for women to reply to:

Which of these statements do you agree with most?

(a) A wife's first concern should be her husband's welfare and happiness.
(b) A wife's first concern should be her children's welfare and happiness.

(c) A wife's first concern should be her own welfare and happiness.

We realize we gave the women a black-and-white choice, whereas choices usually are gray, and life situations are not so arbitrary. Thus, it was not surprising that a few women simply could not or would not choose. For most, the question raised basic conflicts, conflicts between self, husband and children that many never fully resolve. As one woman put it:

There's a conflict between fulfilling myself and spending a great deal of time with my children. Despite women's liberation and all that, we women have been brainwashed to think that if we don't spend most of our time with our kids, we're depriving them. It's awfully hard to break out of this.

Despite the conflict, 94 percent of our respondents did make a choice on this question. Almost two-thirds of those who look to marriage and motherhood for fulfillment are primarily "husband-oriented." They place *his* welfare and happiness first. Altogether they comprise 40 percent of the total wives sampled. Their basic view of marriage is that a wife is fulfilled through her husband's success and happiness. One woman summed it up:

I don't think you should say a woman's job is her family. I think her job is her husband.

When children arrive, the focus may shift temporarily, but the husband-oriented wife generally takes the long view:

Well, I think my husband is there and I'll have him a lot longer than my children. My children will grow away from me. That's why I should keep growing toward my husband and he toward me.

Although American wives have been accused of creating and living in a child-centered world, only 21 percent of our representative sample turned out to be "child-oriented." One woman succinctly expressed this attitude:

I think—I have only one child, another on the way—I cater to my daughter first, and then my husband second and myself third. My husband once asked me, "If we were in a boat that started to sink and you were the only one who could swim, who would you save?" "I'd save you both," I said. "No, I want the truth," he insisted. "You have to pick!" Well, then I admitted I would save Margaret. I would save her because she wouldn't have anybody. Like, I always think of my daughter first. If I go into a shopping center, I don't head for the men's or women's department, I head for the children's department.

Of course, mothers of small children are more likely to be found in this group, just as older women are more likely to be husband-oriented, and young women fit into the self-realizer category. But all three types can be found in every population group. See the table at the bottom of the page for a statistical breakdown by age and presence of children.

How does the "self-realizer" wife differ from those who continue to see themselves

	"Extended Honeymoon" (Under 30, No Children)	"The Family Years"		"Empty Nest" (Over 30, No Children)
		Children Under 6	Children 6–18	
Self-realizers	51 percent	36 percent	33 percent	23 percent
Husband-oriented	37	30	41	51
Child-oriented	10	28	19	19

primarily as wives or mothers? Is she self-centered, domineering, frigid, unable to enjoy marriage or motherhood? Hardly. Despite their search for self-fulfillment outside marriage and motherhood, the overwhelming majority of self-realizers put the welfare and happiness of their family over their own. Sixty-one percent agreed that a wife's first concern should be her husband, while 23 percent put their children first. Only 14 percent indicated that their own welfare and happiness are their first priority.

This last group, a mere five percent of the *total* sample, may indeed fit the stereotype of the self-centered wife, but the typical self-realizer does not. It is not that she rejects her husband and children. Rather, she accepts herself.

And like the majority of all wives we polled, the self-realizer usually sees herself as very happily married. On a standard scale used by many sociologists to obtain ratings of self-perceived marital happiness, self-realizers rated the same as the married women in the survey. Fifty-eight percent rated their marriages as "very happy." Only 20 percent, no more than the average for all wives, placed themselves at the unhappy end of the scale. Husband-oriented wives average out higher on the marital happiness scale, with 62 percent reporting very happy marriages, while the child-oriented (53 percent "very happy") are least so.

It's clear that a reasonably high and roughly equal degree of happiness is common to all three groups of wives. And common to all is a consistent belief in a particular set of attitudes toward their marriage: Altruism and equality, the "Golden Rule" values of unselfishness, tolerance and consideration, the desirability of an equal partnership in decision-making, and, incidentally, a pooling of incomes.

HEALTHY SELFISHNESS

Self-realizers are more likely to believe that "a little healthy selfishness" is beneficial in a marriage, but seven in ten believe that constant consideration for one another's wishes is a better key to happiness. This woman speaks for the majority:

> It is a matter of two people being considerate toward one another, and not being self-centered. If you reach this—a certain amount of maturity, and a lack of self-centeredness—I think that you have a good marriage.

All three groups believe in being tolerant of their husband's habits. And even the self-realizer tends to feel that she should not only tolerate her husband's faults but should also make a real effort to correct her own.

When it comes to decision-making, an overwhelming majority of all three groups believe that the wife should have an equal say.

In some marriages, however, the husband still rules the roost. One of our panelists remarked:

"My sister-in-law is like that. If her husband says this is black, it's black. I mean, she knows in her mind it's not right, but her mother and father fought and she swore when she married she wouldn't fight. And she has to live with him. So if he thinks that's black, then it's black."

But most describe a more equitable process, like this wife:

"We've come to an agreement that we discuss mostly everything he wants done; but if I disagree, he'll listen to my argument and sometimes he'll go along with me and sometimes he won't. But somebody has to make the final decision. You have to come to an agreement or you'll always end up fighting over something."

Not only are wives demanding an equal

say in decision-making, but they're also calling for an equal command over the family's financial resources. Most married women, whatever their orientation, think that their husband's earnings, along with any of their own, should be the joint property of the couple. Even the husband-oriented wife is reluctant to allow her husband to put her on an allowance and dispose of what is left over himself.

Varying life circumstances, what social researchers call "the demographics," have an enormous influence on the likelihood of a woman falling into one or the other of the three orientation groups. Self-realizers, for example, are much better educated than other wives.

Two out of three college graduates see themselves finding ultimate fulfillment in pursuits beyond marriage and motherhood. Among high school graduates, only 36 percent are self-realizers; among those who did not complete 12 years of schooling, the figure is 14 percent. No other characteristics—income, religion, race or geographical location; even, as we have seen, age or presence of children—discriminate so sharply.

Those college graduates who see their ultimate fulfillment in marriage and motherhood are three times more likely to be husband-oriented than to put their children first. Child orientation is concentrated, at 32 percent, among the lowest educational group in this survey.

Religious preference and background also play a role. Jews and, perhaps more surprisingly, Catholics, are self-realizers considerably more often than those of Protestant background. And despite the legend of the Jewish mother, they are the least likely (12 percent) to be child-oriented. Most surprising is the finding that religious activity, as indicated by active membership in a religious congregation, did not contribute to orientation.

Black women, on the average, are much more inclined to be child-oriented. No other group in the population—socioeconomic, geographical or age-related—shows even a roughly similar ratio (8 to 5) of child- to husband-oriented wives. For whites in general, the ratio is strongly the opposite (1 to 2).

PORTRAIT OF THE SELF-REALIZER

A portrait of the self-realizer begins to emerge. She is first of all educated. She tends to be young, urban or suburban—except among the elderly and the most poorly educated, she may be found in considerable numbers throughout the population.

On the fundamental "Golden Rule" values, wives in all three groups are in essential agreement. But on the importance of sex and a number of other issues, those related to the maintenance of an individual, autonomous identity within marriage, and the value placed upon activities and interests outside the home, including a job, the self-realizer differs from other married women.

As mentioned before, most American wives do not consider sexual fulfillment essential to a reasonably happy marriage. But among the self-realizers, interest in sex is higher. Forty-two percent believe that sexual fulfillment is essential to a happy marriage. (Only 32 percent of the national sample agreed with this statement.)

NO TOGETHERNESS

Self-realizers also depart from traditionalists in the value they place on what Nena and George O'Neill, in their recent best-selling book, describe as a more "open marriage." They reject by a two-to-one margin the notion that a couple can be happy only if they share all interests and leisure time.

One self-realizer remarked:

"You have to share some things. If you both like to go out to dinner, so you go out to dinner. But if he likes baseball and you can't stand baseball, why do you have to watch it?"

A second summed up:

"You shouldn't be the same mold as he is or there'll be nothing to talk about at all."

Self-realizers believe that you have to be "an active, interesting person" to hold a husband. To them a good marriage must be lively.

A young, self-realizer mother, obviously very much in love with her husband, put it this way:

"I remember my husband's mother asking him why he wanted to marry me. He didn't say, 'Because I love her'; he said, 'Because we have fun together.' To him that was it. I know he loved me, too, but it was important to him that he had a girl he could have a good time with."

The self-realizer's liberated view of woman's place in the world as well as in the home leads her to value the emotional rewards of work *outside* the home. She believes that a woman will usually be happier when she works not only in her home but at an outside job, as this woman pointed out:

> As soon as my kids started kindergarten, I went out to work. It made a fantastic difference, because I didn't know very many people and I was so confined to home and everything, and it was dull, really dull. At work I met a whole bunch of people, and I would come home and I was alive. I still feel alive and I feel that never again could I ever stand going back to the way things were before, and I'm thinking this has made a whole happier life for everybody.

Clearly the urge to find an identity beyond the roles of wife and mother plays a part in the working-wife phenomenon. Almost half the self-realizers work outside the home, but only a third of the husband-oriented.

WORKING MOTHERS

Child-oriented women, perhaps paradoxically, tend to be represented in the work force in numbers slightly above the average for the population as a whole. The explanation may lie in the statement of this child-oriented working mother we interviewed:

> I work only two days, but I keep thinking to myself, well, with the extra money I am getting, my daughter will have more things than if I'm not working. She's with my mother, in good hands, but I still feel, Is she all right, did anything happen, what did she do, did she ask for me? I wish I could be home with her, but since I have been working there are so many extra things I can get her, that in a way I think it's better. I'm also saving money for when she gets older.

Our study shows the emergence of a new, more independent attitude toward marriage. Even self-realizers, however, are not quite ready to accept complete role equality between husbands and wives. Three out of four in the more traditional groups reject this idea, but so do six out of ten self-realizers. Most wives seem to feel that their husbands are just not ready for equality. One wife told us:

> It sounds groovy . . . that they should share the children and housekeeping and the woman should have her career . . . but it doesn't fit into my home yet.

Another forthrightly remarked:

> My husband hates to babysit. Once, when I went out to the store, the baby went in his diaper. You know what my husband did? He knocked on

the door of a friend of mine in the house and told her: "I'll give you a dollar if you go upstairs and change my baby's diaper."

MARRIAGE AS PARTNERSHIP

And while some women's lib groups have proclaimed that marriage exploits women, the wives in this survey—even the self-realizers—disagree. Rather, despite frustrations felt by many, despite the feeling of some that husbands stand between them and the fulfillment of their dreams, most see marriage as a partnership with equal benefits to wife and husband.

To the husband- or child-oriented wife, marriage still involves a willing sublimation of her own will and identity to that of her husband or children. Although we have seen profound social changes during the past decade, most American wives still cling to the traditions of the past, extolling home and family.

But today, our survey shows, married women are increasingly choosing to be "something more." A third, by our best estimates, are making this choice. While they reject, for the most part, the more negative and radical aspects of women's lib, they nevertheless enthusiastically embrace the positive notion that without abandoning their love for husband and family they, too, can live a life of their own.

54.

THE SWEDES DO IT BETTER

Richard F. Tomasson

As indicated in the preceding selection, the family as a social institution is currently undergoing significant changes. One feature which has altered markedly is the orientation toward, and opportunity for, employment of married women outside the home. The problems raised by working wives have been handled differently in different cultures. In this selection Tomasson contends that Swedish women, as compared with American women, face fewer role conflicts between work and marriage and between a job and bearing children. Numerous arrangements are designed to make the two roles compatible in their industrialized society. And the result, says Tomasson, is a less child-centered society but one with more stable marriages.

Some rational answers to questions that trouble many American women today—and perhaps some illuminating guidelines for the future—can be found in the experience of Sweden. Our countries, to be sure,

Source: Richard F. Tomasson, *Harper's Magazine* 225, no. 1349 (October 1962): 178–80. Copy-

are different in many respects: Sweden is a small nation with a homogeneous population. But both nations are attached to a democratic political philosophy, and Sweden comes closer to matching our high standard of living than any other European country. While there are many resemblances between our two societies, the Swedes have come closer to resolving issues which are still being uneasily debated in the United States.

Why, for instance, is the familiar conflict between work and marriage so much less of a problem in Sweden? One reason —though by no means the only one—is the fact that Swedish women devote less time and energy to child bearing.

Sweden has, in fact, one of the lowest birth rates in the world, fourteen per thousand population in 1960 compared with twenty-four per thousand in the United States. This is not due to any great difference in ability to control family size. . . . Nor are economic factors the heart of the matter. In fact the relative cost of rearing a child is greater in America than in Sweden, where an expanding system of welfare legislation has provided increasing financial benefits to mothers and children. This aid began in the 1930s to spur the low birth rate which was below replacement level for several years.

All Swedish mothers, married or not, [in 1962 received] a grant of $180 when a child was born, as well as free delivery and confinement, grants for postnatal health care for mother and child, and an allowance of $180 a year for each child up to the age of sixteen. (Unmarried mothers receive additional cash compensation in recognition of their greater need when a father does not contribute to the support of the child.) Comprehensive national health insurance makes the child's medical bills negligible and complete dental care is available to all children in the schools. Nor need Swedish parents worry about paying for their children's education. Through the university level, tuition is virtually free and there are generous scholarship and loan programs to help meet students' living costs.

Employers are forbidden by law to discharge a woman employee who gets married or becomes pregnant. She is entitled to a substantial proportion of her pay for a maternity leave of up to six months. With all these inducements one would expect Swedish fertility to exceed ours.

There are, however, important differences in Swedish and American culture which explains the significant disparity in family size. (The Swedish population will probably increase by only 10 percent between 1960 and 1975 while ours will take a 25 or 30 percent leap.)

Of prime importance is the simple fact that Swedes marry about four years later than Americans—the median age for Swedish men in the 1950s was twenty-seven; for women, twenty-four. Americans, in fact, marry earlier than the people of any other industrialized nation. This is, of course, one reason for our population explosion. Very young couples have a longer period of fecundity, more energy to deal with the rigors of child-rearing, and a less realistic picture of the burdens of parent-

---

Sociologist Richard F. Tomasson is professor and chairman in the Department of Sociology at the University of New Mexico, Albuquerque. His fields of study include comparative and political sociology and his areas of interest include social stratification, sociological theory, and Scandinavian societies. He is the author of *Patterns in Negro-White Differential Mortality, 1930–1957* and *Swedish Society*.

hood than those who marry later. It is also true that a girl who goes to marriage directly from her parents' home or the college dormitory adjusts more easily to the confining role of motherhood than one who has had several years of bachelor freedom. And early marriage tends to narrow a woman's horizon to the traditional roles of wife and mother before competing interests have a chance to develop.

Most American wives have worked outside their homes before marriage, a majority do so again some time after marriage, but few—even among college graduates—can be said to have careers. In Sweden, on the other hand, a high proportion of middle-class wives have relatively uninterrupted working lives and there are far more women in the traditionally male occupations than in America.

In Swedish universities, for example, women are now a quarter of the students of medicine, dentistry, and the natural sciences, and 15 percent of those in law school; a majority of the pharmacy students are women. In all these fields in the United States the proportion of women is small or negligible. Few Swedish wives give up careers when they marry; few American wives have careers to give up.

A SHACK IN THE COUNTRY

Family size and behavior are affected too by a difference in attitudes toward city living. Smaller quarters and the distractions and opportunities of the city discourage large families. In all industrial societies urban families have fewer children than those who live in the country. Statistically, Americans are as urbanized as the Swedes but—as William F. Whyte and Jane Jacobs have eloquently charged—we are essentially anticity; if we can afford it we prefer to live in the suburbs despite the difficulties and deprivations that go with commuting.

The Swedes, on the other hand, do not share our feeling that we are not doing right by our children if we bring them up in the city. Families are generally content to live in apartments in Stockholm or Gothenburg, though many wish they were larger and easier to get. A vacation shack in the country satisfies their bucolic longings.

An even more striking difference is in the permissive single standard of sexual behavior which prevails in Sweden. . . . There are social pressures against promiscuity, but on the whole unmarried young women have about the same latitude as young men. Thus there is little of the guilt and moral ambiguity about sex relations among the unmarried which act as such a powerful inducement to early marriage in the United States.

Interestingly, Sweden has a divorce rate lower by a third than ours. Considering how far Sweden has moved along the road to full equality for women, it is perhaps paradoxical that the roles of husband and wife are more specifically defined than in the United States. This is, in fact, generally true of Europeans who feel that American husbands do much "woman's work." Swedish (or Dutch, French, or Austrian) fathers will seldom be found diapering, feeding, or bathing their children; nor are they dish driers, grocery shoppers, or baby-sitters. (But this is changing among younger Swedes.) Only in America is it not surprising for a university professor to feel that he must be home by five o'clock in order to help his wife with the children. And it may be that the amiable cooperation of their husbands in some of the onerous duties of child care is an extra inducement to American mothers to have more babies.

More probably, however, the decision to have a third or fourth child results from the mother's feeling that she is on full-time duty at home anyhow and has no compelling outside involvements. It takes an exceptionally well organized woman with great vitality to flout convention and play the mother and career roles simultaneously against all the obstacles American middle-class culture puts in her way. Certainly the conventional wisdom makes it clear that home is the only place for the mother of small—and even not so small—children. Family, neighbors, and friends urge her to stay there as do such diverse instructors as Dr. Spock, Ann Landers, and Russell Kirk. Even the government conspires by allowing only slight tax exemption for the child-care expenses of working mothers.

Swedish women too are under some pressure to stay home with their babies, and most of them take more than just a few months out to have them. But a relatively high proportion of middle-class wives with small children work outside their homes. Facilities for the daytime care of small children are more readily available than in the United States and so are competent domestic helpers. But the crucial difference is the fact that it is not generally considered strange, anti-social, or immoral for the Swedish mother of young children to work outside her home.

Recent evidence accumulated in the United States suggests that we too may have reason to reverse our stand on these questions. . . . Three diverse studies all came to the conclusion that maternal employment *per se* does not have the adverse effects on children's lives attributed to it. One study which covered more than a thousand children in the public schools of Cedar Rapids, Iowa, indicated that the academic performance and social adjustment of children—from nursery school through high school—had no perceptible connection with their mother's employment. Similarly, a study of some six hundred Michigan high-school girls demonstrated that while an employed mother may be under increased physical strain, her dual role does not affect the mother-daughter relationship adversely. The same conclusions were corroborated by interviews conducted in Spokane with 104 nonemployed mothers, 104 who were employed, and eighty-two mother substitutes. Nothing was found to support the widely held hypothesis that the separation of children from their mothers "has 'bad' psychological, physical, and social effects on children. . . ."

AMERICA'S FERTILITY CHAMPS

Findings of this sort have not yet gained much currency. But as the facts become more widely known, they are bound to contribute to a more rational and less child-centered way of life for American women. There are indeed already signs that our birth rate is declining and that families will be smaller in the years ahead. I have asked hundreds of college students over the past couple of years how many children they wanted. As might be expected they overwhelmingly want two, three, or four. But the interesting fact is that more want two than four. Compared to the 1940s and 1950s, this is a significant change. The uninterrupted decline in the American birth rate between 1957 and 1963 from 25.3 to 21.6 births per 1,000 population may well reflect a real decline in average family size.

It may well be, in fact, that American women born in the early 'thirties will turn out to be the fertility champions of the twentieth century. On the other hand, wives of the 1970s and 1980s may find themselves as free as Swedish women are today from the conflict between the traditional woman's role and the opportunities which an affluent industrial society provides.

The distance still to be bridged is epitomized in two sociological studies. Writing about "Student Culture at Vassar," John H. Bushnell observed . . . :

"The Vassar student's future identity is largely encompassed by the projected role of wife-mother. . . . For these young women the 'togetherness' vogue is definitely an integral theme of future family life with any opportunities for independent action attaching to an Ivy League degree being willfully passed over in favor of the anticipated rewards of close-knit companionship within the home that-is-to-be."

In sharp contrast, . . . a Danish sociologist . . . notes:

"But even if she excels in all these respects [being a good housekeeper and hostess, a loving mother, and an attractive spouse], she will reap slight social esteem, because dominant middle-class opinion will insist on the superior value of choosing a career outside the home and of cultivating literary and artistic interests."

55.

THE DIVISION OF LABOR IN SOCIETY

Émile Durkheim

One of the recurring basic criticisms of modern society is that the "whole man"—the personality—has been weakened because of specialization, or "division of labor." Said one philosopher, "It is a sad commentary that we have come to the point where we never do anything more than make the eighteenth part of a pin." Said another, "Insofar as the principle of the division of labor receives a more complete application, the art progresses, the artisan retrogresses." Many, comparing the life of the modern worker with the "free, bold life of the 'noble' savage," have found the second much preferable to the first. Adoption of such a

Source: Emile Durkheim, "Conclusion," *The Division of Labor in Society* (New York: The Free Press, 1947), pp. 396–409. Copyright 1947 by The Free Press. Reprinted by permission of Macmillan Publishing Co., Inc.

The author (1858–1917) was a French sociologist and philosopher. He taught at the University of Bordeaux and at the Sorbonne, succeeding Auguste Comte. Besides his doctoral dissertation from which this selection is taken, Durkheim's main works are *The Rules of Sociological Method, The Elementary Forms of the Religious Life,* and *Suicide: A Study in Sociology.*

philosophy, carried to its logical conclusion, would lead to drastic changes in all of social life. (Young people of both sexes living in rural and urban communes, wearing patched, embroidered jeans, denim jackets, work shoes, and other simple garb suggest that this idea is still very much alive today.) The result of specialization, in the thinking of Rousseau and others, is the "splintering" of personalities. Emile Durkheim, however, in this conclusion to his *The Division of Labor in Society* argued that specialization was the chief source of social solidarity and was becoming the foundation of the moral order both within and between societies. One result of these conflicting philosophies is that young people may receive contradictory impressions or even contradictory recommendations: Specialize. Do not specialize.

I

If there is one rule of conduct which is incontestable, it is that which orders us to realize in ourselves the essential traits of the collective type. Among lower peoples, this reaches its greatest rigor. There, one's first duty is to resemble everybody else, not to have anything personal about one's beliefs or actions. In more advanced societies, required likenesses are less numerous; the absence of some likenesses, however, is still a sign of moral failure. Of course, crime falls into fewer different categories; but today, as heretofore, if a criminal is the object of reprobation, it is because he is unlike us. Likewise, in lesser degree, acts simply immoral and prohibited as such are those which evince dissemblances less profound but nevertheless considered serious. Is this not the case with the rule which common morality expresses when it orders a man to be a man in every sense of the word, which is to say, to have all the ideas and sentiments which go to make up a human conscience? No doubt, if this formula is taken literally, the man prescribed would be man in general and not one of some particular social species. But, in reality, this human conscience that we must integrally realize is nothing else than the collective conscience of the group of which we are a part. For what can it be composed of, if not the ideas and sentiments to which we are most attached? Where can we find the traits of our model, if not within us and around us? If we believe that this collective ideal is that of all humanity, that is because it has become so abstract and general that it appears fitting for all men indiscriminately. But, really, every people makes for itself some particular conception of this type which pertains to its personal temperament. Each represents it in its own image. Even the moralist who thinks he can, through thought, overcome the influence of transient ideas, cannot do so, for he is impregnated with them, and no matter what he does, he finds these precepts in the body of his deductions. That is why each nation has its own school of moral philosophy conforming to its character.

On the other hand, we have shown that this rule had as its function the prevention of all agitation of the common conscience, and, consequently, of social solidarity, and that it could accomplish this role only by having a moral character. It is impossible for offenses against the most fundamental collective sentiments to be tolerated without the disintegration of society, and it is necessary to combat them with the aid of the particularly energetic reaction which attaches to moral rules.

But the contrary rule, which orders us to specialize, has exactly the same function. It also is necessary for the cohesion of societies, at least at a certain period in their evolution. Of course, its solidarity is different from the preceding, but though it is different, it is no less indispensable. Higher societies can maintain themselves in equilibrium only if labor is divided; the attraction of like for like less and less suffices to produce this result. If, then, the moral character of the first of these rules is necessary to the playing of its role, it is no less necessary to the second. They both correspond to the same social need, but satisfy the need differently, because the conditions of existence in the societies themselves differ. Consequently, without speculating concerning the first principle of ethics, we can induce the moral value of one from the moral value of the other. If, from certain points of view, there is a real antagonism between them, that is not because they serve different ends. On the contrary, it is because they lead to the same end, but through opposed means. Accordingly, there is no necessity for choosing between them once for all nor of condemning one in the name of the other. What is necessary is to give each, at each moment in history, the place that is fitting to it.

Perhaps we can even generalize further in this matter.

The requirements of our subject have obliged us to classify moral rules and to review the principal types. We are thus in a better position than we were in the beginning to see, or at least to conjecture, not only upon the external sign, but also upon the internal character which is common to all of them and which can serve to define them. We have put them into two groups: rules with repressive sanctions, which may be diffuse or organized, and rules with restitutive sanctions. We have seen that the first of these express the conditions of the solidarity, *sui generis,* which comes from resemblances, and to which we have given the name mechanical; the second, the conditions of negative solidarity and organic solidarity. We can thus say that, in general, the characteristic of moral rules is that they enunciate the fundamental conditions of social solidarity. Law and morality are the totality of ties which bind each of us to society, which make a unitary, coherent aggregate of the mass of individuals. Everything which is a source of solidarity is moral, everything which forces man to take account of other men is moral, everything which forces him to regulate his conduct through something other than the striving of his ego is moral, and morality is as solid as these ties are numerous and strong. We can see how inexact it is to define it, as is often done, through liberty. It rather consists in a state of dependence. Far from serving to emancipate the individual, or disengaging him from the environment which surrounds him, it has, on the contrary the function of making him an integral part of a whole, and, consequently, of depriving him of some liberty of movement. We sometimes, it is true, come across people not without nobility who find the idea of such dependence intolerable. But that is because they do not perceive the source from which their own morality flows, since these sources are very deep. Conscience is a bad judge of what goes on in the depths of a person, because it does not penetrate to them.

Society is not, then, as has often been thought, a stranger to the moral world, or something which has only secondary repercussions upon it. It is, on the contrary, the necessary condition of its existence. It is not a simple juxtaposition of individuals who bring an intrinsic morality with them, but rather man is a moral being only because he lives in society, since morality consists in being solidary with a group and varying with this solidarity. Let all social life disappear, and moral life will disappear with it, since it would no longer have any objective. The state of nature of the philosophers of the eighteenth century, if not immoral, is, at least, *amoral.* Rousseau himself recognized this. Through this, however, we do not come upon the formula which expresses morality as a function of social interest. To be sure, society cannot exist if its parts are not solidary, but solidarity is only one of its conditions of existence. There are many others which are no less necessary and which are not moral. Moreover, it can happen that, in the system of ties which make up morality, there are some which are not used in themselves or which have power without any relation to their degree of utility. The idea of utility does not enter as an essential element in our definition.

As for what is called individual morality, if we understand by that a totality of duties of which the individual would, at the same time, be subject and object, and which would link him only to himself, and which would, consequently, exist even if he were solitary,—that is an abstract conception which has no relation to reality. Morality, in all its forms, is never met with except in society. It never varies except in relation to social conditions. To ask what it would be if societies did not exist is thus to depart from facts and enter the domain of gratuitous hypotheses and unverifiable flights of the imagination. The duties of the individual towards himself are, in reality, duties towards society. They correspond to certain collective sentiments which he cannot offend, whether the offended and the offender are one and the same person, or whether they are distinct. Today, for example, there is in all healthy consciences a very lively sense of respect for human dignity, to which we are supposed to conform as much in our relations with ourselves as in our relations with others, and this constitutes the essential quality of what is called individual morality. Every act which contravenes this is censured, even when the agent and the sufferer are the same person. That is why, according to the Kantian formula, we ought to respect human personality wherever we find it, which is to say, in ourselves as in those like us. The sentiment of which it is the object is not less offended in one case than in the other.

But not only does the division of labor present the character by which we have defined morality; it more and more tends to become the essential condition of social solidarity. As we advance in the evolutionary scale, the ties which bind the individual to his family, to his native soil, to traditions which the past has given to him, to collective group usages, become loose. More mobile, he changes his environment more easily, leaves his people to go elsewhere to live a more autonomous existence, to a greater extent forms his own ideas and sentiments. Of course, the whole common conscience does not, on this account, pass out of existence. At least there will always remain this cult of personality, of individual dignity of which we have just been speaking, and which, today, is the rallying-point of so many people. But how little a thing it is when one contemplates the ever increasing extent of social life, and, consequently, of individual consciences! For, as they become more voluminous, as intelligence becomes richer, activity more varied, in order for morality to remain constant, that is to say, in order for the individual to remain attached to the group with a force equal to that of yesterday, the ties which bind him to it must become stronger and more numerous. If, then, he formed no others than those which come from resemblances, the effacement of the segmental type would be accompanied by a systematic debasement of morality. Man would no longer be sufficiently obligated; he would no longer feel about and above him this salutary pressure of society which moderates his egoism and makes him a moral being. This is what gives moral value to the division of labor. Through it, the individual becomes cognizant of his dependence upon society; from it come the forces which keep him in check and restrain him. In short, since the division of labor becomes the chief source of social solidarity, it becomes, at the same time, the foundation of the moral order.

We can then say that, in higher societies, our duty is not to spread our activity over a large surface, but to concentrate and specialize it. We must contract our horizon, choose a definite task and immerse ourselves in it completely, instead of trying to make ourselves a sort of creative masterpiece, quite complete, which contains its worth in itself and not in the services that it renders. Finally, this specialization ought to be pushed as far as the elevation of the social type, without assigning any other limit to it. No doubt, we ought so to work as to realize in ourselves the collective type as it exists. There are common sentiments, common ideas, without which, as has been said, one is not a man. The rule which orders us to specialize remains limited by the contrary rule. Our conclusion is not that it is good to press specialization as far as possible, but as far as necessary. As for the part that is to be played by these two opposing necessities, that is determined by experience and cannot be calculated *a priori*. It is enough for us to have shown that the second is not of a different nature from the first, but that it also is moral, and that, moreover, this duty becomes ever more important and pressing, because the general qualities which are in question suffice less and less to socialize the individual.

It is not without reason that public sentiment reproves an ever more pronounced tendency on the part of dilettantes and even others to be taken up with an exclusively general culture and refuse to take any part in occupational organization. That is because they are not sufficiently attached to society, or, if one wishes, society is not sufficiently attached to them, and they escape it. Precisely because they feel its effect neither with vivacity nor with the continuity that is necessary, they have no cognizance of all the obligations their positions as social beings demand of them. The general ideal to which they are attached being, for the reasons we have spoken of, formal and shifting, it cannot take them out of themselves. We do not cling to very much when we have no very determined objective, and, consequently, we cannot very well elevate ourselves beyond a more or less refined egotism. On the contrary, he who gives himself over to a definite task is, at every moment, struck by the sentiment of common solidarity in the thousand duties of occupational morality.

II

But does not the division of labor by making each of us an incomplete being bring on a diminution of individual personality? That is a reproach which has often been levelled at it.

Let us first of all remark that it is difficult to see why it would be more in keeping with the logic of human nature to develop superficially rather than profoundly.

Why would a more extensive activity, but more dispersed, be superior to a more concentrated, but circumscribed, activity? Why would there be more dignity in being complete and mediocre, rather than in living a more specialized, but more intense life, particularly if it is thus possible for us to find what we have lost in this specialization through our association with other beings who have what we lack and who complete us? We take off from the principle that man ought to realize his nature as man, to accomplish his ὀικεῖον ἔργον as Aristotle said. But this nature does not remain constant throughout history; it is modified with societies. Among lower peoples, the proper duty of man is to resemble his companions, to realize in himself all the traits of the collective type which are then confounded, much more than today, with the human type. But, in more advanced societies, his nature is, in large part, to be an organ of society, and his proper duty, consequently, is to play his role as an organ.

Moreover, far from being trammelled by the progress of specialization, individual personality develops with the division of labor.

To be a person is to be an autonomous source of action. Man acquires this quality only in so far as there is something in him which is his alone and which individualizes him, as he is something more than a simple incarnation of the generic type of his race and his group. It will be said that he is endowed with free will and that is enough to establish his personality. But although there may be some of this liberty in him, an object of so many discussions, it is not this metaphysical, impersonal, invariable attribute which can serve as the unique basis for concrete personality, which is empirical and variable with individuals. That could not be constituted by the wholly abstract power of choice between two opposites, but it is still necessary for this faculty to be exercised towards ends and aims which are proper to the agent. In other words, the very materials of conscience must have a personal character. But we have seen that this result is progressively produced as the division of labor progresses. The effacement of the segmental type, at the same time that it necessitates a very great specialization, partially lifts the individual conscience from the organic environment which supports it, as from the social environment which envelops it, and, accordingly because of this double emancipation, the individual becomes more of an independent factor in his own conduct. The division of labor itself contributes to this enfranchisement, for individual natures, while specializing, become more complex, and by that are in part freed from collective action and hereditary influences which can only enforce themselves upon simple, general things.

It is, accordingly, a real illusion which makes us believe that personality was so much more complete when the division of labor had penetrated less. No doubt, in looking from without at the diversity of occupations which the individual then embraces, it may seem that he is developing in a very free and complete manner. But, in reality, this activity which he manifests is not really his. It is society, it is the race acting in and through him; he is only the intermediary through which they realize themselves. His liberty is only apparent and his personality borrowed. Because the life of these societies is, in certain respects, less regular, we imagine that original talents have more opportunity for free play, that it is easier for each one to pursue his own tastes, that a very large place is left to free fantasy.

But this is to forget that personal sentiments are then very rare. If the motives which govern conduct do not appear as periodically as they do today, they do not leave off being collective, and, consequently, impersonal, and it is the same with the actions that they inspire. Moreover, we have shown above how activity becomes richer and more intense as it becomes more specialized.

Thus, the progress of individual personality and that of the division of labor depend upon one and the same cause. It is thus impossible to desire one without desiring the other. But no one today contests the obligatory character of the rule which orders us to be more and more of a person.

One last consideration will make us see to what extent the division of labor is linked with our whole moral life.

Men have long dreamt of finally realizing in fact the ideal of human fraternity. People pray for a state where war will no longer be the law of international relations, where relations between societies will be pacifically regulated, as those between individuals already are, where all men will collaborate in the same work and live the same life. Although these aspirations are in part neutralized by those which have as their object the particular society of which we are a part, they have not left off being active and are even gaining in force. But they can be satisfied only if all men form one society, subject to the same laws. For, just as private conflicts can be regulated only by the action of the society in which the individuals live, so intersocial conflicts can be regulated only by a society which comprises in its scope all others. The only power which can serve to moderate individual egotism is the power of the group; the only power which can serve to moderate the egotism of groups is that of some other group which embraces them.

Truly, when the problem has been posed in these terms, we must recognize that this ideal is not on the verge of being integrally realized, for there are too many intellectual and moral diversities between different social types existing together on the earth to admit of fraternalization in the same society. But what is possible is that societies of the same type may come together, and it is, indeed, in this direction that evolution appears to move. We have already seen that among European peoples there is a tendency to form, by spontaneous movement, a European society which has, at present, some idea of itself and the beginning of organization. If the formation of a single human society is forever impossible, a fact which has not been proved, at least the formation of continually larger societies brings us vaguely near the goal. These facts, moreover, in no wise contradict the definition of morality that we have given, for if we cling to humanity and if we ought to cling to it, it is because it is a society which is in process of realizing itself in this way, and with which we are solidary.

But we know the greater societies cannot be formed except through the development of the division of labor, for not only could they not maintain themselves in equilibrium without a greater specialization of functions, but even the increase in the number of those competing would suffice to produce this result mechanically; and that, so much the more, since the growth of volume is generally accompanied by a growth in density. We can then formulate the following proposition: the ideal of human fraternity can be realized only in proportion to the progress of the division of labor. We must choose: either to renounce our dream, if we refuse further to circumscribe our activity, or else to push forward its accomplishment under the condition we have just set forth.

III

But if the division of labor produces solidarity, it is not only because it makes each individual an *exchangist,* as the economists say; it is because it creates among men an entire system of rights and duties which link them together in a durable way. Just as social similitudes give rise to a law and a morality which protect them, so the division of labor gives rise to rules which assure pacific and regular concourse of divided functions. If economists have believed that it would bring forth an abiding solidarity, in some manner of its own making, and if, accordingly, they have held that human societies could and would resolve themselves into purely economic associations, that is because they believed that it affected only individual, temporary interests. Consequently, to estimate the interests in conflict and the way in which they ought to equilibrate, that is to say, to determine the conditions under which exchange ought to take place, is solely a matter of individual competence; and, since these interests are in a perpetual state of becoming, there is no place for any permanent regulation. But such a conception is, in all ways, inadequate for the facts. The division of labor does not present individuals to one another, but social functions. And society is interested in the play of the latter; in so far as they regularly concur, or do not concur, it will be healthy or ill. Its existence thus depends upon them, and the more they are divided the greater its dependence. That is why it cannot leave them in a state of indetermination. In addition to this, they are determined by themselves. Thus are formed those rules whose number grows as labor is divided, and whose absence makes organic solidarity either impossible or imperfect.

But it is not enough that there be rules; they must be just, and for that it is necessary for the external conditions of competition to be equal. If, moreover, we remember that the collective conscience is becoming more and more a cult of the individual, we shall see that what characterizes the morality of organized societies, compared to that of segmental societies, is that there is something more human, therefore more rational, about them. It does not direct our activities to ends which do not immediately concern us; it does not make us servants of ideal powers of a nature other than our own, which follow their directions without occupying themselves with the interests of men. It only asks that we be thoughtful of our fellows and that we be just, that we fulfill our duty, that we work at the function we can best execute, and receive that just reward for our services. The rules whch constitute it do not have a constraining force which snuffs out free thought; but, because they are rather made for us and, in a certain sense, by us, we are free. We wish to understand them; we do not fear to change them. We must, however, guard against finding such an ideal inadequate on the pretext that it is too earthly and too much to our liking. An ideal is not more elevated because more transcendent, but because it leads us to vaster perspectives. What is important is not that it tower high above us, until it becomes a stranger to our lives, but that it open to our activity a large enough field. This is far from being on the verge of realization. We know only too well what a laborious work it is to erect this society where each individual will have the place he merits, will be rewarded as he deserves, where everybody, accordingly, will spontaneously work for the good of all and of each. Indeed, a moral code is not above another because it commands in a drier and more authoritarian manner, or because it is more sheltered from reflection. Of course, it must attach us to something besides ourselves but it is not necessary for it to chain us to it with impregnable bonds.

It has been said with justice that morality—and by that must be understood, not only moral doctrines, but customs—is going through a real crisis. What precedes can help us to understand the nature and causes of this sick condition. Profound changes have been produced in the structure of our societies in a very short time; they have been freed from the segmental type with a rapidity and in proportions such as have never before been seen in history. Accordingly, the morality which corresponds to this social type has regressed, but without another developing quickly enough to fill the ground that the first left vacant in our consciences. Our faith has been troubled; tradition has lost its sway; individual judgment has been freed from collective judgment. But, on the other hand, the functions which have been disrupted in the course of the upheaval have not had the time to adjust themselves to one another; the new life which has emerged so suddenly had not been able to be completely organized, and above all, it has not been organized in a way to satisfy the need for justice which has grown more ardent in our hearts. If this be so, the remedy for the evil is not to seek to resuscitate traditions and practices which, no longer responding to present conditions of society, can only live an artificial, false existence. What we must do to relieve this anomy is to discover the means for making the organs which are still wasting themselves in discordant movements harmoniously concur by introducing into their relations more justice by more and more extenuating the external inequalities which are the source of the evil. Our illness is not, then, as has often been believed, of an intellectual sort; it has more profound causes. We shall not suffer because we no longer know on what theoretical notion to base the morality we have been practicing, but because, in certain of its parts, this morality is irremediably shattered, and that which is necessary to us is only in process of formation. Our anxiety does not arise because the criticism of scholars has broken down the traditional explanation we used to give to our duties; consequently, it is not a new philosophical system which will relieve the situation. Because certain of our duties are no longer founded in the reality of things, a breakdown has resulted which will be repaired only in so far as a new discipline is established and consolidated. In short, our first duty is to make a moral code for ourselves. Such a work cannot be improvised in the silence of the study; it can arise only through itself, little by little, under the pressure of internal causes which make it necessary. But the service that thought can and must render is in fixing the goal that we must attain. That is what we have tried to do.

56.

LETTER FROM BIRMINGHAM JAIL

Martin Luther King, Jr.

The power necessary to maintain the social control function of government often encourages those in control to perpetuate special privileges to serve their own ends. In these circumstances the disadvantaged may resort to civil disobedience or even revolution to overcome the inequities. Using a technique which came to be known as passive resistance, Mahatma Gandhi led a weaponless mass of South Asians in their struggle to end British rule. The nonviolent action approach of the black effort to achieve equal rights, led for over a decade (1956–68) by the late Martin Luther King, Jr., followed the same tradition. In this selection King states his case for nonviolence, the "powerful and just weapon" which he called the Sword That Heals. (See also Kelman, Selection 37 and Gregory, Selection 38.)

April 16, 1963

MY DEAR FELLOW CLERGYMEN:

While confined here in the Birmingham city jail, I came across your recent statement calling my present activities "unwise and untimely." Seldom do I pause to answer criticism of my work and ideas. If I sought to answer all the criticisms that cross my desk, my secretaries would have little time for anything other than such correspondence in the course of the day, and I would have no time for constructive work. But since I feel that you are men of genuine good will and that your criticisms are sincerely set forth, I want to try to answer your statement in what I hope will be patient and reasonable terms.

I think I should indicate why I am here in Birmingham, since you have been influenced by the view which argues against "outsiders coming in." I have the honor of serving as president of the Southern Christian Leadership Conference, an organization operating in every southern state, with headquarters at Atlanta, Georgia.

Source: Martin Luther King, Jr., *Why We Can't Wait* (New York: Harper & Row, 1963).

Martin Luther King, Jr. (1929–1968) was president of the Southern Christian Leadership Conference and vice-president of the National Sunday School and Baptist Training Union, Congress of National Baptist Convention. He was awarded the Nobel Peace Prize in 1964 and was the author of *Stride Toward Freedom* and *Where Do We Go From Here: Chaos or Community?*

AUTHOR'S NOTE: This response to a published statement by eight fellow clergymen from Alabama . . . was composed under somewhat constricting circumstances. Begun on the margins of the newspaper in which the statement appeared while I was in jail, the letter was continued on scraps of writing paper supplied by a friendly Negro trusty, and concluded on a pad my attorneys were eventually permitted to leave me. Although the text remains in substance unaltered, I have indulged in the author's prerogative of polishing it for publication.

We have some eighty-five affiliated organizations across the South, and one of them is the Alabama Christian Movement for Human Rights. Frequently we share staff, educational and financial resources with our affiliates. Several months ago the affiliate here in Birmingham asked us to be on call to engage in a nonviolent direct-action program if such were deemed necessary. We readily consented, and when the hour came we lived up to our promise. So I, along with several members of my staff, am here because I was invited here. I am here because I have organizational ties here.

But more basically, I am in Birmingham because injustice is here. . . . Moreover, I am cognizant of the interrelatedness of all communities and states. I cannot sit idly by in Atlanta and not be concerned about what happens in Birmingham. Injustice anywhere is a threat to justice everywhere. We are caught in an inescapable network of mutuality, tied in a single garment of destiny. Whatever affects one directly, affects all indirectly. Never again can we afford to live with the narrow, provincial "outside agitator" idea. Anyone who lives inside the United States can never be considered an outsider anywhere within its bounds.

You deplore the demonstrations taking place in Birmingham. But your statement, I am sorry to say, fails to express a similar concern for the conditions that brought about the demonstrations. I am sure that none of you would want to rest content with the superficial kind of social analysis that deals merely with effects and does not grapple with underlying causes. It is unfortunate that demonstrations are taking place in Birmingham, but it is even more unfortunate that the city's white power structure left the Negro community with no alternative.

In any nonviolent campaign there are four basic steps: collection of the facts to determine whether injustices exist; negotiation; self-purification; and direct action. We have gone through all these steps in Birmingham. There can be no gainsaying the fact that racial injustice engulfs this community. Birmingham is probably the most thoroughly segregated city in the United States. Its ugly record of brutality is widely known. Negroes have experienced grossly unjust treatment in the courts. There have been more unsolved bombings of Negro homes and churches in Birmingham than in any other city in the nation. These are the hard, brutal facts of the case. On the basis of these conditions, Negro leaders sought to negotiate with the city fathers. But the latter consistently refused to engage in good-faith negotiation.

Then, last September, came the opportunity to talk with leaders of Birmingham's economic community. In the course of the negotiations, certain promises were made by the merchants—for example, to remove the stores' humiliating racial signs. On the basis of these promises, the Reverend Fred Shuttlesworth and the leaders of the Alabama Christian Movement for Human Rights agreed to a moratorium on all demonstrations. As the weeks and months went by, we realized that we were the victims of a broken promise. A few signs, briefly removed, returned; the others remained.

As in so many past experiences, our hopes had been blasted, and the shadow of deep disappointment settled upon us. We had no alternative except to prepare for direct action, whereby we would present our very bodies as a means of laying our case before the conscience of the local and the national community. Mindful of the difficulties involved, we decided to undertake a process of self-purification. We began a series of workshops on nonviolence, and we repeatedly asked ourselves: "Are you able to accept blows without retaliating?" "Are you able to endure the ordeal of jail?" We decided to schedule our direct-action program for the Easter season, realizing that except for Christmas, this is the main shopping period of the year. Knowing that a strong economic-withdrawal program would be the by-product of direct action, we felt that this would be the best time to bring pressure to bear on the merchants for the needed change.

Then it occurred to us that Birmingham's mayoral election was coming up in March, and we speedily decided to postpone action until after election day. When we discovered that the Commissioner of Public Safety, Eugene "Bull" Connor, had piled up enough votes to be in the run-off, we decided again to postpone action until the day after the run-off so that the demonstrations could not be used to cloud the issues. Like many others, we waited to see Mr. Connor defeated, and to this end we endured postponement after postponement. Having aided in this community need, we felt that our direct-action program could be delayed no longer.

You may well ask: "Why direct action? Why sit-ins, marches and so forth? Isn't negotiation a better path?" You are quite right in calling for negotiation. Indeed, this is the very purpose of direct action. Nonviolent direct action seeks to create such a crisis and foster such a tension that a community which has constantly refused to negotiate is forced to confront the issue. It seeks so to dramatize the issue that it can no longer be ignored. My citing the creation of tension as part of the work of the nonviolent-resister may sound rather shocking. But I must confess that I am not afraid of the word "tension." I have earnestly opposed violent tension, but there is a type of constructive, nonviolent tension which is necessary for growth. Just as Socrates felt that it was necessary to create a tension in the mind so that individuals could rise from the bondage of myths and half-truths to the unfettered realm of creative analysis and objective appraisal, so must we see the need for nonviolent gadflies to create the kind of tension in society that will help men rise from the dark depths of prejudice and racism to the majestic heights of understanding and brotherhood.

The purpose of our direct-action program is to create a situation so crisis-packed that it will eventually open the door to negotiation. I therefore concur with you in your call for negotiation. Too long has our beloved Southland been bogged down in a tragic effort to live in monologue rather than dialogue.

One of the basic points in your statement is that the action that I and my associates have taken in Birmingham is untimely. Some have asked: "Why didn't you give the new city administration time to act?" The only answer that I can give to this query is that the new Birmingham administration must be prodded about as much as the outgoing one, before it will act.

. . . My friends, I must say to you that we have not made a single gain in civil rights without determined legal and nonviolent pressure. Lamentably, it is an historical fact that privileged groups seldom give up their privileges voluntarily. Individuals may see the moral light and voluntarily give up their unjust posture; but, as Reinhold Niebuhr has reminded us, groups tend to be more immoral than individuals.

We know through painful experience that freedom is never voluntarily given by the oppressor; it must be demanded by the oppressed. Frankly, I have yet to engage in a direct-action campaign that was "well timed" in the view of those who have not suffered unduly from the disease of segregation. For years now I have heard the word "Wait!" It rings in the ear of every Negro with piercing familiarity. This "Wait" has almost always meant "Never." We must come to see, with one of our distinguished jurists, that "justice too long delayed is justice denied."

We have waited for more than 340 years for our constitutional and God-given rights. The nations of Asia and Africa are moving with jetlike speed toward gaining political independence, but we still creep at horse-and-buggy pace toward gaining a cup of coffee at a lunch counter. Perhaps it is easy for those who have never felt the stinging darts of segregation to say, "Wait." But when you have seen vicious mobs lynch your mothers and fathers at will and drown your sisters and brothers at whim; when you have seen hate-filled policemen curse, kick and even kill your black brothers and sisters; when you see the vast majority of your twenty million Negro brothers smothering in an airtight cage of poverty in the midst of an affluent society; when you suddenly find your tongue twisted and your speech stammering as you seek to explain to your six-year-old daughter why she can't go to the public amusement park that has just been advertised on television, and see tears welling up in her eyes when she is told that Funtown is closed to colored children, and see ominous signs of inferiority beginning to form in her little mental sky, and see her beginning to distort her personality by developing an unconscious bitterness toward white people; when you have to concoct an answer for a five-year-old son who is asking: "Daddy, why do white people treat colored people so mean?"; when you take a cross-country drive and find it necessary to sleep night after night in the uncomfortable corners of your automobile because no motel will accept you; when you are humiliated day in and day out by nagging signs reading "white" and "colored"; when your first name becomes "nigger," your middle name becomes "boy" (however old you are) and your last name becomes "John," and your wife and mother are never given the respected title "Mrs."; when you are harried by day and haunted by night by the fact that you are a Negro, living constantly at tiptoe stance, never quite knowing what to expect next, and are plagued with inner fears and outer resentments; when you are forever fighting a degenerating sense of "nobodiness"—then you will understand why we find it difficult to wait. There comes a time when the cup of endurance runs over, and men are no longer willing to be plunged into the abyss of despair. I hope, sirs, you can understand our legitimate and unavoidable impatience.

You express a great deal of anxiety over our willingness to break laws. This is certainly a legitimate concern. Since we so diligently urge people to obey the Supreme Court's decision of 1954 outlawing segregation in the public schools, at first glance it may seem rather paradoxical for us consciously to break laws. One may well ask: "How can you advocate breaking some laws and obeying others?" The answer lies in the fact that there are two types of laws: just and unjust. I would be the first to advocate obeying just laws. One has not only a legal but a moral responsibility to obey just laws. Conversely, one has a moral responsibility to disobey unjust laws. I would agree with St. Augustine that "an unjust law is no law at all."

Now, what is the difference between the two? . . . Any law that uplifts human personality is just. Any law that degrades human personality is unjust. All segregation statutes are unjust because segregation distorts the soul and damages the personality. It gives the segregator a false sense of superiority and the segregated a false sense of inferiority. Segregation, to use the terminology of the Jewish philosopher Martin Buber, substitutes an "I–it" relationship for an "I–thou" relationship and ends up relegating persons to the status of things. Hence segregation is not only politically, economically and sociologically unsound, it is morally wrong and sinful. Paul Tillich has said that sin is separation. Is not segregation an existential expression of man's tragic separation, his awful estrangement, his terrible sinfulness? Thus it is that I can urge men to obey the 1954 decision of the Supreme Court, for it is morally right; and I can urge them to disobey segregation ordinances, for they are morally wrong.

Let us consider a more concrete example of just and unjust laws. An unjust law is a code that a numerical or power majority group compels a minority group to obey but does not make binding on itself. This is *difference* made legal. By the same token, a just law is a code that a majority compels a minority to follow and that it is willing to follow itself. This is *sameness* made legal.

Let me give another explanation. A law is unjust if it is inflicted on a minority that, as a result of being denied the right to vote, had no part in enacting or devising the law. Who can say that the legislature of Alabama which set up that state's segregation laws was democratically elected? Throughout Alabama all sorts of devious methods are used to prevent Negroes from becoming registered voters, and there are some counties in which, even though Negroes constitute a majority of the population, not a single Negro is registered. Can any law enacted under such circumstances be considered democratically structured?

Sometimes a law is just on its face and unjust in its application. For instance, I have been arrested on a charge of parading without a permit. Now, there is nothing wrong in having an ordinance which requires a permit for a parade. But such an ordinance becomes unjust when it is used to maintain segregation and to deny citizens the First-Amendment privilege of peaceful assembly and protest.

I hope you are able to see the distinction I am trying to point out. In no sense do I advocate evading or defying the law, as would the rabid segregationist. That would lead to anarchy. One who breaks an unjust law must do so openly, lovingly, and with a willingness to accept the penalty. I submit that an individual who breaks a law that conscience tells him is unjust, and who willingly accepts the penalty of imprisonment in order to arouse the conscience of the community over its injustice, is in reality expressing the highest respect for law.

Of course, there is nothing new about this kind of civil disobedience. It was evidenced sublimely in the refusal of Shadrach, Meshach and Abednego to obey the laws of Nebuchadnezzar, on the ground that a higher moral law was at stake. It was practiced superbly by the early Christians, who were willing to face hungry lions and the excruciating pain of chopping blocks rather than submit to certain unjust laws of the Roman Empire. To a degree, academic freedom is a reality today because Socrates practiced civil disobedience. In our own nation, the Boston Tea Party represented a massive act of civil disobedience.

We should never forget that everything Adolf Hitler did in Germany was "legal" and everything the Hungarian freedom fighters did in Hungary was "illegal." It was "illegal" to aid and comfort a Jew in

Hitler's Germany. Even so, I am sure that, had I lived in Germany at the time, I would have aided and comforted my Jewish brothers. If today I lived in a Communist country where certain principles dear to the Christian faith are suppressed, I would openly advocate disobeying that country's antireligious laws.

I must make two honest confessions to you, my Christian and Jewish brothers. First, I must confess that over the past few years I have been gravely disappointed with the white moderate. I have almost reached the regrettable conclusion that the Negro's great stumbling block in his stride toward freedom is not the White Citizen's Councilor or the Ku Klux Klanner, but the white moderate, who is more devoted to "order" than to justice; who prefers a negative peace which is the absence of tension to a positive peace which is the presence of justice; who constantly says: "I agree with you in the goal you seek, but I cannot agree with your methods of direct action"; who paternalistically believes he can set the timetable for another man's freedom; who lives by a mythical concept of time and who constantly advises the Negro to wait for a "more convenient season." Shallow understanding from people of good will is more frustrating than absolute misunderstanding from people of ill will. Lukewarm acceptance is much more bewildering than outright rejection.

I had hoped that the white moderate would understand that law and order exist for the purpose of establishing justice and that when they fail in this purpose they become the dangerously structured dams that block the flow of social progress. I had hoped that the white moderate would understand that the present tension in the South is a necessary phase of the transition from an obnoxious negative peace, in which the Negro passively accepted his unjust plight, to a substantive and positive peace, in which all men will respect the dignity and worth of human personality. Actually, we who engage in nonviolent direct action are not the creators of tension. We merely bring to the surface the hidden tension that is already alive. We bring it out in the open, where it can be seen and dealt with. Like a boil that can never be cured so long as it is covered up but must be opened with all its ugliness to the natural medicines of air and light, injustice must be exposed, with all the tension its exposure creates, to the light of human conscience and the air of national opinion before it can be cured.

In your statement you assert that our actions, even though peaceful, must be condemned because they precipitate violence. But is this a logical assertion? Isn't this like condemning a robbed man because his possession of money precipitated the evil act of robbery? Isn't this like condemning Socrates because his unswerving commitment to truth and his philosophical inquiries precipitated the act by the misguided populace in which they made him drink hemlock? Isn't this like condemning Jesus because his unique God-consciousness and never-ceasing devotion to God's will precipitated the evil act of crucifixion? We must come to see that, as the federal courts have consistently affirmed, it is wrong to urge an individual to cease his efforts to gain his basic constitutional rights because the quest may precipitate violence. Society must protect the robbed and punish the robber.

I had also hoped that the white moderate would reject the myth concerning time in relation to the struggle for freedom. I have just received a letter from a white brother in Texas. He writes: "All Christians know that the colored people will receive equal rights eventually, but it is possible that you are in too great a religious hurry. It has taken Christianity almost two thousand years to accomplish what it has. The teachings of Christ take time to come to earth." Such an attitude stems from a tragic misconception of time, from the strangely irrational notion that there is something in the very flow of time that will inevitably cure all ills. Actually, time itself is neutral; it can be used either destructively or constructively. More and more I feel that the people of ill will have used time much more effectively than have the people of good will. We will have to repent in this generation not merely for the hateful words and actions of the bad people but for the appalling silence of the good people. Human progress never rolls in on wheels of inevitability; it comes through the tireless efforts of men willing to be co-workers with God, and without this hard work, time itself becomes an ally of the forces of social stagnation. We must use time creatively, in the knowledge that the time is always ripe to do right. Now is the time to make real the promise of democracy and transform our pending national elegy into a creative psalm of brotherhood. Now is the time to lift our national policy from the quicksand of racial injustice to the solid rock of human dignity.

You speak of our activity in Birmingham as extreme. At first I was rather disappointed that fellow clergymen would see my nonviolent efforts as those of an extremist. I began thinking about the fact that I stand in the middle of two opposing forces in the Negro community. One is a force of complacency, made up in part of Negroes who, as a result of long years of oppression, are so drained of self-respect and a sense of "somebodiness" that they have adjusted to segregation; and in part of a few middle-class Negroes who, because of a degree of academic and economic security and because in some ways they profit by segregation have become insensitive to the problems of the masses. The other force is one of bitterness and hatred, and it comes perilously close to advocating violence. It is expressed in the various black nationalist groups that are springing up across the nation, the largest and best-known being Elijah Muhammad's Muslim movement. Nourished by the Negro's frustration over the continued existence of racial discrimination, this movement is made up of people who have lost faith in America, who have absolutely repudiated Christianity, and who have concluded that the white man is an incorrigible "devil."

I have tried to stand between these two forces, saying that we need emulate neither the "do-nothingism" of the complacent nor the hatred and despair of the black nationalist. For there is the more excellent way of love and nonviolent protest. I am grateful to God that, through the influence of the Negro church, the way of nonviolence became an integral part of our struggle.

If this philosophy had not emerged, by now many streets of the South, would, I am convinced, be flowing with blood. And I am further convinced that if our white brothers dismiss as "rabble-rousers" and "outside agitators" those of us who employ nonviolent direct action, and if they refuse to support our nonviolent efforts, millions of Negroes will, out of frustration and despair, seek solace and security in black-nationalist ideologies—a development that would inevitably lead to a frightening racial nightmare.

Oppressed people cannot remain oppressed forever. The yearning for freedom eventually manifests itself, and that is what has happened to the American Negro. Something within has reminded him of his birthright of freedom, and something without has reminded him that it can be gained.

Consciously or unconsciously, he has been caught up by the *Zeitgeist,* and with his black brothers of Africa and his brown and yellow brothers of Asia, South America and the Caribbean, the United States Negro is moving with a sense of great urgency toward the promised land of racial justice. If one recognizes this vital urge that has engulfed the Negro community, one should readily understand why public demonstrations are taking place. The Negro has many pent-up resentments and latent frustrations, and he must release them. So let him march; let him make prayer pilgrimages to the city hall; let him go on freedom rides—and try to understand why he must do so. If his repressed emotions are not released in nonviolent ways, they will seek expression through violence; this is not a threat but a fact of history. So I have not said to my people: "Get rid of your discontent." Rather, I have tried to say that this normal and healthy discontent can be channeled into the creative outlet of nonviolent direct action. And now this approach is being termed extremist.

. . . . .

. . . The question is not whether we will be extremists, but what kind of extremists we will be. Will we be extremists for hate or for love? Will we be extremists for the preservation of injustice or for the extension of justice?

. . . . .

. . . Perhaps the South, the nation and the world are in dire need of creative extremists.

. . . . .

Yours for the cause of
Peace and Brotherhood,
MARTIN LUTHER KING, JR.

57.

HOW AMERICANS VOTE

Joel Silbey

Like the other basic institutions in human society, the political institutions represent a relatively permanent, systematic framework of folkways, laws, and forms of procedure for satisfying a persistent essential need—in this instance the need to enforce behavior norms considered vital to the welfare of all and to provide certain services felt to be necessary for the general welfare. In American society, the relation between the political institution and the general social structure can be seen in an examination of voting behavior—the means by which the decision is reached as to which party and which policies shall prevail. In this analysis of voting, Silbey combines the cross-sectional approach, typical of many sociologists who engage in public opinion studies, with the long-range perspective which is characteristic of the social his-

Source: Joel Silbey, "How Americans Vote," *Cornell Alumni News* (October 1972): 17–26.

Joel Silbey is professor of American history at Cornell University. His interests include United States political history and he is coauthor of *Voters, Parties, and Elections.*

torian. The method is useful because it shows the way in which the relative rigidity of institutions can change over time.

Professor Silbey, can you isolate any major, overriding premise that historians and political scientists use to think about American elections?

Yes, the basic premise is that any given election, as one student of this matter has written, is never a new throw of the dice. The odds overwhelmingly favor each voter voting in any given election for the same party he supported the election before, and the odds are also quite strong that the same party will win any given national election as won the previous one.

This is true, historians and political scientists have recently come to believe, because most voters vote as they do, most of the time, for reasons little related to their knowledge of specific issues in the campaign or to the leadership qualities of current candidates.

The Survey Research Center at the University of Michigan has been conducting in-depth polls of voters since 1948. They show that most people cannot identify ten things the Democrats stand for, or ten candidates of the Democratic Party other than the presidential candidate. Nevertheless, they vote on party lines, which are in turn based on the ethnic, cultural, or in some cases geographic groups into which they were born.

Election statistics confirm the evidence of the polls. If you take certain towns, wards, and districts over time, the deviation from one election to the next is very slight. The demographic nature of the area remains constant in many places, so the votes don't change. It's extraordinary. No deviation at all for forty years or more. In fact, there are towns in Upstate New York that have voted almost the same percentage Republican since the 1850s.

How do individual people pick up their party allegiances?

It is clear people pick them up the same way they pick up their religious preferences: at home, hearing about it, talking about it. Assuming their parents are Republicans, that is the first thing children hear of a political nature. That kind of identification begins early.

For example, the first things I heard about politics in my home were Democratic. I didn't hear that we were Democrats, but that Roosevelt had saved the country during the Depression. I also came to realize that nearly all Jews were Democrats, I was Jewish and these things were somehow together in me.

Political values are no different from religious values or social values, in the sense that we absorb them early in our lives, and we hold them, and we rarely change them. Before we know *why* we are Democrats or Republicans, we know that we *are* Democrats or Republicans. And to many people in the United States, that is enough. They don't really care why they're Democrats or Republicans.

Most people just follow the party line. Not consciously, but there's a simple reason for it. The cost of knowing a great deal about politics in this country is very high. Most people don't have the time or the inclination. Most of us do look for guides. We do not know a great deal, and the effective guide is quite often a label, a party.

If you keep pressing someone, "Why are you a Republican?" quite often they will say, "My parents are Republicans." But you will press further. "Why? Why?" And you will often get an answer like, "The Republican Party is the party of the Union. It saved the Union." That doesn't refer specifically to the Civil War, but to the image of the Republican Party as the party that created the modern American colossus.

I SUPPOSE WE ALL HAVE TO HAVE PHRASES TO USE IN ARGUING WITH THE GUY AT THE BAR. THERE MUST BE SOME ANSWER. WE CAN'T JUST SAY, "BECAUSE DAD SAYS SO."

Most of us don't say it that way. But we do have statistical evidence that up until very recently about 90 percent of all voters voted exactly the way their parents did.

WHAT ABOUT RECENTLY?

It's changing, but not as much as most people think. I'll get back to that later.

WHAT DOES THIS ANALYSIS MEAN, THEN, FOR A PARTY ENTERING A PRESIDENTIAL ELECTION?

For most of our history, at the time the campaign begins, most of the decision of the electorate is almost already in. The campaign therefore takes on a different function. Very rarely are campaigns intended to convert people from one party to the other. Most of the time they attempt to provide cues that will mobilize people, to remind them of their party loyalty, to get them out to the polls.

The majority party has to get its people out, and the minority party has to get its people out and perhaps enough of the independents that it will have as many people voting for its candidate as the majority party does. That's why campaigns are directed primarily at the independent vote, despite the smallness of that vote.

In the present era, the figures are profound on who identifies himself as a Democrat. There are two people who will call themselves strong Democrats for every Republican.

YOU'D THINK, THEN, THAT THE DEMOCRATS WOULD HAVE EVERY ELECTION LOCKED UP.

Yes, you would. You'd think McGovern and Humphrey could pull out daggers and duel up and down Fifth Avenue and still the Democrats would win, because there are just that many more Democrats.

However, on one hand, and roughly speaking, since the 1930s the Democratic Party has been the party of the working class. Upper class Republicans, lower class Democrats. And therefore the Democrats always have a problem with a differential turnout in elections. The higher a person is on the economic scale and the education scale, which in America are about the same thing, the more likely he is to vote. The less educated, the less likely to vote.

So even though a 2:1 majority of persons say they are Democrats, each party gets about 50 percent of the vote. If you discount the skewing effect of the electoral college we've had extremely close elections in the past few years, with the exception of 1964's landslide.

Secondly, in any given election there are a number of short term, immediate forces which affect a certain proportion of the electorate. Something happens which affects them so directly and powerfully that it is enough to shake their party identification for this one election. For example, in this election [1972], the anger of the people in the Wilkes-Barre, Pennsylvania area against the Republican administration, which they think has dragged its feet on flood relief, may be enough to cause them to cast a protest vote against the Republicans. But they'll be voting Republican again next election.

Another such short-run force was John Kennedy's Catholicism, which drove many Protestant Democrats away from him in 1960; given the plurality of traditional Democrats in the country he should have won a landslide similar to the Democrats' congressional margin of 1958. After 1960, Protestant Democrats returned to the fold, once they observed that the Pope did not move into the White House with Kennedy.

Such issues don't as yet affect large numbers of voters. Only about 10 to 15 percent of the electorate change their vote in a given national election over such short-run factors. But that's enough to be significant in a close election.

The third element that prevents a Democratic landslide each election is that personality has become a greater force, causing people to temporarily abandon their party identification. Television has made this possible, and Dwight Eisenhower was a good example. He came across so powerfully that large numbers of Democrats voted for him, at the same time that they continued to support Democrats for Congress. They were still Democrats, as shown by the fact Eisenhower carried Republicans to control of Congress only in 1952. The Democrats won in 1954, again in 1956 (when Eisenhower was reelected by a greater margin than in 1952), and by a landslide in 1958.

YOUR WHOLE THEORY THAT ONE PARTY IS IN CONTROL FOR LONG PERIODS IS FINE, BUT WE HAVE HAD EXCEPTIONS TO THE APPARENT DEMOCRATIC MAJORITY IN 1946, 1952, 1956, AND 1968. AREN'T THESE AN AWFUL LOT OF EXCEPTIONS?

Good point. Instability is often a sign that a major shift in party dominance is under way. But the steadiness of congressional election results seems to say otherwise, despite the more visible swings in the presidential results.

PARTY IDENTITIES HOLD FIRM NO MATTER WHAT HAPPENS? DESPITE SCANDALS LIKE TEAPOT DOME, BOBBY BAKER, THE ITT?

Even despite scandals. Most people don't think about them or cannot identify who is at fault very specifically.

EVEN A WAR, EVEN THE QUESTION OF WHO GOT US INTO THE WAR, IS NOT STRONG ENOUGH?

Most of the time, no. In fact, that kind of issue only confirms previous ideas. The claim that "Democrats get us into war," for instance. For the Republicans, it may be another reason not to be a Democrat. But the Democrat will say, "That's ridiculous. Nobody gets us into war. It's a configuration of forces."

IF THIS KIND OF ATTACHMENT TO PARTIES HAS ALWAYS BEEN THE CASE, AS YOU SAY, THEN WHY AREN'T WE ALL STILL WHIGS AND TORIES, OR FEDERALISTS AND ANTI-FEDERALISTS?

Every once in a while, and it occurs every forty years or so, some series of cataclysmic shocks produces a significant overturn in party preferences. Or occasionally the coming to fruition of a massive demographic change in the country changes the way elections come out.

These shifts, which occurred in the 1850s, the 1890s, and the 1930s, are called by political scientists "periods of realignment."

The realignment of the 1850s was the major one—it produced the Republican Party. In the 1890s, a less potent realignment stemmed a Democratic growth that threatened Republican dominance. Finally, in the 1930s, many Republicans abandoned the ship that had carried them into the Depression, and became Democrats.

People are suggesting this realignment process is happening again now. It would make a kind of sense, if only in terms of a certain rhythm that is to be noted in the past.

The Wallace movement may be one piece of evidence that we are indeed in a period of realignment, because a third party has usually risen during these periods. It provides a way station for persons leaving one party on the way to the opposite party. People just cannot bring themselves to go over that easily.

WHAT WERE THE CAUSES, SPECIFICALLY, OF THE REALIGNMENTS OF THE PAST? WHAT ABOUT THE REALIGNMENT OF THE 1850s?

In the 1850s, most of our research would seem to indicate that a great number of white Anglo-Saxon Protestant Democrats reacted very strongly to the incredible surge of Irish Catholic immigration into the United States in the years of the early '50s. Three hundred thousand Irish were coming into this country every year. The numbers were overwhelming.

You may have heard the old folk song, "No Irish Need Apply." The prejudice against them, in this basically Anglo-Saxon country, was profound. It was a country with a long tradition of anti-Irish attitudes.

ANTI-IRISH OR ANTI-CATHOLIC?

Both. I think the anti-Catholic feeling was stronger. The U.S. was a Protestant country, and what most people forget is that the U.S. was settled, not by the tolerant wing of Protestantism, not by Anglicans to any great extent—except in the South, where you didn't have this problem of anti-Irish feeling to the same degree—but by the *purifying* wing of Protestantism, the Congregationalists and Presbyterians of the 1800s. And thus you find a very virulent anti-Catholicism.

Look what happened. In the early 1850s, about half the total nineteenth-century Irish immigration occurred in a period of only four or five years. This was a sharp and sudden social shock to many Americans. Crime increased, as did slums, social disorder, and apparent social disintegration.

Most of all, the Irish brought their church and its hierarchy to Protestant America. Before this time, the entire U.S. had been a part of the Montreal Catholic diocese. Now all of a sudden eleven new dioceses were formed. Parochial schools, convents, and many churches were built. There were no native born bishops available, so Italian bishops were sent over. Somehow all these events struck a powerful chord, and we see the first identifiable backlash in American history.

The backlash had two components. The first, obviously, was against the Irish Catholics. The second element was an effort to allocate the blame.

And the early Republicans made it very plain that it was the Democratic Party that was urging immigration, that was bringing these Catholics in, usually for its own electoral purposes. The Democratic leaders, it was said, were political "bosses"—a word quite often used in those days—who were bringing in these voters to maintain Democratic majorities even if the country became Catholic in the process.

AND THE PROTESTANTS BELIEVED THAT?

Apparently. And the result was a shift, an actual shift of people who had long identified themselves as Democrats, who moved over into a new, Republican party.

BEFORE THE 1850S THERE WAS THE WHIG PARTY?

In that period, the United States had a two-party system, Whigs and Democrats. The Democrats had a majority before the 1850s. The former Whigs converted enough disenchanted Democrats that together they came to constitute a new electoral majority after the 1850s.

WHY DID THEY CHANGE THEIR NAME?

One of the things that prevents realignment from taking place more often, and more dramatically when it does take place, is the difficulty experienced by people who have always identified themselves with one party in moving over to the other party. They don't convert easily; conversion involves a lot of emotional turmoil.

That's part of why the Whigs gave up the name, Whig. They wanted to make former Democrats feel at home. In the early 1850s, Whigs joined to form a new political grouping they called the "People's Party," which ultimately was to become the Republican Party.

What the Republicans were trying to do was to say, in effect, "We aren't the Whigs, you're not coming over to the enemy. We are forming a new party." And they took the name "Republican" because that was the name of the Jefferson party, the progenitor of the Democratic Party.

This all illustrates the attachment of people to a party and the name of the party, which is why, as I indicated, realignments are often associated with, and made easier by, the existence of strong third parties. In the 1850s the American or "Know Nothing" Party was just such a vehicle. Most former Democrats who joined the Know Nothing party ultimately went into the new Republican Party.

I would argue, to skip a century, that one of the things that has thus far prevented realignment in the 1970s from benefiting the Republicans has been the Wallace movement. Disaffected Democrats have been able to move over into the Wallace movement, without having to defect to the Republicans. They can still believe they are true Democrats fighting for the old Democratic principles.

One of the interesting things . . . will be to see what happens when the Wallace movement is not there. I suspect many of his followers, those who are very unhappy with the trend of the Democratic Party, are going to vote Republican for the first time.

VOTE, BUT NOT NECESSARILY REGISTER REPUBLICAN?

Yes, and even when asked their party affiliation in the next round of surveys, they will still say they are Democrats. But they may move from considering themselves strong Democrats to considering themselves weak Democrats, and within four or eight years they may call themselves Republicans.

DID THE SPLIT CONTINUE TO BE BETWEEN THE IMMIGRANT CLASSES AND WHITE ANGLO-SAXON PROTESTANTS UNTIL THE NEXT MAJOR REALIGNMENT IN THE 1930s?

Yes, but there were two exceptions: the blacks and the South. When blacks could vote in the South, as they could from about the 1860s to the 1880s, they tended to vote Republican. They voted for the party of Abraham Lincoln.

They were about the only Southern Republicans because, after the Civil War, the South rejected Republicanism. The Republicans had led the nation into the Civil War, so the South as a whole then embraced the Democratic Party.

That movement also highlighted an anomaly in American politics: groups in the same party who don't have very much in common, or who even have antagonistic ideas. The reason is that each group came into the party at a different time, for different reasons. The real point of union is a rejection of the other party. So, from the 1850s to the present, there exists a Democratic Party made up of Northern urban Catholic immigrants and Southern whites, with pockets of pre-1850s Democratic strength because not all Democrats moved over during the Civil War.

WHAT HAPPENED IN THE 1930s?

The Depression. The impact of the Depression was very powerful, although we tend to forget it today. At the time, it was so powerful that people moved over to the Democratic Party regardless of their ethnocultural background.

Low income Americans, regardless of background, regardless of previous party commitment, tended to vote Democratic as the party of reform and recovery.

This didn't happen overnight. It happened gradually, between 1932 and 1936. But by 1936, for the first time in our history, the two parties tended to be at opposite ends of the economic scale. For the first time, if you asked a person simply how much he made a year, you could probably tell his party affiliation.

DOES THIS HOLD TRUE TODAY?

I don't know. The great untested question about the realignment of the 1970s, if it is a realignment, is what happens if the economic issue becomes important—as it still could. If it does, I think we could have a restoration of the Democratic Party to what it has been. In other words, economic trouble could bring back the Democratic blue collar workers who are now so restive.

And it is true, even today, that people at the lower end of the scale think Democratic. They may not think the economy is a major issue now, but they make the identification that "When the Democrats are in, we work; when the Republicans are in, we're laid off." This identification of parties remains very strong.

ISN'T THIS EFFECT TEMPERED IN ANY WAY BY PEOPLE WHO ARE LOWER MIDDLE CLASS OR UPPER WORKING CLASS WHO ASPIRE TO THE THINGS THAT "REPUBLICANS" WANT?

I don't think it's tempered by that as much as by the old ethnocultural factors that I've mentioned. That is, as the worst parts of the Depression passed in the 1930s, you began to see white Anglo-Saxon Protestants moving back to the Republican Party, to some extent. If you look at a chart of the national Democratic vote from 1932 on, it goes up to a height in 1936. From '36 to '48 it falls constantly until, in 1948, the Republicans almost won.

Again, you see the force of tradition: people moved over to the Democratic Party but didn't stay there. The nature of a realignment is that some who moved over *did* stay.

One identifiable group that moved over and stayed over is the blacks. In 1932 blacks who could vote in this country voted Republican, for Hoover. They identified Franklin Roosevelt as the candidate of the South, and they wanted no part of him. By 1936 they had moved over, overwhelmingly, and became more and more Democratic until 1968, when they voted over 90 percent Democratic.

IS THIS A CONSEQUENCE OF WHAT THE DEMOCRATS DID FOR THEM OR OF WHAT THE REPUBLICANS HAD DONE HOSTILE TO THEM IN THE EARLY '30S?

The important thing seems to be that the New Deal was quite color blind. For the first time since Reconstruction days, blacks were being helped by the federal government. The Democratic policy in many areas benefitted the unemployed regardless of color.

A second group that moved over was a large component of Jews. Many Jews had voted Republican. The division in the Jewish community had always been between German Jews, who were here first, and Polish and East European Jews, who came later. Polish and East European Jews typically remained at the lower end of the economic scale and they were Democrats from the very beginning. The German Jews had tended to be identified with the Republicans for many years. But in the 1930s, that division began to crack, and German Jews moved into the Democratic Party.

WHAT WAS THE BASIS FOR THIS MOVE?

No one is quite sure. Part of it seems to be a very powerful phenomenon within the Jewish community of support for liberalism, support for reform. Jews as a culture group, given their long tradition of self-help, of working together because of an unfriendly outside world, seem more likely to support reform and liberal causes than are other groups.

Jews also reacted very positively to the fact that the New Deal brought Jews into positions of power in the administration. The fact that one of Roosevelt's close associates in politics was Herbert Lehman, who replaced him as governor of New York, was very important. In ethnocultural politics, symbolism is very important.

BEING MORE COMFORTABLE WITH ONE OF YOUR OWN?

That's exactly the best way to describe it. Most of us are acculturated to believe there are enemies out there.

. . . . .

I SENSE YOU THINK THE UNIVERSITY AND HIGHER EDUCATION ARE POSSIBLY RESPONSIBLE FOR BREAKING DOWN SOME OF THE TENSIONS BETWEEN CULTURAL GROUPS.

Among those who have gone to college, there has already been the beginning of a decrease of that kind of instinctive ethnic identification. That sort of identification is a form of tribalism, and tribalism is more likely to survive among people who have not been exposed to a broader view of the world.

But, working against this force, it is also true that, for the first time in our history, ethnic identification is becoming acceptable. The blacks did that. The black power movements, followed by the Italian-American Anti-Defamation League, has made tribalism respectable. Leaders in various ethnic communities are now saying the way to power is to unite.

. . . . .

Really what the blacks did was to copy what others had already done. An ethnic bloc which can deliver votes will be potent in a political party, and to maintain an ethnic bloc you also have to maintain ethnic identification.

That was always there, but it was always *sub rosa.* In New York City you usually had a ticket made up of a Catholic, an Irishman, a Jew, and an Italian. Nobody said that was what was being done, but that was the way it was. "The balanced ticket." Now we've simply brought it to the surface, we've articulated it, and once something is articulated more people are likely to do it.

One interesting thing about the kinds of ethnocultural tensions that have been so strong throughout our history is that most of the time they have been acted out on the local level, in terms of who controls the school, or who controls the police.

In the nineteenth century, when the Protestants controlled the school system in this country, they put the Protestant Bible into every school. And it was the Catholics who resisted Bible reading because they had to listen to something they thought was a sin. When the Catholics became powerful in New York State in the 1870s, one of the things they successfully fought for was state support for parochial schools. They wanted their own schools.

The other major area was the police. The great breakthrough for the Irish, so far as they were concerned, was in the 1860s when they began to get control of the New York City police force. At this point the Republican-controlled State Legislature stepped in and took away local control of police and made it a state function.

IN THAT CASE, THE DEMOCRATIZATION OF THE DEMOCRATIC PARTY MAY BE ITS DOWNFALL BECAUSE IT IMPEDES BALANCING. I SEE THE REPUBLICANS, AT THEIR 1972 CONVENTION, ARE RESISTING THIS MOVEMENT. IN NEW YORK STATE, THE REPUBLICAN LEGISLATURE HAD ENCOURAGED A FREE-WHEELING PRIMARY, WITH THE CONSEQUENCE THAT IN 1970 THE DEMOCRATS WOUND UP WITH A TICKET OF FOUR JEWS AND A BLACK.

One virtue of the political boss is that he doesn't make that kind of mistake. He can count; he knows what's what. One could argue, ideologically, that there should be nothing wrong with four Jews and a black on the ticket. Obviously that is the slate the Democrats of the state wanted. But of course, the ticket was wiped out.

WHAT DO YOU THINK IS HAPPENING TO THE PARTY SYSTEM?

I think the basic alignment that was established in the 1930s is being very badly shaken. Whether a whole series of defections will take place, of the sort we saw in the 1850s and 1930s, is still an open question, because most people still think of themselves as Democrats. Or still dislike Republicans.

First, though, the South: the Democratic Party is clearly identified with the black revolution, particularly in the South. As long as the civil rights revolution remained moderate, Southern whites were willing to fight it out within the party. But now Democratic candidates are supporting what many Southerners, and others, consider excesses.

The Southerner isn't going to change his cultural attitude toward blacks, so many have begun to drift out of the party. Without a Wallace third party I suspect they will vote Republican. Not all of them, of course. Even in a major realignment not everyone is affected to the same degree. The traditional Democratic Party will remain strong, but there's a possibility of a wipeout in the South in terms of offices held by Democrats.

WHAT ABOUT THE NORTH?

Two things are affecting the Democrats.

First, the children of the urban immigrants have gone to college and moved out into the suburbs and taken their Democratic heritage with them. The Democratic Party is gaining a powerful, middle-class, educated element. These people have shucked some of the ethnic values they were born into, but most of them prefer the Democrats because most of them started with the kind of liberal credentials that are usually actively reinforced in college, through their peer group and other forces.

The second element is a conversion phenomenon. The defections of John Lindsay and Rep. Ogden Reid, both former Republicans, are not isolated acts. A liberal Republican element is finding its party increasingly inhospitable, just as Southern Democrats are finding *their* party inhospitable. So the liberal, cosmopolitan Republican element, which dates back to the 1850s, is moving over, somewhat, to the Democrats. This process is reinforced in the more liberal suburbs.

A different conversion, benefiting the Republicans, involves the old urban ethnic communities. The Italians and the Irish, particularly, have been in the Democratic Party since the nineteenth century, but they are becoming very restive because they are not liberal on the so-called social issue. They are the ones on the frontier of America's race war; it is into their neighborhoods that blacks are moving. It is not Leonard Bernstein in the suburbs who is threatened by a black moving in, or if it is the black will be Ralph Bunche.

ARE YOU SUGGESTING WE MAY BE GETTING A KIND OF REPETITION OF THE 1850s?

Yes, we're seeing a kind of ethnocultural backlash. How do you resist the black revolution? You vote against the Democrats.

This movement began to be apparent as early as 1964, in the Wallace movement. Then, in the 1968 primaries, Indiana went strongly for Wallace. The Conservative Party in New York State has gained from a strong component of Irish Catholics in the city moving over. Upstate, though, it may be something quite different.

In the city, I think there is an identification of Mayor Lindsay as an extremist on behalf of the blacks.

THESE DEMOCRATS OWN THEIR OWN HOMES. IS IT PROPERTY? IS IT STATUS?

Partly those, but it's also a pervasive, insidious, far reaching prejudice which whites have. It's not something you argue about logically. Many white people hate blacks, as many Protestants hated—or still hate—Catholics.

. . . . .

Under these circumstances, what does the Democratic Party appear to be pushing? Pro-black programs, social welfare programs, quota systems. All creating fears. Why should whites who feel threatened vote Democratic? As long as this issue remains, Democrats are in real bad trouble.

Jews, too, are worried by aspects of this question. They may support welfare programs, but many of them say they started from scratch as immigrants and got ahead without help. Why should blacks have this much help? Besides, quota systems are a red flag. Quota systems mean only one thing to Jews: they lose.

YOU SEEM TO BE SAYING ISSUES CAN INFLUENCE ELECTIONS AFTER ALL.

Yes. Each party seeks to reflect the prejudices of its component groups. At different times, for instance, the Democrats clearly became the spokesmen for the Irish, the Italians, and the Jews.

People are aware there are differences between the parties and that one party is "better" for them. It reflects their values, their attitudes, the things they want.

One thing about realignment periods is that there is an increased consciousness about issues. Suddenly a new issue appears that the voters have never dealt with before. They want to see how their party stands on it. Then they usually accept that opinion. But if something in their ethnocultural background is strongly enough opposed to the position their party comes to adopt, they may eventually leave that party.

Historically, probably the most potent issue in American political life is economics. But since this rarely is a major issue, except in periods of extreme depression such as the 1930s, in the absence of such an issue ethnocultural issues will determine party loyalty.

. . . . .

IS THERE ANYTHING DIFFERENT IN THE POLITICAL MAKEUP OF THE 1970S THAT WOULD LEAD YOU TO SEE MAJOR CHANGES IN THE ROLE OF PARTIES IN AMERICA?

I think there are three things that indicate conditions for change do exist.

First, the voters are more issue-conscious and less bound by ethnocultural traditions than their parents were. Why? Because more Americans go to college, which causes the young to break with some of their family and tribal traditions. Many people think this will be the end of parties, that the great mass of voters will not identify for very long periods with one party or another, and that our elections will swing wildly from party to party and maybe to many parties.

In my opinion the force of tradition is so powerful that, while the present 15 percent of the electorate who move back and forth from one party to another may increase to 25 percent, still 75 percent of the voters will remain steady. The effects of powerful issues and a loosening of the ethnocultural traditions will not sweep the two-party system before it.

However, the media do have a greater impact than thirty years ago, and they do play up change. By reporting shifts of party loyalty, the defections of important political leaders, they may—if McLuhan is correct—encourage some people to change parties simply because others are doing it and they see it happening.

Finally, for the last fifty years the laws have made it more and more difficult to maintain simple party allegiance. Few states still have the old single levers in the voting booth that allowed a straight party ticket. Primaries have removed the power of bosses to control the party ticket and to balance it ethnically, which assured that the party retained the support of its traditional constituents. And crossover voting in primaries, in which Republicans can vote in Democratic primaries and vice versa, has loosened the control even further.

BUT IN FACT, IS THERE EVIDENCE THAT VOTERS ARE LESS LIKELY TODAY TO IDENTIFY WITH PARTIES WHEN THEY COME TO MAKE THEIR POLITICAL DECISIONS?

I would say no, for two reasons.

The most visible group of independent voters today is the young, the under-30s. But young voters have always had the least identification with parties, adopting or resuming earlier associations only in their later years. The percentage of independents among young voters appears to be only a little more in 1972 than our statistics show it was in 1940. And independents and the young have always been those least likely to actually register and then vote.

Further, as I have said already, I don't see that the antiblack feelings of today are any stronger or much different from the anti-Irish feelings of the 1850s. Ethnic identification and prejudice are still very strong. It is not changing among the mass of American people.

Many circumstances have promoted the *idea* that great change is under way, but that may be because the media are so much more powerful today, not because major change is really taking place in the way the American voter behaves.

58. 59.

PYGMALION IN THE CLASSROOM

Robert Rosenthal and Lenore Jacobson

THE TEACHER AS PYGMALION: COMMENTS ON THE PSYCHOLOGY OF EXPECTATION

Peter and Carol Gumpert

The next two selections are presented as a single unit, dealing with important, formal aspects of education as an institution. The first selection summarizes the major findings of a study on the effect of teachers being told that some children in their classroom had high ability and were likely to spurt in their intelligence and achievement. Rosenthal and Jacobson maintain that students are more likely to perform well if teachers believe that they can and expect them to do so. The implications of this for American education are revolutionary. Though critical reviews of the Rosenthal and Jacobson study have identified various weaknesses in the experiment, the Gumperts, in the second selection, indicate that the general findings are supported by different analyses and other research. This has also been reaffirmed by a reexamination of the data in the original study.

A number of scholars have attempted to replicate the Pygmalion study but most have failed to confirm the results of the original research. This is not surprising, for the nature of this study and the results have become widely known among teachers. It is therefore difficult, if not impossible, to carry out such an experiment without the teachers suspecting that they are being given inaccurate information to modify their expectations of students. If this occurs, the design of the experiment is upset and the results will be invalidated. Tests of the effect of expectations on school achievement must, therefore, be devised in other ways.

One of the editors of this volume, Wilbur B. Brookover, and his associates have investigated the effects of teacher, parent, and peer expectations and evaluations as perceived by upper elementary age students and reported by the teachers on the students' achievement. This study indicates that the expectations and evaluations of students directly, and indirectly through the students' sense of futility or mastery, account for much of the differences in the achievement between elementary schools with similar social class and racial composition.*

* W. B. Brookover, Richard Gigliotti, Ronald Henderson, and Jeffrey Schneider, *Elementary School Social En-*

The effects of teacher expectations on students is illustrated by a teacher in an interview with Robert Coles:

Some black children I've taught here these past two years have surprised me by what they've said or done—and then I've realized that I never expected them to be that bright, or that shrewd, or that imaginative or responsive. Now, perhaps they saw the surprise on my face, or felt my surprise. What do you think that would do to them, to their "attitude," as I hear it said? I think we have to learn a lot more about these children, about their assets as well as their liabilities. I think we teachers need help in that; we need to be encouraged to give these children the benefit of a few doubts, to bend as much as we ask them to bend, to learn from them about ourselves, our values and even our prejudices. I'll have to admit one thing: I've learned as much as I've taught the last two years. I've been frustrated and annoyed, but I've also learned.†

Under the present system of education the schools play a major role in allocating students to different strata and positions in society, on the basis of presumed capacities to learn. If the theory of expectations discussed in these two selections were combined with an assumption of sufficient ability to perform well, as indicated in the selection by Boyer and Walsh (Selection 7), the nature of American education would be drastically changed and the social-class allocation function would probably be removed from American schools.

58. Rosenthal and Jacobson

The central idea of this [research is] that one person's expectation for another's behavior could come to serve as a self-fulfilling prophecy. This is not a new idea, and anecdotes and theories can be found that support its tenability. Much of the experimental evidence for the operation of interpersonal self-fulfilling prophecies comes from a research program in which prophecies or expectancies were experimentally generated in psychological experimenters in order to learn whether these prophecies would become self-fulfilling.

The general plan of past studies has been to establish two groups of "data collectors" and give to the experimenters of each group a different hypothesis as to the data their research subjects would give them. In many such experiments, though not in all, experimenters obtained data from their subjects in accordance with the expectancy they held regarding their subjects' responses. Quite naturally, some of the experiments involved expectations held by the experimenters of the intellectual performance of their subjects.

In addition to those experiments in which the subjects were humans, there were studies in which the subjects were animals. When experimenters were led to believe that their animal subjects were genetically inferior, these animals performed more poorly. When experimeters were led to believe that their animal subjects were

vironment and School Achievement (East Lansing: Michigan State University, College of Urban Development, 1973).

† Robert Coles, "Teachers and the Children of Poverty" in *The South Goes North,* vol. 3 of *Children of Crisis* (Boston: Little, Brown, 1971), p. 468.

Source: Robert Rosenthal and Lenore Jacobsen, *Pygmalion in the Classroom* (New York: Holt, Rinehart & Winston, 1958), pp. 74–79.

Robert Rosenthal is professor of social psychology at Harvard University. He is the author, along with others, of *New Directions in Psychology* and coauthor of *Artifact in Behavioral Research.*

Lenore Jacobson was principal of the elementary school in the South San Francisco Unified School District where the research reported here was carried out.

more favorably endowed genetically, their animals' performance was superior. In reality, of course, there were no genetic differences between the animals that had been alleged to be dull or bright.

If animal subjects believed to be brighter by their trainers actually became brighter because of their trainers' beliefs, then it might also be true that school children believed by their teachers to be brighter would become brighter because of their teachers' beliefs. Oak School became the laboratory in which an experimental test of that proposition was carried out.

Oak School is a public elementary school in a lower-class community of a medium-size city. The school has a minority group of Mexican children who comprise about one-sixth of the school's population. Every year about 200 of its 650 children leave Oak School, and every year about 200 new children are enrolled.

Oak School follows an ability-tracking plan whereby each of the six grades is divided into one fast, one medium, and one slow classroom. Reading ability is the primary basis for assignment to track. The Mexican children are heavily overrepresented in the slow track.

On theoretical grounds it would have been desirable to learn whether teachers' favorable or unfavorable expectations could result in a corresponding increase or decrease in pupil's intellectual competence. On ethical grounds, however, it was decided to test only the proposition that favorable expectations by teachers could lead to an increase in intellectual competence.

All the children of Oak School were pretested with a standard nonverbal test of intelligence. This test was represented to the teachers as one that would predict intellectual "blooming" or "spurting." The IQ test employed yielded three IQ scores: total IQ, verbal IQ, and reasoning IQ. The "verbal" items required the child to match pictured items with verbal descriptions given by the teacher. The reasoning items required the child to indicate which of five designs differed from the remaining four. Total IQ was based on the sum of verbal and reasoning items.

At the very beginning of the school year following the schoolwide pretesting, each of the eighteen teachers of grades one through six was given the names of those children in her classroom who, in the academic year ahead, would show dramatic intellectual growth. These predictions were allegedly made on the basis of these special children's scores on the test of academic blooming. About 20 percent of Oak School's children were alleged to be potential spurters. For each classroom the names of the special children had actually been chosen by means of a table of random numbers. The difference between the special children and the ordinary children, then, was only in the mind of the teacher.

All the children of Oak School were retested with the same IQ test after one semester, after a full academic year, and after two full academic years. For the first two retests, children were in the classroom of the teacher who had been given favorable expectations for the intellectual growth of some of her pupils. For the final retesting all children had been promoted to the classes of teachers who had not been given any special expectations for the intellectual growth of any of the children. That follow-up testing had been included so that we could learn whether any expectancy advantages that might be found would be dependent on a continuing contact with the teacher who held the especially favorable expectation.

For the children of the experimental group and for the children of the control group, gains in IQ from pretest to retest were computed. Expectancy advantage was defined by the degree to which IQ gains by the "special" children exceeded gains by the control-group children. After the first year of the experiment a significant expectancy advantage was found, and it was especially great among children of the first and second grades. The advantage of having been expected to bloom was evident for these younger children in total IQ, verbal IQ, and reasoning IQ. The control-group children of these grades gained well in IQ, 19 percent of them gaining twenty or more total IQ points. The "special" children, however, showed 47 percent of their number gaining twenty or more total IQ points.

During the subsequent follow-up year the younger children of the first two years lost their expectancy advantage. The children of the upper grades, however, showed an increasing expectancy advantage during the follow-up year. The younger children who seemed easier to influence may have required more continued contact with their influencer in order to maintain their behavior change. The older children, who were harder to influence initially, may have been better able to maintain their behavior change autonomously once it had occurred.

Differences between boys and girls in the extent to which they were helped by favorable expectations were not dramatic when gains in total IQ were considered. After one year, and after two years as well, boys who were expected to bloom intellectually bloomed more in verbal IQ; girls who were expected to bloom intellectually bloomed more in reasoning IQ. Favorable teacher expectations seemed to help each sex more in that sphere of intellectual functioning in which they had excelled on the pretest. At Oak School boys normally show the higher verbal IQ while girls show the higher reasoning IQ.

It will be recalled that Oak School was organized into a fast, a medium, and a slow track system. We had thought that favorable expectations on the part of teachers would be of greatest benefit to the children of the slow track. That was not the case. After one year, it was the children of the medium track who showed the greatest expectancy advantage, though children of the other tracks were close behind. After two years, however, the children of the medium track very clearly showed the greatest benefits from having had favorable expectations held of their intellectual performance. It seems surprising that it should be the more average child of a lower-class school who stands to benefit more from his teacher's improved expectation.

After the first year of the experiment and also after the second year, the Mexican children showed greater expectancy advantages than did the non-Mexican children, though the difference was not significant statistically. One interesting minority-group effect did reach significance, however, even with just a small sample size. For each of the Mexican children, magnitude of expectancy advantage was computed by subtracting from his or her gain in IQ from pretest to retest, the IQ gain made by the children of the control group in his or her classroom. These magnitudes of expectancy advantage were then correlated with the "Mexican-ness" of the children's faces. After one year, and after two years, those boys who looked more Mexican benefited more from their teachers' positive prophecies. Teachers' preexperimental expectancies for these boys' intellectual performance were probably lowest of all. Their turning up on a list of probable bloomers must have surprised their teachers. Interest may have followed surprise and, in some way, increased watching for signs of increased brightness may have led to increased brightness.

In addition to the comparison of the

"special" and the ordinary children on their gains in IQ it was possible to compare their gains after the first year of the experiment on school achievement as defined by report-card grades. Only for the school subject of reading was there a significant difference in gains in report-card grades. The children expected to bloom intellectually were judged by their teachers to show greater advances in their reading ability. Just as in the case of IQ gains, it was the younger children who showed the greater expectancy advantage in reading scores. The more a given grade level had benefited in overall IQ gains, the more that same grade level benefited in reading scores.

It was the children of the medium track who showed the greatest expectancy advantage in terms of reading ability just as they had been the children to benefit most in terms of IQ from their teachers' favorable expectations.

Report-card reading grades were assigned by teachers, and teachers' judgments of reading performance may have been affected by their expectations. It is possible, therefore, that there was no real benefit to the earmarked children of having been expected to bloom. The effect could very well have been in the mind of the teacher rather than in the reading performance of the child. Some evidence was available to suggest that such halo effects did not occur. For a number of grade levels, objective achievement tests had been administered. Greater expectancy advantages were found when the assessment was by these objective tests than when it was by the more subjective evaluation made by the teacher. If anything, teachers' grading seemed to show a negative halo effect. It seemed that the special children were graded more severely by the teachers than were the ordinary children. It is even possible that it is just this sort of standard-setting behavior that is responsible in part for the effects of favorable expectations.

The fear has often been expressed that the disadvantaged child is further disadvantaged by his teacher's setting standards that are inappropriately low. Wilson has presented compelling evidence that teachers do, in fact, hold up lower standards of achievement for children of more deprived areas. It is a possibility to be further investigated that when a teacher's expectation for a pupil's intellectual performance is raised, she may set higher standards for him to meet (that is, grade him tougher). There may be here the makings of a benign cycle. Teachers may not only get more when they expect more; they may also come to expect more when they get more.

All teachers had been asked to rate each of their pupils on variables related to intellectual curiosity, personal and social adjustment, and need for social approval. In general, children who had been expected to bloom intellectually were rated as more intellectually curious, as happier, and, especially in the lower grades, as less in need of social approval. Just as had been the case with IQ and reading ability, it was the younger children who showed the greater expectancy advantage in terms of their teachers' perceptions of their classroom behavior. Once again, children of the medium track were most advantaged by having been expected to bloom, this time in terms of their perceived greater intellectual curiosity and lessened need for social approval.

When we consider expectancy advantages in terms of perceived intellectual curiosity, we find that the Mexican children did not share in the advantages of having been expected to bloom. Teachers did not see the Mexican children as more intellectually curious when they had been expected to bloom. There was even a slight tendency, stronger for Mexican boys, to see the special Mexican children as less curious intellectually. That seems surprising, particularly since the Mexican children showed the greatest expectancy advantages in IQ, in reading scores, and for Mexican boys, in overall school achievement. It seemed almost as though, for these minority-group children, intellectual competence may have been easier for teachers to bring about than to believe.

Children's gains in IQ during the basic year of the experiment were correlated with teachers' perceptions of their classroom behavior. This was done separately for the upper- and lower-track children of the experimental and control groups. The more the upper-track children of the experimental group gained in IQ, the more favorably they were rated by their teachers. The more the lower-track children of the control group gained in IQ, the more unfavorably they were viewed by their teachers. No special expectation had been created about these children, and their slow-track status made it unlikely in their teachers' eyes that they would behave in an intellectually competent manner. The more intellectually competent these children became, the more negatively they were viewed by their teachers. Future research should address itself to the possibility that there may be hazards to "unwarranted," unpredicted intellectual growth. Teachers may require a certain amount of preparation to be able to accept the unexpected classroom behavior of the intellectually upwardly mobile child.

. . . . .

59. Gumpert and Gumpert

Pygmalion in the Classroom is an important and thought-provoking book; anyone concerned with the problems and practices of education should certainly take the trouble to read it. The study provides a perfectly satisfactory demonstration that the teacher expectation effects hypothesized do indeed take place. Though the Oak School experiment is not as sophisticated as it might be, it was done in a "natural" setting (which, incidentally, usually makes it difficult to do elegant research) rather than under the more artificial circumstances of the laboratory. The fact that the effect can be demonstrated in the actual classroom under very ordinary conditions is convincing. That the effect appears to be quite strong and stable in spite of the subtlety and simplicity of the experimental induction is especially dramatic. The results of the experiment fairly demand that much serious attention, thought, and research be devoted to the effect on children of the beliefs and attitudes held about them by school administrators, supervisors, and teachers. It also points up the crucial importance of conducting research on just *how* people's expectations of children become realities. It is possible that we will learn to change teachers' behavior toward

Source: Peter and Carol Gumpert, *The Urban Review* 3, no. 1 (September 1968): 21–25. Reprinted by permission of the Center for Urban Education.

When this article was written, Peter Gumpert was teaching in the Doctoral Program in Social Psychology at Teacher's College, Columbia University.

Carol Gumpert was a clinical psychologist in the Department of Psychiatry of the Albert Einstein College of Medicine.

children before we learn how to change their attitudes toward them, and thus their expectations of them. It is on this last general consideration—how the expectation of the teacher might have led to modifications of her pupils' performance and classroom behavior—that Rosenthal and Jacobson are weakest in their analysis. Though they do speculate about some aspects of the problem, the heart of the matter remains untouched. In short, they have shown us that teachers' expectations of their students' performances have definite consequences for these (subsequent) performances. But they have not shown us how this process works.

In the remainder of our article, we propose to do some more or less systematic speculating about how the Oak School teachers may have fulfilled the researchers' prophecies. We shall begin by arguing that expectation leads to selectivity of attention, perception, and response, and end by discussing just how increases in interpersonal "warmth" and encouragement might actually lead to superior learning and performance.

SOME PSYCHOLOGICAL EFFECTS OF EXPECTATION

The study of the influence of expectation upon thinking and behavior has been of interest to psychologists for many years in a variety of contexts. There are literally hundreds of studies that are relevant to the notion that a person's attitude, set, or expectation will affect his perceptions and responses. One tentative conclusion that can be drawn from these studies—of particular interest in thinking about expectancy in the classroom—is the following: a person is more likely to perceive a barely perceptible stimulus if he expects it than if he does not. For example, if an experimental subject is given a list from which words are to be presented tachistoscopically, the recognition threshold for words on the list (i.e., the words he is expecting) will be lower than for those not on the list. When shown an ambiguous stimulus which resembled both a letter and a number, for example *B* and *13*, subjects who were told to expect letters saw *B* and those who were told to expect numbers reported seeing *13*. Neither of these results is surprising, possibly because they both confirm what we often observe in our everyday activities—that we are likely to see what we expect to see, and that we tend to interpret ambiguous events in such a way as to confirm our own predictions. Similarly, if a teacher expects to see something, she is likely to find evidence of its occurrence sooner or later.

Further, that a person's expectations exert a powerful influence on the behavior of the people with whom he interacts is a well-documented phenomenon. In the laboratory, for example, if a group of experimenters is told to expect that their subjects will most likely perform well on a particular task, and another group is told to expect their subjects to perform poorly, the subjects in the former group will tend to have significantly higher scores than those in the latter. Expectation effects have even been demonstrated when the experimental subjects were animals. Strupp and Luborsky make the point that a therapist's expectations about the prognosis of treatment may have much to do with its actual outcome. The teacher, similarly, may have a personal stake in seeing what she expects to see in the classroom.

. . . . .

It appears that a person who is in a position to exercise over another the subtle interpersonal influence we have been talking about may do so without being aware either of the content of the message he transmits or the ways he transmits it. The recipient of influence may be equally unaware that any transaction other than the obvious overt one is taking place; he may well do what is expected of him without even realizing that a demand on him is being made. It also appears likely that some people are more effective "covert persuaders" than others. Such things as the physical appearance, confidence, warmth, friendliness, amount of experience or competence, interest, and status of the persuader seem to affect the extent to which expectancies are influential. Some of these personal characteristics are also related to a person's effectiveness as an overt persuader. So it seems plausible that some teachers may be better covert persuaders in the classroom than others. It is also possible that the teacher who is warm, friendly, and sure of herself is a better covert persuader than her less friendly and less competent colleagues, and that the highly skilled and successful teacher is also good at helping make her prophecies come true.

The manner in which one person influences another is not determined entirely in advance by previously existing attitudes and beliefs. Expectation may change, vary, increase, or decrease, depending on the nature of an ongoing social interaction and the reciprocal influence that two people have upon one another. In the classroom, for example, it is likely that a teacher's behavior toward a particular child will not depend consistently on previously existing beliefs about what he can or will do, but may be modified by what occurs between them.

In order to imagine how such variables might affect an interaction, let us construct an oversimplified situation. Imagine that one of Rosenthal and Jacobson's teachers is told that Johnny Second-Grader, an unremarkable-appearing boy, is about to experience a period of intellectual blossoming. Given a situation in which the teacher is trying to communicate a difficult bit of information to Johnny, she is now more likely to expect an indication of comprehension than if she had been told nothing about potential academic progress. (In fact, she might not otherwise have attempted the communication in the first place.) A minor change in Johnny's behavior at this point, say a nod or smile, may be interpreted as a glimmer of understanding so that, encouraged, the teacher intensifies her efforts to reach him. Consequent subtle changes in the teacher's behavior and attitude, such as alterations in her body posture, tone of voice, perceived interest, facial expression, or verbal praise, may similarly interest and encourage Johnny, leading to his increased motivation and attention, and finally to the reward of mastering something new—as well as the fulfillment of his teacher's expectation. The point is that psychological expectation may have a catalytic effect, evoking interactions and leading to events that depend upon much more than the effects of expectation alone, but which might not, and indeed probably would not, have occurred without the belief that such events were possible.

We have discussed something about the effects that a person's expectations may have on his own behavior and thinking and on the behavior and thinking of others. It seems very clear also that the nature of the social structure itself often has similar effects. One of the findings of a study of the British school system reported by Hilde Himmelweit and Judy Wright involved a comparison of two schools with different policies regarding assignment to tracks (or streams, as they are referred to in England). In one school, assignment to a stream was based on ability. In the other, assignment was based on criteria other than intellectual ability. Yet the effect of stream placement on further academic advancement and final performance was identical for the two schools. Thus, the effect of streaming seemed to be a more powerful determinant of performance than were the attributes that led to the pupils' initial placement in streams; streaming turns out to be a potent "leveler" in Britain. This result can be interpreted as indicating that the meaning for an individual of being allocated to a particular stream, and the influence exerted by the experience of stream membership, can be major determinants of his progress. The expectation for a person's behavior that is implicit by virtue of his place in the social structure may exert a powerful influence over what he does, in that he will not only respond to the expectation but may also help to create an environment within which it will be fulfilled.

. . . . .

Let us return now to the teacher who expects to see startling improvement in the performance of a particular pupil. As we have argued above, if she expects a pupil to begin to improve, she may be avidly watching for signs of improvement while ignoring the pupil's usual inadequacies or failures. If she should see something that indicates improvement, she might be especially quick to reward it by her special attention and by her excitement at seeing her expectations begin to be fulfilled. This in turn might give the child new interest in this kind of performance, and might spur him on to new attempts to fulfill an expectation that he might now begin to perceive. Since the teacher is no longer paying as much attention to the child's failures, the child may now feel new room to grow, and indeed might grow with his burgeoning confidence about new learning and new power over his environment. As the child's performance improves, his teacher's standards for his performance may become higher; thus, what Rosenthal and Jacobson term the "benign circle" might develop. And here is an added dividend: a teacher who spends relatively more time rewarding success in the classroom, and therefore relatively less time punishing failure, may be improving the learning environment not only for the few children of whom she expects new things, but for all the children in the room—as is suggested by the results in Rosenthal and Jacobson described above.

Our discussion in this section has been very speculative; certainly, many links are missing in the chain that connects what the teacher expects the student to be able to do and what the student becomes able to do. And, surely, there is not just one thing happening in the entire process, but many things. The phenomenon of subtle interpersonal influence guiding progress in the classroom is as complex as it is fascinating.

. . . . .

60.

ON INSTITUTIONAL NEUTRALITY IN COLLEGES AND UNIVERSITIES

Thomas Ford Hoult

One of the major debates regarding education as a social institution has to do with whether it is responsible only for introducing (indoctrinating) youth into the dominant culture controlling the educational system, thus maintaining the status quo or whether it should consider its mission to be not merely the perpetuation of the existing culture but also to analyze and evaluate it, to raise searching questions about it, and to examine proposals for the maintenance or modification of the society that supports it. Colleges and universities as instrumentalities of the institution of education are subject not only to cross-pressures regarding this issue but also with respect to a related issue: whether universities, as universities, having explored alternative solutions to social problems should commit themselves to the advocacy of one of them. The debate over this question was intensified during the decade of the sixties because of divisive national-political controversies which caused eruptions on many college and university campuses. Some of these controversies precipitated peaceful demonstrations, others resulted in disruptive, sometimes violent, destructive, and even death-dealing confrontations. Inevitably such polarization led to widespread discussion and debate regarding the proper role of institutions of higher learning faced with inescapable controversial issues. The following selection by one of this book's editors, Thomas Ford Hoult, illustrates one position regarding institutional neutrality, that of favoring it, but only because it is impossible to guarantee that the committed institution would favor humanistic values. However, Hoult asserts that the neutrality must be a genuine one and not one of the pseudo-variety found so commonly in educational institutions.

A number of thoughtful people have recently begun to advocate that universities and colleges should abandon their pretense of impartiality regarding controversial social issues. Such take-a-stand proponents make much of the philosophical truism that it is impossible to be genuinely neutral when it comes to ideological questions. This impossibility arises because so-called neutrality almost always gives help to those currently in power and is thus neutrality in name only.

These arguments against neutrality seem compelling to us and we therefore

Source: Thomas Ford Hoult, *AAUP Bulletin* 56, no. 2 (June 1970): 128–29. Reprinted by permission of the American Association of University Professors.

Thomas Ford Hoult is professor of sociology at Arizona State University in Tempe. His major interests include social problems and political sociology. He is the author of *Sociology of Religion, and the Dictionary of Modern Sociology.*

conclude that universities and colleges should cease to claim what cannot be. But we do not then go on to assert, as some do, that the university should become wedded to a particular ideology, although we would even do that if we could be certain that just one condition were met. Our condition is to be assured that the ideology to be served is that which favors an open society where democratic controls, due process, free inquiry, and free speech and press are meaningfully supported. We favor these minimal aspects of the open society, because only to the degree that they prevail can universities *properly so-called* function effectively.

But what are the chances that universities and colleges will support measures necessary for an open society? Take Arizona for example. In this state, we are currently faced with a demand, on the part of a number of purse-string-controlling legislators, that the state Board of Regents take a stand against socialism as represented in the person of a tenured philosophy professor. Joining the cry, the state's largest newspaper editorialized: Arizona State University's radical-in-residence should be dismissed. If such extreme rightest voices prevail, it is clear what "institutional-taking-an-ideological-stand" would mean in practice. It would mean repression of the different; it would mean stifling of free speech and assembly; it would mean the end of academic freedom. And what would the situation probably be if left extremists were in control? A sufficient answer is perhaps suggested by mentioning the American Civil Liberties Union members who want the Union to cease protecting the constitutional rights of anti-Semites because, it is asserted, such persons are not deserving.

The message is clear: All too many of those wanting the university to be ideologically committed are people inclined to assert, "We demand civil liberties for us, and deny them to you, because we are correct and you are wrong." Quite obviously, to the degree that such a spirit prevails on a campus, it would be an "institution of higher learning" only in name.

Thus, we have arrived at a basic principle: when extremists of any sort—left or right, black or white, religious or nonreligious, etc.—take control of any given social situation, on campus or off, the possibility of a pleasant existence is usually ended for all but the prevailing brand of true believers or the selfishly compliant.

But, some may ask, if liberal centrists are in control, is it not possible for an institution to take a stand on particularly crucial issues and still preserve a free marketplace of ideas so that the right to dissent is not impaired? This *is* a possibility—but it seems improbable in the long run. If a given college's *official* stand, as a social organization, is that the Vietnam war is an abomination, is it likely that war proponents, or even those feeling the war is an ugly necessity, will be hired or promoted if such can be avoided? Indeed, isn't it more realistic to expect that, in such a setting, war proponents would soon feel it necessary to temporize, to tone down their remarks? Again, under such circumstances, it is clear that only those sharing the official view would have meaningful academic freedom.

And so we are led to a second principle: the academic setting that officially favors one side of an ideological question almost inevitably degenerates into a propaganda institute (at least so far as the given question is concerned). Therefore, it seems to us that both logic and self-interest demand two things of us. First, we must, as individuals, take a stand on a multitude of relevant social issues so that we may help to change the current frightening trend toward creating a society in which free inquiry is prohibited. And second, we must do whatever is needed to develop our colleges and universities so that they can offer the kind of liberal education that encourages its recipients critically to examine their own lives and that of their society—and thus, as Arnold Kaufman has phrased it, ". . . make trouble for the complacent and the powerful if their complacency and power are undeserved." *

Since we want to encourage skepticism about dogma, it should be clear that we do not advocate neutrality. We feel colleges and universities serve society best when they teach their participants to engage in social criticism and register dissent when needed. Such encouragement is not ideological commitment; but neither is it a fake neutrality in which the university is more neutral in some things than in others, and least of all when it comes to federal money, selective service—and undercover agents ferreting out those arch criminals, our pot-smoking young who want to declare their independence from a repressive society that has masqueraded as "liberal" while it produced the Vietnam war and unspeakable living conditions for multitudes of minority group members.

* Arnold Kaufman, *The Radical Liberal* (New York: Atherton Press, 1968), p. 128.

61.

THE CHURCH TRAP

Arthur Herzog

Sociologists study the structure and function of religion as one of the basic institutions found in every culture. Organized religion, especially as practiced in the United States, has both "individual" and "societal" functions. In the former function, it provides security, comfort, and a sense of certainty to the believer. In its latter function, it attempts to provide guidance and leadership regarding social issues about which a logical extension of the church's moral precepts would seem to require that it take a stand. It is this societal function that produces the "church trap" discussed in the following selection. After examining the failure of church membership and participation to keep pace with our population growth, the author turns to an analysis of the cross-pressures on reli-

Source: Arthur Herzog, *The Church Trap* (New York: Macmillan Company, 1969), pp. 3–22.

Arthur Herzog is a free-lance writer and former magazine editor. His articles have been published in the *New York Times Magazine, Harper's, Esquire, The Catholic Digest,* and *True.* He is the author of *The War-Peace Establishment* and *The B.S. Factor: The Theory and Technique of Faking It in America.*

gious institutions and the consequences of these cross-pressures for church organization and operation, especially for the role of the church's chief functionaries—the clergy.

What on earth is happening out there, in those 320,000 churches across the land? Instead of rejoicing at the altars of the richest, most powerful religious organizations in history, they come to a funeral. Hurry! Change the neon from

J
SAVES
S
U
S

to

G
O
D
GOD IS DEAD
D
E
A
D

"All the Church is in ferment," said Pope Paul VI, who might have been speaking for any major American denomination or creed. But there is no agreement on the nature of the brew. Some people declare that the churches are poised on the brink of a New Reformation, even in a world which has been called post-Christian, post-ideological, post-just-about-everything. Others think the churches will muddle through; but within the churches themselves today also flourish small, highly vocal bands of latter-day Jeremiahs who predict for organized religion that ultimate of tragedies, decay and death with no hope of an afterlife.

The debate is strange, for on paper at least, the churches appear to be marching confidently toward the third millennium. The familiar statistics have often been held up to the world as talismans of American rectitude. Two out of three Americans claim church membership, and 44 percent of the population is said to comply with the promptings of the public service ads to "worship at the church of your choice" by showing up there once a week (a figure which must be viewed with skepticism, since some religious leaders do not believe the churches can hold that many people on Sundays, sitting or standing). "We are a religious people whose institutions presuppose a divine being," wrote Supreme Court Justice William O. Douglas, and so, in theory at least, religion, if not established, is sanctified by the state and is to be found on our coins, in our oaths, on cornerstones, in short almost everywhere. Evidently, too, Americans like the idea of big, strong churches, seeing them as an anchor against too much and too rapid change, a deterrent to crime in the streets, emblems of our souls. So the conventional portrait is that of a churchy America, as the Protestant theologian Gibson Winter puts it, "pious, pure, holy and noble in a wicked world."

Nonetheless, for organized religion in America not all the News is Good. Religious leaders today can be thought of increasingly as ecclesiastical executives who, in spreading the Lord's word, use computers and PERT (Program Evaluation Review Technique) and flow charts and talk about inputs, outputs and cost-effectiveness. (". . . . the almost frantic propagation of modern methods," thought the famous German Protestant, Dietrich Bonhoeffer, who looked with alarm at the

American religious scene, "betrays the dwindling of content.") The churches do not pay cash dividends but they are clearly interested in the management techniques of modern corporations. The Roman Catholic Church employs management consultants, and a leading Protestant denomination plans to hire a long-range planner who, "hopefully," would be a Christian, while a Southern Protestant denomination employed a Jew to make a study of its membership because it wanted objective answers. The information arriving at the major religious administration centers—like the National Conference of Catholic Bishops, in Washington, D.C., or the limited partnership of thirty-four Protestant denominations known as the National Council of the Churches of Christ in the U.S.A., in New York City, which occupies a large, glittering structure irreverently called by its occupants "the Godbox"—indicates that serious trouble may lie ahead.

Within church circles religious statistics are well-known for their inaccuracy, but some credence, it's thought, can be given to trends. The famous "religious revival" of the 1950's—to which the churches attached great hopes, and which prompted serious scholars to predict a genuinely religious America—now appears to have ended before the decade was out; ended, in fact, just as it was receiving maximum publicity. Since then the trends seem to be running against the churches, and for this reason, perhaps, the yearly releases on church membership are no longer headline news. Membership has been leveling off until it has fallen behind the growth of the general population. In 1965 church membership increased 1.3 percent while the population rose 1.5 percent. The Jews considered themselves lucky to hold their own against death, and the "bluechip" Protestant denominations, studying the figures, have begun to wonder if the WASP has lost his sting. "There is," says R. H. Edwin Espy, General Secretary of the National Council of Churches, "the probability of membership leveling off. There is an identifiable trend. It is a critical issue."

"We feel the tide started to flow out in 1958," says John F. Anderson, Executive Secretary of the Board of National Ministries of the Presbyterian Church in the U.S. The denomination has its roots in the South, where the churches are stronger than anywhere else in the country. Evidently the figures were engraved in his mind, for Anderson, a big man in two-toned shoes, was able to rattle off from memory, without hesitation, the statistical course of his million-member denomination. In 1958 the U.S. Presbyterians could show a net increase in membership of 20,000, which went down to 13,000 in 1960; 7,000 in 1964; 4,000 by 1965. In 1966 the increase was up to 5,000, hardly enough for a denominational sigh of relief.

This "decrease in the rate of increase," as it's called, has lasted long enough to be established as an ecclesiastical fact of life. It appears to be affecting almost all churches, regardless of race, color or creed. The possible exceptions to the rule are fundamentalist churches which still claim to be growing faster than the general population, and indeed there might be solid reasons for thinking that conservative religions will grow for the precise reasons that liberal churches will shrink—the former appealing to both the traditionally minded and those afraid of change; the latter, in tailoring themselves to secular society, gradually losing their separate identity and reason for being. Just the same, the less ebullient Northern churchmen don't believe the fundamentalists apply the same rigor to statistics as evangelism. To them, Southern Baptist figures, for instance, are loaded with nonmembers, and it's true, according to one study, that in several largely Southern Baptist counties in Mississippi the reported church membership actually managed to exceed the *total* number of people who lived there.

But it's not simply membership that has the churches concerned. The Roman Catholic magazine *Commonweal,* pointing out that the church in 1967 had fewer educational institutions, parish elementary pupils, converts, nuns, seminarians, infant baptisms (down 84,096, for Catholics a significant statistic) and a very slow growth rate, went on to say, "U.S. Catholics are deep in their reassessment of traditional Catholicism. The Church has only begun to glimpse the consequences." One might expect to find the Protestants of the future in Sunday School, and yet Protestant figures show sharp declines in Sunday School attendance, to the point where some churchmen would like to write off Sunday School altogether. College church programs attract only a miniscule proportion of students, and while once everybody could be depended on to tell the pollsters dutifully that he believed in God, a large and growing number of high school and college students describe themselves with the dread word "agnostic" or even "atheist." The disenchantment is evident even among Catholics, despite their emphasis on the centrality of the church and its teachings. Catholic leaders are said to be seriously worried by polls like one at a Jesuit high school showing that 84 percent of the students disagreed with the church's position on birth control, 39 percent did not pray and 45 percent did not believe in churches.

On the one hand, then, the churches have fewer replacements in sight, while on the other the present church membership contains a high concentration of old people. This realization has led many churchmen to expect that before very long the decrease in the rate of increase will turn into an absolute decline, bottoming no one knows where. "At meetings of ministers in New York," says a well-informed Lutheran pastor, "there is the unspoken fear that the parishes are going under. One minister vies with the next for members. The result is deep suspicion." "It wouldn't surprise me if, by the year 2000, this parish is down to five percent of its present membership," I was told by a gloomy young Episcopal clergyman in the West. "The Episcopal church will shrink and shrink. The church is like a fat woman, with too much water in the tissues."

So far the seepage has been slow, almost imperceptible, and one might think the elimination of excess fluid would be healthy. But the churches are committed to gaining adherents, not losing them, and for institutional as well as evangelical reasons. The twin breasts of American religion are membership and money, and if one sags so does the other. For a decade or more the churches have been embarked on an ambitious, billion-dollar-a-year building crusade. They now have an enormous physical plant to maintain and hopefully fill with parishioners on Sundays. There are steeples to paint, electric organs to repair, ministers to feed.

. . . . .

Were you, say, a high church leader surveying the religious scene, observing a whittling away of your membership, a loss of your power to influence people, and a goodly amount of discontent and leaving among your clergy and intellectuals, you would be bound to think that something was wrong. You might well decide that religion should be more attractive, exciting, meaningful to peoples' lives—in a word, "relevant." You would be perfectly honest in feeling this, but at your back would be the needs, the institutional imperatives, of the church organization.

In fact, relevance—meaning not only such things as masses in English but a churchly participation in large public issues like peace, civil rights and poverty—is the battle cry of the churches today, except for the extremely conservative denominations. But relevance takes money and this is one substance the churchgoers have proved reluctant to give for the purposes of social action. Not only is the contribution of the average churchgoer less, in terms of his income and the value of the dollar, than it was thirty years ago, but almost all of what he does give is retained by the local parishes, in the building fund or for a new Hammond organ or electronic chimes. When a denomination must cut back on its social programs, as the United Presbyterian Church in the U.S.A. has warned its flock it would have to do unless greater generosity was forthcoming, the implications, for the theologians of relevance, are serious.

The specter that haunts an increasing number of ecclesiasts is the realization that, faced with penurious parishioners on the one hand and a strong desire to prove themselves relevant on the other, the churches can only make their brave march into the world with government funds. And this on top of what is potentially the most explosive issue confronting religion today—the surprising extent to which churches, parishes, ministers, colleges, hospitals and almost all the charities on which religion prides itself for "good works," are already heavily underwritten or subsidized by the state, meaning church-members and nonchurch-members alike.

Religion in America is caught in a sociological trap. One jaw represents the fixed expectations of the parishioners who want a solid church organization with all the trimmings, church-as-usual on Sundays, the same old rules by which they've always lived. "I've had ten children," an angry woman told her priest. "If they change the rules on birth control I'm quitting the church." The other jaw is the pressure of a society whose slackening interest in religion brings great pressure on the churches to modernize, to arouse public interest, to get "where the action is," to be vital, to prove that they do have a useful and honest social function. To change in this direction risks alienating the great bulk of church members, while not to change risks becoming ever more isolated from the secular society. Leadership and laity, then, have different ideas about church. The leaders want a platform, a place from which to be heard on social issues. It may well be that the churchly stress on the woes of secular society betrays an inability to talk to their own members in terms meaningful to them. For the laity does not appear to be deeply involved in the pronouncements and judgments the leadership makes to the world. Church members in America look to religion for guidance, support, direction, and help in personal problems, but to individuals churches have less and less to say.

The man in the middle, a principal victim of the church trap, religion's unlucky Pierre, is the minister. As a profession the clergy is at a gravely low ebb. Protestant seminaries report trouble attracting candidates, and those they do get are likely to be at the bottom of the academic pile. A leading Catholic educator, Kenneth M. Reed, S.V.D., calls the decline in Catholic seminarians a "cliff-drop," and, he says, "It is going to continue down and stay down for a long time." Fewer candidates plus more dropouts add up to a decimated clergy. "For us, the problems of the 1970s won't merely be staffing schools and hospitals," says a leading priest-psychologist, "but in finding priests to run the parishes." As it is, even with the free labor of priests and nuns, Catholic schools and hospitals are imploring more and more government support. If the Catholics, with only one priest per eight hundred churchgoers in the U.S., redouble their "prayers for more priests"—it may be an indication of how serious and worldwide a Catholic difficulty this is that the Diocese of Rome, heartland of Catholicism, is presently producing between one and five vocations *per year*—and wonder where the next generation's clergymen are coming from, so must the Jews wonder, with only about a hundred rabbis annually graduating in the U.S., and the Protestants, whose personnel problems are intensified by the desire of new ministers to serve in education, the "inner city," the poverty program, the church bureaucracy, anywhere but in the local parishes.

Word may have filtered down to them that all is not well with the parish minister. "I think between ten and twenty percent of our clergy would quit tomorrow if they had a job option," I was told by a ranking Episcopal bureaucrat, "and many others are dissatisfied." A Presbyterian official, Rev. Edward S. Golden, a sort of minister to ministers, believes that at least 20 percent of Presbyterian clergymen *ought* to quit. "Many ministers," he says, "when they face the reality of church life, rankle at it and may lose their faith, although they go on mechanically, that is as part of the church machine."

In the halcyon days of Protestantism sons of ministers often emulated their fathers and became ministers themselves, but this is less and less the case. "You were the first minister in our family and you will be the last," the son of a successful suburban minister in Detroit told his father. The son had watched his father perform, year after year, a delicate balancing act between what the minister thought was right and what his parishioners expected of him. It is no accident that most Protestant faiths today have begun to provide psychological services for disturbed ministers, where they can discuss their troubles and try to sort out their lives. In the opinion of those who provide psychological counsel for the clergy the pulpit today is an anxious seat, a place where potential neuroses are brought out in the open. And it is a sad commentary on the rigidity of American Protestantism that troubled ministers are often reluctant to look for help, because a minister, both by popular expectation and his own, isn't supposed to be *sick,* because of his connection with the divine.

The new openness of the Catholic Church has not extended to revealing the number of "fallen priests," but those close to the problem agree on its scope. "We sense," says Msgr. George Higgins, "that priests and nuns don't leave for the reasons they always did—authority and sex. There is something new in the air. I would call it a problem in Catholic identity." An abbot refers to the "mass exodus from the religious life," and nuns appear to be defecting in striking numbers—dropouts of 30 or 40 percent in some orders seem to be occurring. Estimates on the number of fallen priests begin at five thousand and go on up—as compared to a priestly population of sixty thousand—but round numbers are only part of the problem. Also important is the shock to the Catholic nervous system—reflected in the interest displayed by the public in the fallen priests themselves, and in the rumors about defections flooding the priestly grapevines—that priests would actually choose to depart the sacred and high terrain of the church. The defectors, moreover, invariably say that they intend to remain Catholic, and to some

Catholic authorities the real danger is that ex-priests, loosely banded together, will form a sort of antiparty within the church, undermining official authority and further confusing an already confused laity.

The Roman Catholic problem is always presented as unique, related to the great internal stresses that have wracked the church since the Second Vatican Council. And yet is Vatican II entirely the cause? Not according to John Cogley, former religion editor of *The New York Times* and now a resident intellect at the Center for the Study of Democratic Institutions at Santa Barbara. "The Council cannot be blamed for all this unrest. . . . The hour for revolutionary change had struck. . . . In other words, with or without the Council, we would have had the present headlines," Cogley, a Catholic himself, told a group of Catholic educators. He went on to predict, "Without rapid and drastic change there is, I think, little hope for the Church."

One finds gloomily parallel prophecies from the other faiths, from Jews who ask if anything will survive of Judaism but Jewish jokes and chicken soup, from Protestants who contributed to an angry symposium entitled *Who's Killing the Church?* (The Churches are, they cry.) The church, declares an Episcopal minister named Malcolm Boyd, who tried to show precisely how hip and relevant a preacher can be by performing at a San Francisco nightclub, "is to be found somewhere in the position of the *Titanic* heading toward an iceberg."

Such judgments can be heard from high in the church structures, off-the-record or conveyed elliptically, but occasionally stated in black and white. "I always tell young ministers," explains an outspoken Episcopal bishop, Daniel Corrigan, "that before they get to the end of the road, this new church, that new rectory just won't be there. But if they know this ahead of time, if they know that other Christians without big, rich churches have lived effectively, they'll be all right." "We're in the rapids right now," says J. L. Sullivan, Executive Secretary of the powerful Southern Baptist Sunday School Board. "Some are upset by the turbulence and lose their sense of direction." "I compare the Church to a pilot running out of gas over the ocean," says John Wright, Bishop of Pittsburgh, a highly influential Catholic. "Either he slows down in the hope of conserving his fuel or speeds up in hope of getting there before it runs out. Both ways, the hope is probably in vain."

Usually each faith is treated parochially, examined under its own lights, so that Catholics are said to stumble over sex, freedom and authority, Protestants over the Death of God and accusations that they are "weak, tardy, equivocal and irrelevant," Jews over the issue of separatism and the survival of Jewish culture. But though we try to individuate the faiths, it appears that each is undergoing a similar crisis, that the malaise of one is common to all, and that such distinctions in symptomatology as do appear on the surface are really gauges of how far the illness has progressed.

The church crisis is deeply bound up with the myths and aspirations of those who make up the bulk of church membership in America, the white middle class, with its position in the country and the world, with its philosophy, and with its perception of the sacred, meaning reality and power which it wants to locate as close as possible to itself, to its communities and to its country. As Mircea Eliade points out, the feeling of I-am-at-the-center is integral to primitive religion and there is every reason to think it is carried over in church organizations today. But if such beliefs were insecurely held, if the person, community or country had begun to doubt that it was indeed at the center, if it had begun to question its own myths and aspirations, a certain confusion in identity would have to result. In fact, religion in America displays the symptoms of a serious crisis in identity, and it is not too much to say that the churches, though still possessed of large resources and reservoirs of good will, are at the moment holding operations, searching for something to do, something for which to live, some clearer conception of just why they are here and what they are here *for*.

. . . . .

"Founded by Jesus Christ, A.D. 33," asserts an early 1900's legend on a church wall in Nashville, Tennessee, and from this simple faith and rocklike certainty one spans half a century to arrive at "WORSHIP GOD IN YOUR CAR, Casually Dressed, Comfortably Seated—Valley Forge Drive-In Theater" (which probably also showed *The Bible* and charged admission). Over this space of time, as the sociologist Daniel Bell puts it, "The old primary group ties of family and local community have been shattered; ancient parochial faiths are questioned; few unifying standards have taken their place." An oleaginous glow may continue to illuminate the altarpieces, but for practical wisdom people look elsewhere, to scientists, psychiatrists, those with professional credentials. Contrary to the hopeful predictions of religious scholars, there is no sign that any large number of secular intellectuals have become "fellow-travelers of faith." It is not because the churches, eternally optimistic that everyone will come to see the light, haven't tried. The United Presbyterian Church in the U.S.A., for instance, started an experimental ministry at Cape Kennedy, with the idea of lending its spiritual insights to the scientists in the space program, but the scientists apparently felt they could aim for the stars—or Peking—without the aid of organized religion. The secular intellectuals not only determine public policy but they give legitimacy to it, replacing the clergy as standardsetters. The churches, denominational leaders and preachers, take positions on war, nuclear weapons, race and the like—indeed, they are *expected* to—but their predictable pronunciamentos on public matters are conveniently ignored, not just by the men in power but by their own constituents. On one issue where organized religion spoke with considerable unity—against the war in Vietnam—there is no indication that churchly protests had any effect on public policy.

A reason the churches are ignored is that, like ladies of high virtue, they can be counted upon to say, "No." "Thou shalt *not*," thunder the churches—make war, fornicate, covet, commit adultery, or as in the actual case of an order of cloistered nuns, die without the Mother Superior's permission. My own memory of church consists mostly of a pink-cheeked gentleman shaking a verbal finger, and what positives he accentuated sounded suspiciously like platitudes even to young ears. The churchly identity thus fostered is almost entirely negative. The Catholic theologian, Gabriel Moran, speaks of the "negations inherent to Protestantism and incorporated into Catholicism. By seeing God's function as the forgiver of sin, by exalting faith at the expense of reason, post-Reformation Christianity could not find God by going beyond man because it could not accept man." The churches have not only defined man in their own terms, but they have rigidly clung to their definitions even when man, as the new society of abundance has made possible, has insisted on defining himself in new ways. By remaining essentially naysayers and conservers—in matters, say, of sex—the churches have paid an enormous price in believability.

All might be well for the churches had they been able to stay with religion as expressed in the local parishes, but change has been pressing hard. Half the population moves every five years and the migration from town to city has hacked away at religion's rural roots. [Former] vice-President Hubert Humphrey once predicted that within not too many years rural America, from the Appalachians to the Rockies, would be virtually deserted except for the cities, occupied only by a few farmers and caretakers. In this atmosphere of dislocation the churches' private vision of the ideal society is still that of a rural communality, in which services are arranged so as not to interfere with milking time and where people had common backgrounds and interests.

"Churches are by definition communal," says the sociologist Norman Birnbaum, "whereas society tends toward privatization. The churches assume there is a sort of unified public which wants guidance, when in fact there is none." The ladies' groups, the church suppers, the bazaars and prize cakes, the socials, the picnics, the inevitable photos of plain people in rimless spectacles singing—although the denominational magazines show that such events still comprise church life, they are clearly images of days past. The newer, more sophisticated parishes in the suburbs are under heavy fire from within the churches for being parochial, inward-looking, a mere social club, selfish and a spiritual luxury. "The attempt," says Gibson Winter, "to perpetuate the local parish or congregation as a basic unit of the Christian church is doomed to failure."

It's not at all surprising, in view of the circumstances in which organized religion finds itself, that the churches should long to attract new people, to appeal to the urbanites and the young, to reclaim their centrality and importance. So we find, presided over by slightly anxious but always smiling "get-with-it" ministers (crammed with Harvey Cox's guidebook to religious urbanity, *The Secular City*), the jazz vespers and beat services, the guitars, the lonely-hearts socials and showings of what looks to the more strait-laced like prurient art—to bring in the customers. But religion's modernity smacks of borrowed gear, as though change does not spring from genuine inner impulse but is imposed from the outside, by external necessity. Walter Kaufmann speaks of the churches' attempts "to balance the imposing archaism of most of their thought with some of the latest jargon," and indeed the churches want so hard to swing. They would like to be "relevant," "where the action is," "at the cutting edge," to "come alive in a church of dialogue" in the "inner city." The goal for themselves and for others is to become "truly human," to all but religious ears a tautology. Repeated endlessly by writer after writer in religious journals, catchwords like these reveal religion's inability to come up with fresh ideas of its own.

One of the brightest aspects of the current church scene is the sincere attempt by most branches of organized religion to take a forthright position on the issue of race. Here, as nowhere else, the churches have been able to exert some leverage, and there are countless examples of heroism among the clergy. And yet, even on the race question, there are signs that the churches are not precisely comfortable as crusaders. For the churches, not believing that civil rights activism was proper for them, were late in joining the fray. The Roman Catholic bishops did not take a stand until 1958, almost a hundred years after the Civil War, the Protestants not much earlier and in some cases later. Many of the famous priests and nuns who marched at Selma, Alabama, would not have gotten there if orders from a certain bishop rescinding permission had arrived on time. In many cities rabbis are still conspicuously absent from civil rights organizations, and the role of many clerics in the history of civil rights could easily be called "profiles in cowardice." Some churches today are badly divided on the race issue, with parishes withholding funds from denominations that move too far, too fast, and acting as a brake on the religious commitment. Particularly depressing for those who want religion to take a passionate stand on race is the fact that Negro clerics within the white denominations are leaving. For them, the churches' progress has been too slow, and the position of the Negro in a white church structure remains ambiguous.

There is, too, a larger issue here. For if, as Reinhold Niebuhr has said, "The race crisis saved the churches from irrelevance," then what can be thought of their relevance beyond it? If the Negro is Christ today, who will He be tomorrow? If the race issue is solved, what else will make religion relevant? Is it true, then, that Christianity has no intrinsic relevance? If as one Christian radical puts it, "Christian faith equals public involvement," then, strictly speaking, there can be no Christian faith outside of public involvement, and what can be said about the panoply of religious liturgies, prayers and services, of religious belief itself? For one can easily have public involvement without the Christian or any other faith, and if good deeds define the Christian then we have no need of churches to define Christians for us.

The evidence suggests that organized religion is moving on exceedingly treacherous waters and whether it can circumnavigate is by no means sure. Caught in a crisis of identity, lacking a clear relationship with society, confronting unrest in its clergy and declines in its growth, the church has three possible futures:

First, churches can respond actively to the gnawing discontent within the religious organizations and a growing disconcern without. To advocates of this way, it means violently wrenching the churches out of their old frames, committing them entirely to social action, progress and the realities of urban life. It means taking churchly eyes off other-worldly horizons and fastening them securely on this one. It means putting church money where its mouth is, and that implies an end to church building funds, probably the abandonment of the local parishes for a geographic, ecumenic, city-wide one. But this, the secularization of religion, carries grave risks. The doctrinal side of religion might hardly exist at all. Already the Episcopal Church has abandoned the notion of heresy, which would seem to indicate that there is little to be heretical about. If it comes to pass that the Pope is not infallible, even in matters of faith and morals, if bishops are elected by popular vote, if priests can marry and nuns serve only a few years before departing to raise families, how will one define the Roman Catholic Church? How will a Catholic be different from a Protestant? How will the Protestant Church, having jettisoned the supernatural, prayer, authority in moral matters, and so on, having committed itself to liberal social causes, differ, say, from Americans for Democratic Action? Why should the individual join one rather than the other? And what *would* a Jew be?

Such developments in the churches, moreover, would alienate the conservative parishioners who populate and largely finance the parishes, confuse the faithful and pious who find in religion a refuge from change, and risk a sharp decline in membership, a serious split between liberals and conservatives, or both. It is a possibility no red-blooded organization could lightly take, and those who threaten the church structure will almost surely be branded as enemies. Indeed, as Patrick Cardinal O'Boyle of Washington, D.C., has already said, "Today the enemies of religion, and of the Catholic Church in particular, are more likely to come from within."

The second possibility, equally repugnant to religion's organization men, is a conscious retreat from denominations back to sects. The sects might (though probably would not) teach a social gospel, but they certainly would put high-minded emphasis on religious doctrine, their separate identity, and would follow their own beliefs and practices, no matter how oddball they seem to the outside world. The general society would hear them in their own genuine and perhaps remote tongue (how significantly aloof and other-worldly the Papal language still sounds). But the sects could not have their holy wafers and eat them too. They would be forced to assent to the proposition that Protestants and Catholics, like Jews, are minority cultures in an irreligious state. Secular man would be recognized for what he is, the dominant social force, and the notion that our institutions are underwritten by an Almighty, in the sense that Fort Knox guarantees our currency, would be abandoned. The churches, standing on their own feet, would be taxed. The sects would have the virtue of being honest, to themselves and others, and on their own example, not overblown religious publicity or attempts to manipulate power, they would rest their case. At least the churches would have a chance to show the validity (or irrelevance) of the religious ideal, and the vague and unpleasant odor of spurious sanctity which still hangs over the United States would be dispelled.

Here, too, risks abound for religion, for the Jews, who have tried to preserve a sect-religion, also face absorption into the American blotter. But the third possibility, to hang, or try to hang, motionless in the tides of change, is the greatest risk. Changelessness, after all, is death.

62.

BORN-AGAIN CHRISTIANS

Anne Roiphe

The established religious institutions are shaken from time to time by new or revived religious sects and cults. The "Jesus Freaks" and other Pentecostal revival groups, which have recently attracted many young Americans, have thus disturbed the complacent participation of others in the established religious institutions. The struggle between, on the one hand, two sisters who have committed themselves to The New Testament Missionary Fellowship and, on the other hand, their parents, who have attempted to persuade them to discontinue this affiliation, vividly personalizes this institutional confrontation. The socialization of the girls in the new religious group and the efforts to resocialize them in the culture of the rather typical middle-class family, that has been dramatically portrayed in a CBS television program, is vividly described by Anne Roiphe.

Having become "born-again" Christians, Elizabeth and Margaret Rogow, sisters 21 and 19 years of age living in Manhattan, sometime last fall joined the New Testament Missionary Fellowship, an extreme form of Pentecostal worship that was to radically alter the direction of their lives. Believing their children to be under a baneful influence, their parents, Lawrence and Jan Rogow of Hamden, Conn., on April 26 tried with the help of three private detectives and a family friend to take them away in a car. When the girls began screaming on the street outside their apartment building, neighbors called the police and all were taken to the precinct house where the daughters denounced the parents for interfering with their religious freedom. Elizabeth Rogow said to reporters and detectives, "When I was living with two boys in California and was taking drugs, my parents didn't say anything. But now that I've been reborn and am straightening out my life working at a 9-to-5 job, they just can't take it."

In their plan to remove their children forcibly, the parents had been hoping for help in "deprograming" them from Ted Patrick, a black community planner from San Diego who claims to have rescued 125 youths from tight-knit, highly controlled, Jesus-loving, Satan-fearing communities across the country. Known in religious circles as "black lightning," Patrick isolates the Jesus-believing children from their group and, by challenging their Biblical interpretations, by shouting, cajoling and provoking, seems to crack their conviction and loyalty to the religious communities. Patrick had already successfully kidnapped and deprogramed one Fellowship member, Wes Lockwood, who had dropped out of Yale and moved to New York to live with the community. Like many young people

Source: Anne Roiphe, "Struggle over Two Sisters," *New York Times Magazine* (June 3, 1973): 17, 69–70, 74–6, 78.

Anne Roiphe is a novelist who has written *Digging Out, Up the Sandbox,* and *Long Division.*

who join such groups, Lockwood had afterward turned on his parents with a hatred that led to a break in relations. After being deprogramed, he said about Mrs. Hannah Lowe, a woman in her 60s who is one of the Fellowship leaders: "I was essentially serving Hannah Lowe. We were taught that the end was near and because of that we had to follow the Bible fanatically—of course, Hannah's interpretation of the Bible—or we wouldn't be saved." Later, Lockwood offered to testify for Patrick, who had been indicted in an unsuccessful attempt to "kidnap" another former Yale student and Missionary member, Dan Voll, whose parents had also asked for Patrick's help.

Some form of parental mourning for the loss of living children is an established tradition of the open American society. It's an old story for immigrant fathers to have lost their Harvard Ph.D. sons through an unbridgeable communications gap. Children have married out of faith or out of race and become dead to despairing and disapproving parents. The very freedom of opportunity we prize so much has always caused grief as children tumble up, down and sideways on our social scales. We have believed that each generation should improve on the last and that parents should easily let go of their children. Some of our lofty ideals have resulted in fragmented, isolated families, in lonely old age and the taint of failure that haunts the relationship of parent and child throughout.

The family dramas in the cases of the Jesus children are just as intense, similarly tragic, and the legal and social questions are complicated and contradictory. Burdened by the knowledge that right and wrong in most such disputes are surrounded by ambiguities, I set out to explore all viewpoints in the Rogow affair, but quickly ran into an obstacle.

The New Testament Missionary Fellowship is reached by calling Hannah Lowe. She did not want me to attend one of the group's meetings, saying that I would feel uncomfortable because I would not know when to cross myself, etc.; moreover, after many phone calls, I was told that the girls had decided they did not want to talk to me either. They were following the District Attorney's advice in the matter, because of a grand-jury investigation into the April 26 incident. I then offered to submit questions that had to do only with the group's religious beliefs, and was told that they would think about it. I left many messages that were unanswered and finally was told that they did not want to talk to me. The Rev. Dean Kelly of the National Council of Churches, who knows the group, told me that Fellowship members knew my stepdaughter at Barnard and, aware of her attitudes and views, felt that I would not be favorable to them. Some missionaries are obviously more selective about whom they'll talk to than others.

The girls' parents were eager to talk. I went to visit Mr. and Mrs. Rogow in their compact, comfortable house, white with black shutters, set on a small suburban lawn in Hamden. Jan Rogow promptly showed me several pictures of her daughters. Betsy and Peggy, as they were always known at home, were clearly beautiful girls; they seemed poised, confident, glowing. There was a picture of Betsy on a horse, others of Peggy in her leotard, Betsy the night of the junior prom in a floor-length white dress, Peggy leading a dance class of small black children in leaps across a gym floor, Betsy as the lead in the senior play. "They've changed so much," said their mother.

Jan Rogow, whose grandfather was a Methodist minister in Arkansas and whose great-uncle was a U.S. Senator, Joseph T.

Robinson, was graduated from Barnard in 1950. She worked in Harlem as a student teacher and after her marriage got a master's in bilingual education. Now she works as assistant principal in an inner-city elementary school and plans programs to aid Spanish-speaking children to adjust more effectively to American life. She still has a kind of Southern-belle quality, combined with the energy and drive of your average Connecticut Yankee. She has always worked, both for economic reasons and because she says she feels challenged by what she does. Mrs. Rogow talks rapidly, smiling and at the same time defending against tears as she describes her daughters. Hannah Lowe, in the initial phone conversation with me, described Mrs. Rogow as "mental." I found her anxious, a little hysterical—an obviously explosive and emotional woman.

Lawrence Rogow, brought up a Catholic in Queens, was trained as an engineer at Columbia University, a place he remembers as exciting, filled with interesting people, groups, things to do. After moving the family seven times in ten years for business reasons, he settled in New Haven, took an advanced degree at Yale and is now a traffic consultant. He talks of his daughters with pride and a gentle kind of love, relating their accomplishments and acknowledging their faults. Confused and overwhelmed by their hostility to him and his wife and by their participation in a group with convictions that seem to him appropriate to the thirteenth century, he went to the Yale bookstore and bought works on religion, psychology, sociology that now cover tables in his home. There is something admirable about the person who studies the molecular make-up of the storm even as he wanders through the rubble of his house. Mr. Rogow is a gray-haired, conventionally dressed, good-looking man, who says he always had long talks with his daughters on everything from civil rights to the boys they dated. "They're such intelligent girls," he says over and over.

The Rogows joined the Unitarian Church when the younger, Peggy, was about five. Lawrence Rogow served on the board of trustees. Jan was pressed into teaching a sixth-grade Sunday school class on the life of Jesus. During her teaching year, she came to the conclusion that his words were even more powerful and moving since they came from a man, not a God. When Betsy and Peggy no longer wanted to go to Sunday school in their early teens, the Rogows drifted away from the church.

Why did the daughters ultimately convert to a Pentecostal sect that believes in the word of the Bible literally, that holds daily meetings and demands total acceptance of doctrine? Did they come from a home that provided them with security and love? There are no obvious signs of deprivation, but it does appear, after gathering the evidence as related by parents and friends, that these are particularly vulnerable girls.

Betsy, as so often happens with the oldest child, appears to have been the more difficult of the two girls. She has always been headstrong, open, determined, and has had her troubles growing. She was the most popular girl in her sixth-grade class and won many school prizes; she was particularly skilled in language and math. However, in the seventh grade, when the dating pressures started, she found herself alienated, without friends, and unable to be a part of things. Many of her former friends had transferred out of the public-school system. At the end of that year, according to Mrs. Rogow, she asked if she could go to a night Little League game and her mother said no, not that evening but perhaps another, and, Betsy, in a fury, took many aspirins. Later, she told her mother what she had done and was rushed to the nearest emergency room. A year of psychotherapy with a young Yale doctor was started.

Betsy did not make many more friends in the eighth grade and was left out of most social events. These events included beginning sex play and experimentation with drugs. She transferred to a private girls' school in New Haven which has a reputation for academic excellence. Here, she was slow to form close friendships, but eventually became an accepted part of the class. She developed her interests in dancing and dramatics, and, despite arguments with her mother, seemed to all who knew her at the time an inquisitive, intelligent, sensitive, talented girl with a certain kind of aloofness and shyness—giving a sense that much more was being felt than was being said. Before she left for college, she decided to change her name to "Ami" (the name of a neighbor's child). This choice suggests she wanted a new identity and experience.

As she went off to Smith, her father rather hoped that Betsy would become a lawyer and her mother expected that the remaining tensions between them would be smoothed. The initial year at Smith seemed a good one. Betsy brought home a friend, spoke of the exciting classes and at no time told her parents of the emptiness it seems now that she must have felt. At one point she dated a wealthy boy who told her that her parents were fools for working so hard for so little all their lives. She agreed with him, and told her parents she would never fall into their trap. Later, she stopped seeing the boy and lost interest in becoming wealthy.

After a summer in California where she took a dance class (she worked to raise the money for the trip), Betsy returned to Smith and in her sophomore year met a young sculptor at Amherst who became her boyfriend—John Swann. Then, suddenly, she decided to go to California and possibly transfer to a college there; she told her parents that she was anxious and uncertain over what to choose for her major at Smith, but one may speculate that her first sexual relationship perhaps had something to do with the anxiety and restlessness. She was accepted at Cal Tech but decided not to go. She thought she might drop out of college and study dance. Her parents, while preferring her to continue, accepted her reasoning that she needed some time to find out what she really wanted.

The next summer in California she shared an apartment with John and a friend of John's brother. John took an art course and she studied dance. She took a job selling jeans in a local boutique and the owner, a former drug addict and motorcycle freak turned fundamentalist Christian, converted Ami/Betsy to Christianity. She, in turn, convinced John, and the two of them became "born-again" Christians. They started to study the Bible and question the careers they had planned for themselves—maybe it was better to give up art and dance and just work for the Lord. John Swann says, "We thought we had found a new meaning for ourselves—our relationship was very loving and we were so much together that summer. I'll always remember it as a beautiful time." This is the same summer experience that Betsy reproached her parents for permitting to happen.

John decided to finish his last year at Amherst, and Betsy came East to look for a job and take dance classes. She became a live-in baby sitter for a young couple near Columbia. John came down on weekends, and he and Betsy made several friends at the Calvary Baptist Church with other young Christians. Her parents were pleased at her independence and yet intended to push her to return to college in the fall. Mr. and Mrs. Rogow accepted their daughter's new religion, since she and John seemed happy and peaceful, but the mother and father expected it was what knowing parents are apt to call "a phase."

Meantime, Peggy, the younger sister, had enrolled at Barnard. After having bought her first Bible with John and Betsy, she met a member of the New Testament Missionary Fellowship on the Barnard campus, Sharon Worthing, whom she introduced to her sister. When John subsequently asked Betsy if she would plan to marry him in the spring, she turned him down, saying she wanted to devote her life to finding God.

After knowing the Missionary people for a while, John says, she discontinued her sexual relationship with him—they were, because of their premarital sex, known in fundamentalist circles as carnal Christians. John then pressed for marriage again, and Ami left her live-in babysitter job and suddenly moved in with the Missionary people. For a while, John couldn't find her at all; she did not even tell him the name of the group she was becoming so deeply involved with.

Last Christmas, she broke off the relationship completely. John, the son of a Knoxville, Tenn., surgeon, has now gone back to sculpture, and doesn't even think he's a Christian anymore—he says he's still questioning and thinking about what meanings to give his life. John says with a kind of gallantry, "The important thing about Ami is she never wanted to have a mediocre life. She wanted something with meaning and purpose. She intended to be special." Who, of course, at 19 years of age, does not?

Peggy had always been the good daughter. Throughout her childhood, she would listen to her mother's fights with her sister, go into her room, close the door, emerge later smiling at everyone. Her academic work, like her sister's was first-rate. She danced five hours a day all through high school. She taught dance at her mother's school in an after-school enrichment program, and she sewed beautiful clothes for her mother, evening dresses, party clothes —Jan Rogow showed me a few—all for a life Peggy would eventually scorn and consider damnation and sin. The summer before she was to enter college her sick 80-year-old grandmother came to live with the family. Eventually, Peggy was to take turns nursing her in the hospital, where the grandmother suffered convulsions. The 18-year-old girl handled the tongue depressors, the intricate nursing care, with total competence and affection. That summer she had gone to Martha Graham's to dance—her father's aunt had paid for the lessons as a graduation present. She wrote home, ecstatically:

"Shall I begin with my every moment's thought that 'I am so happy!' This is such an exciting time . . . each day I recognize more and more how subtle and strong control over this 'instrument' is . . . it is frustrating and discouraging as each day more false assurance is taken away . . . replaced by a realization that perfection is impossible (the body *always* gets in the way), but also replaced by an infinite respect for control . . . the ability to work each pore and muscle together and separately until the body becomes strong, supple, dramatic and alive. . . .

"I *repeat!!* I am *so* amazingly happy. There is nothing more wonderful than pushing yourself, working to your capacity, doing something you love. . . ."

Peggy's happy summer mood had vanished by the time, during her freshman year at Barnard, she returned home after the Yale-Columbia football game for the Rogows' traditional party. She was sullen, and angry at her mother for the first time in her life. She said, "All you ever do is look at yourself in the mirror." At Thanksgiving, she came home only after her parents insisted. She appeared listless and strange to her parents. She had gained weight and developed acne, and mentioned to her mother that she had not menstruated for seven or eight months. Her mother took her to an internist, who decided she was merely under strain. Peggy wept and begged her mother not to send her back to Barnard. The doctor thought she ought to complete the remaining three weeks of the term and that there was no need for a psychiatrist. The mother and father were torn between compassion for their daughter's obvious unhappiness and a practical consideration of the money spent on tuition and a certain value they set on finishing a job, confronting a problem—a morality of achievers. Peggy complained that all the girls on the campus were evil, and the parents, knowing nothing of the New Testament Missionary Fellowship group or Peggy's growing involvement—she did not discuss religion or any of her Missionary friends with them—did not feel this to be a reason to reject the college experience. "Surely," said Lawrence Rogow, "not everyone is evil."

Strongly urged by her parents, Peggy returned to Barnard after that vacation and was not to speak to her mother in an open or friendly way again. She had already, before Thanksgiving, joined the Missionary Fellowship, and, according to Mrs. Rogow, now began to think of her mother as Satan, whose spirit had entered her when the family, at John's and Betsy's suggestion, had held hands around the Thanksgiving table. The spirit of Satan had tempted her to leave the group and remain with her family, and that's her later explanation of why she had not wanted to return to New York.

I think I understand some of what had happened to Peggy since September's orientation week: She was confronted with a heavy drug scene on campus and with a sexual morality that made it difficult for her to remain uninvolved. Although she had had a boyfriend for some time in high school, she told her mother that she felt like a freak at Barnard because of her avoidance of drugs and sex. Her roommate, whom I talked to at some length, had boys in the room at all hours of the night, and Peggy, always somewhat submissive and overly anxious to please others, waited in the bathroom until the early hours of the morning for the sexual encounters to be over. She was obviously frightened by the confusion of those around her, and turned to her sister and her sister's religion for support. According to her roommate, boys called Peggy all the time, and she would go out with them once and then avoid them. Sometime in late October, she wrote to a boy she had met the summer before:

"I had to call to say don't come because this is the first time I've had a lot of work. . . . It was a selfish decision I admit—but I really felt that I would have been hostile about not being able to do the work the way I felt right about doing it—

"Which returns to the whole start of this circle—being my emotional reactions to all sorts of things lately—

"I feel very strange about myself—and I don't know where to start, mostly because it is so hard for me to be self-analytical—I never have, and find that in this past month I have become totally absorbed in myself to the point of being noncommunicative. How can I explain this??

"It's just that when I was living at home, I was a certain person that had a lot of energy and motivation and opinions and biases—and I was supported a lot by my mother—so that I always felt right—that I could hold opinions last year about not liking what the people in my class were doing—smoking every weekend or having huge brawl-type drinking parties—that I could just exclude myself from all of that without ever feeling that I was antisocial and odd and wrong. So I never thought much about myself—I let myself be defined by my actions and what my mother decided that I was. Is this at all clear to you? In other words I did a lot of things, a lot of dance—teaching dance, lots of activities, but I never was alone with myself to figure out who I was, why I couldn't relate to people—was it right to just not *relate,* or was it better to try and understand?

"So here I am at Barnard and I'm really confused—

"This is so hard to explain—I have a real aversion to emotion. My sister all through high school used to think something was wrong with her that she couldn't relate to the strange goings-on in school—that somehow she was queer—when groupies didn't accept her, etc., she used to just cry and blow up and altogether be miserable—until she met John and until this summer when, in coming to Christianity, she feels she can understand that all those people were lost and insecure and hanging on to a self-imposed identity that they held exclusively: afraid of other people saying you're wrong—

"Which is great to hear—that she is happy and that she understands herself somewhat—but I used to be so blind to what she was going through and just say sort of, organize your time, get away from situations like that, don't get so wrapped up in yourself. Don't *be* miserable—

"And my mother especially supported that—

"So here I am—and I can't believe that anymore—I tried at the beginning the first three weeks, and I raced around taking a lot of dance, getting off-campus, just not relating to people at all. But then I started to feel that the reason I didn't like Barnard was that I wasn't ever around—and of course I couldn't understand my friend snorting cocaine or the strange parties where people just didn't relate—and I just started to feel really lonely—that I was so odd and so much like a little girl that acts without thinking, that talks without thinking—that expresses a lot of opinions without feeling convictions—

"I feel very strange about Christianity—I think in a lot of ways I was so confused and so conscious that Ami had attained this peace that I threw myself in also—and yet no one is the grandchild of God—you have to come to Christ by yourself—and I have let myself be led. . . .

"This past weekend was so strange—Ami and I went home, and it just threw me into all sorts of convulsive waves—I don't want to tag along on John's and her feelings of peace and Christianity—yet it was so hard to go home to my mother feeling lost and unhappy, because she doesn't understand. She thinks I had always been self-defined, secure, and therefore, now that I feel lost, she wants me to leave—go away (run away from myself) which is attractive—but I can't."

The sadness of this letter, which had been given by the boy to Peggy's parents, is that it seems so recognizable—a memory of Salinger's Holden Caulfield—it brings back painful memories of my own. Who has not been confronted by a disappearing self, or found that the boundaries and rules that used to serve no longer protect? And how many of us know what it feels like to be alone on a barren landscape, when the empty sky seems like a judgment? This letter comes from the center of the adolescent storm, during which each day demands choices, and each choice, like a heavy finger on the clay, marks the person to be, the life to come. The first separation from home is a traumatic occasion uncelebrated by any rites of passage in our culture.

Betsy's aspirin overdose tells us that she is not without a secret place of self-destruction, of loss of control, and that a great anger rages in her like a brush fire in the California hills. But that in itself could lead her to become a fine painter, a Bernadette Devlin, a scientist—or even a woman with ordinary accomplishments, night terrors or a mild drinking problem.

The Rogow family, as far as I could see, was not unloving or uncaring; they were not without social values, nor did the parents seem to be at odds with each other in some deep way. Like all of us, they probably made compromises and their lives have not been ideal—ambitions must be unfulfilled, regrets are always there. The moving around through the children's early years, coupled with economic uncertainty and the personal struggles of most young married people, may partially explain Betsy's and, to some extent, Peggy's, unsteadiness. However, I saw no major cruelties, no lack of contact, no overly controlling desires, or indifference, or vanity; Mr. and Mrs. Rogow seemed to be parents like most of us, who make mistakes, who feel guilty, who wanted their home to be something very special with special gifts and special hope, and now must accept their daughters' accusations, spoken and unspoken, "Somehow you failed." Somehow, of course, we've all failed.

The daughters don't agree that the Rogows were your average family. "We weren't a communicative family," Betsy Rogow said in an interview with the Associated Press. "We never went on picnics, or to the beach, or [did] anything else families do. My mother had to work and hated it. When she came home from her job, she would go to bed. There were a lot of closed doors around the house."

In an interview with another reporter, the girls accused their mother of being seductive in manner. For Christmas, when they came home, they gave their mother several boxes of sexy lingerie. Mrs. Rogow was at the time somewhat bewildered by these gifts. The reporter was also told by Mrs. Lowe that Dan Voll's mother wore miniskirts (in fact she is a decorous, middle-aged lady). These accusations seem recognizable as part of the religious zealot's obsession with matters of sex and sin. While members of the Fellowship appear to be totally chaste (in their services, I was told, they rebuke the demons that promote their own sexual thoughts), they do seem to project all sorts of sexual wrongdoing onto others.

To some, money, not sex, is the root of all evil, and there is no question that money plays a part in the Rogow family drama. The parents have used it, as parents often do, as a leash, or means of control. For example, they refused to pay the Barnard tuition if Peggy moved off campus. Both girls now work in the Columbia bursar's office, at essentially menial jobs. Betsy has an inheritance coming from her grandmother. But, says Mrs. Rogow, when Betsy asked the parents to write the check in the name of some bank, they refused, insisting that she come home to get it herself. As of this writing, she has not received the inheritance. Money pressures on the family, real or imagined, were a frequent part of the parents' conversation, and the daughters apparently do not want to be poor missionaries.

There is no question that we who offer our children everything provide them with choices so infinite that we terrify them. They may do almost anything, go almost anywhere, and the freedom itself, like the vast Sahara desert, causes a thirst for meaning, a desperation for direction that we so proudly, with our humanistic values, our pride in independence, do not offer. The village bride sold to the neighbors' son for 14 cows does not suffer the fear, loneliness, confusion that clearly stirred the Rogow girls. The trouble came at the time the girls left home. College is the great opportunity to be free of your parents, freedom to be anything you want—but what good is it if you simply feel like a piece of confetti thrown in a ticker-tape parade of whose origins and ends you have no conception?

The New Testament Missionary Fellowship was established in New York in 1963 by six founders. Among them was Mrs. Lowe, who became a born-again Christian at a Billy Sunday rally when she was 19 years old in Maryland. Afterward, she was married to an Episcopal missionary stationed in Colombia. Her husband died in 1941, during tension between Catholics and Protestants that led to bloodshed in Colombia, and Mrs. Lowe told Jan Rogow that he had been poisoned by priests.

The born-again Christianity practiced by the group was described this way by McCandlish Phillips, a reporter in The New York Times cultural department and another founding member: "Once you are born again and have a belief in Jesus, there is a power in your life that was never there before. The Holy Spirit comes to you and helps you resist sin." Members of the group live near each other in the same apartment buildings on Morningside Heights. They meet in small groups every morning and all together three times a week. Charlotte Shenikin, a former group member accused in an unsuccessful kidnap attempt on her sister, Esther DiQuattro, another member, describes the meetings:

"They play tambourines, guitars, other instruments; you sing and sing and the instruments get louder and some dance in the center. Then the rhythm builds up and you begin talking in tongues and some get revelations. Hannah sits in a chair screaming in tongues * and getting visions. Rebuking demons in wayward Fellowship members and long praying sessions are also part of the service."

Parents of young people in the Fellowship have shared the experience of finding their children strangely angry at them. They have reported that the children suddenly seemed apathetic, zombielike, fearful of demons and capable of talking endlessly about Christ and repeating the leaders' words and opinions. "Fellowship members can't evaluate themselves or the group," says Bob Bakker, a former member. "You automatically reject any argument that is critical because you feel guilty and afraid the Devil will take over your brain."

Do parents have a moral right to kidnap their of-age children—put them through a traumatic deprograming, violate their choices of emotional salvation? I'm finally

* A form of prayer or praise in which the believer, filled with the Holy Spirit and overcome with emotion, begins to utter sounds that seem to be a coherent language, normally followed by an "interpretation" in English. "Glossolalia," as it is called, was first described in Acts ii.

not sure. I'm convinced by both sides. The kidnapping seems authoritarian and brutal. At the same time, I would desperately want my children to be free of the fear of damnation, the enclosed world of missionary folk, the obsession with demons, sin and sex. I would want them to experience the ordinary love of an ordinary woman for the man's body she lies next to, for the children she nurses. What would I do? Like the old question of how would one behave in a war, no answer is possible.

The parents' legal case may be weaker, but at least one expert on constitutionality, N.Y.U. law professor Ephraim London, thinks the issues may be more complex. London says: "The free exercise of religion is of course protected by the Constitution, but where religious observances result in harm to society, they may be curbed. Examples are snake worship, religious beliefs opposed to inoculation, and, from what I have been told, the practices of the New Testament Missionary Fellowship. As I understand it, the Fellowship has, by use of improper means, damaged and in some cases destroyed, family relationships. State intervention in such cases is permissible, and in fact may be necessary."

It wasn't until after Christmas when Peggy Rogow, telling her parents that she wanted to move off campus and have nothing to do with anyone at Barnard, brought the family struggle to a new stage. The Rogows, upset by their daughter's hostility to everyone at Barnard, decided they would not allow her to live off campus. But she and Betsy moved to an apartment with another group member and did not, for a while, tell their parents where they were staying. At this time, they learned about the New Testament Missionary Fellowship.

Mr. Rogow went to New York after Christmas and found Peggy working in Salter's bookstore near Columbia. He had consulted a psychiatrist at Yale and wanted Peggy to join him and his wife at this doctor's for a discussion of the anger that had grown to such a pitch between them, according to the father. Peggy willingly got in the car with him and agreed to see the doctor the next day. Early in the evening, she received a call from her sister and then asked for the car to go get some acne medicine. She left and did not return. The car was found abandoned some blocks away. Wes Lockwood, after he was deprogramed by Patrick, told Mrs. Rogow that Hannah Lowe had called him the night Peggy was home with her parents and said, "We're in trouble. We have to get Margaret Rogow away from her parents, who want to find out about the group."

The next acts in the drama were the alleged attempt to spirit the daughters away on April 16, and what Fellowship leaders say was a second try that failed, on May 5 near Columbia, when Esther DiQuattro was seized while walking near the Rogow daughters. Mr. Rogow and Ted Patrick are charged with kidnapping and assault in the DiQuattro case.

The Rogows had been unable to see their children alone for more than a few minutes since they had joined the group. Mrs. Rogow said that Hannah Lowe once told her, "Nothing you've ever given the girls is of any value because you're a sinner." The Fellowship leaders claim the girls would want to reconcile with the parents—if the parents would respect their life choice. After all the bitterness, reunion seems almost impossible.

The parents' perspective on this religious group is naturally affected by the fact that their children have rejected them and their way of life. One who sees the New Testament Missionary Fellowship very differently is John E. LeMoult of the firm of

Karpatkin, Ohrenstein & Karpatkin, who is the lawyer for the group. "They are lovely, sweet, decent, kind people," he says. "They are joyous and have a great sense of love for each other. If we believe in America at all, we believe in religious freedom. Their beliefs are no more absurd than others; they are not Establishment convictions and so people are prejudiced against them. Kidnapping is an ugly thing and no man has a right to force another to believe as he does. The idea these children have been hypnotized or programed is absurd."

. . . . .

I spoke to the Rev. Dean Kelly of the National Council of Churches, who has written a book on conservative churches and why they are growing. He told me that members of the Fellowship are gentle, lovely, kind, people. Mr. Kelly, who a few years ago attended two Fellowship meetings and played the piano for the services, feels very strongly that the attempted kidnappings are a major threat to religious freedom as we know it. He believes that Establishment religions today, in large well-funded churches attended by the middle class on casual Sundays, are only a rumor of our forefathers' religion. We have lost the passionate, total commitment to God that is the only kind of religion that gives meaning, shape, sense to life, he says. The Pentecostal fundamentalist churches whose memberships are growing rapidly, even as the more moderate churches decline, have always caused friction between themselves and the outside community, Mr. Kelly believes. In order to stay together, they must create among their members a suspicion of, and alienation from, secular authorities. They probably do this not with hypnotism or brainwashing, as some of the families have felt, but by offering people an escape from loneliness, from questions and indecision, from the choice of who, what or where they are or should be.

The heavy demands on the time and emotions of the members, Mr. Kelly told me, reward and sustain them, protecting some from their own destructive impulses. Many of the young people involved, he felt, might need protection from drugs, promiscuity and serious depressions. But, with all this, would he, a minister who appeared to be a highly rational, thinking man, want to be a member of such a group? No, he said, he wouldn't want it for himself, or his children, because his way of being was different. Still, he felt they deserve our respect as a most intense form of religious experience.

. . . . .

We demand of our young people that they become individuals, that they find their own way, and we won't tell them what to do, where to go, whom to love. Perhaps the rise in religious groups, and the drug phenomenon, tell us that what we ask is simply overwhelming. Peggy's cry of "Who am I?" is echoed in all of us. In a society where there are no formal answers, we are all somewhat terrorized, and terror is mitigated—even in a religion that frightens you with fears of the Devil—if it takes on a specific form, with specific enemies.

Aristotle, with his means and moderation, will never convert the romantics away from their extremes of feeling and behavior. We must acknowledge that there is a real spiritual hunger that modern society in no way fulfills, a need for ecstasy, for communion with something larger than oneself, for meaning and for a place for oneself within that meaning. Many of the children attracted to these religious groups appear to be among our brightest, most sensitive youth. Their intolerance of our bleak world tells us sharply where we have failed them.

We may in fact have driven them into

madness. R. D. Laing claims that insanity is a kind of religion in whose depths one can discover the true meaning of things. By twentieth-century technological standards, fundamentalist religion, with its paranoid overtones and hysterical practices, may be seen as a kind of group insanity—whether it is the kind that promises truth or not is a matter of opinion, or, I suppose, of faith.

On May 10, a warm spring day, I stood outside Barnard's gates and watched the girls wheel carts filled with pillows and sweaters, posters and plants down to the waiting cars. Fathers and mothers, older brothers, boyfriends and even a grandmother lifted, tugged and pushed. The college year had ended. The girls walked past the yarmulkes, the Afros, the Chinese and little old ladies on Broadway, and drove off with their families, their futures still an open question. I thought of Peggy and Betsy, who had decided everything so soon. As things now stand, they would never see another Fellini film, read the Marquis de Sade, Freud or Proust. They would never argue about Marxism vs. socialism, racism and colonialism. Because their missionary role is foremost, they would never be doctors or lawyers or teachers or psychologists or dancers. They would never drink Pernod in a Paris cafe or May wine in Munich. They would never flirt with becoming a parachutist, or a skier in the Alps. They would never be overwhelmed with a new idea or form an unexpected friendship. They would never make an independent discovery or fall in love with a stranger. They would resolve everything in terms of Christ or anti-Christ.

They do have ecstasy. They may have found inner peace. They are surely lovely, gentle people, but the price of course is very high.

I remember back in the nineteen-fifties when I was in college, we had just discovered existential meaninglessness. We talked of ethics for its own sake, of the absurdity of life, and somehow accepted the idea that we could see no order or purpose to man's existence or condition. Thinking then became a defiant tool against a mocking universe and, in fact, I remain committed to the idea that man can live without dependence on primitive magic, ancient superstition, altered psychic states in which mystical visions are produced. I still believe we can work our way slowly to a better life with the rational tools of the mind, studying and gaining in control and understanding over the dark primitive irrational force, that, as much as the heart or the liver, belongs organically to us.

However, Lionel Tiger, the anthropologist, says that after studying the cultures of man he sees everywhere the use of magic and primitive thought. He thinks we who attempt to be rational are in fact a kind of mutant, "a sport that may not survive." Lawrence Rogow, one of these sports, says, "My wife and I have as a principal parental aim to help the girls to identify, define and attain their *own* appropriate goals and objectives—free of excessive and undue influence from any source. We'll continue to await the moment when they are ready to resume their lives."

I hope his vigil will not be long.

63.

SEARCHING FOR SAGES

Joyce Maynard

Many adult Americans today lack the firm religious faith and confidence in traditional religious beliefs held by their ancestors. But many of the younger generation brought up by permissive parents, especially in this period of moral confusion, religious doubt, and disbelief, seem to feel a deep need for trustworthy authority figures. Joyce Maynard, a member of this disillusioned youthful generation, vividly illustrates the search for certainty now being made by herself and her young peers.

Just about every suburban-born, college-bred boy I know has a hitch-hiking story about "this real great truck driver" he met, the kind of salt-of-the-earth, natural man who hasn't read a book in twenty years but who, his hitch-hiking passengers tell me, "knows what it's all about." He's usually called Joe or Red, this potato- and beef-hauling Everyman, and his life's a little tragic: he sleeps in the cab of his truck and spends Christmas on the road, staring out at colored lights blinking through frosted windows (he's something of a poet too, Red is) but, tough as it is, his life is simple, honest, free. He is a philosopher of the road who has given the boy—because *this* boy is *special*—some parting nugget of Truth as he lets him out at Exit 1 for New Haven or Exit 23 for Cambridge, some words of wisdom the boy now imparts to me, over coffee and deeply inhaled nonfilter cigarettes in the campus grill. I don't mean to sound lofty. I've met my unionized Polonius too and left him convinced at least for a half hour that what he'd told me (Life is like pizza . . . Love is a merry-go-round . . .) was more profound than anything I'd got at school.

TRIVIA

We're all in search of sages—my generation in particular. Information surrounds us. Facts about the number of North Vietnamese dead and grams of carbohydrate in Rice Krispies and points lost on the stock exchange and figures on TV-star divorces are drilled into us like lists of vocabulary words for college boards. Oh, the new trend in education, while we were in school, leaned toward "concepts" and away from what were called "specifics." Vagueness—we called it bullshitting—was often easy on our high-school essay-question exams. But in spite of the generalities we met with at school, there was a feeling of being overwhelmed by details.

Every succeeding generation has just that many more years of history to study

Source: Joyce Maynard, *Newsweek* 80, no. 26 (December 25, 1972): 13.

At the time she wrote this article, Joyce Maynard was studying at Yale University. She is author of the book *Looking Back*.

—more Presidents, more planets (Pluto had not yet been discovered when my parents were in school. Neither had DNA). We were bombarded outside the classroom most of all by a media-blitz of magazines, TV sets and car radios. (Only when they are turned off do we notice they've been on.) A whole new area of expertise has been developed—some day it will be a college major: the field of trivia. TV game shows, awarding cars and minks and garbage compacters to the ones who know the most cereal-box-type information, have glorified it for us. Watching those shows, singing along with the car radio (I can recite the ads, even), I am amazed to discover how much I know, without knowing I knew it. I answer bonus questions without thinking, like the reincarnated Bridie Murphy speaking in a dialect she claimed she'd never heard.

All of which cannot help but clutter the mind. It's an unscientific notion that, like a cupboard, the brain has only so many shelves before things start to crowd and fall out, but I often get the feeling that I haven't space left to spread out my thoughts and see what I have. Loose links clanking in my head, and no chain, I long for—capital W—Wisdom. We all do, I think. Teachers were rarely funds of knowledge for us; they seldom knew more than what the textbooks taught, keeping one step ahead, reading the chapters the day before they were assigned. Parents, cautioned in the age of permissiveness not to overburden with advice, and confused themselves, sometimes to the point of despair, could give little. The venerable God died in our youth. (I still remember the cover of Time magazine one week—IS GOD DEAD?; the phrase and the notion were brand-new then, and though he'd never been alive for me in the first place, the idea of his death, the death of one of the few existing sages—even a mythical one—disturbed me.) Indeed, so many of our childhood authority figures made a point of *not* being profound, wary of being laughed at for seriousness by what they took to be a sharp, tough, unsentimental bunch of smart-aleck cynics.

TEACHERS

Actually, we weren't that way at all. My contemporaries surprise me with what is at times their mushiness—their damp-eyed reading of "Love Story," Kahlil Gibran and the thin best-selling books of Rod McKuen's emaciated poetry; their rejection of their parents' Muzak for a just-as-artificially-sweetened kind of pop; their trust in the occult and all things astrological, following the daily horoscope with a faith they never gave, when they were younger and regarded as more gullible, to fortune-cookie prophecies and tea-leaf aphorisms. The absence of true sages—men and women of deep sensibility—leads us to make false gods of rock poets and B-grade philosophers, injecting comic strips and children's books with significance their authors never knew they had. We, who so hated school, are in search now of *teachers*. An apricot-robed, lotus-folded guru with a name too long to fit on one line of a poster, an old man on a park bench (with a beard if possible), a plain-talking, no-nonsense Maine farmer with a pitchfork in his hand, the author of any slim volume of austere prose or poetry (the fewer words he writes, the more profound each one must be)—we attend their words so abjectly, sometimes even literally sit at their feet, waiting for any crumb of what will pass as wisdom to be offered us.

CREED

I remember a show-and-tell day when I was in fourth grade. I brought in a potholder I'd woven, someone displayed a sea anemone and someone else explained the engine of his model car, and one boy brought his rosary beads and his crucifix and took from his wallet a photograph of his priest and himself beside their church. We were all too stunned to laugh at first, but then the giggling started, until we were all hiccupping and one girl had to run off to the bathroom without waiting for a pass, and even the teacher was smiling, because religion was something shameful, the soft underside some of us had, but kept concealed. (Going to church was OK, like going to Brownies. But to speak, as Ralphie Leveque did, of loving God and of the blood of Christ, and Mary's tears and thorns and nails—that seemed almost dirty.)

Now, while the fourthgraders might still giggle, Jesus has come out of the closet. The disenchanted and the ones never enchanted in the first place are returning to the fold with a passion their once-a-week religious parents never possessed. It is a sign of many things: an attempt to purify the spirit, to be drenched in holy waters after a drug-filled adolescence, a form of the new nostalgia, even—almost *camp*. What's really going on, though, in the Jesus movement is our search for a prophet, for someone who can, for a change, tell us the answers. (The big line I remember from our school days was, "There is no one right answer. What's your *opinion?*") After so many unprofound facts and so much loose, undisciplined freedom, it's comforting to have a creed to follow and a cross to bear.

64.

THE JOB BLAHS: WHO WANTS TO WORK?

Decades ago social scientists were studying the impact of assemblyline job routines on the human beings who performed them. Their pessimistic claims of dehumanization, like most other contentions of establishment critics, were generally denied or at least disregarded. Sustained or increased industrial employment and corporate profits seemed to prove that an expanding and firmly institutionalized American system of mass production needed no drastic changes. But today, as indicated in the following selection, we live in a very different world. Worker disillusionment has generated widespread domestic experimentation to improve the social organization and worker morale in industry. The reader should find this selection from *Newsweek* an interesting and informative analysis of contemporary industrial organization.

The sullen refrain, it sometimes seems nowadays, is heard everywhere—at a Kaiser Steel Corp. plant in Fontana, Calif.,

Source: *Newsweek* 13 (March 26, 1973): 79, 80, 84, 89.

This article was written by the Staff of *Newsweek* magazine.

at a blue-collar saloon in Houston, Texas, at a production workers' conference called in Atlanta by the United Auto Workers union. "The one thing I have is security," says Fidencio C. Moreno, a $5.60-an-hour Kaiser steelworker. "But it's a boring, repetitious job—nasty, hot and dirty work. I go there 'cause I have to." "It's getting to be a bore to me," grumbles J. E. (Andy) Anderson, a $15,000-a-year machine-shop manager in Houston, who seeks companionship over a couple of lunch-hour beers in Jimmie's Bar. "Every day, for eight hours, we fight that black devil-chain [the assembly line]," said R. J. Soptic, a Kansas City, Mo., autoworker at the recent UAW conference in Atlanta. And even James M. Roche, the retired $790,000-a-year board chairman of General Motors, wisecracked recently: "What is more boring than lugging home a big briefcase of papers to be read before going to bed every night?"

Roche, presumably, was just being sardonic. But the other complaints reflect the discontent of an angry new breed that some say is growing faster than the labor force itself. These men and women are the new problem children of the American economy: the "alienated" workers, afflicted with the blue-collar blues, the white-collar woes and the just plain on-the-job blahs. They are bored, rebellious, frustrated; sometimes they're drunk on the job or spaced out on drugs. And though they are the newest darlings of the sociologists and industrial psychologists, they're still largely a mystery to many of the people who should understand them best: their bosses and their union leaders.

Today some 83 million Americans are holding full-time or part-time jobs. Of the total—62 percent of them men—about 19 million are engaged in manufacturing and 1 million of these are tied to the dull, routine tedium of an assembly line like that satirized four decades ago by Charlie Chaplin in "Modern Times." But there are actually more white-collar workers (49 percent of the total) than blue (35 percent)—the rest are service workers and farm workers. There are more women at work in the nation today than ever before, and more young people.

The mood of this vast work force is obviously of tremendous importance to the country as a whole as well as to the individuals themselves. Worker attitudes affect productivity—how competitive the nation is versus nations such as Japan and how high America's standard of living can go. On a more philosophic but no less significant level, a nation's attitude toward work is a reflection of its sense of itself. The work ethic President Nixon is so fond of celebrating involves not only a job but a way of life.

THE "ENRICHMENT" BOOM

While people have been complaining about work since it was invented, there is a widespread feeling that there is something different about today's discontent. As a result, the managers of American business and industry are now coming up with plan after plan—some pure public relations, some quite innovative, but all designed to pacify unhappy workers. From giant General Motors Corp. to a tiny, 50-worker unit of Monsanto Chemical's textile division in Pensacola, Fla., literally hundreds of companies have instituted "enrichment" programs to give workers a sense of satisfaction on the job and send them home with a feeling of accomplishment.

And the movement is growing rapidly. Lyman Ketchum, a manager of organizational development for General Foods and the father of a pioneer enrichment program at GF's Topeka, Kans., Gaines Pet Food plant, has been practically forced to get an unlisted telephone number. "I was getting ten to twelve calls a week from corporation executives who wanted to talk to me about it," Ketchum reports. "I have just had to say no. I have too much of my own work to do."

In the automobile industry, where about 25 percent of the work force assembles cars with robotlike monotony, General Motors is experimenting with a "team" approach to the assembly of its new $13,000 motor home. Rather than having the chassis roll down an assembly line, with each worker performing only one or two functions, teams ranging in size from three to six workers are now building selected coaches from hubcap to horn. Ford is trying a team assembly program at its Saline, Mich., parts plant while Chrysler has given some Detroit-area plants virtual carte blanche to try any experiment they choose. So far, these have ranged from employees operating without a foreman to assigning assembly-line workers the relatively pleasant chore of test-driving the new cars they have just built.

While experiments by the auto industry's Big Three are still inconclusive, others are not. Indiana Bell Telephone, for example, used to assemble its telephone books in 21 steps, each performed by a different clerk. It now gives each clerk individual responsibility for assembling an entire book. One result: employee turnover in recent years has been cut by as much as 50 percent.

At Kaiser Steel in Fontana, Calif., a group of 150 workers literally kept the continuous-weld pipe mill from closing—at least temporarily—when they were given full responsibility for making it competitive with Japanese pipe producers. Recalls Timon Covert, a grievance committeeman for the United Steelworkers union and a leader of the worker group: "I told management, 'Look, we don't believe anybody in the damned world can outproduce us.' I hear all this bunk about how good they do it in Japan and Germany and we told management to let us try some things." The workers overhauled some tools, rearranged the production flow to make it more efficient and worked out changes in the production schedule. The result: production jumped 32.1 percent during the final three months of 1972, while the spoilage rate dropped from 29 percent to 9.

THE SEARCH FOR SOLUTIONS

As another example, the 50 workers at the Monsanto plant in Pensacola set up task forces to restructure certain jobs through automation, and managed to eliminate certain "dirty" chores that nobody wanted or did well. The workers also became their own managers. In the first year of the new deal, waste loss dropped to zero and productivity improved by 50 percent.

. . . . .

But even as businessmen and government officials search for new solutions to worker alienation, a lively debate goes on in business, labor and academic circles over the basic question of whether the whole thing hasn't been blown out of all proportion to begin with.

On one side are such social scientists as Harold L. Sheppard and Neil Q. Herrick, whose book "Where Have All the Robots Gone" * is considered by some to be a definitive work on the subject. After an in-depth study of 400 male union workers, Sheppard and Herrick concluded that one-third of them—particularly the young ones—were alienated from their jobs and could not be assuaged with the typical rewards of more money, shorter hours or longer vacations.

Sheppard and Herrick went on to assert: "Worker dissatisfaction metamorphosed from a hobby horse of the 'tender minded' to a fire-breathing dragon because workers began to translate their feelings of dissatisfaction into alienated behavior. Turnover rates are climbing. Absenteeism has increased as much as 100 per cent in the past ten years in the automobile industry. Workers talk back to their bosses. They no longer accept the authoritarian way of doing things."

'DULL, REPETITIVE, MEANINGLESS'

In large measure, Sheppard and Herrick are supported by a controversial Health, Education and Welfare Department report issued last December. While short on specific evidence, the HEW report indicated that nearly half of American workers are dissatisfied with their jobs and suggested that something had better be done to make work more attractive, interesting and meaningful. According to the 200-page HEW study, the work force in America is changing and more and more workers are growing restless because of "dull, repetitive, seemingly meaningless taks, offering little challenge or autonomy."

These are foreboding words indeed, but they don't pass unchallenged—and the challenge often comes from the very workers who are supposed to be unhappy. "I like it all right," says 30-year-old Rico Veneas of his job as a paint sprayer for a lighting-fixture firm in Inglewood, Calif. "I mean, I know how to do it so it doesn't tire me out." This may seem like an unscientific sample of one when arrayed against the Sheppard-Herrick and HEW studies. But in actual fact, the thesis that most Americans are indeed contented with their jobs finds powerful support among public-opinion specialists and some thinkers.

For example, a Gallup poll reports that, contrary to what HEW and the others say, eight out of ten Americans are satisfied with the work they do. And the situation is getting better, not worse, says Gallup. Back in 1949, "three out of ten whites and nearly half the blacks said they were dissatisfied or had qualifications about the work they were doing," vs. the two out of ten for today, according to Gallup.

More than that, the Sheppard-Herrick and HEW studies start out with preconceived notions and then find statistics and other evidence to "prove" their point, charges Irving Kristol, professor of urban values at New York University. George B. Morris Jr., General Motors' vice president in charge of industrial relations, compares the current debate with the furor over automation a decade or so ago. "The academics started talking about it and pretty soon they were quoting each other. They said people were on their way out, which simply wasn't true," he says. "Well, today the same thing is happening; there is a lot of writing being done on this subject of 'alienation' by people who don't know what they are talking about."

For their part, most union leaders seem to be gingerly skirting the subject, waiting for someone to offer some definitive answers. UAW president Leonard Woodcock concluded a meeting of his union's production workers not too long ago with a blast at "academics" whom he accused of writing "elitist nonsense" that degraded factory workers. "Sure," Woodcock said, "work is dull and monotonous. But if it's useful, the people who do it are entitled to be honored and not degraded, which is what's going on in this day and time." But a few weeks later, UAW vice president

Irving Bluestone said that the blue-collar blues were indeed a problem and called for an intensive search for answers. As one UAW source summed up: "I guess you could conclude everybody's confused about things."

Indeed, perhaps the best sense on the subject these days is being made by observers far removed from the industrial-relations firing line. One is Fred Foulkes, an assistant professor at the Harvard Graduate School of Business and author of the book "Creating More Meaningful Work." As Foulkes sees it: "Jobs haven't changed. People's expectations have, and this has been expressed in high absenteeism, low morale, high turnover, etc." Greater educational achievement has helped raise expectations. The average worker in 1940 had an eighth-grade education, he notes, but now about 80 per cent of the work force has gone beyond high school. Changing life-styles outside the job affect attitudes at world. Says Foulkes: "[Workers] want some sort of participation. There's more freedom around. So why should employees want regimented, autocratic jobs?"

So far, the White House hasn't taken a public position on the alienated-worker issue. But according to insiders, President Nixon has privately expressed displeasure with the HEW report, claiming that it is the work of soft-headed sociologists who don't know much about work and worker motivation. This may be so. The amount of actual discontent and alienation may be limited in scope. But where it exists, it is important, and increasing numbers of companies are trying to do something about it. Among the best-known and most successful are ongoing programs in Topeka, Hartford, Fort Lauderdale and Medford, Mass.

"I used to work as a construction laborer and every morning I hated to get up," 21-year-old Andy Dodge recalled as he relaxed in the comfortably furnished employee lounge at the Topeka Gaines Pet Food plant. "Now, it's different. I'm still just a laborer, but I have something to say about my job. If I get sore about something, I bring it up at the team meeting in the morning. If I want to go to the bathroom or make a phone call, I do it. I just ask someone else on the team to cover. I really feel more like a human being than a worker. After this, there is no way you could get me to go back to regular employment."

Andy Dodge is one of the lucky 72 production workers at the revolutionary, five-story Gaines plant, a brainchild of General Foods' Lyman Ketchum. Until two years ago, pet-food production was limited to the company's plant in Kankakee, Ill., run along conventional lines and plagued by conventional factory problems: a lackadaisical work force, a 5 percent absentee rate and occasional acts of sabotage. (Someone once dumped a batch of green dye into a hopper and spoiled an entire day's production of dog food.) Thus, when the demand for pet food outstripped Kankakee's capacity, Ketchum persuaded his superiors to try something new: a plant designed around people, not jobs. The result is the Topeka facility.

While it is highly automated, the plant is still burdened with a number of menial jobs with a sizable potential for boredom. So, to insure that both the rewarding and unrewarding jobs are shared equally, Ketchum devised a model workers' democracy. The employees are split into semi-autonomous teams, ranging in size from six to seventeen, depending on the operation. Each team selects its own foreman and, at the start of each shift, determines how to meet production quotas, divides up job assignments and airs grievances. Moreover, each worker is trained to do practically any job in the plant, from filling bags on an assembly line to monitoring the complicated controls of machines that cook and mix the pet food.

Even more unusual, the team leaders interview and hire replacements, and the teams discipline malingerers. "If someone is goofing off," says William Haug, 38, "the team members get on him. If this doesn't work, we have a team meeting. If there is a personal or family problem, team members often help. Sometimes it is just a matter of time off to straighten out problems, but we don't have many of them."

To further expand the individual worker's feeling of involvement and responsibility, Ketchum erased most of the lines dividing the white- and blue-collar workers at the Topeka plant. There are no time clocks, no special parking privileges for executives and everybody eats in the same cafeteria. At lunchtime, it is not unusual to see plant manager Ed Dulworth, a 38-year-old graduate of General Motors Technical Institute, playing Ping Pong with a production worker.

Predictably enough, the result is an exceptionally high level of worker contentment. "Everything is left up to the individual to expand himself," sums up 26-year-old Joe Ybarra. "We are responsible for the product we turn out. A guy can come to work here without a feeling that management is on his neck." As one result, the absenteeism rate at Topeka is less than 1 percent, vs. 5 percent at Kankakee.

Even more important to the executives back at General Foods' headquarters in White Plains, N.Y., the Topeka plant is a glowing financial success. "Even after [allowing for the new] technology, we get a productivity rate here that is 20 to 30 percent higher than at Kankakee," says Dulworth. "We need only about two-thirds of the Kankakee work force to get the same production."

Could the Topeka plant work in a larger, more complicated setting? To a degree, says Ed Dulworth. "I think it is transferable in terms of the basics, and the basics are that work can be organized for both business needs and people needs and it pays off both ways," he told *Newsweek's* Tom Joyce. "The problem with this is that managers are looking for models. They want a package you can put in place and have it pay off. Well, the nature of job design is complex and each program must be developed to fit specific situations."

DIVERSITY BOOSTS MORALE

At the huge, 21,000-employee Travelers Insurance Co. headquarters in Hartford, Conn., the raw material is punch cards rather than dog food, but the problem was the same: high absenteeism and low morale and productivity. So three years ago, Travelers hired Roy W. Walters and Associates, a New Jersey management consultant firm, to undertake a job-enrichment program.

As a pilot project, the Travelers selected a key-punch operation involving 100 operators and ten supervisors. "What we attempted to do here is create a structural change for employees and supervisors which forces a behavior change and eventually an attitude change," said Jewell Westerman, second vice president in charge of management services.

Basically, the project involved transferring some supervisory functions to the operators and broadening their jobs so that instead of dealing day after day with only one phase of an operation they carried it through from start to finish. Ordinarily, a worker would handle receipts or collections or any of the separate punch-card functions. But work was rearranged so that one employee is now responsible for the entire punch-card operation for a particular corporate or individual customer and establishes a firm operator-customer relationship. "Typically, work is assigned on the basis of who has the least to do," explains Norm Edmonds, Travelers' director of management services. "So the operator has no commitment to the job. That's been reversed, and people are aligned with their own group of clients."

The first-year results of the pilot project were dramatic: a 26 percent increase in productivity and a 24 percent decline in absenteeism. The enrichment program has since been expanded to cover some 2,000 employees in four departments at Travelers' headquarters and eight branch offices. As Dale Menard, a 27-year-old supervisor in the premium-collection department, sums up his "new" job: "I'm much more involved in decision-making than my peers at other insurance firms. Before, we went down the syndrome of 'the more you specialize the more efficiency you have.' It got to the point where tasks were divided into smaller and smaller bits and pieces. Now, with combining certain jobs, the problem takes care of itself."

STUDIES IN BOREDOM

At the Corning Glass plant in Medford, Mass., the attitude is so gung-ho that work teams give themselves such nicknames as "The Dirty Half Dozen" and stick around after the 4:30 afternoon whistle to discuss the best way to meet their production schedule. At the Motorola Corp. plant in Fort Lauderdale, Fla., the work teams compete in production races and the winning team is treated to a dinner each month by the company.

The Medford plant turns out such products as hot plates, while the Fort Lauderdale facility produces a pocket-size electronic signaling device called the Pageboy, both of them prime candidates for the impersonal attention of an assembly line. However, in each plant, the hot plates and the Pageboys are assembled in their entirety by a member—usually a woman—of work teams that set their own production goals and, in the case of Corning, even decide when they will take some of their holidays.

The results have been highly encouraging. Last year, the Medford plant increased its hot-plate production by 20 percent and it is expecting an even larger increase this year. And while the plant increased its work force by 50 percent last year, efficiency improved by 100 percent. Even though the pay is relatively low ($2.95 an hour), the plant has many more job applicants than it can satisfy. Margie Bell, a 54-year-old mother of three, sums up: "I love this place. It's not like at Raytheon where I used to work. Here you start with nothing and you make something yourself."

At Fort Lauderdale, Motorola officials say that productivity is about 5 percent lower than it would be on a normal assembly line, but that the quality is better and the morale of employees vastly improved. "It's technology having advanced to a state that permits this kind of operation," one official notes. "We're now back to something simple enough for one girl to make a total contribution, and that is very significant, I think."

Admittedly, the experiments at Gaines, the Travelers, Corning and Motorola would be impossible to impose on many operations; it would be ridiculous, for example, to split the 30,000 employees of Ford

Motor's River Rouge plant into work teams and allow them to decide production schedules and assembly-line speeds. However, there is no question but that job enrichment will continue to grow as a subject for both management soul-searching and collective bargaining between companies and their unions. The Ford Foundation has found the subject worthy of further study and plans to spend nearly $500,000 evaluating experiments industry has undertaken to stimulate worker satisfaction. And the conference on "The Changing Work Ethic" in New York . . . enjoyed the full-scale participation of labor for the first time; autoworkers, steelworkers and machinists were all represented.

But all of the conferences, all of the studies, all of the books may be too late to help some workers, such as steelworker Fidencio Moreno. "I should have quit long ago," he said sadly. . . . "Now my dad, he ran a bar. When he'd come home, us kids would run up to him and say, 'How'd it go?' My dad always had pride in his work. He'd talk about all the things the customers would say and do. Me, I go home, they don't understand a damn thing. All I do is dump a little coal into an oven. Why would my wife or my kids be interested in that?"

65.

MULTINATIONAL GIANTS BEYOND FLAG AND COUNTRY

Harvey D. Shapiro

The organized cultural system of a society which is concerned with the production, distribution, and consumption of goods and services is referred to as the economic institution. A significant recent development in this institution has been the establishment of an ever increasing number of "multinational corporations"—complex organizations which not only sell in more than one country but also obtain their raw materials and capital, and produce their goods, in several countries. Moreover, they are commonly managed from a global point of view. This trend has even spread to the Soviet dominated nations. This selection by Harvey Shapiro examines the nature and scope of these new economic forms and explores their ramifying consequences for individual

Source: Harvey D. Shapiro, *New York Times Magazine* (March 18, 1973): 20–4, 29–30, 52–3.

Harvey D. Shapiro is a writer and consultant on governmental affairs. He is a fellow at the Russell Sage Foundation, and on the editorial staff of the *New York Times Magazine.*

governments, international relations, Third World developments, the union movement, and the future of the world community.

. . . . .

According to recent estimates, the gross world product is valued at $3-trillion, of which some $450-billion, or 15 percent, is produced by multinational corporations. This sector is growing at the rate of 10 percent a year, faster than the economies of many nations, and Prof. Howard V. Perlmutter of the Wharton School has estimated that by 1985 some 300 giant multinational firms will produce more than half of the world's goods and services.

About 200 giant U.S.-based corporations are regarded as multinational, while some 3,600 additional American firms already have at least one foreign subsidiary. American-based firms account for nearly half of total multinational output, but many multinational corporations are based in Europe and Japan, including giants like Unilever and British Petroleum, and 500 or so smaller foreign firms have plants in the U.S.

. . . . .

Almost everybody knows Hershey bars come from Hershey, Pa., but where do Nestlé's chocolate bars come from? Well, these days they're made in Pereira, Colombia; Tempelhof, West Germany; Caçapava, Brazil, and Fulton, N.Y., as well as dozens of other places around the world. Though many U.S. shoppers think of Nestlé's as another little American chocolate maker, the Nestlé Company of White Plains, N.Y., is actually a subsidiary of Nestlé Alimentana, S.A. The name does not evoke an image of massive, many-tentacled power like that of I.B.M. or ITT. Nonetheless, the corporation is the twenty-ninth largest in the world in terms of sales, and ranks with Unilever as the largest of the food processors.

The firm had total income of $4.2-billion last year, of which 53 percent came from Europe, 33 percent from the Americas, 11 percent from Asia and 3 percent from Africa. At headquarters in Vevey, Switzerland, on Lake Geneva, a cosmopolitan group of Nestlé executives orchestrates the activities of the firm's hundreds of subsidiaries, which operate 300 factories, maintain 677 sales offices and employ 110,000 people in 60 countries.

Nestlé Alimentana, a direct descendant of the baby-food business launched by Henri Nestlé in 1866, is now a holding company sitting atop a mind-boggling array of subsidiary companies which it has formed or acquired. It controls two other holding companies, Unilac, Inc., of Panama and Nestlé Holdings Ltd. of Nassau, and beneath this superstructure operates dozens of companies using the Nestlé name and selling Nestlé products such as Nescafé and Nesquik cocoa all over the world. It also controls, or is allied with, dozens of other firms which don't fly the Nestlé flag, like Libby, McNeil & Libby, the giant American canner, Bachmann Bakeries of the Netherlands and the United Milk Company of Thailand. These firms sell their products under hundreds of brand names, including such popular labels as Crosse & Blackwell soups and Deer Park Mountain Spring Water.

The actual production of the firm's coffees, chocolates, baby foods, dairy products and frozen foods is highly decentralized. Cocoa, coffee beans and other raw materials are bought in local markets by individual subsidiaries, and "we vary each product according to local tastes," says Gerard J.

Gogniat, chairman of Nestlé's in White Plains. Nestlé companies make their soups thick and creamy in West Germany and thin, like bouillon, in Latin America.

While the products may be adapted locally, the recipes for marketing and operations are written in Vevey. Headquarters receives regular projections on sales and profits from the subsidiaries, along with plans on how they will achieve their goals, and the parent company takes an active part in developing marketing strategies, brand names and even packages to insure success in each market. Some 25 million foreigners visited Spain last year, and while many have been mystified by the local food, Nestlé Alimentana made sure they could find their old friend Nescafé in a familiar package.

When new products, marketing techniques or technologies prove successful in one country, they are transmitted via the parent organization to other subsidiaries. And if a Nestlé affiliate should falter, the trouble shooters at Nestlé Products Technical Assistance Co. Ltd. (Nestec) will parachute onto the scene to straighten things out. Headquarters also keeps an eye on coffee and cocoa markets, where Nestlé is among the world's largest customers, and it scans global political and social developments. Are there threats in Chile? New markets opening in China? A shift to consumer goods in Eastern Europe? A bad cocoa crop in Ghana? A new taste for wine in the U.S.? From listening posts all over the world, reports flow into Vevey. Ultimately, headquarters also coordinates the massive flow of funds among the subsidiaries, lending money to some, drawing down profits from others, always keeping abreast of impending changes in currency exchange rates, and, some say, manipulating the overall flow of funds to minimize the firm's worldwide tax burden and maximize profits.

Nestlé's top executives come from several countries, but they all seem to regard nation-states more like sales territories than sacred ties of blood and history. For example, Nestlé's U.S. chairman, Gerard Gogniat, who is also a director of Libby's, is a native of Switzerland who joined Nestlé Alimentana in 1946. He moved 12 times over the next 20 years, rising through various executive positions with Nestlé affiliates in Canada, Latin America, Stamford, Conn., Vevey and Paris before coming to White Plains in 1966. This summer [1973] the 47-year-old executive, who speaks softly—in five languages—will return to Vevey to become one of the parent company's seven top-level "general managers."

When Gogniat leaves White Plains, Nestlé president David E. Guerrant, an American, will become chief executive of the corporation while remaining chairman of Libby's. His successor as chief executive officer at Libby's was Douglas B. Wells, an American who joined Nestlé's in White Plains in 1949 and served tours of duty with Nestlé affiliates in New Zealand and South Africa before Vevey installed him as president of Libby's last July. To insure a steady crop of good Nestlé men, last fall the parent company converted an old hotel in Rive-Reine to house its International Training Center, at which Nestlé executives from around the world come to prepare for senior management roles. After a little postgraduate training there, one suspects, they go forth to sell chocolates to the world with passports stamped "Swiss" or "French" or "American," but with an outlook marked simply "Nestlé."

The rise of multinational corporations like Nestlé Alimentana is rooted in the logic of economics. Growth is the *sine qua non* of capitalism: As firms saturate their local markets, they broaden their horizons and seek new markets. Instead of expanding existing plants to supply these new markets, it is often more economical to open new factories near them and to buy raw materials in the area. When a new market is in another country, political concerns may require this choice. There are often political dangers for a product labeled "imported," as the Japanese are finding out, but tariffs and quotas on imported goods don't apply to the same goods if they are produced domestically by foreign-owned corporations. So, as the Japanese economist Chiaki Nishiyama notes, "The higher trade barriers become, the more attractive it will be for foreign capital to go into that country for investment." And once a corporation invests in another country, like a person who buys a house in a community, the firm begins an involvement that broadens its interests and its outlook. In contrast to a firm which simply ships in some goods to be sold, a company which makes a direct investment in plant and equipment in another nation becomes an employer and taxpayer, citizen and political participant. It brings in not only goods, but technology and a way of life.

The extractive industries had no choice but to invest wherever natural resources were to be found; so firms like Anaconda, Exxon, British Petroleum and United Fruit were becoming multinational in the nineteenth century. Rising tariffs after World War I led many manufacturing companies abroad for the first time, but this movement was slowed by the Depression and World War II. The development of truly multinational corporations began on a broad front in the late nineteen-forties. The movement was led by American corporations which saw lucrative new markets in countries rebuilding their war-torn economies, as well as opportunities to produce cheaply abroad for sale at home. U.S. overseas direct investment increased from $11.8-billion in 1950 to $32-billion in 1960 and $86-billion in 1971. Two-thirds of this postwar growth was in Western Europe, and most of that was concentrated in such fast-growing, nonextractive industries as chemicals, electronics, autos and computers. The number of foreign subsidiaries of U.S. firms increased from 2,300 in 1950 to more than 8,000 in 1970, while total foreign assets controlled reached $125-billion.

In his 1967 book "The American Challenge," J. J. Servan-Schreiber warned of an impending takeover of the European economy by American-based multinationals. However, Servan-Schreiber sketched only part of the picture. The rise of the Common Market since 1958 has reduced European trade and investment barriers and permitted American-sized economies of scale, while government-encouraged mergers have created a number of trans-European firms that can generate surpus capital. As a result, an impressive number of European firms have been quietly expanding foreign operations recently.

In contrast to the early European investments in raw materials in colonial areas, the recent European foreign investment has been in the U.S., primarily in technologically sophisticated industries such as chemicals and synthetic fibers, as well as consumer goods. These days, the manufacturers of such "all-American" products as 20-Mule Team Borax, Bic pens, Librium, Ovaltine and even Good Humor ice cream are owned by European companies. Two devaluations of the dollar, which have made investments in the U.S. relatively less expensive, serve to accelerate the trend.

Not only are European firms pulled here

by the world's largest and richest market and by the sophisticated R. and D. community, they are also being forced to become multinational by competition from American-based multinational companies. Joseph Rubin of the international accounting firm of Alexander Grant, Tansley, Witt, explains: "In order to remain competitive, European firms in multinational industries have had to obtain a foothold in the world's largest market in order to dilute their overall costs over a greater sales base and lower their per-unit costs."

Japanese companies are also belatedly becoming multinational. Despite its success as an exporter, Japan has only $4.5-billion in overseas direct investments, mainly in raw materials in nearby, less-developed countries. Now that the Japanese Government has eased its stiff controls on the export of capital, however, foreign investment is likely to rise to $10-billion by 1977. Some of this will flow to the U.S., but a significant amount is being directed toward Europe, where Japan's mushrooming export sales totaled $1.6-billion last year and where the kind of protectionist rumblings that have endangered her American markets are beginning to be heard.

Dr. Peter Gabriel, the new dean of Boston University's College of Business Administration, predicts: "The L.D.C.'s [less developed countries] and the Eastern bloc [the Soviet Union, China and Eastern Europe] represent the biggest single growth area for multinational corporations in the remainder of this century." Gabriel, a former partner in McKinsey & Co., an international consulting firm, argues, "The needs of the Third World and the Eastern bloc countries for the resources and capabilities the multinationals possess are almost infinite, but the multinational involvement will be very different from that in the West."

Rising nationalism in the former colonial areas has fostered a suspicion of any new exploitation. Billions of dollars of investments have been expropriated in such countries as Algeria, Argentina, Indonesia and, most recently, Chile. The oil-producing nations have been demanding not only a larger share of profits, but of ownership as well. And in 1970, the Andean Common Market countries stipulated that foreign companies had to turn over ownership of their operations to local control within 15 to 20 years.

"The era of the multinational corporation as a traditional direct investor in the L.D.C.'s is coming to an end," Gabriel says. Instead, firms which once sought 100 per cent ownership of foreign subsidiaries are becoming more flexible. For example, du Pont and American Cyanamid have accepted minority interests in Mexican ventures. Gabriel sees the management contract, in which firms "invest" their skills instead of their money, as an even more likely model for the future. T.W.A. has managed Ethiopian Airlines since World War II, for example, while Goodyear has agreed to operate two state-owned tire companies in Indonesia for a fee based on sales and profits.

Multinationals don't have any opportunities to acquire ownership interests in Eastern bloc countries, except for Rumania and Yugoslavia, but Dr. Gabriel argues these countries will increasingly seek management contracts with multinational firms to obtain the technology, managerial skills and capital they need to compete in the growing East-West trade. These days, a variety of firms have management contracts with the Soviet Union, among them Fiat, which built the Togliatti auto factory in Russia for a reported $50-million, as well as International Harvester and Renault, which have similar arrangements in Eastern Europe.

Some Eastern bloc countries are even

developing their own state-owned multinational enterprises. The Soviet Union has a group of eight banks in Western Europe. In a joint venture with Belgian interests called Society Scaldia-Volga, the Russians have opened a small plant near Brussels where Volgas and Moskvitches are assembled largely for the Belgian market. Meanwhile, in October [1972] several oil-rich sheikdoms began talking about "downstream" investments in refineries or even gas stations; perhaps Europeans will soon be filling up with Faisal Supreme or Saudi Ethyl.

Whether as owners or managers, as senior or junior partners, multinational enterprises seem destined to continue expanding their role. Only such giants, or major governments, can now afford to develop new technologies and new products. Few institutions in the world, public or private, for example, could have mustered the $5-billion I.B.M. spent to develop its 360 series of computers. Moreover, as multinational firms operate in more and more markets, Joseph Rubin points out, firms in one country must either acquire, or be acquired by, competitors in other nations, just as local and regional industries in the U.S. gradually were consolidated into a nationwide economy earlier in this century.

Earlier this year Carl A. Gerstacker, chairman of Dow Chemical, told the White House Conference on the Industrial World Ahead, "We appear to be moving in the direction of what will not really be multinational or international companies as we know them today, but what we might call 'anational' companies—companies without any nationality, belonging to all nationalities." European firms are leading the way in this. S.K.F., a Swedish ball-bearing manufacturer changed its "official language" on all memos and even conversations in its headquarters from Swedish to English, the *lingua franca* of multinational business. Royal Dutch-Shell and Unilever operate companies which, in each case, are controlled by a pair of holding companies, one based in England and the other in the Netherlands; their executives and employees are even more polyglot than their shareholders. Most American-based multinationals still tend to do 70 percent of their business at home, but a few American firms are also submerging their nationalities. More and more firms are staffing overseas subsidiaries with local citizens, and foreigners have become executives and directors of such corporations as I.B.M., H. J. Heinz and Xerox; in addition, shares of G.E., du Pont, Ford, Kodak and Goodyear are sold on stock exchanges in Paris, Amsterdam, Brussels, and Frankfurt or Düsseldorf.

Paralleling the rise of more "anational" firms, the world's major banks have divided themselves into multinational consortia. The largest, Orion Bank Ltd., was founded in October, 1970, by Chase Manhattan, Royal Bank of Canada, Britain's National Westminster Bank, Westdeutsche Landesbank Girozentrale, Credito Italiano and Mitsubishi Bank. Orion is represented in more than 100 countries and headquartered in London, but it has no real "nationality."

Instantaneous global communications, the computer and the rise of professionally trained managers have made control of these far-flung enterprises feasible, though managerial styles vary from tightly controlled empires to loose confederations. When the Cummins Engine Company of Columbus, Ind., launched Kirloskar-Cummins Ltd. as a joint venture in India a decade ago, Cummins vice-president George Thurston recalls, "All the machinery we brought in was based on the concept of a man standing at a machine while doing his work. But we learned the Indian is much more content if he can squat, so we had to re-engineer the machinery and lower the controls so a guy could work squatting." Like many multinationals, Cummins had adopted Nestlé's approach of defining goals but leaving local managers some discretion in how to achieve them. However, the multinational headquarters almost always reserves for itself the tasks of long-range planning, research and development, and finance.

Because they introduce advanced technology and management on a large scale, the corporations have been telescoping the process of development in many countries. In the Third World, Nestlé is teaching new agricultural methods to its suppliers and new child-rearing and health-care practices to mothers to whom it hopes to sell baby food and dairy products. Ultimately, multinational companies "may be a more effective device than foreign trade in improving the standard of living in the L.D.C.'s," says Charles P. Kindleberger, professor of economics at M.I.T. He explains, "You didn't get an equalized standard of living and wage scale in the U.S. until capital moved out through the country, and national companies helped do this, though the populists hated these companies, especially the chain stores." Although multinational firms may move to an area because of its low wages, the firm's payroll may increase local income dramatically. When Cummins opened its Poona, India, plant, George Thurston recalls, "We used to have three buses to pick up the workers. Now our biggest problem is parking space for their cars and bicycles. People have reached that economic level."

A free flow of goods, investments and technology may heighten worldwide productivity and economic efficiency in the long run, but such free movements could also lead to instability and painful dislocations. Higher living standards, moreover, require new styles of living. For instance, when Sears helped introduce mass merchandising in Mexico, its retail stores provided more varied goods and created new jobs and industries to supply the stores. But these stores, with their impersonal cash-and-carry operations, also replaced the social life that surrounded local markets. Thus, multinational corporations hasten and exacerbate the social changes that accompany development, and sometimes sow tensions which lead to their own expropriation.

While Third World nations would like to acquire the managerial expertise, capital markets and research facilities that come along with multinational headquarters, they are more likely—with their uneducated labor force, low wages and uncluttered land—to attract chemical plants, oil refineries and sprawling, messy, labor-intensive industries. This is particularly so, says Dr. John Hackett, executive vice-president at Cummins Engine Company, because "countries like Brazil aren't nearly as concerned about ecology as the U.S. and Japan." Thus, as pollution legislation grows more stringent in the developed countries, multinational corporations are likely to tempt the less-developed nations with incomes approaching New York or Chicago—at the cost of looking and smelling like northern New Jersey or South Chicago.

Trade unions in the industrialized nations are, of course, concerned that the movement of plants to other countries will mean loss of jobs. However, American labor's claim that multinationals "export jobs" from the U.S. is challenged by Prof. Robert B. Stobaugh in a study financed by the U.S. Department of Commerce. Stobaugh and his associates at the Harvard Business School examined nine major overseas investments and concluded they created more jobs for U.S. workers than they eliminated; if these investments hadn't been made, the study asserted, America would have lost 600,000 jobs, since the firms would have been unable to compete successfully. However, the study noted that these investments tended to "displace" production workers, while increasing managerial, research and service jobs.

Union leaders also worry that multinational companies can undermine collective bargaining by threatening to move rather than meet union demands. Henry Ford II, for example, told Prime Minister Edward Heath in 1971 that if striking workers at Ford's Dagenham, England, plant weren't tamed, the company might abandon the factory.

"International bargaining doesn't exist anyplace and I don't see how it can," says Gus Tyler, assistant president of the International Ladies Garment Workers. Garment workers making $3 an hour in the U.S. and 16 cents an hour on Taiwan have little common ground for negotiating with an employer, Tyler says, so to help stanch the flow of jobs abroad American labor is relying for the present on legislation. The A.F.L.-C.I.O. supports the Burke-Hartke bill, which seeks to tighten controls on foreign investment and restrict imports. "In the long run," Tyler admits, "we have to hope wage levels elsewhere will come up."

Perhaps they will, for in an economy dominated by multinational companies, all roads are supposed to lead to equilibrium. In theory, industry would gradually be moved from high-rent, cluttered areas to cheap, vacant land, thus evening out global land use, and global wages, interest and prices would all tend to become more equal. However, the uniformity resulting from thus tying together various national economies is a double-edged sword. Multinationals are making the world's business procedures, measures and standards more uniform, as goods are being made and used in widely varied settings. But they are also fostering a growing sameness in the world's major cities. "It's sad, but work habits are going to become the same everywhere," says Giorgio Della Seta, a vice-president of the Pirelli Tire Corporation, who bemoans the decline of the long Italian lunch break. All the typewriters and radios and toys and underwear in the world sometimes seem to be made in the same Hong Kong factory. An effective marketing program demands that all British Petroleum stations look pretty much alike. McDonald's golden arches will soon be everywhere. And a Hilton is a Hilton is a Hilton.

This growing sameness applies to people as well. Professor Kindleberger sees multinationals as creating a new cadre of international managers who will be committed to the aggrandizement of their firms and to their own salaries and stock options, but to little else. Like the mobile American executives who shuttle among the bedroom suburbs outside U.S. industrial centers, these international managers will be efficient and useful to be sure, but bland and interchangeable as well. They will be the merchants in the Global Village they're helping to create. They will, that is, unless they are checked by political forces.

The sovereignty of the state requires that it be responsible for all that occurs within its borders. But the multinational corporation requires a free flow of capital, goods, and labor as if there were no borders. Which is to govern: the law of the land or the law of supply and demand? Prof. Raymond Vernon, the director Harvard's Center for International Affairs, argues this "asymmetry" between multinational corporations and nations can be tolerated only up to a point; the threat, as he sees it, is reflected in the title of his recent book about multinationals, "Sovereignty at Bay."

. . . . .

Multinational companies might have caused fewer problems in a nineteenth-century night-watchman state concerned only with maintaining order, but modern governments have assumed the obligation of managing the economy and promoting the general welfare. "How can a national government operate a domestic financial and economic policy when it can't control the decisions of all the factors within the economy?" George Ball, a senior partner at Lehman Brothers and a former Under Secretary of State, asks. In a democratic society, the government manipulates the environment in which economic decisions are made. But multinational companies inhabit a different environment. A central bank may raise interest rates to slow inflation, but a multinational corporation may borrow funds in a low-interest country. The Canadian Government may attempt to change its unemployment rate, but the nearly 50 percent of Canada's manufacturing and mining companies controlled by U.S. firms may determine their hiring policies in response to American rather than Canadian economic policies. The U.S. seeks to maintain its military superiority on the basis of its sophisticated weaponry, yet companies like G.E. that build those weapons want to export their military technology through their subsidiaries in other nations.

One alternative is for a nation to lock the door on movements of capital and goods. By taking such a step, however, a country risks falling behind in economic and technological progress in the rest of the world. Despite General de Gaulle's opposition to the American challenge, the French Government found it had to permit G.E. to take over troubled Machines Bull, the principal French computer company. (Honeywell recently acquired it from G.E.) Although the auto industry is often a matter of national pride, France permitted Chrysler to acquire a 77 percent interest in Simca. After U.S. investment was restricted by France in 1963, U.S. companies set up shop in other Common Market countries, ultimately forcing the Pompidou government to relax the restrictions in order to share in the jobs and income gained by its neighbors.

Whatever their benefits, though, multinational corporations cannot simply be left to their own devices. What's good for General Motors is not always good for the U.S., and even when it is, it may not also be good for the people of Norway, Brazil or other countries.

. . . . .

But multinational corporations have shaken off the traditional sources of countervailing power. They've outgrown trade unions, consumer groups, local and state governments. Currently, multinational corporations are responsible to both their home country and their host countries, and the jurisdictions are sometimes overlapping but often absent. The host governments' fear of losing the benefits of multinational operations leaves the companies with sufficient bargaining power to forestall regulation in many areas.

The traditional, good liberal, common-sense solution is clear: Global corporations should be responsible to a global regulatory authority. Despite the United Nations' impotence, many still call for a multinational solution. George Ball, for example, proposes a treaty creating a supernational regulatory authority to charter multinational corporations and specify their rights and obligations, while also standardizing host government regulations and taxes. Such a treaty would begin with the developed nations—"The less-developed countries are too concerned with their nationalism right now," Ball says—and, like the International Monetary Fund or the General Agreement on Tariffs and Trade, it would gain signatories over time.

However, even if the dislocations caused by multinational companies were to be regulated by international agreement and cushioned by some form of financial assistance, many nations might still be reluctant to shift part of their economic fate out of their own hands. The less-developed countries may lead rather than follow the industrialized nations in dealing with multinationals, for the Third World is demonstrating that it can obtain many of the benefits multinational firms offer while retaining national control of its economy. Dr. Gabriel of Boston University foresees a growth in "bilateral relationships" in which corporations and governments will bargain over new and existing investments one by one. "Such a situation would resemble nothing so much as true capitalists in a free market, each seeking his own self-interest," he says. The result would be an untidy and uneven process, as corporations sought outlets for their capital and products and nations looked for corporations to fulfill their plans for national development. When those national aspirations didn't accord with the multinationals' plans—if India wants a steel industry or Norway wants fishermen—then the nation might create *ad hoc* or permanent subsidies and penalties to change the economic landscape and persuade the multinational corporation to do its bidding.

Economic rationality demands that a nation be what it is best equipped to be, but politics holds the promise of being what a nation wants to be. There need not be a conflict, of course, but the nations of managers and researchers and financiers are more likely to accept their lot than those who seem destined to be the world's factory workers and hewers of wood and haulers of water. They may not maximize global economic efficiency that way, but as Professor Kindleberger says: "The political solution to the question of multinational corporations depends on what it is that people want to maximize."

66.

THE FUTURE OF CAPITALISM

Robert L. Heilbroner

Concluding the economics section of this chapter on institutions and associations is a selection by an outstanding economic theorist. Robert Heilbroner claims that the stereotypes of capitalism held by its supporters as well as by its Marxist opponents have led both schools of economists to ignore or fail adequately to appreciate certain "important aspects of reality" which did not support their ideologically distorted expectations. He reviews past errors of interpretation and, by discounting the impact of superficial aspects—the "scenery"—and by probing to discover and plot the underlying structure—the "geology"—of the territory called capitalism through which we are traveling, draws some cogent and innovative conclusions. Heilbroner's provocative essay suggesting probable developments in capitalism takes into account "new elements in our knowledge" which make current prognosis especially hazardous. It is a beautiful illustration of how a talented social-science thinker can increase comprehension of complex sociological realities by uncovering the significance inherent in their neglected but important aspects. Now that the cold war appears to be winding down it seems especially desirable that the reader secure for himself the insights and understanding this selection can provide regarding the complex interacting "family of systems" of sociopolitical-plus-governmental and economic forces we still call "capitalism."

Was ever a generation so uncertain about its destiny as our own? It seems to me that our foresight is indeed clouded in a way that sets us off from previous generations, at least those of fairly recent times. The cloudiness is not the result of our sheer ignorance—that is more or less a constant throughout history. It results rather from our knowledge. Not because we know too little, but precisely because we have learned too much, it has become singularly difficult to answer with assurance the question: Does capitalism have a future?

Anyone who presumes to discuss the outlook for capitalism, that is, must face the following disconcerting fact: The two most cogent predictions with regard to the future of capitalism have both been tried and found wanting. The first of these—never, perhaps, dominant within the Western world—has always provided a powerful current of thought for those who opposed capitalism. This is the theory, basically Marxian in origin, that capitalism is an inherently *self-destructive social order.*

Source: Robert Heilbroner, *World* 1, no. 6 (September 12, 1972): 27–30. Reprinted by permission of World Magazine, Inc. and the author.

Robert L. Heilbroner, economist and author of *The Worldly Philosophers,* is Norman Thomas professor of economics and chairman of the Economics Department of the Graduate Faculty of the New School for Social Research.

I need hardly say that history has not confirmed the seemingly irrefutable "logic" of this apocalyptic view of capitalism. Capitalism teetered in the United States and England, but it did not collapse; and with the exception of Russia, whenever capitalism underwent violent change, as in Germany and Italy, the direction of the movement was to the Right, not to the Left. Even more disconcerting to the believer in the Marxian drama, when the storm of fascism had passed, capitalism reemerged in excellent economic health, as witness the post-World War II histories of West Germany and Japan.

What happened to disconfirm the Marxian prognosis of the future of capitalism? Here we begin to encounter those new elements in our knowledge that make present-day prediction so difficult. The first such element is the realization that the industrial working class is not revolutionary in its temper.

Why did the doctrine of the inevitability of class war fail? The reasons are many. Primary, of course, is that the economic system did not collapse, so that the pressures of economic misery so vividly described by Marx were slowly alleviated. Next in importance is that the combined economic and technological pressures of an expansive capitalism did not serve to swell, but rather contracted, the numbers of the proletariat, opening the way for many to join the ranks of white-collar workers. As a result, the political temper and social outlook of the working class became progressively less "proletarian" and progressively more "bourgeois"—destroying as a further consequence the unity and discipline that Marx had expected of his revolutionary class. And not least in this array of causes must be placed the disillusion that gradually attached itself to the idea of socialism, as the harsh realities of Stalinism brought an end to the hope that the end of capitalism would usher in an instant transition to a new, classless society.

The second of the now-disproven predictions—this one far more widely believed in among Western societies—is the opposite of the first: namely, that some form of capitalism—call it ameliorative, or welfare, capitalism—could continue to sustain and extend its hegemony.

What do I mean when I say this has been disproven? Certainly not that capitalism is incapable of continuing its impressive record of economic growth. Certainly not that capitalism cannot improve the distribution of income, or its provision of social services. What I have in mind is something much more fundamentally shaking, especially for those who hope that the future can be discerned with clarity by projecting the economic trends of the present. *It is that economic success does not guarantee social harmony.*

Of all the elements of knowledge gained in the past generation I can think of none so radically challenging for the social theorist. Let me present as an instance the case of the United States. Had anyone in the 1930s been told that the U.S. Gross National Product in the early 1970s would surpass a trillion dollars—effectively *doubling* the real per capita income within the lifespan of the majority of the population then alive—I am sure he would have felt safe in predicting an era of unprecedented social peace and goodwill.

Yet that enormous economic change has taken place and social harmony has not resulted. Economic growth, in other words, did not prove the great solvent for social difficulties. The economic transformation from the conditions of the 1930s to those of the 1970s has not lessened the potential for racial disturbance, has not headed off the explosion of juvenile disorders, the widespread decay in urban amenities, or a serious deterioration in national morale. Indeed, growth has brought new problems, environmental and other. Nor has such an experience been confined to the United States. Unprecedented growth in France and Germany has not prevented violent outbreaks of dissatisfaction in those countries, particularly among the young. Nor have Sweden or England or the Netherlands—all countries in which real living standards have vastly improved and in which special efforts have been made to lessen the economic and social distance between classes—been spared a share of the expression of profound social discontents.

This inability of a "successful" capitalism to guarantee social harmony adds more than another neutral element of knowledge to our present uncertainty with regard to the future. I think it is fair to say that among the new evidences of social unrest—the drug culture, the cry for participatory democracy, the alienation of students, the new sexual morality, the retreat to the life of the commune—none is congenial with or supportive of those attitudes and behavior patterns on which capitalism has traditionally rested. It is possible, in other words, that we stand at the threshold of an era in which deep-seated changes in lifeways will undermine capitalism in a manner as fatal as the most dramatic proletarian revolution might do, although perhaps less rapidly or romantically.

Yet the fact that we cannot discern the road ahead does not mean that we are hopelessly lost. On the contrary, because we are forced to stop, we are in a position to do something that the motorist cannot—examine the ground beneath us and perhaps derive some better idea of the geology of the region in which we find ourselves. Now, the composition of this ground, which we will call "capitalism," is considerably different from the idea of it that underlay both the pessimistic and optimistic conceptions of the country through which we thought we were traveling. For in both the Marxian and the "liberal" views of capitalism—divergent as they might be otherwise—there was an important common belief. In both schools of thought, capitalism was formerly described as an economic system in which the means of production were privately owned and the marketplace regulated the main currents of economic activity. But that was not the important thing: *both the apocalyptic and the ameliorative views of capitalism saw the economic machinery of the system as dominant, and the political and social accoutrements as subordinate.*

To begin with, then, let us recognize that both views erected stereotypes of capitalism which ignored important aspects of reality. The Marxian concept of governments being "the executive committee of the bourgeoisie" failed to take into account the very wide latitude that, from the early nineteenth century, government was capable of applying to its task of attending to the interests of the economic ruling classes. And on the other side of the ideological divide, those who believed that the inherent economic tendencies of the system should be allowed to work themselves out with a minimum of political interference closed their eyes to the fact that the governing institutions have always intervened to maintain capitalism as a system in good working order—now stepping in to promote economic activity, now curbing excessive competition, now establishing certain social standards of safety and well-being.

Moreover it is also clear as we look back

over the history of capitalism, in particular since World War I, that the range and depth of government penetration into the economic process have undergone a slow, uneven, but in the end, decisive increase.

This fact has two important effects on our thinking. The first is that the rise of the political "superstructure" to a position of much greater equality with—indeed, perhaps superiority to—the economic base leads to ever greater uncertainty in our predictions. For whatever our belief as to the outcome of the economic mechanism of capitalism—whether, again, it be conceived as self-destructive or ameliorative—our ability to project a trajectory for that economic mechanism weakens when the economic machinery no longer works "by itself" but is continuously subject to political direction. Second and equally clear, the "politicization" of capitalism opens all predictions to the vagaries of the political process, or of social currents such as the changes in life-style to which I earlier referred—aspects of the social system with respect to which we possess no predictive capabilities whatsoever.

Yet with the disappearance of the old stereotypes of capitalism comes an awareness of other aspects of the system that may yet enable us to see some little distance into the surrounding gloom.

For instance, despite the persistence of private ownership of the means of production and the market, the system we call "capitalism" turns out in fact to be a *family of systems* capable of a very great variation in political and social (not to mention economic) performance: witness the guaranteed lifetime employment offered by the big Japanese corporations, and on the other hand, the near-indentured labor of the Union of South Africa; the highly developed welfare system of the United States; the "*dolce vita*" of Italy and the Calvinist atmosphere of Germany; the effective government of three language groups in Switzerland, and the extreme difficulties encountered in governing two language groups in Canada.

In the face of such a spectrum of political and social structures, it should be clear that it is no longer possible to declare with assurance what constitutes the "pure" model of capitalism. This is certainly not to say that this broad spectrum of capitalist societies does not display common problems or face similar challenges. But if social prognosis is to offer more than a mere wishful projection, it cannot predict how such problems and challenges will be met by arguing in terms of a stereotyped "capitalism" that never quite existed.

What, therefore, *do* capitalist societies have in common? I imagine that you think I will now recite a familiar list of ailments: inflation, unemployment, foreign exchange difficulties, competition, and the like. But the truth is I see little that can be forecast with regard to this so-standard range of capitalist ills other than that we will cope with them with about the same mixed results of success and failure as we now experience.

Instead, I wish to turn to quite a different set of problems: namely, the deleterious side effects of certain kinds of economic growth. We have all been aware for some time of the specific dangers posed by pollution-generating output. What we are only now becoming aware of is the possibility that pollution may pose a problem of such dire implications that only a global ceiling on production will assure our very survival.

We do not yet know whether drastic production limitations will in fact be imperative; that depends largely on our ability to develop technologies that will permit the detoxification of certain effluents, the recycling of scarce materials, the efficient use of low-grade minerals, etc. But it seems highly probable that within the lifetime of the present generation a degree of social control will have to be exercised over the level and composition of production that far exceeds anything now known in any capitalist country. Whether the basic institutions of the capitalist mechanism—private ownership of resources and plants, and the reliance on the market as a main instrument of allocation—would survive such a severe constraint is at least problematical.

But there is a second problem—of equal gravity and of perhaps more certain advent. This is the challenge of rising affluence. Economic well-being, however little it speaks to the question of social harmony and content, assuredly *does* bring one consequence: the ability of those who enjoy some degree of affluence to withstand the pressures which underlie the smooth operations of all capitalist and (although less publicized) all socialist systems. For, given the fact that most labor is still monotonous and unrewarding, there is only one answer to the question: "Why do men work?" It is: "Because they have to."

But as the general level of affluence rises, there is a corresponding slow decline in the brute necessity of a search for employment at any price or any place. Already in the United States we see the coexistence of large numbers of "unemployed" youths and unfilled jobs of menial kinds which in a former age would have been quickly filled, or the parallel rise of unemployment among women and unfilled opportunities for domestic labor.

It is no doubt a considerable triumph for a society to reach a level of general affluence at which the unemployed person no longer has to accept gratefully whatever dispensations the market makes available. But we must not hide from ourselves the price of this social victory. That price, very simply, is a vastly increased risk of social breakdown. The extreme vulnerability of all urbanized environments to work stoppages leaves us exposed to potential catastrophes whose foretaste has been felt in the United States (and elsewhere) when strikes of garbagemen have left city populations exposed to disease, strikes of teachers have allowed outbursts of juvenile misbehavior, strikes of air controllers have paralyzed transportation systems.

Societies have, of course, always been vulnerable to work stoppages if they lasted very long. But in the past, two factors militated against a real test of society's vulnerability. One was the concentration of the work force in the industrial sectors, where the effect of strikes—for example in steel or coal—was cushioned by the presence of inventories on which the public could subsist for a considerable time. And the second was the general poverty of most workers, which greatly hampered their staying power when on strike.

In the urbanized, increasingly affluent setting of today and tomorrow, these safeguards have been greatly weakened. No inventories can be accumulated of the vital social services that sustain city life. Meanwhile the staying power of the work force has been very greatly increased. What then will provide the social discipline once exerted by the harsh pressure of necessity? We do not know. Appeals to conscience and to patriotism, the bribe of ever-higher wages, the intervention of public agencies, the use of troops, the outright militarization of labor are all more than mere possibilities—they have already been used on more than one occasion. I cannot predict which measures will be used in the future by which nations, or what damage will be done to civil liberties or to the union movement as a result. I can only state that as industrial societies move to even higher levels of affluence, the economic pressures of the marketplace can no longer be counted on to provide its necessary labor as a matter of course.

Thus a consideration of the problems now facing the family of capitalisms brings one to a curious new perspective. More and more of the kinds of problems to which we find capitalism exposed reach over to affect socialism as well—by which I mean reach over to affect that family of societies that rests on an economic base of public ownership and planning.

Two such problems stand preeminently to the fore. One has to do with the common technologies that are used by all industrial societies, capitalist or socialist. By this I do not mean that there is one and only one way of making steel, electric power, or cloth. A considerable variation in production techniques can be observed from one country to the next. Yet in all industrialized countries, these processes have one characteristic in common—they are organized to achieve a more or less continuous flow of outputs. This in turn requires that there be a continuous flow of inputs, usually applied in the sequential form of mass production, as each commodity is gradually transformed from its original to its final state. Unlike the choice that seems to be available in the institutions of government, in social welfare practices, in lifestyle in general, when it comes to economic life, mature capitalism and mature socialism are both forced to use production "styles" whose resemblances to one another far outweigh their differences.

This observation is perhaps commonplace. But from it follow consequences of considerable importance. For the presence of a common style of production imposes a common "style" of social organization. The presence of huge units of production, each requiring internal order and external coordination with other huge units (or with final consumers), brings to all industrial societies a common scaffolding of control-mechanisms that surrounds the central structure of production itself. This scaffolding, visible as the ministries, the planning agencies, the corporate headquarters, the regulatory commissions of capitalist and socialist economies, constitutes the *economic bureaucracy* that is the counterpart of industrial production itself.

No doubt there is a vast deal of difference between the bureaucracy of a central planning board and that of a cartel or a conglomerate corporation. But one resemblance nevertheless seems crucial; *it is that the industrial process imposes on all who come into contact with it, labor and management alike, a necessity to coordinate efforts in ways that must be specified by an industrial bureaucracy.* I do not claim that industrial production cannot eventually be decentralized, democratized, personalized—only that efforts to achieve these ends will have to overcome the "imperatives" of mass production, and that this struggle will be no easier for socialist societies than for capitalist ones.

Another problem is the increasing necessity to establish effective social controls over the generation and application of science and technology in daily life. We are all aware that we have entered a new era of technological capability of which nuclear energy is only the most spectacular example. Genetic engineering, human transplants, the postponement of death, the conditioning of behavior through electrodes implanted in the brain—all these are either actualities or near-term possibilities for medical science. No less extraordinary are new developments or possibilities in the technology of personal surveillance, of weather-control, and still other areas.

What marks all technological change to some degree, marks these developments to an exaggerated degree. That is their capacity to work large-scale social change, often in directions that we distrust or fear. To control the effects of these technologies, perhaps to inhibit or forbid their application, will therefore become a major challenge—perhaps *the* major challenge—for governments of all advanced nations in the future, socialists no less than capitalists.

From what I have said it must be clear that I believe we can dimly discern something about the terrain over which *all* industrial societies will have to make their way. To be sure, this is a "prediction" of a very different kind from that which would tell us the turns and twists of the road on which any particular industrial society will travel. It is one thing to see the obstacles of technology or industrial organization, or the difficulties of ecology or affluence, and quite another to make the guess—for it can only be a guess—that Sweden will succeed and the United States fail, or vice versa; or that the family of socialist nations will surmount the obstacles, while the family of capitalist nations will not.

Capitalism throughout the world is still saddled with the obsolete privileges of inherited wealth, with the dubious force of acquisitiveness as a source of social morale, and with the problems of reconciling powerful vested interests with needed social policies. On the other hand, however, most advanced capitalist governments enjoy some experience with parliamentary forms of government and some subscription to civil rights and liberties. Thereby they provide themselves with channels that may facilitate the necessary restructuring of their economic institutions, and that may serve as safeguards against the abuse of political control.

On the socialist side, we find an array of nations that have the advantage of a socioeconomic system stripped of the mystique of the private "ownership" of the means of production and the presumed legitimacy of the uncontrolled workings of the market. On the negative side is the cumbersomeness of their present planning mechanisms, their failure to develop incentives superior to those of capitalism, and above all their still rudimentary realization of political freedom.

One last word. Throughout the globe, a long period of acquiescence before the fates is coming to an end. The passivity of the general run of men is waning. Where there was resignation there is now impatience. Where there was acceptance there is now the demand for control.

The end of acquiescence poses challenges to all societies, but perhaps in particular to those in which the silent operation of the marketplace has traditionally given rise to the illusion that society requires no controls. Thus I believe the ultimate challenge to the institutions, motivations, political structures, lifeways, and ideologies of capitalist nations is whether they can accommodate themselves to the requirements of a society in which an attitude of "social fatalism" is being replaced by one of social purpose. If this pronouncement is too imprecise for those who like their prophecies clearcut, at least it may offer consolation to those who see in such a vision the necessary stimulus to fight for the eventual attainment of a good society, be it capitalist or socialist.

Part VIII

Social Organization: Community and Ecology

67.

THE TALK IN VANDALIA

Joseph P. Lyford

Sociologists are interested not only in studying discrete groups, organizations, and institutions, but they are also interested in examining these entities as they function and interrelate within a more or less clearly defined geographical territory—a community. Although our attention today tends to focus on "urban communities," because of their increasing prominence in our society and their critical problems, we must not forget that many people still live in smaller communities—in fact, more than 40 percent of the U.S. population still live in communities of less than 10,000 (though they increasingly come under the influence of large urban centers). The following selection examines community life in one of these smaller cities. For many readers this description of Vandalia may seem like a visit to the nineteenth century—to a world that no longer exists. But millions still live in the "Vandalias" of this country and what is described here is rather typical of the kind and quality of interaction found in smaller communities today. A careful reading of this selection should provide a lively and realistic "feeling" for the meaning of the concept of community.

I

Judged by the map, the city of Vandalia (population 5,500) has a fine location. It lies across a junction of the Pennsylvania and the Illinois Central Railroads, appears to be the center of a crisscross of highways, and is on the edge of the Kaskaskia River, which winds its way diagonally downstate to the Mississippi. But the map reader will be deceived. The Kaskaskia, swollen and icy in winter, subsides by summertime into a winding trail of mud and snags; the new superhighways—Routes 40 and 70—pass by to the north, and the only concession by the Pennsylvania's "Spirit of St. Louis" is a raucous bellow as it hurtles through a cut in the center of town an hour before noon. The Illinois Central is more considerate. Occasionally a freight engine shunts back and forth a few blocks outside of town to pick up some crates from one of the small factories along the tracks. "No trains stop here," the stationmaster says. The indifference of the railroads to Vandalia is paid back in full by the town's oldest practicing Democrat, eighty-eight-year-old Judge James G. Burnside. "We don't pay any at-

Source: Joseph P. Lyford, *A Report to the Center for the Study of Democratic Institutions* (Santa Barbara, Calif.: The Center for the Study of Democratic Institutions, 1962), abridged. Reprinted by permission of The Center for the Study of Democratic Institutions.

Joseph P. Lyford has been a reporter and freelance writer. He now teaches journalism at the University of California at Berkeley and is consultant for the Center for Democratic Institutions in Santa Barbara.

tention to the railroads any more," he remarks. "They're just passing acquaintances."

A train traveler from the East can alight at Effingham, thirty miles away, trudge through the snow to the Greyhound Post House, and take the 1:30 P.M. bus, which is always overdue. The driver does not smile when along with a St. Louis ticket he gets a request for a stopover in Vandalia, which means that the express bus has to make a ten-minute detour off the main highway. Route 40 runs straight and flat as a tight ribbon through wide umber plains sheeted with winter rain, past farmhouses four or five to the mile. For a few hundred feet at a time the road will stagger and pitch slightly as the land wrinkles into prairie, creek, and brushwood; then it subsides again to a level as monotonous as the roar of the bus. The seesawing pump of an occasional oil well is the only motion in the fields on a rainy day. There are a few crossroads villages, then the town of St. Elmo, and, finally, a few miles along Alternate Route 40, the city of Vandalia, once the western terminus of the Cumberland Road, capital of Illinois from 1819 to 1839, seat of Fayette County, and country of Abraham Lincoln of the House of Representatives of the State of Illinois.

The Evans is the taller, hotter, and more impressive of the town's two hotels. A fourth-story room offers a view of the magnificent old state house on the common, a tall-windowed white building, now a museum, where Stephen A. Douglas and Lincoln met with their fellow legislators more than a century ago. The first-floor windows are not too far from the ground to have prevented a long-legged politician from swinging his leg over the sill when he wanted to make a quick exit. The town's second most noticeable monument is a huge, sand-colored statue of a pioneer woman who gazes down Gallatin Street's rows of two-story buildings, parking meters, vertical signs over a Rexall Drug Store and the Evans Hotel, past a pair of banks standing face to face at the main intersection, and, finally, across the tracks to the Eakin Hotel, the County Courthouse on the hill, and one of Vandalia's many churches.

Robert O. Hasler points out that the town has thirteen churches and ten lawyers. It is his business to know odd statistics because he is president of the Chamber of Commerce. He is handy to the main source of such information because his office is in the Town Hall just above the city clerk. Some time ago Hasler prepared a typewritten economic profile which begins, "Vandalia, centrally located in the heart of the Midwest, is seventy miles from St. Louis, ninety-five miles west of Terre Haute, 245 miles southwest of Chicago . . . total labor force of county, 7,778, unemployed 276, self-employed 738, oil production 536. . . ." Under the heading of "Resources of Transportation" appears the information that on the Pennsylvania and IC railroads goods are "in transition" from Chicago, St. Louis, and Indianapolis – a politic way of saying that Vandalia is a way station. The figures on the sheets are from 1959, but Hasler says this is not a serious matter. "Things around here don't change very much from one year to another."

The township of Vandalia is grouped in three economic units. On its outer ring are the farms, the town's main support, ranging from sixty or eighty acres to several hundred, the average being somewhere in the middle. The chief crops are corn, soybeans, and livestock – mainly hogs and cattle. The land is worked with modern machinery by farmers who combine their own land with leased acreage – as much as they can get.

On the western edge of town are four factories, which employ altogether about 850 people. They are the Princess Peggy dress factory; United Wood Heel, manufacturers of heels for women's shoes; the Johnson, Stephens and Shinkle shoe factory (the largest single employer with a work force of 475), and the Crane Packing Company, which turns out mechanical seals for automobiles, machines, appliances, etc.

At the core is the town itself—the stores, the banks, professional offices, churches, schools, filling stations, garages, plus the Elk, Mason, Moose, Odd-Fellow and Legion Halls, the Town Hall and County Courthouse, one movie theatre, restaurants, and nine of the only taverns in a county noted for its religion and its aridity. Vandalia's supermarkets are big and modern; its dry-goods stores range from the antique-looking Fidelity Clothiers to the Hub Department Store which has quality merchandise at New York prices. Only one commercial establishment—Radliff's Pool Parlor—remains open for business seven days a week. The local newspaper plant is built of yellow brick and houses the editorial staff of two weekly papers, the *Union* and the *Leader*. Most of the business district lies south of the Pennsylvania tracks except some hardware and feed stores, the Farm Bureau offices, and a cleaning establishment. On the north side of town the streets are lined with small frame houses, and a few large and attractive Victorian homes. Some blocks further out are the new County Hospital, the million-dollar Vandalia High School which is the community's pride, and a new development of luxurious, ranch-type homes. Beyond the high school is the intersection of Route 51 out of town and Route 40, which has given rise to a cluster of motels, restaurants, and filling stations. To the west lie the factories and on the far side of Shoe Factory Hill, along the Pennsylvania Railroad, are patches of dilapidated wooden dwellings which make up the hopeless part of town. To the east is the Kaskaskia River. The southern part of town peters out rather quickly a few blocks below the Post Office and the white frame house which is the home of Charlie Evans.

When he is not in the front parlor of his home, which he uses as his office, Mr. Evans is in the lobby of the Evans Hotel. He built the hotel in 1924, and, along with a hardware business and various real estate dealings, it made him probably the richest man in Vandalia. Last year, his eighty-first, the $106,000 library he gave to the town opened its doors. "We were a money-saving family, all of us," he says. "We're Welsh by descent. I was never a man to sell, I always bought and added to it. When I sold the hotel I'd been saving all the time. I guess I'd saved too much. I didn't have any use for the money, so I built the library. When I built it, I didn't try to cut corners. I didn't try to save as if I was building for myself."

Mr. Evans leans back, and crosses his arms when he talks about his town. "This is a historic city. When they moved the capital from here to Springfield in 1839, our population was only 400. We've gained a little bit all the time. Population-wise we've never had a setback. We've never had a boom. We held our ground. A big percentage of people own their own homes, including a lot who work at the factory. This makes us a good town for a factory. The companies know our workers are not fly-by-nighters. Their employees are here to stay. They have money invested in our town. Homes today build from $12,000 to $18,000, and we have a good building and loan program. Banks will lend money to anybody here who wants to build a building. We have good, sound, sincere bankers. Back in the late 20's, when people were trying to buy more and more land for their farms, the bankers warned them against it. When the crash came, we weren't so badly off as some. We had hard times in 1932, oh mercy.

"I think the town is going to develop pretty well. Rental housing is pretty scarce. The homes here are good ones, and people have made substantial payments on them. I don't know what we're going to have to do to keep our young people here, though. When they go to the city, they don't come back. They want new people to get acquainted with. Industry might be the answer. We should have more opportunities for skilled workers. The Crane Packing Company has been very good. They have a training program for employees and they are expanding. The shoe factory is a shoe factory. Their idea is how much work you can get out of your help. It's as good a shoe factory as there is. It's a good town, but we have one bad problem. It's the farmers. The farmers are in trouble."

Evans is not the only person who worries about the Fayette County farmers. The townspeople think and talk a great deal about them these days. They have always depended on them in the past, and they are no longer sure of them. The uncertainty may explain why the business of farming, traditionally honored in the State of Illinois as an independent way of life, is undergoing rapid sanctification. Probably more speeches are delivered at Kiwanis and Rotary clubs on the virtues and contributions of the tillers of the soil than on any other single subject; it is also the favorite topic of the county's political circuit-riders during campaign season. The community's businessmen prepare banquets in honor of local agriculture; the Junior Chamber of Commerce's first big dinner of 1962 was held to proclaim Siebert Hoover the "Outstanding Young Farmer of the Year" and present him with tickets to a Miami or New York vacation. Agricultural experts from the University of Illinois and the Department of Agriculture, armed with pamphlets on fowl disease and hog pest, crisscross the territory with advice on all phases of scientific farming. Secretary of Agriculture Freeman's emissaries from Washington are available to discuss the farm program at the smallest gatherings. The Farm Bureau offices have special classrooms where experts lecture local farmers and their wives on the economics of farm management. And, in contrast to the days of the Great Depression in other parts of the nation, the banker and the farmer maintain friendly, interdependent relations throughout Southern Illinois. The two bank presidents in Vandalia talk about farmers as if they were business partners and mutual allies under attack by the rest of the nation's economic interests.

The popularity of the farmer in the abstract has not always thawed out farmers in particular, some of whom still harbor ancient resentments against the town. (One farmer says he wants his children to stay in the rural schools because Vandalians think that "farm kids still piss on stumps and never heard of inside plumbing.") But many of the farmers seem to feel closer to the town than before the war, partly because of the knowledge that a lot of other people besides farmers are involved in their economic troubles, and partly because the farmers' own social life has become more and more interlaced with the life of the town. As the one-room rural schoolhouses have dwindled, over the farmers' opposition, from three dozen in the school district to a half dozen, farm mothers have become members of the PTA's of the Washington, Lincoln, and Central elementary schools. There is more talk in the homes of educational problems jointly shared with the townspeople.

Those farmers who work in the factories – "Saturday farmers," J. B. Turner, the county farm agent, calls them – have a growing association with nonfarmers, and some even join labor union locals in the shoe and heel factories. Also, the growing cost of running a farm because of the new machinery required and the rising prices of land have increased the extent of the farmer's dependence on local financial institutions. The farmers buy more and more of their food locally – most of them have disposed of their dairy cows and buy their milk at the Tri-City Supermarket and the A&P. The farmer's machinery is repaired by local mechanics. Feed-dealer Norman Michel, who carries as many as 21,000 people on his credit rolls, is a farmer's banker in his own way. Vandalia shapes its commercial activities to suit the farmers' tastes, and the farmer, his wife and children, and his trucks are a regular part of the scenery on Gallatin Street. This is not to say that the town has been taken over by the farmers: in one sense it is the farmers who have changed their habits and tastes – even in dress – to fit the town.

The farmer has responded in other ways to the town. He participates more in local events. He comes more to the city's churches. One outstanding farmer is chairman of the school district's Board of Education. Many of the more prosperous farm families contribute their women's time to fund drives. The high school's football and basketball teams are getting a little more help from the farm youngsters who used to shy away from extracurricular activities after the last school bell. One still hears complaints from the townspeople that the farmer is hard to reach, but he is less and less remote.

. . . . . .

II

It would be misleading to say that Vandalia takes everything in its stride, because "stride" implies a measured forward movement which has never been a community characteristic. It is also inaccurate to take the community's easygoing manner at face value. Its calm demeanor is sometimes achieved at the cost of suppressing grave internal discontents. Nevertheless, the atmosphere is rarely charged with the type of emotional storms that test the tempers of New York or Chicago suburbanites. The political fracases that periodically rock a Westport, Connecticut, to its foundations, setting commuter against ancient inhabitant, are unknown. Public controversies usually do not get past the stage of fairly low-pressure arguments over personalities or such transient irritations as disintegrating sidewalks and sheriffs. Candidates do not run for municipal office, they file for it, on ballots that do not mention party affiliations. The only lively competition recently was for the job of county sheriff, but the plenitude of aspirants was attributed to a rise in the unemployment rate, adding considerable glamour to the sheriff's $5,000 yearly stipend. The community blood pressure is unaffected by animosities between Republican and Democrat. County administrations alternate between the two with regularity, and the towns do not even have local political organizations.

The campaign for mayor is not usually one of Vandalia's most exciting events.

Last year's canvass was enlivened somewhat when one candidate promised that, if elected, he would fire the police chief. The reformer was elected, but the police chief is still police chief, and there have been no outraged cries from the electorate about broken campaign promises. It is understood that it is pretty hard for a mayor of Vandalia to fire anybody. It is also generally known that Norman Michel didn't really have his heart set on being mayor, anyway. Although he refrains, out of civic pride, from saying so publicly, there is reason to believe that he considers the mayor's job a trivial and unremunerative demand on time that could have been better spent handling the complicated affairs of a successful feed and grain business. In return for enduring the burdens of the town's highest administrative office, Michel receives $1,200 yearly, considerably less than the earnings of each member of the two-man squad that issues from the Town Hall each day to empty nickels from the parking meters. The mayor's perquisites include neither a black limousine nor office space in the Town Hall.

A discussion with Michel in the back office of his feed store is not highly productive of information relating to any riddles and emergencies that may afflict the community. A heavyset, agreeable man, he frankly states that the main function of the mayor seems to be to sign checks. In addition to this activity, Mr. Michel "works with the Chamber of Commerce and other civic organizations when they want my help." Recently he played an important part in the town's successful effort to induce the Ralston Purina Company, feed manufacturers, to set up a new plant in Vandalia to replace one that had burned down in East St. Louis. The mayor also feels that he ought to "check complaints that come in," but this is a full-time job, certainly not one to be discharged by someone whose feed business has a gross income larger than the town's entire annual general budget. The mayor also runs meetings of the City Council (he has never been an alderman himself, or held political office of any sort), attended by aldermen who are paid $20 per meeting. One such meeting recently authorized an aviation photography outfit in St. Louis to photograph land on Bear Creek, where Vandalia hopes to create a lake for a new water supply. The Kaskaskia River has become so polluted with factory-discharged chemicals that treatment by the town waterworks is becoming prohibitively expensive. Another problem that has agitated the City Council was a degree of local indignation over stray dogs. In the absence of a definite policy on this matter, Marie Bennett, the city clerk, told irate telephoners that the best way to handle the mess was to lock up all dogs, homeless or not, until things blew over.

Michel admits that he ran for mayor because "they couldn't get anybody else." Such a basis of selection has been fairly traditional for many years. Nominations for political leadership are bestowed somewhat as they were in certain primitive societies, on persons who are the least skillful at evading the designation. Even lawyers have to be dragooned into running for court positions. An elective post in Vandalia is barren of power, of financial return, and of prospects for subsequent improvement. Given such a situation, the townspeople regard the biennial struggle to seize control of the Town Hall with only a faint display of emotion.

The columns of the *Leader* and the *Union* mirror the general unconcern with politics. Some of this editorial anaemia comes from a slightly stuffy sense of responsibility which dates back to when the Democratic *Leader* acquired the Republican opposition, the *Union.* Charles Mills, the tall, white-haired editor of the two papers, and one of the most overworked men in town, says that "ever since the opposition was bought out, we have had to realize that when we say something unpleasant about someone, he has no other place to go. We have to present both sides of everything. We think we've got an obligation to promote good activities and criticize bad ones regardless of the politics."

. . . . .

III

Lawyer Martin Corbell's comments about the lack of culture in Vandalia are comparatively mild. A school teacher, repeating the views of most of her associates, says, "Let's face it, the place is a desert." The teacher is not exactly exaggerating. The local entertainment palace, the Liberty Theatre, exhibits only the most excruciatingly fourth-rate films, although distribution syndicates, rather than the Liberty's owner, Herman Tanner, may be the real culprit. The town does not have any concert series, theatrical groups, or local FM radio. Vandalians like Corbell can find the theatre, music, or a passable night club only in St. Louis, seventy miles away. The situation is, if anything, much worse for the teen-agers who have little chance to attend concerts or plays and a rather uneventful social life. High school athletic contests are one occasion on which the young people get together, although the usual Midwestern custom of dances after a basketball game does not seem to have caught on. The chief amusement spots are Nevinger's roller-skating rink and a bowling alley across from the high school. Those who want to dance have to go as far afield as Effingham to do it.

Some time ago, a group of high school seniors, frustrated at the lack of a social center, found themselves a small hall and proceeded to decorate it, with ideas of installing a juke box, coke machine, and ping-pong table. But "Teen Town" collapsed when the minister of the First Baptist Church told the young people in his congregation to stay away. For the most part, the common substitute for something to do is for a gang to pile into a car and drive a traditional circuit in and about town, down Gallatin Street, around in the Kroger Parking lot, back up Gallatin, then out Route 51 to Route 40 to stop for a hamburger, then back on the raceway. Saturday night on Vandalia's main thoroughfare is a steady stream of flap-fendered vehicles, hot rods, and family sedans traveling in both directions and honking at familiar cars going in the opposite direction. The effect is weird in a town where, except for the taverns and a couple of coffee shops, everything closes up tight early in the evening. "Where are they going?" one wonders. A young driver might answer, "Nowhere. But we're under way."

Some persistent souls have attempted to invigorate the town, not without resistance, but then again not without success. Many years ago, Anna Ruth Kains, an English and voice teacher at Vandalia High School, undertook a crusade on behalf of good music. She assembled a choral group. "We got together some nice high school girls—Catholics, Methodists, Pentecostals, and a Jewish girl, among others. We thought we'd offer our voices for Lent." The idea worked well for a while. Several congregations heard some well-trained singers, and the girls discovered something about the insides of churches other than their own. Before long, however, Mrs. Kains's effort foundered on the objections of a Lutheran pastor who wanted young Lutheran ladies in his own church if they were going to be in any church on Sunday.

Mrs. Kains had another go, this time at the formation of a group to sing the Messiah during the Christmas season. She was told by almost everyone that the town wouldn't care much for that sort of thing, but she persisted. A place to practice was not easy to find. One Methodist church turned Mrs. Kains down because the elders had just installed a new red carpet and "they didn't want the singers tracking it all up." But finally the Messiah was presented at the Presbyterian Church and was a tremendous success. Later Messiahs drew so many listeners that the audience spilled out into the street and onto the railroad bridge a few yards from the main entrance of the church. So the Messiah moved to bigger quarters. It is now presented on an improvised stage in the gymnasium of the high school, which has no auditorium. The Messiah has become a Christmas institution.

Mrs. Kains also created a musical disturbance in the high school. She asked the superintendent if the glee club, then a rather sickly organization compared to the band, could sing at graduation exercises. Previously graduation had always been held in church, with choral offerings presented by a church group. "After all, if we were going to have a glee club, we had to have something to get ready for." Permission was granted and the glee club has prospered. Mrs. Kains related that in the beginning the band had sixty-five members and the glee club seventeen, while now glee club membership is up to 100 and the band has shriveled to thirty or thirty-five. "Everybody in school who can carry a tune has a chance to sing."

Significant cultural stirrings are also noticeable in the public library donated last year by Charles Evans. A Friends of the Library group has opened an art gallery in what had originally been designed as the Historical Society Room. The shows have been well attended, featuring the work of high and elementary school students, and some of the more practiced adults. This summer the library scheduled a traveling exhibit from New York City's Museum of Modern Art. Vandalians were well accustomed to abstractions by the time the show arrived, since a sizable percentage of local art work leans to the nonobjective. Some credit for this tendency should go to a young art teacher, Bob Barker, who teaches drawing and painting to nearly forty adults in evening classes at the high school.

The library itself has a store of 15,000 volumes, larger than most collections in many bigger and wealthier communities. The library compensates in part for the fact that Vandalia has no bookstore at all. The only local establishment that sells anything above the cheap paper-back level is a local photographic supply house. In defense of Vandalia's reading habits, Mrs. Kitty Kelley, the librarian, reports that Vandalia's average circulation of six books a year per person is four or five times the national average.

. . . . .

Despite the energetic efforts of such people as Mrs. Kains, the Friends of the Library, the town's two librarians, some local teachers, and a few others, it is doubtful if anything but a major upheaval is going to improve the generally doleful character of Vandalia culture. There are some citizens who think a community college might do the trick, and that its establishment is a practical possibility. The college would play many roles. It would bring some higher education within reach of many high school graduates who, for academic or financial reasons, cannot go away to college but who could attend school and work part time while living at home. If, as has been suggested, the college provided training in vocational skills it might become a source of skilled labor that would attract industrial plants considering location in the Fayette County area. In addition, a college adult education program could stimulate whatever latent intellectual resources the town may have. The entry of a new teaching group into community life could make things more attractive to the town's professional people. The high school principal, William Wells, feels that the daily demonstration of a college program would not be lost upon high school students making their own plans for the future. Important people are interested. One, not surprisingly, is Harry Rogier. Others are members of the Board of Education, John Hegg, superintendent of the Crane plant, local ministers like Ralph Smith and Archie Brown. Charles Evans says he would "like to help." The nearby towns of Centralia and Effingham are talking about the community college idea, too. Vandalians don't like to take a back seat to anybody else, so they may just decide to do something about it. After all, Wells says, the town built three factories, why can't it build a college?

. . . . . .

IV

Even such a caustic commentator as Father Gribbin agrees that Vandalia's school system, despite some drawbacks, is a good one. The townspeople are particularly proud of the yellow, two-story high school on the edge of town, built in 1950. For the 500 students there are twenty-seven teachers, and the average class size is eighteen to twenty pupils, considerably less than the averages for the town's less modern elementary schools. With its gleaming corridors, bright, well-equipped classrooms, vast gymnasium, the high school is the most impressive building in the community. In the back of the high school a new one-story shop addition, built with a recent bond issue of $175,000, is nearing completion.

One might expect to find that the principal of the high school was an expansive, cheery man inclined to mellow comments about "what we are trying to do here." No such description would fit Bill Wells. He is slender, dark, bespectacled. He speaks quickly, with an air of preoccupation, and sometimes rubs his forehead in perplexity. He has been principal of the high school for eleven out of his twenty-one years in the Vandalia school system. Whatever satisfactions he may feel about his establishment are buried under his immediate concerns about the future of his students. It takes him little time to get across his points.

"Many pupils in the high school come from families with only a ninth or tenth grade education. Many of these are farm families. It's surprising how many of the parents never graduated from high school. The understanding of what an education means and what an educational system needs isn't something that comes easily to the people of our community. We have been lucky to have good leadership to help bring this about. We have to do things one at a time. We have to vote an addition to a school, then an appropriation for another school, then an appropriation for a shop.

"So far we have come along fairly well.

But, believe me, we have problems. Our college-bound group is facing a much tougher life in college than they have in the past. Colleges are getting more difficult, the competition to get in is much greater. This means that at one end we have to give our students better preparation all the time. Yet we are not able to hold on to our best teachers. Good new teachers get a little training here and then they leave when they get an offer to go some place else where they can make from $500 to $2,500 more a year. We lose two or three of our best teachers every year to the northern communities, the Chicago suburbs for instance.

"There is a great problem of how to finance our educational system here and it is getting worse. It is going to be tough in the next ten years. I think federal aid is so important. We've got to face the fact that in order to keep our teachers we've got to raise their salaries so that we don't have this great disparity with northern Illinois. And if we don't have these teachers, God help our college-bound kids. Can we keep getting another boost of money from the community? We're near the upper limit of our tax rate, which is fixed by law, and I don't know what we are going to do if we have to jump the tax rate—raise that tax limitation.

"Our kids do keep going on to college. We've been able to put about 30 percent of each class, even as high as 40 percent last year, into higher education. This is a good record, particularly when so many families don't have a college background. The parents do encourage them, much of the time. We have real problems with the students who don't go to college, the ones who are going through the vocational program. We know what automation is doing. There are fewer and fewer jobs for ditch-diggers, farmers, and factory workers, people who do semiskilled work. What happens to the children who drop out of our schools and who take the kind of vocational training that prepares them for jobs that are not going to exist much longer?"

. . . . .

V

Although Vandalia may be suffering from other shortages, it is well supplied with churches. A process of simple division reveals that there is one church to every 400 people in town. The townspeople not only join the town's thirteen churches but attend them regularly and support them generously. Like other towns in the "Bible Belt" of Southern Illinois, the churches have always been at the center of the community's life. Therefore, it is not surprising that Vandalia's clergymen should, as a group, be articulate and informed commentators about their community. More than any other group they have accepted the responsibility to be part of almost every phase of community life, and should they ever lose sight of this fact, their parishioners are quick to remind them. On their part, the ministers do not hesitate to lay about them with a sharp tongue whenever they feel a little castigation is appropriate.

Perhaps the most colorful minister in town is the Reverend Henry Allwardt, pastor of the Holy Cross Lutheran Church, with a membership of 300. He lives in a one-story white frame house at some distance from his church, which is north of town near the high school. A tall, bespectacled man with a very thick shock of shining white hair, he works at a big oak desk covered with books and papers. After preaching in Ohio, Wisconsin, and Michigan and serving as a Navy chaplain in

World War II, he came to Vandalia three years ago.

Mr. Allwardt begins with what is almost a standard opening to a Vandalian's conversation:

There are several classes of people in the community. There are quite a few of the self-satisfied old-timers, a lot of them have good businesses and so forth, then there is a certain element, not as big as it is in some communities, of what I would call the decent, driven cattle. There is a kind of nice social life here, it's the best I've seen in a lot of ways. There is a certain amount of scandal, but on the whole things are pretty decent. I would rate it as a relatively pretty churchly town, not untypical of the communities in this area, and I've been around quite a bit. I haven't lived exactly in a locked trunk. I've been a pastor in the dead of the country, also in a big city like Detroit. A lot of people who behave very well in a small town like this fall away from the church when they get to the big city. It's not an entirely unprogressive community. The Chamber of Commerce has done good work getting plants here, for instance the heel factory. Vandalia is a lot better than the last place I was in, which was Arenzville. I also had a church in Marysville, Ohio. We had a 100-year-old church, and it seemed like most of the people in it must have been charter members.

What was wrong with Arenzville? "Why, everybody up there was so envious of everybody else. There was so darned much hatred. The stores would stay open even on Christmas for fear somebody else would sell something. The population was about 500. It was predominantly a German community. When you get into a German community you should understand the history of Germany if you want to understand the people; for instance, whether they come from north or south Germany. Then you have to understand why their ancestors came to America. The people in Arenzville came here because they thought they were going to get rich. Their standards were quite materialistic. For instance, they didn't know a thing about baking cookies on Christmas. You'd never find that going on in Arenzville.

. . . . .

I have a lot of Germans in my congregation. They came to Vandalia for quite a different reason from the Arenzville people. They came because the churches of Germany did not allow decent Lutheran preaching. Our Lutherans were in constant trouble over there because the State was trying to foist all manner of practices on the church that they didn't agree with. The Germans in this area came for what the Pilgrims claim they came for. And, by the way, the Pilgrims came because they wanted to be the dominant church. They are the most intolerant people who ever came here. It's too bad the Plymouth rock didn't land on them instead of the other way around. Our people wanted separation of church and state. They wanted a church that could operate unhampered. One of the troubles with our synod, however, was that our people were rather timid. They came in here with a church that was relatively unknown west of the Alleghenies. They were also a foreign-language church, and they felt that they had to feel defensive about this. But in a hundred years, since we organized our synod, which was in 1847, we've gone from twenty to 4,000 congregations in this area. St. Louis has the largest seminary in the world. We're busy in other countries too. We have eighty-three radio stations in Japan.

What's that about the social activities of the church? I've got you, I'm a jump ahead. You mean, what does the average layman expect of church and what does he do in church? Well, that gets me into one thing. Theology is getting to be sociology these days, which means that a lot of people when they get in the pulpit feel they should never say anything that could be understood. The only trouble with most churches is their pastors. The pulpit has departed so far from what it is here for it isn't even funny. Why do I want to go to church to listen to lectures on prohibition and world affairs? What business has a minister got talking about matters that 30 percent of his congregation know a lot more about than he does? My responsibility to my congregation is to teach the word of God, and if I happen to have some screwball opinions I'll keep them to myself. That's why we have pastoral conferences, to get ourselves unscrewed, we pastors. Another responsibility I have is to live like a Christian gentleman, and I also have the responsibility to bring children into the church with some understanding of it. The church is not a social club.

The trouble with a lot of churches is that the Catholic Church is good for people who want soul insurance and the Protestant Church spends most of its time adding a mellifluous odor to the prevailing winds. Pastors ought to mind their own business and stick to their own responsibilities. Another job of the minister is to comfort and help the sick. This is his duty. You go to such a person when you're needed. You may have an opening with a sick person that you may never have again to bring him into the church and an understanding of God.

I try to instill in the young people the desire to 'seek ye the Kingdom of God in his righteousness.' In these unsettled times this is the job of the church. I think my young people have pretty good moral character. You can't know too easily what they're striving for. The boys especially, though, seem to be serious-minded. The girls don't seem to have anything to talk about but boys when they get into high school.

You ask about material gain, whether that's what people want instead of helping the community. I'll give you a thousand dollars if you can find three people in any community who aren't looking for material gain. Everybody is after it. Everybody all the way up to the President. Everybody is after what he can get.

. . . . .

The corporation of Vandalia is an aggregate of people and properties, but as a community it is nothing more or less than a single idea, very personal and private, in the mind of each of its citizens. Perhaps someone could draw a composite face of all of them if he were to tailor his questions carefully, but there would be no features in the face. Vandalia is not a place to find a "community attitude," which is probably what Judge Burnside means when he makes the remark, "We're not any special sort of a town. People come here from all over," silently adding that this is where their ideas come from, too.

If the people of Vandalia are not entirely unlike other Americans, there may be some importance in the conclusion that they do not have established sets of ideas, even though they may observe fairly rigid rules of social conduct and share a common vocabulary of stock phrases. It can be argued that this is not a discovery, that it is obvious, and that the people of no community—not even in Puritan New England—ever really had a set of standard thoughts, no matter how total the conformity was on the surface. Even if this argument is granted, the people of Vandalia hardly fit into the Main Street folklore which has been built up around the rural Midwestern town. At least when they are pressed they express self-criticism and lively dissent, and anyone who expects to hear them talk like the people of Sinclair Lewis's Sauk Center will either have to ignore half of what he hears or take charge of the conversations and drive them in the direction he believes they ought to take.

The talks in Vandalia do not support the American myth that a rural town today is a landlocked island inhabited by people who share an abiding complacency with each other. There are the surface appearances of unity and its concomitant sterility in Vandalia, and the appearances are sometimes overwhelming. But they do not persist in the face of its own citizens' conflicting testimony. Vandalians today are in some ways in a better position to observe and to feel, sometimes most painfully, the consequences of a changing society than the suburbanite who lives in a bedroom town or the city dweller who hears about the world mainly from his newspaper and who enjoys the protective layers afforded him by his corporation, his union, and his various other institutional affiliations. There is also a special urgency in the air of Vandalia. A town on the edge of Chicago, Los Angeles, or New York City is forced to deal with the problems of sudden and uncontrolled growth, but Vandalia is beset by the much more desperate problem of how to hold on to what it has in order to survive.

Security is not one of the values the

townspeople attach to living in their community. Vandalia families cannot be certain about the future of their community or even their ability to remain in it. The favorable employment statistics in the Chamber of Commerce's brochure do not veil the fact that jobs now held are in constant danger of disappearing, whether they are in the factory, farm, or local store, and that a great percentage of them cannot support a family or offer any hope for advancement. The family that wants to remain in Vandalia, far from being insulated from the tensions and threats of the outer world, is resisting economic, social, and technological forces that could break the community apart and send the pieces flying in all directions.

Whereas many Americans live in or around the great cities unwillingly because that is where the jobs are, Vandalians live in their town because they want to. Their reasons are not new, but they have an added poignancy because the things these people value are becoming harder to hold on to. They like the freedom of association and personal trust they do not believe can be found in a large city. They hope to maintain a school system in which their children receive a common educational experience in small classes with good teachers. Perhaps, as William Deems says, there is something unhealthy about the way Vandalians meet each local problem with a fund drive; nevertheless, they esteem the relationships with each other that make such solutions practicable.

There are many reasons why a man stays in Vandalia when, as Joe Dees puts it, "he could get the paid vacations and fringe benefits in the city," and most of them recur over and over in the talks. Underlying them all seems to be a desire to be able to know the whole of one's town, to be "some kind of a somebody" in it, to be able to circulate in it freely, and to be part of a social arrangement where there are certain justified assumptions about how people will deal with each other. On a freezing day, Mrs. Mark Miller is operating under one of these assumptions when she asks the postmaster who has just sold her some stamps to call a taxi for her. There is nothing trivial about the transaction.

Vandalia's lawyers and doctors and farmers and teachers and businessmen have their difficulties in talking about what they believe themselves and their community to be. Some of their trouble comes from an unconscious absorption of many of the standard myths about small-town complacency, neighborliness, Godliness, stupidity, provincialism, loyalties, unity, freshness. A tale heard often enough sometimes becomes part of the conversation, and a Vandalian does not usually speak of his community without himself introducing some of the stereotyped criticisms. The view that talks with people in their own environment will dispel the myth of their environment can be misleading.

Despite all their advertised contact with their fellow human beings, many Vandalians seem to do much of their thinking in isolation. Perhaps it is because their problems are so closely bound up with personal relationships that many of them are less inclined to speak openly about them. In a community where almost everyone knows everyone else by name and face, and converses with ease and frequency, the citizens for the most part exchange commonplaces. Dan Hockman, a high school history teacher, describes the situation when he says, "People here are interested in what other people are up to, not in what they think." With all their togetherness—the word is not used with disdain—there are many, many isolated people in the community. Sometimes the isolation is by choice. Alenia McCord says apologetically, "We have our standards and we tend to be a little intolerant of other people if they don't agree with us, but we don't try to railroad our standards on others. If somebody doesn't come up to our standards that's all right just as long as they keep a long distance away from us." More often, however, the isolation is neither sought nor enjoyed. Conversations on the most affecting personal and intellectual matters are given freely—to the outsider who asks for them—but when the conversations end, sometimes after many hours of intense exchange, the conclusion is very often a wish that it might happen again and a remark that it almost never happened before.

Perhaps the absence of serious talk with others in their community explains why so many of the townspeople combine their own inner guesses with mixtures of the prevalent myths, and thereby supplement the myths. There are many remarks about the curse of complacency in the town and, taken together, the people who are disturbed about it make up a sizable portion of the population. But, like the Reverend Ralph Smith, they are really annoyed at the nature of the peace, not the peace itself, at the inertia that seems to be responsible for the lack of conflict and motion in the community. If the inertia proceeds from smugness and total satisfaction with the past, anything Mr. Smith has to say in criticism of "Peaceful Valley" seems relatively mild. But if the inertia grows out of confusion and bewilderment, and the clinging to tradition is done in desperation, then Mr. Smith is being harsh, because the peace in the valley is a troubled one.

It is strange to discover that an assembly of people who live together with a decency unheard of in a large city, and whose community efforts have been astonishingly successful, should at the same time lack the sort of serious communication with each other that would seem to be the basis of democratic life. The potential exists. Vandalia has an unusual assortment of sensitive and informed people. They have opinions, ideas, tempers. They would like to make their town better. But, given this, there is a reticence on important matters that is forbidding, and a lack of a forum—a New England style town meeting, for instance—in which regular discussions could proceed.

In some ways, Vandalians leave the impression that they are members of a family in which the main strength of the past has become a problem for the future. They have had the advantage of similar origins and close kinship, but perhaps so close that, as the family grows and disperses, too much of the dependency remains. And, like a family, they have lived and talked with each other steadily over the years but have kept their real thoughts and worries about each other inside. The old bonds that held Vandalia in a sort of perpetual stability are breaking. There are many departures from the family and few arrivals.

If there is to be a new way for the town, it has many assets which do not appear in Robert Hasler's typewritten town biography. Vandalia is not condemned to become a suburb of anything just yet, and it still has transportation facilities that can serve whatever new industrial establishments it may attract. One advantage of its unhurried history is that no huge defense plants have dropped down on the town to crush its character forever and then move on in a few years. Vandalia has natural beauties that make it a place apart. Few towns to the north have spreading elms and maples of such beauty, and in May there is the wild spring blaze of lilac and dogwood. The Kaskaskia is a navigator's nightmare now, but in a few years floodcontrol dams below and above Vandalia will reclaim much valuable farm land, and, not incidentally, provide fishing and boating for local boys and girls and out-of-state tourists.

Obviously, what happens in Vandalia depends on the people who will have to manage these assets, and what improvements they make in their present arrangements of organizing themselves and communicating with each other. One cannot really tell how they will do, even after talking to them for a long, long time. Affairs move slowly. But there are stirrings and there are contradictions. Judge Burnside says nobody pays any attention to the railroads. On the other hand, in his church by the railroad, Mr. Smith has to stop in the middle of his Sunday sermon when he hears the "Spirit of St. Louis" coming down the tracks.

68.

THE URBAN COMMUNITY . . . A CONVERSATION

Robert W. Glasgow and Herbert J. Gans

The preceding selection by Lyford describes the small town which serves its surrounding rural area. In this selection, Robert Glasgow discusses with Herbert Gans some of the issues in the contemporary urban community crisis—planning, poverty, political participation, power, and pluralism. The continuing urbanization of American society with an increasing proportion of the population in metropolitan areas has produced communities that con-

Source: Robert W. Glasgow, "The Ayn Rand Syndrome: A Conversation between Herbert Gans and Robert W. Glasgow," *Psychology Today* (March 1972).

Robert W. Glasgow is a contributor to many periodicals and is on the senior editorial staff of *Psychology Today.*

Professor of sociology at the Massachusetts Institute of Technology and senior associate at the Harvard-MIT Joint Center for Urban Studies, Herbert Gans is deeply involved in both of his major interests—sociology and planning. Along with many essays and articles, he is the author of *The Urban Villagers,* about urban renewal, and *The Levittowners.* He is completing a study of the news media.

trast sharply with the small town. As the following conversation reveals, we have not yet developed the social, economic, or political institutions to meet satisfactorily the human needs of this our urban population. Gans and Glasgow identify some of the major problems in urban communities and examine the role of social scientists in their solution.

ROBERT W. GLASGOW: Is it because you are both a professional planner and a sociologist that your ideas about the effect of environment on behavior are at such variance with those of so many of your fellow planners, architects, and others in the design field?

HERBERT J. GANS: I'm sure it's my background. I'm trained to analyze people and society, while architects and physical planners learn how to work with buildings and land uses. As a result they have a vested personal and occupational interest in the physical environment. Ever since I went into planning, I have thus found myself at odds with their basic assumptions: that the physical environment is very influential in people's lives and that reshaping it is the first priority for achieving the good life. As a sociologist, I, of course, have a vested interest in the social environment, but when I studied people and communities I found that they share that interest. Their idea of the good life has little to do with the things that preoccupy the planners—such as good design, orderly land use, lots of public open space and highly visible landmarks.

GLASGOW: What are they concerned about?

GANS: Oh, such things as work, income, health, family, friends. If they are homeowners, they are also concerned about property values and status and having friendly neighbors with children who can be playmates for their own kids—things like that.

GLASGOW: They must have some concern with how their communities are zoned, what kinds of density are desirable, whether there is enough park space or whether the community has visual appeal.

GANS: Of course, but often people are concerned about zoning only when it has to do with status or property values, and they care about density when they want to keep apartment houses out of single-family housing areas. They also want their communities to be attractive—but their ideas of what is attractive don't often coincide with those of most planners and architects. For instance, most people care little about the skyline, and many enjoy the pseudocolonial housefronts that drive architects up the wall.

GLASGOW: Surely the planners didn't always completely miss the mark.

GANS: No. Physical planners have done a lot of good. Often they see to it that new subdivisions have enough schools and parking space, and they fought for mass transit in days when anything but a new expressway was sheer heresy, just to mention a few things. But still they too often pursued the planners' professional goals, and not the people's goals.

GLASGOW: Can you give examples?

GANS: Well, they might cluster houses around a lot of public open space but not provide decent backyards. Or they might champion low-density single-family housing and ignore the vast numbers who could afford only tenements. You see, in my view, the planners were victimized by their fallacious belief that physical environment was a major determinant of society and culture and, in addition, they mistakenly believed that the good life would grow only in an environment based on the principles of professional planning.

GLASGOW: Every man is quite sure that he knows precisely what makes a good life, and he's firmly fixed on it, but one man's fish is another man's poison, as the saying goes.

GANS: That's part of the professional bias of too many physical planners. For example, they have always believed that parks are very important to the good life, and all master plans provide lots of park acreage. But many people spend more leisure time in indoor facilities, including the neighborhood tavern or the bowling alley, that never appear in master plans. And lakes, beaches and amusement parks are far more popular than other kinds of parks. Also, most people don't use parks the way planners think they ought to; they come in families, or at night to make love. There are definite class differences in the use of parks—as there are in ideas about what makes the good life. The poor, although they use certain kinds of parks a lot, need better jobs and better housing more urgently than they need parks.

GLASGOW: You're not denying that physical environment does have some influence on human behavior, are you?

GANS: No, certainly not, but it has much less influence than people's economic situation, the power they have over their destiny, and the groups within which they live. After all, a building or a "land use" is only a shell in which economic, political and social processes take place.

GLASGOW: Do you suggest that physical planning is useless?

GANS: No, all I suggest is that it is just one part of planning and a small one at that. I believe that the purpose of planning is to meet social goals and to solve social problems, and planning for buildings and space must take its proper role in that purpose. For example, if your goal is eliminating mental illness, you *may* want to build some mental-health clinics, but that comes at the end of the planning process; you don't move directly from the goal to the clinics. First you ascertain the causes of mental illness and then you develop programs that will deal with these causes, and some of these programs may require buildings. But then again, they may not: I personally believe that the single most potent cure for a great deal of mental illness is a higher income—mental illness is much more severe among the poor. But even housing plans don't involve only buildings: such plans also decide who is going to get what kind of shelter at what cost. In fact, the crucial question in all planning, physical or social, is how to allocate money and other resources—in short, who gets what.

GLASGOW: When you speak of who gets what, I assume you are talking about the economic process.

GANS: That's right. Planning is a part-technical, part-political process that deals with public and private expenditures. And the big questions are *who will benefit from the expenditures* and *who pays the costs?* What was so wrong about physical planning was that it ignored this question, and as a result, planned only for the affluent who could afford what was being proposed. And what little the poor got was irrelevant to their central need, which was to escape the poverty trap.

GLASGOW: What about public housing?

GANS: Public housing came into being partly as an antipoverty scheme, the idea being that when people had better housing they'd be less poor, or at least they'd behave less like poor people. But good housing is only good housing—it doesn't attack the causes of poverty. If people are unemployed, moving them into public housing won't give them jobs—or solve their noneconomic problems. Don't get me wrong. I'm not against public housing. The real problem is that there is so pitifully little of it in use or in prospect. You know, there is no place in the world that builds less low-cost housing than we do. In most European countries a large proportion of new housing, even for the middle class, is built by the government: housing there is treated as a utility, just like electricity, which is what it ought to be. Private enterprise simply cannot afford to build for anyone but the rich anymore, anywhere. Unfortunately, here in America we haven't accepted this elementary economic fact. . . . There just has to be a large public subsidy for housing for the poor and for moderate- and middle-income people.

GLASGOW: How do you get political consent for that?

GANS: In the 1970s, as housing costs rise further, fewer and fewer people will be able to afford privately built housing. By 1975, I think, they will make some political sparks fly. They'll be numerous and insistent—and when the system breaks down for the middle classes and they are hurting, the government usually acts.

GLASGOW: It seems to me that behavioral scientists are pushing to get in on the design process one way or another. And, vague as some of their proposals are, it seems to me that psychologists and sociologists would have quite a lot to contribute.

GANS: I'm not sure there's such a push now, and there certainly isn't enough money yet for large-scale research. Also, so far most of the researchers have been psychologists doing studies of how people perceive the environment. That's important, but we need most urgently to know three things: first, how people use the present environment and all its physical and symbolic components: second, what kind of environment they prefer (and the major variations in their preferences): and third, what impact, harmful or beneficial, the environment has on them. We also need to know what parts of the environment have major impact. For example, which components of slum housing are most harmful to their unfortunate inhabitants and which less so, because with the miserly resources available, we must attack the most harmful ones first. I think space in the house is the most important component: people suffer most from lack of it, and overcrowding may even be more harmful in slum housing than rats or holes in the wall. Now that's one hypothesis that badly needs researching.

GLASGOW: What about sociologists?

GANS: It's too early to say what will result from their research, because so far they haven't done that much. What sociologists and the new breed of urban anthropologists can do especially well is study the socioeconomic and cultural differences in what people want in the environment—what the priorities are at different income levels. Actually, I think that most Americans (and Europeans) want the same thing—a suburban house—though they'd like it in the country and five minutes away from all the urban conveniences. But what people can afford shapes their actual priorities in preferences.

GLASGOW: Planners in the cities seem much more aware of the users these days than they used to be. But the metropolitan users are so diverse that what you get is conflict and contradiction, or no involvement at all.

GANS: Yes, planners are more aware of the users because people will no longer accept master plans put together by professionals who know what's best for the city and don't want citizen participation for their plans, only citizen approval. Now the citizens want the plan to express their preferences and some even want to participate in the planning process. This creates new problems for the planner, for every city has so many sub-groups with different incomes and preferences that it is very difficult to get agreement on any plan, and certainly not on a master plan. About all you can get is agreement on a number of specific policies, and the planner's job is to make sure that these policies achieve their intended goal. The idea of a master plan assumes that most citizens want the same kind of community and resource-allocation policy, and it also assumes that city growth is minimal or controllable and that cities can control their physical boundaries and movement in and out. None of these assumptions holds for most growing cities, so that kind of a master plan is absurd. Actually the master plans of the past dealt with only a small portion of the physical environment and paid almost no attention to the economic, social and political environments.

GLASGOW: Last August you published an article in *The New York Times Magazine* arguing that we won't end the urban crisis until we end majority rule. To a lot of people that would sound antidemocratic.

GANS: But my argument was just the opposite—that in today's American society majority rule might well be undemocratic. It seems to me that in our very heterogeneous society we have what I call permanently outvoted minorities, people who always get outvoted by the various Establishments and the majority so that they can never achieve their goals—the poor and the black, for example. The only alternative they have is to disrupt the social order. Though that is sometimes effective in getting political attention—and a bit more has been done in the ghettos since the summer rebellions—it also has severe disadvantages, both for the outvoted and the majority. In my article, I argued that as long as we have majority rule, there would never be a significant antipoverty or desegregation program and that consequently there would never be an effective solution to the urban crisis.

GLASGOW: You came out for what you called pluralistic democracy, didn't you?

GANS: Yes, I argued that America is and has long been a pluralistic society which allows and even encourages cultural and ethnic and religious pluralism. People who like opera get it, and there's rock 'n' roll and acid rock, and Mantovani or Lawrence Welk for the older folks; we don't say that there can only be one kind of music and the majority doesn't decide what this is to be. It seems to me that the time has come to apply the same pluralism to politics to provide effective representation to minority interests and, wherever possible, to establish pluralistic or parallel institutions. Instead of forcing three minorities to shoehorn themselves into a majority in favor of policy A, let's provide three policies, A, B and C, and let people choose. For example, why just have one kind of public school in the community? Why not one for the minority that prefers old-fashioned rote learning, one grounded on Dewey's idea of progressive education—learning through problem-solving and community experience, and one that gives maximum freedom to the students, like the English Summerhill School and so on.

GLASGOW: But isn't majority rule the essence of democracy?

GANS: Yes, it has been; but I don't think it is an inviolable principle. Today America is so heterogeneous that it's really a nation of minorities, and every important political decision requires an intense amount of negotiation so that enough minorities can be found and united to create a temporary majority. And even then, some minorities will always be outvoted and left out.

GLASGOW: Specifically, what would you suggest?

GANS: Basically, two things. One is to make sure that the government is truly representative and responsive to all citizens, including minorities, by establishing a one-man-one-vote rule at all levels of government and political-party structures: abolishing various seniority systems: providing government funds for all election campaigns to end politicians' dependence on affluent contributors; and making bureaucracies and administrative agencies more responsive by electing boards of directors to guide them.

GLASGOW: And the second thing?

GANS: That's increasing the governmental concern with, and the power of, outvoted minorities. Thus I'm for a constitutional amendment to give every American citizen a right to a decent job or an income above the poverty line, and for Cabinet departments to represent the now outvoted. People should also serve on the boards of government agencies that determine their fate—every urban-renewal agency should have a policy-making board that includes slum dwellers. Also, I'd be in favor of extending the principles of the progressive income tax and equalization payments to all governmental programs, so that a poorer community would automatically get higher Federal and state grants for all services than an affluent one. But I think we also need some direct restriction on majority rule. In the essay I suggested a two-step process, with majority rule applying only to the final step. This would be somewhat like the runoffs in some state and municipal elections, and would require that any legislative proposal or other measure that obtains 25 percent of the total vote must be voted on again, perhaps in revised form, until it is either approved by a majority or rejected by 76 percent of the governmental body. For example, if at least 25 percent of a Congressional committee favored a massive job-creation program, it's likely that some sort of job-creation program would survive the second step in the voting, whereas now a majority would vote it down the first time around. Of course that would work only if Congress were truly representative, if a fifth of the Congressmen represented the almost 20 percent of the American people who are poor.

GLASGOW: What exactly is pluralistic about this?

GANS: You're right. It's not orthodox political pluralism, which believes in allocation to each group according to its power. I am arguing for what one might call compensatory pluralism, that is, more government consideration for those groups who get less at the ballot box and in the economy. But I'm also in favor of a political equivalent of cultural pluralism in which, as I suggested before, there is diversity in governmental services to reflect the diversity of our society.

GLASGOW: I can see where it would work for schools, but how could you satisfy both hawks and doves at the same time; you can't have war and peace simultaneously.

GANS: No, you can't, but what if taxpayers were able to tell the Government that their taxes could or could not be used for war? Then the Government couldn't carry out as expensive a war, at least, and more tax receipts would be guaranteed for peaceful purposes. There'd still be war if the majority wanted it, but people who didn't want to participate could opt out.

All I'm trying to propose is that we begin to think about modernizing our democracy, bringing it into line with changes in American society. There are going to be a lot of new demands on government from new minorities, affluent and poor, in the next few years.

GLASGOW: Some examples?

GANS: Well, we already have students wanting more say in the schools and enlisted men questioning officer rule in the military; people who want more protection for the consumer, and those who demand an end to air pollution and exploitation of the physical environment. . . . Also, when people participate they want more than government can supply. The solution to that isn't to oppose more participation, which is useless in this age we're living in, or to blame democracy, but to give governments the needed resources. Otherwise there's sure to be unrest. What happened with the poverty program is that the poor were asked what they wanted—and mostly they wanted more and better jobs—but the jobs and other resources weren't there and that has created a lot of anger. And because that's been the case for many municipal services, there's now a demand for community control of these services, especially in the ghetto.

GLASGOW: Yes, but if the blacks get control over the ghetto, or the whole city government, it seems to me that they will be taking over bankrupt institutions.

GANS: I'm afraid that's true. Still, community control is the right solution for municipal institutions that have been unresponsive to black needs, such as the schools, although they must have more funds as well. Unfortunately even if a black government took over, the improvement in ghetto conditions would still be minor because municipal government just doesn't have that much power to change things. In most cities the businessmen have more power than the government—at least when they're united. But the real problem, regardless of the color of the government, is that the cities just don't have the funds to provide the services that people want these days. Ultimately the money must come from the Federal Government, and everybody knows it. Still, things may have to get worse before they get better; usually people don't support change until there is a serious crisis in their backyard. One major reason that so little has been done for the ghetto is that for the majority of Americans that crisis hasn't arrived yet. For example, the suburbanites and even most city dwellers have experienced the ghetto rebellions only on TV and they've only read about rising crime rates. Also, many are inclined to begin with inexpensive solutions, like voting for law-and-order candidates and police repression, which is much cheaper in the short run than eliminating the poverty that encourages some people to steal.

The trouble is that it takes people a long, long time to discover that the cheap-and-easy solutions don't really work. I get despondent about that, but I still believe in the innate good sense of people and I think eventually they'll do the rational thing most of the time. However, they don't like solutions that cost them money or power, which is why we have to change the political rules and also cut the defense budget, say to five to 10 billion dollars a year.

. . . . .

GLASGOW: One thing that comes through over and over in your writings and conversation is the belief that until we beat poverty our other concerns are not only slight but almost an improper priority of concern.

GANS: Yes, that's how I feel. I think the most serious problems of the cities are ultimately caused by poverty and segregation—such things as delinquency, slums, crime, mental illness, political unrest, the middle-class exodus and the decline of municipal tax income. Until we deal directly with poverty and segregation, none of these problems will be eliminated, and until then, improving the physical appearance of the community is of lower priority.

GLASGOW: I'm still concerned over the role of the behavioral scientist in the design process. We could argue over the extent to which they are getting into the act, but my observation is that certainly more of them seem to be trying. At the same time, students in architecture schools seem much more concerned with the social process than in the past.

GANS: That's true, the students are way ahead of the practitioners and professors in that. I think architects and physical planners have to recognize that they are functioning in a social-political process, that they are designing for some and not others, and the consequences of that. However, I don't think an architect should become a sociologist and vice versa; they are two different roles. One of the troubles with architecture is that some big-name architects have what I call the Ayn Rand Syndrome. They think they are social philosophers with sociological skills; they propose comprehensive schemes for redoing society and they'd like to impose them on people, often through their buildings. Aside from the fact that I don't think anyone has the right to impose his schemes on the world, whether he's an architect *or* a sociologist, most architects don't have the foggiest notion how society works, how people live and how they want to live. They're trained to design buildings and that's what they ought to be doing: to create functioning, attractive and comfortable buildings—to practice humane architecture, if you will. But because of the Ayn Rand Syndrome too many architects shy away from the prosaic and mundane problems that a humane architect ought to solve. For example, take the family with teen-agers who want to entertain their friends with high-decibel acid rock; how do you give them and their parents aural and visual privacy in a house of the size that an average person can afford?

. . . . .

GLASGOW: Let's move to another topic. Many young psychologists and sociologists are demanding that the scholar take a more social-activist role. What's your feeling about that?

GANS: I think it depends on what kind of social activism. I believe strongly that there ought to be more policy-oriented social science, research that will help formulate policy and answer the questions policymakers raise. For example, what kinds of job-creation and job-training schemes are most effective, and what political strategies would best reduce powerlessness among the poor? However, social scientists should also do such research for organizations of the poor, not just for Government agencies and foundations. But if, by activism, you mean becoming a community organizer or a political leader, then I'm not so sure you can also be a social scientist. Research requires a certain amount of detachment. If you become an activist, I think it becomes harder to be a good social scientist on that issue because you can't be detached. You get so involved in the immediate political activities that you have time only for the trees, not for the forest. It wouldn't be true for all social scientists and even if it were, I think every social scientist has the right to choose his role. When I was doing research in the Boston West End and realized what the bulldozer was about to inflict on the West Enders, I felt like quitting my study and working with the organization that was fighting the renewal project. I debated it for a while, but then decided not to, (a) because it was too late to stop the project, (b) because I'm not a good political organizer and wouldn't have done much good, and (c) I didn't want to endanger the long-term study of the effects of relocation that was planned to follow mine. I thought that study would have national significance by demonstrating the harmful effects of bulldozer renewal, and would help bring an end to it.

GLASGOW: You did give a critical report to the Boston Redevelopment Authority.

GANS: Yes, I wrote a sociological analysis of what I thought renewal and relocation would do to the West Enders, and appended some policy proposals to undo as much of the damage as was still possible—which the B.R.A. ignored. Later I published the full report in the *Journal of the American Institute of Planners* and in *The Urban Villagers,* and I'm told it helped to change the Federal urban-renewal program and cut down the role of the bulldozer. I think writing that report made me an activist, but some of the young people are asking why social scientists don't get on the barricades and fight for what they think is right. My answer to that is, I think I can be more useful as a policy-oriented social scientist than as just another body on the barricades.

GLASGOW: Whether you are a social activist or not, many young activists admire you and I gather you also admire the radicals.

GANS: I do. I like their passion and perseverance. I like the pressure they put on various Establishments, and I find myself benefiting from the way they pose issues: they make me rethink my own values and assumptions. I also share their impatience with the lack and slowness of change. What I disagree with the radicals about is their belief in the need to overturn the whole system.

GLASGOW: Why?

GANS: For one thing, I don't believe in the desirability or feasibility of revolution in America right now, and I can't know enough about the future to favor long-range revolutionary strategies that radicalize a few, but also alienate a lot more who would otherwise support some specific change now. This isn't always the case, of course, and we owe the radicals a great deal for initiating popular pressure against the war in Vietnam.

Also I don't agree with those radicals who believe that the poor and the blacks should take over; I think there should be equality, and power should be divided among all Americans. I'm for equitable class conflict, if you will. Finally, I don't think there is a cohesive system here that can be overturned in one fell swoop.

American society is composed of many interest groups and institutions that compete for power and resources. True, the major political, social and economic institutions are essentially conservative, but that's so for all institutions. Once established they seek to preserve their own status quo, even radical institutions. Moreover, the dominant groups and institutions are not united; they often have conflicting interests and they fight each other, though of course not in behalf of the poor.

What I think is wrong is that additional power and resources usually go to those already well supplied with both. But that is not inevitable in a democracy, for even now the dominant political institutions respond to political pressure. Thus, there's no reason that these institutions can't change more radically and quickly than they do; all it takes is sufficient political pressure. The trouble is that it now takes more pressure than minorities can muster, which is why I'm in favor of changing many of the political rules. Still, the dominant institutions aren't organized into a single system that can be overturned by a revolution, as was the case in Cuba and still is in most Latin American countries.

Also, even the most dissatisfied Americans are not revolutionary; what they want is to be admitted as equals into our almost affluent society. If you had a revolution here you'd have to kill an awful lot of nonrevolutionary people, or else they'd reassert themselves after the revolution and force it to adapt itself to the previous social structure, which is what happened in Russia.

Of course, if the revolutionaries here continue their strategy, the dominant institutions may unite in self-defense to create the very system that revolutionaries think already exists, and then that system would quickly crush them, using far more undemocratic methods than are now being used against them. That in turn *might* radicalize many more Americans and eventually create support for a popular revolution, as in Cuba, but I just don't see it happening in America.

Moreover, I still have faith that basic change is possible here without revolution and that a more democratic and equalitarian society can be created by radical but piecemeal change. This must be brought about by diverse methods, including some favored by radicals. In other words, I continue to believe in the possibility of more drastic and rapid change by democratic methods, liberal and radical, and I'm not ready to wait for the millennium when the dominant institutions may perhaps be overturned all at once.

69.

THE "LIBERATION" OF GARY, INDIANA

Edward Greer

Gary, Indiana, is an industrial community composed of diverse racial and ethnic populations and characterized by great industrial and labor organizations with all the evidence of racism and struggles for power that may be found in such American communities. In this selection, Greer analyzes the processes by which a black man, Richard Hatcher, became mayor, and power was wrested from the previously controlling groups in the community. The ecology, social structure, political processes, and nature of power in such a community are vividly illustrated by this description of Gary during a major transition period.

. . . . .

In silhouette, the skyline of Gary, Indiana, could serve as the perfect emblem of America's industrial might—or its industrial pollution. In the half-century

Source: Edward Greer, *TRANS-Action* (January 1971): 30, 39, 63. Reprinted by permission of TRANS-Action Magazine.

Edward Greer is a free-lance writer on subjects of social and political significance. He has had articles published in several magazines, including the *Nation*.

since they were built, the great mills of the United States Steel Corporation—once the largest steel complex on earth—have produced more than a quarter-trillion tons of steel. They have also produced one of the highest air pollution rates on earth. Day and night the tall stacks belch out a ruddy smoke that newcomers to the city find almost intolerable.

Apart from its appalling physical presence, the most striking thing about Gary is the very narrow compass in which the people of the city lead their lives. Three-quarters of the total work force is directly employed by the United States Steel Corporation. About 75 percent of all male employment is in durable goods manufacture and in the wholesale-retail trades, and a majority of this labor force is blue-collar. This means that the cultural tone of the city is solidly working-class.

But not poor. Most Gary workers own their own homes, and the city's median income is 10 percent above the national average. The lives of these people, however, are parochial, circumscribed, on a tight focus. With the exception of the ethnic clubs, the union and the Catholic church, the outstanding social edifices in Gary are its bars, gambling joints and whorehouses.

COMPANY TOWN

The city of Gary was the largest of all company towns in America. The United States Steel Corporation began construction in 1905, after assembling the necessary parcel of land on the Lake Michigan shore front. Within two years, over $40 million had been invested in the project; by now the figure must be well into the billions.

Gary was built practically from scratch. Swamps had to be dredged and dunes leveled; a belt-line railroad to Chicago had to be constructed, as well as a port for ore ships and of course a vast complex of manufacturing facilities including coke ovens, blast furnaces and an independent electrical power plant. The city was laid out by corporation architects and engineers and largely developed by the corporation-owned Gary Land Company, which did not sell off most of its holdings until the thirties. Even though the original city plan included locations for a variety of civic, cultural and commercial uses (though woefully little for park land), an eminent critic, John W. Reps, points out that it "failed sadly in its attempt to produce a community pattern noticeably different or better than elsewhere."

The corporation planned more than the physical nature of the city. It also had agents advertise in Europe and the South to bring in workers from as many different backgrounds as possible to build the mills and work in them. Today over fifty ethnic groups are represented in the population.

This imported labor was cheap, and it was hoped that cultural differences and language barriers would curtail the growth of a socialist labor movement. The tough, pioneer character of the city and the fact that many of the immigrant workers' families had not yet joined them in this country combined to create a lawless and vice-ridden atmosphere which the corporation did little to curtail. In much more than its genesis and name, then, Gary is indelibly stamped in the mold of its corporate creators.

LABOR AND THE LEFT

During the course of the First World War, government and vigilante repression broke the back of the Socialist party in small-town America, though it was not very strong to begin with. Simultaneously, however, the Left grew rapidly as a political force among the foreign-born in large urban centers. As the war continued, labor peace was kept by a combination of prosperity (full employment and overtime), pressures for production in the "national interest," and Wilsonian and corporate promises of an extension of democracy in the workplace after the war was over. The promises of a change in priorities proved empty, and in 1919 the long-suppressed grievances of the steelworkers broke forth. Especially among the unskilled immigrant workers, demands for an industrial union, a reduction of the workday from twelve to eight hours and better pay and working conditions sparked a spontaneous movement for an industry-wide strike.

For a time it appeared that the workers would win the Great Steel Strike of 1919, but despite the capable leadership of William Z. Foster the strike was broken. The native white skilled labor aristocracy refused to support it, and the corporation imported blacks from the South to scab in the mills. This defeat helped set back the prospect of militant industrial trade unionism for almost a generation. And meanwhile, racism, a consumer-oriented culture (especially the automobile and relaxed sexual mores) and reforms from above (by the mid-twenties the eight-hour day had been voluntarily granted in the mills) combined to prevent the Left from recovering as a significant social force.

It was in this period between World War I and the depression that a substantial black population came to Gary. Before the war only a handful of black families lived there, and few of them worked in the mills. During World War I, when immigration from abroad was choked off, blacks were encouraged to move to Gary to make up for the labor shortage caused by expanding production. After the war this policy was continued, most spectacularly during the strike, but rather consistently throughout the twenties. In 1920 blacks made up 9.6 percent of the population; in 1930 they were 17.8 percent—and they were proportionately represented in the steel industry work force.

When the CIO was organized during the depression, an interracial alliance was absolutely essential to the task. In Gary a disproportionate number of the union organizers were black; the Communist party's slogan of "black and white unite and fight" proved useful as an organizing tactic. Nevertheless, it was only during World War II (and not as the result of the radicals' efforts) that black workers made a substantial structural advance in the economy. Demography, wartime full employment and labor shortages proved more important to the lot of black workers than their own efforts and those of their allies.

As after the First World War, so after the second, there came a repression to counter the growth of the Left. The Communist component of the trade union movement was wiped out, and in the general atmosphere of the early cold war black people, too, found themselves on the defensive. At the local level in Gary, the remaining trade union leaders made their peace with the corporation (as well as the local racketeers and Democratic party politicians), while various campaigns in the forties to racially integrate the schools and parks failed utterly.

Finally, in the early fifties, the inherently limited nature of the trade union when organized as a purely defensive institution of the working class—and one moreover that fully accepts capitalist property and legal norms—stood fully revealed. The Steelworkers Union gave up its right to strike over local grievances, which the

Left had made a key part of its organizing policy, in return for binding arbitration, which better suited the needs and tempers of the emerging labor bureaucrats.

CORPORATE RACISM

The corporation thus regained effective full control over the work process. As a result, the corporation could increase the amount of profit realized per worker. It could also intensify the special oppression of the black workers; foremen could now assign them discriminatorily to the worst tasks without real union opposition. This corporate racism had the additional benefit of weakening the workers' solidarity. For its part, the union abolished shop stewards, replacing them with one full-time elected "griever." This of course further attenuated rank-and-file control over the union bureaucracy, aided in depoliticizing the workers and gave further rein to the union's inclination to mediate worker/employer differences at the point of production, rather than sharpen the lines of struggle in the political economy as a whole.

The corporate and union elites justified this process by substantial wage increases, together with other benefits such as improved pension and welfare plans. For these gains a price was paid. Higher product prices, inflation and a rising tax burden on the workers all ensued from the union's passive acceptance of corporate priorities.

There were extremely important racial consequences as well. For as the union leadership was drawn further and further into complicity with corporate goals, a large segment of the industrial working class found itself in the apparently contradictory position of opposing the needs of the poorest workers for increased social welfare services. A large part of the material basis for white working-class racism originates here. Gary steelworkers, struggling to meet their home mortgage payments, are loath to permit increased assessments for additional municipal services which they view as mostly benefitting black people.

UNITED STATES STEEL

Needless to say, the corporation helped to develop, promote and protect the Gary working class's new ways of viewing itself and its world.

In the mill, the corporation systematically gave the black workers the dirtiest jobs (in the coke plants, for example) and bypassed them for promotion—especially for the key skilled jobs and as foremen. Nor has that policy changed. Although about a third of the employees in the Gary Works are black, and many of them have high seniority, and although virtually all the foremen are promoted directly from the ranks without needing any special qualifications, there are almost no black (or Spanish-speaking) foremen. According to figures submitted by the United States Steel Corporation to the Gary Human Relations Commission, as of 31 March 1968, out of a total of 1,011 first-line supervisors (foremen) only 22 were black.

The corporation not only practices racism directly, it also encourages it indirectly by supporting other discriminatory institutions in Gary. Except for some free professionals and small business, the entire business community is a de facto fief of the corporation. The Gary Chamber of Commerce has never to my knowledge differed from the corporation on any matter of substance, though it was often in its economic self-interest to do so. This has been true even with regard to raising the corporation's property assessment, which would directly benefit local business financially. And in its hiring and sales practices, as well as in its social roles, this group is a leading force for both institutional racism and racist attitudes in the community. For instance, it is well known that the local banks are very reluctant to advance mortgage money in black areas of town, thus assuring their physical decline. White workers then draw the reasonable conclusion that the movement of blacks into their neighborhoods will be at the expense of the value of their homes and react accordingly. The local media, completely dependent financially on the local business community, can fairly be described as overtly racist. The story of the voting fraud conspiracy to prevent the election of the present mayor, Richard Hatcher, a black man, didn't get into the local paper until days after it made the front page of the *New York Times.*

The newspaper publisher is very close to the national Catholic hierarchy and the local bishop, who in turn is closely linked to the local banks. The church is rhetorically moderately liberal at the diocesan level, but among the ethnic parishes the clergy are often overtly racist.

POLITICAL CONSIDERATIONS

While the United States Steel Corporation has an annual budget of $5 billion, the city of Gary operates on some $10 million annually. (The figure applies only to municipal government functions; it excludes expenditures by the schools, welfare authorities, the Sanitary Board and the Redevelopment Commission.)

And the power of the city government, as is usually the case in this country, is highly fragmented. Its legal and financial authority is inadequate to carry out the public functions for which it bears responsibility. The power of the mayor is particularly limited. State civil service laws insulate school, welfare, fire and police personnel from the control of City Hall. Administrative agencies control key functions such as urban renewal, the low income housing authority, sanitation, the park system and the board of health. Appointive boards, with long and staggered terms of tenure, hire the administrators of these agencies; and although in the long run a skillful mayor can obtain substantial control over their operations, in the short run (especially if there are sharp policy differences) his power may well be marginal.

Two other structural factors set the context in which local government in Gary—and in America generally—is forced to operate. First, key municipal functions increasingly depend upon federal aid; such is the case with the poverty program, urban renewal, low income housing and, to a substantial degree, welfare, education and even police and sanitation. Thus, the priorities of the federal government increasingly shape the alternatives and options open to local officials, and their real independence is attenuated.

Second, the tax resources of local governments—resting for the most part on comparatively static real estate levies—are less and less able to meet the sharply rising costs of municipal services and operations. These costs reflect the increased social costs of production and welfare, costs that corporations are able to pass on to the general public.

This problem is particularly acute in Gary because of the ability of the corporation to remain grossly underassessed. As a result, there are implacable pressures to resist expansion of municipal services, even if the need for them is critical. In particular, since funds go to maintain existing services, it is virtually impossible for a local government to initiate any substantive innovations unless prior funding is assured. In this context, a sustained response to the urban crisis is prevented not only by a fragmentation of power but also by a lack of economic resources on a scale necessary to obtain significant results.

For the city of Gary, until the election of Mayor Hatcher, it was academic to talk about such considerations as the limits of local government as an instrument of social change and improvement of the general welfare. Before him, municipal government had been more or less content simply to mediate between the rackets on the one hand and the ethnic groups and business community on the other.

The Democratic party, structured through the Lake County machine, was the mechanism for accomplishing a division of spoils and for maintaining at least a formal legitimacy for a government that provided a minimum return to its citizenry. Left alone by the corporation, which subscribed to an inspired policy of live and let live where municipal politics were concerned, this political coalition governed Gary as it saw fit.

In return for the benevolent neutrality of the corporation toward its junior partner, the governing coalition refrained from attempting to raise the corporation's tax assessments or to otherwise insinuate itself into the absolute sovereignty of the corporation over the Gary Works. Air pollution activities were subjected only to token inspection and control, and in the entire history of the city the Building Department never sent an inspector into the mill. (These and other assertions about illegal or shady activities are based on reports from reliable informants and were usually verified by a second source. I served under Mayor Hatcher as director of the Office of Program Coordination until February 1969.)

In this setting—particularly in the absence of a large middle class interested in "good government" reform—politics was little more than a racket, with the city government as the chief spoils. An informal custom grew up that representatives of different ethnic minorities would each hold the mayor's office for one term. The mayor then, in association with the county officials, would supervise the organized crime (mostly gambling, liquor and prostitution) within the community. In effect, the police force and the prosecutor's office were used to erect and centralize a protection racket with the mayor as its director and organized crime as its client. Very large sums of money were involved, as indicated by the fact that one recent mayor was described by Internal Revenue officials as having an estimated annual income while in office of $1.5 million.

Besides the racket of protecting criminal activity, other sources of funds contributed to the large illicit incomes of city officials. There were almost 1,000 patronage jobs to distribute to supporters or sell to friends. There were proceeds from a myriad of business transactions and contracts carried out under municipal authority. Every aspect of municipal activity was drawn into the cash nexus.

For instance, by local ordinance one had to pass an examination and pay a $150 fee for a contractor's license to do repair or construction work within city limits. The licensing statute was enacted to maintain reasonable standards of performance and thus protect the public. In reality, as late as 1967, passing the exam required few skills, except the ability to come up with $1,200 for the relevant officials, or $1,500 if the applicant was unfortunate enough to have black skin.

Gary municipal affairs also had a racist quality. The black population continued to rise until in the early sixties it composed an absolute majority. Yet the benefits of the system just outlined were restricted to the less scrupulous of the leaders of other ethnic groups, which constituted altogether only 40 percent of the population. The spoils came from all; they were distributed only among whites.

And this was true not only for illegal spoils and patronage but also for legitimate municipal services. As one example, after Hatcher became mayor, one of the major complaints of the white citizenry concerned the sharp decline in the frequency of garbage collection. This resulted, not from a drop in efficiency of the General Services division, as was often charged, but from the fact that the garbage routes were finally equalized between white and black areas.

In short, the city government was itself just another aspect of the institutionalized structure of racism in Gary. To assure the acquiescence of Gary's blacks to the system, traditional mechanisms of repression were used: bought black politicians and ward leaders, token jobs, the threat of violence against rebels and the spreading of a sense of impotence and despair. For instance, it was a Gary tradition for the Democratic machine to contribute $1,500 each week to a black minister's alliance for them to distribute to needy parishioners—with the tacit understanding that when elections came around they would help deliver the vote.

Hatcher's Campaign

The successful insurgency of Richard Gordon Hatcher destroyed the core of this entire relationship.

Hatcher developed what can best be described as a black united front, inasmuch as it embraced all sectors of the black community by social class, occupation, ideology and temperament. The basis of this united front was a commonly held view that black people as a racial group were discriminated against by the politically dominant forces. Creating it required that Hatcher bridge existing divisions in the black community, which he did by refusing to be drawn into a disavowal of any sector of the black movement either to his left or right—except for those local black politicians who were lackeys of the Democratic machine. Despite immense public pressure, for example, Hatcher refused to condemn Stokley Carmichael, even though scurrilous right-wing literature was widely circulated calling him a tool of Carmichael and Fidel Castro. Actually, the rumor that hurt Hatcher the most was the false assertion that he was secretly engaged to a white campaign worker—and it was so damaging in the black community that special pains had to be taken to overcome it.

Muhammad Ali was brought to the city to campaign for Hatcher, but Hubert Humphrey was not invited because of the bitter opposition of white antiwar elements within his campaign committee. It is worth noting that a substantial portion of Hatcher's financial and technical assistance came from a very small group of white liberals and radicals, who, while they played a role disproportionate to their numbers, suffered significant hostility from their white neighbors for involving themselves openly with Hatcher. Their support, however, made it possible for the campaign to appeal, at least rhetorically, to all the citizens on an interracial basis.

Of course, this support in the white community did not translate into votes. When the count was complete in the general election, only 13 percent of Gary's overwhelmingly Democratic white voters failed to bolt to the Republicans; and if one omits the Jewish professional and business section of town, that percentage falls to 6 percent (in blue-collar Glen Park)—a figure more explicable by polling booth error than goodwill.

Even in the Democratic primary against the incumbent mayor, Hatcher barely won, although he had the support of a large majority of the Spanish-speaking vote and overwhelming support (over 90 percent) of the black vote. His victory was possible, moreover, only because the white vote was split almost down the middle due to the entry of an insurgent and popular "backlash" candidate.

Hatcher's primary victory was particularly impressive given the obstacles he had to face. First, his entire primary campaign was run on less than $50,000, while the machine spent an estimated $500,000 in cash on buying black votes alone. Second, the media was openly hostile to Hatcher. And third, efforts were made to physically intimidate the candidate and his supporters. Death threats were common, and many beatings occurred. Without a doubt, the unprecedented action of the Hatcher organization in forming its own self-defense squads was essential in preventing mass intimidation. It was even necessary on primary day for armed groups to force open polls in black areas that would otherwise have remained inoperative.

These extraordinary methods demonstrated both how tenuous are the democratic rights of black people and what amazing organization and determination are necessary to enforce them when real shifts of power appear to be at stake. When the primary results came in, thousands of black citizens in Gary literally danced in the streets with joy; and everyone believed that the old Gary was gone forever.

HATCHER'S TEMPTATIONS

Immediately after the primary victory, the local alignment of forces was to some degree overshadowed by the rapid interposition of national ones. Until Hatcher won the primary, he was left to sink or swim by himself; after he established his own independent base of power, a new and more complex political process began: his reintegration into the national political system.

The county Democratic machine offered Hatcher a bargain: its support and $100,000 for the general election campaign in return for naming the chief of police, corporation counsel and controller. Naturally Hatcher refused to accept a deal that would have made him a puppet of the corrupt elements he was determined to oust from power. Thereupon the county machine (and the subdistrict director of the Steelworkers Union) declared itself for, and campaigned for, the Republican.

But the question was not left there. To allow the Democratic party to desert a candidate solely because he was black would make a shambles of its appeal to black America. And dominant liberal forces within the Democratic party clearly had other positive interests in seeing Hatcher elected. Most dramatically, the Kennedy wing of the Democratic party moved rapidly to adopt Hatcher, offering him sorely needed political support, financial backing and technical assistance, without any strings attached. By doing this, it both solidified its already strong support from the black community and made it more reasonable for blacks to continue to place their faith in the Democratic party and in the political system as a whole.

As a necessary response to this development (although it might have happened anyway), the Johnson-Humphrey wing of the Democratic party also offered support.

And this meant that the governor of Indiana and the Indiana State Democratic party endorsed Hatcher as well—despite the opposition of the powerful Lake County machine. Thus Hatcher achieved legitimacy within the political system—a legitimacy that he would need when it came to blocking a serious voting fraud plot to prevent his winning the election.

Despite clear evidence of what was happening, the Justice Department nevertheless refused to intervene against this plot until Hatcher's campaign committee sent telegrams to key federal officials warning them that failure to do so would result in a massive race riot for which the federal officials would be held publicly responsible. Only by this unorthodox maneuver, whose credibility rested on Hatcher's known independent appeal and constituency, was the federal executive branch persuaded to enforce the law. Its intervention, striking 5,000 phony names from the voters rolls, guaranteed a Hatcher victory instead of a Hatcher defeat.

The refusal of the Justice Department to move except under what amounted to blackmail indicated that the Johnson-Humphrey wing of the party was not enthusiastic about Hatcher, whose iconoclastic and often radical behavior did not assure that he would behave appropriately after he was in power. But its decision finally to act, together with the readiness of the Kennedy forces to fully back Hatcher, suggests that there was a national strategy into which the Hatcher insurgency could perhaps be fitted.

My own view of that national strategy is that the federal government and the Democratic party were attempting to accommodate themselves to rising black insurgency, and especially electoral insurgency, so as to contain it within the two-party system. This strategy necessitated sacrificing, at least to a degree, vested parochial interests such as entrenched and corrupt machines.

Furthermore, black insurgency from below is potentially a force to rationalize obsolete local governments. The long-term crisis of the cities, itself reflecting a contradiction between public gain and private interest, has called forth the best reform efforts of the corporate liberal elite. Centered in the federal government, with its penumbra of foundations, law firms and universities, the political forces associated with this rationalizing process were most clearly predominant in the Kennedy wing of the Democratic party.

The economic forces whose interests are served by this process are first the banks, insurance companies and other sections of large capital heavily invested in urban property and, more generally, the interests of corporate capital as a whole—whose continued long-range profit and security rest on a stable, integrated and loyal population.

Thus the support given to Hatcher was rational to the system as a whole and not at all peculiar, even though it potentially implied economic and political loss for the corporation, United States Steel, whose operations on the spot might become more difficult. The interests of the governing class as a whole and of particular parts of it often diverge; this gap made it possible for Hatcher to achieve some power within the system. How these national factors would shape the amount and forms of power Hatcher actually obtained became quite evident within his first year of office.

MOSAIC OF BLACK POWER

When I arrived in the city five months after the inauguration, my first task was to aid in the process of bringing a semblance of order out of what can fairly be described as administrative chaos.

When the new administration took over City Hall in January 1968 it found itself without the keys to offices, with many vital records missing (for example, the file on the United States Steel Corporation in the controller's office) and with a large part of the city government's movable equipment stolen. The police force, for example, had so scavenged the patrol cars for tires and batteries that about 90 percent of them were inoperable. This sort of thing is hardly what one thinks of as a normal process of American government. It seems more appropriate to a bitter excolonial power. It is, in fact, exactly what happened as the French left Sekou Toure's Guinea.

There were no funds available. This was because the city council had sharply cut the municipal budget the previous summer in anticipation of a Hatcher victory. It intended, if he lost, to legislate a supplemental appropriation. But when he won without bringing in a council majority with him, its action assured that he would be especially badly crippled in his efforts to run the city government with a modicum of efficiency. Moreoever, whenever something went wrong, the media could and did blame the mayor for his lack of concern or ability.

Not only did Richard Hatcher find his position sabotaged by the previous administration even before he arrived, but holdovers, until they were removed from their positions, continued to circumvent his authority by design or accident. And this comparatively unfavorable situation extended to every possible sphere of municipal activities.

Another problem was that the new administrators had to take over the management of a large, unwieldy and obsolete municipal system without the slightest prior executive experience. That there were no black people in Gary with such experience in spite of the high degree of education and intelligence in the black community is explicable only in terms of institutionalized racism—blacks in Gary were never permitted such experiences and occupational roles. Hatcher staffed his key positions with black men who had been schoolteachers, the professional role most closely analogous to running a government bureaucracy. Although several of these men were, in my view, of outstanding ability, they still had to learn everything by trial and error, an arduous and painful way to maintain a complex institution.

Furthermore, this learning process was not made any easier by the unusually heavy demands placed on the time of the mayor and his top aides by the national news media, maneuvering factions of the Democratic party, a multiplicity of civil rights organizations, universities and voluntary associations and others who viewed the mayor as a celebrity to be importuned, exploited or displayed. This outpouring of national interest in a small, parochial city came on top of and was almost equal to, the already heavy work load of the mayor.

Nor were there even clerical personnel to answer the mail and phone calls, let alone rationally respond to the deluge. The municipal budget provided the mayor with a single secretary; it took most of the first summer to make the necessary arrangements to pay for another two secretaries for the mayor's own needs. One result was that as late as June 1968 there was still a two-month backlog of personal mail, which was finally answered by much overtime work.

In addition to these problems there were others, not as common to American politics, such as the threat of violence, which had to be faced as an aspect of daily life. The problem of security was debilitating, especially after the King and Kennedy assassinations. In view of the mayor's aggressive drive against local organized crime, the race hatred whipped up during and after the campaign by the right wing and the history of violence in the steel town, this concern with security was not excessive, and maintaining it was a problem. Since the police were closely linked with the local Right, it was necessary to provide the mayor with private bodyguards. The presence of this armed and foreboding staff impaired efficiency without improving safety, especially since the mayor shrugged off the danger and refused to cooperate with these security efforts.

In addition, the tremendous amounts of aid we were offered by foundations, universities and federal officials proved to be a mixed blessing. The time needed to oversee existing processes was preempted by the complex negotiations surrounding the development and implementation of a panoply of new federal programs. There had never been a Concentrated Employment Program in Gary, nor a Model Cities Program, nor had the poverty program been locally controlled. Some of these programs weren't only new to Gary, they hadn't been implemented anywhere else either. The municipal bureaucracy, which under previous administrations had deliberately spared itself the embarassment of federal audits, didn't have the slightest idea as to how to utilize or run these complex federal programs. Moreover, none of the experts who brought this largesse to Gary had a clear understanding of how it was to be integrated into the existing municipal system and social structure. These new federal programs sprang up overnight—new bureaucracies, ossified at birth—and their actual purposes and effects bore little relation to the legislative purposes of the congressional statutes that authorized them.

Needless to say, ordinary municipal employees experienced this outside assistance as a source of confusion and additional demoralization, and their efficiency declined further. Even the new leadership was often overwhelmed by, and defensive before, the sophisticated eastern federal bureaucrats and private consultants who clearly wanted only to help out America's first black mayor. The gifts, in other words, carried a fearful price.

BUREAUCRATIC ENEMIES

Except for the uniformed officials and the schools, which were largely outside the mayor's control, the standing city bureaucracy was a key dilemma for Mayor Hatcher.

The mayor had run on a reform program. His official campaign platform placed "good government" first, ahead of even tax reform and civil rights. Hatcher was deeply committed to eliminating graft and corruption, improving the efficiency of municipal government—especially the delivery of services to those sectors of the citizenry that had been most deprived—and he did not view his regime as merely the substitution of black faces for white ones in positions of power.

But he also had a particular historic injustice to rectify: the gross underrepresentation of blacks in the city government, and their complete exclusion from policy-making positions. Moreover, implicit in his campaign was a promise to reward his followers, who were mostly black. (At least most participants in the campaign assumed such a promise; Hatcher himself never spoke about the matter.)

Consequently, there was tremendous pressure from below to kick out everyone not covered by civil service protection and substitute all black personnel in their places. But to do so would have deepened the hostility of the white population and probably weakened Hatcher's potential leverage in the national Democratic party. He resisted this pressure, asserting that he believed in an interracial administration. However, in addition to this belief (which, as far as I could determine, was genuine), there were other circumstances that dictated his course of action in this matter.

To begin with, it was always a premise of the administration that vital municipal services (police and fire protection, garbage collection, education, public health measures) had to be continued—both because the people of Gary absolutely needed them and because the failure to maintain them would represent a setback for black struggles throughout the country.

It also appeared that with a wholesale and abrupt transition to a totally new work force it would be impossible to continue these services, particularly because of a lack of the necessary skills and experiences among the black population—especially at the level of administration and skilled technical personnel. In this respect Hatcher faced the classic problem faced by all social revolutions and nationalist movements of recent times: after the seizure of power, how is it possible to run a complex society when those who traditionally ran it are now enemies?

The strategy Hatcher employed to meet this problem was the following. The bulk of the old personnel was retained. At the top level of the administration (personal staff, corporation counsel, chief of police, controller) new, trustworthy individuals were brought in. Then, gradually, new department heads were chosen, and new rank-and-file people included. If they had the skill already, they came at the beginning; if they didn't, they were brought in at a rate slow enough to provide for on-the-job training from the holdovers, without disrupting the ongoing functions of the particular department.

The main weakness of this gradualist strategy was that it permitted the old bureaucracy to survive—its institutional base was not destroyed.

The result was that the new political priorities of the administration could not be implemented with any degree of effectiveness in a new municipal political practice. City government remained remarkably like what it had been in the past, at least from the perspective of the average citizen in the community. While the political leadership was tied up with the kinds of problems I noted earlier, the bureaucracy proceeded on its own course, which was basically one of passive resistance. There were two aspects to this: bureaucratic inertia, a sullen rejection of any changes in established routine that might cause conflicts and difficulties for the employees; and active opposition based on politics and racism, to new methods and goals advocated by the mayor.

To cite just one example, the mayor decided to give a very high priority to enforcement of the housing codes, which had never been seriously implemented by preceding administrations. After much hard work, the Building Department was revamped to engage in aggressive inspection work. Cases stopped being "lost," and the number of inspections was increased by 4,000 percent while their quality was improved and standardized. Then it was discovered that cases prepared for legal enforcement were being tabled by the Legal Department on grounds of technical defects.

I personally ascertained that the alleged legal defects were simply untrue. I then assumed that the reason for the legal staff's behavior was that they were overburdened with work. Conferences were held to explain to them the mayor's priorities so they could rearrange their work schedule. Instead, a series of bitter personal fights resulted, culminating in my removal from that area of work since the staff attorneys threatened to resign if there were continued interference with their professional responsibility. In the course of these disputes, both black and white attorneys expressed the opinion that they did not consider themselves a legal aid bureau for Gary's poor, and furthermore the root of the city's housing problem was the indolent and malicious behavior of the tenants. In their view, it was therefore unjust to vigorously enforce the existing statutes against the landlords. Thus, despite the administration's pledge, black ghetto residents did not find their lives ameliorated in this respect.

Gradually, then, the promise of vast change after the new mayor took office came to be seen as illusory. Indeed, what actually occurred was much like an African neocolonial entity: new faces, new rhetoric and people whose lives were scarcely affected except in their feelings towards their government.

This outcome was not due to a failure of good faith on the part of the Hatcher administration. Nor does it prove the fallacious maximalist proposition that no amelioration of the people's conditions of life is possible prior to a revolution. Instead, it was due to the decline of the local mass base of the Hatcher administration and the array of national political forces confronting it.

Most black people in Gary were neither prepared nor able to take upon themselves the functions performed for them by specialized bureaucracies. They relied upon the government for education, welfare, public health, police and fire protection, enforcement of the building codes and other standards, maintenance of the public roads and the like. Unable to develop alternative popularly based community institutions to carry on these functions by democratic self-government, the new administration was forced to rely upon the city bureaucracy—forced to pursue the option that could only result in minor changes.

ABORTED LIBERATION

The most significant consequence of the Hatcher administration's failure to transcend the structural terrain on which it functioned was political, the erosion of popular support after the successful mobilization of energies involved in the campaign. The decline of mass participation in the political process contributed in turn to the tendency of the new regime to solve its dilemmas by bureaucratic means or by relying on outside support from the federal government.

The decline in mass support ought not to be confused with a loss of votes in an election. Indeed, Hatcher is now probably as secure politically as the average big city mayor. The point is that the mass of the black population is not actively involved in helping to run the city. Thus, their political experiences are not enlarged, their understanding of the larger society and how it functions has not improved, and they are not being trained to better organize for their own interests. In short, the liberating process of the struggle for office was aborted after the initial goal was achieved—and before it could even begin to confront the profound problems faced by the mass of urban black Americans.

For example, after the inauguration, old supporters found themselves on the outside looking in. For the most part, since there was no organized effort to continue to involve them (and indeed to do so could not but conflict with the dominant strategy of the administration), they had to be content to remain passive onlookers. Moreover, the average citizen put a lot of faith in the mayor and wanted to give him an opportunity to do his job without intruding on the process.

Even among the most politicized rank-and-file elements there was a fear of interfering. Painfully conscious of their lack of training and experience, they were afraid of "blowing it." Instead they maintained a benevolent watchfulness, an attitude reinforced by the sense that Hatcher was unique, that his performance was some kind of test of black people as a race. (Whites were not the only people encouraged by the media to think in these terms.) There were of course some old supporters who were frankly disillusioned: they did not receive the patronage or other assistance they had expected: they were treated rudely by a bureaucratic holdover or were merely unable to reach the ear of a leader who was once accessible as a friend.

The ebbing away of popular participation could be seen most markedly in the Spanish-speaking community, which could not reassure itself with the symbolic satisfaction of having a member of its group in the national spotlight. With even less education and prior opportunity than the blacks, they found that the qualifications barrier to municipal government left them with even less patronage than they felt to be their due reward. This feeling of betrayal was actively supported by the former machine politicians and criminal elements, who consciously evoked ethnic prejudices to isolate the mayor and weaken his popular support.

What happened in the first year of the new administration, then, was a contradiction between efficiency and ethnic solidarity. At each point the mayor felt he had to rely upon the expert bureaucracy, even at the cost of increasing his distance from his mass base. And this conflict manifested itself in a series of inexorable political events (the appointment of outside advisors, for example), each of which further contributed to eroding the popular base of the still new leadership.

As Antonio Gramsci pointed out, beneath this contradiction lies a deeper one: a historic class deprivation—inflicted on the oppressed by the very structure of the existing society—which barred the underclass from access to the skills necessary for it to run the society directly in its own interests and according to its own standard of civilization. Unless an oppressed social group is able to constitute itself as what Gramsci characterizes as a counterhegemonic social bloc, its conquest of state power cannot be much more than a change in leaders. Given the overall relations of forces in the country at large, such an undertaking was beyond the power of the black community in Gary in 1968. Therefore, dominant national political forces were able quickly to reconstitute their overall control.

NATIONAL POWER

What happened to Richard Hatcher in Gary in his first year as mayor raises important questions—questions that might be of only theoretical interest if he were indeed in a unique position. He is not. Carl Stokes [1971], a black, is mayor of Cleveland. Charles Evers, a black, is mayor of Fayette, Mississippi. Thomas Bradley, a black, very nearly became mayor of Los Angeles.

Kenneth Gibson, a black, is now mayor of Newark. The list will grow, and with it the question of how we are to understand the mass participation of blacks in electoral politics in this country and the future of their movement.

I believe that until new concepts are worked out, the best way of understanding this process is by analogy with certain national liberation movements in colonial or neo-colonial countries. Of course, the participants—in Gary as in Newark—are Americans, and they aren't calling for a UN plebiscite. But they were clearly conscious of themselves as using elections as a tool, as a step toward a much larger (though admittedly ill-defined) ultimate goal—a goal whose key elements of economic change, political power, dignity, defense of a "new" culture and so forth are very close to those of colonial peoples. It is because Hatcher embraced these larger objectives (without, of course, using precisely the rhetoric) that his campaign can be thought of as part of a nationalist process that has a trajectory quite similar to that of anti-colonial liberation movements.

In its weakened local posture, the Hatcher administration was unable to resist successfully a large degree of cooption by the national political authorities. Despite a brave vote at the Democratic National Convention for Reverend Channing Philips, Hatcher was essentially forced to cooperate with the national government and Democratic party—even to the extent of calling on the sheriff of Cook County to send deputies to reinforce the local police when a "miniriot" occurred in the black ghetto.

Without either a nationally coordinated movement or an autonomous base of local insurgency—one capable of carrying out on a mass scale government functions outside the official structure—Hatcher's insurgency was contained within the existing national political system. Or, to express it somewhat differently, the attempt by black forces to use the electoral process to further their national liberation was aborted by a countervailing process of neocolonialism carried out by the federal government. Bluntly speaking, the piecemeal achievement of power through parliamentary means is a fraud—at least as far as black Americans are concerned.

The process by which the national power maintained itself, and even forced the new administration to aid it in doing so, was relatively simple. As the gap between the popular constituency and the new government widened, like many another administration, Hatcher's found itself increasingly forced to rely upon its "accomplishments" to maintain its popularity and to fulfill its deeply held obligation to aid the community.

Lacking adequate autonomous financial resources—the mill remained in private hands, and it still proved impossible to assess it for tax purposes at its true value—accomplishments were necessarily dependent upon obtaining outside funds. In this case, the funds had to come from the federal government, preferably in the form of quick performance projects to maintain popular support and to enable everyone to appear to be doing something to improve matters.

These new programs injected a flow of cash into the community, and they created many new jobs. In his first year in office, the mayor obtained in cash or pledges more federal funds than his entire local budget. Hopes began to be engendered that these programs were the key to solving local problems, while the time spent on preparing them completed the isolation of the leadership from the people.

Then, too, the stress of this forced and artificial growth created endless opportunities for nepotism and even thievery.

Men who had never earned a decent living before found themselves as high-paid executives under no requirement to produce any tangible results. Indeed, federal authorities seemed glad to dispense the funds without exercising adequate controls over their expenditures. A situation arose in which those who boasted of how they were hustling the system became prisoners of its largesse.

Even the most honest and courageous leader, such as Mayor Hatcher, could not help but be trapped by the aid offered him by the federal authorities. After all, how can any elected local executive turn down millions of dollars to dispense with as he sees fit to help precisely those people he was elected to aid? The acceptance of the help guaranteed the continuation of bonds of dependence. For without any real autonomous power base, and with new vested interests and expectations created by the flow of funds into the community, and with no available alternate path of development, the relation of power between the local leader and the national state was necessarily and decisively weighted toward the latter.

In Gary, Indiana, within one year after the most prodigious feat in the history of its black population—the conquest of local political power—their insurgency has been almost totally contained. It is indeed difficult to see how the existing administration can extricate itself from its comparative impasse in the absence of fresh national developments, or of a new, more politically coherent popular upsurge from below.

There is, however, no doubt that the struggle waged by the black people of Gary, Indiana, is a landmark on their road to freedom; for the experiences of life and struggle have become another part of their heritage—and thus a promise for us all.

70.

ON RECOVERING OUR SENSE OF CONTINUITY

Vance Packard

One of the major points of debate among those specializing in the study of community is the extent to which it is important to individuals to have a sense of involvement in a collective community, to have, as Packard says in this selection, a "geographical sense of place"—to at least "know where you are from." Some would argue that this is unimportant, that it is the network of relationships that one establishes at any one time which is of value and not one's physical origins or surroundings. Packard, in a recent work from which this selection is taken, supports the opposing view and here explores some of the means by which such a sense of community might be achieved.

Source: Vance Packard, *A Nation of Strangers* (New York: David McKay Co., 1972), pp. 275–83, 287–88.

Vance Packard has written extensively on technological progress and some of the problems it brings. He is the author of *The Hidden Persuaders, The Status Seekers,* and the *Waste Makers.*

If the modern middle-class man does not know who he is, that is in part because he does not know where he is from.—ANTHONY LEWIS, INTERNATIONAL CORRESPONDENT.

Knowing, in a deep-down sense, where you are from contributes not only to your sense of identity but to your sense of continuity. Psychologist Abraham Maslow in his famed hierarchy of human needs places among the four main ones the social need to attain a sense of security through belonging, through association, through being accepted, through giving and receiving close friendship.

If one's life has continuity, one can look back upon it in his twilight years and see a "continuous whole," to use the dictionary phrase, rather than a long series of disjointed moves, many barely worth remembering. Some psychiatrists believe that for our well-being and sense of continuity we need to have roots in a specific geographic place, to have a sense of place.

Some people feel that simply *knowing* where you are from is enough. A wife who had moved fifteen times in three decades of marriage was deeply concerned that her children were growing up without such knowledge. She explained:

"Although I can only occasionally return to the town where I was born, the knowledge that it is there and that my sisters and several of my relatives are there lies inside me like a little, warm, furry thing and is comforting. I can go back there and see the people I grew up with and know *home.* But where will my children go?"

Better than "knowledge" of having a home somewhere is living *now* in the area that you identify with sufficiently to think of it as home. That means, for example, that merchants know you well enough to trust you. They don't ask for identification when you give them a check. Jane Wayne, wife of actor David Wayne, has led an extraordinarily high-mobile life, attending dozens of schools and living in dozens of places. Now for a number of years she and her family have lived in the same house in Fairfield County, Connecticut, despite pressures or temptations to move on. It is going to take something pretty compelling to get her to move again. She explained to me that she had finally achieved a *home* and likes very much the sense of roots it gives. When she calls the plumber about an ailing faucet he will say, "Mrs. Wayne, is that the faucet in the back bathroom you had trouble with three or four years ago?" She thinks such interchanges are marvelous.

American society has an urgent need for remedies that will reduce the feeling of so many people that they are in the midst of relative strangers. Achieving a sense of continuity is one major way to shed feelings of strangeness. But where do we begin to gain more sense of continuity?

Ideally, you begin by finding a reasonably congenial area to live in and making a point of sinking roots there for at least a few years. You can of course occasionally sample different houses or apartments but you should stay within the area of familiarity. An exception should be made for young adults under, say, twenty-six. They are still testing themselves, broadening personal horizons and learning as they respond to the challenges of adapting to new environments. Mobility—but not chronic nomadism—may possibly be helpful to them.

But assuming that we are talking about people who are past twenty-six and who find themselves feeling rootless because of mobility or living in a barren metropolized environment, where do we begin, beyond sending Christmas cards to everyone we can remember? Here are some possibilities.

One obvious place for us to begin is to

reexamine the built-in assumption of organizations that they can feel free to shift personnel about the landscape purely on the basis of what seems at the moment to be the most efficient utilization of that personnel. Such shifting—by both business and governmental organizations—is often not only mindless but frequently heartless. The social needs of the individuals involved, and of their families, are viewed as noneconomic and therefore irrelevant in the decision-making process. It is just assumed that the jobholder and his or her family will *want* to move if they wish to be known as team players within the system.

Such assumptions, unfortunately, are just one aspect of the rising importance of institutions in American life and the corresponding decrease in the seeming importance of the individual. Institutions have reached such size and power that increasingly they are controlling our lives, dictating where and for how long we should live in any one area, and to a larger extent controlling our way of life.

Corporations have been making assumptions about employee movability just as casually as they have assumed that communities where they have plants will be happy to put up with the polluting practices at the plants since the plants provide jobs in the area.

Recently corporations have been getting some warnings and admonitions to proceed more thoughtfully in their transfer policies. Urie Bronfenbrenner, the child psychologist, in a report to the White House Conference on Children recently urged business to cut back on both job travel and job transfers. The National Industrial Conference Board found in a survey that reluctance of managers to move was becoming a nationwide phenomenon. The reluctance was undoubtedly intensified by the increased difficulties transferees began to have in the early 1970s in selling the old house and raising mortgage money to buy a house at the new location. A survey by Louis Harris & Associates on attitudes of young people asked: "Would you like a job that involves being transferred to different places?" Sixty-three percent said no. And a nationwide firm that helps transferred executives locate homes finds that more and more of them are stating that their current moves are absolutely their last. A spokesman told me, "They have moved so many times that they are putting their feet down and saying that their children have to have some successive years in a town to build up a foundation. They are worried not only about the hardships of moving but about the fact that they don't seem to have time to develop roots."

Some companies are listening. And meanwhile they have been adding up the dollar costs to themselves of their own increasingly liberal policies designed to reassure nervous transferees that any move would not create an undue financial hardship for the transferee and his family. A number have been cutting back on transfers.

One company that has been listening to the rumbles of protests and caution is International Business Machines, whose initials, as indicated, had come to mean "I've Been Moved" to many of the company's families. First the company made some surveys of employee attitudes toward moving. These revealed that, though most employees still wanted the *option* of making a move if a really good opportunity presented itself, employees in general were concerned about not only the costs of moving but the effects upon their families. The latter concern was particularly prevalent among families with school-age children.

Out of the rethinking at IBM has come a

specific program designed to force both the company and its employees to be more cautious about transfers. Orders have gone out throughout the company that a relocation should be considered only when really necessary and when it is in the best interests of the employee's career development. Will the new post give him "room to grow"? An employee is to be given more time to think things over before he accepts a relocation. He and his wife are now allowed to visit the new location at company expense *before* deciding whether or not they want to move.

To assure that division managers are taking a conservative approach to transfers, the company now asks each division to estimate the number of transfers that will be necessary during the coming year. A company spokesman advised me that as a result of the new policies "our divisions have informed us that the number of relocations is down and employee concern over moving has subsided."

IBM has also been giving thought to the impact on communities of any large-scale moves of personnel and facilities it is considering. As a result of its thinking, the spokesman said, IBM now tries "to avoid any abrupt turnover in community population."

Boeing, the aerospace firm, is another giant company that is taking a much closer look at a man and his family before moving him. It became concerned by reports that frequent moves were creating an "aerospace syndrome."

Another approach to improving a family's sense of continuity is to work near home. This applies not only to the father but to the mother if she works. Children whose parents work near home have a better understanding of who their parents are—and thus who they themselves are. Their own sense of place will be reinforced.

It is often not economically feasible, however, in today's society to do this. The place of work may be located in an expensive area. Corporations, if they are to be socially responsible, should show more resolve than they have heretofore to locate facilities only in areas that can provide homes for the total range of their employees. And town and city planners should also bear this consideration in mind when encouraging or discouraging companies that want to build facilities in their areas. In many parts of the United States considerable sentiment is building up to force such a viewpoint upon planners.

If a family leads a relatively rootless existence much of the time, because of mobility or because it is surrounded by urban strangers, it still can enjoy some sense of continuity by having a fixed second home to which it can always return. This can be a summer seaside or lakeside cottage, a mountain chalet, a once abandoned farmhouse in the country, a rural townhouse, or a place in a vacation community. Interstate highway systems make such places reasonably accessible if they are within five hundred miles. Approximately two million Americans now have second homes.

The futuristic architect and thinker Buckminster Fuller, who has a professorship in Illinois, is a globe-hopper who scorns national boundaries and applauds today's youth as being "wonderfully uprooted." Yet, as writer Barry Farrell has noted, Mr. Fuller admits there is one place he retreats to that he confesses does give him a deep feeling of belonging. It is an island off the Maine coast that his family has owned for almost seventy years.

I suspect that one reason the island of Martha's Vineyard, Massachusetts, commands such intense loyalty from its summer residents is that the Vineyard has become a substitute—or real—home for many high-mobile or metropolized Americans. Thousands of summer people there maintain year-round subscriptions to the *Vineyard Gazette* even though they get to the Vineyard only for a few summer weeks or months, and perhaps for Thanksgiving or Christmas holidays. I find that my off-island acquaintances who subscribe read each issue intently during the winter. My family, now scattered, gets back together for a while every summer on the Vineyard, where we have been going for twenty-two years, while renting our Connecticut house. Almost all of our neighbors in the part of the Vineyard where we stay have been coming there for at least fifteen years; yet many of them have lived in several parts of the country or world during the same fifteen years. To many, the Vineyard is their real home. There they have come to know their druggist, the hardware clerks, and the First Selectman better than they do the equivalent in the mainland towns or cities where they currently reside. And many seem to feel more intensely about Vineyard issues than they do about issues of their official areas of residence. My wife Virginia was chatting with a fairly new girl at the checkout counter of the A&P when the girl startled her by asking, "How is your mother?" Virginia's mother had broken her hip while visiting us a couple of months earlier. As they continued chatting the girl said, "Did you know Mrs. K—— broke her hip too yesterday?" Mrs. K—— is a friend but this was the first Virginia had heard about the accident.

In our increasingly estranged, uprooted world such small talk—and such a neighborly grapevine—can be very gratifying.

Still another promising approach to promoting continuity would be to greatly encourage the present trend toward developing really good four-year community colleges within commuting distance of every talented young person in the land. This would reduce the "brain drain" felt by many communities and tend to keep young people closer to their families, friends, and geographical roots.

If achieving a geographic sense of place is an impossible dream because of one's career pattern, one may still achieve some sense of continuity that is unrelated to geographic locations.

It is possible to maintain ties to a network of widely separated friends or colleagues. Family life specialists—a breed I have observed—are located on campuses or in offices or clinics all across the country, yet many know one another better than they know their neighbors. They get together several times a year at conferences, they invite one another to be guest lecturers at their own places of employment, they correspond, and they argue with one another in the pages of their journals. These colleagues may make contact ten or twenty times a year.

A lawyer I know who for years has been involved in causes related to civil liberties and women's rights happens to have roots geographically in New York City but she also flies off to meetings in various parts of the globe several times a month and is on the phone to distant colleagues many times a week. Her colleagues probably mean more to her in terms of a sense of continuity in her life than do her social friends where she lives and relaxes, although she and her husband do attach great importance to having a weekend retreat in the country and get there despite blizzards.

Even enthusiasts can form networks that become meaningful to them over the years though the network members live hundreds of miles apart. Skiing enthusiasts get together for reunions at resorts on many weekends during the winter months, and such networks can remain substantially intact over many years.

From the typical American's viewpoint, however, such networks are exceptional. Often they can be sustained only by the expenditure of a great deal of energy and money.

A strong family solidarity can also help provide one with a sense of meaningful continuity when the world about you is changing. This includes strong ties to spouse, children, and one's parents, brothers, sisters, and close relatives. Much of our geographic and psychological rootlessness is caused by the malfunctioning or breakup of marriages. If there is a breakup —and half of all marriages now do result in divorce, separation, desertion, or annulment—geographic rootlessness often occurs as the wife and children move elsewhere.

In these rootless times marriages are increasingly held together by emotional rather than functional bonds. Many people today feel an urgent need for warmth and stability. One important role of the wife-mother in a mobile family is, in the words of sociologist Warren Bennis, "to provide continuity, the portable roots." It is becoming urgent that we as a society move to place a higher value on family solidarity. One simple way to begin doing so is to require that couples applying for a marriage license wait for a month in order to reflect upon their decision before the license is actually issued. This would greatly reduce the proportion of impulsive or ill-considered unions.

. . . . .

A final important step the people of the United States should take to promote stability and a personal sense of continuity is to stop glorifying growth for growth's sake. At the top of my hometown newspaper is the slogan "Grow or Go." The town has doubled in size in twenty years. Happily the slogan is now in very small type. The grow-or-go philosophy long cherished by Chamber of Commerce boosters is at the heart of much of our urban turmoil. It has encouraged rapid, sprawling growth which is overwhelming established communities and recreational facilities.

City and state planners are starting to become wary of uncontrolled growth. They used to assume that more people meant more prosperity and more tax revenues. But now they are finding that as they get many more people those people tend to demand more services than they pay for. One of the fastest-growing regions in the U.S., Santa Clara County, California, down the peninsula from San Francisco, is near bankruptcy. And the county, once made up of visible small towns and cities, has become a sad example of urban sprawl.

The first step to getting uncontrolled growth in hand is to stabilize the nation's population by taking advantage of conception control techniques now readily available. Until population stabilization is achieved Americans should think in terms of establishing viable communities—both by starting fresh and by developing them within existing metropolitan areas.

71.

ECOLOGY AND SOCIAL JUSTICE: IS THERE A CONFLICT?

Sam Love

Years ago the almost invisible but inexorably escalating pollution costs of American industrialization impressed the visitor to only a few of our largest cities. Today the local air pollution count is a familiar component of the daily news in almost all cities throughout the country. The recent ecology crisis and the resulting remedial movement has created deep concern among disadvantaged minority group members who fear that correction of their injustices will be delayed by attention to ecological problems. In the selection which follows, Love presents convincingly the evidence which causes him to believe that there is no necessary conflict between the movements for social justice and ecological purification. The convergence of these movements, then, not only should but, according to Love, do lead to hitherto unimaginable results in both domestic peace and purity of our natural environment.

During its Denver hearing on the 1972 Democratic Party platform, the platform committee heard Colorado state Senator George Brown, one of the Senate's black members, unleash an all-too-familiar attack on the environmental movement. After listening to testimony from environmental advocates about what planks should be in the platform, Brown blasted the environmentalists as diverting attention from the real issues. He then proceeded to tick off a list of black demands which ran the gamut from community control of police to guaranteed annual income.

The distrust of the environmental movement which surfaced in Denver runs deep in the minority communities. The basis for the mistrust stems from a long history of affluent whites spending millions to preserve natural areas while children suffer the pangs of hunger. Put simply, minorities are concerned by what they see as a series of distorted priorities being pursued by environmentalists. Furthermore, they are frightened by the genocidal tinge to some of the more common population control arguments. This legacy of our movement cannot be ignored; yet, as an understanding evolves that many minority and ecological problems have common causes, the gap between the social justice and ecology movements is closing.

West Virginia Congressman Ken Hechler articulated the interrelationship in his pronouncements on strip mining during his 1972 reelection campaign. "I told them I was against the exploitation of land because it was also the exploitation of people," Hechler said. His analysis is really not new. In *Capital,* Karl Marx said

Source: Sam Love, *Environmental Action,* newsletter (August 5, 1972): 3–6. Reprinted by permission of Environmental Action and the author.

Sam Love is coordinator of the national organization called Environmental Action and has served as the coeditor of the organization's publication. He served as one of the original coordinators of Earth Day and is the editor of *Earth Tool Kit* and *Ecotage.*

that labor and land (by which he also meant resources) are the sources of wealth and that the capitalist would abuse both in the pursuit of profit.

Many conditions have changed since the 1860s from which Marx drew his analysis, but exploitation of resources and humans still occurs because our social system places a higher priority on profit than on human or natural welfare. The blatancy of the human exploitation which occurred in the factories and fields has been curbed by an organized labor force, but more sophisticated forms of exploitation abound. Because today's workers wear white collars and labor in air-conditioned offices does not mean that exploitation disappeared with the sweatshop. It may be harder to spot, but it still exists and the struggle to create a just society is still underway by civil rights, minority, labor, and women's groups.

The government and industry's handling of the supersonic transport contract vividly illustrates the nature of the modern profiteering. The SST contract which Boeing and the subcontractors secured from the government provided for full repayment of the research and development investment of the private corporations in the event that the government decided to terminate the project. After a fight which pitted environmentalists and budget cutters against the aerospace industry and their unions, Congress did vote to stop the SST and the contractors recovered from Uncle Sam their $85-million investment in the project. Because the SST contractors had been writing off each year for tax purposes their share of the research and development costs, the refund was merely added to the corporations' normal profits. Thus, in the Boeing situation alone, the company's executives laid off almost 7,000 workers in the same fiscal quarter that they beefed up their reserve fund by declaring a 91-cents-per-share extra credit on their stock.

Exploitation doesn't end inside the corporation. The corporation's resource acquisition activities (such as mining, drilling for oil or cutting down forests), production (factory air or water pollution), and market manipulation (conspiring to keep prices high or advertising to stimulate sales) have an impact on the ecology and the society—not to mention the problems stemming from consumer use of a company's products. And this impact is not always equitably distributed.

Until now the ecology movement has operated on the assumption that everyone breathes the same air and drinks the same water; therefore, it is in everyone's interest to take care of the air and water. The harsh reality that our movement must accept is that the rich have a cleaner environment than the poor and the middle class. Let's take a look at some of the day-to-day differences in the rich man and the poor man's lives.

The average man does not breathe the same air that the rich man breathes. The Council on Environmental Quality's 1971 report to the Congress breaks down air pollution exposure by income. Utilizing data from industrialized areas, such as Chicago, and nonindustrial areas, such as Washington, D.C., the report reveals that the lowest income neighborhoods are in the areas of highest air pollution concentrations. The report's exposure charts document the fact that lower-income people are exposed to higher amounts of air pollutants. These results can be explained by the fact that residential real estate values are lower near polluting factories and in the central city; therefore, people with lower incomes, forced into houses and apartments with cheaper rents, are exposed to more pollutants. So if air pollution continues to get worse, the rich will produce the gas masks but they will not be the first to have to buy them.

After air, the Council considered water. The report does not contain much information on who gets the dirtiest water, but it does point out that residents in older buildings can get large doses of lead from the cementing compounds which seal their water pipes. This type of compound is no longer used in construction; consequently, those who live in newer houses will get lower doses of lead in their water.

Residents in lower income areas are also more likely to be uprooted by freeway construction. The Council's report says that federally aided highway projects have displaced an average of 60,000 people from their homes and businesses each year. Of those "dislocated," three-fourths were urban dwellers, most of whom lived in middle- or low-income housing units that cost less than $15,000 or rented for less than $110 per month. Those who are displaced may be lucky in comparison to the lot of those who are left to live next to a freeway and continuously face high levels of noise and air pollution.

Even though bombardment by noise and air pollution may make the average man's home approach the intolerable, it is a monument to pristine purity in comparison to his work environment. A 1968 U.S. Public Health Service study among one million workers in the Chicago area found that 46 percent were exposed to "serious and urgent" health hazards. This situation exists because the government has consistently allowed workers to be exposed to higher levels of dangerous pollutants than citizens in the communities surrounding the industrial facilities. For example, workers are allowed to breathe 50 parts per million (ppm) of carbon monoxide (it was 100 ppm until recently) though the Environmental Protection Agency's general carbon monoxide standard for a 24-hour period is 8 ppm (it is allowed to rise to 35 ppm for a single day in any year). Workers, then, are permitted to take in five times more carbon monoxide every day on the job than the citizen walking down the streets.

The impact of such lax policies on the production worker's health is undeterminable because the corporations and the government have not conducted adequate tests or maintained proper health records. In one of the few studies which have been conducted, Dr. Irving J. Selikoff of the Mount Sinai School of Medicine found that among 230 textile factory workers exposed to asbestos between 1941 and 1946 the death rate from lung cancer is five times normal.

Equally startling statistics are coming to light with coal miners who have contracted black lung from breathing coal dust, textile workers who have developed brown lung from inhaling cotton fibers, and uranium miners who have gotten cancer from exposure to radiation. The recent emergence of this health and mortality data helped persuade Congress to pass the nation's first Occupational Health and Safety Law in 1970. Although the law marks a breakthrough in the concept of worker protection, most experts consider it inadequate to do the job, and labor leaders are fond of pointing out that we have more fish and game wardens than occupational health specialists who can identify workplace environmental problems.

With a socioeconomic system which blesses the rich with profits and the poor with pollution, we should not be surprised at minority and poor communities' skepticism of our Earth Day-type admonitions to all link arms and fight pollution. Our stress should be on social justice, because the fact that the poor live in a worse environment means that they have more to gain from a clean-up.

We must be concerned with much more than just stopping pollution. We must take a hard look at clean-up costs and at who will pay them. Corporations can only meet the costs of pollution by raising prices, getting a government subsidy, or taking a cut in profits. Corporate history is not rich with examples of corporations cutting profits for altruistic reasons, so it may be safe to assume that without public pressure the money for pollution control will either come from raising prices or securing a government subsidy.

Generally, government policies have placed responsibility for preserving and cleaning up the environment on the corporations which degrade it; therefore, the government is sanctioning a general policy of product pricing which will reflect the clean-up costs. This allows the corporations to pass pollution control costs on to consumers by raising the price. The Council on Environmental Quality's 1971 annual report states that higher prices which result from pollution control will force the costs to be "borne disproportionately by those with lower incomes because they spend a larger percentage of their incomes on such products." "Borne disproportionately" is an economic euphemism for giving someone the shaft.

The CEQ's economists estimate that meeting the standards of the Clean Air Act and making reasonable progress against water pollution will cost private industry over $35 billion between 1969 and 1975. "Most of that will be passed on to consumers in the form of higher prices," the report states. The costs of putting air pollution control devices on each car will be $350 according to a study by the government's Office of Science and Technology. Auto industry estimates put the cost per vehicle at over $500. Thus, if we allow the auto industry to tack the cost boost on each car, the average man's $3,000 sedan will get a disproportionately higher cost increase than the same increase on the $5,000 luxury car.

Raising prices can also serve the function of discouraging customers in most cases. In Denver, development pressures are so great that a $500 fee is required to hook up to the city's water and sewerage system. A real need exists to limit consumption of many products and steeper prices can be an effective curb on sales. Unfortunately, the maldistribution of wealth which exists in America and the world creates a situation in which higher costs are used to exclude the have-nots. And for this reason our movement must not blanketly embrace present policies which finance pollution controls by upping the price. A reduction in profits offers a more just answer to the question of who will pay the clean-up costs.

Our efforts to shift the burden of clean-up costs from the consumer to the stockholder must be matched by a movement to redistribute wealth. A society with a reasonably fair distribution of wealth could use cost increases as a fair limiter of consumption. Redistribution also offers an added benefit to us in our fight to reduce consumption levels and create an equilibrium state. It can help reduce the lure of wealth which tempts all of us to want more from a planet that can increasingly produce less.

In 1848 John Stuart Mill described a "stationary state" economy in which people would not be addicted to wanting more. He wrote: "Most fitting, indeed, is it, that while riches are power, and to grow as rich as possible the universal object of ambition, the path to its attainment should be open to all, without favour or partiality. But the best state for human nature is that in which, while no one is poor, no one desires to be richer, nor has any reason to fear being thrust back, by the efforts of others to push themselves forward."

Mill believed that the creation of such a state required redistribution of wealth and a "restraint of population." To redistribute wealth he suggested that people be allowed to keep what was earned "with the final fruits" of their industry, but that there should be a "limitation of the sum which any one person may acquire by gift or inheritance, to the amount sufficient to constitute a moderate independence."

Mill's work is reverberating through history. With the publication of works such as *Limits to Growth,* a renewed interest is evolving in the stationary state and equilibrium economics. Critics, such as Vice-President Spiro Agnew, may denounce it as "antiprogress," but Mill anticipated Agnew by over a hundred years. In *Principles of Political Economy* he wrote:

> It is scarcely necessary to remark that a stationary condition of capital and population implies no stationary state of human improvement. There would be as much scope as ever for all kinds of mental culture, and moral and social progress; as much room for improving the Art of Living, and much more likelihood of its being improved, when minds cease to be engrossed by the art of getting on. Even the industrial arts might be as earnestly and as successfully cultivated, with this sole difference, that instead of serving no purpose but the increase of wealth, industrial improvements would produce their legitimate effect, that of abridging labour.

The achievement of a stationary state or even a move in that direction threatens today's economic status quo. Indian Prime Minister Indira Gandhi touched upon the radical critique that our movement offers when she addressed the U.N. Environment Conference. "All of the 'isms' of the modern age—even those which in theory disown the private profit principle—assume that man's cardinal interest is acquisition. The profit motive, individual or collective, seems to overshadow all else. This overriding concern with Self and Today is the basic cause of the ecological crisis."

As we challenge the basic tenet of capitalism that happiness and success can be found through the acquisition of more material goods we will promote the ultimate act of subversion—nonconsumption. And it is important for us to remember that the abuses associated with consumption occur at the top rungs of the economic ladder, not the bottom.

The convergence of the ecology and social justice movements places within our grasp the creation of a society that could only have been dreamed about in the past. This society will exist in harmony with nature and be at peace with itself.

72.

LIKE IT IS IN THE ALLEY

Robert Coles

Peter, a remarkably mature, intelligent, and articulate nine-year-old Boston ghetto black boy proved to be a "very good teacher" for Robert Coles, a Harvard University faculty member and psychiatrist doing research in the College of Medicine. If the reader is like Coles—not black and not living in the ghetto—he can likewise learn much that is crucially important about the costs of survival in the hostile northern urban world where many American blacks exist today. They suffer with frighteningly hazardous living conditions, unmet health care needs that are almost endless, school teachers who do not care about the children, municipal government bureaucrats who are neither friendly nor helpful, and token programs for blacks that are ineffective, inappropriate, or inadequate. Such conditions reinforce the hostility and distrust of whites by blacks, especially those who are talented, young, poor, and ambitious for a better life. White people who do not understand why there is black rage against whites, and black separatism, would do well to consider the insights gained from statements such as "Like It Is in the Alley," and then try to do what needs to be done.

In the alley it's mostly dark, even if the sun is out. But if you look around, you can find things. I know how to get into every building, except that it's like night once you're inside them, because they don't have lights. So, I stay here. You're better off. It's no good on the street. You can get hurt all the time, one way or the other. And in buildings, like I told you, it's bad in them, too. But here it's o.k. You can find your own corner, and if someone tries to move in you fight him off. We meet here all the time, and figure out what we'll do next. It might be a game, or over for some pool, or a coke or something. You need to have a place to start out from, and that's like it is in the alley; you can always know your buddy will be there, provided it's the right time. So you go there, and you're on your way, man.

Like all children of nine, Peter is always on his way—to a person, a place, a "thing" he wants to do. "There's this here thing we thought we'd try tomorrow," he'll say; and eventually I'll find out that he means there's to be a race. He and his friends will compete with another gang to see who can wash a car faster and better. The cars belong to four youths who make their money taking bets, and selling liquor that I don't believe was ever purchased, and pushing a few of those pills that "go classy with beer." I am not completely sure, but I think they also have something to do with other drugs; and again, I can't quite be sure what their connection is with a "residence" I've seen not too far from the alley Peter describes so possessively. The women come

Source: Robert Coles, "The Conscience of the City," *Daedalus, Journal of the American Academy of Arts and Sciences* 97, no. 4 (Fall 1968): 1315–30. Reprinted by permission of *Daedalus, Journal of the American Academy of Arts and Sciences,* Boston, Mass.

See biographical note for Selection 31, page 222.

and go—from that residence and along the street Peter's alley leaves.

Peter lives in the heart of what we in contemporary America have chosen (ironically, so far as history goes) to call an "urban ghetto." The area was a slum before it became a ghetto, and there still are some very poor white people on its edges and increasing numbers of Puerto Ricans in several of its blocks. Peter was not born in the ghetto, nor was his family told to go there. They are Americans and have been here "since way back before anyone can remember." That is the way Peter's mother talks about Alabama, about the length of time she and her ancestors have lived there. She and Peter's father came north "for freedom." They did not seek out a ghetto, an old quarter of Boston where they were expected to live and where they would be confined, yet at least some of the time solidly at rest, with kin, and reasonably safe.

No, they sought freedom. Americans, they moved on when the going got "real bad," and Americans, they expected something better someplace, some other place. They left Alabama on impulse. They found Peter's alley by accident. And they do not fear pogroms. They are Americans, and in Peter's words: "There's likely to be another riot here soon. That's what I heard today. You hear it a lot, but one day you know it'll happen."

Peter's mother fears riots too—among other things. The Jews of Eastern Europe huddled together in their ghettos, afraid of the barbarians, afraid of the *Goyim,* but always sure of one thing, their God-given destiny. Peter's mother has no such faith. She believes that "something will work out one of these days." She believes that "you have to keep on going, and things can get better, but don't ask me how." She believes that "God wants us to have a bad spell here, and so maybe it'll get better the next time—you know in Heaven, and I hope that's where we'll be going." Peter's mother, in other words, is a pragmatist, an optimist, and a Christian. Above all she is American: "Yes, I hear them talk about Africa, but it don't mean anything to us. All I know is Alabama and now it's in Massachusetts that we are. It was a long trip coming up here, and sometimes I wish we were back there, and sometimes I'd just as soon be here, for all that's no good about it. But I'm not going to take any more trips, no sir. And like Peter said, this is the only country we've got. It you come from a country, you come from it, and we're from it, I'd say, and there isn't much we can do but try to live as best we can. I mean, live here."

What is "life" like for her over there, where she lives, in the neighborhood she refers to as "here"? A question like that cannot be answered by the likes of me, and even her answer provides only the beginning of a reply:

> Well, we does o.k., I guess. Peter here, he has it better than I did, or his daddy. I can say that. I tell myself that a lot. He can turn on the faucet over there, and a lot of the time, he just gets the water, right away. And when I tell him what it was like for us, to go fetch that water—we'd walk three miles, yes sir, and we'd be lucky it wasn't ten—well, Peter, it doesn't register on him. He thinks I'm trying to fool him, and the more serious I get, the more he laughs, so I've stopped.
>
> Of course it's not all so good, I have to admit. We're still where we were, so far as knowing where your next meal is coming from. When I go to bed at night I tell myself I've done good, to stay alive and keep the kids alive, and if they'll just wake up in the morning, and me too, well then, we can worry about that, all the rest, come tomorrow. So there you go. We do our best, and that's all you can do.

She may sound fatalistic, but she appears to be a nervous, hardworking, even hard-driven woman—thin, short, constantly on the move. I may not know what she "really" thinks and believes, because like the rest of us she has her contradictions and her mixed feelings. I think it is fair to say that there are some things that she can't say to me—or to herself. She is a Negro, and I am white. She is poor, and I am fairly well off. She is very near to illiterate, and I put in a lot of time worrying about how to say things. But she and I are both human beings, and we both have trouble—to use that word—"communicating," not only with each other, but with ourselves. Sometimes she doesn't tell me something she really wants me to know. She has forgotten, pure and simple. More is on her mind than information I might want. And sometimes I forget too:

> Remember you asked the other day about Peter, if he was ever real sick. And I told you he was a weak child, and I feared for his life, and I've lost five children, three that was born and two that wasn't. Well, I forgot to tell you that he got real sick up here, just after we came. He was three, and I didn't know what to do. You see, I didn't have my mother to help out. She always knew what to do. She could hold a child and get him to stop crying, no matter how sick he was, and no matter how much he wanted food, and we didn't have it. But she was gone—and that's when we left to come up here, and I never would have left her, not for anything in the world. But suddenly she took a seizure of something and went in a half hour, I'd say. And Peter, he was so hot and sick, I thought he had the same thing his grandmother did and he was going to die. I thought maybe she's calling him. She always liked Peter. She helped him be born, she and my cousin, they did.

Actually, Peter's mother remembers quite a lot of things. She remembers the "old days" back South, sometimes with a shudder, but sometimes with the same nostalgia that the region is famous for generating in its white exiles. She also notices a lot of things. She notices, and from time to time will remark upon, the various changes in her life. She has moved from the country to the city. Her father was a sharecropper and her son wants to be a pilot (sometimes), a policeman (sometimes), a racing-car driver (sometimes), and a baseball player (most of the time). Her husband is not alive. He died one year after they all came to Boston. He woke up vomiting in the middle of the night—vomiting blood. He bled and bled and vomited and vomited and then he died. The doctor does not have to press very hard for "the facts." Whatever is known gets spoken vividly and (still) emotionally:

> I didn't know what to do. I was beside myself. I prayed and I prayed, and in between I held his head and wiped his forehead. It was the middle of the night. I woke up my oldest girl and I told her to go knocking on the doors. But no one would answer. They must have been scared, or have suspected something bad. I thought if only he'd be able to last into the morning, then we could get some help. I was caught between things. I couldn't leave him to go get a policeman. And my girl, she was afraid to go out. And besides, there was no one outside, and I thought we'd just stay at his side, and somehow he'd be o.k., because he was a strong man, you know. His muscles, they were big all his life. Even with the blood coming up, he looked too big and strong to die, I thought. But I knew he was sick. He was real bad sick. There wasn't anything else, no sir, to do. We didn't have no phone and even if there was a car, I never could have used it. Nor my daughter. And then he took a big breath and that was his last one.

When I first met Peter and his mother, I wanted to know how they lived, what they did with their time, what they liked to do or disliked doing, what they believed. In the back of my mind were large subjects like "the connection between a person's moods and the environment in which he lives." Once I was told I was studying "the psychology of the ghetto," and another time the subject of "urban poverty and mental health." It is hoped that at some point large issues like those submit themselves to lives; and when this is done, when particular but not unrepresentative or unusual human beings are called in witness, their concrete medical history becomes extremely revealing. I cannot think of a better way to begin knowing what life is like for Peter and his mother than to hear the following and hear it again and think about its implications:

No sir, Peter has never been to a doctor, not unless you count the one at school, and she's a nurse I believe. He was his sickest back home before we came here, and you know there was no doctor for us in the county. In Alabama you have to pay a white doctor first, before he'll go near you. And we don't have but a few colored ones. (I've never seen a one.) There was this woman we'd go to, and she had gotten some nursing education in Mobile. (No, I don't know if she was a nurse or not, or a helper to the nurses, maybe.) Well, she would come to help us. With the convulsions, she'd show you how to hold the child, and make sure he doesn't hurt himself. They can bite their tongues real, real bad.

Here, I don't know what to do. There's the city hospital, but it's no good for us. I went there with my husband, no sooner than a month or so after we came up here. We waited and waited, and finally the day was almost over. We left the kids with a neighbor, and we barely knew her. I said it would take the morning, but I never thought we'd get home near suppertime. And they wanted us to come back and come back, because it was something they couldn't do all at once—though for most of the time we just sat there and did nothing. And my husband, he said his stomach was the worse for going there, and he'd take care of himself from now on, rather than go there.

Maybe they could have saved him. But they're far away, and I didn't have money to get a cab, even if there was one around here, and I thought to myself it'll make him worse, to take him there.

My kids, they get sick. The welfare worker, she sends a nurse here, and she tells me we should be on vitamins and the kids need all kinds of check-ups. Once she took my daughter and told her she had to have her teeth looked at, and the same with Peter. So, I went with my daughter, and they didn't see me that day, but said they could in a couple of weeks. And I had to pay the woman next door to mind the little ones, and there was the carfare, and we sat and sat, like before. So, I figured, it would take more than we've got to see that dentist. And when the nurse told us we'd have to come back a few times—that's how many, a few—I thought that no one ever looked at my teeth, and they're not good, I'll admit, but you can't have everything, that's what I say, and that's what my kids have to know, I guess.

What *does* she have? And what belongs to Peter? For one thing there is the apartment, three rooms for six people, a mother and five children. Peter is a middle child with two older girls on one side and a younger sister and still younger brother on the other side. The smallest child was born in Boston:

It's the only time I ever spent time in a hospital. He's the only one to be born there. My neighbor got the police. I was in the hall, crying I guess. We almost didn't make it. They told me I had bad blood pressure, and I should have been on pills, and I should come back, but I didn't. It was the worst time I've ever had, because I was alone. My husband had to stay with the kids, and no one was there to visit me.

Peter sleeps with his brother in one bedroom. The three girls sleep in the living room, which is a bedroom. And, of course, there is a small kitchen. There is not very much furniture about. The kitchen has a table with four chairs, only two of which are sturdy. The girls sleep in one big bed. Peter shares his bed with his brother. The mother sleeps on a couch. There is one more chair and a table in the living room. Jesus looks down from the living room wall, and an undertaker's calendar hangs on the kitchen wall. The apartment has no books, no records. There is a television set in the living room, and I have never seen it off.

Peter in many respects is his father's successor. His mother talks things over with him. She even defers to him at times. She will say something; he will disagree; she will nod and let him have the last word. He knows the city. She still feels a stranger to the city. "If you want to know about anything around here, just ask Peter," she once said to me. That was three years ago, when Peter was six. Peter continues to do very poorly at school, but I find him a very good teacher. He notices a lot, makes a lot of sense when he talks, and has a shrewd eye for the ironic detail. He is very intelligent, for all the trouble he gives his teachers. He recently summed up a lot of American history for me: "I wasn't made for that school, and that school wasn't made for me." It is an old school, filled with memories. The name of the school evokes Boston's Puritan past. Pictures and statues adorn the corridors—reminders of the soldiers and statesmen and writers who made New England so influential in the nineteenth century. And naturally one finds slogans on the walls, about freedom and democracy and the rights of the people. Peter can be surly and cynical when he points all that out to the visitor. If he is asked what kind of school he would *like,* he laughs increduously.

Are you kidding? No school would be my first choice. They should leave us alone, and let us help out at home, and maybe let some of our own people teach us. The other day the teacher admitted she was no good. She said maybe a Negro should come in and give us the discipline, because she was scared. She said all she wanted from us was that we keep quiet and stop wearing her nerves down, and she'd be grateful, because she would retire soon. She said we were becoming too much for her, and she didn't understand why. But when one kid wanted to say something, tell her why, she told us to keep still, and write something. You know what? She whipped out a book and told us to copy a whole page from it, so we'd learn it. A stupid waste of time. I didn't even try; and she didn't care. She just wanted an excuse not to talk with us. They're all alike.

Actually, they're all *not* alike, and Peter knows it. He has met up with two fine teachers, and in mellow moments he can say so:

They're trying hard, but me and my friends, I don't think we're cut out for school. To tell the truth, that's what I think. My mother says we should try, anyway, but it doesn't seem to help, trying. The teacher can't understand a lot of us, but he does all these new things, and you can see he's excited. Some kids are really with him, and I am, too. But I can't take all his stuff very serious. He's a nice man, and he says he wants to come and visit every one of our homes; but my mother says no, she wouldn't know what to do with him, when he came here. We'd just stand and have nothing to talk about. So she said tell him not to come; and I don't think he will, anyway. I think he's getting to know.

What is that teacher getting to know? What *is* there to know about Peter and all the others like him in our American cities? Of course Peter and his friends who play in the alley need better schools, schools they can feel to be theirs, and better teachers, like the ones they *have* in fact met on occasion. But I do not feel that a reasonably good teacher in the finest school building in America would reach and affect Peter in quite the way, I suppose, people like me would expect and desire. At nine Peter is both young and quite old. At nine he is much wiser about many things than my sons will be at nine, and maybe nineteen. Peter has in fact taught me a lot about his neighborhood, about life on the streets, about survival:

I get up when I get up, no special time. My mother has Alabama in her. She gets up with the sun, and she wants to go to bed when it gets dark. I try to tell her that up here things just get started in the night. But she gets mad. She wakes me up. If it weren't for her shaking me, I might sleep until noon. Sometimes we have a good breakfast, when the check comes. Later on, though, *before* it comes, it might just be some coffee and a slice of bread. She worries about food. She says we should eat what she gives us, but sometimes I'd rather go hungry. I was sick a long time ago, my stomach or something—maybe like my father, she says. So I don't like all the potatoes she pushes on us and cereal, all the time cereal. We're supposed to be lucky, because we get some food every day. Down South they can't be sure. That's what she says, and I guess she's right.

Then I go to school. I eat what I can, and leave. I have two changes of clothes, one for everyday and one for Sunday. I wait on my friend Billy, and we're off by 8:15. He's from around here, and he's a year older. He knows everything. He can tell you if a woman is high on some stuff, or if she's been drinking, or she's off her mind about something. He knows. His brother has a convertible, a Buick. He pays off the police, but Billy won't say no more than that.

In school we waste time until it's over. I do what I have to. I don't like the place. I feel like falling off all day, just putting my head down and saying good-bye to everyone until three. We're out then, and we sure wake up. I don't have to stop home first, not now. I go with Billy. We'll be in the alley, or we'll go to see them play pool. Then you know when it's time to go home. You hear someone say six o'clock, and you go in. I eat and I watch television. It must be around ten or eleven I'm in bed.

Peter sees rats all the time. He has been bitten by them. He has a big stick by his bed to use against them. They also claim the alley, even in the daytime. They are not large enough to be compared with cats, as some observers have insisted; they are simply large, confident, well-fed, unafraid rats. The garbage is theirs; the land is theirs; the tenement is theirs; human flesh is theirs. When I first started visiting Peter's family, I wondered why they didn't do something to rid themselves of those rats, and the cockroaches, and the mosquitoes, and the flies, and the maggots, and the ants, and especially the garbage in the alley which attracts so much of all that "lower life." Eventually I began to see some of the reasons why. A large apartment building with many families has exactly two barrels in its basement. The halls of the building go unlighted. Many windows have no screens, and some windows are broken and boarded up. The stairs are dangerous; some of them have missing timber. ("We just jump over them," says Peter cheerfully.) And the landowner is no one in particular. Rent is collected by an agent, in the name of a "realty trust." Somewhere in City Hall there is a bureaucrat who unquestionably might be persuaded to prod someone in the "trust"; and one day I went with three of the tenants, including Peter's mother, to try that "approach." We waited and waited at City Hall. (I drove us there, clear across town, naturally.) Finally we met up with a man, a not very encouraging or inspiring or generous or friendly man. He told us we would have to try yet another department and swear out a complaint; and that the "case" would have to be "studied," and that we would then be "notified of a decision." We went to the department down the hall, and waited some more, another hour and ten minutes. By then it was three o'clock, and the mothers wanted to go home. They weren't thinking of rats anymore, or poorly heated apartments, or garbage that had nowhere to go and often went uncollected for two weeks, not one. They were thinking of their children, who would be home from school and, in the case of two women, their husbands who would also soon be home. "Maybe we should come back some other day," Peter's mother said. I noted she didn't say *tomorrow,* and I realized that I had read someplace that people like her aren't precisely "future-oriented."

Actually, both Peter and his mother have a very clear idea of what is ahead. For the mother it is "more of the same." One evening she was tired but unusually talkative, perhaps because a daughter of hers was sick: "I'm glad to be speaking about all these things tonight. My little girl has a bad fever. I've been trying to cool her off all day. Maybe if there was a place near here, that we could go to, maybe I would have gone. But like it is, I have to do the best I can and pray she'll be o.k."

I asked whether she thought her children would find things different, and that's when she said it would be "more of the same" for them. Then she added a long afterthought:

Maybe it'll be a little better for them. A mother has to have hope for her children, I guess. But I'm not too sure, I'll admit. Up here you know there's a lot more jobs around than in Alabama. We don't get them, but you know they're someplace near, and they tell you that if you go train for them, then you'll be eligible. So maybe Peter might someday have some real good steady work, and that would be something, yes sir it would. I keep telling him he should pay more attention to school, and put more of himself into the lessons they give there. But he says no, it's no good; it's a waste of time; they don't care what happens there, only if the kids don't keep quiet and mind themselves. Well, Peter has got to learn to mind himself, and not be fresh. He speaks back to me, these days. There'll be a time he won't even speak to me at all, I suppose. I used to blame it all on the city up here, city living. Back home we were always together, and there wasn't no place you could go, unless to Birmingham, and you couldn't do much for yourself there, we all knew. Of course, my momma, she knew how to make us behave. But I was thinking the other night, it wasn't so good back there either. Colored people, they'd beat on one another, and we had lot of people that liquor was eating away at them; they'd use wine by the gallon. All they'd do was work on the land, and then go back and kill themselves with wine. And then there'd be the next day—until they'd one evening go to sleep and never wake up. And we'd get the Bossman and he'd see to it they got buried.

Up here I think it's better, but don't ask me to tell you why. There's the welfare, that's for sure. And we get our water and if there isn't good heat, at least there's some. Yes, it's cold up here, but we had cold down there, too, only then we didn't have *any* heat, and we'd just die, some of us would, every winter with one of those freezing spells.

And I do believe things are changing. On the television they talk to you, the colored man and all the others who aren't doing so good. My boy Peter, he says they're putting you on. That's all he sees, people "putting on" other people. But I think they all mean it, the white people. I never see them, except on television, when they say the white man wants good for the colored people. I think Peter could go and do better for himself later on, when he gets older, except for the fact that he just doesn't *believe.* He don't believe what they say, the teacher, or the man who says it's getting better for us—on television. I guess it's my fault. I never taught my children, any of them, to believe that kind of thing; because I never thought we'd ever have it any different, not in this life. So maybe I've failed Peter. I told him the other day, he should work hard, because of all the "opportunity" they say is coming for us, and he said I was talking good, but where was my proof. So I went next door with him, to my neighbor's, and we asked her husband, and you know he sided with Peter. He said they were taking in a few here and a few there, and putting them in the front windows of all the big companies, but that all you have to do is look around at our block and you'd see all the young men, and they just haven't got a thing to do. Nothing.

Her son also looks to the future. Sometimes he talks—in his own words—"big." He'll one day be a bombardier or "something like that." At other times he is less sure of things: "I don't know what I'll be. Maybe nothing. I see the men sitting around, hiding from the welfare lady. They fool her. Maybe I'll fool her, too. I don't know what you can do. The teacher the other day said that if just one of us turned out o.k. she'd congratulate herself and call herself lucky."

A while back a riot excited Peter and his mother, excited them and frightened them. The spectacle of the police being fought, of white-owned property being assaulted, stirred the boy a great deal: "I figured the whole world might get changed around.

I figured people would treat us better from now on. Only I don't think they will." As for his mother, she was less hopeful, but even more apocalyptic: "I told Peter we were going to pay for this good. I told him they wouldn't let us get away with it, not later on." And in the midst of the trouble she was frightened as she had never before been:

> I saw them running around on the streets, the men and women, and they were talking about burning things down, and how there'd be nothing left when they got through. I sat there with my children and thought we might die the way things are going, die right here. I didn't know what to do: if I should leave, in case they burn down the building, or if I should stay, so that the police don't arrest us, or we get mixed up with the crowd of people. I've never seen so many people, going in so many different directions. They were running and shouting and they didn't know what to do. They were so excited. My neighbor, she said they'd burn us all up, and then the white man would have himself one less of a headache. The colored man is a worse enemy to himself than the white. I mean, it's hard to know which is the worst.

I find it as hard as she does to sort things out. When I think of her and the mothers like her I have worked with for years, when I think of Peter and his friends, I find myself caught between the contradictory observations I have made. Peter already seems a grim and unhappy child. He trusts no one white, not his white teacher, not the white policeman he sees, not the white welfare worker, not the white storekeeper, and not, I might add, me. There we are, the five of us from the 180,000,000 Americans who surround him and of course 20,000,000 others. Yet, Peter doesn't really trust his friends and neighbors, either. At nine he has learned to be careful, wary, guarded, doubtful, and calculating. His teacher may not know it, but Peter is a good sociologist, and a good political scientist, a good student of urban affairs. With devastating accuracy he can reveal how much of the "score" he knows; yes, and how fearful and sad and angry he is: "This here city isn't for us. It's for the people downtown. We're here because, like my mother said, we had to come. If they could lock us up or sweep us away, they would. That's why I figure the only way you can stay ahead is get some kind of deal for yourself. If I had a choice I'd live someplace else, but I don't know where. It would be a place where they treated you right, and they didn't think you were some nuisance. But the only thing you can do is be careful of yourself; if not, you'll get killed somehow, like it happened to my father."

His father died prematurely, and most probably, unnecessarily. Among the poor of our cities the grim medical statistics we all know about become terrible daily experiences. Among the black and white families I work with—in nearby but separate slums—disease and the pain that goes with it are taken for granted. When my children complain of an earache or demonstrate a skin rash I rush them to the doctor. When I have a headache, I take an aspirin; and if the headache is persistent, I can always get a medical check-up. Not so with Peter's mother and Peter; they have learned to live with sores and infections and poorly mended fractures and bad teeth and eyes that need but don't have the help of glasses. Yes, they can go to a city hospital and get free care; but again and again they don't. They come to the city without any previous experience as patients. They have never had the money to purchase a doctor's time. They have never had free medical care available. (I am speaking now of Appalachian whites as well as southern blacks.) It may comfort me to know that every American city provides some free medical services for its "indigent," but Peter's mother and thousands like her have quite a different view of things:

> I said to you the other time, I've tried there. It's like at City Hall, you wait and wait, and they pushes you and shove you and call your name, only to tell you to wait some more, and if you tell them you can't stay there all day, they'll say "lady, go home, then." You get sick just trying to get there. You have to give your children over to people or take them all with you; and the carfare is expensive. Why if we had a doctor around here, I could almost pay him with the carfare it takes to get there and back for all of us. And you know, they keep on having you come back and back, and they don't know what each other says. Each time they starts from scratch.

It so happens that recently I took Peter to a children's hospital and arranged for a series of evaluations which led to the following: a pair of glasses; a prolonged bout of dental work; antibiotic treatment for skin lesions; a thorough cardiac work-up, with the subsequent diagnosis of rheumatic heart disease; a conference between Peter's mother and a nutritionist, because the boy has been on a high-starch, low-protein, and low-vitamin diet all his life. He suffers from one attack of sinus trouble after another, from a succession of sore throats and earaches, from cold upon cold, even in the summer. A running nose is unsurprising to him—and so is chest pain and shortness of breath, due to a heart ailment, we now know.

At the same time Peter is tough. I have to emphasize again *how* tough and, yes, how "politic, cautious and meticulous," not in Prufrock's way, but in another way and for other reasons. Peter has learned to be wary as well as angry; tentative as well as extravagant; at times controlled and only under certain circumstances defiant: "Most of the time, I think you have to watch your step. That's what I think. That's the difference between up here and down in the South. That's what my mother says, and she's right. I don't remember it down there, but I know she must be right. Here, you measure the next guy first and then make your move when you think it's a good time to."

He was talking about "how you get along" when you leave school and go "mix with the guys" and start "getting your deal." He was telling me what an outrageous and unsafe world he has inherited and how very carefully he has made his appraisal of the future. Were I afflicted with some of his physical complaints, I would be fretful, annoyed, petulant, angry—and moved to do something, see someone, get a remedy, a pill, a promise of help. He has made his "adjustment" to the body's pain, and he has also learned to contend with the alley and the neighborhood and *us,* the world beyond: "The cops come by here all the time. They drive up and down the street. They want to make sure everything is o.k. to look at. They don't bother you, so long as you don't get in their way."

So, it is live and let live—except that families like Peter's have a tough time living, and of late have been troubling those cops, among others. Our cities have become not only battlegrounds, but places where all sorts of American problems and historical ironies have converged. Ailing, poorly fed, and proud Appalachian families have reluctantly left the hollows of eastern Kentucky and West Virginia for Chicago and Dayton and Cincinnati and Cleveland and Detroit, and even, I have found, Boston. They stick close together in all-white neighborhoods—or enclaves or sections or slums or ghettos or whatever. They wish to go back home but can't, unless they are willing to be idle and hungry all the time. They confuse social workers and public officials of all kinds because they both want and reject the city. Black families also have sought out cities and learned to feel frightened and disappointed.

I am a physician, and over the past ten years I have been asking myself how people like Peter and his mother survive in mind and body and spirit. And I have wanted to know what a twentieth-century American city "means" to them or "does" to them. People cannot be handed questionnaires and asked to answer such questions. They cannot be "interviewed" a few times and told to come across with a statement, a reply. But inside Peter and his brother and his sisters and his mother, and inside a number of Appalachian mothers and fathers and children I know, are feelings and thoughts and ideas—which, in my experience, come out casually or suddenly, by accident almost. After a year or two of talking, after experiences such as I have briefly described in a city hall, in a children's hospital, a lifetime of pent-up tensions and observation comes to blunt expression:

> Down in Alabama we had to be careful about ourselves with the white man, but we had plenty of things we could do by ourselves. There was our side of town, and you could walk and run all over, and we had a garden you know. Up here they have you in a cage. There's no place to go, and all I do is stay in the building all day long and the night, too. I don't use my legs no more, hardly at all. I never see those trees, and my oldest girl, she misses planting time. It was bad down there. We had to leave. But it's no good here, too, I'll tell you. Once I woke up and I thought all the buildings on the block were falling down on me. And I was trying to climb out, but I couldn't. And then the next thing I knew, we were all back South, and I was standing near some sunflowers—you know, the tall ones that can shade you if you sit down. No, I don't dream much. I fall into a heavy sleep as soon as I touch the bed. The next thing I know I'm stirring myself to start in all over in the morning. It used to be the sun would wake me up, but now it's up in my head, I guess. I know I've got to get the house going and off to school.

Her wistful, conscientious, law-abiding, devoutly Christian spirit hasn't completely escaped the notice of Peter, for all his hard-headed, cynical protestations: "If I had a chance, I'd like to get enough money to bring us all back to Alabama for a visit. Then I could prove it that it may be good down there, a little bit, even if it's no good, either. Like she says, we had to get out of there or we'd be dead by now. I hear say we all may get killed soon, it's so bad here; but I think we did right to get up here, and if we make them listen to us, the white man, maybe he will."

To which Peter's mother adds: "We've carried a lot of trouble in us, from way back in the beginning. I have these pains, and so does everyone around here. But you can't just die until you're ready to. And I do believe something is happening. I do believe I see that."

To which Peter adds: "Maybe it won't be that we'll win, but if we get killed, everyone will hear about it. Like the minister said, before we used to die real quiet, and no one stopped to pay notice."

Two years before Peter spoke those words he drew a picture for me, one of many he has done. When he was younger, and when I didn't know him so well as I think I do now, it was easier for us to have something tangible to do and then talk about. I used to visit the alley with him, as I still do, and one day I asked him to draw the alley. That was a good idea, he thought. (Not all of my suggestions were, however.) He started in, then stopped, and finally worked rather longer and harder than usual at the job. I busied myself with my own sketches, which from the start he insisted I do. Suddenly from across the table I heard him say he was through. Ordinarily he would slowly turn the drawing around for me to see; and I would get up and walk over to his side of the table, to see even better. But he didn't move his paper, and I didn't move myself. I saw what he had drawn, and he saw me looking. I was surprised and a bit stunned and more than a bit upset, and surely he saw my face and heard my utter silence. Often I would break the awkward moments when neither of us seemed to have anything to say, but this time it was his turn to do so: "You know what it is?" He knew that I liked us to talk about our work. I said no, I didn't—though in fact the vivid power of his black crayon had come right across to me. "It's that hole we dug in the alley. I made it bigger here. If you fall into it, you can't get out. You die."

He had drawn circles within circles, all of them black, and then a center, also black. He had imposed an X on the center. Nearby, strewn across the circles, were fragments of the human body—two faces, an arm, five legs. And after I had taken the scene in, I could only think to myself that I had been shown "like it is in the alley"—by an intelligent boy who knew what he saw around him, could give it expression, and, I am convinced, would respond to a different city, a city that is alive and breathing, one that is not for many of its citizens a virtual morgue.

73. 74. 75.

WHAT MAKES MAO A MAOIST?

Stuart R. Schram

REPORT ON AN INVESTIGATION OF THE PEASANT MOVEMENT IN HUNAN, MARCH, 1927

Mao Tse-tung

MAO'S CHINA IN 1972

Herbert A. Simon

The average American probably knows very little about the peoples, societies, and cultures which constitute the reality called the Third World or the Less Developed Countries which contain about two-thirds of the world's population. Of all these nations, the People's Republic of China is outstanding for its size, potential significance, and as the world's largest communist nation. In view of these facts it seems particularly unfortunate that most Americans have had little or no opportunity, until very recently, to learn first-hand about post-World War II China. This situation is now rapidly changing due to a growing recognition of the urgent need for a drastic about-face in U.S. relations with China. The following three selections constitute the editors' efforts to give the interested reader an opportunity to learn a bit more about "Mao's China." In the first of these Stuart Schram, a British China scholar, analyzes some of the factors that led to the Communist revolution, and the development of the People's Republic of China under Mao Tse-tung's leadership. This provides a background for the second selection by Mao himself. The excerpt is taken from one of Mao's early reports and is his reply to critics of the Chinese peasants' revolutionary activities. It illustrates the revolutionary process of destroying the old and creating new political institutions in China's predominantly rural areas. In a letter to one of this book's editors, the late Edgar Snow characterized the report from which this selection by Mao is taken as follows:

> . . . the whole content of the Report is so down to earth, so full of the flavor of rural life and toil, and the deeps of murderous passions of the landlord-peasant class struggle, which Mao understood and succeeded in articulating and mobilizing, that it helps us to comprehend the revolution better than "mature" theorizing of a later period.

The third item is an American social scientist's account, in part whimsical, in part deadly serious, of his recent brief visit to China. He concludes with a thought-provoking summary of what impressed him as most important for us to learn.

73. Schram

In May, 1853, a correspondent for The New York Tribune by the name of Karl Marx, who regularly wrote for that newspaper on the European workers' movement, contributed an article called "Revolution in China and in Europe." In it he discussed the possible impact of "rebellion" in China on England — then the leading world power — and through England on the European order as a whole, venturing the "very paradoxical assertion" that events in China might well prove to be the most important single cause of revolutionary change in Europe. He found in this a striking illustration of the views of that "most profound yet fantastic speculator," Georg Friedrich Hegel, who was "wont to extol as one of the ruling secrets of nature what he called the law of the contact of extremes."

"It would," wrote Marx, "be a curious spectacle, that of China sending disorder into the Western world while the Western powers, by English, French and American war-steamers, are conveying 'order' to Shanghai, Nanking and the mouths of the Great Canal." Of such a curious spectacle we are today the witnesses — but the details of the picture diverge substantially from those foretold by Marx. America now comes first rather than last in the list of the

Source: Stuart R. Schram, "What Makes Mao a Maoist," *New York Times Magazine* (March 8, 1970): 32–82 passim. Copyright © 1970 by The New York Times Company. Reprinted by permission of the publisher.

Stuart R. Schram is professor of politics and head of the Contemporary China Institute of the School of Oriental and African Studies at The University of London. He is author of *Protestantism and Politics in France, The Political Thought of Mao Tse-Tung,* and *Mao Tse-Tung.*

"European" powers intervening in the Far East, weapons more modern than "war-steamers" are employed, and the action takes place well to the south of Shanghai. But these are merely external and superficial differences compared to the change in the nature of the Chinese "disorder," and the way it is transmitted to the West. If there was one thing Marx thought Asians were incapable of producing, it was ideas relevant to the modern world. In his view, China would contribute to revolution in Europe only by disrupting British commerce. And yet today the Little Red Book, containing the words of a peasant from Hunan Province, is read and quoted by students from Berkeley to the Sorbonne. What is the explanation for this "contact of extremes"?

The response that Mao's ideas have found in the West must be understood in the context of developments within our own society, but the ideas themselves have been shaped by half a century's experience of the Chinese revolution. It would be exceedingly rash to assert that Mao's contribution to the theory and practice of revolution has now been finally and definitively spelled out, and that he has no more surprises in store for us. Nevertheless, the Ninth Congress of the Chinese Communist party in April, 1969, marked, if not the end of the cultural revolution, at least the end of one major phase, and in the intervening months the broad contours of the pattern that Mao is endeavoring to establish have become increasingly clear. It is therefore an appropriate moment to sum up his life's work.

The inhabitants of Mao's native province have long been renowned in China for their military and political talents. When Mao was born in 1893, Hunan was already in the forefront of the strivings toward intellectual and political renewal that were to lead to the Reform Movement of 1898. This attempt to modernize the political system was soon crushed by the reactionary Empress Dowager, but the problems it had raised remained. China was in danger, not merely from the incursions of the foreigners, Western and Japanese, who had been trampling on the country and carving out spheres of influence ever since the Opium War of 1840, but above all from her own weakness and failure to adapt to the modern world. Only if a remedy could be found for the lack of political and economic dynamism that lay at the root of Chinese military inferiority would there be a future for Mao Tse-tung's generation at all, or in any case a future worthy of their ambitions for their country and themselves.

Mao has recounted that he first began to have "a certain amount of political consciousness" when, as an adolescent, he read a pamphlet beginning: "Alas, China will be subjugated." He has spent a lifetime endeavoring to transform the Chinese people in such a way as to defeat this prophecy—and in his own eyes the task is not yet done.

Mao Tse-tung grew to manhood in the first and second decades of the twentieth century, at a time when the most progressive Chinese revolutionaries or reformists were seeking in the West the secrets of the strength which would make it possible to resist the West. It was characteristic of Hunan, however, that the older generation of scholars, who were Mao's teachers and models, did not restrict themselves to the "new learning" from abroad, but at the same time promoted the study of China's own tradition, and especially of the philosophers who, at the time of the Manchu conquest three centuries earlier, had exhorted the Chinese to revive the pragmatism and martial spirit of their ancestors. Such ideas were more immediately accessible to Mao than those of foreign origin. His first published article, written in 1917 when he was twenty-three, is filled with references to the "heroes, martyrs and warriors" of old, and quotes admiringly from a poem attributed to the unsuccessful rival of the founder of the Han Dynasty: "My strength uprooted mountains, my energy dominated the world." Thus, while preaching the need to influence people's "subjective attitudes" in order to promote "self-awareness," Mao was still concerned at this time above all with the self-discipline and strength of will that should be cultivated by an élite.

Already Mao had been exposed, both through reading and the instruction of his teachers, to the basic ideas of Western liberalism, and for two or three fleeting years he came to share its ideals. "Wherever there is repression of the individual," he wrote in 1918, "there can be no greater crime." The traditional social order, with its ingrained respect for authority, both political and parental, must therefore be destroyed, together with the Confucian philosophy that buttressed it, in order that individual freedom might prevail.

By 1920 Mao had been converted to Communism, under the impact of the Russian revolution. Henceforth, he was persuaded that the liberation of every Chinese could only be a collective liberation resulting from victory over the foreign oppressors and the domestic reactionaries. Nevertheless, he retained the conviction that men themselves and their attitudes had to be transformed if society was effectively to be changed. A genuine revolutionary movement had to be made up of individuals consciously carrying out tasks accepted of their own free will. This enterprise could only appear to skeptics like squaring the circle, but the cultural revolution demonstrates that Mao has still not given up trying.

Mao Tse-tung and his comrades now regarded themselves as Marxists, and they did their best to learn how to be "Marxist-Leninists" as well (though the term had not yet been coined). In other words, they set about assimilating the modifications in Marxist theory that Lenin had made in order to adapt it to conditions in Asiatic Russia and in the even more backward lands to the east. There, Lenin had proclaimed, the patriotic capitalists were not necessarily (at least in the first instance) the enemies of the Communist revolutionaries, but could even be their allies for a time in the struggle for national liberation and independent economic development. Moreover, the peasants and not the workers would provide the main strength of the revolutionary movement, though they would, of course, require the leadership of the workers' party—i.e. of the Communists—not to mention the "international proletariat," as incarnate in the representatives of the Comintern.

Even with these modifications, Marxism (or Marxism-Leninism) remained a fundamentally urban-centered philosophy. Progress and enlightenment would radiate outward from the cities to the backward countryside. Mao Tse-tung himself had become thoroughly impregnated during his student days with the traditional contempt of the Chinese intellectuals for physical labor. And though as a Communist he could no longer retain an attitude of superiority toward manual workers in general, his early experience as a trade-union organizer fostered in him the snobbish disdain for the dirty and ignorant peasants that has characterized Marxist thinking since Marx himself first stigmatized "the class that represents barbarism in the midst of civilization."

Then, almost accidentally, while resting in his native village, Mao suddenly found himself confronted with an extremely militant peasant movement which had sprung up in the Chinese countryside in the wake of the nationalist outburst provoked by the massacre of a number of Chinese by the foreign police in Shanghai on May 30, 1925. At one stroke, the urban intellectual turned back to the countryside, and grasped that there China's fate would be decided. The peasants were (as he put it in early 1927) "like a tornado or tempest—a force so extraordinarily swift and violent that no power, however great, will be able to suppress it." Mao set out to organize that power. He was forced to desist momentarily in the spring of 1927, when Stalin ordered the Chinese Communists to refrain from actions that might jeopardize the alliance with the Kuomintang, and thereby menace the security of his Siberian frontier. But soon this policy led to bloody catastrophe and the utter destruction of the urban workers' movement in China. Mao took refuge in the mountain range known as the Chingkangshan, and there began a long search for revolutionary methods better adapted to the realities of the Chinese countryside.

In these gropings Mao endeavored to take as a guide the principles of Marxism as he understood them, including the dogma of working-class leadership; but inevitably, being thus plunged once more into the peasant world of his youth, he thought again of the legends that had been the companions of his youth. The organ of the Chinese Communist party was soon accusing him of emulating the Robin Hood-like bandit heroes of "Water Margin" (translated by Pearl Buck under the title "All Men are Brothers"), and a few years later he was ridiculed for deriving his military tactics from the famous novel of war and statecraft, "The Romance of the Three Kingdoms."

It would, of course, be absurd to suggest that Mao had simply fallen back into the intellectual universe of his adolescence. He already had, when he went to the Chingkangshan, some knowledge of Marxist theory, and considerable experience with and mastery of the organizational principle of Leninism. A decade later, when more Soviet books had been translated into Chinese, and he had the leisure in his headquarters in Yenan to engage in reading and study, he greatly deepened and extended his knowledge of Marxism. Nevertheless, both Mao and the revolution he led remained most profoundly marked by the rural environment in which the revolutionary process was taking place.

Much has been written about the originality (or lack of originality) of the Chinese revolution, and the crucial points have long since been identified: a revolution from the bottom up rather than from the top down; protracted warfare in the countryside rather than a rapidly victorious urban insurrection; the Red Army rather than the armed workers as the spearhead. In all of these respects, the Soviet pattern, with its stress on the workers and the cities, was far more in conformity with the basic precepts of Marxism than was the Chinese pattern. But perhaps the most un-Marxist thing that Mao did was to reject the need for Soviet guidance. Marx regarded Asia as hopelessly backward and stagnant until prodded into action by the impact of the West. Such backward societies and cultures were quite incapable, in his view, of modernizing in their own way; the only salvation for them lay in "Europeanization." Moreover, they would require the Europeans to tell them "how it is done." Soviet insistence that the revolution in the agrarian lands of the East, where there was hardly any indigenous working class, must be carried out under the guidance of a "proletarian" International dominated by the Europeans, was thus solidly rooted in Marx's own thinking about Asia. (The fact that the most influential of these Europeans turned out to be Russians would have been less satisfying to Marx, since he regarded Russia herself as an Oriental despotism.)

Mao had seen in 1927 the fruits of such guidance—and therefore, while endeavoring to keep in the good graces of Stalin in order to forestall Russian intervention on the side of his rivals, he progressively asserted the right and the ability of the Chinese to solve their own problems without European tutelage. Asked by Edgar Snow in 1936 whether, if the Chinese revolution were victorious, there would be "some kind of actual merger of governments" with the Soviet Union, Mao replied abruptly, "We are certainly not fighting for an emancipated China in order to turn the country over to Moscow!" And in 1943, hailing the dissolution of the Comintern, he declared that, although the International had not meddled in the affairs of the Chinese Communist party since 1935, that party had "done its work very well, throughout the whole anti-Japanese war of national liberation."

Mao himself recognized, in 1949, that his road to power was an unorthodox one, but he declared that henceforth these tendencies would be reversed:

"From 1927 to the present the center of gravity of our work has been in the villages—gathering strength in the villages, using the villages in order to surround the cities and then taking the cities. The period for this method of work has now ended. The period of 'from the city to the village' and of the city leading the village has now begun. The center of gravity of the party's work has shifted from the village to the city."

In the first few years of the existence of the Chinese People's Republic, an effort was indeed made to follow the Soviet pattern. Large numbers of urban workers were recruited into the Chinese Communist party – which had functioned for two decades primarily as a soul or parasite in the body of Mao's peasant army in the countryside – in order to make of it a "proletarian" party not only in theory but in fact. Simultaneously, a beginning was made toward planned economic development on the Soviet model, with the active participation of Soviet advisers. But these attempts at following the orthodox path soon clashed head-on with Mao's conception of what revolution was all about.

Chinese society in 1949 was overwhelmingly rural. Perhaps the most important single question presenting itself to Mao as he assumed control of the nation's destiny was whether the key to the transformation of the Chinese countryside lay within the villages themselves or without. The answers to this question dictated by Marxist theory and Soviet practice were diametrically opposed to those drawn from his own experience.

Marx had regarded the peasants as totally incapable of independent political action, and this view had dictated the approach of his Soviet disciples to collectivization and agricultural development. Stalin had dispatched élite workers from Moscow and Leningrad at the beginning of the collectivization drive of 1929–30 to provide the political consciousness, organizing capacity and technical knowledge that the peasants were, in his view, incapable of generating themselves. And today [1970], forty years later, a patronizing attitude toward people in the countryside still prevails in the Soviet Union.

Mao's experience, on the other hand, was that of a revolution which not only took place in the countryside, but which (despite the lip service paid to Marxist slogans about "proletarian hegemony") derived its leadership largely from the countryside, and its strength from the fact that it genuinely reflected the aspirations of the peasantry. To be sure, Mao and his comrades cherished ultimate goals, such as collectivization and the introduction of modern technology, which did *not* correspond to what the peasants themselves spontaneously wanted. But the twenty years of symbiosis between Mao's guerrilla forces in the countryside and the peasants who provided the "ocean" in which the "fish" of the revolutionary army could swim, had laid the basis for a relationship between the Communists and the peasants totally different from that in the Soviet Union.

Instead of ordering the rural people – from without and from above – to accept a complete upheaval in their way of life, the Chinese Communists were in a position to communicate with them through men within the villages enjoying their confidence, and to obtain their adhesion to a much greater degree than had been possible in Russia. This was, of course, partly the result of the unbelievable degree of exploitation to which the Chinese peasantry had been exposed at the hands of the landlords – exploitation which for centuries had lent to their revolts, whenever they finally burst out, the "violence of a hurricane" noted by Mao in 1927. But the ability of the Chinese Communists to communicate with the peasants and to channel their bitterness to revolutionary ends was greatly increased by their political methods, and by their physical and moral presence in the countryside over a long period.

Although Mao and his comrades have, on the whole, been closer to the peasants than

Lenin or his successors ever were, there have been significant fluctuations in this respect. In the early nineteen-fifties, when the Chinese were making a conscious effort to learn from the Soviet example (the more so as the Russians considered such conformity to be only the normal price of continued economic aid), Mao himself appeared to accept the principle that the really fundamental developments were taking place in the cities, where the heavy industry necessary to further economic growth was being created. But such an emphasis in fact contradicted his most cherished beliefs: that revolution was above all a matter of changing the patterns of thought and behavior of human beings, and that ideological indoctrination and social mobilization were more important than technical factors in bringing about such changes.

Mao's speech of July, 1955, advocating a speed-up in the formation of rural cooperatives marked the first decisive step toward reversing the order of priorities that characterized not only the Soviet model, but the logic of Marxism itself. Discussing the relationship between collectivization and mechanization, Mao declared: "The country's economic conditions being what they are, the technical transformation will take somewhat longer than the social." In other words, the potential for reshaping the Chinese peasantry was to be found in the revolutionary virtue of the peasants themselves, and not in mere material instruments produced by a minority of technical specialists and skilled workers.

These tendencies had their culmination in the Greap Leap Forward of 1958. The foundations of Socialism, and even of Communism, were to be laid in the countryside, where the "people's communes" provided the best form for the transition to the future ideal society. Progress toward social and moral transformation would be somewhat slower in the cities, where "bourgeois ideology" was still prevalent.

Not surprisingly, the Great Leap Forward, with its emphasis on the revolutionary capacity of the "poor and blank" Chinese people, was accompanied by a growing skepticism regarding the utility either of the Soviet example or of Soviet assistance. In a speech of June, 1958, Mao declared that, while it was necessary to obtain Soviet aid, the main thing was for China to develop her economy by her own efforts. Nor should the Chinese blindly copy Soviet methods, either economic or military.

"Some people have suggested that if our comrades, the Soviet advisers, see we are not copying from them, they will complain or be discontented. Well, I might ask these [Soviet] comrades, 'Are you copying from China?' If they say they are not copying from us, then I could say, 'If you don't copy from us, we won't copy from you either.' "

Summing up the problem of learning from the Soviet Union, Mao declared that the slogan for internal use should be "Study critically," while the slogan for public consumption put it somewhat more tactfully as "Study selectively."

The Great Leap policies led to grave economic difficulties, not only because Mao had overestimated the technical capacity of the rural population at that particular stage, but also because he deliberately flouted the need for effective coordination of the economy. This much Mao admitted himself in a speech delivered in July, 1959, in which he assumed responsibility for the failure of the planners to attend to the plans:

"What I mean by saying that they didn't attend to planning is that they rejected comprehensive balances—they completely failed to calculate the amounts of coal, iron and transport required. Coal and iron cannot walk by themselves. They must be transported in carriages. This point I had not foreseen. . . . Prior to August of last year I devoted most of my energy to the revolutionary side of things. I am fundamentally incompetent on economic construction, and I do not understand industrial planning."

The pendulum therefore swung back toward an emphasis on technical factors and the role of the manager and the expert. This was clearly most distasteful to Mao, but he was forced to bow to circumstances and to the opinions of the "capitalist roaders" in the Chinese Communist party. At the same time, he had learned from the experience of the Great Leap. Therefore, when, beginning in 1963, he made a new attempt to change the temper of society, he did not limit himself, as in 1955–58, primarily to the rural sector. This time, on the contrary, he attached greater importance to remolding urban intellectuals, as well as the party and state bureaucrats in the cities, so as to make use of them in modernizing the countryside.

The cultural revolution has been, as everyone now knows, to a very considerable extent a struggle for power between Mao and his partisans on the one hand, and the proponents of a more orthodox brand of Communism, such as Liu Shao-ch'i and Teng Hsiao-p'ing, on the other. But it has also been a great and wide-ranging debate about the nature of revolution, and at the center of this debate has been the problem of the role to be played by "intellectuals" in society.

The Chinese, like the Soviets, use this term in a far wider sense than is commonly imparted to it in the West, to designate any literate person with a modicum of specialized knowledge who makes use of this training in his work. In China, however, the word has resonances quite different from those in Russia, because of the traditionally high social status of the intellectuals and the fact that in the past many of them actually exercised political power as scholar-officials. This offered a unique opportunity for the Chinese Communists to fill the void left by the collapse of the old imperial bureaucracy (as the Kuomintang had tried and failed to do), but it also concealed a most dangerous snare in the temptation to imitate the arrogance and contempt for the common people that often characterized the old imperial officials.

It is because he had become convinced, by 1964 at the latest, that party cadres in general (and not merely a corrupt minority) were all too prone to succumb to this temptation, that Mao proceeded to discipline the party from without, with the support of the army, rather than undertaking another "rectification" campaign within the party, as he had done in the past.

Such campaigns had long been a characteristic feature of Mao's leadership style. The greatest and most memorable of them had taken place during World War II, in 1942 and 1943. When the United States Army mission came to Yenan in August, 1944, Mao described rectification as a manifestation of the democratic spirit of the Chinese Communists, declaring to John S. Service:

"Of course, we do not pretend that we are perfect. We still face problems of bureaucracy and corruption. But we do face them. We welcome observation and criticism—by the Americans, by the K.M.T. or by anyone else. We are constantly criticizing ourselves and revising our policies toward greater efficiency and effectiveness."

The results of these and other policies, Mao continued, were visible in the areas then ruled by the Communists: "You can see the difference in our areas—the people are alive, interested, friendly. They have a human outlet. They are free from deadening repression."

Even at the time this was something of an idealization—though the reports of many visitors to Yenan during the war years attest that there was much truth in it. But Mao did express in simple language, in these remarks to an American diplomat, the two basic aims of this and all subsequent rectification movements: to combat the bureaucratic tendencies of the party cadres by subjecting them to mass criticism, thus developing at the same time a sentiment of participation and therefore of freedom among the people.

Similar campaigns were conducted in the early nineteen-fifties, and again in 1957, after the outcome of the "Hundred Flowers" experiment, in which all citizens were invited freely to criticize the party and the Government, had revealed to Mao that the Chinese had not yet been as thoroughly reeducated as he imagined. Although they involved mass criticism sessions that were often highly traumatic for the individuals concerned, all such campaigns prior to the cultural revolution remained clearly under the control of the Chinese Communist party, which was expected to reform itself from within, under the stimulus of outside criticism.

Although the bureaucratic tendencies of those enjoying even a small parcel of authority are a particular source of concern to Mao, the problem with which he has been grappling in recent years is, as already suggested, much broader, involving not merely that small fraction of "intellectuals" who constitute the party apparatus, but the relation between all those who possess modern skills and the other members of society.

In the long run, of course, Mao is persuaded that the gulf between the educated and the uneducated will disappear, with the progressive effacement of differences between town and countryside and between mental and manual labor. But for the time being it persists, and nourishes attitudes on the part of those who do have some "book learning" of which Mao is all the more wary, since he once entertained them himself. "I began as a student and acquired the habits of a student," he declared in 1942. "Surrounded by students who could neither fetch nor carry for themselves, I used to consider it undignified to do any manual labor, such as shouldering my own luggage. At that time it seemed to me that the intellectuals were the only clean persons in the world; next to them the workers and peasants seemed rather dirty." It was only after becoming a revolutionary, Mao continued, and living together with the workers and peasants of the revolutionary army, that he divested himself of the "bourgeois and *petit bourgeois* feelings" implanted in him by the bourgeois schools, and came to feel that "it was those unreconstructed intellectuals who were unclean . . . , while the workers and peasants were after all the cleanest persons . . . , even though their hands were soiled and their feet smeared with cow dung."

No doubt it is a mixture of guilt resulting from his own past feelings, and resentment by a man partly self-taught who never took a proper university degree (though he has an excellent grounding in traditional Chinese history and philosophy) that has led Mao to adopt an increasingly hostile and patronizing attitude toward the intellectuals. "Throughout history," he declared in 1964, "no highest graduate of the Hanlin Academy has been outstanding. . . . The reading of too many books is harmful, and one with too much education cannot be a good emperor. . . . We must read Marxist books, but we should not read too many of them either. It will be enough to read a few dozen of them."

The culmination of Mao's suspicions regarding both the uselessness and the inherently narrow and selfish outlook of the intellectuals was first of all the assault by the young students constituting the Red Guards on the "reactionary bourgeois academic authorities," who had hitherto regarded themselves as indispensable, and ruled the universities according to their own pleasure. Mao himself, though he had launched the movement, was startled by the violence of the first outburst in the autumn of 1966. At the end of October he declared, "I did not foresee that as soon as the big-character poster from Peking University was broadcast [on Mao's orders], the whole country would be in an uproar. . . . Red Guards in the whole country were mobilized, and charged with such force as to throw you into dismay. I myself had stirred up this big trouble, and I can hardly blame you if you have complaints against me."

But if he had not realized that events would take quite this turn, Mao set out deliberately to accomplish the end which was in fact accomplished, namely to make sure that henceforth no one in China (except himself) would dare to demand unquestioning obedience by virtue of either official status or specialized knowledge. His chosen instrument for this purpose was a highly ambiguous one. Seen in relation to the party, the Red Guards appeared as "masses," attacking the ruling élite from outside. But at the same time, in relation to the real masses of the Chinese people, they themselves were very much élite. And so, once the students had accomplished their function of humiliating the "authorities" in the cities, they were packed off to the countryside, there to learn humility by listening to the tales of the peasants about the hardships and oppression of former days, and to discover thus how little they knew of real life.

The ambiguous role of the Red Guards is, of course, only one facet of the ambiguous and contradictory nature of the cultural revolution as a whole. On the one hand, it has involved opening wide the floodgates of criticism, and turning what was, four years ago, a tightly organized political system entirely in the hands of party leaders into the world's biggest experiment in direct democracy, where at any moment those theoretically in charge of a certain sector—be it a school, a factory, or a government department—might find things taken out of their hands by a mass meeting or a group of Red Guards or "revolutionary rebels." On the other hand, the whole movement originated not spontaneously, but at Mao's command, and under the guidance of the army—even though, as Mao later said, the results surprised even him. Subsequently, these anarchistic tendencies were brought under control by the network of "Revolutionary Committees" which are (despite the lip service paid to party leadership since the Ninth Congress) effectively dominated by the army. And above the whole scene towers the figure of the Great Leader, Chairman Mao, who decides in accordance with his infallible historical vision which groups, movements and ideas are genuinely proletarian and revolutionary.

This ambiguity of Mao's own personality and of the revolution he leads explains the singularly disparate nature of the groups that have rallied around his name in today's "contact of extremes" between China and the West. The first phase of the cultural revolution, when young people shouting the slogan "To rebel is justified!" attacked all received opinions and all established authority, called forth a profound echo among students of Europe and America in search of new political and social forms whereby small groups can shape their own lives. At the same time, Mao's defense of Stalin against "modern revisionism," and his vigilance in unmasking one after the other as counterrevolutionaries all those who venture to oppose his "correct proletarian line," have drawn to the pro-Chinese splinter parties in the West a number of unrepentant and unregenerate Stalinist bureaucrats and hacks filled with nostalgia for the reassuring certainties of a world dominated by the "Father of the Peoples."

The picture just sketched—two halves of Mao's personality, corresponding to two categories among his supporters—is of course an oversimplified one, for anarchist and authoritarian tendencies are linked, both in Mao and in his disciples. The thirst for absolute purity that characterizes much of the New Left today inclines one to view all those who differ as evil men who must be prevented from leading others astray. And the denial of the collective authority of the party, on the grounds that any organization whose members automatically enjoy power over others is by definition a bureaucracy, leads necessarily to the exaltation of the personal authority of chairman Mao as the only instrument for deciding who is evil and must be suppressed.

In a speech of January, 1958, Mao claimed that one day China would teach the West the true meaning of democracy:

"If we are to exert our utmost efforts, if we are to leave the West behind us, must we not rectify and get rid of bourgeois thinking? No one knows how long it will take the West to get rid of bourgeois thinking. If Dulles wanted to get rid of his bourgeois style, he too would have to ask us to be his teacher."

It would be all too easy to dismiss these pretensions, in the light of Mao's doubtful success in rooting out selfishness and creating a new humanity in China herself. But there may be something to be learned from the experience of the cultural revolution, precisely because it has taken place in a preindustrial society. In the last analysis, Mao's aim is to prevent the emergence in China of tendencies that he calls "capitalist," and which characterize, in fact, advanced industrial societies: the progressive alienation of the individual in an economic system that has become a vast impersonal machine, and in which it is hard to find out who is responsible for the decisions affecting people's lives; increasing functional specialization and economic inequality; and, as a result of all this, the tendency for people to bury themselves in the pursuit of self-interest and personal satisfaction.

Mao's declared aim is to prevent such a society from taking shape in China (as, in his view, it has already done in the Soviet Union—hence the term "capitalist restoration"). Read literally, such fears are groundless, or at least premature, for China has not yet reached the economic and technological level where she could begin to be threatened by phenomena of this kind. There is servitude enough in China, but it is of a different type, rooted less in technology and more in the arbitrariness of human beings. But Mao, who has always shown the strongest interest in laying the economic foundations for China's status as a great power, is, as he has repeatedly stated, looking to the future—to the fate of the Chinese revolution in the decades and centuries to come. He sees his fellow countrymen, from the highly paid bureaucrats and technicians to the moderately well-off peasants, all too preoccupied with their own material well-being, and asks himself whether things would not become much worse if there were more wealth to covet.

However inadequate are Mao's answers to these questions (as already pointed out, his utopia is in fact run by the army), he is the first major political leader to have raised them with such urgency. This in itself is enough to explain the sympathy he has aroused among many students in the West, who find in his statements and policies an echo of their own most fundamental conviction: that the principal concern of men should be with the quality of human life, rather than with the accumulation of things as an end in itself. On the other hand, though the experience of a nation on the verge of large-scale industrialization can provide a stimulus to self-examination, the real solution to the problem of the human use of technology and of the material wealth it produces can only be devised by those who are themselves the victims of technology.

Marx would, of course, have found outrageous the suggestion that Europeans could learn anything from Asians at all. In any case, he was persuaded that detachment from material possessions could flourish only in highly industrialized societies where an abundance of products was available to all. The experience of the U.S.S.R. and of other "Socialist" countries in Europe does not provide evidence of any such tendency, but this does not mean that salvation must come from the East. Mao's project for regenerating the West by the example of Chinese virtue is no more viable in the twentieth century than was Marx's project for the Europeanization of Asia in the nineteenth. The "contact of extremes" must remain a two-way street.

74. Mao Tse-tung

During my recent visit to Hunan I made a first-hand investigation of conditions in the five counties of Hsiangtan, Hsianghsiang, Hengshan, Liling and Changsha. In the thirty-two days from January 4 to February 5, I called together fact-finding conferences in villages and county towns, which were attended by experienced peasants and by comrades working in the peasant movement, and I listened attentively to their reports and collected a great deal of material. Many of the hows and whys of the peasant movement were the exact opposite of what the gentry in Hankow and Changsha are saying. I saw and heard of many strange things of which I had hitherto been unaware. I believe the same is true of many other places, too. All talk directed against the peasant movement must be speedily set right. All the wrong measures taken by the revolutionary authorities concerning the peasant movement must be speedily changed. Only thus can the future of the revolution be benefited. For the present upsurge of the peasant movement is a colossal event. In a very short time, in China's central, southern and northern provinces, several hundred mil-

Source: Mao Tse-tung, *Selected Works of Mao Tse-tung* 1 (Peking: Foreign Language Press, 1944), pp. 23–34 passim.

Mao Tse-tung is a Chinese Communist political leader and Chairman of The People's Republic of China. He was chairman of the first All-China Congress of Soviets, which formed the Soviet Republic of China in 1931. He was also chairman of the Central People's Government. He is author of *Selected Works of Mao Tse-Tung* (four volumes).

lion peasants will rise like a mighty storm, like a hurricane, a force so swift and violent that no power, however great, will be able to hold it back. They will smash all the trammels that bind them and rush forward along the road to liberation. They will sweep all the imperialists, warlords, corrupt officials, local tyrants and evil gentry into their graves. Every revolutionary party and every revolutionary comrade will be put to the test, to be accepted or rejected as they decide. There are three alternatives. To march at their head and lead them? To trail behind them, gesticulating and criticizing? Or to stand in their way and oppose them? Every Chinese is free to choose, but events will force you to make the choice quickly.

GET ORGANIZED!

The development of the peasant movement in Hunan may be divided roughly into two periods with respect to the counties in the province's central and southern parts where the movement has already made much headway. The first, from January to September of last year, was one of organization. In this period, January to June was a time of underground activity, and July to September, when the revolutionary army was driving out Chao Heng-ti, one of open activity. During this period, the membership of the peasant associations did not exceed 300,000–400,000, the masses directly under their leadership numbered little more than a million, there was as yet hardly any struggle in the rural areas, and consequently there was very little criticism of the associations in other circles. Since its members served as guides, scouts and carriers of the Northern Expeditionary Army, even some of the officers had a good word to say for the peasant associations. The second period, from last October to January of this year, was one of revolutionary action. The membership of the associations jumped to two million and the masses directly under their leadership increased to ten million. Since the peasants generally enter only one name for the whole family on joining a peasant association, a membership of two million means a mass following of about ten million. Almost half the peasants in Hunan are now organized. In counties like Hsiangtan, Hsianghsiang, Liuyang, Changsha, Liling, Ninghsiang, Pingkiang, Hsiangyin, Hengshan, Hengyang, Leiyang, Chenhsien and Anhua, nearly all the peasants have combined in the peasant associations or have come under their leadership. It was on the strength of their extensive organization that the peasants went into action and within four months brought about a great revolution in the countryside, a revolution without parallel in history.

DOWN WITH THE LOCAL TYRANTS AND EVIL GENTRY! ALL POWER TO THE PEASANT ASSOCIATIONS!

The main targets of attack by the peasants are the local tyrants, the evil gentry and the lawless landlords, but in passing they also hit out against patriarchal ideas and institutions, against the corrupt officials in the cities and against bad practices and customs in the rural areas. In force and momentum the attack is tempestuous; those who bow before it survive and those who resist perish. As a result, the privileges which the feudal landlords enjoyed for thousands of years are being shattered to pieces. Every bit of the dignity and prestige built up by the landlords is being swept into the dust. With the collapse of the power of the landlords, the peasant associations have now become the sole organs of authority and the popular slogan "All power to the peasant associations" has become a reality. Even trifles such as a quarrel between husband and wife are brought to the peasant association. Nothing can be settled unless someone from the peasant association is present. The association actually dictates all rural affairs, and, quite literally, "whatever it says, goes." Those who are outside the associations can only speak well of them and cannot say anything against them. The local tyrants, evil gentry and lawless landlords have been deprived of all right to speak, and none of them dares even mutter dissent. In the face of the peasant associations' power and pressure, the top local tyrants and evil gentry, have fled to Shanghai, those of the second rank to Hankow, those of the third to Changsha and those of the fourth to the county towns, while the fifth rank and the still lesser fry surrender to the peasant associations in the villages.

"Here's ten yuan. Please let me join the peasant association," one of the smaller of the evil gentry will say.

"Ugh! Who wants your filthy money?" the peasants reply.

Many middle and small landlords and rich peasants and even some middle peasants, who were all formerly opposed to the peasant associations, are now vainly seeking admission. Visiting various places, I often came across such people who pleaded with me, "Mr. Committeeman from the provincial capital, please be my sponsor!"

In the Ching Dynasty, the household census compiled by the local authorities consisted of a regular register and "the other" register, the former for honest people and the latter for burglars, bandits and similar undesirables. In some places the peasants now use this method to scare those who formerly opposed the associations. They say, "Put their names down in the other register!"

Afraid of being entered in the other register, such people try various devices to gain admission into the peasant associations, on which their minds are so set that they do not feel safe until their names are entered. But more often than not they are turned down flat, and so they are always on tenterhooks; with the doors of the association barred to them, they are like tramps without a home or, in rural parlance, "mere trash." In short, what was looked down upon four months ago as a "gang of peasants" has now become a most honourable institution. Those who formerly prostrated themselves before the power of the gentry now bow before the power of the peasants. No matter what their identity, all admit that the world since last October is a different one.

"IT'S TERRIBLE!" OR "IT'S FINE!"

The peasants' revolt disturbed the gentry's sweet dreams. When the news from the countryside reached the cities, it caused immediate uproar among the gentry. Soon after my arrival in Changsha, I met all sorts of people and picked up a good deal of gossip. From the middle social strata upwards to the Kuomintang right-wingers, there was not a single person who did not sum up the whole business in the phrase, "It's terrible!" Under the impact of the views of the "It's terrible!" school then flooding the city, even quite revolutionary-minded people became downhearted as they pictured the events in the countryside in their mind's eye; and they were unable to deny the word "terrible." Even quite progressive people said, "Though terrible, it is inevitable in a revolution." In short, nobody could altogether deny the word "terrible." But, as already mentioned, the fact is that the great peasant masses have risen to fulfil their historic mission and that the forces of rural democracy have risen to overthrow the forces of rural feudalism. The patriarchal-feudal class of local tyrants, evil gentry and lawless landlords has formed the basis of autocratic government for thousands of years and is the cornerstone of imperialism, warlordism and corrupt officialdom. To overthrow these feudal forces is the real objective of the national revolution. In a few months the peasants have accomplished what Dr. Sun Yat-sen wanted, but failed, to accomplish in the forty years he devoted to the national revolution. This is a marvellous feat never before achieved, not just in forty, but in thousands of years. It's fine. It is not "terrible" at all. It is anything but "terrible." "It's terrible" is obviously a theory for combating the rise of the peasants in the interests of the landlords; it is obviously a theory of the landlord class for preserving the old order of feudalism and obstructing the establishment of the new order of democracy, it is obviously a counterrevolutionary theory. No revolutionary comrade should echo this nonsense. If your revolutionary viewpoint is firmly established and if you have been to the villages and looked around, you will undoubtedly feel thrilled as never before. Countless thousands of the enslaved – the peasants – are striking down the enemies who battened on their flesh. What the peasants are doing is absolutely right; what they are doing is fine! "It's fine!" is the theory of the peasants and of all other revolutionaries. Every revolutionary comrade should know that the national revolution requires a great change in the countryside. The Revolution of 1911 did not bring about this change, hence its failure. This change is now taking place, and it is an important factor for the completion of the revolution. Every revolutionary comrade must support it, or he will be taking the stand of counterrevolution.

THE QUESTION OF "GOING TOO FAR"

Then there is another section of people who say, "Yes, peasant associations are necessary, but they are going rather too far." This is the opinion of the middle-of-the-roaders. But what is the actual situation? True, the peasants are in a sense "unruly" in the countryside. Supreme in authority, the peasant association allows the landlord no say and sweeps away his prestige. This amounts to striking the landlord down to the dust and keeping him there. The peasants threaten, "We will put you in the other register!" They fine the local tyrants and evil gentry, they demand contributions from them, and they smash their sedan-chairs. People swarm into the houses of local tyrants and evil gentry who are against the peasant association, slaughter their pigs and consume their grain. They even loll for a minute or two on the ivory-inlaid beds belonging to the young ladies in the households of the local tyrants and evil gentry. At the slightest provocation they make arrests, crown the arrested with tall paper-hats, and parade them through the villages, saying "You dirty landlords, now you know who we are!" Doing whatever they like and turning everything upside down, they have created a kind of terror in the countryside. This is what some people call "going too far," or "going beyond the proper limits in righting a wrong," or "really too much." Such talk may seem plausible, but in fact it is wrong. First, the local tyrants, evil gentry and lawless landlords have themselves driven the peasants to this. For ages they have used their power to tyrannize over the peasants and trample them underfoot; that is why the peasants have reacted so strongly. The most violent revolts and the most serious disorders have invariably occurred in places where the local tyrants, evil gentry and lawless landlords perpetrated the worst outrages. The peasants are clear sighted. Who is bad and who is not, who is the worst and who is not quite so vicious, who deserves severe punishment and who deserves to be let off lightly – the peasants keep clear accounts, and very seldom has the punishment exceeded the crime. Secondly, a revolution is not a dinner party, or writing an essay, or painting a picture, or doing embroidery; it cannot be so refined, so leisurely and gentle, so temperate, kind, courteous, restrained and magnanimous. A rural revolution is an insurrection, an act of violence by which one class overthrows another. A rural revolution is a revolution by which the peasantry overthrows the power of the feudal landlord class. Without using the greatest force, the peasants cannot possibly overthrow the deep-rooted authority of the landlords which has lasted for thousands of years. The rural areas need a mighty revolutionary upsurge, for it alone can rouse the people in their millions to become a powerful force. All the actions mentioned here which have been labelled as "going too far" flow from the power of the peasants, which has been called forth by the mighty revolutionary upsurge in the countryside. It was highly necessary for such things to be done in the second period of the peasant movement, the period of revolutionary action. In this period it was necessary to establish the absolute authority of the peasants. It was necessary to forbid malicious criticism of the peasant associations. It was necessary to overthrow the whole authority of the gentry, to strike them to the ground and keep them there. There is revolutionary significance in all the actions which were labelled as "going too far" in this period. To put it bluntly, it is necessary to create terror for a while in every rural area, or otherwise it would be impossible to suppress the activities of the counterrevolutionaries in the countryside or overthrow the authority of the gentry. Proper limits have to be exceeded in order to right a wrong, or else the wrong cannot be righted. Those who talk about the peasants "going too far" seem at first sight to be different from those who say "It's terrible!" as mentioned earlier, but in essence they proceed from the same standpoint and likewise voice a landlord theory that upholds the interests of the privileged classes. Since this theory impedes the rise of the peasant movement and so disrupts the revolution, we must firmly oppose it.

THE "MOVEMENT OF THE RIFFRAFF"

The right-wing of the Kuomintang says, "The peasant movement is a movement of the riffraff, of the lazy peasants." This view is current in Changsha. When I was in the countryside, I heard the gentry say, "It is all right to set up peasant associations, but the people now running them are no good. They ought to be replaced!" This opinion comes to the same thing as what the right-wingers are saying; according to both it is all right to have a peasant movement (the movement is already in being and no one dare say otherwise), but they say that the people running it are no good and they particularly hate those in charge of the associations at the lower levels, calling them "riffraff." In short, all those whom the gentry had despised, those whom they had trodden into the dirt, people with no place in society, people with no right to speak, have now audaciously lifted up their heads. They have not only lifted up their heads but taken power into their hands. They are now running the township peasant associations (at the lowest level), which they have turned into something fierce and formidable. They have raised their rough, work-soiled hands and laid them on the gentry. They tether the evil gentry with ropes, crown them with tall paper-hats and paade them through the villages. (In Hsiangtan and Hsianghsiang they call this "parading through the township" and in Liling "parading through the fields.") Not a day passes but they drum some harsh, pitiless words of denunciation into gentry's ears. They are issuing orders and are running everything. Those who used to rank lowest now rank above everybody else; and so this is called "turning things upside down."

VANGUARDS OF THE REVOLUTION

Where there are two opposite approaches to things and people, two opposite views emerge. "It's terrible!" and "It's fine!" "riffraff" and "vanguards of the revolution"—here are apt examples.

We said above that the peasants have accomplished a revolutionary task which had been left unaccomplished for many years and have done an important job for the national revolution. But has this great revolutionary task, this important revolutionary work, been performed by all the peasants? No. There are three kinds of peasants, the rich, the middle and the poor peasants. The three live in different circumstances and so have different views about the revolution.

. . . . . .

The poor peasants have always been the main force in the bitter fight in the countryside. They have fought militantly through the two periods of underground work and of open activity. They are the most responsive to Communist Party leadership. They are deadly enemies of the camp of the local tyrants and evil gentry and attack it without the slightest hesitation. "We joined the peasant association long ago," they say to the rich peasants, "why are you still hesitating?" The rich peasants answer mockingly, "What is there to keep you from joining? You people have neither a tile over your heads nor a speck of land under your feet!" It is true the poor peasants are not afraid of losing anything. Many of them really have "neither a tile over their heads nor a speck of land under their feet." What, indeed, is there to keep them from joining the associations? According to the survey of Changsha County, the poor peasants comprise 70 percent, the middle peasants 20 percent, and the landlords and the rich peasants 10 percent of the population in the rural areas. The 70 percent, the poor peasants, may be subdivided into two categories, the utterly destitute and the less destitute. The utterly destitute, comprising 20 percent, are the completely dispossessed, that is, people who have neither land nor money, are without any means of livelihood, and are forced to leave home and become mercenaries or hired labourers or wandering beggars. The less destitute, the other 50 percent, are the partially dispossessed, that is, people with just a little land or a little money who eat up more than they earn and live in toil and distress the year round, such as the handicraftsmen, the tenant-peasants (not including the rich tenant-peasants) and the semitenant-peasants. This great mass of poor peasants, or altogether 70 percent of the rural population, are the backbone of the peasant associations, the vanguard in the overthrow of the feudal forces and the heroes who have performed the great revolutionary task which for long years was left undone. Without the poor peasant class (the "riffraff," as the gentry call them), it would have been impossible to bring about the present revolutionary situation in the countryside, or to overthrow the local tyrants and evil gentry and complete the democratic revolution. The poor peasants, being the most revolutionary group, have gained the leadership of the peasant associations. In both the first and second periods almost all the chairmen and committee members in the peasant associations at the lowest level were poor peasants (of the officials in the township associations in Hengshan County the utterly destitute comprise 50 percent, the less destitute 40 percent, and poverty-stricken intellectuals 10 percent). Leadership by the poor peasants is absolutely necessary. Without the poor peasants there would be no revolution. To deny their role is to deny the revolution. To attack them is to attack the revolution. They have never been wrong on the general direction of the revolution. They have discredited the local tyrants and evil gentry. They have beaten down the local tyrants and evil gentry, big and small, and kept them underfoot. Many of their deeds in the period of revolutionary action, which were labelled as "going too far," were in fact the very things the revolution required. Some county governments, county headquarters of the Kuomintang and county peasant associations in Hunan have already made a number of mistakes; some have even sent soldiers to arrest officials of the lower-level associations at the landlords' request. A good many chairmen and committee members of township associations in Hengshan and Hsianghsiang Counties have been thrown in jail. This mistake is very serious and feeds the arrogance of the reactionaries. To judge whether or not it is a mistake, you have only to see how joyful the lawless landlords become and how reactionary sentiments grow, wherever the chairmen or committee members of local peasant associations are arrested. We must combat the counterrevolutionary talk of a "movement of riffraff" and a "movement of lazy peasants" and must be especially careful not to commit the error of helping the local tyrants and evil gentry in their attacks on the poor peasant class. Though a few of the poor peasant leaders undoubtedly did have shortcomings, most of them have changed by now. They themselves are energetically prohibiting gambling and suppressing banditry. Where the peasant association is powerful, gambling has stopped altogether and banditry has vanished. In some places it is literally true that people do not take any articles left by the wayside and that doors are not bolted at night. According to the Hengshan survey, 85 percent of the poor peasant leaders have made great progress and have proved themselves capable and hard-working. Only 15 percent retain some bad habits. The most one can call these is "an unhealthy minority," and we must not echo the local tyrants and evil gentry in indiscriminatingly condemning them as "riffraff." This problem of the "unhealthy minority" can be tackled only under the peasant associations' own slogan of "strengthen discipline," by carrying on propaganda among the masses, by educating the "unhealthy minority," and by tightening the associations' discipline; in no circumstances should soldiers be arbitrarily sent to make such arrests as would damage the prestige of the poor peasants and feed the arrogance of the local tyrants and evil gentry. This point requires particular attention.

. . . . . .

75. Simon

Some years ago, on the basis of careful research, I announced a theorem which, slightly simplified, reads:

Anything that can be learned by travel, can be learned faster, cheaper, and better in a good library.[1]

The accumulation of evidence supporting the travel theorem is now overwhelming. What, then, can one report about China on the basis of a 19-day visit? Very little from the travel itself, but a great deal from the library trips that the travel stimulated. I should like, therefore, to testify here as a China Expert Twice Removed—once removed because my expertness derives from reading the works of China Experts; removed once again because most of those experts are themselves Experts Once Removed, veterans of painstaking China-watching from Hong Kong, Taiwan, Tokyo, or Ann Arbor.

On second thought, I am exaggerating my remoteness from the facts. The *Little Red Book* is as much a fact of China as is a stone of the Great Wall. It is available at your local bookstore, as are other relevant documents, as well as eyewitness accounts of recent China by perceptive observers—e.g., Klaus Mehnert's *China Returns.* I am much better off than an archaeologist, who has only bones and physical artifacts to go by in reconstructing a civilization. I am as well off as a historian, with whom I share those most important artifacts of all—the words that members of a civilization use to communicate with each other.

On third thought, I have even further qualifications as a China Expert. Observations, to produce facts, must be skilled observations, by qualified observers. The description of a moon rock by a layman produces very little, if anything, in the way of fact. Only a geologist can extract a fact from a rock. Only a social scientist can extract a fact from a social artifact or a social communication. Hence, I will claim the status of Qualified Observer of facts about China. What I see and, more important, what I read will be sifted through the mesh of theory that I hold in my mind, will be winnowed.

Perhaps that is enough to qualify the witness (and to comfort those who would otherwise see in this essay a betrayal of the travel theorem). What about China, Mao's China in 1972? Perhaps, even if I am going to talk mainly about what I have read and not what I have seen, I should first mention the circumstances of our journey.

Nearly two years ago, some computer scientists of my acquaintance agreed—perhaps over cocktails, and stirred by the

[1] For a more exact version of the theorem, in place of "travel" read "a journey of less than six months' duration." The theorem has been attacked by persons who wantonly and persistently misunderstand it. For example, it is often confused with the patently false proposition: "Travel is not enjoyable." To suggest that opposition to the travel theorem stems from guilt produced by conflict between enjoyment of travel and the Protestant ethic would be to argue *ad hominem*—something I should not like to do.

Source: Herbert A. Simon, *Social Science Research Council Items* 27, no. 1 (March 1973): 1–4. Reprinted by permission of the author and the Social Science Research Council.

The author is a social scientist and professor of computer sciences and psychology at Carnegie-Mellon University in Pittsburgh. He received a grant to travel to China under the program of the Committee on Scholarly Communication with the People's Republic of China.

table tennis match in Peking—that it would be a fine thing to arrange for a scientific interchange between American computer scientists and their counterparts in the People's Republic of China. Two of them volunteered to visit the Chinese Embassy in Ottawa to see if a trip could be arranged. The proposal was received politely but coolly, and nothing more was heard through the subsequent period of the Kissinger and Nixon trips. In the middle of April, 1972, a cordial invitation was received for six of us (of our own selection) and our wives to visit China as guests of the People's Republic. A larger party would not be feasible, we were told, because of limits on accommodations and interpreters. . . . All six, and two of the five wives who completed the party, were experts in one aspect or another of computer science; only my wife and I also had social science training.

The trip, taken in July, as previously remarked, gave us some 19 days in China. The time was spent mainly in Canton, Shanghai, and Peking, with plane transit between those cities. We saw rural China from the ground only on the train from the border to Canton, and in brief excursions by automobile, e.g., to a commune, to the Great Wall, and to a temple in a city near Canton. We were free to wander unescorted in the cities, and two of us who had enough rudiments of spoken and written Chinese to read and ask directions and to shop made extensive use of that opportunity. About half of the time was spent in working sessions with Chinese computer scientists, in lectures (by both sides, but mainly by us), and in smaller discussion groups. Only two of the scientists we encountered (and I think none of our other hosts) spoke usable amounts of English, so our communication (except in our urban wanderings) was entirely mediated by the half-dozen interpreters who traveled with our group.

The hospitality was overwhelming. In spite of, or because of, our unofficial and apolitical status, our accommodations and travel arrangements were excellent, red tape was absent, and the food was unbelievably good. (Some of our compatriots soon backslid to eating Western breakfasts, but I enjoyed my morning soup and dumplings through the final day.) We were dually hosted by the Chinese Agency for Travel and Tourism (CATT) and the Chinese Academy of Science, the former handling the travel arrangements, the cars and drivers in each city, the interpreters, and (we surmise) the budget that paid for our trip.

It is not clear that any agreements had been reached before our arrival between CATT and the Academy as to how we would spend our time. This was the subject of much negotiation with the CATT representatives who (we thought) wished to take us to the usually visited monuments of the revolution (e.g., Yennan and Mao's birthplace), with only token and ceremonial meetings with scientists, while we opted for a heavy work schedule. Since the scientists were not party to these initial discussions, we do not know how they felt about it. The CATT official doctrine was: "In China, we believe we must meet several times before we become friends," which we countered with "We Americans are queer, hasty folk. We say that people become friends by working together." In the end the work ethic triumphed, but probably at the sacrifice of the visits to Yennan and Shaoshan. We believe our stance was appreciated by the Chinese scientists and came to be respected by the CATT administrators. Though it caused some tense early moments, it is our *guess* that it made a net positive contribution to the goodwill objectives of our trip.

The interchanges with our colleagues in computer science were extensive and meaningful. We found an impressive computer technology in China, lagging, perhaps, some four to six years behind ours, but roughly comparable in quality to the Russian technology. We saw both the computers and the factories in which they were made. Everything, from components to systems, appears to be produced in China without direct foreign assistance. The computer scientists are well read in the Western literature, but no foreign technicians or imported hardware are in evidence. Although the factories are small, China appears to be producing several hundred medium-large, modern solid-state computers per year. The computers appear to be used mainly for scientific and engineering calculations; we learned nothing of applications to economic planning or management.

There appears to be very close cooperation among the Computer Technology Institute of the Chinese Academy, the universities (e.g., Tsinghua University in Peking), and the factories. There is evidently considerable interchange of personnel among them, and the scientists, professors, and engineers appear to be well known to each other.

The discussions, arranged with the Institutes in Shanghai and Peking, were lively and attended by some dozens of researchers, teachers, and students. (The formal lectures were attended by 100 or more in each city.) Our Chinese colleagues showed strong interest in learning about recent developments in time-sharing (which they do not yet use) and so-called extensible programming languages; and they were eager to tell us, in turn, about the design of their computers, and the ALGOL compiler they had produced for one of them. They responded warmly—and the warmth seemed more than mere politeness—to all of our comments on the desirability of continuing two-way exchange of information and visits. They were very open in answering our technical questions (obviously, we did not ask them about military applications of computers). The fact that Kuo Mo-Ro, President of the Chinese Academy, entertained us at a dinner before we left Peking suggests that our hosts were not displeased with the interchange. A toast I offered to closer relations between the Academies of Science of the two countries received a cordial but thoroughly noncommittal response from our host.

But enough of this travel gossip. What are the facts about Mao's China in 1972? The first fact, supported by all of the eyewitness evidence we have from travelers, is that the China watchers have been essentially accurate in their analyses of what is going on. Certainly, I made no concrete observations that contradicted anything the experts had led me to expect. . . .

When I say that the China watchers are accurate, I refer especially to their observations about the economic situation and the political situation. Of course, they do not know just how much grain, for instance, China is producing. No traveler could find that out either. It is not obvious that the Chinese government knows. In all likelihood, one lesson the Chinese experience may teach us is that it is possible to run an economy, even a planned economy of sorts, with very rudimentary statistics. It is possible, on the other hand, that the Chinese government *does* know, but succeeds in keeping that knowledge from everyone—Chinese or foreign—who does not demonstrate a need to know.

However, the China watchers have been right when they have told us that the Chinese are not impoverished and that they are not affluent—that they have been making steady, but not spectacular, economic progress. Nothing that eyewitnesses report challenges that conclusion; and it has the further virtue that it fits very well the predictions that economic theory would make. The China watchers have been equally right in telling us that the doctrine of Mao is not only prescriptive but also descriptive of large aspects of Chinese behavior. There is a total absence of public evidence (e.g., in the theatre, in bookstores, in conversation) of even the most elementary freedoms of political, intellectual, and artistic expression—exactly as we would expect from official doctrine that makes a point of placing all manipulation of symbols in the service of society. Social control of personal dress seems slightly less complete than at the end of the Cultural Revolution; some colored blouses and shirts could be seen on the streets of Peking, but not to an extent that would allow you to mistake where you were.

With respect to economic equality, the picture is less simple—as the China watchers have also observed. I have nothing new to report on wage inequalities, but the contrast between urban commuters on bicycles (one in every two with a wrist watch), and peasants on a showpiece commune near Peking (austerely neat) was quite visible—as visible, perhaps, as the corresponding contrast would be in this country. Thus the picture fits together. There are no major pieces of discrepant evidence to explain away. What the casual traveler, the eyewitness, sees is what others have been seeing before him, and what the China watchers have told him he would see.

But why should we expect it to be otherwise? A society is fundamentally a simple system, not a complex one. In organization, it is more akin to a mass of colonial algae than to a highly synchronized machine. Its main regularities are statistical regularities, and its parameters statistical aggregates. These aggregates—their rough magnitudes at least—cannot be long hidden either from the members of the society or from distant observers. The general level of life is revealed by the artifacts that dot the landscape—buildings, tools, means of transport—and by the visible physical condition of people.

The most sophisticated component of social structure is its system of symbol flows, its communications. But these too are extremely difficult to disguise. The *Renmin Ribao* is not published to give foreigners false notions about China; it is published as a major medium for official communication of public policy to the masses of the population. For certain purposes, and within severe limits, it can lie to the Chinese people, but it cannot tell a different story at home and abroad.

The channels of communication used to organize and manage the Cultural Revolution, until the army was called in in its latter phases, were primarily newspapers, television, and the big-character wall posters—the mass media. Hence, while interpretation of what is happening at any time in China may be difficult (substitute "the United States" for "China" and the statement is still true), and prediction may be impossible, the difficulty has little to do with the inaccessibility of data. The populace of China, of any society, finds many things about its own society difficult to understand and predict. The Chinese citizen, too, is a China watcher. What is mainly lacking is accurate social theory, rather than information.

What about the power struggles in the Inner Circle: the fall of Liu Shao Chi, and subsequently of Lin Piao? Here, the relevant communications are largely private and restricted, not public. But a China watcher, citizen or foreigner, stationed in Tien An Men Square is in no better position to intercept these communications than one reading translations of the Chinese press in his local public library. I can only conclude that China watching, as it has been practiced over the past two decades, is as good a way of doing social science on a societal scale as any I know; and by and large, the China watchers have done it well. Except for some specifics about computer technology, they had already described for me almost everything I saw on that 19-day trip to China, and more. (Which didn't spoil my enjoyment of the trip one bit.)

And so let me turn to the summing up; for tourism to a part of the world where important events are occurring always calls for a summing up. The Chinese people, except for a very few of them, are better off than they have ever been in modern times —and by no small margin. (I guess this is what Galbraith, a 10-day expert, meant when he wrote in the *New York Times* that the system "works.") The Chinese people are almost totally deprived of every kind of freedom we hold important—freedom of political and artistic expression, of choice of occupation or residence—and have no visible prospect of attaining any of these freedoms under a government that does not regard them as social goods. Do these two sentences, so juxtaposed, making a contradiction—a Hegelian, Marxist, Maoist, or just plain garden-variety contradiction? They cannot make a contradiction, because they are facts about the world; and the world is as it is, and cannot contradict itself.

If we feel the confrontation of economic well-being with absence of freedom to be a contradiction, the contradiction must stem not from the facts, but from our values applied to them. History and politics would be simpler if there really were good guys to love and reward and bad guys to hate and punish. The real world presents us with very mixed bundles of goods and bads —lovable villains and hateful heroes.

Nothing I have learned about China has simplified for me the decisions with which we shall be confronted in the years ahead. My admiration for genuine economic progress does not blind me to the fact that achievement of the messianic Maoist mission—not our version of it, but Mao's version—would destroy the human values I place highest in my scale. My genuine concern for that prospect—or rather for the damage that can be done by attempts to realize it—does not blind me to both the undesirability and the unrealizability of changes in Chinese society that would destroy its economic and social gains. I do not wish for counterrevolution, although I might be gratified at signs of that middle-left deviationism which the far-left Maoists *brand* counterrevolution.

What then? The slim, or not so slim, hope that in a longer run human beings in China will find the same things valuable that are valued by human beings in the United States. The hope that we can avert apocalyptic confrontations between two messianic visions—for ours is that too—until those visions are moderated by a third vision, the vision of tolerance for human diversity. Vietnam has reminded us, as if we needed that reminder, of the human costs of confrontation. On the more hopeful side, coexistence between the West and Russia has been managed, short of disaster, for a half century. Perhaps with that experience behind us, the next half century will be easier.

Part IX

Social Processes

76.

LIFE, LIBERTY AND THE PURSUIT OF PRIVACY

Alan F. Westin

It has seemed fitting to the editors to begin this section on the "social processes" with an examination of the problems involved in the maintenance of privacy, of *avoiding* social interaction—what might be referred to as the "nonsocial processes." In this selection Alan Westin perceptively reviews the various ways in which privacy is treated in many societies. He then analyzes the major functions privacy fulfills for individuals and groups in Western democratic nations. The reader will find here a thorough and detached assessment of the need for balance between the right of privacy and the necessity for some mechanism to oversee conduct in order to maintain social order. In these days of increasingly sophisticated electronic devices for surveillance and intensified insistence that all steps in public decision-making be open to public scrutiny, Westin's ideas should receive our most careful consideration.

To its profound distress, the American public has recently learned of a revolution in the techniques by which public and private authorities can conduct scientific surveillance over the individual. In chilled fascination, the press, television programs and popular books have described new means of telephone tapping, electronic eavesdropping, hidden television-eye monitoring, "truth measurement" by polygraph devices, personality testing for personnel selection, and growing dossiers of personal data about millions of citizens. As the late 1960s arrived, it was clear that American society had developed a deep concern over the preservation of privacy under the new pressures from surveillance technology.

In my view, the modern claim to privacy derives first from man's animal origins and is shared, in quite real terms, by men and women living in primitive societies.

One basic finding of animal studies is that virtually all animals seek periods of individual seclusion or small-group intimacy. This is usually described as the tendency toward territoriality, in which an organism lays private claim to an area of land, water or air and defends it against intrusion by members of its own species. A meadow pipit chases fellow pipits away from a

---

Source: Alan F. Westin, *Think* 35, no. 3 (May–June 1969): 12–21. Reprinted by permission of the author.

Alan F. Westin is professor of public law and government and Director of the Center for Research and Education in American Liberties at Columbia University. He is also director of a National Academy of Sciences nationwide study of the problems computerized data banks pose for individual privacy and due process of law. He is a member of The District of Columbia Bar and the National Board of Directors of The American Civil Liberties Union. He is the author of *Privacy and Freedom*.

private space of 6 feet around him. Except during nesting time, there is only one robin on a bush or branch. Antelopes in African fields and dairy cattle in an American farmyard space themselves to establish individual territory. For species in which the female cannot raise the young unaided, nature has created the "pair bond," linking temporarily or permanently a male and a female who demand private territory for the unit during breeding time. Studies of territoriality have even shattered the romantic notions that when robins sing or monkeys shriek, it is solely for the "animal joy of life." Actually, it is often a defiant cry for privacy, given within the borders of the animal's private territory.

Ecological studies have demonstrated that animals also have minimum needs for private space without which the animal's survival will be jeopardized. Since overpopulation can impede the animal's ability to smell, court or be free from constant defense reactions, such a condition upsets the social organization of the animal group. The animals may then kill each other to reduce the crowding, or they may engage in mass suicidal reductions of the population, as lemmings do. Experiments with spacing rats in cages showed that even rats need time and space to be alone. When they were deliberately crowded in cages, patterns of courting, nest building, rearing the young, social hierarchies and territorial taboos were disrupted. Studies of crowding in many animals other than rats indicate that disruption of social relationships through overlapping personal distances aggravates all forms of pathology within a group and causes the same diseases in animals that overcrowding does in man —high blood pressure, circulatory diseases and heart disease.

THE VEIL OF THE TUAREG

Anthropological studies have shown that the individual in virtually every society engages in a continuing personal process by which he seeks privacy at some times and disclosure or companionship at other times.

A sensitive discussion of this distance-setting process has been contributed . . . by Robert F. Murphy of Columbia University. Murphy noted that the use of "reserve and restraint" to provide "an area of privacy" for the individual in his relations with others represents a "common, though not constant" factor in all social relationships. The reason for the universality of this process is that individuals have conflicting roles to play in any society; to play these different roles with different persons, the individual must present a different "self" at various times. Restricting information about himself and his emotions is a crucial way of protecting the individual in the stresses and strains of this social interaction. Murphy also notes that creating social distance is especially important in the individual's intimate relations, perhaps even more so than in his casual ones.

Murphy's work among the Tuareg tribes of North Africa, where men veil their faces and constantly adjust the veil to changing interpersonal relations, provides a visual example of the distance-setting process. Murphy concluded that the Tuareg veil is a symbolic realization of the need for privacy in every society.

Another element of privacy that seems universal is a tendency on the part of individuals to invade the privacy of others, and of society to engage in surveillance to guard against antisocial conduct. At the individual level, this is based upon the propensity for curiosity that lies in each individual, from the time that as a child he seeks to explore his environment to his later conduct as an adult in wanting to know more than he learns casually about what is "really" happening to others. Gossip, which is only a particular way of obtaining private information to satisfy curiosity, seems to be found in all societies.

Curiosity is only half of the privacy-invading phenomenon, the "individual" half. There is also the universal process of surveillance by authorities to enforce the rules and taboos of the society. Any social system that creates norms—as all human societies do—must have mechanisms for enforcing those norms. Since those who break the rules and taboos must be detected, every society has mechanisms of watching conduct, investigating transgressions and determining "guilt."

The importance of recognizing this "social" half of the universal privacy-invading process is similar to the recognition of the individual curiosity—it reminds us that every society which wants to protect its rules and taboos against deviant behavior must have enforcement machinery.

PRIVACY IN DEMOCRACIES

It is important to realize that different historical and political traditions among contemporary democratic nations have created different types of overall social balances of privacy. Britain has what might be called a "deferential democratic balance," based on England's situation as a small country with a relatively homogeneous population, strong family structure, surviving class systems, positive public attitude toward government, and elite systems of education and government services. This combination has produced a democracy in which there is a great personal reserve between Englishmen, high personal privacy in home and private associations, and a faith in government that bestows major areas of privacy for government operations. There is also a tradition of tolerating nonconformism which treats much deviant political and social conduct as permissible private action.

West Germany today has what might be called an authoritarian democratic balance. The Bonn Republic defines privacy in a nation where the traditions of democratic self-government came late; authoritarian patterns are deeply rooted in German family structure and social life; both law and government are permeated by high public respect for officialdom and experts; and neither German law nor government showed high capacity, until the post-World War II period, to enforce a meaningful system of civil liberties restraints on government surveillance practices or harassment of dissent. The result is a democratic state in which privileged elements having the authority of family, wealth and official position often enjoy substantial privacy and government enjoys great rights of secrecy; but the privacy of the critic and the nonconformist is still not secure in West German life.

Where does the United States fall in this spectrum?

American individualism—with its stress on unique personality in religion, politics and law—provides a major force for privacy in the United States. This attitude is derived from such factors in American national experience as frontier life, freedom from the feudal heritage of fixed class lines, the Protestant religious base of the nation, its private property system, and the English legal heritage. Along with the individualist stress has gone a complementary trait of associational life—the formation of numerous voluntary groups to pursue private and public goals. An outcome partly of our heterogeneous immigrant base and partly of the American's search for group warmth in a highly mobile, flexible-status society, associations have long been a distinctive aspect of our culture, with well-established rights of privacy against government surveillance or compulsory public disclosure. A final value supporting privacy is the American principle of civil liberty, with its belief in limits on government and private power, freedom of expression and dissent, and institutionalized mechanisms, particularly the legal system and independent courts, for enforcing these rights.

Were these the dominant values of the American sociopolitical tradition, the privacy balance in the United States might be called wholly libertarian. But, from colonial days down to the present, foreign and native analysts have observed other powerful tendencies in American life that press against privacy and support restrictive rules of disclosure and surveillance. The classic American belief in egalitarianism and "frontier democracy" gives rise to several trends: a denial of various "status rights" to privacy that once were attached to European aristocratic classes and are now claimed by elite groups of culture, intellect and science; a propensity toward "leveling curiosity" in social and political life that supports inquisitive interpersonal relationships; and a demand for external conformity of a high order, in the name of a middle-class system in which the blessings of equality and opportunity carry with them a heavy burden of ideological and social conformity.

The United States is thus a democracy whose balance of privacy is continually threatened by egalitarian tendencies demanding greater disclosure and surveillance than a libertarian society should permit.

PRIVACY AND THE SENSES

Privacy also differs from nation to nation in terms of the impact of culture on interpersonal relations. The most extensive recent work, on this theme comes from the cultural anthropologist Edward Hall, who states that people in different cultures experience the world differently not only in terms of language, but also with their senses. They "inhabit different sensory worlds," affecting the way they relate to one another in space, in matters ranging from their concepts of architecture and furniture arrangement to their setting of social distance and interpersonal contact.

To compare these differences, Hall studied a number of contemporary cultures to see how their notions of sensory pleasure and displeasure affected their definitions of interpersonal space. First, he compared the dominant norms of American society, as set by the white middle and upper classes, with three European cultures with which the American middle and upper classes are most closely linked historically and culturally—Germany, England and France.

Germans, Hall found, demand individual and enclosed places to achieve a sense of privacy. This need is expressed in closed doors to business and government offices, fenced yards and separate closed rooms in the home, discomfort at having to share facilities with others, and strict "trespass" rules regulating the person-to-person distance on social, business and ceremonial occasions.

In contrast, Americans are happy with open doors in offices, do not require fencing or screening of their homes to feel comfortable, and are far more informal in their rules of approach, order and distance. An American does not feel that a person walking close to a group or a home has "intruded" on privacy; Germans, on the other hand, will feel this a trespass.

English norms of privacy, Hall found, lie between the American and the German. The English accomplish with reserve what Germans do with doors, walls and trespass rules. Because English children in the middle and upper classes do not usually have separate rooms but share in the nursery with brothers and sisters until they go away to boarding school and live in dormitories, the Englishman grows up with a concept of preserving his individual privacy within shared space rather than by solitary quarters. He learns to rely on reserve, on cues to others to leave him alone. This habit is illustrated in later life by the fact that many English political and business figures do not have private offices; members of Parliament, for example, do not occupy individual offices, and they often meet their constituents on the terrace or in the lobbies of the House of Commons. Englishmen speak more softly and direct the voice more carefully so that it can be heard, only by the person being spoken to, and the eyes are focused directly during conversation. Where an American seeking privacy goes to a private room and shuts the door, an Englishman stops talking, and this signal for privacy is respected by family, friends and associates. By contrast, when an American stops talking, it is usually a sign that something is wrong among the persons present.

Hall found that the influence of Mediterranean culture set the French apart from the American, English and German patterns. Mediterranean peoples pack more closely together in public, enjoy physical contact in public places, and are more involved with each other in sensory terms than more northern peoples. On the other hand, while the American brings friends and acquaintances into his home readily, the French home is reserved for family privacy and is rarely opened to outsiders, even coworkers of long standing or social acquaintances.

INDIVIDUAL PRIVACY

Recognizing the differences that political and sensory cultures make in setting norms of privacy among modern societies, it is still possible to describe the general functions that privacy performs for individuals and groups in Western democratic nations. These functions can be grouped conveniently under four headings: personal autonomy, emotional release, self-evaluation, and limited and protected communication. Since every human being is a whole organism, these four functions constantly flow into one another, but their separation for analytical purposes helps to clarify the important choices about individual privacy that American law may have to make in the coming decade.

Personal Autonomy

Each person is aware of the gap between what he wants to be and what he actually is, between what the world sees of him and what he knows to be his much more complex reality. In addition, there are aspects of himself that the individual does not fully understand but is slowly exploring and shaping as he develops. Every individual lives behind a mask in this manner; indeed, the first etymological meaning of the word "person" was "mask," indicating both the conscious and expressive presentation of the self to a social audience. If this mask is torn off and the individual's real self bared to a world in which everyone else still wears his mask and believes in masked performances, the individual can be seared by the hot light of selective, forced exposure. The numerous instances of suicides and nervous breakdowns resulting from such exposures by government investigation, press stories, and even published research constantly remind a free society that only grave social need can ever justify destruction of the privacy which guards the individual's ultimate autonomy.

The autonomy that privacy protects is also vital to the development of individuality and consciousness of individual choice in life. Leontine Young has noted that "without privacy there is no individuality. There are only types. Who can know what he thinks and feels if he never has the opportunity to be alone with his thoughts and feelings?" This development of individuality is particularly important in democratic societies, since qualities of independent thought, diversity of views, and nonconformity are considered desirable traits for individuals. Such independence requires time for sheltered experimentation and testing of ideas, for preparation and practice in thought and conduct, without fear of ridicule or penalty, and for the opportunity to alter opinions before making them public. The individual's sense that it is he who decides to "go public" is a crucial aspect of his feeling of autonomy.

Emotional Release

Life in society generates such tensions for the individual that both physical and psychological health demands periods of privacy for various types of emotional release. At one level, such relaxation is required from the pressure of playing social roles. Social scientists agree that each person constantly plays a series of varied and multiple roles, depending on his audience and behavior situation. On any given day, a man may move through the roles of stern father, loving husband, car-pool comedian, skilled lathe operator, union steward, water cooler flirt, and American Legion committee chairman. Like actors on the dramatic stage, individuals can sustain roles only for reasonable periods of time, and no individual can play indefinitely, without relief, the variety of roles that life demands. There have to be moments "off stage" when the individual can be "himself": tender, angry, irritable or dream-filled. Such moments may come in solitude; in the intimacy of family, peers or woman-to-woman and man-to-man relaxation; in the anonymity of park or street; or in a state of reserve while in a group. Privacy in this aspect gives individuals, from plant workers to presidents, a chance to lay their masks aside for a rest. To be always "on" would destroy the human organism.

Self-Evaluation

Every individual needs to integrate his experiences into a meaningful pattern and to exert his individuality on events. For such self-evaluation, privacy is essential.

At the intellectual level, individuals need to process the information that is constantly bombarding them, information that cannot be processed while they are still "on the go."

The evaluation function of privacy also has a major moral dimension. While people often consider the moral consequences of their acts during the course of daily affairs, it is primarily in periods of privacy that they take a moral inventory of ongoing conduct and measure current performance against personal ideals. For many persons this process is a religious exercise. Even for an individual who is not a religious believer, privacy serves to bring the conscience into play, for, when alone, he must find a way to continue living with himself.

A final contribution of privacy to evaluation is its role in the proper timing of the decision to move from private reflection or intimate conversation to a more general publication of acts and thoughts. This is the process by which one tests his own evaluations against the responses of his peers. Given the delicacy of a person's relaxations with intimates and associates, deciding when and to what extent to disclose facts about himself—and to put others in the position of receiving such confidences is a matter of enormous concern in personal interaction, almost as important as whether to disclose at all.

MENTAL DISTANCE

Limited and Protected Communication

The greatest threat to civilized social life would be a situation in which each individual was utterly candid in his communications with others, saying exactly what he knew or felt at all times.

In real life, among mature persons, all communication is partial and limited, based on the complementary relation between reserve and discretion that has already been discussed. Limited communication is particularly vital in urban life, with its heightened stimulation, crowded environment, and continuous physical and psychological confrontations between individuals who do not know one another in the extended, softening fashion of small-town life. Reserved communication is the means of psychic self-preservation for men in the metropolis.

Privacy for limited and protected communication has two general aspects. First, it provides the individual with the opportunities he needs for sharing confidence, and intimacies with those he trusts—spouse, the family, personal friends and close associates at work. The individual discloses because he knows that breach of confidence violates social norms.

In its second general aspect, privacy through limited communication serves to set necessary boundaries of mental distance in interpersonal situations ranging from the most intimate to the most formal and public. In marriage, for example, husbands and wives need to retain islands of privacy in the midst of their intimacy if they are to preserve a saving respect and mystery in the relation. Successful marriages usually depend on the discovery of the ideal line between privacy and revelation and on the respect of both partners for that line. In work situations, mental distance is necessary so that the relations of superior and subordinate do not slip into an intimacy which would create a lack of respect and an impediment to directions and correction. Thus, physical arrangements shield superiors from constant observation by subordinates, and social etiquette forbids conversations or off-duty contacts that are "too close" for the work relationship.

The balance of privacy and disclosure will be powerfully influenced, of course, by both the society's cultural norms and the particular individual's status and life situation. In American society, for example, which prefers "activism" over contemplation, people tend to use their leisure time to "do things" rather than to rest, read and think in privacy. And, in any society, differences in occupation, socioeconomic level and religious commitment are broad conditioning factors in the way each person allots his time and tunes his emotional wavelength for privacy.

In general, however, all individuals are

constantly engaged in an attempt to find sufficient privacy to serve their general social roles as well as their individual needs of the moment. Either too much or too little privacy can create imbalances which seriously jeopardize the individual's well-being.

. . . . .

IDEALIZED PORTRAITS

Just as individuals need privacy to obtain release from playing social roles and to engage in permissible deviations from social norms, so organizations need internal privacy to conduct their affairs without having to keep up a "public face." This involves, in particular, the gap between public myth and organizational reality.

For the same basic reasons that standards of moral expectation are set for individuals, churches, labor unions, corporations and government agencies ought to operate. These idealized portraits are usually based on notions of rational decision-making, fair-minded discussion, direct representation of membership viewpoints by the leadership, dedication to public over personal interest, and orderly control of the problems assigned to the organization's care. In fact, much of the behavior of both private and public organizations involves irrational decision-making procedures, harsh and/or comic discussion of "outside" people and causes, personal motivations for decisions, and highly disorderly procedures to cope with problems seen by the organizations as intractable or insoluble. Despite press and social-science exposures of the true workings of organizations, society at large persists in believing that these are departures from a norm and that properly led and dedicated organizations will adhere to the ideal procedures.

Given this penchant of society for idealized models and the far different realities of organizational life, privacy is necessary so that organizations may do the divergent part of their work out of public view. The adage that one should not visit the kitchen of a restaurant if one wants to enjoy the food is applied daily in the grant of privacy to organizations for their staging processes. Privacy affords the relaxation which enables those who are part of a common venture, public or private, to communicate freely with one another and to accomplish their tasks with minimum of social dissembling for "outside" purposes. Without such privacy the operations of law firms, businesses, hospitals, welfare agencies, civic groups, and a host of other organizations would be seriously impaired.

Of course, society decides that certain phases of activity by some organizations are so charged with public interest that they must be carried out in the open. This is illustrated by rules requiring public agencies or private organizations to conduct certain proceedings in public (such as regulatory-agency hearings or union elections), to publish certain facts about their internal procedures (such as corporate accounting reports and other public-record requirements for private groups), and to open their premises to representatives of the public for periodic inspections of procedures (such as visiting committees of universities and government inspectors checking safety practices or the existence of discrimination in personnel policies).

. . . . .

The other aspect for organizational decision-making is the issue of timing—when and how to release the decision—which corresponds to the individual's determination whether and when to communicate about himself to others. Groups obviously have a harder time keeping decisions secret.

The large number of persons involved increases the possibility of leaks, and the press, competitors and opponents often seek energetically to discover the decision before the organization is ready to release it. Since most organizational decisions will become known eventually, privacy is a temporary claim—a claim of foundations, university administrations, political parties and government agencies to retain the power of deciding for themselves when to break the seal of privacy and "go public."

While the timing problem is not unique to government (advance news of a corporate decision is worth a great deal in the stock market and may harm the company's plans), its scope is greatest in governmental life. A major need is to prevent outsiders from taking unfair advantage of a government decision revealed through secret surveillance, careless leaks, or deliberate disclosure by a corrupted employee.

The basic point is obvious; privacy in governmental decision-making is a functional necessity for the formulation of responsible policy, especially in a democratic system concerned with finding formulas for reconciling differences and adjusting majority-minority interests. Nevertheless, drawing the line between what is proper privacy and what becomes dangerous "government secrecy" is a difficult task. Critics have complained that the public often has a right to know what policies are being considered and, after a decision is taken, to know who influenced the result and what considerations moved the government leaders.

THE PEOPLE WATCHERS

Surveillance is obviously a fundamental means of social control. Parents watch their children, teachers watch students, supervisors watch employees, religious leaders watch the acts of their congregants, policemen watch the streets and other public places, and government agencies watch the citizen's performance of various legal obligations and prohibitions. Records are kept by authorities to organize the task of indirect surveillance and to identify trends that may call for direct surveillance. Without such surveillance, society could not enforce its norms or protect its citizens, and an era of everincreasing speed of communication, mobility of persons, and coordination of conspiracies requires that the means of protecting society keep pace with the technology of crime. Yet one of the central elements of the history of liberty in Western societies has been the struggle to instill limits on the power of economic, political and religious authorities to place individuals and private groups under surveillance against their will. The whole network of American constitutional rights—especially those of free speech, press, assembly and religion; forbidding the quartering of troops in private homes; securing "persons, houses, papers and effects" from unreasonable search and seizure; and assuring the privilege against self-incrimination—was established to curtail the ancient surveillance claims of governmental authorities. Similar rules have evolved by statute, common law and judicial decision to limit the surveillance powers of corporations and other private agencies.

WHY WORRY?

Though this general principle of civil liberty is clear, many governmental and private authorities seem puzzled by the protest against current or proposed uses of new surveillance techniques. Why should persons who have not committed criminal acts worry whether their conversations might be accidentally overheard by police officers eavesdropping on public telephone booths or at public places used by suspected criminals? Why should truthful persons resist verifying their testimony through polygraph examination? Shouldn't anyone who appreciates the need for effective personnel placement accept personality testing? And aren't fears about subliminal suggestion or increased data collection simply nervous response to the new and the unknown? In all these instances, authorities point to the fact that beyond the benefits of the surveillance for the organization or the community, the individual himself can now prove his innocence, virtue or talents by "science" and avoid the unjust assumptions frequently produced by "fallible" conventional methods.

The answer, of course, lies in the impact of surveillance on human behavior.

. . . . .

SOMETHING IS TAKEN AWAY

The right of individuals and organizations to decide when, to whom, and in what way they will "go public" has been taken away from them. It is almost as if we were witnessing an achievement through technology of a risk to modern man comparable to that primitive men felt when they had their photographs taken by visiting anthropologists: a part of them had been taken and might be used to harm them in the future.

American society now seems ready to face the impact of science on privacy. Failure to do so would be to leave the foundations of our free society in peril.

77.

EXPERIMENTS IN GROUP CONFLICT

Muzafer Sherif

This selection not only illustrates aspects of the concept "conflict" but also demonstrates the "experimental method" of research used by many social scientists. By providing a relatively natural setting in which interaction can take place, while at the same time introducing an inconspicuous but effective manipulation of certain crucial elements or variables, Sherif has been able to obtain new evidence about the behavior of individuals and groups in conflict situations. The reader should be cautioned, of course, not to assume that the conclusions drawn from such an experimental setting are applicable without further testing to all kinds of groups under all circumstances.

Source: Muzafer Sherif, *Scientific American* 195, no. 5 (November 1956): 54–8.

Muzafer Sherif is a social psychologist and is professor of sociology at Pennsylvania State University. Born in Turkey and educated there and in the United States, he is the author of *The Psychology of Social Norms* and the coauthor of *An Outline of Social Psychology*.

Conflict between groups—whether between boys' gangs, social classes, "races" or nations—has no simple cause, nor is mankind yet in sight of a cure. It is often rooted deep in personal, social, economic, religious and historical forces. Nevertheless it is possible to identify certain general factors which have a crucial influence on the attitude of any group toward others. Social scientists have long sought to bring these factors to light by studying what might be called the "natural history" of groups and group relations. Intergroup conflict and harmony is not a subject that lends itself easily to laboratory experiments. But in recent years there has been a beginning of attempts to investigate the problem under controlled yet lifelike conditions, and I shall report here the results of a program of experimental studies of groups which I started in 1948. Among the persons working with me were Marvin B. Sussman, Robert Huntington, O. J. Harvey, B. Jack White, William R. Hood and Carolyn W. Sherif. The experiments were conducted in 1949, 1953 and 1954; this article gives a composite of the findings.

We wanted to conduct our study with groups of the informal type, where group organization and attitudes would evolve naturally and spontaneously, without formal direction or external pressures. For this purpose we conceived that an isolated summer camp would make a good experimental setting, and that decision led us to choose as subjects boys about 11 or 12 years old, who would find camping natural and fascinating. Since our aim was to study the development of group relations among these boys under carefully controlled conditions, with as little interference as possible from personal neuroses, background influences or prior experiences, we selected normal boys of homogeneous background who did not know one another before they came to the camp.

They were picked by a long and thorough procedure. We interviewed each boy's family, teachers and school officials, studied his school and medical records, obtained his scores on personality tests and observed him in his classes and at play with his schoolmates. With all this information we were able to assure ourselves that the boys chosen were of like kind and background: all were healthy, socially well-adjusted, somewhat above average in intelligence, and from stable, white, Protestant, middle-class homes.

None of the boys was aware that he was part of an experiment on group relations. The investigators appeared as a regular camp staff—camp director, counselors and so on. The boys met one another for the first time in buses that took them to the camp, and so far as they knew it was a normal summer of camping. To keep the situation as lifelike as possible, we conducted all our experiments within the framework of regular camp activities and games. We set up projects which were so interesting and attractive that the boys plunged into them enthusiastically without suspecting that they might be test situations. Unobtrusively we made records of their behavior, even using "candid" cameras and microphones when feasible.

We began by observing how the boys became a coherent group. The first of our camps was conducted in the hills of northern Connecticut in the summer of 1949. When the boys arrived, they were all housed at first in one large bunkhouse. As was to be expected, they quickly formed particular friendships and chose buddies. We had deliberately put all the boys together in this expectation because we wanted to see what would happen later after the boys were separated into different groups. Our object was to reduce the factor of personal attraction in the formation of groups. In a few days we divided the boys into two groups and put them in different cabins. Before doing so, we asked each boy informally who his best friends were, and then took pains to place the "best friends" in different groups so far as possible. (The pain of separation was assuaged by allowing each group to go at once on a hike and camp-out.)

As everyone knows, a group of strangers brought together in some common activity soon acquires an informal and spontaneous kind of organization. It comes to look upon some members as leaders, divides up duties, adopts unwritten norms of behavior, develops an *esprit de corps.* Our boys followed this pattern as they shared a series of experiences. In each group the boys pooled their efforts, organized duties and divided up tasks in work and play. Different individuals assumed different responsibilities. One boy excelled in cooking. Another led in athletics. Others, though not outstanding in any one skill, could be counted on to pitch in and do their level best in anything the group attempted. One or two seemed to disrupt activities, to start teasing at the wrong moment or offer useless suggestions. A few boys consistently had good suggestions and showed ability to coordinate the efforts of others in carrying them through. Within a few days one person had proved himself more resourceful and skillful than the rest. Thus, rather quickly, a leader and lieutenants emerged. Some boys sifted toward the bottom of the heap, while others jockeyed for higher positions.

We watched these developments closely and rated the boys' relative positions in the group, not only on the basis of our own observations but also by informal sounding of the boys' opinions as to who got things started, who got things done, who could be counted on to support group activities.

As the group became an organization, the boys coined nicknames. The big, blond, hardy leader of one group was dubbed "Baby Face" by his admiring followers. A boy with a rather long head became "Lemon Head." Each group developed its own jargon, special jokes, secrets and special ways of performing tasks. One group, after killing a snake near a place where it had gone to swim, named the place "Moccasin Creek" and thereafter preferred this swimming hole to any other, though there were better ones nearby.

Wayward members who failed to do things "right" or who did not contribute their bit to the common effort found themselves receiving the "silent treatment," ridicule or even threats. Each group selected symbols and a name, and they had these put on their caps and T-shirts. The 1954 camp was conducted in Oklahoma, near a famous hideaway of Jesse James called Robber's Cave. The two groups of boys at this camp named themselves the Rattlers and the Eagles.

Our conclusions on every phase of the study were based on a variety of observations, rather than on any single method. For example, we devised a game to test the boys' evaluations of one another. Before an important baseball game, we set up a target board for the boys to throw at, on the pretense of making practice for the game more interesting. There were no marks on the front of the board for the boys to judge objectively how close the ball came to a bull's-eye, but, unknown to them, the board was wired to flashing lights behind so that an observer could see exactly where the ball hit. We found that the boys consistently overestimated the performances by the most highly regarded members of their group and underestimated the scores of those of low social standing.

The attitudes of group members were even more dramatically illustrated during a cookout in the woods. The staff supplied the boys with unprepared food and let them cook it themselves. One boy promptly started to build a fire, asking for help in getting wood. Another attacked the raw hamburger to make patties. Others prepared a place to put buns, relishes and the like. Two mixed soft drinks from flavoring and sugar. One boy who stood around without helping was told by the others to "get to it." Shortly the fire was blazing and the cook had hamburgers sizzling. Two boys distributed them as rapidly as they became edible. Soon it was time for the watermelon. A low-ranking member of the group took a knife and started toward the melon. Some of the boys protested. The most highly regarded boy in the group took over the knife, saying, "You guys who yell the loudest get yours last."

When the two groups in the camp had developed group organization and spirit, we proceeded to the experimental studies of intergroup relations. The groups had had no previous encounters; indeed, in the 1954 camp at Robber's Cave the two groups came in separate buses and were kept apart while each acquired a group feeling.

Our working hypothesis was that when two groups have conflicting aims—i.e., when one can achieve its ends only at the expense of the other—their members will become hostile to each other even though the groups are composed of normal well-adjusted individuals. There is a corollary to this assumption which we shall consider later. To produce friction between the groups of boys we arranged a tournament of games: baseball, touch football, a tug-of-war, a treasure hunt and so on. The tournament started in a spirit of good sportsmanship. But as it progressed good feeling soon evaporated. The members of each group began to call their rivals "stinkers," "sneaks" and "cheaters." They refused to have anything more to do with individuals in the opposing group. The boys in the 1949 camp turned against buddies whom they had chosen as "best friends" when they first arrived at the camp. A large proportion of the boys in each group gave negative ratings to all the boys in the other. The rival groups made threatening posters and planned raids, collecting secret hoards of green apples for ammunition. In the Robber's Cave camp the Eagles, after a defeat in a tournament game, burned a banner left behind by the Rattlers; the next morning the Rattlers seized the Eagles' flag when they arrived on the athletic field. From that time on name-calling, scuffles and raids were the rule of the day.

Within each group, of course, solidarity increased. There were changes: one group deposed its leader because he could not "take it" in the contests with the adversary; another group overnight made something of a hero of a big boy who had previously been regarded as a bully. But morale and cooperativeness within the group became stronger. It is noteworthy that this heightening of cooperativeness and generally democratic behavior did not carry over to the group's relations with other groups.

We now turned to the other side of the problem: How can two groups in conflict be brought into harmony? We first undertook to test the theory that pleasant social contacts between members of conflicting groups will reduce friction between them. In the 1954 camp we brought the hostile Rattlers and Eagles together for social events: going to the movies, eating in the same dining room and so on. But far from reducing conflict, these situations only served as opportunities for the rival groups to berate and attack each other. In the dining-hall line they shoved each other aside, and the group that lost the contest for the head of the line shouted "Ladies first!" at the winner. They threw paper, food and vile names at each other at the tables. An Eagle bumped by a Rattler was admonished by his fellow Eagles to brush "the dirt" off his clothes.

We then returned to the corollary of our assumption about the creation of conflict. Just as competition generates friction, working in a common endeavor should promote harmony. It seemed to us, considering group relations in the everyday world, that where harmony between groups is established, the most decisive factor is the existence of "superordinate" goals which have a compelling appeal for both but which neither could achieve without the other. To test this hypothesis experimentally, we created a series of urgent, and natural, situations which challenged our boys.

One was a breakdown in the water supply. Water came to our camp in pipes from a tank about a mile away. We arranged to interrupt it and then called the boys together to inform them of the crisis. Both groups promptly volunteered to search the water line for the trouble. They worked together harmoniously, and before the end of the afternoon they had located and corrected the difficulty.

A similar opportunity offered itself when the boys requested a movie. We told them that the camp could not afford to rent one. The two groups then got together, figured out how much each group would have to contribute, chose the film by a vote and enjoyed the showing together.

One day the two groups went on an outing at a lake some distance away. A large truck was to go to town for food. But when everyone was hungry and ready to eat, it developed that the truck would not start (we had taken care of that). The boys got a rope—the same rope they had used in their acrimonious tug-of-war—and all pulled together to start the truck.

These joint efforts did not immediately dispel hostility. At first the groups returned to the old bickering and name-calling as soon as the job in hand was finished. But gradually the series of cooperative acts reduced friction and conflict. The members of the two groups began to feel more friendly to each other. For example, a Rattler whom the Eagles disliked for his sharp tongue and skill in defeating them became a "good egg." The boys stopped shoving in the meal line. They no longer called each other names, and sat together at the table. New friendships developed between individuals in the two groups.

In the end the groups were actively seeking opportunities to mingle, to entertain and "treat" each other. They decided to hold a joint campfire. They took turns presenting skits and songs. Members of both groups requested that they go home together on the same bus, rather than on the separate buses in which they had come. On the way the bus stopped for refreshments. One group still had five dollars which they had won as a prize in a contest. They decided to spend this sum on refreshments. On their own initiative they invited their former rivals to be their guests for malted milks.

Our interviews with the boys confirmed this change. From choosing their "best friends" almost exclusively in their own group, many of them shifted to listing boys in the other group as best friends. They were glad to have a second chance to rate boys in the other group, some of them remarking that they had changed their minds since the first rating made after the tournament. Indeed they had. The new ratings were largely favorable.

Efforts to reduce friction and prejudice between groups in our society have usually followed rather different methods. Much attention has been given to bringing members of hostile groups together socially, to communicating accurate and favorable information about one group to the other, and to bringing the leaders of groups together to enlist their influence. But as everyone knows, such measures sometimes reduce intergroup tensions and sometimes do not. Social contacts, as our experiments demonstrated, may only serve as occasions for intensifying conflict. Favorable information about a disliked group may be ignored or reinterpreted to fit stereotyped notions about the group. Leaders cannot act without regard for the prevailing temper in their own groups.

What our limited experiments have shown is that the possibilities for achieving harmony are greatly enhanced when groups are brought together to work toward common ends. Then favorable information about a disliked group is seen in a new light, and leaders are in a position to take bolder steps toward cooperation. In short, hostility gives way when groups pull together to achieve overriding goals which are real and compelling to all concerned.

78.

YOU HAVE TO GROW UP IN SCARSDALE TO KNOW HOW BAD THINGS REALLY ARE

Kenneth Keniston

One of the pervasive social movements in contemporary society is the student demand for change in the educational institutions as well as in many other aspects of society. In this selection Kenneth Keniston provides an analysis of the causes of the widespread student revolt. Other scholars have proposed alternate explanations for both the development of the student movement and its apparent decline in recent months. Keniston's analysis of the causes and targets of the student revolt provides a useful basis for discussion of both the movement and its decline. Harry Edwards' advice to rebels in Selection 95 may add to an understanding of the student revolt.

. . . . .

We have learned to expect students in underdeveloped countries to lead unruly demonstrations against the status quo,

Source: Kenneth Keniston, *New York Times Magazine* (April 27, 1969): 27–8, 122–30.

Kenneth Keniston, educator and psychologist, is on the faculty of the Yale Medical School. He is director of the Behavioral Sciences Study Center and author of *Young Radicals: Notes on Committed Youth, The Uncommitted: Alienated Youth in American Society,* and *Youth and Dissent.*

but what is new, unexpected and upsetting to many is that an apparently similar mood is sweeping across America, France, Germany, Italy and even Eastern European nations like Czechoslovakia and Poland. Furthermore, the revolts occur, not at the most backward universities, but at the most distinguished, liberal and enlightened—Berkeley, the Sorbonne, Tokyo, Columbia, the Free University of Berlin, Rome and Harvard.

This development has taken almost everyone by surprise. The American public is clearly puzzled, frightened and often outraged by the behavior of its most privileged youth. The scholarly world, including many who have devoted their lives to the study of student protest, has been caught off guard as well. For many years, American analysts of student movements have been busy demonstrating that "it can't happen here." Student political activity abroad has been seen as a reaction to modernization, industrialization and the demise of traditional or tribal societies. In an already modern, industrialized, detribalized and "stable" nation like America, it was argued, student protests are naturally absent.

Another explanation has tied student protests abroad to bad living conditions in some universities and to the unemployability of their graduates. Student revolts, it was argued, spring partly from the misery of student life in countries like India and Indonesia. Students who must live in penury and squalor naturally turn against their universities and societies. And if, as in many developing nations, hundreds of thousands of university graduates can find no work commensurate with their skills, the chances for student militancy are further increased.

These arguments helped explain the "silent generation" of the nineteen-fifties and the absence of protest, during that period, in American universities, where students are often "indulged" with good living conditions, close student-faculty contact and considerable freedom of speech. And they helped explain why "superemployable" American college graduates, especially the much-sought-after ones from colleges like Columbia and Harvard, seemed so contented with their lot.

But such arguments do not help us understand today's noisy, angry and militant students in the advanced countries. Nor do they explain why students who enjoy the greatest advantages—those at the leading universities—are often found in the revolts. As a result, several new interpretations of student protest are currently being put forward, interpretations that ultimately form part of what Richard Poirier has termed "the war against the young."

Many reactions to student unrest, of course, spring primarily from fear, anger, confusion or envy, rather than from theoretical analysis. Governor Wallace's attacks on student "anarchists" and other "pinheaded intellectuals," for example, were hardly coherent explanations of protest. Many of the bills aimed at punishing student protesters being proposed in Congress and state legislatures reflect similar feelings of anger and outrage. Similarly, the presumption that student unrest *must* be part of an international conspiracy is based on emotion rather than fact. Even George F. Kennan's discussion of the American student left is essentially a moral condemnation of "revolting students," rather than an effort to explain their bevior.

If we turn to more thoughtful analyses of the current student mood we find two general theories gaining widespread acceptance. The first, articulately expressed by Lewis S. Feuer in his book on student movements, "The Conflict of Generations," might be termed the "Oedipal Rebellion" interpretation. The second, cogently stated by Zbigniew Brzezinski and Daniel Bell, can be called the theory of "Historical Irrelevance."

The explanation of Oedipal Rebellion sees the underlying force in all student revolts as blind, unconscious Oedipal hatred of fathers and the older generation. Feuer, for example, finds in all student movements an inevitable tendency toward violence and a combination of "regicide, parricide and suicide." A decline in respect for the authority of the older generation is needed to trigger a student movement, but the force behind it comes from "obscure" and "unconscious" forces in the child's early life, including both intense death wishes against his father and the enormous guilt and self-hatred that such wishes inspire in the child.

The idealism of student movements is thus, in many respects, only a "front" for the latent unconscious destructiveness and self-destructiveness of underlying motivations. Even the expressed desire of these movements to help the poor and exploited is explained psychoanalytically by Feuer. Empathy for the disadvantaged is traced to "traumatic" encounters with parental bigotry in the students' childhoods when their parents forbade them to play with children of other races or lower social classes. The identification of today's new left with blacks is thus interpreted as an unconscious effort to "abreact and undo this original trauma."

There are two basic problems with the Oedipal Rebellion theory, however. First, although it uses psychoanalytic terms, it is bad psychoanalysis. The real psychoanalytic account insists that the Oedipus complex is universal in all normally developing children. To point to this complex in explaining student rebellion is, therefore, like pointing to the fact that all children learn to walk. Since both characteristics are said to be universal, neither helps us understand why, at some historical moments, students are restive and rebellious, while at others they are not. Second, the theory does not help us explain why some students (especially those from middle-class, affluent and idealistic families) are most inclined to rebel, while others (especially those from working-class and deprived families) are less so.

In order really to explain anything, the Oedipal Rebellion hypothesis would have to be modified to point to an unusually *severe* Oedipus complex, involving especially *intense* and unresolved unconscious feelings of father-hatred in student rebels. But much is now known about the lives and background of these rebels—at least those in the United States—and this evidence does not support even the modified theory. On the contrary, it indicates that most student protesters are relatively *close* to their parents, that the values they profess are usually the ones they learned at the family dinner table, and that their parents tend to be highly educated, liberal or left-wing and politically active.

Furthermore, psychological studies of student radicals indicate that they are no more neurotic, suicidal, enraged or disturbed than are nonradicals. Indeed, most studies find them to be rather more integrated, self-accepting and "advanced," in a psychological sense, than their politically inactive contemporaries. In general, research on American student rebels supports a "Generational Solidarity" (or chip-off-the-old-block) theory, rather than one of Oedipal Rebellion.

The second theory of student revolts now being advanced asserts that they are a reaction against "historical irrelevance." Rebellion springs from the unconscious awareness of some students that society has left them and their values behind. According to this view, the ultimate causes of student dissent are sociological rather than psychological. They lie in fundamental changes in the nature of the advanced societies—especially, in the change from industrial to postindustrial society. The student revolution is seen not as a true revolution, but as a counterrevolution—what Daniel Bell has called "the guttering last gasp of a romanticism soured by rancor and impotence."

This theory assumes that we are moving rapidly into a new age in which technology will dominate, an age whose real rulers will be men like computer experts, systems analysts and technobureaucrats. Students who are attached to outmoded and obsolescent values like humanism and romanticism unconsciously feel they have no place in this postindustrial world. When they rebel they are like the Luddites of the past—workers who smashed machines to protest the inevitable industrial revolution. Today's student revolt reflects what Brzezinski terms "an unconscious realization that they [the rebels] are themselves becoming historically obsolete"; it is nothing but the "death rattle of the historical irrelevants."

This theory is also inadequate. It assumes that the shape of the future is already technologically determined, and that protesting students unconsciously "know" that it will offer them no real reward, honor or power. But the idea that the future can be accurately predicted is open to fundamental objection. Every past attempt at prophecy has turned out to be grievously incorrect. Extrapolations from the past, while sometimes useful in the short run, are usually fundamentally wrong in the long run, especially when they attempt to predict the quality of human life, the nature of political and social organization, international relations or the shape of future culture.

The future is, of course, made by men. Technology is not an inevitable master of man and history, but merely provides the possibility of applying scientific knowledge to specific problems. Men may identify with it or refuse to, use it or be used by it for good or evil, apply it humanely or destructively. Thus, there is no real evidence that student protest will emerge as the "death rattle of the historical irrelevants." It could equally well be the "first spark of a new historical era." No one today can be sure of the outcome, and people who feel certain that the future will bring the obsolescence and death of those whom they dislike are often merely expressing their fond hope.

The fact that today's students invoke "old" humanistic and romantic ideas in no way proves that student protests are a "last gasp" of a dying order. Quite the contrary: *All* revolutions draw upon older values and visions. Many of the ideals of the French Revolution, for example, originated in Periclean Athens. Revolutions do not occur because new ideas suddenly develop, but because a new generation begins to take *old* ideas seriously—not merely as interesting theoretical views, but as the basis for political action and social change. Until recently, the humanistic vision of human fulfillment and the romantic vision of an expressive, imaginative and passionate life were taken seriously only by small aristocratic or Bohemian groups. The fact that they are today taken as real goals by millions of students in many nations does not mean that these students are "counterrevolutionaries," but merely that their ideas follow the pattern of every major revolution.

Indeed, today's student rebels are rarely opposed to technology *per se*. On the contrary, they take the high technology of their societies completely for granted, and concern themselves with it very little. What they *are* opposed to is, in essence, the worship of Technology, the tendency to treat people as "inputs" or "outputs" of a technological system, the subordination of human needs to technological programs. The essential conflict between the minority of students who make up the student revolt and the existing order is a conflict over the future direction of technological society, not a counterrevolutionary protest against technology.

In short, both the Oedipal Rebellion and the Historical Irrelevance theories are what students would call "put-downs." If we accept either, we are encouraged not to listen to protests, or to explain them away or reject them as either the "acting out" of destructive Oedipal feelings or the blind reaction of an obsolescent group to the awareness of its obsolescence. But if, as I have argued, neither of these theories is adequate to explain the current "wave" of student protest here and abroad, how can we understand it?

. . . . .

One factor often cited to explain student unrest is the large number of people in the world under thirty—today the critical dividing line between generations. But this explanation alone, like the theories just discussed, is not adequate, for in all historical eras the vast portion of the population has always been under thirty. Indeed, in primitive societies most people die before they reach that age. If chronological youth alone was enough to insure rebellion, the advanced societies—where a greater proportion of the population reaches old age than ever before in history—should be the *least* revolutionary, and primitive societies the *most*. This is not the case.

More relevant factors are the relationship of those under thirty to the established institutions of society (that is, whether they are engaged in them or not); and the opportunities that society provides for their continuing intellectual, ethical and emotional development. In both cases the present situation in the advanced nations is without precedent.

. . . . .

Only as industrial societies became prosperous enough to defer adult work until after puberty could they create institutions—like widespread secondary-school education—that would extend adolescence to virtually all young people. Recognition of adolescence also arose from the vocational and psychological requirements of these societies, which needed much higher levels of training and psychological development than could be guaranteed through primary education alone. There is, in general, an intimate relationship between the way a society defines the stages of life and its economic, political and social characteristics.

Today, in more developed nations, we are beginning to witness the recognition of still another stage of life. Like childhood and adolescence, it was initially granted only to a small minority, but is now being rapidly extended to an ever larger group. I will call this the stage of "youth," and by that I mean both a further phase of disengagement from society and the period of psychological development that intervenes between adolescence and adulthood. This stage, which continues into the 20s and sometimes into the 30s, provides opportunities for intellectual, emotional and moral development that were never afforded to any other large group in history. In the student revolts we are seeing one result of this advance.

I call the extension of youth an advance advisedly. Attendance at a college or university is a major part of this extension, and there is growing evidence that this is, other things being equal, a good thing for the student. Put in an oversimplified phrase, it tends to free him—to free him from swallowing unexamined the assumptions of the past, to free him from the superstitions of his childhood, to free him to express his feelings more openly and to free him from irrational bondage to authority.

I do not mean to suggest, of course, that all college graduates are free and liberated spirits, unencumbered by irrationality, superstition, authoritarianism or blind adherence to tradition. But these findings do indicate that our colleges, far from cranking out only machinelike robots who will provide skilled manpower for the economy, are also producing an increasing number of highly critical citizens—young men and women who have the opportunity, the leisure, the affluence and the educational resources to continue their development beyond the point where most people in the past were required to stop it.

So, one part of what we are seeing on campuses throughout the world is not a reflection of how bad higher education is, but rather of its extraordinary accomplishments. Even the moral righteousness of the student rebels, a quality both endearing and infuriating to their elders, must be judged at least partially a consequence of the privilege of an extended youth; for a prolonged development, we know, encourages the individual to elaborate a more personal, less purely conventional sense of ethics.

What the advanced nations have done is to create their own critics on a mass basis—that is, to create an everlarger group of young people who take the highest values of their societies as their own, who internalize these values and identify them with their own best selves, and who are willing to struggle to implement them. At the same time, the extension of youth has lessened the personal risks of dissent: These young people have been freed from the requirements of work, gainful employment and even marriage, which permits them to criticize their society from a protected position of disengagement.

But the mere prolongation of development need not automatically lead to unrest. To be sure, we have granted to millions the opportunity to examine their societies, to compare them with their values and to come to a reasoned judgment of the existing order. But why should their judgment today be so unenthusiastic?

What protesting students throughout the world share is a mood more than an ideology or a program, a mood that says the existing system—the power structure—is hypocritical, unworthy of respect, outmoded and in urgent need of reform. In addition, students everywhere speak of repression, manipulation and authoritarianism. (This is paradoxical, considering the apparently great freedoms given them in many nations. In America, for example, those who complain most loudly about being suffocated by the subtle tyranny of the Establishment usually attend the institutions where student freedom is greatest.) Around this general mood, specific complaints arrange themselves as symptoms of what students often call the "exhaustion of the existing society."

To understand this phenomenon we must recognize that, since the Second

World War, some societies have indeed begun to move past the industrial era into a new world that is postindustrial, technological, postmodern, posthistoric or, in Brzezinski's term, "technectronic."

In Western Europe, the United States, Canada and Japan, the first contours of this new society are already apparent. And, in many other less-developed countries, middle-class professionals (whose children become activists) often live in postindustrial enclaves within preindustrial societies. Whatever we call the postindustrial world, it has demonstrated that, for the first time, man can produce more than enough to meet his material needs.

This accomplishment is admittedly blemished by enormous problems of economic distribution in the advanced nations, and it is in terrifying contrast to the overwhelming poverty of the Third World. Nevertheless, it is clear that what might be called "the problem of production" *can,* in principle, be solved. If all members of American society, for example, do not have enough material goods, it is because the system of distribution is flawed. The same is true, or will soon be true, in many other nations that are approaching advanced states of industrialization. Characteristically, these nations, along with the most technological, are those where student unrest has recently been most prominent.

The transition from industrial to postindustrial society brings with it a major shift in social emphases and values. Industrializing and industrial societies tend to be oriented toward solving the problem of production. An industrial ethic—sometimes Protestant, sometimes Socialist, sometimes Communist—tends to emphasize psychological qualities like self-discipline, delay of gratification, achievement-orientation and a strong emphasis on economic success and productivity. The social, political and economic institutions of these societies tend to be organized in a way that is consistent with the goal of increasing production. And industrial societies tend to apply relatively uniform standards, to reward achievement rather than status acquired by birth, to emphasize emotional neutrality ("coolness") and rationality in work and public life.

The emergence of postindustrial societies, however, means that growing numbers of the young are brought up in family environments where abundance, relative economic security, political freedom and affluence are simply facts of life, not goals to be striven for. To such people the psychological imperatives, social institutions and cultural values of the industrial ethic seem largely outdated and irrelevant to their own lives.

Once it has been demonstrated that a society *can* produce enough for all of its members, at least some of the young turn to other goals: for example, trying to make sure that society *does* produce enough and distributes it fairly, or searching for ways to live meaningfully with the goods and the leisure they *already* have. The problem is that our society has, in some realms, exceeded its earlier targets. Lacking new ones, it has become exhausted by its success.

When the values of industrial society become devitalized, the élite sectors of youth—the most affluent, intelligent, privileged and so on—come to feel that they live in institutions whose demands lack moral authority or, in the current jargon, "credibility." Today, the moral imperative and urgency behind production, acquisition, materialism and abundance has been lost.

Furthermore, with the lack of moral legitimacy felt in "the System," the least request for loyalty, restraint or conformity by its representatives—for example, by college presidents and deans—can easily be seen as a moral outrage, an authoritarian repression, a manipulative effort to "co-opt" students into joining the Establishment and an exercise in "illegitimate authority" that must be resisted. From this conception springs at least part of the students' vague sense of oppression. And, indeed, perhaps their peculiar feeling of suffocation arises ultimately from living in societies without vital ethical claims.

Given such a situation, it does not take a clear-cut issue to trigger a major protest. I doubt, for example, that college and university administrators are in fact *more* hypocritical and dishonest than they were in the past. . . . The conditions for students in America have never been as good, especially, as I have noted, at those élite colleges where student protests are most common.

But this is *precisely* the point: It is *because* so many of the *other* problems of American society seem to have been resolved, or to be resolvable in principle, that students now react with new indignation to old problems, turn to new goals and propose radical reforms.

So far I have emphasized the moral exhaustion of the old order and the fact that, for the children of postindustrial affluence, the once-revolutionary claims of the industrial society have lost much of their validity. I now want to argue that we are witnessing on the campuses of the world a fusion of *two revolutions* with distinct historical origins. One is a continuation of the old and familiar revolution of the industrial society, the liberal-democratic-egalitarian revolution that started in America and France at the turn of the eighteenth century and spread to virtually every nation in the world. (Not completed in any of them, its contemporary American form is, above all, to be found in the increased militancy of blacks.) The other is the new revolution, the postindustrial one, which seeks to define new goals relevant to the twentieth and twenty-first centuries.

In its social and political aspects, the first revolution has been one of universalization, to use the sociologist's awkward term. It has involved the progressive extension to more and more people of economic, political and social rights, privileges and opportunities originally available only to the aristocracy, then to the middle class, and now in America to the relatively affluent white working class. It is, in many respects, a *quantitative* revolution. That is, it concerns itself less with the quality of life than with the amount of political freedom, the quantity and distribution of goods or the amount and level of injustice.

As the United States approaches the targets of the first revolution, on which this society was built, to be poor shifts from being an unfortunate fact of life to being an outrage. And, for the many who have never experienced poverty, discrimination, exploitation or oppression, even to *witness* the existence of these evils in the lives of others suddenly becomes intolerable. In our own time the impatience to complete the first revolution has grown apace, and we find less willingness to compromise, wait and forgive among the young, especially among those who now take the values of the old revolution for granted—seeing them not as goals, but as *rights*.

A subtle change has thus occurred. What used to be utopian ideals—like equality, abundance and freedom from discrimination—have now become demands, inalienable rights upon which one can insist without brooking any compromise. It is noteworthy that, in today's student confrontations, no one requests anything. Students present their "demands."

So, on the one hand, we see a growing impatience to complete the first revolution. But, on the other, there is a newer revolution concerned with newer issues, a revolution that is less social, economic or political than psychological, historical and cultural. It is less concerned with the quantities of things than with their qualities, and it judges the virtually complete liberal revolution and finds it still wanting.

"You have to have grown up in Scarsdale to know how bad things really are," said one radical student. This comment would probably sound arrogant, heartless and insensitive to a poor black, much less to a citizen of the Third World. But he meant something important by it. He meant that *even* in the Scarsdales of America, with their affluence, their upper-middle-class security and abundance, their well-fed, well-heeled children and their excellent schools, something is wrong. Economic affluence does not guarantee a feeling of personal fulfillment; political freedom does not always yield an inner sense of liberation and cultural freedom; social justice and equality may leave one with a feeling that something else is missing in life. "No to the consumer society!" shouted the bourgeois students of the Sorbonne during May and June of 1968—a cry that understandably alienated French workers, for whom affluence and the consumer society are still central goals.

What, then, are the targets of the new revolution? As is often noted, students themselves don't know. They speak vaguely of "a society that has never existed," of "new values," of a "more humane world," of "liberation" in some psychological, cultural and historical sense. Their rhetoric is largely negative; they are stronger in opposition than in proposals for reform; their diagnoses often seem accurate, but their prescriptions are vague; and they are far more articulate in urging the immediate completion of the first revolution than in defining the goals of the second. Thus, we can only indirectly discern trends that point to the still-undefined targets of the new revolution.

What are these trends and targets?

First, there is a revulsion against the notion of quantity, particularly economic quantity and materialism, and a turn toward concepts of quality. One of the most delightful slogans of the French student revolt was, "Long live the passionate revolution of creative intelligence!" In a sense, the achievement of abundance may allow millions of contemporary men and women to examine, as only a few artists and madmen have examined in the past, the quality, joyfulness and zestfulness of experience. The "expansion of consciousness"; the stress on the expressive, the aesthetic and the creative; the emphasis on imagination, direct perception and fantasy—all are part of the effort to enhance the quality of this experience.

Another goal of the new revolution involves a revolt against uniformity, equalization, standardization and homogenization—not against technology itself, but against the "technologization of man." At times, this revolt approaches anarchic quaintness, but it has a positive core as well—the demand that individuals be appreciated, not because of their similarities or despite their differences, but because they *are* different, diverse, unique and noninterchangeable. This attitude is evident in many areas: for example, the insistence upon a cultivation of personal idiosyncrasy, mannerism and unique aptitude. Intellectually, it is expressed in the rejection of the melting-pot and consensus-politics view of American life in favor of a posthomogeneous America in which cultural diversity and conflict are underlined rather than denied.

The new revolution also involves a continuing struggle against psychological or institutional closure or rigidity in any form, even the rigidity of a definite adult role. Positively, it extols the virtues of openness, motion and continuing human development. What Robert J. Lifton has termed the protean style is clearly in evidence. There is emerging a concept of a lifetime of personal change, of an adulthood of continuing self-transformation, of an adaptability and an openness to the revolutionary modern world that will enable the individual to remain "with it"—psychologically youthful and on top of the present.

Another characteristic is the revolt against centralized power and the complementary demand for participation. What is demanded is not merely the consent of the governed, but the involvement of the governed. "Participatory democracy" summarizes this aspiration, but it extends far beyond the phrase and the rudimentary social forms that have sprung up around it. It extends to the demand for relevance in education—that is, for a chance for the student to participate in his own educational experience in a way that involves all of his faculties, emotional and moral as well as intellectual. The demand for "student power" (or, in Europe, "codetermination") is an aspect of the same theme: At Nanterre, Columbia, Frankfurt and Harvard, students increasingly seek to participate in making the policies of their universities.

This demand for participation is also embodied in the new ethic of "meaningful human relationships," in which individuals confront each other without masks, pretenses and games. They "relate" to each other as unique and irreplaceable human beings, and develop new forms of relationships from which all participants will grow.

In distinguishing between the old and the new revolutions, and in attempting to define the targets of the new, I am, of course, making distinctions that students themselves rarely make. In any one situation the two revolutions are joined and fused, if not confused. For example, the Harvard students' demand for "restructuring the university" is essentially the second revolution's demand for participation; but their demand for an end to university "exploitation" of the surrounding community is tied to the more traditional goals of the first revolution. In most radical groups there is a range of opinion that starts with the issues of the first (racism, imperialism, exploitation, war) and runs to the concerns of the second (experimental education, new life styles, meaningful participation, consciousness-expansion, relatedness, encounter and community). The first revolution is personified by Maoist-oriented Progressive Labor party factions within the student left, while the second is represented by hippies, the "acid left," and the Yippies. In any individual, and in all student movements, these revolutions coexist in uneasy and often abrasive tension.

Furthermore, one of the central problems for student movements today is the absence of any theory of society that does justice to the new world in which we of the most industrialized nations live. In their search for rational critiques of present societies, students turn to theories like Marxism that are intricately bound up with the old revolution.

Such theories make the ending of economic exploitation, the achievement of social justice, the abolition of racial discrimination and the development of political participation and freedom central, but they rarely deal adequately with the issues of the second revolution. Students inevitably try to adapt the rhetoric of the first to the problems of the second, using concepts that are often blatantly inadequate to today's world.

Even the concept of "revolution" itself is so heavily laden with images of political, economic and social upheaval that it hardly seems to characterize the equally radical but more social-psychological and cultural transformations involved in the new revolution. One student, recognizing this, called the changes occurring in his California student group, "too radical to be called a revolution." Students are thus often misled by their borrowed vocabulary, but most adults are even more confused, and many are quickly led to the mistaken conclusion that today's student revolt is nothing more than a repetition of Communism's in the past.

Failure to distinguish between the old and new revolutions also makes it impossible to consider the critical question of how compatible they are with each other. Does it make sense—or is it morally right—for today's affluent American students to seek imagination, self-actualization, individuality, openness and relevance when most of the world and many in America live in deprivation, oppression and misery?

The fact that the first revolution is "completed" in Scarsdale does not mean that it is (or soon will be) in Harlem or Appalachia—to say nothing of Bogotá or Calcutta. For many children of the second revolution, the meaning of life may be found in completing the first—that is, in extending to others the "rights" they have always taken for granted.

For others the second revolution will not wait; the question, "What lies beyond affluence?" demands an answer now. Thus, although we may deem it self-indulgent to pursue the goals of the new revolution in a world where so much misery exists, the fact is that in the advanced nations it is upon us, and we must at least learn to recognize it.

Finally, beneath my analysis lies an assumption I had best make explicit. Many student critics argue that their societies have failed miserably. My argument, a more historical one perhaps, suggests that our problem is not only that industrial societies have failed to keep all their promises, but that they have succeeded in some ways beyond all expectations. Abundance was once a distant dream, to be postponed to a hereafter of milk and honey; today, most Americans are affluent. Universal mass education was once a Utopian goal; today in America almost the entire population completes high school and almost half enters colleges and universities.

The notion that individuals might be free, en masse, to continue their psychological, intellectual, moral and cognitive development through their teens and into their 20s would have been laughed out of court in any century other than our own; today, that opportunity is open to millions of young Americans. Student unrest is a reflection not only of the failures, but also of the extraordinary successes of the liberal-industrial revolution. It therefore occurs in the nations and in the colleges where, according to traditional standards, conditions are best.

But for many of today's students who have never experienced anything but affluence, political freedom and social equality, the old vision is dead or dying. It may inspire bitterness and outrage when it is not achieved, but it no longer animates or guides. In place of it, students (and many who are not students) are searching for a new vision, a new set of values, a new set of targets appropriate to the post-industrial era—a myth, an ideology or a set of goals that will concern itself with the quality of life and answer the question, "Beyond freedom and affluence, what?"

What characterizes student unrest in the developed nations is this peculiar mixture of the old and the new, the urgent need to fulfill the promises of the past and, at the same time, to define the possibilities of the future.

79.

GETTING USED TO MUGGING

Andrew Hacker

An important aspect of social processes—the subject of this part of the book—is the element of "social control"—the force that inclines the individual to behave in a culturally specified manner, often for fear of legal reprisal. In this selection Andrew Hacker examines criminal behavior, especially "street crime," and alternative means for controlling it. He also offers some hypotheses as to why social control seems to be less effective today. The reader might also find this selection valuable in further illustrating some aspects of our governmental (political) institutions.

The most urgent issue in American cities, we are told, is the fear of crime. Yet if this is true, writers and politicians no longer speak confidently on the subject, only reuttering commonplaces we already

Source: Andrew Hacker, *New York Review of Books* (April 19, 1973): 9–14.

The author is a professor of political science at Queens College, New York. He has consulted for the Brookings Institution and is author of *The End of the American Era*.

know. (The age-old recourse to draconian punishments is a case in point.) But perhaps most exasperating is the unwillingness of too many of us to follow through on the implications of our arguments. Let us suppose, for example, that we wish to have crime-free cities, or at least some approximation of that condition. The standard solutions run as follows:

(1) That we change the basic conditions which turn people into criminals: slum housing, bad schools, absent fathers, lack of employment opportunities. But the unpursued implication here is not the cost itself (anyone can conjure up a figure) but rather the extent to which the rest of us would have less money to spend and would lead quite different lives were this aim to be achieved.

(2) That the police be so omnipresent that would-be criminals would forebear from assaulting anyone, in view of the extremely high chances of getting caught. Here the undiscussed issue (over and above the cost) is the impact such expanded policing would have on everyone's private habits and pursuits. We now have about one policeman for every 380 citizens. Do we really want a lower ratio than that?

(3) That all persons who commit crimes be caught, convicted, and imprisoned until the rest of us are assured that, upon release, they will lead law-abiding lives. Here, too, leave to one side the costs of more efficient apprehension, streamlined courts, and additional prisons. What is implied is the assumption that some young toughs had better be kept behind bars until they are at least seventy. Some people prefer to suppose that the places we call prisons will remove criminal tendencies, that there *must* be some correctional arrangements which will effect changes in the attitudes of inmates. Suggestions range from more highly paid and psychologically sensitive professionals to community-controlled institutions to no prisons at all. But apart from gouging out a criminal's eyes, no one has any convincing proposals on how to prevent his reversion upon release.

Indeed no politician I have heard has a "plan" for dealing with crime, including the President of the United States, various governors, and former policemen who seek or have gained municipal office. Variations on one or another of the proposals I have just cited do not contain strategies for reducing criminality, for they shy away from specific suggestions. The fear of crime has produced more snake-oil merchants than we have seen in a long time, ranging from the domestic armaments industry to university-based rip-off artists who reroof their summer cottages with research grants. Several thousand criminals have succeeded in terrorizing several tens of millions of their fellow citizens. What are we, the public, to do? People who have had all sorts of bright ideas on everything from curing schizophrenia to bringing peace to Southeast Asia content themselves with reciting the "causes" of crime. Why have we reached this impasse?

Certainly crime tests the limits of liberalism. It is one thing to express compassion for women and children on welfare or underpaid agricultural workers. But it is quite another to regard the man nudging a knife into your ribs as someone to whom society offered no other choice. The tough position on crime is no longer a monopoly of the right. Even while opposing a return to capital punishment or mandatory life sentences, many of us wonder whether we can still afford to treat our street-corner gunslingers as sociological casualties. Writing off any human being certainly seems wrong, but then our New Deal parents never faced Saturday Night Specials.

I will deal here mainly with street crime, and particularly robbery. In fact the phrase "street crime" is a misnomer, at least in New York. Most robberies now occur inside: in hallways, elevators, shops, or subways. You are safer out on the sidewalk. I realize that muggers take much less from us than do corporate, syndicate, and white-collar criminals. I have little doubt that the average executive swindles more on his taxes and expense account than the average addict steals in a typical year. Moreover I am well aware that concentrating on street crime provides yet another opportunity for picking on the poor, a campaign I have no wish to assist. It is a scandal that a bank embezzler gets six months while a hold-up man is hit with five years. Yet it is not entirely their disparate backgrounds that produce this discrimination.

A face-to-face threat of bodily harm or possibly violent death is so terrifying to most people that the $20 or so stolen in a typical mugging must be multiplied many times if comparisons with other offenses are to be made. I have a hunch that a majority of city-dwellers would accept a bargain under which if they would not be mugged this year they would be willing to allow white-collar crime to take an extra ten percent of their incomes. Of course we are annoyed by corporate thievery that drives up prices, but the kind of dread induced by thuggery has no dollar equivalent or, if it does, an extremely high one.

How pervasive is street crime? There are more than enough people prepared to attest that "almost everyone on this block has been held up at least once." Even so, there is only one official statistic. In the case of New York City, citizens reported a total of 78,202 robberies to the police during 1972. The immediate reply, of course, is that some (many? most?) robberies are not reported to the authorities. But do reported crimes represent half or a tenth or a twentieth of the actual offenses? It is a case of pick your expert, and I happen to have picked Sydney Cooper, the former Chief of Inspectional Services in the New York Police Department and an almost-hero in the Frank Serpico story, who has been keeping track of various studies for the Rand Institute's research on cities.

In Cooper's judgment there are at most about three unreported robberies for every one divulged to the police, and in most cases the nonreporting victim will be poor and disillusioned about any increase in his safety. On this speculation—and that is all that it is—300,000 robberies took place in New York throughout 1972. As the city has approximately six million residents aged sixteen and over, a New Yorker stands a chance of being robbed about once every twenty years. While the odds are clearly greater in the South Bronx, the Lower East Side, and Bedford-Stuyvesant, ironically the most noise about crime comes from Parkchester, Bay Ridge, and Staten Island, where the likelihood of being held up in an average lifetime is almost nil.

Even the most confident experts will refuse to hazard a guess about how many people commit most of a city's robberies. I will be arguing that every large city contains a stratum of people I will call its criminal class. But estimating its size depends on a string of suppositions, none of which can be grounded on reliable data. Until recently, police officials have asserted that half of all robberies are committed by addicts. (In fact there is reason to believe that addicts prefer burglary and shoplifting.) In New York, this would mean they are responsible for about 150,000 such crimes each year.

This may sound plausible until we remember that the average addict needs $50 a week to support his habit, and perhaps another $50 for food and other expenses. Suppose that he can obtain this sum, or merchandise that will yield its equivalent, with one robbery a week and a few burglaries on the side. This means that if a typical addict performs about fifty holdups per year, it takes only 3,000 addicts to account for the 150,000 robberies attributed to persons on drugs. This seems a bit odd, since the head of the New York Police Department's narcotics division talks about the city having 200,000 drug addicts; and even the *New York Times*'s specialist on the question writes that "there are 150,000 to 300,000 heroin addicts and users in the city, according to prevailing estimates."

What seems to emerge is that the number of addicts who commit robberies is a very small proportion of the total. Apparently many addicts raise their cash by selling drugs to each other and by noncriminal means. More likely, most so-called "addicts" can actually take it or leave it alone and do not want or need a dose every day. Reducing the incidence of addiction would clearly cut down the level of crime. Still, I am not persuaded that slavery to a drug habit is the major cause of holdups, especially when we look at the number of robberies committed by people who are not addicted. At all events, it does not take many thugs to terrorize a city the size of New York. My guess is that they are fewer than 10,000.

How much better a job the police might be doing, no one knows. Cities have no choice but to work on the assumption that a uniformed policeman, pounding a beat or patroling in a car, deters would-be robbers. Hence the demand that the number of men on patrol, particularly on foot, be substantially increased. Still, no one is willing to predict how many fewer robberies we might have were there a police officer on every corner. (Back in 1969 the New York department estimated that such a deployment would cost $2.5 billion a year.) In theory, the presence of the police makes a potential criminal realize the high odds of getting caught.

John Conklin's informative and unpretentious study of 1,240 robberies committed in Boston in 1964 and 1968 shows that only sixty-two of these were "discovered by an officer sighting the offense in progress." He also cites an estimate of the President's Commission on Law Enforcement and the Administration of Justice (1967) that the chance of a patrolman happening on a robbery while it was actually taking place is about once in every fourteen years. Perhaps some sympathy should be extended to police commanders who have to decide which proportions of their force they will assign to walking beats, riding patrol cars, and staking out likely locations in plainclothes. A good case can be made for putting the entire force in mufti and letting it wander unrecognized throughout the city. But how many of us are willing to give up even an infrequent glimpse of a blue uniform.

If prevention is moot, then the alternative must be apprehension. Catch those who have committed crimes (that is what plainclothesmen do best) and put them where they will not be able to harm the rest of us for some time to come. I won't pursue here the question whether prison terms can ever rehabilitate criminals or even if such punishment can discourage subsequent lawbreaking. Nor can I consider, now, the propensity of courts to suspend sentences, accept reduced pleas, and throw out cases they consider too flimsy for convictions. I will merely note that New York City's criminal courts apparently cannot handle more than about 600 felony trials in a year, and that New York State's prisons have fewer than 22,000 beds in less-than-ideal conditions, where the annual cost of keeping an inmate comes to $6,000. I think it will be more useful to explore how the police go about catching criminals, which after all is one of their jobs, whatever happens further along in the judicial process.

In 1972, New York's police force of about 30,000 men and women made 19,227 robbery arrests. In other words, the average police officer goes a full year without making an arrest. Compared with 78,202 reported robberies, a record of 19,227 arrests is not the worst imaginable. Compared with what some say is a more realistic figure of 300,000 robberies, the arrest ratio looks less auspicious.

However arrest figures are tricky. To begin with, 19,227 robbery arrests signify the number of times that policemen charged citizens. Thus contained within those 19,227 arrests may be only 5,000 or 10,000 people, some of whom were arrested twice or more times during the year. The New York Police Department says it does not have the resources to keep track of how many people are arrested each year. Second, if two or more people are arrested for performing a single robbery, each person is recorded as a separate arrest. Third, and clearly most worrisome, at least some of those citizens arrested for robbery are in fact innocent of any such crime. The police have been known to bring in the wrong man, who may even plead guilty on a reduced charge out of despair of ever establishing his innocence. At the same time, many of the persons represented by the 19,227 arrests may have committed robberies in addition to the one for which they were arrested. According to Conklin, after a man is taken in by the Boston police, he "usually understands that if he confesses to other crimes, he will not be charged with these offenses and may even receive more lenient treatment in court."

Still, it seems strange that a police force the size of New York's can make fewer than 20,000 robbery arrests in a year. To be sure, we are continually told that they are doing their best in an impossible situation. In addition to the reported robberies, the police had to deal with reports of 356,101 other crimes ranging from 1,691 murders to 75,865 auto thefts. One detective lamented to me that on a given weekend, thirty such reports could land in his lap. He claimed that he could solve a lot more robberies if he were able to give a full week to each such incident, particularly in tramping the streets searching for informants. For example, *modus operandi* files are still kept, a holdover from the days when detectives had the leisure for detecting. If, on being questioned, you recall that the man who held you up used a white-handled revolver, the police can make up a list and then produce mug shots of men who seem attached to such weapons.

But this takes time. In Conklin's Boston study, only nineteen of the 304 street robbery victims he interviewed were asked to examine mug shots, although others were asked to come to the station house to look at line-ups of men arrested for other reasons. There seems reason to believe that in large cities only murder cases are treated with a full investigation, with a wide search for witnesses and rounding up of suspects.

But it is better to have no arrests at all than ones based on perfunctory investigations. This is something the police themselves acknowledge. Unlike civilian law-and-order buffs, the police still realize that a person can be arrested only for having committed a particular crime. John Smith cannot be charged simply with "being a criminal." It is not enough to protest that everyone in his neighborhood "knows" that Smith is an addict and that he supports his habit by stealing. The police can only arrest Smith if he can be convincingly connected with a specific holdup. If householders demand of their precinct that something be done about Smith, they will be told that the police cannot act until evidence is adduced linking him with an actual crime. If this seems frightening or frustrating, consider the consequences of not permitting Smith the presumption of innocence. If it is your wish that the police lock up all the "known" muggers in the city, such a street-clearing strategy should also indicate how it will ensure that innocent persons do not fall in the net.

. . . . .

Earlier I suggested that we should be wary of attributing too many robberies to drug addicts. The suspicion arises that even if most addicts shook off their habits, many of them would steal for a living. Suppose that through methadone or some other treatment, an addict manages to kick his craving for drugs; even suppose he can get heroin legally and cheaply, as in England. He may then join the ranks of those who engage in robbery to get money for their food, rent, clothing, and other amenities. Certainly many former addicts have found jobs and stopped performing criminal acts. Drug programs justify themselves even if they lead only a handful of their participants out of the nether world of stalking their fellow citizens. Even so, the options for the young man who has gone off heroin are not much different from what they were before he got hooked. The jobs available to him still mostly involve washing other people's dirty dishes, parking cars, mopping floors, or pushing handtrucks for a take-home wage of about $80 per week. In short, wearying and dead-end jobs. Most poor people take such positions. Crime results from those who prefer theft.

When I say that each American city now contains a criminal class, I refer to its citizens who have few misgivings, perhaps none at all, about stealing from other people. Their thefts differ from those of other dishonest persons in that they are prepared to scare the daylights out of their victims in face to face confrontations. (They can also be distinguished from organized killers, whose homicides are largely intramural.) The "crime problem," as every city defines it, centers on the existence and exactions of this class, which consists chiefly of young men who are unwilling to work at the kinds of jobs our economy offers them. (Of course they are not the only ones unwilling to work at the minimum wage. But their middle-class counterparts have college as an option; and even in a tight market a BA can get you a selling job at Gimbels.) Above all else this is a violent class, its members ready to traumatize anyone from old women to people of their own background and economic standing.

London, Paris, and America's large cities have all contained such a class in the past. We have heard of the men who would as soon slit your throat for a shilling, of neighborhoods where policemen walked only in pairs or not at all. But that was supposed to be the history, now past, of slums and stews which reduced men to little better than beasts. Indeed by 1900 that period had passed in most cities. For the first five or six decades of this century America's cities were remarkably orderly, with little violent crime and safe streets in most lower-class neighborhoods. These were the generations in which most adult Americans were raised, and their memory is one of relative tranquility. In fact that half-century or so now emerges as exceptional in urban history. Its placidity depended chiefly on the modest ambitions and self-estimates of the poorer citizens. European immigrants and arrivals from our own rural areas displayed the duty and deference of an urban peasantry. Those were the good old days.

When I speak of a criminal class they need not be lifetime criminals. I have had good students who, in earlier incarnations, held up shopkeepers and taxicab drivers. And there is a continual supply of recruits. Has anyone ever wondered from what source fifteen-year-olds in the slums are supposed to obtain their spending money? If their fathers are poorly paid or their mothers are on welfare, they must raise their own cash for clothing, records, and other entertainments. Not all do so by delivering groceries. Despite all the research into delinquency, no one can say why one brother turns to mugging and the other labors in a laundry. All we know is that more choose the first today than in the recent past, and there are enough of them to terrorize whole cities.

Certainly upswings and downswings of the economy no longer show a significant relation to crime rates. For this reason some skepticism should be directed at those asserting that we must create more "job opportunities" if we are to deal with crime in a serious way. It would be well to wonder what kinds of jobs might induce the average hoodlum to abandon his current occupation. If he rejects a stupefying job at $80 a week, will the offer of $125 move him to give up robbery? Or will it take closer to $175, which raises the question of the kind of work he could do that would merit such a stipend. None of these questions is meant invidiously, but only to suggest that robbery is one way some Americans assert that they deserve better than the economy has offered them.

Nowadays members of the criminal class blend into the general population. (They probably always did. Bill Sikes must have looked much like an average London laborer.) It is likely that some of the young men we pass on the street or see in the subway held up someone the night before. But which ones should we fear? Without knowing for sure, many of us fear them all. A student of mine told me that when he is on an elevator others about to enter often draw back on seeing him there. Some finally enter and, according to his account, he can almost hear their hearts pounding until they alight. Interestingly, one police method operates on the premise that the city contains a quota of persons who can be counted on to commit crimes. To discover who they are, plainclothes policemen dress up as old men and shamble down slum streets on the expectation that they will eventually be jumped. Fairly soon they usually are, at which point backup men dash in to help with the arrest.

Is this in fact provoking a crime that would not otherwise have occurred? The obvious reply is that had the decoy not been there, his assaulter would have attacked a real old man later that evening; thus the trap saved an actual citizen from a mugging, and also put a criminal behind bars, sparing the rest of us from his depredations for a while. Still, buying this argument shows how desperate we have become for we have blotted from our minds the possibility that dangling a decoy may tempt some teenagers who would not otherwise have considered committing a crime. The case is obviously different from putting a box of dollar bills outside a store and then pouncing on anyone who helps himself. Even so, provocation of any sort is a risky business.

If "law and order" has served as a code phrase for racism, then proposals that we unleash to the police have a somewhat more specific result in mind. Both black and white robbery victims would probably settle for protection from the black part of the criminal population. In other words, both would be willing to take their chances on encountering a white criminal. Orde Coombs, a Harlem writer, is saying as much when he agonizes that "we stand menaced by our kith and kin." Crimes by blacks against blacks have become so debilitating that Coombs will support any hard line. ("If the liberals cry about constitutional rights, chase them back to Scarsdale. . . .") Needless to say, many whites join him in this sentiment. So let's get it out in the open.

According to the 1970 census, New York City has 187,146 black men between the ages of fifteen and twenty-nine. The only way to make a dent in street crime (and by this I simply mean getting the criminals off the streets) is by withdrawing the constitutional presumption of innocence from these 187,146 citizens. Within their number lurk most of the city's criminals. The entire stratum will have to endure harsh and humiliating treatment if the dangerous members are to be ferreted out. That is what is being said, or at least whispered, with increasing stridency.

Take, for example, the matter of weapons. Most robbers carry a gun or at least a knife that seems somewhat sharper than needed to cut string. Every patrolman now has the authority to stop and frisk any citizen he has cause to believe may be carrying a felonious item. However the courts have ruled that the officer must be able to give an explicit reason for conducting that frisking. Simply stating that the individual looked "suspicious" is not enough. Many city-dwellers would like nothing better than for the police to stop various persons, as a matter of routine, and pat them down. Perhaps several times a day. Those who harbor such daydreams do not extend them to businessmen's attaché cases being opened or housewives' handbags being subjected to scrutiny. Rather the target would be those 187,146 young men who are statistically most suspect.

Such a procedure might well round up a major share of the city's illegal weapons and also provide an excuse for putting their bearers behind bars. Still, these round-ups would have to be sweeping and indiscriminate. Black muggers and murderers seldom dress in rags. Most of them are quite indistinguishable from black Columbia students and Chase Manhattan trainees, so that those subject to fairly frequent friskings would include people like Percy Sutton and Nigerian UN delegates, along with black ministers, shoe shiners, schoolteachers, and writers. Would Orde Coombs show that added patience and put up with public humiliation so that his criminally inclined brothers might be more readily apprehended?

I doubt it, and for a good reason, the one which makes residents of even the most vulnerable black neighborhoods show little enthusiasm for Governor Rockefeller's plan to jail pushers for life. Middle-aged slum-dwellers may live in terror of local muggers, but they also have sons of their own, who they realize would be subject to round-ups were the police truly unleashed. Black wives, mothers, and sisters have no great confidence in the ability of the police to distinguish a string-cutting knife from one intended for throats. Nor are any criminals currently being "coddled." The most one can say is that some of those arrested are given a chance to show that the police caught the wrong man. Certainly, once caught in the criminal justice system not a few innocent persons have pleaded guilty on reduced charges as the only way of ever getting home.

To put it very simply, the tougher the police the closer we get to imposing martial law on those 187,146 citizens. Most of those young men are as law-abiding as the rest of us. But all would be treated as presumptive criminals, and some would end up in detention because they were wrongly identified or someone was suspicious of them. All of this should be obvious and in no need of reiteration. But apparently code-talk about crime needs continual deciphering, particularly when that talk comes from circles that should know better. If people have something in mind other than round-ups based on race, they ought to say so.

The "street crime" problem should be understood chiefly as one created by a criminal class of young men, a class that we are going to be living with for a long time. The major cause of street crime is not heroin, as we shall discover once we get every addict either unhooked or onto a substitute. (In fact, someone who is not half-incapacitated by hard drugs should make a more efficient mugger.) My own considered—and by no means capricious—view is that we ought to count ourselves fortunate that so small a part of our population has taken to thievery. That so many Americans remain honest, while being treated so shabbily, has never ceased to amaze me.

80.

SOCIAL CONTROL AND NON-CONFORMITY IN A SOUTHERN TOWN

Edgar A. Schuler and Robert L. Green

In this selection Schuler and Green have edited an extended interview that the senior author had with a prominent educator in a southern town. In the interview Dean Gordon Moss relates how shunning and other processes of social control operated in efforts to force his compliance with the local norms regarding segregated schools. This case study also illustrates how belief in educational opportunity for all, and other values acquired in the larger society, produced the nonconformity of a respected community leader. The analysis of the conflicting social forces with his resolution of them and the stages of nonconformity and ostracism in the community is an insightful documentation of these social processes.

Prince Edward County, located in south-central Virginia, is a predominantly rural area containing approximately 8,000 whites and 5,000 Negroes. Both the County and the town of Farmville, its County seat, manifest the cultural, social, economic, and inter-

racial situations typical of many southern counties and towns. The children of both Negro and white families come primarily from lower and lower-middle class socio-economic backgrounds, and the same social and racial barriers exist as are normally found in comparable southern communities.

For the past thirteen years Prince Edward County has exhibited a pattern of growing interracial conflict, emerging openly in 1951 in a strike engineered by Negro high school students to obtain more adequate educational facilities.

During this period the Negro citizens of Prince Edward County began to perceive the issue of equal school facilities and education as being integrally related to the more basic problem of school desegregation. After a number of lawsuits had been initiated by local Negro citizens, the County Board of Supervisors in 1959 closed both the white and Negro public schools rather than comply with court-ordered desegregation. Shortly thereafter certain members of the white community established privately financed segregated schools for their children. Since 1959 approximately 1,300 of the 1,700 Negro children of school age who live in Prince Edward County have had almost no formal, and very little informal, education. In the summer of 1963 and continuing through September of 1965 a team of social scientists under the direction of Robert L. Green of Michigan State University has been involved in a research project in Prince Edward County, Virginia, supported by the U.S. Office of Education. The major objective of the project is to assess what effect four years of nonschooling has had upon the achievement and aptitude levels of the Negro school-age children in this county. Furthermore, an analysis is being made of the social impact of the schools' closing upon the community.

As the school issue developed and gained in momentum a number of prominent Prince Edward County residents became involved in the school controversy. Outstanding among these individuals has been C. G. Gordon Moss, Dean of Longwood College, a State-supported institution of higher education located in Farmville, which enrolled only white students up to the time of the interview. In connection with initiation of the field activities of the research team the senior author of this paper, a faculty member in the Colleges of Education and Social Science at Michigan State University and sociological consultant to the research project, interviewed Dean Moss at Farmville, Virginia, in May of 1963 in an attempt to gather information pertinent to the research

---

Source: Edgar A. Schuler and Robert L. Green, *Interview with Dean Gordon Moss, Dean of Longwood College, Farmville, Va.* (May 23, 1963). Conducted and recorded by Edgar A. Schuler in connection with a study directed by Professor Green, which was financed by the U.S. Office of Education, Grant 2321. The interview was reprinted substantially without change in *Phylon* 28, no. 1: 28–40, under the title "A Southern Educator and School Integration: An Interview." Reprinted by permission of the authors.

Edgar A. Schuler is professor emeritus of education and sociology at Michigan State University. From 1959 to 1962 he was senior adviser of the Pakistan Academy for Village Development at Comilla.

Robert L. Green is dean of the College of Urban Development at Michigan State University and a professor of educational psychology. He was the administrator of the Citizenship Education Program for the Southern Christian Leadership Conference during 1965–66. He reported the study of Negro children in Prince Edward County, Virginia, in *The Educational Status of Children in a District without Public Schools,* and edited *Racial Crisis in American Education.*

project. Except for the italicized paragraphs and the topical subheadings, the following is an edited version of the transcribed recording of what Dean Moss had to say.

PERSONAL BACKGROUND

We are getting to a sort of impasse here in Farmville, insofar as our local situation is concerned. We have been in such an impasse for some months now, since we are really awaiting court decisions and neither side can do anything one way or the other until the legal situation is clarified.

With regard to my own background, I should begin with the fact that I am just fifty miles away from my birthplace. I was born in Lynchburg, Virginia, at the end of the nineteenth century, and I have lived in Virginia all my life except some three years of residence in New Haven when I did my graduate work at Yale and the one year that I taught in North Carolina. Other than those four years, I have spent my entire life in Virginia: in Lynchburg, in Fredericksburg to the north, in Alexandria for three years back at the beginning of my teaching career, and here in Farmville. I certainly grew up in the normal, the average, and the traditional southern atmosphere. I can remember, as a child, having several Negro friends—one, in particular, was a close friend. But, of course, as I grew up, I was unconsciously subjected to the normal nineteenth century southern attitudes regarding the Negro. I can remember having jumped right over a seat in a streetcar in Washington when a Negro sat down beside me. That must have been around 1912 or 1913—when I was a very young boy.

I can remember avoiding eating with Negroes at various public meetings and conferences into my adult life. But I can also remember that in my home there was never any hatred or fear of Negroes, and that we maintained an attitude that was normal in the era—the kindliest possible relationship with the Negro servants. I did not become aware, and certainly not intensely aware, of any major issue in regard to Negroes until this situation developed here in Prince Edward County.

I have no recollection of even being aware of the difficulties Negroes were having with regard to education until at least the 1940s. The only thing I do remember was my relief when my mother-in-law sold some Negro residential property that she had inherited down in the slum areas of the town. I felt relieved because it was perfectly obvious that the property was being used for economic exploitation. By "economic exploitation" I mean that it was the cheapest, slummiest, scummiest type of property on which she had spent nothing in the way of improvement and consequently all of the rent was pure profit to her. She spent nothing on physical improvements, neither as an investment nor in improving her inheritance, and I couldn't have been a normal rational human being if I hadn't realized that such disinterest was not the best way to behave.

PATERNALISM AS A SALVE FOR THE TROUBLED WHITE CONSCIENCE

If I may attempt to summarize as briefly as possible, first the developments in Prince Edward County, but more particularly, my reaction and relationship to the developments, it would have to begin with the fact that as a normally sensitive person, I have been aware at least subconsciously for as long as I have known anything about Farmville in Prince Edward County—and that would go back to 1926—of the most paternalistic attitude maintained by the ruling white majority toward the Negro in this community. This was and is an attitude of love for the Negro, if the Negro will accept everything from the white rulers—if he will, to use common southern language, "stay in his place." But I would say that this paternalistic attitude toward the Negro is probably stronger in this particular locality than generally throughout Virginia.

I believe this attitude represents an unconscious salving of the conscience of the white man in this community. The white men have known that the Negroes who made up almost 50 percent of the population were uneducated, patient, and willing to remain in their low situation. They wanted that Negro population for the dirty work of raising tobacco on farms or laboring in the local tobacco processing plants. The housewives of the County wanted the Negro population for household servant work. And, whether they were able to consciously admit it to themselves or not, I believe that they have known that by keeping the Negro uneducated, poor, available for what they wanted from him was unjust to the Negro, and as a result they had to in some manner protect their own consciences against what they were doing. Consequently, they have developed the feeling that they were the benefactors of the Negro. They treated Negroes personally and individually in a friendly and kindly way, and were helpful to them in their personal problems—give or lend the Negro who is becoming a drunkard money when he needs to buy another bottle of cheap wine, pay his fine so he can get out of jail in order that he can work your garden for you again. This protective position or attitude was both beneficial to the Negro and to the white man in easing the latter's conscience with regard to what he was doing to the Negro. This preserves the kind of image that we like to hold of ourselves . . . that we are kindly masters concerned with the personal life of our servants (no longer our slaves but now our servants) and that we want to make them as happy as possible, always assuming that they can be entirely happy in this totally subservient status.

INFERIOR EDUCATION FOR NEGROES

The paternalistic attitude as a salve for the white man's conscience had its most specific social reaction and implication in terms of the educational system maintained by the County for the Negroes. All through the 1930s and into the 1940s an admittedly inferior school system for the Negroes was manifested in the buildings, in the teachers, and in the school administration, and as a result, in inferior educational content. But the white man eased his conscience by thinking and by assuming that this very modicum of education was all that the Negro wanted, and that he was entirely satisfied with it. When, in the 1930s and on into the 1940s, the schools for the Negroes—particularly in the town of Farmville in contrast to the surrounding County community—became severely overcrowded, the white people were not willing to spend the necessary money to relieve the crowded condition in any reasonable and effective manner. They were only willing to do this inch by inch, as they were forced to do so, and to do it in the cheapest way possible, such as putting up temporary buildings—tar paper shacks.

I recall now that around 1945 a friend of mine from Longwood College was asked to give a science lecture at the Negro high school. When he came back, he told me how impossibly crowded the high school building was, that he could barely get to the platform to deliver the lecture because every square inch of space was taken up by the students. I believe that this was my first concrete, specific realization of the crowded conditions.

NEGRO EFFORTS TO IMPROVE NEGRO EDUCATION

I am aware that throughout the 1940s the Negroes through their Parent-Teachers Association were persistently and continuously urging the School Board to build adequate structures for the education of their children. There was no effort then to build for integration. It was merely an effort to increase the physical facilities for the admittedly "Negro" schools. The whites resisted any such obligations to provide such needed facilities. As a result, if I recall correctly, the Negro children by 1951 had become utterly disillusioned and thought that there would never be any schools.

So in the spring of 1951, the Negro children initiated on their own, without any adult help or even knowledge, a strike in the Negro high school. They went out on strike and declared that they were going to stay out on strike until the School Board agreed to build a structure. The strike brought in the N.A.A.C.P. led by Reverend L. Francis Griffin who was the local Baptist Negro minister and President of the local and state N.A.A.C.P. This group sought to help the Negro children in their endeavors and led to the initiation of a legal suit originally designed, I believe, to promote more adequate physical facilities for the Negro children, but eventually demanding that segregation in the school system be abandoned. I am quite certain that suit was in the Federal Courts in 1952, and it was the beginning of the combination of suits which reached the Supreme Court in 1954.

With the above threat hanging over the heads of the ruling whites of the County they *did* go ahead and find the money they had previously said they were unable to find. They found the money, and borrowed to build an entirely adequate high school for the Negro children of the town and the County. This new school, the Moton High School located on the southern outskirts of the town, is far and away the best school building in the entire County, white or Negro. The white people were trying to "buy the Negroes off" by giving them more than they had asked for in the way of physical facilities and thus hoped to stop the desegregation suit. The new school was in use when the Supreme Court decision of May 1954 was handed down.

POPULAR REACTIONS TO THE SUPREME COURT DECISION

The next milestone to be considered is the reaction of the people of the County to the Supreme Court decision of 1954. I believe the white community's reaction was originally one of utter confusion and dismay, and then, very rapidly, of anger and determination to resist to the utmost the decision and all of its implications. This feeling resulted in the formation of the so-called Defenders of State Sovereignty—a southside Virginia organization, not merely a Prince Edward County organization—an organization that was determined to resist by all possible legal means, as they said, any end of segregation whatsoever.

My reaction to the decision was one that I did not have to make publicly for a while. However, when the occasion arose, I did make it known whenever possible—that the County should open the white schools immediately to the Negro children and abandon segregation at once. The schools would be crowded with Negroes for the first week or two or for a brief interval of time, and then it would become difficult to find even a single Negro—certainly not more than a bare sprinkling—who would be able to persist in the white schools with the latter's higher standards and the difficult social situation for the Negro children. No consideration was given to my proposal by anybody in authority whatsoever.

Then after the second Supreme Court decision of 1955, with its implementation of the 1954 decision, there was the immediate local reaction—a public county-wide meeting to consider action. Undoubtedly careful preparation was made for that meeting in terms of speakers and proposals. The attendance was just about as large as one could expect—it overflowed the 1,200 seat auditorium of Longwood College. There was essentially no opposition voice raised in the meeting at all, and it was at that meeting that they organized their Prince Edward Educational Foundation Corporation to conduct private schools for the white children if and when that became necessary. That was in the spring of 1955. I had no opportunity to participate at that time since I was in the hospital with coronary thrombosis and under doctor's orders not to become involved in the local controversy until well into 1956.

I believe that my first public statement was at a meeting of the high school Parent-Teachers Association when I was the only person who voted "No" on a resolution that the P.T.A. would resist integration of schools by all possible means. I had to ask specifically for the opportunity to cast my negative vote—the chairman did not think it was necessary even to ask for the negative vote. From that time, which was probably somewhere in the spring of 1956, until 1959, there has been really no opportunity for public protest whatsoever. I became known throughout the community as a proponent for public schools and for whatever integration was necessary to maintain the public schools. I doubt that I had developed my own thinking to any appreciable point beyond merely believing that the Negroes should be allowed to continue to have the right to education, and for those Negroes who wanted it, integrated education.

REFUSAL TO COMPROMISE LEADS TO PRIVATE SCHOOL FOR WHITES, 1959

Finally in May 1959 the Board of Supervisors refused to adopt a budget providing for the continuance of public schools because the Federal District Court decision had been rendered, demanding that such schools would have to be integrated in the fall of 1959. In June of 1959 the Board of Supervisors decided to hold a public hearing on that action of May 1959. The public hearing was the occasion of my first real public expression of opinion. At that time I protested against the closing of schools and insisted that there was no necessity for such closing even to preserve segregation (if they wanted to preserve segregation) because not a single Negro had applied for admission to the white schools in June of 1959 for the subsequent September opening of the schools. There were several white citizens that did make such protests in that public meeting, but it was an entirely futile action because the Board of Supervisors merely went through the motions but not the reality of listening to us. I recall definitely that Henry Bittenger, a colleague of mine on the Longwood College faculty, also spoke. Possibly, he and I were the only two white people at the first to protest.

After the public hearing, upon realizing that there was no possible local way of preventing the closure of the schools, Bittenger and I, wondering if there was anything else we could do, began to meet from time to time. By September 1959 we succeeded in finding two Negro leaders who were willing to meet with us to explore the possibilities of maintaining free public education. We proposed that they, speaking for the Negroes, accept voluntary segregation for three years with the possibility of continued voluntary segregation beyond that point as the only possible way to having schools in the County in the year 1959–1960. They agreed to this proposal, but admitted that their agreement did not necessarily mean that all of the Negroes of the County would go along with them. We carried that agreement to the State Government, as well as to . . . , the outstanding spokesman of the white supremacists in the County. [He] . . . refused to consider it at all. He said that he would not discuss anything with the two Negro leaders and that he would only discuss private education with Negroes of his own choice, but that he would not discuss resumption of public education with anyone.

I consider it highly significant to call attention to this situation in the fall of 1959—that the white supremacists were determined to have no public schools at all, segregated or integrated. They rejected the opportunity to have segregated schools, as I have indicated. It was only after their Prince Edward Foundation had begun to operate the white private schools that they organized a separate group, claiming that this would assist the Negroes in establishing a private school for the Negro children in the County. They attempted to get an academic friend of mine, a sort of "academic son" of mine of the Longwood College faculty, to head the organization for private schools for Negroes—a move, I assume, to undercut any opposition on my part. I did succeed in persuading that young man not to accept the position. Late in the fall of 1959—it was possibly as late as December 1, I am not certain—they issued what in a sense was an ultimatum to the Negroes: they would give them until the first of January to accept the idea of these private schools, and if the Negroes did nothing about it, the project would be dropped. This ultimatum was delivered, and if I recall correctly, in the form of a circular letter to every parent requesting their replies as to whether or not they would send their children to the private school system if established. January 1, 1960, arrived with only one Negro family having indicated that it would place its children in such a school—and within two weeks time the white Foundation had made an official request to the School Board to rent the white public school buildings for the private school system. I do not think there is a mere coincidence involved in those dates. It is definitely known that during the fall of 1959 they had found the lack of adequate buildings to be the greatest difficulty in running the white private school system. They realized their desperate need for the public white schools, and saw that if they could get the Negroes to accept the token of a private school system and the use of Negro public schools, then they would have no difficulty whatsoever in obtaining the use of the white schools for the white private school system.

I am stressing the above point at considerable length because ever since the winter of 1959–1960, recurrently until it has become virtually a monotonous singsong, they keep on repeating that they offered the Negroes a private school system, that they offered it honestly, that the Negroes refused it, and therefore the whites were absolved from any guilt caused by the Negro children not having an education. The offer was a mere paper offer and nothing was done in any sense to actually organize the private schools such as obtaining school teachers or determining the location of the buildings or of acquiring money to operate them. It was a paper offer made by and for the white people in an effort to be able to use the white schools.

I personally did not sense any real criticism, or hatred by the white people of the County, until I spoke in strong opposition at a public meeting of the School Board in late January or early February of 1960 held to consider whether or not to grant the request for the use of the white school buildings by the private school system. The School Board members turned down the request. I believe they had decided to do so before they even held the public meeting. They simply wanted to show at least some support from the public for such an action.

EMERGENCE OF THE NEW VIEW: NEGROES ARE FELLOW HUMAN BEINGS

My next personal crisis in the conflict came in January and February of 1961 when I attended the national annual meeting at Williamsburg of the Episcopal Society for Cultural and Racial Unity. The incidents and details of the matter are not of any public concern, but the local people used them in an attempt to pin on me the label of a total integrationist—even to the extent of believing in intermarriage of the two races. This resulted in a turmoil in my own church and in strained relations for me there ever since.

I have talked every time, every year—1959, 1960, 1961, 1962—when the Board of Supervisors held their annual public meeting with regard to a budget to include schools. I have, I think, gone through a very definite progression in my own thinking. I believe I have already referred to the fact that in 1959, at that first Board of Supervisors meeting at which I spoke, I was initially simply a proponent for public education for Negroes and whites regardless of whether it involved integration or not. But during the four years of the non-school system, as a result of my continuous private biracial conferences that had begun in 1959 between the two Negro leaders and Bittenger and myself, my thinking regarding the issue has changed. The conferences have become more frequent, with meetings approximately once a month from 1959 to the present, the spring of 1963. As a result, I have had to reexamine my own thoughts on the racial situation, and I think I have grown.

To me, the question of integrated schools is a very minor part of the problem in even so peaceful a county as Prince Edward. The real issue has grown beyond the mere question of integration to nothing more nor less than whether or not the white people are going to accept the Negroes as fellow human beings. And I doubt very much if even 10 percent of the white population of the County would consider looking at the issue in so fundamental a form as that. And among the 10 percent, one would be more likely to find the better educated (for example, members of the faculties of the two colleges in the County).

I do not believe that religion, however, would be a factor in determining whether one would look at Negroes as fellow human beings. Essentially all of the white churches and the white ministers of the County have refused to look at what has happened as a moral issue. One Presbyterian preacher was driven away at the beginning of the controversy in 1956 or 1957 because he insisted upon recognizing the problem as a moral issue. There is one Presbyterian minister out in the County now—has been there since 1962—who accepts it as such. But with the exception of those two men,

I do not know of any white minister anywhere in the town or County who, in the last ten or twelve years, has ever been brave enough to accept it as such.

We have also had one physician who from the first has been very sympathetic to the Negroes, but who has not been willing to take a public and open stand, although he has allowed his wife to do so with moderation. Another physician was originally sympathetic and started out admitting that the Negroes had been grossly mistreated. However, he had now succeeded in rationalizing his withdrawal from the issue and his acceptance of the status quo. A third physician did accept the chairmanship of the County School Board in 1961, at the time the previous chairman and most of the School Board resigned. He was a very beloved physician who unfortunately has since died, and I never had the opportunity to discuss the matter with him. I believe he accepted the position with the hope that he could do something constructive by working from within with those who controlled the situation. He certainly never made any public statement advocating integration or advocating that we ought to do something for the Negroes in the County.

As to those who controlled the situation, I have already mentioned one person.

The open, entirely known, active leaders of the movement are, however, few in number but without them I don't believe the situation would have developed, and I doubt very much if, without them, there would have been any controversy and concrete issue here at all.

Whether or not it is true that one man, or several men, are behind these recognized leaders has always been a question in my own mind. I have very strong reasons to believe that there is one person, but I have no proof of it and so I will not even name that person. But it is altogether likely that in the final analysis the County's actions have resulted from one person's beliefs and ideas.

The local bar has not supported the cause of the Negroes. One member of that bar was legal counsel for the School Board at the beginning of the case. That was W. Cabell Fitzpatrick. He was gravely mistreated at the time when the lease or sale of the school buildings was an active issue. But he has never taken any open stand. Only one other person, who was trained for the law (but did not actively practice it) for a time took an active stand in favor of the Negro.

SOCIAL MECHANISMS TO MAINTAIN CONFORMITY

Though Dean Moss has not himself referred to this, Reverend L. Francis Griffin, the local Negro minister, has described the kind of ostracism to which Dean Moss has been exposed. This is a kind of punishment the community has imposed on him because he spoke out and purportedly advocated not only integrated education but also intermarriage.

The senior author notes, in passing, that this kind of social control, i.e., ostracism, operates in much the same manner in the East Pakistani villages he had occasion to visit. There the mechanism was called "outcasting." The ruling group of old men led by the headman would investigate a case and tell the individual what he must do if he would accept their control. If the individual refused to conform to the traditional ideals of this local leader and the others comprising the village power group, there was a formal outcasting procedure after the completion of which he was cut off from any communication and all social contacts within the village. This process of social action is known as "Ek ghore," i.e., "keeping the person in solitary confinement." In rural East Pakistan, where everyone depends on others for almost all types of daily services, this is the most severe type of punishment which the village community can impose. No one will speak to him. The grocer will not sell his merchandise to him. The banker will not offer his services. Teachers will not instruct his children. The religious leader will not give his blessings. The rickshaw puller will not transport him. In other words, all types of specialized skills and services available in the villages are denied to him. At the same time, no one will buy his services, thus imposing on him an economic boycott. In addition, a type of social stigma is attached to his personality. If any villager sees him in the morning before breakfast that villager will refrain from taking breakfast himself as evidence of protest at his nonconformity. According to Dean Moss, in general terms, his experience and that of other people in the Farmville community could be used as illustrations of the mechanism presented above.

Here I am, a native of Virginia, born in Lynchburg, only 50 miles to the west of Prince Edward County. My ancestors on both sides of my family have been in Virginia since the seventeenth century. I came to Farmville, Virginia, in 1926 to begin my college teaching. I married a native of Farmville in 1929. I returned to Farmville to teach in 1929 and 1930 and left only because the substitute position I took in 1929 and 1930 did not develop into the permanent position I had hoped it would. I was continuously visiting in the town from 1930 until my return to the faculty of Longwood College in 1944. I have been associated with various civic organizations, such as the Rotary Club and so forth.

However, because I do not accept the Farmville interpretation of the racial issue, I am a foreigner, as much of a foreigner as if I had come from Iowa or even East Pakistan, I expect. On the contrary, one of the principal spokesmen for the white supremacists is a native of Pennsylvania and is the mouthpiece of the publisher of the *Farmville Herald* and is a member of the Board of Supervisors. He married, not a native of Prince Edward County, but the widow of a native of Prince Edward County. But because he goes along with the ruling clique, he is a native and not a foreigner.

My sin, really, is that I am a scalawag: a native but a nonconformist. The Foundation people have continuously argued that this matter should be settled by natives of Farmville, but look at this situation: When they needed legal counsel, they took a lawyer from Blackstone, Virginia, as their principal legal counsel. Blackstone is 35 miles to the east, which is almost as far as Lynchburg, 50 miles to the west; however, I suppose the eastward direction is all-important! And furthermore, when they needed additional legal counsel, they took another outsider, a lawyer from Richmond, Virginia, and became very much incensed when, in the public hearing on school leases, I insisted upon establishing the fact that their principal counsel was not a native. I was accused of being most impolite to a person who had been invited into the County. It is not who you are or where you are from; it is whether or not you go along with the rules that determines your nativity.

I do not think that I have particularly suffered, personally, because of my criticism of the local situation. I have been snubbed on Main Street by virtually lifetime friends. I sit in a pew by myself every Sunday. I am not allowed to serve on the vestry although they are quite willing to accept my work as treasurer of the church.

On the positive side, let me add this. When the schools were closed in 1959, I had one remaining child in public school. He was ready for the eighth grade and I publically refused to allow him to go to the Prince Edward County school even though it was going to have the same faculty it had had for years as a public school, for the County school was, according to my views, based upon evil principles. So I refused to allow my son to go to that school and sent him away at the age of 13 to a boarding school much against his personal wishes, and he has been away from the local schools throughout the four years. Nevertheless, that boy has retained all of his friends in the Prince Edward Academy and his principal desire throughout these four years has been to get home as frequently as possible in order to be with his friends. So far as I know, he has never been snubbed in any way by any of his age peers.

I would therefore like to think that the attitudes of the adolescents differ from their parents and thus make the future look more hopeful, and that is what I thought for a good while—possibly for the first two years of the school system.

It would be a bit difficult to prove, but I have increasingly gotten the impression for the past two years that the white children in the private school systems are beginning to inherit and adopt their elders' ideas and that they are beginning to develop in themselves positive attitudes of hatred toward the Negroes. That is difficult to prove, and I would not attempt to do so now.

FOUNDATIONS OF A PHILOSOPHY OF TOTAL INTEGRATION

Actually, I have prevented any too strong personal attack being launched upon myself since I have always insisted that my opposition was based upon, first, my belief that public education was an absolutely necessary foundation stone for America if America was going to be a leading world nation.

Second, I have insisted that my opposition was based upon my belief in democracy, and that in democracy you cannot have second-class citizens.

And, finally, I based my opposition and insisted that it be so recognized, on Christianity—on the principle that Christianity forbade the mistreatment of any subordinate group in the society.

Accordingly, I have virtually defied people and insisted that if they wanted to criticize me, they would have to admit that they did not believe in public education, that they did not believe in democracy, and that they did not believe in Christian principles. Even so, it has threatened my life professionally and economically. Within a matter of days after my first public speech for public schools, a delegation was in the office of the president of Longwood College demanding that I be fired.

In the winter of 1961, an attempt was made to circulate a petition to the State Board of Education to fire me. They could not get enough signatures on the petition to make it of any weight, but they did carry it privately to the State Board of Education. An effort was made at that time to shut me up with the threat that if I did not stay quiet, I might lose my job. I guess what rankles the leaders of the opposition most is that in 1956–1959, when I began my opposition, I was merely Chairman of the History Department of Longwood College, but since then I have been promoted to Associate Dean and finally to the position of Academic Dean of the College, which is a rather bitter pill for most people in the community to take.

PRESENT STATUS OF PUBLIC SCHOOLS

A private foundation known as the Prince Edward Free School Association was organized in September 1963. It made available elementary and secondary education to all Prince Edward County children on a desegregated basis. The Free School Association was financed by grants and contributions from foundations and private citizens. Although approximately 1,500 Negro youngsters attended the Free Schools, only four out of approximately 2,000 white school-age children were enrolled. Among the four white children was a 17-year-old senior named Richard Moss, the son of Dean Gordon Moss.

A court order which directed the reopening of public schools in the county on an integrated basis in the Fall of 1964 rendered unnecessary continuation of the Free School Association's educational operation. Most white children of school age in Prince Edward County, however, are still attending—in 1967—the segregated private academy.

81.

PICTURES IN OUR HEADS

Otto Klineberg

More than fifty years ago Walter Lippmann made a classic analysis of what he referred to as the stereotypes that people hold of other persons and groups. He termed those stereotypes "pictures in our heads" and indicated how these images, often based on inadequate knowledge and overgeneralized ideas, provide the basis for our behavior in relation to others. Here Otto Klineberg examines some of the stereotypes commonly held of several national groups and discusses the consequences of spuriously based images.

About a year ago I was in London at the invitation of British psychologists and sociologists in order to lecture on "National

Source: Otto Klineberg, *The Unesco Courier* 8, no. 6 (June 1955): 5–9. Reprinted by permission of *The Unesco Courier.*

Otto Klineberg, psychologist noted for his work on race differences and national differences and attitudes, was professor of psychology at the University of Paris after he retired from the psychology department at Columbia University. He was Director of Research for the "Tensions Project," UNESCO. He was author of *Race Differences, Social Psychology,* and *Tensions Affecting International Understanding.*

Stereotypes." Throughout the preceding day, during which I was undoubtedly made more sensitive by my preoccupation with this topic, I kept running into examples of such stereotyped thinking.

In my hotel, I heard someone say, "Oh, she has that Scottish stubbornness, you know." A book review in a newspaper used the phrase, "With true Gallic wit." At the theatre that evening, during the interval, I caught part of a conversation in which a pretty girl said to her escort, "I know that all Americans have a 'line' "; and in a mystery story that I read before retiring, there was a reference to "typical German thoroughness."

These are all instances of those "pictures in our heads" to which Walter Lippmann gave the name of stereotypes. They are typical of the ease with which most of us generalize about national or ethnic groups, usually without even stopping to think where such "information" comes from, and whether it represents the truth, the whole truth, or anything like the truth.

There are certainly very few, if any, among us who have not succumbed to the temptation to stereotype nations. One might almost describe the tendency as inevitable, or at least very nearly so. We *know* that Englishmen are reserved, and Irishmen pugnacious; we have heard it all our lives; besides most people agree with us. If we are asked, however, *how* we know, we would not easily find a suitable answer.

One of the earliest careful studies of this tendency was made by Katz and Braly, in 1932, in connexion with the stereotypes held by Princeton University students. The technique was simple.

Each student was given a list of traits, and a list of nationalities; from the first list he chose the five traits which he regarded as characteristic of each national or racial group.

The results showed a fair degree of unanimity, e.g. out of 100 students, 78 described the Germans as "scientifically minded," and 65 described them as "industrious"; 53 students used the adjective "artistic" for the Italians; the same percentage described the English as "sportsmanlike"; 79 agreed that the Jews were "shrewd" and 54 stated that the Turks were "cruel"; 84 regarded Negroes as "superstitious," and 75 described them as "lazy."

We may summarize the results in a slightly different manner by indicating the three or four characteristics most commonly ascribed to each nationality. These included, for the Germans, scientifically-minded, industrious, stolid; the Italians, impulsive, artistic, passionate; Negroes, superstitious, lazy, happy-go-lucky, ignorant; the Irish, pugnacious, quick-tempered, witty; the English, sportsmanlike, intelligent, conventional; the Jews, shrewd, mercenary, industrious; the Americans, industrious, intelligent, materialistic, ambitious; the Chinese, superstitious, sly, conservative; the Japanese, intelligent, industrious, progressive; the Turks, cruel, religious, treacherous.

A recent study of the stereotypes of German students at the Free University of Berlin by Sodhi and Bergius showed a similar willingness to stereotype nations and, on the whole, comparable results. Americans, for example, were described as sportsmanlike, democratic, materialistic; the Italians as warmblooded, musical, lighthearted; the Chinese as poor, inscrutable, modest; the German as conscious of duty, loving their homeland, intelligent; the English as proud of their nation, bound by traditions, sportsmanlike. There were some variations between the German and the American stereotypes, but on the whole the overlapping is considerable.

On a more extensive scale, a study conducted in 9 countries under the auspices of UNESCO in 1948 and 1949, showed that such stereotyped thinking could easily be elicited almost anywhere. In each country approximately 1,000 respondents, representing a cross-section of the population, were given a list of 12 traits, and asked to choose those which they thought were most applicable to themselves, to Americans, to Russians, and in some cases, to two or three other national groups as well. They could choose as many of the traits as they wished.

The British, for example, thought of Americans as primarily progressive, conceited, generous, peace-loving, intelligent, practical. The Americans regarded the British as intelligent, hard-working, brave, peace-loving, conceited and self-controlled. The Norwegians described the Russians as hard-working, domineering, backward, brave, cruel and practical. The full results can be found in the volume by Buchanan and Cantril, "How Nations See Each Other."

The "self-image" is also revealing. The British saw themselves as peace-loving, brave, hard-working, intelligent; the French saw themselves as intelligent, peace-loving, generous, and brave; the Americans saw themselves as peace-loving, generous, intelligent and progressive. All the groups agreed on one item: their own nation was the most peace-loving of all!

Few people realize how much the existence of stereotypes may colour our relations with other people, even to the extent of seeing them differently as a result. Psychologists have long known that our perceptions of the external world, and particularly of human beings, are determined not only by what is *out there,* but also by what is *in ourselves.* What we see is determined in part by what we expect to see. If we believe, for example, that Italians are noisy, we will have a tendency to notice those Italians who are indeed noisy; if we are in the presence of some who do not fit the stereotype, we may not even realize that they, too, are Italian. If someone points that fact out to us and says: "Look, those people are Italians, and they are not noisy," we can always dismiss them as exceptions.

Since there is no limit to the number of cases that can be so dismissed, we may continue to cling to the pictures in our heads, in spite of all the facts to the contrary. This does not always happen. Stereotypes do sometimes change in the light of new experiences, and evidence for this is presented later. If we have had them for a long time, however, we surrender them with great reluctance.

A number of significant investigations have shown in a very dramatic manner how our stereotypes may determine our perceptions. Some years ago Allport and Postman, psychologists at Harvard University (Cambridge, U.S.A.) studied some of the phenomena associated with the spread of rumours, making use of a technique known as "serial reproduction," a very simple device which anyone can use with a group of friends in his own home. They showed a picture to one student, and he described to a second student what he saw in the picture. The second then told a third what the first had told him; the third told the fourth, and so on, through a series of 8 to 10 reproductions. Then a comparison was made between the final result and the original presentation.

One of the pictures used in this investigation showed a scene in a subway in which, in addition to a number of people seated, there were two men standing, one a white man, the other a Negro. The white man was dressed in working clothes, with an open razor stuck in his belt. It so happens that the stereotype of the Negro held by some people in the USA includes the notion that

Negroes carry with them an open razor, of which they make ready use in an argument.

The psychologists were able to demonstrate that in half of the groups who served as subjects in these experiments, before the end of the series of reproductions had been reached, the razor had "moved" from the white man to the Negro. In some instances, the Negro was even represented as brandishing the razor violently in the face of the white man. This does not mean that half of the subjects in the experiment saw the Negro with the razor, since if only one person in the chain made this error, it would be repeated by those that followed. Interestingly enough, this did not occur when the subjects were Negroes (who rejected the stereotype), or young children (who had not yet "learned" it).

Another study conducted by Razran in New York points in the same direction. A group of college students in the USA were shown photographs of 30 girls, and asked to judge each photograph on a 5-point scale, indicating their general liking of the girl, her beauty, her intelligence, her character, her ambition, and her "entertainingness." Two months later, the same students were again shown the same photographs, but with surnames added. For some of the photographs Jewish surnames were given, such as Rabinowitz, Finkelstein, etc.; a second group received Italian names, such as Scarano, Grisolia, etc.; a third group Irish surnames, such as McGillicuddy, O'Shaughnessy, etc.; a fourth, "old American" names like Adams and Clark.

The investigator was able to demonstrate that the mere labeling of these photographs with such surnames definitely affected the manner in which the girls were perceived. The addition of Jewish and Italian names, for example, resulted in a substantial drop in general liking, and a similar drop for judgments of beauty and character. The addition of the same names resulted in a rise in the ratings for ambition, particularly marked in the case of the Jewish surnames. It seems clear that the same photographs *looked different* just because they could now be associated with the stereotype held by these students.

If a great many people agree that a particular trait is associated with a particular nation, does that make it true? There is a fairly widespread theory to the effect that "where there's smoke there's fire"; or, in other words, that the very existence of a stereotype is, to some extent at least, an argument in favour of its truth. Otherwise, the argument runs, where does the stereotype come from? How would it come into existence?

There is, however, a good deal of evidence as to the possibility that stereotypes may develop without any kernel of truth whatsoever. We all know how widespread is the notion that intelligent people have high foreheads, yet scientific investigation in this field has failed to reveal any such relationship. The stereotype of the criminal as bearing in his features the mark of his criminality is widely accepted, but it is equally without foundation; the famous British criminologist, Sir Charles Goring, was able to demonstrate that a composite photograph, representing criminals in British gaols, bore no resemblance to the accepted stereotype of the criminal.

Stereotypes frequently change. In some cases it may be argued that this corresponds to a real change in the characteristics of the people; in others, however, it seems much more likely to be due to external circumstances which have little or nothing to do with the group concerned. The Dutch sociologist, Shrieke, has, for example, made a collection of some of the descriptive phrases applied to the Chinese during the course of their residence in the state of California, U.S.A.

When the Chinese were needed in California, in order to carry on certain types of occupation, they were welcome there; during that period, newspapers and journals referred to them as among "the most worthy of our newly adopted citizens"; "the best immigrants in California"; they were spoken of as thrifty, sober, tractable, inoffensive, law-abiding. This flattering picture prevailed over a considerable period of time, but around 1860, presumably because economic competition had grown much more severe, there was a marked change in the stereotype of the Chinese. The phrases now applied to them included: "a distinct people," "unassimilable," "their presence lowered the plane of living," etc. They were spoken of as clannish, criminal, debased, servile, deceitful, and vicious.

This startling change can hardly be accounted for by any real modification of the characteristics of the Chinese population of California. The most acceptable explanation is that when it became advantageous to reduce the competition from the Chinese, the stereotype was altered in a direction which would help to justify such action. In this historical case it seems reasonable to conclude that the change in the characteristics ascribed to the Chinese throws doubt on the notion that stereotypes must necessarily contain some truth.

Another Dutch sociologist, Den Hollander, has studied the historical changes in the stereotype of the Hungarians in Europe. He points out that for centuries after the migration of Hungarians to Central Europe, they had a bad reputation, and were regarded as culturally different, and therefore inferior, to Europeans generally. During the fifteenth and sixteenth centuries, however, when they joined in the war against the Turks, they were pictured as a brave, devout, and chivalrous people.

By the second half of the eighteenth century their popularity had again declined, and they were described as savage, lazy, egotistical, unreliable, and tyrannous. This picture changed again a little later, when the Hungarians became romanticized and idealized. Den Hollander believes that the image followed the pattern of political interrelationships; it seems unlikely that there was sufficient transformation in the character of the people to justify the change in the national image.

One of the most amusing examples of a stereotype which has apparently developed without any kernel of truth emerges from an investigation by Schoenfeld on stereotypes associated with proper names. Here again the technique used was a simple one. The American students who served as subjects in this study were given a list of eight proper names and a list of eight adjectives; their task was to "match" or pair each name with the adjective regarded as most appropriate.

Since there were 120 students, and eight names, the results to be expected by chance alone, that is to say, if no stereotype existed, would be 120 divided by eight, or 15 for each name. The actual results showed that 63 out of the 120 judges matched Richard with "good looking"; 58 judged Herman to be "stupid"; 59 judged Rex as "athletic"; 71 associated Adrian with "artistic"; and 104 agreed that Cuthbert was "a sissy." In a similar experiment with American girls judging feminine names, 54 regarded Minnie as stupid; 60 saw Linda as sophisticated; 69 said that Mary was religious; 58 that Maisie was talkative; and 73 that Agatha was middle-aged.

Although this study was done with American students, it seems quite certain that comparable stereotypes would be found in languages other than English.

In any case, it can hardly be argued that Richard is really better looking than John, or Herman more stupid than Cuthbert. To return to ethnic stereotypes, one significant study may be cited which demonstrates the manner in which stereotypes may develop without any basis in truth. The American sociologist, La Piere, studied the attitudes of residents of California towards first and second generation Armenian immigrants in Fresno County in that State. There was almost complete agreement that these Armenians had more than their share of faults, and the general attitude toward them was relatively unfriendly.

La Piere proceeded to question non-Armenians as to the reasons for their antipathies, and he was able to classify the answers into three stereotypes. In the first place, it was stated that Armenians were treacherous, lying, deceitful. In actual fact, when measured by the criterion of business integrity, the Armenian merchants turned out to be equal and frequently superior to others. In the second place, they were alleged to be parasites, making excessive demands upon charitable organizations, free clinics, etc. Actually, such demands by them were less than half of what would be expected in terms of their proportion of the population.

Finally, it was said that they had an inferior code of morality, and they were always getting into trouble with the law. In fact, police records showed that they appeared in only 1.5 percent of Police Court cases, although they constituted approximately 6 percent of the population. La Piere concludes that all of these stereotypes have one factor in common, viz. that they are definitely false. This does not mean that stereotypes *never* contain any truth. It does mean that they *can* develop without any truth whatsoever.

There is, however, the possibility that a little truth may enter into a stereotype through the back door, so to speak. A Frenchman, with considerable experience of international meetings, once said that when he had occasion to address such a meeting he usually did so in a rather oratorical, flowery, "Latin" style. He said that otherwise his Anglo-Saxon colleagues would be disappointed! When he was with other Frenchmen, he reverted to a quieter, more matter-of-fact, "un-Latin" manner, which really suited him personally much better.

In this case, the stereotype itself determined his behavior under certain circumstances, and undoubtedly reinforced the conviction of the Anglo-Saxons that they really knew what Frenchmen were like. More rarely, the stereotype may operate in reverse. A member of a group with the reputation for frugality may go out of his way to spend freely, and tip lavishly; if the stereotype calls for lack of punctuality, he may make it a point to arrive at his destination well before the hour specified. Since, in that case, as was indicated above, he will probably be regarded as an exception, the stereotype will still prevail.

Stereotyped thinking may be *almost* inevitable, but there is good evidence that it can at least be reduced, if not eliminated. Eighteen years after the Katz and Braly study, another psychologist (Gilbert) applied the same technique to a new generation of Princeton students. He found that there was some persistence of stereotypes, but also a very important change which he describes as "a fading effect."

There is much less agreement among the students in 1950 than in 1932; any specific trait is usually checked by a much smaller proportion of students in the later study. In 1932, for example, 84 percent of the students described the Negroes as lazy; in

1950 the percentage had dropped to 31. The description of Italians as artistic drops from 83 to 28.

In London, a UNESCO study conducted by H. E. O. James and Cora Tenen showed how specific personal experiences might affect the nature and content of stereotypes. What they did was to obtain from schoolchildren their opinions of other ethnic groups, particularly of African Negroes, and then bring them into contact with two able African women teachers who spent a few weeks in the schools.

The "before and after" picture is very striking. As an example, a child before the experience stated that "I do not like black people; it's the colour; it makes me nervous; they might be savage . . . they are different in nature to us, more savage and cruel sometimes, so you don't trust them ever." The same child after the experience said: "Miss V. and Miss W. were nice people . . . there does not seem any difference between them and us except the colour. I think that Negroes are like that—just like us, except for the colour. I like them. They are nice people."

The authors give many examples of similar changes that occurred. Stereotypes cannot always be modified so strikingly nor so fast, but the fact that they can be changed at all as a result of experience is itself encouraging.

Sometimes just growing older helps. In a study sponsored by UNESCO, Plaget and Weil report the results of a series of interviews with Swiss children of different ages. One interview with a little girl aged eight years ran as follows:

"Have you heard of foreigners?—Yes, there are Germans and French.—Are there any differences between these foreigners?—Yes, the Germans are bad, they are always making war. The French are poor and everything is dirty there. Then I have heard of Russians, but they are not at all nice.—Do you have any personal knowledge of the French, Germans, or Russians, or have you read something about them?—No.—Then how do you know?—Everyone says so."

On the other hand, a boy aged thirteen years, after having mentioned a large number of foreign countries of which he had heard, was asked, "Are there any differences between all those countries?", and his answer was, in part, "*you find all types of people everywhere.*" We are not all as "mature" as this 13-year-old boy, but perhaps we can move in that direction. Or is it possible that the Swiss are . . . ? Oh no! No stereotypes!

The understanding of national characteristics represents an important task for all of us. . . . The difficulties in the way are great: nations are made up of many different kinds of individuals, and generalizations are dangerous if they do not give adequate consideration to the range of individual variations.

An important first step will be taken if we treat "the pictures in our heads" with a strong dose of scepticism, and if we keep our minds closed to stereotypes and open only to facts. No one is denying the existence of national characteristics.

A knowledge of them can aid our understanding of people, as well as our enjoyment of the varieties of behaviour and personality that are found in different parts of the world. We need to make sure, however, that the "pictures in our heads" correspond as closely as possible to reality.

82.

TEA AND SYMPATHY: LIBERALS AND OTHER WHITE HOPES

Lerone Bennett, Jr.

The processes by which societies change vary from drastic revolutionary changes on the one hand to maintenance of a relatively stable society with little or no change on the other. Advocates of various types of change have often been classified as radicals, liberals, and conservatives. This selection by Lerone Bennett, Jr., focuses on the position of liberals in contemporary society. Bennett analyzes the liberal position on contemporary changes in the status of blacks in American society, and identifies the limitations of this position in the present situation that demands more rapid and more drastic change than liberals are likely to accept. This perception of the liberal from the point of view of those who have long been oppressed is in striking contrast to that held by the white liberal of himself.

. . . . .

Who is *our,* who is man's, who is freedom's friend?

The white liberal answers; let us begin with him. The white liberal is a man who finds himself defined as a white man, as an oppressor, in short, and retreats in horror from that *designation.* But – and this is essential – he retreats only halfway, disavowing the title without giving up the privileges, tearing out, as it were, the table of contents and keeping the book. The fundamental trait of the white liberal is his desire to differentiate himself psychologically from white Americans on the issue of race. He wants to think and he wants others to think he is a man of brotherhood.

The white liberal talks brotherhood; he writes about it, prays for it, and honors it. But:

> Between the idea
> And the reality
> Between the motion
> And the act
> Falls the shadow.

The white liberal is Augustine praying before his conversion, "Give me chastity and continency, but not yet."

He is Andrew Johnson saying to Negroes in 1864, "I will be your Moses," and taking, in 1865, the posture of Pharaoh.

He is Abraham Lincoln biting his lip, as he put it, and keeping silent.

The white liberal is the man who was not there in Montgomery and Little Rock and Birmingham; the white liberal is the man who is never there. The liberal, as Saul Alinsky, the brilliant white radical

Source: Lerone Bennett, Jr., *The Negro Mood* (Chicago: Johnson Publishing Co., 1964), pp. 122–28, 142–48.

Lerone Bennett, Jr., is a senior editor of *Ebony* Magazine. He has received many awards for his publications. Among his many books are *Confrontation: Black and White, The Negro Mood, Before the Mayflower: A History of the Negro in America, 1619–1964,* and a biography of Martin Luther King, Jr., entitled *What Manner of Man.*

said, is the man who leaves the meeting when the fight begins.

It was of the white liberal, or someone like him, that men were thinking when they invented the phrase: he wants to have his cake and to eat it, too. The essential point here is that the white liberal is of no color or race or creed. He is Everyman. "For the good that I would I do not; but the evil which I would not, that I do."

That is it, precisely:

> Between the desire
> And the spasm
> Between the potency
> And the existence
> Between the essence
> And the descent
> Falls the Shadow.

The Shadow of safety, the Shadow of comfort, the Shadow of greed, the Shadow of status. This is the white Liberal: a man of Shadows, a friend of freedom who pauses, calculates, hesitates.

The dancing waves of revolt and rebellion have exposed with pitiless clarity the dark shadows of the white liberal soul. As a result, the reputation of white liberals in the Negro community is at an all-time low. This is not, as some claim, a perverse spasm of a frustrated folk. The Negro senses dimly that white liberals, despite their failings, are the best America has to offer. And he clings to the white liberal, as a drowning man clings to a plank in a raging sea, not because the plank offers hope of salvation but because it is the very best he has.

The plank is rotten; the sea is choppy—the plank must be made better or we shall all drown.

Let us look closer at the white liberal.

What characterizes the liberal, above all, is his inability to live the words he mouths. The white liberal cannot bear the great white whale of guilt that rises from the sea of Negro degradation and he joins groups and assumes postures that permit him and others to believe something is being done. The key word here is *believe*. The white liberal believes something should be done, but not too soon and not here. He is all negation, the white liberal: now is not the time, this is not the place, the weapon you have is too large or too small. He is all ceremony, all ritual. He pretends, he postures, he resolves. Always, everywhere, in every age, the white liberal flees the principle made black flesh. He wants results without risks, freedom without danger, love without hate. He affirms tomorrow, denies yesterday, and evades today. He is all form, all means, all words—and no substance.

The white liberal is *sui generis*. Men of similar tone and texture exist in South Africa and other countries. But the breed, white liberal, is peculiar to America. No other country has felt called upon to create this office, for it is an office, if not a profession. Lévi-Strauss reminds us that "in any society it is inevitable that a percentage . . . of individuals find themselves placed, as it were, outside of any system or between two or more irreducible systems. The group asks and even requires that these individuals represent certain forms of compromise which cannot be achieved on the collective level, that they stimulate imaginary transitions and embody incompatible syntheses."

To "simulate imaginary transitions," to embody incompatible syntheses: this is the function of white liberals. They are ordained to stand in the middle, to sustain hope, to personify an "impossible ideal," and to suffer. They serve the same purpose in the Negro community as token Negroes serve in the white community: they are public monuments of racial progress. In a period of real crisis, white liberals are shoved into the breach between the contending groups to perform four key functions: 1) symbolic flames (tokens of white interest and white good faith); 2) flagellants (whipping boys and deflectors of Negro discontent); 3) channels of communications between separate communities; and 4) expendable platoon leaders of the most advanced positions of the white camp. White liberals are charged, above all, with preventing the coagulation of a massive black clot of Negro discontent. In the March on Washington, it was considered significant that white people participated, thereby preventing an all-Negro demonstration against all white people. In all crises, at all times, white liberals have two basic aims, to prevent polarization and to prevent racial conflict.

Because their aims are so narrow, white liberals are of limited value to Negro leadership. The basic postulates of the white liberal are that bigotry is caused by ignorance and that changes must be carried out quietly, surreptitiously, as it were, so white people will not notice. These assumptions ignore basic considerations of interest and power and permit white liberals to nibble at the edges of the problem without mounting basic assaults on structures of influence and affluence. As Ralph J. Bunche pointed out in the forties, white liberals "are attempting to work within a system which is opposed to any basic change, and they do not try nor do they desire to change that system in any of its fundamentals."

By word and by deed, white liberals insist that Negroes subordinate their claims to the emotions of racists. In the liberal rhetoric, it is considered a provocative act to irritate white racists. It never seems to occur to white liberals that irritated or not they are still the same old racists.

The modern version of this paternalistic theory is that demonstrations enrage white people and imperil the advance of democracy. This statement contains two wholly unacceptable premises. It assumes, first, that white people have some freedom to give and, secondly, that they can dole it out based on the smiles or lack of smiles of the victims. This is a nursery rhyme approach to the historical process and it explains, in part, the continuing distrust of liberals and other white hopes.

White liberals are much given to victim analysis. Nothing pleases the average liberal more than a long and leisurely contemplation of the defects of the victim. The liberal sees quite clearly that the Negro has been robbed, but in violation of all logic and all law he insists that the robbed instead of the robber make restitution. It is not a pretty picture, this, to see the robber lecturing his victims on the virtues of thrift. Silence were better.

But silence is not the liberal's strong point. Refusing, like practically all other white Americans, to accept Negroes as serious social actors, liberals lecture Negroes on cleanliness, godliness and the duty of obeying laws which white Americans, with white liberal help, have violated for more than one hundred years. Liberals, like practically all other Americans, are paternalistic, patronizing, condescending; they think they can tell Negroes how to frame their posture of protest, how to scream and how to cry or, indeed, whether they should cry at all.

The word *masses* separates Negro activists from Negro militants; the word *conflict* separates white liberals and Negroes. Liberals want orderly change; Negroes want change, orderly if possible, disorderly if necessary. Above all else, the liberal recoils from the shock of conflict. He tends to study much and to pray much. He accepts the goals, but disagrees on the method. The liberal is an aesthete, much preoccupied with form and means and techniques. He looks out on a raging battlefield and sees error everywhere, and he thinks he can find the truth by avoiding error. He is reasonable, the liberal; he preaches and surveys while men are burning churches and rats are biting children.

Prejudice is irrational to its core, but liberals insist that the Negro fight rationally. The Negro is fighting a barroom brawler who knees in the clinches and gouges between rounds; but liberals, standing on the edge of the ring, hold the Negro to *Robert's Rules of Order*.

Moderation: that is the dominant liberal value. Liberals are moderately for the Fourteenth Amendment; they are moderately for Negro freedom, and they think Negroes ought to be moderate. This means almost always that Negroes must dilute their demands, that they must wait, that they must not rock the boat. On every question involving Negro rights, the liberal is moderate—on every question except two: Negro hate and Negro violence. This man, so moderate, so reasonable, so content, becomes an extremist when Negroes hate and hit back. Why? From whence comes this obsession with Negro violence? It stems from an unconscious perception of the ambiguity of the liberal position. Liberals fear Negro violence more than anything else because Negro violence, more than anything else, illuminates the precarious ledge of their posture. White violence, though deplorable, is endurable, and white liberals endure it amazingly well. But Negro violence creates or threatens to create a situation which forces white liberals to choose sides; it exposes their essential support of things as they are.

. . . . .

In order for Negroes and white liberals to communicate they must break out of the glass cage of caste and hate that contains them. Negroes have a duty to assimilate their situation, to accept it and transmute it so they can view white liberal approaches with greater objectivity. But the power and the glory are the white man's; and so is the responsibility. An act to the end is a minimum requirement. Anything else is silence, evasion, and untruth. The Negro hates his role in America and he hates white liberals who approach him in the aspect of *white* liberals and remind him, however obliquely, of his situation. For white people to pretend surprise at this fact is not only naive but downright cynical. And to pretend, as many do, that Negro hate is of the same tone and texture as white hate is ludicrous. As Arnold Rose pointed out—and I use Rose because he is a perceptive non-Negro—"[Negro] hatred of white people is not pathological—far from it. It is a healthy human reaction to oppression, insult, and terror. White people are often surprised at the Negro's hatred of them, but it should not be surprising.

"The whole world knows that the Nazis murdered millions of Jews and can suspect that the remaining Jews are having some emotional reaction to that fact. Negroes, on the other hand, are either ignored or thought to be so subhuman that they have no feelings when one of their number is killed because he was a Negro. Probably no week goes by in the United States that some Negro is not severely beaten, and the news is reported in the Negro press. Every week or maybe twice a week almost the entire Negro population of the United States suffers an emotional recoil from some insult coming from the voice or pen of a leading white man. The surviving Jews had one, big, soul-wracking 'incident' that wrenched them back to group identification. The surviving Negroes experience constant jolts that almost never let them forget for even an hour that they are Negroes. In this situation, hatred of whites and group identification are natural reactions."

There are hundreds of ways of hating the white man in America, including imitating him. But the harsh fact is that the choice for most Negroes is not between hating or loving but between hating and hating, between hating themselves or hating their oppressors.

This should surprise no literate man. You cannot deny people the basic emotions of rage, resentment and, yes, hate. Only slaves or saints or masochists love their oppressors. If you humiliate a man, if you degrade him, if you do this over and over for hundreds of years, he will either hate you or hate himself. This is a basic fact of humanity, and Negroes are human. At best, you will get that strange kind of love Camus spoke of—the love of Jesus and Gandhi, a love that expresses itself in creative resentment, in the cursing of fig trees and the driving of money changers from temples.

A strange kind of love or a strange kind of hate.

Martin Luther King, Jr., or Malcolm X.

Either/or.

It would help enormously in America if there were a ten-year moratorium on the use of the word love. Love and hate are not mutually exclusive phenomena; they are two sides of the same coin and they are found almost always in different degrees in the same relation. The Negro loves white Americans but he also hates white Americans and there is nothing that can be done about it until the white liberal addresses himself to conditions that breed love, hate, and desperation. It is not required, finally, that we love each other. What is required is something infinitely more difficult, for us to confront each other.

But this is what the white liberal refuses to do. The white liberal is fleeing the truth of his, of *our* situation. He is seeking personal salvation not justice. He is moved not only by a vision of the future but by a horror of the past, not by the Negro, but by himself. What moves him is guilt. What the liberal seeks is his lost innocence. What the liberal wants, paradoxically, is for the Negro to tell him that he is not as white and as cold as snow.

83.

BLACK PROGRESS AND LIBERAL RHETORIC

Ben J. Wattenberg and
Richard M. Scammon

The processes of social change frequently generate much debate over the extent and speed of the change. Those desirous of rapid revolutionary change are dissatisfied with any slower pace while conservatives condemn any significant pace. In the previous selection, Lerone Bennett, Jr., analyzes what he believes to be the very moderate and wholly inadequate change in the status of blacks, advocated by liberals. In this selection liberals are condemned by Wattenberg and Scammon for not recognizing the changes that the authors believe have occurred in the black status.

This article has generated another debate over the claim that 50 percent of American blacks have now achieved middle-class status. Citing data showing upward change in the income, occupation, and education of blacks, the authors claim the evidence shows rapid progress in the 1960s. In the subsequent article, Joe Darden uses the same data to demonstrate that compared to whites, the change in blacks' status has been very slight.

A remarkable development has taken place in America over the last dozen years: for the first time in the history of the republic, truly large and growing numbers of American blacks have been moving into the middle class, so that by now these numbers can reasonably be said to add up to a *majority* of black Americans—a slender majority, but a majority nevertheless.

This development, which has occurred against a historical backdrop of social and economic discrimination, is nothing short of revolutionary. Despite the fact that Southern blacks are economically still significantly worse off than Northern, and older blacks than younger, and despite the fact too that the economic and social gap separating whites and blacks is still a national disgrace, "middle class" has now become an accurate term to describe the social and economic condition of somewhat more than half of black Americans.

What does "middle class" mean in this context? Obviously any line that is drawn in the sociological sand must have about it

---

Source: Ben J. Wattenberg and Richard M. Scammon, *Commentary* (April 1973): 35–44.

Ben J. Wattenberg served as an aide to President Lyndon B. Johnson and worked on the government publication, *Social and Economic Condition of Negroes in the United States,* in 1967 and 1968. He has also been a political aide on the staff of Senator Hubert H. Humphrey and, earlier, Senator Henry Jackson. He is the coauthor of *This U.S.A.* and *The Real Majority.*

Richard M. Scammon is a political scientist and director of the elections research center of the Governmental Affairs Institute. He has studied patterns of immigration and voting.

something of the arbitrary and the artificial, yet there are a number of statistical criteria—notably in the areas of income, job patterns, and education—that serve to measure the relative standing of groups (as well, of course, as individuals) in society, and these indices have an unambiguous tale to tell about the recent economic and social movement of American blacks. Obviously, too, "middle class" as used here does not refer to a condition of affluence, to a black population made up of doctors, lawyers, and businessmen with cabin cruisers (although such blacks certainly do exist). It refers rather to the condition of that vast majority of working-class Americans who, although often hard-pressed, have safely put poverty behind them and are now looking ahead, no longer back; it refers not only to engineers and teachers, but also to plasterers, painters, bus drivers, lathe operators, secretaries, bank tellers, and automobile assembly-line workers: the kinds of people who, when they are white, are described as "Middle Americans" or members of the silent, real, or new American majorities. It refers, in the words of the economist Thomas Sowell, who is himself black, to "black men and women who go to work five days a week, pay their bills, try to find some happiness for themselves, and raise their children to be decent people with better prospects than they had. . . ."

To belong to this "middle class" means, first, to have enough to eat, to have adequate, if not necessarily expensive, clothes to wear, and to be able to afford housing that is safe and sanitary. But that is only the beginning. The advent of a majority of blacks into the middle-income class has triggered a dominolike movement throughout American society. Once the necessities of food, shelter, and clothing are provided for, a vast flow of secondary desires follows. A middle-income family wants not only a house that is safe and sanitary but one in a safe and sanitary neighborhood. Middle-income parents want their children to go to good schools, to stay in high school and graduate and, they hope, then go on to college. The young adults who come out of high school and college want better jobs than those their parents have held, the kinds of jobs that have always been available to whites in an equivalent socioeconomic position.

The middle-income blacks have made much headway toward satisfying all these traditional middle-class desires. Their progress has hardly been trouble-free; as is the case with all forms of sharp economic movement, it has been accompanied by considerable social turbulence, much of it occasioned by race prejudice, and it has had a tremendous impact on the political life of the nation at large. But it is real progress, a massive achievement; and to all appearances it is here to stay.

This is a phenomenon of enormous portent for the future of American society. That it should have come about, as it has, at a time when many civil-rights leaders and liberals alike have insisted that conditions for American blacks are not improving at all, but actually deteriorating, is not the least astonishing aspect of the entire episode. It will be a great and tragic irony if this insistence on failure should in the end prove a hindrance to the continued upward progress of American blacks.

I

The first and most basic index of status in American life is money, and it is therefore to comparative income statistics that we must turn first to show the broad outlines of black upward mobility in the 1960s. According to the 1970 census figures, income for white families in America went up by 69 percent in the 1960s, while income for black families * went up by 99.6 percent. If we round off the 99.6 percent figure it can be stated that black family income actually doubled during a single decade! †

The *ratio* of black family income to white family income also changed dramatically in the period, climbing from 53 percent in 1961 to 63 percent in 1971. It might be argued—and rightly—that 63 percent is a long way from 100 percent and still scandalously low, but what is open to little argument is that there has been sharp progress—a catching up—during recent years which was not at all apparent during the previous decade (the ratio of black to white family incomes was the same in 1961 as it had been in 1951). And the changing percentage of black families earning above $10,000 is even more startling, jumping from 13 percent in 1961 to 30 percent in 1971 (from 1951 to 1961 the percentage had increased from 3 to 13); these figures are in 1971 constant dollars, the effects of inflation having been factored out.

The median family income in the United States in 1971 was $10,285; today, it can be estimated at $11,000. This figure represents the middle-of-the-middle of family income distribution. Some lower figure—say, $8,000 outside the South—may be said to represent the bottom-of-the-middle or the beginning of middle-income status in America. In the South, where median income averages almost $2,000 lower, and where a disproportionate number of blacks still lives, the bottom-of-the-middle line may be drawn at $6,000. By these criteria, and again adjusting for recent income increases, just over half of black families in the United States are by now economically in the middle class (about 52 percent).

The march of blacks across the invisible line into the lower-middle and middle classes may be seen even more clearly by looking at the data on the regional rather than on the national level, and by breaking down the figures by age and family characteristics. Thus, there is a sharp difference between black income in the South and black income elsewhere. Whereas in 1970 black family income in the South was 57 percent of white family income, outside the South the corresponding figure was 74 percent. A second variable affecting black-white income ratios is family status. As we shall note later, black families are much more likely than white families to be "female-headed," but when they are *not*—when the families are "husband-wife" families—income is much likelier to approach equality with comparable white family incomes. Among black husband-wife families all over America in 1970, income was 73 percent of white family income. Outside the South it was 88 percent. But perhaps the most encouraging, and most significant, cross-tabulation of the income data concerns the economic status of young blacks. These young men and women have made striking educational gains in recent years; they have made gains in "occupation" as well, i.e., in the

* These figures are for "Negroes and other races." Throughout this essay the data used are either for "Negroes" or, when not available, for "Negroes and Other Races" as defined by the Census Bureau. Since "Negroes" comprise 90 percent of this latter category, the index may be considered relatively reliable for American blacks as a whole.

† The statement, however, would be accurate only if inflation had not eroded *everyone's* income. Taking inflation into account we find that the actual income increases come out to 34 percent for whites and 59 percent for blacks.

sorts of jobs they hold; and they have made gains in the amounts of money they earn. Black males aged 25–34, for example, earn 80 percent of white levels of income on a national basis.

When one combines all these factors—youth, non-Southern residence, and an unbroken family—a truly striking statistic emerges. The median income of black husband-wife families, in the North and West, with the head of family under 35 years of age, rose from 78 percent of white income in 1959 to *96* percent in 1970. There is a word to describe that figure: parity. And if we add a fourth variable to the equation, and examine families in which both the husband and wife work, the figures come out to 85 percent in 1959, and in 1970—104 percent! For such families, parity has not only been achieved, it has even been surpassed: young, married blacks, outside of the South, with husband and wife both working, earn as much as or a trifle more than comparable whites.‡

II

If income statistics are the most basic index of economic mobility in the United States, employment patterns follow closely behind. For the last two decades the reality of the black-white employment situation can be summed up, bleakly, as follows: black unemployment rates have been twice as high as white rates. But in recent years a massive shift has occurred in the identity of the black unemployed. A cross-tabulation of married men over age 20 reveals a far sharper *drop* in unemployment among blacks than for the population as a whole, as is shown by this comparison of two early years of the 60s with two early years of the 70s:

Unemployment Rate and Black-to-White Ratio for Married Men, 20 Years and Over, with Spouse Present, 1962 to 1972

	Negro & Other Races %	*White* %	*Ratio*
1962	7.9	3.1	2.5 to 1
1963	6.8	3.0	2.3 to 1
1971	4.9	3.0	1.6 to 1
1972	4.4	2.6	1.7 to 1

The drop in the ratio from 1962 to 1972 is 53 percent (from 2.5 to 1, to 1.7 to 1—with 1 to 1 representing parity). Here, too, then, we see a steady and powerful movement into the middle class. Black family men are, like white family men, "at work," that is, at least 95 out of 100 of them are, even during recessionary times.

At the same time, teenage unemployment has gone up. Among the 1.9 million black teenagers (age 16–19), unemployment rates in 1960 were 24 percent; by 1970, the rate had climbed to 29 percent, and by 1971 to 32 percent. The rate for white teenagers fluctuated between 13 and 15 percent in the same years.

. . . . .

On balance, then: teenage unemployment rates are up, adult male rates are down, particularly among married males. Black teenagers are mostly in school, adults are mostly supporting families. The net result would seem to be an important social and economic plus, despite the unfortunately large and continuing dis-

‡ Some, but by no means all, of these remarkable husband-wife family gains are due to the fact that young black wives outside of the South are somewhat more likely to work year 'round than young white wives (52 percent versus 36 percent). However, it is important to note that in those same families the husbands were also making progress. They earned 76 percent of comparable white husbands in 1959—and 90 percent of comparable white husbands in 1970.

proportion in black-white employment rates.

III

The overall employment pattern, of course, is made up of more than the statistics of who is at work and who is without work. Of equal significance is what *kinds* of jobs people hold. And here again we see major progress by blacks in gaining access to middle-class occupations, especially in the categories of "white-collar workers," "craftsmen," and "operatives":

Numbers of White-Collar Workers, Craftsmen, and Operatives, in Millions

	Negro	*White*
1960	2.9	46.1
1970	5.1	57.0
Percentage increase	*76*	*24*

Over the same decade the numbers of Negroes in "other" work—primarily low-paying jobs in private households, as service workers, farm workers, and laborers—decreased from 4 million to 3.5 million. Comparing, then, the balance of occupational status for blacks in America in 1960 and 1970, we find that in 1960 blacks in "good" jobs totaled 2.9 million while blacks in "not good" jobs totaled 4 million; by 1970 the number of blacks with "good" jobs totaled 5.1 million, while those with "not good" jobs totaled 3.4 million—in short, a reversal, and then some. In 1960, 42 percent of blacks held "good" (i.e., middle-class) jobs—less than half. By 1970 the rate had climbed to 64 percent—almost two-thirds.

. . . . .

Along with higher incomes and better jobs the 1960s also saw a great breakthrough in the area of education. Thus in 1960 only 36 percent of young black males finished four years of high school, the educational level that seems to separate Americans into "middle class" and "non-middle class." By 1970 the rate was more than half—54 percent. Among young black women the increase was even greater—from 41 percent in 1960 to 61 percent in 1971. If we take a longer range view, say over the last thirty years, the great educational leap forward of young American blacks becomes even more impressive:

Median School Years Completed, Negroes, Aged 25–29

1940	7.0 years
1950	8.6 years
1960	10.8 years
1970	12.2 years

In 1940 the young black was typically an elementary-school dropout; a decade later he could be described only as an elementary-school graduate. Not until 1960 did the young American black typically reach even the level of high-school dropout, and not until 1970 did he typically become a high-school graduate—a bona-fide member of the educational middle class. To give a sense of the speed with which educational parity—in terms of years of school completed for young Americans *—came about,

* To be sure, many of those who were in school or at home wanted, and needed, work, particularly part-time work, and could not get it. They needed money to help support themselves through school, to provide a second income to make ends meet, to help out their parents and siblings struggling at home with too little money and too many mouths to feed. But they were not the primary breadwinners, and their relative position has to be judged accordingly.

For Americans of all ages there is still a disparity, reflecting earlier years of inequity. Median school years completed for all adult Negroes was 10.1 years in 1971 as compared with 12.2 years for all adult whites.

we may note that the gap between young whites and young blacks in 1950 was 3.5 years; twenty years later the gap was .4 of one year. The significance of these data cannot be discounted by arguments, however valid, that blacks are behind whites in reading levels, or by the view that education has little to do with economic success. In the real world, a young man cannot even get interviewed for a job as a bus driver unless he has a high-school diploma.

Finally, the leap into the educational middle class can be seen in college-enrollment statistics. In 1970, there were over half a million young blacks in college, slightly more than 9 percent of the total. Over a short six-year period—from 1965 to 1971—the comparative figures are as follows:

Percent of Persons, Aged 18–24, Enrolled in College 1965–1971

	1965 %	*1971* %
Negro	10	18
White	26	27
"Gap"	16	9

Again, there is a gap and it is still large—but it has narrowed considerably.

IV

By most of the standards by which Americans measure middle-class status, then, blacks in the last decade have made mighty strides—both absolutely and relative to whites—and the time has come for this fact to be recognized. The image of the black in America must be changed, from an earlier one of an uneducated, unemployed, poverty-stricken slum-dweller, to that of an individual earning a living wage at a decent job, with children who stay in school and aspire to still-better wages and still-better jobs, living not in a slum (but still in a ghetto), in a decent if unelaborate dwelling, still economically behind his white counterpart but catching up.

But to say all this, while indeed correct, is *not* to say that the situation is uniformly good; that all blacks are in the middle class; that blacks as a whole have achieved parity with whites; that poverty is largely a thing of the past; or, last but not least, that there is cause for complacency in the realm of social and economic policy. None of these conclusions, in fact, is valid.

The high incidence of broken families among blacks—regarded by some observers as the key to the pathology of the black slums—has increased substantially in recent years. The figures chronicling the rise in the number of black female-headed families are stark:

Percent Female-Headed Familes

	White %	*Black* %
1950	8.5	17.6
1960	8.9	22.4
1970	9.1	26.8
1971	9.4	28.9
1972	9.4	30.1

Today, close to a third of black families are headed by females; twenty-odd years ago it was about a sixth. The white rate has changed only marginally in the same period.

. . . . .

As the numbers and relative percentages of black female-headed families soared, so too did the numbers and rates of blacks on welfare.* In 1960, there were 3.1 million total welfare recipients in the United States. Of that number it is estimated that 41 percent—roughly 1.3 million—were black, or about 7 percent of the 18.8 million Negroes in America in 1960. As the decade progressed, the overall figures rose precipitously:

Recipients, Aid to Dependent Children, 1960–1971

1960	3,073,000
1965	4,396,000
1967	5,309,000
1968	6,086,000
1969	7,313,000
1970	9,659,000
1971	10,651,000

Of the 10.6 million on welfare in 1971, 45 percent were black—4.8 million. Of the total black population of 23 million, 21 percent were on AFDC—up from 7 percent only eleven years earlier.

It would be blinding ourselves to reality to deny the seriousness of these figures. The rise in female-headed black families living in poverty, and the concomitant increase in the number of blacks on welfare, is a deplorable situation from whatever angle it is viewed.

. . . . .

And the situation is also deplorable because of what it does to our politicians and our politics—particularly liberal politicians and liberal politics. Middle-class voters—including many black middle-class voters—don't want to pay the bill for families they believe are "shiftless," for families they believe ought to be cared for by the (absent) man of the house. They especially resent paying when they believe that the standard of living they are providing for families on welfare has begun to approach their own, a standard they have toiled long and hard to reach. Politicians with liberal instincts feel compassion for the poor and the needy, but they also feel the hot breath of the voters on their necks. Caught between compassion and self-interest, liberal politicians also face torment from more conservative candidates who are perfectly willing, even anxious, to exploit the situation further.

Yet the welfare figures alone, deplorable as they are, do not tell the full story. For the increase in the percentage of blacks on welfare has occurred during a time when the rate of blacks in poverty has sharply decreased. The meaning of this apparent paradox is simply that those blacks still in poverty are more likely than they once were to be receiving aid. The percentage of blacks in poverty has gone sharply down from 48 to 29 percent in the years from 1959 to 1971. That is an enormous change. At the same time, as we have seen, the percentage of blacks on welfare has gone sharply up—by about three times, from 7 to 21 percent: another enormous change. A black person in the poverty range, then, is far more likely to be receiving welfare now than in the early 60s, perhaps as much as five times as likely.

. . . . .

What do all these figures on poverty and dependency tell us? First of all, there are fewer blacks in poverty. Secondly, those blacks in poverty are far more likely to be receiving help than was formerly the case. And finally, poor blacks are rising to levels closer to the line dividing poverty from non-poverty than before.

. . . . .

* "Welfare" as the term is generally used refers primarily to aid disbursed under the category "Aid to Families with Dependent Children" (AFDC)—and numbers for that program are the ones used here.

VI

Judging progress is of necessity a cold and comparative discipline. We believe, however, that on the basis of the statistics we have examined, it is fair to say that for American blacks *generally* in the 1960s a huge amount of progress was made—although there is still a substantial and necessary distance to traverse before some rough level of parity is reached. Moreover, those three in ten blacks who remain trapped in poverty also made statistical economic progress in these years, although on balance this progress may with justice be considered nullified by the stunning rise of violence in the worst areas of our nation.

Now, is all this better than what it replaced? The answer is an uncompromising "yes." In a society that prides itself on being middle class, blacks are now moving into the middle class in unprecedented numbers. In a society that scorns the high-school drop-out and offers work to the high-school graduate, blacks are now finishing high school and significant numbers are going on to college. In a culture that has a clear idea of what is a good job and what is not, blacks are now moving into good jobs. There can be little doubt that all these socioeconomic developments are better than what they replaced.

But what of the future?

. . . . .

Insofar as it can be measured sketchily over a short period of time, progress in the Nixon years of 1969, 1970, and 1971 was less dramatic than in the Kennedy-Johnson years. True, the slowdown was not aimed at blacks; there was a national economic recession, and if the sinking rate of blacks in poverty stopped sinking, so, roughly, did the rate for whites. The rates of black families earning $10,000 a year or more in fact continued to climb, although more slowly than earlier. Black income viewed as a fraction of white income seemed to reach a plateau. Unemployment rates climbed for both blacks and whites—somewhat more so for whites. On some fronts progress continued strong—very strong—despite the recession: high-school drop-out rates for black males fell markedly from 1970 to 1971 (for 18-years-olds the rate fell from 30 percent to 23 percent; for 19-year-olds from 44 to 29 percent).

The record of the first three Nixon years cannot be called much better than mixed. The key question, of course, is whether these three years signal a general and continuing slowdown or merely a partial and temporary one. The answer will have to wait until the economy heats up again, but according to the second scenario the 1970s will begin to bear a structural resemblance to the economic plateau of the 1950s, rather than to the sharp ascent of the 1960s.

Aside from the recent figures . . . , there is further reason to be concerned about the new Nixon budget for fiscal 1974. That budget has been described as the death knell of the Great Society, and while the description is no doubt overly dramatic, it is clear that if the President has his way many of the Great Society programs will be cut back or cut out. If these programs were indeed what was responsible for the great progress made by blacks in the 1960s, it follows that progress will decrease as the programs are eliminated or starved. Doing away with the programs, in effect, will presumably do away with some if not all of the relative gains that are likely to accrue from structural forces alone.

. . . . .

Things for blacks will get relatively worse in the 70s according to this scenario.

In our judgment this is an improbable prognosis. President Nixon neither wants to, nor could, undo all the progress of the 60s. No one, for instance, has proposed repealing the Voting Rights Act, which wields enormous political clout. No one has proposed repealing the Public Accommodations Law. Nor the new minimum wages. Nor Medicaid. Nor aid to higher education. In addition, while no one can accurately quantify the impact of the New Frontier and Great Society, we believe it a mistaken analysis that the programs alone were responsible for the progress of the 60s. A key antipoverty remedy in the past, and one likely to remain so in the future, is a steadily strong economy. The Great Society programs were a central ingredient of progress, but not so central that repeal of some of them now would actually reverse the tide.

VII

It has been our contention, and one which we have attempted to document, that enormous progress has been made by American blacks in the past decade, so much so that a thin majority of American blacks now belong to the middle class. But we noted early in this essay that a blanket of silence seems to envelop the liberal community on this point, so that the economic and social advances made by blacks, far from being trumpeted or even acknowledged, are simply ignored when they are not actually denied. In the face of all the evidence to the contrary, not a few liberal spokesmen and civil-rights activists have claimed that blacks are in fact worse off now than they were ten years ago.

. . . . .

Julian Bond, in noting the current statistical condition of blacks in America, said, incredibly:

> . . . We are no longer slaves. Secondly, we can sit at lunch counters, sit downstairs at movie theaters, ride in the front of buses, register, vote, work, and go to school where we once could not. But in a great many ways, we are constantly discovering that things have either not changed at all, or have become much worse. A quick look at all of the facts and figures that measure how well, or how poorly, a people are doing—the kinds of statistics that measure infant mortality, unemployment, median family income, life expectancy—demonstrates clearly that the average black American, while better off in comparison than his father was, is actually worse off when his statistics are measured against similar ones for white people. It is as though black Americans are climbing a molasses mountain in snowshoes, while the rest of the country rides a rather leisurely ski-lift to the top. It is these depressing figures, and the accompanying pathology which results from them, that causes so much discontent and depression in black communities today. The realization is that separately over the years the diverse strategies of Booker T. Washington and Dr. W. E. B. Du Bois and Marcus Garvey and Martin Luther King and Malcolm X have not appreciably improved the material lot of the masses of black folk.

Why have the data of black advancement been kept secret by those who presumably have an interest in making them known? After all, the black man-in-the-street is perfectly aware of the gains that have been made. A Potomac Associates/Gallup Poll taken in 1972, for instance, revealed that whereas whites on the whole said life in America had gotten worse in recent years, blacks said things were getting better (they were the only group of 31 subcategories who thought so). The answer is of course that civil-rights leaders do know what has happened, and even acknowledge it in private; but they have elected as a matter of policy to mute any public acknowledgment or celebration of black accomplishments in order to maintain moral and political pressure on the administration and on public opinion.

This strategy, we submit, is a mistaken one, counterproductive of its goal; the only people who have been kept under pressure by it are liberals themselves. As has been the case with many aspects of the liberal agenda in the last half-century, civil-rights leaders who refuse to claim credit for the successes they have earned only lend themselves to the purposes of those who declare the bankruptcy of liberalism altogether as a political strategy.

Here is the dilemma in which liberals find themselves. Forty years have passed since they became the driving force of American politics, frequently occupying the White House, always influential in the Congress. In this period of time a remarkable body of legislation has been placed on the statute books, as a result of which great economic and social progress has been made in the country at large, from which all Americans have benefited. And this progress liberals now deny, claiming that the programs for which they fought and lobbied have not worked (but at the same time denouncing Richard Nixon when *he* says they haven't worked).

In short, the liberal battle-cry has become, "We have failed; let us continue!"

A classic illustration of this tendency was provided by Senator Edmund Muskie in a speech delivered at the Liberal party dinner in New York in October 1971:

> We meet tonight in a time of failure of American liberalism. You can see the failure everywhere in this city and across the country. For too long, the sound of liberal alarms has been answered by little more than the echo of our own voices. . . . The blunt truth is that liberals have achieved virtually no fundamental change in our society since the end of the New Deal. We have made strong efforts, some of them even inspiring. We have made good speeches, some of them great. And we have even made some advances . . . too many of them half-measures. So in 1971, we continue to live with institutions . . . that serve the few who are comfortable at the expense of the many who truly are in need. How have we gained so little after so long a time and so much work? It is easy to blame others. But the fault is not primarily in others . . . it is in ourselves. Too often, we have assumed that we would win because we should win. Too often, we have equated a hard fight for progress with the hard fact of progress.

Now let us suppose that, instead of the institutionalized gloom pervading liberal thought today, a different analysis—an *accurate* analysis—were substituted, and a different rhetoric adopted to conform to it. Of what would it consist? It would begin, first of all, in the recognition that in 1960 and in 1964, the nation elected Presidents who were pledged to get America moving again, to give a better deal to the poor and the black, to break a decades-old legal, political and social logjam. Thanks to these Presidents, thanks to a liberal impulse in the Congress in the mid-1960s, thanks to the tireless efforts of liberals all over America, the legislation was passed to fulfill that pledge: manpower programs, poverty programs, and a stunning array of health, education, and legal services. Now, more than a decade later, we can look back and see—results. The census and the other statistical indices of our time show success in many crucial areas; in particular, a better deal has been given to the poor and the black to the point where many of them are now in the middle class, just as the Presidential pledges and the legislation promised. The confirming data have been presented above. To be sure, we cannot say absolutely that the legislation was *totally* responsible for the progress made, but we can say absolutely that it was crucial. Liberalism worked.

Normally, given a situation such as the one we have described, the political burden of proof would be on him who wished to deny it, in this case a Republican President with an analysis and a strategy of his own to promote. He would be the one forced to show that life in America has deteriorated, or at least that liberal programs had failed. Instead—at a moment when history and data show victory for their ideas—liberals loudly compete with each other to do his work. Instead of proclaiming success, liberals can only assert that America is a failure, that things are as bad as ever and maybe worse. And President Nixon smiles in agreement.

84.

BLACK INEQUALITY AND CONSERVATIVE STRATEGY

Joe T. Darden

In this selection, written at the editors' invitation, Joe T. Darden shows how the processes of change may be viewed quite differently by different observers. Here a black social scientist examines the data on changes in black income, occupation, and education compared to whites and arrives at a conclusion quite different than the white authors of the previous selection. For the white authors the change in black status has been a "remarkable development," while for Darden the gap between the status of blacks and whites has not been significantly reduced. Since both use census data, the different conclusions emerge from the differences in data selected for analysis, or in the interpretation of what the data show. The reader may wish to study both to decide which analysis and interpretation is more valid.

Angry reaction from the NAACP, the Urban League, other civil rights organizations and blacks throughout America is

Source: This article appears for the first time in this volume.

Joe T. Darden is an assistant professor at Michigan State University working jointly in the Urban and Metropolitan Studies and Geography departments.

justified when such published statements appear as (1) "middle class has now become an accurate term to describe the social and economic condition of somewhat more than half of black Americans," and (2) "civil rights leaders know what has happened and even acknowledge it in private; but they have elected as a matter of policy to mute any public acknowledgement or celebration of black accomplishments in order to maintain moral and political pressure on the administration and on public opinion." Such statements of black advancement into the middle class and charges of lack of public acknowledgement by civil rights organizations were made by Wattenberg and Scammon.[1]

Needless to say, this is an old conservative strategy designed to maintain the status quo, i.e., black inequality, by directing public opinion toward complacency, social inaction and the cessation of any commitment to total racial equality. As usual, such strategic statements are highly subjective and are made with little or no specific reference to the source of data. This procedure is followed for fear that any point by point check for verification may result in part truths, half truths or no truth at all.

The purpose of this paper is to determine the changes if any in the level of black inequality from 1960 to 1972. Examination of the changes in the level of black inequality is the most effective way to measure black progress. The extent of black inequality will be examined by using the following variables: income, employment patterns and education.

Let me emphasize from the beginning that true black progress can be adequately measured only within the context of racial inequality. For example, if the black median income in 1960 were $6,000 and the white median income were $8,000, and by 1970 the black median income increased to $8,000 while the white median income increased to $10,000, this is not true black progress. Even though black median income increased, so did white median income at the same rate, leaving their ratios unaffected. Thus, true black progress must be measured in terms of changes in the "socioeconomic gap" between whites and blacks. Therefore, regardless of increases in black median income, regardless of improvements in black employment patterns, regardless of increases in the black median educational level, if the socioeconomic gap between blacks and whites does not narrow, it is not true black progress. Furthermore, if the gap widens, it is indeed retrogression.

Contrary to the view of Wattenberg and Scammon, I will argue that while there has been a slight relative improvement in the socioeconomic condition of blacks since 1960, the absolute socioeconomic gap between blacks and whites, as measured by income, has actually increased. I will not waste time discussing what does or does not constitute middle-class status or whether a majority of blacks are now middle class, since such definition (as defined by Wattenberg and Scammon) is merely arbitrary and is based on their perception.[2] Instead I will focus on the more objective socioeconomic indices associated with class, in order to determine the extent of black progress.

INCOME

The first and I believe the most important index associated with class is income. Contrary to the argument of Wattenberg

[1] See Ben J. Wattenberg and Richard M. Scammon, "Black Progress and Liberal Rhetoric," *Commentary* (April 1973), pp. 35–44.

[2] I, for example, would set the income level for "middle class" at $11,446, the Bureau of Labor Statistics "intermediate family budget." Using that figure, not a majority, but only about 30 percent, of the black families in the United States would be considered middle class.

and Scammon, my analysis of the census data reveals little black progress in recent years. Instead the absolute gap between black and white incomes has actually increased. What Wattenberg and Scammon have called "sharp progress" on the part of blacks during the sixties is merely a 4 percentage point increase, probably the result of fluctuation in the economy (Table 1). Such a 4 percentage point increase is not unique, as Wattenberg and Scammon imply. Similar increases have occurred in the past. For example, for 1949 to 1952, a three-year period, the ratio of black to white median income jumped from 51 percent to 57 percent, an increase of 6 percentage points, reaching only 2 points less than the 1972 ratio of 59 percent.[3] In other words, when the relative level of black progress in 1952 is compared to the level in 1972, there is a difference of only 2 percentage points. The ratio of black to white median income reached its peak in 1969 and the usual decline is already evident (see Table 1).

Furthermore, in an economy of rising incomes, even decreasing *relative* differences are compatible with increasing *absolute* differences.[4] The income gap between blacks and whites has continued to increase decade by decade (Table 2). In 1950, the gap between black and white incomes was only $2,738. By 1960, the gap was $3,703. By 1972, the gap had increased to $4,443, almost doubling the 1950 income gap. Why would anyone interpret such increasing income gaps between blacks and

Table 1 *Ratio of Black to White Median Incomes*

Year	Percent	Percentage Point Change
1960	55*	
1963	53*	−2
1965	54	+1
1966	58	+4
1967	59	+1
1968	60	+1
1969	61	+1
1970	61	0
1971	60	−1
1972	59	−1

Source: U.S. Bureau of the Census, Current Population Reports, Series P-23, No. 42, *The Social and Economic Status of the Black Population in the United States, 1971,* p. 29; and the U.S. Bureau of the Census, Current Population Reports, Series P-60, No. 87, *Money Income in 1972 of Families and Persons in the United States,* U.S. Government Printing Office, Washington, D.C., 1973, p. 1.

* Includes other races.

whites as "black progress," when there is in fact retrogression? One of two reasons may account for this. Either the truth is known and understood by the proponents and they chose to follow the conservative strategy of public deception, in order to stifle efforts toward black social and economic progress and consequent elimination of racial inequality; or the proponents do not know the truth and do not understand what has happened to the social and economic conditions of blacks vis-a-vis whites over the years. For example, the small relative income gains by blacks in recent years have not necessarily been due to liberalism or liberal legislation, as Wattenberg and Scammon have implied.[5] The ma-

[3] U.S. Bureau of the Census, *Current Population Reports,* Series P-60, no. 75, "Income in 1969 of Families and Persons in the United States," Washington, D.C.: U.S. Government Printing Office, 1970, p. 25.

[4] U.S. Congress Joint Economic Committee, *The American Distribution of Income: A Structural Problem,* by Lester C. Thurow and Robert E. B. Lucas, Joint Committee Print (Washington, D.C.: U.S. Government Printing Office, 1972), p. 7.

[5] I do not mean to imply that liberal legislation is not and was not needed. Small groups, like young black male college graduates, may have progressed as a result of liberal social programs. However, if racial equality is ever to be realized in the near future, enforcement efforts must be greatly increased or more legislation drafted.

Table 2 *Difference in Median Family Income, 1950 and 1960 to 1972 – in Constant Dollars by Race of Head (in 1972 Dollars)*

Year	White	Black[a]	Difference or Gap
1950	$ 5,986	$3,248	$2,738
1960	8,267	4,564	3,703
1961	8,390	4,461	3,929
1962	8,631	4,608	4,023
1963	8,946	4,751	4,195
1964	9,256	5,183	4,073[b]
1965	9,612	5,349	4,263
1966	10,042	6,008	4,034[b]
1967	10,319	6,380	3,939[b]
1968	10,741	6,718	4,023
1969	11,179	7,062	4,117
1970	11,030	7,018	4,012[b]
1971	11,025	6,936	4,089
1972	11,549	7,106	4,443

Source: Calculated from U.S. Bureau of the Census, Current Population Reports, Series P-60, No. 87, *Money Income in 1972 of Families and Persons in the United States,* U.S. Government Printing Office, Washington, D.C., 1973, p. 6.

[a] Includes other races.

[b] Decrease in income gap.

Table 3 *Race and Unemployment Rates: 1960–1972* *

Year	Black and Other Races	White	Ratio: Black and Other Races to White
1960	10.2	4.9	2.1 to 1
1961	12.4	6.0	2.1 to 1
1962	10.9	4.9	2.2 to 1
1963	10.8	5.0	2.2 to 1
1964	9.6	4.6	2.1 to 1
1965	8.1	4.1	2.0 to 1
1966	7.3	3.3	2.2 to 1
1967	7.4	3.4	2.2 to 1
1968	6.7	3.2	2.1 to 1
1969	6.4	3.1	2.1 to 1
1970	8.2	4.5	1.8 to 1
1971	9.9	5.4	1.8 to 1
1972	10.0	5.0	2.0 to 1

Source: U.S. Bureau of the Census, Current Population Reports, Series P-23, No. 46, *The Social and Economic Status of the Black Population in the United States, 1972.* U.S. Government Printing Office, Washington, D.C., 1973, p. 38.

* The unemployment rate is the percent of the civilian labor force that is unemployed.

jor source of income gains for blacks has probably been geographic migration. Blacks have increasingly moved out of the south, where relative incomes are low, to the north and west, where black incomes are higher. Based on the geographic movements that have actually taken place among blacks between 1950 and 1970, geographic movement more than accounts for the observed relative increase in black incomes.[6]

However, contrary to the predictions of Wattenberg and Scammon that black incomes will continue to rise relative to white incomes (as I stated previously, a decline is already evident), geographic migration as a tool for black-white income parity is inherently limited. Even if all black families were to move out of the south, black incomes would still only be about 75 percent of white incomes.[7]

OCCUPATION

A second index associated with class is occupation (including the presence or absence of employment and the kinds or types of jobs people possess). In both categories, widespread black inequality continued during the sixties. Examination of the total black civilian labor force reveals that the

[6] Ibid., p. 10.

[7] Ibid., p. 10.

Table 4 *Unemployment Rates by Sex, Race and Age, 1960 and 1970 to 1972 (Annual Averages)*

	Black and Other Races				White			
Subject	1960	1970	1971	1972	1960	1970	1971	1972
TOTAL	10.2	8.2	9.9	10.0	4.9	4.5	5.4	5.0
ADULT MEN	9.6	5.6	7.2	6.8	4.2	3.2	4.0	3.6
ADULT WOMEN	8.3	6.9	8.7	8.8	4.6	4.4	5.3	4.9
TEENAGERS *	24.4	29.1	31.7	33.5	13.4	13.5	15.1	14.2

Source: U.S. Bureau of the Census, Current Population Reports, Series P-23, No. 46, *The Social and Economic Status of the Black Population in the United States, 1972,* p. 39.

* "Teenagers" include persons 16 to 19 years old.

disparities in unemployment rates of blacks to whites remained relatively unchanged during the sixties. The *ratio* was 2.1 to 1 in 1960 and was 2.0 to 1 in 1972 (Table 3). Therefore, regardless of remarks by Wattenberg and Scammon that tremendous gains by blacks occurred during the sixties, the total black civilian labor force did not progress toward equality with whites.

Furthermore, unemployment rates for black teenagers increased from 24.4 percent in 1960 to 33.5 percent in 1972. On the other hand, the unemployment rate for white teenagers increased from 13.4 percent in 1960 to 14.2 percent in 1972 (Table 4). Black teenage girls experienced particularly severe unemployment in 1971. Their rate of 35.5 percent – up from 34.4 percent in 1970 – was almost two and one half times that of white teenage girls.[8]

In summary, unemployment rates for blacks are still almost double those for whites in most categories. Not since 1953 has the black unemployment rate been below the 6.0 percent "recession" level widely regarded as a sign of *serious* economic weakness when prevalent for the entire work force. While the black unemployment rate remains high in relation to the white rate, the number of additional jobs needed to lower this to the level of white unemployment is small and getting smaller, especially in the central cities, as more and more jobs move to the predominately white suburbs.

As in the case of black and white unemployment rates, racial disparities also persist in the occupational structure. Black workers are still highly concentrated in the lowest skilled and lowest paying occupations such as service, private household and farm and laboring jobs. These jobs often involve substandard wages, great instability and uncertainty of tenure, extremely low status in the eyes of both employer and employee, little or no chance for meaningful advancement and unpleasant or exhausting duties. In 1972, black and other races still comprised a disproportionately small share of employed persons holding high-paying, high-status jobs. About 4 percent of black and other races compared to 11 percent of whites were employed as managers and administrators, and about 10 percent of black and other races versus 15 percent of whites were employed as professional and technical workers. Similarly, a smaller proportion of black and other races than white

[8] U.S. Department of Labor, Employment Standards Administration, *Facts on Women Workers of Minority Races* (Washington, D.C.: U.S. Government Printing Office, 1972), p. 2.

workers were employed as craftsmen or in related skilled trades. However, on the lower end of the occupational structure, the proportionate racial percentages are reversed. The proportion of black and other races employed in the lower-paying, lower-status occupational categories (service, farm and nonfarm laborer jobs combined) was about double that of the comparable group of whites – 40 percent compared with 20 percent.

These selected statistics give some indication that despite any progress by blacks over the past years, the present black occupational distribution still does not approximate equality with the white distribution. Of course these differences are the consequences of discrimination (past and present) and differences in educational achievement, with the latter being largely the result of social and economic discrimination.[9] As racial discrimination declines, racial differences in the occupational distribution of blacks and whites should also decline. Few would dispute the fact that the decade of the sixties was one in which great "pressure" toward reducing racial discrimination occurred. The impact of that "pressure" should be reflected in the changes in the racial differences in occupations in 1960 and 1972. If there has been a decrease in the percent of racial difference in occupations, it is logical to assume that the "pressure" toward reducing racial discrimination in employment did make an impact (albeit not yet successful since success means the total elimination of discrimination and consequent racial differences in the pattern of occupations).

To examine the progress toward the elimination of racial differences in the pattern of employment over the past decade or so, an index of racial difference has been constructed. The index can be expressed mathematically as:

$$RD = \sum \frac{x_1 - y_1}{2}$$

where x_1 is the percent of the employed white population residing in a given occupation and y_1 is the percent of the employed black population residing in the same occupation. The derived value indicates the percentage of either race that would have to change occupations to make the percentages equal.

There is little doubt that there has been some progress made in decreasing the percent of racial difference in occupations from 1960 to 1972. In 1960, the racial difference index was 38.2 percent (Table 5). This means that a 38.2 percent change in occupations by either race would have been necessary in 1960 to eliminate racial inequality. The question then is how much racial change in occupations occurred between 1960 and 1972? Examination of the index of racial difference revealed that by 1972, the index had declined to 26.2 percent, a reduction of 12 percentage points (Table 6).

Sure, there was black occupational progress from 1960 to 1972 but not nearly enough. During the sixties, the greatest pressure (e.g., demonstrations, legislation, enforcement) against racial discrimination in employment occurred since Reconstruction. However, in spite of the "pressure," the average rate of racial change in the occupational structure was only one percentage point per year. At this rate, assuming that the "pressure" remained intact (and there is already some indication that it has

[9] U.S. Bureau of the Census, *Changing Characteristics of the Negro Population*, by Daniel O. Price (a 1960 Census Monograph). U.S. Government Printing Office, Washington, D.C., 1969. p. 241.

Table 5 *Racial Differences by Occupation in 1960*

	Percent Distribution		
Occupation	White (x_1)	Racial Difference ($x_1 - y_1$)	Black * (y_1)
White-Collar Workers . . .	46.6	30.5	16.1
Professional and technical workers . . .	12.1	7.3	4.8
Managers and administrators, except farm . . .	11.7	9.1	2.6
Sales Workers . . .	7.0	5.5	1.5
Clerical Workers . . .	15.7	8.4	7.3
Blue-Collar Workers . . .	36.2	3.9	40.1
Craftsmen and kindred workers . . .	13.8	7.8	6.0
Operatives, except transport; transport equipment operatives . . .	17.9	2.5	20.4
Nonfarm laborers . . .	4.4	9.3	13.7
Service Workers . . .	9.9	21.8	31.7
Private Household . . .	1.7	12.5	14.2
Other . . .	8.2	9.3	17.5
Farm Workers . . .	7.4	4.7	12.1
RACIAL DIFFERENCE (RD)		38.2	
TOTAL EMPLOYED, PERCENT	100.0		100.0

Source: Calculated by the author from data derived from U.S. Bureau of the Census, Current Population Reports, Series P-23, No. 46, *The Social and Economic Status of the Black Population in the United States, 1972.* U.S. Government Printing Office, Washington, D.C., 1973. P. 49.

* Includes other races.

not),[10] it would take at least another 26 years to eliminate racial inequality in the occupational structure. Therefore, while it seems clear that the "pressure" against racial discrimination in employment should be doubled, it is the strategy of the conservative to put out the word that "parity has been reached," or nearly so, "the majority of blacks are now middle class." As the white masses read such statements and blacks demand more "pressure," the typical white reaction is "What *more* do *you people* want?" The ultimate action by the decision makers is a reduction of pressure.

[10] It appears that the Nixon Administration is already decreasing the pressure against discrimination in employment and my prediction is that the relative occupational gains if any by blacks during the seventies will be substantially *less* than the gains during the sixties.

EDUCATION

Along with income and occupation, widespread disparities continue to exist in education. In 1971, among blacks 20 to 34 years old, 35 percent were high school dropouts, compared to only 18.5 percent for whites of the same age group.[11] For blacks,

[11] U.S. Bureau of the Census, Current Population Reports, Series P–20, no. 241, *Social and Economic Characteristics of Students: October 1971,* U.S. Government Printing Office, Washington, D.C., 1972. p. 2.

Table 6 *Racial Difference by Occupation in 1972*

Occupation	Percent Distribution		
	White (x_1)	Racial Difference ($x_1 - y_1$)	Black * (y_1)
White-Collar Workers . . .	50.0	20.2	29.8
Professional and technical workers . . .	14.6	5.1	9.5
Managers and administrators, except farm . . .	10.6	6.9	3.7
Sales Workers . . .	7.1	4.9	2.2
Clerical Workers . . .	17.8	3.4	14.4
Blue-Collar Workers . . .	34.4	5.5	39.9
Craftsmen and kindred workers . . .	13.8	5.1	8.7
Operatives, except transport; transport equipment opperatives . . .	16.0	5.3	21.3
Nonfarm laborers . . .	4.6	5.3	9.9
Service Workers . . .	11.8	15.4	27.2
Private Household . . .	1.2	5.6	6.8
Other . . .	10.5	10.0	20.5
Farm Workers . . .	3.8	0.8	3.0
RACIAL DIFFERENCE (RD)		26.2	
TOTAL EMPLOYED, PERCENT	100.0		100.0

Source: Calculated by the author from data derived from U.S. Bureau of the Census, Current Population Reports, Series P-23, No. 46, *The Social and Economic Status of the Black Population in the United States, 1972.* U.S. Government Printing Office, Washington, D.C., 1973. P. 49.

* Includes other races.

14 to 19 years old, the dropout rate was 11.1 percent compared to only 7.4 percent for whites of the same age group.

Contrary to statements by Wattenberg and Scammon, there was no "progress" in reducing the "racial difference gap"[12] between young black males and young white males from 1960 to 1970. In 1960, the "racial difference gap" was 27 percent. By 1970, the racial difference was still 27 percent. At the college level, the "racial difference gap" even increased from 1960 to 1972. In 1960, the "racial difference gap" between blacks and whites 25 to 34 years old who completed four years of college or more was 7.8 percent (Table 7). By 1972, the "racial difference gap" had increased to 10.9 percent, black-oriented recruitment programs, financial aid and tutorial assistance notwithstanding.

Furthermore, Wattenberg and Scammon failed to consider the fact that when measuring black educational progress, "college completion statistics" are much more reliable indicators than "college enrollment statistics," since the black college dropout

[12] The concept of "racial difference gap" as used above refers to the difference in the percent of white males and black males 25 to 29 years old who completed four years of high school or more. It is my view that a reduction in the percent of racial difference in the educational level of blacks and whites is a much more important indicator of black educational progress than a mere increase in the black educational level, along with an increase in the level of the total population.

Table 7 *Percent Racial Difference in Population 25 to 34 Years Old Who Completed 4 Years of College or More: 1960, 1967, 1970 and 1972*

Year	Black	White	Racial Difference Gap
1960	4.1	11.9	7.8
1967	5.4	15.0	9.6
1970	6.1	16.6	10.5
1972	7.9	18.8	10.9

Source: Calculated from U.S. Bureau of the Census, Current Population Reports, Series P-23, No. 46, *The Social and Economic Status of the Black Population in the United States, 1972*. P. 65.

rate is extremely high. Many predominately white institutions have used a "revolving door policy," i.e., enrolling large numbers of blacks to inflate their minority enrollment statistics in order to meet federal equal opportunity guidelines. Several of the enrolled blacks fail to graduate.

On a final note, Wattenberg and Scammon's claim that a black high school graduate is a "bona-fide member of the educational middle class" reflects a gross unawareness of the racial differences in the amount of socioeconomic rewards for educational achievement. For example, in America the average white elementary graduate is rewarded with as much or more socioeconomic status (income) than the average black high school graduate. Likewise, the average white high school graduate is rewarded with as much or more socioeconomic status (income) than the average black college graduate. These inequities are of course due primarily to racism and racial discrimination. Therefore, as long as racial discrimination and racism exist, on the average, a black person in America must be a college graduate before he or she is rewarded with the socioeconomic status (income) to become a bonafide member of the educational middle class.

SUMMARY AND CONCLUSIONS

In summary, blacks have made socioeconomic progress in some areas over the last decade. But so has the total American population. What is more significant is the fact that blacks have made little relative progress toward reducing racial inequality in income, employment and education. In most instances in which relative progress was made, there was absolute retrogression. In other words, the socioeconomic gap between blacks and whites remains almost as wide today as it was in 1960. Until the gap is reduced, true black progress is not a reality; until the gap is completely eliminated, true success does not exist.

The apparent confusion over the socioeconomic condition of the black population probably lies in the fact that the black population, as the white population, is diverse in income, occupation and education. Three black economic groups are readily distinguishable. The first group (31.5 percent) consists of middle and upper income blacks whose occupational and educational characteristics are similar to those of middle and upper income white groups.[13] This group had incomes of over $10,000 in 1972. The second group (35.5 percent) contains blacks whose incomes are above the "poverty level" of $4,275 for a nonfarm family of four but less than $10,000, who have *not* attained the occupa-

[13] I have no disagreement about the middle class status or economic gains of *this* group during the sixties. This segment of the black population continued to make economic gains.

tional or educational status typical of "middle class" Americans. It is the condition of this group that Wattenberg and Scammon have misconstrued by assigning it middle class status. The third group (33 percent) has very low occupational and educational attainments and lives below the "poverty level." If racial equality is ever to occur, more attention and concern must be given to this poorest black group, whose numbers seem to be increasing. Examination of recent census statistics reveals that about 24.5 million persons were below the low-income level in 1972, according to the results of the Current Population Survey (CPS) conducted in March 1972 by the Bureau of the Census. The survey revealed that the number of low-income white persons declined by about 9 percent between 1971 and 1972, but there was a small *increase* in the number of low-income blacks.[14] In 1972, the low-income or poverty threshold, i.e., the income level which separates "poor" from "nonpoor" was $4,275 for a nonfarm family of four; it was $4,137 in 1971 and $2,973 in 1959.[15] These thresholds are updated every year to reflect the changes in the Consumer Price Index (CPI). Since 1959, the first year for which data on poverty was available, there has been a sizable reduction in the number and percent of persons in poverty—from about 22 percent of the population in 1959 to 12 percent in 1972. However, in 1972 as in previous years a widespread disparity continued to exist between the percent of all white persons in poverty and the percent of all black persons in poverty. In 1972, only 9 percent of all white persons were in poverty as compared to 33 percent for blacks.[16] Furthermore, poverty tends to strike a higher proportion of young blacks (the hope of the black future) than young whites. In 1972, children under 18 years accounted for about 36 percent of all white persons in poverty, as compared to 52 percent of all black persons.

What is the probability then of these poor blacks breaking out of poverty in the future and becoming "middle class"? Studies of poverty families indicate that about 70 percent of the families that were in poverty the preceding year are in poverty the following year. Of the remaining 30 percent, 11 percent were usually dissolved from death and other causes and 19 percent escaped from poverty. Of the 19 percent who escaped, 8 percent were still within $1,000 of the poverty line, 4 percent were within $2,000 of the poverty line, and 7 percent were only more than $2,000 away from the poverty line.[17] Families who escape from poverty in any one year also have a significant probability of falling back into poverty in succeeding years. As a consequence, poverty data would seem to indicate a low degree of economic mobility among the black poor population. As for the remainder of the black population, a rise in incomes relative to white incomes will depend heavily on continued geographic movements from the south to the north and west. To the extent that this trend continues, black incomes will rise relative to white incomes. To the extent that it slows down, black incomes will

[14] U.S. Bureau of the Census, Current Population Reports, Series P-60, no. 88, *Characteristics of the Low-Income Population: 1972.* U.S. Government Printing Office, Washington, D.C., 1973. p. 1.

[15] For a more detailed definition of the concept of poverty, see *Current Population Reports,* Series P-23, no. 28 and Series P-60, no. 86.

[16] U.S. Bureau of the Census, *Current Population Reports,* Series P-60, No. 88, p. 1.

[17] *Report of the Council of Economic Advisors, 1965.* Washington, D.C.: U.S. Government Printing Office. P. 164.

cease rising relative to whites.[18] Additional changes in black incomes will depend heavily on the future impact of equal opportunity programs and enforcement of antidiscrimination laws, i.e., stepped-up "pressure." As yet these programs do not seem to be having a noticeable impact on relative incomes of a substantial number of blacks on a national level. However, some changes seem to be visible for small groups of college-educated blacks.

In the final analysis, I see a more unstable and less optimistic future for black progress than that outlined by Wattenberg and Scammon. First, women's liberation and consequent improvements in female incomes and job opportunities will tend to lead to a widening gap between black and white family incomes in the future. For example, in 1969 53 percent of all black wives were working in the paid labor force, while only 38 percent of all white wives were doing so. At high incomes, the difference is even more extreme. Seventy-three percent of all black families with incomes over $15,000 had a wife in the paid labor force, while only 48 percent of all white families with incomes over $15,000 per year had a wife in the paid labor force. As a consequence, better income opportunities for existing female workers would tend to equalize black and white incomes, but better income and job opportunities that succeeded in attracting more female workers into the labor force would tend to *increase* the gap between black and white incomes. There are simply more white wives remaining to be attracted into the labor force.

Second, a firm commitment to altering the present unequal distribution of income does not exist among American decision-makers. For example, the poverty program, a program for altering the distribution of income, is presently being dismantled. Third, equal opportunity programs, programs designed to bring nonwhite minority and white majority income distributions into conformity, are presently not being enforced at a maximum level. Fourth, black public education, which is to some extent also designed to improve black economic mobility, is continuing to deteriorate. Until a firm commitment to income redistribution exists, and the necessary "pressure" applied to carry out that commitment, black inequality will continue to exist and black success will not be a reality.

[18] U.S. Congress Joint Economic Committee, *The American Distribution of Income,* p. 14.

85.

WHY BLACK SEPARATISM?

John Howard Griffin

When violence, burning, and destruction were added to protest and peaceful demonstration against the injustices imposed on blacks by a racist society, whites began to prepare for widespread racial conflict. In this period of crisis, many blacks came to feel that their survival required replacement of white leaders in the movement for racial equality by trustworthy and capable blacks. John Howard Griffin, a 40-year-old white native of Texas convincingly changed his appearance of racial identity to find out for himself what it means to be black in some Southern states. The publication of his *Black Like Me* in 1960 made him an unwilling racial "expert." In this selection, he gives his enlightening explanation of the blacks' rejection of traditional white liberal leadership. This should help the reader to understand the demand for black control of the black community and the desire for a separate social system.

Source: John Howard Griffin, *Sepia* 22, no. 4 (April 1973): 26–8, 30, 32, 34, 36. Copyright © 1973 by John Howard Griffin. Reprinted by permission of the author and *Sepia*.

Author-photographer John Howard Griffin has received many awards for his work. He was corecipient of Pope John XXIII Pacem in Terris Peace and Freedom Award in 1964. He is the author of *Black Like Me,* for which he won the Anisfield Wolf Award in 1961. More recently he is the author of *The Church and the Black Man,* and *A Hidden Wholeness: The Visual World of Thomas Merton.*

As a person who lived alternately in both white and black communities, I could forsee nothing but trouble in years of the 60s after my book, "Black Like Me," had been published and shocked many whites by what I had discovered while passing as a black. Suddenly I was looked upon as some kind of "racial expert," although I well knew that to be far from the truth.*

I was called into cities where "racial difficulties" surfaced, by perfectly sincere community leaders, usually mayors or college presidents or city councils. They wanted me to study their situation and report to them on it.

First I would have meetings and be briefed by white men on the conflicts, often

* Where did civil rights go wrong in the years since author John Howard Griffin wrote his best-selling book, "Black Like Me," which first appeared in SEPIA magazine as a series of articles recounting his experiences in passing for black on a journey through four Dixie states? In the first part of his account of what he observed in the immediate years after publication of his book, Griffin told of the trials of whites who tried to help in the rights struggle. In his concluding article, Griffin relates what happened in black communities when frustrations poured over in the vain battle for racial decency and how black separatism was born, thrived and has shocked an increasing number of white liberals.

Much of Griffin's findings are based on people and audiences he met around the nation as he was called upon to speak at college campuses and community meetings as a "racial expert" because of the acclaim and publicity for his book, which has gone into 39 printings and is now used in many schools as a standard text in race relations. A native Texan born in 1920, Griffin has lived in Texas most of his life, looks at the racial scene as an enlightened Southerner and rejects any notion of being a "racial expert." For several years he was blind as a result of wartime injuries, and when he regained his sight he learned to become color blind, as his books and his articles in SEPIA demonstrate.

in close touch with trained white social scientists. Then I would be taken into the black community where again I would be briefed by black leaders and sometimes black social scientists.

In no city did these two briefings coincide. In St. Louis, Rochester, Detroit, Kansas City, Los Angeles and many others this occurred. In every city there was this different view of the same situation by perfectly sincere men.

. . . . .

Black spokesmen like Dr. Martin Luther King, Roy Wilkins, Whitney Young, James Farmer, Dick Gregory, Stokely Carmichael and many others warned that the inner cities were becoming powder kegs and would certainly explode. In every city I was brought in to study (and often I returned again and again) I would live in the black ghetto with black families. I would come out and give a most detailed analysis to the whole city and to community leaders, warning them that they were sitting on powder kegs and one day some little insignificant event would occur and produce an explosion that would astound the whole community. "We are like children tossing matches toward that keg," I said. "One of them will detonate it, and the tragedy will occur, and you will not have wanted it and no black person will have wanted it."

In every city the local community leaders who had brought me in nevertheless felt that they lived there and knew better and said that I was being "unduly pessimistic." In some cities I was called "unduly pessimistic" only weeks before the explosions occurred. And when those cities exploded into turmoil, men who had not believed me would telephone to tell me I had been right and they had been wrong.

. . . . .

This was perhaps the most terrible time in modern history insofar as civil rights were concerned in this land. Black people began to believe in greater numbers that this country was really moving toward genocide, and from the point of view of black America, the evidence was alarming. That year [1967], in President Johnson's televised State of the Union message, his appeals for social justice and civil rights met with absolute silence from Congress—not a single lone handclap of approval broke that silence.

His appeal for saving the California Redwood trees, which followed immediately, got an ovation of wild handclapping approval from Congress. The message was clear and desolating. It showed this country's priorities and mood. It said to every black man: "Save the redwood forests and to hell with you."

In my dismay, I wired the President: "AM TIRED OF BEING A LOSER. FROM NOW ON I'M GOING TO FORGET HUMANITY AND WORK FOR THE TREES"

The patterns of these exploding inner cities began to emerge. From the black man's viewpoint it often looked as though black people were being driven to a flare-up which would then justify suppression by white men on the grounds of "self-defense."

In those terrible days of open conflict, I was being taken into the inner cities, usually by black militants, as an observer. I hardly ever opened my mouth. The day was past when black people wanted any advice from white men.

I was taken in simply to view it from the inside, so that in the event we did come to open genocidal conflict, there would be someone to give another view to history. And another view I got. I attended rage meetings where black men, women, children, students discussed their experiences. Everyone was saying the turmoil was the work of the young black. That was not true.

Middle-aged and elderly black people attended those meetings everywhere, and burned with rage.

In Wichita, I heard a young college student say the kinds of things that were being said in all the cities. He recounted an injustice done him in that community. He showed wounds where he had been beaten by white men.

"We've tried everything decent," he said loudly.

"Yes," the audience responded. "Yes. Who can doubt that?"

"We asked for justice and they fed us committees," he shouted.

"Yes."

"They've even got committees to decide how much self-determination we're going to have."

"Take ten!" someone shouted from the back of the room.

"Take ten!" a few responded.

After he had spoken, the young man came over to my chair, almost sobbing with frustration. He looked into my eyes with eyes that were wild with anguish and whispered while we shook hands, "When you go back, will you do me a favor?"

"Yes, if I can," I said.

"When you go back out there, will you tell your friend, Jesus Christ, and your friend, Martin Luther King—'shit!' . . ." He spat out the word with the deepest despair I ever heard in a human voice.

On the streets, young black men would call out, "Take ten!" to one another. Whites thought they were talking about a ten-minute coffee break. What they were really saying was that this country was moving toward the destruction of black people, and since the proportion was ten whites to every black, then black men should take ten white lives for every black life taken by white men.

Certainly the news reports and coverage, given largely by white interpreters outside the ghettos and widely and sincerely believed by horrified whites, had no credibility within the ghettos because it did not coincide with what black men were experiencing. In the heat of emotions, few white men could penetrate the troubled areas, and the media had not yet hired many black reporters who could have given a more balanced view.

As black men began to compare notes with me around the country, a strange pattern began to emerge. If it did not hold true for all the exploding communities, it held true for many of them. In these, someone in a high place—the mayor, chief of police or other official—would receive information that a neighboring city was already in flames and that carloads of armed black men were coming to attack this city.

This happened in Cedar Rapids where Des Moines was allegedly in flames. It happened in Ardmore, Oklahoma, and in in Ft. Worth, Texas, when it was alleged that Oklahoma City was in flames and carloads were converging on those two cities. It happened in Reno and other western cities, when Oakland, California, was supposed to be in flames. It happened in Roanoke when Richmond, Virginia, was supposed to be in flames. And in many other communities.

In no instance were these reports true or were any of these cities actually in flames. But the result was immediate action on the part of the white officials. They got in contact with important community and industrial leaders. Riot control measures were ordered into effect. Civilians armed themselves for the coming attack and stationed themselves at strategic points.

. . . . .

I traveled from city to city in those days and the view from within the ghettos was terrible and terrifying. While white people in the periphery were arming themselves against the day when they would have to defend themselves from attack by blacks (and really believed someone was fomenting a racial war in which black people would rise up and attack them), black people mostly without arms huddled inside the ghettos feeling that they were surrounded by armed whites.

Black parents tried to keep a closer watch on their children. Black men spoke of the old "licensed blood lust" which allowed racists to do anything to black people and get away with it.

Local white leadership was discredited in the eyes of black people, too, by their insistence on asking me, when we met to discuss the local events (usually with black people present), if I had discovered who was the traveling black agitator who had come in and stirred up their "good black people." And had I discovered if there were any communists behind the disruptions. Black people just could not believe local white officials, who surely must be aware of local conditions, could really think the explosion had been caused by "outside agitators" or communists. And the white officials were viewed as completely insincere. Sadly enough, I knew the white officials really and sincerely did believe the causes lay elsewhere than in their own backyards.

. . . . .

Three weeks before the assassination of Martin Luther King, I met on the West Coast with a group of black leaders to compare notes. Almost simultaneously many black people had become convinced that every time a black community was goaded into such an explosion, it served only the cause of racists and brought us closer to a genocidal situation.

The word went out not to let racists manipulate the communities into flare-ups. This is certainly one of the reasons why Dr. King's murder did not unleash massive violence as might have been anticipated. There were, of course, scattered pockets of retaliatory violence in some of the Eastern cities and Washington, D.C., but it was not the all-out race war that it could have been.

What reconciliation was possible then? If whites looked on blacks with distrust, it was nothing compared to the vast distrust with which blacks regarded whites.

Almost ironically the person of Martin Luther King in life and in death became the touchstone for a whole new evaluation among black thinkers. This evaluation led to alternatives to violent confrontation. So, in a bizarre sense, Dr. King, who had seemed so defeated and who had died without much hope that his philosophy of nonviolent resistance had accomplished anything, became the mainspring for a whole new way of thinking among black people and in the long run averted violent head-on collision between the citizens of this country. As a result of this new thinking, the "Take-ten!" call faded. Black men began to see other ways out. A whole new dynamism was put into play at the time of Dr. King's martyrdom.

Up until that time black thinking had been focused on the dream of an integrated society as the ultimate solution to discrimination and racial injustice. It was a dream held also by many whites, a dream for which many whites and blacks had already died. This dream was so deep, so cherished, and seemed to be such an unqualified good that no one really questioned it.

It took men of great mental toughness to begin to ask if that dream had not carried in its wake certain weaknesses for the black American. When this painful line of thought was opened up, it became apparent that at least some of that dream had kept black men weak. For example if a black man set up a business, he might very well hear his black potential clients say: "After all this struggle for integration, I'm not going to self-segregate," and refuse to patronize his business.

Also it was generally believed, though the belief was fading, that most "good whites" lived in the North and most "bad whites" lived in the South. Certainly many northern cities deplored what was going on in the South. But when Martin Luther King, who had been so praised in the North for the work he did in the South, came to work in the cities of the North, the very officials who had praised him sometimes led opposition to his work locally.

This revealed to black people that there was no basic difference between attitudes in the North and South. A white-imposed separation had always existed in both areas. Dr. King's trips into the North showed that even in the friendliest cities there would always rise up out of the local community sufficient opposition to any attempt to bridge this separation. It became bitterly apparent that this separation was going to go on existing into the foreseeable future.

What then? Black leaders and thinkers began to stand back and review the situation. Their conclusions were harsh. The old dream, and the constant hope in one solution—that of an integrated society—had not worked and had little chance of working now. Black people were jammed together in ghettos and were going to have to stay there.

All the apparent progress had not changed the problems of black people living in the ghettos of this land. Black men were still not able to function as men, as leaders of their households, as self-determining and self-respecting human individuals.

What were the possible alternatives to these exhausting and violent cycles of hopes built up and then dashed through the moods of white society?

Black leaders pondered. They must find the genius to turn a seemingly hopeless situation into an advantageous one. The first step was to accept the realities of the situation and act on them rather than on some nebulous dream of a future when all men would come to the realization that racial justice was for the good of all society, not just for the good of the oppressed.

Once viewed from this perspective, some startling facts become clear. Black thinkers, discarding the old dream, began to expose the weaknesses that had been built into the system. The first of these weaknesses was called "fragmented individualism" by the philosophers. As soon as it was defined, it was understood by black people, and recognized. "Fragmented individualism" concerned what happened to a black man who tried to make it in this society. In order to succeed, he had to become an imitation white man: dress white, talk white, think white, express the values of middle class white culture (at least when he was in the presence of white men). Implied in all this was the hiding, the denial of his selfhood, his Negritude, his culture, as though that were somehow shameful.

If he succeeded he was an alienated marginal man, alienated from the strength of his culture, from fellow black men, and never able, of course, to become that imitation white man because he bore the pigment that made the white man view him as intrinsically other. The instant the term "fragmented individualism" was understood, it was completely understood by black men who had lived it in all its nuances. And as soon as it was understood, black men could do something positive to counter it.

The "Brother" and "Sister" concept swept in. Black people deliberately stopped trying to imitate white men in dress, speech and etiquette. Black men reversed the weaknesses of "fragmented individualism" by studying black history, developing black pride, even using words like "black" which had been oppressive before, hammering them home until they stood for the symbol of the New Black and became beautiful.

Black thinkers spoke of turning the ghettos into gardens, taking over their own schools, building a "nation within a nation."

They pointed out the economic weaknesses of the old system. Most businesses in black areas were owned by white men, particularly the big chain grocery stores. Black people were shown that their dollars lost strength when spent in those stores because the profits went into white banks which would not discriminate against black people for TV and car loans, but would discriminate against them in small-business or housing loans.

With this understanding, black people in Chicago began to make the rounds of such stores, saying in effect that if the stores expected to sell another leaf of lettuce to black people, the stores had to hire black personnel, including black people at management level; and furthermore had to bank the proceeds of that particular ghetto operation in black banks which would not discriminate against black people in loans. The stores had to comply and this was so successful in Chicago that the techniques began to spread across the country.

At more personal levels it began to be understood, and was then quickly understood, that black society must work to salvage the black male child. Always before there had been concern for the black girl child. It was not pointed out that the black male child, even in a black school using white textbooks, could early come to the conclusion that all the heroes in history were white men. Furthermore, with the exception of nationally-known black civil rights leaders like Martin Luther King, Roy Wilkins, James Farmer and others, the black male child frequently saw the adult black male as ineffectual and defeated.

The old picture of the white man leading the black man by the hand toward the solution to his problems again gave the black male child a view of the adult black male as something not worth becoming. It killed his spirit and his will to become an adult, problem-solving individual. This perception swept the nation. Black parents began to demand changes in textbooks and to insist that black people be visibly involved in the solutions to all problems that concerned them.

A few white men who had worked long and hard in civil rights saw the immense importance of this new perception. Men like Saul Alinsky and Father Groppi and others who were regarded as heroes of the civil rights movement began to fade from public view, although continuing to work privately. They felt, as many blacks now felt, that for the sake of that black male child, black men should be seen as the problem-solvers and leaders, and that whites should stay out of the spotlight.

Some whites who had never really understood, were offended by this sudden death of their role as the "good white leading the poor black out of the jungle." Many of these were among the saddest people of our time, good-hearted whites who had dedicated themselves to helping black people become imitation whites, to "bringing them up to our level," without ever realizing what a deep insult this attitude can be.

White perception of these rapid changes in black concepts lagged. Whites, in general, could not keep up with the progress of black thinking of black men.

Black students were particularly aware that they had to give the black child the view of black men standing on their own, and to erase all hints of the old view of "being led by whites." College students formed black student unions and excluded white students. Few white students understood. White college students, after all, had been one of the great bulwarks in the battle for racial justice, and many had dedicated themselves heroically to this cause.

But part of that incipient racism had always led whites to assume the leadership positions which perpetuated the view that whites rather than blacks were the heroes of the movement. Really sincere and informed whites were thanked for what they had done and advised to go and work in their own communities, to combat the racism there which could ultimately be as oppressive to nonracist whites as to blacks. Some did this and continue to do it, though it is perhaps more onerous than working with blacks.

The same principle held in black universities where students demanded more and more black teachers. White professors who had virtually dedicated their lives and their academic careers as historians, anthropologists, sociologists to the problems of racism and its cures, thinking they did this for the good of the oppressed victims of racism (and often suffering social and academic insults as a result) were asked to leave schools in favor of black teachers. Some of them turned very bitter.

Some who were eminent authorities in their disciplines and were recognized as such by black authorities in the same disciplines, were told by students that their work was not relevant because they were not black. To have one's life's work dismissed in such a frivolous manner by people who have never yet studied it was a severe insult.

One elderly scholar who had been a thundering advocate of civil rights now speaks of "those black punks." Another, a sociologist, still involved in the study of discrimination in medicine and medical schools, told a professor at a California medical school who was proud of the achievement of black medical students there, "Well, I hope when you get sick you call one of them."

Such men, deeply offended to be excluded from participation with black men in the solutions to the problems of racism, sometimes begin to look for symptoms of inferiority as a means of self-defense. We are seeing a recrudescence of these contentions by scientists, even the recent suggestion that men with lower IQs (by white-oriented tests) be paid to have vasectomies, one thousand dollars for each point lower than 100 – so that a man with an IQ of 90 would get ten thousand dollars to have himself sterilized. This has been viewed as another example of genocidal thinking.

All of this is part of the current scene. Some people call it polarization, and many of us, white and black, still lament the old days of the early and mid-60s when we were all working together, singing "We Shall Overcome" and thinking that success was just around the corner.

But now, though we can still bungle into fratricide, there is really more hope than in the past. In the past, hope was based on the moods of the majority – a fragile and slippery basis. That is gone now and a realism, harsh, full of contradictions, has replaced it as something more solid on which to build – a basis which says that black people will continue to move toward being fully-functioning and self-determining people. And this is irreversible.

Polarization. Separation. No one has wanted this, white or black. It has come because the things we dreamed of did not materialize. Many still hold the old dreams, all the while accepting today's realities.

A couple of years ago I was seated in an auditorium in Detroit where Reverend Cleage was explaining to a conference of priests that what they called "black separatists" were in reality men who recognized the implacability of a white-imposed separation.

Afterward, one of the priests got up and asked: "But aren't you advocating an un-Christian way—the way of accepting as a reality this white-imposed separation? You are a minister. Are not all of us who are ministers obligated to bring men together in love?"

"Yes," Reverend Cleage said. "And because you have not preached that long enough and loudly enough, we are faced with accepting the separation."

Eventually, some black thinkers believe, this "separation" may be the shortest route to an authentic communication at some future date when blacks and whites can enter into encounters in which they truly speak as equals and in which the white man will no longer load every phrase with unconscious suggestions that he has something to "concede" to black men, or that he wants to help black men "overcome" their blackness.

86.

HOME FROM THE WAR

Robert Jay Lifton

This selection is an examination of certain aspects of the social process called "conflict," which Lewis Coser defines as "a struggle over values and claims to scarce status, power and resources in which the aims of the opponents are to neutralize, injure or eliminate their rivals." The classic, traditional, and extreme form of conflict between major social systems (nation-states) has been called "war." The entire subject of conflict, and especially its extreme form—war—is so important as to merit much more attention than can possibly be given to it in the space available in this book. However, the reader will find several selections which touch on

Source: Robert Jay Lifton, *Home From the War* (New York: Simon & Schuster, 1973), pp. 59–71.

Robert Jay Lifton is professor of psychiatry at the Yale Medical School and has consulted as a behavioral scientist for the National Institute of Mental Health. He has written on the problems of nuclear weapons and their impact on death symbolism and has worked extensively in the Far East. Among his publications are *Death in Life: Survivors of Hiroshima.* He coauthored *Crimes of War* in 1971.

such aspects of the subject as the inevitability of conflict because it is biologically inherent in the human species (Selection 16, Ascher), the vested interests of big business which encourages investment in the military machine (Selection 90, Lebow), and approaches to the control of conflict between nation-states (Selection 96, Boulding). Of all the other elements of conflict with which this book might deal, we have chosen to examine the consequences for some of the participants, and *via* them, though perhaps to a lesser extent, *all* Americans, of having taken part in a lengthy, brutal, and an increasingly "unpopular" war. The author of this selection, a psychologist by training and an activist by socialization, bases his analysis on an admittedly specialized "sample" (a group of antiwar veterans) but develops his case logically, as well as vividly, with respect to the pervasive and corrupting effects upon all. This examination of "the psychology of My Lai"—an activity that no doubt has immortalized the name of what would otherwise have been just another tiny village in Vietnam—demonstrates the price that conflict (war) exacts not only in broken bodies and lives lost, not only in natural resources squandered and lands devastated, but also in the potential socialization to violence that can permanently brutalize and can discipline the mind to view whole peoples as less than human and hence as "objects" to be destroyed.

A key to understanding the psychology of My Lai, and of America in Vietnam, is the body count. Nothing else so well epitomizes the war's absurdity and evil. Recording the enemy's losses is a convention of war, but in the absence of any other goals or criteria for success, counting the enemy dead can become both malignant obsession and compulsive falsification. For the combat GI in Vietnam killing Vietnamese is the entire mission, the number killed his and his unit's only standard of achievement, and the falsification of that count (on many levels) the only way to hold on to the Vietnam illusion of noble battle. Killing *someone,* moreover, becomes necessary for overcoming one's own death anxiety. We have seen how, at My Lai, killing Vietnamese enabled men to cease feeling themselves guilty survivors and impotent targets, and become instead omnipotent dispensers of death who have realized their mission. Only killing, then, can affirm power, skill, and worth.

And there is a way of measuring: one counts, scores points, competes with one's fellow soldiers, or collectively with another unit, for the highest score. One kills "for the record." Indeed, there is now considerable evidence confirming earlier suspicions that My Lai was largely a product of the numerical (body count) ambitions of high-level officers. That "record" could determine their promotions and profoundly affect their future careers. For instance, Colonel Oran K. Henderson, a non-West Pointer who had previously suffered a number of frustrations in his efforts to become a general, "followed the usual commander's practice of emphasizing body counts"; as did the Task Force Commander, Colonel Frank A. Barker, an unusually aggressive and ambitious officer, whose units were known for their high body counts and their capacity to "gun down a lot of people." The hunger for a high body count on the part of these two officers, and of course on the part of their superiors as well, was passed along to Medina at the earlier briefing, and so on down the line—everyone, from President of the United States on down to the lowliest GI caught up in this malignant mix of pressure and need.

There was a troublesome disparity between body count and the number of captured enemy weapons, a disparity which, if honestly evaluated, would have made it clear that bodies counted were mainly those of civilians. Instead, Colonel Henderson, during his briefing, attributed the disparity to GIs having been insufficiently aggressive in the past in "closing with the enemy," thereby permitting women and children in the area to pick up the weapons before the GIs "arrived to where they had killed a VC." Again illusion is more compelling than actuality. In different men and in different degrees, the illusion is sustained by genuine self-deception, conscious lying, or, probably most common, a kind of "middle knowledge" within which one both knows the truth about body counts (the reason for the disparity between bodies and weapons) and does not know—resists knowing—that truth.* But the image of women and children picking up the weapons of dead VC also contains still another informal message that killing women and children was, therefore, "okay." The body count illusion thus carries its logic full circle—the falsification of the evidence that civilians were being killed leading in turn to a further reason—and motivation—for killing still more civilians. All this happens because so much rides on the body count: the conquest of death anxiety, one's sense of skill, worth, and manhood—and for many, one's future as a professional soldier and long-range claim to the immortalizing status of warrior-hero.

*The term "middle knowledge" was used by Avery Weisman and Thomas Hackett to describe the state of mind of fatally ill patients in relationship to their impending death. Within the psychoformative perspective . . . , we may say that middle knowledge becomes necessary where one can neither find a place for the painful death-linked truth within one's overall formulation of self and world nor deny the pressing evidence of that truth. The problem is solved by evolving (at least) two contradictory images, the extent to which the accurate one can be covered over by the illusory one depending largely upon the degree to which the environment supports illusion.

The official body count that day for Task Force Barker (of which Charlie Company was a part), operating in and around My Lai, was "128 Vietcong." Nobody seemed certain just how that number was arrived at, but a discussion Calley recalled, in his testimony at his trial, between himself and Medina gives us something of a clue:

CALLEY: He asked me about how many—basically what my body count—how many people we had killed that day. And I told him I had no idea and for him to just go on and come up with an estimate, sir. . . .

DANIEL (prosecuting attorney): Just any body count? Just any body count, is that what you are saying?

CALLEY: Basically, yes, sir.

DANIEL: Captain Medina could just put in any body count that he wanted to put?

CALLEY: Any body count that was reasonable. I would imagine he would put in the highest acceptable body count that he would. . . .

DANIEL: Did he give an actual count?

CALLEY: Yes and no. I don't remember exactly what it was. I remember that I took fifty, sir. . . .

DANIEL: Did you tell Captain Medina that you had shot the people in the ditch?

CALLEY: Yes sir, I did. . . .

DANIEL: How did you tell him about it?

CALLEY: He asked . . . what the percentage of civilians was.

DANIEL: What did you tell him?

CALLEY: I told him he would have to make that decision, sir.

Calley and Medina, in other words, were groping for the maximum figure that could be considered "reasonable"—that could be constructed or rationalized from the events of the day—that could support the logic of illusion. Calley thus made an estimate "off the top of my head" that came to "between thirty and forty," but Medina preferred fifty. Medina then radioed an overall body count (for all the units) of 310, but somewhere along the line this was pared down to the figure of 128.

Again the disparity between body count (128) and weapons captured (3)* was troublesome, this time to the GI in the public information office who had to write up the action. One form of compromise was combining the figure of "128 Vietcong" with that of "24 civilians." The "middle knowledge" of the situation was reflected in the duality of response to the final figure. On the one hand there was "great excitement" at the base area because it was "the largest for the task force since it had begun operations forty days earlier." On the other, there was a certain amount of embarrassment and uneasiness reflecting considerable awareness of what had actually happened—as expressed in such comments as "Ha ha, they were all women and children," and in what one observer called "a general feeling that this was a bad show, that something should be investigated." To examine the complex web of cover-up and pseudoinvestigation is to be impressed with the sustaining power of the My Lai illusion. While the cover-up, as Seymour Hersh has demonstrated, can be attributed to specific high-ranking officers, it must also be understood as part of a vast military and civilian collusion to maintain the war's justifying fictions of order and nobility in the face of its fundamental corruption, false witness, and absurd evil.

In the end, Charlie Company was credited with only fourteen of the 128 "kills," and the majority of these attributed to "artillery fire" as a way of giving the incident a greater aura of combat. The official report referred to "contact with the enemy force," and the colonel in command of the task force was quoted as saying that "the combat assault went like clockwork." We may thus say that the body count serves the psychological function of making concrete the whole illusionary system; it is the locus of falsification.

One learns more about this phenomenon from other impressions of how the bodies were counted. The My Lai survivor told me that the prevailing standard was:

> The ones that could walk they counted as bodies. The ones that couldn't walk they counted as, you know, sort of, they didn't count them. Because they couldn't have been Vietcong. They thought about this later.

He went on to say that he had heard talk of a body count of over 300 (undoubtedly the early count made by Medina) and was never clear about why it was reduced to 128. But the distinctions he describes, the informal attempts to impose a standard according to which one counts some bodies and not others, all this suggests the need to hold on to fragmentary aspects of actuality and logic in the service of the larger illusion.

Needless to say, these standards varied greatly. I heard descriptions of totals inflated in every conceivable way: by counting severed pieces of corpses as individual bodies; by counting a whole corpse several times on the basis of multiple claims for credit (by the man or unit doing the killing, the patrol encountering the body, the headquarters outfit hearing about the killing, etcetera); and by counting murdered civilians, animals, or nonexistent bodies according to the kinds of need, ambition, and whim we have already encountered. Once a corpse has been identified (or imagined)

*One might ask why there is not more falsification of the number of weapons captured as a way of eliminating the disparity. The answer is probably that the captured-weapons figure is much more difficult to falsify, because one is dealing with concrete, gathered objects concerning which accuracy or falsification can readily be proven, as opposed to corpses that, in their repellent distance, lend themselves to every kind of admixture of exaggeration, fantasy and falsification.

it *becomes* that of a slain "enemy," and, therefore, evidence of warrior prowess—as the My Lai survivor makes clear:

If it's dead it's VC. Because it's dead. If it's dead it *had* to be VC. And of course a corpse couldn't defend itself anyhow.

He went on to place the body count into a frame of corrupt competitiveness—a company commander "obsessed with the body count" who "wanted a body count that would just beat all," that would "satisfy him . . . [and] satisfy higher headquarters . . . even if he knows this body count is a big dirty old lie." For, "Probably higher headquarters knows also. So they're fooling each other and theirselves as well." The whole thing, as he goes on to explain, resembles a cheater's golf game:

There was A Company over on the other side. They were counting bodies too. . . . He [the Company Commander] did sort of envy those people counting their bodies, keeping score. . . . Expressing sort of a disbelief that they had actually got that many. Which is like playing golf with somebody and carrying your own strokes and having some guy say, "I'm on [the green] in three." "You're on in *three?*" If it didn't matter to you how many *you* were on in, it wouldn't matter to you how many *he* was on in.

I am convinced that the ethically sensitive historians of the future will select the phenomenon of the body count as the perfect symbol of America's descent into evil. The body count manages to distill the essence of the American numbing, brutalization, and illusion into a grotesque technicalization: there is something to count, a statistic for accomplishment. I know of no greater corruption than this phenomenon: The amount of killing—any killing—becomes the total measure of achievement. And concerning that measure, one lies, to others as well as to oneself, about why, who, what, and how many one kills.

The atrocity-producing situation, the illusions that surround it, and the military arrangements that further it—all these have their origins in a malignant spiral of parallel illusion, deception, and self-deception surrounding the entire American relationship to the war in Vietnam.

By extending the analysis outward in a psychohistorical direction, we recognize that the murderous false witness of GIs in the Vietnamese countryside results directly from a more extensive false witness on a national scale. Propelling that false witness is a totalistic cosmology—reaching its height during the post-World War II Cold War years but persisting even now—that contrasts absolute American purity with absolute communist depravity. Joining that cosmology, indeed becoming part of it, is an equally pervasive technicism that leads Americans to view Vietnam as no more than a "problem," a "job to be done" by applying "American know-how"—and to ignore psychological and historical forces surrounding the long-standing Vietnamese struggle against Western invaders, and Chinese invaders before that. When the "problem" persistently resists the American "solution," when the job will not get done, the assumption is that still more "know-how" is needed—greater fire-power, more "scientific" computerized studies of "safe hamlets," better "techniques" for improving the always-inadequate South Vietnamese military "leadership." This marriage of totalistic cosmology and all-pervasive technicism, amply documented in the Pentagon Papers, has prevented fundamental questions from being raised, while perpetuating three overall psychohistorical illusions around which the war has been pursued.

The first of these illusions concerns the nature of the war, and converts a fifty-year-old anticolonial revolution, nationalist and communist from its inception, into an "outside invasion" of the South by the North. The second concerns the nature of the government we have supported, and converts a despotic military regime without standing among its own people into a "democratic ally." The third illusion, partly a product of fatigue over maintaining the first two, holds that we can "Vietnamize" the war (leave and still keep the present government in power in the South) by turning it over to a regime that lacks legitimacy and an army that has shown little will to fight—through a program that is American rather than Vietnamese, and one that few if any Vietnamese really want to implement. Bound up with this last illusion is a seemingly pragmatic Machiavellian effort (which may itself turn out to be infused with illusion) to create in Vietnam an urbanized "consumer society" under American and Japanese corporate hegemony. In all, it is not too much to say that the illusions surrounding an aberrant American quest for immortalizing glory, virtue, power, control, influence, and know-how are directly responsible for the more focused My Lai illusion.

This new version of American "manifest destiny" has been rudely subverted, not by a formidable adversary, but by people of no standing in the world, small people from a tiny, obscure, technologically backward country, employing hit-and-run guerrilla tactics that not only frustrate and defeat American military power but at the same time mock in the extreme the vision of American grandeur. Most humiliating of all, those very guerrillas—defined by official America as the carriers of the communist infestation—emerge (for most of the world, including many American civilians and soldiers) as the anointed ones of this war. Only they can be said to have approached the myth of the warrior-hero—in their ability to relate killing and dying to an immortalizing vision as well as in their extraordinary prowess and continuous sense of ultimate victory. Americans, in contrast, have suffered from the absence of both cause and sense of victory. For victory in itself tends to *feel* immortalizing, and has been perceived since antiquity as a favorable judgment of the gods, a confirmation of anyone's virtuous quest and equivalent of manifest destiny.

In earlier work, I found that survivors of the Hiroshima holocaust experienced what I described as "a vast breakdown of faith in the larger human matrix supporting each individual life, and therefore a loss of faith (or trust) in the structure of existence." The same is true not only for large numbers of Vietnam veterans but, perhaps in more indirect and muted ways, for Americans in general. This shattered existential faith has to do with remaining bound by the image of holocaust, of grotesque and absurd death and equally absurd survival. Even Americans who have not seen Vietnam feel something of a national descent into existential evil, a sense that the killing and dying done in their name cannot be placed within a meaningful system of symbols, cannot be convincingly formulated. The result is widespread if, again, vague feeling of lost integrity at times approaching moral-psychological disintegration.

What distinguishes Vietnam veterans from the rest of their countrymen is their awesome experience and knowledge of what others merely sense and resist knowing, their suffering on the basis of that knowledge and experience, and, in the case of antiwar veterans, their commitment to telling the tale. That commitment, especially for rap group participants, meant asking a question very much like that of Remarque's hero in *All Quiet on the Western Front:* "What would become of us if everything that happens out there were quite clear to us?" "Out there" means Vietnam, their own minds, and in the end, American society as well.

As part of their survivor mission, antiwar veterans seek understanding of and liberation from the political and military agents of their own corruption. Their constant probing of these and other aspects of American society is less in the spirit of calm reflection than of anxious and pressured need. Amid their confusions and touchiness, they have shared with one another a bond of brotherhood around their holocaust, their corruption, and their struggle against both. There is a sense in which they can fully trust only those who share their experience and their mission—though in each this trust may live side by side with suspicion toward one another, related to suspicion of oneself.

They are loath to judge other veterans whose corruption has been much greater than their own. I recall a very tense moment during a psychiatric meeting at which a group of veterans described some of their experiences. When they had finished, a questioner from the floor asked them what they thought of a promise made by Lieutenant Calley (who was then still on trial) that, should he be acquitted, he would go on a speaking tour throughout the country on behalf of peace. The men visibly stiffened and answered in a series of terse phrases, such as "I can't judge him," "I have nothing to say about him," and "It could have been any of us." They knew too much about their corruptibility and everyone's within that specific atrocity-producing situation to be able to pass judgment upon a man in whom the disintegrative process had gone still further. They were not only trying to cope with their own guilt but with their overall formulation of their holocaust.

For they have taken on a very special survivor mission, one of extraordinary historical and psychological significance. They are flying in the face of the traditional pattern of coping with survivor emotions by joining organizations of veterans that not only justify their particular war but embrace war-making and militarism in general. Contemporary antiwar warriors are turning that pattern on its head and finding their survivor significance in exposing precisely the meaninglessness—and the evil—of their war. They do so, not as individual poets or philosophers (who emerged, for instance, from World War I) but as an organized group of ordinary war veterans. The psychological rub in the process is the necessity to call forth and confront their own warlike selves, or, as they sometimes put it, "the person in me that fought the war."

For a number of them, and at varying intervals, political activities become inseparable from psychological need. Telling their story to American society has been both a political act and a means of psychologically confronting an inauthentic experience and moving beyond it toward authenticity. For such people not only is protest necessary to psychological help—it *is* psychological help. At one moment one sees confused youngsters struggling to put together their shattered psychological selves—at another, young people with premature wisdom. As one of them expressed this uneasy combination to me, "I feel bitter because I'm a pretty young guy and the things I had to do and see I shouldn't have to in a normal lifetime." Still, they feel they have come to difficult truths that adult American society refuses to face. Indeed, in their eyes most of adult America lives in illusion. They describe others saying such things to them as, "You're different from other people," or "You seem to know things that other people don't know." Since that knowledge has to do with death and pain, they have a double view of themselves in another way as well. They see themselves sometimes as a victimized group unrecognized and rejected by existing society and sometimes as a special elite who alone can lay claim to a unique experience of considerable value in its very extremity and evil.

There is an additional paradox as well: that of an antimilitary group creating itself around its military experience, an antiwar group made up of those who fought the war now opposed. This means that their war-linked death anxiety and death guilt are constantly at issue. Merely to be in one another's presence is a reminder of the conflict and pain around which their group takes shape. No wonder they are wary of their own identity as antiwar veterans. As one of them said during a rap group: "Our life is being against the war. When the war ends, then we end as people." While ostensibly referring only to his antiwar organization, he unconsciously revealed his own sense of depending totally upon—and being consumed by—the identity of the antiwar warrior.

By a number of criteria, the group I have worked with represents a small minority of Vietnam veterans. For one thing, most saw active combat, as opposed to the majority of men stationed there in support assignments. For another, they emerged with an articulate antiwar position, in contrast to the majority who take no public stance on the war, and to another minority who emerge strongly supporting it. Concerning the first issue, my impression was that the intensity of residual conflicts were roughly parallel to one's degree of involvement in (or closeness to) combat, but that the sense of absurd evil radiated outward from the actual killing and dying, and that every American in Vietnam shared in some of the corruption of that environment. Hence, Polner's finding that no Vietnam veteran was free of doubt about what he had been called upon to do.

Similarly, even those who later come to insist that we should have gone all-out to win the war—should have "nuked Hanoi" or "killed all the gooks"—are struggling to cope with their confusions and give some kind of form and significance to their survival. There is much evidence that antiwar and prowar veterans (the categories are misleading, and the latter hardly exists in a public sense) are much closer psychologically than might be suspected—or to put the matter another way, take different paths in struggling to resolve the same psychological conflicts. Clearly the great majority of Vietnam veterans struggle silently, and apolitically, with that specific constellation of survivor conflict associated with Vietnam's atrocity-producing situation. So that one antiwar veteran could comment:

> I hear a lot of people say, "We know Vietnam veterans and they don't feel the way you do." My immediate reaction to that is, "Wait and see. If they are lucky they will. If they are lucky, they will open up."

The likelihood is that relatively few of the three million Vietnam veterans will be able to "open up" in the way he means. Yet there is a very real sense in which those few are doing symbolic psychological work for all veterans, and indeed for all of American society.

Part X

Social and Cultural Change: Disorganization, Planning, and Values

87.

DEATH BY DIESELIZATION: A CASE STUDY IN THE REACTION TO TECHNOLOGICAL CHANGE

W. Fred Cottrell

We in America tend to place a positive value on "change." We seem to welcome all kinds of miracles of modern scientific technology: spacecraft carrying men to the moon and to space labs, communication satellites that link the nations of the world in instantaneous video and audio contact, and the atom-splitting capabilities that provide new sources of power (for good or evil). When a new development is generally accepted as "good," the public commonly takes the position that any side effects in the way of "costs" (negative spillover) to small segments of the population are more than offset by the benefits to "society as a whole." We may even consider it unpatriotic, immoral, or selfish for groups unfavorably affected by technological changes to petition for reparations for the losses they suffer. This selection dramatizes the widespread side effects of an invention and helps us to understand something of the position of those on whom the social costs of that invention fell most directly.

In the following instance it is proposed that we examine a community confronted with radical change in its basic economic institution and to trace the effects of this change throughout the social structure. From these facts it may be possible in some degree to anticipate the resultant changing attitudes and values of the people in the community, particularly as they reveal whether or not there is a demand for modification of the social structure or a shift in function from one institution to another. Some of the implications of the facts discovered may be valuable in anticipating future social change.

The community chosen for examination has been disrupted by the dieselization of the railroads. Since the railroad is among the oldest of those industries organized around steam, and since therefore the social structure of railroad communities is a product of long-continued processes of adaptation to the technology of steam, the sharp contrast between the technological requirements of the steam engine and those of the diesel should clearly reveal the changes in social structure required. Any one of a great many railroad towns might have been chosen for examination. However, many railroad towns are only partly dependent upon the railroad for their existence. In them many of the effects which take place are blurred and not easily dis-

Source: W. Fred Cottrell, *American Sociological Review* 16, no. 3 (June 1951): 358–65. Reprinted by permission of the author and The American Sociological Association.

W. Fred Cottrell is emeritus professor of sociology and government at Miami University in Oxford, Ohio. His interests include the effects of technology upon society and he has written *The Railroader, Men Cry Peace,* and *Technological Change and Labor in the Railroad Industry.*

tinguishable by the observer. Thus, the "normal" railroad town may not be the best place to see the consequences of dieselization. For this reason a one-industry town was chosen for examination.

In a sense it is an "ideal type" railroad town, and hence not complicated by other extraneous economic factors. It lies in the desert and is here given the name "Caliente" which is the Spanish adjective for "hot." Caliente was built in a break in an eighty-mile canyon traversing the desert. Its reason for existence was to service the steam locomotive. There are few resources in the area to support it on any other basis, and such as they are they would contribute more to the growth and maintenance of other little settlements in the vicinity than to that of Caliente. So long as the steam locomotive was in use, Caliente was a necessity. With the adoption of the diesel it became obsolescent.

This stark fact was not, however, part of the expectations of the residents of Caliente. Based upon the "certainty" of the railroad's need for Caliente, men built their homes there, frequently of concrete and brick, at the cost, in many cases, of their life savings. The water system was laid in cast iron which will last for centuries. Business men erected substantial buildings which could be paid for only by profits gained through many years of business. Four churches evidence the faith of Caliente people in the future of their community. A twenty-seven bed hospital serves the town. Those who built it thought that their investment was as well warranted as the fact of birth, sickness, accident and death. They believed in education. Their school buildings represent the investment of savings guaranteed by bonds and future taxes. There is a combined park and play field which, together with a recently modernized theatre, has been serving recreational needs. All these physical structures are material evidence of the expectations, morally and legally sanctioned and financially funded, of the people of Caliente. This is a normal and rational aspect of the culture of all "solid" and "sound" communities.

Similarly normal are the social organizations. These include Rotary, Chamber of Commerce, Masons, Odd Fellows, American Legion and the Veterans of Foreign Wars. There are the usual unions, churches, and myriad little clubs to which the women belong. In short, here is the average American community with normal social life, subscribing to normal American codes. Nothing its members had been taught would indicate that the whole pattern of this normal existence depended completely upon a few elements of technology which were themselves in flux. For them the continued use of the steam engine was as "natural" a phenomenon as any other element in their physical environment. Yet suddenly their life pattern was destroyed by the announcement that the railroad was moving its division point, and with it destroying the economic basis of Caliente's existence.

Turning from this specific community for a moment, let us examine the technical changes which took place and the reasons for the change. Division points on a railroad are established by the frequency with which the rolling stock must be serviced and the operating crews changed. At the turn of the century when this particular road was built, the engines produced wet steam at low temperatures. The steel in the boilers was of comparatively low tensile strength and could not withstand the high temperatures and pressures required for the efficient use of coal and water. At intervals of roughly a hundred miles the engine had to be disconnected from the train for service. At these points the cars also were inspected and if they were found to be defective they were either removed from the train or repaired while it was standing and the new engine being coupled on. Thus the location of Caliente, as far as the railroad was concerned, was a function of boiler temperature and pressure and the resultant service requirements of the locomotive.

Following World War II, the high tensile steels developed to create superior artillery and armor were used for locomotives. As a consequence it was possible to utilize steam at higher temperatures and pressure. Speed, power, and efficiency were increased and the distance between service intervals was increased.

The "ideal distance" between freight divisions became approximately 150 to 200 miles whereas it had formerly been 100 to 150. Wherever possible, freight divisions were increased in length to that formerly used by passenger trains, and passenger divisions were lengthened from two old freight divisions to three. Thus towns located at 100 miles from a terminal became obsolescent, those at 200 became freight points only, and those at 300 miles became passenger division points.

The increase in speed permitted the train crews to make the greater distance in the time previously required for the lesser trip, and roughly a third of the train and engine crews, car inspectors, boiler-makers and machinists and other service men were dropped. The towns thus abandoned were crossed off the social record of the nation in the adjustment to these technological changes in the use of the steam locomotive. Caliente, located midway between terminals about six hundred miles apart, survived. In fact it gained, since the less frequent stops caused an increase in the service required of the maintenance crews at those points where it took place. However, the introduction of the change to diesel engines projected a very different future.

In its demands for service the diesel engine differs almost completely from a steam locomotive. It requires infrequent, highly skilled service, carried on within very close limits, in contrast to the frequent, crude adjustments required by the steam locomotive. Diesels operate at about 35 percent efficiency, in contrast to the approximately 4 percent efficiency of the steam locomotives in use after World War II in the United States. Hence diesels require much less frequent stops for fuel and water. These facts reduce their operating cost sufficiently to compensate for their much higher initial cost.

In spite of these reductions in operating costs the introduction of diesels ordinarily would have taken a good deal of time. The changeover would have been slowed by the high capital costs of retooling the locomotive works, the long period required to recapture the costs of existing steam locomotives, and the effective resistance of the workers. World War II altered each of these factors. The locomotive works were required to make the change in order to provide marine engines, and the costs of the change were assumed by the government. Steam engines were used up by the tremendous demand placed upon the railroads by war traffic. The costs were recaptured by shipping charges. Labor shortages were such that labor resistance was less formidable and much less acceptable to the public than it would have been in peace time. Hence the shift to diesels was greatly facilitated by the war. In consequence, every third and sometimes every second division point suddenly became technologically obsolescent.

Caliente, like all other towns in similar plight, is supposed to accept its fate in the name of "progress." The general public, as shippers and consumers of shipped goods, reaps the harvest in better, faster service and eventually perhaps in lower charges. A few of the workers in Caliente will also share the gains, as they move to other division points, through higher wages. They will share in the higher pay, though whether this will be adequate to compensate for the costs of moving no one can say. Certain it is that their pay will not be adjusted to compensate for their specific losses. They will gain only as their seniority gives them the opportunity to work. These are those who gain. What are the losses, and who bears them?

The railroad company can figure its losses at Caliente fairly accurately. It owns 39 private dwellings, a modern clubhouse with 116 single rooms, and a twelve-room hotel with dining-room and lunch-counter facilities. These now become useless, as does much of the fixed physical equipment used for servicing trains. Some of the machinery can be used elsewhere. Some part of the roundhouse can be used to store unused locomotives and standby equipment. The rest will be torn down to save taxes. All of these costs can be entered as capital losses on the statement which the company draws up for its stockholders and for the government. Presumably they will be recovered by the use of the more efficient engines.

What are the losses that may not be entered on the company books? The total tax assessment in Caliente was $9,946.80 for the year 1948, of which $6,103.39 represented taxes assessed on the railroad. Thus the railroad valuation was about three-fifths that of the town. This does not take into account tax-free property belonging to the churches, the schools, the hospital, or the municipality itself which included all the public utilities. Some ideas of the losses sustained by the railroad in comparison with the losses of others can be surmised by reflecting on these figures for real estate alone. The story is an old one and often repeated in the economic history of America. It represents the "loss" side of a profit and loss system of adjusting to technological change. Perhaps for sociological purposes we need an answer to the question "just who pays?"

Probably the greatest losses are suffered by the older "nonoperating" employees. Seniority among these men extends only within the local shop and craft. A man with twenty-five years' seniority at Caliente has no claim on the job of a similar craftsman at another point who has only twenty-five days' seniority. Moreover, some of the skills formerly valuable are no longer needed. The boilermaker, for example, knows that jobs for his kind are disappearing and he must enter the ranks of the unskilled. The protection and status offered by the union while he was employed have become meaningless now that he is no longer needed. The cost of this is high both in loss of income and in personal demoralization.

Operating employees also pay. Their seniority extends over a division, which in this case includes three division points. The older members can move from Caliente and claim another job at another point, but in many cases they move leaving a good portion of their life savings behind. The younger men must abandon their stake in railroad employment. The loss may mean a new apprenticeship in another occupation, at a time in life when apprenticeship wages are not adequate to meet the obligations of mature men with families. A steam engine hauled 2,000 tons up the hill out of Caliente with the aid of two helpers. The four-unit diesel in command of one crew handles a train of 5,000 tons alone. Thus, to handle the same amount of tonnage required only about a fourth the manpower it formerly took. Three out of four men must start out anew at something else.

The local merchants pay. The boarded windows, half-empty shelves, and abandoned store buildings bear mute evidence of these costs. The older merchants stay, and pay; the younger ones, and those with no stake in the community will move; but the value of their property will in both cases largely be gone.

The bondholders will pay. They can't foreclose on a dead town. If the town were wiped out altogether, that which would remain for salvage would be too little to satisfy their claims. Should the town continue there is little hope that taxes adequate to carry the overhead of bonds and day-to-day expenses could be secured by taxing the diminished number of property owners or employed persons.

The church will pay. The smaller congregations cannot support services as in the past. As the church men leave, the buildings will be abandoned.

Homeowners will pay. A hundred and thirty-five men owned homes in Caliente. They must accept the available means of support or rent to those who do. In either case the income available will be far less than that on which the houses were built. The least desirable homes will stand unoccupied, their value completely lost. The others must be revalued at a figure far below that at which they were formerly held.

In a word, those pay who are, by traditional American standards, *most moral.* Those who have raised children see friendships broken and neighborhoods disintegrated. The childless more freely shake the dust of Caliente from their feet. Those who built their personalities into the structure of the community watch their work destroyed. Those too wise or too selfish to have entangled themselves in community affairs suffer no such qualms. The chain store can pull down its sign, move its equipment and charge the costs off against more profitable and better located units, and against taxes. The local owner has no such alternatives. In short, "good citizens" who assumed family and community responsibility are the greatest losers. Nomads suffer least.

The people of Caliente are asked to accept as "normal" this strange inversion of their expectations. It is assumed that they will, without protest or change in sentiment, accept the dictum of the "law of supply and demand." Certainly they must comply in part with this dictum. While their behavior in part reflects this compliance, there are also other changes perhaps equally important in their attitudes and values.

The first reaction took the form of an effort at community self-preservation. Caliente became visible to its inhabitants as a real entity, as meaningful as the individual personalities which they had hitherto been taught to see as atomistic or nomadic elements. Community survival was seen as prerequisite to many of the individual values that had been given precedence in the past. The organized community made a search for new industry, citing elements of community organization themselves as reasons why industry should move to Caliente. But the conditions that led the railroad to abandon the point made the place even less attractive to new industry than it had hitherto been. Yet the effort to keep the community a going concern persisted.

There was also a change in sentiment. In the past the glib assertion that progress spelled sacrifice could be offered when some distant group was a victim of technological change. There was no such reaction when the event struck home. The change can probably be as well revealed as in any other way by quoting from the Caliente *Herald:*

> . . . [over the] years . . . [this] . . . railroad and its affiliates . . . became to this writer his ideal

of a railroad empire. The [company] . . . appeared to take much more than the ordinary interest of big railroads in the development of areas adjacent to its lines, all the while doing a great deal for the communities large and small through which the lines passed.

Those were the days creative of [its] enviable reputation as one of the finest, most progressive—and most human—of American railroads, enjoying the confidence and respect of employees, investors, and communities alike!

One of the factors bringing about this confidence and respect was the consideration shown communities which otherwise would have suffered serious blows when division and other changes were effected. A notable example was . . . [a town] . . . where the shock of division change was made almost unnoticed by installation of a rolling stock reclamation point, which gave [that town] an opportunity to hold its community intact until tourist traffic and other industries could get better established—with the result that . . . [it] . . . is now on a firm foundation. And through this display of consideration for a community, the railroad gained friends—not only among the people of . . . [that town] . . . who were perhaps more vocal than others, but also among thousands of others throughout the country on whom this action made an indelible impression.

But things seem to have changed materially during the last few years, the . . . [company] . . . seems to this writer to have gone all out for glamor and the dollars which glamorous people have to spend, sadly neglecting one of the principal factors which helped to make. . . [it] . . . great: that fine consideration of communities and individuals, as well as employees, who have been happy in cooperating steadfastly with the railroad in times of stress as well as prosperity. The loyalty of these people and communities seems to count for little with the . . . [company] . . . of this day, though other "Big Business" corporations do not hesitate to expend huge sums to encourage the loyalty of community and people which old friends of . . . [the company] . . . have been happy to give voluntarily.

Ever since the . . . railroad was constructed . . . Caliente has been a key town on the railroad. It is true, the town owed its inception to the railroad, but it has paid this back in becoming one of the most attractive communities on the system. With nice homes, streets and parks, good school . . . good city government . . . Caliente offers advantages that most big corporations would be gratified to have for their employees—a homey spot where they could live their lives of contentment, happiness and security.

Caliente's strategic location, midway of some of the toughest road on the entire system has been a lifesaver for the road several times when floods have wreaked havoc on the roadbed in the canyon above and below Caliente. This has been possible through storage in Caliente of large stocks of repair material and equipment—and not overlooking manpower—which has thus become available on short notice.

. . . But [the railroad] or at least one of its big officials appearing to be almost completely divorced from policies which made this railroad great, has ordered changes which are about as inconsiderate as anything of which "Big Business" has ever been accused! Employees who have given the best years of their lives to this railroad are cut off without anything to which they can turn, many of them with homes in which they have taken much pride; while others, similarly with nice homes, are told to move elsewhere and are given runs that only a few will be able to endure from a physical standpoint, according to common opinion.

Smart big corporations the country over encourage their employees to own their own homes—and loud are their boasts when the percentage of such employees is favorable! But in contrast, a high [company] official is reported to have said only recently that "a railroad man has no business owning a home!" Quite a departure from what has appeared to be [company] tradition.

It is difficult for the *Herald* to believe that this official however "big" he is, speaks for the . . . [company] . . . when he enunciates a policy that, carried to the letter, would make tramps of [company] employees and their families!

No thinking person wants to stand in the way of progress, but true progress is not made when it is overshadowed by cold-blooded disregard for the loyalty of employees, their families, and the communities which have developed in the good American way through the decades of loyal service and good citizenship.

This editorial, written by a member of all the service clubs, approved by Caliente business men, and quoted with approbation by the most conservative members of the community, is significant of changing sentiment.

The people of Caliente continually profess their belief in "The American Way," but like the editor of the *Herald* they criticize decisions made solely in pursuit of profit, even though these decisions grow out of a clear-cut case of technological "progress." They feel that the company should have based its decision upon consideration for loyalty, citizenship, and community morale. They assume that the company should regard the seniority rights of workers as important considerations, and that it should consider significant the effect of permanent unemployment upon old and faithful employees. They look upon community integrity as an important community asset. Caught between the support of a "rational" system of "economic" forces and laws, and sentiments which they accept as significant values, they seek a solution to their dilemma which will at once permit them to retain their expected rewards for continued adherence to past norms and to defend the social system which they have been taught to revere but which now offers them a stone instead of bread.

IMPLICATIONS

We have shown that those in Caliente whose behavior most nearly approached the ideal taught are hardest hit by change. On the other hand, those seemingly farthest removed in conduct from that ideal are either rewarded or pay less of the costs of change than do those who follow the ideal more closely. Absentee owners, completely anonymous, and consumers who are not expected to cooperate to make the gains possible are rewarded most highly, while the local people who must cooperate to raise productivity pay dearly for having contributed.

In a society run through sacred mysteries whose rationale it is not man's privilege to criticize, such incongruities may be explained away. Such a society may even provide some "explanation" which makes them seem rational. In a secular society, supposedly defended rationally upon scientific facts, in which the pragmatic test "Does it work?" is continually applied, such discrepancy between expectation and realization is difficult to reconcile.

Defense of our traditional system of assessing the cost of technological change is made on the theory that the costs of such change are more than offset by the benefits to "society as a whole." However, it is difficult to show the people of Caliente just why *they* should pay for advances made to benefit others whom they have never known and who, in their judgment, have done nothing to justify such rewards. Any action that will permit the people of Caliente to levy the costs of change upon those who will benefit from them will be morally justifiable to the people of Caliente. Appeals to the general welfare leave them cold and the compulsions of the price system are not felt to be self-justifying "natural laws" but are regarded as being the specific consequence of specific bookkeeping decisions as to what should be included in the costs of change. They seek to change these decisions through social action. They do not consider that the "American Way" consists primarily of acceptance of the market as the final arbiter of their destiny. Rather they conceive that the system as a whole exists to render "justice," and if the consequences of the price system are such as to produce what they consider to be "injustice" they proceed to use some other institution as a means to reverse or offset the effects of the price system. Like other groups faced with the same situation, those in Caliente seize upon the means available to them. The operating employees had in their unions a device to secure what they consider to be their rights. Union practices developed over the years make it possible for the organized workers to avoid some of the costs of change which they would otherwise have had to bear. Featherbed rules, make-work practices, restricted work weeks, train length legislation and other similar devices were designed to permit union members to continue work even when "efficiency" dictated that they be disemployed. Members of the "Big Four" in Caliente joined with their fellows in demanding not only the retention of previously existing rules, but the imposition of new ones such as that requiring the presence of a third man in the diesel cab. For other groups there was available only the appeal to the company that it establish some other facility at Caliente, or alternatively a demand that "government" do something. One such demand took the form of a request to the Interstate Commerce Commission that it require inspection of rolling stock at Caliente. This request was denied.

It rapidly became apparent to the people of Caliente that they could not gain their objectives by organized community action nor individual endeavor but there was hope that by adding their voices to those of others similarly injured there might be hope of solution. They began to look to the activities of the whole labor movement for succor. Union strategy which forced the transfer of control from the market to government mediation or to legislation and operation was widely approved on all sides. This was not confined to those only who were currently seeking rule changes but was equally approved by the great bulk of those in the community who had been hit by the change. Cries of public outrage at their demands for make-work rules were looked upon as coming from those at best ignorant, ill-informed or stupid, and at worst as being the hypocritical efforts of others to gain at the workers' expense. When the union threat of a national strike for rule changes was met by government seizure, Caliente workers like most of their compatriots across the country welcomed this shift in control, secure in their belief that if "justice" were done they could only be gainers by government intervention. These attitudes are not "class" phenomena purely nor are they merely occupational sentiments. They result from the fact that modern life, with the interdependence that it creates, particularly in one-industry communities, imposes penalties far beyond the membership of the groups presumably involved in industry. When make-work rules contributed to the livelihood of the community, the support of the churches, and the taxes which maintain the schools; when featherbed practices determine the standard of living, the profits of the business man and the circulation of the press; when they contribute to the salary of the teacher and the preacher; they can no longer be treated as accidental, immoral, deviant or temporary. Rather they are elevated into the position of emergent morality and law. Such practices generate a morality which serves them just as the practices in turn nourish those who participate in and preserve them. They are as firmly a part of what one "has a right to expect" from industry as are parity payments to the farmer, bonuses and pensions to the veterans, assistance to the aged, tariffs to the industrialist, or the sanctity of property to those who inherit. On the other hand, all these practices conceivably help create a structure that is particularly vulnerable to changes such as that described here.

Practices which force the company to spend in Caliente part of what has been saved through technological change, or failing that, to reward those who are forced to move by increased income for the same service, are not, by the people of Caliente, considered to be unjustifiable. Confronted by a choice between the old means and resultant "injustice" which their use entails, and the acceptance of new means which they believe will secure them the "justice" they hold to be their right, they are willing to abandon (in so far as this particular area is concerned) the liberal state and the omnicompetent market in favor of something that works to provide "justice."

The study of the politics of pressure groups will show how widely the reactions of Caliente people are paralleled by those of other groups. Amongst them it is in politics that the decisions as to who will pay and who will profit are made. Through organized political force railroaders maintain the continuance of rules which operate to their benefit rather than for "the public good" or "the general welfare." Their defense of these practices is found in the argument that only so can their rights be protected against the power of other groups who hope to gain at their expense by functioning through the corporation and the market.

We should expect that where there are other groups similarly affected by technological change, there will be similar efforts to change the operation of our institutions. The case cited is not unique. Not only is it duplicated in hundreds of railroad division points but also in other towns abandoned by management for similar reasons. Changes in the location of markets or in the method of calculating transportation costs, changes in technology making necessary the use of new materials, changes due to the exhaustion of old sources of materials, changes to avoid labor costs such as the shift of the textile industry from New England to the South, changes to expedite decentralization to avoid the consequences of bombing, or those of congested living, all give rise to the question, "Who benefits, and at whose expense?"

The accounting practices of the corporation permit the entry only of those costs which have become "legitimate" claims upon the company. But the tremendous risks borne by the workers and frequently all the members of the community in an era of technological change are real phenomena. Rapid shifts in technology which destroy the "legitimate" expectations derived from past experience force the recognition of new obligations. Such recognition may be made voluntarily as management foresees the necessity, or it may be thrust upon it by political or other action. Rigidity of property concepts, the legal structure controlling directors in what they may admit to be costs, and the stereotyped nature of the "economics" used by management make rapid change within the corporation itself difficult even in a "free democratic society." Hence while management is likely to be permitted or required to initiate technological change in the interest of profits, it may and probably will be barred from compensating for the social consequences certain to arise from those changes. Management thus shuts out the rising flood of demands in its cost-accounting only to have them reappear in its tax accounts, in legal regulations or in new insistent union demands. If economics fails to provide an answer to social demands then politics will be tried.

It is clear that while traditional morality provides a means of protecting some groups from the consequences of technological change, or some method of meliorating the effects of change upon them, other large segments of the population are left unprotected. It should be equally clear that rather than a quiet acquiescence in the finality and justice of such arrangements, there is an active effort to force new devices into being which will extend protection to those hitherto expected to bear the brunt of these costs. A good proportion of these inventions increasingly call for the intervention of the state. To call such arrangements immoral, unpatriotic, socialistic or to hurl other epithets at them is not to deal effectively with them. They are as "natural" as are the "normal" reactions for which we have "rational" explanations based upon some pre-scientific generalization about human nature such as "the law of supply and demand" or "the inevitability of progress." To be dealt with effectively they will have to be understood and treated as such.

88.

STEEL AXES FOR STONE AGE AUSTRALIANS

Lauriston Sharp

The preceding selection describes the seriously disruptive effects of the introduction of a new invention on an American community. This selection deals with a similar problem, but in a primitive setting where the introduction of the new culture trait is almost completely destructive rather than merely disruptive. The destructive results—demoralization of the individual, disintegration of the culture, and perhaps even dissolution of the society as a viable, distinct entity—appear to have been unavoidable once the trait was widely adopted. One writer has referred to this particular article as the story of "The Steel Axe That Destroyed a Tribe." It is important to note that a similar story could hardly be written about a complex and less integrated society such as ours. But problems that are only quantitatively (not qualitatively) different from those faced by the Yir Yoront appear in every society that undergoes change.

Source: Lauriston Sharp, *Human Problems in Technological Change,* ed. Edward H. Spicer (New York: Basic Books, 1952), pp. 69–90. Copyright 1952 by the Russell Sage Foundation, New

THE PROBLEM

Like other Australian aboriginals, the Yir Yoront group at the mouth of the Coleman River on the west coast of tropical Cape York Peninsula originally had no knowledge of metals. Technologically their culture was of the old stone age or paleolithic type; they supported themselves by hunting and fishing, obtaining vegetable foods and needed materials from the bush by simple gathering techniques. Their only domesticated animal was the dog, and they had no domesticated plants of any kind. Unlike some other aboriginal groups, however, the Yir Yoront did have polished stone axes hafted in short handles, and these implements were most important in their economy.

Toward the end of the nineteenth century metal tools and other European artifacts began to filter into the Yir Yoront territory. The flow increased with the gradual expansion of the white frontier outward from southern and eastern Queensland. Of all the items of western technology thus made available, none was more acceptable, none more highly valued by aboriginals of all conditions than the hatchet or short-handled steel axe. . . .

RELEVANT FACTORS

If we concentrate our attention on Yir Yoront behavior centering about the original stone axe, rather than on the axe—the thing—we should get some conception of the role this implement played in aboriginal culture. This conception, in turn, should permit us to foresee with considerable accuracy some of the results of the displacement of stone axes by steel axes acquired directly or indirectly from Europeans by the Yir Yoront.

The production of a stone axe required a number of simple skills. With the idea of the axe in its various details well in mind, the adult men—and only the adult men—could set about producing it, a task not considered appropriate for women or children. . . .

The use of the stone axe as a piece of capital equipment for the production of other goods indicates its very great importance in the subsistence economy of the aboriginal. Anyone—man, woman, or child—could use the axe; indeed, it was used more by women, for theirs was the onerous, daily task of obtaining sufficient wood to keep the campfire of each family burning all day for cooking or other purposes and all night against mosquitoes and cold (in July, winter temperature might drop below forty degrees). In a normal lifetime any woman would use the axe to cut or knock down literally tons of firewood. Men and women, and sometimes children, needed the axe to make other tools, or weapons, or a variety of material equipment required by the aboriginal in his daily life. . . .

While the stone axe helped relate men and women and often children to nature in technological behavior, in the transformation of natural into cultural equipment, it also was prominent in that aspect of behavior which may be called conduct, primarily directed toward persons. Yir Yoront men were dependent upon interpersonal relations for their stone axe heads, since the flat, geologically recent alluvial country over which they range, provides no stone

---

York. Reprinted by permission of Basic Books, Inc.

The author is professor of anthropology at Cornell University. He has worked extensively in the areas of Oceania and Southeast Asia. Among his publications are *Siamese Rice Village, Some Principles of Cultural Change,* and *The Dream Life of a Primitive People.*

from which axe heads can be made. The stone they used comes from known quarries four hundred miles to the south. It reached the Yir Yoront through long lines of male trading partners, some of these chains terminating with the Yir Yoront men, while others extended on farther north to other groups, having utilized Yir Yoront men as links. Almost every older adult man had one or more regular trading partners, some to the north and some to the south. His partner or partners in the south he provided with surplus spears, and particularly fighting spears tipped with the barbed spines of sting ray which snap into vicious fragments when they penetrate human flesh. For a dozen spears, some of which he may have obtained from a partner to the north, he would receive from a southern partner one stone axe head. . . . Thus trading relations, which may extend the individual's personal relationships out beyond the boundaries of his own group, are associated with two of the most important items in a man's equipment, spears and axes, whether the latter are of stone or steel. Finally, most of the exchanges between partners take place during the dry season at times when the great aboriginal fiestas occur, which center about initiation rites or other totemic ceremonials that attract hundreds and are the occasion for much exciting activity besides trading.

Returning to the Yir Yoront, we find that not only was it adult men alone who obtained axe heads and produced finished axes, but it was adult males who retained the axes, keeping them with other parts of their equipment in camp, or carrying them at the back slipped through a human hair belt when traveling. Thus, every woman or child who wanted to use an axe—and this might be frequently during the day—must get one from some man, use it promptly, and return it to the man in good condition. While a man might speak of "my axe," a woman or child could not; for them it was always "your axe," addressing a male, or "his axe."

This necessary and constant borrowing of axes from older men by women and children was done according to regular patterns of kinship behavior. A woman on good terms with her husband would expect to use his axe unless he were using it; a husband on good terms with his wives would let any one of them use his axe without question. If a woman was unmarried or her husband was absent, she would go first to her older brother or to her father for an axe. Only in extraordinary circumstances would she seek a stone axe from a mother's brother or certain other male kin with whom she had to be most circumspect. A girl, a boy, or a young man would look to a father or an older brother to provide an axe for her or his use, but would never approach a mother's brother, who would be at the same time a potential father-in-law, with such a request. Older men, too, would follow similar rules if they had to borrow an axe.

It will be noted that these social relationships in which the stone axe had a place are all pair relationships and that the use of the axe helped define and maintain the character of the relationships and the roles of the two individual participants. Every active relationship among the Yir Yoront involved a definite and accepted status of superordination or subordination. A person could have no dealings with any other on exactly equal terms. Women and children were dependent on, or subordinate to, older males in every action in which the axe entered. Among the men, the younger was dependent on the older or on certain kinds of kin. The nearest approach to equality was between brothers, although the older was always superordinate to the younger. Since the exchange of goods in a trading relationship involved a mutual reciprocity, trading partners were usually a kind of brother to each other or stood in a brotherly type of relationship, although one was always classified as older than the other and would have some advantage in case of dispute. It can be seen that repeated and widespread conduct centering on the axe helped to generalize and standardize throughout the society these sex, age, and kinship roles, both in their normal benevolent and in exceptional malevolent aspects, and helped to build up expectancies regarding the conduct of others defined as having a particular status.

The status of any individual Yir Yoront was determined not only by sex, age, and extended kin relationships, but also by membership in one of two dozen patrilineal totemic clans into which the entire community was divided. A person's names, rights in particular areas of land, and, in the case of a man, his roles in the totemic ceremonies (from which women are excluded) were all a function of belonging to one clan rather than another. Each clan had literally hundreds of totems, one or two of which gave the clan its name, and from any of which the personal names of clan members were derived. These totems included not only natural species or phenomena like the sun, stars, and daybreak, but also cultural "species": imagined ghosts, rainbow serpents, heroic ancestors; such eternal cultural verities as fires, spears, huts; and such human activities, conditions, or attributes as eating, vomiting, swimming, fighting, babies and corpses, milk and blood, lips and loins. While individual members of such totemic classes or species might disappear or be destroyed, the class itself was obviously ever present and indestructible. The totems therefore lent permanence and stability to the clans, to the groupings of human individuals who generation after generation were each associated with one set of totems that distinguished one clan from another.

Among the many totems of the Sunlit Cloud Iguana clan, and important among them, was the stone axe. The names of many members of this clan referred to the axe itself, or to activities like trading or wild honey gathering in which the axe played a vital part, or to the clan's mythical ancestors with whom the axe was prominently associated. When it was necessary to represent the stone axe in totemic ceremonies, it was only men of this clan who exhibited it or pantomimed its use. In secular life the axe could be made by any man and used by all; but in the sacred realm of the totems it belonged exclusively to the Sunlit Cloud Iguana people.

Supporting those aspects of cultural behavior which we have called technology and conduct is a third area of culture, including ideas, sentiments, and values. These are most difficult to deal with, for they are latent and covert or even unconscious and must be deduced from overt actions and language or other communicating behavior. In this aspect of the culture lies the "meaning" of the stone axe, its significance to the Yir Yoront and to their cultural way of life. The ideal conception of the axe, the knowledge of how to produce it (apart from the purely muscular habits used in its production) are part of the Yir Yoront adult masculine role, just as ideas regarding its technical use are included in the feminine role. These technical ideas constitute a kind of "science" regarding the axe which may be more important in relation to behavioral change than are the neurophysiological patterns drilled into the body by years of practice. Similarly there are normative ideas regarding the part played by the axe in conduct which constitute a kind of "morality" of the axe, and which again may be more important than the overt habits of social interaction in determining the role of the axe in social relationships. More than ideas regarding technology, ideas regarding conduct are likely to be closely associated, or "charged," with sentiment or value. Ideas and sentiments help guide and inform overt behavior; in turn, overt behavior helps support and validate ideas and sentiments. . . .

Important for an understanding of the Yir Yoront culture is a system of ideas, which may be called their totemic ideology. A fundamental belief of the aboriginal divided time into two great epochs, a distant and sacred period at the beginning of the world, when the earth was peopled by mildly marvelous ancestral beings or cultural heroes who in a special sense are the forebears of the clans; and a second period, when the old was succeeded by a new order that includes the present. Originally there was no anticipation of another era supplanting the present; the future would simply be an eternal continuation and reproduction of the present, which itself had remained unchanged since the epochal revolution of ancestral times.

The mythical sacred world of the ancestors with which time began turns out on investigation to be a detailed reproduction of the present aboriginal world of nature, man, and culture altered by phantasy. In short, the idea system expressed in the mythology regarding the ancestral epoch was directly derived from Yir Yoront behavior patterns—normal and abnormal, actual and ideal, conscious and unconscious. The important thing to note, however, is that the native believed it was just the other way around, that the present world, as a natural and cultural environment, was and should be simply a detailed reproduction of the world of the ancestors. He believed that the entire universe "is now as it was in the beginning" when it was established and left by the ancestors. The ordinary cultural life of the ancestors became the daily life of the Yir Yoront camps, and the extraordinary life of the ancestors remained extant in the recurring symbolic pantomimes and paraphernalia found only in the most sacred atmosphere of the totemic rites.

. . . . . .

ANALYSIS

The introduction of the steel axe indiscriminately and in large numbers into the Yir Yoront technology was only one of many changes occurring at the same time. It is therefore impossible to factor out all the results of this single innovation alone. Nevertheless, a number of specific effects of the change from stone axes to steel axes may be noted; and the steel axe may be used as an epitome of the European goods and implements received by the aboriginals in increasing quantity and of their general influence on the native culture. The use of the steel axe to illustrate such influences would seem to be justified, for it was one of the first European artifacts to be adopted for regular use by the Yir Yoront; and the axe, whether of stone or steel, was clearly one of the most important items of cultural equipment they possessed.

The shift from stone to steel axes provided no major technological difficulties. While the aboriginals themselves could not manufacture steel axe heads, a steady supply from outside continued; and broken wooden axe handles could easily be replaced from bush timbers with aboriginal tools. Among the Yir Yoront the new axe never acquired all the uses it had on mission or cattle stations (carpentry work, pounding tent pegs, use as a hammer, and so on); and indeed, it was used for little more than the stone axe had been, so that it had no practical effect in improving the native standard of living. It did some jobs better, and could be used longer without breakage; and these factors were sufficient to make it of value to the native. But the assumption of the white man (based in part on a realization that a shift from steel to stone axe in his case would be a definite regression) that his axe was much more efficient, that its use would save time, and that it therefore represented technical "progress" toward goals which he had set for the native was hardly borne out in aboriginal practice. Any leisure time the Yir Yoront might gain by using steel axes or other western tools was invested, not in "improving the conditions of life," and certainly not in developing aesthetic activities, but in sleep, an art they had thoroughly mastered.

Having acquired an axe head through regular trading partners of whom he knew what to expect, a man wanting a stone axe was then dependent solely upon a known and an adequate nature and upon his own skills or easily acquired techniques. A man wanting a steel axe, however, was in no such self-reliant position. While he might acquire one through trade, he now had the new alternative of dispensing with technological behavior in relation with a predictable nature and conduct in relation with a predictable trading partner and of turning instead to conduct alone in relation with a highly erratic missionary. If he attended one of the mission festivals when steel axes were handed out as gifts, he might receive one simply by chance or if he had happened somehow to impress the mission staff that he was one of the "better" bush aboriginals (their definition of "better" being quite different from that of his bush fellows). Or he might—but again almost by pure chance—be given some brief job in connection with the mission which would enable him to earn a steel axe. In either case, for older men a preference for the steel axe helped create a situation of dependence in place of a situation of self-reliance and a behavior shift from situations in technology or conduct which were well structured or defined to situations in conduct alone which were ill defined. It was particularly the older ones among the men, whose earlier experience or knowledge of the white man's harshness in any event made them suspicious, who would avoid having any relations with the mission at all, and who thus excluded themselves from acquiring steel axes directly from that source.

The steel axe was the root of psychological stress among the Yir Yoront even more significantly in other aspects of social relations. This was the result of new factors which the missionary considered all to the good: the simple numerical increase in axes per capita as a result of mission distribution; and distribution from the mission directly to younger men, women, and even children. By winning the favor of the mission staff, a woman might be given a steel axe. This was clearly intended to be hers. The situation was quite different from that involved in borrowing an axe from a male relative, with the result that a woman called such an axe "my" steel axe, a possessive form she never used for a stone axe. (Lexically, the steel axe was differentiated from the stone by an adjectival suffix signifying "metal" the element "axe" remaining identical.) Furthermore, young men or even boys might also obtain steel axes directly from the mission. A result was that older men no longer had a complete monopoly of all the axes in the bush community. Indeed, an old man might have only a stone axe, while his wives and sons had steel axes which they considered their own and which he might even desire to borrow. All this led to a revolutionary confusion of sex, age, and kinship roles, with a major gain in independence and loss of subordination on the part of those able now to acquire steel axes when they had been unable to possess stone axes before.

The trading partner relationship was also affected by the new situation. A Yir Yoront might have a trading partner, in a tribe to the south whom he defined as a younger brother, and on whom as an older brother he would therefore have an edge. But if the partner were in contact with the mission or had other easier access to steel axes, his subordination to his bush colleague was obviously decreased. Indeed, under the new dispensation he might prefer to give his axe to a bush "sweetheart" in return for favors or otherwise dispose of it outside regular trade channels, since many steel axes were so distributed between natives in new ways. Among other things, this took some of the excitement away from the fiestalike tribal gatherings centering around initiations during the dry season. These had traditionally been the climactic annual occasions for exchanges between trading partners, when a man might seek to acquire a whole year's supply of stone axe heads. Now he might find himself prostituting his wife to almost total strangers in return for steel axes or other white men's goods. With trading partnerships weakened, there was less reason to attend the fiestas, and less fun for those who did. A decline in one of the important social activities which had symbolized these great gatherings created a lessening of interest in the other social aspects of these events.

Not only did an increase in steel axes and their distribution to women change the character of the relations between individual and individual, the paired relationships that have been noted, but a new type of relationship, hitherto practically unknown among the Yir Yoront, was created in their axe-acquiring conduct with whites. In the aboriginal society there were almost no occasions outside the immediate family when one individual would initiate action to several other people at once. For in any average group, while a person in accordance with the kinship system might be superordinate to several people to whom he could suggest or command action, at the same time he was also subordinate to several others, in relation with whom such behavior would be tabu. There was thus no overall chieftainship or authoritarian leadership of any kind. Such complicated operations as grass-burning, animal drives, or totemic ceremonies could be carried out smoothly because each person knew his roles both in technology and conduct.

On both mission and cattle stations, however, the whites imposed upon the aboriginals their conception of leadership roles, with one person in a controlling relationship with a subordinate group. Aboriginals called together to receive gifts, including axes, at a mission Christmas party found themselves facing one or two whites who sought to control their behavior for the occasion, who disregarded the age, sex, and kinship variables among them of which they were so conscious, and who considered them all at one subordinate level. Or the white might impose similar patterns on a working party. (But if he placed an aboriginal in charge of a mixed group of post hole diggers, for example, half of the group, those subordinate to the "boss," would work while the other half, who were superordinate to him, would sleep.) The steel axe, together, of course, with other European goods, came to symbolize for the aboriginal this new and uncomfortable form of social organization, the leader-group relationship.

The most disturbing effects of the steel axe, operating in conjunction with other elements also being introduced from the white man's several subcultures, developed in the realm of traditional ideas, sentiments, and values. These were undermined at a rapidly mounting rate, without new conceptions being defined to replace them. The result was a mental and moral void which foreshadowed the collapse and destruction of all Yir Yoront culture, if not, indeed, the extinction of the biological group itself.

From what has been said it should be clear how changes in overt behavior, in technology and conduct, weakened the values inherent in a reliance on nature, in androcentrism or the prestige of masculinity, in age prestige, and in the various kinship relations. A scene was set in which a wife or young son, his initiation perhaps not even yet completed need no longer bow to the husband or father, who was left confused and insecure as he asked to borrow a steel axe from them. For the woman and boy the steel axe helped establish a new degree of freedom which was accepted readily as an escape from the unconscious stress of the old patterns, but which left them also confused and insecure. Ownership became less well defined, so that stealing and trespass were introduced into technology and conduct. Some of the excitement surrounding the great ceremonies evaporated, so that the only fiestas the people had became less festive, less interesting. Indeed, life itself became less interesting, although this did not lead the Yir Yoront to invent suicide, a concept foreign to them.

The whole process may be most specifically illustrated in terms of the totemic system, and this will also illustrate the significant role which a system of ideas, in this case a totemic ideology, may play in the breakdown of a culture.

In the first place, under pre-European aboriginal conditions in which the native culture has become adjusted to a relatively stable environment in which there can occur few, if any, unheard of or catastrophic crises, it is clear that the totemic system must serve very effectively to inhibit radical cultural changes. The closed system of totemic ideas, explaining and categorizing a well-known universe as it was fixed at the beginning of time, presents a considerable obstacle to the adoption of new or the dropping of old culture traits. The obstacle is not insurmountable and the system allows for the minor variations which occur about the norms of daily life, but the inception of major changes cannot easily take place.

Among the bush Yir Yoront the only means of water transport is a light wood log, to which they cling in their constant swimming of rivers, salt creeks, and tidal inlets. These natives know that forty-five miles north of them are tribes who have a bark canoe. They know these northern tribes can thus fish from midstream or out at sea, instead of clinging to the river banks and beaches, and can cross coastal waters infested with crocodiles, sharks, sting rays, and Portuguese-men-of-war without the recurring mortality, pain, or anxiety to which they themselves are constantly subjected. They know they lack any magic to do for them what the canoe could do. They know the materials of which the canoe is made are present in their own environment. But they also know, as they say, that their own mythical ancestors lacked the canoe, and therefore they lack it, while they assume that the canoe was part of the ancestral universe of the northern tribes. For them, then, the adoption of the canoe would not be simply a matter of learning a number of new behavioral skills for its manufacture and use. The adoption would require at the same time a much more difficult procedure, the acceptance by the entire society of a myth, either locally developed or borrowed, which would explain the presence of the canoe, associate it with some one or more of the several hundred mythical ancestors (and how decide which?), and thus establish it as an accepted totem of one of the clans ready to be used by the whole community. The Yir Yoront have not made this adjustment, and in this case we can only say that ideas have for the time being at least won out over very real pressures for technological change. In the elaborateness and explicitness of the totemic ideologies we seem to have one explanation for the notorious stability of Australian cultures under aboriginal conditions, an explanation which gives due weight to the importance of ideas in determining human behavior.

At a later stage of the contact situation, as has been indicated, phenomena unaccounted for by the totemic ideological system begin to appear with regularity and frequency and remain within the range of native experience. Accordingly, they cannot be ignored (as the "Battle of the Mitchell River" was apparently ignored), and an attempt is made to assimilate them and account for them along the lines of principles inherent in the ideology. The bush Yir Yoront of the mid-1930s represent this stage of the acculturation process. Still trying to maintain their aboriginal definition of the situation, they accept European artifacts and behavior patterns, but fit them into their totemic system, assigning them as totems to various clans on a par with original totems. There is an attempt to have the myth-making process keep up with these cultural changes so that the idea system can continue to support the rest of the culture. But analysis of overt behavior, of dreams, and of some of the new myths indicates that this arrangement is not entirely satisfactory; that the native clings to his totemic system with intellectual loyalty, lacking any substitute ideology; but that associated sentiments and values are weakened. His attitudes toward his own and toward European culture are found to be highly ambivalent.

All ghosts are totems of the Head-to-the-East Corpse clan. They are thought of as white, and are, of course, closely associated with death. The white man, too, is white and was closely associated with death, so that he and all things pertaining to him are naturally assigned to the Corpse clan as totems. The steel axe, as a totem, was thus associated with the Corpse clan. But it is an "axe," and is clearly linked with the stone axe, which is a totem of the Sunlit Cloud Iguana clan. Moreover, the steel axe, like most European goods, has no distinctive origin myth, nor are mythical ancestors associated with it. Can anyone, sitting of an afternoon in the shade of a ti tree, create a myth to resolve this confusion? No one has, and the horrid suspicion arises that perhaps the origin myths are wrong, which took into account so little of this vast new universe of the white man. The steel axe, shifting hopelessly between one clan and the other, is not only replacing the stone axe physically, but is hacking at the supports of the entire cultural system.

The aboriginals to the south of the Yir Yoront have clearly passed beyond this stage. They are engulfed by European culture, in this area by either the mission or cattle station subcultures, or for some natives a baffling, paradoxical combination of both incongruent varieties. The totemic ideology can no longer support the inrushing mass of foreign culture traits and the myth-making process in its native form breaks down completely. Both intellectually and emotionally a saturation point is reached, so that the myriad new traits which can neither be ignored nor any longer assimilated simply force the aboriginal to abandon his totemic system. With the collapse of this system of ideas, which is so closely related with so many other aspects of the native culture, there follows an appallingly sudden and complete cultural disintegration and a demoralization of the individual such as has seldom been recorded for areas other than Australia. Without the support of a system of ideas well devised to provide cultural stability in a stable environment but admittedly too rigid for the new realities pressing in from outside, native behavior and native sentiments and values are simply dead. Apathy reigns. The aboriginal has passed beyond the reach of any outsider who might wish to do him well or ill. . . .

89.

DESCENT TO ANOMY

Robert M. MacIver

Our social ties, the values by which we live, and our sense of "belonging" are so much a part of most of our lives that we have little conception of their deep significance to us and to our society. Hence, with some dramatic recent exceptions, such as the value conflicts and distortions over Vietnam and over the maintenance of integrity in government, as evidenced in events surrounding Watergate, we have been able to take social cohesion pretty largely for granted. But this social cohesion through which the unity of our personalities is secured and maintained always rests in delicate balance. In a complex society, even under the most favor-

Source: Robert M. MacIver, *The Ramparts We Guard* (New York: Macmillan Co., 1950), pp. 84–92. Reprinted by permission of Macmillan Publishing Co., Inc. and the author.

Robert M. MacIver (1882–1970) was Lieber Professor Emeritus of Political Philosophy and Sociology, Columbia University. He was former chancellor of the New School for Social Research and founder of the New School's Center for New York City Affairs. He was also a former president of the American Sociological Association. Among his many books are *Society: Its Structure and Changes, The Web of Government, Life: Its Dimensions and Its Bounds,* and *As a Tale That Is Told.*

able conditions, there are individuals who fall into anomie (here spelled anomy) a condition where the sense of "belonging" to the group is lost and the norms or values of society are ignored or rejected. In times of crisis "whole groups are exposed to the malady." In this selection MacIver describes three types of anomic persons and examines the problems faced by democracies if they are to deal with anomie "as a disease and not as a sin."

Let us look next at *anomy,* the other malady of democratic man that becomes most virulent in times of crisis and turbulent change, the breakdown of the individual's sense of attachment to society, to all society. Anomy is not simply lawlessness. A gangster or a pirate or a mere law-evading rogue is not as such, indeed is not likely to be, anomic. He has his own code of law against law and is under strong sanctions to obey it. He need not be the victim of that inner detachment, of that cleavage between the real self and the projected self, of that total rejection of indoctrinated values that characterizes the anomic person. Anomy signifies the state of mind of one who has been pulled up from his moral roots, who has no longer any standards but only disconnected urges, who has no longer any sense of continuity, of folk, of obligation. The anomic man has become spiritually sterile, responsive only to himself, responsible to no one. He derides the values of other men. His only faith is the philosophy of denial. He lives on the thin line of sensation between no future and no past.

In any times particular individuals may fall into anomy. It happens when sensitive temperaments suffer without respite a succession of shocks that disrupt their faith. And not a few men have temporary moods that resemble anomy, periods when the spirit of denial rules them, after they have experienced some grave bafflement. But there are times of profound disturbance when whole groups are exposed to the malady. The soldiers in Mailer's novel, *The Naked and the Dead,* talk the language of anomy. They have been torn in youth from their environments, their careers, their dreams, their hopes, to face laborious tedium and the ugliest forms of death. They have been bereft of the sustaining ways of their culture. They are thrust back on the immediate needs and demands of each perilous hour. The present offers nothing but sensations; there are periods of boredom and drudgery, and then they are alone with nature and sudden death. So they use the language of sensation—there is nothing else to express. It means little but there is nothing else to mean. The livid, gory, sexy words they utter soon convey precisely nothing, nothing but the denudation they feel. For them, however, for those who survive, there is a return to nearly all the things they have lost. For most of them anomy wears away in their restoration to their society. But there are others, the hopelessly displaced, the totally uprooted, the permanently insecure, those who need the support of authority and have lost it without hope of recovery, the oversophisticated who find that the challenges of life cannot be met by sophistication—among such people anomy takes full command.

Anomy is a state of mind in which the individual's sense of social cohesion—the mainspring of his morale—is broken or fatally weakened. In this detachment of the anomic person from social obligation his whole personality is injured. He has lost the *dynamic unity* of personality. The anomic fall into various types, though we do not have so far the psychological researches necessary for the adequate classification of these types. We can, however, broadly distinguish the following.

First, there are those who, having lost

altogether, or in great measure, any system of values that might give purpose or direction to their lives, having lost the compass that points their course into the future, abandon themselves to the present, but a present emptied of significance. They resort, in other words, to a sophisticated cynicism, by aid of which they rationalize their loss. They live by the hour, seeking immediate gratification on whatever level it is available. They tend to be sensationalists and materialists. It is their defense against the ghosts of perished values.

Second, there are those who, having lost their ethical goals, having no longer any intrinsic and socialized values to which they can harness their drive to action, transfer this drive to extrinsic values instead, to the pursuit of means instead of to the pursuit of ends beyond them, and particularly to the pursuit of power, so far as that lies within their reach. It has been claimed that there is a "strain toward anomy" in modern capitalistic society, with its emphasis on competitive success measured by the purely extrinsic standard of money-making. There can be little doubt that engrossment in the competitive struggle, especially when it is carried on under the aegis of the "soulless bodyless" corporation, diverts men from the search for intrinsic satisfactions and erodes their recognition of the common interests of their society, the inclusive more abiding interests that bind men in the responsible fellowship of their community. At the same time, the experience of the past two generations suggests that it requires the violence of change, the deeper perturbations that disorient and displace men from their former ways, their former goals, their former faiths, to bring anomy to its full being, and in particular this second type of anomy. Those who exhibit it tend to be domineering, sadistic, ruthless, irascible, vain, inherently destructive. Unlike the first type, they live for a future, they have objectives that bind today to the further tomorrow, but these objectives are self-centered, ego-glorifying, bereft of social obligation. Often they profess adherence to some intrinsic faith or value, but primarily because that profession enhances their private designs. They are then like Machiavelli's prince, who must appear to be religious and high-minded if he is to retain his prestige and power. Moreover, they make the creeds of other men the instruments of their own aggrandisement, the utilitarian myths of their authority. On another level they are racketeers, buccaneers of industry or finance, unprincipled exploiters of whatever position, privilege, or power they acquire. All men or nearly all men cherish their private interest and frequently enough they allow it to overcome their public obligation. But they are restrained within certain limits set by loyalties of one kind or another, and when they transgress they are conscious of dereliction. But the truly anomic man has no limit short of necessity and no conscience that is more than expediency.

Third, we may distinguish a type of anomy that is characterized above all by a fundamental and tragic insecurity, something that cuts deeper than the anxieties and dreads that beset other men. It is the insecurity of the hopelessly disoriented. They have lost the ground on which they stood, the ground of their former values. Usually it happens when they have lost also their former environment, their former connections, their social place, their economic support. In the profoundest sense they are "displaced persons." The displacement, however, may not be physical. There is, for example, the social alienation of those who feel themselves rejected and become the victims of a persecution complex. This is perhaps the bitterest of all forms of anomy. There is a crushing sense of indignity, of exclusion, of injustice, of defeat, arousing feelings of intense hate, counter-aggressiveness, total revulsion from things as they are, sometimes accompanied by unquiet introspection and self-torture.

This cursory review is intended to suggest types, not to classify them. In any event there is a considerable overlapping of attributes between our types. We should also remember that many people approach the full bent of anomy in various degrees. As we have already suggested, the conditions of our civilization create some predisposition to it and when our kind of civilization is racked by abrupt and violent change anomy grows rampant. Anomy is a disease of the civilized, not of the simpler peoples. As Durkheim pointed out, one index of anomy is the number of suicides, and suicide is much more frequent among the civilized.

It is noteworthy that modern doctrines of violent social change are initiated by those who have at least a tendency to anomy. Let us take for example the case of Karl Marx. He was from his early youth subjected to some of the conditions that breed anomy. His family belonged to the rabbinical elite in Germany. While he was still an infant his father, to the general surprise, announced his conversion to the Protestant Evangelical Church. This was the cause of a bitter dispute between his father and his mother. In the end, when Karl was six years old, his father had his way, and Karl, along with the six other children of the family, was baptized into the new faith. We know from modern studies how deeply disturbing it is to the mind of a child to have his first indoctrinations shattered by a "culture clash" on the hearth. The secret churning of the young boy's mind was the first preparation of the revolutionist-to-be, greatly heightening that sense of aloofness and disorientation that is the lot of many a Jewish boy in a society that stupidly clings to its hoary prejudices. The first obvious effect on Karl Marx was his loathing of all religions.

He grew into an impetuous, irascible, opinionated, and still idealistic youth. Then his ambitions suffered a series of reverses and frustrations. At this stage he fell in with the "communist rabbi," Moses Hess. He was ripe for the new gospel. He embraced it avidly, inclining at first toward the French socialists but soon repudiating and scorning them to assert his own truly scientific brand. It was the culmination of a process that began in the disorientation of childhood. Marx had become completely alienated from the society in which he lived, not its economic order particularly but its whole being and all the culture it nourished. In the background of his mind there flickered visions of an ideal society. But his love of the ideal was pale and distant compared with his hatred of the actual. He turned early to dreams of power, of lonely mastery. He was at enmity with the world. He denounced with incredible bitterness his own best friends the moment they ventured to question in any way his authority.

A man may condemn the society in which he lives without being himself anomic. But only if he is sustained by the engrossing vision of a better society, only if he is working to hasten the coming of some "new Jerusalem," only if he lives in fellowship with some brotherhood of the faithful who share his vision, only, in the last resort, if he is already, prophetically, a member of the society for which he yearns. There are those who believe the main inspiration of Marx was just some such redemption of mankind, that he was filled with the vision of a world in which men would be liberated from exploitation and injustice, from the gross oppression of every form of power. To the present writer that seems a mistaken interpretation. In the voluminous writings of Marx there are only one or two most fleeting references to "the good society." There is no evidence that he really cared for his fellowmen. He never uses kindly language except for those who looked upon him as their infallible leader. He hated those of his own party who showed any independence of thought. He was venomous toward all whom he could not dominate.

Marx focused his sharp intelligence on the worst sore of the society he hated. A new industrial system had been growing up. It was being exploited with callous disregard for the welfare of the workers. In the "dark Satanic mills," as the poet Blake called them, men, women, and young children labored endlessly long days, under the worst conditions, for subsistence wages or less. There were riots and threats of revolution. The French Revolution had shown how a class system could be overthrown. Here Marx found his opportunity. With immense vigor and remarkable propagandistic skill he proclaimed the inevitable victory of the proletariat. Marx had never mixed with any proletarians. He was himself a bourgeois. He never showed any interest in proletarians as human beings—only as a class. As he himself said, he found in the proletariat the "material weapon of philosophy," of his philosophy, of his revenge on society, of his triumph. He was the wrathful divider. The "bourgeoisie" became the fixed objective of his hate, the source of all evil. He identified it with the society that had rejected him. It was anathema. He devoted his being to its destruction.

The presence of anomy in modern society is evidenced by the spread of violently divisive doctrines, doctrines of all-or-nothing, doctrines that loudly preach a reactionary or a revolutionary authoritarianism, doctrines that appeal to men not as human beings but as deindividualized masses in motion. The anomic and near-anomic persons of the second and third types are particularly prone to such doctrines. For they offer a congenial release from anomy, a drastic remedy for its bitterness and frustration, a refuge from its insecurity, a means of reconciling its destructive tendencies with its secret need for social reintegration.

All these doctrines are enemies of democracy. They reject its tolerance, its acceptance of difference, its respect for the individual, its faith in the healing processes of free opinion. The anomic man has lost the balance of social health, mostly through no fault of his own. In his alienation he seeks a quick and false prescription. The anomic who cannot be masters are often ready to be slaves. They cry out for the superman to save them, for some equivalent of a Providence, a God, the ineluctable authority who will end their alienation by saying, "I command you to follow," making his command ring with the magic of a lost obligation.

What then can democracy do to meet these two perils that threaten it in this age of violent change—group anarchy and individual anomy? We remarked in passing that we should not blame the anomic for their plight; they are suffering from a disease incident to our civilization. The remark may seem at best a truism—of what other social ailment might not the same be said? But it was said to call attention to the proper ways in which democracy can safeguard itself against these dangers. When we seek to heal a social ailment—or a physical one—we should always treat it as a disease and not as a sin. Unfortunately we often proceed on the latter assumption, as we have been doing, for example, in our "denazification" policies, with mostly unhappy consequences. To protect democracy against anomy or against group anarchy we must endeavor to get at and to remove their causes.

In the first place we should realise that all our efforts to protect democracy against these and other dangers are wholly futile unless we can protect it first against the catastrophe of war. For war has now become so immeasurably ruinous that the shaken and impoverished survivors would be driven to desperate measures that might be fatal to the very existence of democracy. Therefore while we still possess the inestimable spiritual heritage of democracy we must assure it against the very possibility of war, showing an alertness and a forethought that in the past two generations the democratic world most deplorably failed to show.

To achieve this end democracy must be strong in its quality as democracy, not only in its arms. The spiritual weakness of democracy is the strength of its enemies. In some respects we still make only a pretence at democracy. Ask the Mexican-Americans within our borders, whom we do not permit to sit at the same table with our noble Nordics. Ask the Negroes, whom we segregate as pariahs, so that we may not be contaminated by the social presence of a lower caste. Ask the Jewish people, who cannot live in the same hotels, sometimes cannot even be treated in the same hospitals as their democracy-loving fellow-Americans. Ask the Eastern Europeans, who are still frequently treated as second-class citizens, especially if their names have a Slavic sound. Ask the Chinese among us, the Japanese, the Filipinos, the Hindus—and remember that by our treatment of these people we are betraying our democracy before the greater part of the human race; remember also that the Orient is now stirring to new political life and that its decision between democracy and dictatorship will profoundly affect our future and the future of all mankind. Ask these questions, remember these things, and you must see that *our* failure to be true to *our* democracy is in the last resort the main reason why democracy is in danger.

The diseases of group anarchy and of personal anomy are peculiarly incident to modern democracies. The unfree systems are authoritarian; by authority and by sheer compulsion they suppress such manifestations. Democracy places responsibility in the individual and in the group—it asks their free allegiance, their free cooperation. But it must on that account assure its citizens the conditions in which they can exercise their freedom. It must guard them from haunting economic insecurity or their civic freedom becomes a mockery. It must guard them against the rank prejudice that cuts them off from the equal partnership of democratic society. Otherwise democracy will breed the seeds of its own destruction.

Lastly, it must make its own meaning, its own philosophy, its own spirit, positive and vital. It cannot rest in the outworn liberalism that never rose above the negative of nonintervention. No vague negative faith can meet men's needs in this age where dogmatic authoritarian creeds deride the democratic ideal, and promise men, however falsely, a greater security and a greater reward. Democracy must become self-conscious of its own worth. Here we reach a theme that needs our most earnest attention.

90.

SATELLITES AND SURROGATES—THE SYSTEM OF POWER

Victor Lebow

An examination of "social and cultural change" and an exploration of the role of "value systems" in supporting our national priorities would not be complete without a look at what has been called our "national security bureaucracy" and the long-standing anti-Communist ideology which supports it. The following selection by Victor Lebow, a successful businessman recently turned academic, illustrates in extensive detail the complex interactions among many types of institutionalized organizations—including economic, political, military, religious, educational, and the media—resulting from our recently diminishing but still perhaps dominant anti-Communist obsession. As the author points out, though President Eisenhower, in his valedictory, warned against the influence of the "military-industrial complex," we seem still to be enmeshed in what may well not be a conspiracy but, fully as bad in its consequences, an enormous, self-perpetuating institutional organism. And though J. Edgar Hoover, who is viewed by Lebow as having played a significant role in developing the anticommunist phobia, is now dead, the heritage of his, and others', ideology still seems to persist and to feed that organism.

To fight "The System" is to battle with an array of encrusted interests which are devoted unreservedly to the system of private profit, regardless of any disagreements among themselves. A typical satellite system combines organization, wealth, propaganda, the power to benefit its constituents and to punish its opponents, and often the ability to impose discipline and penalties upon recalcitrants.

The American Medical Association is such a system. For years it has been fierce in its opposition to most social legislation, particularly in the field of health. With their commitment to the business system, the Hippocratic Oath has become "un-American" and subsersive to the leaders of American medicine. The critical shortage of doctors is the result of their opposition to the building of more medical schools and the training of more physicians. Through the state and county medical associations, the AMA controls the profession, determines hospital accreditation, and can deprive a dissenting physician of much of his livelihood.

Take the National Rifle Association which combines the lovers of hunting with the interests of the firearms and ammunition manufacturers, and the right-wing groups who want to keep arms to protect the nation from "subversion." The NRA is able to impose its veto on legislation designed to limit and license gun sales. This is a society which is suffering increasingly from the use of weapons in individual and

Source: Victor Lebow, *Free Enterprise: The Opium of the American People* (New York: Oriole Editions, 1973), pp. 86–102.

See biographical note for Selection 25.

mob violence. These *afficionados* of the gun have been able to defeat outstanding members of the House and Senate who sponsored antiweapons legislation.

The American Farm Bureau Federation has proclaimed itself the voice of the farmer, but in fact it represents the largest, wealthiest and most influential farm operators, bankers, machinery and agricultural supply manufacturers. It has espoused every reactionary cause, opposed every piece of legislation which promised increased aid to the poor, the underpaid, the sick, or which benefitted the workingman. It has throttled minimum wage legislation for farm workers as well as any move to recognize the right of farm workers to organize. The Federation does not concern itself with the well-being or needs of the small farmer and the family-sized farm. That is why the poor farmer, when he thinks of "The System" which oppresses him, wants to see this Federation demolished along with its hold on the Department of Agriculture, its influence with the county agents, its cozy partnership with all the forces which help keep him in penury.

These pressure groups with their special interests include the trade associations, most of the labor organizations, the various organized religions, the United States Chamber of Commerce, the National Association of Manufacturers, and hundreds of others. Their lobbyists constitute a "shadow" Congress, providing advice, guidance, largesse, junkets, and importunity for the elected members of the House and Senate, as well as those in the State legislatures and administrations, and reaching the ears of strategically placed officials in the executive branch. The military-industrial complex is probably the most effective of all in terms of the spectacular profits and power it has won for its cohorts.

All of these are satellites of business because they are committed to the private enterprise economy, to the profit system, and because their existence and power are predicated upon the continued dominion of business in our society. The response of these special interest groups to critics who denounce "The System" is to align themselves with all the forces that oppose the dissatisfied, the dispossessed, the disinherited, the dissenters, the revolutionaries.

The role of the surrogate differs from that of the satellite, but is even more important. The Congress acts in that relationship to business, as the whipping boy for the impositions it enacts upon the rank and file citizens of the land. When it is forced by the excesses of private enterprise to pass laws which appear to abridge the rights of business, it does so to protect and perpetuate the private enterprise system, not to destroy it. The political establishment is wed to the proposition that all efficiency, all dependability reside in the private sector.

From the politicians who fancy themselves beatified by their badge of "liberal," to the know-nothing Rightists, all call for private enterprise to undertake the cure of our social and economic ills. For them, it would seem, a special magic is commanded by the system of private profit.

Perhaps one should recall to the business leaders who deliver the homilies on the social responsibility of business, and remind their political sycophants as well, of what old August Bebel once told a meeting of their counterparts in the Germany of his day:

"Gentlemen," he said, "you are not the doctors. You are the disease."

In a most literal sense, the armament of the private enterprise system, its defense and its guard as business and investments expand all over the world, is the military establishment. The Pentagon is often viewed as a separate power, as a bureaucracy independent of business and, in fact, the beneficent patron of corporate makers of planes and guns and missiles. A former commandant of the United States Marine Corps, Major General Smedley D. Butler, after his retirement made very clear the relationship between the corporations and the military. He wrote:

"I spent thirty-three years in the Marines and during that period I spent most of my time being a high-class muscle man for Big Business, for Wall Street and the bankers. In short, I was a racketeer for capitalism . . . I helped make Mexico and especially Tampico safe for American oil interests in 1914. I helped make Haiti and Cuba a decent place for the National City Bank to collect revenues in. I helped purify Nicaragua for the international banking house of Brown Brothers in 1908–1912. I brought light to the Dominican Republic for American sugar interests in 1916. I helped make Honduras 'right' for the American fruit companies in 1903. In China, in 1927, I helped see to it that Standard Oil went on its way unmolested."

If the dates General Butler's memoirs mention seem in the distant past, the role of the military can be brought up to the recent years and the present. One need only mention Guatemala, the Dominican affair of 1965, the attempts at overthrow of Fidel Castro in Cuba, the military aid program which provides bonus business for American armaments manufacturers on top of their domestic sales to the Pentagon. The National Interest, which is the translation in political terms of the concerns and interests of American private enterprise, is what the military is sworn to protect and defend, and for which it is prepared to wage war.

Business benefits from war and the preparations for war. But only the ignorant can believe that American business itself exhibits the loyalty and patriotism which it expects of the American people. In fact, there is a long record of instances of trading with the enemy, of disloyalty, of passing military information to actual or potential enemies, of acts bordering on treason, by major American corporations.

Yet one must face the fact that the "little people" have a stake in military preparations. Their role was summed up by Dr. Arthur F. Burns when he was president of the National Bureau of Economic Research. He pointed out that the scale of defense expenditures has become a self-reinforcing process. It does not depend for its momentum entirely upon the energy of military planners, contractors, scientists, and engineers. "To some extent it is abetted also by the practical interests and anxieties of ordinary citizens . . . With a large part of our economy devoted to defense activities, the military-industrial complex has acquired a constituency including factory workers, clerks, secretaries, even grocers and barbers . . . The vested interest that numerous communities have acquired in defense activities may therefore continue to run up costs on top of the rising budgets generated by the momentum of competing military technologies."

Thus, the military-industrial complex has not only succeeded in persuading the American people that preparations for war are preparations for "defense," but has also enlisted the self-interest of workers and small business people in support of the swollen appropriations for the Department of Defense. In effect, this is a subtle form of corruption; essentially, it constitutes bribery of a whole people. ("In 1967, defense-generated activity was responsible for 7,500,000 jobs, representing 10 percent of total United States employment.")

The valedictory message of President Eisenhower included a warning: "In the councils of government," he said, "we must guard against the acquisition of unwarranted influence, whether sought or unsought, by the military-industrial complex. The potential for the disastrous rise of misplaced power exists and will persist." According to Malcolm C. Moos, who drafted the speech for the President, the employment of retired officers in defense industry played a direct role in the formulation of this message. In 1959, there were 768 officers of the rank of colonel or above employed by the hundred largest contractors. In 1969, there were 2,072. The seven largest aerospace contractors alone employed over seven hundred.

The examples are legion of Congressional action to protect cozy industry-Pentagon relationships. Thus, when a bill for uniform accounting systems by defense contractors passed the House, the Senate watered it down by substituting an act which provided for an eighteen month study of the "feasibility" of applying uniform standards, although it had already been proved by the outgoing Renegotiation Board that it had been able to recapture almost two billion dollars in excess profits, and more could be uncovered if contractors could be prevented from hiding these excess profits by juggling figures.

Forced to testify before a committee of the United States Senate, a Pentagon official admitted that he had not revealed how grossly underestimated had been the cost of the C-5A aircraft because he feared that the news might depress the value of Lockheed Aircraft shares on the stock market! A retired Navy captain, who had been director of the procurement control and contract clearance division in the office of the Chief of Naval Matériel, testified that there was serious waste and inefficiency in defense spending because of the relationship between the defense industry and high-ranking Defense Department officials. Of one Assistant Secretary of the Air Force he told the Congressional Committee (in 1969), ". . . he will tell you that he believes no defense contractor should be allowed to lose money on a Government contract." When a contractor had failed to live up to the terms of his contract, this Secretary asked, "Could any other contractor in that industry have done better?"

As the physicist, Ralph Lapp, has said, "Our commitment to weapons-making has distorted the free-enterprise system of our economy into a kind of 'defense socialism,' a system in which the welfare of the country is permanently tied to the continued growth of military technology and the continued stockpiling of military hardware." The steady production of armaments and their rapid rate of obsolescence keep the defense manufacturers busy and require constant pruning of the inventory. In addition, it has become part of our foreign policy to use armaments to help tie other nations to our apron strings. When war broke out between India and Pakistan over Kashmir, the former ambassador to India, John Kenneth Galbraith, testified before the Senate Foreign Relations Committee: "The arms we supplied . . . caused the war between India and Pakistan . . . If we had not supplied arms, Pakistan would not have sought a military solution."

So anxious is the Pentagon to create business for defense contractors that it will even order armaments which it will never use. Thus, in March, 1970, it invited eight aerospace companies to compete on the design and development of a jet fighter plane, to be known as The International Fighter, for sale to other countries. As *Forbes Magazine* has written, "Arms and military equipment are one of the United States' major export items. Without them, few defense companies would be earning the kind of money they do." . . .

. . . . .

. . . Of course, the United States by no means has a monopoly of the trade in armaments. In the Middle East, for example, besides the United States, Great Britain, France, the Soviet Union, Czechoslovakia, Belgium, Sweden, Italy, Switzerland, Poland, Bulgaria, Japan and both Chinas have plugged in. "On top of this are the independent arms dealers, many of whom have long believed that the Middle East is their own private market."

American arms have played an important role in the Congo, in Indonesia, in the civil war in Nigeria, in the slaughter of East Pakistanis by West Pakistanis, to say nothing of the suppression of the peoples in the countries to which we sell arms: Greece, Portugal, the "Banana Republics" of Central America, Brazil, Taiwan, South Africa, and many more. By 1966 we had seventy countries on the list of those receiving arms from the United States, which included, of course, the nations which have given us rights to establish military bases on their territory.

"In the quarter century since the end of World War II," reported *Business Week,* "some $66 billion worth of conventional arms have been pumped into world markets. Close to $50 billion of those weapons have come from the United States, which achieved its status mainly through military aid programs bolstering allies during the Cold War." This is a measure of the "bonus" which the Pentagon bestows upon its contractors.

The late Representative Mendel Rivers (D. So. Car.) was chairman of the House Armed Services Committee. According to Senator Proxmire, Rivers once told a colleague, "I could defeat Strom Thurmond any day in the week. But I don't want to be a South Carolina senator. I've got the most powerful position in the U.S. Congress." His campaign slogan was, "Rivers delivers," and his constituency was blessed with what has been described as a microcosm of the military-industrial complex. The corporations which sought his approval upon their contracts for the Defense Department have been happy to locate new installations in his district. Not only does the Charleston area benefit from the many Army, Navy, and Air Force installations—the Charleston Air Force Base, the Marine Corps Recruit Depot at Parris Island, the Naval Weapons Station, and a Polaris missile facility—but duPont operates the 315-square mile Savannah River plant of the Atomic Energy Commission, and plants have been built in the district, in the years since Rivers became chairman, by General Electric, Avco, J. P. Stevens & Co., McDonnell-Douglas, and Lockheed. United Aircraft is to build a new helicopter plant in Charleston. The payrolls of the military installations alone pump $317 million a year into the economy of the Charleston area.

Serving both as satellites and as surrogates for the system of private enterprise are the veteran and superpatriotic groups, the American Legion, the Veterans of Foreign Wars, the Navy League, the Air Force Association, the Daughters of the American Revolution, the Minutemen, and the John Birch Society, among others. For these organizations, their nationalistic code, their patriotism, and their support of the military, are all consistent with their identification of private enterprise with the Flag.

The most potent ideological support for business has come from the institutions dedicated to the Cold War, to the anti-Communist phobias, to the rooting out of dissenters. These have included the House Committee on un-American Activities, now renamed to be consistent with its Senate counterpart, the Committee on Internal Security, and, most important, the Federal Bureau of Investigation. For these, ideas which question established institutions produce repugnance, horror, and hate, and the counteractions of repression, censorship, violence, imprisonment, treason trials, and even executions.

When measures are proposed that might constrain or control business, we have seen how it marshalls its battalions. It is therefore not surprising that it should convert the entire society into its bastion and defense when any question its right to exist. We have not seen in the whole history of this country, so prolonged, so pervasive, and so powerful a campaign as has been waged against Communism, real and imagined, and against all who could be accused of being Communists, whether by association or by the nature of the proposals they have advocated. As one examines this phenomenon, it becomes evident that the tendency has been to label any idea "Communistic" if it offended the interests of business.

The consensus has been wide indeed, ranging from the Americans for Democratic Action to the John Birch Society, and enlisted in this national brain washing have been the churches, schools, newspapers, magazines, radio and television, State legislatures, the House of Representatives, the Senate, the Department of Justice. Many men have made careers out of the Red-hunt; some have reached high office, and Richard M. Nixon the highest in the land.

In *The Paranoid Style in American Politics,* the late Professor Hofstadter italicized his finding that the rhetoric and activities which he characterized as paranoid have been limited, in the past, to *minority* groups. But American anti-Communism has been a paranoia which affected the overwhelming majority of the population. University professors have embraced the creed, as do John Birchers whose bumper stickers read, "Kill a Commie for Christ."

This is not to say that business itself has held aloof from this campaign. The United States Chamber of Commerce inspired the postwar Red-hunts. Millionaires of the stripe of H. L. Hunt, Patrick Frawley, William Loeb, and others have contributed funds and support to the anti-Communist crusades. Support for Senator Joe McCarthy came from thousands of businessmen.

The United States has now celebrated a full half-century of anti-Communism. It has become a doctrine as American as apple pie. But it is not merely a doctrine, it is also an establishment. As doctrine it is a creed and a dogma, and it dies hard. As establishment it is most securely rooted. It permeates the State Department, animates the Congress, dominates all manner of organizations. It is gospel for both the National Association of Manufacturers and the CIO-AFL, the liberal left and the extremist right, the Catholic hierarchy and the secular universities, lurid comic strips and respectable syndicated columnists. Every political candidate is committed to it. After these five decades of blind acceptance, it has been sanctified. Only recently and reluctantly is it now being questioned. How the foreign policy of the Government has been shaped by this doctrine is all too evident. The bloated military budgets, the race in space, the adventures in many lands, have all been dictated by anti-Communism: Greece, Iran, Lebanon, Guatemala, Cuba, the Congo, the Dominican Republic, Korea, Vietnam.

It would be naive to ascribe the actions of a world power, jealous of its dominion, to motives purely ideological. It is clear that the military-industrial complex would have had to invent Communism if it did not have it ready to hand. For aided by this American obsession, the makers of armaments and the seekers for imperial power have won opportunities for both enormous power and enormous profits.

. . . . .

This obsession has wrought havoc not only with national policy but with the morality of the American people. How calmly Americans have taken slaughter and destruction, watching it on evening television, when the killed were labelled Communists. The result of this half-century of anti-Communist indoctrination has made Americans a people unable to grasp this country's dangerous role in the world. Even the labor movement, once a proud and militant institution, today gives lip service to its social and political aims, and eagerly seeks largesse from defense contracts. In less than twenty years it has been castrated by the anti-Communism it has embraced.

All this serves business well. Of course, it arises out of ground already well fertilized. The frenetic character of American anti-Communism is only partly the product of its usefulness to business. It is also a result of deep frustrations in American life and society. We tend to think of democracy in terms of the New England town meeting when, as a matter of cold fact, the individual citizen has long lost his voice. Frustrated people need scapegoats. The more rational havens for the dissenters have long ago been destroyed by the prevailing anti-Communism and the Red-hunts. The result has been a new high level of violence and a dangerous, destructive nihilism which tends to overshadow disciplined dissent and principled opposition.

It is in the American tradition to subscribe to a Mephistophelian interpretation of history. We have been addicted to it for one hundred and seventy years or more. From the time when Citizen Gênet came to this country on behalf of the French Revolution, to the calamitous visit of Fidel Castro, Americans have reacted with fear, horror, and hate to new thinking that related to property and government.

Perhaps one key to the hysteria and passion over Communism lies in a tradition peculiar to the United States among all the great industrialized nations of the world. It is in the roles of dogma and heresy in American life. Others have documented the history of violence in this country. What has not been accorded similar study is the predilection for dogmatic creeds and the unceasing cruelty to heretics which runs through our history. The Puritan heritage, acceptance of the Bible as irrefutable proof, the regionalism, the provincialism, the xenophobia which passes for patriotism—these have been among the influences which have stirred up furious hatreds and fears of the sceptic, the dissenter, the opponent, the stranger, the foreigner, and particularly when any fiercely held dogma is questioned. In a sense, the ready use of violence is itself often a concomitant of the embraced dogma, for the true believer, when he faces any reasoned critique of his opinions and attitudes, seeks refuge in force to relieve his frustration.

The intensity of the anti-Communist obsession in the United States can actually be measured. It is represented by our capacity for "overkill" with nuclear weapons. As Professor Melman has calculated our power, the United States has the nuclear warheads and the delivery capability to wipe out all of the 370 cities with populations of over 100,000 in the entire Sino-Soviet world—not once but *fifty times over!* We have a stock of atomic weapons which would have permitted this country to detonate one bomb of the Hiroshima type every day from the birth of Christ to the present—and have some left over.

American anti-Communism is not the complete explanation of the prevalence and power of the antiintellectual forces in this country. But they are reinforced by our over-reaction to an ideology which opposes our own. This combination of the provincial, the fearful, the uninformed, combined with his long record of anti-

Communism put Richard M. Nixon in the White House.

When the Church and the bishops taught their flock to accept the divine right of kings, they helped maintain the rule of absolute monarchs for one thousand years, an epoch of which we now characterize the greater part as the Dark Ages. Today, in the United States, the politicians, the organs of the State, the legislators, the communications media, and the schools perform a similar function in preserving the rule and power of business. Of all these, the role of the politicians most closely resembles that of the Church. And over us, too, hangs the portent of dark ages.

For business, these satellites and surrogates provide "full coverage" insurance. Critics may bemoan the life of the white collar man, and the organization man, and the full-time commitment to profit-making of the executive ranks, but the institution itself, this system of private enterprise, rides untouched—controlling our economy, our politics, and our minds.

91.

AGRARIAN REVOLUTION AND ECONOMIC PROGRESS

Rainer Schickele

Major social and cultural changes are occurring in the non-Western world. The emergence of independent nations in Asia and Africa and the modernization of their economic and social systems are parallel aspects of this movement. In the following selection Rainer Schickele, who has assisted several countries in the modernization process, examines the motivation for, and processes of change in, these societies. He places his analysis in an historical perspective through a comparison with the Western industrial revolution.

Source: Rainer Schickele, *Agrarian Revolution and Economic Progress: A Primer for Development* (New York: Praeger Publishers, 1968), pp. 1–9. Reprinted by permission of the publisher.

Rainer Schickele, now retired, worked in the field of agricultural economics. He formerly served with the United Nations Food and Agriculture Organization and as an associate of the Agricultural Development Council, Inc., of New York. His interests have focused upon the processes of economic development in newly developing nations. He is the author of many publications.

We are witnessing a drama of breathtaking sweep throughout the newly developing world.

We are in the second act on which the curtain rose after World War II. The first act started in the wake of the French and American revolutions, around the year 1800. The center of the stage was Europe and North America. In the second act, it has shifted from the West to the East and South, to Asia, Africa and Latin America.

The central protagonist is the worker, the peasant, the small craftsman, the clerk, the poor man working in the factory, field, workshop, and office. The plot of the drama deals with his frustrations and triumphs as he struggles along his way from subservience to human dignity and citizenship, from poverty to wealth, under the guiding spirit of humanist ideology, of democracy and the equality of man.

THE INDUSTRIAL REVOLUTION OF THE WEST

In the first act, during the Industrial Revolution up to World War II, technology brought about a tremendous increase in productivity. Application of science to the production processes increased the capacity of people to produce so much that, for the first time in the history of mankind, it became possible to wipe out hunger and poverty. The humanist ideology taught people that the purpose of an economic system is the creation of wealth for the satisfaction of human wants, and that men are created equal. This means that men of all races and creeds have a basic human right to equality of opportunity and civic dignity, that the satisfaction of the human wants of the poor is as important as that of the rich, and that degrading poverty is incompatible with the principle of human rights in a modern democracy.

The economic system during the Industrial Revolution was based mainly upon private entrepreneurs. Although producers were always subject to various public policies and regulations, these were in the beginning formulated in the interest of industrial producers and of commerce with no regard for expanding also the opportunities for the millions of poor workers employed at starvation wages and working under most horrible sweatshop conditions. During the nineteenth century, many people became rich, but many, many more people remained extremely poor. As late as the middle of the twentieth century, the richest of the Western industrial countries still had far too many families living in poverty, in the midst of plenty.

This weakness of the private enterprise system in distributing its rising output to also meet the needs of the poor became apparent as early as the middle of the nineteenth century. Our drama's hero, the worker, farmer and small craftsman, with the help of philosophers and economists, came forth with the proposal of an alternative economic system, that of state enterprise, whose purpose was to create wealth for the satisfaction of human wants according to physical and social need rather than ability to pay. It was, however, only as late as the 1920s, and only in one country, Russia, that a centralized state enterprise system was actually put into practice during the first act of our drama. It performed well in reducing abject poverty among the masses of the people, but was much less successful in the task of increasing productivity, particularly in agriculture.

The hero, when he saw more than half a century go by without any Western country adopting the state enterprise system, began struggling for a fundamental reform, for a reorientation of the private enterprise system which would strengthen its performance in satisfying the human wants of the poor, without weakening its performance in producing wealth. In their political ascendancy, people assigned to the state the responsibility for guiding the private enterprise economy with social and economic welfare policies so as to reduce poverty and give equal opportunities to the poor for education, health and bargaining power in the market. These policies compensated, at least in part, for the lack of the market system's response to the needs of the poor, and still preserved the incentives and initiatives of private enterprise in production.

This "mixed economy" where private enterprise produces and trades within a framework of public policies and controls designed to promote the economic welfare of people as a whole, and particularly of the poor and disadvantaged, achieved a dramatic breakthrough in most of the Western industrialized countries during the 1920s and 30s. In the Scandinavian countries, poverty has almost been wiped out, private enterprise is producing efficiently and profitably, and living standards are among the highest in Europe. Also, in many of the other Western industrialized countries, the extent of poverty has been reduced more or less depending on the scope and efficiency of the public policies for equalizing opportunities and reducing poverty. There remains no economic or moral justification for poverty in an industrially developed affluent society where excess production capacity and surpluses are more troublesome than shortages. So our drama's hero continues his struggle in the West, but with a strong stance which promises to bring him soon within reach of his economic goal—the abolition of poverty.

This is the state of affairs, the scenery and the stage of the plot at the end of the drama's Act I, the Industrial Revolution of the West.

THE AGRARIAN REVOLUTION OF THE NEWLY DEVELOPING WORLD

As the curtain rises on Act II around the year 1950, the Agrarian Revolution of the East and South has started. The scene is the vast region of Asia, Africa, and South America, a rural region where most people live on farms and in villages and derive their livelihood from agriculture. Here, 800 to 900 million people achieved political independence from colonial rule in recent years, and another 400 million people are bringing about fundamental changes in their old traditional governments. Of the 1.25 billion people in this newly developing part of the world, 90 percent live in countries with an average per capita income of less than $200 per year. This simply means that the vast majority of the people are very poor indeed.

The people want to consummate their newly won political independence and strive toward their new aspirations of human dignity, freedom as responsible citizens, and equality of opportunity. This means they must raise their production and do so for the main purpose of reducing poverty.

The hero finds himself in a state of deep and widespread poverty. His trials deal with finding ways of harnessing the wealth-creating drive of private enterprise within a framework of governmental policies that satisfy the human wants of the poor, in order to unleash the pent-up capacities and energies of the people which are now stunted, suppressed by lack of education, health, food, and other bare necessities of life.

The drama's hero is not a heroic character. He takes on the shape of many different persons in all walks of life. He appears as an Indian farmer, overlooking his fields parched by the drought of the failing monsoon, with his wife, children and grandparents. Where will the food come from to keep his family alive? He appears as an office clerk in Nigeria who was fired by the manager to make room for a cousin, and who cannot find another job because he comes from the wrong tribe. He appears as a woman in a textile factory in Malaysia, a fisherman in Haiti, a blacksmith in the Northeast of Brazil—and whenever some little thing goes wrong he is down and out. There are so many little things over which he has no control and which can go wrong for him, because he has no influence over his environment, no influence with his employer, landlord or creditor in the conduct of public and community affairs. But he knows that if he is given a chance, if he can get education, food, and other prime necessities of life, he can do well, and he has proven it again and again on the rare occasions when he did get a chance. He is determined to get this chance for the multitude of poor people everywhere.

There are leaders emerging who articulate the aspirations of the people, who educate them in political and economic matters, who organize them into cooperative groups and political parties, who are rapidly learning the art and science of modern politics and government. Some of these leaders come from poor families, from peasant farms and shantytowns; but many come from well-to-do families, from educated classes, from professional and civil service ranks and landed aristocracies. Gandhi, whose father and grandfather were chief ministers of several Indian states, shared the life of the poor voluntarily in the service to their cause. Nyerere was a teacher, Senghor a philosopher and poet, Cardenas a general, before they became great leaders of their people. They identified themselves with them, they came to political power with their support and held their confidence. This emergence of progressive leaders of the common people is proceeding everywhere, slowly in some places, faster in others. There is today no government, no group of rulers and wealthy merchants and landowners who do not sense the political ascendancy of the poor.

This pervasive spirit of the times is our drama's hero. This spirit is energized by the vision of man coming into his own, as an individual on equal terms with his brethren of all races, creeds and nations, with equal opportunities to develop his talents, to apply his productive efforts, and to be treated with respect by other persons and by his government. This is the freedom aspect of this ideology; its counterpart, fully as indispensable, is the responsibility aspect—the vision of man as a member of the community, who accepts the obligation to serve the needs of society, who participates in public affairs as a responsible citizen with the community's interest at heart.

The practical meaning of this ideology, this spiritual credo of our time, is that the individual has the right to choose and act freely within the limits of compatibility with community welfare; and that the government, in its promotion and safeguarding of the community's welfare, exercises its power with the consent of the people at large, and within the limits of compatibility with individual freedom and dignity.

Who is the villain in our drama? The plantation owner with a whip? The feudal prince in his palace with wives in silk brocades and thousands of peasants in rags and abject servitude? The colonial administrator backed by mercenaries?

These characters are disappearing rapidly with the demise of colonial empires, the achievement of political independence and the creation of representative democratic governments, although there are still areas where they are fighting covertly, but ruthlessly, for their power and social status.

The real antagonist is the old traditional spirit of privilege and power of the few over the many, of the elite over the "innately inferior," of the born aristocrat over the plebs, of the wealthy over the poor. This antagonist still has great strength which is rooted in past traditions of thousands of years. He also takes on the shape of many different persons in all walks of life. He appears as a peasant who has no respect for the dignity of his wife and mistreats her as a slave. How can his children grasp the belief in human dignity when they see their own mother mistreated? He appears as a government official who abuses the power of his office, who intimidates people and demands bribes. He appears as a landowner who keeps his tenants and laborers ignorant and poor and in debt to him, or as a foreman in a factory who bars his workers from advancement and keeps them in constant fear of dismissal.

This metaphoric prologue symbolizes the essence of the forces underlying modern economic development problems. For the first time in mankind's history, technology offers the possibility of producing enough for every man, woman, and child to live in decency, free from hunger and stultifying want. This constitutes the material base upon which a democratic society can be built embracing all the people rather than only a small elite.

GENERATORS OF PROGRESS

These are two powerful generators of economic development: the humanist ideology, and science and technology.

The great moral force which ushered in the American and French revolutions of the late eighteenth century and shaped the concept of a modern democratic social system was rooted in the belief that men are created equal before God, or in worldly terms, that men are equal before the law and have equal rights for opportunities to develop their capacities, to reap the fruits of their productive efforts, and to participate in the shaping of their communities, in the molding of their institutions and governments. This idea is still an infant in world history's perspective, and is very new indeed to the traditional cultures of two thirds of the world population. But this humanist idea is on the march everywhere, is stirring in the minds and hearts of people throughout the world, and will continue to shape the history of mankind throughout the current and the coming centuries.

In the West, this humanist ideology transformed a feudal elite society into a democratic society of citizens in which universal suffrage, one-man, one-vote, became the revolutionary invention for making government responsible to the people. It transformed a highly restrictive and esoteric educational system for the privileged few into a universal, largely free educational system for everyone. It abolished slavery and established a code of law and a system of courts before which every man was considered equal in his rights and responsibilities. It created the goal of people's economic welfare, of equitable sharing of the nation's wealth and opportunities, of abolition of hunger and poverty—a logical sequel to the abolition of slavery. These were tremendously powerful innovations which triggered a revolution of rising aspirations and unleashed pent-up energies of people for building a new society, new institutions and standards of behavior, new laws and forms of government. Even after 150 years of political potency in the Western industrial world, no one claims that this humanist ideology has found its full realization in modern Western society; it is still far from it. But since the middle of the current century, it has become the dominant world spirit and driving force. It is giving the direction, the orientation for progress throughout the world, in the industrial West and newly developing agrarian countries alike.

Science and technology transformed the traditional production processes in industry, agriculture, and trade into instruments of amazing power for making the natural resources of the earth the servants of the material needs of man. In the industrial West, during the last hundred years, output per worker increased manyfold in every line of production. It created a large variety of new goods and services which were not even conceivable a hundred years ago. This application of a rapidly expanding science to practical production processes is now beginning to spread throughout the developing world, and is bringing about new attitudes of people toward their work, new forms of organization and group activities in production techniques, in market structures and government functions. Science and technology has given man the power to abolish poverty, for the first time in history—but also to destroy himself by instantaneous mass-murder. The greatest challenge to mankind in the coming centuries is to uphold the mastership of the humanist ideology, of the spiritual and moral values of modern society, over the application of technology, over the use of science in human affairs. This applies to the use of atomic energy as well as to the use of mechanization and automation.

These two great generators of progress, the humanist ideology and the scientific technology, are the West's constructive legacy to the newly developing regions of the world; they have to adapt them to their own peculiar conditions, but they need not invent them anew. Herein lies the hope for a victorious outcome of the race against time.

If progress lags too much, there is real danger of mankind losing control over technology. A serious disintegration of the spiritual power which the idea of the equality and dignity of man holds over our hearts and minds may readily lead to an atomic holocaust, or to a technocratic society of robots along the alpha-beta-gamma lines of Huxley's *Brave New World* or the nightmare of Orwell's *1984*.

The *material aspect* of the race against time is that between food and population, between production and poverty. Will we succeed in abolishing hunger and poverty fast enough to prevent a world-wide breakdown of interhuman and international relations, of national and world peace?

The *ideological aspect* is the question: Will people's faith in the humanist idea of the respect for our fellowman's and neighbor-nation's dignity and right of self-government withstand the frustrations and trials on the road to progress, or will this faith falter in us before a modicum of realization is reached?

These are the two basic disturbing aspects of the race against time which leaders must ponder honestly, at all levels, in all walks of life, in all countries throughout the world.

92.

THE ALTRUISTIC IMPULSE AND THE GOOD SOCIETY

Charles K. Warriner

The preceding selections in this section have, for the most part, provided a pessimistic view of the consequences of social change. The author of this selection, however, like Schickele in the preceding one, still sees hope of a better world through the systematic efforts of mankind. Here Warriner explores the individual and shared values he feels are essential if we are to achieve a better world for everyone without, on the one hand, becoming so bogged down with specifications and procedures that we lose the "common touch," or on the other hand, becoming so imbued with an ideology as to be willing to sacrifice many people today in order to achieve a vaguely outlined Utopia tomorrow. His analysis of the role of the various forms of altruism, and especially what he refers to as collective altruism, in improving man's condition is especially insightful.

Source: Charles K. Warriner, *Voluntary Action Research: 1972,* eds. David Horton Smith, Richard Reddy and Burt R. Baldwin (Lexington, Mass.: Lexington Books, D. C. Heath and Co., 1972), pp. 343–52. Abridged. Reprinted by permission of the publisher.

The author is professor of sociology at the University of Kansas. He has studied in the Philippines on a Fulbright grant.

. . . . .

Progress toward the good society involves two elements of which the amelioration of certain of men's conditions is only one. Whatever the sources of our pain and of the torments imposed upon us by our particular world, we can live with these and surpass them in a satisfying and even joyful human life only as others participate in our lives through empathy and sympathy. It is only as others, touched by the altruistic impulse, come to our side that life is fully worthwhile.

The material aid given by the altruistic impulse, directly and personally expressed, may have little effect upon the lot of the sufferer. His fate is unchanged. But what he gains, what both gain, is a reaffirmation of their humanness and the destruction of their isolation and loneliness. No matter what the nature of our material condition, no matter what the burden, it is tolerable only when we know that others care about us, only when we know that others feel what we are feeling, only when we know that ours is a shared and not a lonely burden. Men cannot long survive as humans without the kind of interpersonal relationships that break their isolation.

In our search for the good society we have emphasized the first of these elements of progress and have neglected the second. *We have been more concerned with the external material conditions of people's lives than with the subjective conditions of their lives*—their quality of life, to use a popular phrase. Our philanthropy has lost the human touch. If we are to make the most of our opportunities for effective altruism, if we are to make our voluntary associations and our volunteer activities effective means toward attaining the good society, we must learn how to improve the human touch.

There are at least four major expressions of the altruistic impulse. Each is necessary and each must be in some ways consonant with the others if we are to make real progress toward the better society. Each of these forms contributes in a different way to changing the circumstances of our lives and to our ability to bear the circumstances we cannot change.

EMPATHY AND PERSONAL ALTRUISM

In every time and in every place some men are especially touched by the sufferings of their neighbors. By their empathy with others they are particularly attuned to and receptive of the altruistic impulse. Such men have helped to carry the other's burden, have offered sympathy and love in times of grief, have given their own, often meager goods to ameliorate another's greater need. They have walked with the other through the lonely hours and down the lonely miles, though their own paths called them other ways.

Such altruistic acts stem from the capacity to *be* for a moment the other person, to stand in his shoes not as one's self merely transposed, but as if he himself is standing there. And empathy is more than a product of communication in the sense of message sending, it is active communing. I have elsewhere argued that such communication is the unique attribute of humanness and is essential if men are to surpass the bounds of their isolation and alienation, and to create a society in which they are more than merely parts of the environment with little relationship to one another.

The practice of this form of communication is at a low ebb in our modern urban, chaotic society and as a result this form of the altruistic impulse is stifled. Some would trace this loss to the kinds of personalities which we build and . . . seek the personality traits and capacities which engender the altruistic impulse in its various forms. If, on the other hand, we recognize that humans may be continuously emergent and that their personalities are a function of the continuity of their experiences with others, then we must look to the forms and patterns of the society for an explanation of the loss of the human touch. Many such sources could be identified, but three appear to be of central importance.

A. The Death of Cultural Norms of Personal Altruism

At most times and in most, though not all societies—our own urban, heterogeneous, symbiotic society especially excepted—culturally established patterns of personal altruism have been apparent. The frontier custom of hospitality to the traveling stranger, the rural community custom of plowing and planting for a sick man or the new widow, and the neighborly food and presence at times of illness and death were such cultural patterns of personal altruism. These cultural patterns are important for they do not depend upon the altruistic impulse or the capacity for empathy that any particular person may have. One brought food to the wake, opened the door to the stranger, and lent a hand at the harvest even if burdened with the soul of a misanthrope. These normatively supported patterns not only ensure that those in need receive help, but through the self-fulfilling processes engender the altruistic impulse.

Although instances of personal altruism may be found in the crowded urban street and in the lonely institutional corridor, the normative sanction for these has been lost. Much more widespread are the opposing norms of avoiding involvement, staying out of other people's business, and leaving it up to the police or social workers (an example being the fatal stabbing of Kitty Genovese in New York City while forty uninvolved citizens looked on). The older norms have been lost because the situations by which they were defined no longer exist. The objective conditions of life have changed and we have not developed new norms for the new situations.

B. The Increasing Rationalization of Activities

Ever since the industrial revolution, there has been a growing rationalization of work and other activities so that the paramount criteria for guiding action have become differentiation, specialization, and efficiency in the achievement of limited productive goals. Work has been ripped out of the context of interpersonal relations so that men at work become parts of productive machines rather than parts of a network of social relations. Our churches and our schools, affected by the same forces, have evolved out of the context of human interaction. Large congregations and large classes produce audiences rather than participants in an interpersonal system. Even the family has been stretched apart by the individuated claims upon the time of family members.

These patterns of the present world reduce for all of us the opportunities for communion with others and turn interaction into a superficial information exchange. Many persons are left in the backwash of society, isolated by secondary relations at work and in leisure. They have neither families nor other small associations in which their needs for communion can be satisfied.

That such interpersonal relations are not available to many is dramatically shown by the men and women who cry out for the human touch. The growth of the hippie communes, the appeal of the "Jesus-freak" community, the rapid adoption of "group-grope therapies," and in less dramatic form, the rising incidence of psychiatric needs all demonstrate that many are isolated and alone. The synthetic euphoria of the "trip," individuated, isolating, and lonely, cannot replace the practice of humanistic altruism.

C. The Growth of the Chaotic Society

Philip Hauser has described ours as a "chaotic society," as a result of the population explosion, implosion, and differentiation. Although there may be other causes, we do have a society in which collective patterns of action are crumbling, in which coordination of action is weak or coerced by either convenience or force in which our relations with most people is symbiotic and informed only by temporary expediency. We use language gestures as bludgeons, manipulating others, rather than as tools of communication and communion. In such a society the exploitive, self-serving, and self-aggrandizing attitude is the norm for men who are isolated, alienated, and alone. Empathy is seldom possible for we are not usually involved in the kinds of continuing interaction in which we are permitted or encouraged to identify with another's experience.

Throughout the years preachers and prophets, poets and philosophers, from the Chinese to the Egyptian, from the Mohammedan to the Judeo-Christian, from the pagan to the sophisticated, have seen the necessity for love. They have known that our lives are bleak, barren, and brutish without the communion with others that leads to the altruistic impulse. But love is not enough to build the good society. *Love does not change the human condition, it only makes it human.*

SYMPATHY AND COOPERATIVE ALTRUISM

In every society there are occasions of crisis and catastrophe and painful yokes common to many men. Floods and fires, epidemics and pestilential invasions, subjugation, and poverty attack many men at once. Though these are common conditions, men will often treat them as unique individual problems and seek a solution for themselves alone, suffering not only from their problems but also from "pluralistic ignorance." These may be occasions when each seeks only his own small advantage.

However, sometimes men recognize that theirs is not a unique situation and that others too are suffering as they are suffering. Because they are able, as themselves, to stand in the other's shoes and know something of what the other feels they are able to sympathize with him. They know that they suffer in common and so they may be struck by the altruistic impulse to invite the other to join in a mutual search for some advantage in the situation.

Such cooperative endeavors are found in all societies and at all times. Some cultures have emphasized this approach to life problems and provide models and normative sanctions to promote such action. Other cultures treat life as a zero-sum game in which there is no increase in the total value to be obtained by cooperative effort. Sociologically, we are most aware of cooperative altruism when it is expressed in formal voluntary associations such as the Rochdale Cooperatives formed by the weavers in England in the last century, the mutual benefit societies of the American community, or the attenuated form of legally sanctioned benefit districts. However, the latter may lose their character as cooperative endeavors and become institutional agencies serving clients, their former members.

The essential element in the successful formation of cooperative altruistic efforts is the capacity for sympathy, the ability to stand in each others' shoes, the ability to play the role of the other. Without sympathy there is no possibility of subordinating one's own small advantage to the collective welfare. Thus, the scope of such cooperative organization is limited by both the commonality of the life situation and by the existing patterns of interaction and identity.

The obvious value and success of such organizations in improving the common conditions of life have often led to attempts to generate this form of altruism in similar situations. I am told that in Honduras officials in one government agency were particularly struck by the success of indigenous cooperative farming by the peasants on a certain neglected banana plantation. These officials wanted to promote this form of self-help in other areas and persuaded others to take on the form of this endeavor. However, these subsequent induced cooperatives were beset by "selfish" patterns: individual farmers failed to put their effort into the common enterprise and managers absconded with the funds. The same failures can be found in the United States and in any other locale where the imposition of synthetic cooperative endeavors has been attempted. These failures stem, I believe, from the lack of a common recognition of a common problem among the members of the created group, and from the lack of sympathy and the altruistic impulse which it engenders. When sympathy is lacking, no matter how good the organization looks on paper, each man will use the organization for his own ends, exploiting it for his own purposes and small advantages.

. . . . .

Cooperative altruism, when it does occur, makes three major contributions toward the good society. It changes the material situation and thus alters the process of history, for this particular group at least. The peasants on the banana plantations, the weavers in England, and the small farmers in America were economically better off through the success of their cooperative endeavors. Secondly, by involving coordinate action and patterns of interaction, it reduces for this group the impact of the chaotic, symbiotic society. And finally, by providing opportunities for communication and communion, it increases the opportunity for empathy and the human touch.

ANTHROPOPATHY AND PHILANTHROPY

Empathy occurs when men recognize their common feelings and attitudes and are thus able to sorrow *as one*. *Sympathy* occurs when men share a common situation and thus are able to sorrow *together*. *Anthropopathy* occurs when men are different but recognize the capacity for suffering in others, thus they sorrow *for* others.

Recognizing that others may suffer, some men are struck by the altruistic impulse to do something *for* them, and so they send aid or attempt to organize general programs of relief or assistance to make changes in the other's circumstances—they then express the philanthropic form of altruism.

In contrast to other forms, philanthropy is based upon and increases the separation between those giving and those receiving aid. *Where personal altruism serves primarily to maintain a common identity, and where cooperative altruism increases the strength of the interpersonal relationships, philanthropy serves to widen the gulf between people. Doing for is not doing with or being with.* The very nature of the aid, the fact that it does not necessarily fit the scheme of needs of the receiver, as well as the impersonal and chauvinistic way in which it is presented, often serve as a symbolic affirmation of the differences in situation and circumstances.

Although philanthropy may alter the objective situation of others, it often does so without understanding the nature of their sorrow, the sources of their discomfort, or the character of their conception of the good society. Because of our peculiar folk-psychologies and our implicit beliefs that the poor and others are in trouble because of some motivational or moral failure of their own, we often impose conditions to our philanthropy: to get soup one must first be converted, to secure aid for one's children one must avoid men, to get assistance for the elderly, one must sign away the home of a lifetime. At the very least, one must tug his forelock and bowing low offer humble thanks to his benefactor.

As a result philanthropy, directly or indirectly, often imposes new strands in the spider web of history in which people are caught. We add to the constraints, the forces and impositions over which they have no control. Is it no wonder then that the welfare mothers, the blacks in the ghettos and the natives on the other islands say "whitey (or Uncle or welfare worker) go home, leave us alone!"

I must admit to a jaundiced view of philanthropic efforts for I believe that, as Willie says, "the ideas and attitudes of the subdominants . . . [tend to be] ignored or forgotten." Unless touched by sympathy and empathy, anthropopathy leads to separation and differentiation between those in need and those who aid. The typical anonymity of philanthropy (as for example in giving to the United Fund or Community Chest), is a means of avoiding interaction, of avoiding involvement and its consequences—sympathy and empathy. Most philanthropic efforts probably do more for the philanthropist than for those he purports to aid. The delusion of most philanthropy is that it does good for others. At the very least, we must admit that adequate evaluations are lacking to demonstrate the objective value of philanthropy to the recipients.

Not all philanthropy has been exclusively dominated by anthropopathy. When it has been touched by sympathy and empathy, when those giving aid have become in part those being aided, then such assistance takes on some of the elements of cooperative altruism. But most frequently our philanthropy has become organized and rationalized, bureaucratized and institutionalized. Welfare agencies become more concerned with their domains than with the character of their altruism; and thus become an extension of the problem rather than a solution. Even at best they have focused more upon the objective conditions of men's lives than on their human needs.

But, philanthropy is a necessary element in a society where men are more dissimilar in circumstance and point of view than they are alike. Some are more vulnerable than others to the special disabilities of their time and these disabilities become self-perpetuating and expanding without outside help. If so, then we must learn, more clearly than we have, the appropriate and necessary scope of philanthropy, and how such efforts can be leavened by sympathy and empathy, and how they can be tied to and generate the cooperative and personal forms of altruism.

THE ALTRUISTIC IMPULSE, SOCIAL CHANGE, AND COLLECTIVE ALTRUISM

Altruism in most of its expressions has little impact upon the larger forces and processes that lead to men's sorrows. Personal altruism at best relieves only the very immediate and temporary conditions of men's lives, cooperative altruism can ameliorate broader situational factors and improve the relative advantage of the participants, philanthropy may help remove special disabilities and provide basic sustaining conditions, but none of these forms of altruism as we have described them attack or try to change the fundamental laws, the basic forces, or the global processes that constrain these situations. Although the peasant's lot may be improved through cooperative farming, it does not alter the economic, political, and social forces which produce peasantry. Although philanthropy may sustain life in the poor, it does nothing about the sources of poverty. In sum, much altruistic activity can only purport to deal with the *symptoms* of a problem rather than the problem per se.

In the person of imagination, the concern for others—whether stemming from empathy, sympathy or anthropopathy—takes on an especially poignant form, for he sees one man's catastrophe multiplied by all men. For him the despot's lash on the prisoner's back is a thousand lashes on a thousand backs; the death of a neighbor from puerperal fever is the death of thousands of women in childbirth; the starving child of the street is a million children of neglect.

The arms of such a person cannot succor all these lonely children of God and so he seeks to find a new world in which pain and suffering no longer exist. His altruistic impulse leads him to seek a change in the conditions of pain and sorrow for all, not just to alleviate the burden of those present or to share the sorrow of those he knows.

Some of these men remain dreamers and draftsmen, content to portray their vision of the world-that-should-be in poems and pictures. But other men of imagination seek more active expressions of their concern. They attempt to take action upon the sources of man's difficulties; such men seek to change the world by re-forming it, either by revolution or reformation.

When the gap between his vision of the good and the present condition of man is blatant, and when his world view is apocalyptic and cataclysmic, such a man will turn to revolution and attempt the total destruction of the present social world. He feels that only through the ashes of the present can the eden of the future be built.

Although this position may genuinely stem from the altruistic impulse, it is often difficult to see the altruism; for such a position requires the willingness to sacrifice many men today in order to hope for the future. It is a view that only the most alienated and impatient of us can afford to accept because it requires the rejection of empathy and sympathy.

There are others, however, whose vision and impatience for the good society are tempered by sympathy for the man who is living today. He is unwilling to pay the present cost for a dramatic new world tomorrow. He therefore seeks re-formulation of the world through less drastic processes. It is true that often such men would have much to lose by putting the present world to the torch for they are not without hope. And because they are hopeful, they can afford sympathy and empathy.

This form of collective altruism leads to a variety of movements, programs, and associations designed to change in some large or small measure the process of history for all men. Sometimes these efforts are misguided for lack of knowledge or for mistaken belief; sometimes they fail for lack of leverage and the means to achieve the ends sought. Success, furthermore, is often hard to perceive or lies only in a vision of the future. Despite these limitations, there appears to have been a significant increase in this form of collective altruism in recent years—the Zero Population Growth programs, the attacks on pollution, and Common Cause are among the more recent manifestations of collective concern leading to collective action. These collective actions often seem a long way from the altruistic impulse. Men may use such movements and organizations for their own purposes. Kooks, firebrands, and misanthropes may play out their own nightmares within the shelter of new movements. On the other side, programs may be caught up in bureaucratic forms and self-serving, self-sustaining practices which lose sight of the altruistic collective goals with which they started.

The frequent failure of such programs from lack of knowledge leads some to believe that we can achieve this part of the search for the good society only through improved knowledge of the basic processes and principles of the world. This often leads to the expression of the altruistic impulse by the turning toward science and the search for knowledge. I suspect that for many . . . , as for myself, the humanitarian sentiment was at least one factor in our career decisions. . . .

It is often difficult to mobilize men to act in collective altruistic movements. The immediate improvement for their own and others' lives appears small and the future seems a long way off. More importantly, participation depends upon confidence in the knowledge which specifies the relation between the latent, hidden and abstract forces and the particulars which we wish to change. Most of all, there must be a vision of and confidence in the better society as emerging from the present.

But without effective, informed, and visionary collective altruism we shall be unable to get out of the constraint of the web of history. It is for this reason that we must learn how to organize and sustain such efforts, whether through already established institutions (whether voluntary, commercial, or of government) or through new organizations and new kinds of collective behavior.

93.

IGNORANCE IS STRENGTH

George Orwell

Lightened in part by a boy-meets-girl theme, the novel *1984* from which this selection is taken is, nevertheless, a deadly serious, satirical exposition of life as it might become in a totalitarian society. Its author, George Orwell, develops to their logical limits the characteristics of the institutions in modern authoritarian cultures. In this excerpt, Orwell sets forth the rationale and method of operation of his 1984 society. He begins with the contention that modern science and mass production have made it technically possible to eliminate the great class differences in material and mental well-being that have heretofore characterized the major so-

Source: George Orwell, *1984* (New York: Harcourt, Brace and Jovanovich, 1949), pp. 208–18.

George Orwell (1903–1950), a nom de plume for Eric Arthur Blair, was a British novelist and essayist. He was born in Motihari, India, of Anglo-Indian parents. He served on the Republican side in the Spanish Civil War, and one result of his time as a soldier was his book *Homage to Catalonia.* He also wrote *Down and Out in Paris and London, Burmese Days,* and *Animal Farm.*

cieties of the world. Orwell then describes how, in the face of this possibility, a ruling class can still maintain itself in power through carefully calculated strategies such as the use of "doublethink" and the firm guidance of "Big Brother."

Throughout recorded time, and probably since the end of the Neolithic Age, there have been three kinds of people in the world, the High, the Middle, and the Low. They have been subdivided in many ways, they have borne countless different names, and their relative numbers, as well as their attitude toward one another, have varied from age to age; but the essential structure of society has never altered. Even after enormous upheavals and seemingly irrevocable changes, the same pattern has always reasserted itself, just as a gyroscope will always return to equilibrium, however far it is pushed one way or the other. . . .

The aims of these groups are entirely irreconcilable. The aim of the High is to remain where they are. The aim of the Middle is to change places with the High. The aim of the Low, when they have an aim—for it is an abiding characteristic of the Low that they are too much crushed by drudgery to be more than intermittently conscious of anything outside their daily lives—is to abolish all distinctions and create a society in which all men shall be equal. Thus throughout history a struggle which is the same in its main outlines recurs over and over again. For long periods the High seem to be securely in power, but sooner or later there always comes a moment when they lose either their belief in themselves, or their capacity to govern efficiently, or both. They are then overthrown by the Middle, who enlist the Low on their side by pretending to them that they are fighting for liberty and justice. As soon as they have reached their objective, the Middle thrust the Low back into their old position of servitude, and themselves become the High. Presently a new Middle group splits off from one of the other groups, or from both of them, and the struggle begins over again. Of the three groups, only the Low are never even temporarily successful in achieving their aims. It would be an exaggeration to say that throughout history there had been no progress of a material kind. Even today, in a period of decline, the average human being is physically better off than he was a few centuries ago. But no advance in wealth, no softening of manners, no reform or revolution has ever brought human equality a millimeter nearer. From the point of view of the Low, no historic change has ever meant much more than a change in the name of their masters.

By the late nineteenth century the recurrences of this pattern had become obvious to many observers. There then arose schools of thinkers who interpreted history as a cyclical process and claimed to show that inequality was the unalterable law of human life. This doctrine, of course, had always had its adherents, but in the manner in which it was now put forward there was a significant change. In the past the need for a hierarchical form of society had been the doctrine specifically of the High. It had been preached by kings and aristocrats and by the priests, lawyers, and the like who were parasitical upon them, and it had generally been softened by promises of compensation in an imaginary world beyond the grave. The Middle, so long as it was struggling for power, had always made use of such terms as freedom, justice, and fraternity. Now, however, the concept of human brotherhood began to be assailed by people who were not yet in positions of command, but merely hoped to be so before long. In the past the Middle had made revolutions under the banner of equality, and then had established a fresh tyranny as soon as the old one was overthrown. The new Middle groups in effect proclaimed their tyranny beforehand. Socialism, a theory which appeared in the early nineteenth century and was the last link in a chain of thought stretching back to the slave rebellions of antiquity, was still deeply infected by the Utopianism of past ages. But in each variant of Socialism that appeared from about 1900 onwards the aim of establishing liberty and equality was more and more openly abandoned. The new movements which appeared in the middle years of the century, Ingsoc in Oceania, Neo-Bolshevism in Eurasia, Death-worship, as it is commonly called, in Eastasia, had the conscious aim of perpetuating *un*freedom and *in*equality. These new movements, of course, grew out of the old ones and tended to keep their names and pay lip-service to their ideology. But the purpose of all of them was to arrest progress and freeze history at a chosen moment. The familiar pendulum swing was to happen once more, and then stop. As usual, the High were to be turned out by the Middle, who would then become the High; but this time, by conscious strategy, the High would be able to maintain their position permanently.

The new doctrines arose partly because of the accumulation of historical knowledge, and the growth of the historical sense, which had hardly existed before the nineteenth century. The cyclical movement of history was now intelligible, or appeared to be so; and if it was intelligible, then it was alterable. But the principal, underlying cause was that, as early as the beginning of the twentieth century, human equality had become technically possible. It was still true that men were not equal in their native talents and that functions had to be specialized in ways that favored some individuals against others; but there was no longer any real need for class distinctions or for large differences of wealth. In earlier ages, class distinctions had been not only inevitable but desirable. Inequality was the price of civilization. With the development of machine production, however, the case was altered. Even if it was still necessary for human beings to do different kinds of work, it was no longer necessary for them to live at different social or economic levels. Therefore, from the point of view of the new groups who were on the point of seizing power, human equality was no longer an ideal to be striven after, but a danger to be averted. In more primitive ages, when a just and peaceful society was in fact not possible, it had been fairly easy to believe in it. The idea of an earthly paradise in which men should live together in a state of brotherhood, without laws and without brute labor, had haunted the human imagination for thousands of years. And this vision had had a certain hold even on the groups who actually profited by each historic change. The heirs of the French, English, and American revolutions had partly believed in their own phrases about the rights of man, freedom of speech, equality before the law, and the like, and had even allowed their conduct to be influenced by them to some extent. But by the fourth decade of the twentieth century all the main currents of political thought were authoritarian. The earthly paradise had been discredited at exactly the moment when it became realizable. Every new political theory, by whatever name it called itself, led back to hierarchy and regimentation. And in the general hardening of outlook that set in round about 1930, practices which had been long abandoned, in some cases for hundreds of years—imprisonment without trial, the use of war prisoners as slaves, public executions, torture to extract confessions, the use of hostages and the deportation of whole populations—not only became common again, but were tolerated and even defended by people who considered themselves enlightened and progressive.

It was only after a decade of national wars, civil wars, revolutions and counter-revolutions in all parts of the world that Ingsoc and its rivals emerged as fully worked-out political theories. But they had been foreshadowed by the various systems, generally called totalitarian, which had appeared earlier in the century, and the main outlines of the world which would emerge from the prevailing chaos had long been obvious. What kind of people would control this world had been equally obvious. The new aristocracy was made up for the most part of bureaucrats, scientists, technicians, trade-union organizers, publicity experts, sociologists, teachers, journalists, and professional politicians. These people, whose origins lay in the salaried middle class and the upper grades of the working class, had been shaped and brought together by the barren world of monopoly industry and centralized government. As compared with their opposite numbers in past ages, they were less avaricious, less tempted by luxury, hungrier for pure power, and, above all, more conscious of what they were doing and more intent on crushing opposition. This last difference was cardinal. By comparison with that existing today, all the tyrannies of the past were half-hearted and inefficient. The ruling groups were always infected to some extent by liberal ideas, and were content to leave loose ends everywhere, to regard only the overt act, and to be uninterested in what their subjects were thinking. Even the Catholic Church of the Middle Ages was tolerant by modern standards. Part of the reason for this was that in the past no government had the power to keep its citizens under constant surveillance. The invention of print, however, made it easier to manipulate public opinion, and the film and the radio carried the process further. With the development of television, and the technical advance which made it possible to receive and transmit simultaneously on the same instrument, private life came to an end. Every citizen, or at least every citizen important enough to be worth watching, could be kept for twenty-four hours a day under the eyes of the police and in the sound of official propaganda, with all other channels of communication closed. The possibility of enforcing not only complete obedience to the will of the State, but complete uniformity of opinion on all subjects, now existed for the first time.

After the revolutionary period of the Fifties and Sixties, society regrouped itself, as always, into High, Middle, and Low. But the new High group, unlike all its forerunners, did not act upon instinct but knew what was needed to safeguard its position. It had long been realized that the only secure basis for oligarchy is collectivism. Wealth and privilege are most easily defended when they are possessed jointly. The so-called "abolition of private property" which took place in the middle years of the century meant, in effect, the concentration of property in far fewer hands than before; but with this difference, that the new owners were a group instead of a mass of individuals. Individually, no member of the Party owns anything, except petty personal belongings. Collectively, the Party owns everything in Oceania, because it controls everything and disposes of the products as it thinks fit. In the years following the Revolution it was able to step into this commanding position almost unopposed, because the whole process was represented as an act of collectivization. It had always been assumed that if the capitalist class were expropriated, Socialism must follow; and unquestionably the capitalists had been expropriated. Factories, mines, land, houses, transport—everything had been taken away from them; and since these things were no longer private property, it followed that they must be public property. Ingsoc, which grew out of the earlier Socialist movement and inherited its phraseology, has in fact carried out the main item in the Socialist program, with the result, foreseen and intended beforehand, that economic inequality has been made permanent.

But the problems of perpetuating a hierarchical society go deeper than this. There are only four ways in which a ruling group can fall from power. Either it is conquered from without, or it governs so inefficiently that the masses are stirred to revolt, or it allows a strong and discontented Middle Group to come into being, or it loses its own self-confidence and willingness to govern. These causes do not operate singly, and as a rule all four of them are present in some degree. A ruling class which could guard against all of them would remain in power permanently. Ultimately the determining factor is the mental attitude of the ruling class itself.

After the middle of the present century, the first danger had in reality disappeared. Each of the three powers which now divide the world is in fact unconquerable, and could only become conquerable through slow demographic changes which a government with wide powers can easily avert. The second danger, also, is only a theoretical one. The masses never revolt of their own accord, and they never revolt merely because they are oppressed. Indeed, so long as they are not permitted to have standards of comparison they never even become aware that they are oppressed. The recurrent economic crises of past times were totally unnecessary and are not now permitted to happen, but other and equally large dislocations can and do happen without having political results, because there is no way in which discontent can become articulate. As for the problem of overproduction, which has been latent in our society since the development of machine technique, it is solved by the device of continuous warfare, which is also useful in keying up public morale to the necessary pitch. From the point of view of our present rulers, therefore, the only genuine dangers are the splitting-off of a new group of able, underemployed, power-hungry people, and the growth of liberalism and skepticism in their own ranks. The problem, that is to say, is educational. It is a problem of continuously molding the consciousness both of the directing group and of the larger executive group that lies immediately below it. The consciousness of the masses needs only to be influenced in a negative way.

Given this background, one could infer, if one did not know it already, the general structure of Oceanic society. At the apex of the pyramid comes Big Brother. Big Brother is infallible and all-powerful. Every success, every achievement, every victory, every scientific discovery, all knowledge, all wisdom, all happiness, all virtue, are held to issue directly from his leadership and inspiration. Nobody has ever seen Big Brother. He is a face on the hoardings, a voice on the telescreen. We may be reasonably sure that he will never die, and there is already considerable uncertainty as to when he was born. Big Brother is the guise in which the Party chooses to exhibit itself to the world. His function is to act as a focusing point for love, fear, and reverence, emotions which are more easily felt toward an individual than toward an organization. Below Big Brother comes the Inner Party, its numbers limited to six million, or something less than two percent of the population of Oceania. Below the Inner Party comes the Outer Party, which, if the Inner Party is described as the brain of the State, may be justly likened to the hands. Below that come the dumb masses whom we habitually refer to as "the proles," numbering perhaps eighty-five percent of the population. In the terms of our earlier classification, the proles are the Low, for the slave populations of the equatorial lands, who pass constantly from conqueror to conqueror, are not a permanent or necessary part of the structure.

In principle, membership in these three groups is not hereditary. The child of Inner Party parents is in theory not born into the Inner Party. Admission to either branch of the Party is by examination, taken at the age of sixteen. Nor is there any racial discrimination, or any marked domination of one province by another. Jews, Negroes, South Americans of pure Indian blood are to be found in the highest ranks of the Party, and the administrators of any area are always drawn from the inhabitants of that area. In no part of Oceania do the inhabitants have the feeling that they are a colonial population ruled from a distant capital. Oceania has no capital, and its titular head is a person whose whereabouts nobody knows. Except that English is its chief lingua franca and Newspeak its official language, it is not centralized in any way. Its rulers are not held together by blood ties but by adherence to a common doctrine. It is true that our society is stratified, and very rigidly stratified, on what at first sight appear to be hereditary lines. There is far less to-and-fro movement between the different groups than happened under capitalism or even in the preindustrial ages. Between the two branches of the Party there is a certain amount of interchange, but only so much as will ensure that weaklings are excluded from the Inner Party and that ambitious members of the Outer Party are made harmless by allowing them to rise. Proletarians, in practice, are not allowed to graduate into the Party. The most gifted among them, who might possibly become nuclei of discontent, are simply marked down by the Thought Police and eliminated. But this state of affairs is not necessarily permanent, nor is it a matter of principle. The Party is not a class in the old sense of the word. It does not aim at transmitting power to its own children, as such; and if there were no other way of keeping the ablest people at the top, it would be perfectly prepared to recruit an entire new generation from the ranks of the proletariat. In the crucial years, the fact that the Party was not a hereditary body did a great deal to neutralize opposition. The older kind of Socialist, who had been trained to fight against something called "class privilege," assumed that what is not hereditary cannot be permanent. He did not see that the continuity of an oligarchy need not be physical, nor did he pause to reflect that hereditary aristocracies have always been shortlived, whereas adoptive organizations such as the Catholic Church have sometimes lasted for hundreds or thousands of years. The essence of oligarchical rule is not father-to-son inheritance, but the persistence of a certain world-view and a certain way of life, imposed by the dead upon the living. A ruling group is a ruling group so long as it can nominate its successors. The Party is not concerned with perpetuating its blood but with perpetuating itself. *Who* wields power is not important, provided that the hierarchical structure remains always the same.

All the beliefs, habits, tastes, emotions,

mental attitudes that characterize our time are really designed to sustain the mystique of the Party and prevent the true nature of present-day society from being perceived. Physical rebellion, or any preliminary move toward rebellion, is at present not possible. From the proletarians nothing is to be feared. Left to themselves, they will continue from generation to generation and from century to century, working, breeding, and dying, not only without any impulse to rebel, but without the power of grasping that the world could be other than it is. They could only become dangerous if the advance of industrial technique made it necessary to educate them more highly; but, since military and commercial rivalry are no longer important, the level of popular education is actually declining. What opinions the masses hold, or do not hold, is looked on as a matter of indifference. They can be granted intellectual liberty because they have no intellect. In a Party member, on the other hand, not even the smallest deviation of opinion on the most unimportant subject can be tolerated.

A Party member lives from birth to death under the eye of the Thought Police. Even when he is alone he can never be sure that he is alone. Wherever he may be, asleep or awake, working or resting, in his bath or in bed, he can be inspected without warning and without knowing that he is being inspected. Nothing that he does is indifferent. His friendships, his relaxations, his behavior toward his wife and children, the expression of his face when he is alone, the words he mutters in sleep, even the characteristic movements of his body, are all jealously scrutinized. Not only any actual misdemeanor, but any eccentricity, however small, any change of habits, any nervous mannerism that could possibly be the symptom of an inner struggle, is certain to be detected. He has no freedom of choice in any direction whatever. On the other hand, his actions are not regulated by law or by any clearly formulated code of behavior. In Oceania there is no law. Thoughts and actions which, when detected, mean certain death are not formally forbidden, and the endless purges, arrests, tortures, imprisonments, and vaporizations are not inflicted as punishment for crimes which have actually been committed, but are merely the wiping-out of persons who might perhaps commit a crime at some time in the future. A Party member is required to have not only the right opinions, but the right instincts. Many of the beliefs and attitudes demanded of him are never plainly stated, and could not be stated without laying bare the contradictions inherent in Ingsoc. If he is a person naturally orthodox (in Newspeak, a *goodthinker*), he will in all circumstances know, without taking thought, what is the true belief or the desirable emotion. But in any case an elaborate mental training, undergone in childhood and grouping itself round the Newspeak words *crimestop, blackwhite,* and *doublethink,* makes him unwilling and unable to think too deeply on any subject whatever.

A Party member is expected to have no private emotions and no respites from enthusiasm. He is supposed to live in a continuous frenzy of hatred of foreign enemies and internal traitors, triumph over victories, and self-abasement before the power and wisdom of the Party. The discontents produced by his bare, unsatisfying life are deliberately turned outwards and dissipated by such devices as the Two Minutes Hate, and the speculations which might possibly induce a skeptical or rebellious attitude are killed in advance by his early acquired inner discipline. The first and simplest stage in the discipline, which can be taught even to young children, is called, in Newspeak, *crimestop. Crimestop* means the faculty of stopping short, as though by instinct, at the threshold of any dangerous thought. It includes the power of not grasping analogies, of failing to perceive logical errors, of misunderstanding the simplest arguments if they are inimical to Ingsoc, and of being bored or repelled by any train of thought which is capable of leading in a heretical direction. *Crimestop,* in short, means protective stupidity. But stupidity is not enough. On the contrary, orthodoxy in the full sense demands a control over one's own mental processes as complete as that of a contortionist over his body. Oceanic society rests ultimately on the belief that Big Brother is omnipotent and that the Party is infallible. But since in reality Big Brother is not omnipotent and the Party is not infallible, there is need for an unwearying, moment-to-moment flexibility in the treatment of facts. The key word here is *blackwhite.* Like so many Newspeak words, this word has two mutually contradictory meanings. Applied to an opponent, it means the habit of impudently claiming that black is white, in contradiction of the plain facts. Applied to a Party member, it means a loyal willingness to say that black is white when Party discipline demands this. But it means also the ability to *believe* that black is white and more, to *know* that black is white, and to forget that one has ever believed the contrary. This demands a continuous alteration of the past, made possible by the system of thought which really embraces all the rest, and which is known in Newspeak as *doublethink.*

The alteration of the past is necessary for two reasons, one of which is subsidiary and, so to speak, precautionary. The subsidiary reason is that the party member, like the proletarian, tolerates present-day conditions partly because he has no standards of comparison. He must be cut off from the past, just as he must be cut off from foreign countries, because it is necessary for him to believe that he is better off than his ancestors and that the average level of material comfort is constantly rising. But by far the more important reason for the readjustment of the past is the need to safeguard the infallibility of the Party. It is not merely that speeches, statistics, and records of every kind must be constantly brought up to date in order to show that the predictions of the Party were in all cases right. It is also that no change of doctrine or in political alignment can ever be admitted. For to change one's mind, or even one's policy, is a confession of weakness. If, for example, Eurasia or Eastasia (whichever it may be) is the enemy today, then that country must always have been the enemy. And if the facts say otherwise, then the facts must be altered. Thus history is continuously rewritten. This day-to-day falsification of the past, carried out by the Ministry of Truth, is as necessary to the stability of the regime as the work of repression and espionage carried out by the Ministry of Love.

The mutability of the past is the central tenet of Ingsoc. Past events, it is argued, have no objective existence, but survive only in written records and in human memories. The past is whatever the records and the memories agree upon. And since the Party is in full control of all records, and in equally full control of the minds of its members, it follows that the past is whatever the Party chooses to make it. It also follows that though the past is alterable, it never has been altered in any specific instance. For when it has been recreated in whatever shape is needed at the moment, then this new version *is* the past, and no different past can ever have existed. This holds good even when, as often happens, the same event has to be altered out of recognition several times in the course of a year. At all times the Party is in possession of absolute truth, and clearly the absolute can never have been different from what it is now. It will be seen that the control of the past depends above all on the training of memory. To make sure that all written records agree with the orthodoxy of the moment is merely a mechanical act. But it is also necessary to *remember* that events happened in the desired manner. And if it is necessary to rearrange one's memories or to tamper with written records, then it is necessary to *forget* that one has done so. The trick of doing this can be learned like any other mental technique. It *is* learned by the majority of Party members, and certainly by all who are intelligent as well as orthodox. In Oldspeak it is called, quite frankly, "reality control." In Newspeak it is called *doublethink,* although *doublethink* comprises much else as well.

Doublethink means the power of holding two contradictory beliefs in one's mind simultaneously, and accepting both of them. The Party intellectual knows in which direction his memories must be altered; he therefore knows that he is playing tricks with reality; but by the exercise of *doublethink* he also satisfies himself that reality is not violated. The process has to be conscious, or it would not be carried out with sufficient precision, but it also has to be unconscious, or it would bring with it a feeling of falsity and hence of guilt. *Doublethink* lies at the very heart of Ingsoc, since the essential act of the Party is to use conscious deception while retaining the firmness of purpose that goes with complete honesty. To tell deliberate lies while genuinely believing in them, to forget any fact that has become inconvenient, and then, when it becomes necessary again, to draw it back from oblivion for just so long as it is needed, to deny the existence of objective reality and all the while to take account of the reality which one denies—all this is indispensably necessary. Even in using the word *doublethink* it is necessary to exercise *doublethink.* For by using the word one admits that one is tampering with reality; by a fresh act of *doublethink* one erases this knowledge; and so on indefinitely, with the lie always one leap ahead of the truth. Ultimately it is by means of *doublethink* that the Party has been able—and may, for all we know, continue to be able for thousands of years—to arrest the course of history.

All past oligarchies have fallen from power either because they ossified or because they grew soft. Either they became stupid and arrogant, failed to adjust themselves to changing circumstances, and were overthrown, or they became liberal and cowardly, made concessions when they should have used force, and once again were overthrown. They fell, that is to say, either through consciousness or through unconsciousness. It is the achievement of the Party to have produced a system of thought in which both conditions can exist simultaneously. And upon no other intellectual basis could the dominion of the Party be made permanent. If one is to rule, and to continue ruling, one must be able to dislocate the sense of reality. For the secret of rulership is to combine a belief in one's own infallibility with the power to learn from past mistakes.

It need hardly be said that the subtlest practitioners of *doublethink* are those who invented *doublethink* and know that it is a vast system of mental cheating. In our society, those who have the best knowledge of what is happening are also those who are furthest from seeing the world as it is. In general, the greater the understanding, the greater the delusion: the more intelligent, the less sane. One clear illustration of this is the fact that war hysteria increases in intensity as one rises in the social scale. Those whose attitude toward the war is most nearly rational are the subject peoples of the disputed territories. To these people the war is simply a continuous calamity which sweeps to and fro over their bodies like a tidal wave. Which side is winning is a matter of complete indifference to them. They are aware that a change of overlordship means simply that they will be doing the same work as before for new masters who treat them in the same manner as the old ones. The slightly more favored workers whom we call "the proles" are only intermittently conscious of the war. When it is necessary they can be prodded into frenzies of fear and hatred, but when left to themselves they are capable of forgetting for long periods that the war is happening. It is in the ranks of the Party, and above all of the Inner Party, that the true war enthusiasm is found. World-conquest is believed in most firmly by those who know it to be impossible. This peculiar linking-together of opposites—knowledge with ignorance, cynicism with fanaticism—is one of the chief distinguishing marks of Oceanic society. The official ideology abounds with contradictions even where there is no practical reason for them. Thus, the Party rejects and vilifies every principle for which the Socialist movement originally stood, and it chooses to do this in the name of Socialism. It preaches a contempt for the working class unexampled for centuries past, and it dresses its members in a uniform which was at one time peculiar to manual workers and was adopted for that reason. It systematically undermines the solidarity of the family, and it calls its leader by a name which is a direct appeal to the sentiments of family loyalty. Even the names of the four Ministries by which we are governed exhibit a sort of impudence in their deliberate reversal of the facts. The Ministry of Peace concerns itself with war, the Ministry of Truth with lies, the Ministry of Love with torture, and the Ministry of Plenty with starvation. These contradictions are not accidental, nor do they result from ordinary hypocrisy: they are deliberate exercises in *doublethink.* For it is only by reconciling contradictions that power can be retained indefinitely. In no other way could the ancient cycle be broken. If human equality is to be forever averted—if the High, as we have called them, are to keep their places permanently—then the prevailing mental condition must be controlled insanity.

But there is one question which until this moment we have almost ignored: It is: *why* should human equality be averted? Supposing that the mechanics of the process have been rightly described, what is the motive for this huge, accurately planned effort to freeze history at a particular moment of time?

Here we reach the central secret. As we have seen, the mystique of the Party, and above all of the Inner Party, depends upon *doublethink.* But deeper than this lies the original motive, the never-questioned instinct that first led to the seizure of power and brought *doublethink,* the Thought Police, continuous warfare, and all the other necessary paraphernalia into existence afterwards. This motive really consists. . . .

94.

AFTER THE COUNTERCULTURE, WHAT?

Doug Campbell

This brief selection examines social change from the perspective of a student who has, as he contends, lived through the era of the counterculture and now sees us standing on the threshold of a new "social contract." He sees the need for a new arrangement of special importance with regard to sexual roles, the social obligations of industry, and property rights. The reader who has explored the principles of social and cultural change should read this selection not only with those ideas in mind but also in the light of his own experiences in contemporary society. Especially significant are Campbell's questions about the possibility of acquiring common goals and values as a basis for the moral order needed to establish and maintain the new social contract.

Religious standards, sexual roles, property rights, the social obligations of industry, and the proper nature of patriotism were the kinds of issues not discussed much in this country until the later 1960s. Before that time, people who spoke against the status quo were either ignored or thoroughly condemned as misfits, pinkos, and bohemian deviates. But somehow – maybe it was the war – the nonconformists gained the offensive and began to intimidate those who held traditional attitudes. And wasn't it disturbing to see how ineffective the defenses for the status quo were, and how many hypocrisies and injustices the dissidents could find in it? And one was regularly surprised to find yet another clean-cut kid from an affluent New Jersey high school deserting the traditional ranks to join the oncoming, beaded enemy. Suddenly "straight" became a pejorative description. Nonconformity was exalted, and to be counted a "freak" was dandy. Misfits, pinkos, and bohemian deviates had won social momentum.

Nowhere was the change more visible than on college and university campuses. Here at Carnegie-Mellon University, for example, in 1970, the year Strom Thurmond was pelted with marshmallows, the yearbook expressed the then dominant attitude towards Education, God, Mom, Society, and the Government through an illustrated dialogue between two characters – one real, one fictional – who characterized themselves respectively as "a bearded commie-pinko-anarchist radical," and as a "clever reprobate, the sultan of obscenity, the pharaoh of degeneracy, the prince of the put-on, the down-and-out king of the ego-trippers, the lion of sloth and the recipient of numerous awards and citations for bad taste and many other derelictions," the final and summary word from these two characters was, "Higher education is a fraud! You've been trained to equate elitist

Source: Doug Campbell, *Chronicle of Higher Education* (October 16, 1972). Reprinted by permission of Carnegie Alumni News.

At the time this article was written, the author was a senior English major at Carnegie-Mellon University in Pittsburgh, Pa.

snobbery with culture—stay at this expensive trade school, if you want, you linear fools! I'm heading for the West Coast." In contrast, the editor of the first CMU yearbook, in 1906, wrote simply, "C-A-R-N-E-G-I-E RAH! RAH! RAH! TECH!"

But today, only two or three years since what we labeled the "counterculture" indisputably dominated the campus, it has lost social momentum. The counterculture has become an ill-defined thing, increasingly more difficult to discern from what it supposedly "counters." It has gained some concessions and made some, and in this manner its former polar relationship to the old culture is being synthesized, gradually, into a new, single culture.

A wound is healing. Students are more flexible socially than they were a decade ago. Individual freedom is this generation's proclaimed common value, and it has necessitated a general increase in social tolerance. Consequently, society's authority over the individual has decreased and, so too, has the individual's concern with the standards of society.

In the college community the results of increased individuality are visible. Student activities are fewer and less ambitious. Involvement in the campus community has dwindled and student organization is dissolving. There is no longer a BMOC sort here—in fact, I'd say that the name or face of no student in this university would be recognized by more than 50 percent of the student body. The need for a yearbook has ceased, and so has the yearbook. Peer pressure has lessened considerably. People seem more relaxed (much more than they were just two years ago) and lend themselves less to being stereotyped.

If we describe what happened during the late '60s as a breakdown in the social contract, then we are presently negotiating a new one. And while I'm certain that the breakdown was not only necessary but inevitable and that our society will be stronger and better for having been through it, I'm not certain what the terms—the values and goals—of the new social contract will be. I do know that they will not be the same as they were.

The old social contract for women is chiseled around the inside of the Margaret Morrison rotunda, now overgrown with ivy:

> To make and inspire the home . . .
> To lessen suffering and increase happiness . . .
> To aid mankind in its upward struggles . . .
> To enable and adorn life's works, however humble . . .
> These are women's high prerogatives.

It told women what they had to do, how important it was that it be done, and that someone would appreciate them if they did it. Andrew Carnegie, after all, attributed a large proportion of his success to his mother. Yet today, the "high prerogative" of making and inspiring the home suggests little more to most university women than cleaning the johns. It is inconceivable that the women of this university will ever again write as they did in 1907, "Here we are going to put into practice our knowledge of the Home Making Arts . . . ; and when all is said and done this is the one thing that appeals most to us."

Perhaps the new role of women will be one of total equality with men. But in recent years the traditional roles and goals of men, too, have been discredited, or at least belittled. Traditionally this university has given its men a liberal-professional education which would enable them to produce and succeed in the world of industry. The 1907 yearbook contains an illustration of a young man, soon to graduate, standing with his wise and paternal professor at the top of a hill, about to start down a path through a giant arched gate. And beyond the gate lies the outside world the eager boy has so long prepared to enter, a world characterized by scores of billowing industrial smokestacks.

But in the course of the last half-dozen years, all industry, no matter how innocuous, has somehow come to be implicitly associated with napalm bombs, exploitation, and piggishness. And although most of our recent graduates have continued to go into industry, they have gone into it quietly, not wishing to attract an activist's self-righteous scorn, and wondering if perhaps they *had* sold out to their corporate masters and really *were* nothing more than insensitive 9-to-5 linear fools, out to exploit the resources of the Third World.

Antiindustrialism is waning now, yet it did succeed in pressuring most businesses to demonstrate a social conscience.

But if the people are to demand that business continue displaying a social conscience, then the people must also recognize the certain property rights that business has. Our morals concerning property have been unclear ever since the misfits, pinkos, and bohemian deviates convinced some of the otherwise intelligent and honest people here that there is a moral distinction between stealing and "ripping-off."

"Ripping-off" has politico-economic connotations. When you "rip-off," you steal from people you think should afford it, people who you feel have taken advantage of less fortunates. It's the Robin Hood syndrome, except in this case Robin isn't giving the booty to the poor, he's just taking it from the corporate, the rich, and the large, and keeping it for himself. And although I do recognize that industry has more than once excused a colossally immoral practice in the name of free enterprise, I find the counterculture's "rip-off" as shamelessly euphemistic as the military's "protective reaction strikes."

In any case, property rights, sexual roles, and the social obligations of industry are among some of the major issues that will be resettled in the new social contract.

Kurt Vonnegut has said that the most frightening moment in his life was when he realized that his high school classmates were running the world. I suppose that's why *Newsweek* starts taking notes every time a Harvard student sneezes. For when today's students are running the world as adults, their present characteristics will no doubt emerge in some recognizable form as the characteristics of established American society. Pacifism, drugs, Eastern philosophy, zero population growth, liberalized sexual mores, yoga, and yogurt—the kinds of things that interested only misfits, pinkos, and bohemian deviates just ten years ago—are now the concerns and life-styles of future civil engineers, technical writers, doctors, metallurgists, architects, biochemists, and lawyers, and even of non-university graduates, such as bricklayers, professional athletes, secretaries, and cab drivers.

From their common goals and values will evolve a new moral order, from which a commonly acceptable social contract will be produced. But in saying this I am supposing that a moral order can be established without a basis in religion or, at least, in fear. That is a large supposition. I don't know that humanistic morality can hold the great masses of society together for very long.

Maintaining general participation in the social contract without the aid of organized religion or fear, especially with a continued valuing of maximum individual freedoms, will be the most significant, critical, and difficult challenge facing today's students as adults. And should they fail, I fully expect that misfits, brown shirts, and theological fanatics, will rile up the young, gain the social momentum, declare that the individual's rights are selfish and must be secondary to society's rights, and finally impose a rigid moral order upon general society which will exact its participation in a new social contract of their own design.

95.

TO DROP OUT, OR NOT TO

Harry Edwards

The student revolution of the last decade, analyzed by Keniston in Selection 78, is challenged by a black sociologist, Harry Edwards, in this selection. Dr. Edwards maintains student activists have been ineffective as change agents. Rather they have contributed to elitist and reactionary changes in America. He proposes an alternative "revolutionary conformity" as a more effective avenue for social change.

Antiestablishment activity is not conducive to either immediate or long-range humanitarian change merely because it confronts the establishment, violates established order or is destructive of traditional processes and procedures. In fact, at the student movement's present stage, the more productive of change any given action is, the greater the likelihood is that

Source: Harry Edwards, *Intellectual Digest* (September 1972): 20–21. Copyright © 1972 by Communications/Research/Machines, Inc. Reprinted by permission of *Intellectual Digest*.

Harry Edwards is professor of sociology at the University of California at Berkeley. Edwards led the 1968 Olympic boycott.

such change can be more expeditiously implemented through established channels.

Because of the unique character of academic life and the relatively vague, nondescript roles, responsibilities and liabilities of the "students" in communities bordering upon the campus, not only is there potential for highly visible, aberrant, unproductive—though invariably well-intentioned—activity by this group, but students are behaving in a manner irrelevant to and destructive of not only the students' immediate concerns but also of their expressed goals of humanity and brotherhood. The responsibility for this tragic waste of human potential cannot be laid *in toto* upon the blatant discrepancy between what America as a nation claims to be or ought to be and what this country in fact *is*. The hypocrisy and the insanity of America are *the* chief problems facing any group desiring progressive change.

I would say to students that ultimately the waste in human potential, in terms of the difference between what you as a generation have become and what you could be, must be measured by the difference between what you are doing and what you can do. In the years to come, it will wax increasingly clear that the most vocal, activist elements of the "turned-on generation" have not in 1972 turned on to the fact that great challenges to mankind historically have not been confronted and conquered because given social and political conditions did or did not hold sway. Rather, truly dedicated people have met moral challenges *despite* the adversities and obstacles characteristic of the situations they confronted.

Equally tragic is that activist students have not been able to see the sophistry underlying their definitions of what constitutes legitimate bases from which to launch constructive attacks aimed at change. Despite their awareness and sophistication—unmatched by any comparable age group within any past generation—students continue to couch much of the rationale for their activities in rhetoric, in explanations that don't explain anything, in answers that answer nothing. Everything becomes simplistic. You are either in or you are out. You are here or you are there; either you are absolutely part of the solution or you are absolutely part of the problem.

The real choice for the student dedicated to constructive and progressive change is not between working within the system and outside of it, but between revolutionary conformity and renunciatory or reactionary radicalism.

As a result of speaking tours to more than 200 college campuses over the last five years (speaking engagements that eventually earned me a position on Congressman Richard Ichord's House Internal Security Committee list of 57 radical and/or revolutionary campus speakers), I have concluded that many of the various forms that student radicalism have taken have been extremely elitist, renunciatory and reactionary.

What could be more irrelevant to the professed goals of the humanitarian, anti-establishment generation, including bringing about more positive outcomes for the oppressed, than the trend toward living in communes—a style of life that can be pursued by the few only as long as it is beyond the reach of the masses?

My observations of the college campuses have led me to another conclusion. Student demonstrations and physical confrontations with authority have been, all too often, ill conceived, poorly organized (or not organized at all), misguided and a tragic expenditure of effort and energy. They could not have been more reactionary in impact or more destructive of progressive potential and goals if they had been planned, organized and implemented by Barry Goldwater, James Eastland and the Daughters of the American Revolution.

The political establishment and the news media have played prominent roles in the perpetuation of this paradox. Nothing makes better grist for the political mills than the specter of students running amuck. In the mind of the nine-to-five American neanderthal, nothing is more reprehensible than the thought that *his* tax money is supporting a generation of freeloaders who have chosen to bomb, riot, show disrespect for established authority and denigrate the flag rather than pursue the purely educational goals that *he* never had an opportunity to achieve. Here one must consider the question of whether the goal of this generation is to convince and persuade or to alienate the masses of Americans.

Student radicals have taken the assumption that anything of importance is at some point reported on TV, and they have twisted it into the presumption that, unless something receives TV coverage, it is unimportant, and even more significantly, it is unproductive of change.

Students have confused significance with sensationalism, goal-directedness and productivity with publicity (or more accurately, with notoriety). Finally, they have managed to precipitate what all the Nixons, Reagans and Hoovers of the last two decades could never have accomplished—the perversion of the energies, progressive intentions and humanitarian values of America's most activist, best educated and empathetic generation into one of the most reactionary forces on the political scene today. For lest we forget Chicago, not only did radical students contribute to the dumping of Johnson, but also in large part they precipitated the election of Nixon and the establishment of the most reactionary federal administration of the last two decades.

Alternatives to renunciatory and reactionary radicalism must be defined and pursued, not only so that we can salvage what remains of our activist energies but also so that we can realize the degree of visible, enduring goal achievement sufficient to sustain and nurture our humanitarian efforts. Unless such an alternative is arrived at, the next stage of the student movement is all too clear.

Already manifest are the insidious insignia of a defeated order, a people whose efforts and intentions have been perpetually thwarted, whose spirit has been broken by a succession of hopes destroyed, dreams that turned into nightmares and plans never realized. I do not feel it to be coincidental that the look and manner of many of my most radical, intelligent and concerned students are greatly reminiscent of the demeanor with which I became so familiar in the black ghetto of East St. Louis, Illinois.

Neither do I feel that drug abuse, overdoses, the degradation of the human body, the various escapist trips and the overnight conversions to all manner of new-found religious sects to be coincidental. I have seen it all before in the ghetto—and as any competent sociologist can tell you, when such self-defeating phenomena as these are found to be peculiar to a particular group in American society, they usually result from dreams deferred too long, efforts negated.

For students and this generation of young in general, however, there remains an alternative and as yet unexplored avenue: they owe it to both themselves and humanity to develop it into a full-fledged movement of the scope of the peace and civil rights movements or the New Left.

This avenue I call "revolutionary conformity." Its main feature is that rather than dropping out or engaging in the most ludicrous kinds of confrontation since the lions ate lunch at the Colosseum, you get involved in the system, you use established channels.

But rather than going with the prevailing power flow from the top to the bottom of the social order, your efforts are aimed primarily against the flow; you swim upstream, so to speak.

This tack is hard work. Revolutionary conformity involves twice the effort conformity per se does, and it consumes the amount of energy expended in reactionary radicalism, not to speak of such forms of renunciatory radicalism as the commune movement. But the potential for reward is immensely greater and, overall, the cost is less.

Two of the most productive antiestablishment people in America today have nothing approaching long hair; neither wears even a mustache; and neither would be caught outside his bedroom without his drab business suit, his white shirt and tie or his attaché case.

These two individuals are Ralph Nader and Charles Garry.

Charles Garry must know the law better than his adversaries do, because although he is moving through established channels, he is moving against the current of the system that the inequitable application of the law maintains.

Ralph Nader must be able to bring at least as much factual information to bear on the professed, as opposed to the actual, functioning, quality and durability of consumer goods as General Motors, General Foods or the Ford Motor Company can.

Securing such information involves not only a thorough knowledge of what the establishment knows and desires to perpetuate but also a rational and functional grasp of alternatives to established structures, means and products. I have never read an irrelevant book or taken an irrelevant course. The reason is simply that everything I have encountered in the course of my education has been either something that I can use or something that eventually I would have to deal with—whether it is an idea, an attitude or sheer incompetence or ignorance. The same is true for the revolutionary conformist.

If there has been a single ubiquitous fact of your lives, it has been change itself. The question for you has always been not whether change will come about in any particular sphere, but only *what direction that change will take.* Now it is your chief task to control that change through rational and constructive efforts, and I believe that revolutionary conformity is the means.

You do not need a long line of letters after your name to be effective. Any number of properly credentialed functionaries would gladly front for students and guide them through the necessary channels until enough of you are properly credentialed. The only difference between a lawyer and a law student, a sociologist and a sociology student, a medical doctor and a medical student, a political scientist and a political science student, a city planner and a city-planning student, is a matter of credentials. And lack of credentials need not limit competence at feeding information to those sources that can best use it in pursuit of humanitarian social change.

Students have pioneered many of the tactics that became milestones. I hope you will take this next and potentially most productive step toward a more just, humane and tolerant American society.

Right on.

96.

THE PREVENTION OF WORLD WAR III

Kenneth E. Boulding

The preceding selection examines the need for change in America and suggests methods for moving toward "a more just, humane, and tolerant American society." This selection examines the need for change not at the national but at the international level—specifically with regard to the threat of conflict between nation-states. Though significant changes for the better have taken place in the relationship among the great powers recently, Boulding's basic points, made more than a decade ago, remain as urgent as before. He suggests five stages which he feels we need to move through if we are to avert the complete extinction of civilization which another major war could bring about.

When we talk about preventing something we imply two things. We imply, first, that there is a dynamic system which is now proceeding that, if allowed to proceed unchanged, will result in an event which is regarded as undesirable and which, therefore, we want to prevent. We imply also that it is possible to change the dynamic system in question and replace it by another dynamic system in which the unwanted event does not occur. Thus, suppose we find ourselves driving towards a railroad crossing and suddenly we see the red lights flashing and a train approaching. Our dynamic system at the moment consists simply of velocity and direction. We are proceeding, say at 50 miles per hour, towards the crossing. The distant early warning system of our eyes informs us the crossing is dangerous. The knowledge which we have of our existing dynamic system informs us that if it continues we will arrive at the crossing at the precise moment when the train is there. The combination of a distant information system coupled with the simple dynamics of automobiles enables us, however, to prevent the disaster. We do this by putting on the brakes long before we get to the crossing. This in effect changes the dynamic system under which we have been operating. It introduces a new variable into it, indeed a new dimension, deceleration. Because of this, we are able to avoid simultaneous occupancy of the crossing by ourselves and the train.

We must be careful, of course, in applying the analogy of a simple psycho-mechanical system like a man driving a car to the enormous complexities and uncertainties of the international system. However, the international system is still

Source: Kenneth E. Boulding, *The Virginia Quarterly Review* 38, no. 1 (Winter 1962): 1–12. Reprinted by permission of the publisher.

Kenneth E. Boulding is a professor of economics at the University of Colorado, Boulder. He is director of the program on general social and economic dynamics at the Institute for Behavioral Science. Among his many published works are *Economics of Peace, Disarmament and the Economy,* and *Peace and the War Industry.*

a system, even though it has important random elements in it. Because it is not entirely random, it has elements of predictability. One of the greatest difficulties lies precisely in the stochastic nature of the system. We are driving a car, as it were, that may or may not respond to brakes according to whether dice held by the driver indicate "respond" or "fail." The situation is made all the more difficult by the fact that we face here a stochastic system with a very small universe, that is, a very small number of cases. Stochastic systems with a large number of cases can be treated by the theory of probability. We have a pretty fair idea, for instance, how many people are going to die in automobile accidents next year, although we do not know exactly who they are.

The problem of reducing the total number of automobile accidents is a very diffierent kind of problem from the one that faces the driver of the preceding paragraph. Nevertheless, even with our present knowledge it would not be difficult to design an automobile and a road system which would kill, let us say, 20,000 people a year instead of 40,000. What we would be doing here would be to reduce the probability of disaster on the part of a single individual. It is by no means impossible to think of the international system in a rather similar way, and to talk about the things we can do to reduce the probability of disaster. What we mean by this is that if we had a very large number of planets roughly identical with our own we could postulate changes in the system which would reduce the number of cases in which disaster occurred. This would be the analogue of treating road deaths as a public health problem and seeking to reduce their probability. As far as we know, however, we do not have a large number of planets like ours and for our purposes at least there is only one. Hence, reducing the probability of disaster does us very little good if the disaster actually occurs. The problem of stochastic systems with a small number of cases has received insufficient attention in the theoretical literature. It is precisely this kind of system, however, with which we have to deal in international affairs.

I believe the present international system to be one which has a significant probability built into it of irretrievable disaster for the human race. The longer the number of years we contemplate such a system operating, the larger this probability becomes. I do not know whether in any one year it is one percent, ten percent, or even fifty percent. I feel pretty sure, however, that it is of this order of magnitude, not, shall we say, of the order of magnitude of .01 percent. The problem of system change, therefore, is urgent and desperate, and we are all in terrible danger. This is largely because of a quantitative change in the parameters of the international system under which we now live. This is still essentially the system of unilateral national defense in spite of the development of the United Nations and certain international organizations. Unilateral national defense is workable only if each nation can be stronger than its potential enemies in its home territory. This is possible under two circumstances. The first is that the nations must be far enough away from each other, and the extent to which their power declines as they operate further away from home bases must be sufficiently great. Then each nation can be stronger than the other *at home* with on-the-spot forces because of the fact that in a nation's home territory the enemy operates at a certain disadvantage. There is a second condition, however, which is that each nation must be able to dominate an area around its home base equal in depth to the range of the deadly missile. Because of quantitative changes in these conditions even in the last few years the system of unilateral national defense has become infeasible on a world scale. No nation is now far enough away from potential enemies to be sure that it can dominate even its own territory. Furthermore, the range of the deadly missile is rapidly reaching 12,500 miles, which means that the second condition cannot possibly be fulfilled. The condition which unilateral national defense attempts to establish, therefore, which I call *unconditional viability,* is now no longer possible.

The urgent and desperate nature of the present situation is created by the universality of the disaster with which we are threatened. The system of unilateral national defense has never given permanent security. The rise and fall of nations and empires is a testament to this fact. Indeed, looking with a large historical eye, one may say that unconditional viability has never existed except perhaps for brief periods and the best that unilateral national defense could do for any society was to postpone disaster. The situation of the individual society, that is, is rather analogous to that of the individual, whose life, on this earth at any rate, must also end in irretrievable disaster, that is, in death. Where we have a large number of individuals, however, death for the individual is not death for the race. In fact death for the individual is necessary if the race is to survive. Where the number of individuals becomes smaller and smaller, however, there comes to be a critical point where death for the individual is also death for the race and the irretrievable disaster which the individual suffers is likewise irretrievable disaster for the species. The unilaterally defended national state now seems to me to have got to this state in its development. It is no longer appropriate as a form of organization for the kind of technical society in which we live. Its death throes, however, may destroy the whole human race. The age of civilization out of which we are passing was characterized by a large number of nation-states or independent political organizations practicing unilateral national defense. Because of the large number of these organizations there were always some being born and always some ready to rise into the places of those which suffered disaster. With the number of effectively independent nation-states now reduced to two or perhaps at most three, the possibilities of irretrievable disaster become much greater.

The problem which we face, therefore, is how to effect a system change in the international order, or perhaps we should say the world political order, sufficient to lower the probability of disaster to a tolerable level. The critical problem here might be described as that of "system perception." To revert again to the analogy of the car and the railroad crossing, if the driver of the car does not see that he is approaching the crossing, if the warning lights are not working, and if he cannot see the train approaching, he will naturally not take any steps to avert the disaster. The world problem here is perhaps psychological rather than mechanical. There is a fairly widespread sense abroad of impending doom. The doom, however, is so large that we do not really believe it and we go about our daily actions as if it did not exist. This is the mechanism, as Jerome Frank has pointed out, known to the psychologists as "denial." Up to a point this is actually healthy. We all know that we are going to die sometime and we may die tomorrow; but we act pretty much as if we are going to live forever. We do not spend much time in taking tearful farewells and in writing out last wills and testaments. We plan ahead for months and even for years, in spite of the fact that these plans may never come to fruition. This perfectly legitimate response to uncertainty becomes pathological when it prevents us from taking steps which would postpone disaster or make it less likely. The man who is afraid that he has a cancer but who will not go to a doctor because he might find out that he has one is a good example. Where the prospect of disaster, therefore, is so vague or so uncertain that it merely results in pathological denial, it is necessary to bring the actor to a more realistic appraisal of the system within which he is acting.

If the problem of "denial" is to be overcome, it is necessary to do more than merely scare people with horrendous pictures of the possible future. Indeed, the more horrendous the picture which is drawn, the more it is likely to result in denial and pathological inactivity. The future which faced our driver at the railroad crossing was also horrendous, but instead of denying this and continuing on his way he presumably applied the brakes, that is, initiated a system change. The problem in the international system is that we seem to have no brakes. That is, it is hard for people to visualize the nature of the system change which is necessary for survival. This, then, is one of the major tasks today of the political scientist, the philosopher, the journalist, and the prophet: to give the people an image of changes in the international system which seems small enough to be feasible yet large enough to be successful. It is not useful to picture Utopias which seem utterly unattainable—this perhaps is the main difficulty with the World Federationists—even though the function of Utopias in providing a constant driving force in social dynamics should not be underestimated. The present situation, however, calls not for Utopia, but for political solutions. Indeed, one of our great difficulties today is that we have too many Utopias. We need to think, therefore, in terms of a world social contract: that is, a minimum bargain between the contending parties which will give the world a sufficient system change to relieve it from the intolerable burden which it now bears. This social contract does not even have to be explicit or contractual. It can begin by being tacit; indeed, one can argue that a world social contract already exists in a tacit embryo form. We can visualize perhaps the following five stages of development.

I. The stage of tacit contract. In systems which have an inherent instability, such as duopoly in the relations of firms, or a bipolar system of mutual deterrence in the relations of states, it is often possible to maintain a quasi-stable position for a long time through tacit contract: that is, through mutually consistent unilateral behavior on the part of each party. A quasi-stable position is like that of an egg on a golf-tee—it is stable for small disturbances but not for large. For considerable periods of time, however, the disturbances may be small enough so that Humpty-Dumpty does not fall. Comes a slightly larger disturbance, however, and all the King's horses and men cannot put him together again. The international system under the Eisenhower administration exhibited this kind of quasi-stability. An important element in that stability was a tacit agreement between the United States and the Soviet Union to do nothing effective about civil defense. We agreed, in effect, that our civilian populations should be mutually exchanged as hostages, for we each had the power to destroy large numbers—at least half—of each other's civilians. This meant that the chance of deliberate nuclear war was very small, though the chance of accidental war was appreciable; indeed, the missiles almost went off on at least two occasions. A natural accident, such as a large meteor, or an electronic breakdown, or a social accident, such as a mad pilot, or a political accident, such as an unwise commitment to an irresponsible third party, could under these circumstances easily set off a mutual exchange of nuclear weapons, so that the system could not be regarded as more than a temporary expedient.

Another example of tacit contract was the mutual suspension of nuclear tests, recently broken by the Soviet Union. Here the fear, perhaps, of world opinion, and the fear also of the technical consequences of an uncontrolled race for technical development of weapons, created a temporary tacit agreement. We have had similar tacit agreements in regard to spheres of influence and intervention in third-party quarrels. The United States did not interfere in Hungary, nor the Soviet Union in Egypt during the Suez crisis. The Russians allowed themselves to be thrown out of the Congo, and are not threatening to be more than a nuisance in Cuba. The conflicts in Korea and Viet Nam were temporarily settled by latitudinal partitions. The Arab-Israeli conflict does not become an arena of the cold war. All these represent systems of mutuality of conduct which might be classified as tacit agreement.

II. The fate of the tacit agreement on nuclear testing, and what looks like the impending fate of the tacit agreement on civil defense, is a testimony to the inherent instability of the tacit agreement in the long run. It is something like the gentleman's agreement in economic competition, which suffers from the defect that not all people are gentlemen. The danger is that in the absence of organization between contending parties their only means of communication is by a "threat system." A threat system, which is characteristic of unilateral national defense, is based on the proposition, "If you do something bad to me I will do something bad to you," by contrast with an exchange system, which is based on "If you do something good to me I will do something good to you." Both systems tend to lead to consummation, but whereas the consummation of exchange is an increase of goods, the consummation of threats is an increase of "bads." War is mainly the result of the depreciation in the credibility of threats in the absence of their consummation; and hence a threat system has a basic instability built into it, which tacit contract may postpone but cannot ultimately avoid. The great problem, therefore, is how to get rid of threat systems. This, I suspect, happens historically mainly by their being overlaid with other systems of relationship—trade, communication, organization—until they fall so much to the bottom of the pile that they are no longer significant.

The essential instability of threat systems and the weakness of tacit agreements, therefore, make it highly desirable to pass into the second stage of formalized agreement, and the building of what might be called "peace-defending" organizational structures. The first of these obviously is an arms control organization designed at first perhaps only to limit the present arms race but capable of the ultimate hope of policing genuine disarmament. We could begin, perhaps, with an organization for the prevention of accidental war. This will be a joint organization of the major armed forces of the world. Once this has been accomplished, a major system change is under way. It is the organizational disunity of the armed forces of the world which constitutes the real threat to humanity. If they were united they might threaten us with a great many disagreeable consequences but they would not threaten us with extinction. An arms control organization, therefore, would be the beginning of a very powerful social change. It would constitute the formal recognition of the fact that unilateral national defense is no longer possible. Once this initial break is made, system change may be expected to take place quite rapidly. It may be that we shall have to look forward to a substantial separation of the armed forces organization from the states which they are supposed to defend, and which they can no longer defend. Just as we solved the problem of religious wars by the separation of church and state, so we may be able to solve the problem of nuclear war by the separation of the armed forces from the state. The plain fact is that today the threat which the armed forces of the world present to their own civilian populations is much greater than any conflict among the nations. Arms control will be the beginning of the recognition of this social fact.

III. Arms control must move fairly rapidly into disarmament; otherwise it will be unstable. The organization of the world armed forces will be a loose and unstable one at first, and it will always threaten to break up. It may be, of course, that the major pressure towards disarmament will come from the economic side. Once the threat of war is removed by arms control and by organizational unity of the world armed forces, the economic burden of maintaining these monstrous establishments will seem intolerable, especially in view of the fact that it is the arms burden (equal to the total income of the poorest half of the human race!) which perhaps prevents the world from really tackling the problem of economic development and which condemns hundreds of millions of people and their descendants to live in misery. One looks forward, therefore, to the third stage of rapid and total disarmament, under the arms control organization. There are many difficult problems involved in this which have not been worked out and on which research desperately needs to be done. These problems, however, are difficult rather than insoluble.

IV. Even universal total disarmament, however, is not enough, for this too is likely to be unstable even though disarmament itself will reduce many of the sources of conflict, especially those which arise out of strategic considerations. It will not eliminate all conflicts by any means. In a world as divided as this, ideologically and economically, we may expect serious conflicts continually to arise. These conflicts will constantly present the temptation to the losing side to resort to violence and to redevelop organized armed forces. If disarmament is to be stable, therefore, there must be a system of conflict control. Conflict control is one of the essential functions of government. It is not, however, the only function. In thinking of world government, this is probably where we ought to begin. In the early stages it is more important to establish conflict control than to establish justice or to solve all social problems. Conflict control as a function of government has been inadequately studied and identified. This is perhaps because the study of conflict systems themselves is still in its infancy. However, this is a rapidly developing body of social science and one hopes that it may be possible in the not-too-distant future to develop a substantial body of knowledge on the identification and control of conflict systems. The problem, of course, is the identification of conflict processes in early stages before they become pathological. There are very difficult problems here in the definition of the pathology of conflict, as this, of course, goes very deep into our value systems. Conflict which is regarded as pathological by one person may not be so regarded by another. If, however, we regard violence as generally a sign of pathological conflict, we may be able to identify the processes of social dynamics which lead towards it, and we may therefore be able to interpose counterweights which will correct these processes. We may revert once more to the analogy of the car at the crossing. We need to develop both perception of dangers ahead and also organizations which can act as brakes. These processes have been fairly well worked out in industrial relations, where a whole profession of mediators and conciliators and personnel experts has come to being. There is no reason why these principles should not be applied in other fields of social life and especially to the conflict of states.

V. The last stage, of course, is true world government, capable not only of controlling conflict but of expressing and developing the common concerns and aims of mankind. At the moment this seems to be a long way off. Fortunately, the prevention of war does not depend, I think, on the establishment of full world government. If the stages of development which I have outlined can be pursued rapidly enough, war may be postponed for longer and longer periods until the postponement becomes indefinite by the establishment of a true world government. We must therefore find half-way houses and quarterway houses which are moderately habitable. We must not allow Utopian longings to deprive us of political bargains. The actual negotiation of the world social contract is going to be a long and arduous business. We need to put many more resources into this than we are now doing. Nevertheless, there is something here which can be done. There is a road which leads somewhere. If we are to break out of the apathy, irrationality, and despair which beset us, we must gain a vision of that road of escape and make at least one step along it. This is the great significance of the growing movement for peace research. Just as we no longer accept depressions as "acts of God," wholly unpredictable and uncontrollable, so we need no longer accept mass violence as unpredictable and uncontrollable. The fact that we cannot yet predict or control it should stir us to a great intellectual effort in this direction, for this way lies hope. The only unforgivable sin in the present crisis of mankind is despair.

97.

KEY CHOICES OF THE NEXT TWO DECADES

Willis W. Harman

It is the firm hope of the editors of this volume that its readers share our concern over the well-being of mankind and that they will view the study of sociology as one means to increase their sensitivity toward injustice and to be aroused to action by it, to understand what correctives need to be applied and where and how to apply them, to be able to distinguish the "truly important" from the "merely urgent," and to develop the skill to act on this distinction. We feel it is fitting, therefore, to end this volume with a selection which addresses itself to the challenges that lie before all of us during the next two decades. The reader may not agree with the position taken here by Harman that we can no longer permit humanistic values to be a mere luxury superimposed on our economic values. But if the selection serves to do no more than stimulate the reader to think through his own position and make plans to act on it, we will feel amply rewarded for our efforts.

ALTERNATIVE PATHS TO 1990

Few informed persons now doubt that technically advanced societies like the United States are undergoing a major historical transformation to some sort of postindustrial age. This is characterized by diminishing dominance of industrial production as a social function, by increasing prominence of service activities, and by increasing concern with value questions related to quality of life. The differences among opinions lie on how rapid and extreme this change will be in values, perceptions, and institutions. I forecast that the shift is likely to be rapid, extreme, and hazardous.

This forecast is in distinct contrast to the view that the available alternative futures comprise modest deviations from a "long-term multifold trend," with slow changes in social institutions and cultural values. It is not possible now to demonstrate which view is the more correct. Five years hence the situation may be clearer. Today both views are held by groups of reasonable men.

RAPID, DRASTIC CHANGES AHEAD

I propose to examine the arguments suggesting that forces toward an abrupt and drastic modification of the long-term multifold trend may lead to a revolutionary social change within the next two decades. Further, this revolutionary change may free up the system so that satisfactory answers to the questions raised above can be found.

I say this soberly. History gives us little reason to take comfort in the prospect of

---

Source: Willis W. Harman, *A Look at Business in 1990: A Summary of the White House Conference on the Industrial World Ahead,* proceedings (Washington, D.C.; Government Printing Office, November 1972).

Willis W. Harman is the director of the Educational Policy Research Center, Stanford Research Institute in Menlo Park, California.

fundamental and rapid social change—little reason to think we can escape without the accompanying threat of economic decline and disruption of social processes considerably greater than anything we have experienced or care to imagine. If indeed a fundamental and rapid change in basic perceptions and values occurs, such a chaotic period seems inevitable as the powerful momentum of the industrial era is turned in a new direction, and as the different members and institutions of the society respond with different speeds.

Accurate interpretation of this disorder is crucial. The form—and the success—of the nation's policies will depend a great deal on whether the disruption is seen as accompaniment to a change toward a more workable system, or is perceived as essentially destructive. Or, alternatively, whether it is seen as a rather bothersome episode as a result of which things will be neither particularly better nor worse, just different.

INDICATORS OF REVOLUTIONARY CHANGE

Several clues indicate that the industrialized world may be experiencing the beginning phase of a sociocultural revolution as profound and pervasive in its effects on all segments of the society as the Industrial Revolution, the Reformation, or the Fall of Rome. I am not speaking of *The Greening of America,* or of the achieving of any of the popularly promoted Utopias. The shape of the future will no more be patterned after the hippie movement and the youth revolution than the industrial age could have been inferred from the "new-age" values of the Anabaptists.

The transformation that we call the Protestant Reformation affected all aspects of the society, from the nascent science to the new capitalist commercial structure. Similarly, in the present case, we should expect impacts on the economic system, on science, on government, and on community and work life. As we look back at the Reformation, the most fundamental change appears to be in those tacitly agreed on, largely unquestioned basic premises on which every culture is based. Only a half dozen or so times in the history of Western civilization did this basic paradigm undergo revolutionary change. The Reformation was the most recent of these. It was characterized by a shift from the otherworldly, inner-directed, teleological paradigm of the Middle Ages to this worldly, outer-directed, relatively nontelelogical paradigm of the industrial age. These characteristics are summarized as follows:

Development and application of scientific method; wedding of scientific and technological advance
Industrialization through organization and division of labor; machine replacement of human labor
Acquisitive materialism; work ethic; economic-man image; belief in unlimited material progress and in technological and economic growth
Man seeking control over nature; positivistic theory of knowledge; manipulative rationality as a dominant theme
Individual responsibility for own destiny; freedom and equality as fundamental rights; nihilistic value perspective, individual determination of the "good"; society as an aggregate of individuals pursuing their own interests

Thus we are talking about an event that is historically improbable because of its rarity. It is a transformation that has not yet occurred; therefore, we can make only an informed guess at the main characteristics of the substitute paradigm. If this interpretation begins to appear more or less correct, the consequences for economic and political decision making are profound. Hence we can ill afford not to take the possibility seriously.

The Reformation period lasted about a

century. Earlier major transformations, such as the agricultural revolution, were far more dispersed in both space and time. How can such a profound shift as we are contemplating take place in the space of a decade or two? One reason is the general speedup of change. Another, of course, is the impact of modern communication media. Still another reason may lie, as we shall see, in the acceptability of the paradigm that may be replacing the beliefs and values of the industrial age.

This impending revolutionary-change view is plausible for three major reasons. 1—The complex of social problems confronting the developed world appears to require changes in cultural values for their satisfactory resolution; 2—a competitor to the industrial-state paradigm, embodying the requisite kinds of value shifts, may be arising spontaneously; and 3—various "lead indicators" that have preceded historic cultural-change periods have been prominent during the past decade.

New values required. It is almost a truism that most of our severe social problems are essentially the consequence of our technological and industrial successes. For example, success in reducing infant mortality has contributed to excessive population growth. Technology-created affluence poses resource-depletion problems. New materials (e.g., plastics, detergents, aluminum) have interfered with natural recycling processes. Machine replacement of manual and routine labor has exacerbated unemployment and poverty problems. Development of nuclear, biological, and chemical weapons has led to the potential worldwide decimation. And so on.

The nature of these problems is such that many analysts have seriously questioned whether those basic values and premises that have served to build up our present technological and industrial capabilities are now suitable for the humane application or even rational control of those Faustian powers. As long as this remains a question, values that appear more suitable will be able to mobilize social power. We will return to this point later.

Emerging paradigm. Several signs visible here and in other industrialized nations point to the possible emergence of a new dominant paradigm:

Surveys and polls indicate significant value shifts among certain elite groups, such as students and corporate executives. Increased emphasis is placed on humanistic and spiritual values, quality of life, community person-centered society, and so forth. Emphasis on materialistic values, status goals, and unqualified economic growth is diminished.

Numerous cultural indicators (e.g., books read, voluntary associations, rock lyrics, themes of plays and motion pictures, content of magazine articles, "New Age" subculture) show greatly increased interest in and tolerance for the transcendental, religious, esoteric, occult, suprarational, mystical, and spiritual.

New scientific interest in exploring subjective states, altered consciousness, partly as a consequence of new tools relating inner experience to physical and physiological correlates (e.g., galvanic skin response, body electric fields, EEG components, biofeedback signals), is resulting in a new legitimation of studies of religious beliefs, psychic phenomena, mystical experiences, and meditative states.

From these indicators, particularly the last, we can infer something about the direction in which values, and the dominant vision of man-in-the-universe, are likely to shift. Wherever the nature of man has been probed deeply, the paramount fact emerging is the duality of his experience. He is found to be both physical and spiritual, both sides being real, and neither describable in terms of the other. At various times and places the spiritual or the material has been temporarily dominant. A fundamental characteristic of the candidate paradigm is the relationship of complementarity in which it places such troublesome opposites as spirit/body, science/religion or determinism/free will, in much the same way as modern physics reconciles the previously opposing wave and particle theories of light. Suggested characteristics of the emergent paradigm are:

Complementarity of physical and spiritual experience; recognition of all "explanation" as only metaphor; use of different noncontradicting "levels of explanation" for physical, biological, mental, and spiritual reality.
Teleological sense of life and evolution having direction/purpose; ultimate reality perceived as unitary, with transcendent order.
Basis for value postulates discoverable in own inner experience of a hierarchy of "levels of consciousness"; potentiality of supraconscious as well as subconscious influence.
Goals of life—aware participation in individual growth and the evolutionary process, individual fulfillment through community; integration of work, play, and growth.
Goals of society—to foster development of individuals' transcendent and emergent potentialities. Economic growth, technological development, design of work roles and environments, authority structures, and social institutions all are to be used in the service of this primary goal.
"New naturalism, holism, immanentism" (V. Ferkiss); "re-discovery of the supernatural" (P. L. Berger); "The counterculture is essentially an exploration of the politics of consciousness" (T. Roszak).

Thus the challenging paradigm assumes some sort of transcendent spiritual order, discoverable in human experience, and against which human value choices are assessed. Ultimately reality is unitary. There is a teleological sense of life and evolution having direction or purpose. Other levels of consciousness than the usual are explorable, with different appropriate levels of explanation. Hence the scientific explanation of the level of sensory experience is in no way contradictory to religious, philosophical, or poetic interpretations of suprasensory experience. Rather, it is complementary to them.

The candidate paradigm extends, rather than contradicts, the modern scientific world view, much as relativity theory extended Newtonian mechanics. Moreover, it is in its essence not new at all, having formed a central stream of thought in the humanities, in Western political tradition, in "transcendentalist" movements in our own history. (However, never has anything like it been the guiding paradigm of an entire society. Popular religions, East and West, have been at best some watered-down version.) Part of the growing acceptability of the New Age world view undoubtedly has been due to this drawing on what is already well established in the culture, together with the bridging of the "two cultures" of science and the humanities.

Lead indicators of revolutionary change—From studies of historical occurrences of revolutionary cultural and political change come the following list of typical occurrences in the period leading up to that change:

Decreased sense of community
Increased sense of alienation and purposelessness
Increased occurrence of violent crime
Increased frequency of personal disorders and mental illness
Increased frequency and severity of social disruptions
Increased use of police to control behavior
Increased public acceptance of hedonistic behavior
Increase in amount of noninstitutionalized religious activities

To anyone who has read the newspapers over the last decade, the list alone makes the point, without the necessity of further comment.

A FUNDAMENTAL PROBLEM

All the above is not to say that such a revolutionary change and paradigm shift will inevitably occur. Rather, the three assertions listed argue that among the alternative "future histories" to be considered, needs to be included this possibility. Whether or not the social forces for such a transition are gathering sufficient strength to bring it about remains to be seen. The probability is not negligible at any rate.

Consider the first of these three propositions—namely, that the nature of society's problems necessitates significant value change for satisfactory resolution. At the risk of seeming to oversimplify, I will make this assertion much more explicit:

> Industrial societies in general, and this nation in particular, are faced with one fundamental problem that is so pervasive and so pernicious that the related societal problems (e.g., poverty, unemployment, inflation, environmental deterioration, crime, alienation) will defeat all attempts at solution until that fundamental problem is satisfactorily resolved. Such resolution hinges on value change.

The problem to which I refer has puzzled Adam Smith and most economists since his time. It is this: individuals, corporations, government agencies in the course of their activities make microdecisions (e.g., to buy a certain product, to employ a man for a particular task, to enact a minimum-wage law) that interact to constitute a set of macrodecisions of the overall society (e.g., a five-percent growth rate, failing cities, polluted air and water). The problem is that perfectly reasonable microdecisions currently are adding up to largely unsatisfactory macrodecisions.

Some specifics will illustrate:

The tragedy of the commons—Microdecisions regarding utilization of resources (e.g., land, air, water, fuels, minerals), which are reasonable from the viewpoints of corporate management and stockholders, developers, and local governments, but result in macrodecisions of resource depletion, environmental degradation, urban crowding, which are unsatisfactory to society at large.

Insufficient work opportunity—People need opportunities to contribute meaningfully to the society and be affirmed in return (commonly with wages). Individual decisions to create and accept jobs fail to result in a satisfactory full-employment policy, and thus lead to the incongruity that work opportunity becomes considered as a scarce commodity that needs to be rationed.

Unintended technological impact—Even with technology assessment we do not know how to preserve market microdecision making regarding technological innovation and yet achieve satisfactory macrochoices with regard to technological disemployment, quality of the environment, infringements of human rights, interference with natural recycling processes, and resource depletion.

Inflation—Decisions to pass productivity increases from technological innovation on to workers in the form of increased wages, rather than apply them to reducing prices to consumers (plus demands for similar increases for service-sector workers whose productivity is not appreciably increasing), have contributed to persistent inflation.

State of the economy—Decisions of hundreds of U.S.-based corporations to transfer manufacturing operations to low-labor-cost countries, while economically sound as individual decisions, collectively constitute a serious temporary threat to U.S. economy and industrial capability.

Alienation—Individual, corporate, and government decisions are widely believed to have been guided by such principles as economic growth as a self-justifying end, "the business of business is business," the affluent society, the underdeveloped world as supplier of raw materials for that affluent society, and the "technological imperative" that any technology that can be developed and applied should be—and that this fact is leading the world toward an intolerable future. Further, individuals feel themselves forced by pressures of "the system" to act in ways that they perceive as neither what they want to do, nor what would be in general social good. The result is a serious alienation from the society and its institutions.

This fundamental problem is not simply a matter of trade-offs—as a recent cartoon quip had it, "There's a price tag on everything. You want a high standard of living, you settle for a low quality of life." Rather, it is a flaw in the decision-making system such that individuals are encouraged to choose on the basis of their own short-term, imprudent self-interest, instead of their long-term, enlightened self-interest.

Classical economic theory attempted to explain how the market mechanism could operate to constitute, from individual self-interest microdecisions, macrodecisions that would operate for the general good. As time went on, the invisible hand clearly needed a little help in the form of government rule-making and umpiring, from antitrust laws to Keynesian manipulations of the money supply and interest rate. Yet the basic dilemma of unsatisfactory macrodecisions worsens, as illustrated above.

Why is the system in such trouble now when it worked satisfactorily before? Some of the contributing factors are:

Interconnectedness, so that laissez-faire approaches are less workable

Reduction of geographical and entrepreneurial frontier opportunities

Approaching limits of natural recycling capabilities

Sharpened dichotomy between "employed" and "unemployed" (e.g., virtual elimination of the small farmer, partially or sporadically employed)

More adequate supplying of deficiency needs (improved diet, material advance) plus more education, resulting in higher expectations and keener perception of the gap between actualities and potentialities

Transition from a basic condition of labor scarcity to one of job scarcity

Approaching limits of some resources (e.g., natural gas, domestic petroleum, fresh water)

Faustian powers of technology and industrialization that have reached the point where they can have a major impact on the physical, technological, sociopolitical, and psychological environment

Expanded political power of labor that, forcing industrial wages to follow increasing productivity, constitutes an inflationary force

Weakening of the force of "American civil religion," partly through the eroding effect of positivistic science, and hence a weakening of the will to self-regulation in the interest of the whole.

A CRUCIAL CHOICE

If this is the diagnosis, what then is the prescription?

A key characteristic of the future of this society lies in the way in which the nation handles this fundamental dilemma. By and large, two significantly different approaches can be considered.

One of these is a continuation of the collectivist trend that has characterized the past four decades. If this path is taken, as the kinds of problems mentioned earlier grow more severe, they will be turned over to an expanding public sector to handle. Individual decisions will increasingly be regulated by government, through coercive controls and manipulative incentives. That this outcome is intrinsic is emphasized in John Galbraith's 1967 analysis of *The New Industrial State,* in which he predicted that ". . . a system of wage and price restraints is inevitable in the industrial system . . . neither inflation nor unemployment are acceptable alternatives." On this path of deprivatization it will be difficult to avoid the well-known disadvantages of centralized control and bureaucratic giantism. Nevertheless, many today seem inclined to accept the inevitability of this drift.

The other direction is toward a reversal

of the collectivist trend and a revitalized role for the private sector. However, it will not return to some previous state—it will move forward to something we have never known.

The "entrepreneurial capitalism" of the nineteenth century involved a view of economic man in a freemarket society, a state of scarcity, and minimal governmental intervention. Over the past few decades, it has been replaced by "managerial capitalism," picturing man as consumer in an affluent industrial state, with government regulating growth, employment, and wage-price stability. The alternative to which I am alluding might be termed "humanistic capitalism."

Again it is necessary to oversimplify to make the point easily. If the basic problem concerns unsatisfactory macrodecisions arising from self-interest-directed microdecisions, then the almost obvious thing to do is to turn the situation upside down. That is, select appropriate macrodecisions —which is to say, national and planetary goals—that are in accord with the best available knowledge regarding human fulfillment. Then see what patterns of microdecisions would be necessary to achieve those goals.

But there is a catch. The means used to obtain those necessary individual actions have to be compatible with the ends. This nation affirms the goal to ". . . guard the rights of the individual . . . enhance the dignity of the citizen, promote the maximum development of his capabilities, stimulate their responsible exercise, and widen the range and effectiveness of opportunities for individual choice . . . to build a nation and help build a world in which every human being shall be free to dedicate and develop his capacities to the fullest." However, if we take this seriously, then the necessary patterns of microdecisions cannot be obtained through coercion, as in a totalitarian state, nor through manipulative behavior-sharing as in B. F. Skinner's version of a technocratic state. The only means compatible with goals such as those declared above is through reeducation toward appreciation of wholesome goals and understanding of the microdecisions necessary for reaching them.

In sum, the more unsatisfactory the macrodecisions, the stronger the government required. Thus we have two routes—stronger government or changed culture.

SOME CHARACTERISTICS OF "HUMANISTIC CAPITALISM"

The basic characteristic of the political economics I am referring to with the term humanistic capitalism is that society would be what Robert Hutchins describes as *The Learning Society,* one that will have transformed "its values in such a way that learning, fulfillment, becoming human, had become its aims and all its institutions were directed to this end." Postindustrial society, whatever its other characteristics, must answer the question of how men shall occupy the portion of their time that is not required to provide goods and services and keep the essential processes of the society functioning. Learning is the major such activity that is nonpolluting, nonstultifying, humane, and social beneficial.

Large privately owned and managed corporations, we may assume, will continue to be the dominant economic institutions in American society. If their modes of operation move toward humanistic capitalism, corporate goals would broaden to include, besides the present economic and institutional goals, authentic social responsibility and the personal fulfillment of those who participate in the corporate activity. This would not be as a gesture to improve corporate image or as a moralistically undertaken responsibility, but as operative goals on a par with profit making and institutional security. With humanistic capitalism not production, but productiveness in human life would be the goal.

The manpower concept of contemporary business management has resulted in job structuring for efficient production and incentive structuring to shape the men to fit the jobs. Among the consequences of this policy have been "unemployable" welfare recipients, overtrained aerospace engineers, underutilized employees, and alienated production and office workers. The policy is basically analogous to approaching the problem of air pollution by breeding smog-resistant humans. Under humanistic capitalism jobs would be structured to fit people. Production processes would be designed to reinstill pride of craftsmanship. Goods and services would be tailored to fit consumers' needs and desires, not consumer wants shaped by manipulative advertising to meet the needs of business. Employees would work for pay, of course, but also because they believed in and identified with the operative goals of their employing corporation.

Government would probably remain the organizer and regulator of large, complex systems (e.g., for transportation, communication, health care, energy supply, financial operations, food production, education) composed of relatively autonomous self-organizing and self-monitoring subsystems, coordinated mainly by shared values and goals. Adequate governmental regulation would be required to ensure that future social costs and benefits are adequately represented in private decision-making procedures. However, government would tend to reduce its role in the direct provision of goods and services (e.g., education, health insurance, property protection, welfare services) and instead adjust incentives to encourage supply of these from the private sector.

In short, private-sector institutions would assume a significantly expanded range of responsibilities in the implementation of new postindustrial values. Large institutions that retained narrow self-serving goals, be they corporations or labor unions, would find their legitimacy questioned.

Does this sound like idealism? I mean it to be intensely practical. Let me mention three reasons why I think a humanistic capitalism is completely feasible, assuming that recent trends in shifting cultural values continue:

The public can exert tremendous power through engaging in political buying, stock purchase, and job seeking, favoring those corporations of whose operative values they approve. Thus the balance could easily shift to where it is the corporations that display serious social responsibility, which have the competitive advantage, not the reverse. (Recent truth-in-lending and truth-in-advertising pressures exemplify the principle.) Changes in tax laws, antitrust provisions, corporate charters, and so forth, might be introduced to encourage broader corporate responsibilities.

Requirements for effective functioning of large, complex systems naturally support such values as personal honesty, openness, (to ensure accurate information flow); responsibility (hence self-actualization); and cooperative trust. The values required in the team that puts a man on the moon and gets him back are a far cry from those that suffice for operation of a used-car lot. Thus as the production and service tasks of the society become more complex, humane values become not only moral but also functional imperatives.

As such institutions as industrial conglomerates, multinational corporations, and international labor unions, not directly accountable to the public, become larger and more powerful relative to representative governments, their operative goals have to become more congruent with those of the overall society—else the goals of the society will become distorted toward those of the dominant institutions. Thus, political pressure will urge corporate goals toward personal fulfillment of participants, public good, and social responsibility. If multinational corporations are to be dominant social institutions in the future, the fate of the world will hinge on the operative goals and values of those corporations.

THE ROLE OF VALUE CHANGE

Thus we have postulated a direction toward resolution of the fundamental dilemma that the resultant of the microdecisions is so typically an unsatisfactory macrodecision. It does not depend on Adam Smith's "invisible hand," or on the manipulation of motivations and behavior by a technocratic elite, or on the socialist solution of the private sector abdicating to the public. Rather, it depends on reeducation to perceive suitable macrodecisions and appropriate microdecisions to lead toward them, and on a shift in cultural values to support the process.

This last point is key. A modern banking, checking, and credit-card system requires for its operation that the trust level in society be above a threshold value. The quality of good family life rests on shared values that would not be present if a number of people with diverse self-interests were living together. Institutional change requires value change for its support—just as new institutions may be required to implement new values.

Earlier arguments about the nature of social problems strongly indicate that the decision-making system will break down without an increase in the amount of caring for fellowman, for future generations, for nature, and for planet earth. No doubt it would have been nice all along if we had more of the traditional values of integrity, humility, and caring—now it may be a necessity if the system is to work at all.

But to have power over men's actions, values cannot stand in isolation or be arbitrarily chosen. They must be rooted in some sort of "vision of reality," some guiding philosophy. A recent book by Victor Ferkiss argues, from an analysis of the present predicament of the technological-industrial state, that an adequate new guiding philosophy would have to incorporate three basic elements. First is what he terms a "new naturalism," which affirms that man is absolutely a part of a nature, a universe, that is always in process of becoming. The second element, a "new holism," recognizes that "no part can be defined or understood save in relation to the whole." The third, a "new immanentism," sees that the whole is "determined not from outside but from within." Men's actions and the forces they set in motion are all part of the developing whole; "every part of the whole has power and influence; every living particle is a source of direction and life." If man is to acquire the necessary sense of responsibility for the impact of his own actions on the shaping of the whole, he "must so internalize these ideas and make them so much a part of his instinctive world view that they inform his personal, political, and cultural life."

But these characteristics are precisely those found in what we described earlier as an emerging "new paradigm." They are the characteristics that would make the candidate paradigm socially useful, and give it staying power. And this is why the historically improbable paradigm shift and cultural revolution is even plausible as a future alternative worthy of consideration.

CONCLUSION

Among the future alternatives to be considered is one that comprises a rapid and drastic break with trends of the recent past, characterized essentially by a change in that basic vision of man-in-the-universe in which the operative values of the society have their origins. The main reason it is of interest, and that it seems plausible at all, is that the change would be in such a direction as to assist in the resolution of the society's most serious problems—particularly the central problem that reasonable actions according to the rules seem to be leading us toward such an unacceptable future.

In this view, *contemporary political, military, economic, ecological, and social crises are reflections of an underlying moral and spiritual crisis of civilization, and their resolution depends on the resolution of that deeper crisis.* The underlying dilemma is that somehow humanistic and transcendental values have come to be a luxury superimposed on economic values, rather than being the measure of the appropriateness of economic values. The result is that, rather than reinforcing the best we know, the economic institutions of the society seem to be at odds with the society's highest values. Further alienation, economic decline, and social disruption are likely to occur before this situation is corrected.

The extent to which our deliberate actions can affect the future is undoubtedly limited. Continuity of cultural change, institutional inertia, unexpected events, and subliminal social forces conspire to shape the course of history and to thwart attempts to design the future. Quite apart from our desires, the transformation postulated in these remarks is either upon us or it is not—it is not our choice to make. However, we can choose either to understand and move with the tides of history, whatever they may be—or to attempt to resist them.

Appendix

Correlation of *Readings in Sociology* with Sociology Texts

In the table that follows, the principal sociology texts are arranged alphabetically by authors' last name. For each text, chapter numbers are printed in boldface on the left, and the selections from *Readings in Sociology* that best relate to each text chapter are listed in lightface on the right.

Abrahamson

Sociology: An Introduction to Concepts, Methods, and Data

Van Nostrand, Reinhold, 1969

1	Prologue, 4, 6, 49, 96, 97
2	1-3, 5, 77
3	4, 9, 10, 15, 16, 73–75
4	25, 26, 37, 39, 40, 42, 56, 57, 66, 71, 82, 87, 88, 91, 92, 94–96
5	25, 26, 31, 36, 39, 40–42, 44–46, 65, 66, 68, 72, 78, 79, 90
6	18, 40–51, 58, 59, 72, 83–85
7	5-9, 16–18, 21–24, 27, 58, 59, 62, 89
8	2, 9, 12, 13, 53, 54
9	Prologue, 7, 40, 41, 44, 46, 47–50, 58–60, 78, 80, 83, 84, 95
10	5, 10, 13, 79, 95

Acuff, Allen, and Taylor

From Man to Society

The Dryden Press, 1973

1	4, 6
2	1-3, 5, 77
3	24, 55
4	9-13, 16, 75, 81
5	5-9, 16–18, 21, 23, 24, 27, 58, 59, 62, 89
6	9, 12, 13, 92, 97
7	19–21, 54
8	27–29, 32, 33
9	18, 40–51, 58, 59, 72, 83–85
10	20, 21, 34–39, 56, 62, 73, 78, 95
11	16, 77, 86, 90, 96
12	25, 26, 37, 39, 40, 42, 56, 57, 66, 71, 82, 87, 88, 91, 92, 94–96
13	2, 13, 53, 54
14	Prologue, 7, 47–50, 58–60, 78, 80, 95
15	10, 35, 61–63
16	25, 26, 31, 40, 55, 64–66, 75, 91
17	51, 52
18	29, 67–70, 89
19	2, 14, 31
20	8, 18, 39, 43, 45, 46, 49, 50, 56, 58, 59, 68, 72, 80–85, 95
21	55, 64, 65, 89
22	5, 10, 13, 25, 31, 42, 45, 69, 72, 78, 79, 81, 82, 87–90, 95, 97
23	15, 67–72

Anderson

Toward a New Sociology: A Critical View

Dorsey Press, 1971

1	16, 22, 23, 27–30, 32, 33, 76, 77, 86, 90, 96
2	2, 5, 9–13, 16, 19–21, 29, 54, 57, 75, 76, 79–81, 90, 93, 95
3	55, 65, 66, 73–75, 89, 91
4	71, 72, 78, 87
5	44, 67–69
6	40, 41, 43, 44, 46–49, 58, 59, 64, 83, 84, 95
7	42, 45, 46, 72
8	4, 18, 31, 36, 41, 44, 49, 51, 52, 57, 60, 65, 66, 74, 76, 79, 82, 86, 90, 93, 96
9	25, 26, 31, 40, 55, 64, 65, 75, 91

10 10, 29, 35, 44, 61–63, 70
11 8, 18, 39, 43, 50, 56, 68, 72, 80, 82–85, 95
12 2, 13, 14, 31, 53, 54
13 73–75, 88, 91
14 Prologue, 49, 92, 96, 97

Berger and Berger

Sociology: A Biographical Approach

Basic Books, 1972

1 24, 55
2 4, 6
3 5–9, 16–19, 21, 23, 24, 27, 58, 59, 62, 89
4 35, 52, 57
5 2, 13, 53, 54
6 29, 67–70, 89
7 18, 40–51, 58, 59, 72, 83–85
8 19–21, 54
9 Prologue, 2, 7, 29, 47–50, 58–60, 76, 78, 79, 80, 90, 93, 95
10 51, 52
11 13, 18, 25, 47, 58, 59, 63, 72
12 25, 30, 40, 41, 45, 48, 64
13 2, 29, 76, 79, 80, 90, 93
14 5, 10, 13, 79, 95
15 25, 26, 37, 39, 40, 42, 56, 57, 66, 71, 82, 87, 88, 91, 92, 94–96
16 19, 63, 89
17 9, 10, 12, 13, 35, 61–63, 92, 97
Postscript Prologue, 4, 6, 49, 96, 97

Bierstedt

The Social Order, 3d ed.

McGraw-Hill, 1970

1 4, 6
2 15, 16
3 15, 67–72
4 2, 14, 31
5 9–13, 16, 75, 81
6 9–13, 16, 75, 81
7 5–9, 16–18, 21, 23, 24, 27, 58, 59, 62, 89
8 9, 12, 13
9 19–21, 54
10 27–29, 32, 33
11 24, 25, 57
12 29, 30, 51, 73–75
13 18, 42–44, 49, 65, 68, 90
14 13, 20, 21
15 2, 13, 53, 54
16 9, 27–29, 32, 33, 40, 41, 44, 46–49, 83, 84
17 18, 40–51, 58, 59, 72, 83–85
18 8, 18, 39, 43, 45, 46, 49, 50, 56, 58, 59, 68, 72, 80–85, 95
19 4, 24, 44, 57, 60, 66, 68, 74, 76, 79, 82, 86, 90, 93, 96
20 25, 26, 37, 39, 40, 42, 56, 57, 66, 71, 82, 87, 88, 91, 92, 94–96

Biesanz and Biesanz

Introduction to Sociology,
2d ed.

Prentice-Hall, 1973

1 4, 6
2 1–3, 5, 77
3 9, 12, 13
4 13, 18, 41, 82
5 7, 10, 76
6 9–12
7 19–21, 24, 54, 55
8 27–29, 32, 33
9 18, 40–48, 49–51, 58, 59, 72, 83–85
10 8, 18, 39, 43, 45, 46, 49, 50, 56, 58, 59, 68, 72, 80–85, 95
11 17, 18, 22–24
12 5–9, 16–18, 21–24, 27, 58, 59, 62, 89
13 5, 10–13, 16, 75, 81
14 25, 26, 37, 39, 40, 42, 56, 57, 66, 71, 82, 88, 91, 92, 94–96
15 75, 91
16 67–70
17 2, 14, 15, 31, 67–72
18 20, 21, 34–39, 56, 62, 73, 78, 95
19 Prologue, 2, 7, 13, 35, 47–50, 53, 54, 58–63, 78, 80, 95

20 4, 9, 25, 26, 31, 40, 44, 55, 57, 64–66, 69, 72, 75, 78, 81, 82, 87–93, 96, 97

Broom and Selznick
Sociology, A Text With Adapted Readings, 5th ed.
Harper and Row, 1973

1 1–6, 57, 77
2 2, 5, 10, 13, 19–22, 29, 30, 32, 33, 51, 54, 76, 79, 80, 90, 93, 95
3 9–13, 16, 75, 81
4 5–9, 16–18, 21, 23, 24, 27, 58, 59, 62, 89
5 27–29, 32, 33
6 18–21, 40–51, 54, 58, 59, 72, 83, 85
7 2, 24, 25, 29, 51, 52, 76, 79, 80, 90, 93
8 20, 21, 25, 26, 34–40, 42, 56, 57, 62, 66, 71, 73, 78, 82, 87, 88, 91, 92, 94–96
9 2, 14, 31
10 2, 13, 53, 54
11 Prologue, 47–50, 58–60, 78, 80, 95
12 10, 35, 61–63
13 5, 10, 13, 79, 95
14 8, 18, 39, 43, 45, 46, 49, 50, 56, 58, 59, 68, 72, 80–85, 95
15 15, 67–72
16 15, 25, 26, 31, 40, 55, 64–72, 75, 91
17 4, 18, 31, 36, 41, 44, 49, 57, 60, 65, 66, 68, 74, 76, 79, 82, 86, 90, 93, 96

Caplow
Elementary Sociology
Prentice-Hall, 1971

1 Prologue, 4, 6
2 1–3, 5, 77
3 1–3, 5, 77
4 4, 6, 51, 55
5 2, 14, 31
6 67–70
7 18, 40–51, 58, 59, 72, 83–85
8 41, 42, 44, 46, 55
9 51, 52
10 2, 13, 53, 54
11 5, 10, 13, 79, 95
12 16, 77, 86, 90, 96
13 25, 26, 37, 39, 40, 42, 56, 57, 66, 71, 82, 87, 88, 91, 92, 94–96
14 Prologue, 2, 3, 97

DeFleur, D'Antonio, DeFleur
Sociology: Man in Society
Scott, Foresman, 1971

Prologue Prologue, 1–6, 49, 77, 96, 97
1 9, 12, 13, 16, 19–21, 54, 77, 86, 90, 96
2 24, 25, 27–29, 32, 33, 51, 52, 67–70, 89
3 9–13, 16, 75, 81
4 7, 8, 13, 18–23
5 5–9, 16–18, 21, 23, 24, 27, 58, 59, 62, 89
6 25, 26, 37, 39, 40, 42, 56, 57, 66, 71, 82, 87, 88, 91, 92, 94, 95, 96
7 40–51, 58, 59, 72, 83–85
8 2, 14, 15, 31, 67–69, 70–75
9 25, 26, 29, 30, 40–46, 63, 65, 66, 70–72
10 8, 18, 39, 43, 45, 46, 49, 50, 56, 58, 59, 68, 72, 80–85, 95
11 20, 21, 34–39, 56, 62, 73, 78, 95
12 5, 10, 13, 79, 95
13 3, 34, 36, 38, 56, 57, 73, 74, 76, 82, 93
14 4, 44, 57, 60, 66, 68, 74, 76, 79, 82, 86, 90, 93, 96
15 25, 26, 31, 40, 55, 64–66, 75, 91
16 2, 13, 53, 54
17 10, 35, 61–63
18 Prologue, 7, 47–50, 58–60, 78, 80, 95
Epilogue Prologue, 4, 6, 49, 96, 97

Doby, Boskoff, and Pendleton
Sociology, The Study of Man in Adaptation
D. C. Heath, 1973

Introduction 1, 6
1 6, 7, 9
2 5–7, 9
3 9, 12, 13, 30, 32, 33

4	19, 20, 30, 55
5	19–21, 27, 28, 30, 54, 55
6	5–9, 16–18, 21, 23, 24, 27, 58, 59, 62, 89
7	2, 13, 53, 54
8	18, 40–51, 72, 83, 84
9	29, 67–70, 89
10	2, 14, 31
11	2, 14, 31
12	87, 88, 91, 96
13	4, 49, 90, 93
14	16, 77, 86, 90, 96
15	91, 96, 97
16	25, 26, 37, 39, 40, 42, 56, 57, 66, 71, 82, 87, 88, 92, 94, 95
17	–
18	87, 88, 91

Douglas, et al.

Introduction to Sociology

The Free Press, 1973

1	4, 6
2	1, 5, 12, 51, 55
3	4, 27–29, 32–34
4	22, 23, 27
5	9–13, 16, 75, 81
6	2, 13, 53, 54
7	5–9, 16–18, 21, 23, 24, 27, 58, 59, 62, 89
8	17, 18, 22–24
9	22, 30, 32, 33, 76
10	1–3, 5, 77
11	22, 30, 32, 33, 76
12	34, 36
13	4, 44, 57, 60, 66, 68, 74, 76, 79, 82, 86, 90, 92, 96
14	18, 40–51, 58, 59, 72, 83–85
15	25, 26, 31, 40, 55, 64–66, 75, 91
16	24, 51, 52, 55
17	1–3, 5, 77, 87, 88, 93
18	8, 18, 25, 31, 39, 42, 43, 45, 46, 49, 50, 56, 58, 59, 68, 69, 72, 78, 80–85, 87–90, 95, 97
19	14, 26, 36, 40, 42, 44–46, 69, 70, 72, 79, 90, 97
20	2, 5, 10, 13, 29, 76, 79, 80, 90, 93, 95
21	Prologue, 49, 96, 97

Dressler and Carns

Sociology, The Study of Human Interaction, 2d ed.

Knopf, 1973

1	Prologue, 4, 6, 49, 96, 97
2	1–6, 77
3	9–13, 16, 24, 55, 75, 81
4	9, 92, 97
5	9–13, 16, 25, 26, 37, 39, 40, 42, 56, 57, 66, 71, 75, 81, 82, 87, 88, 91, 92, 94–96
6	2, 9, 12, 13, 29, 76, 79, 80, 90, 93
7	9, 12, 13
8	5–9, 16–18, 21, 23, 24, 27, 58, 59, 62, 89
9	9–13, 16, 17, 24, 55, 75
10	19–21, 54
11	5, 10, 13, 79, 95
12	27–29, 32, 33
13	24, 25, 27–29, 32, 33, 51, 52
14	34–39
15	18, 40–51, 58, 59, 72, 83–85
16	29, 67–70, 89
17	24, 25, 51, 52, 57
18	4, 25, 26, 31, 40, 44, 55, 57, 60, 64–66, 68, 74–76, 79, 82, 86, 90, 91, 93, 96
19	2, 13, 53, 54
20	10, 35, 61–63
21	25, 31, 42, 45, 69, 72, 78, 81, 82, 87–90, 97
22	8, 18, 39, 43, 45, 46, 49, 50, 56, 58, 59, 68, 72, 80–85, 95
23	2, 14, 15, 31, 67–72

Green

Sociology, 6th ed.

McGraw-Hill, 1972

1	Prologue, 4, 6, 49, 96, 97
2	15, 67–72
3	24, 55
4	22, 30, 32, 33, 76

5	9, 12, 13, 16
6	10–12, 75, 81
7	5–9, 16–18, 21–24, 27, 58, 59, 62, 89
8	17–24
9	2, 14, 31, 67–72
10	18–21, 40–51, 54, 58, 59, 72, 83–85
11	20, 25, 40–42, 46, 55
12	8, 18, 39, 43, 45, 46, 49, 50, 56, 58, 59, 68, 72, 80–85, 95
13	29, 67–70, 89
14	2, 13, 53, 54
15	2, 13, 53, 54
16	Prologue, 7, 47–50, 58–60, 78, 80, 95
17	10, 35, 61–63
18	4, 44, 57, 60, 66, 68, 74, 76, 79, 82, 86, 90, 93, 96
19	9, 12, 13
20	34, 64
21	25, 26, 37, 39, 40, 42, 56, 57, 66, 71, 82, 87, 88, 91, 92, 94–96

Hardert, Parker, Pfuhl, Anderson

Sociology and Social Issues

Rinehart Press, 1974

1	4, 6
2	10, 24, 25, 30, 51, 52
3	9–13, 16, 75, 81, 89
4	5–9, 16–18, 21–24, 27, 58, 59, 62, 89
5	18, 40–51, 58, 59, 72, 83–85
6	2, 14, 15, 31, 67–69, 70–72
7	4, 13, 25, 26, 53, 54, 57, 61–66, 74, 75, 86, 90, 91, 96
8	8, 18, 39, 43, 45, 46, 49, 50, 56, 58, 59, 68, 72, 80–85, 95
9	20, 21, 34–39, 56, 62, 73, 78, 95
10	5, 10, 13, 76, 79, 80, 93, 95
11	1–3, 5, 77
12	Prologue, 49, 92, 96, 97

Hodges

Conflict and Consensus, An Introduction to Sociology

Harper and Row, 1971

1	4, 6
2	1–3, 5, 77
3	9–13, 16, 75, 81
4	5–9, 16–18, 21–24, 27, 58, 59, 62, 89
5	27–29, 32, 33
6	29, 67–70, 89
7	2, 14, 31
8	18, 40–51, 58, 59, 72, 83–85
9	2, 13, 53, 54
10	25, 26, 31, 40, 55, 64–66, 75, 91
11	4, 44, 57, 60, 66, 68, 74, 76, 79, 82, 86, 90, 93, 96
12	10, 35, 61–63
13	Prologue, 7, 47–50, 58–60, 78, 80, 95
14	25, 26, 37, 39, 40, 42, 56, 57, 66, 71, 82, 87, 88, 91, 92, 94–96
15	8, 18, 39, 43, 45, 46, 49, 50, 56, 58, 59, 68, 72, 80–85, 95
16	1, 60, 94

Horton and Hunt

Sociology, 3d ed.

McGraw-Hill, 1972

1	1, 5, 6
2	Prologue, 2, 4, 49, 77, 96, 97
3	9, 12, 13, 81
4	10, 11, 16, 75, 81
5	5–9, 16–18, 21, 23, 24, 27, 58, 59, 62, 89
6	19–21, 54
7	2, 5, 10, 13, 29, 76, 79, 80, 90, 93, 95
8	27–29, 32, 33
9	4, 26, 35, 44, 47–50, 55, 57, 61, 62, 64–66, 75, 76, 90, 91, 95, 96
10	2, 13, 53, 54
11	5, 52
12	18, 42, 45, 49–51, 58, 59, 72, 85

13 40, 41, 44, 46–48, 83, 84
14 16, 77, 86, 90, 92, 96
15 4, 18, 31, 36, 41, 49, 65, 90, 93
16 8, 18, 39, 43, 45, 46, 49, 50, 56, 58, 59, 68, 72, 80–85, 95
17 20, 21, 34, 36, 38, 39, 78
18 2, 14, 31
19 29, 67–70, 89
20 25, 26, 37, 39, 40, 42, 56, 57, 66, 71, 82, 87, 88, 91, 92, 94–96
21 35, 37, 56, 62, 73, 95

Hoult
Sociology for a New Day
Random House, 1974

Introduction Prologue, 49, 92, 96, 97
1 6–9, 16–18, 21–24, 27, 58, 59, 62, 89
2 5, 10, 13, 19, 79, 95
3 Prologue, 4, 6, 49, 60
4 1–3, 5, 77
5 9–13, 16, 24, 27–29, 32, 33, 55, 77, 80, 81, 86, 90, 92, 96
6 19, 20, 30, 42, 43, 45, 50, 51
7 40, 41, 44, 46–48
8 35, 51, 52, 57
9 2, 13, 35, 47, 48, 50, 53, 54, 58–63, 95
10 4, 25, 40, 44, 57, 64–66, 68, 74, 76, 82, 86, 90, 91, 93, 96
11 2, 14, 15, 67–71
12 34–39, 56, 62, 73, 82, 87, 88, 92, 94, 96, 97

Lenski
Human Societies
McGraw-Hill, 1970

1 Prologue, 18, 19
2 2, 5–7, 16–18
3 6, 16
4 2, 4, 6, 18, 88
5 2, 6, 20, 21, 37, 53, 61, 73–75, 87–91
6 26–28, 51
7 9, 16, 88
8 9, 10, 15, 16
9 9, 10, 15, 16, 74, 91
10 10, 15, 27
11 25, 26, 31, 40, 55, 64–66, 75, 91
12 2, 4, 14, 31, 44, 51, 52, 57, 60, 68, 74, 76, 79, 82, 86, 90, 93, 96
13 18, 25, 26, 31, 40–51, 55, 58, 59, 64–66, 72, 75, 83–85, 91
14 2, 9, 12, 13, 35, 53, 54, 61–63
15 42, 45, 55, 74, 91
16 25, 26, 37, 39, 40, 42, 56, 57, 66, 71, 82, 87, 88, 91, 92, 94–96

Leslie, Larson, and Gorman
Introductory Sociology
Oxford University Press, 1973

1 Prologue, 4, 6, 49, 96, 97
2 1–3, 5, 77
3 22, 30, 32, 33, 76
4 16, 77, 86, 90, 92, 96
5 9, 12, 13, 92, 97
6 24–26, 37, 39, 40, 42, 55–57, 66, 71, 82, 87, 88, 91, 92, 94–96
7 9–13, 16, 75, 81
8 5, 6, 7–9, 16–18, 21, 23, 24, 27, 58, 59, 62, 89
9 5, 10, 13, 79, 95
10 27–29, 32, 33
11 20, 21, 34–39, 56, 62, 73, 78, 95
12 24, 25, 51, 52
13 2, 14, 31
14 15, 29, 67–72, 89
15 18–21, 40–51, 54, 58, 59, 72, 83–85
16 8, 18, 39, 43, 45, 46, 49, 50, 56, 58, 59, 68, 72, 80–85, 95
17 2, 13, 53, 54
18 35, 61–63
19 Prologue, 7, 47–50, 58–60, 78, 80, 95
20 25, 26, 31, 40, 55, 64–66, 75, 91
21 4, 44, 57, 60, 66, 68, 74, 76, 79, 82, 86, 90, 93, 96

Lowry and Rankin

Sociology, The Science of Society

Scribners, 1969

1 Prologue, 1–6, 49, 77, 96, 97
2 5–9, 16–18, 21, 23, 24, 27, 58, 59, 62, 89
3 9–13, 16, 75, 81
4 16, 22, 27–30, 32, 33, 76, 77, 86, 90, 96
5 20, 21, 34–36, 38, 39, 56, 62, 73, 77, 78, 95
6 18–21, 41–51, 54, 58, 59, 72, 83–85
7 24, 25, 35, 51, 52, 61–63
8 15, 29, 67–72, 89
9 2, 13, 35, 51–54, 57, 60, 74, 90
10 5, 10, 13, 79, 95
11 25, 26, 37, 39, 40, 42, 56, 66, 71, 82, 87, 88, 91, 92, 94–96

McGee

Points of Departure (alternate edition)

The Dryden Press, 1972

1 Prologue, 4, 6
2 9–13, 16, 75, 81
3 5–9, 16–18, 21, 23, 24, 27, 58, 59, 62, 89
4 24, 25, 35, 52, 57
5 18, 40–51, 58, 59, 72, 83–85
6 5, 10, 13, 79, 95
7 4, 6, 9, 55
8 67–70, 72, 85

Mack and Pease

Sociology and Social Life, 5th ed.

D. Van Nostrand, 1973

1 4, 6
2 18, 40–51, 58, 59, 72, 83–85
3 22, 30, 32, 33, 76, 92
4 9–13, 16, 75, 81
5 5–7, 35, 52
6 5–9, 16–18, 21, 23, 24, 27, 58, 59, 62, 89
7 29, 67–70, 89
8 51, 52
9 2, 14, 31
10 15, 67–72
11 18, 40–51, 58, 59, 72, 83–85
12 8, 18, 39, 43, 45, 46, 49, 50, 56, 58, 59, 68, 72, 80–85, 95
13 25, 26, 31, 40, 55, 64–66, 75, 91
14 4, 44, 57, 60, 66, 68, 74, 76, 79, 82, 86, 90, 93, 96
15 2, 13, 53, 54
16 Prologue, 7, 47–50, 58–60, 78, 80, 95
17 10, 35, 61–63
18 25, 26, 37, 39, 40, 42, 56, 57, 66, 71, 82, 87, 88, 91, 92, 94–96
19 20, 21, 34–39, 56, 62, 73, 78, 95
20 5, 10, 13, 25, 31, 42, 45, 69, 72, 78, 79, 81, 82, 87–90, 95, 97

McKee

Introduction to Sociology

Holt, Rinehart, and Winston, 1969

1 4, 6
2 Prologue, 4, 5
3 1–3, 5, 77
4 22, 30, 32, 33, 76
5 9–13, 16, 75, 81
6 5–9, 16–18, 21, 23, 24, 27, 58, 59, 62, 89
7 27–29, 32, 33
8 51, 52
9 29, 67–70, 89
10 18–21, 40–51, 58, 59, 72, 83–85
11 8, 18, 39, 43, 45, 46, 49, 50, 56, 58, 59, 68, 72, 80–85, 95
12 19–21, 54
13 2, 13, 53, 54
14 Prologue, 7, 47–50, 58–60, 78, 80, 95
15 25, 26, 31, 40, 55, 64–66, 75, 91
16 4, 44, 57, 60, 66, 68, 74, 76, 79, 82, 86, 90, 93, 96
17 1, 6, 60
18 10, 35, 61–63
19 20, 21, 34–39, 56, 62, 73, 78, 95
20 35, 37, 56, 62, 73, 95

21 2, 14, 31
22 25, 31, 42, 45, 69, 72, 78, 81, 82, 87–90, 97
23 2, 3, 49, 92, 96, 97

McNall

The Sociological Experience, 3d ed.

Little, Brown, 1974

1 Prologue, 4, 6
2 1, 3, 4
3 6, 9
4 5, 9–13, 16, 75, 81
5 23, 30, 32, 33
6 5–9, 16–18, 20–24, 27, 58, 59, 62, 89
7 24, 25, 27–29, 32, 33, 51, 52
8 2, 14, 31
9 29, 67–70, 89
10 18, 40–51, 58, 59, 72, 83–85
11 16, 77, 86, 90, 96
12 20, 21, 34–39, 56, 62, 73, 78, 95
13 60, 63, 94, 95
14 8, 18, 39, 43, 45, 46, 49, 50, 56, 58, 59, 68, 72, 80, 82–85, 95
15 2, 13, 53, 54
16 18, 31, 36, 41, 44, 57, 60, 65, 66, 68, 74, 76, 79, 82, 86, 90, 93, 96
17 10, 35, 61–63
18 1–3, 5, 77
19 Prologue, 49, 96, 97

Mercer and Wanderer

The Study of Society

Wadsworth, 1970

1 1–7, 77
2 9–13, 16, 75, 81
3 5–9, 16–18, 21, 23, 24, 27, 58, 59, 62, 89
4 19–21, 54, 92
5 5, 10, 13, 25, 31, 42, 45, 69, 72, 78, 79, 81, 82, 87–90, 95, 97
6 27–29, 32, 33
7 18–21, 40–51, 54, 58, 59, 72, 83–85
8 8, 18, 39, 43, 45, 46, 49, 50, 56, 58, 59, 68, 72, 80–85, 95
9 2, 13, 53, 54
10 10, 35, 61–63
11 Prologue, 7, 47–50, 58–60, 78, 80, 95
12 4, 44, 57, 60, 66, 68, 74, 76, 79, 82, 86, 90, 93, 96
13 25, 26, 31, 40, 55, 64–66, 75, 91
14 2, 14, 31
15 29, 67–70, 89
16 25, 26, 37, 39, 40, 42, 56, 57, 66, 71, 82, 87, 88, 91, 92, 94–96

Merrill

Society and Culture, An Introduction to Sociology, 4th ed.

Prentice-Hall, 1969

1 22, 27–30, 32, 33, 76
2 27–29, 32, 33
3 24, 25
4 9, 12, 13, 27–29, 32, 33
5 9–13, 16, 75, 81
6 5–9, 16–18, 21, 23, 24, 27, 58, 59, 62, 89
7 19–21, 54
8 5, 10, 13, 79, 95
9 8, 18, 39, 43, 45, 46, 49, 50, 56, 58, 59, 68, 72, 80–85, 95
10 18, 40–51, 58, 59, 72, 83–85
11 19–21, 54
12 40, 41, 44, 46–49, 83, 84
13 35, 52, 57
14 2, 13, 53, 54
15 51, 52
16 29, 67–70, 89
17 25, 26, 37, 39, 40, 42, 56, 57, 66, 71, 82, 87, 88, 91, 92, 94–96
18 20, 21, 34–39, 56, 62, 73, 78, 95
19 20, 21, 34–39, 56, 62, 73, 78, 95
20 34–39
21 25, 31, 42, 45, 69, 72, 78, 81, 82, 87–90, 97

Nisbet

The Social Bond: An Introduction to the Study of Society

Knopf, 1970

1 Prologue, 1–7
2 Prologue
3 12, 13, 19–21, 27–30, 55, 89
4 22, 23, 30, 32, 33, 76
5 27–29, 32, 33
6 4, 18, 31, 36, 41, 49, 65, 73, 90, 92, 93
7 19–21, 54
8 19–21, 54
9 9, 12, 13, 61, 62
10 5, 10, 13, 79, 89, 95
11 35, 52
12 2, 37, 39, 87, 88
13 25, 26
14 35, 55, 73, 74
Epilogue Prologue, 49, 92, 96, 97

Phillips

Sociology, Social Structure and Change

Macmillan, 1969

1 1–7, 22, 25–30, 32, 33, 37, 39, 40, 42, 56, 57, 66, 71, 76, 82, 87, 88, 91, 92, 94–96
2 1–3, 5, 7, 22, 30, 32, 33, 76
3 24, 27–29, 32, 33, 35, 52, 55, 57
4 5–9, 16–18, 20, 21, 23, 24, 27, 34–39, 56, 58, 59, 62, 73, 78, 89, 95
5 2, 5–9, 13, 16–18, 21, 23, 24, 27, 53, 54, 58, 59, 62, 89
6 24, 25, 51, 52
7 19–21, 54
8 18, 40–51, 58, 59, 72, 83–85
9 8, 16, 18, 39, 43, 45, 46, 49, 50, 56, 58, 59, 68, 72, 77, 80–86, 90, 95, 96
10 2, 14, 15, 31, 67–72
11 25, 26, 31, 40, 55, 64–66, 75, 91
12 10, 35, 61–63
13 Prologue, 7, 47–50, 58–60, 78, 90, 95
14 4, 18, 31, 36, 41, 44, 49, 57, 60, 65, 66, 68, 74, 76, 79, 82, 86, 90, 93, 96
15 29, 67–70, 89
16 20, 21, 34–39, 56, 62, 73, 78, 95
17 25, 26, 37, 39, 40, 42, 56, 57, 66, 71, 82, 87, 88, 91, 92, 94–96

Popenoe

Sociology

Appleton-Century-Crofts, 1971

Introduction Prologue, 49, 96, 97
1 19, 24, 29, 55, 76, 79, 80, 90, 93
2 9–13, 16, 75, 81
3 5–9, 16–18, 21–24, 27, 58, 59, 62, 89
4 2, 13, 27–29, 32, 33, 53, 54
5 24, 25, 51, 52
6 18–21, 40–51, 58, 59, 72, 83–85
7 8, 18, 39, 43, 45, 49, 50, 56, 58, 59, 68, 72, 80–85, 95
8 Prologue, 7, 48–50, 58–60, 78, 80, 95
9 10, 35, 61–63
10 15, 67–72
11 2, 5, 10, 13, 29, 76, 79, 80, 90, 93
12 20, 21, 34–39, 56, 62, 73, 78, 95
13 25, 26, 31, 40, 55, 64–66, 75, 91
14 4, 44, 57, 60, 66, 68, 74, 76, 79, 82, 86, 90, 93, 96

Remmling and Campbell

Basic Sociology, An Introduction to the Study of Society

Littlefield, Adams, 1970

1 Prologue, 1, 5, 6
2 1, 5, 6
3 1–3, 5, 77
4 9–13, 16, 75, 81
5 9–13, 16, 75, 81
6 2, 29, 35, 52, 57, 76, 79, 80, 90, 93
7 2, 13, 53, 54
8 2, 13, 53, 54
9 7, 10, 35, 47–50, 58, 59, 60–63, 78, 80, 95

10	25, 26, 31, 40, 44, 55, 57, 60, 64–66, 68, 74–76, 79, 82, 86, 90, 91, 93, 96
11	30, 32, 33, 97
12	24, 25, 29, 67–70, 89
13	8, 18–21, 39, 40–51, 54, 56, 58, 59, 68, 72, 80–85, 95
14	24, 25, 27–29, 32, 33, 51, 52
15	20, 21, 34–39, 56, 62, 73, 78, 92, 95
16	25, 26, 31, 37, 39, 40, 42, 45, 56, 57, 66, 69, 71, 72, 78, 81, 82, 87–97
17	5-9, 16–18, 21, 23, 24, 27, 58, 59, 62, 89
18	–
19	Prologue, 49, 92, 96, 97
20	–
21	–

Rose

Introduction to Sociology

Rand McNally, 1971

1	4, 6
2	1–3, 5, 77
3	9–13, 16, 75, 81
4	25, 26, 37, 39, 40, 42, 56, 57, 66, 71, 82, 87, 88, 91, 92, 94–96
5	24, 55
6	27–29, 32, 33
7	19–21, 54, 84
8	2, 13, 53, 54
9	35, 61–63
10	4, 44, 57, 60, 66, 68, 74, 76, 79, 82, 86, 90, 93, 96
11	18, 40–51, 58, 59, 72, 83–85
12	8, 18, 39, 43, 45, 46, 49, 50, 56, 58, 59, 68, 72, 80–85, 95
13	2, 29, 76, 79, 80, 90, 93
14	5, 10, 13, 79, 95
15	22–24
16	34, 36, 38, 39
17	35, 37, 56, 62, 73, 78
18	2, 14, 31
19	29, 67–70, 89
20	15, 67–72

Rose and Rose

Sociology: The Study of Human Relations

Knopf, 1969

1	4, 6, 15, 67–72
2	9–13, 16, 75, 81
3	7, 8, 16–18, 22, 23
4	2, 9, 29, 76, 79, 80, 90, 92, 93, 97
5	51, 52, 57
6	2, 13, 53, 54
7	27–29, 32, 33
8	4, 25, 26, 31, 35, 40, 44, 55, 57, 60–66, 68, 74–76, 79, 82, 86, 90, 91, 93, 96
9	24, 25
10	18, 40–51, 58, 59, 72, 83–85
11	20, 21, 34–39, 56, 62, 73, 78, 95
12	2, 14, 31
13	29, 67–70, 89
14	25, 26, 37, 39, 40, 42, 56, 57, 66, 71, 82, 87, 88, 91, 92, 94–96
15	16, 77, 86, 90, 96

Society Today, 2d ed.

CRM Books, 1973

1	Prologue, 4, 6, 49, 96, 97
2	1–3, 5, 77
3	9–13, 16, 24, 55, 75, 81
4	6
5	5–8, 20
6	5–9, 16–18, 58, 59
7	19–21, 54
8	27–29, 32, 33
9	51, 52
10	21, 23, 24, 27, 62, 89
11	5, 10, 13, 79, 95
12	18, 19, 40–51, 54, 58, 59, 72, 83–85
13	40, 41, 44, 46–49, 83, 84
14	36, 45, 56, 68, 72
15	41–44, 48
16	8, 18, 39, 43, 45, 46, 49, 50, 56, 58, 59, 68, 72, 80–85, 95

17 13, 20, 21
18 2, 13, 53, 54
19 Prologue, 7, 47–50, 58–60, 78, 80, 95
20 10, 35, 61–63
21 4, 44, 57, 60, 66, 68, 74, 76, 79, 82, 86, 90, 93, 96
22 25, 26, 31, 40, 55, 64–66, 75, 91
23 2, 14, 31
24 29, 67–70, 89
25 15, 67–72
26 25, 26, 37, 39, 40, 42, 56, 57, 66, 71, 82, 87, 88, 91, 92, 94–96
27 20, 21, 34, 36–39, 56, 62, 73, 78, 95
28 35, 37, 56, 62, 73, 95
29 91, 92, 94, 97

Steward and Glynn

Introduction to Sociology

McGraw-Hill, 1971

1 Prologue, 4, 6, 49, 96, 97
2 27–29, 32, 33
3 9–13, 16, 75, 81
4 5–9, 16–18, 21, 23, 24, 27, 58, 59, 62, 89
5 18–21, 40–51, 54, 58, 59, 72, 83–85
6 8, 18, 39, 43, 45, 46, 49, 50, 56, 58, 59, 68, 72, 80–85, 95
7 20, 21, 34–39, 56, 62, 73, 78, 95
8 2, 14, 31
9 15, 67–72, 91, 92, 94, 97
10 2, 13, 53, 54
11 10, 35, 61–63
12 Prologue, 7, 47–50, 58–60, 78, 80, 95
13 25, 26, 31, 40, 55, 64–66, 75, 91
14 4, 44, 57, 60, 66, 68, 74, 76, 79, 82, 86, 90, 93, 96
15 25, 26, 37, 39, 40, 42, 56, 57, 66, 71, 82, 87, 88, 91, 92, 94–96

Toby

Contemporary Society, 2d ed.

Wiley, 1971

1 4, 6, 9, 12, 13, 19–21, 54
2 1–3, 5, 77
3 9–13, 16, 75, 81
4 7, 8, 13, 18, 58, 59
5 9, 21, 23, 24, 27, 62, 89
6 25, 26, 31, 40, 55, 64–66, 75, 91
7 14, 31, 40, 44, 46, 53, 66, 69, 72, 75, 79, 86, 90, 94
8 10, 35, 61–63
9 4, 44, 52, 60, 66, 68, 74, 76, 79, 82, 86, 90, 93, 96
10 24, 25, 51, 52
11 Prologue, 7, 47–50, 58–60, 78, 80, 95
12 18, 40–51, 58, 59, 72, 83–85
13 5, 10, 13, 79, 95
14 25, 26, 37, 39, 40, 42, 56, 57, 66, 71, 82, 87, 88, 91, 92, 94–96
15 9, 92, 97

Tumin

Patterns of Society: Identities, Roles, Resources

Little, Brown, 1973

1 4, 6
2 9, 12, 13, 19–21, 54, 92, 97
3 42, 45, 47, 48, 58, 59
4 40, 41, 55
5 4, 18, 31, 36, 41, 49, 65, 90, 93
6 43, 45, 46, 48
7 24, 44, 46, 50
8 40, 41, 44, 46–49, 83, 84
9 20–23
10 7, 8, 43, 50, 82–84
11 18, 39, 43, 45, 58, 59, 72, 78, 80, 82, 85
12 20, 21
13 13, 18, 29, 62, 63, 94, 95
14 5, 10, 13, 79, 95
15 9–13, 16, 24, 55, 57, 75, 81
16 2, 13, 53, 54
17 10, 35, 61–63
18 2, 14, 31
19 25, 26, 31, 40, 55, 64–66, 69, 75, 91
Epilogue 5–9, 16–18, 21–24, 27, 58, 59, 62, 89

Vander Zanden

Sociology: A Systematic Approach, 2d ed.

Ronald Press, 1970

1	1–3, 5, 77
2	9–13, 16, 75, 81
3	5–9, 16–18, 21, 23, 24, 27, 58, 59, 62, 89
4	5, 10, 13, 79, 95
5	19–21, 54
6	24, 25, 27–29, 32, 33
7	18, 40–51, 58, 59, 72, 83–85
8	8, 18, 39, 43, 45, 46, 49, 50, 56, 58, 59, 68, 72, 80–85, 95
9	20, 21, 34–39, 56, 62, 73, 78, 95
10	25, 26, 37, 39, 40, 42, 56, 57, 66, 71, 82, 87, 88, 91, 92, 94–96
11	2, 13, 53, 54
12	10, 35, 61–63
13	25, 26, 31, 40, 55, 64–66, 75, 91
14	4, 44, 57, 60, 66, 68, 74, 76, 79, 82, 86, 90, 93, 96
15	Prologue, 7, 47–50, 58–60, 78, 80, 95
16	2, 14, 31
17	67–70

Vernon

Human Interaction: An Introduction to Sociology, 2d ed.

Ronald Press, 1972

1	Prologue, 4, 6
2	1–3, 5, 77
3	30, 32, 33
4	27–29, 32, 33
5	5, 7, 8, 15, 16, 88
6	9–13, 16, 75, 81
7	9, 92, 97
8	9, 12, 13
9	19–21, 54
10	22–24
11	–
12	9, 16, 17, 22, 30, 32, 76
13	9, 92, 97
14	5–9, 16–18, 21, 23, 24, 27, 58, 59, 62, 89
15	19–21, 54
16	5–9, 16–24, 27, 54, 58, 59, 62, 89
17	27–29, 32, 33
18	18, 40–51, 58, 59, 72, 83–85
19	8, 18, 39, 43, 45, 46, 49, 50, 56, 58, 59, 68, 72, 80–85, 95
20	25, 26, 37, 39, 40, 42, 56, 57, 66, 71, 82, 87, 88, 91, 92, 94–96
21	20, 21, 34–39, 56, 62, 73, 78, 95
22	5, 10, 13, 79, 95
23	16, 77, 86, 90, 96
24	24, 55
25	2, 14, 15, 31, 67–72
26	2, 13, 53, 54
27	51, 52
28	10, 35, 61–63
29	–

Wilson

Sociology: Rules, Roles, Relationships, rev. ed.

Dorsey Press, 1971

1	4, 6
2	2, 14, 31
3	9–13, 16, 75, 81
4	5–9, 16–18, 21, 23, 24, 27, 58, 59, 62, 89
5	27–29, 32, 33
6	19–21, 27–29, 32, 33, 54
7	15, 67–72
8	18–21, 40–51, 54, 58, 59, 72, 83–85
9	Prologue, 7, 19–21, 47–50, 54, 58–60, 78, 80, 95
10	25, 26, 31, 40, 55, 64–66, 75, 91
11	4, 35, 44, 57, 60–63, 66, 68, 74, 76, 79, 82, 86, 90, 93, 96
12	5, 10, 13, 79, 95
13	26, 38–40, 66, 71, 82, 87, 88, 91
14	25, 37, 40, 42, 56, 57, 71, 94–96
15	Prologue, 4, 6, 49, 96, 97

Name Index

D

E

F

G

H

I

J

K

L

M

R

S

Subject Index

A

B

D

E

F

G

H

I

J

K

L

M

N

O

P

R